The
MANAGERIAL MIND
Science and Theory in Policy Decisions

The
MANAGERIAL MIND
Science and Theory in Policy Decisions

CHARLES E. SUMMER

Professor
Graduate School of Business
Columbia University
and
Institut pour l'Etude des Méthodes
de Direction de l'Entreprise
Lausanne, Switzerland

JEREMIAH J. O'CONNELL

Assistant Professor
Wharton School of Finance and Commerce
University of Pennsylvania

With the Collaboration of **BORIS YAVITZ**

Associate Professor of Management
Graduate School of Business, Columbia University

Revised Edition • 1968
Richard D. Irwin, Inc., Homewood, Illinois
Irwin-Dorsey Limited, Nobleton, Ontario

Revised Edition

First Printing, May, 1968

Library of Congress Catalog Card No. 67–30241

Printed in the United States of America

To Our Parents
Edgar and Emily Summer
Jerry and Mary O'Connell

PREFACE

Since our original work on this book in the period 1960 through 1963, there has been an accelerated use of fundamental knowledge in the administration of corporations here and abroad. Under various rubrics from applied mathematics and the behavioral sciences especially, theoretical materials have increasingly affected the policy formulation and implementation processes. Many managers seem more sensitive to the old saw: "Ten years of experience may simply be one year of experience repeated ten times." So that experience will be a better teacher, demands are made of a wide range of academic disciplines to provide (a) explanations for past events, (b) conceptual schemes to serve as strategies for experiencing the richness of the here-and-now, and (c) models to aid in achieving at least probabilistic predictions of the consequences of present decisions. We see a growing intolerance for solution by analogy, and expanded interest and energy directed to process analysis or critical introspection at the individual, group, and even organizational level. One index of the trends noted here is the mounting concern for the management of knowledge within corporations. Many corporations are finding they must rethink several structural features of their organizations in order to capitalize on the increased availability of relevant conceptual materials and the eagerness for their use. There is heightened tension, too often quite creative tension—in the classic conflict between science and judgment in policy decisions.

During this same period of the sixties the curricula of business schools have continued to introduce more and more substantive content from related disciplines. The search has been intensified for pedagogies which bridge the gap between this substantive content and the decision-making practice which is present in one form or another in professional programs in business.

In our teaching at the executive development, graduate, and undergraduate levels we found the first edition helpful in responding to these evolving educational needs. Happily, scores of our colleagues in this and three other countries found the book a useful teaching aid. Eighty percent of the book's adopters generously responded to an extensive questionnaire which gave us substantial guidance for the revision of the book. Cases and readings which have proven valuable and whose issues and content are not dated have been retained. The new cases emphasize internal issues in corporations more so than relations-with-environment issues. The kinds of case data presented lend themselves to more rigorous and intensive inquiry. In the same spirit, the new readings are somewhat longer than those in the first edition. All these changes reflect the constructive criticism of those who shared our experience of exercising ourselves and students with the first edition.

It may be appropriate here to explain the genesis of this book by repeating part of the Preface to the first edition.

*   *   *   *   *

This book is the joint effort of two people, and its concept grew out of certain experiences that we have had in teaching, in studying the social sciences, and in working in business organizations. Some of these experiences are reported in the beginning chapter, in the form of our reflections on, and observations of, situations in which social science and operations research came into contact with the practice of management—in which scholars and applied scholars came into contact with businessmen.

At this point, we shall simply recount some of the specific settings in which these situations took place.

First was our formal educational experience. We owe to the healthy churning and ferment of the doctoral program at Columbia a special debt. We were caught up in a period of change, in which the rigor of economics, plus advanced work in more practical technologies such as finance and management theory, stood in danger (it appeared at times) of being rendered technologically obsolete. Since 1956, there was first the addition of behavioral sciences, particularly sociology and cultural anthropology, later joined by increased emphasis on applied mathematics, in addition to what had already been a rigorous exposure to statistics. At about the same time came emphasis on the humanities and social philosophy in business administration. This confusion, painful at times, has resulted in a healthy balance in the curriculum among all of these things, and the baby (economics and the technical fields) did not get thrown out with the bath water (he is simply being updated).

Secondly, we observed in this process, both as students and then teachers, a healthy conflict between people of diverse disciplines which led to many of the conclusions in this book. Underlying much of the curriculum ferment, we noticed that different people, including ourselves, had vastly different ideas about what ought to go into the education of a practicing businessman, and what issues, or areas of research, should be undertaken to advance the state of the . . . (art? science?). We saw mathematicians and economists and management theorists (who have much in common with political scientists) wondering about how important human behavior, studied rigorously, is. We saw people oriented to one type of human organization philosophy wondering about the value of other types, and wondering about whether one philosophy might be more applicable at the firm level while another might be more applicable at the level of the national economic society. We also saw some who felt that practice and case work were more important in terms of both teaching time and research; while others felt that study of fundamental disciplines was more important, in these terms. Perhaps somewhere in between in this latter case, some people felt that study of technologies, usually referred to as the functional fields of business, were more important.

A third factor was our exposure to business institutions and business-men—our employment experience, in manufacturing firms and consulting firms, as full-time employees and later as part-time consultants. At points in these experiences, we were called upon to utilize behavioral science, economics, mathematics, and the technologies, such as management theory, or capital budgeting, or marketing. The problem of making sense out of company problems, we found, led many times to admiration for theories we had learned; but on the other hand led many times to the full impact of the fact that no theory ever fits any problem in the sense of giving com-pletely accurate predictions, or in indicating action solutions. In some cases, we found either that there were apparently no theories covering certain aspects of problems, or that those theories which gave the impres-sion of being relevant were, in fact, useless in the particulars of the prob-lem, in that specific situation.

A fourth and very valuable experience was working with students. An advanced seminar, started in 1957, resulted in major changes in our thinking. For one thing, it started as an attempted application of philo-sophical theories and basic values to policy problems. Ernest Nagel, for example, addressed himself to the question "What is truth?" and what does it mean in business decisions? The following week, students and in-structor took policy cases and tried to apply what Nagel had said, in the difficult process of relating it to cases in their buzzing confusion. The late Lyman Bryson addressed himself to "What is beauty and what does it mean in business institutions or policy systems?" The following week pro-duced cases in which these ideas were related to practice. Over the years, this approach was abandoned in favor of more formal or more empirical theories from various disciplines in the social sciences. In the sense that values and ideals *do* get mixed into social science, which Chapter III will explain, the initial experience in trying to apply deep, basic, "pure" values influenced us greatly when trying to make sense out of applying social science to cases.

The authors are indebted to the General Electric Advanced Manage-ment program, and its director, Mr. James Shipton, for the opportunity to do research with cases and theories, and later to publish two volumes and use these as teaching devices in that school, working with business-men. In the process of that research, we were groping our way with theories and cases. Lawrence Klein, from the Columbia Law School; Paul Jonas, who has degrees in economics from both Budapest and Columbia; and Samuel Gluck, a philosopher on the faculty of City College, aided in gathering concepts. That procedure went something like this: One of the authors would read the cases and then ask naïve questions of the three specialists. For example, to Klein: "Why do people obey laws (or com-pany policies)?" Or, to Jonas: "Why is this company moving its plant from Chicago to Buffalo?" Or, to Gluck: "Why is this bank president using a committee, and letting the subordinates make this decision?"

The researchers would come back with a series of abstracts of theories and conceptual schemes. We would then try to eliminate bias in the total spread of readings by asking: Is there an important opposing point of view? Can we get an abstract which gives a different answer to the question?

This process was repeated two years later in research in connection with the Columbia curriculum, for which we express appreciation to Deans Brown and Walton for their support, and to the Ford Foundation for its support. This time, we had excellent help from our colleagues. Boris Yavitz gave us help in the field of engineering and operations research. Kirby Warren helped in writing three cases, and lent expertise in managerial economics and financial planning. John Hutchinson wrote one of the cases in which a great deal of knowledge of manufacturing and labor relations was necessary. Fred Abrahams, of the Bureau of Applied Social Research, provided suggestions in the field of sociology.

We also acknowledge the contributions of former students in the Seminar Science and Philosophy in Policy Decisions for nine of the readings, and help on research for four of the cases in this book. Messrs. Rooks, Beck, Sansone, Steindler, Rosenbaum, Stockbridge, Easton, Turko, Garrity, Worth, Sauer, and Kisch are all now practicing businessmen or teachers from San Francisco to Zurich.

*   *   *   *   *

In this revised edition we are indebted for case materials to two Wharton School colleagues, Richard Swersey and Wayne Howard, and to Messrs. Jerome Schnee, Avrel Mason, and Charles Gautschi.

*   *   *   *   *

Because so much indication of how this book might be used is given in the individual case introductions, little need be said here about what the individual teacher may want to do in this respect. We do not claim to have been either exhaustive or comprehensive in selecting which theories apply to a given case. In fact, the teacher may want to take other theories, in his experience found useful, which illuminate the fundamental forces at work in any given case situation.

In most instances, the questions included in the case introduction to tie theories to the case situation are, at least in one sense, "nondirective." They ask a practical question, referring to a theory which is useful, but without indicating how a theory would indicate the answer. Thus, instead of asking, "How do long-run cost curves of the firm determine whether or not a firm will move its plant location?" we ask, "From the viewpoint of economic theory, why is the Apex Company moving its plant to Ferndale?" and "From the viewpoint of economic theory, what effect does this decision of Apex management have on gross national product?" or "From the viewpoint of psychology, why are the employees of Apex Company joining a labor union and engaging in a strike?"

One can easily perceive that any teacher or student may see theories, events, or causes of problems that the authors have not included. Far from being a diversion in class or a source of confusion, this would represent a very constructive course of events. So long as the teacher bears in mind that the main goal of the instruction is clear, deep, precise thinking, and practice in relating theory to cases in action decisions—and so long as he makes this known through example in the classroom—he will not be thought of by students as conducting a confused, purposeless, nonsystematic discussion. Why? First, because the world does not come in neat formulas, and the cases are miniature representations of reality. Second, theories and conceptual schemes do not fit together—there is no universal common language or way of predicting the world between economics and psychology. The resulting class discussions will therefore tend to be highly creative and highly motivated, all the while referring to concepts and theories which have meaning to the business school student in terms of his problems in business, and at the same time have more precision and power than cases used without the benefit of theory.

We have found it necessary to devote two to six class meetings to each individual case unit, depending on the complexity of the case itself, and the complexity of the theoretical readings with that particular case. The kinds of managerial policy attitudes and methods we try to develop cannot be developed if only one class period, inevitably leading to superficial discussion, is used.

The method we prefer for structuring class discussions is to divide total class time into two parts; to make an arbitrary split between (1) the time devoted to analysis and diagnosis (questions and theoretical readings are labeled that way in the case introductions), and (2) the time devoted to solutions—to managerial and policy questions. For example, if a complex case requires four class meetings, three might be devoted to the first decision-making phase and one to the second phase. While the teacher's manual will give some suggestion of the time that might be allotted to each case, the individual instructor would do well to experiment with time allocations, making his own guess as to how much effort is involved.

A second method for approaching class work is to start first with solutions or policy questions (alternative courses of action), bringing in the analytical and theoretical work as action solutions are proposed. If this plan is used, it requires much more intensive and high quality individual student study *before* class. It also requires some precision on the part of the instructor in listing advantageous and disadvantageous consequences to various alternative solutions, based on the underlying predictions from theoretical readings.

The advantage of this approach lies in the fact that less class time, and fewer numbers of class meetings, are required for rigorous analysis and solution. We recommend this as a possibility in advanced courses. In more elementary courses, unless rigorous individual preparation is in fact carried out, one may jump to conclusions, and produce serious unintended consequences, if he starts with solutions and an assumed statement of the problem.

We also want to call attention to the five cases for original analysis at the end of the book. These have not been structured in any way, but ask the student to duplicate, in terms of his own creativity, insight, and prior education, the kind of work done by the authors. In an advanced seminar at Columbia, we have found this to be one of the most stimulating intellectual experiences we have had. Each student is asked to read the case, and to reflect on important theories or ideas from any discipline which *he* "sees" as relevant to "what is going on in the case." He is then asked to come to class with one abstract of an underlying theory or concept, and to explain how this basic view illuminates the actions and phenomena (technological, economic, behavioral, etc.) going on in the real-world facts of the case. The instructor and fellow students, in our experience, have been stimulated and intellectually impressed with how different minds can come up with differing viewpoints and powerful arguments, based on important theories, that have important bearing on analysis and solution to action problems.

Actually, any case in the whole book can be treated in this manner. The first 23 case introductions include, as the final two questions, instructions to the student to repeat the process which the authors performed in drawing up the case introduction framework for analysis and solution. We have also had success in a second seminar in which the first one third of the course was devoted to casework according to the authors' questions and supporting readings. This provided a training in the attitudes and methodologies of the managerial mind—of relating back and forth from facts in the real world to ideas in the realm of theory. At this point, the remainder of the course changed to completely nondirective and original work by students, using not only the last five cases in the book, but any case throughout the book as explained in the preceding paragraph. This kind of course is particularly recommended for smaller, seminar-type classes, when different students have had exposure to differing educations in the sciences, the humanities, or business administration. It is not necessary that any one student have wide exposure to all three areas, since students and instructor educate each other, based on their prior specializations, education, and life experience.

As a final point from our teaching experience, we believe that the fact that no case can be solved in a discussion of limited time, with comprehensiveness and clear agreement, should be recognized clearly. The clock runs out on all case discussions, and this has educational value too. In the business world, decisions could be researched and talked about, with enormous amounts of data being gathered, and in the end someone must use judgment at some point of time to stop the decision-making process. Therefore, students and teacher alike may do well to recognize and accept this fact. Policy-makers and managers need courage and a willingness to face ambiguity, in their decisions, where there is no overall conceptual scheme which gives them certainty and predictability.

*   *   *   *   *

Finally, we express our appreciation to Carol Summer, Pat O'Connell, and Camilla Koch who did an excellent job of collecting, reproducing, cataloging, and cross-referencing all of the materials. Without this help we could not have accomplished our work.

April, 1968   C. E. S.

                                                                          J. J. O'C.

CONTENTS I

Plan of the Book

INTRODUCTORY

The Relation between Theory and Policy Decisions. The Managerial Mind, the Scholarly Mind, and the Applied Scholarly Mind. This Book as a Textbook. This Book as a Practice Laboratory. This Book as a Research Document. This Book as the Basis for Further Research. The Problematic Situation. Technology and Central Planning in Modern Institutions. Technological and Sociological Concentration (Interdependence). Complexity and Unintended Consequences. The Law of Subdisciplinization. Reactions of Executives and Theorists. "Responsibility" of the Executive. What This Book Will Not Do.

Concepts and Abstraction. Theory and Conceptual Schemes. Physical Science and Physical Scientists. Repetitive versus Divergent Phenomena. Operationalism in Science. The Lesson of Physical Science for Policy Makers.

Theory Formulation in the Social Sciences: An Example from Sociology. Theory Construction: An Example from Social Psychology. Theory Construction: An Example from Economics and Industrial Engineering. Ceteris Paribus in Social Science. Who Has the Final Answer for Policy Determination? Social Science and Social Philosophy. The Value of Social Science in Policy Decisions.

CASE MATERIALS

CASE MATERIALS: CASES, READINGS, CONNECTIVE TISSUE

Less Complex Cases:

APPENDIX

INDEXES

CONTENTS II

CASES RELATED TO DISCIPLINES AND CONCEPTS IN READINGS

Case				
6. THE WHITE HOUSE OF EL PASO p. 177	Technology and employment Technological change and gross national product	Profit maximization Marginal productivity of labor Marginal productivity of capital Theory of firm Economics and organization structure Wage theory under competition	Function of standardized work rules Ideologies of social control of technology Functions of entrepreneur in society Sources of social innovation	Formal organization planning Organization and outside forces Reasons for government control	Motivations of the entrepreneur
7. PHOTOGENERAL OPTICAL COMPANY p. 198	Probability theory Subjective and objective probability Decision-making rules (uncertainty, risk, conflict) Expected monetary value criterion Expected utility criterion Quantification and clarity of objectives	Oligopolistic pricing Premium versus penetration pricing Market structure and competition Innovation and the entrepreneur	Calculated risk and social goal attainment Specialists and the hierarchical organization Innovation and organizational constraints Status and role conflicts	Technological competence and the democratic process Authority to decide and ability to decide Legitimacy of specialists power	Knowledge, certainty, and probability Judgment, belief, and probability Knowledge, verbal expression, and quantification Expertise, leaders, and group decisions
8. BECK PLASTICS CORPORATION p. 229	Nature of technological systems Rational planning of decision system	Paramount position of production	Theory of technocracy Rational planning of organization	Legislative law versus common law Theory of legal authority Theory of government discipline	Motivation of executives Perception Defense mechanisms Theory of human needs Dependency
9. NATIONAL MOTOR PARTS p. 257	Quantitative standards for output Money units in engineering decisions Input-output analysis of production Models and quantification: use and limits	Performance standards and profit maximization The labor union as power organization The labor union as market-ing organization	The paramount position of production Science and the social order Technical competence and social organization Knowledge as power Indispensability as power Legitimate and hierarchical authority	Organization adjustment to environment Philosophy of central planning Unity of command Necessity for law and order Private property as source of authority Sanction as power	Motivations to obey a rule system Psychological concept of authority Participative leadership
10. FABRICATED STEEL PRODUCTS p. 284	Inventory control models Forecasting models Information systems design Suboptimization Relevant costs Science versus judgment	Increasing returns to scale Economics of standardization Economics of system decoupling	Conflict between specialist and operating manager Implementation of change Bureaucracy and the sanctification of means Information and power Organization as a socio-technical system	Multiple firm goals Organization structure and control	Interpersonal conflict Uncertainty as basis for resistance to change

16. ELECTRONICS INTERNATIONAL CORPORATION p. 477	Decision theory and competitive bidding Risk management	Cost estimation Sealed bid competition Fixed price bidding Cost plus incentive fee bidding	The organization's needs for action-oriented roles	Unity of command Functional authority Departmentation and coordination Project management Matrix organization De jure versus de facto authority	Personal influence and organization authority Human needs Laws of perception Leadership styles
17. MIDWEST HARDWARE MANUFACTURING COMPANY p. 556	Internal generation of funds Mathematical inventory models Suboptimization Balance of forces in technical system Benefits of science and mathematics	Firm size, specialization, economies of scale Indivisibility of units Diminishing returns Marginal productivity of specialist	Knowledge as power Limits to participation in decision making Organization structure and personality Pressure as stimulus to group formation Hierarchical differentiation and decision making Role of the expert	Unity of command Staff expert and line authority Controls and performance standards Central intelligence and efficiency Democracy and scientific management Autocratic versus democratic leadership	Response to tension and pressure Anxiety and social support Conflicts of interest and dialectical change Self-confidence and participation Personality differences of expert and manager Unstable interaction patterns and stress
18. APEX WIRE AND CABLE COMPANY p. 588	The concept of line balancing	Determinants of resource allocation National income accounting Cost-output functions Planned versus market-directed economy Price system: two way circular flow	Social values and economic efficiency The common good and individual self-interest Money payments and prices as social communication system Appropriate inclusion in organization decisions	The price of democracy Property rights and freedom The metrocorporation Social responsibility syndrome	Motivation for informal group formation Translation of needs into monetary demands Dynamics of attitude change Defense mechanisms Emotions, logic, and value conflicts
19. MISSISSIPPI VALLEY EQUIPMENT CORPORATION p. 618	Technological expertise and planning Application of science for efficiency Value of quantification and models	Profit maximization The invisible hand Function of the entrepreneur Economies of scale and organization structure Marginal productivity Effects of specialization	Science and the social order Necessity for roles and rational planning Sociological concepts of authority Conflict of hierarchy and free communication	Multiple goals of the firm Organization and external forces Evolution of government and organization Effects of decentralization Legislative law versus common law	Decisiveness, action, and innovation Informal organization Motivation to chaos or cooperation Competence, central planning Directive leadership Human needs and organization

CASE AND PAGE NUMBER	TECHNOLOGY ENGINEERING AND MANAGEMENT SCIENCE	ECONOMIC SCIENCE AND PHILOSOPHY	SOCIOLOGY AND SOCIAL PHILOSOPHY	POLITICAL SCIENCE LEGAL THEORY MANAGEMENT PHILOSOPHY	PSYCHOLOGY SOCIAL PSYCHOLOGY GROUP DYNAMICS
20. UNITED STATES STEEL CORPORATION p. 647	Profit, depreciation, cash flow analysis Bounded rationality in decision making Optimization of multiple objectives	Capacity utilization and costs Price leadership in oligopoly The invisible hand Cost push, profit push, ratchet inflation Productivity related to factor payments	Power, legitimacy, and functional analysis Communication networks, images, roles, and values Differential skills in role attainment and role performance Social cohesion: product of competition or cooperation Functional versus hierarchical status	Source of managerial authority Semantics in formation of public opinion Public interest and corporate objectives The price of freedom Legitimate power and authority	Motivation for obedience to authority Knowledge: images of fact and value Messages, value systems, and perception
21. CONTINENTAL ELECTRIC COMPANY p. 699	Quantitative measurements and self-control Limitations of the average as a statistical criteria for action Power of mathematics Suboptimization	Profit center accounting Difference in profit and cash flow Cash flow as investment criterion	Knowledge as power Conflict of specialist and manager Technology as cause for divergence between authority and ability The monocratic model	Results of decentralization Conflict of long- and short-term objectives Conflict of multiple objectives The right versus the ability to decide Conditions for participative leadership	Structural factors in perception Functional factors in perception Group decision making Joint setting of performance standards Motivations for lack of cooperation
22. GENERAL AMERICAN STEEL COMPANY p. 724	Technological competition Complexity of the technological system Technology and rational planning	Price system as allocation of resources Principle of specialization	Unintended consequences of rational planning Symbolic influence Compensation, prestige, and normative influences Behavior patterns of foremen	Organization response to environment Forces producing labor unions Function of executive in the firm	Psychological effects of specialization Engineering logic Human needs Formal organization and human behavior Motivation of managers
23. LINCOLN ROCHESTER TRUST COMPANY p. 758	Marginal productivity: the production function Optimization of long- and short-run costs	Economies of scale Managerial specialization Operating specialization Theory of the firm National income accounting Forms of competition Size, concentration, and power	Complexity of the technological system Role of the expert Function of the innovator in society Individualism in the social order Status and role	Origins of government Political order versus chaos	Motivations of the executive Human needs and initiative
24. DAYTON METAL WORKS					
25. GENERAL MOTORS CORPORATION					
26. THE GLIDDEN COMPANY					
27. MORRIS AIRWAYS COMPANY					
28. NORTH EUROPEAN REGION OCEAN TRANSPORTATION DIVISION					

These cases are for original student analysis. The authors have therefore not classified them either by disciplines in Contents II, or by action problems in Contents III.

CONTENTS III
Cases and Interrelated Action Problems

Management of Technical Operations and Work Flow	Personnel, Labor Relations Employee Motivation and Behavior	Planning Technological Change, Long-Range Planning, Capital Investment Planning	Executive Motivation, Behavior, Personal Leadership (Including Line-Staff Relations)	Designing the Structure of Duties, Standards and Controls	External Relationships: Economic, Legal, Social, National-International	
*	*	—	**	**	—	1
—	—	**	—	—	**	2
*	**	—	*	**	*	3
—	*	*	**	**	*	4
**	—	**	—	*	—	5
**	*	**	—	*	*	6
—	—	*	*	—	*	7
**	**	**	**	—	—	8
**	*	**	*	**	*	9
**	—	**	**	**	—	10
*	**	**	*	—	*	11
*	*	—	**	**	—	12
*	**	**	*	—	*	13
—	—	—	*	—	**	14
*	*	*	*	—	*	15
*	—	*	**	**	**	16
**	*	*	**	**	—	17
—	**	*	**	—	**	18
**	**	—	**	**	—	19
—	*	*	*	—	**	20
—	*	**	**	**	—	21
**	**	—	**	*	*	22
—	—	**	**	*	**	23

* Problems of less emphasis and subsidiary issues.
** Problems of major emphasis or multiple issues of a particular problem classification.

I. INTRODUCTORY

1. THEORY AND PRACTICE IN GENERAL MANAGEMENT

The Relation between Theory and Policy Decisions

It is one of the central theses of this book that *theories* are powerful aids to decision making by general managers in policy systems of today—in large complex institutions of the second half of the twentieth century. They are powerful in that they help in diagnosis and identification of managerial (action and policy) problems, in the clarification of goals which managers are attempting to reach, and in the prevention of harmful unintended consequences which managers might overlook without the use of theory. They are powerful, also, because they call attention to a wide variety of forces at work in the managerial system—technological forces, economic forces, sociological forces, political forces, and psychological forces. They prevent the executive from unknowingly making decisions which satisfy one goal while seriously compromising another, and from concentrating on good technological and economic subsystems (within the larger policy system) while doing damage to the human subsystems.[1] Conversely, they prevent him from concentrating on satisfying and harmonious human subsystems while doing damage to efficient technological and economic subsystems.[2] Finally, theories are valuable to the general manager in assembling, organizing, and allocating physical resources in the policy system, and in organizing and influencing the behavior of human beings in that system.

The second central thesis of this book is that theories have serious, sometimes even dangerous, limitations for managers who must make decisions in large complex policy systems of today. Stated in a reciprocal way, *judgment* or *intuition* (often referred to as "art," as opposed to "sci-

---

[1] The term "human system," as we use it, refers to any frame of reference which describes or predicts how human beings will act or behave. Thus political science and legal philosophy undertake this kind of explanation as well as sociology, psychology, and small group theory. The term "technological and economic system," as we use it, refers to the sum total of all structures and dynamic events that are of a nonhuman nature. Plants, machines, flow of goods in process, inventories of goods, money inventories, cash flows, accounting systems, formal organization structures, job descriptions, and the like, fall within the meaning of this concept.

[2] This is not meant to imply that technological systems are, or are not, ends in themselves. They satisfy human needs through production of goods and services, through provision of employment, and in some cases through provision of a psychologically secure place to "belong" in a large-scale society.

ence" of management) has a powerful place in decision making by general managers.

Any one theory, or any group of theories in a discipline, does not represent reality in the *total* policy system, and may lead the manager to suboptimize, or overemphasize, one part of the system to the exclusion of another. For example, political forces may be overlooked while economic forces are stressed, or political forces may be stressed and psychological forces minimized.

It may seem a paradox that theories seemingly have contradictory effects on the decision-making mind at the same time: they prevent unintended consequences on the one hand, but they encourage such consequences on the other. The answer to this, to be more fully explained later, hinges on how theories are used—in the degree of comprehensiveness in their use, in the open-minded entertainment of diverse views, and in the judgmental courage to pick, choose, test, and modify theory in action situations. Another limitation in the use of theories is that they often do not suggest alternatives in terms of things that are operational for the executive—in terms of things he can take hold of and change in the world of action. Though theories may be operational for the scientist in terms of his controlled and measured experiments, practicing managers react to this limitation by calling them "longhair" ideas, "up in the clouds."

A third and final thesis held by the authors is that there is such a concept as "the managerial mind," or "the policy orientation," which bridges the gap between the power of science and theory on the one hand and the limitations of theory in practice on the other. This particular orientation is characterized by—

>   —*Managerial or Policy Attitudes and Methodology.* These consist of a
>   cluster of attitudes about the nature of policy systems and policy makers,
>   and a philosophy of general management as an endeavor in life, as con-
>   trasted with scholarship (science or philosophy) or applied science.
>   —*Substantive Theory of Policy Decision and Management.* This theory is of
>   two kinds: first, recognition of the major policy issues faced by leaders in
>   policy systems which are enduring through changing times and which are
>   faced by leaders in all types of institutions (government, business, medical,
>   voluntary associations), and at varying levels of hierarchy (divisions, de-
>   partments, whole industries); and second, selected key disciplines and key
>   concepts within these disciplines which are of high relevance to the major
>   policy issues.

A tentative formulation of the first of these ideas (managerial attitudes and methodology) is presented in Chapters 1 through 3 of this book. Evidence for this concept as well as practice in its application is provided in the cases, the theoretical readings, and the case introductions. Regarding the attitudinal-methodological aspects of the managerial mind, the authors make no claim that the statements on these pages are the last word, or even that the attitudes and methodologies are in final, systematic form.

Our only claim is that this is the first time these two attributes have been presented from the viewpoint of the general manager or the policy-making executive, *his problems,* and the *goals of a policy system* instead of from the viewpoint of a scholar, his problems, and the goals of scholarly schemes of thought.

The Managerial Mind, the Scholarly Mind, and the Applied Scholarly Mind

While the following ideas will be made more explicit throughout the introductory chapters, some notion of what we mean when we say "the managerial mind" or "the policy orientation" is necessary at the very outset.

These terms should not be confused with "the scientific mind" or "the philosophical mind." In briefest terms, the scientist and philosopher are engaged in thought rather than action; in understanding the environment rather than controlling it;[3] in selecting out facts for study which meet *their* problems rather than those which meet someone else's (e.g., the general manager's). They are not as much concerned with the *time* or *costs* involved in their decision-making process. Scientists and philosophers thus share common attributes on the basis of which both can be termed, on a higher level of abstraction, *scholars.*

Neither should the terms "managerial mind" and "policy orientation," as used in this book, be confused with the ideas of "the policy orientation" as used by some authors. A "general manager" or "policy maker" is not the same as a "technologist" or "practitioner." Technologists are people who are interested first and foremost in applying concepts from some particular nonhuman-oriented disciplines (physics, engineering, certain branches of economics such as material-goods-machine structures and dynamics) to the action problems of the world.

"Practitioners," on the other hand, are interested first and foremost in applying a discipline, or group of disciplines, from "human sciences" and "human philosophy" to the action problems of the world.[4]

Applied scholars (technologists and practitioners) share one common attribute with scholars (scientists and philosophers). Their life endeavor gives them a high interest value in one body of knowledge, in some branch of theory, in a limited network of conceptual schemes. Thus they pick and choose problems, pick and choose facts to study, and bring a

---

3 With the exception of some scholars in moral and ethical philosophy.

4 For an idea of the orientation of applied social scientists, see Daniel Lerner and Harold D. Lasswell, *The Policy Sciences* (Stanford, Calif.: Stanford University Press, 1951); Warren G. Bennis, Kenneth D. Benne, and Robert Chin, *The Planning of Change* (New York: Holt, Rinehart & Winston, Inc., 1961); and Ronald Lippitt, Jean Watson, and Bruce Westley, *Planned Change* (New York: Harcourt, Brace & Co., 1958). For an excellent example of the clinical method of a practitioner, see Paul R. Lawrence, *The Changing of Organizational Behavior Patterns* (Boston: Harvard University, Graduate School of Business Administration, 1958).

bias to their final conclusions based upon the knowledge in their area of study.

But technologists and practitioners have another characteristic which distinguishes them from scientists and philosophers and which they hold in common with general managers or policy makers—they have an interest in the problems of the world. They have an interest in choosing problems for study and selecting facts for observation which leads them to *prescriptions* for action rather than, as in the case of the scientist, description and understanding of nature.

Finally, technologists and practitioners have one other attribute which separates them from policy makers and general managers. The latter begin with (1) the policy system in its totality as it exists in the buzzing confusion of the world—in an "open system," and (2) the goals of the organization. In the sense that policy makers choose problems to study which are relevant to the goals of policy systems, they close their system of thought. But in the sense that they pick and choose facts and theories, regardless from which discipline of scholarship they originate, they deal with an "open system." Technologists and practitioners start first with theories from some discipline or group of disciplines and move in the other direction. They pick problems in the total policy system which can be attacked by their disciplines and look for and deal with facts which can be fitted into theories in their area of study. In this sense, the applied scholars have a primary interest in *some* of the problems of the world. It is in this sense, too, that they deal with a system which is more "open" than the scientist's system but is more "closed" or "biased" than that of the policy maker or general executive.

This Book as a Textbook

This book has four goals. We intend it to serve (1) as a textbook in the traditional meaning of imparting knowledge; (2) as a practice laboratory in the sense of reinforcing this knowledge with meaning and providing the active experience that develops the attitudes and methodologies of the managerial mind; (3) as a research document to show how we arrived at our concept of the managerial mind; and (4) as the basis for research in further clarification of the attitudinal and methodological aspects of the managerial mind, and in beginning the accumulation of the substantive issues and underlying concepts of most relevance to policy makers and general executives.

As a textbook, Chapters 1–3 present fundamental ideas about scholarly theories, about policy making, and about the way in which these two are related in the making of policy decisions by general managers in policy systems.

Chapter 1   presents a preliminary overview of the central relationships between theory and practice of general management, sets forth the authors' beliefs about how managerial knowledge and skill are developed, and describes the symptomatic conflicts in society that have led the authors to study the relationship of theory to policy making.

Chapter 2   presents something of the nature of concepts in general, of scientific theories in the physical sciences, and of the way such theories are generated by the scientist. Inferences are drawn as to the power of science in action problems and its limitations.

Chapter 3   presents the nature of theory in social science and social philosophy, and the way such theory is generated by the minds of social scientists. Inferences are drawn as to the power and limitations of social science in total policy systems.

This Book as a Practice Laboratory

But knowledge, verbalized, written down, and read is not enough in the managerial orientation. It lacks two things. Reading words cannot convey real meaning in terms of being operational to the person who is to use the words. One can read a book on playing baseball, flying an airplane, or driving a car. But until this knowledge is reinforced—until one *understands* the *meaning* of terms by playing, flying, or driving, and attaches an emotional belief to the fact that *it* (the knowledge) *works*—knowledge is not operational in the sense of being able to use it. This is the pragmatic attitude. Meaning, and the pragmatic attitude, must be developed through practice.

A second thing that verbalized knowledge, read by the learner, lacks in being operational (usable) to the man of action, is skill. It is very difficult to jump back and forth from ideas and theory, on the one hand, to action problems and their solution, on the other—from the world of abstract thought to the world of reality in its buzzing confusion. The first time one plays golf it is difficult to apply the rules (words). One may "know the grip" but it "feels unusual"; you "know" the course the swing should follow, but it "doesn't connect." Only after practice, during which knowledge is tempered with intuition, and during which it is incorporated as habit, is the knowledge operational or useful.

Thus, a second goal of the book is the development of reinforced, meaningful, operational knowledge, modified by intuition and judgment, and the development of an ability or skill in applying it. The remainder of the book—cases, case introductions, and theory readings—is devoted to this second goal. In this part, the material is not a "textbook" in the traditional sense. It is not a body of orderly, verbalized ideas put down in printed words. It corresponds more closely to a laboratory in physics and chemistry. You can study concepts like "acceleration," which is measured by "foot-pounds per second per second," but when you repeat an experiment in the physics laboratory which records amounts of acceleration, you not only *understand* more deeply the meaning of the word symbol "acceleration" but you learn something about the rigorous methods required in the practice of science, and develop attitudes regarding the "proper" practice of science and the practice of experiments in the laboratory.

The case introductions help the student to use the theories (readings) in the practice of policy decision making, or synonymously, in the practice of general management. They ask questions which help to bridge the gap between theory and practice. The diagnostic and predictive questions refer the student to aspects of the practical problem which can be understood in terms of underlying theories from different disciplines; the policy questions refer him to action problems and practical solutions; and the major policy issues refer him to key problems of lasting importance to any manager.

This Book as a Research Document

A third goal of the book is the authors' hope that it will serve as a research document. This has nothing to do with the training or education of general managers. To anyone concerned about how we arrived at the concept of the managerial mind presented in the introductory chapters, or concerned as to whether this concept is valid or true, we say, "Try it yourself; attempt to diagnose policy problems or arrive at action solutions with theories, using our readings and questions, or choices of your own. Then judge the validity of the concept in the introductory chapters."

To those more practical minded who may question the usefulness of theory in action problems, whether in the business world or in the case method of instruction in business schools, we say, "Study the introductory chapters, go through the experience of merging theory and practice with the cases, and then judge the validity of the managerial orientation."

To those more scientifically or technologically oriented who may question the way in which theory is limited in the practice of general management, or policy making, we say, "There is no conceptual scheme or theory which can be applied directly, and without modification, to decisions regarding total policy systems. If you wish to know how we arrive at this, and other concepts of the managerial mind, take any such schemes and try them in case situations."

This Book as the Basis for Further Research

The authors believe that the conceptual scheme which is formulated in the introductory chapters is subject to much further research.

Regarding the attitudes and methodology of the policy orientation, we believe that these are set down in a form which is of value to general managers and policy makers working in the complex and rapidly changing world of the mid-twentieth century. They are preliminary, however, in the sense that they are not formulated as precisely, nor organized as systematically, as we hope that they can be in the future.

When it comes to the substantive aspects of the policy orientation, we believe that the cataloging of major policy issues—those issues faced by all policy makers and leaders in policy systems—and the selection of key underlying theories which are of most relevance to these issues is something which can only occur slowly, over many years in the future. We have not even attempted to give *systematic* or comprehensive treatment to these two substantive types of knowledge.

What the book does do is to give a nonsystematic and highly tentative treatment in these ways:

—It presents certain major policy issues faced by executives in each particular case situation. These are included as questions at the end of that case. For example, in the Mississippi Valley Equipment Corporation case, we ask: "Is there inevitable conflict between technological and economic goals in an organization, on the one hand, and human motivations, on the other?" and "Under what conditions, if any, can such conflicts be reconciled (or) minimized?"

—It catalogs five major discipline groups which bear importantly on policy problems. These can be seen as the column headings of Contents II in the form of such classifications as "Technology, Engineering, and Management Science"; "Economic Science and Philosophy"; "Sociology and Social Philosophy"; "Political Science, Legal Theory, and Management Theory"; and "Psychology, Social Psychology, and Group Dynamics."

—It selects important theories and concepts within these disciplines which are of relevance to specific cases and to groups of cases. These can be seen, cross-referenced to both case situations and to major discipline fields, in the squares of the matrix in Contents II. They also can be seen in the diagnostic and predictive questions and the connected theory readings given in each case introduction.

—These concepts, for example, range from the concept of "role conflict" (sociology) to that of "pluralism" (political philosophy), to "probability theory" and "expected utility criterion" (technology and management science), or "marginal productivity" (economics) and "functional versus structural factors in perception (social psychology). There are 152 abstracts in the book which include somewhat over 200 conceptual schemes or theories that are related to 23 case situations.

—Finally, the very last questions in each case introduction ask the advanced student to do exactly what the authors have done: to analyze cases, picking, choosing, or discarding theories from his own experience, and conceptualizing, independently and creatively, his own idea of major policy issues and the underlying theories of most relevance and importance to these issues.

The Problematic Situation

Before any person studies a problem, strains his mind to understand it, and to put it into some meaningful order, he faces something which John Dewey has called a "problematic situation." Particularly before a human being can become interested enough to do research and devote significantly large amounts of work and thought to a subject, there must be something in the environment that is "interesting" him or "bothering" him, and/or some internal desire which prompts him to engage in such work. We suspect that it is both. This is true in the case of all of the authors of all of the theoretical readings reproduced in this book, and it is also true in the case of the authors of this book.

For several reasons, it will be helpful to the reader if we can describe the problematic situation which led to conceptualization of the managerial mind in the introductory chapters, to the compiling of the case introductions, and to the writing of the "connective tissue" between theories and cases. Such an exposition will point up the importance of having a rationale for general managers and policy makers. It will also aid in understanding the underlying reasons for controversy between businessmen and scholars over what place theory occupies in the practice of policy making. Third, an exposition of our problematic situation will help in understanding the underlying reasons for controversy between different scholars in business education as to what is the "best" way to train people for positions of leadership in the world of action.

A fourth reason for describing the situation that interests and bothers the authors, and prompts this book, has some training value to the reader. In doing so, we will be illustrating one of the most significant ideas in the relationship of theory to practice; that is, that every person who develops a theory or conceptual scheme, such as the one we develop regarding the managerial mind, selects his concepts and explains the facts on the basis of his interest in the problematic situation. This is particularly true of those whose interest is in the *social* sciences and *social* philosophy. It is less true in the physical sciences in general, and it is somewhat irrelevant in the matter of astronomy—the mother of physical science. Incidentally, problematic situations do not come in orderly form, or neatly laid out in formulae and clear outlines. They are confused, often interrelated, descriptions of problems, conflicts, and the like. They have something of the "buzzing confusion" of the world even in their verbalized form on the printed page.

We will be describing the problematic situation in symptomatic terms, that is, describing surface problems which we have seen around us, and in our own endeavors. The deeper explanation of these surface problems is to be found in Chapters 2 and 3 which deal with the inherent differences in science, philosophy, applied science, and practice; and in the inherent differences in the attitudes and methodologies of scientists, philosophers, technologists, practitioners, and policy makers.

We can bring some order out of the more chaotic situations we saw and were interested in over the last several years by viewing the problematic situation according to the outline as presented in section headings. The following discussion, including the conclusions we reach about policy systems and policy decision making, is a halfway house between the world of confusion the authors originally faced and the analytical reasons for the confusion which are pointed out in Chapters 2 and 3.

Technology and Central Planning in Modern Institutions

Beginning roughly in World War II, and continuing in an accelerated fashion from 1950 to the present time, there has been a great increase in the size of organizations and in their complexity. In that war, the United States marshalled a military establishment of over twelve million men, and the technological machines and dynamic logistic movements to fight a war on a scale never before undertaken. This was supported by an industrial organization with a degree of central planning which represented greater control of the economic sector of our nation than had ever been experienced before. The planning, the allocation of inputs and outputs of the firms of the nation, and the regulation of consumer demand resulted in an *efficient* flow of goods to the civilian sector and the military sector and in the chain of production from industry to industry. In other words, the timing of flows, the quality of flows (e.g., steel, sugar, gasoline, etc.), and the quantity of flows (how many pounds of sugar, how many tons of iron ore, how much steel, how many tanks of gasoline) were synchronized in such a way that the final output—the quantity of civilian consumption and external output of national defense—was accomplished in quick enough time to win a war against another formidable opponent.

In this instance, the United States engaged in a form of central planning for the goal of technological efficiency, in contradiction to another goal of our culture, freedom of individual firms. If we should have another war, the input-output analysis which will be carried out in Washington with planning formulae, plus the hardware to process data (electronic computers), will dwarf any planning that we have heretofore witnessed. The economic society will be *managed* because that is the way to technological efficiency—achieving output of defense effort in a limited time—at least in the short run.

Whether or not such planning in detail results in greater technological and economic efficiency *in the long run* is a question open to debate. Political and economic philosophy in the Western world holds that in the long run loss of initiative and creativity under such planning will mean that it is less efficient. The invisible hand, whereby what is good for an independent firm pursuing its selfish interest is good for the gross national product *and* for the freedom of individuals, will eventually render inefficient such an industrial society, according to this economic science and economic philosophy. The industrial system of the Soviet Union might, in one respect, be viewed as a massive experiment in which there is rational planning of technology which is based on clearly defined national goals and planned in terms of subgoals for industrial segments down to the individual firm. Officials in that society suppose that a higher level of national technological efficiency will be reached, not through the invisible hand but through the highly visible hand of the planners in the central planning body (Gosplan), the area councils, industry councils, and the plant hierarchy—all aided by new devices for information processing and communication.

We see an attempt to raise the level of technological efficiency in western European countries such as France through industry-government cooperation in allocating materials, manpower, and outputs of various segments of the economy as they become inputs to other segments in the dynamic flows of goods. We even see many examples in the United States which attempt to regulate technological activities. These central plans—decisions—take many forms. The report of the President's Commission on the National Goals is an attempt to think through and put down in rational form a set of balanced goals—both technological and human goals —in the hope that decisions made by semiautonomous executives in suborganizations in society will be more nearly coordinated. Many of the growing number of governmental laws and regulations relative to industrial organizations are attempts to influence the flow of goods, the movement of workers, the wages of labor, the income of corporations, or similar matters. They tend toward central planning in the case of the freedom allowed to merge corporations into horizontally or vertically integrated companies, or the formal approval by such bodies as the Federal Reserve Board and the Interstate Commerce Commission to merge banks, railroads, and airlines. In other instances, they move toward central planning at the government level, but against central planning at the corporate level—trustbusting larger units which result in divesting of certain operations.

Between units in our semifree technological society, we see evidence of increasing complexity and of increasing degrees of central planning. All government contracts, for example, specify that prime contractors use Program Evaluation and Review Technique (PERT) to link together sometimes as many as a thousand separate contracting companies into a flow diagram of jobs to be accomplished (subobjectives), the time of completion of each job, the time it takes to do the job, and the quality and quantity of resources needed for each job. Each separate firm then takes its part in the overall plan and breaks this down into more detailed PERT diagrams within divisions, departments, sections, and down to individual production lines. The resulting complex total plan may contain hundreds of thousands of technological events, specifying the quantity, quality, and timing of inputs and outputs.

At the individual firm level, central planning is not new. Traditionally, the internal operation of an individual firm has not been viewed as a social democracy by practical men or by scholars, even in the United States. The free enterprise economists, stressing autonomy and freedom, were addressing themselves to freedom of the owners and managers of firms, not freedom of employees to elect their bosses, determine production runs, and the like. In fact, the economist's value of freedom disappeared in the micro or firm side of the analysis (as contrasted with the macro or social level). The executive was viewed as an expert rational planner who allocated resources and planned production runs, acting as a rational computer of supply, demand, marginal costs, marginal revenues, and then gave orders to execute these centrally and expertly reasoned decisions.

In more recent years, the traditional view of the firm has been challenged by several forces, each explained by readings in this volume. Behavioral scientists have suggested that the firm *ought* to be viewed as a social system where workers *do* determine production runs. Labor unions have worked out customs whereby pluralistic decision making, jointly practiced by labor and management, *are* a fact of reality. Some businessmen stress *de*centralization as a political alternative to central planning.

In spite of these views, with the advent of more and more technological specialists, the United States in the second half of the twentieth century has witnessed acceleration of the trend to central planning *inside* corporations. The crude functional planners in Frederick Taylor's steel mill have been supplanted by operations researchers, market researchers, applied psychologists, computer programmers, organization analysts, research and development administrators, labor experts, or executive compensation specialists; or, and this is the epitome of rational planning, people who are given the full-time job of long-range planning at divisional levels or company levels.

To cope with the enormous complexity of operations, there is a distinct trend toward the establishment of specialists whose full-time day is spent in long-range planning, in drawing up the *substance* of plans, utilizing expertise and skill in the *methodology* of such planning.[5]

Each of these specializations, resulting in the establishment of a staff department at some organizational level, at the top or in the middle echelons of a company represents a trend toward central planning at that level. The movement toward decentralization in American companies has not stopped the trend toward central planning, in our opinion, for more than one reason. First, the march toward more and more specialization is not stopped. The specialists are lodged in another echelon of the organization which itself becomes a centrally planned unit and is by the act of decentralization enabled to grow much larger in terms of size and complexity. Second, we have observed a move to re-centralization in most of the large companies which had moved to decentralization in the mid-fifties. These companies apparently judge that the gradual addition of new staff departments at the top level of the company is a technological necessity.[6]

Underlying all of these tendencies toward centralization—whether at

---

[5] See Charles E. Summer, Jr., "The Future Role of the Corporate Planner," *California Management Review*, Winter 1961.

[6] *Idem.*

the level of national society, or at the level of interindustry groups, or at the level of internal firm operations—are several powerful factors. The increasing size, complexity, and interdependence of subparts of policy systems, facilitated by developments in science, technology, and rapid communication devices which represent part of the scientific explosion since World War II, is probably the most important factor.

The necessity for rapid change of the whole complex structures in the face of outside forces (political forces such as the U.S.S.R. and technological forces such as scientific discovery) is another important cause for the trend to centralization. It implies speed of change, which in turn implies the use of authority or power. Evidence of this cause is the willingness of the United States to plan and manage the economy through political power in Washington, when the goal of technological efficiency in national defense superseded the ideology of freedom.

A third cause, interconnected with the other two, is the rigidity and difficulty of quick change in large bureaucratic and technologically rigid structures. In the American Telephone and Telegraph Company, for example, the process of changing from the letter exchange code dialing system to an all-number code involved changing literally hundreds of thousands of pieces of technological equipment, as well as in changing the behavior and habits of thousands of people inside the company and outside (customers). This particular process of change in a technological-social pattern is now in its sixth year, and will be completed only after the elapse of more than ten years from the time of the inception of the idea to the time when the change will have been accomplished.

These trends, and the factors which produce them, are in evidence in many of the cases in this book. At the highest level, the case on the defense of Queymoy and Matsu illustrates the paradox of centralized decision making in a world populated by experts on weapons systems, military science, and political science in which speedy decision by general executives in Washington was deemed a necessity. The attention given by governments in Washington and London to the acquisition of Ford of England by Ford of Detroit is an example of the rational planning these two governments were willing to undertake to coordinate the production (technological) and financial (economic) systems between, and within, nations.

At the industry level, the Lincoln Rochester case illustrates the clash of technological and economic forces tending toward centralized planning of formerly (legally) independent banks, against psychological and political forces tending toward maintenance of legally independent decentralized banks.[7]

Virtually every case in the book dealing with internal operations of a

---

[7] The question here is legal or political independence. The banks are technologically and communicationally *interdependent,* whether we "like" it or not.

company illustrates the same tendencies toward central planning, caused by technological and economic forces, and the dilemma of such planning, presented by psychological, sociological, and ideological forces. The problem exists at top company levels (e.g., in the Continental Electric Company problem of centralization-decentralization). It exists at middle management levels (e.g., in the Kansas City branch of the Mississippi Valley Equipment Corporation). And it exists at the lowest levels (e.g., the typing pool within one plant of the multiplant General American Steel Company).

In summary, there are powerful forces of technology and economics which result in a tendency to central planning in our society. These forces are in part created, and accentuated, by increasing size and complexity of our sociotechnological institutions. They seem to operate at the national social level (one policy system) as well as at suborganizational levels within that larger system: at the level of industries, at the level of firms, at intermediate middle-level departments, and at the lowest, small work group, level. Given such a tendency, and given the increasing availability of science and theory to understand and cope with (make policy decisions for) our complex environment, the authors began to wonder about the extent to which science and theory really are useful in policy decisions, the extent to which their use is limited or dangerous, and about some of the things general managers ought to know regarding *how* to use them. The latter, we thought, would result in some approximation to a methodology for decision making by general executives in complex policy systems.

Technological and Sociological Concentration (Interdependence)

Closely allied to the problems of size and complexity in today's institutions is a phenomenon which can be called interdependence, mutual dependence, reciprocal dependence, or, in a particular sense, concentration.

In its most traditional sense, the term "concentration" implies closeness in space, as in the concentration of population. The term is also used in phrases such as "concentration of power in Washington." In this latter usage, the term does not mean that the people of Iowa or the commercial bank in Louisiana are any closer in geographic space to the Department of Agriculture or the Federal Reserve headquarters. One attribute that population and power concentration have in common is the fact that the relationships *between* people, or *between* banks across the nation, occur in greater frequency or duration (time concentration), or increasing uniformity in quality (quality concentration). For example, the Federal Reserve Bank of Atlanta or the Federal Reserve Board in Washington have communications with the Whitney National Bank in New Orleans more frequently than ever before regarding actions carried out by both units. These are informational or communicational attributes of concentration.

On the other hand, there appears to be increasing concentration or interdependence in technological (physical) phenomena. The frequency of cash flows, for example, is increasing between Atlanta and New Orleans, and the frequency of technological work flow such as accounting entries is increasing. These impersonal work interconnections may also be expected to be carried out by human beings, or they may be carried out by teletype machines and electronic communications devices which connect bookkeeping machines or electronic computers. Thus the time concentration, in the form of frequency and duration of technological contact, appears to be increasing, and it is facilitated by advance in the sciences of physical work flow, in the sciences of decision-making machines, and in the sciences of communications devices to connect the decision points.

As will be seen in many of the cases in this book, quality concentration (interdependence) is also increasing. For example, the national government has seen fit to establish across the nation a minimum wage law which has been gradually extended first to manufacturing and then to commercial (retail store) enterprises; or, as a second example, the Civil Aeronautics Board has determined that only aircraft of a certain quality are licensed for flying anywhere in the nation. In these instances, it is not the timing but the quality of technological phenomena which appears to be concentrated into a pattern of uniformity.

In the internal affairs of a company, as opposed to the national economy, the increasing sociological and technological interdependence is apparent on many dimensions. We see technological information such as orders for goods being summarized or processed inside one human brain or computer and the output of summaries fed to other human brains or computers which then perform internal computations and summarize the output as a complex of schedules for manufacturing plants, for the purchase of raw materials, and so on. We find that in any given organization unit, the number of operating personnel or staff specialists which must be consulted, or who contribute facts, in any given decision is increasing. This appears to be true even in companies which operate on a so-called decentralized basis—both within the divisions of the company and between the various divisions and the central headquarters. In a decision as to whether or not to introduce a new product, for example, both the timing and the quality of actions within a company must occur in great detail so that all facets of the program—market research, advertising, packaging, product characteristics research, cash flows, production line design, machine operations, patent and legal characteristics, unit costs, and a host of other details, right down to the artist who must make a silk screen from which to print different colors and designs on the label —must coordinate in timing of outputs from one job to the next, and in the quality of output from one job to the next, and in the spatial delivery of outputs from one physical location to another.

The enormous concentration or interdependence of such sociotechnological systems is beyond the comprehension of the human mind. Perhaps the PERT diagrams, referred to above, come closest to depicting such systems, since they include more events and interrelated activities than most simulation models drawn up by systems theorists. The sum total of all paper-work systems, policy manuals, job description manuals, and budgetary plans (showing manpower and materials and dollar derivatives of these) in any one company, though never collected in any one place for the entire system from top to bottom, would give some indication of this concentration or structure of interdependence. All of these devices show either timing relationships between inputs-outputs, or quality relationships between inputs-outputs, or spatial locations between which the dynamic process flows.

Bear in mind that we are not talking about increasing complexity in the sense of multiplication of the technological and human *parts* of a system. We are talking about complexity of interdependence *between* parts—not the "plugs and bulbs" but the "wires."

At the very lowest level, that of the face-to-face work group, the same increasing concentration is noted. Suppose we have a group of three people in a small department where one person types offset stencils, a second runs these on an offset press, and a third proofreads and binds documents. The timing of both technological and informational interconnections may be increased by the addition of faster electric typewriters, or by addition of faster press or mimeograph machines. In this case changes in science and technology (different machines) generated the greater frequency of interaction or, viewed in another way, the technological concentration of the system. A new type of printed form, or greater diversity of printed forms required by customers (outside the company or outside the group but inside the legal organization by other departments), or a more frequent change in forms could lead to more interactions between the three people who must work together to change the whole system (final output). If enough of this kind of speed of change is required in the environment (by customers) across many industries, this, too, might stimulate increased development of faster machines, thus more time interdependence when the machines are developed. In this case, the root cause was generated by a practical problem first (more work faster), whereas in the previous case it was generated by science and technology (someone creates a new machine).

This kind of interdependence was visualized by Max Weber, the sociologist, when he saw that his bureaucracy must be rationally connected by procedures, paper work, work rule uniformities, and the like. It was seen by the economists who stressed the complexities of "roundabout production." It is seen much more clearly, in greatly increased complexity and concentration, by the automation engineers, PERT analysts, capital budgeting experts, and job-description writers of today, and by systems analysts in the concept of suboptimization.

Complexity and Unintended Consequences

Faced with increasing complexity in the form of different specializations, with concentration-interdependence whereby everything in social dynamics and the technological dynamics seems to depend partly on everything else, with increasing size of institutions, and with an apparent tendency to central planning in practice, the authors reasoned to other points. The central planning is done by general managers who legitimize or approve recommendations and information contributions of many specialists in and outside the company. These plans, or policy decisions, are themselves becoming more complex. Unless the manager[8] has some acquaintance with the vast array of forces at work in the policy system, which theories can provide, plus some attitudes about or skill in the difficult task of *applying* these theories (jumping back and forth from theory to practice), it is likely that he will face unintended consequences after the decision is made.

The theory of unanticipated consequences arose in the behavioral sciences. It implies that the executive who looks only (or more closely) at technological, political, and economic goals of his organization is likely to find that there are some human forces at work which he overlooked and which have consequences such that his original goals are, in effect, not reached. They may be sabotaged, for example, by a hostile group or a labor union. Decisions made and passed on may cause human beings to do something that the executive wants, but also to do something that he doesn't want. In many of the cases in this book this will be seen to be true—in the operating affairs inside a company or in the governing of the affairs in a nation. In the department store case (White House), for example, the federal government passed a minimum wage law. In doing this, it hoped to raise the standard of living of workers. It did not intend, however, that the law would cause a number of workers to be dismissed from their jobs altogether, which is exactly what happened.

There is, however, another side to the theory of unanticipated consequences which has received little attention and which bothered the authors. As we studied the theories of the behavioral sciences and then tried to relate them to case situations and to our experience in the business world, we found that many of the things which behavioral scientists imply strongly to executives, *in themselves* would result in unanticipated and

---

8 This book is addressed to general managers who perform decision functions. Some may be heavily involved in gathering facts and reasoning; some may be involved only in putting the stamp of approval on decisions made by teamwork of a number of specialists. In either of these two cases, our conclusion is the same. This book is also addressed to a third kind of manager—the specialist who forms part of the influential leadership group. In short, at any given organizational level, there is a group of decision makers (the relatively few) whose mental efforts influence the relatively many. Political science has referred to such a system as an oligarchy. Sociology refers to the smaller group as the influentials or simply as the leaders. Management theory refers to them as executives or managers.

(to the executive) harmful consequences in terms of the executive's economic and technological goals. Any one conceptual scheme from social psychology, it seemed (including, for example, democratic leadership as implied executive behavior), might have serious unanticipated technological or economic consequences for the survival and growth of the organization, depending on the individual departmental, company, or national situation. It also seemed from our study of theories of small group dynamics or from our actual participation in training groups that the technological or economic variables (e.g., time) were ignored. Furthermore, various aspects of technological and economic efficiency may be adversely affected to a serious degree if one attempted to operate on such theories in large complex organizations. In this sense, the behavioral scientist is as apt to be a victim of unanticipated consequences as is the executive, the engineer, or the economist.

The Law of Subdisciplinization

When writing articles or books for the businessman market, it is highly probable that technologists and social scientists will imply certain courses of action which should be taken in view of the types of more basic phenomena they study. The psychologist will imply that, though there are other important factors, human needs and motivations are most important, and therefore that such alternative decisions as participative leadership or job enlargement are the things that any intelligent businessman will seek. The political theorist will imply that, though there are other factors involved, law and order, based on what the "reasonable man" will see, obviously means that the intelligent businessman will seek a workable authority delegation system. The operations researcher, while including other important factors as assumptions or constraints on his model, gives the impression that the intelligent businessman will optimize the technological flows in his plant location or inventory system, "if other factors don't prevent this."

This kind of impression, conveyed by so-called "pure" scientists, and to a lesser but nevertheless important extent by technologists in the physical realm and practitioners in the social realm, is a phenomenon that can be called "subdisciplinization." These individuals need not necessarily become company employees, or do consulting work, or even leave the university, though each of these degrees of involvement determines how conscious and explicit they will be about the "other things" in a policy decision-making situation. In the social sciences, where values are more likely to enter scientific theory and where social science frequently merges into social philosophy, scholars frequently develop highly complex and "factual" theories, where subdisciplinization is likely to be hidden in assumptions. This will be more clearly understood and illustrated in Chapter 3.

We are not saying that this is right or wrong, good or bad. It simply exists. It is a natural thing for people who become highly interested in one view of part of the world to exaggerate the influence of this view in the total scheme of things. Read, for example, the introductions to books explaining such divergent theories as those dealing with human groups, industrial dynamics and cybernetics, capital budgeting, or management principles.

This is simply one of the outcomes of the phenomena of specialization. It is more particular than the generic term "trained incapacity" in that we are relating it to (1) the failure of scholars to be fully aware of, or clearly explicit about, the unintended consequences if executives follow their implications; and (2) those specialists in science, technology, or practice who imply to the leadership group in companies, either explicitly or implicitly, that one set of forces in the company is so important that the executive's time, attention, or analytical power should be devoted to these in great detail, in making decisions, where time is scarce in making the decision.

Reactions of Executives and Theorists

Another factor in the problematic situation which seemed important was the feelings of two parties who, by all counts, should work together a great deal for the mutual benefit of both. Executives, both in our work contacts with them and in the Columbia Executive Program at Arden House, express feelings ranging from admiration for the application of science, to suspicion of the actual results, to a feeling of threat that the "buzz boys will take over." We see this too, for example, in feelings of company executives toward some business school graduates when they enter employment; or, when we read in the newspapers that officials in the Defense Department have these same feelings about the greatly accelerated rate with which planners, systems men, and a wide variety of specialists, using techniques of powerful analysis, are being given decision-making responsibility.

On the other side of the fence, it is not uncommon to find people from various disciplines in science—technologists who engineer physical science or practitioners who apply social science—who are ambiguous in their feelings toward policy systems and executives who manage them. These range from the feeling that, somehow, executives can't understand the truth and importance attached to their theories, to a feeling of admiration for an executive who has the personality and physical stamina to make complex and definite decisions in the face of ambiguity. As above, there is sometimes the feeling that "uninformed people will take over" (the reverse of the feeling that buzz boys will take over).

In both cases, there is the implicit threat to the individual that the other person has something which will depreciate the life work and product of his endeavors. Consciously or unconsciously, the specialist in theory knows that there is no policy system, no real world problem or situation, in which a given theory will work. To that extent, a policy decision is threatening. Consciously or unconsciously, the executive knows that there are many things in the complex problem he faces that he may not see or understand, and that the theories may point up something that he is not knowledgeable about. To this extent, a conceptual scheme is threatening.

It has become a cliché to say that much of science has grown out of technology, and that it is in trying to solve the problems of the world that some of our most important discoveries (theories) are made, and further, that scholars can therefore reap benefit by studying policy problems and communicating with policy makers. It is also a cliché to say that many of our machines and social systems of today could never have been constructed if some scholar had not generated some theory which allowed such structures. The power of science in controlling nature, as well as the power of ideas in shaping nations and companies, is great.

We conclude that, in view of the need for interchange between ideas and people, and in view of the feelings on both sides which inhibit interchange, something might be done to adjust the latter. Thus, (1) in Chapters 1–3, we put into words some of the causes of such feelings, and (2) in the remainder of the book, we provide practice in the difficult task of using theory in the light of both its advantages and disadvantages.

"Responsibility" of the Executive

In recent years, there has been much talk to the effect that business executives either *do, don't, or should* have something which is loosely referred to as "responsibility." Many writers have addressed themselves to the thesis that executives today are responsible, while many have argued that they are not. Others have tried explicitly to say what this responsibility is: some say business executives are (should be) responsible for profits, and that everything else will fall in line; still others have expressed they are not (should not be) responsible for profits, in the absolute sense, but that they are responsible for the production of other values in society. One group holds that the philosophy of equilibrium (the invisible hand) does not work in today's complex society, nor does the philosophy of human-technological integration work inside a company. To this group, what's good for the nation is not necessarily good for General Motors (and vice versa); what's good for the company is not necessarily good for a department or subgroup (and vice versa); and what's good for the group is not necessarily what's good for the individual person (and vice versa).

Finally, another group of writers have attempted to say what the businessman owes to different groups, implying a balance or compromise between the stockholders, department heads, individual employees, suppliers, customers, and so on.

The readings in this book, we believe, are balanced in terms of presenting various points of view on this subject. In this sense, one can examine the meaning of various conceptual schemes, from the "scientific" analysis of equilibrium economics and psychology to the "philosophical" conceptual schemes of political philosophy.

Confronted with this great interest in current society on the subject of "responsibility," we wondered why the interest developed, why there should be so much talk about it. We concluded that it is partly due to the increasing size and complexity of policy systems. In smaller systems, with few human beings, and with less complex machines, the problem of balancing the needs for technological efficiency and the needs of human subparts or organizations was less formidable. Not only could the leaders in small organizations see what was going on and have time, through personal observation of facts and communication with people, to make decisions or react with enlightened wisdom, but the organizations themselves were more flexible. The lesser rigidity of technological and social systems, due to size, enabled the "long run" to be a relatively short period of time. In this way, the theories of equilibrium tended to work in practice: what was good for any part of the organization did, through the process of correction by common sense, human feeling, and wisdom, correspond roughly to the good of the whole organization, and vice versa.

In our own value system, we believe that a human being will more nearly "be responsible"—acting on his own moral and ethical values, in accordance with those values developed by his culture—if he can "be informed." He will see what is going on in the system, both in terms of human needs and in terms of the technological constructs in society, if he can comprehend what is happening. He will act responsibly if he can predict what effects his policy decisions will have "out there in the world," on other people, other groups, and on the technological systems which societies have set up in the world as institutions for the service of man.

Here is where the power of theory and conceptual schemes comes into the more value-laden *feeling* of responsibility which lies within the individual executive. We shall see that theories are the result of scholars exerting enormous amounts of time, human effort, and creativity in order to see the fundamental forces operating in nature which are not seen by other people who do not have the time, the effort, or the interest in that *particular* phenomenon. Furthermore, the theories do something which is vital in a world as enormously complex as our world is today. They produce *abstractions,* in that they simplify and reduce the world to manageable ideas which the human mind can handle. They report on *regularities,* or patterns of events over time, so that much decision-making time is saved by not dealing with masses of events and detail. In a particular sense, then, one who can apply theories to policy decisions is more informed, and therefore more responsible, in a world of increasing complexity: (1) he utilizes the congealed experience from other brains, and

(2) he receives this in a form which comprehends the complexity in generalized bundles—in concepts and abstraction, and in predictable regularity. These ideas will be developed more explicitly in the following chapters.

There is another side of responsibility which must be emphasized with equal weight in comparison with our first value of keeping informed. "Informed," as used above, implies the study of, and an ability to apply, the rational conceptual schemes developed by the minds (logic) and experiments (experiences) of the social sciences, industrial engineering, and operations research. In addition, we believe that there are two other responsibilities which fall on the executive of today. One has to do with reasonableness and rationality in that part of the policy system that cannot be reduced to regularity and prediction. Working with the cases in this book, or in actual policy problems, one sees constantly that *irregularity,* or what in the next chapter Langmuir calls "divergent phenomena," is a matter which the executive must face with courage, and with a willingness to attack ambiguous problems. He must be willing to think deeply about these problems, put subjective weights on alternative solutions, and otherwise cope with the factors in a problem that cannot be put precisely into words or reduced to quantitative measurement. A second interconnected responsibility of the businessman is to deal with the fact in policy problems that rationality is not the only cause of human behavior. Feelings, sentiments, and nonrational responses are part of the executive's own behavior, as well as that of those around him (including the behavior of theorists, logicians, specialists of various kinds, and scientists). We believe that an understanding of the limitations of science and theory, and a deeper understanding which is associated with practice in relating these to policy problems, particularly in group discussion, generates these two kinds of responsibilities.

What about the more substantive attitudes of morality represented by religious and moral philosophies? So far, we have taken a position of intellectual morality about the way the executive should use his mind in the solution of problems. In regard to the former, the authors have their own convictions regarding individual human morality and regarding the kind of social structures which man creates that in turn can be judged as good or bad. However, we have not dealt with these value positions in any way except, perhaps, that they influence to some degree the selection of theoretical readings and the values of the theorists who developed the theories. We doubt that preaching a philosophy, at least in the brief pages of this book, can have any real impact on the behavior of most readers. In this belief we have been influenced by the seemingly lifeless (in terms of changing anyone's behavior, as opposed to talking) nature of speeches which say that management has a responsibility to the community, to stockholders, to employees, and the like. What the cases in this book do, in many instances, is to show precisely this problem: that people often verbalize noble ideals, but their actions tell a different story.

For example, insofar as there is a discrepancy between one's *ideas* about democracy and anyone's *actions* which jeopardize democratic institutions, case practice brings to a conscious level the problem and helps one to clarify just what one's ideals are.

What This Book Will Not Do

As a final note to this first chapter, we need to be clear about certain limitations to the present book. The attempted merger of theory and practice involves certain costs.

First, we do not believe that study of the abstracts of theoretical readings, even though in the author's original words, is a substitute for studying more deeply and comprehensively the theories of social science and technology. The study in depth of economics, operations research, financial accounting, psychology, organization theory, and many other areas of inquiry, is a valuable thing in the world of today. Abstracts frequently cannot give the total context, or complete understanding, of the author's conceptual scheme. This does not mean, we hasten to say, that such abstracts, and practice in using them, is not valuable. One cannot be a philosopher king, nor can he or should he know everything about everything. On the other hand, it is intended that the student draw on his entire educational experience, which hopefully has been developed in considerably more power and detail than is presented in the readings in this book. Certain of the questions in case introductions are phrased to encourage this.

A second price we pay is the fact that study of theories does, in one sense, stifle the creativity and initiative of the problem solver. Just as the advocates of John Dewey's progressive education argue that injection of too much arithmetic and too little playing with clay in the first grade inhibits the growth of children, certain advocates of the pure nondirective case method have argued that injection of theories in case problems interferes with a learner's hard drive, tough thinking, and creative analysis and solution of problems. That there is truth in this viewpoint cannot be denied. Perhaps in answer we can say only what we have already said in regard to the complexity of modern institutions, and add the comment that this is the age of Sputnik and the Soviet Union, not the age of the power loom and Victorian England.

2. CONCEPTUAL SCHEMES AND SCIENCE

In this chapter we will examine the nature of concepts, of scientific conceptual schemes or theories, and something of the nature of how these are generated by the minds of scientists. By doing this, we set the stage for understanding their power as an aid to men of action—policy makers and general executives—and for understanding their limitations in the control of policy systems.

Concepts and Abstraction

A concept is an invention of the mind, a product of the imagination, which enables human beings to make sense out of the world about them. Around us at all times, in our environment, are thousands of objects and dynamic events which give stimulus to the sense organs—eyes, ears, nose, touch—in profusion. After infancy, the human being would be helpless to cope with these unless he has some means of cataloging them into terms that have meaning in dealing with day-to-day problems.

Some of these are cataloged as "good" or "bad," as to whether they satisfy or penalize a person's basic desires. These are normative or value concepts, and we label them "attitudes" or "values." Others are relatively neutral in emotional value; they simply *are*. These are descriptive concepts.

As I sit in my office, I see an object with four legs, two arms, and an upright back and I catalogue this as a "chair." The semantic symbol "chair" does not need to be spoken, since I cannot think without conceptualizing and without the power of word symbols. Somewhere along the line in our cultural development, the symbol "chair" was *conceptualized* to denote the particular constellation of characteristics of legs, back, and arms. The process which the human mind uses to conceptualize the enormous complexity of the world into ideas is known as the process of abstraction.

But the chair in my office is really a particular object—it is not exactly like any other chair in the world. It may have a solid back or a cane back. It may have a round seat or square seat. It may have round legs or square legs, or it may even have a big scratch on the back whereas the chair across the hall is new and unblemished. These are particular character-

25

istics, rather than general characteristics, similar to what scientists refer to as divergent phenomena. The point to be made here is that, in the process of abstraction, we select certain abstract characteristics, divorced from the total reality of hard cold facts in the world. Only in this way can we make sense out of the buzzing confusion around us. Thus, legs plus arms plus back equals chair—three abstract characteristics are cataloged into a larger concept or idea. The pigeon-hole system in the mind eliminates irrelevant details if we simply want something to sit upon and do not want other attributes. Notice that the concepts we select for thinking depend on what our problem is.

This process of abstraction can proceed to higher and higher levels of abstract concepts. I have another concept in my mind labeled "table," another labeled "bookcase," another labeled "file cabinet." If my purpose is to construct a new "building" for the business school, I know that one of the things I will have to direct my attention to is "furniture," a concept which abstracts on another characteristic or dimension. This concept eliminates, for purposes of this specific decision, the difference between divergent furniture objects (bookcases don't have arms) because the myriad of details are not relevant to certain decisions, and because one would literally go crazy if every detail in the environment were to be entertained in the mind in every thought or decision.

When we face problems of achieving our goals and subgoals in life, of building buildings, going to work in public transportation, furnishing houses, managing business corporations, deciding on what to have for dinner, getting tired of standing upright, we pick and choose concepts which are useful in understanding the world (analysis), in predicting what will happen "out there" (prediction), and what we might do to get what we want (control). Concepts are therefore powerful mechanisms for thought and action.

Value (attitudinal) abstraction is even more powerful to us in these three respects. We learn that "fire" is "bad" for sticking hands in, but "good" for cooking. We do not have to make decisions over and over about what to do around, or with, fire because we have built in policies (values and attitudes) in the mind which enable us to react (1) in quick time, and (2) without cluttering our minds with new decisions and facts every time we face similar situations.

Finally, concepts have one other very powerful use to society and to individuals. Semantic symbols or concepts not only aid the individual person to think, predict, and in some measure control things around him; they also enable one human being to pass on *experience, learned* from prior actions, to other human beings. You may have never been bitten by a "snake," but somewhere along the line someone either told you what a snake it (described it in terms of abstract characteristics such as "long" and "round"), pointed one out to you, or showed you a picture. They then gave you a predictive statement: snakes bite; their bites cause sickness or death.

In the conceptual or semantic sense, then, concepts enable cultures to develop. They enable people to control others' behavior; they enable one person to learn and get help from the congealed experience of someone else.

Value (attitudinal) concepts, in fact, are one of the primary ways in which societies control the behavior of divergent individuals and groups. In certain societies, for example, alcoholic beverages are "bad," and this is conveyed through families to children. This is a form of "conscience control." Social pressures, and social penalties, or even the formal codification of value concepts into prohibition laws, are added means of control. But even these could not exist without the existence of concepts and the power of abstraction.

Theory and Conceptual Schemes

So far, we have used the term "concept" to denote any meaningful idea which exists in the mind and which *partially* (in the sense of selecting certain abstract characteristics) describes reality—what is "out there" in the world.

A theory is a form of conceptualization in that it (1) is more precise than the garden variety of ideas generated by common sense, (2) it was arrived at by a process of thought which is more rigorous than common sense and day-to-day action, and (3) it therefore is more likely to describe what is reality and what will happen "out there."

Let us look for a moment at the second of these. For our purposes, theories can be classified in two ways, depending on (*a*) whether they were developed for the purpose of understanding nature versus controlling nature, or (*b*) whether they were arrived at with the aid of observation or experiment[1] or with the aid of logic and reason alone. The first of these dimensions separates scientific and philosophical theories on the one hand from technological theories on the other. The second dimension separates scientific theories from philosophical theories.

Physical Science and Physical Scientists

Scientific theory is one form of conceptualization which is aimed primarily at understanding the operation of nature, not in controlling nature. This has very important implications for policy makers because many of the ideas generated by scientists either seemingly are beyond

---

[1] The phrase "with the aid of" is very important. Later discussion will show that in many scientific theories, particularly in the social sciences, the theories are not generated *by* observation and experiment alone. The scientist's values, needs, and subjective preconditioning leads him to "speculate" or to "imagine" an hypothesis, the hypothesis being a concept which exists in the mind, not solely in the facts.

the control of the policy maker at the time of his decision, or because they actually are beyond his control (regardless of timing), or because they are irrelevant to his problems and goals.

Additionally, scientific theories are arrived at in a very special way: through observation (or experiment), by the imagination of a hypothesis which explains why things happen, and then by a testing of that hypothesis.

In the science of astronomy, many years of patient observation of "planets" (note that someone distinguished these from "stars") enabled astronomers to speculate that a planet's orbit was determined by several forces, one of which is the "gravitational force" of other planets (in addition to the gravitational force of the sun). Another factor is the size and mass of both the planet under study and the size and mass of the other heavenly bodies within the field of influence or force of the planet under study.

The following record of the observations and hypotheses that led to the discovery of Neptune serves as an example to show (1) how the scientist, with great concentration of time and effort, is able to come up with understandings of nature which laymen could not attain through common sense; (2) how *measurement* enables the scientist to prove the truth of his hypotheses; and (3) how great amounts of creative imagination, as well as brute facts and observations, are involved in the development of a theory.[2]

1820   The first attempt to chart and predict the motions of the three outer planets (Uranus, Saturn, Jupiter) was developed by the French mathematician Laplace in the *Mechanique Celeste*. This theory, based on the mutual perturbations of these planets, was used by Bovard of Paris to construct highly accurate tables of their past and predicted future positions. Jupiter and Saturn moved very satisfactorily according to prediction, but the observations of Uranus showed it to move well outside the tolerable limits of error of the predictions. The outstanding difference noted between the prediction and the observation was one minute of arc (one minute equals one sixtieth of a degree which equals about one one-hundred-eightieth of the sky).

In the light of these circumstances, mathematicians and astronomers of the time approached the problem in two different ways. First they tried to make a generality of all observations of Uranus and thus render the tables of prediction clearly erroneous. Secondly, they tried discarding all older observations, using only the most recent ones. A few years of observation showed that both these methods were inadequate to describe the deviations of Uranus from any predicted path. Past history and fact was of no avail. The question was put forth that perhaps the mass of Saturn had been miscalculated: a rapid calculation showed that the mass necessary to create the noted deviations of Uranus would have to be so enormous as to be impossible.

1834   An English amateur astronomer offered the solution to the problem of an ultra-Uranian planet beyond the orbit of Uranus. He offered to search for it in a general sort of way if the Royal Academy would supply estimates of its

---

[2] From B. A. Gould, *Report to the Smithsonian Institution on the History of the Discovery of Neptune* (Washington, D.C.: Smithsonian Institution, 1850), *passim*.

position. Sir George Airy, the respondent to this letter, doubted that the deviations were caused by such a planet, believing firmly that the deviations were caused by miscalculation of Uranus' orbit. His main support of this thesis was a calculation he presented showing the size of Uranus to be in error as well as its heliocentric longitude. Nothing was done.

1843   The Royal Society of Science in Gottingen (Germany) offered a prize of fifty ducats to whomever would offer the best solution to the problem of Uranus' orbit.

The question having now exhausted all known proofs, combined with the incentives of the prize money, it remained for an astute mathematician to work upon the only remaining hypothesis: that of the ultra-Uranian planet. In England, J. C. Adams undertook such work, and within several years was able to prove that the deviations could be fairly well represented by the gravitational effects of an unknown planet of which he then calculated the motion and orbital elements. The planet he described from his derivations is only one and a half degrees in error from the actual position of the heliocentric longitude as it is now known, and only one-half degree in error from the position along the ecliptic.

But Airy, in replying to all this information presented to him by Adams, merely inquired if the assumed perturbation would also explain the error of the radius vector of Uranus. Adams, incensed, made no reply.

Meanwhile, in France, the mathematician Leverrier had drawn the same conclusion as Adams. His investigations were more thorough, though, in that he proved by scientific demonstration and logical deduction that there was no known admissible solution to the problem except that of an ultra-Uranian planet.

1846   At this point, both groups began searching the skies for the new planet. Airy, being convinced that it might be possible, set an assistant to sweeping the sky in the neighborhood of the area predicted by Adams. The plan required the comparison of two sweeps, of all stars noted down to the sixth magnitude, in order that the new planet might be detected by its motion. Nothing was found, after this had been carried out.

On August 31, 1846, Leverrier wrote to the Berlin Observatory that now-famous letter stating that if they would but train their telescopes on a certain point in the sky, comparing their results over several nights, they would discover the presence of a new planet. By chance the proper chart for comparison had just been completed; the new planet was discovered two evenings later as an eight-magnitude body whose movements could be shown. The existence of the new planet was thus established.

In the above example, note how the scientists involved could not possibly have imagined the hypothesis that Neptune was out there without the concepts of "size," "mass," "heliocentric longitude," and "gravitational effects." These concepts of the mind had already been arrived at through generations of other scientists devoting all of their time, all of their energies, and all of their intellectual and creative power to the understanding of celestial movements. This was an example of deductive thinking, or reasoning from certain concepts (force, mass), to prove facts that were not known. It is the opposite of inductive thinking, or the mental process that produced the original theory of force and mass as determinants of planets' orbits. This theory, and these concepts, were formulated from observation of the facts. It is in this sense that science, being the result of efforts of many people, with different mental powers[3] than laymen, have much to offer to the latter in the solution of everyday problems.

Notice also that to the policy maker in the mid-twentieth century, there is not much usefulness in knowing that Neptune is there. Neither the President of the United States nor the Chairman of the Communist Central Committee of the U.S.S.R. is going to change its orbit. But the conceptual scheme of "mass," "size," "heliocentric longitude," and "gravitational effect"—the theory of cause and effect—is very much a policy matter. Laplace, charting Jupiter in 1820, probably did not think that President James Monroe would put a man on Jupiter, or the moon. In our century, until recently, a man on the moon was a matter for comic books and science fiction writers. Today, however, any intelligent citizen, or any president of a corporation which makes rockets, metals, or electronic equipment for the space industry, or who sells food supplies or builds houses for personnel at the missile base in Cape Kennedy, might well recognize that part Laplace had in shaping their lives, determining the products they sell, or, in the case of the space industry, determining the processes and operations which must take place in their companies.

Repetitive versus Divergent Phenomena

In a powerful chapter on "The Origins of Modern Science,"[4] Alfred North Whitehead, the eminent mathematician-philosopher, points out that "there can be no living science unless there is a widespread instinctive conviction in the existence of an *order of things"*—that is, scientists believe instinctively that events will repeat themselves, and that the events can be observed (in the skies, in the laboratory) as forming a repetitive pattern. This pattern is described in terms of lower order facts, and then general laws or principles are stated at higher levels of abstraction. For example, repeated observations are made and recorded, and then conceptualized into concepts such as "force," "mass," and "orbit."

Orbit is a pattern, and the forces producing it continue to operate, year in and year out. There are no "divergent" phenomena, no outside disturbances or forces which interrupt the pattern.

Yet there is a paradox here. Whitehead goes on to point out that even in the physical sciences, "nothing ever really occurs in exact detail. No two days are identical, no two winters. What has gone, has gone forever. Accordingly, the practical philosophy of mankind has been to expect

---

3 The word "different" is used here rather than "superior." Viewed in one way, scientists are specialists who devote their lives to a certain pursuit. Whether this is "superior power" depends upon what one's criteria for "superior" is. For instance, if we measure superiority by the degree of complexity of problems on which a human mind works, policy decisions in policy systems can be distinctly more complex than scientific systems.

4 Alfred North Whitehead, *Science and the Modern World*, Lowell Lectures, February, 1925 (New York: The Macmillan Co., 1925), chap. i.

broad recurrences, and to accept the details as emanating from the inscrutable womb of things beyond the ken of rationality."

In sciences such as astronomy, in which the systems are in reality (as well as the mind) relatively simple, with no disturbing forces, the assumption of repeated patterns seems to yield theories which are true, from year to year and century to century.

Today in the physical sciences, when we get away from astronomy, scientists are discovering that their laws are quite tentative, and that the study of change, differences in detail, and disruptions to the system or pattern are as important as recurring patterns. These divergent phenomena, as opposed to convergent phenomena (patterns), in the modern world of intellectual and cultural complexity are extremely important in the social sciences, and they are even more important in the world of policy making and managerial action. Why? Because, as we shall see later, there are many disturbances in an action system or policy system.

For the present, the following statement by the retiring president of the American Association for the Advancement of Science should help to understand the paradox to which Whitehead refers.[5] In one way, this paradox is caused by the fact that scientists, in their process of abstraction, leave out important details which, as Langmuir points out, "are important in altering the course of human history" and "profoundly affect human lives."

Up to the beginning of the present century one of the main goals of science was to discover natural laws. This was usually accomplished by making experiments under carefully controlled conditions and observing the results. Most experiments when repeated under identical conditions gave the same results.

The scientist, through his own experiments or from previous knowledge based on the work of others, usually developed some theory or explanation of the results of his experiments. In the beginning this might be a mere guess or hypothesis which he would proceed to test by new types of experiments. . . .

. . . The usefulness of the theory lies just in its ability to predict the results of future experiments. The extraordinary accomplishments of the great mathematical physicists in applying Newton's Laws to the motions of the heavenly bodies gave scientists of more than a century ago the conviction that all natural phenomena were determined by accurate relations between cause and effect. If the positions, the velocities and the masses of the heavenly bodies were given it was possible to predict with nearly unlimited accuracy the position of the bodies at any future time. The idea of causation, or a necessary relation of cause and effect, has long been embedded in the minds of men. The recognized responsibility of the criminal for his acts, the belief of the value of education and thousands of words in our language all show how implicitly we believe in cause and effect. The teachings of classical science, that is, the science up to 1900, all seem to reinforce this idea of causation for all phenomena.

*　　*　　*　　*　　*

[5] Irving Langmuir, "Science, Common Sense and Decency," *Science*, Vol. 97, No. 2505 (January 1943), pp. 1–7, reprinted from *Science* by permission. The authors are indebted to Professor Joseph Bailey of the Harvard Business School for calling attention to the importance of Langmuir's ideas in the practice of administration.

The theories or explanations which were developed in connection with the natural laws usually involved a description in terms of some kind of a model. In general, instead of thinking of the whole complex world we select only a few elements which we think to be important and concentrate our minds on these. Thus, the chemist developed the atomic theory according to which matter was made up of atoms of as many different kinds as there are chemical elements. These were thought of as small spheres, but no thought was given as to the material of which they were made. When later theories indicated that these atoms were built up of electrons and positive nuclei this made very little difference to the chemist, for he had not needed previously to consider that aspect of the model.

*   *   *   *   *

The essential characteristic of a model is that it shall resemble in certain desired features the situation that we are considering. On this basis we should recognize that practically any theory has many arbitrary features and has limitations and restrictions imposed by the simplifications that we have made in the development of the theory or the construction of our model.

Beginning with Einstein's relativity theory and Planck's quantum theory a revolution in physical thought has swept through science. Perhaps the most important aspect of this is that the scientist has ceased to believe that words or concepts can have any absolute meaning. He is not often concerned with questions of existence; he does not know what is the meaning of the question, "Does an atom really exist?" The definition of "atom" is only partly given in the dictionary. Its real meaning lies in the sum total of knowledge on this subject among scientists who have specialized in this field. No one has been authorized to make an exact definition. Furthermore, we can not be sure just what we mean even by the word "exist." Such questions are largely metaphysical and in general do not interest the modern scientist. Bridgman has pointed out that all concepts in science have value only in so far as they can be described in terms of operations or specifications. Thus it doesn't mean much to talk about length or time unless we agree upon the methods by which we are to measure length and time.

For many years, up to about 1930, the new physics based on the quantum theory seemed to be fundamentally irreconcilable with the classical physics of the previous century. Through the more recent development of the uncertainty principle, developed by Bohr and Heisenberg, this conflict has now disappeared. According to this principle it is fundamentally impossible to measure accurately both the velocity and the position of any single elementary particle. It would be possible to measure one or the other accurately but not both simultaneously. Thus it becomes impossible to predict with certainty the movement of a single particle. Therefore, Ampere's estimate of the scope of science has lost its basis.

According to the uncertainty principle, which is now thoroughly well established, the most that can be said about the future motion of any single atom or electron is that it has a definite probability of acting in any given way. Probability thus becomes a fundamental factor in every elementary process. By changing the conditions of the environment of a given atom, as, for example, by changing the force acting on it, we can change these probabilities. In many cases the probability can be made so great that a given result will be almost certain. But in many important cases the uncertainty becomes the dominating feature just as it is in the tossing of a coin.

The net result of the modern principles of physics has been to wipe out almost completely the dogma of causation.

How is it, then, that classical physics has led to such definite clean-cut laws?

The simplest answer is that the classical physicist naturally chose as the subjects for his studies those fields which promised greatest success. The aim of the scientist in general was to discover natural laws. He therefore carried on his experiments in such a way as to find the natural laws, for that is what he was looking for. He was best able to accomplish this by working with phenomena which depended upon the behavior of enormous numbers of atoms rather than upon individual atoms. In this way the effects produced by individual atoms averaged out and become imperceptible. We have many familiar examples of this effect of averaging—the deaths of individual human beings can not usually be predicted but the average death rate in any age group is found to come close to expectation.

Since the discovery of the electron and the quantum and methods of detecting or even counting individual atoms, it has been possible for scientists to undertake investigations of the behavior of single atoms. Here they have found unmistakable experimental evidence that these phenomena depend upon the laws of probability and that they are just as unpredictable in detail as the next throw of the coin. If, however, we were dealing with large numbers of such atoms the behavior of the whole group would be definitely determined by the probability of the individual occurrence and therefore would appear to be governed by laws of cause and effect.

Just as there are two types of physics, classical physics and quantum physics, which have for nearly twenty-five years seemed irreconcilable, just so must we recognize two types of natural phenomena. First, those in which the behavior of the system can be determined from the average behavior of its component parts and second, those in which a single discontinuous event (which may depend upon a single quantum change) becomes magnified in its effect so that the behavior of the whole aggregate does depend upon something that started from a small beginning. The first class of phenomena I want to call *convergent phenomena,* because all the fluctuating details of the individual atoms average out giving a result that converges to a definite state. The second class we may call *divergent phenomena,* where from a small beginning increasingly large effects are produced. In general then we may say that classical physics applies satisfactorily to convergent phenomena and that they conform well to the older ideas of cause and effect. The divergent phenomena on the other hand can best be understood on the basis of quantum theory of modern physics.

*   *   *   *   *

The formation of crystals on cooling a liquid involves the formation of nuclei or crystallization centers that must originate from discrete, atomic phenomena. The spontaneous formation of these nuclei often depends upon chance.

At a camp at Lake George, in winter, I have often found that a pail of water is unfrozen in the morning after being in a room far below freezing, but it suddenly turns to slush upon being lifted from the floor.

Glycerine is commonly known as a viscous liquid, even at low temperatures. Yet if crystals are once formed they melt only at 64° F. If a minute crystal of this kind is introduced into pure glycerine at temperatures below 64° the entire liquid gradually solidifies.

During a whole winter in Schenectady I left several small bottles of glycerine outdoors and I kept the lower ends of test-tubes containing glycerine in liquid air for days, but in no case did crystals form.

My brother, A. C. Langmuir, visited a glycerine refinery in Canada which had operated for many years without ever having any experience with crystalline glycerine. But suddeny one winter, without exceptionally low temperatures, the pipes carrying the glycerine from one piece of apparatus to another froze up.

The whole plant and even the dust on the ground became contaminated with nuclei and although any part of the plant could be temporarily freed from crystals by heating above 64° it was found that whenever the temperature anywhere fell below 64° crystals would begin forming. The whole plant had to be shut down for months until outdoor temperatures rose above 64°.

Here we have an example of an inherently unpredictable divergent phenomenon that profoundly affected human lives.

Every thunderstorm or tornado must start from a small beginning and at least the details of the irregular courses of such storms across the country would be modified by single quantum phenomena that acted during the initial stages. Yet small details such as the place where lightning strikes or damage occurs from a tornado may be important to a human being.

*   *   *   *   *

As the implications of the uncertainty principle, especially as applied to divergent phenomena, are more generally recognized the limitations of the idea of causality should have profound effects on our habits of thought. The science of logic itself is involved in these changes. Two of the fundamental postulates of logic are known as the law of uniformity of nature and the law of the excluded middle. The first of these laws is equivalent of the postulate of causality in nature. The second law is simply the familiar postulate that a given proposition must be either true or false. In the past these so-called laws have formed the basis of much of our reasoning. It seems to me, however, that they play no important part in the progress of modern science. The cause and effect postulate is only applicable to convergent phenomena. The second postulate in assuming that any proposition must be true or false implies that we attach absolute meanings to words or concepts. If concepts have meanings only in terms of the operations used to define them we can see that they are necessarily fuzzy. Take, for example, this statement, "Atoms are indestructible." Is this true or false? The answer depends upon what aspect of atoms is considered. To the chemist the statement is as true as it ever was. But a physicist, studying radioactive changes, recognized that some atoms undergo spontaneous disintegration or destruction. The fact is that the chemist and the physicist have no exact definition of the word "atom" and they also do not know in any absolute sense what they mean by "indestructible."

Fortunately such questions no longer occupy much of the time of scientists, who are usually concerned with more concrete problems which they endeavor to treat in common-sense ways.

It is often thought by the layman, and many of those who are working in so-called social sciences, that the field of science should be unlimited, that reason should take the place of intuition, that realism should replace emotions and that morality is of value only so far as it can be justified by analytical reasoning.

Human affairs are characterized by a complexity of a far higher order than that encountered ordinarily in the field of science.

To avoid alternating periods of depression and prosperity economists propose to change our laws. They reason that such a change would eliminate the cause of the depressions. They endeavor to develop a science of economics by which sound solutions to such problems can be reached.

I believe the field of application of science in such problems is extremely limited. A scientist has to define his problem and usually has to bring about simplified conditions for his experiments which exclude undesired factors. So the economist has to invent an "economic man" who always does the thing expected of him. No two economists would agree exactly upon the characteristics of this hypothetical man and any conclusions drawn as to his behavior are of doubtful application to actual cases involving human beings. There is no logical scientific method for determining just how one can formulate such a problem or what factors one must exclude. It really comes down to a matter of common sense or good judgment. All too often wishful thinking determines the formulation of the problem. Thus, even if scientifically logical processes are applied to to the problem, the results may have no greater validity than that of the good or bad judgment involved in the original assumptions.

Some of the difficulties involved in a scientific approach to economic problems is illustrated by the following: If we wish to analyze the cause of a depression (or for example, a war) we should ask ourselves what we mean by the word "cause" in this connection. In terms of operations the usual meaning of the word cause is something as follows: It is a common experience, in a study of convergent phenomena, that if a given set of physical conditions are brought about repeatedly at different times, the same result occurs in each case. Except in so far as it is possible to repeat the experiment and get the same result it is impossible to give a definite meaning to the word cause.

In the case of a depression or a war, we logically need to produce, or at least to observe, a given set of possible antecedent conditions and to see whether they are always followed by depressions. Since we can not produce experimental depressions, nor have we sufficient observational data to enable us by statistical means to unravel the enormous number of factors involved, we must conclude that the word "cause" as applied to a depression has an extremely fuzzy meaning.

When we consider the nature of human affairs it is to me obvious that divergent phenomena frequently play a role of vital importance. It is true that some of our historians cynically taught most of our college students from 1925 to 1938 that wars, the rise and fall of a nation, etc., were determined by nearly cosmic causes. They tried to show that economic pressure, and power politics on the part of England or France, etc., would have brought the same result whether or not Kaiser Wilhelm or Hitler or any other individual or group of individuals had or had not acted the way they did. Germany, facing the world in a realistic way, was proved, almost scientifically, to be justified in using ruthless methods— because of the energy and other characteristics of the German people they would necessarily acquire and should acquire a place in the sun greater than that of England, which was already inevitably on the downward path.

I can see no justification whatever for such teaching that science proves that general causes (convergent phenomena) dominate in human affairs over the results of individual action (divergent phenomena). It is true that it is not possible to prove one way or the other that human affairs are determined primarily by convergent phenomena. The very existence of divergent phenomena almost precludes the possibility of such proof.

Operationalism in Science

In Dr. Langmuir's article, he asks why it was that classical physicists could find such clean-cut laws. The answer is that "the classical physicist naturally chose as the subjects for his studies those fields which promised greatest success" (that is, chose subjects and imagined concepts of a kind that did show recurring patterns).

Today, even with quantum thinking in the natural sciences and emphasis on probability in social sciences such as economics and sociology, we must note one more characteristic of science which bears on its usefulness in the formulation of policy problems and the analysis and solution of policy decisions.

The individual scientist will not select problems to work on nor will he select concepts to investigate unless they are operational to him—unless they fit his method. The two things which determine this are (1) the concepts and events must be repetitive in observation, or reproducible in the laboratory; and (2) they must be things that can be quantified. Only in this way can the scientist test the reality of his "imagined" concepts and hypotheses. Numbers and mathematics are the one thing on which different human minds can agree. If phenomena are not repetitive in an absolute sense, they must be in the statistical sense, so that probability figures can be attached.

For example, chemists have discovered through patient experiment that "hydrogen" (note the concept) has an "atomic weight" of 1, and that oxygen has an atomic weight of 16, and that the "valence" (combining power) of hydrogen is 1 while the valence of oxygen is 2. From these, he can predict that of any amount of water (H_2O), say 200 pounds, 11% will be made up of hydrogen and 89% of oxygen. He does this by dividing the total of the molecular weight $[(2 \times 1) + (1 \times 16)]$ into the atomic weights of the individual elements $(1 \div 18)$. If you do not "believe" this, he can take you into the laboratory, weigh the water sample, reduce it to hydrogen and oxygen, and then weigh them under repetitive, experimental conditions.

J. W. N. Sullivan, one important philosopher of science, states that this predisposition to select out of the universe only those things that could be *measured* experimentally or observationally was due simply to a *faith* on the part of Copernicus, Kepler, and Galileo "that mathematics is the key to the universe . . . a belief which was very proper to born mathematicians . . . (which) gave the mathematical aspects of the universe a much more exalted position than they occupied in the current Aristotelian outlook. . . ."

"(Kepler's) deepest conviction was that nature is essentially mathematical, and all his scientific life was an endeavor to discover nature's hidden mathematical harmonies. Galileo, also, had no doubt that mathematics is the one true key to the universe. It was this persuasion that gave these men their criterion for selection amongst the total elements of the universe."[6]

Whitehead, on the other hand, gives a slightly different reason for the scientist's willingness to deal only with problems which can be reproduced, quantitatively, in experiment or by observation. To him it was a loss in faith, by scholars, in the dogmatic speculation of the Middle Ages, when philosophy and truth were laid down, speculatively, without reference to facts in the world. Copernicus, for example, felt a great anxiety

---

6 J. W. N. Sullivan, *The Limitations of Science* (New York: New American Library Edition), pp. 128–29. Copyright, 1933, Viking Press, Inc., reprinted by permission.

because he knew that the Ptolemaic theory of the universe was not true. That theory, with the earth as the center, and stationary at that, was a current conceptual scheme of the mind, which explained how the stars rotated around the earth. Copernicus had "heard" that some of the great Greek philosophers had put forward the hypothesis that the earth was in motion. Copernicus then took the sun as his center of reference (he imagined a new theory or conceptual scheme) and proceeded to collect data.

It is significant that in 1964 the concept of operationalism (experiment-quantification) is important in physical science, in some social science, and in the current application of mathematics in business administration, that is, in the field of operations research. One of the better recent textbooks on operations research states:

> The goals of individuals have been the subject of discussion and debate for many centuries. To say that happiness is the goal of the individual . . . does not solve any problem. We cannot define happiness in operational terms. Operationalism is an important concept for understanding operations research. It implies concreteness, the ability to observe, measure, and analyze. . . . We cannot treat happiness as an operational term.[7]

Facts which are operational to the scientist and statistician in the laboratory, quantified and under controlled experimental (repetitive and abstract) conditions, are not always operational to the policy maker; or they may be relevant to his problems, but not of high relevance in terms of his goals; or they may be relevant, but uncontrollable in terms of executive action. Finally, they may be highly relevant, and controllable by the executive, but subject to overriding importance of *other* forces than explained by any one theory.[8]

The Lesson of Physical Science for Policy Makers

Why have we spent time discussing the nature of science, the idea of divergent phenomena, and the idea of operationalism in science? First, because it helps the policy maker, the man of action, to recognize that the great power of creativity and the enormous amounts of time and energy expended add to the value of many scientific concepts. It also helps to see that the very bias of scientists—their preconditioning and their attitudes—is one of the factors that enable them to see things that laymen may overlook. Secondly, some of the characteristics of science, divergent phenomena, and operationalism have contradictory implications in policy systems—they put a limitation on the degree to which science can be used

---

[7] David Miller and Martin Starr, *Executive Decisions and Operations Research* (Englewood Cliffs, N.J.: Prentice-Hall, Inc., 1960).

[8] In many of the cases in the latter part of the book, one of these three limitations can be seen. For example, see the following cases: Queymoy and Matsu, Midwest Hardware Manufacturing Company, National Motor Parts Company, and Continental Electric Company.

in policy formation. They indicate that the practicing executive must pick and choose his theories, must test them, modify them, use them, or discard them, depending on how they operate in the world of action, where experimental conditions cannot be met, where divergent phenomena are many times as important as convergent phenomena, and where everything cannot be measured by mathematics.

Finally, many social scientists, whether rightly or wrongly, try, with varying degrees of success, to adopt the methods of the physical sciences. To the extent that they do, this chapter has set the stage for understanding the nature and methods of social sciences discussed in the next chapter.

3. SOCIAL SCIENCE AND APPLIED SOCIAL SCIENCE

Theory Formulation in the Social Sciences: An Example from Sociology

In the last chapter, we looked at the nature of conceptual schemes, as formulated by those scientists whose main interest is understanding non-human objects in the environment, for the purpose of explaining how one object or event causes another.

The social sciences occupy a special place in policy making by general executives. In fact, "management" has been defined by some as "getting results through human organizations."[1] Such a definition implies that the proper study of decisions by men of action—military, governmental, legal —should be based on political philosophy, or political science, or one of the so-called behavioral sciences—psychology and certain branches of sociology and anthropology.

In this chapter, we will be looking at the nature of social science, its concepts, and the way they are derived (its methods), in the hope that the reader himself, in both reading these words and working with the cases, will gain an appreciation for the value of social science, and its limitations, in the world of policy-making action.

We will begin by using an explanation of "The Theory Construction Function of Science" put forth by Ernest Greenwood.[2] The example he cites, that of Durkheim's theory of suicide, is a classic one, often used by social scientists to illustrate their methods:

---

[1] This, of course, is a conceptual idea which puts the relationships between people, and their governance or management, in the center of analysis, rather than the relationships between machines, goods, money flows, and the like. Neither is true: the policy system, as we shall see, is a very complex conglomerate of human structures and dynamics, and technological-economic structures and dynamics.

[2] From Ernest Greenwood, "The Practice of Science and the Science of Practice," presented as a University Lecture at Brandeis University, October 1959, and published as one of the Brandeis University Papers in Social Welfare by the Florence Heller Graduate School for Advanced Studies in Social Welfare, 1960. This Lecture is also abridged in *The Planning of Change*, edited by Warren Bennis, Kenneth D. Benne, and Robert Chin (New York: Holt, Rinehart & Winston, 1962). The latter is considered an excellent collection of writings from the viewpoint of the practitioner— the applied social scientist who is interested in planned change (control) in the environment rather than simply in understanding the operation of nature.

[L]et me describe in more specific language the nature of the scientific activity. The end product of the collective efforts of scientists within a given discipline is a system of internally consistent propositions which describe and explain the phenomena that constitute the subject matter of that discipline. This system is called a body of *theory*. The function of all science is to construct theories about the what, the how, and the why of the natural world. There is some current misunderstanding regarding this function of science, many laymen believing that only philosophers theorize and that scientists "stick close to facts." I wish to dwell a bit on the theory-construction focus of science. In this connection it will prove clarifying if I were to distinguish between two levels of knowledge with which scientists are concerned. On the first level are first-order facts called *empirical generalizations;* on the second and higher level are the explanations or interpretations of these facts called *theory*. These constitute two orders of abstraction.

NATURE OF EMPIRICAL GENERALIZATIONS

To make clear the distinction between these two orders of abstraction, let me present you with a few examples of an empirical generalization. Thus:

a. In Western societies, Jews commit fewer suicides than Gentiles, and Catholics commit fewer suicides than Protestants.

b. American middle-class wives participate in communal health and welfare activities more than their husbands.

c. In cities key commercial facilities concentrate at point of convergence of transportation lines.

d. Juvenile delinquency rates are higher in urban census tracts with lower median monthly rentals.

An empirical generalization may be defined as a proposition about a class of units which describes the uniform recurrence of two or more factors among them. As the term empirical implies, such generalizations are derived inductively by actual observation of the class members. The procedures pursued in their derivation can be operationalized and textbooks on research method are written to describe them; these involve scaling, sampling, controlled observation, data manipulation, application of statistical tests, et cetera. Given time and patience, there is no limit to the number of hitherto unsuspected empirical generalizations, or first-order facts, that one could discover about the social world. The body of knowledge of a science, however, consists of more than empirical generalizations.

DESCRIPTION VERSUS EXPLANATION

That shrewd critic of the sociological scene, Robert Bierstedt, in a brilliant article, entitled "A Critique of Empiricism in Sociology," puts the matter in the following form.[3] Surveys, he states, have amassed an assortment of facts about bread consumption in the United States. Thus: Americans are consuming decreasing amounts of home-made and increasing amounts of factory-made bread. Most Americans prefer white to dark bread. Men consume more bread than women. Adolescents consume more bread than other age groups. Negroes consume more bread than Whites. Rural dwellers consume more bread than urban dwellers. Low income families consume more bread than high income families. This factual list might be extended without adding significantly to our compre-

---

3 Robert Bierstedt, "A Critique of Empiricism in Sociology," *American Sociological Review,* Vol. 14 (October 1949), pp. 584–92.

hension of the American bread consumption phenomenon. To achieve the latter requires a formulation that will tie together these discrete generalizations and will explain their interrelationships. Such a formulation would constitute a theory of American bread consumption.

The function of social scientists is to develop theories which will explain such social phenomena as bread consumption, alcoholism, class conflict, crime, drug addiction, juvenile delinquency, marital discord, population migration, suicide, technological change, urban growth, et cetera. In constructing theory, the scientist uses empirical generalizations as building blocks.

AN EXAMPLE OF THEORY BUILDING

I would like to present an idealized description of theory construction taken from Durkheim's work on the social aetiology of suicide. Although now over a half century old, it still remains an impeccable model of theory construction.[4] I have deliberately selected an example at a relatively simple level of theory, thereby ignoring so-called grand and all-embracing theories.

Durkheim begins his search for the societal cause of suicide by casting his net far and wide, garnering all the available facts about the problem. The data yield him a series of empirical generalizations. Careful scrutiny of Durkheim's volume reveals over three dozen such generalizations which assume a wide variety. Let me present some of them.

a. Countries predominantly Protestant in population have higher suicide rates than countries predominantly Catholic.

b. Christians have higher suicide rates than Jews.

c. Countries with high literacy rates have higher suicide rates than countries with low literacy.

d. The liberal professions as a group have a higher suicide rate than the manual occupations.

e. The unmarried have a higher suicide rate than the married.

f. The divorced have a higher suicide rate than the married.

g. The childless married have a higher suicide rate than the married with children.

h. Average size of family is inversely related to the suicide rate.

Having extracted these empirical generalizations from the data, Durkheim next, in essence, asks the question: What common thread runs through these generalizations? What do Protestants, high literacy countries, liberal professions, the unmarried, the divorced, the childless, have in common that should make for higher suicide rates among them than in their opposite classes? At this point Durkheim begins to speculate, and his speculation bears recapitulation.

If Protestants are more prone to suicides than Catholics, religious differences must be held accountable. Protestantism permits individualism and free inquiry, while Catholicism brooks no scrutiny by the faithful. The more binding the creed, the more unified the religious group and the more attached is the individual to the group. The atmosphere permitted by Protestantism weakens the traditional beliefs that solidify the religious group. That group discipline exerts a preservative influence is borne out by the case of the Jews, a cohesive minority living in compact communities, with a low suicide rate. Attachment to a group

---

[4] Emile Durkheim, *Suicide. A Study in Sociology* (New York: The Free Press of Glencoe, 1951). Translation by John A. Spaulding and George Simpson. Durkheim's theory of suicide presented in this paper is a highly abstracted version of the original, necessitated by space requirements. Any distortions in the theory are the responsibility of this writer.

must be a potent factor in the suicide phenomenon as indicated by the marital correlates of suicide. Note how the unmarried state encourages suicide and how the disruption of marriage by divorce and death increases its chances. Close examination of the facts reveals that even more preservative than the conjugal relationship between the spouses is the familial relationship between parents and children. In fact, the more children the better. The common thread that runs through these empirical generalizations is clear. A well-integrated group holds its members by strong bonds, preventing them from evading their social obligations by self-elimination, at the same time providing them the support to enable them to perform their obligations in the face of otherwise disabling personal stress. Where group solidarity is weak, the individual feels detached from the group and is thrown on his own feeble resources to sustain him in his personal frustrations.

This, highly condensed, is Durkheim's theory of the social cause of suicide. The theory may now be summarized into a single proposition, *i.e.*, a law of suicide: *Suicide is a function of the degree of group integration which provides the psychic support to group members for handling acute stress.*

NATURE OF THEORY BUILDING

Durkheim's method epitomizes the scientific process. From a host of apparently disconnected first-order facts he theorizes to a law. He moves from the facts to an abstract proposition which interprets the interrelationship among them. Note the difference in levels of abstraction between the law and the empirical generalizations. Note how much more abstract is the proposition with which he terminates the theorizing process from the propositions with which he initiates it. Theory may thus be defined as a systematic interpretation in abstract terms of a generalizable trend that prevails within a set of varied facts, explaining the interrelationship among them. Law is the summarization of the theory in causal terms.

As indicated earlier, the derivation of empirical generalizations can be operationalized, but I have yet to find a textbook that will operationalize the theorizing process. The interpretive process, the development of a formulation which will account for a series of facts, is essentially a free-wheeling, speculative one. It is an inferential process whereby the inquiring mind churns the available information over and over, employing all the logical devices and bringing to bear upon it any and all kinds of relevant knowledge. The process allows for a considerable play of the imagination, and the final formulation bears the personal imprint of its formulator.

In this example of fact gathering and speculation-theory construction in the social sciences, the policy maker might well take note of some of the characteristics of the theory itself and of its formulator, Durkheim.

First, the final law of suicide contains two concepts or variables which Durkheim "saw." By the process of abstraction, he simplified the world: "suicide," as an event or occurrence, and "group integration," which determines the suicide rate. These two concepts are, at one and the same time, products of his imagination, and representative of the underlying facts. The intermediate variables with which he reasoned (the other concepts he imagined and formulated) are "psychic support" for handling "acute stress." Thus, we get these cause-and-effect relationships: low degrees of group participation cause a feeling of lack of psychic support in the individual which cause him to be unable to handle problems of acute stress, which in turn cause him to commit suicide.

Second, to test the theory, one can reason deductively from the theory to other facts, just as in the case of the prediction that Neptune was "out there" (Chapter 2). One can look for groups with low degrees of "group integration," and without experiment, deductively predict that members of that group would have a higher suicide rate; further, one can then test to see if the members of that group *in fact* have a higher suicide rate.

Third, Durkheim's central theory does not refer to any other causes of suicide. He assumes that group integration is the uniformly constant and most important cause, and that other causes are either less important, or are simply deviant, random events, not relevant to scientific study and rational explanation. He treats suicide as a repetitive, convergent phenomena (in Langmuir's term), a pattern which varies with one central cause—group integration.

Fourth, Durkheim had an interest in studying suicide. He was not interested in making automobiles, winning a war, setting the discount rate of the federal reserve banks, influencing the behavior of subordinate personnel in a factory, or explaining the rise and fall of governments.

If he were interested in a very broad range of problems and events and variables in a policy system, he could not have conceptualized in precise enough terms to produce the power of thought and the understanding of nature, which he did.

Finally, the principle itself (any principle is a statement of explanation —of cause and effect) is not "engineered"—it does not prescribe to a government official *how* to provide group integration. Only by re-studying the underlying facts, as to how the various groups provided (or did not provide) integration, can the policy maker infer what they did in a practical sense to influence the suicide rate. This is an important difference in science, technology, and practice.

Theory Construction: An Example from Social Psychology

In order to understand the use of theories in policy formulation more deeply, we need another example—one from a practitioner whose interests are nearer to the business organization. This time, we will look at a theory which explains the ways in which "organizations" have certain effects on "individual behavior" and "group behavior" and how the latter two variables reciprocally affect "organizations." This theory, that explained by Chris Argyris in *Personality and Organization*,[5] has received wide attention.

---

[5] New York: Harper & Bros., 1957. The presentation of the theory here is a highly abstracted version of Professor Argyris' book. Responsibility for abstraction is assumed by the authors. A longer version, in Professor Argyris' own words, appears as a reading in this volume. The theory is also highly controversial—see the review of Argyris' later work by Mason Haire, *Management Science*, April 1963, p. 505.

In formulating this conceptual scheme, Argyris utilizes six hundred and forty footnotes, many of which draw on empirical research in the social sciences. He draws on a breadth of experimental and observed situations—from studies of motivation in children, of personality tests in business, and of rational behavior in large bureaucracies to studies of why people join trade unions. Argyris is *primarily interested* in how large organizations affect human personality and how they affect informal group behavior. At the highest level, he is interested in what causes conflict between organizations, on the one hand, and the rank-and-file members of organizations, on the other.

With these interests, he proceeds to conceptualize meaning from a wealth of diverse facts which have "come to his attention." The overall theory and its intermediate concepts can be stated in briefest terms as follows:

1. All human beings have a capacity for "self-actualization" (growth), for developing from infancy in terms of interests, abilities, and activities. Such development satisfies needs, and it is the continuing striving for such development which gives us energy.

2. The formal organization has four characteristics: jobs are split up and specialized, there is a chain of command, everyone has only one boss, and there is a long hierarchy or pyramid of command.

3. These characteristics of formal organization severely limit the self-actualization, development, and growth of the human being.

4. Rank-and-file members of the organization, thus confronted with a block to their growth and development, either quit, become apathetic (lose their energy), or become aggressive against the organization.

5. The leaders of organizations see the rank and file behaving this way, develop beliefs that they are lazy or hostile, and tighten up on the characteristics of formal organization (step [2]). They define jobs more minutely, stress the chain of command, and rigidify the hierarchical pyramid.

6. This causes the apathy and aggression of employees who remain in the organization to intensify: they become lethargic and devote less energy to their work; or they increase their aggression in the form of cliques to "get around" the rules; or they even form formal labor unions to fight back.

7. The vicious circle continues, with steps (5) and (6) reinforcing the conflict.

Argyris' interest in organization-personality conflict led him to conceptualize a series of cause-and-effect relationships between two highly abstract concepts: "the organization" and "personality." In order to think about these, however, his original interest dictated that he had to formulate some lower order concepts about what a "human being" is and about what an "organization" is. What did he do about these two variables? What did he see? In effect, he said, "A personality (human being) is first and foremost an organism which has an almost unlimited capacity for self-actualization and growth"; and "an organization is a construct with specialized jobs, chain of command, and a hierarchical pyramid."

The choice of these two larger abstractions, "personality" and "organization" with their lower order abstractions, "growth," "chain of command," etc., enabled him to reason the further cause-and-effect relationships pointed out above.

Theory Construction: An Example from Economics and Industrial Engineering

The founder of the discipline of economics, Adam Smith, had as his main interest exactly what the title of his famous book implies: *An Inquiry into the Nature and Causes of the Wealth of Nations.* He was interested in the national balance sheet, the assets and liabilities of a nation, and the national income and gross national product which produces the national wealth. Thus motivated in terms of interest, Smith conceptualized the first and most important cause of the productivity of a nation as the "principle of specialization"—the division of work into smaller parts which produced efficiency of the whole.[6]

This is the same "specialization" which Argyris refers to as one of the characteristics of organizations, in step (2) in the preceding section, except that the two scholars derived different meanings from it. To Adam Smith, it is the foremost cause of the productivity of an industrial system, yet to Argyris it is one of the causes of apathy or aggression in organizations. Even today, in modern economics, the principle of specialization has important implications for creating larger organizations, for creating staff departments for central planning in organizations, and for realizing "increasing returns to scale."[7]

In the field of industrial engineering and in operations research models, there is implied a certain physical division of labor between parts of the system (including locations, such as jobs, factories, and warehouses). If this division of labor produces the greatest job output in the case of industrial engineering or the optimum balance between the inputs and outputs of an inventory system (in operations research), then the engineers or researchers tend either to ignore the motivational effects of specialization,[8] or to assume that they have less importance than the

---

[6] The relevant argument is presented in this volume as pages 4–15 of *The Wealth of Nations.*

[7] Study particularly the Lincoln Rochester Trust Company case, and the Mississippi Valley Equipment Company case, plus the readings, for insight into the meaning of the term "specialization" in relation to internal organization planning (Mississippi Valley Equipment Company) and the planning of a merger (Lincoln Rochester Trust Company).

[8] That is, in their formal models. They cover such divergent phenomena in their assumptions when they study a technological system, but these generally receive less rigorous analysis and proof than the phenomena of primary focus.

rational planning of jobs and the flow of material. In this sense, the *interests* of industrial engineers, or operations researchers, simply cause them to select certain variables which are more important in their view of the world.[9] This, incidentally, does not mean that all industrial engineers, operations researchers, and economists ignore the meaning of "specialization" as it occurs to Argyris. It simply means that they must, if they are to accomplish their principal objectives of inquiry, devote their greatest attention to their own expertise and logic, as based on what they are trying to accomplish.[10] In the process of building their models or conceptual schemes, they are exercising the prerogative of a scholar or technologist: to derive meaning from facts *as they see them.*

Ceteris Paribus in Social Science

Even in the pure version of social science, such as is directed toward the understanding of nature rather than the controlling of nature through technology, and as exemplified in the Durkheim theory, the scientist sees certain important, central meanings to a wide variety of facts. Though Durkheim's theory seems the "very model of theoretic and methodologic sophistication . . . (indicating his stature) as a pure social scientist,"[11] there is no assurance that another social scientist will not one day set out to derive different meanings from different orders of facts, thus showing another important cause of suicide, and a different conceptual scheme. In this sense, even in pure varieties of social science, the social scientist assumes *ceteris paribus,* or "other things being equal." Operations researchers and Chris Argyris, because of their choice of when to close the system—of what other things would be assumed to be equal—arrive at totally different meanings of the same phenomenon, specialization.

As one moves nearer and nearer to the control of the environment—when one becomes a technologist, or even more a policy maker—he must realize that "other things" are present in the policy system: that divergent or assumed phenomena can be of lesser importance, equal importance, or greater importance than the convergent phenomena presented by the scientist.

Economics has traditionally been concerned, in part, with control of the environment. As scholars who reason, *a priori,* from "supply" and "demand," economists assume, for example, that all men are motivated by

9 For more detailed examples of these views of the world, see the following cases and their collateral readings: Midwest Hardware Manufacturing Company, Photogeneral Optical Company, and National Motor Parts Company.

10 Many students of Adam Smith, being interested in his major thesis, will not have been "interested" enough to remember his later passages which state, in a powerful way, the harmful effects of specialization on human beings. These are reproduced herein as pages 734–35 of *The Wealth of Nations.* Smith did not consider these as important as the opposite principle when he formulated economic theory.

11 Alvin W. Gouldner, "Theoretical Requirements of the Applied Social Sciences," *American Sociological Review,* Vol. 22, No. 1 (February 1957), p. 98.

"competition," and they are very careful to state their principles in terms of *other things being equal.* This is a signal to men of action that they are studying only parts of a policy system at any one time.

What we are saying here is that in a policy decision made by a general executive in a policy system, each theory (from each discipline) may predict a certain outcome, in absolute terms, if a given course of action (policy, decision, and strategy) is decided upon. But when many theories, from many disciplines, predict different outcomes, the *absolute* result predicted by each theory must be given a *weight* by the general executive. From the standpoint of any one individual theory, other outcomes from other theories may be weighted lower, the same, or higher, depending on the goals of the policy system as interpreted by the manager. These weights based on goals which the executive is trying to accomplish *are not necessarily the same* as the weight that a psychologist would assign to psychological outcomes based on the goals of psychologists. They are not necessarily the same as the weights an applied mathematician would assign to technological performance, such as the quantities in an inventory control and product planning system, when he expresses this system in a mathematical, operations research model.

Who Has the Final Answer for Policy Determination?

In philosophy of knowledge, the term "validity" means that a conceptual scheme of concepts linked together in an explanation of cause and effect is internally consistent. That is, terms are defined precisely and reasoning proceeds according to rules, either the older Aristotelian syllogistic rules or the newer rules of general semantics.

There is no such thing as this kind of "validity" in a policy decision. There may be validity in each of the separate theories, but that is because scholars used methods to simplify the world which yielded this kind of validity.

In the world of theory, "truth" (reliability) means that the conceptual schemes generated by the human mind through scientific method have been (and can be) verified by repeating the observation or by reproducing an experiment. Thus, Leverrier verified the scheme of "force, mass, heliocentric longitude, orbit" when he predicted that Neptune was there, looked through his telescope, and saw it.

One might also verify the scheme of "suicide-group integration" by observing groups in the real world. The scientist would then go out and look for groups with high or low integration and, using statistical probability, prove that the higher suicide rate could not have been caused by random factors. It therefore must have been caused by the variable or concept of group integration. In this case, the theory of group integration caused the researcher to measure group characteristics only on this scale. He closed out the rest of the world, so to speak.

In the other means of verification (experimentation), were it not for our social mores regarding experimenting with human beings, one might set up two experimental groups, controlled in the sense that (1) the two groups have different degrees of the independent variable, group integration, and (2) in all other respects, the groups are alike. By changing the degree of group integration in one group, one then would measure the difference in the suicide rates which result and subject them to tests of statistical probability. The scientist has deliberately created a factual situation "out there" which eliminates the world in its confusion and simplifies it into a controlled experiment, abstracted from the world. In one sense, then, he is creating a situation, by controlling reality, which produces the very phenomena which his imagination created in the first place. In Langmuir's sense, he is setting up a factual situation in which divergent phenomena are deliberately kept out.

Thus in both the observations and in the reproducible experiments of social science, *ceteris paribus,* other things being equal, presents a special problem. In astronomy, an observational science where the phenomena under study are literally "in a vacuum" and where other things are equal in the reality of day-to-day dynamics, conceptual schemes and reality approximate the same thing. In social science, where controlled conditions create artificial vacua or where choosing of facts to study "closes the system" and where other things in the complexity of day-to-day events are such that other things are *not* equal, theory and total reality are not necessarily the same thing. Such theories are creations of the human mind.

In answer to our question, who has the final answer for policy determination, the answer is: probably nobody. An executive may seem to question the validity and truth of theories as he evaluates them for his policy making. Not so! Because the executive has moved away from the closed system of the scholar to the open policy system, he must apply another criterion: does the theory work? No one theory fits the policy system with its multitude of interacting variables. As we have said, theories come to grips with a slice of reality, burying the remainder of reality in the *ceteris paribus* assumption. The executive recognizes that a theory may have validity and truth within the closed system of the scholar's purpose. If Durkheim's purpose is to understand suicide, there may well be validity and truth in his statement of its cause. If Argyris' purpose is to understand conflict in organizations, there may well be validity and truth in his more elaborate scheme. If the applied mathematician's purpose is to minimize the cost of holding inventory, there may also be validity and truth in his mathematical formula for the optimum lot size, based on a number of technological and economic variables. But when the executive comes to policy determination, he must eclectically draw from valid and true theories, those aspects which are relevant to *his* problems, and which aid in his analysis and his decisions.

Roethlisberger, in a book reporting on one of the most significant research projects undertaken in social science, points out that there is within sociology and anthropology today a controversy over the "historical" versus the "functional" conceptual schemes. He clearly points out that neither is true nor false, but "more or less convenient or useful for certain purposes . . . [and] its usefulness can only be decided after it has been used."[12] He then cites a rather powerful passage from a book by Thurman Arnold:

> The eye of the artist or poet looking at the human body is different from the eye of the physician looking for pathological symptoms. Neither one has the "true" nor the "false" view of the body. The physician, however, is the better person when therapy rather than decoration is demanded.[13]

Social Science and Social Philosophy

The social scientist's study of *certain problems* in the environment is complicated by the fact that he cannot isolate his own emotional needs from the hypothesis he generates. In the physical sciences, an astronomer is not necessarily mad or happy when he finds Neptune in a certain orbit. He does not think this is good or bad.

In the social sciences this is not necessarily true, particularly in the study of organizations. Every social scientist has been living in organizations from birth (the family), and shall be in organizations until death (government, universities, business). As he performs the scientific operations noted in the preceding section, selection of facts to observe, interpretation of meanings, setting up of experiments, these value predispositions (positive-negative) influence the total intellectual process in each of its stages.

In this sense, social "science" has something in common with social "philosophy." Faced with limitations on the methods the astronomer uses to leave his emotions out of his observations in a pure, simplified system, the social scientist in one sense reasons *a priori*, i.e., from a combination of assumptions and facts, rather than from facts alone. He is denied the very conditions (a simple, closed system) which would have been a check on his deeper, unconscious assumptions.

Still other scholars, social philosophers, attack large social issues where measurement, observation, reproducible experiment, and validation are not possible. These people reason from assumptions freely and employ logic (philosophy) rather than a combination of fact and logic (science) to explain their concepts. The individual scholar's values are even more likely to influence such theories in these cases. A good example of how different values create different conceptual schemes is to be found in the apparent contradiction between traditional management theory based on

---

12 F. J. Roethlisberger, *Management and Morale* (Cambridge: Harvard University Press, 1941), p. 69.

13 *The Symbols of Government* (New Haven: Yale University Press, 1935), p. 30.

economics and political science and certain forms of management theory based on psychology.

Management theory, based primarily on economic principles such as specialization, and interested primarily in the necessity of technological coordination of the inputs and outputs between operating and staff functions, proceeds to reason out such concepts as "division of work," "delegation of authority," and "unity of command (power)." In this sense, management theory is quite akin to political philosophy. It starts with assumptions similar to John Locke's[14]—that "all men are biased" (note that it does not start with "growth") and that men need and want an "indifferent judge," with "authority," so that chaos and anarchy will not prevail (note that there is no reference to the fact that the "indifferent judge" will stifle the "growth" of men). Management theory also has some unconscious assumptions similar to engineering and operations research. That is, the importance of technological coordination in the production of goods—between the timing, quality, and quantity of work flow, with the aid of central, rational planning—is of paramount concern.

On the other hand, theories based on psychology and small group dynamics imply that, in order to liberate the largest amount of human energy and creativity in the organization, a maximum amount of participation, by group members, is a desirable type of managerial and subordinate behavior. Most of these theories do not refer to the increment of efficiency due to technological coordination by central planners, or expert staff personnel such as engineers and operations researchers, or to the time consumed in patient, "two-way communication" (one of their central concepts). Rather, such theories highlight the fact that such communication arrives at the best decisions on how to structure the business, and at the same time produce the most harmonious human system. (Note that these theories do not deliberately reason with Locke that all people need authority, or with the economists, that all people are competitive.[15] Nor do they say that anarchy would prevail without some legalized authority.)

Obviously, we could go on and on in giving examples of differences in conceptual schemes, due to differences in the deeper values of the scholars who formulate them. The point to be made is that in the study of mankind, as opposed to the study of nonhuman objects and phenomena, values do get into the picture in more than one way. For philoso-

---

14 Reproduced herein as pages 53–54 of John Locke, *Concerning Civil Government*.

15 Note, also, that the assumptions of scholars vary according to the nature of the institution they are studying. Classical economists were "in favor of" freedom of the firm's management to do as it wished, but they never implied that *within* the firm there should be "free enterprise." They imply quite the contrary: that the executive, either as an expert computer of economic data, or as a deterministic agent, should determine jobs and specializations, and allocate resources up to the margin. The applied economists, such as budget analysts, financial planners, and the like, imply even more explicitly that people and other resources should be managed on the basis of expert calculation of marginal revenues, cash flows, break-even charts, and the like.

phers, who use assumptions and reasoning, the values can clearly influence what they see, both in terms of selecting assumptions from which to reason and in showing relationships. For applied social scientists, the practitioners who study large complex organizations, and particularly those who study matters of human individuality and organizational attributes, these values influence the choice of facts to observe, the way experiments are set up, and derivation of meaning from those facts.

The Value of Social Science in Policy Decisions

In this chapter we have seen some of the methods used by social scientists and social philosophers to arrive at their theories and conceptual schemes.

If there is anything which should stand out to the policy maker, to the man of action, it is the fact that social science provides an enormous pool of experience from a wide variety of people who spend their lives looking for meaning of events within their field. The very bias with which they approach their subjects, occasioned by different viewpoints or preconceptions, or, as in the Durkheim case, occasioned by their interest in a certain problem, means that they see people, organizations, and events in a light not available to laymen. To the policy maker these theories are valuable in determining managerial goals, in creatively formulating alternative courses of action, and in predicting what will happen if policy makers make decisions one way or another. Most important, *in all three* of these steps, they help to prevent a decision being made which later is discovered to have adverse unintended consequences.

For further insight into how the executive uses theory in his policy decisions, see "The Managerial Mind" in the Appendix.

CASE MATERIALS:

Less Complex Cases

MANCO CORPORATION

I Case Introduction

Synopsis

During the formative years of the management systems department of a consumer specialties manufacturing and marketing company, the staff witnesses three major reorganizations. In the three years from 1963 to 1966, the organization moves from a specialization by function (systems analysts and programmers) to specialization by customer (internal operating divisions like Marketing, Finance, Manufacturing, and R.&D.). The "generalists" in management systems serve the operating divisions in project groups headed by systems project administrators. This latter position evolves from a liaison and coordination role to a formal, supervisory role with accountability for the project itself and the project personnel involved in the new, integrated, staff service.

A former specialist, who is promoted to the systems project administrator position, seems to resist the newly integrated approach. He leaves the organization, and one of his former subordinates runs into serious trouble with an important EDP system for an operating division. A systems project administrator who had not previously been involved with the faulty system nor its designer assumes responsibility for both. Arrangements are made to correct the system. The systems project administrator "is very troubled" over what to do with the system's designer in view of his superior's statement: "I'm not sure where he fits in . . . do what you have to do."

Why This Case Is Included

The brief history of the management systems department records the interplay between the individual and organization structure. It is instructive to trace the development of role demands and the relationship between such role demands and perceived roles of those involved in the case. The history of the management systems department also points to the interdependence of people, structure, and technology—no one of the factors is altered in an organizational change effort without affecting the other two. There is opportunity to explore the degree of openness in interpersonal relationships and how this affects executive decisions. Finally, the case poses the issue of due process for the white-collar or management employee—that is, the degree of protection the employee has from unilateral behavior of superiors, especially when he works for a succession of different superiors with seemingly different criteria for acceptable performance.

Diagnostic and Predictive Questions

In answering the following diagnostic and predictive questions, remember that these questions apply theories and conceptual ideas from certain disciplines. Such theories are valuable to understand basic forces at work in the policy system (diagnosis) and to predict what will happen in the system in the future (prediction). Since each reading abstracts from the total policy system certain factors or variables into the closed or partial viewpoint of one theory or discipline, no one reading gives answers to the practical policy problems of the case. In diagnosis and prediction, the parts of the problem are studied with "other things being equal."

Following each question are listed readings which will be helpful in answering the question. The readings included with this case are marked (*). By referring to the author index at the end of this book, you may locate the other readings listed.

1. In an economic sense, what was Manco trying to accomplish in the 1963 reorganization of the management systems department? Keeping in mind the two concepts of specialization and coordination, trace the impact of the reorganization on the customer account computer system.

Read: *O'Connell, "Beyond Economics: Coordinomics," Part I.

2. Trace the interdependencies of people and structure during the 1963–66 period of growth and change in the management systems department of the Manco Corporation. Should top management have been able to predict the "people impact" of the structural changes and the "structure impact" of the personnel changes?

Read: *Leavitt, *Managerial Psychology*, pp. 317–25.

3. Using the social psychology conceptual schema for role development, trace the impact of the 1963 reorganization on the behavior (role performance) of the specialists in programming and the specialists in systems. What were the new role demands for each class of specialist? For the newly appointed systems project administrators?

Read: *Levinson, "Role, Personality, and Social Structure in the Organizational Setting"; Abrahams, "Status, Role, and Conflict."

4. Using the theoretical model of interpersonal relations analyze the relations between the following pairs as they are pictured and as they develop in the case: Carson-Wallace, Wallace-Roberts, Roberts-Carson, Behrens-Wallace, Behrens-Jonas, Jonas-Roberts, Carson-Jonas. Do you find perception "errors" in any of these relationships? If so, why do the individuals misperceive one another?

Read: *McGrath, *Social Psychology*, pp. 50–52.

5. Trace the development of Wallace's self-concept and Roberts' self-concept. Relate each self-concept to role performance by using the bridging construct of role concept.

Read: The readings assigned in the two previous questions.

6. After Behrens announces the departure of Wallace, Jonas asks: "Why don't you call a spade a spade?" How can you explain Behrens' behavior on this occasion? How explain Carson's behavior in his last interview with Jonas?

Read: *Carr, "Is Business Bluffing Ethical?"

7. When Wallace's job was eliminated in a reorganization of Behrens' unit, Jonas raised the issue of the "very involved system for placing unsatisfactory performers on warning. . . ." He said: "That system's supposed to protect the employee." Does Jonas voice a legitimate concern? What are the consequences of

what Jonas calls "a completely arbitrary system?" Does Roberts have due process protection?

Read: *Evan, "Organization Man and Due Process of Law."

Policy Questions for This Specific Case

In answering the following policy questions, the results of diagnosis and prediction are used to reduce the amount of guesswork, or judgment, in designing action solutions. However, since certain parts of the total case situation cannot be reduced to science, and since "other things are not equal," judgment must still be used to fill in the factors not accounted for by readings. You will also need a second kind of judgment as you put value weights on different scientific predictions, since different theories may point to conflicting solutions.

8. From what has happened to Wallace and Roberts in the Manco Company do you find cause to revise the appraisal system? If so, what would you recommend?

9. Would you have planned or implemented the Manco reorganizations any differently? If so, how?

10. If you were Behrens, what would you do at the end of the case? If you were Carson? If you were Jonas?

Major Policy Issues: Tentative Generalizations about Any Policy System

In arriving at conclusions for the following questions, generalize from the facts in the case and use your own ideas to (a) confirm, (b) modify, or (c) test the workability of the concepts and theories from readings. As an executive or professional, use wisdom to merge theory, on the one hand, with "brute facts" and practice, on the other.

11. As we plan reorganizations do we really understand all the dimensions of the relationship between the degree of specialization and the kind and degree of coordination?

Read: The reading attached to Question 1.

12. Is it true that relations in business firms are governed by the rules of poker?

Read: The reading attached to Question 6.

13. Have business organizations adequately faced the due process issue for white-collar workers, especially in light of the realities surrounding the economic assumption about free mobility in the labor market?

Read: The reading attached to Question 7.

Questions for Original Student Work in Analysis and Policy

The methods of viewing this case as represented by the authors' questions and selection of readings are not exhaustive. There are other relevant ideas for diagnosis and prediction. Furthermore, there are other ways of stating policy questions. More powerful analyses and wiser solutions will result by drawing on your own training and experience for (a) relevant concepts and theories, and (b) creative ways for asking policy questions. The following questions are designed to help you acquire this skill.

14. While reflecting on case facts, what additional theories from prior education give you insights as to "what is going on" in the Manco Corporation? As to what might be predicted to happen in the future?

15. Other than the policy questions asked by the authors, what pragmatic ways can you think of to state the practical problems faced by executives in the case?

II Manco Corporation

The Manco Corporation serves the consumer field with a broad line of high-quality specialty products. Most of the corporation's 6,000 employees work in Saginaw, Michigan, the headquarters and main plant location. Manco, with the other nine leading companies in its field, invests heavily in R.&D. and relies more on product innovation than on the protection of its numerous patents. Manco's $200 million sales volume is made up of about 75 per cent domestic sales and 25 per cent foreign sales. Growth over the past half-dozen years has averaged somewhat over 5 per cent a year, and profit margins have stayed well in excess of 10 per cent before tax.

One of the staff support groups serving the expanding and ever more sophisticated management is the management systems department. The partial organization chart of the Manco Corporation in Exhibit 1 shows the position of this department as of June 1966.

THE MANAGEMENT SYSTEMS DEPARTMENT

The 55 professional people in the management systems department serve all the operating divisions of the corporation as part of the central staff reporting to Elkin Parker, the vice president of Manco's Administrative Division, through Harold Simken, the director of administrative services.

The department is responsible for performing a broad range of internal consulting activities. The management systems department's major efforts are concentrated in the design and maintenance of computer-based information systems. Project work is also conducted in the areas of organization planning, operations research, general systems design, and standard operating procedures.

All management systems work is conducted on a project request basis. An appropriate manager in one of the company's divisions must request assistance before project work may be initiated. The project request is jointly reviewed by the management systems department manager and his five unit supervisors so that a priority may be assigned to the project. The considerable project backlog has made it necessary for departmental management to devote substantial time to identifying the most important project requests.

The organization of management systems (Exhibit 1) reflects Harold Simken's and Walter Davis' strong interest in maintaining satisfactory and stable relationships with all company divisions. Three systems units —the international-marketing unit, the financial-manufacturing unit,

Exhibit 1

PARTIAL MANCO ORGANIZATION CHART
(June 1966)

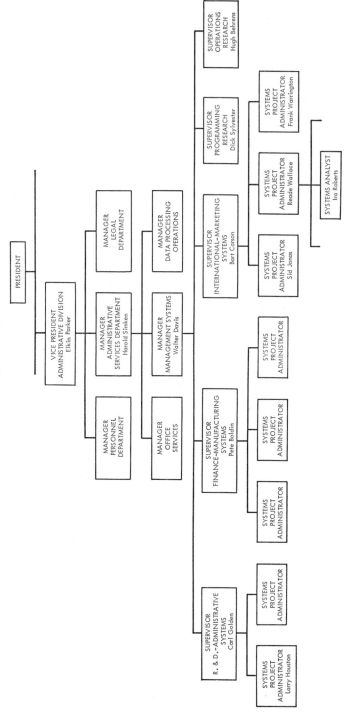

and the R.&D.-administrative unit—form the core of the department. Each unit performs work for two company divisions on a continuing basis. The operations research and programming research units provide technical support to the three systems units. Operations research and programming research personnel often work on those systems projects which require very specialized skills, and they are frequently involved in nonproject development work.

The mix of project work and personnel within each of the three systems units is determined by the pattern of project requests made by the various Manco divisions. The potential for meaningful systems design work and the receptivity of key managers vary from division to division. These differences create demands for divergent sets of skills in the three systems units. Project requests from the Research and Development Division, for example, involve the computerized retrieval of scientific information on laboratory experiments. On the other hand, systems work for the Administrative Division primarily consists of issuing and revising standard operating procedures. As a result of these project demands, the R.&D.—administrative unit has two distinct types of analysts—programmers and standard procedure specialists.

The requests made by the International and Marketing Divisions demand a still wider set of skills in the international-marketing systems unit. This unit has been involved in large-scale simulations of domestic and international distribution networks, organizational studies of the Marketing Division and several international branches, and other complex systems studies. Since these projects usually require skills different from either programming or procedure work, the international-marketing systems unit employs management scientists and organization planning specialists, as well as programmers and systems analysts.

Within each systems unit, there are two or three systems project administrators, who handle the day-to-day administrative activities of the systems units. Each project administrator is responsible for specific departments in one or two Manco divisions. Thus, in the international-marketing systems unit, one project administrator is responsible for projects in the market research and promotion planning departments, while another supervises project work for the sales, advertising, and general promotion departments. The systems project administrator is, in essence, a working first-line supervisor. From a supervisory standpoint, the project administrators supervise client project requests, plan and schedule work loads, administer salary, and appraise performance of their subordinates. In addition, they spend approximately one third of their time actually performing some of the more complex project work.

The present management systems department was formed during a June 1963 reorganization, which combined all systems and programming activities. Prior to the reorganization, separate Systems and Programming Sections existed. Most of the analysts believed that the reorganization was precipitated by management's dissatisfaction with the divided responsibility for projects, which so often called for both systems and programming work. There had been an increasing number of complaints concerning the inability of the two sections to meet deadlines for converting systems from manual to computer processing. The systems analysts believed that the programmers were at fault for not adhering to schedules. The programmers contended that the systems analysts did not appreciate the magnitude and complexity of the programming task. Because of this lack of understanding, argued the programmers, the systems analysts made unrealistic calendar commitments to the divisional managers responsible for the particular system.

The reorganization was also designed to eliminate the discontent among systems analysts and programmers over advancement opportunities. As a result of the reorganization, the positions of management systems manager and unit supervisor were upgraded to higher salary classifications. The new position of systems project administrator was created one level below the unit supervisor level. Between June 1963 and June 1966, eight former senior system analysts and senior programmers were elevated to systems project administrators.

In the spirit of the 1963 reorganization, the systems analysts working for each systems project administrator were expected to perform both systems and programming activities. Initially the interests and assignments of most analysts corresponded to their previous specialty—systems or programming. Salary increases and promotions in the new organization, however, were designed to reward the generalist—the man who was able and willing to do both systems and programming and demonstrated this in project work. The hiring and training of new employees were also geared to produce this new breed of systems analysts.

THE INTERNATIONAL-MARKETING SYSTEMS UNIT

The supervisor of the international-marketing systems unit (see Exhibit 1) is Bart Carson. Carson, who had transferred into systems from the Manufacturing Division in 1958, is generally considered by his peers to be the most experienced and talented systems supervisor. Although his (pre-1963) experience had been confined to the Systems Section, he has been very positive about the new integrated approach of the 1963 reorganization. Carson has made conscious efforts to give his analysts diversified exposure and gradually has begun to develop what is regarded as a well-rounded unit within the context of the new management systems job responsibilities.

One of the three systems project administrators reporting to Carson in the summer of 1966 was Reade Wallace. Carson had given Wallace responsibility for project work in the International Division and the distribution department of the Marketing Division. Wallace, who had joined the company in 1959 after obtaining his MBA degree, had been regarded as a mainstay of the pre-1963 Systems Section. He had specialized in organization planning, standard operating procedures, and general systems work. Wallace's associates noted that his diplomacy and tact had enabled him to establish excellent rapport with several key managers in the company, in general, and in the International Division, in particular. Harold Simken, manager of administrative services, and Walter Davis, manager of management systems, were keenly interested in generating new international project work, and they both often spoke of how much they valued Wallace's interpersonal skills.

After the 1963 reorganization but before his promotion to systems project administrator, Wallace had made it clear to Bart Carson, systems supervisor, that he had no desire to get involved in EDP or management science projects. He preferred to continue his concentration in organizational planning and general administrative systems and said so publicly. Wallace was, in fact, the only analyst after the 1963 reorganization who overtly resisted Carson's plan for development. Consequently, Wallace's promotion to systems project administrator in October 1964 had been a very controversial move. To many analysts, the promotion represented a flagrant violation of the criteria established for the systems project administrator position. Some analysts attributed the move to pressure exerted on Carson by Simken and/or Davis.

MANAGEMENT SYSTEMS DEPARTMENT EXPANDS

The management systems department experienced rapid growth between June 1963 and June 1965, expanding from a personnel complement of 30 analysts to one of 55 analysts. One source of new people was the company's management training program, a rotational program consisting of several six- to eight-week assignments in various Manco divisions.

Among the trainees in this program was Ira Roberts, a former high school teacher who had taught for four years. As he completed the program in December 1965, Roberts' record showed he had created favorable impressions throughout the company during his rotational assignments. Roberts' first permanent position was as management systems analyst in Bart Carson's international-marketing unit, reporting to Reade Wallace. Roberts had performed poorly on the programming aptitude test administered to all prospective management systems employees. He had received a B— on the exam, lower than anyone currently in the department. The independent psychological consulting firm, which administers the test, placed Roberts in the "Not Recommended" category on the analysis accompanying his test score. Since Roberts' principal work was to be in the general systems area, Carson and Wallace agreed that Roberts' personal strengths offset his relatively weak performance on the aptitude test. Carson and Wallace planned to increase Roberts' exposure to programming at some later date.

Roberts' first assignment was to develop a small-scale system to centralize information on grants to foundations and charities made by various company departments. His second project involved procedural work with various company divisions to insure company-wide compliance with new federal legislation affecting the sale of company products. After some training in network scheduling techniques, Roberts performed admirably in developing a PERT chart to plan and schedule the introduction of Manco's first product in the Australian market. Co-workers observed Roberts working yeoman's hours, and the manager of the new Australian Branch was unstinting in his praise of Roberts and his network schedule.

Roberts' performance during his first year in systems was formally appraised by Wallace in January 1967. He noted the following strengths:

1. Quick mind.
2. Ability to shoulder responsibility.
3. Works well with others.
4. Loyal and excellent attitude towards the company.
5. Documents work well and is both cost and profit conscious.

Wallace listed project planning as Roberts' major area for improvement. He rated Roberts satisfactory overall and concluded the appraisal by discussing his potential:

Roberts handles work very well and has high potential. Could develop into one of our better senior analysts with a bit more programming experience.

At the bottom of the appraisal sheet in the section entitled "Promotability," Wallace checked off "Promotable within two years." The only rating superior to this was "Promotable immediately." The appraisal was reviewed and signed by Carson, in accordance with company policy.

During the early part of 1967, the personnel department notified Roberts that several managers in the company were interested in offering him positions in their departments. These offers of employment in the public relations, distribution, and personnel departments were transmitted through the company's formal system for recruiting internal candidates. Each of these opportunities represented a promotion for Roberts. While these advancement opportunities all appeared attractive, Roberts expressed enthusiasm for his work in systems and was reluctant to leave. When he discussed the situation with Wallace and Carson, they both spoke optimistically about his future progress and their plans for him. Roberts decided to turn down the various internal opportunities and remain in management systems.

On April 1, 1967 Wallace and Carson jointly announced that Roberts had been promoted from management systems analyst to senior management systems analyst.

THE CUSTOMER ACCOUNT COMPUTER SYSTEM (CACS) PROJECT

As part of his plan to increase Roberts' programming experience, Wallace assigned him in April 1967 to a major EDP project, under the direction of another analyst. The basic purpose of this project was to create a computerized information system of all retail and wholesale accounts that distributed a major section of the product line. The system was designed to assist in processing orders during the hectic fall and winter sale periods. A secondary objective was to use the system for recording salesmen's call activities. The system was scheduled to go "online" in the fall of 1967.

In May 1967, the project was dealt a serious setback when the senior systems analyst leading the project resigned from the company. Wallace decided to have Roberts direct the project and assigned a new analyst to assist him. Between May and September, Roberts worked feverishly to complete the system. He worked a considerable amount of overtime each week, including six Saturdays during the summer months. Throughout this period, he assured Wallace and Carson and the management of the distribution department that the system would be ready to go into operation by September 1, 1967.

In the midst of Roberts' efforts on the CACS project, corporate organization changes affected the management systems department.

THE CORPORATE REORGANIZATION

In July 1967, a major corporate reorganization was announced. The objectives of the reorganization were the separation of planning activities from operations and the introduction of a strong profit center philosophy.

As a result of the reorganization, some key management changes occurred in the management systems department. Walter Davis, manager of the department, was appointed director, organization and policy planning, on the new corporate staff. Carl Golden, supervisor of the R. & D.—administrative systems unit, joined Davis' staff as manager of organization planning.

Bart Carson replaced Davis as management systems manager (see Exhibit 2). Dick Sylvester, previously supervisor, programming research, was named to direct a new Management Research Group. The three systems units were merged into two new units, reporting to Pete Boldin and Hugh Behrens. Behrens, who had previously served as supervisor, operations research, assumed responsibility for Carson's international–marketing systems unit and for all R. & D. systems. The administrative systems would henceforth be designed by the new corporate staff group

Exhibit 2

PARTIAL MANCO ORGANIZATION CHART
(August 1967)

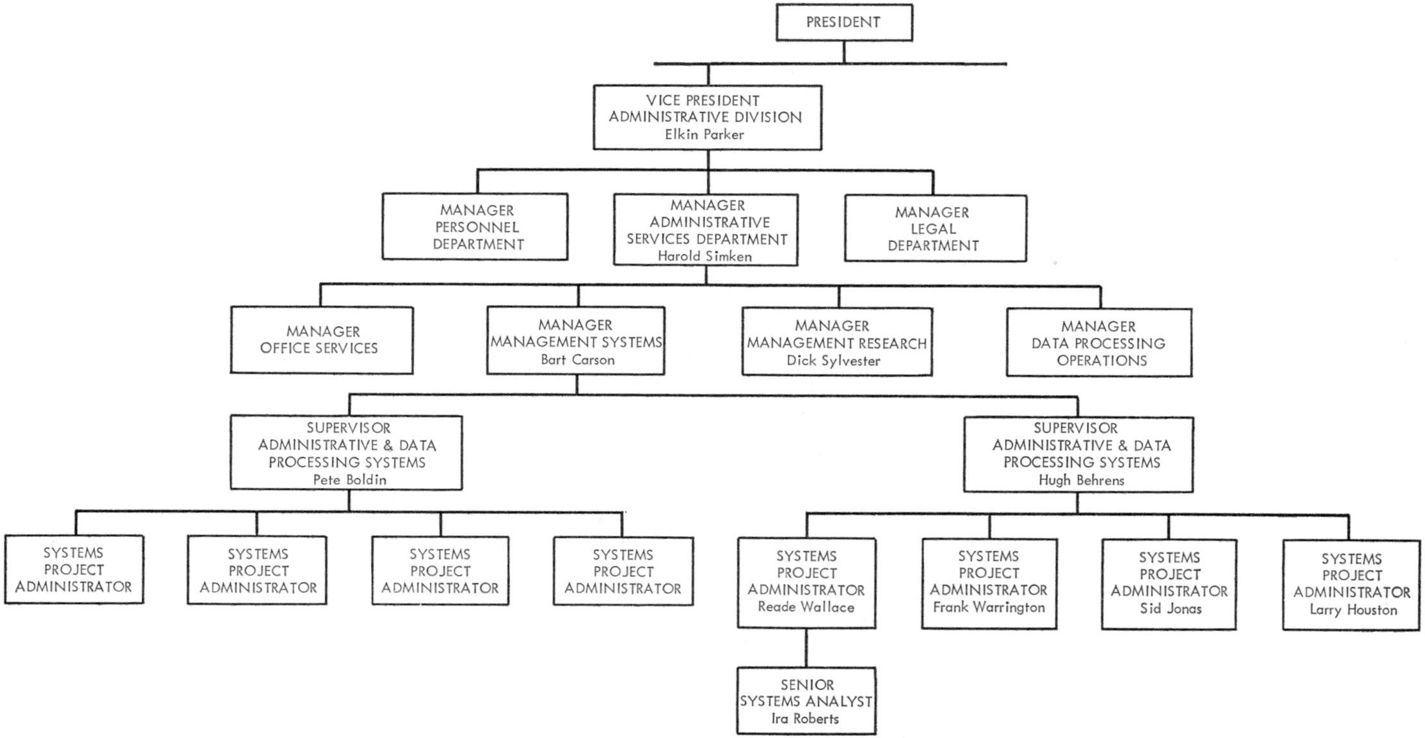

headed by Walter Davis and Carl Golden. Boldin retained responsibility for all financial and manufacturing systems.

THE JULY 1967–OCTOBER 1967 PERIOD

After the initial excitement generated by the announcement of management appointments, management systems activities continued with no major changes in direction. Carson and his two direct subordinates, Boldin and Behrens, conferred regularly to establish project objectives for 1968, plan the impending conversion to a 360 computer, and develop a new project control system.

Behrens' four systems project administrators (Sid Jonas, Frank Warrington, Larry Houston, and Reade Wallace) found him more conservative and less communicative than Carson, and yet by late summer they felt they had good rapport with him. Behrens started with Manco as a programmer in 1960, and had since served in various capacities in the Programming Section, Systems Section, and Operations Research Section. He was credited with conducting the company's most successful operations research effort—a large-scale simulation of the entire Manco distribution network. His several diverse skills had enabled him to establish an excellent reputation throughout the corporation.

Behrens called informal meetings of his four systems project administrators whenever he felt it necessary to review plans or communicate information. These hour-long meetings occurred about every two weeks during the late summer and early fall.

On October 18, Behrens called a 1:30 meeting of his systems project administrators. The only unusual aspect of the scheduling was the short two-hour notice. When the group assembled, they noted that Behrens, who was typically a very calm individual, seemed upset. Warrington, Jonas, and Houston were also surprised to see that Wallace was not present. Behrens began the meeting by announcing:

I've called you together to tell you that our unit has been reorganized as of this afternoon. Reade Wallace's job has been eliminated and he is leaving the company today. Sid Jonas will pick up Reade's responsibilities for all systems and management science projects in International. Ira Roberts will report to you, and we'll continue to recruit for a replacement for Ira's predecessor on the CACS project. Frank will handle all EDP projects for International. Barbara Mellor and Murray Hankins [Wallace's other analysts] will report to you.

Jonas was the first to speak after a long silence. "Does that mean that Reade was fired due to unsatisfactory performance?" "No," replied Behrens, "Reade was doing a satisfactory job, but we no longer had a position for him in our organization." Jonas reacted sharply to Behrens' answer:

Now, how can you do a thing like that? We have a very involved system for placing unsatisfactory performers on warning for 30 to 90 days and advising them that they will be canned if they don't shape up. You just subverted the whole system by reorganizing him out of a job. That system's supposed to protect the employee. Now all of the analysts will think that this is a completely arbitrary system and the axe can fall on them any time. We all know that Reade was deficient in certain respects. Why don't you call a spade a spade?

Interrupting, Behrens said:

Hold on a minute, Sid. Some of your points are valid, but you don't have all the facts. First of all, Wallace did get severance pay amounting to over $5,000. More important, we talked to all the personnel experts, and they said it would be in his best interest to do it this way. The company can give him a good reference without any black marks on his record. And, as an aside, we tried to place him elsewhere in the company. Distribution and International were interested, but because of the budget cutbacks throughout the company, they couldn't afford someone at his salary level. It's been my most traumatic experience since I've been with the company. What more can I say?

Jonas was preparing to resume the verbal battle but thought better of it and added, "I'm sorry, Hugh, but I don't agree. I'm probably unfair arguing with you over this since Reade only worked for you for three months. It's Bart Carson who's responsible, and I plan to tell him that I think the whole situation was handled poorly." With that the meeting was adjourned.

THE CUSTOMER ACCOUNT COMPUTER SYSTEM FAILS

Following the announcement of Wallace's departure, Jonas and Warrington met with their newly assigned analysts to review work loads and project plans. The main topic during the first meeting between Jonas and Roberts on October 20 was the CACS project. Roberts first explained the system to Jonas, pointing out its objectives and major features. He explained that the system began operating in September, although a few "bugs" still had to be ironed out. Roberts expressed confidence that the system would be operating smoothly before too long.

The CACS project seemed to be moving toward final completion when Jonas was called into Behrens office on Thursday, November 9. Behrens informed Jonas that one of the scheduled computer runs for the CACS project had produced incorrect results and Ned O'Donnell, the distribution department manager, had phoned a complaint to Bart Carson. Behrens expressed the fear that there might be some major problem with the entire system. Jonas suggested they speak to Roberts. Behrens phoned Roberts, requesting that he come to his office. Roberts explained that the error in sales totals resulted from 50 duplicate records on the master file. He had scheduled a computer printout of the master file so that the clerks in the distribution department could correct the errors. He assured Jonas and Behrens that he would take care of the problem.

The master file printout was checked by the distribution clerks on Monday, November 13, and Tuesday, November 14. On the 15th, Ned

O'Donnell asked Harold Simken, manager of administrative services, to come to his office. When Simken arrived, he saw that O'Donnell had several hundred pages of a computer report on his desk. O'Donnell began to shout at Simken, "Harold, you see this printout? You know how much it's worth? This much!" And with that O'Donnell stuffed the printout in the waste basket. O'Donnell continued, "What's wrong with your damn department. If it's not one kind of mistake, it's another. Now that guy has gone and dropped all of our accounts in Northern California from the file. I can't make any sense out of this."

Simken returned to his office and asked to see Jonas, since Carson and Behrens were both out of the office. Carson was at a week-long management training session, and Hugh Behrens was attending a seminar in operations research. Simken gave Jonas a monotone hello when he entered and asked him what he was doing about the CACS situation. Jonas identified the various problems as best he could and reviewed the instructions he had given Roberts. Simken listened without comment until Jonas was through and then began to speak in a very stern voice. "Sid, I know you weren't involved in this system from the start, and you aren't responsible for these problems. But, it's yours now, and I'm holding you responsible for correcting this mess. Now, get busy on this and keep me informed of your progress."

When Behrens returned to the office the following morning, he was treated to a similar—in his words—"severe harangue," from Simken. Behrens decided to form a task force of himself, Pete Boldin, Jonas, and Roberts to conduct a comprehensive review of the system. After a three-day review, Behrens submitted a report to Carson and Simken, outlining the various technical problems and the proposed remedial action. The review had made it clear to Jonas and Behrens that Roberts did not have the technical EDP expertise to direct a project as complex as CACS. Moreover, some aspects of the system were misrepresented to marketing management in that the system was touted as a panacea for all of distribution's information problems. The cost of the system was vastly underestimated. Original estimates for development costs and annual operating costs were $14,000 to $19,000 and $8,500 to $14,000. Actual development costs exceeded $32,000, while annual operating costs zoomed to $30,000.

When Jonas and Behrens reviewed the report, Behrens began to discuss Roberts' capabilities:

Sid, we really gave you a personnel problem. That review convinced me that Roberts is not capable of senior analyst performance. There's no question about his technical deficiencies as far as I'm concerned. We know he wasn't a technical whiz but, if that wasn't bad enough, he did a terrible job of directing the project. There's no evidence of any planning. He missed every deadline, and I'm not sure he properly represented the critical status of the system to marketing or us. He probably didn't know how bad off he really was. You better think about how you're going to use him in the future. Given the type of things we expect from you in the future, I'm not sure where he fits in.

Jonas raised some questions about the apparently poor supervision and direction which Roberts had received from Wallace. Behrens agreed that this was a consideration. Behrens' secretary interrupted to remind him of a meeting, and he abruptly ended the discussion, "Well, give it some thought, Sid, and let's discuss it in a few days."

On Wednesday, November 22, Jonas arranged a session with Carson and Behrens to discuss the Roberts situation. Jonas opened the discussion by summarizing his position for Carson:

Bart, I've given this issue considerable thought, and I'm very troubled by it. I'm not reluctant to be a so-called "tough-minded manager" and place Roberts on warning for unsatisfactory performance. The problem with this approach is that it's the easy way out because it avoids the real troubling issues. Someone in this organization has to accept responsibility for the things that were said to Roberts six months ago. We told him that his future was very bright in systems and dissuaded him from accepting other jobs in the company. In fact, we promoted him in a relatively short span of time. In retrospect, that was the wrong decision. He's better suited for less technical work, such as personnel or public relations. So far, he hasn't demonstrated that he can perform at a senior level. And, don't forget, one big reason for his poor performance was the lack of proper supervision from Wallace.

If you want me to, I'll try to compensate for our past errors by getting back to basics and developing Roberts the right way. But I can't do this if you're not willing to adjust your expectations of my group. Hugh thinks that Roberts doesn't fit into my operation. So now it seems that if I try to develop one of my less adequate subordinates, I don't meet my technical responsibilities. If I stick to the technical goals, I ship Roberts out the door.

Carson answered:

Sid, I don't want you to worry about things that were said to Roberts before he started working for you. Perhaps we were premature in promoting him. I'll accept responsibility for all of that. We expect big things of you, and you need the proper blend of skills in your group. It's very easy for Hugh and me to sit here and tell you what to do. But, if we did that, we'd impair your development as a supervisor. All I can say is do what you have to do.

III Selected Readings

From: Jeremiah J. O'Connell
BEYOND ECONOMICS: COORDINOMICS*

(PART I)

The word economics is taken from the two Greek words *oikos* and *nemein*. *Oikos* means "household" and *nemein* means "to manage." The root meaning of the word economics, therefore, is "to manage a household." In the economics of business enterprise we concentrated on the specialized segments or segmented departments of the corporation. Historically, the emphasis has been on efficiency within functional departments—a concentration on the area described by each of the boxes on the organization chart. Each box was a household, so to speak, to be managed in such a way that, within the confines of that functional box on the organizational chart, we achieved all the efficiencies produced by specialization and derived all the benefits from economies of scale or size. Now, in the mature business enterprise it seems we are approaching the point of diminishing returns to our efforts at managing these segmented compartments of the organization. We are at a point now where the emphasis is shifting in the quest for efficiency to inter-departmental cooperation and coordination—that is, to a concentration on managing the spaces between the boxes on the organization chart. We are at the point where there are greater returns to an investment spent on achieving coordination among the functional departments of an organization than to an investment spent on improving the operations in any one of the functional departments.

Historically, when we spoke of systems, we behaved as if the organization were a mechanical system, that is, that the whole was nothing other than and nothing different from the sum of the several, functionally specialized, parts of the organization. Systems today have come to mean something organic rather than mechanical—that is, the whole is something other than and something in addition to the sum of the functionally specialized parts. In this sense, then, we have moved beyond economics—the management of separate households—to coordinomics—the management of the process of coordination. Economics had us focus on the compartments of the organization; coordinomics would have us focus on the spaces between the compartments in the organization. . . .

*   *   *   *   *

* Excerpt from Keynote Address at the Eighth Annual Systems Conference of the Southwest, Dallas, Texas, May 9, 1966.

From: Harold J. Leavitt

THE VOLATILE ORGANIZATION:
EVERYTHING TRIGGERS EVERYTHING ELSE*

In this first chapter in Part IV, we have just one purpose—to encourage the reader to think about organizations not just as simple, static charts or as milling collections of people or as smoothly oiled man-machine systems but as rich, volatile, complicated but understandable systems of *tasks, structures, tools,* and *people* in states of continuous change.

Toward that purpose, consider the following example:

If, as a manager, you have a rather complicated problem, you may want to call in a consultant for help. Suppose the problem is a typically hard one: one of your larger field units is turning in much poorer results than all your forecasts had predicted.

So you call in the partner in charge of the local office of one of the reputable older consulting firms—the largest in town. They contract to take on the problem and send some people out to the unit to collect information.

When they finally come in with a report, you scan it and then turn to the recommendations. They recommend the following: (1) You need tighter controls. (2) Job relationships need to be reorganized and redefined; job descriptions need to be rewritten with greater precision (to get rid of squabbles about overlapping authority). (3) The functional form of organization they now have down there ought to be switched over to a product form. (4) In fact, that unit has grown so big that it ought to go through a partial decentralization itself, with a lot more authority given to the product managers. (5) You need a thorough methods analysis. The number of reports that are being generated now is excessive. There is wasteful duplication of effort and communication. You ought to streamline the organization's procedures. (6) And you may have to move a few people out, too. There is too much fat in the organization, and so on.

If you are a manager with an experimental turn of mind and a pocket full of money, you will decide not to act on this consultant's report yet. You decide, instead, to knock on the door of another consultant and get a second independent assessment.

You had gotten to know the first firm by now. You had found that the people in it were active in the Society for the Advancement of Management, and highly experienced in business organization. You note, with some discomfort, that this second firm professes different allegiances and displays other pedigrees. This second group is active in the Operations Research Society, and the Institute for Management Sciences. Its experiences in industry really are not as extensive as those of number-one firm, but it has done a lot of recent military work, and its senior people all have Ph.D's. It looks like a group of whiz kids. But they have cut their hair and they sound reasonable, so you hire them to look into the same problems.

They send their people out to the unit, and they, too, come up with a report. But their conclusions are different. Instead of recommending

* Chapter 21, from Harold J. Leavitt, *Managerial Psychology* (Chicago, Ill.: University of Chicago Press, 1964), pp. 317–25. Reprinted by permission.

modifications in the *structure* of the organization, they recommend modifications in the *technical* and *analytic* methods being used. They are technologists who think technological improvement is the means to the best of all possible worlds. They want to linear program the inventory control methods being used in that division, and to automate the purchasing operation. They want to modify the information flows, so that decisions can be made at different points in the organization, and faster. And instead of job descriptions and organization charts as their tools, their pockets are full of computers and long equations. You will have to hire some hot-shot college boys if you want to carry out their recommendations; because neither you nor any of your top people can fully understand them.

But if you are *really* an experimental manager, and if your pockets are really full of gold, and if you don't satisfy easily, you call in the only other consulting firm in town. Its members are Ph.D. types, too. Their offices aren't very elaborate, either. Their affiliations are different, again. They are members of the American Psychological Association, and/or members of the consultant network of the National Training Laboratories. They are clinical or social psychological types. And they view the world from the human side. They don't carry computers in their back pockets, or write job descriptions, or draw organization charts. Their favorite tools are the meeting, the discussion, the face-to-face group, and the open-ended interview.

So you hire them and let them take a look at your difficult unit. And they too come up with a report. But their report is different again. It argues that the solution to unit X's problem lies in changing the attitudes and interrelations of the people in that unit. Morale is low, they say. Apathy is high. People are constricted and anxious, afraid to speak up or take risks. What your organization needs is more *openness,* more *participation,* more *involvement,* more *creativity.*

So their recommendation is that you work on the people end of the problem. They want you to set up a series of "laboratory" training programs, in which you take groups of your people from division X out to a country club for a week at a time to talk things over; to open up valid communication among themselves; to express what they really feel; and to develop much more mutual trust and confidence.

Probably you could go on experimenting, but the board members are giving you strange looks by now, and the people in unit X are really up in the air. So you decide to stop there and take a look at what you have. Which of the three firms' recommendations should you follow up? Since you are the manager, we'll leave it to you to answer that question.

But though we can't answer it, let's not leave it quite there. As of right now we have a situation that looks like this:

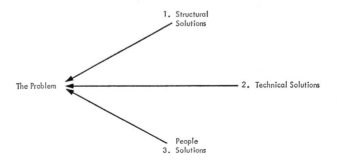

We have one group that wants to solve the problem of unit X by working on *structure*, by changing the organization chart and the locations of authority and responsibility. We have another group that's going to solve the same problems *technologically*, by improving the analytic quality of decisions and applying new techniques for controlling and processing information. And we have a third group that's going to solve the very same problems humanly, by working on persons and interpersonal relations. But there is one more important point that needs to be made here, before you decide which one of these to use. They aren't mutually exclusive. The point is that the diagram above is incomplete. Because no one of these actions will affect the way the task of division X gets done without also involving each of the other points on that chart. *Structure* and *technology* and *people* are not separable phenomena in organizations. If we hire the structurally oriented firm, and if we decentralize the unit, or if we change the present allocation of responsibilities, it will not only affect the problem but will also affect (perhaps adversely) people's attitudes and interpersonal relations. We will have to draw an arrow like this:

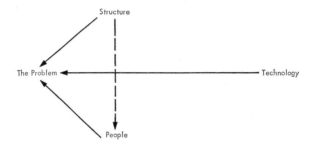

If you tighten controls, for example, some people may get angry or uncomfortable. If you switch from a functional to a product organization form, there will be new problems of interpersonal relations.

And if we play with the organization structure we will also get some effects on *technology*. The kinds of techniques that are now appropriate in a highly decentralized scheme—the accounting techniques for example—may have to be very different than those appropriate for highly centralized organizations.

And similarly, if we hire the technically oriented consulting firm, and go on to introduce the computer and new information flows, then we can darn well expect effects not only on the way the job gets done but also on structure and on people. If we can centralize information in locations where we couldn't centralize before, we will find decisions being made and responsibilities being taken in different places than they were being taken before. And while we may be talking about *de*centralization, that new information system may be pushing us toward centralization. We may also find that the kinds and numbers of people we need in our new, technically sophisticated organization may be quite different from the kind and number of members we needed before. Moreover some things that were done judgmentally and thoughtfully are now pretty well programed, so that essentially they can be done by the machine—with some consequent effects on the attitudes and feelings of persons.

Finally, if we move in on the people side, hiring the human relations firm, we will encourage people to be more open and more valid in their communication, encourage people to take more responsibility, and encourage people to interact more with other members of the organization. If we do these things, let us not for a moment think that we can do them without exerting great pressure on our existing organizational structure. The authority system will change and so will the status system. And we will exert pressure on technology too. The newly freed-up people may want new tools or the abolition of old ones that have been technically useful but are psychologically frustrating.

And so we end up with a diagram that looks like this:

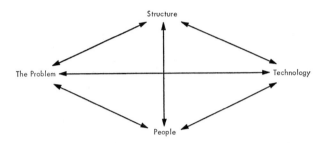

In this one everything feeds back on everything else, so that although we started out to worry only about the relationship between structure and task, or technology and task, or people and task, we must end up worrying about the effects of changes in any one on all of the others. Some of those changes may be very helpful, but some may be negative. And the manager has to somehow diagnose the secondary and tertiary effects of action in any one of these areas.

For organizations do not stand still. If we inject something into one part of the system bells begin to ring and lights begin to go on all over the system, often in places we hadn't counted on and at times we hadn't expected.

This is not to say that the complexity of the organization is so great that we can never tell what will happen when we do something. It is only to say that an organization is complex enough to make any simple structural or technical or human model inadequate. But we have made a lot of progress in understanding the complexities in the last few decades. We now know a good deal more about ways of acting on structure or people or technology; and we know somewhat more about how they are wired to one another. There is real progress in the organizational world. The three classes of consulting firms in our example should not be taken as an indication that things have gone to pot. On the contrary they are an indication of how much we have learned about organizations. And about how much we now know of ways to change or modify them.

The practitioner in each of these three realms may be oversold on his own product. He may be overly enthusiastic about all that can be done by changing structure, or technology, or people. Each may be partially and understandably blind to the perspectives of the others. But the manager need not be blind. He has lots more to work from than he did in the days when we so naïvely believed that the simple line drawing on the organization chart actually did capture the essence of our live, volatile organization.

In Summary

Organizations can be thought of as lively sets of interrelated systems designed to perform complicated tasks. We can try to manipulate at least three dimensions of those systems in order to get the performance of tasks changed or improved. We can manipulate the organization structure—which means we can manipulate the communication system or the authority and power system, or the system of work flows and processes. We can manipulate the tools and techniques used in the system—which means we can provide new and better hammers or new and better information-processing devices. And we can enter from the people side, to change bodies, or attitudes, or interpersonal relations—which means we can change the training and skills of our people, or the numbers of people involved, or the kinds of people we hire.

But we must never for a moment forget that when we tamper with any one of these three variables, structure or technology or people, we are likely to cause significant effects on the others, as well as on the task.

From: Daniel J. Levinson
*ROLE, PERSONALITY, AND SOCIAL STRUCTURE IN THE ORGANIZATIONAL SETTING**

[EDITOR'S NOTE: The author is Professor of Psychology at Yale University. In this article Professor Levinson adds balance to the literature on role theory by giving emphasis to personality as well as environmental determinants of role concept and role performance. The excerpts reproduced here do not present the richness or detail of Professor Levinson's theoretical position. Those interested in going further should consult the original article.]

*   *   *   *   *

"SOCIAL ROLE" AS A UNITARY CONCEPT

The concept of role is related to, and must be distinguished from, the concept of social position. A position is an element of organizational autonomy, a location in social space, a category of organizational membership. A role is, so to say, an aspect of organizational physiology; it involves function, adaption, process. It is meaningful to say that a person "occupies" a social position; but it is inappropriate to say, as many do, that one occupies a role.

There are at least three specific senses in which the term "role" has been used, explicitly or implicitly, by different writers or by the same writer on different occasions.

a) Role may be defined as the *structurally given demands* (norms, expectations, taboos, responsibilities, and the like) associated with a given social position. Role is, in this sense, something outside the given individual, a set of pressures and facilitations that channel, guide, impede, support his functioning in the organization.

b) Role may be defined as the member's *orientation* or *conception* of the part he is to play in the organization. It is, so to say, his inner definition of what someone in his social position is supposed to think and do about it. Mead (1934) is probably the main source of this view of social role as an aspect of the person, and it is commonly used in analyses of occupational roles.

c) Role is commonly defined as the *actions* of the individual members—actions seen in terms of their relevance for the social structure (that is, seen in relation to the prevailing norms) . In this sense, role refers to the ways in which members of a position act (with or without conscious intention) *in accord with*

* This abridgment from the article of the same title is reprinted by permission from *Journal of Abnormal Psychology,* Vol. 58 (1959) , pp. 171–80.

or in violation of a given set of organizational norms. Here, as in (*b*), role is defined as a characteristic of the actor rather than of his normative environment.

Many writers use a definition that embraces all of the above meanings without systematic distinction, and then shift, explicitly or implicitly, from one meaning to another. The following are but a few of many possible examples.[1]

*   *   *   *   *

In short, the "unitary" conception of role assumes that there is a 1:1 relationship, or at least a *high degree of congruence,* among the three role aspects noted above. In the theory of bureaucratic organization, the rationale for this assumption is somewhat as follows. The organizationally given requirements will be internalized by the members and will thus be mirrored in their role-conceptions. People will know, and will want to do, what is expected of them. The agencies of role socialization will succeed except with a deviant minority—who constitute a separate problem for study. Individual action will in turn reflect the structural norms, since the appropriate role-conceptions will have been internalized and since the sanctions system rewards normative behavior and punishes deviant behavior. Thus, it is assumed that structural norms, individual role-conceptions and individual role-performance are three isomorphic reflections of a single entity: "the" role appropriate to a given organizational position.

It is, no doubt, reasonable to expect some degree of congruence among these aspects of a social role. Certainly, every organization contains numerous mechanisms designed to further such congruence. At the same time, it is a matter of common observation that organizations vary in the degree of their integration; structural demands are often contradictory, lines of authority may be defective, disagreements occur and reverberate at and below the surface of daily operations. To assume that what the organization requires, and what its members actually think and do, comprise a single, unified whole is severely to restrict our comprehension of organizational dynamics and change.

*   *   *   *   *

ORGANIZATIONALLY GIVEN ROLE-DEMANDS

The role-demands are external to the individual whose role is being examined. They are the situational pressures that confront him as the occupant of a given structural position. They have manifold sources: in the official charter and policies of the organization; in the traditions and ideology, explicit as well as implicit, that help to define the organization's purposes and modes of operation; in the views about this position which are held by members of the position (who influence any single member) and by members of the various positions impinging upon this one; and so on.

*   *   *   *   *

In attempting to characterize the role-requirements for a given position, one must therefore guard against the assumption that they are unified and logically coherent. There may be major differences and even contradictions between official norms, as defined by charter or by administrative authority, and the "informal" norms held by various groupings within the organization. Moreover,

---

[1] An argument very similar to the one made here is presented by Gross, Mason, and McEachern (1958) in a comprehensive overview and critique of role theory. They point up the assumption of high consensus regarding role-demands and role-conceptions in traditional role theory, and present empirical evidence contradicting this assumption. Their analysis is, however, lese concerned than the present one with the converging of role theory and personality theory.

within a given-status group, such as the top administrators, there may be several conflicting viewpoints concerning long range goals, current policies, and specific role-requirements. In short, the structural demands themselves are often multiple and disunified. Few are the attempts to investigate the sources of such disunity, to acknowledge its frequency, or to take it into conceptual account in general structure theory.

It is important also to consider the specificity or *narrowness* with which the normative requirements are defined. Norms have an "ought" quality; they confer legitimacy and reward-value upon certain modes of action, thought and emotion, while condemning others. But there are degrees here. Normative evaluations cover a spectrum from "strongly required" through various degrees of qualitative kinds of "acceptable," to more or less stringently tabooed. Organizations differ in the width of the intermediate range on this spectrum. That is, they differ in the number and kinds of adaptation that are normatively acceptable. The wider this range—the less specific the norms—the greater is the area of personal choice for the individual. While the existence of such an intermediate range is generally acknowledged, structural analyses often proceed as though practically all norms were absolute prescriptions or proscriptions allowing few alternatives for individual action.

There are various other normative complexities to be reckoned with. A single set of role-norms may be internally contradictory. In the case of the mental hospital nurse, for example, the norm of maintaining an "orderly ward" often conflicts with the norm of encouraging self-expression in patients. The individual nurse then has a range of choice, which may be narrow or wide, in balancing these conflicting requirements. There are also ambiguities in norms, and discrepancies between those held explicitly and those that are less verbalized and perhaps less conscious. These normative complexities permit, and may even induce, significant variations in individual role-performance.

The degree of *coherence* among the structurally defined role-requirements, the degree of *consensus* with which they are held, and the degree of *individual choice* they allow (the range of acceptable alternatives) are among the most significant properties of any organization. In some organizations, there is very great coherence of role-requirements and a minimum of individual choice. In most cases, however, the degree of integration within roles and among sets of roles appears to be more moderate.[2] This structural pattern is of especial interest from a sociopsychological point of view. To the extent that the requirements for a given position are ambiguous, contradictory, or otherwise "open," the individual members have greater opportunity for selection among existing norms and for creation of new norms. In this process, personality plays an important part. . . .

Role-Facilities

In addition to the demands and obligations imposed upon the individual, we must also take into account the techniques, resources, and conditions of work— the means made available to him for fulfilling his organizational functions. . . .

*   *   *   *   *

[2] The reduced integration reflects in part the tremendous rate of technological change, the geographical and occupational mobility, and the diversity in personality that characterize modern society. On the other hand, diversity is opposed by the standardization of culture on a mass basis and by the growth of large-scale organization itself. Trends toward increased standardization and uniformity are highlighted in Whyte's (1956) analysis.

PERSONAL ROLE-DEFINITION

INDIVIDUAL (AND MODAL) ROLE-CONCEPTIONS

The nature of a role-conception may perhaps be clarified by placing it in relation to an ideology. The boundary between the two is certainly not a sharp one. However, ideology refers most directly to an orientation regarding the entire organizational (or other) structure—its purposes, its modes of operation, the prevailing forms of individual and group relationships, and so on. A role-conception offers a definition and rationale for one position within the structure. If ideology portrays and rationalizes the organizational world, then role-conception delineates the specific functions, values, and manner of functioning appropriate to one position within it.

*   *   *   *   *

. . . After all, individual role-conceptions are formed only partially within the present organizational setting. The individuals' ideas about his occupational role are influenced by childhood experiences, by his values and other personality characteristics, by formal education and apprenticeship, and the like. The ideas of various potential reference groups within and outside of the organization are available through reading, informal contacts, etc. There is reason to expect, then, that the role-conceptions of individuals in a given organizational position will vary and will not always conform to official role-requirements. Both the diversities and the modal patterns must be considered in organizational analysis.

INDIVIDUAL (AND MODAL) ROLE-PERFORMANCE

This term refers to the overt behavioral aspect of role-definition—to the more or less characteristic ways in which the individual acts as the occupant of a social position. Because role-performance involves immediately observable behavior, its description would seem to present few systematic problems. However, the formulation of adequate variables for the analysis of role-performance is in fact a major theoretical problem and one of the great stumbling blocks in empirical research.

Everyone would agree, I suppose that role-performance concerns only those aspects of the total stream of behavior that are structurally relevant. But which aspects of behavior are the important ones? And where shall the boundary be drawn between that which is structurally relevant and that which is incidental or idiosyncratic?

One's answer to these questions probably depends, above all, upon his conception of social structure. Those who conceive of social structure rather narrowly in terms of concrete work tasks and normative requirements, are inclined to take a similarly narrow view of role. In this view, role-performance is simply the fulfillment of formal role-norms, and anything else the person does is extraneous to role-performance as such. Its proponents acknowledge that there are variations in "style" of performance but regard these as incidental. What is essential to *role*-performance is the degree to which norms are met.

A more complex and inclusive conception of social structure requires correspondingly multi-dimensional delineation of role-performance. An organization has, from this viewpoint, "latent" as well as "manifest" structure; it has a many-faceted emotional climate; it tends to "demand" varied forms of interpersonal allegiance, friendship, deference, intimidation, ingratiation, rivalry, and the like. If characteristics such as these are considered intrinsic properties of social structure, then they must be included in the characterization of role-performance. My own preference is for the more inclusive view. I regard social structure as having psychological as well as other properties, and I regard as intrinsic to role-performance the varied meanings and feelings which the actor communicates to those about him. Ultimately, we must learn to characterize organizational behavior in a way that takes into account, and helps to illuminate, its functions for the individual, for the others with whom he interacts, and for the organization.

It is commonly assumed that there is great uniformity in role-performance among the members of a given position. Or, in other words, that there is *a dominant, modal pattern of role-performance corresponding to the structural requirements.* The rationale here parallels that given above for role-conceptions. However, where individual variations in patterns of role-performance have been investigated, several modal types rather than a single dominant pattern were found (Argyris, 1957; Greenblatt *et al.,* 1957) .

Nor is this variability surprising, except to those who have the most simplistic conception of social life. Role-performance, like any form of human behavior, is the resultant of many forces. Some of these forces derive from the organizational matrix; for example, from role-demands and the pressures of authority, from informal group influences, and from impending sanctions. Other determinants lie within the person, as for example his role-conceptions and role-relevant personality characteristics. Except in unusual cases where all forces operate to channel behavior in the same direction, role-performance will reflect the individual's attempts at choice and compromise among diverse external and internal forces.

*   *   *   *   *

ROLE-DEFINITION, PERSONALITY, AND SOCIAL STRUCTURE

*   *   *   *   *

Clearly, individual role-conception and role-performance do not emanate, fully formed, from the depths of personality. Nor are they simply mirror images of a mold established by social structure. Elsewhere (Levinson, 1954) , I have used the term "mirage" theory for the view, frequently held or implied in the psychoanalytic literature, that ideologies, role-conceptions, and behavior are mere epiphenomena or by-products of unconscious fantasies and defenses. Similarly, the term "sponge" theory characterizes the view, commonly forwarded in the sociological literature, in which man is merely a passive, mechanical absorber of the prevailing structural demands.

Our understanding of personal role-definition will remain seriously impaired as long as we fail to place it, analytically, in *both intra-personal and structural-environmental contexts.* That is to say, we must be concerned with the meaning of role-definition both for the individual personality and for the social system. A given role-definition is influenced by, and has an influence upon, the *psyche* as well as the *socius.* If we are adequately to understand the nature, the determinants, and the consequences of role-definition, we need the double perspective of personality and social structure. The use of these two reference points is, like the use of our two eyes in seeing, necessary for the achievement of depth in our social vision.

*   *   *   *   *

From: Joseph E. McGrath

THE PERCEPTION OF OTHER PEOPLE*

Oliver Wendell Holmes (1809–1894) once described a famous conversation between John and Henry in which six "persons" took part: John, as John knew himself; John, as he was known to Henry; the "true" John, as he was known only to God; and the equivalent trio of Henrys.

This same basic insight into the special nature of interpersonal perception was reflected in the work of early sociologists, notably in Cooley's (1902) concept of the "looking-glass self" and in George Mead's (1934) concepts of the two selves, the "I" and the "me." Both men pointed out that the child first develops an awareness of himself as an entity separate and distinct from his environment because *other people* respond to him as a separate, autonomous object. If there were no other people, we would have no self concept. As an individual develops a concept of "self," he becomes aware of himself as an object of his own perception (Mead's "me"), as distinct from himself as the perceiver (Mead's "I"). Furthermore, his own evaluation of himself arises as a *reflection of others' evaluation of him.* Thus, argued Mead and Cooley, the very heart of the individual's personality, his own self concept, arises in the first instance and develops through time by the process of social interaction with other people.

Since these early formulations, there has been much research and theory on the nature and consequences of interpersonal perceptions. One whole school of psychotherapy (see Rogers, 1942) is built upon Mead's premise that the self concept is crucial to adjustment and that self evaluation changes in response to changes in others' evaluations of oneself. On this premise, the crux of therapy is to provide the patient with a consistently warm and accepting social environment, thus providing a proper climate for him to reorient his self concept. Recently, Fiedler and his coworkers (1959) have shown that interpersonal perceptions are related to the individual's adjustment. In a large study of both military and college living groups, they found that individuals who see themselves as similar to others with whom they have close associations and who are seen as similar by those "significant others" show better personal adjustment than persons for whom this is not the case.

Newcomb (1953) points out that our perceptions of other people are closely tied to our attitudes on matters related to those people. We tend to agree with those we like and like those with whom we agree. We also tend to disagree with those we dislike and dislike those with whom we disagree. Newcomb has formalized these ideas in a theoretical model that summarizes many of the concepts in this area. Newcomb's model deals with two persons (A and B) engaged in interaction about one or more objects (X's), which can be ideas, physical objects, or other people. The set of attitudes which A and B have about each other and about the X's constitutes a system of interrelated parts. This set of attitudes is a system because the parts are interdependent, and when one part changes other parts are likely to show compensating changes. In fact, Newcomb postulates that there are certain states of the system (patterns of attitudes) which constitute *balanced* or *equilibrium* states. These balanced states are: mutual attraction between *A* and *B,* along with agreement about *X*'s; and mutual rejection between *A* and *B* along with disagreement about *X*'s. All other states (such as disagreement with mutual attraction) are unstable states and will tend toward one or another of the equilibrium patterns.

FIGURE 1

The Objective System

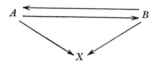

A's attitudes toward *B* and *X*
and *B*'s attitudes toward *A* and *X*

The Subjective Systems

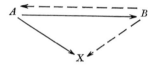

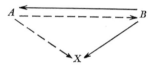

From *A*'s point of view

From *B*'s point of view

A's attitudes toward *B* and *X*
and *A*'s perceptions (estimates)
of *B*'s attitudes toward *A* and *X*

B's attitudes toward *A* and *X*
and *B*'s perceptions (estimates)
of *A*'s attitudes toward *B* and *X*

Diagram of Newcomb's *A-B-X* Model of Systems of Interpersonal Relationships. *A* and *B* represent two persons; *X* represents an object about which *A* and *B* are communicating or toward which *A* and *B* are co-orienting. Solid arrows represent actual attitudes of one person toward the other or toward *X*. Arrows run from holder of the attitude to target of the attitude. Broken-line arrows represent estimates by one person of the other persons' attitudes; for example, *B* — — — — — → *X* represents *A*'s estimate of *B*'s attitude toward *X*.

Underlying this "objective" system or pattern of attitudes are two "subjec-tive" *A-B-X* systems, one for *A* and one for *B*. *A*'s subjective system includes his attitudes toward *B* and toward *X* and his *perceptions* (estimates) of *B*'s attitudes toward himself (*A*) and toward *X*. *B*'s subjective system includes the correspond-ing attitudes and perceptions. The same kinds of balanced states (perceived agreement with positively attractive others, and perceived disagreement with negatively attractive others) and the same tendency toward system balance hold for the subjective systems as for the objective *A-B-X* system. These systems of interpersonal relationships are shown in Figure 1.

Thus, Newcomb is saying that the famous John and Henry conversation includes two other "persons" besides the six listed by Holmes, namely: John as John believes Henry sees him; and Henry's perception of how John sees Henry. Newcomb is also postulating that these interpersonal perceptions are interde-pendent with John's and Henry's own attitudes about the topics of their inter-action and with their perceptions of each other's attitudes. Thus, at a more general level, he postulates that interpersonal attitudes, interpersonal perceptions, and attitudes toward other objects are all interdependent with one another, tend to be compatible, and tend to change together as a system.

From: Albert Z. Carr

IS BUSINESS BLUFFING ETHICAL?*

[NOTE: Mr. Carr was Assistant to the Chairman of the War Production Board during World War II and later served on the White House staff and as a Special Consultant to President Truman. He is now writing full-time. Among his books is *John D. Rockefeller's Secret Weapon*, a study of corporate development. This article is adapted from a chapter in his newest book, *Business As a Game,* to be published by New American Library in March 1968.]

A respected businessman with whom I discussed the theme of this article remarked with some heat, "You mean to say you're going to encourage men to bluff? Why, bluffing is nothing more than a form of lying! You're advising them to lie!"

I agreed that the basis of private morality is a respect for truth and that the closer a businessman comes to the truth, the more he deserves respect. At the same time, I suggested that most bluffing in business might be regarded simply as game strategy—much like bluffing in poker, which does not reflect on the morality of the bluffer.

I quoted Henry Taylor, the British statesman who pointed out that "falsehood ceases to be falsehood when it is understood on all sides that the truth is not expected to be spoken"—an exact description of bluffing in poker, diplomacy, and business. . . .

*   *   *   *   *

PRESSURE TO DECEIVE

Most executives from time to time are almost compelled, in the interests of their companies or themselves, to practice some form of deception when negotiating with customers, dealers, labor unions, government officials, or even other departments of their companies. By conscious misstatements, concealment of pertinent facts, or exaggeration—in short, by bluffing—they seek to persuade others to agree with them. I think it is fair to say that if the individual executive refuses to bluff from time to time—if he feels obligated to tell the truth, the whole truth, and nothing but the truth—he is ignoring opportunities permitted under the rules and is at a heavy disadvantage in his business dealings.

But here and there a businessman is unable to reconcile himself to the bluff

---

* An abridgment of the article of the same title as it appeared in *Harvard Business Review*, Vol. XLVI, No. 1 (January–February 1968), pp. 143–53. © Harvard Business Review.

in which he plays a part. His conscience, perhaps spurred by religious idealism, troubles him. He feels guilty; he may develop an ulcer or a nervous tic. Before any executive can make profitable use of the strategy of the bluff, he needs to make sure that in bluffing he will not lose self-respect or become emotionally disturbed. If he is to reconcile personal integrity and high standards of honesty with the practical requirements of business, he must feel that his bluffs are ethically justified. The justification rests on the fact that business, as practiced by individuals as well as by corporations, has the impersonal character of a game—a game that demands both special strategy and an understanding of its special ethics.

The game is played at all levels of corporate life, from the highest to the lowest. At the very instant that a man decides to enter business he may be forced into a game situation. . . .

*   *   *   *   *

THE POKER ANALOGY

We can learn a good deal about the nature of business by comparing it with poker. While both have a large element of chance, in the long run the winner is the man who plays with steady skill. In both games ultimate victory requires intimate knowledge of the rules, insight into the psychology of the other players, a bold front, a considerable amount of self-discipline, and the ability to respond swiftly and effectively to opportunities provided by chance.

No one expects poker to be played on the ethical principles preached in churches. In poker it is right and proper to bluff a friend out of the rewards of being dealt a good hand. A player feels no more than a slight twinge of sympathy, if that, when—with nothing better than a single ace in his hand—he strips a heavy loser, who holds a pair, of the rest of his chips. It was up to the other fellow to protect himself. In the words of an excellent poker player, former President Harry Truman, "If you can't stand the heat, stay out of the kitchen." If one shows mercy to a loser in poker, it is a personal gesture, divorced from the rules of the game.

Poker has its special ethics, and here I am not referring to rules against cheating. The man who keeps an ace up his sleeve or who marks the cards is more than unethical; he is a crook, and can be punished as such—kicked out of the game or, in the Old West, shot.

In contrast to the cheat, the unethical poker player is one who, while abiding by the letter of the rules, finds ways to put the other players at an unfair disadvantage. Perhaps he unnerves them with loud talk. Or he tries to get them drunk. Or he plays in cahoots with someone else at the table. Ethical poker players frown on such tactics.

Poker's own brand of ethics is different from the ethical ideals of civilized human relationships. The game calls for distrust of the other fellow. It ignores the claim of freindship. Cunning deception and concealment of one's strength and intentions, not kindness and openheartedness, are vital in poker. No one thinks any the worse of poker on that account. And no one should think any the worse of the game of business because its standards of right and wrong differ from the prevailing traditions of morality in our society.

*   *   *   *   *

CAST ILLUSIONS ASIDE

*   *   *   *   *

The illusion that business can afford to be guided by ethics as conceived in private life is often fostered by speeches and articles containing such phrases as,

"It pays to be ethical," or, "Sound ethics is good business." Actually this is not an ethical position at all; it is a self-serving calculation in disguise. The speaker is really saying that in the long run a company can make more money if it does not antagonize competitors, suppliers, employees, and customers by squeezing them too hard. He is saying that oversharp policies reduce ultimate gains. That is true, but it has nothing to do with ethics. The underlying attitude is much like that in the familiar story of the shopkeeper who finds an extra $20 bill in the cash register, debates with himself the ethical problem—should he tell his partner?—and finally decides to share the money because the gesture will give him an edge over the s.o.b. the next time they quarrel.

I think it is fair to sum up the prevailing attitude of businessmen on ethics as follows:

We live in what is probably the most competitive of the world's civilized societies. Our customs encourage a high degree of aggression in the individual's striving for success. Business is our main area of competition, and it has been ritualized into a game of strategy. The basic rules of the game have been set by the government, which attempts to detect and punish business frauds. But as long as a company does not transgress the rules of the game set by law, it has the legal right to shape its strategy without reference to anything but its profits. If it takes a long-term view of its profits, it will preserve amicable relations, so far as possible, with those with whom it deals. A wise businessman will not seek advantage to the point where he generates dangerous hostility among employees, competitors, customers, government, or the public at large. But decisions in this area are, in the final test, decisions of strategy, not of ethics.

THE INDIVIDUAL AND THE GAME

An individual within a company often finds it difficult to adjust to the requirements of the business game. He tries to preserve his private ethical standards in situations that call for game strategy. When he is obliged to carry out company policies that challenge his conception of himself as an ethical man, he suffers.

It disturbs him when he is ordered, for instance, to deny a raise to a man who deserves it, to fire an employee of long standing, to prepare advertising that he believes to be misleading, to conceal facts that he feels customers are entitled to know, to cheapen the quality of materials used in the manufacture of an established product, to sell as new a product that he knows to be rebuilt, to exaggerate the curative powers of a medicinal preparation, or to coerce dealers.

There are some fortunate executives who, by the nature of their work and circumstances, never have to face problems of this kind. But in one form or another the ethical dilemma is felt sooner or later by most businessmen. Possibly the dilemma is most painful not when the company forces the action on the executive but when he originates it himself. . . .

        *   *   *   *   *

. . . If an executive allows himself to be torn between a decision based on business considerations and one based on his private ethical code, he exposes himself to a grave psychological strain.

This is not to say that sound business strategy necessarily runs counter to ethical ideals. They may frequently coincide; and when they do, everyone is gratified. But the major tests of every move in business, as in all games of strategy, are legality and profit. A man who intends to be a winner in the business game must have a game player's attitude.

The business strategist's decisions must be as impersonal as those of a surgeon performing an operation—concentrating on objective and technique, and sub-ordinating personal feelings. . . .

* * * * *

If a man plans to take a seat in the business game, he owes it to himself to master the principles by which the game is played, including its special ethical outlook. He can then hardly fail to recognize that an occasional bluff may well be justified in terms of the game's ethics and warranted in terms of economic necessity. Once he clears his mind on this point, he is in a good position to match his strategy against that of the other players. He can then determine objectively whether a bluff in a given situation has a good chance of succeeding and can decide when and how to bluff, without a feeling of ethical transgression.

To be a winner, a man must play to win. This does not mean that he must be ruthless, cruel, harsh, or treacherous. On the contrary, the better his reputation for integrity, honesty, and decency, the better his chances of victory will be in the long run. But from time to time every businessman, like every poker player, is offered a choice between certain loss or bluffing within the legal rules of the game. If he is not resigned to losing, if he wants to rise in his company and industry, then in such a crisis he will bluff—and bluff hard.

Every now and then one meets a successful businessman who has conveniently forgotten the small or large deceptions that he practiced on his way to fortune. "God gave me my money," old John D. Rockefeller once piously told a Sunday school class. It would be a rare tycoon in our time who would risk the horse laugh with which such a remark would be greeted.

In the last third of the twentieth century even children are aware that if a man has become prosperous in business, he has sometimes departed from the strict truth in order to overcome obstacles or has practiced the more subtle deceptions of the half-truth or the misleading omission. Whatever the form of the bluff, it is an integral part of the game, and the executive who does not master its techniques is not likely to accumulate much money or power.

From: William M. Evan

ORGANIZATION MAN AND DUE PROCESS OF LAW*

[EDITORS' NOTE: The author is Professor of Sociology and Industry, Wharton School of Finance and Commerce, University of Pennsylvania.]

The ideology of the "organization man," as it bears on industrial organizations, has at least two irrelated structural sources: (a) the unstructured character of the work of junior and middle managers which is conducive to the use of subjective criteria of performance appraisal, and (b) an authority structure devoid of a mechanism to insure "procedural due process of law." It is hypothesized that this ideology has largely dysfunctional consequences from the viewpoint of the individual executive, the industrial organization, and society as a whole. Two potential countervailing forces are considered:

* Reprinted from *American Sociological Review*, Vol. XXVI, No. 4 (August 1961).

the professionalization of management and the institutionalization of norms of procedural due process. Some research implications of this analysis are noted.

*   *   *   *   *

By comparison with the unionized manual worker, whose occupational rights are protected by the grievance machinery provided by the collective bargaining agreement, the junior or middle manager is at a distinct disadvantage: lacking the right of appeal, he is at the mercy of the decisions of his immediate superior who, in his decisions regarding his subordinates, may function simultaneously as judge, jury, and prosecutor.[1] From this perspective, the organization man appears to be a member of a "new proletariat" in present-day American industry. He does not have the protection of an outside occupational organization, such as unionized employees do; nor does he have a code of professional ethics to govern his relationships with his superordinates, his peers, and his subordinates; nor does he have the protection of "colleague control," as professionals do, to counteract "hierarchical control." Since the nature of his work makes objective evaluation of performance difficult, and since he lacks the right of appeal, he is, therefore, highly motivated to fulfill his superior's expectations—even at the expense of his own ideas and wishes—in order to insure a positive appraisal and the associated rewards. However, to fulfill his superior's expectations, which are often ambiguous, he learns to avoid any actions which he suspects might displease his superior. Such actions may range from joining or not joining the Masons[2] to the choice of style of clothing. The organization man's process of adapting himself to the expectations and behavior patterns of his superior and of relinquishing, if necessary, his own preferences and judgments may be likened to the conformity patterns experimentally observed by Sherif and Asch. Subjects faced with an ambiguous and unstructured situation—as in the case of the auto-kinetic effect—tend to adjust their statements of perceptions to one another;[3] and some subjects faced with an unambiguous and structured situation relinquish their true statement of perceptions of reality in favor of a false statement of perceptions made by others.[4]

In brief, the ideology of the organization man has at least two interrelated sources: occupational and organizational. Occupationally, the amorphous character of managerial work encourages the use of subjective criteria for evaluating performance, including a pattern of sponsorship or patronage and a concern for the organizational loyalty of subordinates. Organizationally, in the absence of norms of procedural due process of law, such as the right to appeal the decision of a superordinate, junior and middle managers are encouraged to become "conformists," developing an over-sensitivity to the expectations of superordinates in order to insure positive appraisal and corresponding rewards. Otherwise put, the ideology of organization man is an adaptation to certain normless elements in the work situation of junior and middle managers.

---

1 "There is no final escape from dependency if the superior is the ultimate authority, with no appeal beyond his interpretation or ruling. Unless there is some outside authority to which the subordinate can appeal, he never can be entirely safe in his dependency or quite able to develop a real independence." Mason Haire, *Psychology in Management* (New York: McGraw-Hill Book Co., 1956), p. 67.

2 Cf. Melville Dalton, *Men Who Manage* (New York: John Wiley & Sons, Inc., 1959), pp. 178–81.

3 Muzafer Sherif, "Group Influences upon the Formation of Norms and Attitudes," in Eleanor E. Maccoby, Theodore M. Newcomb, Eugene L. Hartley (eds.), *Readings in Social Psychology* (New York: Henry Holt & Co., 1958), pp. 219–32.

4 Solomon E. Asch, "Effects of Group Pressure upon the Modification and Distortion of Judgments," in Maccoby, Newcomb and Hartley, *op. cit.*, pp. 174–83.

SOME CONSEQUENCES OF THE IDEOLOGY
OF THE ORGANIZATION MAN

The consequences of the ideology of the organization man are presumably—in the absence of systematic data—largely dysfunctional from the viewpoint of the individual executive as well as from the viewpoint of the industrial organization and society at large. Several illustrative and hypothetical dysfunctions will be considered.

From the standpoint of the individual executive as well as the organization, the ideology tends to inhibit original and creative effort which, by definition, departs from prevailing practices, and hence runs the risk of not being approved by a superordinate. Accordingly, the industrial organization must increasingly rely on staff specialists for new ideas rather than on line management. This entails a loss to the organization of a potential source of valuable innovations—which is not to gainsay the advantages of having staff specialists concern themselves principally with problems of innovation.

Another consequence of this ideology for the individual as well as for the organization is the paradoxical combination of high job immobility with high job insecurity. By definition, the organization man's loyalty induces him to devote his entire career to his organization. He has a "local" rather than a "cosmopolitan" orientation; in other words, his reference group is his organization rather than the occupation of management which transcends a given organization. This tends to result in a high degree of job immobility among executive personnel. From the point of view of the organization, low turnover may be highly advantageous, provided the manager's performance is judged to contribute to the organization's effectiveness. In the event that his performance is judged to interfere with the organization's attainment of its goals, the organization may transfer him to an innocuous position, induce him to resign, or dismiss him.[5] In the absence of due process of law for junior and middle managers, and we might even add top managers, those who are judged undesirable for whatever reasons—relevant or irrelevant—may be discharged without an opportunity for a fair hearing.

Another consequence of the ideology which is dysfunctional for the organization is the tendency of the organization man to restrict upward communication to material which is calculated to enhance his self-image and simultaneously not threaten the superordinate in any way. On the basis of studies of experimentally created hierarchies, we would expect that organization men who are upwardly mobile—and this is presumably true of the bulk of junior and middle managers—would be strongly motivated to censor upward communication to insure positive appraisal and corresponding rewards.[6] Such action, of course, complicates the planning and coordination problems of top management.

Yet another effect of the ideology on the individual executive, related to job insecurity and the pressures for restriction of upward communication, is the tendency for discrepancies to develop between overt and covert behavior. Covert nonconformity occurs provided the probability of the discovery of such action is low. Where covert nonconformity does not occur, we may expect to find covert disbelief in the legitimacy of the authority exercised by the superior together

---

[5] Cf. Perrin Stryker, "How to Fire an Executive," *Fortune,* Vol. L (October 1954), pp. 116–17, 178–92.

[6] Cf. Harold H. Kelley, "Communication in Experimentally Created Hierarchies," *Human Relations,* Vol. IV (February 1951), pp. 39–56; Arthur R. Cohen, "Upward Communication in Experimentally Created Hierarchies," *Human Relations,* Vol. XI (February 1958), pp. 41–53.

with overt behavioral conformity. The resulting degree of cognitive dissonance, due to the discrepancy between overt conformity and covert disbelief, on the part of the organization man may be considerable. To reduce the resulting dissonance, the organization man can convince himself that his overt behavior is quite satisfactory after all, i.e., by changing his cognitions so that they are consonant with his overt behavior.[7]

The effect of the ideology of the organization man on society as a whole is probably more elusive than its effects on the individual manager and on the industrial organization, though nonetheless real. As a result of the premium put on cautious behavior calculated not to offend the preferences and expectations of a superior, the organization man may tend to transfer this behavior pattern and principle of behavior to his community life and engage in only "conformist" activity. This approach to community life lessens the chances of successfully coming to grips with new and complex social problems requiring innovative rather than "conformist" behavior. The consequences of this ideology for society as a whole may be especially marked in view of the recent efforts by corporations to encourage management to increase their participation in community affairs.

A related effect of the ideology may be observable in family values and child-rearing patterns of the organization man. The values of seeking approval from superiors, of "teamwork," and of "togetherness" may be transplanted from the corporation to the family.[8]

POTENTIAL COUNTERVAILING FORCES TO THE IDEOLOGY OF THE ORGANIZATION MAN

Two potential countervailing forces to the ideology of the organization man are the institutionalization of norms of procedural due process of law for corporate management and the professionalization of management.

As yet it is difficult to discern any evidence for the institutionalization of norms of due process within corporate management. It is possible, however, that such a development may be stimulated by the need for resolving conflicts between staff and line management. The high frequency of such conflicts, in the absence of unionization among staff specialists, may be conducive to the growth of norms of procedural due process. Such a development could pave the way for the extension of this institution to all corporate management.

Another source of influence favoring an extension of procedural due process is external to the corporation. There is a growing awareness of the need for restricting the powers of the corporation. In particular, it is being argued that the courts and the legislatures should extend constitutional guarantees of procedural due process to the corporation[9] or that corporations should develop their own "supplementary constitutional systems."[10] The venerable doctrine of due process, which dates back at least to the Magna Carta, includes a complex of procedural safeguards against the exercise of arbitrary and unlimited power.[11] These norms seek to insure that disputes are resolved impartially and fairly.

---

[7] Leon Festinger, *A Theory of Cognitive Dissonance* (Evanston, Ill.: Row, Peterson & Co., 1957), pp. 1–31.

[8] Daniel R. Miller and Guy E. Swanson, *The Changing American Parent: A Study in the Detroit Area* (New York: John Wiley & Sons, Inc., 1958).

[9] Adolph A. Berle, Jr., *The 20th Century Capitalist Revolution* (New York: Harcourt, Brace & Co., 1954), pp. 77 ff.

[10] Benjamin M. Selekman, "Power and Morality in Business," in Dan H. Fenn, Jr., *Management's Mission in a New Society* (New York: McGraw-Hill Book Co., 1959), pp. 317–19.

[11] Rodney L. Mott, *Due Process of Law* (Indianapolis, Ind.: Bobbs Merrill Co., 1926), pp. 1–29.

This complex of norms includes the right of all parties to a conflict to be heard, the right to confront witnesses, to cross-examine them, and to introduce evidence in one's behalf. . . . Another potential countervailing force to the ideology of the organization man is the professionalization of management. In spite of the plethora of discussions for several decades about the professionalization of management, there has been very little progress in this direction. . . .[12]

*   *   *   *   *

Either of the two potential countervailing forces to the ideology of the organization man may be conducive to the development of the other. As between these two possible developments it appears more likely that professionalization of management will be conducive to the institutionalization of norms of due process than the reverse.

Short of the institutionalization of the norms of procedural due process for junior and middle management, several other mechanisms may upon inquiry prove to have an equivalent function. The first is the institutionalization of the right of job transfer within a company. This would enable a manager, finding himself in an unsatisfactory authority relationship with his superior, to overcome this problem without suffering the consequences of adjustment to an arbitrary superior.

A related mechanism is "job rotation." To the extent that this becomes an institutionalized procedure, it affords the executive an opportunity to manifest his abilities to more than one superior and in different organizational situations, which in turn increases the chances of a more objective appraisal of his talents.

A third mechanism which might be a functional substitute for the norms of due process is an increase in the opportunities for intercompany mobility. One of the major impediments to such mobility is the absence of vested pension rights. This discourages job changes because of the financial loss entailed. The vesting of pension rights for executives—such as already exists among university professors—if it should ever develop, would probably betoken a significant measure of progress toward the professionalization of management. Only an occupation with "cosmopolitan" values would encourage the institutionalization of such a practice.

*   *   *   *   *

---

[12] See, for example, Henry C. Metcalf (ed.), *Business Management as a Profession* (Chicago: A. W. Shaw Co., 1927); Howard R. Bowen, "Business Management: A Profession?" *Annals of the American Academy of Political and Social Science,* Vol. 297 (January 1955), pp. 112–17.

FORD MOTOR COMPANY

I Case Introduction

Synopsis

The parent Ford Motor Company in America proposes to acquire 100% ownership of its British subsidiary by offering about 75% more than the current market price for the minority interest. Mr. Henry Ford II has to weigh the expected benefits of "increased operational flexibility" against competitive accusations at home and abroad of "economic imperialism," the British laborites' fear for employment security, and the concern of some in the United States over the impact of the $360 million purchase on our worsening international balance of payments picture.

Why This Case Is Included

The establishment and maintenance of a multinational corporation introduce a whole new dimension into business policy making. This case presents the opportunity to see how efforts at serving the worldwide interest of a single business unit force management to weigh the responsibilities of corporate citizenship against the economic benefits of supranational policy making. Classical economists theorized that the common good could best be served by the uninhibited, individual pursuit of economic gain and that comparative advantage should rule in international trade. In this case, these theories can be tested for their relevance as guides to corporate policy making in a worldwide economic system.

Diagnostic and Predictive Questions

In answering the following diagnostic and predictive questions, remember that these questions apply theories and conceptual ideas from certain disciplines. Such theories are valuable to understand basic forces at work in the policy system (diagnosis) and to predict what will happen in the system in the future (prediction). Since each reading abstracts from the total policy system certain factors or variables into the closed or partial viewpoint of one theory or discipline, no one reading gives answers to the practical policy problems of the case. In diagnosis and prediction, the parts of the problem are studied with "other things being equal."

Following each question are listed readings which will be helpful in answering the question. The readings included with this case are marked (*). By referring to the author index at the end of this book, you may locate the other readings listed.

1. What did Henry Ford II hope to gain for the Ford Motor Company by the purchase of the minority interest in British Ford? Why did he choose November 14, 1960 as the time to make the move? It might help to review the case facts about financial, marketing, competitive, and administrative matters.

2. In what sense, if at all, does Adam Smith's doctrine of individual economic self-interest serving the common good apply to the activities of the Ford Motor Company as an individual firm in the worldwide economic system?

Read: *Smith, *Wealth of Nations,* pp. 423, 508.

3. In what way does the theory of comparative advantage in international trade give, or deny, foundation to the rationale offered by U.S. Ford for its purchase of the minority interest of British Ford?

Read: *Blaug, *Economic Theory in Retrospect,* pp. 114–16.

4. What impact will the $360 million private investment have on the United States balance of payments picture? Trace the change in the accounts for the fourth quarter 1960 on the United States balance of payments and the change in accounts on the last half 1960 of the United Kingdom balance of payments. Does a longer-range view of the balance of payments give a different perspective on the impact of the proposed U.S. Ford investment?

Read: *Kindleberger, *International Economics,* pp. 17, 19–21, 23, 26, 28–29, 47–48, 54. *Benoit, "The Balance of Payments Payoff of Direct Foreign Investments."

5. Does the offer to purchase the minority interest of British Ford fit into your conception of the policies required of a multinational corporation?

Read: *Lilienthal, "The Multinational Corporation."

Policy Questions for This Specific Case

In answering the following policy questions, the results of diagnosis and prediction are used to reduce the amount of guesswork, or judgment, in designing action solutions. However, since certain parts of the total case situation cannot be reduced to science, and since "other things are not equal," judgment must still be used to fill in the factors not accounted for by readings. You will also need a second kind of judgment as you put value weights on different scientific predictions, since different theories may point to conflicting solutions.

6. Had you been Henry Ford II would you have made the purchase offer on November 14, 1960? Why? Or, why not?

7. How would you, as chief executive officer of U.S. Ford, respond to the criticism of economic imperialism and disregard for national boundaries? (See Questions 2, 3, and 5.)

8. How would you respond to the allegation that the $360 million purchase would hurt the United States balance of payments position? (See Question 4.)

9. What answer would you have for those critics who insist that 100% ownership is not necessary to "obtain greater operational flexibility and enable us better to coordinate our European and American operations on a worldwide basis"? (See Questions 1 and 5.)

10. After having seen the reaction at home and abroad to the initial purchase offer would you, as the chief executive of the Ford Motor Company, go ahead with the purchase? Would you modify the terms of the offer in any way or change the timing of your move?

Major Policy Issues: Tentative Generalizations about Any Policy System

In arriving at conclusions for the following questions, generalize from the facts in the case and use your own ideas to (a) confirm, (b) modify, or (c) test the workability of the concepts and theories from readings. As an executive or professional, use wisdom to merge theory, on the one hand, with "brute facts" and practice, on the other.

11. "The action of the supranational entity, called a multinational corporation, in which some sovereign state suffers detriment is analogous to the action of an American corporate giant which harms a competitor but fosters the general well-being of the larger economic system." Comment. (Refer to Questions 2 and 5.)

12. As a general rule, no American citizen may simultaneously be a citizen of a foreign nation. The multinational corporation is a *de facto* "citizen" of many nations. What does this mean in practical terms for the administration of multinational corporations? (See Question 5 and its attached reading.)

Questions for Original Student Work in Analysis and Policy

The methods of viewing this case as represented by the authors' questions and selection of readings are not exhaustive. There are other relevant ideas for diagnosis and prediction. Furthermore, there are other ways of stating policy questions. More powerful analyses and wiser solutions will result by drawing on your own training and experience for (a) relevant concepts and theories, and (b) creative ways of asking policy questions. The following questions are designed to help you acquire this skill.

13. While reflecting on case facts, what additional theories from prior education give you insights as to "what is going on" in Ford Motor Company? As to what might be predicted to happen in the future?

14. Other than the policy questions asked by the authors, what pragmatic ways can you think of to state the practical problems faced by executives in the case?

II *The Ford Motor Company**

On Monday, November 14, 1960 the Ford Motor Company of England announced that the parent company in Dearborn, Michigan, had offered to purchase the publicly held common shares of British Ford. American Ford already holds 54.6% of its British subsidiary. The proffered purchase price for the minority interest of some 17.7 million shares is $20.50 per share. Since about 85% of this minority interest is held within the British Isles, the new net foreign investment for American Ford will amount to $300 million.

---

* Copyright 1964 by the Graduate School of Business, Columbia University.

Henry Ford II and the management of American Ford have to weigh generally adverse reaction to the proposed purchase from both sides of the ocean against the long-run economic benefit to the international operations of the whole Ford Motor Company.

COMPANY PROFILE

Ford Motor Company (United States)

Henry Ford incorporated the original Ford Motor Company in 1903. Today Ford holds the second position (behind General Motors) in the domestic automobile industry, having sold over two million units in 1959 for $5,357 million in dollar volume. (See Exhibit 1 for financial summary.) In addition to its 31.1% market share in cars and trucks, Ford ranks third among United States corporations in terms of combined asset size ($3,462 million) and average number of employees (159,541). Ford produces its three lines of cars, its trucks, and some diversified products (automobile accessories and farm equipment) in 36 manufacturing plants and 21 assembly plants throughout the United States.

In addition to Ford of England, Canadian and West German subsidiaries manufacture and market Ford vehicles. The Ford Motor Company of Canada—74.9% owned by the parent company—ranks second to General Motors in Canada's auto industry (33% market share in cars and 27% market share in trucks). American Ford owns 99% of Germany's fourth largest producer (9% of market share). Besides marketing subsidi-

Exhibit 1

FORD MOTOR COMPANY

Financial Summary

(Millions of Dollars)

	1959	1958	1957	1956	1955	1954
Sales	$5,356.9	$4,130.3	$5,771.3	$4,647.0	$5,594.0	$4,062.3
Income	842.8	182.5	580.6	490.4	985.6	510.7
Taxes	391.4	66.3	286.6	242.2	531.4	268.1
Net income	451.4	116.2	294.0	248.2	454.2	242.6
Dividends paid	153.5	109.4	130.7	129.6	174.7	89.8
Retained income	297.9	6.8	163.3	118.6	279.5	152.8
Capital expenditures	75.0	89.0	328.7	486.9	214.0	279.9
Cash; securities	666.3	451.6	265.1	215.1	568.3	327.6
Current assets	1,357.7	1,102.6	1,091.3	967.2	1,269.0	869.2
Current liabilities	528.5	532.1	656.2	683.1	643.6	445.9
Property, plant, and equipment	2,574.0	2,598.7	2,623.3	2,335.4	1,754.0	1,601.0
Depreciation	1,037.7	925.4	781.0	649.3	561.6	474.9
Long-term debt	249.5	250.0	250.0	58.6	—	—
Total assets	3,462.2	3,133.5	3,265.3	2,932.2	2,713.3	2,194.2
Equity	2,614.8	2,312.9	2,300.3	2,127.0	1,996.2	1,704.0

Source: 1959 Annual Report.

aries in many other countries, Ford has 12 assembly plants in the Commonwealth, Europe, Latin America, and the Middle East. Today 17.4% of Ford's earnings come from overseas.

Ford Motor Company (England)

The British subsidiary, in operation since 1911, manufactures and assembles six lines of passenger cars, trucks, and tractors in the British Isles. Besides the domestic market it serves Autralia, New Zealand, South Africa, various European countries, and the United States. Half the units produced—some 276,000—are exported (about 53,000 to the United States). Actually, British Ford earns more United States and Canadian dollars by its exports than are remitted back to the United States in profits by all the United States manufacturing companies in Britain put together. British Ford's sales volume of $652 million places it in second place in the auto industry behind the British Motor Company. Since 1950, sales have increased 150% compared to the 50 to 60% increase for the United States built Fords. British Ford's return on assets is 14.9% compared to 10.7% for the worldwide Ford company. British Ford's market share is 27% in cars, 23% in commercial vehicles, and 28% in tractors.

British Ford's total assets in dollars are about $504 million (see Exhibit 2 for the financial summary). The company employs an average of 50,000 workers in its five plants.

Exhibit 2

FORD MOTOR COMPANY LIMITED

FINANCIAL SUMMARY

(Millions of U.S. Dollars)

	1959	1958	1957	1956	1955	1954
Sales	$652.0	$579.0	$464.0	$407.5	$424.0	$356.0
Income	95.0	73.9	54.3	28.8	46.8	54.0
Taxes	39.8	36.7	23.2	10.6	21.0	26.6
Net income	55.5	37.2	31.1	18.2	25.8	27.7
Dividends paid	14.0	6.2	5.9	5.0	5.0	4.8
Retained income	41.5	31.1	25.2	13.2	20.9	23.0
Capital expenditures .	35.8	51.2	54.6	39.2	26.6	12.3
Cash; securities	191.0	139.5	104.8	89.0	132.0	126.2
Current assets	308.0	238.2	217.0	190.4	224.3	204.5
Current liabilities ...	223.5	181.7	160.0	118.5	139.0	121.3
Property, plant, and equipment (net) ...	196.5	183.3	151.0	111.1	84.0	67.5
Long-term debt	—	—	—	—	—	—
Total assets	504.5	421.5	368.0	301.5	308.3	272.0
Preferred stock	8.1	8.1	8.1	8.1	8.1	8.1
Common stock	109.2	109.2	109.2	109.2	109.2	109.2
Equity	281.0	239.8	208.0	183.0	169.3	150.7

Source: 1959 Annual Report. Conversion of pounds to dollars—slide rule accuracy—@ one pound = $2.80.

Though American Ford owns the majority interest, only three of British Ford's 12 directors are also employed by the parent company. The chief executive officer of British Ford is Sir Patrick Hennessy.

TRENDS IN THE AUTO INDUSTRY

In Market Structure

Maturing markets and changing tastes have begun to affect the entire structure of the international auto industry. The statistics in Exhibit 3 indicate the pressure on the United States market. What some observers called a softening domestic market was being increasingly tapped by foreign imports until the advent of the compact car. It is likely that the 1960 dollar volume of car imports into this country will be approximately 30% under the $735 million total of last year. Dealers of imported cars are now carrying a 2½-month supply of cars—two months is the usual supply. Prices of used imports are down, and there has been a decline in

Exhibit 3

PRODUCTION, EXPORTS, IMPORTS OF U.S., CANADA, AND MAJOR
COUNTRIES OF WESTERN EUROPE AUTOMOTIVE
VEHICLES, 1955–59

	1955	*1956*	*1957*	*1958*	*1959*
United States:					
Production	9,169,292	6,920,590	7,220,520	5,121,269	6,723,556
Exports	386,973	372,442	335,851	268,092	266,318
Imports	58,425	110,991	276,775	446,138	690,833
Canada:					
Production	454,182	470,674	411,884	359,777	368,858
Exports	18,431	19,034	20,120	16,434	11,763
Imports	57,949	89,232	80,001	113,377	165,564
Belgium:					
Production	1,625	383	320	382	343
Exports	24,564	39,380	27,536	40,057	62,094
Imports	129,975	146,231	136,659	148,253	188,012
France:					
Production	725,061	827,048	925,882	1,127,761	1,283,251
Exports	162,681	176,245	215,920	359,328	603,248
Imports	10,812	11,488	36,063	10,229	13,961
Germany:					
Production	908,742	1,075,188	1,212,232	1,495,321	1,718,544
Exports	403,959	484,598	584,274	733,222	870,817
Imports	17,000	21,655	27,866	N.A.	117,074
United Kingdom:					
Production	1,238,384	1,006,203	1,150,964	1,189,943	1,560,427
Exports	531,174	463,164	549,555	599,410	696,937
Imports	12,161	7,813	10,062	12,266	28,323

Source: Automobile Facts and Figures.

the number of dealers and a switch from private to factory-owned distributorships.

On the other side, United States exports are running at an annual average rate which will substantially top last year's total of 104,000 cars and 157,000 trucks. Demand is on the upswing especially in western Europe. (See Exhibit 3.) United States producers are utilizing assembly plants within these growing markets as well as foreign manufacturing subsidiaries to capture a market segment. Investment abroad since 1955 has been heavy. From the beginning of 1955 to the end of 1959, General Motor's foreign investment rose from $287.2 million to $679.2 million. During the same period Ford's foreign investment grew from about $200 million to over $500 million. The two companies plan to spend a total of almost $500 million abroad next year—exclusive of the purchase of the minority interest in British Ford.

Some foreign producers fear that the United States manufacturers will begin wholesale production of small cars right in the European market. "Pierre Dreyfuss, president of France's largest auto maker, Renault, has begged Detroit not to build a tiny car in Europe. He has reported rumors a Big Three company was planning such a vehicle and called the product 'an atomic bomb' for the European car industry. Mr. Dreyfuss has even hinted it would weaken the West's economic alliance. Henry Ford II called Mr. Dreyfuss' plea disgraceful."[1]

Tariff Prospects and Quotas

The chief changes in the tariff picture come from the Common Market countries—France, West Germany, Italy, Belgium, Luxemburg, and the Netherlands. These countries, within the European Economic Community, plan to cut their internal tariffs to 70% of their 1957 level by December 31, 1960. The E.E.C. is also working toward the target of a common external tariff of 27 to 29% on assembled cars. Comparative external tariffs now in effect are:

	Assembled Cars
United States	$8\frac{1}{2}\%$
United Kingdom	30 %*
Germany	17–21 %
France	30 %
Italy	35–45 %
Benelux	24 %

*20% on imports from Commonwealth's Preference area.

Ownership Pattern in Foreign Affiliates

As has been pointed out, Ford owns 99% of its West German subsidiary and 74.9% of its Canadian subsidiary. The British Vauxhall, the

---

[1] *Wall Street Journal,* November 25, 1960.

West German Opel, and the Canadian General Motors companies are all wholly owned subsidiaries of General Motors Corporation (United States). The Chrysler Corporation follows a different pattern. While it does own its own manufacturing facilities in England and Australia, it has minority interests in Mexico, Argentina, and France (Simca). American Motors hasn't made any moves in foreign operations beyond some expansion of assembly plants. Studebaker-Packard is in the same position. Willys Motors (a Kaiser Industries corporation) holds minority positions in its several South American manufacturing plants.

DETAILS OF THE FORD OFFER

The minority interest in British Ford amounted to 45.4% of the outstanding common shares, or 17,718,900 shares. At $20.50 a share this would mean American Ford was planning a $363,219,185 investment to gain full ownership of its British subsidiary. If the minority stockholders agree to sell their shares, the British Treasury would net about $300 million for its gold and dollar reserves. The net figures allow for the estimated number of shares already held by Americans. The impact on the United States balance of payments will be partially discounted by the annual dividends to be paid by British Ford to the new American owners.

The offer is conditional on the acceptance by at least 75% of the minority holders, representing not less than 90% of the value of the shares not held by American Ford. If this condition is met, American Ford can require the sale of the rest of shares withheld. American Ford must also secure the permission of the British government for the proposed purchase.

Clarifications of the Proposal by American Ford

On November 15, 1960 Henry Ford II issued the following statement:

I should like to comment on yesterday's announcement that Ford Motor Company U.S.A. intends to make an offer to the stockholders of its English Subsidiary, Ford Motor Company Limited of Dagenham, to acquire the publicly held shares in the English company, at a price of $20.50 a share. As stated in the announcement, our objective is to obtain greater operational flexibility and enable us better to coordinate our European and American operations on a world-wide basis.

In recent years, competition in world automotive markets has become broader and more intense. The development of the Common Market and the European Free Trade Area in the years ahead is likely to accentuate this trend. In these circumstances, we believe that it is important for us, as a world manufacturer, to pursue the objective I mentioned if we are to be able to continue to compete effectively.

In my view, the results of the proposed transaction should be beneficial to the economies of both the United States and the United Kingdom. Obviously, one of our major objectives is to achieve greater operational efficiency and greater marketing effectiveness in both countries. If we are successful in attaining this objective, we shall have a product position and a cost position which should enable us to compete more effectively throughout the world. This should benefit not only both companies, but also their employes, their suppliers, their dealers and the public.

I should like to repeat what was said in the announcement, namely that, so far as we are concerned, we intend that Ford Motor Company Limited's operations shall continue under the able direction of Sir Patrick Hennessy without change in its employment policy or in its development program.

Four days later Mr. Ford reiterated the company's motivation in the planned acquisition:

Since the announcement on November 14th regarding our intention to make an offer to the stockholders of Ford of England to acquire the minority shares of that company, we have had an opportunity to discuss the terms of the proposed offer with H.M. Treasury.

It has developed that because of U.K. exchange control regulations, it is necessary that an offering of this kind be made in sterling. We therefore intend to make the offer in sterling at 145 shillings, 6 pence per share (equal to between approximately $20.15 and $20.50 at rates prevailing during 1960), subject to the consent of H.M. Treasury.

If the plan is carried out the American company's stake in the English company would far exceed its interests in all other operations outside the U.S. combined. In these circumstances I think it should be agreed that we would have added incentive to promote the interests, the well-being, and the prosperity of Ford of England in every way practicable, as we have always done in the past and intend to continue to do in the future.

In the intensely competitive battle that we see ahead in the world automotive markets, we believe that Ford of England is especially well fitted to play an important role in the European operations—and in fact the world operations—of the Ford group. Full ownership of the English company would provide the operational flexibility to make this completely feasible.

In recent years competition in the European and in the world markets has become constantly broader and, in our view, this competition is likely to become more intense, not less. The development of the European Free Trade Area and the Common Market in the years ahead is likely to accentuate this trend.

Our major objective in proposing to acquire the minority shares of Ford of England is to obtain greater operational flexibility and to coordinate better our American and European operations so that the Ford group may be able to compete more effectively in world markets. Successful completion of the proposed transaction would permit full coordination of the operations of the English company with those of the American company.

We believe sincerely that full ownership of the English company will make it possible for both companies to obtain benefits that could not be obtained otherwise.

During the year Sir Patrick Hennessy, Chairman of Ford-England, has announced a program of substantial expansion by his company on Merseyside, at Basildon, in Essex, and elsewhere involving expenditures estimated at 70 million pounds. This is going ahead and commitments have already been entered into for more than half this sum. The Chairman has indicated that further large sums may be spent on tooling for new models, replacements, and on engineering and administrative buildings. The Chairman has also stated that it is expected that the English company's present financial resources and the plow-back of earnings during the period of expansion will be sufficient to finance these large developments.

The proposed acquisition by Ford–U.S.A. of the minority shareholdings in Ford-England will not have any effect on this program. Although from time to time Sir Patrick and his associates may wish to make some changes in these plans in the normal course of events, the amount to be spent and the employment which will result from the developments will not be substantially affected.

As we said a few days ago the company's operations will continue under the direction of Sir Patrick Hennessy with continuity in its employment policy. Ford of England will continue as a British company, and it will continue to make a substantial contribution toward the British economy.

REACTION TO THE PROPOSED ACQUISITION

In the United States

The stock market reflected part of the reaction as can be seen in the price movement of American Ford on the New York Stock Exchange and British Ford on the American Stock Exchange from November 14 to December 1:

	AMERICAN FORD				BRITISH FORD			
	Sales 100's	High	Low	Close	Sales 100's	High	Low	Close
11/14	225	65½	63⅞	64	35	12¾	12⅝	12⅝
15	97	64⅛	63⅝	64	1001	18¾	18⅜	18⅝
16	115	64⅛	62⅞	63⅛	526	18⅞	18½	18⅞
17	162	63¾	62¾	63¾	274	19¼	18⅞	19
18	320	64¼	63½	64	283	19¼	18⅞	19
21	176	65⅛	64¼	64½	227	19⅞	19¼	19½
22	196	65¼	64	64¼	95	19⅝	19½	19⅝
23	153	64¾	64	64½	123	19⅝	19½	19⅝
25	113	65⅛	64⅜	64⅞	113	19¾	19⅝	19¾
28	137	65⅜	64⅞	65	91	19¾	19⅝	19⅝
29	109	64⅞	64½	64⅝	80	19¾	19⅝	19¾
30	93	64⅜	63½	63½	60	19⅝	19½	19½
12/ 1	127	63⅜	62½	63	131	18⅞	18	18⅞

Business Week[2] commented:

Industry people on both sides of the Atlantic accept (Ford's statement) as far as it goes, but they say there must have been more urgency than Ford admits. Otherwise, they say, Ford would not have chosen this timing when signs are unpropitious on two points:—The British auto industry is slowing down, and the Unions are quick to pin the blame on Detroit, its compact cars and its export sales campaign. Ford's announcement was greeted with distrust by unions that represent British Ford's 50,000 workers of whom 40,000 are at Dagenham.— The trend in U.S. private investment abroad has been running opposite from the direction of Ford's proposed move, toward joint enterprise with citizens of a foreign land.

Unlike G.M.'s taut empire, Ford's foreign set-up contains the element of

2 *Business Week,* November 19, 1960.

friction. With only minority influence from Dearborn, British Ford has conceivably been working at cross purposes with other Ford interests, particularly the German company. Under a global master plan, Ford Motor Company may well wish to define marketing areas more precisely and more enforceably.

The British company is rounding out a $216 million expansion program that started in 1955, and it has announced plans for $196 million more including a $78 million automobile plant near Liverpool that U.S. Ford is said to oppose as not fitting in with its European planning.

In this same issue of *Business Week* the article immediately preceding the Ford article is entitled "Attacking the Payments Deficit." It outlines President Eisenhower's proposals to halt the gold outflow (see Exhibit 4) and goes on to say:

The third quarter's balance of payments figures make gloomy reading. The deficit ran at a $4.3 billion annual rate compared to $2.9 billion and $2.6 billion during the second and first quarters respectively. Gold losses rose to about $637 million from $94 million in the second quarter and $50 million in the first quarter. . . .

It has been noted that shortly before the U.S. Ford purchase offer the Detroit papers reported persistent rumors that the United States might be forced to devaluate the dollar.

The following headline appeared in the November 26, 1960 *Business Week:* "Canada Hits At U.S. Influence. Diefenbaker government seeks to curb U.S. 'domination' of industry, plans legislation to encourage greater Canadian ownership, requires reports by U.S. subsidiaries." Special mention was made of the auto and magazine industries. (In 1959 American Ford faced much Canadian criticism when it extended its stock control of Canadian Ford from 56.8 to 74.8%.)

The *New York Times*[3] reported:

This is the price (Ford) is prepared to pay with the aim of coordinating European and American manufacturing facilities and integrating output on a world wide basis.

Wall Street sources, in discussing the Ford offer, tied it in part to a drive by the American auto industry to snare a greater share of the European car market.

There is also the factor that production costs are lower overseas than here.

Then there is the matter of continued dollar flow from this country now considered a major problem. If the Ford deal would go through, the British treasury would gain about $300 million.

But with 100 per cent ownership of its British subsidiary, the parent Ford company would be in a better position to use retained earnings overseas for expansion there and thus avoid any new dollar drain or shipment abroad.

George Romney, president of American Motors Corporation, had a somewhat different perspective in his press conference on December 15, 1960:

Let's take a look at what's happening to the world vehicle situation. In 1951—that's only 9 years ago—United States auto production accounted for 72

---

3 *New York Times,* November 15, 1960.

Exhibit 4

UNITED STATES: BALANCE OF PAYMENTS SUMMARY,*
1958–THIRD QUARTER 1960

(In Millions of U.S. Dollars)

			1960		
	1958	*1959*	*Jan.– Mar.*	*Apr.– June*	*July– Sept.*
Goods and services:†					
Exports of merchandise f.o.b. ...	16,263	16,282	4,607	4,994	4,676
Imports of merchandise f.o.b. ...	−12,951	−15,294	−3,830	−3,857	−3,550
Military expenditures	−3,412	−3,109	−767	−756	−798
Other services†	1,650	1,502	376	294	67
Total	1,550	−619	386	675	395
Government grants and capital ...	−2,587	−1,986	−605	−804‡	−562
Private long-term capital:					
U.S. direct investment	−1,094	−1,372	−303	−331	−327
U.S. portfolio investment	−1,444	−926	−258	−229	−149
Foreign capital	24	555	187	150	23
Total	−2,514	−1,743	−374	−410	−453
Balance on goods and services,† long-term capital, and aid ..	−3,551	−4,348	−593	−539	−620
Balance, seasonally adjusted			*−491*	*−481*	*−360*
Short-term capital:					
U.S. private	−306	−77	−90	−164	−448
Foreign private	119	330	−107	−4	−63
International nonmonetary institutions	283	144	83	61	97
Total	96	397	−114	−107	−414
Net errors and omissions	380	528	49	−128	−117
Change in gold and liquid liabilities to foreign officials and banks:					
Liabilities to foreign banks	48	1,140	457	132	5
Liabilities to foreign official holders	752	1,552	151	548	509
U.S. gold holdings (increase −) ..	2,275	731	50	94	637
Total	3,075	3,423	658	774	1,151
Memorandum item: change in gold holdings and liquid liabilities, seasonally adjusted	3,477	3,897	614	706	1,106

* Excluding military aid and transfers financed by it. No sign indicates credit; minus sign indicates debit.

† Including remittances and pensions.

‡ Including subscriptions to the Inter-American Development Bank ($80 million) in the second quarter and the International Development Association ($74 million) in the fourth quarter.

Sources: U.S. Department of Commerce, *Survey of Current Business,* and Fund staff estimates.

per cent of the total world automobile production; world output was 9,400,000. By 1959, the U.S. share had dropped to 48 per cent; the world output had reached 13,900,000. You'll note that the *unit* output in the United States hasn't

Exhibit 4—Continued

UNITED KINGDOM: BALANCE OF PAYMENTS SUMMARY,
1958–FIRST HALF 1960

(In Millions of U.S. Dollars)

		1959		1960
	1958	*First Half*	*Second Half*	*First Half*
Goods, services, and donations:				
Exports f.o.b.	9,497	4,833	4,992	5,339
Imports f.o.b.	−9,324	−4.844	−5,174	−5,693
Trade balance	173	−11	−182	−354
Services and donations	641	255	81	132
Total	814	244	−101	−222
Long-term capital:				
Repayment of Export-Import Bank loan	—	—	−249	—
Other official long-term	−137	−6	−187	−106
Private long-term:				
Abroad (net)	−904	−456	−432	−381
In United Kingdom (net)	540	255	235	176
Total	−501	−207	−633	−311
Balance on goods and services and long-term capital	313	37	−734	−533
Balance excluding two special transactions	*313*	*37*	*−485*	*−533*
Private short-term capital	6	67	−45	115
Net errors and omissions	277	186	−6	396
Changes in sterling holdings:				
Of nonsterling area	428	−241	216	350
Of sterling area	−249	364	154	−84
Total	179	123	370	266
Reserve movements (increase −):				
Net IMF position	−16	−356	−22	−90
EPU debit balance	−28	25	—	—
Official holdings:				
Nonconvertible currencies	64	22	—	3
Gold and convertible currencies	−795	−104	437	−157
Total	−775	−413	415	−244
Memorandum item: change in reserves and sterling balances plus two special transactions		−290	536	22

Source: International Monetary Fund.

changed particularly from 1951. Expansion in other countries has been tremendous.

Expansion outside certainly was going to occur, but this expansion of vehicle production outside is greater than it would have been if the American automobile manufacturers had faced the people of this country with the issues involved in keeping the American automobile business as a basis of a world automobile business—because we had that position. The American automobile business is the pre-eminent industrial development of the free economy in this country.

One of the points I want to make here is that the investment of American capital abroad, both in the Automobile business and in other industries, is *in excess* of that required to meet the needs of foreign markets. It's intended importantly for the penetration of our domestic market from abroad. That's what is taking place.

Here's the G.M. and Ford world-wide operation. . . [pointing to a map]. G.M. is located around the world. . . . . Ford also has located pretty well around the world—not quite to the extent of G.M., but just about.

Now, why? Has this been required to meet foreign markets? Yes, to some extent. But not just for that purpose. Why is Ford currently seeking 100 per cent control of its Ford subsidiary in England—why is it extending such control over its other subsidiaries? Let me read what *Business International*, weekly report to management of business abroad, had to say in its November 18 issue. The article was headlined "Metamorphosis of Ford Motor Company Girds Firm for Explosive World Competition." It said, in part: "In a nutshell, Ford is gearing up to treat the world market, including the U.S., exactly as it does the U.S. market today; i.e., to evolve a system of production and distribution based squarely on where supplies can best be obtained and customers best served, with as little regard to national boundaries as political realities of time and place will permit.

"The revolution, for Ford, is starting as it must with purchasing. About half of an automobile is bought from independent suppliers, and inevitably these components are made cheaper and better in some countries than in others. Ford is taking increasing advantage of this fact on a European-wide, and indeed Atlantic-wide, scale." (I insert, on a *worldwide* scale.)

What this really means is that G.M. and Ford are establishing a world network to permit them to procure parts, vehicles, anything else from whatever point will be most meaningful from the standpoint of the sheer, cold economics of the situation. I mean *sheer, cold economics* of the situation.

[Mr. Romney modified this statement by saying: In the verbatim account at the New York press conference on December 15, there is a seriously inaccurate assertion. General Motors is charged with intention to use its facilities abroad for importation of components into the United States, and for the purpose of disregarding national boundaries and policies. Such facilities were not established for that purpose, and there is no evidence of that intention now.]

Now, let me continue with another excerpt or two:

". . . the firm that starts side-stepping national boundaries . . . today is the one that will wind up at the top of the heap."

And another one:

"An immediate problem is that of equity ownership of the company's overseas manufacturing facilities. The administrative and operational flexibility necessary to a purchasing, production and distribution system that ignores national boundaries demands complete centralization of control *and* ownership. Local stockholders of local subsidiaries, even when they have only a minority interest, can seriously impair management's freedom to effect the most economical and profitable arrangement. Ford's swift use of its Antwerp and Cork plants to assemble the British Anglia during the peak of U.S. demand for this model illustrates the need for flexibility through full ownership."

*   *   *   *   *

The automotive industry is the highest economic expression of the effort of a free people. Thirty years ago the U.S. automobile industry was exporting 8 to

10 per cent of our total output. That pattern has changed, and Ford has permitted it to be indicated that their small-car Cardinal program is based on a combination of foreign and domestically produced components for cost reasons.

*   *   *   *   *

I believe America has a great role to play in the economic development of the world. I am absolutely certain that that role cannot be played on the basis of 100 per cent ownership of operations abroad. It will sooner or later result in resentment and expropriation programs.

One of our men sat in on a meeting I couldn't attend just a few weeks ago in Chicago, attended by one of our country's ambassadors from a Latin American country that is friendly to us. This Latin American U.S. ambassador pleaded with us: "When you go into those countries, don't go in on the basis of complete control. Let them control—go in and help them."

One firm's representative present said: "We are planning such and such investments in that country and we expect to own them 100 per cent. Are you saying to me we shouldn't do that?" And he said: "I can't tell you that in an official capacity, but unofficially, don't do it. Those people consider that market *theirs*, not our market."

This pattern is not limited to the automobile industry. We have certain American industries which through foreign investment have made foreign companies the principal source of components and some finished products for the purpose of *this* market, not the world market.

The U.S. Department of Commerce in a report released this week said that United States corporations' investments abroad have increased from $11.7 billion in 1950 to $29.8 billion in 1959. The Department of Commerce indicated in its press release that this investment was in excess of that required to meet foreign market needs and was intended importantly for the purpose of competing for *this* market.

I think this approach is wrong. . . . We believe on the basis of experience that an international program that is based on ignoring national boundaries and establishing 100 per cent ownership and avoiding foreign partnerships is unsound. It represents economic imperialism, and it will so be labeled as we move forward—and you mark my words—because this a cold, calculated effort to become exempt from national policy and national boundaries, in exactly the same way that vast national corporations in this country have become exempt in effect, or at least flexible, in relationship to state policy and state boundaries.

It represents economic imperialism because it means that the control of those operations is centered at one point—and that is economic imperial power. At one point the decision is made how to use the vast worldwide organization. The cold facts are—whether we want to recognize it or not in America—that probably the best friends we have in the world, the Canadians, are currently expressing as vigorously as they can their resentment of this 100 per cent ownership and direction of economic activities in their country by firms located in this country, and their direction on the basis of American national policy rather than on the basis of Canadian national policy.

. . . The other peoples of the world want our help, but they don't want our domination and control economically any more than they want it politically.

When we set up organizations with 100 per cent control in America on a worldwide basis, that is economic imperialism in their thinking. If you look up the definition in the dictionary you will find that that is what the word means. We must not forget that they consider their markets *their* markets—not ours.

Reaction in England

British reaction ranged from the *Evening Standard* headline "Kill This Sellout!" to the sober comment of the *London Times:* "Britain is hardly in a position to take a rigid attitude when her own stake abroad is so large."

Though the offer price was some 75% higher than current market price for the stock and despite the assurances of Henry Ford II concerning the continuity of development and employment policy in the British subsidiary, protests were voiced on both counts. Said Mr. Cleaver, a Conservative: "I do not think the offer was good enough. It was made at a good time for a buyer. This is possibly the secret reason that the Opposition is try to unearth. Ford has certainly not made it at the top of the market. No doubt the City is preparing a case that would justify an increase in the figure."

The *London Economist* commented on November 19, 1960:

Ford regards this deal against one time-horizon; the British minority owner has to consider his own. The price offered looks generous against the depressed level of these Ford shares immediately before the offer was made, though not so generous against the 120s. to which they rose earlier this year on rumours, repeatedly and strenuously denied, that a bid for the minority holding was in the offing. . . .

. . . Certain investors may be inclined to wonder if this is really the top price that Ford would be prepared to pay for it.

British Ford Stock on the London exchange followed the pattern of the shares on the American Stock Exchange, rising from $12.80 to $19.25 on November 15.

The Labor party representatives were most disturbed about the ramifications of the purchase for the 50,000 Ford employees in England. Said Harold Wilson, Labor party:

If this deal goes through, there will be real danger that production and employment in this country would be sacrificed not only to Detroit but also to the West German subsidiary of Ford.

Said Mr. Edelman, Labor party:

The assurances given by Henry Ford to the Chancellor were not worth the breath with which they were spoken. No one . . . could predict with confidence what the future development of the American motor industry was likely to be.

Said Tom Driberg, Labor party:

The Americans have bases in this country, and now they seem quite prepared to take over the whole country.

There were dissenting voices. The *Manchester Guardian Weekly* editorialized on November 17, 1960:

. . . It is surely inconceivable that Detroit would invest such a sum in Britain unless it expected to get a good return on the capital. If there is danger for employment in the British motor industry, it is much more likely to arise in the smaller companies which are struggling to survive in a world of increasingly standardised mass production. . . .

Other political and economic issues were raised by the proposed Ford purchase. Noting that the permission required from the British government was the product of an administrative decision by the Chancellor of the Exchequer, Selwyn Lloyd, many in parliament were disturbed. "What clearly worried and indeed angered a large part of the House, Labour and Tories alike, was the fact that such momentous moves can be made without its having any say in the matter."[4]

The concern for fundamental issues is shown in the following exchange. The *Evening Standard* said:

For the Government to allow the Ford takeover to succeed would be an abdication of responsibility for one of the key sectors of the British economy. The gain in dollars would be only temporary, for it would soon be outweighed by the increased burden of interest payments.

British Ford's chairman countered:

There is no reason the offer should be opposed by the Treasury. After all, we are encouraging investment, and there is no doubt the British end of the organization would benefit. Fears about the labor situation being controlled from Detroit are groundless.

Mr. Selwyn Lloyd remarked:

Such a movement helps our balance of payments and adds to our resources for investment overseas. [See Exhibit 4.]
    I believe that the United Kingdom has a permanent interest in the freest possible movement of capital. We want capital to move freely; we don't want other governments to impose restrictions or to be too nationalistic in their approach to the movement of capital.
    We have been steadily building up our position as a creditor nation over the past ten years, and it would be silly for us of all people to raise difficulties or impose restrictions unless it was absolutely necessary.
    The next point to be balanced against these other matters is are there to be limits to this process of foreign capital coming in here? What matters is control. It can be said that in any industries which are important for national security, or those which are a major factor in our economy, obviously there must be limits to which control should be allowed to pass to foreign countries. Each transaction has to be considered on its merits.

---

[4] *Manchester Guardian Weekly,* November 17, 1960.

III Selected Readings

From: Adam Smith
*THE WEALTH OF NATIONS**

[EDITORS' NOTE: Adam Smith (1723–90) is generally considered to be the father of classical economic theory, an archenemy of mercantilism and a proponent of laissez-faire capitalism.]

. . . [E]very individual necessarily labours to render the annual revenue of the society as great as he can. He generally, indeed, neither intends to promote the public interest, nor knows how much he is promoting it. By preferring the support of domestic to that of foreign industry, he intends only his own security; and by directing that industry in such a manner as its produce may be of the greatest value, he intends only his own gain, and he is in this, as in many other cases, led by an invisible hand to promote an end which was no part of his intention. Nor is it always the worse for the society that it was no part of it. By pursuing his own interest he frequently promotes that of the society more effectually than when he really intends to promote it. I have never known much good done by those who affected to trade for the public good. It is an affectation, indeed, not very common among merchants, and very few words need by employed in dissuading them from it.

*   *   *   *   *

. . . The natural effort of every individual to better his own condition, when suffered to exert itself with freedom and security, is so powerful a principle, that it is alone, and without any assistance, not only capable of carrying on the society to wealth and prosperity, but of surmounting a hundred impertinent obstructions with which the folly of human laws too often incumbers its operations; though the effect of these obstructions is always more or less either to encroach upon its freedom, or to diminish its security. . . .

* Published by Random House, Inc., in the Modern Library Series, 1937 (pp. 423, 508).

From: M. Blaug
*ECONOMIC THEORY IN RETROSPECT**

[EDITORS' NOTE: Professor Blaug teaches economics of education at University of London Institute of Education.]

. . . Ricardo was virtually the first economist to advocate a separate theory of international as against intranational trade. The basis of this separate theory is the relative immobility of capital between nations. The labor theory of value cannot pertain to goods traded across national boundaries because the rate of profit does not tend to equality between countries. But, in that case, what determines the movement of goods between countries, and on what basis will the barter terms of trade be decided? The answer to both questions, of course, is comparative cost advantages.

There are three kinds of differences in cost ratios for pairs of goods between countries: equal differences, absolute differences, and comparative differences. Supposing that both cloth and wine are produced in two countries, England and Portugal, by labor alone, the distinction is set out in the accompanying table.

LABOR HOURS REQUIRED TO PRODUCE A UNIT OF

	Equal Differences			*Absolute Differences*			*Comparative Differences*		
	Cloth	*Wine*	*Relative Prices* pw/pc	*Cloth*	*Wine*	pw/pc	*Cloth*	*Wine*	pw/pc
England	100	88	0.88	100	60	0.6	100	120	1.2
Portugal	90	80	0.88	90	80	0.88	90	80	0.88

Even Adam Smith knew that no foreign trade could arise when the cost ratios for two goods between two countries were equal. He thought that trade took place only when both countries had an absolute cost advantage in one good: in our example, England has an absolute advantage in wine, and Portugal in cloth. In the eighteenth century a few authors began to advance the rule that each country would find it profitable to import those goods which could be obtained in exchange for exports at less cost than their home production would entail. But almost no one, not even Adam Smith, realized that this meant that under free trade all goods are not necessarily produced in countries where their real costs of production are lowest: it might pay a country to import a product even though it could be produced at less cost at home than abroad. The doctrine of comparative cost is simply a rigorous statement of the informal eighteenth-century rule.

* Reprinted by permission of Richard D. Irwin, Inc., Homewood, Illinois, 1962 (pp. 114–16).

In Ricardo's example Portugal has a comparative advantage in wine, since the cost-difference here is relatively greater than in the case of cloth: $80/120 < 90/100$. What has to be compared is not costs but ratios of costs, and it does not matter whether we compare cost ratios of producing the same good in different countries or of producing different goods within the same country. An obscure pamphlet published in 1818 gave a simple algebraic statement of the necessary conditions. Let W and C denote the number of labor hours required to produce one unit of wine and cloth, the subscripts p and e identifying the respective countries. Then:

(1)   Equal cost-differences: $W_p/W_e = C_p/C_e.$
(2)   Absolute cost-differences: $W_p/W_e < 1 < C_p/C_e.$
(3)   Comparative cost-differences: $W_p/W_e < C_p/C_e < 1.$

To return to Ricardo's example: it is clearly to Portugal's advantage to send wine to England, where a unit of it commands 1.2 units of cloth, as long as 1 unit of wine can be traded with England for more than 0.88 units of cloth; it is to England's advantage to specialize in cloth if less than 1.2 units of cloth must be given for 1 unit of wine. Hence, the comparative-cost doctrine states the upper and lower limits within which exchange can take place between countries to their mutual benefit. If 1 unit of British cloth were exchanged for 9/8 units of Portuguese wine, all gains from trade would go to England. If, instead, the ratio were 1:9/8 all gains would go to Portugal. Ricardo assumes a 1:1 ratio. England produces cloth with 100 man-hours and receives 1 unit of wine, which would have cost her 120 man-hours, and Portugal obtains cloth for 80 man-hours, which would have cost her 90 man-hours. Clearly, the comparative-cost case is much subtler than the absolute-cost case. In the latter it is self-evident that an international division of labor leads to an increase in total output. The "gains of trade" in Ricardo show up as an over-all saving in cost per unit of product; before trade, it took 390 labor days for England and Portugal each to produce one unit of cloth and wine; after trade, these four units require only 360 labor days. The point of Ricardo's analysis is to show that the conditions that make international trade possible are quite different from the conditions under which domestic trade will rise. If England and Portugal were two regions in the same country, all capital and labor would migrate to Portugal and both goods would be produced there. Within a nation, trade between two places requires an absolute difference in costs, but a comparative difference is a sufficient condition for the existence of international trade.

Ricardo's doctrine is incomplete: it shows how nations may gain by trade but it fails to tell us how the gain from trade is divided among the trading countries. The actual barter terms of trade, as John Stuart Mill was soon to show, depend not only on the cost conditions but also on the patterns of demand. Since Ricardo's theory requires that all goods are produced at constant costs— there is only one factor of production—one may wonder why demand has anything to do with international prices, when, under the same conditions, domestic prices are entirely determined by supply. The reason lies in the fact that goods are produced at constant cost *within* countries but not *between* countries.

From: Charles P. Kindleberger

INTERNATIONAL ECONOMICS*

[EDITORS' NOTE: Professor Kindleberger teaches economics at Massachusetts Institute of Technology.]

The balance of payments of a country is a systematic record of all economic transactions between the residents of the reporting country and residents of foreign countries. . . .

*   *   *   *   *

Let us now consider the mechanics of balance-of-payments accounting. In theory, the balance of payments is kept in standard, double-entry bookkeeping under which each international transaction undertaken by residents of a country will result in a credit and a debit entry of equal size. Let us suppose that a company in the United States exports $100 worth of goods to a customer in Britain. This will call for two entries in the balance of payments in each country. In the United States, exports will be credited $100:

BALANCE OF PAYMENTS OF THE UNITED STATES

	Credit	Debit
Exports	$100	

because transactions which give rise to receipts are recorded as credits. In Britain, the importation of $100 worth of merchandise will be recorded as a debit because transactions which give rise to payments to residents of foreign countries are debits:

BALANCE OF PAYMENTS OF THE UNITED KINGDOM

	Credit	Debit
Imports		$100

But there should be two entries for each transaction in each country, a credit and a debit. What the other entry is will depend upon how the transaction is financed. To take only the United States view of the matter, the other side of the transaction can be an increase in the American company's open-book account in Britain; a reduction in an old obligation to the British company; the accumulation of a sterling balance in a London bank; the acquisition of dollars from the sale of sterling to an American bank which holds it; the receipt of dollars from a reduction in the dollar balances of the British company; or a gift by the United States company to the British. In all but the gift, the debit entry is

---

*Reprinted by permission of Richard D. Irwin, Inc., Homewood, Illinois, 1958 (pp. 17, 19–21, 23, 26, 28–29, 47–48, 54).

"Capital Outflow." If the goods are given to the British recipient, the debit entry is "Donation."

A capital outflow from the United States, which is a debit entry in its balance of payments, may consist in an increase in United States claims on foreigners or a reduction in United States liabilities to foreigners. The transaction which gives rise to the claim is a credit; the increase in claims (or the reduction in liabilities) itself is a debit. In ordinary, domestic bookkeeping, one credits Sales and debits Cash. In the balance of payments, one records a credit for Exports and a debit for the Capital Outflow.

The student will do well to pause here and make sure that he takes due note of this complex fact: An increase in claims of foreigners (foreign assets) or a reduction in liabilities to foreigners is a capital outflow and is a debit in the balance of payments; a decrease in claims on foreigners (foreign asset) or an increase in liabilities to foreigners is a capital inflow and is a credit in the balance of payments.

Let us suppose that there are two transactions: one an export of goods from the United States worth $100 against payment out of a British importer's account in New York; the other an import of goods valued at $100 by an American buyer from an English exporter, settled by a payment into the account of the latter in New York. The reduction in the English account in New York in the first transaction is a decrease in American liabilities to foreigners or a capital outflow or a debit. The increase in the English account in New York in the second transaction is an increase in American liabilities to foreigners or a capital inflow or a credit.

The balance of payments after the first transaction looks like this:

BALANCE OF PAYMENTS OF THE UNITED STATES

	Credit	Debit
Exports	$100	
Capital Outflow		$100

The balance of payments for the second transaction alone looks like this:

BALANCE OF PAYMENTS OF THE UNITED STATES

	Credit	Debit
Exports		$100
Capital Inflow	$100	

When both are added together, the capital transactions cancel out, and it is recorded that exports paid for imports:

BALANCE OF PAYMENTS OF THE UNITED STATES

	Credit	Debit
Exports	$100	
Imports		$100

This elementary exercise in balance-of-payments accounting indicates a fundamental point. In theory, the balance of payments is devised on the basis of double-entry bookkeeping.

*   *   *   *   *

Of all the items in the current account, merchandise or visible trade is almost always the most important. The difference between credits and debits (exports and imports) is frequently called the balance of trade, and this is often regarded as "favorable" when exports exceed imports and "unfavorable" when imports exceed exports. For some purposes, the balance of trade has significance and furnishes a shorthand indication of the position of the current account as a whole. . . .

The service items in the current account, sometimes called "invisible" exports and imports, include a number of things which are services pure and simple and some which are included under the rubric for convenience and for lack of anything better to call them. Insurance, which is generally net (or premiums less expenses and losses), banking, freight, film rentals, royalties (authors' and patent), and expenses of tourist travel are clearly payments tendered for services performed. Interest on investment is also properly regarded as a return for some service rendered by the capital loaned; and profits may, with some stretching, be regarded as the return for the efforts of entrepreneurs.

* * * * *

The capital account records changes in the claims of residents of a country or residents of other countries, and changes in liabilities owed. For ease of exposition, it is handier to talk of claims of one country on the rest of the world, and vice versa, leaving out mention of the residents in both cases. This is permissible only if we remember that an accurate statement would require us to bring the residents back in.

The recording of movements in the capital account sometimes gives the student (and even the teacher) difficulty. It seems strange, for example, that a capital outflow should be a debit in the balance of payments when it makes the country a creditor. But such is the case, and the student must master it. An inflow is a credit, and a capital outflow a debit.

Some writers, and occasionally an official compiler of balances of payments, will try to make things easier by pointing out that a capital inflow involves the export of securities, bank deposit books, or IOU's. By analogy, with an export of merchandise, and export of securities (bankbooks, IOU's) is a credit. And an import of securities (an export or outflow of capital) becomes a debit. This device, though cumbersome, may be helpful to remember.

Another way of keeping in mind that an export of capital is a debit, and inflow a credit, is to concentrate on the direction of payment. An export of capital gives rise to a payment to foreigners—just as does an import of merchandise. Both are debits. An inflow of capital, however, means that foreigners make payments to the reporting country and that the country is "collecting receipts" such as would be the case with an export of goods. It may be helpful to think more narrowly in terms of the exchange market: capital exports and goods imports add to the supply of a country's currency on the foreign-exchange market; capital imports and goods exports add to the demand.

* * * * *

In the final analysis, a country pays for its imports with its exports. But it is also true that the exporters in any given country receive payment in the domestic currency from the country's importers, who are thereby enabled to pay domestic currency for their purchases from abroad. Goods and credit instruments move across the border, but payment in domestic currency takes place within the country as part of the clearing process. Fig. 3.1 provides a highly stylized illustration of this basic proposition. The exporter in the United States ships goods to the importer in Britain; and the importer in the United States acquires goods

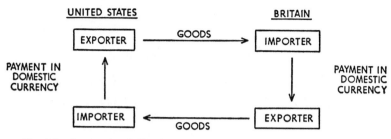

FIG. 3.1. International Clearing through the Foreign-Exchange Market.

from the exporter in Britain. The United States exporter is presumably paid by the British importer, and the British exporter is the United States importer. But in an ultimate sense the United States importer pays the United States exporter and the British importer the British exporter. The detailed way in which this is done will depend upon the way in which the transactions are organized.

Suppose the British importer buys dollars to pay his obligation to the United States exporter. How are dollars produced in the London market? Evidently by British exports to the United States for dollars. Dollars paid by the United States importer to the British exporter are bought by the British importer and paid to the United States exporter.

Or the transaction can proceed in sterling through the medium of the New York exchange market. The United States exporter draws a sterling bill on his British customer and discounts it with his bank. The bank then sends it to London for rediscount, selling the resulting sterling to the United States importer who needs it to discharge his debts for goods bought in Britain.

*　　*　　*　　*　　*

. . . The rate of foreign exchange, and with it the domestic value of a given amount of foreign money, can change. What brings it about that the pound is worth $4.00 in 1948 and $2.80 in 1950? Why does the market anticipate that the Deutschemark is likely to go up, despite the denials of the Economics Minister and the officials of the Deutsche Bundes bank?

The answer to these questions is demand and supply. The sterling exchange rate falls from $4.00 to $2.80 because the supply of sterling at $4.00 to the pound exceeded the demand at that price. This statement can be put the other way. The dollar rose from $4.00 to the pound to $2.80 because the demand for dollars at $4.00 to the pound exceeded the supply at that price.

From: Emile Benoit

"THE BALANCE OF PAYMENTS PAYOFF OF DIRECT FOREIGN INVESTMENTS"*

[EDITORS' NOTE: Professor Benoit teaches International Business in the Graduate School of Business, Columbia University.]

The Administration has proposed to raise the effective taxes on certain U.S. companies by taxing the profits of their foreign subsidiaries as earned and before their receipt by the United States taxpayer. A major announced purpose is to reduce the outflow of U.S. foreign investment, at least to the developed areas, in order to strengthen the U.S. balance of payments.[1]

*   *   *   *   *

The assumption that foreign investment burdens the balance of payments has appeared to some as self-evident, since foreign investment appears as a payment or debit item in the balance of payments. However, the purely conventional character of the balance of payments accounts, and the considerable degree of interrelation of the various items, both concurrently and over time, should be kept in mind.

Mr. Walther Lederer, Chief, Balance of Payments Division, U.S. Department of Commerce, in a speech before the American Statistical Association in New York City on December 28, 1961, discussing the balance of payments, stated as follows:

"First of all, it is important to understand that balance of payments compilations are done on the principle of double entry accounts, in which each transaction is shown as a credit as well as a debit item in exactly the same magnitude.

"Consequently, the total of all transactions also results in an equality of the total credit and debit entries. The balance of payments is always in balance. This concept generally is not followed in the collection of the data and it is often forgotten in the interpretation of the account itself.

---

* Reprinted by permission of *Michigan Business Review*, University of Michigan, School of Business Administration, Ann Arbor, Michigan, July 1962 (pp. 9–14).

1 "Concluding that deferral damages the balance of payments, it (the Treasury) decided that the time was most appropriate to end a tax preference that could no longer contribute to national objectives. Deferral should not have been ended right after the war, as the United States was then concerned to aid in European reconstruction by promoting an outflow of private American capital. It should not be ended now for the less developed countries as the United States is now concerned to promote development in those countries. But there can be no justification for continuing deferral for the developed countries, and there is every reason to anticipate that ending it now would strengthen the balance of payments." *Statistical Data and Economic Issues Involved in Treasury's Testimony on Tax Deferral*, submitted by the Secretary of the Treasury to the House Ways & Means Committee under letter of June 29, henceforth referred to as "The Treasury Memorandum." See *Hearings on the President's 1961 Tax Recommendations*, p. 3522.

"Second, the transactions included in the balance of payments presentations are not limited to those involving international payments in 'money,' usually consisting of gold, dollars, or other freely usable currencies, during any single period. The data cover all transactions involving transfers of resources, both real and financial."

*   *   *   *   *

. . . [M]uch direct foreign investment is closely tied to the export of capital equipment and, in addition, earns dividends (also, sometimes royalties and fees) which represent receipts in the balance of payments, offsetting the capital out-flow. Earnings remitted to the U.S. from direct foreign investment have exceeded net capital outflows into such investment in every year between 1950 and 1960, and to a total amount of $8.5 billion. Even Europe, taken alone shows a sur-plus of earnings over outflows between 1950 and 1959.

A private study by 19 leading companies of their foreign investments showed exports of capital equipment and materials for further processing to their foreign subsidiaries of $677 million over the 4 years 1957 through 1960, plus $812 million of net exports to foreign subsidiaries for resale, plus $691 million of other exports attributed to the existence of the foreign investments.[2]

In addition, these companies remitted a total of $289 million in dividends and earned $117 million in royalties and management fees and other service fees. Thus, the total earnings on their investments in this period, together with the net export sales directly and indirectly generated by them—deducting im-ports of finished goods from the subsidiaries—totaled $2.6 billion, enormously exceeding the actual outflow of new capital funds into the investments which totaled only $148 million in the corresponding period. While part of this $2.6 billion might have been gained in exports and royalties even without foreign investment, this would be true of only a small part of the total.

*   *   *   *   *

. . . [O]ver a period of years, a successful or profitable U.S. direct foreign investment may contribute handsomely to the balance of payments, by (1) earn-ing dividends, (2) earning royalties and fees, (3) financing exports of capital equipment, components and materials, etc., (4) building up a foreign marketing potential capable of expanding sales of the products both of the parent and of the subsidiary, and (5) raising foreign income and thereby imports of U.S. prod-ucts.

The difficult and relevant question that remains is, how long these favorable balance of payments effects take. This question cannot be answered by compari-sons between the outflow of capital investment over any short period of years and the reflows from dividends, interest, royalties, fees, and induced exports during that same period of years. This is because part of the reflows during the period investigated are attributable to the investment made in an earlier period, and part of the potential returns to the investment would not be fully manifested during the reference period. The shorter the reference period, and the more uneven the flow of investment and the rate of earnings, the more serious the dis-tortion that is introduced by any such comparison.[3]

*   *   *   *   *

---

[2] This study to which the present writer served as technical consultant . . . was presented by Mr. H. J. Heinz, II, for the Industry Committee on Foreign Investments to the House Ways and Means Committee on June 8, 1961. Hearings on the Presi-dent's 1961 Tax Recommendations, Volume 4, No. 70510, pp. 3185 ff.

[3] The Treasury initially tried to develop a case that direct foreign investment burdened the balance of payments by this type of comparison of capital outflows and

As an alternative approach, light has been sought by the construction of simplified models, based on reasonable or plausible or historically-based assumptions concerning such matters as rates of investment, profits, dividends, etc.

*   *   *   *   *

A model prepared by us, using historically-based parameters adopted by the Treasury in its own presentation, suggests that a direct investment in Europe will show a full return of dollars in less than seven years, and that the average dollar so invested will be outstanding for only $3\frac{1}{3}$ years. Moreover, it indicates that within a decade the investment will be earning almost 50% of its original value per year: 30% in dollars and 20% in local currencies being reinvested and generating additional dollar reflows in later years. Thus direct foreign investment would appear to provide strong support to the balance of payments rather than to burden it, except in the fairly short run.

From: David E. Lilienthal

"THE MULTINATIONAL CORPORATION"*

[EDITORS' NOTE: Mr. Lilienthal is Chairman of the Board and President of Development and Resources Corporation, New York, New York.]

Many large and even medium-sized American corporations are already operating in other countries, in one way or another. By *operating* I do not mean merely that they have a financial stake, like a portfolio investment, in business in other countries than their own; nor do I refer only to sales agencies or distributors. I have particularly in mind industrial or commercial operations abroad which directly involve corporate managerial responsibility.

Such corporations—which have their home in one country but which operate and live under the laws and customs of other countries as well—I suggest be called *multinational corporations*.

*   *   *   *   *

RELATIONS WITH GOVERNMENTS

The most serious problems confronting the multinational corporation are those concerned in its relations with governments. These must be the everyday business of the corporation manager. If he handles them with skill and patient

---

earnings reflows over a fixed span of years. Because the reflows have greatly exceeded the outflows over the last decade, such a case could be made only by concentrating attention on Europe and Canada separate from the rest of the world and for the limited period 1957 through 1960—a period marked by unusual acceleration of investment and distorted by the exceptional $370 million re-purchase of the British Ford interest in 1960.

 * By permission from *Management and Corporations 1985,* by Melvin Anshen and George L. Bach. Copyright 1960. McGraw-Hill Book Company, Incorporated. (Excerpts from pp. 119, 121–28, 135–36, 139–42, 146–47, 154–57.)

attention, his company should prosper; if he underestimates their importance, if he fails to bring the full force of his training and resources to bear on them, then he is risking disaster.

MULTIPLICITY OF GOVERNMENTS

As we all know, a corporation is an artificial person, created by government. It is thus the offspring of a government. We also know how an ordinary corporation in the United States must relate to its government from its birth through its creative existence and ultimately to its death or dissolution. But the multinational corporation has multigovernments. It will come from the territory of one government and it will incorporate and live under the laws of another. More than that, it may incorporate and live under the laws of many governments.

*   *   *   *   *

. . . [E]ven in the simplest of examples—in which a corporation comes from country A to live and work in country B—the multiplicity of governments will be a perplexing complication. The immigrant corporation must learn to live with its new legal parent and yet honor its real parent, the government of the country of its origin. Legally, it cannot call on its true parent for protection and support, as can the traveler abroad. Yet it must be able to rely on that parent to some extent without at the same time offending its new parent. Thus one can see how delicately the relationship between the old and the new governments must be balanced.

The problem grows more complicated when the origins of the multinational corporation are multifarious. . . . Which country is the "protecting power" of such an entity? Certainly not one and one only of the several countries which have participated.

REGIONAL BLOCS

There is still a further complication for the managers of multinational corporations. They must learn to live not only with two or more different national governments, but also with regional associations, or blocs. The formation of these groups will multiply the already burdensome problems of government relations, for a regional body is essentially a kind of new government or community, though of limited powers, created by its members.

*   *   *   *   *

While this is all going on, from the period of raw newness through the growth of central power, the multinational corporations will be prominent citizens living under the developing systems. They will have to contend with both the reality and the form. The old state sovereignty will govern, the new federal authority will govern and, perhaps, contradictorily. Conflicts and contradictions must be anticipated as inescapable. Accommodating to these conflicts will become a part of the multinational corporate manager's daily tasks. . . .

MULTIPLICITY OF REGULATIONS AND LIAISON

Whether the corporate manager has to deal with one foreign government or with several—perhaps including a supranational regional group—he will need the services of government, the protection of government, and an intimate knowledge of the facilities of government far more than will the man who manages a purely domestic business. Even for domestic operations, the weight of government relations has grown heavy. With the increased complexity of economic life, government regulation has naturally become intensified. Compliance with government regulations is a large and indispensable part of the corporate activity, and relations with governmental authorities are a primary duty of the corporate manager.

For the multinational corporation, government regulations and relations will be multiplied. Here the manager must deal not with one government but with two, or even more. He will, at times, have detailed and often subtle and complex relations with his home country. He will, for example, be governed by his nation's tax laws and economic and social controls affecting the operations abroad of its nationals or its corporations. Every government enforces some of its laws extraterritorially. On the most mundane level there are, say, the social security laws applicable to citizens employed abroad. On more complex levels there are neutrality laws, nationality laws, antitrust laws, and there may yet be other types whose precise nature is not now predictable.

Then the corporate manager will face the even more difficult problem of understanding and complying with the requirements of the foreign country or countries in which he has established his enterprise. These requirements may be many times as involved and onerous as those imposed in his home country. It is here—in his relations with governments overseas—that the manager will need the most guidance, the most services, the most contact with officialdom.

He and his compeers must maintain constant liaison with ministries of the government or governments under whose laws they operate. If there is no appropriate machinery in these ministries to provide the managers with the services or guidance they need, then they must encourage its development. They must, if need be, foster the growth of governmental bureaus of overseas trade. More than this, they must also maintain contact with the international bodies which in public life parallel their private ventures. . . .

Managers of multinational private corporations also have a responsibility to keep abreast of the rapidly moving events in the public sector which may affect their own operations. . . .

There should follow, as well, the creation of joint governmental machinery for the encouragement and protection of the multinational corporation. Private national activity should have parallel multinational administrative and governmental support. For instance, there should be not only a British board of trade to foster British trade and activity abroad, there should be international boards of trade. We should have also international economic agencies of governments ready to help if and when—and it is well-nigh inevitable—the multinational private venture is in a controversy with the government of the scene of operations.

We will not achieve this without the most active effort by those primarily interested, the managers of the multinational corporations. If the multinational corporation is to be sufficiently protected and serviced, it will have to join in creating its protectors and servicers.

WORKING UNDER FOREIGN GOVERNMENTS

But the big job of government relations for the multinational corporation will be its relations with the individual government overseas. The American business executive who thinks of his own government as ubiquitous will be surprised at how pervasive relations with governments abroad can be.

First, the multinational corporation, though it be incorporated in the country of operations, will face the problem of being a foreigner. The status of a foreigner has a very tangible significance in law and business. Emotionally, the progression of some forms of nationalism goes something like this—foreigner, alien, stranger, suspect. Legally, it is somewhat the same. There are separate laws for aliens—immigration and similar laws which govern only aliens or travelers. There are separate laws governing alien corporate registration, owner- ship of land and stock by foreign corporations, and always, special tax laws. Finally there are all the laws governing international business relations, financial and informational. All these require understanding, compliance, and continuing government relations. Frequent and seemingly interminable negotiations and relations with governments and their bureaucracies will be the lot of the execu- tive in a country not his own. . . .

* * * * *

Antitrust Laws—American and Foreign

The American antitrust law affects both the American corporation operating abroad and the foreign corporation which comes here. There is also a body of antitrust law abroad, actual or potential, affecting every corporation operating within its jurisdiction.

The American corporation which goes abroad to become a multinational corporation may run head on into its own antitrust laws, perhaps for the first time, and usually where least expected, for our antitrust laws apply to restraints, from abroad, on the foreign commerce of the United States. American or other corporations may, in combination, so operate abroad as to violate the American antitrust laws at home.

Since the multinational corporation will usually incorporate abroad, there will thus be two (or more) corporations where there was one before. The two may find themselves engaged in the combination which is an essential ingredient of most antitrust violations. That is, one company may refuse to sell in certain areas, or refuse to sell except upon certain conditions, or apportion territories among its salesmen and divisions. Two companies, if they agree to do this, may very well be engaged in a violation of the American antitrust laws by restraining the foreign commerce of the United States. This consequence may be avoided by retaining the singleness of the corporate structure, but this may be impractical for many other reasons.

* * * * *

Managers of multinational corporations will need the assistance of specialists in this complicated field of antitrust law. But the effective corporate manager must himself become, in his multinational operations, at least as familiar with antitrust and trade regulations as he is with labor relations.

* * * * *

Political Activity

* * * * *

Should the multinational corporation go into politics? Certainly not the kind of politics which in an earlier day took the form of secretly subsidizing rebel leaders or keeping cabinets on a payroll. But can a multinational corporate management possibly avoid action—economic or business action—that has politi- cal consequences? I think not. . . .

. . . [A] corporate manager overseas must not be content simply to master the intricacies of a government's tax law. He must also study the political forces which shaped that law—and which may modify it or even strike it from the books tomorrow.

The corporate manager who is politically alert and knowledgeable will be in a position to form broad and sound judgments about the course of his firm's career. A lively awareness of politics in the broadest sense can be the key to constructive relations with governments, and these relations, in turn, have a definite bearing on the success of his business enterprise.

MULTINATIONAL OWNERSHIP, MANAGEMENT AND LABOR

*　　　*　　　*　　　*　　　*

As industrialization increases and living standards rise, there will be increasingly wider ownership of stock in large corporations around the world, not merely in the United States. The pattern is fairly familiar. . . .

It seems fairly clear that the phenomenon of wider ownership of stock in large corporations will spread. . . .

Just as more ownership of corporate shares in more countries seems certain, so will it surely be more multinational. First, multinational corporations are on the increase. A share in Lever Brothers or ICI, owned by an English worker today, is already a share in a multinational corporation. A share of Montecatini owned by an Italian technician is today a share in Italian wealth. But tomorrow that same share may represent enough American or Argentine assets to be properly described as a piece of world, not provincial, wealth.

*　　　*　　　*　　　*　　　*

. . . The day is past when a Western corporation operating in a less developed country could reserve the top-echelon jobs for its own nationals. The bitter rewards of this wasteful and myopic policy are only too well known to us. It surely has been made painfully clear by now that the multinational corporation which ignores the legitimate aspirations of the people who live in the country of operations will destroy itself. The contrary should also be clear. The multinational corporation which works toward the ultimate ideal of management and operation by the people of the country concerned will succeed the best.

Thus, in the less developed countries the foreign manager must honestly seek to work himself out of his job. He must strive to hasten the day when he can turn his desk over to a man of local citizenship. This is not sheer altruism (although there would be no reason to be ashamed of it if it were); it is symbolic of the posture which the multinational corporation must conscientiously adopt in order to prosper. . . .

*　　　*　　　*　　　*　　　*

SOME LONG-RANGE EFFECTS

*　　　*　　　*　　　*　　　*

It is not out of the question that multinational corporate operations also will give us the beginnings of a world-wide system of business ethics. This system would govern business dealings between competitors, regulate sharp business practices, unfair competition, and even what we call "commercial bribery." Laws and attitudes opposed to venality in government office or to conflicts of interest by government officials, which are generally accepted as right in the West, will come to be introduced in other areas. In the main, I would guess that in Asia, Africa, and Latin America the leaders of business will come to adopt the best of Western business ethics. In consequence, the treaties on trade practices and perhaps even the new foreign laws on commercial bribery and business expense deductions will imitate the most enlightened Western standards.

The various nations' laws—not to speak of good public relations—will generally require that there be separate corporations in the separate countries. The task will thus be to secure the benefits of centralized effort and understanding while engaged in separate ventures in the different countries. . . .

*   *   *   *   *

Multinational corporations will influence exports and imports of institutions other than those directly related to their business. They will export not only the technology of the countries of their origin, but also to a great extent the concepts of social justice of these countries.

*   *   *   *   *

There is still another significant contribution of the multinational corporation. It is patent that the multinational corporation is an exercise in international, in binational, and in multinational activity. Financiers, businessmen, managers, technicians, and laborers will work together. Governments and government officers will work together in settling the large and small problems incident to multinational corporate activities. This ferment will necessarily improve both the climate and the techniques for binational and multinational political activity. Thus with an increase in natural, functional multinational corporate activity, it is possible—perhaps inevitable—that there will be more and more likelihood that comparable efforts on the political side will be made and will succeed.

THE SELLERS MACHINE COMPANY

I Case Introduction

Synopsis

A relatively small subsidiary of a nationally known machine manufacturer experiences a sudden upsurge in orders in the spring of 1965. Exercising its rather broad autonomy, local management decides the only way to meet the increased demand, in the short run at least, is to institute a third shift. The third shift is planned to begin in the machinery department on June 7. On June 1, management posts six job openings for the third shift and announces details of the plan to union officials. What have been "excellent" union-management relations heretofore become strained as the union files a grievance against the "unilateral action of the company in establishing a third shift in violation of the present working Agreement." The grievance process quickly reaches the third step, with the union eventually employing a labor attorney and the local management being represented by the manager of industrial relations from the parent company. On June 10, the union announces plans to seek immediate arbitration if the issue is not settled. One more joint meeting is planned for June 15, but meanwhile management has to decide whether or not to institute the once-delayed third shift on June 10 as announced.

Why This Case Is Included

This case offers the opportunity to observe conflict between union and management within the bounds of the contractually established grievance procedure. The reader can trace the causes of the conflict and the reasons for its escalation, and the stakes each party has in the confrontation. Knowing the traditional arena (no strike clause in the contract, the grievance procedure, and the possibility of submission to arbitration), the reader can explore strategies for both parties that will satisfy individual and mutual objectives. The case may be viewed from at least two levels: conflict of individuals and conflict of institutions.

Diagnostic and Predictive Questions

In answering the following diagnostic and predictive questions, remember that these questions apply theories and conceptual ideas from certain disciplines. Such theories are valuable to understand basic forces at work in the policy system (diagnosis) and to predict what will happen in the system in the future (prediction). Since each reading abstracts from the total policy system certain factors or variables into the closed or partial viewpoint of one theory or discipline, no one reading gives answers to the practical policy problems of the case. In diagnosis and prediction, the parts of the problem are studied with "other things being equal."

Following each question are listed readings which will be helpful in answering the question. The readings included with this case are marked (*). By referring to the author index at the end of this book, you may locate the other readings listed.

1. By sifting case facts identify the logic that led the local management to the decision to establish a third shift.

2. Considering the complex of objectives of the union as bargaining agent for the Sellers Machine Company employees, how do you think the union would have decided if it processed the same facts used by management in its determination of the need for a third shift? In what way, if any, would the union logic differ from management's?

  Read: *Slichter, Healy, and Livernash, *The Impact of Collective Bargaining on Management,* pp. 211–12, 221–23, 241–43, 692–96, 732–36.

3. Knowing what transpired in the May 27, 1965, meeting between management (Harker, plant superintendent, and Kraus, personnel manager) and the local union officials, could you have predicted a change in the "cooperative attitude" and in the "excellent" relations between management and the union? Look especially at the Harker-Bruder interaction on May 27.

  Read: McGrath, *Social Psychology,* pp. 50–52.

4. Think carefully about institutional as well as interpersonal factors and identify the reasons for the filing of the grievance on June 1, 1965.

  Read: *The readings assigned in Question 2.

5. Does the psychology of human needs help explain the differences in behavior of Wilson and Kraus as they interact with union representatives?

  Read: Gellerman, *Motivation and Productivity,* pp. 109–18; Maslow, *Motivation and Personality,* pp. 80–94.

6. Does the psychology of perception aid in understanding how both local and corporate management could have overlooked the crucial issues raised by the union counsel on June 10 so that the management team had to "plead surprise?"

  Read: Leavitt, *Managerial Psychology,* pp. 27–33; Boulding, *The Image,* pp. 11–14; Krech and Crutchfield, *Theory and Problems of Social Psychology,* pp. 81–83, 87–89, 94–96, 98, 102–3.

7. What motivations does management have to settle the grievance before it is submitted to arbitration? Where do you think the union stands on the desirability of settling before submission to arbitration?

  Read: *The readings assigned in Question 2.

8. In the presence of a no-strike clause, the Agreement provides a mechanism for conflict resolution—a three-step grievance process with ultimate recourse to arbitration. Examine this mechanism in light of the relevant conceptual schemes from political philosophy.

  Read: *Eells and Walton, *Conceptual Foundations of Business,* pp. 360–63; Follett, "Constructive Conflict."

Policy Questions for This Specific Case

In answering the following policy questions, the results of diagnosis and prediction are used to reduce the amount of guesswork, or judgment, in designing action solutions. However, since certain parts of the total case situation cannot be reduced to science, and since "other things are not equal," judgment must still be used to fill in the factors not accounted for by readings. You will also need a second kind of judgment as you put value weights on different scientific predictions, since different theories may point to conflicting solutions.

9. What should local management do as regards its announced plans to institute the third shift at midnight on June 10? If management decides to go ahead with the third shift now, what are the probable implications for settling the grievance through continued negotiation? What would be the likely impact on an arbitration decision?

10. Should management stand firm in its position and take its chances on arbitration or attempt to negotiate a settlement? (Review your answer to Question 7.)

11. What can management afford to give up if it negotiates further? Are there any unimportant issues?

12. What should management use as bargaining strategy if it negotiates further? What items go first on the agenda? What arguments should be used?

13. If management negotiates further, who should represent management? Why? From management's point of view who would best represent the union? Why? How might management influence who represents the union?

14. How should local management relate to Wilson, the corporate manager of industrial relations?

Major Policy Issues: Tentative Generalizations about Any Policy System

In arriving at conclusions for the following questions, generalize from the facts in the case and use your own ideas to (a) confirm, (b) modify, or (c) test the workability of the concepts and theories from readings. As an executive or professional, use wisdom to merge theory, on the one hand, with "brute facts" and practice, on the other.

15. Are there institutional imperatives which may prompt a union to act (for example, file a grievance) contrary to the current and perceived interests of its members? If so, what are the implications for management? For society?

(Review the reading attached to Question 2.)

16. Is the conflict resolution mechanism built into so many union agreements (a grievance process with ultimate recourse to binding arbitration) a helpful model for designing some institutionalized form of due process for nonunion, exempt employees.

Read: Evan, "Organization Men and Due Process of Law."

Questions for Original Student Work in Analysis and Policy

The methods of viewing this case as represented by the authors' questions and selection of readings are not exhaustive. There are other relevant ideas for diagnosis and prediction. Furthermore, there are other ways of stating policy questions. More powerful analyses and wiser solutions will result by drawing on your own training and experience for (a) relevant concepts and theories, and (b) creative ways of asking policy questions. The following questions are designed to help you acquire this skill.

17. While reflecting on case facts, what additional theories from prior education give you insights as to "what is going on" in the Sellers Machine Company? As to what might be predicted to happen in the future?

18. Other than the policy questions asked by the authors, what pragmatic ways can you think of to state the practical problems faced by executives in the case?

II The Sellers Machine Company*

The Sellers Machine Company produces electrical machinery in a rural plant in eastern Pennsylvania. Its primary customer is the paper industry. Employing about 150 workers, it is much smaller than its major competitors and relies upon its long-established reputation for quality work and upon its flexibility in operations which frequently permits it to quote earlier delivery dates than its competitors.

The day-to-day direction of the company is vested in a general manager, sales manager, plant superintendent, and personnel manager. No formal delineation of duties or authority exists. Where decisions may impinge on several areas of the business, they are arrived at by informal consensus among the managers. All of the managers and a majority of the employees are of native Pennsylvania-Dutch stock and have known each other most of their lives.

The employees were organized by the International Union of Electrical Radio and Machine Workers in 1946, and relations between the company and the union have been described as excellent by company and union. Both parties take pride in the fact that they have never experienced a strike. As an indication of its cooperative attitude with the union, the company each month holds information meetings with the five union officers who composed the local union leadership to discuss various subjects, such as order backlogs, new products, and recruitment needs, many of which transcend the usual matters of collective bargaining.

Late in the year 1964, the Sellers Company was merged into a large nationally known machinery manufacturer. The parent company retained the local management to operate the company as an independent division with relatively broad autonomy. One change introduced in the labor relations function was the parent company's insistence upon having its representative present at third-step grievance meetings.[1]

During the spring of 1965, the company experienced a substantial increase in orders, and sales forecasts indicated that the increase in orders would continue at least through 1967. A general management meeting was called to determine means of accommodating the increase without major additions to plant or equipment, for a general modernization

---

* Case written by Wayne E. Howard, Wharton School of Finance and Commerce.

[1] The contract-established grievance procedure provides for three steps: first, discussion between the employee and/or the shop steward and the departmental foreman; second, discussion between the chief steward and the personnel manager; third, discussion between the international representative of the union and the general manager. If satisfactory settlement of grievances cannot be reached after the above procedure has been exhausted, either party may appeal the dispute to arbitration.

program had been budgeted for the plant by the parent company for the year 1967. Moreover, it was recognized that additional machinery could not be placed in operation quickly enough to accommodate to the sudden surge in orders.

The plant superintendent pointed to two particular problems in adding new employees. Recruitment of skilled hands would be difficult in the rural area surrounding the plant. He pointed out that existing employees were working a six-day week, and in some cases a seven-day week. Secondly, the two shifts currently operating were scheduled over a 17-hour period (7 A.M. to 3:30 P.M., 3:30 P.M. to 12 A.M.), since each shift was entitled under the labor agreement to a half-hour unpaid lunch break. Were the company to add a third shift, it could only effectively operate six and one-half hours, since in all likelihood employees would demand a lunch break. The sales manager suggested the idea of over-lapping shifts but was convinced by the other managers that neither parking facilities nor plant facilities could support doubling up of shifts and that only chaos would result, should that alternative be tried.

It was decided that the plant superintendent would attempt to work out plans or a third shift for the machining department on a trial basis, since operations within that department were currently the most critical from a scheduling standpoint. The personnel manager brought up the advisability of notifying the union, but the consensus of the management group was that notification should be delayed until the feasibility of adding a third shift could be determined and the details of the manning schedule could be worked out.

On May 27, 1965, the plant superintendent and personnel manager held a regular information meeting with local union officers, at which time they discussed certain quality problems in production and the sub-stantial increase in forecasted business. According to company minutes of the meeting, the company discussed the latter problem as follows:

To meet the forecast we will add 10 or 12 people as soon as possible. Unfortu-nately, there is a shortage of skilled help in the valley and we have to depend to a great extent on green hands. As you know, we have a class for upgrading our skilled classifications which fits into this program.

At the conclusion of this meeting, Mr. Jacob Bruder, chief steward of the union asked, "Is there any truth to the rumor that the company intends to establish a third shift?"

Mr. L. G. Harker, the plant superintendent, replied, "We should keep this an information meeting." Mr. Bruder said, "But the guys in the shop have been asking about this rumor all week." Mr. Harker stated, "All I'm interested in is getting enough machinery to have a full complement of personnel on the second shift."

On Tuesday, June 1, at 9 A.M., Personnel Manager Robert Kraus called the union Grievance Committee into the personnel office and handed them seven job postings.[2] Six of these postings were for a newly created third shift in the machinery department to be established on Monday, June 7, with the shift hours running from midnight Monday until 7 A.M. Tuesday morning.[3]

Chief Steward Bruder raised his voice and said, "You can't do this to us; you got to sit down and bargain the wages, hours, and conditions first. There can't be any third shift without us agreeing to it." Personnel Manager Kraus replied, "Look, Jake, we're going to do it. Why can't we discuss it sensibly?"

"What about a lunch period?"

"We'll give them a paid lunch period."

"What about a shift differential?"

"They'll get the same shift differential as those on the second shift, 10 per cent."

After about a 30-second pause and without any inflection, Jake Bruder said, "We'll think it over." The committee then left the personnel office, but later in the day filed the following grievance:

The Union is grieving the unilateral action of the Company in establishing a 3rd shift in violation of the present working Agreement (Art. I, Sec. 1 and Art. III, Sec. 1).[4]

Recognizing the policy nature of the grievance, Bob Kraus immediately contacted Plant Superintendent Harker and General Manager Koch. All agreed that the corporate manager of industrial relations should be notified, and Kraus placed a conference call to the parent company.

The corporate manager of industrial relations, Warren Wilson, after hearing the background of the dispute suggested the position the company should take in denying the grievance and suggested that the company attempt to set up a third-step grievance meeting for June 9, at which time he would personally attend. From notes taken during the telephone conversation, Bob Kraus framed the following answer to the union's grievance:

This letter is in reply to your Grievance #792 relative to the establishment of a third shift in our plant.

The establishment of a third shift to meet the production needs of our plant is clearly within the rights of Management in accordance with our working agreement.

---

[2] Article VII, Section 1 of the Agreement provides: "Whenever a vacancy occurs in the plant, it shall be posted for a period of three (3) working days and filled on the basis of seniority for those applicants who are qualified to perform the posted job."

[3] Because the third shift would be likely to be composed of less experienced employees, the company believed that greater efficiency could be achieved by having this shift follow the existing shifts and merely carry forward work initiated on the existing shifts. Therefore, they scheduled the workweek for this shift to begin at midnight Monday, rather than the more common workweek schedule starting at midnight Sunday.

[4] See Exhibit 1, at the end of this case, for the relevant provisions in the collective bargaining agreement.

We specifically recognize the Union as the sole and exclusive bargaining agent for the production and maintenance employees whom we would employ on the third shift, and we are willing to bargain with you in accordance with Article I, Section 1 of our Contract. Meeting our production needs is solely and exclusively the responsibility of the Company as covered under Article II of our Labor Agreement.

With respect to your reference to Article III, Section 1, we believe that our proposal is consistent with the provisions contained therein.

Therefore your grievance is denied.

After reading the company response, Bruder agreed with Kraus that a third-step grievance meeting should be scheduled for June 9. Since this date was only two days after the planned establishment of the third shift, Kraus convinced Koch and Harker that the establishment of the third shift should be deferred pending the results of the grievance meeting.

At the meeting of June 9, Warren Wilson acted as spokesman for the company group and presented the following points to the union committee and to International Union Representative John Barker:

1. Under the labor agreement, the company has the right to unilaterally establish a third shift.
2. The establishment is necessary because of the sudden upsurge in business.
3. The use of a seven-hour shift is necessary to avoid the chaos of overlapping shifts.
4. The company is willing to discuss any details of the third shift, its hours, conditions, and pay, but will not entertain any discussion of changes in the existing shifts, their hours, conditions, or rates of pay.
5. Regardless of the outcome of the meeting, the third shift will be placed in operation at midnight on June 10.

John Barker who had apparently expected the meeting to be one of general negotiation was enraged. "Of all the double-dealing tricks," he shouted. "Let's get the hell out of here and take the men with us!"

"You do and you'll be saddled with a nice fat damage suit," Wilson retorted. "Our agreement has an ironclad no-strike clause in it."[5]

Barker and Wilson shouted at one another for the next few minutes. Barker accused the company of bad faith, and Wilson accused the union of attempting to pressure the company into renegotiation of the contract in the middle of its term. The union committee, however, made no move to leave the meeting.

Bob Kraus caught the eye of Jake Bruder, and they left the meeting for a conversation in the corridor outside the conference room. "Look, Jake," Bob pointed out, "we're not getting anywhere here today, and we're not likely to with both sides in this frame of mind. Why not get your side to recess, and I'll work on my guys, and we'll try to thrash this thing out tomorrow. Nothing's going to be done before then anyway."

Jake Bruder agreed, and the two men returned to the conference room to find Barker and Wilson still shouting. A short time later, however, Bob Kraus requested a short recess and broached his idea to Warren

---

[5] See Exhibit 1 for the relevant provisions of the collective bargaining agreement.

Wilson, who agreed to stay over for another day in an effort to settle the dispute. Jack Bruder was equally successful with his committee, and the parties arranged to meet the following morning.

After leaving the meeting, John Barker felt that the local union should have the benefit of legal counsel on the points raised by the company. Jake Bruder at first felt that it was a waste of local union funds, but was won over when John Barker pointed out that Wilson had taken an adamant and legalistic position and that if the union did not make a strong showing on this issue, the parent company would, in all likelihood, "force other decisions down the local's throat." Accordingly, International Representative Barker contacted a nearby attorney who frequently represented the international union or labor matters. The committee met with him that evening. After hearing the facts as presented by the local committee, he agreed to represent them at the meeting the following morning, but cautioned the committee not to take precipitate action, regardless of the outcome of the meeting.

On Thursday morning, June 10, the union committee again met with company representatives, and the union counsel, Louis Somerson, acted as spokesman. Somerson immediately took the initiative. "Gentlemen," he stated, "I've examined the position you took at yesterday's meeting, and there's no question in my mind, and there should be none in your own minds, that you have committed a deliberate violation of the agreement." He spelled out the union's present position with the following arguments:

1. The right of the company to establish a third shift does not encompass an establishment on some basis other than it is applied to the first and second shifts, nor in a manner contrary to the plain langauge of the agreement.
2. Establishment on a basis different from what the current agreement provides must be negotiated with the union. Failure to negotiate infringes on the union's rights as the collective bargaining representative of the employees and violates Article I, Section 1 of the agreement.[6]
3. Third-shift employees under the company's plan will receive numerous benefits not available to first- and second-shift employees: a paid lunch period; eight hours of pay for six and one-half hours of work; premium overtime pay after six and one-half hours of work. Thus, the company has discriminated in favor of certain employees and against other employees.
4. Moreover, if the company establishes the shift on a regular Monday midnight through Saturday 7 A.M. basis, without specific negotiation with the union, it will be liable for premium overtime payments for all time worked by the third shift after midnight Friday under Article III, Section 2 of the agreement.[7]
5. Since the union was taken by surprise by the job posting for the third shift and immediately filed a grievance, employees who otherwise might have availed themselves of this opportunity did not do so because of uncertainty over how the grievance would be resolved. Therefore, the union

---

[6] See Exhibit 1.
[7] See Exhibit 1.

demands that once the issue is finally resolved, the company repost the jobs.

6. Finally, if the issue is not resolved at this meeting the union will seek immediate arbitration of the grievance.

The company mangement team pleaded surprise over items 4 and 5, above, and asked for a recess to consider them. During the recess, Warren Wilson was contacted by the parent company and was asked to return to the home office. He requested that he be kept informed of all developments. The company team again convened with the union committee, pointed out that the team needed further time to consider the union position, and requested that the group convene again on Tuesday, June 15. The union agreed to meet again on that date.

On the evening of June 10, General Manager Koch called a meeting of company management to determine the course of action the company should pursue.

Exhibit 1

APPLICABLE CONTRACT PROVISIONS

Article I—Union Recognition

Section 1. The Company recognizes the Union as the sole and exclusive bargaining agent for all production and maintenance employees with regard to rates of pay, hours of employment, and other conditions of employment.

Article II—Management Rights

Section 1. It is the responsibility of the Management of the Company to maintain discipline and efficiency in the plant. The Management has the sole right to hire and to lay off employees, in accordance with the terms of this Agreement. The right of the Management to discipline and discharge employees for just cause and relieve employees from duty because of inefficiency is expressly recognized subject to the right of appeal through the Grievance Procedure provided in Article XV. In addition, the products to be manufactured, the schedule of production, the methods, processes, and means of manufacturing are solely and exclusively the responsibility of the Company. Previous rights of the Management in the past history of labor relations between the Company and the Union shall be continued.

Article III—Hours and Overtime

Section 1.

(*a*) The regular workweek shall consist of forty (40) hours, five (5) days from Monday to Friday inclusive, consisting of eight (8) hours each day.

(*b*) Any changes in the regular workday and/or week as referred to in Section 1 (a) of this Article shall not be made effective until mutually agreed to by both parties.

Section 2. All work performed in excess of eight (8) hours in any single day, or in excess of forty (40) hours in any week and all work performed on Saturdays shall be paid at the rate of time and one half.

Article VIII—Wages

Section 7. All employees working on shifts other than the regular day shift shall receive a rate of pay which will be ten per cent (10%) above the day hourly rates.

Article XIV—Grievance Procedure

Section 1. There shall be no suspension of work by the Union or lockout by the Company on account of any differences, grievances, or disputes that may arise between the Company and the Union, its members, or any employees covered by the bargaining unit.

III Selected Readings

From: Sumner H. Slichter, James J. Healy, and E. Robert Livernash

*WORK SCHEDULING**

When a union is certified or recognized as the sole collective bargaining agent by a company, one of its acknowledged responsibilities is to bargain hours of employment. It might be inferred from this and from a casual inspection of the terms of agreements that a union's impact on work-scheduling is limited to a definition of the workday and workweek. This is not the case. Collective bargaining in the past twenty years has introduced many indirect, devious, and subtle influences on scheduling.

*   *   *   *   *

NATURE AND SCOPE OF THE CONFLICT

Quite apart from any union influences, managements do not always have complete freedom to decide how work is to be scheduled. Sometimes the range of managerial discretion is surprisingly narrow. Influences beyond management's direct control and beyond the union's ability to regulate are constantly at work. Large groups of workers are called upon to work unusual hours on a regular basis or from time to time even though both the employer and the union would prefer an orthodox schedule.

INFLUENCES OUTSIDE OF COLLECTIVE BARGAINING

The origin and often the form of union interest in the scheduling of work become much more meaningful if the variety of factors that influence scheduling are understood. Among the several work scheduling determinants other than collective bargaining, the following will illustrate the problems encountered by managements and unions in their efforts to systematize or regularize the hours of work.

HABITS OF CONSUMING PUBLIC . . .

*   *   *   *   *

NATURE OF PRODUCT OR SERVICE . . .

*   *   *   *   *

NATURE OF PROCESS . . .

*   *   *   *   *

NATURE OF CAPITAL INVESTMENT . . .

*   *   *   *   *

---

* Excerpts from Chapter 8, Sumner H. Slichter, James J. Healy, and E. Robert Livernash, *The Impact of Collective Bargaining on Management* (Washington, D.C.: Brookings Institution, 1960) , pp. 211–12, 221–23, and 241–43.

SEASONAL INFLUENCES . . .

           *   *   *   *   *

NATURE OF JOB . . .

           *   *   *   *   *

INFLUENCE OF WEATHER AND EMERGENCIES . . .

           *   *   *   *   *

INFLUENCE OF LAW . . .

           *   *   *   *   *

GENERAL ECONOMIC DETERMINANTS . . .

           *   *   *   *   *

INFLUENCES OF TECHNOLOGY . . .

           *   *   *   *   *

PERSONNEL CONSIDERATIONS . . .

           *   *   *   *   *

UNION AND EMPLOYEE INTERESTS

Union interests, as we shall see throughout this chapter, is often at odds with the practical considerations that influence management's scheduling decisions. At least six, sometimes conflicting, factors help to explain union and employee interest: (1) a desire for leisure time, (2) health considerations, (3) personal convenience, (4) additional money, (5) job security, and (6) increased job opportunities.

It is emphasized that these desires of employees are by no means consistent from one group to another or from one period of time to another. To illustrate, while employees generally are interested in a shorter workweek, they are often equally anxious to avail themselves of overtime work opportunities because of the premium pay involved. The very success of the union in achieving the shorter workweek with penalty payments for hours scheduled beyond a certain number has often stimulated employees to want longer hours and to compete for the privilege of working longer hours. Employees in an industry suffering from a cyclical or secular decline will want a short week with no reduction in take-home pay. Scheduling becomes an issue in combating unemployment.

The conflict of interest between leisure and added income is sometimes heightened by the time factor. Employees who normally are eager to work all available overtime will suddenly become convinced of the sanctity of the regular work schedule when asked or ordered to work overtime during the hunting or fishing season or during summer months. The employee who is plagued at the moment by installment plan obligations or unexpected drains on his income will find the remunerations of an irregular schedule far more desirable than the convenience and planned leisure permitted by a predictable, orthodox schedule. The dichotomy of employee preference does not permit generalizations, but it can be explained rationally in terms of time and the circumstances of each individual.

Sometimes the interests of employees are not compatible with those of the union as an institution. Many employees would prefer to have added work handled by overtime scheduling than by the addition of a second shift or by the employment of more persons for the existing shift. The union, in turn, may favor greater employment, either to rationalize its traditional argument for a shorter workweek or to gain institutional strength through more members. One of the difficult tasks of union leadership is the reconciliation of the short-run, occasionally shortsighted, desires of its members with the long-run goals and interests of the union and its membership.

As a consequence, anomalous situations arise. Employers who have yielded reluctantly to a reduced schedule of work and have agreed to the payment of premiums for overtime, call-in, or other scheduling irregularities are often confronted by union grievances on behalf of those who want to enjoy the gains of these irregularities. This is an irritant to many employers. Sophisticated employers have learned to recognize that the union's attitude in negotiations does not necessarily reflect its attitude in the processing of a particular grievance.

In summary, the conflict of interests in scheduling is considerable. What a company might want or need to do because of one or more of the eleven determinants described does not coincide with union and employee desires, explained in terms of the six factors listed. The further conflict arising between union long-term and employee short-term interests serves to heighten the problem for the employer.

UNION MEASURES TO DEAL WITH THE CONFLICT

It is difficult to classify the many ways in which unions have affected the scheduling of work. Some union policies and achievements are concerned directly with this subject. Others, however, involve very different matters, yet have a significant influence on how work is scheduled. The influences, therefore, are both *direct* and *indirect*.

DIRECT MEASURES

The *direct* measures, in general, seek to accomplish three objectives: to limit departure from normality, to make departure from normality a function of joint agreement, and finally, to penalize the use of abnormal arrangements by premium pay requirements. The concept of normality has been fairly stable in the past twenty years. In the discussion that follows, these direct measures will be considered: (1) definition of the regular workweek, (2) definition of the regular workday, (3) control of starting and quitting times, (4) scheduling and manning of shifts, (5) penalty payments for irregular work scheduling.

*   *   *   *   *

IMPLICATIONS OF UNION POLICY

In a book such as this it is impossible to describe the thousands of scheduling arrangements that have evolved under collective bargaining in American industry. As in the case of seniority arrangements, this is a subject that even the parties can handle only by general statements of principle in the basic agreement. In multiplant companies under a master agreement, local supplements are used to develop the skeletal concepts. Understandably the grievance procedure and arbitration are relied upon extensively for the development of scheduling guides. Innumerable special situations arise that cannot be anticipated in contract negotiations.

For this reason it is difficult to generalize concerning the impact of union policy. We know that it has been considerable. In a few instances, where direct controls have been imposed, the union may exercise a strong veto power over scheduling decisions. This is true where the agreement expressly forbids any work beyond a specified number of hours or during certain hours of the day. It may also occur where the union requires that any schedules deviating from the normal be agreed to by the union.

In most cases the union's impact has been to add considerably to the cost of irregularity and unorthodoxy in scheduling. Undoubtedly the original union proponents of overtime and special premium payments were sincere in arguing that such payments would have the salutary effect of regularizing the work schedule. They hoped that the added costs of working employees for extra hours or at abnormal hours would be a strong incentive to management to add shifts or otherwise rearrange schedules so that work outside the norm could be avoided. A lesser consideration in their campaign was the argument that *if* such work was necessary, the employee was entitled to special payment for the inconvenience and the irregularity of the hours. Seldom were premium payments advocated on the ground that they offered greater earnings opportunity for employees.

The fact is that these payments are viewed by employees primarily is an excellent opportunity to increase their take-home pay. Only when the irregular work is excessive on any given occasion or when it becomes a schedule pattern day in and day out, does resistance arise. The following sampling of comments reflects the dominant attitude. The die sinkers in a forge shop are said to "just love overtime and Saturday work because of the high earnings involved." A large drug company experienced a strike in which one of the issues was the subcontracting of work, which deprived maintenance men of Saturday overtime work. A paper company found that, in spite of what it considered to be a "grueling" 56-hour weekly schedule in a newly-acquired plant, the workers still wanted Sunday work because of the large overtime earnings. In fact, some employees resented the establishment of a 6-day schedule.[1] The earnings opportunity theory is sometimes deliberately fostered by management in promoting overtime as a substitute for basic wage increases. One well-known company admits freely that it has scheduled week-end overtime in part to offset the fact that its machinist and tool and die rates were below the area average, a differential that had led to unrest among the craftsmen. The New York plant of a large chemical company says that while it has low base rates, the high overtime of a 56-hour weekly schedule provides "good earnings relative to the area." One of the most extreme cases of the use of overtime as a revenue measure is to be found among Pacific Coast longshoremen. In their 1959 agreement with the Pacific Maritime Association they gained a guarantee of 8 hours of work, which had to be provided between 8 A.M. and 6 P.M. However, overtime is paid after 6 hours of work. The straight time rate for longshoremen is $2.74 an hour, and the overtime rate is $4.11 an hour. The average hourly earnings have been $3.70, showing clearly the significance of overtime in take-home pay.

The conclusions stated should not be interpreted to mean that employees necessarily want to work overtime or at irregular hours. Instead, the evidence seems to indicate that the prevailing premium pay arrangements are a satisfactory—perhaps more than adequate—supply price to induce people to give up leisure time and personal convenience. If the overtime is excessive or if it falls on days when the preference for leisure is very high, the supply price exacted is likely to be greater. Undoubtedly this accounts for the growth in double-time payments on Sunday and after a certain number of hours of overtime and the use of triple-time payment for work on holidays.

An important consequence of the attractiveness of premium pay work is the competition among employees for such work. This has led unions to seek from management a commitment that, wherever possible, overtime will be shared equally. The right to be called in at irregular hours is often claimed by those with the greatest seniority. Administering these systems for allocating irregular

---

[1] There are notable exceptions. Some employees for health or family reasons or because they are holding two jobs dislike overtime or irregular call-in at any price. Where the Scanlon Plan is in effect . . . , there is union and employee opposition to overtime and other premiums because of their adverse effect on bonus levels.

work opportunities has become a difficult problem for many companies and is a significant source of grievances.

Except in rare cases management has retained considerable freedom in scheduling work to meet normal or unexpected business needs. But collective bargaining has imposed a stiff price for this freedom, either in the form of requiring the employment of additional workers or in the form of premium payments. This price has been an incentive to many managements to avoid irregular scheduling wherever possible.

From: Sumner H. Slichter, James J. Healy, and
E. Robert Livernash

THE PROBLEM OF GRIEVANCES*

The arrangements for handling grievances have been well described as the heart of union-management contracts. They are the heart because their effectiveness determines in large measure how well the terms of the contract are observed.

ROLE OF UNIONS IN ADJUSTING GRIEVANCES

It is extremely difficult for management to operate a grievance procedure effectively in nonunion plants. In these plants a few individuals may voice complaints or suggest changes, but in general the employees are not heard from, and their complaints rarely go beyond the foremen.[1] Attempts to set up arrangements for handling grievances in plants where there are no unions have generally failed. Many managements have tried it, some by establishing employee representation plans to handle grievances. The employee committees were intended to be safety valves—to prevent the building up of discontent by giving workers a regular and management-approved procedure for bringing their problems to the attention of supervision. A high proportion of them failed. Usually the representation committee was active for a few months, but after a while the employees made less and less use of their committees. Often the meetings with management became purely social affairs, and in many instances the plans ceased to operate.[2] Of the employee representation plans that sur-

---

* From Chapter 23, Sumner H. Slichter, James J. Healy, and E. Robert Livernash, *The Impact of Collective Bargaining in Management* (Washington, D.C.: Brookings Institution, 1960), pp. 692–96 and 732–36.

[1] An exception to this generalization is an eastern scientific instrument manufacturer whose employees have asserted their interests and have questioned almost every job description in the job evaluation plan. Because the workers speak out on their own behalf, unions have not been able to organize them. The workers do not feel the need of a union. Several similar exceptions are known to the authors.

[2] The National Industrial Conference Board found that of 715 employee representation plans started prior to 1932, 389 were abandoned during the 13-year period from 1919 to 1932. *Collective Bargaining through Employee Representation* (1933), Table I, p. 16. Of considerable interest is the following observation in the report of the NICB on the activity of employee councils. The report states: "At first they served primarily as

vived, most remained in existence only because management went out of its way to stimulate interest in them.

Trade unions change all this. They give the workers machinery for presenting complaints to management, and they protect workers who make complaints from being victimized. Furthermore, unions negotiate contracts that impose obligations on management, thus creating the basis for grievances. Finally, the union itself may be the source of grievances. It may be interested as an organization in enforcing certain parts of the agreement that do not interest the employees. Or the union may seek to enforce an interpretation of the agreement different from that accepted by the workers in the plant. In a few cases the union may stir up grievances as a matter of union policy to harass management or to foster interest in the union. And political rivalries within the union may produce grievances.

* * * * *

THE NATURE OF GRIEVANCES

Fairness and reasonableness on the part of both management and union do not assure that the grievance rate will be low—although they assist in the speedy and unemotional settlement of cases. An important reason is that most grievances relate to matters on which reasonable men easily differ. Furthermore, the nature of many grievances is such that unions have a wide choice in the number of grievances they bring; the grievance rate is very much within the control of the union.

Grievances should be distinguished from complaints. Any behavior of the employer that an employee or the union does not like (what he has done or what he has failed to do) may be the basis for a complaint. Some complaints are also grievances. The essence of a grievance is a charge that the union-management contract has been violated. It should be emphasized that the union has great latitude in charging contract violations on almost any complaint. Therefore, it follows that some grievances discussed in the grievance procedure may not be arbitrable. This subject is discussed in the chapter on the arbitration procedure.

Grievances are usually thought of as involving charges by employees or the union against the employers, but occasionally employers have grievances against employees and the union. The latter are rare, however, since management as a rule is able to act on its own interpretations of the union-management contract.

Grievances may be divided into five main groups:

---

grievance boards. The mechanics of the system permitted the employee who harbored a real or fancied grievance to bring it before the council through his representative and secure an unprejudiced hearing. But after a time these matters were disposed of, conditions that may have led to them were corrected, and cases for adjustment by the council steadily diminished. This was the critical period in the council's existence. If nothing of a constructive character was provided to occupy the council's attention, it was likely to drift into disuse ending in abandonment. When, however, its possibilities for bringing management and working force together in united effort for the success of the enterprise were realized, the works council usually made for itself a permanent place in the company organization. As grievances claimed a diminishing share of the council's attention, they were replaced by subjects affecting the operating efficiency of the plant and the general welfare of the employees." The same, pp. 13, 14.

The Conference Board's explanation that the activity of many employee representation plans diminished because the employee councils cleaned up grievances may be questioned. Experience with unions shows that new sources of grievance are constantly arising. A more likely reason for the decline in grievance activity is that the unorganized workers gradually became timid about bringing complaints and that the foremen were increasingly successful in discouraging them.

(1) Cases arising out of plain violations of the agreement by the employer. No dispute over the meaning of the agreement or over facts is involved—the employer for some reason (ignorance, carelessness, or some other reason) has simply violated the agreement.

(2) Cases arising essentially out of disagreements over facts, as when a worker is discharged for an offense that he denies having committed. Another example is a charge that an employer altered the working hours of a chef in a cafeteria for the sole purpose of avoiding payment of overtime, in violation of a prohibition in the agreement. The umpire upheld the employer, finding that avoiding payment of overtime was only one of several reasons for changing the chef's working hours. Some agreements prohibit managements from changing "established practices" except under certain conditions. Hence, there may be differences as to what is the established practice in a given department or plant.

(3) Cases in which the essential issue is the meaning of the agreement between the union and the employer. These include cases where the scope of the agreement is in dispute. Even plainly written agreements may give rise to a multitude of disputes over what the agreement means in specific situations. Included in this group are grievances that arise from omissions in the agreement. For example, an agreement may contain no provision against the employer's contracting out work, but include a wage scale for various occupations. Does inclusion of the wage scale mean that the employer is prohibited from contracting out work done by the crafts for which the agreement includes a wage scale? Must a plant with a tool and die shop and a wage scale for its tool and die workers do all of its own tool and die work? May it abolish its tool and die shop and contract out all of its tool and die work? The job evaluation plan in a plant contains descriptions of the various jobs. Are the descriptions merely a means of identifying the various jobs, or are they a complete and limiting definition of the duties that go with the job? If some duties are added to a job, must the job be reevaluated? An agreement specifies rates of pay for overtime but is silent on the obligation of employees to work overtime. May the employer require them to do so? The agreement provides that employees who report for work at their regularly scheduled time are guaranteed four hours pay unless the employer has given them a certain number of hours' notice not to come in, or unless he has been prevented from giving work by "an act of God." What is an act of God?

Now infrequently the ambiguities in the union-management contract are deliberate; the language is purposely indefinite because it is all the negotiators can agree to. Making a section of the agreement ambiguous may represent a decision by the negotiators to "pass the buck" to those charged with administering the agreement.

(4) Cases involving the method of applying the agreement. For example, an agreement provides that overtime shall be divided equally among the employees who do a given kind of work. But the agreement does not say during how long a period management must make an equal division of overtime.

(5) Cases involving differences of opinion as to the reasonableness or fairness of various actions. Cases of this sort give the union great discretion in influencing the grievance rate. The union, while admitting that a worker was at fault, may contend that the discipline imposed is too severe. Or workers may complain that a standard is too high or a piece rate too low. In a plant making electrical goods, production standards may be changed whenever there is a "significant" change in the time required to do the job. There is no agreement on the meaning of "significant," but there is an informal understanding that it means 3 per cent or more. There may be a difference over the evaluation of a newly-created job and of the rate that it should pay. An airline agrees that it will not contract out services unless it is uneconomic or impracticable for the company to do the work. Differences of opinion may easily develop over what is uneconomic

or impracticable. In the absence of express provisions in the agreement, does management have the right to impose discipline for failure to meet standards on measured daywork? Under a step rate system based on production, may management reduce the hourly wage of a man who has earned a given rate for good production and then dropped back to a lower level of output?

A common cause for grievance under seniority rules is whether a given worker who would like to be promoted to a vacancy has "sufficient ability" to do the job. What is meant by "sufficient" ability? Is it ability to do the job at once, ability to attain a satisfactory level of output within a week, a month, or some other period, or ability to learn the job? Differences over these issues may go on for years and produce many grievances.

*   *   *   *   *

STEP AT WHICH GRIEVANCES ARE SETTLED

Statistics indicating at what step grievances are settled should be interpreted carefully. One large company and the union settle a very large proportion of grievances at the first and second steps. The second step in this procedure, however, is at the level of the plant manager and plant industrial relations director. In the following discussion the first two steps are used to indicate first line supervision and one appeal to a level below the plant manager and plant industrial relations director. The level of the plant manager and plant industrial relations director is considered to be a crucial higher step though not necessarily in large organizations the step immediately prior to arbitration.

One often hears the opinion that grievances should be settled as near the point of origin as possible, namely by the worker's immediate supervisor at the first step. However, routine grievances—minor discipline, for example—frequently require one appeal for settlement. Complaints that can be settled by the immediate supervisor often do not become formal grievances. Union stewards or first-level committeemen are not considered to be fulfilling their jobs if they don't take at least one appeal above the immediate supervisor. Technical grievances often require one appeal for adequate discussion and explanation. A grievance procedure that settles a large proportion of routine grievances at the first two steps is functioning very well.

Grievances involving interpretation of the contract or applications of the contract to several departments or perhaps the entire plant obviously cannot be settled at the lower steps. Such grievances might concern, for example, management's right to require employees to work overtime, or its right to contract out work. The higher steps are appropriate for settlement of such policy questions. It has already been pointed out that some contracts permit discussion of these plantwide issues to be started at the top. If not started at the top, discussion is bound to move there. The company's views may be presented to the union by the plant manager or the director of industrial relations, but management's position on these general issues will probably be made by top management—the president or executive vice-president or the administrative committee, if there is one.

With these exceptions, it is desirable to settle as large a proportion of grievances as possible at the lower steps. The reasons, generally inadequately stated, have been listed as follows by a division director of labor relations in a large company: (1) to maintain the authority and status of first line supervision, (2) to prevent the grievance from changing in character, and (3) to gain meaningful employee acceptance. . . . Substantially enlarging the authority of the foremen is not a feasible solution. Of great significance is the development of a satisfactory labor relations policy at the operating level to create first-step settlements that are acceptable in the light of policy and practice.

Many grievances change in character as they move through the grievance procedure—a fact not always realized. A production standard grievance on the factory floor has real significance to the employee and to the operating management. It involves the basic question of how much work the employee should do in a given time. As such a grievance advances up the grievance procedure, it loses its operating flavor and content. It becomes a "paper grievance" on the way the job was timed, on whether the proper allowances were given, and on other technical questions. Other types of grievances change in character as they are appealed. This point is in turn related to the third point—securing meaningful employee acceptance. Discussion and settlement of a large proportion of grievances in their operating environment by those most immediately concerned in the outcome go much farther to create a satisfactory employee relations environment than do higher-step settlements. A top-step settlement of an individual employee grievance, no matter which side wins, creates no meeting of minds of those most immediately concerned. Reflection on these reasons for seeking a high proportion of lower-step settlements shows the importance of the goal.

Consider briefly the functioning of the grievance procedure in three different plants of the same company under the same master contract with an international union. In the first plant, with from 5,000 to 9,000 employees, the grievance procedure functioned very satisfactorily. Statistics on grievances covering a four-year period have been consolidated. There were no significant differences among the years. The grievance rate was somewhat high, but not significantly so in the light of circumstances. Grievances were written at the first step (first line supervision) and averaged 22 grievances per 100 employees per year for the four years. The plant was a new one, having operated for less than six months prior to the period surveyed. It grew from 5,000 to 9,000 employees over the first three of the four years. A new and growing plant with inexperienced local union leadership is expected to have a fairly high grievance rate. The pattern of settlement is of primary interest. Of 6,747 grievances over the four years, 51.2 per cent were settled at the first step (immediate supervisor), 37.1 per cent were settled at the second step (labor relations supervisor), 10.3 per cent were settled at the third step (labor relations director, plant manager, and union grievance committee), and 1.4 per cent were arbitrated. A clear pattern of settling most grievances at the lower steps was established.

For the other plants of the company statistics will be given for only one year, but the pattern has been similar in recent years. The grievance rate in the second plant with grievances again written at the first step was 49.8 grievances per 100 employees per year. There can be no question that the grievance rate was very high in this plant although again the pattern of settlement is of primary interest. What was happening in this plant can best be seen by considering the number of denials. Of 710 grievances denied at the first step, 689 were appealed to the second. Of 638 grievances denied at the second step, 617 were appealed to the third. Of 228 grievances denied at the third step, 162 were carried to arbitration. In the third plant the grievance rate was 34 per 100 employees per year. Of 1,242 grievances denied at the first step, 1,079 were appealed to the second. Of 531 denied at the second, 381 were appealed to the third. Of 210 denied at the third step, 143 were carried to arbitration. In both of these plants the company granted, wholly or in part, 60 to 65 per cent of all grievances, and denials at lower steps were reversed in a high proportion of cases at later steps. The chances of favorable action on routine grievances at the third step were so good in the last two plants that the union would have been negligent if it did not appeal unfavorable lower-step decisions. In the first plant the number of modifications of decisions on appeal was very low.

The difference between a pattern of settlement at the lower steps and a pattern of constant appeal to the top has been made clear in the examples. The reasons for differences in patterns will be explored briefly. It will be recognized at once that most of the determinants of grievance rates dicussed in Chapter 23 apply, sometimes with a different emphasis, to patterns of settlement. The state of relations between the parties, the degree of experience of the parties, the personalities of key union and company representatives, changes in operating methods or conditions, union policies, union politics, some features of the grievance procedure, and management policies are all pertinent, and the earlier discussion need not be repeated to introduce small differences in emphasis. Conditions that produce instability within the union or management or both and lead to a high grievance rate are also likely to mean that most grievances will be brought to the top.

As with grievance rates, caution is required in judging the significance of a particular pattern of settlement. It is easy to get a pattern of settlement in the lower steps if decisions unfavorable to employees and the union are rare. It is easy to get low-step settlements if the union is weak. More important, sometimes top plant management, line or staff, does not really want a pattern of settlement at lower steps. Real grievance decisions are made only at the top. Denials at lower steps are only trial balloons—a way of playing it safe. It is generally recognized that real decisions are made only when a grievance reaches a key man at the top. The same situation may exist on the union side. While this is frustrating to lower management and to lower union representatives, it does not necessarily indicate inconsistent or poor management policy or highly disturbed union-management relations. It is amusing, however, to hear a top company official complain vigorously because lower management can't settle grievances and he must spend an inordinate amount of time on them, when it is perfectly clear that the real trouble is that the executive in question would no more give up the personal privilege of making the decisions than he would stop complaining about the consequences. Such situations, however, should be distinguished from that in plants where policy is inadequately developed and not made effective at lower levels with the result that lower-level decisions are inconsistent and of poor quality. An effective pattern of lower-step settlements must rest on a high proportion of good decisions at the first step. . . .

*   *   *   *   *

From: Richard Eells and Clarence C. Walton

*CONCEPTUAL FOUNDATIONS OF BUSINESS**

[EDITORS' NOTE: Richard Eells heads Richard Eells and Associates, Inc., and Clarence C. Walton is Dean, School of General Studies, Columbia University.]

Pluralism always implies multiplicity, frequently diversity, and sometimes conflict. It is as much the generator as the result of freedom. Pluralism is

* Reprinted by permission of Richard D. Irwin, Inc., Homewood, Illinois, 1961 (pp. 360–63).

intimately associated with toleration as opposed to bigotry, with voluntarism as opposed to coercion, and with a happy blending of individualism and associationism. This reflects those differences of interests that characterize the large, modern nation-state. Indeed, James Madison's claim to immortality rests mainly on his anticipation of the growth of parties and other voluntary organizations at a time when the former were unknown and the latter few in number. His prophetic observation (in No. 10 of *The Federalist*) [1] that the existence of many autonomous groups makes tyranny by the majority less likely has an important place in any theory of "countervailing power."

Pluralism is concerned with the roles that these autonomous associations can play as a result of the power they enjoy, with the interplay of forces among these various groups as they enhance or diminish a specific group's power, and with the effect of power blocs on individual freedom and creativity.

*   *   *   *   *

Pluralism encompasses an aim (wide diffusion of power) and a structure (voluntary groups operating between the national government and the citizen in a manner that neither subordinates nor dominates the individual), but it also involves a method for evaluating results. This method does not seek to construct broad social programs on the basis of prior fixed dogma but relies on the consequences flowing from various groups' actions for the emergence of policy. Pluralism is less concerned with the lack among Americans of a "public philosophy"—to use Lippmann's apt phrasing—than it is with the loss of a "sharp perception of consequence" by the leaders of these various private sectors in American society. . . .

*   *   *   *   *

From a political standpoint, pluralism seeks to build a bridge connecting the traditions of liberalism and conservatism in American history. In the liberal tradition, pluralism is marked by references to problems rather than solutions, by faith in change rather than a change of faith. Whether it is Wilson's New Freedom, Roosevelt's New Deal, or Kennedy's New Frontier, this liberalism insists that transformation and reformation are the natural products of a pluralistic and creative society. Pluralism's conservative lineaments show in its skepticism of state power and centralized state planning, on the one hand, and in its esteem of local responsibility and states' rights, on the other. . . .

*   *   *   *   *

Pluralism seeks to diffuse power into many organizations and groupings and thus to prevent the development of imbalances of power and to assure the freedom of the individual from the tyranny of the one, the few, or the many. It constitutes a continuing challenge to totalitarianism of every kind, whether the rule be held by a political dictator, by a business or labor oligarchy, or by the masses themselves. It is suspicious of claims to omniscience, and omnipotence and is therefore as much opposed to the ambitious pretenses of a James Stuart (the king can do no wrong), as it is to the Rousseauian version of democracy (the collectivity can do no wrong). . . .

---

[1] James Madison, *The Federalist: A Collection of Essays* (New York: John Tiebout, 1799).

SEABOARD CHEMICAL CORPORATION

I Case Introduction

Synopsis

Auditors from the Cleveland headquarters of Seaboard Chemical Corporation visit the Los Angeles Plant, where they judge certain items in the equipment inventory to be ruined. On return to Cleveland, they advise the controller of their judgment, who in turn requests the plant manager to write off the equipment's value ($45,000) from the asset accounts, which make up the company's balance sheet. There is disagreement between various people at the plant and at headquarters as to whether the equipment is, in fact, ruined. Actions of the parties involved are described as they relate to other individuals, and to the company organization structure.

Why This Case Is Included

The Seaboard situation shows how the necessity for central planning (by experts) and the necessity for uniformity often conflict with the necessity for decision-making freedom at lower operating levels. The executive is faced with theories which prescribe different solutions to this problem; the "technology school" of management gives one answer, the "political school" gives another, and the "psychology school" gives a third.

In this case, a conflict appears between staff executives and line executives, and between parts of the organization structure (position descriptions of the executives involved). The various theories mentioned above all have some truth in them, and one must judge which ones apply to the specific situation.

Diagnostic and Predictive Questions

In answering the following diagnostic and predictive questions, remember that these questions apply theories and conceptual ideas from certain disciplines. Such theories are valuable to understand basic forces at work in the policy system (diagnosis) and to predict what will happen in the system in the future (prediction). Since each reading abstracts from the total policy system certain factors or variables into the closed or partial viewpoint of one theory or discipline, no one reading gives answers to the practical policy problems of the case. In diagnosis and prediction, the parts of the problem are studied with "other things being equal."

Following each question are listed readings which will be helpful in answering the question. The readings included with this case are marked (*). By referring to the author index at the end of this book, you may locate the other readings listed.

1. From the standpoint of finance (management of cash flow), why is Mr. Turner interested in having the book figures at headquarters be an accurate "symbol" or "picture" of the assets which actually exist in the real world? Or, assuming that the physical equipment will actually be needed in the following accounting period, and that company headquarters must provide funds, why is he interested in such accuracy?

Read: Anthony, *Management Accounting*, pp. 290–92, 306. (Remember that the equipment is part of the capital equipment inventory.) Summer, "Profit, Flow of Funds, and Depreciation."

2. From the standpoint of the company's legal position with stockholders, and the fiduciary function of controllership, why was Turner's job description written the way it was?

Read: From standard texts on accounting, or auditing, study the concept of fiduciary relationship. Or, study the job description and draw your own conclusions from case facts.

3. From the viewpoint of the status and role of both the plant manager and the controller, what influence do their respective job descriptions have on their actions in the case? Why did they act as they did?

Read: Abrahams, "Status, Role and Conflict."

4. From the viewpoint of perception theory, and certain sociological processes, why is there disagreement between the plant personnel and the headquarters personnel in Seaboard Corporation? Why might each party rely on his own job description?

Read: *Merton, "Bureaucratic Structure and Personality." Krech and Crutchfield, *Theory and Problems of Social Psychology*, pp. 81–83, 87–89, 94–96, 98, 102–3. Thompson, *Modern Organization*, pp. 4–6, 12–13, 19–21, 61, 63–65, 77–78.

5. The problem of assets might be solved partially if each plant had its own corrosion engineer to appraise assets, rather than having one corrosion engineer at headquarters who works in all three plants. Why would such an organization structure not be feasible in the Seaboard Chemical Company?

Read: Summer, "Economies of Scale and Organization Structure."

6. From the viewpoint of that management theory which stresses technological excellence, who do you predict is most capable to make the final decision in the matter of asset condition?

Read: *Taylor, "Shop Management," pp. 92–96, 98–100. Veblen, *The Engineers and the Price System*, chap. v. *Smith, *The Wealth of Nations*, pp. 4–15.

7. From the viewpoint of that management theory which stresses political science and "law and order," who do you predict is the most competent person (or position) to make the final decision on asset conditions?

Read: *Fayol, *General and Industrial Management*, pp. 24–25, 68–70. *O'Donnell, "The Source of Managerial Authority." Locke, *Concerning Civil Government*, chap. ix.

8. From the viewpoint of that management theory which stresses initiative, freedom, and autonomy of individual people, who in the whole hierarchy (from president to storehouse supervisor) is most qualified to make the decision on asset conditions?

Read: Curtice, "General Motors Organization Philosophy and Structure." McGregor, *The Human Side of Enterprise,* pp. 3–10, 47–48, 53–54.

Policy Questions for This Specific Case

In answering the following policy questions, the results of diagnosis and prediction are used to reduce the amount of guesswork, or judgment, in designing action solutions. However, since certain parts of the total case situation cannot be reduced to science, and since "other things are not equal," judgment must still be used to fill in the factors not accounted for by readings. You will also need a second kind of judgment as you put value weights on different scientific predictions, since different theories may point to conflicting solutions.

9. Do you think any one person in the organization should decide on the condition of the equipment in the storage yard? If so, whom? If so, explain why the person you designate would have the most valid, or true, decision.

10. What specific changes would you recommend for the job descriptions of the controller and the plant manager? For any other job descriptions in the Seaboard organization?

11. Suppose answer to Question 9 is "no." What other means are available for getting a decision made which is valid or accurate?

Read: Follett, "Constructive Conflict." Eells and Walton, *Conceptual Foundations of Business,* pp. 361–63. McGregor, *The Human Side of Enterprise,* pp. 124–31, 172–75

Major Policy Issues: Tentative Generalizations about Any Policy System

In arriving at conclusions for the following questions, generalize from the facts in the case and use your own ideas to (a) confirm, (b) modify, or (c) test the workability of the concepts and theories from readings. As an executive or professional, use wisdom to merge theory, on the one hand, with "brute facts" and practice, on the other.

12. In complex organizations, is any one person ever capable of making accurate decisions? If so, how does one identify that person or position? If not, what about the principle of unity of command, so popular in political science and management theory?

13. Do, or should, specialists and experts have the real authority and power in modern corporations? If so, does this mean that line-staff conflict is inevitable? If not, do generalists (line) executives have the competence to make accurate decisions which involve specialist knowledge?

Questions for Original Student Work in Analysis and Policy

The methods of viewing this case as represented by the authors' questions and selection of readings are not exhaustive. There are other relevant ideas for diagnosis and prediction. Furthermore, there are other ways of stating policy questions. More powerful analyses and wiser solutions will result by drawing on your own training and experience for (a) relevant concepts and theories, and (b) creative ways of asking policy questions. The following questions are designed to help you acquire this skill.

14. While reflecting on case facts, what additional theories from prior educa-

tion give you insights as to "what is going on" in the Seaboard Chemical Corporation? As to what might be predicted to happen in the future?

15. Other than the policy questions asked by the authors, what pragmatic ways can you think of to state the practical problems faced by executives in the case?

II Seaboard Chemical Corporation*

Seaboard Chemical Corporation is a producer of sulphuric acid, employing a total of 1,640 people, with headquarters in Cleveland, Ohio. Plants are operated at Cleveland; Marcus Hook, Pennsylvania; and Los Angeles. The company is one of the older firms that produce this basic chemical.

This case concerns a problem that has arisen in the work performed at the Los Angeles plant and the work performed by the controller's department in Cleveland. Excerpts from job descriptions of the Plant Manager and the Controller appear in Exhibits 1 and 2. The general duties of other people in the plant and in the controller's department are mentioned later in the case. A simplified organization chart of the company appears in Exhibit 3.

Exhibit 1 *
POSITION DESCRIPTION OF PLANT MANAGER,
LOS ANGELES

1. The Plant Manager shall be responsible for operating the Plant profitably.
6. The Plant Manager shall attempt at all times to keep costs to a reasonable minimum, and to prevent waste of monetary and physical resources.
8. The Plant Manager's responsibility covers all operations within the plant, including direct production lines, maintenance work, and construction operations.
10. The Plant Manager shall have such authority over all personnel in the plant as is necessary to carry out the other responsibilities enumerated herein.

* Taken from page 16, Organization Manual, excerpt of certain numbered items.

It is the practice of Seaboard to do most of the construction of acid-processing units at each of its plants, rather than to farm out the construction of such machinery to outside construction firms. At each plant, a construction department, headed by a process (chemical) engineer, designs and constructs the various mixing vessels, pipe lines, agitators, and

* William H. Newman and Charles E. Summer, Jr., *The Process of Management: Concepts, Behavior, and Practice.* © 1961. Reprinted by permission of Prentice-Hall, Inc., Englewood Cliffs, New Jersey.

Exhibit 2 *

POSITION DESCRIPTION OF CONTROLLER,
HEADQUARTERS STAFF

1. The Controller shall have the responsibility of conserving all assets of the Company, and of protecting them from misappropriation, abuse or other conditions prejudicial to the interests of the owning stockholders.
5. The Controller shall personally, or through his appointed representatives, make a periodic audit to determine the condition of company land, buildings, plants, warehouses and other fixed and current assets, and their accurate valuation.
8. The Controller shall gather totals of all company assets from various locations, and all company liabilities from various locations, and consolidate these into the company-wide balance sheet at the end of the year.

   ° Taken from page 8, Organization Manual, excerpt of certain numbered items.

Exhibit 3

PARTIAL ORGANIZATION CHART OF SEABOARD CHEMICAL
CORPORATION

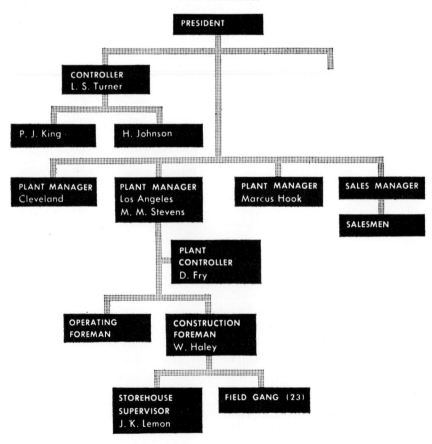

other equipment through which raw materials are converted to finished acid. Because the materials are so corrosive, some units of machinery must be replaced as often as once a year, and many others must be replaced after a useful life of one to five years. Replacement of depreciated equipment is continuous, and construction work is treated as routine, rather than as major addition to the plant.

In order to carry out the actual building and construction of processing units, each plant has a construction department, headed by a foreman. The specifications for this position state that the man who holds the job must be a graduate process (chemical) engineer, with at least five years' experience in actual construction operations. The incumbent at Los Angeles is Bill Haley. M. M. Stevens, the plant manager at Los Angeles, says that, "Haley is unusually competent in his job, having been with us for eight years. He hasn't practiced design engineering since graduation, but he knows a lot about the practical side of construction."

Haley schedules the work, and watches the progress, of 23 construction laborers. He is also responsible for the storage of materials used in construction, though this activity has been delegated to J. F. Lemon, supervisor of the storehouse department. This department operates a warehouse for storing the hundreds of parts used regularly in the construction of units. These range from pumps worth $1,200, down to nuts and bolts worth a few cents, up to large heat exchangers that may cost $20,000 or more. In addition to warehouse space, there is a storage yard adjoining the warehouse, surrounded by a steel security fence, where large equipment is maintained in open storage.

Last August, P. J. King, a CPA and financial auditor in the controller's department in Cleveland, accompanied by Harry Johnson, an engineer-auditor employed in the same department, made their yearly visit to Los Angeles for the purpose of verifying the capital equipment on hand. This procedure had been set up so that the company controller, L. S. Turner, could have an accurate consolidated picture of the company's asset accounts to put on the balance sheet at the end of the year. King and Johnson spot-check the physical equipment in the plant, compare the equipment they inspect with the accounts kept in the plant Controller's office, and either verify that the dollar amount in the account represents certain physical equipment, or advise plant personnel when they are unable to locate the specific physical equipment (asset) in the warehouse that should match a monetary asset carried on the books by the Controller.

In performing this spot-check and comparison, King and Johnson found in the storage yard certain items that they inspected with close scrutiny and later decided were damaged to the point where they should be physically salvaged (sold for junk or second-hand equipment) and subtracted from the assets on the books of the plant. These items, supposedly new, cost a total of $45,000. Johnson, a specialist in metals, corrosion, and condition of equipment, drafted the following memorandum to Mr. Fry, the plant controller. The memo was signed by King as well as by Johnson.

Our visit to Los Angeles this year has been a pleasant one, and we particularly want to thank you for the cooperation shown us by yourself and the men in your department. The only account which we believe should be adjusted is the storehouse materials account, in the amount of $45,000, and supported by the attached list. Messrs. Lemon and Haley have discussed this with us and state that the equipment is certainly in questionable condition, but that they may be able to use it in some way next year. We have, in turn, explained to them that it is in the interest of the company as a whole to have an accurate balance sheet. Only in this way can the President have the accurate information with which to run the company, and do his own planning. Since the equipment is in fact ruined, the Cleveland headquarters must provide for its replacement in next year's budget, but we cannot do this unless the accounts show the need for it. With this information, Mr. Haley said that he will go along with the decision to salvage.

After returning to Cleveland, Johnson gave a copy of this memorandum to Mr. Turner, company controller, and explained the problem of the ruined equipment. Mr. Turner then sent a routine memorandum to Mr. Fry, the last paragraph of which read:

Would you therefore be kind enough to adjust the storehouse account downward in the amount of $45,000, so that when, in December, you send the totals in each account to Cleveland, the Controller here will have accurate figures to combine with assets of other plants for entry on the year-end balance sheet.

Fry studied the memorandum and brought up the problem with M. M. Stevens, the plant manager, at a regular Monday morning conference Stevens had set up so that he could keep abreast of financial and cost matters at the plant. Stevens had been a foreman of the blending operation for 12 years before becoming plant manager, and for the remainder of his 30 years with the company had risen from a mixer's helper up through the production operations to foreman. He had not worked in the construction department. He says, however, that, "I have watched an awful lot of construction in this plant the last 30 years, and I have a good general knowledge of the whole operation."

Stevens visited the maintenance yard along with Haley, and both men agreed that the equipment listed in the Cleveland memo was "in not too good condition." They also agreed that, "We may be able to use it next year, but we'll have to wait until then to know what shape it is in." Stevens then told Fry that an additional reason for not writing off the equipment is that, "This $45,000 will be looked at as a deduction from the profitability of this plant, and we shouldn't be blamed for it until we know definitely whether it is usable." On instruction from Stevens, Fry, on November 6th, sent the following note to Turner:

Mr. Stevens has asked me to not write off the $45,000 worth of equipment specified in your September 14 memorandum. Therefore, the asset accounts which are listed in the attached report for balance sheet purposes reflect the fact that we are still carrying this equipment on our books.

At the writing of this case, on December 15, this is where the matter stands. In effect, the company controller, Turner, has taken the information supplied by his staff men, Johnson and King, and has requested Fry, the plant controller, to write down the equipment. Fry, on the other hand, has taken the information given him by Stevens, and the information given him by Johnson and King, and written to Turner the above memo.

III Selected Readings

From: Robert K. Merton

"BUREAUCRATIC STRUCTURE AND PERSONALITY"*

[EDITORS' NOTE: Professor Merton teaches sociology at Columbia University.]

. . . The chief merit of bureaucracy is its technical efficiency, with a premium placed on precision, speed, expert control, continuity, discretion, and optimal returns on input. The structure is one which approaches the complete elimination of personalized relationships and nonrational considerations (hostility, anxiety, affectual involvements, etc.). . . .

*   *   *   *   *

The Dysfunctions of Bureaucracy. In these bold outlines, the positive attainments and functions of bureaucratic organization are emphasized and the internal stresses and strains of such structures are almost wholly neglected. The community at large, however, evidently emphasizes the imperfections of bureaucracy, as is suggested by the fact that the "horid hybrid," bureaucrat, has become an epithet, a *Schimpfwort.* The transition to a study of the negative aspects of bureaucracy is afforded by the applications of Veblen's concept of "trained incapacity," Dewey's notion of "occupational psychosis" or Warnotte's view of "professional deformation." Trained incapacity refers to that state of affairs in which one's abilities function as inadequacies or blind spots. Actions based upon training and skills which have been successfully applied in the past may result in inappropriate responses *under changed conditions.* An inadequate flexibility

---

* Reprinted by permission of *Social Forces,* Vol. XVII (1940), pp. 560–68, by permission of the author and the publisher. (Copyright, 1940, by the University of North Carolina Press.)

in the application of skills will, in a changing milieu, result in more or less serious maladjustments. Thus, to adopt a barnyard illustration used in this connection by Burke, chickens may be readily conditioned to interpret the sound of a bell as a signal for food. The same bell may now be used to summon the "trained chickens" to their doom as they are assembled to suffer decapitation. In general, one adopts measures in keeping with his past training and, under new conditions which are not recognized as *significantly* different, the very soundness of this training may lead to the adoption of the wrong procedures. Again, in Burke's almost echolalic phrase, "people may be unfitted by being fit in an unfit fitness"; their training may become an incapacity.

Dewey's concept of occupational psychosis rests upon much the same observations. As a result of their day to day routines, people develop special preferences, antipathies, discriminations and emphases. (The term psychosis is used by Dewey to denote a "pronounced character of the mind.") These psychoses develop through demands put upon the individual by the particular organization of his occupational role.

The concepts of both Veblen and Dewey refer to a fundamental ambivalence. Any action can be considered in terms of what it attains or what it fails to attain. "A way of seeing is also a way of not seeing—a focus upon object A involves a neglect of object B." In his discussion, Weber is almost exclusively concerned with what the bureaucratic structure attains: precision, reliability, efficiency. This same structure may be examined from another perspective provided by the ambivalence. What are the limitations of the organization designed to attain these goals?

For reasons which we have already noted, the bureaucratic structure exerts a constant pressure upon the official to be "methodical, prudent, disciplined." If the bureaucracy is to operate successfully, it must attain a high degree of reliability of behavior, an unusual degree of conformity with prescribed patterns of action. Hence, the fundamental importance of discipline which may be as highly developed in a religious or economic bureaucracy as in the army. Discipline can be effective only if the ideal patterns are buttressed by strong sentiments which entail devotion to one's duties, a keen sense of the limitation of one's authority and competence, and methodical performance of routine activities. The efficacy of social structure depends ultimately upon infusing group participants with appropriate attitudes and sentiments. . . .

. . . There is a margin of safety, so to speak, in the pressure exerted by these sentiments upon the bureaucrat to conform to his patterned obligations, in much the same sense that added allowances (precautionary overestimations) are made by the engineer in designing the supports for a bridge. But this very emphasis leads to a transference of the sentiments from the *aims* of the organization onto the particular details of behavior required by the rules. Adherence to the rules, originally conceived as a means, becomes transformed into an end-in-itself; there occurs the familiar process of *displacement of goals* whereby "an instrumental value becomes a terminal value." Discipline, readily interpreted as conformance with regulations, whatever the situation, is seen not as a measure designed for specific purposes but becomes an immediate value in the life-organization of the bureaucrat. This emphasis, resulting from the displacement of the original goals, develops into rigidities and an inability to adjust readily. Formalism, even ritualism, ensues with an unchallenged insistence upon punctilious adherence to formalized procedures. This may be exaggerated to the point where primary concern with conformity to the rules interferes with the achievement of the purposes of the organization, in which case we have the familiar phenomenon of the technicism or red tape of the official. . . .

Structural Sources of Overconformity. Such inadequacies in orientation which involve trained incapacity clearly derive from structural sources. The process may be briefly recapitulated. (1) An effective bureaucracy demands reliability of response and strict devotion to regulations. (2) Such devotion to the rules leads to their transformation into absolutes; they are no longer conceived as relative to a given set of purposes. (3) This interferes with ready adaptation under special conditions not clearly envisaged by those who drew up the general rules. (4) Thus, the very elements which conduce toward efficiency in general produce inefficiency in specific instances. Full realization of the inadequacy is seldom attained by members of the group who have not divorced themselves from the "meanings" which the rules have for them. These rules in time become symbolic in cast, rather than strictly utilitarian.

Thus for, we have treated the ingrained sentiments making for rigorous discipline simply as data, as given. However, definite features of the bureaucratic structure may be seen to conduce to these sentiments. The bureaucrat's official life is planned for him in terms of a graded career, through the organizational devices of promotion by seniority, pensions, incremental salaries, *etc.*, all of which are designed to provide incentives for disciplined action and conformity to the official regulations. The official is tacitly expected to and largely does adapt his thoughts, feelings, and actions to the prospect of this career. But *these very devices* which increase the probability of conformance also lead to an over-concern with strict adherence to regulations which induces timidity, conservatism, and technicism. Displacement of sentiments from goals onto means is fostered by the tremendous symbolic significance of the means (rules).

Another feature of the bureaucratic structure tends to produce much the same result. Functionaries have the sense of a common destiny for all those who work together. They share the same interests, especially since there is relatively little competition insofar as promotion is in terms of seniority. In-group aggression is thus minimized and this arrangement is therefore conceived to be positively functional for the bureaucracy. However, the esprit de corps and informal social organization which typically develops in such situations often leads the personnel to defend their entrenched interests rather than to assist their clientele and elected higher officials. . . .

It would be much too facile and partly erroneous to attribute such resistance by bureaucrats simply to vested interests. Vested interests oppose any new order which either eliminates or at least makes uncertain their differential advantage deriving from the current arrangements. This is undoubtedly involved in part in bureaucratic resistance to change but another process is perhaps more significant. As we have seen, bureaucratic officials affectively identify themselves with their way of life. They have a pride of craft which leads them to resist change in established routines; at least, those changes which are felt to be imposed by coworkers. This nonlogical pride of craft is a familiar pattern found even, to judge from Sutherland's *Professional Thief,* among pickpockets who, despite the risk, delight in mastering the prestige-bearing feat of "beating a left breech" (picking the left front trousers pocket).

. . . [T]here may ensue, in particular vocations and in particular types of organization, the *process of sanctification* (viewed as the counterpart of the process of secularization). This is to say that through sentiment-formation, emotional dependence upon bureaucratic symbols and status, and affective involvement in spheres of competence and authority, there develop prerogatives involving attitudes of moral legitimacy which are established as values in their own right, and are no longer viewed as merely technical means for expediting administration. One may note a tendency for certain bureaucratic norms, originally introduced for technical reasons, to become rigidfied and sacred, although, as Durkheim would say, they are *laïque en apparence.* . . .

Primary vs. Secondary Relations. Another feature of the bureaucratic structure, the stress on depersonalization of relationships, also plays its part in the bureaucrat's trained incapacity. The personality pattern of the bureaucrat is nucleated about this norm of impersonality. Both this and the categorizing tendency, which develops from the dominant role of general, abstract rules, tend to produce conflict in the bureaucrat's contacts with the public or clientele. Since functionaries minimize personal relations and resort to categorization, the peculiarities of individual cases are often ignored. But the client who, quite understandably, is convinced of the "special features" of *his* own problem often objects to such categorical treatment. Stereotyped behavior is not adapted to the exigencies of individual problems. The impersonal treatment of affairs which are at times of great personal significance to the client gives rise to the charge of "arrogance" and "haughtiness" of the bureaucrat. . . .

Still another source of conflict with the public derives from the bureaucratic structure. The bureaucrat, in part irrespective of his position with*in* the hierarchy, acts as a representative of the power and prestige of the entire structure. In his official role he is vested with definite authority. This often leads to an actually or apparently domineering attitude, which may only be exaggerated by a discrepancy between his position within the hierarchy and his position with reference to the public. Protest and recourse to other officials on the part of the client are often ineffective or largely precluded by the previously mentioned esprit de corps which joins the officials into a more or less solidary in-group. This source of conflict *may* be minimized in private enterprise since the client can register an effective protest by transferring his trade to another organization within the competitive system. But with the monopolistic nature of the public organization, no such alternative is possible. . . .

From: Frederick Winslow Taylor
*"SHOP MANAGEMENT"**

[EDITORS' NOTE: The author was an Engineer at Bethlehem Steel and became consultant for many leading industries.]

. . . One of the most difficult works to organize is that of a large engineering establishment building miscellaneous machinery, and the writer has therefore chosen this for description.

Practically all of the shops of this class are organized upon what may be called the military plan. The orders from the general are transmitted through the colonels, majors, captains, lieutenants and noncommissioned officers to the men. In the same way the orders in industrial establishments go from the man-

---

* From *Scientific Management* by Frederick Winslow Taylor. Copyright © 1947. Reprinted by permission of Harper & Row, Publishers, Inc. (Excerpts from pp. 92–96, 98–100.)

ager through superintendents, foremen of shops, assistant foremen and gang bosses to the men. In an establishment of this kind the duties of the foremen, gang bosses, etc., are so varied, and call for an amount of special information coupled with such a variety of natural ability, that only men of unusual qualities to start with, and who have had years of special training, can perform them in a satisfactory manner. . . .

* * * * *

In the writer's experience, almost all shops are under-officered. Invariably the number of leading men employed is not sufficient to do the work economically. Under the military type of organization, the foreman is held responsible for the successful running of the entire shop, and when we measure his duties by the standard of the four leading principles of management above referred to, it becomes apparent that in his case these conditions are as far as possible from being fulfilled. His duties may be briefly enumerated in the following way. He must lay out the work for the whole shop, see that each piece of work goes in the proper order to the right machine, and that the man at the machine knows just what is to be done and how he is to do it. He must see that the work is not slighted, and that it is done fast, and all the while he must look ahead a month or so, either to provide more men to do the work or more work for the men to do. He must constantly discipline the men and readjust their wages, and in addition to this must fix piece work prices and supervise the time-keeping.

The first of the four leading principles in management calls for a clearly defined and circumscribed task. Evidently the foreman's duties are in no way clearly circumscribed. It is left each day entirely to his judgment what small part of the mass of duties before him it is most important for him to attend to, and he staggers along under this fraction of the work for which he is responsible, leaving the balance to be done in many cases as the gang bosses and workmen see fit. The second principle calls for such conditions that the daily task can always be accomplished. The conditions in his case are always such that it is impossible for him to do it all, and he never even makes a pretence of fulfilling his entire task. The third and fourth principles call for high pay in case the task is successfully done, and low pay in case of failure. The failure to realize the first two conditions, however, renders the application of the last two out of the question.

The foreman usually endeavors to lighten his burdens by delegating his duties to the various assistant foremen or gang bosses in charge of lathes, planers, milling machines, vise work, etc. Each of these men is then called upon to perform duties of almost as great variety as those of the foreman himself. The difficulty in obtaining in one man the variety of special information and the different mental and moral qualities necessary to perform all of the duties demanded of those men has been clearly summarized in the following list of the nine qualities which go to make up a well rounded man:

Brains.
Education.
Special or technical knowledge; manual dexterity or strength.
Tact.
Energy.
Grit.
Honesty.
Judgment or common sense and Good health.

Plenty of men who possess only three of the above qualities can be hired at any time for laborers' wages. Add four of these qualities together and you get a higher priced man. The man combining five of these qualities begins to be hard to find, and those with six, seven, and eight are almost impossible to get. . . .

*   *   *   *   *

It is evident, then, that the duties which the ordinary gang boss is called upon to perform would demand of him a large proportion of the nine attributes mentioned above; and if such a man could be found he should be made manager or superintendent of a works instead of gang boss. However, bearing in mind the fact that plenty of men can be had who combine four or five of these attributes, it becomes evident that the work of management should be so subdivided that the various positions can be filled by men of this caliber, and a great part of the art of management undoubtedly lies in planning the work in this way. This can, in the judgment of the writer, be best accomplished by *abandoning the military type of organization* and introducing two broad and sweeping changes in the art of management:

(*a*) As far as possible the workmen, as well as the gang bosses and foremen, should be entirely relieved of the work of planning, and of all work which is more or less clerical in its nature. All possible brain work should be removed from the shop and centered in the planning or laying-out department, leaving for the foremen and gang bosses work strictly executive in its nature. Their duties should be to see that the operations planned and directed from the planning room are promptly carried out in the shop. Their time should be spent with the men, teaching them to think ahead, and leading and instructing them in their work.

(*b*) Throughout the whole field of management the military type of organization should be abandoned, and what may be called the "functional type" substituted in its place. "Functional management" consists in so dividing the work of management that each man from the assistant superintendent down shall have as few functions as possible to perform. If practicable the work of each man in the management should be confined to the performance of a single leading function.

Under the ordinary or military type the workmen are divided into groups. The men in each group receive their orders from one man only, the foreman or gang boss of that group. This man is the single agent through which the various functions of the management are brought into contact with the men. Certainly the most marked outward characteristic of functional management lies in the fact that each workman, instead of coming in direct contact with the management at one point only, namely, through his gang boss, receives his daily orders and help directly from eight different bosses, each of whom performs his own particular function. Four of these bosses are in the planning room and of these three send their orders to and receive their returns from the men, usually in writing. Four others are in the shop and personally help the men in their work, each boss helping in his own particular line or function only. Some of these bosses come in contact with each man only once or twice a day and then for a few minutes perhaps, while others are with the men all the time, and help each man frequently. The functions of one or two of these bosses require them to come in contact with each workman for so short a time each day that they can perform their particular duties perhaps for all of the men in the shop, and in their line they manage the entire shop. Other bosses are called upon to help their men so much and so often that each boss can perform his function for but a few men, and in this particular line a number of bosses are required, all performing the same function but each having his particular group of men to help. Thus the grouping of the men in the shop is entirely changed, each workman belonging to eight different groups according to the particular functional boss whom he happens to be working under at the moment.

The following is a brief description of the duties of the four types of executive functional bosses which the writer has found it profitable to use in the active work of the shop: (1) gang bosses, (2) speed bosses, (3) inspectors, and (4) repair bosses. . . .

From: Adam Smith
*THE WEALTH OF NATIONS**

[EDITORS' NOTE: Adam Smith, 1723–1821, Professor of Moral Philosophy at the University of Glasgow, is considered the founder of the Science of Economics.]

OF THE DIVISION OF LABOUR

The greatest improvement in the productive powers of labour, and the greater part of the skill, dexterity, and judgment with which it is anywhere directed, or applied, seem to have been the effects of the division of labour.

The effects of the division of labour, in the general business of society, will be more easily understood, by considering in what manner it operates in some particular manufactures. It is commonly supposed to be carried furthest in some very trifling ones; not perhaps that it really is carried further in them than in others of more importance: but in those trifling manufactures which are destined to supply the small wants of but a small number of people, the whole number of workmen must necessarily be small; and those employed in every different branch of the work can often be collected into the same workhouse, and placed at once under the view of the spectator. In those great manufactures, on the contrary, which are destined to supply the great wants of the great body of the people, every different branch of the work employs so great a number of work-men, that it is impossible to collect them all into the same workhouse. We can seldom see more, at one time, than those employed in one single branch. Though in such manufactures, therefore, the work may really be divided into a much greater number of parts, than in those of a more trifling nature, the division is not near so obvious, and has accordingly been much less observed.

To take an example, therefore, from a very trifling manufacture; but one in which the division of labour has been very often taken notice of, the trade of the pin-maker; a workman not educated to this business (which the division of labour has rendered a distinct trade), nor acquainted with the use of the machinery employed in it (to the invention of which the same division of labour has probably given occasion), could scarce, perhaps, with his utmost industry, make one pin in a day, and certainly could not make twenty. But in the way in which this business is now carried on, not only the whole work is a peculiar trade,

---

* Published by Random House, Inc., in the Modern Library Series, 1937 (pp. 4–15). This citation is taken from the 1789 edition of the book.

but it is divided into a number of branches, of which the greater part are likewise peculiar trades. One man draws out the wire, another straights it, a third cuts it, a fourth points it, a fifth grinds it at the top for receiving the head; to make the head requires two or three distinct operations; to put it on is a peculiar business, to whiten the pins is another; it is even a trade by itself to put them into the paper; and the important business of making a pin is, in this manner, divided into about eighteen distinct operations, which, in some manufactories, are all performed by distinct hands, though in others the same man will sometimes perform two or three of them. I have seen a small manufactory of this kind where ten men only were employed, and where some of them consequently performed two or three distinct operations. But though they were very poor, and therefore but indifferently accommodated with the necessary machinery, they could, when they exerted themselves, make among them about twelve pounds of pins in a day. There are in a pound upwards of four thousand pins of a middling size. Those ten persons, therefore, could make among them upwards of forty-eight thousand pins in a day. Each person, therefore, making a tenth part of forty-eight thousand pins, might be considered as making four thousand eight hundred pins in a day. But if they had all wrought separately and independently, and without any of them having been educated to this peculiar business, they certainly could not each of them have made twenty, perhaps not one pin in a day; that is, certainly, not the two hundred and fortieth, perhaps not the four thousand eight hundredth part of what they are at present capable of performing, in consequence of a proper division and combination of their different operations.

In every other art and manufacture, the effects of the division of labour are similar to what they are in this very trifling one; though, in many of them, the labour can neither be so much subdivided, nor reduced to so great a simplicity of operation. The division of labour, however, so far as it can be introduced, occasions, in every art, a proportionable increase of the productive powers of labour. The separation of different trades and employments from one another, seems to have taken place, in consequence of this advantage. This separation too is generally carried furthest in those countries which enjoy the highest degree of industry and improvement; what is the work of one man in a rude state of society, being generally that of several in an improved one. In every improved society, the farmer is generally nothing but a farmer; the manufacturer, nothing but a manufacturer. The labour too which is necessary to produce any one complete manufacture, is almost always divided among a great number of hands. How many different trades are employed in each branch of the linen and woolen manufactures, from the growers of the flax and wool, to the bleachers and smoothers of the linen, or to the dyers and dressers of the cloth! . . .

This great increase of the quantity of work, which, in consequence of the division of labour, the same number of people are capable of performing, is owing to three different circumstances; first, to the increase of dexterity in every particular workman; secondly, to the saving of the time which is commonly lost in passing from one species of work to another; and lastly, to the invention of a great number of machines which facilitate and abridge labour, and enable one man to do the work of many.

First, the improvement of the dexterity of the workman necessarily increases the quantity of the work he can perform; and the division of labour, by reducing every man's business as some one simple operation, and by making this operation the sole employment of his life, necessarily increases very much the dexterity of the workman. A common smith, who, though accustomed to handle the hammer, has never been used to make nails, if upon some particular occasion he is obliged to attempt it, will scarce, I am assured, be able to make above two or three hundred nails in a day, and those too very bad ones. A smith who has been accustomed to make nails, but whose sole or principal business has not been that of a nailer, can seldom with his utmost diligence make more than eight hundred or a thousand nails in a day. . . .

Secondly, the advantage which is gained by saving the time commonly lost in passing from one sort of work to another, is much greater than we should at first view be apt to imagine it. It is impossible to pass very quickly from one kind of work to another, that is, carried on in a different place, and with quite familiar tools. A country weaver, who cultivates a small farm, must lose a good deal of time in passing from his loom to the field, and from the field to his loom. When the two trades can be carried on in the same workhouse, the loss of time is no doubt much less. It is even in this case, however, very considerable. A man commonly saunters a little in turning his hand from one sort of employment to another. When he first begins the new work he is seldom very keen and hearty; his mind, as they say, does not go to it, and for some time he rather trifles than applies to good purpose. . . .

Thirdly, and lastly, everybody must be sensible how much labour is facilitated and abridged by the application of proper machinery. It is unnecessary to give any example. I shall only observe, therefore, that the invention of all those machines by which labour is so much facilitated and abridged seems to have been originally owing to the division of labour. Men are much more likely to discover easier and readier methods of attaining any object, when the whole attention of their minds is directed towards that single object, than when it is dissipated among a great variety of things. But in consequence of the division of labour, the whole of every man's attention comes naturally to be directed towards some one or other of those who are employed in each particular branch of labour should soon find out easier and readier methods of performing their own particular work, wherever the nature of it admits of such improvement. A great part of the machines made use of in those manufactures in which labour is most subdivided, were originally the inventions of common workmen, who, being each of them employed in some very simple operation, naturally turned their thoughts towards finding out easier and readier methods of performing it. . . .

All the improvements in machinery, however, have by no means been the inventions of those who had occasion to use the machines. Many improvements have been made by the ingenuity of the makers of machines, when to make them becomes the business of a peculiar trade; and some by that of those who are called philosophers or men of speculation, whose trade it is not to do any thing, but to observe every thing; and who, upon that account, are often capable of combining together the powers of the most distant and dissimilar objects. In the progress of society, philosophy or speculation becomes, like every other employment, the principal or sole trade and occupation of a particular class of citizens. Like every other employment too, it is subdivided into a great number of different branches, each of which affords occupation to a peculiar tribe or class of philosophers; and this subdivision of employment in philosophy, as well as in every other business, improves dexterity and saves time. Each individual becomes more expert in his own peculiar branch, more work is done upon the whole, and the quantity of science is considerably increased by it.

It is the great multiplication of the productions of all the different arts, in consequence of the division of labour, which occasions, in a well-governed society, that universal opulence which extends itself to the lowest ranks of the people. Every workman has a great quantity of his own work to dispose of beyond what he himself has occasion for; and every other workman being exactly in the same situation, he is enabled to exchange a great quantity of his own goods for a great quantity, or, what comes to the same thing, for the price of a great quantity of theirs. He supplies them abundantly with what they have occasion for, and they accommodate him as amply with what he has occasion for, and a general plenty diffuses itself through all the different ranks of the society.

OF THE PRINCIPLE WHICH GIVES OCCASION TO THE DIVISION OF LABOUR

This division of labour; from which so many advantages are derived, is not originally the effect of any human wisdom, which foresees and intends that general opulence to which it gives occasion. It is the necessary, though very slow and gradual, consequence of a certain propensity in human nature which has in view no such extensive utility; the propensity to truck, barter, and exchange one thing for another.

As it is by treaty, by barter, and by purchase, that we obtain from one another the greater part of those mutual good offices which we stand in need of, so it is this same trucking disposition which originally gives occasion to the division of labour. In a tribe of hunters or shepherds a particular person makes bows and arrows, for example, with more readiness and dexterity than any other. He frequently exchanges them for cattle or for venison with his companions; and he finds at last that he can in this manner get more cattle and venison, than if he himself went to the field to catch them. From a regard to his own interest, therefore, the making of bows and arrows grows to be his chief business, and he becomes a sort of armourer. Another excels in making the frames and covers of their little huts or moveable houses. He is accustomed to be of use in this way to his neighbours, who reward him in the same manner with cattle and with venison, till at last he finds it his interest to dedicate himself entirely to this employment, and to become a sort of house-carpenter. In the same manner a third becomes a smith or brazier; a fourth a tanner or dresser of hides or skins, the principal part of the clothing of savages. And thus the certainty of being able to exchange all that surplus part of the produce of his own labour, which is over and above his own consumption, for such parts of the produce of other men's labour as he may have occasion for, encourages every man to apply himself to a particular occupation, and to cultivate and bring to perfection whatever talent or genius he may possess for that particular species of business.

The difference of natural talents in different men is, in reality, much less than we are aware of; and the very different genius which appears to distinguish men of different professions, when grown up to maturity, is not upon many occasions so much the cause, as the effect of the division of labour. The difference between the most dissimilar characters, between a philosopher and a common street porter, for example, seems to arise not so much from nature, as from habit, custom, and education. When they came into the world, for the first six to eight years of their existence, they were, perhaps, very much alike, and neither their parents nor play-fellows could perceive any remarkable difference. About that age, or soon after, they come to be employed in very different occupations.

From: Henri Fayol
*GENERAL AND INDUSTRIAL MANAGEMENT**

[EDITORS' NOTE: The author was Managing Director of Commentry-Fourchambault-Decazeville (French mining combine). He formed the Centre of Administrative Studies in Paris.]

For any action whatsoever, an employee should receive orders from one superior only. Such is the rule of unity of command, arising from general and ever-present necessity and wielding an influence on the conduct of affairs, which to my way of thinking, is at least equal to any other principle whatsoever. Should it be violated, authority is undermined, discipline is in jeopardy, order disturbed and stability threatened. This rule seems fundamental to me and so I have given it the rank of principle. As soon as two superiors wield their authority over the same person or department, uneasiness makes itself felt and should the cause persist, the disorder increases, the malady takes on the appearance of an animal organism troubled by a foreign body, and the following consequences are to be observed: either the dual command ends in disappearance or elimination of one of the superiors and organic well-being is restored, or else the organism continues to wither away. In no case is there adaptation of the social organism to dual command.

Now dual command is extremely common and wreaks havoc in all concerns, large or small, in home and in State. The evil is all the more to be feared in that it worms its way into the social organism on the most plausible pretexts. For instance—

(*a*) In the hope of being better understood or gaining time or to put a stop forthwith to an undesirable practice, a superior S^2 may give orders directly to an employee E without going via the superior S^1. If this mistake is repeated there is dual command with its consequences, viz., hesitation on the part of the subordinate, irritation and dissatisfaction on the part of the superior set aside, and disorder in the work. It will be seen later that it is possible to by-pass the scalar chain when necessary, whilst avoiding the drawbacks of dual command.

(*b*) The desire to get away from the immediate necessity of dividing up authority as between two colleagues, two friends, two members of one family, results at times in dual command reigning at the top of a concern right from the outset. Exercising the same powers and having the same authority over the same men, the two colleagues end up inevitably with dual command and its consequences. Despite harsh lessons, instances of this sort are still numerous. New colleagues count on their mutual regard, common interest, and good sense to save them from every conflict, every serious disagreement and, save for rare exceptions, the illusion is short-lived. First an awkwardness makes itself felt, then a certain irritation and, in time, if dual command exists, even hatred. Men cannot bear

---

* Reprinted by permission of Sir Isaac Pitman & Sons, Ltd., London, 1959 (pp. 24–25, 68–70). (This translation is published by permission of Dunod, Editeur, 92 Rue Bonaparte (VI), Paris, owners of the French copyright.) (Translated by Constance Storrs.)

dual command. A judicious assignment of duties would have reduced the danger without entirely banishing it, for between two superiors on the same footing there must always be some question ill-defined. But it is riding for a fall to set up a business organization with two superiors on equal footing without assigning duties and demarcating authority.

(c) Imperfect demarcation of departments also leads to dual command: two superiors issuing orders in a sphere which each thinks his own, constitutes dual command.

(d) Constant linking up as between different departments, natural inter-meshing of functions, duties often badly defined, create an ever-present danger of dual command. If a knowledgeable superior does not put it in order, foot-holds are established which later upset and compromise the conduct of affairs.

In all human associations, in industry, commerce, army, home, State, dual command is a perpetual source of conflicts, very grave sometimes, which have special claim on the attention of superiors of all ranks.

*   *   *   *   *

Such is the system of organization as conceived by Taylor for running the workshops of a large mechanical engineering concern. It turns on the two following ideas—

(a) Need for a staff to help out shop foremen and foremen.

(b) Negation of the principle of unity of command.

Just as the first seems to me to be good, so the second seems unsound and dangerous.

(a) Need for a Staff to Help out Shop Foremen and Foremen

Taylor, better than anyone else, demonstrated the complexity and weight of the responsibility laid upon the men in charge of a large mechanical engineering shop. They cannot carry out their work satisfactorily unless given help. To attain his objective, Taylor devised and carried out the foregoing procedure: sundry specialists are attached to the foreman, who absolve him from having to have special knowledge at his command, and relieve him of the innumerable interruptions which would occupy too great a part of his time. This is the work of the staff. . . . Hitherto the need has been met in a variety of ways, but rarely satisfactorily. I consider that Taylor has rendered great service in drawing attention to the importance of such a mechanism and to the manner of instituting it.

(b) Negation of the Principle of Unity of Command

According to Taylor the ordinary type of organization referred to somewhat scornfully by him as "military," wherein workers receive instructions from one man only—shop foreman or gang-boss—is to be abandoned. . . . According to Taylor himself some adherents to the principle of unity of command would not abjure it even at his instance. For myself I do not think that a shop can be well run in flagrant violation of this. Nevertheless, Taylor successfully managed large-scale concerns. How, then, can this contradiction be explained? I imagine that in practice Taylor was able to reconcile functionalism with the principle of unity of command, but that is a supposition whose accuracy I am not in a position to verify. In business matters, day in and day out, from top to bottom of the scalar chain, functonalism has to be reconciled with unity of command. Considerable ability is demanded and this Taylor must have had in good measure.

I think it dangerous to allow the idea to gain ground that unity of command is unimportant and can be violated with impunity. So, until things change, let us treasure the old type of organization in which unity of command is honoured. It can, after all, be easily reconciled, as recommended by Taylor, with the assistance given to superintendents and foremen.

My reservations as regards Taylor's scientific or functional management do not prevent me from admiring the inventor of high-speed steel, the pioneer of minute and precise methods in conditions of work, the energetic and adept industrialist who, having made discoveries, shrank from no effort nor spared any pains to make them of practical application, and the tireless propagandist who meant the world to profit from his trials and experiments.

From: Cyril J. O'Donnell

"THE SOURCE OF MANAGERIAL AUTHORITY"*

[EDITORS' NOTE: The author is Professor of Business Organization and Policy, University of California at Los Angeles.]

For four decades none of the writers in the management field inquired into the nature of authority, not even into its source. This is not strange, of course, when one considers that their main interest was in the specialization of enterprise tasks. But it is significant that none seemed to think that the right of managers to give orders would be questioned. Seeing all about them that business men, in fact, did give orders and that they were generally obeyed, that the state promulgated laws and that these were generally obeyed also—seeing these things, the facts seemed to point to acceptance of the idea that the right to issue orders must certainly rest with the business managers. Indeed, if the question had been put to them they probably would have agreed with Petersen and Plowman, who state that

"Under our democratic form of government the right upon which managerial authority is based has its source in the Constitution of the United States through the guaranty of private property. Since the Constitution is the creature of the people, subject to amendment and modification by the will of the people, it follows that society, through government, is the source from which authority flows to ownership and thence to management."[1]

*　　*　　*　　*　　*

First among the writers in the field of management theory to question this accepted doctrine was Chester I. Barnard, Harvard graduate, successful top manager of large-scale enterprises, and the author of *The Functions of the Executive*.[2] Apparently reading widely in the fields of philosophy and psychology, and being much impressed by the political theory of Harold Laski,

---

* Reprinted by permission of the *Political Science Quarterly*, Vol. 67, No. 4 (December 1952), pp. 573–88.

[1] Elmore Petersen and E. Grosvenor Plowman, *Business Organization and Management* (Chicago, 1949), p. 62. This is a very restricted view of the source of authority.

[2] Cambridge, 1950. Succeeding quotations from Barnard are from his chapter xii.

Barnard postulates that a correct theory of authority must be consistent with the facts and then proceeds to enumerate several instances wherein the members of an organization have refused to obey persons in authority. On the basis of these "facts" he states that ". . . the decision as to whether an order has authority or not lies with the persons to whom it is addressed, and does not reside in 'persons of authority' or those who issue these orders." This concept means, if anything, that the source of authority lies in the members of an organization, that they confer authority upon their superior by deigning to accept and act upon commands, that they may, if they wish, decide, to accept orders seriatim, and that they may withdraw conferred authority at any time by refusing to obey the commands of their superiors.

*   *   *   *   *

. . . Robert Tannenbaum[3] dubs as "formal" the authority of a manager when it is viewed as "originating at the top of an organization hierarchy and flowing downward therein through the process of delegation." He thinks of "informal" authority as a right conferred upon a manager by his subordinates. Thus, informal authority is equated with Barnard's complete concept. But Tannenbaum, as a practical matter, does not actually differ from Barnard because he says,

"The real source of the authority possessed by an individual lies in the acceptance of its exercise by those who are subject to it. It is the subordinates of an individual who determine the authority which he may wield. Formal authority is, in effect, nominal authority. It becomes real only when it is accepted."

In order to substantiate this conception of authority, Tannenbaum quotes approvingly from Barnard, Kardiner, Benne, and Simon. . . . And I may add that Selekman[4] simply cannot make up his mind on the subject so he says:

"It is true enough that the management executive must, directly or indirectly, obtain consent to his decisions from the men under him; the importance of such consent now receives ever-increasing recognition. Nonetheless, the manager still wields authority over his workers as of right—a right delegated to him by the owners of the business."

*   *   *   *   *

Authority is the right to command or to act. It implies the possession of the power to coerce, for obviously if there were no way to enforce an order the enterprise would become disorganized and unable to achieve its purpose. To realize how clear this is, the reader should imagine what would happen in a business if workers failed to adhere to the opening and closing hours of work; if individual players on a football team decided to engage their opposites in competition at any time; . . .

*   *   *   *   *

Now, the *order* in organized behavior implies authority—the right to command coupled with the right to coerce. Malinowski is emphatic in saying that "submission to laws as well as the power to enforce laws and rules are indispensable in human behavior."[5] Otherwise, there will only be anarchy. West is of the opinion that

"The prime requisite and firm creator of any community life is a law or order

---

[3] Robert Tannenbaum, "Managerial Decision-Making," *The Journal of Business,* XXIII, 1 (January 1950).

[4] Benjamin M. Selekman, *Labor Relations and Human Relations* (New York, 1947), pp. 175–76.

[5] Bronislaw Malinowski, *Freedom and Civilization* (New York, 1944), p. 27.

maintained by force. For human nature is such that, in all its most necessary social relationships, it is subject to the permanent threat of the self-assertive impulse, which misinterprets facts, misjudges events, and then, through consequent self-justificatory passion, breaks the social bond, unless it be externally restrained. We may claim this as adequately confirmed. Nursery studies and family life confirm it. Social and natural history confirm it. Modern psychology confirms it. And finally, our common sense tends to confirm it—for all others except ourselves, which is in itself a final confirmation. Individual, group or nation-state, we cannot judge our own cause. And if we try to do so, we shall be reduced again and again to fighting for a supposed "right" against a supposed "wrong," for one set of illusions against another."[6]

*   *   *   *   *

In the case of private business enterprise the authority relationships operate in much the same way. Americans have not deprived themselves of their common-law freedom to engage in business activity. It is true that elaborate safeguards for the rights of others have been spelled out in ordinance, rule, law and constitution, but within this framework anyone can engage in business as an individual proprietorship or on a partnership basis without special permission. Since corporations are legal persons created by law, their managers exercise authority which has reached them through the chain of delegation from the people to their constitution and thence through government to its creature. But whether a manager is operating an incorporated enterprise or not, his subordinates are obliged to obey his lawful orders, as long as the employer-employee relationship exists, because the right to command issues ultimately from the collective will of the people. Neither the individual subordinate nor the trade union to which he may belong is in a position to disobey those commands. . . .

---

[6] Ranyard West, *Conscience and Society* (London, 1942), p. 240.

SEA BREEZE MOTEL, INC.

I Case Introduction

Synopsis

A graduate of a University program in Hotel Administration builds a new motel on Cape Cod. During the first season's operation, there is a considerable problem of "no-shows"—people who make reservations and then do not honor them. This often results in loss of revenues. In order to overcome this problem, the owner of the motel employs a consultant in operations research who recommends an optimum strategy, that of taking 12 reservations for a 10-room facility. During the second season's operation, the motel operates under this strategy. However, in the judgment of the owner, the formula or model is not working, and he wonders whether to use it in the third season.

Why This Case Is Included

The Sea Breeze case enables one to see both the power of scientific approaches in the practice of management and the limitations of this approach. It forces the policy maker to decide whether a management science approach will be utilized in the formulation of firm policy or whether he will place more reliance on judgment or intuition.

Diagnostic and Predictive Questions

In answering the following diagnostic and predictive questions, remember that these questions apply theories and conceptual ideas from certain disciplines. Such theories are valuable to understand basic forces at work in the policy system (diagnosis) and to predict what will happen in the system in the future (prediction). Since each reading abstracts from the total policy system certain factors or variables into the closed or partial viewpoint of one theory or discipline, no one reading gives answers to the practical policy problems of the case. In diagnosis and prediction, the parts of the problem are studied with "other things being equal."

Following each question are listed readings which will be helpful in answering the question. The readings included with this case are marked (*). By referring to the author index at the end of this book, you may locate the other readings listed.

1. From the viewpoint of economics, why is it so important to Heenan to have the rooms filled to capacity at all times?

   Prepare: Using your own analytical ability, think about the fixed costs such as investment in buildings and furnishings. Convert these costs to a formula that will yield fixed cost per unit of output.

2. Why did Heenan "decide right then and there that there must be a way for me to solve the problem more reliably than just by guessing"? Why did

Imhoff have inner self-confidence that he could solve the problem by mathematics or "management science"?

Read: Barber, *Science and the Social Order,* pp. 7–8, 12–13, 18, 21. Also, the concept of "convergent phenomena" and the section on "physical science" in Chapter 2 of *The Managerial Mind.* Not included in this volume, but an excellent source for understanding of the nature of science as uncovering an orderliness in dynamic events is Alfred N. Whitehead, *Science and the Modern World* (New York: Macmillan Co., 1925; now available in paperback by Mentor), chap. i.

3. Why do you think that Heenan "obeyed" Imhoff—or, in what sense did Imhoff have "authority" over Heenan? The same question might be asked as to why the journal article had "authority" or "influence" over Heenan.

Read: *General Electric Co., *Professional Management in General Electric.* *Moore and Tumin, "Specialists and the Ignorance of Non-Specialists." Simon, Smithburg, and Thompson, *Public Administration,* pp. 182, 189–200.

4. Why didn't the facts of the real world correspond to the mathematical prediction—that is, why did the motel units fill less than predicted in June and more than predicted in July? Why did Heenan consider Shields as part of the "model" which didn't work?

Read: Chapter 2 of *The Managerial Mind,* and the section on Ceteris Paribus in Chapter 3.

Policy Questions for This Specific Case

In answering the following policy questions, the results of diagnosis and prediction are used to reduce the amount of guesswork, or judgment, in designing action solutions. However, since certain parts of the total case situation cannot be reduced to science, and since "other things are not equal," judgment must still be used to fill in the factors not accounted for by readings. You will also need a second kind of judgment as you put value weights on different scientific predictions, since different theories may point to conflicting solutions.

5. If you were in Heenan's place, what would you do about the reservation policy in the coming season?

Major Policy Issues: Tentative Generalizations about Any Policy System

In arriving at conclusions for the following questions, generalize from the facts in the case and use your own ideas to (a) confirm, (b) modify, or (c) test the workability of the concepts and theories from readings. As an executive or professional, use wisdom to merge theory, on the one hand, with "brute facts" and practice, on the other.

6. Are probability estimates valid for a decision which is not repeated often enough to take advantage of the "law of averages"? (I.e., are probabilities of guest arrivals valid for making decisions on taking or turning away customers for one season?)

Questions for Original Student Work in Analysis and Policy

The methods of viewing this case as represented by the authors' questions and selection of readings are not exhaustive. There are other relevant ideas for diagnosis and prediction. Furthermore, there are other ways of stating policy questions. More powerful analyses and wiser solutions will result by drawing on your own training and experience for (*a*) relevant concepts and theories, and (*b*) creative ways of asking policy questions. The following questions are designed to help you acquire this skill.

7. While reflecting on case facts, what additional theories from prior education give you insights as to "what is going on" in the Sea Breeze Motel, Inc.? As to what might be predicted to happen in the future?

8. Other than the policy questions asked by the authors, what pragmatic ways can you think of to state the practical problems faced by executives in the case?

II Sea Breeze Motel, Inc.*

Since his graduation from the Cornell University School of Hotel Administration, Dave Heenan had been the owner-manager of the Sea Breeze Motel in Harwichport, Massachusetts, on Cape Cod. With funds furnished from an administered inheritance, Heenan initiated the construction of the lavish, 10-suite complex in the late autumn of 1965. An early completion date of March 23, 1966, further enabled Heenan to solicit customers for the oncoming season—beginning June 1 and terminating September 10. Heenan intended to supplement his seasonal earnings at Sea Breeze by assisting his cousin in the management of the Royal Palms Hotel during the winter months.

Since the rate per suite was set at $40 a day, and because the motel has only 10 units, Heenan sought to segment the motel's market to upper-income families and to make his accommodations conducive to repeat trade over the years. Although competition on the Cape was fierce for this type of clientele, Heenan initiated measures to appeal to the appropriate market.

First, Heenan—with the assistance of experienced classmates and friends of his father—sought out and received the highest possible rating, "AAA," from the Certification Board of the New England Hotel and Motel Association (NEHMA). Knowledgeable persons in the hotel-motel industry had pointed out to Heenan that the possession and maintenance of "AAA" would be probably the most important factor in attracting desirable occupants. Frequently, these experts noted that customers will generalize the qualitative attributes of a service establishment to its most recent classification.

In addition, Heenan embarked on a promotional campaign designed to attract wealthy vacationers. By advertising in the travel sections of the *Boston Globe,* the *Christian Science Monitor,* and appropriate national and regional media and by personally selling a carefully selected group of

---

* Copyright 1968 by the Graduate School of Business, Columbia University. Names of persons, associations, firms, and places have been disguised.

travel agents, Heenan felt that he had made significant headway in promoting the Sea Breeze image.

However, upon returning to Harwichport in May 1966, Heenan soon became aware that full-season occupancy of individual customers would be most difficult to achieve in the early stages of operations. The majority of early reservations received were for various periods ranging from three nights to two months. Moreover, the average duration appeared to be somewhere between one to two weeks. With this in mind, Heenan readied the Sea Breeze for the reception of its first guest in June.

While he considered the first summer's operations as favorable for the most part, Heenan realized that if his existing facilities were to be expanded annually, greater revenues and/or reduced operating costs would have to be generated. What bothered Heenan most was the so-called "no-show" problem. In a significant number of instances, people who had previously reserved a specific Sea Breeze suite neither arrived to fill their reservations nor notified management in advance of their cancellations.

Initially, Heenan thought about establishing a minimum advance deposit to protect against "no-show" losses, but he soon dropped the idea after recognizing that such a requirement would foster a host of inhibitory effects in the minds of potential upper-income occupants. As a result, Heenan adopted a policy of holding reservations until 3 P.M. of the specified day to protect against possible losses. This arbitrary deadline, he thought, would best afford sufficient customer convenience while, at the same time, hopefully enable management ample time within which to rent the rooms of canceled reservations. But in practice over a period of weeks, marked customer irritation was voiced by those unable to reach Harwichport by early afternoon, and since it was extremely difficult to rent "no-show" rooms late in the day, it soon became evident that such a policy was unwise. Nevertheless, feeling that "no-shows" were making serious inroads on the motel's profitability, Heenan saw no other course of action but to retain the 3 P.M. deadline.

It was not until Heenan's attendance at the Annual Assembly of Hotelmen in the late fall of 1966 that a workable solution to the "no-show" dilemma seemed imminent. Originated some years ago to serve the dual role of congregating hotel executives and informing them of updated managerial methods and techniques, the Assembly provided a forum for the discussion—formally and informally—of a wide variety of operational problems.

In his association with other managers, Heenan found that an ever increasing percentage of hotelmen minimized the risk of "no-shows" with a procedure of accepting more reservations than the number of rooms available. The strategy is directed at placing the motel in the optimal position of receiving sufficient reservations to fill available rooms after "no-show" reservations are deducted. Moreover, the motel's calculated demand for rooms, based on the "estimated valid" reservations (those remaining after the elimination of an estimated percentage of "no-shows"), is equated to the fixed supply of rooms.

In practice, there are costs associated with the adoption of such a strategy. For example, if the demand for rooms is underestimated, there will result vacant rooms with a consequential loss of rental revenues. Or, if the demand for rooms is overstated, there will no doubt be a loss of those highly dissatisfied customers who are rejected lodging in spite of their reservations.

Bob Fuller, manager of the Pine Manor Lodge in Lake Placid, New York, and one of Heenan's most respected classmates from Cornell, suggested that Heenan should make use of some modern operations research techniques for solving the "no-show" problem. He explained that, in operations research terms, the proprietor of a motel might adopt various "strategies" or alternatives of action. These strategies, in the last analysis, are different numbers of reservations the proprietor might wish to accept. For example, given the fixed number of 10 suites at Sea Breeze, Heenan might have one strategy of accepting 11 reservations, a second strategy of accepting 12 reservations, or a third strategy of accepting 13 reservations. In Heenan's later calculations, when he drew up a decision matrix (Table II), these strategies were listed down the left column as row headings.

Fuller went on to explain that the other critical determinant of what he should do about "no-shows" were various "states of nature" that he might encounter—things over which he has little control. "You can control the number of reservations, through your strategy, but you cannot control what all of those customers will do—whether they will cancel or simply not show up. Therefore, why not view the actual number of customers which in fact arrive as various states of nature, and then calculate which strategy will yield the least cost to Sea Breeze due to 'no-show' customers."

Fuller also recommended that Heenan read an article entitled "Decision Theory Applications to the No-Show Problem" in a recent edition of a hotel trade publication. After reading this article, Heenan said, "I decided right then and there that there must be a way for me to solve this problem more reliably than just by guessing. I got in touch with a large consulting firm in Boston, and they referred me to Jim Imhoff, an individual who does operations-research-type consulting. The big firm frankly said my project was not as large or complex as they generally take on."

Heenan arranged to return from Florida in the spring of 1967, and he arranged with Imhoff to come to Harwichport to gather data from his records. This Imhoff did, and according to Heenan, "We worked well together. Jim kept asking questions and I would supply what I could. I even enlisted the help of three other motels out here to furnish data, in return for which we agreed to let them read the report." Imhoff's memorandum to Heenan appears as Exhibit 1 (see page 170).

According to the recommendation, the Sea Breeze Motel should accept 12 reservations for any given period, so long as the facility contains 10 suites. Imhoff explained over the telephone, after Heenan had received the report, that no solution "will allow you to eat your cake and have it, too. You can't have completely satisfied every single customer and at the same time satisfied your desire for every dollar of profit. But 12 reservations will give the best balance—the optimum profit."

Assured that this policy would remedy the "no-show" predicament at Sea Breeze, Heenan announced his intention of accepting 12 reservations for 10 suites during single time intervals of the oncoming seasons. For the first few weeks of the motel's 1967 operations, Heenan was pleased with the relative effectiveness of his newly stated reservations program. It was true that customers were turned away on some occasions because of over-acceptance, while on others, vacant rooms resulted because of under-estimated "no-shows." However, Heenan believed that these costs would be exceeded by the additional revenues gained in reserving the two extra suites.

During the remaining months of the 1967 season, however, a series of incidents occurred which caused considerable trouble, in Heenan's words, "for the smooth operations of Sea Breeze Motel, and for its reputation."

In July, Cape Cod was plagued with an unusually bad weather situation. Fog, haze, and below normal temperatures resulted in a decreased tourist business for the entire area and in a high rate of cancellations and "no-shows" for Sea Breeze. Given 10 motel units, and 31 days in July, the motel would be fully occupied if the management received payment for 310 unit/days. However, for the month as a whole, paying guests occupied units only for 186 unit/days. This is the equivalent of having 6 units occupied for the 31-day period, instead of the full 10 units. On inspection of his records, Heenan found that almost exactly half of these unoccupied unit/days were accounted for by "no-shows"—in other words, of the four units remaining unoccupied throughout July, two of these could be traced to occasions when people did not cancel their reservations. On numerous occasions, because of the quality of his property, Heenan had the opportunity of renting to tourists who, defying the weather, stopped in between 10 a.m. and 2 p.m. to see if they could stay overnight. Believing in his reservation system, he turned these potential guests away.

Just the opposite happened in August. Instead of having many cancellations and "no-shows," the Sea Breeze found that everyone seemed to want to carry through his vacation plans. Even though Table I in Imhoff's report indicates that there is only a 3 percent chance that there will be no "no-shows" if 12 reservations are accepted, there were in fact nine days on which reservation guests arrived for all 12 reservations.

One additional event in August troubled Heenan a great deal. On the weekend of August 14th, one of those nine times when all 12 reservations appeared for actual occupancy, a particularly important guest was refused his room. Mr. Foster Shields, Executive Secretary of the New England Motel Managers Association, arrived with a reservation made in May. He arrived just before the latest reservation hold time (3 P.M.). The desk clerk apologized for the error in bookings, and offered to help him obtain suitable accommodations elsewhere.

Shields later wrote to Heenan and informed him that the committee on certifications could lower his rating from "Triple A" to a lower category, possibly "BCC." Heenan knew that with the luxury nature of his property, such an action would seriously impair the image of his motel, and he knew that loss of qualitative status is reported in trade journals which are read widely by travel agencies.

On closing the Sea Breeze and going to Florida, Heenan took with him the day-by-day records of the 1967 season. He wanted to study the records and compare them with the Imhoff report, to see what to do about a reservation policy for the motel in the 1968 season.

As of the time this case is written, in early 1968, Heenan states:

I have got to decide whether to try to operate under this system this year, whether to junk the whole thing and accept only 10 reservations to match my facilities, or whether to hire Jim Inhoff again to see if he can work the bugs out of the system. Somehow I know that the thing can be solved better than just by guessing—I had faith in what Bob Fuller said, what I read in the journal, and what Jim Imhoff can do as a man with knowledge I don't have. At the same time, I think I fell between the chairs last summer. I alienated guests in August too much, I lost too much profits in July, and that problem with Shields is a sticky one. Incidentally, I did visit with Shields personally and things are temporarily OK. He is thoroughly pleased with everything he knows or has seen regarding Sea Breeze. That's the one thing that saves us. I showed him all of the calculations and tried to explain what I'm trying to do—to match a really excellent facility with good management. I don't think he understood what I was talking about but he agreed to let me inform him this month (March) what I intend to do regarding customer satisfaction through a good reservation system. One thing is certain: I've got to decide what to do about reservations for this season; 1968 is a better year for tourist and vacation expenditures than ever.

Exhibit 1

Mr. David Heenan
Sea Breeze Motel
Harwichport, Massachusetts

DEAR DAVE:

I know that you are anxious to receive this final report, so that you can proceed with accepting reservations for the 1967 summer season. I have enjoyed working on this project, and hope that you will feel free to call on me again if you have further questions. I have discussed the problem with my partner before coming to the final conclusion.

The purpose of this report is to give you our final recommendation as to how many reservations you should accept, and to explain how we arrived at this figure. Let me, therefore, begin with this recommendation:

Exhibit 1—Continued

Sea Breeze Motel should accept 12 reservations for the existing 10-suite facility, if optimum season profit is to be realized.

I know that you have been referring to this final figure as "the magic number." Here it is. But I should like to explain how we arrived at this so that it won't seem like magic. Rather, it is an orderly attempt to gather concrete factual information and then to use certain mathematical techniques to arrive at costs, revenues, and final profit. I'm fully aware that you know much of what we're doing from our past conversations. However, let me devote the rest of this report to summarizing the steps we went through.

Essentially, two different cost figures had to be determined: (*a*) the cost of a vacant room (given a "no-show"); and (*b*) the cost of the anticipated lifetime loss of a good customer if he is denied admission, even with a reservation (because of an overstated demand estimate). The former statistic was easily derived; it was simply the daily loss of revenues of a single vacant suite, or $40. However, to determine the latter expense, we had to analyze the financial records of the past season. Initially required was the average customer stay at Sea Breeze, which was found to be 10 days. At the set rate of $40 per day, we calculated that some $400 in rentals were generated during this period. Furthermore, desirous of a 10% profit return on gross rentals, we calculated a net profit of $40 for any base period.

To project the expected lifetime customer value, it was necessary to determine the probability of one's returning to Sea Breeze in the following year. Although the infancy stage of your operations did not provide available historical information, files of the NEHMA revealed that approximately an 80% probability of return could be anticipated for motels comparable to the Sea Breeze. Stated otherwise, the probability that a guest will return for n years is $(0.80)^n$—or Lifetime value of a customer = (Net profit base) + (Pr. return next year)

$$\text{(Net profit base)} + \ldots + (\text{Pr. return } n \text{ years}) \cdot (\text{Net profit})$$

For Sea Breeze then—

$$\text{Lifetime value} = \$40 + (0.80) \cdot (40) + (0.64) \cdot (40) + \ldots$$
$$+ (0.80)^n \cdot (40) = \$200$$

In summary, the expected lifetime revenue stream at Sea Breeze for the average customer was found to be $200. However, recognizing the present value of money, we discounted the above statistic (by 10% yearly) in order to establish the true present worth to the motel.

$$\text{Lifetime value adjusted} = \$40 + \frac{(0.80) \cdot (40)}{1.10} + \frac{(0.64) \cdot (40)}{1.21} +$$
$$\ldots \frac{(0.80)^n \cdot (40)}{(1.10)^n} = \$90.09$$

Moreover, Sea Breeze would probably lose the entire $90.09 for any customer who, despite a reservation, has been turned away for his vacation stay.

Exhibit 1—Continued

To calculate the probabilities of the requisite states of nature, we first determined the probability of a "no-show" and then the total number of reservations. You were able to obtain "no-show" statistics over a five-year period from three comparable motels on Cape Cod. These records indicated that 25% of all reservations were of a "no-show" variety. Given the total number of reservations, we utilized the binomial probability distribution to calculate the probabilities of the various numbers of "no-shows."

For R (reservations), the probability of n ("no-shows") is:

$$\frac{R\ (R-1)\ (R-2)\ .\ .\ .\ .\ (R-n+1)}{n\ (n-1)\ (n-2)\ .\ .\ .\ .\ (2)\qquad(11)}\qquad (0.25)^n\ (0.75)^{R-n}$$

For example, given 10 suites, we considered how many reservations over 10 you might best be advised to accept. If 11 reservations were taken, the probability of one "no-show" (the optimal solution) could be determined as follows:

$$\text{Pr. 1 no-show} = \frac{11}{1}\ (0.25)^1\ (0.75)^{10} = 0.1459 = 15\%$$

Simply stated, there is roughly a 15% chance that if one "extra" reservation were accepted, the two ever present costs—loss of rentals and loss of lifetime customer value—would be erased.

Proceeding in this manner, we computed the probabilities of "no-shows" under various acceptance strategies, letting R equal the number of reservations:

Table I

PROBABILITY

"No-Shows"	$R = 11$	$R = 12$	$R = 13$
0	0.0422	0.0317	0.0238
1	0.1549	0.1267	0.1029
2	0.2581	0.2323	0.2059
3	0.2581	0.2581	0.2517
4	0.1721	0.1936	0.2097
5	0.0803	0.1032	0.1258
6	0.0268	0.0401	0.0559
7	0.0064	0.0115	0.1186
8	0.0011	0.0024	0.0047
9	0.0001	0.0004	0.0009
			0.0001
	1.000	1.000	1.000

Finally, having computed the probabilities of the various states of nature (the number of "no-shows," over which you have no control), and the necessary costs, we calculated the resultant payoffs. By utilizing the matrix in Table II which blends the costs and probabilities of selected reservation strategies, we found that the minimum expected cost—hence, the optimal solution—was attained when $R = 12$.

By adopting a policy of accepting 12 reservations for 10 rooms, the Sea Breeze would follow the safest and surest possible course of action. In short, the least cost (over time) of such a policy would be $63.69 as compared with the more costly strategies of $R = 11$ and $R = 13$.

Table II

"No-Shows"	0	1	2	3	4	5	6	7	8	9	Expected Cost US$
					States of Nature						
Probability strategy: $R = 11$	0.0422 $ 90.09	0.1549 0	0.2581 $40	0.2581 $80	0.1721 $120	0.0803 $160	0.0268 $200	0.0064 $240	0.0011 $280	0.0001 $320	$75.75
Probability strategy: $R = 12$	0.0317 $180.18	0.1267 $ 90.09	0.2323 $ 0	0.2581 $40	0.1936 $ 80	0.1032 $120	0.0401 $160	0.0115 $200	0.0024 $240	0.0004 $280	$63.69
Probability strategy: $R = 13$	0.0238 $270.27	0.1029 $180.18	0.2059 $90.09	0.2517 $ 0	0.2097 $ 40	0.1258 $ 80	0.0559 $120	0.0186 $160	0.0047 $200	0.0009 $240	$73.66

Note: If there are zero "no-shows" with one reservation too many, the cost is the lifetime value of a customer ($90.09).

III Selected Readings

From: Professional Management in General Electric
MEASURING*

Of the four elements of the work of a professional manager, the element of measuring has been given too little inventive attention. Conversely, this is an area in which rapid advances will be made if the area is given the attention which it deserves. The feed-back of adequate measurements into the other areas of a manager's work closes the cycle and makes dynamic progressive achievement possible. What would a sailor on the high seas do without a compass? How can a manager make wise decisions if he does not have adequate, timely facts about the working situation? The more completely, accurately, and promptly he can be kept informed, the wiser and surer his decisions can be.

*   *   *   *   *

The work of managing inherently involves exercising judgment as a basis for making decisions. Judgment, which is in essence appraisal, is in turn a function of the facts and information on which it is based. It is the manager's task, in a business enterprise, or component, to make decisions as occasion requires, and on the best information available at the time. If only qualitative appraisal, rooted in general experience or beliefs, is feasible, it is still essential to weigh and to decide. But the professional manager's job is to function through the authority of knowledge rather than of rank. Hence, the more he can "measure," the more he can ask sound, balanced, objective, and persuasive questions and when appropriate, make decisions of corresponding clarity and acceptability. As a manager develops professional skill, the advantages of seeking "measured facts" in more and more areas is increasingly realized. With modern knowledge of mathematics and statistics, and with modern tools and machines or computers to apply them, the opportunities to "measure" increasingly more complex situations are simultaneously enhanced. Hence, the areas can be minimized where reliance is on opinion and qualitative judgment alone because the appraisal factors can be stated and worded in terms which are more and more measurable.

*   *   *   *   *

In *The New York Times* for January 31, 1954, Secretary of the Treasury George M. Humphrey is quoted as saying, "There are no hard decisions, just insufficient facts. When you have the facts, the decisions come easy."

The scientific method involves analysis and synthesis that are directed toward the simplification of concepts and the statement of generalizations or principles. The situations in which we find ourselves tend to become unmanageable, unless the simplification process keeps pace with the rapidly growing volume and complexity of observed facts. The first four chapters of this book give an orderly arrangement of the ideas that appear pertinent and of significant importance in

* By permission from *Professional Management in General Electric*, Book Three, *The Work of a Professional Manager*, copyright 1954 by the General Electric Company. (Excerpts from pp. 109–10; 142–43.)

the WORK OF A PROFESSIONAL MANAGER. By the very arrangement of these ideas, simplification of concept is achieved.

Zay Jeffries has observed that if the simplification processes keep pace with the complicating processes, "individuals with a given ability can expect to go forward indefinitely without becoming casualties of their own complexity."

The true search of the people of the world is for order, not chaos. Managing should be the science of bringing the kind of order which nature exhibits all about us; and of doing so by applying a process of rational organization to the relationships in which men associate. This is our deep need. As individuals, we show little or no more capacity or ability or emotional steadiness than the able men among our forebears. Yet, unfolding science brings new complexities, and it is the manager's job to match them with patterns of simplicity, which will win the comprehension and the acceptance of the individual men whose work is being managed. . . .

From: Wilbert E. Moore and Melvin M. Tumin
*"SPECIALISTS AND THE IGNORANCE OF NON-SPECIALISTS"**

The function of ignorance that is most obvious, particularly to the cynical, is its role in preserving social differentials. However, a purely cynical view is likely to overlook the extent to which the continuity of any social structure depends on differential access to knowledge in general, and, *a fortiori,* to specialized knowledge of various kinds. In many instances, of course, the counterpart of ignorance on the part of the outsider is *secrecy* on the part of the possessor of knowledge. Some of the outstanding examples of this general function of ignorance are summarized in the following paragraphs.

The Specialist and the Consumer. Ignorance on the part of a consumer of specialized services (for example, medical or legal advice) helps to preserve the privileged position of a specialized dispenser of these services. This is in some measure a by-product of the division of labor, and theoretically the same persons may occupy super-ordinate or subordinate positions as one or another service or skill is demanded. However, there are both theoretical and empirical bases for concluding that some persons whose skills are both scarce and functionally important will occupy a generalized superior position.[1] Although that status is not solely the product of the ignorance of others, in concrete instances it is partially maintained by such ignorance.

One evidence of the function of ignorance as a preservative of privileged position lies in the situation where the consumer acquires, through continuous exposure to the services of the specialist, a sense of his own ability to deal with his problems, and thus to dispense with the services of the specialist (*e.g.,* when we learn how to treat common colds, simple fevers, and bruises, and where we

---

* By permission from "Some Social Functions of Ignorance," *American Sociological Review,* Vol. 14 (December 1949) , pp. 788–89. Copyright by the American Sociological Society.

[1] Kingsley Davis and Wilbert E. Moore, "Some Principles of Stratification," *American Sociological Review,* Vol. 10 (April 1945) , pp. 242–49.

learn how to send stern notes concerning contractual obligations). Thus the range of situations in which the special services are believed to be required is altered from the original position.

On the other hand, the specialist commonly develops devices to protect himself against this sort of attrition. A common device is that of specialized and possibly esoteric vocabulary, or the use of instruments and techniques not intrinsically required for the solution but seemingly so.

However, the central point remains that real or presumed differential knowledge and skills are inherently necessary to maintain mutually satisfactory relationships between specialist and consumer. . . .

THE WHITE HOUSE OF EL PASO

I Case Introduction

Synopsis

Management of this department store is faced with an increase in wages for many employees of the store, due to the extension of the Fair Employment Act $1.00 per hour minimum wage to cover retail stores. As one way to offset this tendency to decrease profits, new cash registers were purchased which enabled salespeople to ring up sales and wrap packages. This more efficient machine technology and organization structure eliminated twenty-five jobs of cashier-wrappers in the main store and a potential twenty-five more in a new branch to be opened.

Why This Case Is Included

This case shows the various forces which management must reconcile in a top decision—the political forces originating in government, the psychological forces of morale and human motivation, and the economic forces of cost and profit (as they derive from technological ways of organizing personnel and equipment). It can also be used to examine the theory by which wages are set in a free enterprise system, versus a system with government control. Finally, the case helps to understand the value of technological innovation in the economy; the motivating forces which produce it; and some of its effects on Gross National Product, firm profits, and individual employees.

Diagnostic and Predictive Questions

In answering the following diagnostic and predictive questions, remember that these questions apply theories and conceptual ideas from certain disciplines. Such theories are valuable to understand basic forces at work in the policy system (diagnosis) and to predict what will happen in the system in the future (prediction). Since each reading abstracts from the total policy system certain factors or variables into the closed or partial viewpoint of one theory or discipline, no one reading gives answers to the practical policy problems of the case. In diagnosis and prediction, the parts of the problem are studied with "other things being equal."

Following each question are listed readings which will be helpful in answering the question. The readings included with this case are marked (*). By referring to the author index at the end of this book, you may locate the other readings listed.

1. Analyze the following ways in which the organization structure of the store was changed by top management:

    a) List the duties of salesmen prior to, and after, the change.

    b) List any difference in duties, responsibilities, and authority of the buyers (sales supervisors).

    c) List any difference in the duties of personnel who operate I.B M. equipment under the controller.

    d) List any positions that were dropped from the organization.

    e) List any work (function) that formerly was performed by people which under the new system is produced by machines.

2. What, from the viewpoint of technology and economics, was top management of the store trying to achieve?

    a) In the way of efficiency of capital (output of store service per unit of capital input, or fixed cost per sale made).

    b) In the way of efficiency of labor (output of store service per unit of labor employed, or variable cost per sale made).

    c) In the way of allocating resources (the mixture of capital and labor) necessary to make sales or render the service of the store.

    Read: Anderson, *An Organization Appraisal,* pp. 1–2. *McGuire, *Interdisciplinary Studies in Business Behavior,* pp. 3–6. Summer, "Economies of Scale and Organization Structure."
               (Optional, advanced work: Spencer and Siegelman, *Managerial Economics: Decision Making and Forward Planning,* pp. 242–48, 202–12.)

3. From the viewpoint of sociology of the firm, what was management trying to do by standardizing "work rules"—that is, by specifying standard job classifications based on new duties occasioned by installation of the new cash register system?

    Read: Dubin, *Human Relations in Administration,* pp. 218–19.

4. According to economics of pure competition, what would set the wages of the employees—both cashier-wrappers and salesmen—in the store?

    Read: *Harriss, *The American Economy,* pp. 468–74.

5. Why did the government intervene in the wage-setting process? That is, why did not the government let free competition economic laws (Question 4) operate, without injecting political laws into the process?

    Read: *Berle, "The Corporation in a Democratic Society." *Heilbroner, *The Future as History,* pp. 158–59.

6. What other effects (than in Question 4) from the viewpoint of society, did the new law have which were "unintended consequences," or possibly disadvantageous? Would these be short-run, or more lasting, consequences? Think of both the cashier-wrappers and the salesman-wrappers, and their wages.

    Read: *Etzioni, *A Comparative Analysis of Complex Organizations,* pp. 31–39, 80–82.

7. What happens to the following factors in the economy when technological innovation results in machines replacing workers?

    a) To total production of goods and services (Gross National Product) in the long run?

    b) To total employment levels in the whole economy in the long run?

    c) To displaced workers, such as the cashier-wrappers, in the long and the short run?

    Read: Heilbroner, "The Impact of Technology: The Historic Debate." *Cordiner, "Automation in the Manufacturing Industries." *Morgan,

Labor Economics, pp. 238–41.

8. What was the basic cause of the cost-cutting campaign? Who or what basic forces were responsible for automation of the cash registers and other changes, including automation of the elevators in the store?

Read: Schumpeter, *The Theory of Economic Development,* pp. 84–94, and add your own conclusions from facts in the case.

Policy Questions for This Specific Case

In answering the following policy questions, the results of diagnosis and prediction are used to reduce the amount of guesswork, or judgment, in designing action solutions. However, since certain parts of the total case situation cannot be reduced to science, and since "other things are not equal," judgment must still be used to fill in the factors not accounted for by readings. You will also need a second kind of judgment as you put value weights on different scientific predictions, since different theories may point to conflicting solutions.

9. If you were president of The White House, what, if anything, would you have done differently in the management of the store, particularly regarding (a) decision making and planning, and (b) implementation of decisions?

10. What lessons might be learned for planning and implementing the operation of the store in the future?

Major Policy Issues: Tentative Generalizations about Any Policy System

In arriving at conclusions for the following questions, generalize from the facts in the case and use your own ideas to (a) confirm, (b) modify, or (c) test the workability of the concepts and theories from readings. As an executive or professional, use wisdom to merge theory, on the one hand, with "brute facts" and practice, on the other.

11. What are the effects of technology on society, on individual firms, and on persons employed? What should individual company management do about these effects?

Read: Heilbroner, *The Future as History,* pp. 158–59.

12. To what extent, if any, should the government enter the economic process (a) in setting of wages, and (b) in dealing with technological unemployment?

Questions for Original Student Work in Analysis and Policy

The methods of viewing this case as represented by the authors' questions and selection of readings are not exhaustive. There are other relevant ideas for diagnosis and prediction. Furthermore, there are other ways of stating policy questions. More powerful analyses and wiser solutions will result by drawing on your own training and experience for (a) relevant concepts and theories, and (b) creative ways of asking policy questions. The following questions are designed to help you acquire this skill.

13. While reflecting on case facts, what additional theories from prior education give you insights as to "what is going on" in The White House of El Paso? As to what might be predicted to happen in the future?

14. Other than the policy questions asked by the authors, what pragmatic ways can you think of to state the practical problems faced by executives in the case?

II The White House of El Paso*

The White House is one of the two largest department stores in El Paso, Texas. Founded in 1900 by an El Paso family, it is today principally family owned. Annual sales volume amounts to $6,000,000 at the downtown store, and it is expected that this will be increased significantly (perhaps by as much as 50%) by the opening of a branch in nearby Bassett, Texas, in March of 1962. At the time of writing of this case in September 1962, there are 290 employees in the downtown store and 152 in the Bassett branch.

This case concerns certain changes in the technology of doing work in the store, and further changes in the organization of personnel.

Prior to May 1961, the store employed cashier-wrappers—people who received merchandise and cash from the salesclerk, put the customer's money in the cash drawer, wrapped the merchandise, and either redelivered it to a salesperson or routed it to the delivery department. There were 25 cashier-wrappers in the main store, and management estimates that an additional 25 would have been necessary for the Bassett branch, had a similar system been installed there. The cashier-wrappers worked 38½ hours a week, and were paid a weekly salary ranging from $25 to $45.

Management of the store recognizes certain benefits of having cashier-wrappers perform the function mentioned above. Miss Strauss, secretary to the president, states that they provide an extra check against inventory losses by requiring the wrapper to check the sales ticket against the price tag on the merchandise, and to check the number of items listed on the sales ticket against the actual number of items wrapped. In addition, Miss Strauss points out that the wrappers "provide a beautiful free gift wrap —since the Mexican girls, though poorly educated, have a definite artistic flair. Our competitors also hire these girls, and wrapping becomes a definite competitive practice." Finally, the wrappers kept accurate records of merchandise in transit to other departments—delivery, C.O.D., layaway, and alteration departments.

Sometime prior to May 1961, Mr. Richard Miller, president of the store, became concerned about the fact that many of the wages paid to employees in the store would increase sharply in September, when the federal minimum wage law would be extended to cover, for the first time, retail stores. This law specifies that no person may be hired at a wage less than $1.00 per hour. "In our particular case, geography has a

---
* Copyright 1964 by the Graduate School of Business, Columbia University.

great deal to do with the problem. We are on the Mexican Border and, therefore, have an abundance of inexpensive labor. This labor, though abundant, is, happily, inexpensive—but, unhappily, it is unskilled."

Because of the impending wage increases, Mr. Miller instituted a study of the entire organization to determine what might be done to hold or reduce costs, and thus to eliminate the adverse affect of the wage increases on profits.

One of the projects investigated, and instituted in May, is a change from the cashier-wrap to a clerk-wrap system. Under this system, the salesperson rings up the sale on especially designed cash registers, wraps the merchandise, and delivers it to the customer. Thirty-five of these registers were purchased for the main store and 32 for the Bassett Branch, at a total cost of $150,000. Mr. Miller expects, after a study of the new system, that this cost will be recovered in a period of three to five years by saving an equivalent amount in wage costs.

The controller of the store states that there are two other factors in connection with the new cash registers which mean greater efficiency.

First, the registers keep a total of sales made by departments (notions, housewares, etc.), and by individual salesclerks. At the end of the day, these totals are fed into central data processing machines. At the same time, the cash from each register is counted and fed into the same machines. If a mistake has been made so that the total sales (less charge sales) does not equal the cash received, the machine signals this, and a check can be made of the proper department and various salespeople.

A second economy results from the fact that the store needs expensive I.B.M. equipment for other accounting and analysis work. If the above work can also be performed, the capital cost of this equipment can be spread over more units and types of work performed.

There are today 156 people selling in the downtown store. In ready-to-wear departments, they make, on the average, about $215 per month. However, in some of the marginal producing departments, such as accessories, the salespeople made (prior to the new law) considerably less than did the salesclerks in the ready-to-wear, linens, etc. Salesclerks in the marginal departments gained about $8.50 per week per person in extra wages after the Fair Labor Standards Act minimum was extended to retail stores. The average amount of wage increase for all 290 employees of the downtown store has been about $6.00 per week per person.

Prior to the wage change, salespeople were on an incentive system—they got $25 to $40 a week salary, plus a percentage of what they sold (this varied by department). Now, they all receive a dollar an hour minimum, and in the opinion of the president, this eliminates some of the incentive to sell, because it increases the base salary of all people to around $40 a week.

At the time the change was made, 13 of the 25 cashier-wrappers were discharged. Ten were retrained for other jobs in the store, and two were maintained as wrappers in china, crystal, and gifts. A representative of the management states that "we had a real morale problem at first when people thought that 25 people were being eliminated at one stroke. This caused a great deal of comment amongst the other Mexican employees when they first heard of the plan. Some complaints came to the president, and some to the controller (to whom the cashiers reported). Of course, in the 13 cases that we decided weren't capable of being retrained for other positions in the store, we also have some problems. A few of these people told us they did not know how they would make a living now that The White House couldn't employ them. Others asked us if we would help them get jobs. There were naturally some cases where the cashier girls were contributing to the support of their families, and this made it tough for us in one way."

In the 15 months since the system was changed, salespeople have been trained on the more complicated cash register system, and in gift wrapping. Buyers (sales supervisors) have been trained to accept responsibility for checking for inventory losses and maintaining wrapping service to the customers.

One representative of management states that "the customer did not seem to mind the fact that the salesperson rings up the sale and then wraps the package. In fact, I believe that they feel they are getting a more personal service.

"We have found that no additional salespeople are needed to do the selling and wrapping; in fact, we have reduced the number of salespersons.

"One overriding factor played the most important part in the decision to change systems—and caused us to face the problem in a hard-nosed fashion. We were faced with increasing wage costs which would adversely affect profit of the store. We recognized that if we did not eliminate the poorly educated or substandard help, the raise in salary of these people would cause employees in higher jobs to make increased wage demands, and this would cost still more in the total wage bill. So, instead of jacking up all wage scales, we eliminated the lowest category workers.

"You may be interested to know that we are now in the process of automating our three elevators, which will eliminate the equivalent of the time of five operators.

"Perhaps these kinds of changes are necessary for the good operation of the store. All changes could have been done, and probably should be made, even if it were not for the new extension of the minimum wage law to our store. This merely brought the problem into focus immediately. In any event, they are the direct result of severe government interference in business."

III Selected Readings

From: Joseph W. McGuire

*INTERDISCIPLINARY STUDIES IN BUSINESS BEHAVIOR**

[EDITORS' NOTE: The author is Dean, School of Business, University of Illinois.]

There is no one economic theory of the firm which is universally acceptable to all economists. There is, nevertheless, ample evidence in the form of articles and books to indicate that some economic consensus of opinion exists. Briefly, the "traditional" theory of the firm postulates a goal—maximum profits, and then describes how this objective may be attained through the process of marginal analysis.

*   *   *   *   *

. . . [T]he firm in economic theory is an entity. By this we mean that the business concern is viewed as a single unit, or person, dealing with problems of marketing, pricing, and production. We really never observe the internal relationship of the firm in economic theory, but we do know that it acts rationally toward its prime goal of maximum profits. This notion of a "black box" with predictable actions but irrelevant mechanisms for action has led some economists to consider the firm as though it were, for theoretical purposes, a single person— the entrepreneur.[1] The firm (entrepreneur) is therefore looked upon as a transformation unit, taking in inputs and altering these in some way to outputs, with the limits of its activities set by a specific market situation and restrained by its goal of profit maximization.

*   *   *   *   *

In order to maximize profits, it is necessary that business concerns produce at those levels of output where the "gap" between revenues and costs is greatest, for at this point net revenues (or profits) will be as large as possible. It is evident, therefore, that two of the most vital factors in this theory are revenues and costs, which are ordinarily expressed in monetary terms. Both revenues and costs depend, in turn, upon two variables: the price and number of units involved. For example, gross revenue consists of the prices at which each unit of output is sold multiplied by the number of units sold; and total cost equals the prices of all inputs times the number of inputs.

---

* Reprinted by permission of South-Western Publishing Co., Cincinnati, Ohio, 1962 (pp. 3–6).

[1] Cf., James H. Strauss, "The Entrepreneur: The Firm," *Journal of Political Economy*, Vol. 52 (June 1944), pp. 112–127, and R. H. Coase, "The Nature of the Firm," *Economica*, New Series, Vol. 4 (November 1937), pp. 386–405.

The task of the entrepreneur, then, is twofold: (1) to minimize costs and, (2) to maximize revenues, and to do both in such a manner as to maximize net revenues. It is assumed that the entrepreneur is rational and that he possesses perfect knowledge of his costs and revenues so that he is enabled to accomplish these goals through the use of marginal analysis.

It is conventional to depict the firm in economic theory as confronted with a known demand schedule and known costs over a feasible range of inputs. The prime decision made by the firm, given these conditions, is to select that specific output which will maximize its profits. This decision involves others on the number and mix of inputs and outputs. The primary and all secondary decisions are made through an examination of pertinent variables at the "margin." The use of marginal analysis in the economic theory of the firm ordinarily involves the comparison (in money terms) of additions to more than one of the pertinent variables. Marginal cost, for example, consists of the cost of producing an additional unit of output, while marginal revenue is the income which is received from the sale of additional units of output. If the production of an additional item will return more additional revenue than it costs to produce, then entrepreneurs will increase output. On the other hand, should marginal costs exceed marginal revenue, production will not be expanded. The optimum profit, then, will be at that level of output where a further increase in production will add more to costs than to revenue, while a reduction in output will subtract more from revenue than from costs. In other words, profit will be maximized where marginal cost and marginal revenue are equal.

The entrepreneurial decisions on inputs are made in similar fashion. If the costs of hiring or buying additional inputs are less than their value to the firm, these units will be purchased or hired (as with labor) until their costs are equal to their value to the firm at the margin. In the same way, the ratios of the marginal values to the marginal costs of particular inputs will be equated to the similar ratios of other inputs. These conditions insure that the costs of production will be minimized.

This, then, is the skeleton of the economic theory of the firm, presented as simply as possible, which has been so violently attacked and so staunchly defended in recent years. In fact, between the attacks and the defense, the exact nature of the theory has become confused and its separate parts somewhat obscured. What began many years ago as a relatively simple blend of the goal of maximum profits and the means of marginal analysis has turned out to be considerably more complex. Among other questions to which conflicting answers have been given by economists are the following: Is the theory supposed to be a description of modern business behavior? Or is it a prescription for business operations? Or is it perhaps a description of how firms would act *if* they were rational and *if* they maximized profits? Affirmative answers to the first two questions raise so many further questions that they seem completely unpalatable to the authors of this volume. The last, which reduces the theory of the firm to a mere exercise in logic, is of little utility to serious students of business.

From: C. Lowell Harriss

THE AMERICAN ECONOMY*

[EDITORS' NOTE: The author is Professor of Economics in Columbia University. In the passages below, he is considering the basic forces that determine wage rates for labor: the forces of supply of labor and demand for labor. He states: "Some people feel that it is inhumane to analyze wages as we do the prices of commodities. People certainly are not commodities. The services they sell, however, are essentially commodities and must be analyzed as such."]

Supply of Labor as a Whole. The total population, of course, limits the supply of labor; but any population has large possible variations in the amount of work it will do. Excluding involuntary unemployment, the time people will work freely varies tremendously. Whether one looks at the number of hours per week (or really minutes per hour if we allow for the "coffee break" and other interruptions) or years per life, the variations in choices expressed freely are not small. The forces that make the differences are complex, partly subjective, partly arising outside the individual—from such trivialities as the attractiveness of the person at the next desk to rules about child labor and the age of retirement.

One example is the "working wife." In some cultures, married women, especially of the upper or middle classes, rarely work outside the home; a job outside is an index of the husband's "failure." In this country, however, women commonly hold jobs until the first baby is on the way. . . .

The more years we customarily spend in school, the smaller the fraction of the total population that will be holding full-time jobs. Another influence is government regulation of working hours and other policies which restrict the amount of time one may work for someone else, or impose burdens upon the employer if he offers jobs beyond certain hours, such as 40 per week. The condition of health, wage rates, the state of transportation, the number of holidays, and sports events, are a few things that influence the amount of labor that will be supplied effectively from any given population. So, too, are opportunities for supplementary jobs, the "moonlighting" (a term derived from night work on a second job) that millions of workers welcome, or accept, to help meet expenses.

What about subsistence and the supply of labor? In some parts of the world, income is about at the level of subsistence. Any appreciable decline in real income would, in true Malthusian fashion, reduce population and the supply of labor. Incomes in the Western world, however, are as a rule so much above the subsistence level that total labor supply has little relation to the needs of minimum existence. . . .

An employer's *demand* for labor, of course, is derived from the demand for his product. As a rule the demand for the output of his firm does not depend upon the wage rates he pays; whether a hat factory pays its bookkeepers $60 or

---

* Reprinted by permission of Richard D. Irwin, Inc., Homewood, Illinois, 1959 (pp. 468–74).

$70 a week has an insignificant effect on the demand for its hats. The employer has some idea of the demand for his product. His best adjustment, we know, is the output where marginal revenue equals marginal cost; he should hire labor that will produce this output. His demand for workers will depend upon the marginal productivity of labor (the marginal revenue product) that is, what he can get from the sale of additional (marginal) units of output. With workers of essentially uniform productivity and with a given demand for his product, the number he can afford to hire will depend upon the wage rate—the higher the rate, the smaller the amount of labor he will buy. Other employers of the same kind of labor will also have their demand schedules. All of these together make up the *total market demand* for such labor. This demand schedule, however, does not tell how much labor will be employed, or the wage rate. To get such answers, we must also know supply conditions.

What determines the market *supply* of a particular kind of labor? Just as the supply of a commodity is determined by cost, the supply of labor for any type of work, is determined by a cost—*opportunity cost* or the best alternative sacrificed. Generally this cost is the wage that might have been earned in another occupation. The cost of taking one job is the loss of the best thing (opportunity) sacrificed.[1] Some people have few alternatives, and none of which are very good; they will accept jobs at relatively low rates. Others have more attractive alternatives and so will not work on a specific job except at higher rates than the first group. A smaller number have much better opportunities and so need still higher inducements to take any particular job. As we take account of all potentialities, we arrive at a supply schedule that, when graphed, slopes upward. The higher the remuneration (wage rates plus other considerations), the more labor of the specific type that will be offered.

A demand curve sloping downward and a supply curve sloping upward create the conditions for an equilibrium (price-quantity adjustment) in the market—a balance of conditions such that no one can benefit by a change so long as the underlying factors are unaltered. If this a purely competitive market, each firm will be able to hire as much of the labor of this type as it wants at the market price; and everyone who is qualified and who wants to work at the price will be able to get a job. The quantities demanded and supplied will come to balance as employers and workers seek their maximum advantage. Not everyone may be happy, but no one can do better. The equilibrium will change, however, when underlying conditions of demand or supply change for any of the reasons we now examine.

Changes in Demand for a Type of Labor. . . . [1.] Any changes in the demand for the product will change the employer's demand for labor. An increase in demand for motorboats will increase the demand for labor in motorboat factories and for servicemen. A decline in the demand for movies will cut the demand for Hollywood extras and perhaps for growers of popcorn.

2. A change in productivity will alter the demand for a type of labor. . . . Assume that workers produce more per hour; then, for the same wage rate, the employer will find it profitable to hire more labor (assuming that the demand for the product does not change). Lower labor costs per unit of output (*a*) induce him to substitute labor for other factors and also (*b*) permit him to sell more units at the lower price which competition will bring. If workers' productivity falls, however, the employer's most profitable output is one of smaller employment. He will wisely cut out the labor whose marginal revenue product is less than the wage rate.

---

[1] The sacrifice may include desired leisure, greater safety, more congenial work conditions, and other nonmonetary factors, welcome and unwelcome.

3. Changes in the prices of other productive factors can alter the demand curve for a type of labor. Suppose that, with two pilots needed for each transport airplane, the price of planes falls considerably; and the airline companies buy more planes because the lower cost makes expansion profitable. They must also hire more pilots. If the price of planes rises, on the other hand, the opposite would be true; higher plane costs would reduce the demand for pilots. The demands for pilots and for planes are *complementary.* Sometimes, however, demands for productive factors are *substitutive,* one factor replaces another. Suppose that by adding new planes which are faster, the airlines cut the number of meals they must serve. The demand for labor to provide airline meals then drops. In deciding whether the expense of faster planes is justified, the airlines would consider the saving on meals. In short, the demand for labor of any particular type will depend upon the prices of the other factors of production which are used in the same process. If another factor can be *substituted* directly for man-hours, a rise in its price will tend to increase the demand for labor, and vice versa. If, however, the other factor is *complementary,* a rise in its price will reduce the demand for the labor. . . .

Changes in the Supply of a Particular Type of Labor. The supply of any particular type of labor depends largely upon the relative attractiveness of this and other kinds of work. As in the supply of commodities, however, the difference between the long run and the short run is important. Supply may be relatively fixed in the short run,[2] but the long-run elasticity is likely to be far higher.

Let us suppose that the wage rate of TV repairmen has risen substantially. The work, we assume, requires skills that many persons can acquire in 3 months. The higher wage will attract some people from other jobs and induce them to learn the skill; for 3 months, there may be little change in the number of competent repairmen, but thereafter more and more will qualify. As they seek work, the wage rate will gradually fall (assuming no upward shift in demand) until it is no longer high enough to attract newcomers. On the other hand, suppose that the equilibrium wage rate has settled at a low level; the best wage obtainable at the moment is unattractive for the long pull. Many workers will continue on the job because they have no better alternative; but newcomers will not get involved in such a fix. Repelled by the poor terms, they will seek jobs somewhere else. As time passes, some workers retire or die; and some gradually find better jobs. Supply shrinks; as it does, wage rates will gradually rise, assuming no changes in other conditions.

Or, let us assume, the demand for some types of labor rises substantially; gradually the supply of labor of other types will drop as workers, after getting the necessary training, move to the jobs now relatively more attractive. Important changes may occur almost before they are recognized. . . .

A Commentary on Wage Adjustment. Although an economy never adjusts perfectly, we should note the basic forces that operate. Income is so important to the earner that most people will try to obtain more. They are hindered and helped by many things—from a wife's prodding to their own skillful bargaining. On the other hand, wages are a large enough element of business cost that employers will generally resist requests for higher rates and try to obtain less, rather than more, expensive labor. Yet employers will benefit from hiring workers up to the point where wages equal marginal revenue product; an employer's own interest is in employing people at the right price.

Fundamental elements of competition exist. People will seek out jobs where

---

[2] The *amount* supplied in the short run may vary considerably, depending upon the wage rate (a movement along the supply curve); but, at any given wage rate, the amount offered will change more slowly (the shift of the curve).

total remuneration is relatively high, while employers will search for ways to economize labor costs. The forces of supply and demand thus operate with both sides gaining more from employment than from unemployment, and hence desiring a settlement. At some wage rate, the amout of labor of a specific kind supplied will equal the amount demanded. . . .

From: Robert L. Heilbroner

*THE FUTURE AS HISTORY**

[EDITORS' NOTE: Mr. Heilbroner is an economic historian, especially well known for his book, *The Worldly Philosophers*.]

What precise form the technology of the future may take, we do not know. But we can at least observe the salient directions in which industrial development is moving. One such direction, in which we have barely begun to explore, is the widespread automation of industry. Another is the mechanization, not of factory work, but of the simplest and most traditional tasks within the home. Yet another, still further removed from the industrial base, is the refinement of the arts of communication and persuasion. These general avenues of advance, diverse as they are, nonetheless present a common aspect to the private person. In one fashion or another, they weaken his solitary capacity to cope with life, whether as a job-seeker faced with the threat of technological displacement, or as a home-owner unable to make the most elementary repairs on his personal equipment without outside assistance, or as an individual mind treated as part of a mass audience. All impel the individual to define his existence in terms of an ever wider, more demanding engagement with his society. And this effect can be demonstrated in virtually every aspect of life with which modern technology comes into contact.

To a large extent this loss of personal mastery is an inescapable—and perhaps an increasing—condition of an age in which science has progressed far beyond the reach of any but the most highly trained minds. But what is at stake is not only a loss of personal mastery, of intellectual grasp. It is a loss of social mastery, of control over our own habitat. We are in the unpleasant position of watching our *society* change under the impact of its own technology while we stand impotently by to suffer the consequences for better or worse. And this loss of social mastery cannot be blamed only on the complexity of the technological process. It also lies with the fact that the main control we exercise over the social incursion of technology is that of economics.

It is at this point that our economic growth comes directly into contact with the historic shaping of the age of science. For our growth not only rests on technological advance, but is itself the regulator of the entrance of technology into our social system. We all realize that the speed with which automation will

---

be introduced depends primarily on the *economic* advantages which it will bring, and that the main use of television is that which best lends itself to economic exploitation. In similar fashion, the rate at which the mechanical duplication of human skills is integrated into our homes likewise rests with the salability of the relevant devices. In a word, with few exceptions, we allow the products of science and technology, like half-tamed genii from Aladdin's lamp, to work their social will without hindrance, so long as they are economically obedient. As a result our economic growth steadily adds to our social involvement in technology in a manner which is essentially capricious and haphazard. We have narrowed our control over the incursion of scientific technology into our lives to the main and often to the single criterion of its profitability.

From: Ralph J. Cordiner
*"AUTOMATION IN THE MANUFACTURING INDUSTRIES"**

[EDITORS' NOTE: Mr. Cordiner was at one time Chairman of the Board of the General Electric Company.]

1. *Technological progress sets off a sort of chain reaction of economic growth:* more productive machines reduce costs and prices; this increases volume of business, creating a need for more workers. The period between the installation of new machines and the build-up of business is generally very short. It has to be, or the company could not afford to invest in the machinery.

The reverse is also true: if a company fails to modernize, it will lose business, and *fewer* workers can be employed. A company *owes* it to its customers, share owners, *and* employees to modernize and thus remain competitive.

2. *The service industries provide new employment.* Our economy, as it progresses toward greater automation, spends less of its effort (proportionately) in making things and more in selling, servicing, and using things. . . . Technological progress creates more leisure and wealth for cultural and educational activities. Hobbies, sports, travel, entertainment, and retail trade are increasingly important sources of employment.

3. *The industries supplying automation and technological advance also create new employment opportunities.* We have what might be described as a "bow-wave" theory of technological employment. When a boat moves at high speed, the water it displaces piles up in *front* of the boat, in what is called the "bow-wave." In an analogous manner, there is a wave of new employment opportunities that runs in front of automation and technological change—the employment involved in designing, selling, building, and installing the new

---

* Reprinted by permission of the Philosophical Library, New York, 1959. From *Automation and Society,* edited by Howard Boone Jacobson and Joseph S. Roucek (pp. 30–31).

machinery and controls, along with the new buildings required. In addition, there is additional employment required to maintain and service the equipment after it is installed—and to sell and service its increased output.

This "bow-wave" of technological employment has not yet been adequately studied, statistically, and deserves the attention of interested economists.

4. *Entire new industries, employing thousands, are created by the new automation technologies.* The great chemical, petroleum, and electrical industries, among the fastest growing industries in America, simply could not exist without mechanization and automation. You cannot make chemicals, gasoline, and electricity by hand.

On the horizon we see an atomic energy industry, a transistor and semiconductor industry, an industry for the production of the supermetals like titanium and zirconium, and even the man-made diamonds that came out of the General Electric Research Laboratory. . . .

From: Chester A. Morgan

*LABOR ECONOMICS**

[EDITORS' NOTE: The author is Chairman of the Department of Labor Economics at the University of Iowa.]

While technological unemployment is frequently defined in terms of the displacement of human labor by the introduction of labor-saving technology, it should also include loss of employment resulting from the use of new methods or processes of production, new materials, and improved methods of industrial management. It is probable, however, that the major portion of technological unemployment does stem from the introduction of labor saving machinery as is implied in the designation given this type of unemployment.

The question of the effects of technology upon employment has been debated with varying degrees of intensity ever since industrialization began. Members of the working class as well as its spokesmen have been convinced on occasion that machines destroy more jobs than they create. Others, notably economists and employer representatives, have argued that machines create more jobs than they destroy.

. . . In the long debate over the employment effects of technology, a great deal of confusion has been generated owing to the fact that the short-run specific (micro) effects of the introduction of technology are quite different from the long-run aggregative (macro) effects thereof. In the short-run specific situation, workers are laid off when labor saving machinery is introduced. In the long-run a good deal of evidence seems to indicate that the total demand for labor in general within the economy is not apparently hurt by the increased use of technology, even though the demand for specific grades or types of workers may be affected negatively, even in the long run.

Economists of the nineteenth century and also of the present century have

---

* Reprinted by permission of Richard D. Irwin, Inc., Homewood, Illinois, 1962 (pp. 238–41).

often advanced what might be termed the "automatic absorption" theory to minimize the seriousness of technological unemployment. In this connection, it is insisted that workers displaced by technology will rather quickly be absorbed by the economy in employment elsewhere or by re-employment in their original industry. Thus, in a given industry for whose output the demand is highly elastic, the advent of technology, by decreasing production costs and lowering the commodity price, will occasion such an increase in the demand for the industry's output that workers laid off at the time the machinery was installed will be quickly re-employed. On the other hand, in an industry where product demand is highly inelastic, relatively few laid-off workers, if any, will be re-employed; but the extra consumer dollars released from this industry by the machine-induced decline in price will be spent elsewhere, assuming no change in the consumption function. Hence, the workers who were laid off will gradually be absorbed in employment by other industries which have experienced an increase in demand. In most situations, in actuality, some combination of re-employment and employment elsewhere of laid-off workers probably would take place, rather than either of the extremes just noted.

As a result of the reasoning above, most economists of the classical school especially, have argued traditionally that any unemployment occasioned by the use of technology would be brief and unimportant. In addition, it allegedly would be quickly self-erasing and should not be thought of as constituting a problem requiring governmental action. Other economists, starting with John Stuart Mill as early as the mid-nineteenth century, have contended that even though the unemployment under discussion might resolve itself in time, it did constitute a serious problem for families affected, who should, in turn, be objects of protective consideration by legislative bodies.

*   *   *   *   *

In actuality, a number of factors will operate to determine the seriousness of the effects of technology upon employment, in a given situation. These factors would include the elasticity of product demand, the ultimate effects of technology upon product price, the flexibility of wage rates, whether the technology actually displaces labor or merely reallocates labor, whether the technology involves a new method of producing an existing good or the production of an entirely new good, the general state of the labor market and the level of over-all economic activity and the average age level and mobility of the workers displaced. The influence of each of the factors noted can briefly be summed up as follows:

1. The more elastic the product demand, the less serious will be the effects upon employment.
2. The more marked the downward influence upon product price, the less serious will be the effects upon employment.
3. The greater the flexibility in wages, the less serious will be the employment effects.
4. Technology which merely reallocates labor—say, from skilled to semi-skilled jobs and the like—will have less serious employment effects than technology which entirely displaces many workers.
5. Technology involving new ways of producing an existing good would probably have more serious effects upon employment than technology for producing a new good.
6. The lower the level of employment in a given labor market and/or in general, the more serious the employment effects of technology.
7. Finally, the higher the average age level of workers displaced the more serious the employment effects would tend to be.

From: Adolf A. Berle

"THE CORPORATION IN A DEMOCRATIC SOCIETY"*

[EDITORS' NOTE: The author is a Professor Emeritus of Law at Columbia Law School, a corporate lawyer, corporate director, and government official.]

. . . The conventional objections to reasonable planning (we can all recite them by heart) already have boiled down to the residual platitudinous dregs propounded for corporation presidents and chamber-of-commerce orators by public relations counsel.

Ineluctable fact here meets obsolete shibboleth. The fact is that the profit motive, organized through great corporations, can do many things and do them extremely well. But it does not do and apparently cannot do many things which are essential if a modern economy (and business as an essential part of it) is to progress. The profit motive, like all social devices, has certain limits. Specifically, while it can produce without apparent limit, it cannot allocate resources to certain kinds of need. . . .

. . . [T]here is one national American economic system and . . it rises and falls as a unit. A stiff miscalculation by the automobile industry in Detroit can throw off balance as large an essential industry as steel, incidentally forcing hardships on distributors, dealers, and small suppliers literally in every village. Shifts in the technique of national defense—like the prospective change from aircraft to rockets—could make a shambles of the economic life of Long Island and Connecticut, of California and substantial parts of the Northwest. The indirect effects, though not readily calculable, could be very great, eventually impinging on a large sector of the population. In these contingencies, we think, to be sure, about "dangers to business"—but that thought will be secondary. The end of an economic system is to serve life: and life would be in travail.

In the next phase, the complaint will not be, as in 1933, that the unplanned system is financially unsound. Rather, it will be that the fluctuations of the unplanned system are unbearably inhuman. In extreme, the verdict might be still worse: the unplanned system is inadequate. That would be the last word in damnation. The unforgivable sin of any government, economic as well as political, is inability to govern.

It follows that the first brush in the evolving conception of state-corporate relations will be on the subject of planning for stability. As always, the choice will lie between taking the evolution as light—or as lightning.

The allied subject of this evolution will relate to allocation of resources. Already it is clear to economists and is dawning on financial writers that mere "production" is not an answer. Production differs in valence. Creation of a good housing development has a higher valence than production of plastic toys or

---

electric cocktail shakers, whatever the dollar figures may be. . . . The economic cliché has always been that the public showed what it wanted by what it paid for. The fact is that it buys what it can, often taking something it wants less because it cannot get at a viable price certain goods or services it wants far more. In pleasanter theoretical terms, the unguided profit economy is showing a number of air pockets in which vivid wants go unfilled, while lesser wants are taken care of.

Third in this list will be allocation of resources to those human activities which are not, and perhaps never have been, carried on within a private profit system. Medical care, good teaching, creation of an adequate supply of public servants who are scientists, doctors, or engineers—not to mention reasonable provision of decent instead of meretricious drama and art—all fall within this field. . . .

*   *   *   *   *

Social accounting, a new subject and a new device, will be a developed and accepted tool in this future towards which we are looking. Let us suppose the case of a company transferring a plant from, say, central New York to Alabama (as General Electric might do with its Schenectady plant). This operation leaves, at best, a trail of human and community damage behind it. The operation conceivably might yield the transferring company a higher profit—indeed this calculation would have lain behind the transfer. But this does not eliminate the losses. It merely means that the social expenses are paid in some other form or by someone else. The men thrown out of work would draw from unemployment insurance. Some families would draw relief. First-rate managements endeavor to minimize these losses now—but they are never wholly avoidable. Mortgages or other debt in the area would go unpaid or only partly paid; the losses would be borne by the banks, the tradesmen, the creditors, the community tax rolls, and Social Security funds. Savings of some families would be wiped out; they would thus pay part of the expense. If all the bills thus paid were added up, it might well be discovered that the transfer, whatever its impact on the financial account of the company, on balance worked out a net loss to the entire community. At this point, financial planning enters. It might literally be cheaper to work out tax relief or government orders or other form of aid than to allow the plant to move. A generation from now considerations of this kind will be adequately briefed and sufficiently calculated so that labor unions and corporations as well as local, state, and Federal government units will understand them. With understanding there should come a measure of capacity to handle forces and events with greater efficiency.

In all these and similar operations, the state necessarily enters. Meeting its own assignment—that of developing a planning mechanism insulated from conventional political influences, and of maintaining separation of the all too compulsive state from the private business mechanism—will take a good bit of doing. Yet the outlines of the problem are fairly clear even today. They are briefly these:

1. The economic system, not being an end in itself, must reflect the value system on which the public generally agrees.

2. Economic planning in a democracy in essence consists of reducing to concrete form the values on which the community agrees, and applying them, where needed, to the economic system.

3. In accordance with that system, it determines priorities. Some things (national defense, public health, and the like) must be done in any event. Others must be done to some extent. Still others may be left to the catch and toss of private choice.

4. Resources must be available for the top priorities. A measure of allocation may be needed to provide for other sectors.

5. If adequate resources are not available, it becomes a priority to assure that they can be increased through increased productivity.

. . . A planning group could not consult individuals. In a democracy, it would have to consult the highest common denominator of the public consensus, leaving to private individuals the task of transcending it at their own risk and with their own resources.

Within the influence of such a system (my impression is that it would operate by influence rather than by crude decree), the corporations of the next generation will have to operate. Wisdom would suggest that they meet the problem with pleasure rather than with anger. Unfulfilled value systems held by the public historically have eventually imposed themselves—and the process of their imposition over massed economic opposition can be bitter to the last degree.

From: Amitai Etzioni
*A COMPARATIVE ANALYSIS OF COMPLEX ORGANIZATIONS**

[EDITORS' NOTE: Dr. Etzioni is Associate Professor of Sociology in Columbia University.]

Utilitarian organizations are organizations in which remuneration is the major means of control over lower participants and calculative involvement (i.e., mild alienation to mild commitment) characterizes the orientation of the large majority of lower participants. Utilitarian organizations are commonly referred to as industries. . . . Thus, for our purposes, industries and divisions of industrial organizations can be classified into three main categories: those whose lower participants are predominantly *blue-collar* workers, such as most factories and mines; those whose lower participants are predominantly *white-collar* employees, such as offices, whether private (insurance companies and banks) or public (various governmental agencies); and those whose lower participants are *professionals,* such as research organizations, planning organizations, and law firms (these, as we will see, are normative organizations).

Statements made about one category of industry also hold, though to a lesser degree, for employees of the same type in subdivisions of other categories of organizations. Thus, statements about white-collar industries apply to office employees in factories; statements about professional organizations are also true for professional divisions in blue-collar industries, as in research and development divisions; and statements about blue-collar industries hold for janitors in a university. . . .

Remunerative power—such as the manipulation of wages, salaries, commissions, fringe benefits, working conditions, and similar rewards—constitutes the

* Reprinted with permission of the publisher from *A Comparative Analysis of Complex Organizations* by Amitai Etzioni. Copyright 1960 by The Free Press, A Corporation. (Excerpts from pp. 31–39, 80–82.)

predominant source of control in blue-collar industries. These sanctions also constitute the predominant means of control in white-collar industries, but they are less pronounced there than in blue-collar industries; and they constitute an important though secondary power in professional organizations. Normative controls play a relatively limited role in blue-collar industries; an important though secondary role in white-collar industries; and they constitute the predominant means of control in professional organizations. In other words, professional organizations are not a remunerative but a normative "industry." Hence their compliance structure is examined in the subsequent chapter, with other normative organizations.

*   *   *   *   *

Remuneration is the predominant means of control of blue-collar workers. Its allocation and manipulation make these employees conform to regulations governing the required level and quality of production, the use and treatment of organizational property, tardiness, absenteeism, and the like. It may not be the central factor determining their orientation to work in general, or their choice of a particular line of work, but it seems to be central in affecting their orientation to particular jobs and many job-norms, and to the organization as a control structure.

It is true that other factors, including their basic values, degree of unionization, intrinsic satisfaction from work, prestige and esteem derived from it, and, to some degree, social relations on the job, also influence the job orientation and performance of workers. We suggest, however, that when the relative weight of these various factors is established, remunerative rewards and sanctions will turn out to play a more important part in control of blue-collar workers than other factors.

Some relevant material is supplied in a study of the method of control preferred by workers in an electric power company, and the method of control considered effective by their supervisors (Mann and Dent, 1954) . . . .

*   *   *   *   *

Further evidence is supplied by a study of workers who chose to work on an assembly line in the automotive industry (Walker and Guest, 1952) . An examination of their previous jobs indicates that by six criteria of job satisfaction, the workers were much better off on their previous job; 87.4 per cent had formerly held a job where pace was determined individually; 72 per cent had had non-repetitive jobs; about 60 per cent had had jobs requiring some skills and training; and 62.7 per cent had been entirely or partly free to determine how their jobs ought to be done *(ibid.,* pp. 34ff.) . They chose to leave these jobs and take the frustrating assembly-line jobs basically because the new jobs offered a higher and more secure income. Three quarters of the workers reported that the reasons bringing them to the new plant were primarily economic. Wage differences were about 30 per cent—$1.51 per hour compared with $1.05 *(ibid.,* p. 91) .

Social scientists studying industries have emphasized that the earlier image of the worker as a rational machine, from whom greater effort can be elicited when more incentives are introduced, is not valid. By now this point is widely accepted; indeed, it seems at times to be overstressed. Students of industries should be reminded that attempts to increase the normative elements of supervision are in some cases reported to lead only to small increases in productivity; whereas in other cases they cause an increase in "morale" (i.e., job satisfaction) but none in productivity. On the other hand, reports from industry and surveys by government bureaus generally attest to the effectiveness of wage-incentive plans in increasing productivity and achieving other objectives. A government survey of 514 wage-incentive plans in the United States reported in 1945 that, under such plans, production increases averaged 38.99 per cent; unit labor costs were decreased on the average by 11.58 per cent (Viteles, 1953, p. 27). Argyris reviews a large number of studies, all supporting the same point.

*   *   *   *   *

White-collar employees are predominantly controlled by remunerative means, but less so than blue-collar workers. Normative controls, though secondary, seem to play a more important role among white-collar employees, and commitment to the organization is higher.

*   *   *   *   *

Morse's meticulous study (1953) of white-collar employees supplies information on what 742 employees "like best about working in the company" studied, and thus casts some light on the relative importance of various rewards and sanctions. Morse's findings suggest the overriding importance of remunerative rewards for white-collar employees, and support our suggestion that the compliance of lower-ranking white-collar employees is predominantly remunerative.

A study of salesgirls by Lombard (1955, esp. pp. 124–30) points out many of the phenomena usually considered typical of manual workers. He reports, for instance, that the work group restricts "output," limits competition among the girls, and enforces other norms which are in direct contrast to those supported by management.

At the same time the manipulation of esteem and prestige symbols, which as a rule has a limited effect on blue-collar workers, seems to be more effective among white-collar employees (Homans, 1953). This point is illustrated in a study of salesgirls which emphasized the role of nonremunerative "symbolic" controls. Salesgirls who made mistakes in writing out sales slips had the slips returned to them, marked with a red rubber band, to be opened and corrected in the presence of the section manager and other salesgirls. These red bands "do not result in fines or punishments of any sort, and yet the clerks feel that to get one is a disgrace" (Donovan, 1929, p. 64). Similarly, "all sorts of honors are bestowed upon the capable and efficient. . . . To be ace—the best saleswoman in your department—is a compensation enough in itself" (*ibid.*, p. 192).

*   *   *   *   *

. . . There are several reasons why organizations that have economic goals function more effectively when they employ remuneration than when they employ coercion or normative power as their predominant means of control. Production is a rational activity, which requires systematic division of labor, power, and communication, as well as a high level of coordination. It therefore requires also a highly systematic and precise control of performance. This can be attained only when sanctions and rewards can be readily measured and allocated in close relation to performance. Remunerative sanctions and rewards are the only ones that can be so applied, because money differentials are far more precisely measurable than force, prestige, or any other power differentials.

Much production requires some initiative, interest, "care," responsibility, and similar attributes of the lower participants. Engineers and personnel people frequently describe the great damage caused when workers carry out orders to the letter but ignore the spirit of the directive, in order to "get even" with a supervisor. . . .

*   *   *   *   *

The use of normative power in organizations serving economic goals may lead to highly effective performance, but in general only for work of a particularly gratifying nature, such as research and artistic performance, or for limited periods of time, particularly in crises. Thus, for example, the work of transferring the defeated British army home from Dunkirk, under the pressure of the approaching German army, was conducted by a fleet of volunteers under normative command. Similar efforts on the industrial front take place in the early stages of war.

Normative compliance can be used to conduct "services" of a dramatic nature (in the sense that they have a direct relation to ultimate values), such as fighting fires, helping flood victims, searching for lost children, or collecting money for the March of Dimes and similar causes. But production engaged in by lower participants in typical blue-collar or white-collar industries lacks such qualities. Its relation to ultimate goals is indirect; it is slow to come to fruition; the worker is segregated from the fruits; and activities are highly routinized, spread over long periods of time, and evoke little public interest. Hence production as a rule cannot rely on the moral commitments of lower participants and the normative power of organizational representatives; for example, when a relatively "dramatic" service such as searching for lost children requires continued, routinized activity, the number of volunteers and the level of normative compliance tend to decline rapidly. This is one of the reasons such activities are often delegated to permanent utilitarian organizations, such as the fire department and "professional" fund raisers. In summary, effective production of commodities and services is carried out almost exclusively by utilitarian organizations.

PHOTOGENERAL OPTICAL COMPANY

I Case Introduction

Synopsis

Faced with increasing foreign and domestic competition in the post-war years, Photogeneral decides to diversify its product line outside its traditional field of cameras and accessories. Photogeneral's management is trying to determine the price at which to introduce its newly developed photoelectric burglar deterrent, the Auto-Switch. Marketing forecasts have been projected for the three most probable prices. With no more than some general feelings as to the probable success of its introductory advertising campaign, management must decide the kickoff price for the Auto-Switch.

Why This Case Is Included

The Photogeneral case offers a lesson in how certain external (market structure and competitive picture) and internal (cash needs) economic realities affect a pricing decision. There is much to be learned too about the clarity of objectives needed for mathematical decision making. Sufficient data is available in the case to set up a payoff matrix and figure out the optimal strategies with the various decision rules. This might be a mere pencil-pushing exercise if there weren't challenges to the use of two integral facets of the mathematical techniques—the expected (monetary) value criterion and subjective probabilities. Finally, it becomes obvious in the course of the group decision that the scientific approach may divide the management team instead of help them toward a group decision.

Diagnostic and Predictive Questions

In answering the following diagnostic and predictive questions, remember that these questions apply theories and conceptual ideas from certain disciplines. Such theories are valuable to understand basic forces at work in the policy system (diagnosis) and to predict what will happen in the system in the future (prediction). Since each reading abstracts from the total policy system certain factors or variables into the closed or partial viewpoint of one theory or discipline, no one reading gives answers to the practical policy problems of the case. In diagnosis and prediction, the parts of the problem are studied with "other things being equal."

Following each question are listed readings which will be helpful in answering the question. The readings included with this case are marked (*). By referring to the author index at the end of this book, you may locate the other readings listed.

1. Why is Photogeneral planning to introduce the Auto-Switch? What is the management specifically seeking? Are the objectives long or short run?

2. What assumptions about competitive behavior does the Photogeneral management seem to be making in its pricing approach? Are they realistic? What are the factors which limit Photogeneral's discretion in price setting?

Read: *Stonier and Hague, *A Textbook of Economic Theory*, pp. 123–26, 162–64, 182–83, 189, 197–99, 201, 204–5, 208.

3. What line of economic and/or marketing reasoning would lead the Photogeneral management to favor a relatively high price (premium pricing) for the Auto-Switch? A relatively low price (penetration pricing)?

Read: *Beckman and Davidson, *Marketing*, pp. 689–91.

4. What is meant by probability? What is an objective probability? What is a subjective probability? What function do probabilities serve in decision making? Do subjective probabilities serve as well as objective probabilities in decision making? Any distinctions or exceptions? Is it appropriate to use subjective probabilities in the Photogeneral pricing problem?

Read: *Morris, *Management Science in Action*, pp. 265–68, 272–78, 280. (Additional reading, not in this volume: C. West Churchman, *Prediction and Optimal Decision* [Englewood Cliffs, N.J.: Prentice-Hall, Inc., 1961], chap. vi. See also the readings cited in footnote 1 in Morris' selection.)

5. Did Mr. Edwards' (controller) objection receive the hearing it deserved? Recall that he valued the first quarter of a million in profits more than the second quarter million. Note that the rule for decisions under risk (cf. O'Connell, "Decision Making Rules and Computational Techniques") is to choose the strategy with the highest expected (monetary) value. Edwards is objecting to the applicability of that rule for this specific decision because the procedure is not capable of discriminating between strategies (various prices) which differ in riskiness. The reader should observe that this criterion would have the decision maker prefer a 50/50 chance of getting $100 or 0 to a sure chance for $49, despite the fact that A is riskless and B is a gamble.

	.5	.5	
A	49	49	$49(.5) + 49(.5) = 49$
B	100	0	$100(.5) + 0(.5) = 50$

Is the expected (monetary) value criterion valid for this Photogeneral pricing decision?

Read: *Miller and Starr, *Executive Decisions and Operations Research*, pp. 60–65. (Additional readings, not in this volume: Robert Schlaifer, *Probability and Statistics for Business Decisions* [New York: McGraw-Hill Book Co., Inc., 1959], chap. ii. R. Duncan Luce and Howard Raiffa, *Games and Decisions* [New York: John Wiley & Sons, Inc., 1958], chap. ii.)

6. Which decision-making technique fits the needs of Photogeneral—one of the four techniques (taking into account the differing attitudes toward risk they represent) for decision making under uncertainty, or playing the percentages by using the techniques for decision making under risk? Or, none of these? Why? In using the mathematical techniques recommended by Minor, which do you

think is the weakest (or most uncertain) link in the data or computations from which the optimum price is derived? Explain your doubts and reservations and outline any ways you might overcome the difficulties.

    Read: O'Connell, "Decision Making Rules and Computational Techniques." *Bross, *Design for Decision,* pp. 29, 38–41, 85–87, 89, 92–94, 102–6, 108–9, 128–29, 255–57.

7. From the way Magnus, the president, has acted in the group meeting, how would you predict he will act when it comes down to the necessity of making the final pricing decision? Will his lack of competence with the mathematical techniques favor or jeopardize getting the full benefit for Minor's expertise?

    Read: Thompson, *Modern Organizations,* pp. 4–6, 12–13, 19–21, 61, 63–65, 77–78. Barnard, *Organization and Management,* pp. 48, 85–87, 89–90, 94. Schumpeter, *The Theory of Economic Development,* pp. 84–94.

Policy Questions for This Specific Case

In answering the following policy questions, the results of diagnosis and prediction are used to reduce the amount of guesswork, or judgment, in designing action solutions. However, since certain parts of the total case situation cannot be reduced to science, and since "other things are not equal," judgment must still be used to fill in the factors not accounted for by readings. You will also need a second kind of judgment as you put value weights on different scientific predictions, since different theories may point to conflicting solutions.

8. Are there cogent enough economic (factors external as well as internal to the firm) and/or marketing arguments to make you, as Photogeneral's president, favor either premium or penetration pricing without going through the mathematical decision-making procedures? If so, which would you favor, a high or a low price, and why?

(See Questions 1, 2, and 3 with their attached readings.)

9. Determine the best strategy using the rules for decision making under uncertainty. (Note that the ideas expressed by Messrs. May, Medicus, Leeds, Shurr, and Lucas can be reduced to the rules under Section I in O'Connell, "Decision Making Rules and Computational Techniques." Hint: May's approach is a variation of the maximin—the maximax—in which the highest of the maximum payoffs is preferred.) Be sure to take account of the advertising expense in setting up the payoff matrix. (See Question 6.)

Determine, also, the optimal strategy, using the rules for decision making under risk. (See Questions 4 and 6.)

(Optional: Convert Edward's money values to utilities as best you can with the information available and find the best strategy by using the expected utility technique for decision making under risk. [See Question 5 and its attached readings. Appropriate procedures are found in the Schlaifer reading cited.])

10. What price would you choose if you were Magnus? Defend your method for arriving at that price.

Major Policy Issues: Tentative Generalizations about Any Policy System

In arriving at conclusions for the following questions, generalize from the facts in the case and use your own ideas to (a) confirm, (b) modify, or (c) test the workability of the concepts and theories from readings. As an executive or professional, use wisdom to merge theory, on the one hand, with "brute facts" and practice, on the other.

11. Had Photogeneral's management clearly enough defined their objectives in introducing the Auto-Switch before they attempted to set the price with mathematical techniques? (See Question 1.) Did you find the objectives being clarified as the discussion about mathematical decision making proceeded or did you sense that the efforts at quantification tended to stifle vigorous management by objective? On balance, does the use of mathematical decision making help or hinder in clarifying objectives?

12. "The use of subjective probabilities is a sham—just a gimmick to lull the executive into thinking he has been scientific in his decision making when all he has done is quantify hunches and decide the way he *wanted* to decide, not the way he *should* have decided!" Comment. (See Question 4 and its readings.)

13. When technology gets beyond the competence of a chief executive (Magnus in this case), does that very fact dictate a change in his behavior pattern as a manager? In such a situation, how can the chief executive modify his approach to managing in order not to stifle creativity and innovation and in order to take full advantage of the skills of subordinates? (See Question 7.)

Questions for Original Student Work in Analysis and Policy

The methods of viewing this case as represented by the authors' questions and selection of readings are not exhaustive. There are other relevant ideas for diagnosis and prediction. Furthermore, there are other ways of stating policy questions. More powerful analyses and wiser solutions will result by drawing on your own training and experience for (*a*) relevant concepts and theories, and (*b*) creative ways of asking policy questions. The following questions are designed to help you acquire this skill.

14. While reflecting on case facts, what additional theories from prior education give you insights as to "what is going on" in Photogeneral Optical Company? As to what might be predicted to happen in the future?

15. Other than the policy questions asked by the authors, what pragmatic ways can you think of to state the practical problems faced by executives in the case?

II Photogeneral Optical Company*

Company History

The Photogeneral Optical Company is a comparatively small manufacturer of cameras and photographic accessories. Founded in the 1920's in Schenectady, in its first decade of operations Photogeneral was a leading producer of still picture cameras with annual sales reaching a level of $21,000,000.

Increased competition, expiration of patents, and the depressed economic conditions of the early 1930's brought Photogeneral to the verge

---

* Copyright 1964 by the Graduate School of Business, Columbia University.

of bankruptcy in 1934. The company was saved when a controlling share of its stock was purchased by George Magnus, who at that time was the president and chief stockholder of the Magnus Motion Picture Studios.

Magnus, a wealthy and energetic young man of thirty-two, indicated later that he had bought Photogeneral primarily to obtain several patents which he felt had wide application in the growing motion-picture industry. He was also interested in acquiring the imaginative engineering talents of Rene Foche, founder and then president of the company.

Foche, who was then a man in his late forties expressed little interest in continuing as president of the company and told Magnus that he wished he could "get out from under the burden of administering the business and get back to my drawing board."

Foche, nevertheless, continued as president for two years, until 1936, when Magnus Motion Picture Studios went into bankruptcy as a result of several costly motion-picture failures and George Magnus assumed the presidency of Photogeneral. Rene Foche stayed on as director of research, and the company sold its Schenectady plant and moved to San Diego where it hoped to compete more favorably in the motion-picture camera industry.

Several patentable features developed by Foche allowed the company to flourish in the late 1930's, reaching an annual sales level of $40,000,000 in 1939.

Throughout the war years much of Photogeneral's efforts were directed to military products, and by 1945 sales had risen to an annual level of $62,000,000. With a return to peace and a market demand that had not been satisfied because of war rationing, Photogeneral's sales remained near the $60,000,000 level for the next three years.

By 1949, however, competition from the larger camera manufacturers and some Japanese and German imports made itself felt on Photogeneral sales. The company shifted its line as best it could to avoid this competition since it lacked the resources to meet it head on. Up to the time of his death in 1952, Rene Foche had succeeded in keeping the company supplied with new products and new features which were added to existing products. In addition to his creative ability, Foche had great success in attracting and effectively utilizing talented research people.

Management Philosophy

In the past decade Magnus had been approached by several of Photogeneral's largest competitors and asked to consider the possibility of a merger, but Magnus had turned down each offer.

"I have been offered some very attractive terms," he said, "but frankly I don't know what I would do if I sold out. The companies that want to acquire us are after our patents, processes, and the people who produce them—our research department. Our plant and marketing channels offer them little, and I don't see any place for me in any of these outfits.

"We have a good business here even though we live under the shadow of lower-cost foreign competition and powerful domestic competition. This forces us to live by our wits and stay one jump ahead.

"While it makes for a tough and tenuous life, it's the kind of life we are all accustomed to at Photogeneral. It breeds a kind of *esprit de corps* that you can sense throughout the company."

The present director of research, Edward Shurr, seconded Magnus' statement:

"I have been with the company for almost 20 years now. I have six key men in my department, and they average 14 years with Photogeneral. None of these men would want to work for one of the bigger outfits. If they did, they'd have left us long ago."

Present Position

Despite these sentiments which seemed to be held throughout the company, Photogeneral's economic position seemed indeed tenuous. From 1949 to 1957 annual sales declined from roughly $60,000,000 to $38,000,-000. In 1958 the introduction of a low-cost 8mm motion-picture camera called the "Sightseer" brought sales up to $43,250,000, and revenues through 1961 had remained at approximately the same level. The recent introduction of a higher-quality Japanese camera at a considerably lower price, however, convinced management that it would be virtually impossible for Photogeneral to sell its Sightseer model at a profit. Accordingly, a decision has been made to discontinue production of this model.

The discontinuance, it is estimated, will result in a loss in annual sales volume of more than $5,000,000 and a decline in profits of almost $600,000. To offset this drop, Magnus has intensified the company's efforts to bring a new automatic light switch to market as quickly as possible. The switch was developed almost 18 months ago but has been kept from the market while Magnus was seeking a reliable subcontractor to provide a timing mechanism needed in its operation.

Auto-Switch

The switch, which is protected by several patents and is to be marketed under the name of "Auto-Switch," operates on a simple photoelectric cell which can be attached inconspicuously to any window. One or more table or floor lamps can be readily plugged into the Auto-Switch which, when set to "automatic," will automatically turn the lamps on when the natural light falls below a predetermined level.

Commenting on the Auto-Switch, Shurr explained, "such a device is not just a trick novelty, but has great practical value in preventing home burglaries. For example, if I go out for the day and return late at night or perhaps leave my house on a trip or vacation, a sure sign to burglars that the house is empty is darkened rooms. With the Auto-Switch, at nightfall any light so equipped goes on automatically.

"There are similar switches on the market, but they all have one major drawback; once the light goes on at night, it stays on until sunrise. A smart burglar, seeing a light burning at 4:00 or 5:00 A.M. takes this as an almost certain sign that the house is empty.

"In the Auto-Switch we have incorporated a timing device which will automatically override the photocell after a given number of hours and turn the light off. Thus, knowing when dark will fall and adding a reasonable number of hours before 'bedtime,' the switch will turn the light on at dusk and off after say, the 11:00 P.M. news. It's really a remarkable little gadget, and the only thing that has held us up is finding someone to supply us with the kind of timer we want."

Ken May, Photogeneral's director of marketing, agrees that the switch has great potential:

"While it's a little out of our line," he said, "I've been able to arrange for effective distribution and have worked out what should be an extremely effective advertising and promotion campaign to back up sales.

"Our competition will come in part from a less expensive switch which has no timing device and sells for just under $9.00, and a more expensive switch which does not work on a photocell but is controlled entirely by a clock mechanism. This one, called the 'Time-a-Lite,' works very much like a clock radio and can do everything the Auto-Switch will do. However, it's a larger device using a much more costly timing mechanism, and it now retails at $24.95."

Market Forecasting

The task of forecasting the first year's sales of the Auto-Switch was assigned to Dave Minor, director of market research. Dave joined the company as a sales analyst eight years earlier after completing a Master's degree in Business Administration. He advanced steadily and rapidly in the company, and two years ago was given the newly created title, director of market research.

"Dave is great with figures," May explained. "At times he goes overboard and acts as if the numbers he manipulates tell the whole story, but he has been an enormous help to us. He helped our manufacturing people revise their inventory policy by use of linear programming techniques which saved the company close to $14,000 a year."

In making forecasts for the Auto-Switch, Minor developed several sets of five-year sales projections based on different assumptions of market acceptance, competition, price, and advertising success.

After careful analysis of these projections, Magnus decided to go ahead with the Auto-Switch and asked for a more specific forecast of first-year sales.

Minor presented a tabulated summary of his first-year projections (Exhibit 1), which he explained to Magnus, as follows:

Exhibit 1

SALES FORECASTS FOR ALTERNATIVE PRICES
AND SUCCESS DEGREES OF ADVERTISING

Price	Promotion Success	Sales Volume	Sales Revenue
$15.00	Excellent	420,000	$6,300,000
15.00	Good	400,000	6,000,000
15.00	Poor	360,000	5,400,000
17.50	Excellent	340,000	5,950,000
17.50	Good	270,000	4,725,000
17.50	Poor	180,000	3,150,000
20.00	Excellent	270,000	5,400,000
20.00	Good	150,000	3,000,000
20.00	Poor	40,000	800,000

"We are definitely going to have to underprice the clock timer, and from the cost figures Nelson [Nelson Edwards, controller] has worked up, it looks like we'll have to price at least $4.00 or $5.00 above the cheaper photocell switches.

"I have worked up all sorts of linear and curvilinear demand functions under various price and market assumptions, and for the first year the key determinants will be: First, the price we set, and second, the degree of success Ken has with his advertising and sales promotion. From the discrete nature of the functions and pricing practices in the industry, it looks as if our best price will be either $15.00, $17.50, or $20.00, and these are the prices I projected in my tabulation. Of course those revenue projections only tell half the story. To get the whole picture we have to look at them in conjunction with Nelson's cost figures to see the profit potential."

Nelson Edwards, the company controller, presented Magnus with the cost information shown in Exhibit 2. It is based on data supplied by

Exhibit 2

ESTIMATED UNIT PRODUCTION COSTS

Annual Volume Units	Average Unit Production Cost*
25,000–100,000	$18.00
100,000–225,000	16.00
225,000–350,000	15.00
350,000–450,000	14.00
450,000–500,000	14.50

* Includes all manfacturing costs, cost of timer, appropriate overhead, and a $1.50 dealer discount.

Photogeneral's plant manager and the contract cost of varying volumes of timers bought from Photogeneral's expected supplier.

Advertising and sales promotion expense, on which Ken May anticipates spending almost $100,000 during the first year, are not included in the above unit costs.

Pricing Decision Criteria

Magnus next turned to Minor and said, "Well, here's the other half of the information you need. Can you now go back to your calculator and come up with the 'right' price for us to set? It'll sure save us a lot of time and argument if there's a price-picking mathematical technique in your bag of tools, Dave."

"I'm afraid it's not quite that simple," Minor replied. "Sure, I could take my projections and Nelson's cost estimates and compute them into a neat little three-by-three matrix which would show the estimated profit under all nine possible combinations of price and degree of advertising success. It'd make a nice Exhibit 3, but I couldn't put my finger on which price any one of you would pick as 'best.' We'd be faced with what's described as decision making under uncertainty, which means that quite different solutions could be considered 'best,' depending on the *criteria* any one of you wants to adopt. In practice the degree of optimism or pessimism you may feel about the success of Ken's advertising campaign and your basic attitude as to the risks we can take will determine which price you'd pick as 'best.' I'd have to know your personal criteria for selection before I could recommend the price you'd want. Perhaps if we exchanged points of view on the subject we could determine some common criteria."

From the general discussion which followed, it is possible to summarize the essence of each participant's comments as follows:

KEN MAY: My position is simple, we have to go for broke. Let's go for the price that presents the highest profit opportunity. Sure there's risk involved, but our best chance to survive is to take the calculated risk. We're too small, and our position is too tenuous to be ultraconservative. We'll survive by moving faster and more boldly than our big competitors or we won't survive at all.

PHIL MEDICUS (*plant manager*): My position is even simpler. Dave wants to know how optimistic I am; well I'd put myself down as a 40% optimist when it comes to new product introduction. Not that I'm a pessimist, or that I have doubts about the cost figures we projected—I think these are pretty good—but projections of sales volumes always leave me a little uneasy. And how can you predict the success of an advertising campaign?

BOB LEEDS (*advertising manager*): I frankly have an axe to grind. I think most of you tend to oversimplify the effect of advertising in the success or failure of a new product. It may sound strange coming from me, but very often technical matters such as design, quality, etc., can outweigh all the advertising gimmicks in the world. I'd frankly pick a technically sound price at which the relative degree of advertising success will have the least influence. Don't forget this is a brand-new product area for us and we'll be feeling our way into the right advertising technique. This is no buck-passing in advance, but I'd hate to see you pick a price which could either throw us into a huge loss or a fat profit just because of the so-called success of our advertising program. I can hear you now beefing about the profits we *could* have made—instead of this loss—if only those advertising people had done their job right.

NELSON EDWARDS (*controller*): I can't equate profits and losses quite so directly as Bob is doing. Of course I'd like to see as fat a profit as possible. But let's be realistic. We're going to be in tough financial shape next year unless we bring in at least a quarter of a million in additional profits to make up for the profits we had on the "Sightseer." Our credit lines are strained now, we have notes coming due, and I say we're in no position to gamble on a loss just to try and make a bigger killing. I tend to place a much higher premium on the first $250,000 in profits than I do on the next $250,000, $500,000, or even a potential million dollar profit. I don't know how Dave can handle my objections, but I just can't see that in our situation the first $250,000 is only half as valuable as a $500,000 profit; I put a much higher value on it.

ED SHURR (*director of research*): I've seen too many brilliant ideas go up in smoke. My philosophy is simple: you can hope and strive for the best, but in laying out your plans assume the worst. Consider what might happen under the worst possible conditions, and act accordingly.

JOHN LUCAS (*assistant to the president*): Ed is probably too pessimistic; I'd sooner rely on averages. At each price we pick Dave can figure out three possible profit outcomes, since we're guessing anyway, why assume the best or the worst? Let's take an average of the three and select the highest average profit potential. Or is this too simple for Dave's computer?

After listening to the six views summarized above, Minor observed that he would have to apply a distinctly different selection criterion to reflect each individual philosophy expressed: "With the exception of Nelson's beliefs, I think I can satisfy all five of you by using pretty standard criteria for picking the 'best' price. What Nelson is saying is that the value of a dollar is not always constant for him, and that a dollar at, say, the $100,000 profit level has a much different value than a dollar at the million level. In other words, a dollar of profits has different values or 'utilities' at different levels. We can handle this kind of a problem without too much trouble if we seek to maximize Nelson's *utilities* rather than dollars; or we can make use of Bernoulli's theorem to translate dollars into utilities and . . ."

At this point Magnus interrupted saying, "Dave, I think you're getting too complicated and theoretical for all of us—certainly for me. I know you can do the darndest things with numbers, but I think we've got enough troubles without going into variable-valued dollars and their utilities. Can you come up with an optimal price based on the other views you heard?"

"I certainly can," replied Minor, "but chances are I'll pick a different optimum price to meet each view, so I'll probably end up picking all three possible prices as 'best.' Which of the philosophies we've heard would you want me to use?"

After some reflection Magnus answered that he believed there was some merit in each view he'd heard: "My own inclination is somewhat similar to John's, only I'd feel better playing the *percentages* rather than the averages he was talking about. When I bet on a horse I don't as a rule feel that all the horses in a race have an equal chance of winning. Is there any way of doing some smart handicapping to pick the most likely winner here?"

Introduction of Probabilities

Minor reacted quickly to Magnus' question: "There sure is a way of doing just that. If Ken—or any of you, for that matter—would give me the probabilities of his advertising campaign coming out excellent, good, or poor, the rest is simple arithmetic. In technical terms, this would switch our problem from decision making under uncertainty to decision making under risk, which is a way of 'playing the percentages' on this one."

Ken May objected. He did not believe it was possible to put a numerical probability on something as unpredictable as an advertising campaign —not for a new product, anyway. Minor continued to argue, "You may not be able to call the exact turn, Ken, but I'm sure you have some feeling about the prospects of success. Do you think, for instance, that it's equally likely that the campaign will be a flop as that it will be good or excellent?"

> MAY: Of course I don't, or I wouldn't be pushing it.
> MINOR: Well, do you think there's about one chance in a hundred that it will be good?
> MAY: Oh, no, much better than that.
> MINOR: How about 80 chances in a hundred.
> MAY: That's being *too* optimistic, Dave.
> MINOR: O.K., so we bracketed it now between 10 and 80. How about 20? Or 70? You see, Ken, you do have a feeling that can be quantified if I push you hard enough.

The probable success of the proposed advertising campaign was discussed for some time, with the group finally settling on the following probabilities: excellent, 30%; good, 50%; poor, 20%. Minor was pleased. "Good. What we've done is 'sneak up' on the probabilities of success or failure, and as a result we're able to use a single and more rational criterion for picking the optimum price for the Auto-Switch. Let me work this one out and see how it comes out."

May was still unhappy. "I don't see how Dave can pick a price by formula. I've got to see the result of his calculations and see if it makes sense to me. Other things being equal I know I'd favor the top price— $20. If we've got a good item let's cash in on it; if we later find that we have to change our price, it's always easier to lower than to raise." Leeds believed that the *lowest* possible price made sense on the new Auto- Switch—on the assumption that a high initial sales volume would carry its own word-of-mouth advertising for future sales. Edwards similarly was not convinced, "I still feel it makes no sense to play the percentages, even if they reflect real probabilities, when we're so severely pressed for that first quarter of a million profit. What you are telling us, Dave, is that if we had to make this pricing decision a hundred times we should take probabilities into account. But we won't make the decision a hundred times—we'll only do it once, so we don't have the safety factor implicit in averages." Edwards reminded Minor of the man, six-foot tall, who drowned crossing a stream whose *average* depth was only four feet.

Magnus closed the discussion: "All right, Dave, you get your figures worked up, and we'll all get together tomorrow for a final discussion on the Auto-Switch price. We've wasted enough time talking about it, let's wrap it up tomorrow."

III Selected Readings

From: Alfred W. Stonier and Douglas C. Hague
*A TEXTBOOK OF ECONOMIC THEORY**

[EDITORS' NOTE: A. W. Stonier is Senior Lecturer in Political Economy, University College, London. D. C. Hague is Newton Chambers Professor of Economics in the University of Sheffield.]

PURE AND PERFECT COMPETITION

. . . We spoke in Chapter V of *pure competition* where demand for the product of the individual firm was infinitely elastic, so that the firm could sell all it wished at the existing market price, but was unable to alter the price by its own actions. . . . There are three fundamental prerequisites for the existence of pure competition between producers. These are as follows:

(a) LARGE NUMBERS

The first condition for pure competition in an industry is that there must be a large number of firms in the industry. This is essential, because only when there are many firms in an industry can each firm be sure that any action on its own part will have no noticeable effects on the price and output of the whole industry. . . .

---

* Reprinted with permission from Alfred W. Stonier and Douglas C. Hague, *A Textbook of Economic Theory*, 1953, John Wiley & Sons, Inc. (pp. 123–26, 162–64, 182–83, 189, 197–99, 201, 204–5, 208).

(b) Homogeneous Products

Second, each of the firms in a "purely" competitive industry must be making a product which is accepted by customers as being identical, or *homogeneous,* with that made by all the other producers in the industry. . . .

*   *   *   *   *

It is probably worth pointing out here that we have so far assumed, and shall continue to assume until further notice, that there is always pure competition *between buyers.* We have taken it for granted that the total number of buyers is very large, and that each one takes so small a proportion of the total sales of any good that no one buyer can alter the price of a good by his own actions. Buyers must therefore take prices as given. . . .

(c) Free Entry

The third fundamental condition which must be fulfilled if there is to be pure competition in an industry is that anyone who wishes to enter the industry must be allowed to do so. . . .

*   *   *   *   *

These three conditions, large numbers of firms, homogeneous products and free entry, between them ensure that there is pure competition in the sense that there is competition which is completely free from any monopoly elements. . . . One can, however, distinguish also between pure competition, which we have just defined, and "perfect" competition—a concept frequently used by economists. For there to be "perfect" competition, it is necessary to make some additional assumptions. In particular, it is necessary to assume that there is perfect knowledge on the part of all buyers and of all sellers about conditions in the market. In addition it is usual to assume complete mobility of factors of production between industries. It is also convenient when discussing perfect competition to make the assumption that all producers work sufficiently close to each other for there to be no transport costs. . . .

*   *   *   *   *

[IMPERFECT COMPETITION]

. . . We turn now . . . to a study of . . . imperfect competition. . . .

We shall continue to assume that there is perfect competition *between buyers.* . . . We shall also continue to assume that each consumer is "rational," . . .

So far as the individual firm is concerned we shall continue to assume that the sole aim of its entrepreneur is to earn maximum profits. . . . When competition is imperfect, there are no longer sufficient firms in the industry for a change in the output of any one of them to have a negligible effect on the output of the industry as a whole. . . .

*   *   *   *   *

. . . We shall discuss these various narrower types of imperfect competition in turn. . . .

Monopoly

Strictly interpreted, a "monopolist" is the sole producer of his product, and the distinction between the firm and the industry, both producing the same product, so important in perfect competition, goes. The firm of the monopolist is not only a firm, it is an industry. It is the only firm producing the product in question. . . .

* * * * *

MONOPOLISTIC COMPETITION

* * * * *

In the real world, . . . imperfect competition does not usually mean only one producer who has no closely related goods competing with his own—as we suggest when we talk of a monopolist. The great majority of imperfectly competitive producers in the real world produce goods which are very similar to those made by their rivals. It follows that such producers must always be very concerned about the way in which the actions of these rivals affect their own profits. This kind of situation is dealt with in economic theory by the analysis of what is called *monopolistic competition.* . . .

It is reasonable to suppose that in these circumstances the shape of the firm's average revenue curve will be determined not only by the tastes and whims of consumers, but also by the price-output decisions of rival producers. The problems of monopolistic competition are therefore more complicated than those of perfect competition. In perfect competition there is at any rate only one homogeneous commodity. In monopolistic competition there is differentiation of products. Products are not homogeneous, as in perfect competition, but neither are they only remote substitutes, as in monopoly. What this really means is that in monopolistic competition there are various "monopolists" competing with each other. These competing "monopolists" do not produce identical goods. Neither do they produce goods which are completely different. Product differentiation means that products are different in some ways, but not altogether so. "Branding," the use of attractive packets and wrappers, and the use of trade-marks and of trade-names will be the most usual methods by which products are differentiated, even if physically they are identical, or almost so. In addition, of course, it will be possible to make slight improvements or alterations in the physical constitution of a product to persuade consumers that it is rather superior to other similar products.

* * * * *

. . . [T]he more closely competitive substitutes there are, the more elastic the demand for the product of any one firm in the "group" will be.

* * * * *

OLIGOPOLY

. . . Oligopoly . . . occurs where there are only a few sellers. It differs both from monopoly, where there is only one seller, and from perfect and monopolistic competition, where there are many. . . .

The simplest case of oligopoly occurs when there are only two sellers and is known as *duopoly.* Duopoly analysis raises all the fundamental problems of oligopoly.

* * * * *

OLIGOPOLY WITHOUT PRODUCT DIFFERENTIATION

. . . The important feature of duopoly, with or without product differentiation, is that the individual producer has to consider very carefully what the indirect effects of his own decision to change price or output will be. Since, in duopoly without product differentiation, there are only two producers of identical goods, any price or output change by the first producer is bound to affect the second, whose reactions will in turn change the position of the first, and so on. The individual producer therefore has to acknowledge that he may change the whole situation in which he is producing in this indirect way if he changes his own price-output policy.

*   *   *   *   *

. . . Both firms are producing identical goods. So, if we continue to assume (as we must) that consumers are indifferent which producer they patronize when prices are the same for each firm's good, we cannot say how many consumers will go to A except on some assumption about what B's price is. . . . It will be a matter of pure accident whether *individual* consumers go to A or to B.

*   *   *   *   *

OLIGOPOLY WITH PRODUCT DIFFERENTIATION

Where there is oligopoly *with* product differentiation in any market, not only is the number of firms small but their products are also differentiated. . . .

. . . [I]n oligopoly *with* product differentiation the fact that products are somewhat different means that it may be possible for one producer to raise or lower his price without needing to fear either the loss of all his customers on the one hand, or an immediate response by his rival on the other.

In such a situation it is possible for consumers to be attached more or less firmly to one product rather than the other. So, the assumption that the producers will share the market equally, which we could make for duopoly without product differentiation, need no longer hold. . . .

*   *   *   *   *

A CLASSIFICATION OF MARKET SITUATIONS

	Type of Market Situation	
Number of Firms	*Homogeneous Products*	*Differentiated Products*
Many firms	Perfect competition	Monopolistic competition
Few firms	Oligopoly without product differentiation	Oligopoly with product differentiation
One firm	Monopoly	————

From: Theodore N. Beckman and William R. Davidson
*MARKETING**

[EDITORS' NOTE: The authors are both Professors of Marketing at Ohio State University.]

Low-Price Policies. Some vendors follow a policy of underselling competitors. A notable historical example is the famous R. H. Macy & Company department store in New York. Over a number of generations, its policy has been to sell at less than the shopped price for comparable items. More recently, this policy has been used by various discount houses, especially Masters, Inc., and E. J. Korvette, Inc., both of which operate a number of establishments in eastern markets, and Polk Bros. of Chicago. This price policy is by no means confined to the field of retailing. In the wholesaling of goods, arrangements are frequently made whereby the vendor agrees to supply his customers with merchandise at or below the lowest price quoted by competitors, thus following the policy of "meet or beat" competitors' prices.

There are some manufacturers who believe in and follow a low or lowest price policy. In some cases a low-price policy may be a relatively temporary expedient to meet conditions in an unsettled market. For example, the St. Joseph Lead Co. attracted considerable attention in 1960 with a policy announcement that it would discount any competitive posted price for zinc by one-half cent per pound.[1] This policy was adopted when prices for the commodity were very unsettled, and all suppliers were making special concessions of one form or another to customers. Buyers were uncertain about alternative costs available to them. Hence the policy announcement of this major supplier was a means of communicating to the trade that a customer could not likely do better by buying elsewhere. When market conditions become more settled in early 1961, and discounting of base selling prices diminished, St. Joseph rescinded its lowest price policy and reverted to its previous policy of selling at the market level.

A low-price policy, pursued on a continuing basis, is likely to succeed in markets in which there are considerable latent demands at lower prices, and the manufacturers most likely to do so are those with a relatively high physical efficiency. Such a policy tends to widen the market and to give the seller the opportunity of utilizing his facilities to best advantage. A bold and imaginative policy of low or greatly reduced prices can sometimes reach such broader bases of potential demand involving new applications that the low price becomes in itself a product innovation. This has been aptly illustrated as follows:[2]

"A new synthetic fiber, for example, may be so costly and high priced that it is used only for surgical and other very limited purposes. By dropping the price in anticipation of reduced costs, the hosiery and fine apparel markets may be

---

* Theodore N. Beckman and William R. Davidson, *Marketing*, Seventh Edition. Copyright © 1962, The Ronald Press Company. (Excerpts from pp. 689–91.)

1 "Zinc Breathes Easier—and Hopes," *Business Week*, January 28, 1961, p. 103.

2 Clare E. Griffin, "When Is Price Reduction Profitable?" *Harvard Business Review*, September–October, 1960, p. 129.

reached; still further down the price scale, the rug, carpet, and industrial markets may be tapped."

There are definite limits, however, to what may be deemed desirably low prices for any period of time. Unless the reduction is a matter of competitive necessity, no businessman can be expected to reduce his prices materially in the face of a belief that he would not be compensated by sufficient increases in sales volume and satisfactory profitability on the basis of cost and revenue factors applying to the larger volume marketed. Assuming a homogeneous product, the price of the product may be constant at a given time and no firm may be able to sell above the ruling price. No lower price, therefore, need be quoted in order to get the business. In fact, a further lowering of price may bring retaliatory action from competitors or at best may result in a permanent lowering of prices by all of them. In any event, when the basic policy is to sell at relatively low prices this is assigning to pricing a major and an offensive role in the marketing mix.

*   *   *   *   *

Selling at Relatively High Prices. Some firms find it possible to market products at a relatively high price. This is not ordinarily practical on a sustained basis unless there is a strong degree of market control. Such control may be achieved by significant differentiation in the physical attributes or the functioning of products which are protected by patents or which are manufactured according to complex or secret processes that are difficult to duplicate. In some cases significant differentiation may exist as a result of unusually successful promotional effort which has created an exceptional favorable enterprise or brand image. If the product is a complicated durable good, either consumer or business equipment, differentiation may exist in the form of an outstanding reputation for installation or maintenance service, which may be more important to the user than initial cost.

Selling at a relatively high price level may also be a temporary expedient under certain conditions. For example, a firm brings out a product which is entirely new in its class in some distinctive way, but feels that competitors will follow with similar product modifications after some period of time. The decision may be to price at a relatively high level initially, to recover product research, developmental, and promotional costs as quickly as possible, before it becomes necessary to meet intensive competition. As another example, relatively high price levels are sometimes established on new products or substantial product modifications in order "to try the market." The firm may be totally lacking in information about the nature of elasticity of demand. If it must actually experiment, it is much easier to start with a price that is too high and lower it later, if necessary, than to do the opposite.

When a firm decides to sell at relatively high prices, the assumption is that price is not a very important factor in getting or retaining business. The role of price in the marketing mix is nearly a negative one, having been subordinated almost completely to product development, advertising, or other ingredients. There remains, nevertheless, the major management problem about deciding just what specific price to establish.

From: William T. Morris

*MANAGEMENT SCIENCE IN ACTION**

[EDITORS' NOTE: The author is Professor of Industrial Engineering, The Ohio State University.]

For our purposes it will suffice to consider three rough types of interpretations of the term "probability," although there are more.[1]

1. *Relative frequency.* The probability of an event A is the limit of the relative frequency with which A is observed when an experiment is repeated an indefinitely large number of times. This is ordinarily what is meant when it is asserted that the probability of heads when a fair coin is flipped is one half. It is an unhandy kind of an operational definition since the notion of a limit is quite imaginary. In practice, however, we are perfectly willing to make an induction from a large number of replications as to what would happen in the limit. The class of all possible experiments or instances is called a reference class, and the occurrences of the event A form a subclass of the reference class. Sometimes the reference class is finite (the number of customers now served by the firm) and the probability of an event (sales of $1,000 or more to a customer) can in principle be learned by examining every member of the reference class. The trouble comes, as we shall see, not when we want to make statements about large or infinite reference classes but when decision making requires something be said about very small reference classes containing perhaps one or two members.

2. *Personalistic or subjective.* The probability of the event A in this view is a measure of a person's "degree of belief" in the statement, "The outcome of the experiment will be A." It measures his confidence in the assertion or his conviction of its truth. This interpretation is itself the subject of considerable confusion. We will shortly explore more carefully its meaning and the ways in which it may be made operational. Personalistic or subjective probabilities are not, in spite of their name, products of unbounded flights of whim and fancy. The interpretation is appealing because of the possibility of dealing with a manager's confidence in assertions like, "Our chief competitor is coming out with a new model this year." Managers having feelings of certainty or uncertainty about such assertions, and these feelings can in no useful way be dealt with by means of the relative frequency interpretation.

3. *Everyday language.* This is not really an interpretation of probability, but a category into which are placed all the known and unknown, vague and precise, consistent or inconsistent, meanings which attach to the term "probability" in ordinary conversation. What do managers mean when they talk about probabil-

* Reprinted by permission of Richard D. Irwin, Inc., Homewood, Illinois, 1963 (pp. 265–68, 272–78, 280).

[1] L. J. Savage, *The Foundation of Statistics* (New York: John Wiley & Sons, Inc., 1954), pp. 56–57; R. Duncan Luce and Howard Raiffa, *Games and Decisions* (New York: John Wiley & Sons, Inc., 1957); Robert Schlaifer, *Probability and Statistics for Business Decisions* (New York: McGraw-Hill Book Co., Inc., 1959); and Harry V. Roberts, "The New Business Statistics," *Journal of Business,* Jan. 1960.

ity in discussing their decisions? What is a businessman's notion of "running a calculated risk"? Do these meanings have any useful relationship to the interpretations already mentioned?

There is ample evidence that many of the difficulties which arise between adviser and manager are in some way related to a divergence between meanings assigned to words in everyday language and the operational interpretations made of them by management science.

*   *   *   *   *

Here, all at once, are a considerable variety of misunderstandings about what the "laws of probability" promise. The more common of these difficulties include the following:

1. "The probability of this coin coming up heads *on its next flip* is one half." Here is a problem which troubles not only the manager but the analyst as well. A businessman faces the same predicament when he tries to relate the evidence, "One half of all new business enterprises fail during their first two years" to a decision about investing in one particular new enterprise.

In the case of the coin, it is clear the next flip will come up either heads or tails. The number "one half" has no direct meaning in description of what will happen on a particular flip. We do not know what the coin will do, except to say it will land on one side or the other. The relative-frequency interpretation may hold that one half is the number approached by the long-run ratio of heads to flips, if the experiment is repeated an indefinitely large number of times. The personalistic interpretation may suggest that one half is a number which somehow measures a person's degree of belief in the truth of the statement, "The next flip of this coin will result in heads." These ideas may turn out to be useful in decision making, but not because of anything they assert about what will actually happen on a given flip. More of this later.

2. Mistaken beliefs based on "the law of averages" are popular. What does this law promise about things that will happen in the long run? "If a coin has come up heads ten times in a row, it is almost sure to come up tails on the eleventh flip." Flips of a coin are independent events, with each outcome quite unrelated to what has happened in the past. The coin, after all, cannot remember. To some extent this may parallel the thought behind such remarks as, "The law of averages requires that this decision be right because the last two (or ten, or twenty) have been wrong."

The law of averages is not at all the kind of imperative seemingly assumed by such statements. Poisson called it a "law," and thus led many astray. Its originator, Bernoulli, was careful to call it a "theorem." It promises nothing in the short run, and not what is commonly supposed in the long run. One version of it roughly stated says, "As the number of flips grows larger, the *probability* that the observed relative frequency of heads will differ from one half by more than a specified amount, grows smaller. As the number of flips approaches infinity, this probability approaches zero."

3. The common decision maker's remark, "We took a calculated risk," is seemingly meant most often as an ex post facto rationalization of a decision rather than as a description of what was done. In the majority of cases nothing resembling the calculating of a risk was carried on. Perhaps at the time the decision was made it was recognized that things might not turn out well. Actually calculating the risk is, as has been noted, the chief contribution of management science.

How little use is made of any of the statistical evidence which is widely available and potentially relevant to decisions. Vast amounts of data exist which decision makers might translate into probabilities, both in their business and personal choices, but they are little used, at least in any explicit fashion. It may even be argued that the probabilities thus derived are not relevant—say, for example, the use of a mortality table by a man buying insurance—but the reasons that support such an argument are not well known.

4. Continued interest and belief in the possibility of gambling systems suggest further this irrationality and inability to calculate the risk in reasonable ways. Hunches, which experiments in extrasensory perception suggest are not to be sneered at, are one thing, but a system which will improve one's chances in a straight gambling game is not to be found. Most are based on false impressions of the nature of independent events and the law of averages. Gamblers may feel they are challenging fate in order to conquer it, or that fate will somehow be especially kind to them, but if this happens it is not a result of their own calculations.

5. Sampling, the process of drawing inferences about a population on the basis of evidence from a sample, is a particularly difficult concept for many to accept. The *theory* of sampling is, of course, a deductive result of the theory of probability. It may be that management's difficulties with sampling are natural ones for those who often deal only with the end products of the process. It may be that the self-confidence of experienced executives manifests itself in a contempt for statistics, especially when the results disagree with their own views.

*   *   *   *   *

Relative-frequency probability is thus sometimes called "objective probability" to contrast it with the subjective or personalistic interpretation. "Objective" here may give the impression of a method of making probability operational which does not depend *in any way* on a person's state of mind but reflects some fact to which all must agree. Carefully examined, "objective probability" is not so objective as all that, since in practice it requires a number of judgments which different people may well make in different ways.

*   *   *   *   *

The data used to obtain probabilities represent nearly always a sample of the population to which the probabilities are intended to refer. Thus, probabilities are usually based upon inferences. As has been seen, judgment is involved in making such inductions. Perhaps all that can ultimately be said about objective probabilities is that the data upon which they are based and the judgments involved in their production are (or can be) made explicit for all to see and question. This is not the case with personalistic or subjective probabilities.

The more troublesome shortcoming of this interpretation is that it provides no way of dealing with one-time events or situations which are repeated only a small number of times. Unfortunately, it is the case that many business decisions, especially those of great consequence, are not what can be usefully or reasonably viewed as repeatable situations. A "repeatable" event means that it can be classed with other events into a reference class in a way which is informative and of some use for decision-making purposes. Thus a strict relative-frequency interpretation leaves one without guidance except in the long run. It makes no logical sense to talk about the probabilities of outcomes in a one-time decision.

This, however, has not prevented people from doing so. Probabilities are used widely in decisions without regard to the number of times the decision is to be repeated. Various arguments have been used to justify this, although in actual practice the necessity for justification is hardly ever appreciated.

1. Although the decision situation is not, in the view of the decision maker, to be repeated, he stipulates an imaginary problem in which it is to be repeated

many times. He then uses the probabilities which would be useful guides to action for the imaginary problem in exactly the same way for the real problem. This is supposed to "explain" the use of probabilities in the one-time case.

2. The decision maker stipulates that what he is doing is illogical but goes ahead anyway on the premise that being a little bit illogical does only a little bit of harm.

3. The probabilities are redefined so as to be regarded as measures of "degree of belief" in truth of propositions and are thus somehow relevant without regard to the repeatability of the situation. More of this shortly.

4. The decision maker proposes to use probabilities in all decisions, thus taking advantage of long-run effects in the reference class of all decisions rather than in a more restricted reference class.

*   *   *   *   *

In two general situations the relative-frequency position may lead to a model which does not reflect all the evidence available to and used by a manager. Ordinarily an experienced manager will have a large amount of accumulated information or background data which is not duplicated by the explicit evidence obtained by the staff. In a simple case, suppose a sample of a lot of a product is inspected and the resulting inference is that the lot is of acceptable quality. Suppose, however, that a manager has some information to the effect that the supplier was having a good deal of trouble with his process at the time the lot was produced. He might decide, and wisely so, to hold off on acceptance of the lot until a much larger sample can be inspected. . . .

The second case is that in which no relative-frequency data at all are available, and the evidence is solely that which the decision maker himself stipulates. Suppose a new and radically different product is to be launched and no test marketing is to be made. Clearly, the decision must be based on experience which cannot be made explicit in the staff analysis. If the staff operates without any stipulation from the manager it can only view the volume of sales for the new product as a matter of uncertainty. The manager himself may be quite unwilling to take this view, and thus he calls up from this memory all the experience he feels is relevant.

The net effect of a strict relative-frequency interpretation is to restrict staff work to those situations in which relative-frequency evidence is available, or to exclude from explicit consideration by the staff any evidence not of a statistical nature. . . .

*   *   *   *   *

It is clear that, in many important decisions, relative-frequency evidence alone will not seem to the manager a sufficient basis for choice. He will indeed add to and modify this evidence, a process loosely called judgment. To what extent should one try to reflect these judgments or applications of experience explicitly in the analysis of a decision? To put it another way, if one is really serious about the involvement of the manager in the staff analysis, why not reflect the executive's rich background and experience, together with his ability to guess at the future, directly in the model of the decision? . . .

*   *   *   *   *

To transform a manager's beliefs into personalistic probabilities and to integrate them with other evidence in the analysis would doubtless be a considerable task. What would be the advantages of doing this? It would provide one way of explicitly involving the decision maker in the work of the staff. It would help the manager impart to the staff in a careful manner some aspects of his own estimates of the decision situation. It would show the manager that his own

thinking was expressly included in the model. Thus the resulting recommendations would be consistent with his beliefs, and indeed partly of his own creation.
It would provide a possible means of taking advantage of both the manager's
rich background of experience and the data obtained by the staff. If the practice
became well developed and generally accepted, it might offer the staff a wider
field of operation, including decision problems on which relative-frequency
evidence was not available. It might exploit the usefulness of the staff in connection with decisions at higher management levels. It would permit the adviser
to extend in a consistent fashion the choice processes of the manager. . . .

Not the least benefit of this program would be to make these probabilities
explicit so they could be checked for consistency, criticized by others, and revised as new experience is obtained. . . .

* * * * *

The case in favor of subjective probabilities may include arguments such as
the following:

1. All probabilities are to some extent subjective, and thus nothing new in
principle is being proposed.

2. Different people, in situations where relative-frequency evidence may
eventually be obtained, may have quite different subjective probabilities, but
these get modified through further experience. With the aid of the staff, this
modification may take place in accordance with Bayes' theorem. If this happens,
then in the long run all the different subjective probabilities will converge to
the relative-frequency probabilities. The effects of the initial a priori probabilities are soon washed away by the accumulation of evidence.

3. It is foolish to waste the experience of decision makers, especially when
little other evidence is available. Here is a way to use and to extend it by
deducing useful consequences from it.

4. It is assumed, by those who favor this approach, that reasonable men having similar experience will not differ greatly in their personalistic probabilities.
This assumption may indeed be true.

* * * * *

From: David W. Miller and Martin K. Starr

EXECUTIVE DECISIONS AND OPERATIONS RESEARCH*

[EDITORS' NOTE: The authors are Professors at the Columbia University
Graduate School of Business.]

EXPECTED VALUE

. . . This idea is not complex. Expected value is simply the old fashioned
arithmetic average. It can be expressed in mathematical symbols by using W's
(W_1, W_2, and so forth) to represent the possible numerical outcomes, and

---

* *Executive Decisions and Operations Research,* David W. Miller and Martin K.
Starr. © 1960 by Prentice-Hall, Inc., Englewood Cliffs, New Jersey (pp. 60–65).

p's (p_1, p_2, and so forth) to represent the probability that each of the W's will occur. Thus, for two possible outcomes, we have

$$\text{Expected value} = W_1 p_1 + W_2 p_2$$

where $p_1 + p_2 = 1$, since either W_1 or W_2 necessarily has to occur.

The W's may be positive or negative, and occur in combinations, depending on the problem. For example, consider the executive who is certain to get one or the other of two possible bonuses, the first representable as W_1, the second as W_2. If we know for each the probability of his getting that bonus, our equation represents the executive's expected value of bonus. Both the W's are, in this case, positive. . . .

. . . For example, what is the expected value of a coin toss upon which two players each bet $100? Here we can let W_1 represent the gain of $100 ($W$ is positive), and W_2 the loss of $100 ($W$ is negative). Then we have $100(\frac{1}{2}) - $100(\frac{1}{2}) = 0$ as the expected value. What is your advantage if the other player puts $200 against your $100? Simply $200(\frac{1}{2}) - $100(\frac{1}{2}) = 50. Under these conditions you should average $50 gain on each play; if you play 1000 times you should have $50,000 to show for it.

. . . We can use expected values of any quantities whatsoever; in particular, we can directly take the expected value of total capital. For example, assume you have a total capital of $500 and you are offered the coin toss of $200 against your $100. Then we can identify the W's with total capital. If you win you will have $700, and if you lose you will have $400. Therefore we have $700(\frac{1}{2}) + $400(\frac{1}{2}) = 550, which is the expected value of your capital after one toss. Let us consider how one might more broadly use this concept of expected value.

Suppose you have the choice of making two investments of $1000 each. Presume that the return on investment A will be $4\frac{1}{2}$ per cent and the return on investment B will be 6 per cent. Granted the certainty of these statements and assuming that you are motivated by the objective of getting the greatest possible return you will undoubtedly invest in B. This conclusion follows because your return from B will be $60 compared to only $45 return from A. But now suppose that you are informed that both of the investments are risky and that the risk is greater on investment B. Suppose, to be precise, that you are told that the probability of a return on investment A is 0.90 (90 per cent) and the probability of a return on B is 0.65 (65 per cent). We will assume that either you will get the full stated percentage return or else no return at all. How would you choose between the investments?

We could calculate the expected values for the two investments in accordance with our equation. We will assume that the capital invested will remain secure in any event and the only question is whether there is a return or not. In this case the amounts won will be the return on the investment and the amounts lost will be 0—simply the fact of not receiving a return. In accordance with our equation, the expected value for investment A will be $45(0.9) - 0(0.1) = 40.50. The expected value of investment B will be $60(0.65) - 0(0.35) = 39. This means that if we made a number of different investments identical in every respect to investment A we would expect an average return of $40.50 on each of them. For a number of investments similar to investment B we could expect an average return of only $39. We could, therefore, conclude that we should invest in A because our expected return from A is larger than it is from B.

Note that we said "could conclude" rather than "must conclude." The reasoning we followed is perfectly logical and affords complete justification for choosing investment A. However, it is clear that one might prefer to play a hunch and invest in B and that he might be right and we might be wrong. This in no way changes the fact that our reasoning is impeccable, granting the probabilities as given and the objective as stated. . . .

In this reasoning concerning expected values we have ignored the very point with which we started—namely, that individuals do not have the same utility for money. We calculated above the considerable advantage accruing to the individual who receives $200 in the coin-tossing game for each $100 he wagers. Yet we have previously stated that under certain conditions (our so-called second case) we wouldn't accept this handsome offer. There is no contradiction. Instead of expected value we need only calculate the expected utility, using precisely the same procedure except that some measure of the utility of the amounts involved is used instead of the amounts themselves. This kind of calculation will be illustrated when we return finally to Bernouilli's problem of self-insurance.

SELF-INSURANCE

What is the problem of self-insurance? Individuals or organizations faced with the risk of loss of assets can either assume the risk themselves or pay an insurance company to assume the risk for them. The question is: When is it reasonable to do one or the other?

Let us take as an example a shipment of goods worth $10,000 which has a probability of 0.10 (10 per cent) of being destroyed or lost in transit. What is the expected value of such a shipment? Using our equation we have $10,000(0.90) + 0(0.10) = 9000, reflecting the fact that out of 100 shipments only 90 will arrive. Put in another way, the shipper can expect that on the average he will sustain a $1000 loss in value for each shipment. It would follow on this basis that the shipper should be prepared to pay up to $1000 for each shipment as premium on insurance. In this way, he will suffer no loss on his merchandise value, but he will pay the same amount as his expected loss to the insurance company. If he paid $1000 for each shipment then he would pay a total of $10,000 in premiums for ten shipments and this would be repaid him for the one that was lost or destroyed. Thus, he would break even. The lower the premium, below $1000, the more advantageous it would be for the shipper to insure. But from the standpoint of the insurance company a premium of $1000 per shipment would only enable them to break even and they would demand a higher premium say $1500. Viewed in the same light as gambling games, if the shipper takes insurance at a $1500 premium, then he has a negative expected value. That is, he loses on each play (shipment). Yet, under exactly this kind of circumstance, people continually insure themselves against loss. Why? Are they all being irrational? Of course the answer is no. They are not.

The explanation resides in the fact that the parties to the insurance contract have different utilities for money. There is diminishing utility for money (the more one has, the less an additional amount will contribute to utility). That the diminishing utility should take precisely the form of the logarithm of the amount of money, as Bernouilli assumed, is unlikely but it will serve to illustrate the logic of the situation. Suppose the shipper has total assets of $15,000, including the shipment which must arrive safely that the shipper be paid. Then, according to Bernouilli's assumption of a logarithmic measure of utility, if he does not take insurance, the shipper will have a utility of the logarithm of $15,000 or 4.17609 with probability of 0.90 and a utility of the logarithm of $5000 or 3.69897 with probability of 0.10. His expected utility in this case is simply $4.17609(0.90) + 3.69897(0.10) = 4.12838$ (the utility of $13,439, since 4.12838 is the logarithm of $13,439). If he insures for a premium of $1500 he will always end up with $15,000 − $1500 = $13,500$ and his utility will be the logarithm of $13,500 or

4.13033. Thus, the shipper's total expected utility is higher if he insures so this is the course of action he should take.

From the standpoint of the insurance company it is rational to offer the insurance because the company has so much money that its total utility is increased by accepting the insurance. Assume that the insurance company has assets of only $100,000. If it doesn't accept the insurance its utility will be measured by the logarithm of $100,000 or 5. If it does accept the insurance it will have the utility of $101,500 or 5.00647 with probability of 0.90 and the utility of $91,500 or 4.96142 with probability of 0.10. Its expected utility if it accepts the insurance will therefore be $5.00647(0.90) + 4.96142(0.10) = 5.00196$, the utility of $100,454. The insurance company should, therefore, accept the insurance for a premium of $1500. Thus, both parties are acting with complete rationality—once account is taken of the differences in the utility of money.

What, then, is the answer to the problem of whether to insure or not? It clearly depends on the amount of assets the shipper has. From the equation for his expected utility it can be calculated that he has equal utility whether he insures or not if his total assets are about $16,000. If he has more than this it is to his advantage to bear the risk himself. If he has less he should insure. Perhaps the shipper would scoff at the idea that with only $16,000 he should carry this risk himself. If so, it should be realized that this only means that the logarithm is not a good representation of the diminishing utility of money, a fact which we have already noted. If we had, for a specific shipper, the correct representation of his utility for money, we could use precisely the same approach to determine exactly at what point it was to his advantage to self-insure. Our use of the logarithm, we repeat, was only to illustrate the idea that it is utility that is important—not the amount of money.

The point of all this discussion is that even for objectives with a natural measure of degree of achievement it is still necessary to recognize that the natural measure may not coincide with the utility the decision-maker receives from the degree of achievement of his objective. And, if it doesn't, it is the *utility* that governs the decision problem, not the natural measure.

But there are many decision problems for which the amount of money involved does satisfactorily measure the utility. This would tend to be true where the amount of money involved is small relative to total assets. Can this be made more precise? Only if the real relation of the utility of additional increments of money to the amount of money possessed is known. For example, if the true relationship between utility and money is expressed by the logarithm of the amount of money, as Bernoulli suggested, then decision problems involving changes in money of no more than 2 to 3 per cent of the total amount possessed can be approximated with sufficient accuracy by assuming that the utility is represented by the amount of money. In short, the amounts of money involved could be used directly without worrying about the utility of the money. For decision problems involving greater amounts of money than this it would be necessary to attempt to determine the utility of the sums involved.

It is important to note that problems arise at the other end of the scale, too. Even if the logarithm, as used, were a correct representation of the utility for money under most circumstances, difficulties arise as soon as a decision problem includes any risk of total loss, i.e., bankruptcy. The difficulty is indicated by the logarithm itself, since the logarithm of zero is negative infinity. For some people, negative infinity, which is an infinite loss, would properly represent the situation. Other individuals, with suitable temperaments, don't look upon bankruptcy as the end of the road. For these people, it wouldn't be accurate to suppose that a small chance of complete failure would deter them. . . .

From: Irwin D. Bross
*DESIGN FOR DECISION**

[EDITORS' NOTE: The author is statistical consultant at Cornell University Medical College and New York and Memorial Hospitals.]

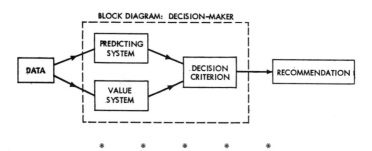

BLOCK DIAGRAM: DECISION-MAKER

*   *   *   *   *

When we are faced with a specific forecasting problem, we may have to study the subject intensively in order to see what prediction techniques are applicable. After making a choice, we must then decide what information or data will be needed for the operation of this technique. Next this data must be collected. Sometimes the information may be obtained from available records, but often existing records are inadequate for the purpose, and it may be necessary to go out and make our own observations. The prediction techniques can be tested on this data and perhaps modified in the light of the additional experience. If we are clever or lucky, we may wind up with forecasts that will be sufficiently accurate for our particular purposes. This whole process, from data to forecast, will be called a Predicting System.

Sooner or later in this process we are bound to run into the problem of error. Few things are so disheartening, embarrassing, and (alas) inevitable as a "busted" forecast. What can be done about this problem?

The first step that can be taken is to face up to the problem, to meet it honestly. This means admitting, to others and to ourselves, that the Predicting System is fallible. This means abandoning face-saving alibis and acknowledging that incorrect predictions are not accidents but are as much a part of the Predicting System as the correct predictions themselves.

The second step is to abandon all-or-none prediction. If any one of several outcomes may occur the possibilities should be explicitly stated. Whenever possible a list or range of outcomes should be given.

Some device for stating the chance of occurrence of each outcome is now necessary. One such device is that used on a racing sheet where the chance of each horse is described verbally. Thus a horse may be a "favorite," a "contender," a "longshot," or "just out for the exercise."

A more conventional verbal *scale* would be to employ such words as "likely"

* Reprinted with permission of the publisher from *Design for Decision* by Irwin D. Bross. Copyright 1953 by The Macmillan Company. (Excerpts from pp. 29, 38–41, 85–87, 89, 92–94, 102–6, 108–9, 128–29, 255–57.)

or "unlikely" and perhaps modify them with adverbs such as "very." In this way the Predicting System becomes a device for *classifying* the possible outcomes.

*   *   *   *   *

The verbal scale, though a step in the right direction, is not very satisfactory. The word "likely" is not precise; it may mean different things to different people. Some might feel that if events classed as "likely" actually occurred more than half of the time the classification was all right; others might feel that an event should happen oftener than this to deserve the classification "likely."

*   *   *   *   *

It has long been recognized that words are inadequate tools for really precise description, that disagreements over definitions are likely to arise, and that manipulation of words is subject to a variety of pitfalls that are hard to avoid. I will not labor the point—the semanticists have made a profession of it.

While it is easy to criticize language as a tool, it is a much more difficult matter to suggest a substitute means of communication. It took mankind several thousand years to come up with a workable replacement.

The introduction of this new tool coincides with the birth of modern science. Galileo transformed physics by substituting numerical measurements for verbal descriptions and mathematical derivations for verbal arguments. Since then, one field of science after another has made the slow and painful transition from words to numbers. Some scientists regard this step as the distinction between scientific and unscientific study. Said Lord Kelvin:

"When you cannot measure what you are speaking about, when you cannot express it in numbers, your knowledge is of a meager and unsatisfactory kind; it may be the beginning of knowledge, but you have scarcely in your thoughts advanced to the stage of a *science,* whatever the matter may be."

The third step that we shall take in dealing with the problem of uncertainty is to go from a verbal scale (such as likely—unlikely) to a numerical one. In taking this step we shall be in accord with scientific tradition. Moreover, it is a step that often leads to important results.

How can a verbal scale be replaced by a numerical one? First of all, the Prediction System must be modified so that it associates a number instead of a word with each outcome. It is customary to use for this purpose either a common or a decimal fraction, i.e., a number between zero and one. This number is to be regarded as a measure of the chance that a particular outcome will actually occur.

The Predicting System is still engaged in classifying the outcomes, but now the classification is a numerical one. Once again we want to know how good a job of classification is being performed.

A predicting system which leads to probabilities will be called a Probability Prediction System. . . .

. . . [S]uch a system is an integral feature of the process of Statistical Decision. In fact, it is essentially this particular component that distinguishes Statistical Decision from the other theories of decision that exist at present.

*   *   *   *   *

. . . Now I want to consider the second component in the decision-maker— the Value System. Like the Prediction System, the Value System also assigns a number to each possible outcome but this second number measures the desirability of the outcome rather than the chance that the outcome will occur. We shall be concerned here with Values only in this limited sense.

Even in this restricted sense, however, the problem of Values is a very difficult one. Insofar as the Prediction System is concerned there is substantial agreement among experts on the broad principles. Furthermore, the theory of probability provides powerful and well-tested tools for the construction of predicting systems in fairly simple situations. Even then, as I have emphasized before, the actual job of constructing a predicting system is no easy matter.

When we turn to the Value System the situation is much worse. There is a very little agreement among experts on general procedures—in fact, there is not even agreement as to what constitutes an expert in *this* field. There is no comparable theoretical development or theory of desirabilities to assist in the actual construction process.

In the field of Values the transition from words to numbers has been accomplished only in a very limited area. . . .

. . . If, as I have insisted, the decision is to be based on the consequences of the possible actions, then these consequences must be evaluated and hence a Value System must be incorporated in the Decision-Maker.

*　　*　　*　　*　　*

Not only do we distinguish good and bad but further we acknowledge degrees of goodness and badness. In practice we no more use the two-point scale good or bad for desirabilities than we use the corresponding two-point scale true or false for probabilities. As in the case of probabilities, there seems to be a continuous scale for values. In verbal terms we indicate this scale by such phrases as "very bad" or "extremely good."

Various attempts have been made to convert this intuitive scale to a quantitative one. The Utilitarians, such as J. S. Mill, have discussed the pain-pleasure scale and have suggested that numerical measurements would be nice to have. Unfortunately most such discussions carry the suggestion only to this stage, and no attempt is made to construct a procedure for measurement of desirabilities.

A majority of scholars have insisted that Values cannot be measured numerically. The only effective rebuttal to this argument is to present a quantitative system which deals with Values. Since no such system exists at present (except for very special situations), the only answer that can be made is that many of the quantities which we now regard as being measured fairly well were formerly considered to be unmeasurable. . . .

*　　*　　*　　*　　*

. . . [I]t is the unscientific folks in the workaday world who have provided the principal value scale currently available for use in a decision system. In short, let us get down to dollars and cents.

*　　*　　*　　*　　*

There is a large class of events for which I would be willing to specify the desirabilities numerically. For example, I could quote a number which would seem to be the appropriate desirability for such events as receiving a new suit or title to a new Chevrolet. The numerical value I would choose would be the *market value* of the item.

Because market values are so much a part and parcel of our everyday life, we may be inclined to overlook the remarkable features of this particular Value System. In the first place it assigns a numerical value to a very wide range of commodities and services. There is not much in common between a new car and a bushel of apples, but both are evaluated on the same scale; that is, in terms of dollars and cents. This in itself is a noteworthy accomplishment.

But even more surprising is the widespread acceptance of this Value System by people in all conditions of life and various backgrounds. . . . In view of the diversity of backgrounds and tastes of individuals and the tendency for differences in value systems to produce emotional reactions, this widespread acceptance of market values gives us some hope that it is possible to construct other value systems which will also be acceptable to a majority of the people.

*   *   *   *   *

The contribution of the economists lies in the conception of an alternative value scale to the dollar-and-cents scale—the Utility scale (Utility has a specialized meaning here). The process of constructing this scale is similar to the process which determines market values. The resemblance is not surprising since the concept Utility grew out of attempts to explain market values. However, the Utility scale is an *individual's* value scale rather than a consensus.

*   *   *   *   *

In principle, at least, this procedure could be extended to study the intuitive Value System of any individual and to measure the Utility of goods or services on some single scale. . . .

Let me emphasize that Utility has so far been employed as a handy *conceptual* tool only. The process for the determination of Utilities as *numbers* needs much more development.

*   *   *   *   *

In looking for rules for action it is well to realize at the very beginning that no rules can be constructed which will lead to the most favorable results in every case. Since both prediction systems and value systems are imperfect, it follows that the rules for actions which spring from these systems must likewise be imperfect.

It is true that most authors who have laid down rules for action have not taken this view, that they regard actions as right or wrong in an absolute sense. This authoritarian attitude is popular with politicians, moralists, and editorial writers but the long, sad history of failures of the infallible has led to widespread skepticism in our times. People with the courage to look at the world about them as it is, rather than as they would like it to be, have realized that all action is attended by risk.

More and more one hears the phrase calculated risk in connection with decisions, especially at the international level. When this is used to justify a choice of action it implies that the favored action is not guaranteed to lead to a desired end, but rather that it seems more likely to do so than the alternative actions. Moreover the word "calculated" implies that this conclusion is reached by a deliberate analysis of the situation and historical precedents.

This attitude of calculated risk underlies Statistical Decision. However, Statistical Decision carries this viewpoint one stage further and translates the uncertainties and values into numbers rather than words. Hence in Statistical Decision the risks are, quite literally, *calculated.*

The preceding chapters have discussed the quantification of values and uncertainties and the determination of desirabilities and probabilities. When this has been done we have a list of possible actions, a list of possible outcomes for each action, the numerical consequences of each outcome, the probability associated with each outcome, and the costs associated with each line of action. What is needed now is some way of putting all of these numbers together in such a way that the choice of action can be determined. I have previously called such a rule a *criterion for decision.*

*   *   *   *   *

SOME POSSIBLE RULES

... *1.* Consider the most probable outcome for each action (the outcome which has the largest probability) and the desirabilities associated with these most probable outcomes. Choose the action for which the desirability of the most probable outcome is as large as possible.

* * * * *

... *2.* (Optimistic.) Choose the action which *could* lead to the *most* favorable outcome.

* * * * *

... *3.* (Pessimistic.) Consider the *least* favorable outcome possible for each action. Of this set of least favorable outcomes one will be more favorable than others. Take the action associated with this outcome.

* * * * *

... *4.* Choose the course of action which has the largest mathematical expectation.

* * * * *

... *5.* Select the action associated with the largest of the least favorable expectations.

[EDITORS' NOTE: See, J. J. O'Connell, "Decision Making Rules and Computational Techniques," for further information on decision rules.]

* * * * *

In the past, and even today, it is not uncommon for scientists to disagree violently on the conclusions to be drawn from a given body of data. But although there may be a complete deadlock at the data level, it may be possible for the scientists to agree at the next higher level, i.e., on the *rules* for drawing inferences from data. If agreement is reached on these rules, and these rules are applied to the data, then agreement on the interpretation of the data may be obtained.

I think that Statistical Decision can play much the same role outside the boundaries of science; that is, it *could* be a method for reaching group decisions. The agreement of two or more individuals is often an important aspect of everyday decisions.

It may be easier for a group to agree on probabilities and desirabilities than on actions considered per se. If probabilities and desirabilities are still too controversial then it may be possible to agree on the next level—Prediction and Value Systems. In any case, these concepts of Statistical Decision may at least serve to break down the main problem into a number of smaller, and possibly simpler, problems. The attempt to think in terms of numbers instead of words may in itself help to clear the atmosphere. Somehow the use of words always seems to inject irrelevant or emotion-charged issues into a discussion. . . .

* * * * *

Some readers, I'm sure, have felt that the Decision-Maker is a cold-hearted—even grim—method of making decisions. These readers might be willing to admit that a machine may be all right for making the scientific decisions which I have largely emphasized in the text, or even for commercial decisions, but they may feel that Statistical Decision has no place in their own world, that it is meaningless insofar as personal, governmental, or international decisions are concerned.

I disagree with this view point. I think that Statistical Decision can play a useful role in a wider class of decisions and in particular in those decisions which have a direct influence on all of us.

I certainly do not consider Statistical Decision to be a panacea. It is one method among many methods of reaching decisions. It is not necessarily the best method; there are situations in which intuitive procedures lead to more effective decisions than any existing Decision-Maker. . . .

. . . I do think that the principles which underlie the Decision-Maker can also be used, informally, to arrive at effective choices of actions to be taken in everyday situations. In fact, I think that most people with common sense have already used many of the principles in making their decisions. All that the statisticians have done is to borrow these notions and dress them up in the symbolic language.

You may have felt that such concepts as mathematical expectation were new and unfamiliar. However, if you scrutinize the concept itself closely you will find antecedents in everyday experience. In the symbolic notation, mathematical expectation may look esoteric, but I'm sure that you can recall occasions when you have had to make decisions on the basis of expectations, when you have had to combine probabilities and desirabilities (though you probably did not use these names or make the combination in the same manner as a mathematical expectation).

Laplace once described probability as "common sense reduced to calculation" and I think this applies equally well to the whole of Statistical Decision.

In the process of reducing common sense to calculation, we are doing a job of translation. The mere *attempt* to make a translation into the symbolic language may be very useful. Even if the translation is only partially completed it may serve to bring into focus—or even resolve—problems which are almost insurmountable in the verbal language.

BECK PLASTICS CORPORATION

I Case Introduction

Synopsis

Under the leadership of the production vice president, C. T. Vincent, two staff executives, W. W. John and R. L. Davidson, have devised a production system which specifies what operations are necessary to produce plastic products. They have also designed a decision system by which customer orders are translated into a detailed plan by three levels of management—each breaking down the overall plan handed to him into more specific plans for those working under him.

The plan does not work in practice, as evidenced by quality or quantity deviations when customer delivery time arrives. The production vice president diagnoses the cause of the trouble, and passes his decision to the production manager, who in turn talks with the foreman.

Why This Case Is Included

The case shows the necessity for rational planning of production in terms of input-output synchronization of the primary operations. It also shows how a decision elaboration system is necessary to implement this plan. The actions of the various executives reveal something of executive motivation (why executives believe as they do). The case offers opportunity to study the very subtle relationship between (a) the logic of rational planning versus the immediate motivation of subordinates, and (b) the logic of rational planning versus the development of executives. Finally, the way in which leadership style affects subordinate development can be studied.

Diagnostic and Predictive Questions

In answering the following diagnostic and predictive questions, remember that these questions apply theories and conceptual ideas from certain disciplines. Such theories are valuable to understand basic forces at work in the policy system (diagnosis) and to predict what will happen in the system in the future (prediction). Since each reading abstracts from the total policy system certain factors or variables into the closed or partial viewpoint of one theory or discipline, no one reading gives answers to the practical policy problems of the case. In diagnosis and prediction, the parts of the problem are studied with "other things being equal."

Following each question are listed readings which will be helpful in answering the question. The readings included with this case are marked (*). By referring to the author index at the end of this book, you may locate the other readings listed.

1. Why does Mr. Beck express great pride in the company's engineering plan? Why are Davidson and Walt John motivated to compile such a plan?

Read: Galbraith, *The Affluent Society*, pp. 121–24, 126. Veblen, *The Engineers and the Price System*, pp. 439–40. Friedman, *Law in a Changing Society*, pp. 3–6, 22–23. Beard, *Public Policy and the General Welfare*, p. 148. *Hampton, Summer, and Webber, *Organizational Behavior*, chap. x.

2. Why do Vincent and Peabody feel *intellectually* committed to follow Davidson's and John's engineering plan?

Read: *Locke, *Concerning Civil Government*, chap. x. O'Donnell, "The Source of Managerial Authority." Fayol, *General and Industrial Management*, pp. 24–25, 68–70. Simon, Smithburg, and Thompson, *Public Administration*, pp. 182, 189–200.

3. What dormant emotional feelings on the part of Peabody and Vincent might the engineering plan of Davidson and John arouse?

Read: *Leavitt, *Managerial Psychology*, pp. 16–21, 24–26.

4. Why did the warehouseman "forget to snap the bin catch"? Why did the drillers "make a mistake" and drill only 6,000 parts for Rankin Company? In other words, why did these men not obey "legitimate" authority?

Read: Argyris, *Personality and Organization*, pp. 27–28, 157.

5. Why did the four men in finishing ask for a transfer? Why did they later request a pay raise? Why did they engage in union activity? Why might other workers in the plant become interested in the union?

Read: Argyris, *Personality and Organization*, pp. 27–28, 157. *Maslow, *Motivation and Personality*, pp. 80–94.

6. When Bergstrom told the four men that he didn't "know about the transfer situation," what effect did this have on their feelings and attitudes?

Read: *Leavitt, *Managerial Psychology*, pp. 16–21, 24–26.

7. Recall that Vincent appointed Davidson to investigate the situation, that Davidson then reported to Vincent the facts from Tom Sullivan, and that Vincent then showed Peabody the facts and told him what responsibility seemed to lie in two places.

   a) In a decision-making sense, whose "minds" are learning to be interested in, and to *feel* responsible for, integrating human factors and technological factors into balanced, wise, company decisions?

   b) Whose mind is being denied the day-to-day experiences that develop such interests, feelings, and abilities?

   c) Write a few paragraphs on the effect of Vincent's and Davidson's actions on the development of Peabody as an executive, his interests, abilities, and attitudes. Explain what caused Peabody to say, "Now that this has come up, there is no need for me in the act. . . . I hope that Vincent and the others continue to hold such meetings."

Preparation: There are no specific reading assignments for these questions. Use your own common sense and thoughtful analysis, and you will discover some insights which otherwise might have been included in readings from learning theory.

8. When Peabody thought about the problem of the four workers and then "told Ralph to remind them that Beck is paying above average," what effect did this kind of behavior have on:

a) Bergstrom's development (in interests, attitudes and decision-making capabilities) as a manager?

b) Bergstrom's later behavior—when he said that if he has any more trouble out of them that he will ask *Peabody* to handle it, and when he told the four workers that he did not know anything about the transfer situation?

Read: Same Leavitt reading as in Question 3, but use your own creative analysis and judgment to add factors about Bergstrom's interests, attitudes, and decision capabilities. Think about his *feelings* of competence and responsibility, and his actual competence, abilities, and interests.

Policy Questions for This Specific Case

In answering the following policy questions, the results of diagnosis and prediction are used to reduce the amount of guesswork, or judgment, in designing action solutions. However, since certain parts of the total case situation cannot be reduced to science, and since "other things are not equal," judgment must still be used to fill in the factors not accounted for by readings. You will also need a second kind of judgment as you put value weights on different scientific predictions, since different theories may point to conflicting solutions.

9. In terms of company efficiency and profits, state the key problems of the Beck Corporation in these three areas:

a) The morale and commitment of workers.

b) The decision system—who thinks carefully about technological plans, about human motivations, and then judges or weighs these and arrives at balanced, wise decisions for the company.

c) The morale, capabilities, interests, and attitudes of middle executives—the Bergstroms, Peabodys, and Vincents.

10. What longer-range action program might you design that would develop the middle executives—have them feel responsible for wise decisions, and give attention to the kinds of problems in Question 9?

11. If you were Vincent, how would you act tomorrow morning with Peabody in order to "develop" him? If you were Peabody, how would you act tomorrow morning with Bergstrom in order to "develop" him? It will help greatly if you sit down with another member of the class, each of you playing one of these parts, and act out the situation. At the end of the role play, ask yourselves: What were your goals at the beginning of the role play—what effects on knowledge, attitudes, or skills were you trying to achieve with Peabody (or Bergstrom)? At completion, ask: How successful was the interview in terms of original objectives?

Major Policy Issues: Tentative Generalizations about Any Policy System

In arriving at conclusions for the following questions, generalize from the facts in the case and use your own ideas to (*a*) confirm, (*b*) modify, or (*c*) test the workability of the concepts and theories from readings. As an executive or professional, use wisdom to merge theory, on the one hand, with "brute facts" and practice, on the other.

12. What is meant by the term "executive development," that is, what kinds of knowledge, feelings and attitudes should be the goals of development?

13. What does the term "delegation of responsibility" mean? How is this achieved in an organization,
   —in terms of legal status?
   —in terms of function in the organization?
   —in terms of feelings within the individual?

Questions for Original Student Work in Analysis and Policy

The methods of viewing this case as represented by the authors' questions and selection of readings are not exhaustive. There are other relevant ideas for diagnosis and prediction. Furthermore, there are other ways of stating policy questions. More powerful analyses and wiser solutions will result by drawing on your own training and experience for (a) relevant concepts and theories, and (b) creative ways of asking policy questions. The following questions are designed to help you acquire this skill.

14. While reflecting on case facts, what additional theories from prior education give you insights as to "what is going on" in Beck Plastics Corporation? As to what might be predicted to happen in the future?

15. Other than the policy questions asked by the authors, what pragmatic ways can you think of to state the practical problems faced by executives in the case?

II Beck Plastics Corporation

Beck Plastics Corporation is engaged in the manufacture and sale of plastic parts to a wide variety of manufacturing companies located principally in Michigan, Ohio, Illinois, and Indiana. With headquarters in Cleveland, the company has experienced considerable growth over the last 10 years, to the point where it employs 1,850 people. A. F. Beck, president and principal owner, estimates that the company will double in size in the next six years; plans are being made to open an additional plant in Illinois, and eventually to "go national," marketing Beck products throughout the United States.

Industrial customers use Beck products either as external trim for their own products or as internal components for these products. In the former case, products are first injection molded and then buffed to smooth out irregularities on the surface caused by the molding process. This is usually followed by a process of drilling holes in the product, and by painting. In the case of internal components, the molded product is usually routed directly to the drilling operation, or directly to shipping inventory, without being buffed and painted. Exhibit 1 shows both the work flow (input-output process between departments) and the authority structure of the Production Division. It will be seen that, for authority and managerial purposes, the eight primary operations at the bottom of the organization are grouped under four foremen and that these are in turn grouped

Exhibit 1

ORGANIZATION STRUCTURE, BECK PLASTICS CORPORATION

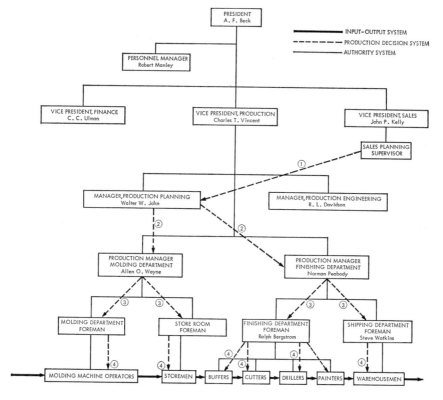

under two production managers, one for Molding and one for Finishing and Shipping.

The "Permanent" Operating Plan: Production Division

Mr. Beck expresses great pride in the company's engineering plan. This has been worked out primarily by the manager of production engineering who, according to Beck,

. . . is a staff man who designs the plant layout and management structure on a more or less permanent basis. He knows machinery and plastics processes and has been responsible for laying out our physical production line and the jobs to match it, including the organization of foremen and department managers for Molding and Finishing. Bob Davidson has been with the company 11 years since getting out of the military service. Before that he graduated from Purdue in engineering. As the company grew, he took our projected product line and capacity estimates and designed both the physical flows and the boxes on the chart I have given you. [Mr. Beck is referring to both the light lines, boxes, dotted lines, and heavy lines in Exhibit 1.] This has resulted in a series of job responsibilities for all concerned. At the lowest level these responsibilities take the form of work activities of machine operators and warehousemen, often devised with the help of time and motion studies, or the industry standards we get from the Methods Engineering Council of Pittsburgh. These show the proper job methods for, say, a buffer or molding machine operator, regardless of whether in our company or in a company in Kalamazoo. At the middle-management levels, these responsibilities show that each foreman's job responsibility is to receive production requirement information from the two department managers (Wayne and Peabody) and then to devise their own schedules for the different operators under them. Peabody and Wayne, on the other hand, get their master schedule from Walt John, manager of current production and inventory planning. His work is to receive the sales orders from John Kelly's sales planning supervisor, and translate them into a superschedule which coordinates all of our complicated manufacturing jobs with the sales department and the customer.

So you see, a company like ours cannot do without a man like Davidson. In competition with others who are doing a good planning job, we must do a *better* one for two reasons. We have to keep our customers satisfied as to timing and quantity, and we have to prevent waste of time and manpower in the production process so that we can be efficient and charge reasonable prices.

The "Current" Operating Plan

Walter John, manager of production planning, executes the above plan on a monthly and weekly basis. Whereas Davidson sets the structure or standing procedure for planning (deciding on production), John and the line executives execute the dynamic decision making. John receives sales orders on Mondays, works out a schedule on Tuesday and Wednesday showing qualities and quantities of items, and forwards these to Wayne and Peabody on Wednesday afternoon. The latter two men prepare subplans on Thursday for delivery to foremen on Friday morning. The foremen in turn translate these into schedules for their workers to begin on Monday morning. There is thus a week of planning activities being performed by the various levels of supervision (for next week) at the same time that the operators at the bottom of the organization are executing work during the current week.

Problems in Supplying Customers

Over the past year, there have been a number of times when customer trucks would arrive at the shipping platform when their orders were not ready in the warehouse. John Kelly, sales vice president, has studied this problem and estimates that Beck has lost one large customer and five smaller customers because of "repetition of our failure to deliver on time."

As an illustration of the problem, the case writer was present when John Kelly came into Vincent's office to report some trouble with a present customer, Lawrence Manufacturing Company. This company purchases approximately $540,000 in products from Beck each year.

KELLY: Charlie, I just got another call from the purchasing agent at Lawrence. His trucker came back to his plant with an incomplete load for the second time in three weeks. Believe me, he sounded sore, and it sounds like the way we lost the Dodge account.

VINCENT: John, I've done as much as I can to stop this. I've hinted to Norm Peabody a dozen times this year that things are not well in the finishing end of the business. You and I both have impressed on him several times the absolute necessity for producing products on time, according to the master schedule.

KELLY: Have you found out what's wrong?

VINCENT: I think I have. And I don't like it. I started investigating about three months ago. I figured it could be the production plan, as devised by Walt John, further elaborated by Norm Peabody himself, and still further broken down by his two foremen. *Or,* it could be that Peabody and the foremen aren't getting the workers to execute this plan. Well, I told Norm that we were going to do a thorough study. Bob Davidson was assigned a project to check up on how the workers were performing. His report shows one thing: We have a good inventory plan but Peabody isn't giving enough attention to employee motivation and discipline.

KELLY: Well, something has got to be done. If we lose a Lawrence or two, A.F. will be on everybody's necks. I can hear him now—"We've simply got to determine where the responsibility lies."

VINCENT: I am going to have another talk with Peabody. The operations have got to be shaped up or else. I'm afraid he is in trouble.

The Davidson Report

Two months ago, at the end of a one-month project, Bob Davidson issued a report on some of the things he had observed in the Finishing and Shipping Department. Davidson, whose responsibility has been specified as a staff man to Vincent, issued his report to the latter who discussed it with Norm Peabody. Here are some of Davidson's comments.

When Tom Sullivan [warehouseman] was asked of there were difficulties in filling orders, he replied: "Difficulties? Have you been up in the warehouse recently? Yesterday, Steve Watkins [shipping foreman] sent me up there to get out an order, and a whole pile of carbons had fallen in the aisle. It seems that one of the other warehousemen had forgotten to snap the bin catch after he finished. Then when I found the parts for Rankin Company, I found also that there were only 6,000 of them when the master plan showed that there should be 8,000. Steve phoned over and chewed out Ralph Bergstrom, the finishing foreman. They finally found that the drillers had made a mistake and drilled only 6,000. The other 2,000 raw moldings were found in the molding storeroom, waiting for somebody to pick them up for delivery to the Finishing Department."

Later, Vincent showed this incident to Peabody. He told Peabody that responsibility seemed to lie in two places—the warehousemen were not interested enough in their jobs to maintain the warehouse properly, thus causing delays with spilled products; and the drillers obviously lacked motivation to read the production schedules correctly and take pride in producing what is called for. He suggested that Peabody should give more attention to morale of his men, and that this would pay off in better production.

Problems in Finishing Operations

Products may flow through four operations in the Finishing Department: buffing, cutting, drilling, and painting. In addition, there is a grinding operation at the end of the lines where rejected moldings are ground up into plastic chips to be returned to the Molding Department, melted down, and fed into the molding machines.

Buffing removes marks left on the parts by the molding machine, the buffer holding the part against a buffing wheel and being careful to hold the part firmly so that the wheel does not pull it from his hands. Cutting insures that a part is the proper length or that some unwanted part is removed. The cutter places the part in a prealigned gripping device while a circular blade cuts the plastic. In drilling, the operator also places the part in a gripping device and pushes a button. The drill bit descends, drills a hole, ascends, and a jet of compressed air blows away excess plastic. Painting involves placing parts on trays in an enclosure and turning on the sprayers. After moving through at a predetermined speed, parts emerge, and the sprayers automatically turn off.

Five months ago, four workers came to Ralph Bergstrom to ask if they could get transferred either to molding machine positions or to warehouseman positions. Bergstrom told them that he did not know about the transfer situation, since Peabody handled the shipping section. Bergstrom said that he did not know who handled transfers to the Molding Department—"Maybe Thompson or Vincent or Davidson. Why don't you see them?"

These same four men have been, according to Bergstrom,

. . . real troublemakers. Other men in the department do a fair day's work, except they goof too often in following the schedule. But these guys—they are always griping. After I suggested they see Vincent or somebody about transfers, they sat around as usual a few weeks and then came to say that they had just as soon have a pay raise, and that I ought to go to Peabody about this.

Well, about a week ago, I went to Peabody but good, and the situation was so hot that he went straight to Vincent. I hear that they even got hold of Beck within an hour. You see, for about two months we have been finding some literature about labor unions lying around the plant. Well, over in one side of the drilling area, neatly wrapped in boxes, I found a whole supply of leaflets printed by the union that organizes in the plastics industry. One of the first I opened was a pamphlet called "What a Seniority System Can Do for You." It went on to say how the union could bargain out a plan that would force the company to transfer men to different jobs they might want—that any man could bid on any opening in any department, and if he has enough seniority he will get the job and the company has to give him a training period.

Within two days, Vincent and Bob Manley, the personnel manager, held three identical meetings, so that they could talk to every man in the plant.

Interviews with Vincent and Peabody

Norman Peabody is 38 years old, married, and has two children in high school. He has been with Beck Corporation 11 years, having graduated from Kent State University, served two years in the Air Force as a noncommissioned officer, and worked for another company two years. For his first year with the company, he rotated between all seven major jobs as a production worker. Peabody's parents lived in the same neighborhood in Cleveland as the Vincent family, and Charlie Vincent got to know him well while he was in high school. Vincent states that because the company has a difficult time finding younger men for positions in management, particularly men who are willing to work hard in their careers, and accept responsibility, he recognized Norm Peabody as potentially successful. He [Vincent] felt that he could do a favor for both the company and for Norm if he provided a place for him to further his career. Peabody subsequently became foreman of the Finishing Section for three years, shipping foreman for three years, and has been in his present position for five years. As manager of Finishing and Shipping, he is the highest paid person in the Manufacturing Division except for Davidson and Vincent. Until about a year ago, Vincent says, he was sure that Peabody would take his place when he retires and that he might even be president, since A. F. Beck has no relatives who are interested in the company.

Norman Peabody seemed genuinely interested in reporting the problems in the department to the case writer. He expressed his willingness to discuss frankly the recent situation involving union pamphlets, as well as other problems the company faces.

We have a really tough problem in finding workers today who have sufficient interest in their own future, and who believe in good work. I've read in the papers that younger people are changing in their outlook, and I can certainly verify it. You take those four that Bergstrom is having trouble with. Ralph came to me several weeks ago and said they had asked him for a raise. I try to make it a point to keep up with the wage structure that Bob Davidson sets on the basis of rather scientific job evaluation and surveys of what our competition is paying.

I told Ralph to remind them that Beck is paying slightly above the average for the plastics industry in the Midwest, and that we are higher than some neighboring industries in Cleveland which are not in our industry. I knew that, given Davidson's extensive and expert wage analysis, it was no use to bring up the issue of raising the whole pay structure in the company.

Ralph said that if he had any more trouble out of them he will ask me to talk to them. I told him I would. Now that this has come up, there is no need for me in the act, since Vincent and Manley have gone to great pains, with a lot of patience, to hold meetings and explain thoroughly our pay structure, employee benefits such as retirement and group insurance, and a whole host of other matters of interest to the men. Maybe our company should have been doing this all along. In fact, I hope that Charlie Vincent, Manley, and Davidson will continue to hold such meetings as a regular procedure. It seems to me that somehow we have got to educate the men in the plant as to what the company's competitive situation is, and what the company is doing in the way of personnel practices.

III Selected Readings

From: David Hampton, Charles Summer, and Ross Webber

ORGANIZATIONAL BEHAVIOR AND THE PRACTICE OF MANAGEMENT*

[EDITORS' NOTE: The authors are Professors at San Diego State University, Columbia University, and the University of Pennsylvania, respectively.]

THE MOTIVATION OF EXECUTIVES TO POLITICAL ACTION

The motivations which cause executives to design technological systems, to convert them to systems of authority, and (in some cases) to engage in strategic actions intended to influence others can be further analyzed into (1) the value (attitude) of technological necessity, (2) the desire to be head of an organization, (3) the competitive urge and the will to conquer, (4) the urge to creative action, (5) the need for symmetry as a means to security, and (6) the pragmatic position—"it works." Each of these will be discussed separately.

THE ATTITUDE OF TECHNOLOGICAL NECESSITY

Technological necessity was discussed in Chapter 7. Without being repetitious, let us recall that phenomenon.[1] We start with the fact that in industrially developed societies, specialization has progressed to a profound degree. Man and his family are dependent on the roundabout production process for almost everything they require in the form of material needs. The days of the nearly sufficient Vermont farm are gone forever, and one of society's great unwritten mores is what Galbraith has called "the paramount position of production." Whether in the United States or in Soviet Russia, the society has provided both "ethical" and "monetary" institutions which reward the executive when his organizational system is efficient, and which punish him when it is inefficient. Granted that there are sometimes other motivations which operate to prevent him from striving for *maximum* organizational efficiency, there are nevertheless powerful material and non-material pressures which cause him to put a high value on organizational efficiency.

This means, among other things, that the internal technological system of the firm or department—the rational division of this system into parts (specializa-

---

* Reprinted by permission of Scott, Foresman & Company, Chicago, Illinois, 1968 (chap. x).

[1] The description of the technological system in Chapter 7 of *Organizational Behavior and the Practice of Management,* including the powerful statements of Veblen, Friedman, and Beard, gives added emphasis to the necessity for both technological planning and political action.

tions) and the rational relating of one of these parts to others (planning the input-output system) —must be (1) designed (an act of rule formulation) and that (2) it must be cloaked with the symbols of authority and legitimacy.

In addition to this social belief in production and prevention of waste, together with rewards and penalties which cause executives to *learn* this value, there is undoubtedly the factor of training and education of the man himself. Stated simply, if one goes to business school or engineering school and learns finance, operations research, marketing, or any of the sub-fields of administration, this stored knowledge with its symbolic representation is a form of "invested capital" in one's own life and career. It represents one's functional importance in society—his repertoire of actions that help him cope with life in an industrial and economic world. This commitment no doubt reinforces the original social value attached to planning and implementing an efficient, "well run," "high quality" organization.

THE DESIRE TO BE HEAD OF AN ORGANIZATION

Some people, particularly those who rise to high positions in organizations, have found that the way to get what they want and to be secure in getting it in the future, is to rely on getting into positions of status and power. This is where we get the familiar phrase "empire building." Schumpeter, the great sociologist-economist, characterized the entrepreneur this way:

"In the breast of one who wishes to do something new . . . there is the dream and the will to found a private kingdom. . . . The modern world really does not know any such positions, but what may be attained by industrial or commercial success is still the nearest approach to medieval lordship possible to modern man. Its fascination is specially strong for people who have no other way of achieving social distinction. The sensation of power and independence loses nothing by the fact that both are largely illusions."[2]

Of course, this motivation comes to different people in degrees. In moderation, it is functional for the individual executive and functional for the organization. Running throughout much of the more accepted management literature is an implication that the executive has a degree of this motivation. When Chester Barnard . . . gives us the principles of cooperative action, we can see at least his self-confidence in creating a system for large numbers of people to live in and to follow in their behavior. This same might be said of Fayol's explanation of discipline and unity of command, of the casual way in which Newman lays out the purposes of standing policies and procedures, and of the tone in which Cordiner presents General Electric's vast philosophy for governing the behavior of 281,000 employees. Even Wilfred Brown, head of Glacier Metal Company in England, who brought industrial psychologists from Tavistock into his company, shows a high degree of self-confidence in his role as the most important single person responsible for instituting a specific "new order" for governing behavior within the firm.

In extreme cases, this desire to achieve a position of status and power can be dysfunctional for both the executive and for the organization. In literature, we have the "King Lear" syndrome, in which the desire for keeping one's status and prerogatives was so strong that decisions made by the King were finally unworkable with resulting disintegration of his own personality and rebellion by his subjects. Or, we need look only to Hitler in Germany to see the results of one

---

[2] Joseph A. Schumpeter, *Theory of Economic Development* (Cambridge, Mass.: Harvard University Press, 1934) , pp. 84–94.

imbued with maintaining personal office and power—resulting in organizational decisions which would not work.

A number of modern sociologists have cited cases where executives so focused on the rule system and the prerogatives of office, that they almost ignore changing needs of customers, of technology, or of other *facts* which should be considered in dynamic decision-making. . . .

COMPETITION AND THE WILL TO CONQUER

But Schumpeter gives us another set of motivations, which have some verification in subsequent studies in clinical psychology:

> "Then there is the will to conquer: the impulse to fight, to prove oneself superior to others, to succeed for the sake, not of the fruits of success, but of success itself. From this aspect, economic action becomes akin to sport—there are financial races, or rather boxing matches . . ."[3]

This motivation, too, comes parceled to differing executives in differing degrees. And here, too, moderation may well be functional for both the organization and the individual executive.

We recall from Gellerman's summary of "The Power Motive" as conceptualized by the psychoanalyst, Adler . . . , that all men may have some of this type of motivation. And in economics, the very essence of "free enterprise" has been the competitive instinct. Too little of this motivation may result in one's being a follower but not a leader, and too much may result in pathological or dysfunctional outcomes. . . . Bennis and Shepard . . . clearly [show] that, in their orientations toward authority, some people tend to have formed habitual behavior patterns of dependency, others of counter-dependency, and still others of "independency."

In extreme cases, we should not discount the possibility that the *executive* can be the one who plays Berne's deadly game, "Now I've Got You You Son of a Bitch." . . . If he plays for the rules *per se,* without regard for the reality of decisions, and if his primary motivational repertoire consists of the one strategy to check up on people, to "place the blame," this seems the proper diagnosis.

THE URGE TO CREATIVE ACTION

A third executive motivation often cited in the literature is aptly put by Schumpeter:

> "[In addition to the dream of a private kingdom, and the will to conquer] there is the joy of creating, of getting things done, or simply of exercising one's energy and ingenuity. . . . Our [executive] type seeks out difficulties, changes in order to change, delights in ventures."[4]

Schumpeter goes on to explain that there *would be no leaders* if there were not some people who possess certain mental characteristics which enable them to get outside of their routine way of living in the organization. There are three reasons why, for many human beings, it is difficult to create new things and get things done. First, there is great risk—mental risk—in doing something new, in which the outcome is unknown. Action must be taken without working out all of the details, and success depends partly upon *Intuition.* Therefore, there is a lack

---

3 *Idem.*
4 *Idem.*

of objective information "out there." Secondly, even if there were not objective insecurity out there, there is subjective insecurity for the human mind to do something new. "In the breast of one who wishes to do something new, the forces of habit rise up to bear witness against the embryonic project. A new and *another kind* of effort of will is necessary. This mental freedom presupposes a great surplus force over the everyday demand and is something peculiar and by nature rare."[5] Thirdly, even if one can overcome the two obstacles above, there is a reaction of the social environment against one who wishes to do something new. For all of these reasons, we take the position in the present chapter that the men who actually engage in political action—who actively make rules, and who engage in dynamic action to get them instituted—are motivated in part by these kinds of feelings. Remembering the Maslow theory of human motivation . . . , we see that such men are engaging in a kind of self-fulfillment—and they have found a way of life to do this, that of political action.

At a number of points in this book, we have seen that there is another kind of executive who relies on the existing rules to achieve security and status, who "goes by the book," who is satisfied by the feeling of importance of office and title, and whose mental reactions are similar to the less innovating individual described above. That there are such executives cannot be denied. They are motivated by the two first of Schumpeter's forces (empire ruling and the will to conquer), but not especially by the third.

SYMMETRY AS A MEANS TO SECURITY

Mental security—"peace of mind"—results in part when a person lives in an orderly world, in which "everything is in its place," and in which there are few unexpected events. If you expect that your class will begin at 10 o'clock and that there will be an examination on Chapters 3–7 in the book, think what it does to your feelings of security if the professor shows up at 10:30, or if he gives the examination on Chapters 5–8!

This kind of motivation operates for both general (line) executives and for specialist (staff) executives. In the former case, sociologists have pointed out that many executives have "a demand for control," and that this causes them to make rules for uniformity, or standards for measuring results. Given the necessity for technological coordination, the executive is much more secure if he can predict what people will do in the organization, and if he has uniform standards and policies so that all parts and people don't have to be viewed individually. Throughout the readings by Barnard . . . , Newman, Cordiner, and Brown, we see the need expressed in orderly procedures, policies and standards.

In the case of staff specialist executives, this need is expressed in the desire to formulate business operations on the basis of certain *known* bodies of knowledge. The finance specialist is much more secure in his thinking if he has tools of marginal analysis or discounted cash flow to apply to investment decisions or pricing problems. The marketing specialist's mind is much more at ease if there are known ways of predicting consumer motivation or of choosing advertising media. And the Operations Research specialist, through use of formulas for inventory control, can do his work much more securely than if he had to face entirely new projects, without models for approaching them. This kind of motivation is clear . . . when staff men are sometimes given "functional authority."

Thus, both general executives and specialist executives have an additional reason for formulating standing plans and rules, and for instituting them in organizations. Such rules enable them to pursue their careers, and use their

---

[5] *Idem.*

minds, with less mental strain and frustration than if there were no systems, rules, and order.

THE PRAGMATIC POSITION—"IT WORKS"

A final reason why executives engage in political action is that all human beings need law and order in an interdependent organization, and the executive recognizes either explicitly or intuitively that he *can* take such action.

This has already been explained . . . on more than one level analysis. Locke's philosophical explanation of human passion, Presthus' emphasis on reduction of anxiety among peers, and Gouldner's explanation of how rule systems reduce anxiety between superiors and subordinates all confirm that the executive can, if he does so wisely, govern human behavior through formulation of systems of law and order.

The many other studies in this book which show that people react to authority systems in ways which are dysfunctional should, however, serve as a warning. The phrase "if he does so wisely" is an important one. Later in this chapter, we will examine how the technological rule system is converted to legitimate law and order.

DESIGNING THE TECHNOLOGICAL SYSTEM

It may seem odd that in a chapter on political action, we begin with a section called "Designing the Technological System." Does this not sound like engineering or economics instead of politics? The answer lies in the fact that the technological system—the organizational output goals, the system of working parts, and the input-output relationships between them—are at one and the same time the technical work operations to be performed by each part of the organization, and the rules of human conduct which the part (person, department) should follow. . . .

From: John Locke
*CONCERNING CIVIL GOVERNMENT**

The great and chief end, therefore, of men uniting into commonwealths, and putting themselves under government, is the preservation of their property; to which in the state of Nature there are many things wanting.

Firstly, there wants an established, settled, known law, received and allowed by common consent to be the standard of right and wrong, and the common measure to decide all controversies between them. For though the law of Nature be plain and intelligible to all rational creatures, yet men, being biased by their interest, as well as ignorant for want of study of it, are not apt to allow of it as a law binding to them in the application of it to their particular cases.

Secondly, in the state of Nature there wants a known and indifferent judge,

---

* Encyclopaedia Britannica, Inc., William Benton, Publisher, Chicago, 1952, The Great Ideas, Vol. 35 (pp. 53–54).

with authority to determine all differences according to the established law. For every one in that state of being both judge and executioner of the law of Nature, men being partial to themselves, passion and revenge is very apt to carry them too far, and with too much heat in their own cases, as well as negligence and unconcernedness, make them too remiss in other men's.

Thirdly, in the state of Nature there often wants power to back and support the sentence when right, and to give it due execution. They who by any injustice offended will seldom fail where they are able by force to make good their injustice. Such resistance many times makes the punishment dangerous, and frequently destructive to those who attempt it.

Thus mankind, notwithstanding all the privileges of the state of Nature, being but in an ill condition while they remain in it are quickly driven into society. Hence it comes to pass, that we seldom find any number of men live any time together in this state. The inconveniences that they are therein exposed to by the irregular and uncertain exercise of the power every man has of punishing the transgressions of others, make them take sanctuary under the established laws of government, and therein seek the preservation of their property. It is this makes them so willingly give up every one his single power of punishing to be exercised by such alone as shall be appointed to it amongst them, and by such rules as the community, or those authorised by them to that purpose, shall agree on. And in this we have the original right and rise of both the legislative and executive power as well as of the governments and societies themselves.

For in the state of Nature to omit the liberty he has of innocent delights, a man has two powers. . . .

The first power—viz., of doing whatsoever he thought fit for the preservation of himself and the rest of mankind, he gives up to be regulated by laws made by the society, so far forth as the preservation of himself and the rest of that society shall require; which laws of the society in many things confine the liberty he had by the law of Nature.

Secondly, the power of punishing he wholly gives up, and engages his natural force, which he might before employ in the execution of the law of Nature, by his own single authority, as he thought fit, to assist the executive power of the society as the law thereof shall require. For being now in a new state, wherein he is to enjoy many conveniencies from the labour, assistance, and society of others in the same community, as well as protection from its whole strength, he is to part also with as much of his natural liberty, in providing for himself, as the good, prosperity, and safety of the society shall require, which is not only necessary but just, since the other members of the society do the like. . . .

. . . And so, whoever has the legislative or supreme power of any commonwealth, is bound to govern by established standing laws, promulgated and known to the people, and not by extemporary decrees, by indifferent and upright judges, who are to decide controversies by those laws; and to employ the force of the community at home only in the execution of such laws, or abroad to prevent or redress foreign injuries and secure the community from inroads and invasion. . . .

From: Harold J. Leavitt

MANAGERIAL PSYCHOLOGY*

[EDITORS' NOTE: The author is Professor of Psychology at Stanford University.]

DEPENDENCY AND THE DEVELOPMENT OF PERSONALITY

The most important issue seems to be this one: Can we, with as few assumptions as possible, account for the development of individually different adult personalities? For the back-slapping sales manager and the quick, methodical comptroller?

A theory, it has been said, is as good as its ratio of predictions to assumptions. To economize on assumptions, we may assume here that only the basic physical needs are inherited and then go on from there. It is then possible to account broadly for the elaborate complex of needs that exists in a twenty-year-old while assuming that all he had to begin with were (1) his basic physical needs and (2) his body. In his "body" we must include his sense organs, plus his memory—a mechanism for retaining information picked up by the sense organs—plus a decision-making mechanism, plus a tendency to be stingy in the expenditure of energy, plus a muscular system that allows the person to move and act upon his environment. If that is the person's original basic equipment, it is almost enough to account for the accessories he will have added by the time he is ten or twenty or forty. But he still needs one more characteristic, a characteristic that is not so much a part of the person as of the relationship between the person and the world. This additional characteristic is *dependency*—the dependency of the newborn infant on parents for the satisfaction of his needs; the dependency of the growing child on parents, teachers, and friends; of husband on wife; and of people in industry on their bosses; and vice versa.

If the human infant came into the world with almost complete physical development, like some other animal young, then we might have to devise quite a different theory to account for the adult personality. In fact, if the infant could fend for himself from the start, the adult personality would be noticeably different from what it is.

But any infant who survives to adulthood has necessarily passed through a period in which he was almost entirely dependent upon other peope for the satisfaction of his basic physical needs. And this dependency, coupled with the presence of physical needs and a good but incomplete physical plant, may give us the leverage to account for the development of a great many secondary and tertiary mental needs. To see how this dependency lever might work, consider this entirely hypothetical illustration:

> Suppose that you suffer from a magical ailment. The major symptom of the ailment is paralysis—complete paralysis. But though you are paralyzed, your head is perfectly clear and your senses are perfectly keen. You can hear, you can see, you can feel, and you can think—but you can't move.

---

* Reprinted by permission of the University of Chicago Press, Chicago, Illinois, 2d. ed., 1964 (pp. 16–21; 24–26).

You have a brother who possesses a magical gift. Whenever his hand is on your shoulder you are cured; you can move as well as anyone else. But when he takes his hand away the paralysis immediately returns.

Assume that your brother is a nice guy; he spends a good deal of his time with his hand on your shoulder, and he goes through considerable inconvenience to do this. Through his help you can lead something approximating a normal life. You have not had this disease very long, but by now you have gotten over the shock that it entailed, and you are trying to settle down to the best life you can work out.

This morning you awake, but of course you cannot move. You lie in bed until your brother comes in to put his hand on your shoulder. Whereupon you rise, dress, and wash. You have breakfast, chat, and read the morning paper. You do everything that you may have done before you had the disease.

Over breakfast your brother announces that he forgot to tell you he has a dentist's appointment this morning. He will have to leave the house about ten. He probably will not be back until noon. This is a matter of no great concern to you, since it's just a two-hour absence.

With his hand on your shoulder you arrange a comfortable place in which you can sit while your brother is gone. You set an easy chair by the window, put your feet on an ottoman, and tune in a radio to a program you particularly like. You open the window to let the warm air and sun in and to see what's going on outside. You settle down for the two-hour absence.

Your brother leaves.

For half an hour or so, as you expected, things are fine. You are perfectly comfortable; there's enough activity outdoors to keep you interested; and the radio program is good.

At ten-thirty the program changes to the thing you hate most—hillbilly music—but that's of no major concern. A fly manages to get through a hole in the screen and begins to buzz around your nose—but this is just one of those inconveniences you have now learned to bear.

By eleven o'clock there's a little itch from a rough place in the chair, but that's bearable, too. The fly is still around. The hillbilly music goes on. At eleven-thirty the sky clouds over. The air gets cold and windy. At a quarter to twelve it's raining hard. You're getting wet and cold. If you could shiver, you would. The itches increase. Your bladder begins to get a little too full for comfort.

But you reassure yourself: fifteen minutes more.

At noon you're waiting hopefully for your brother's step, but you don't hear it. He doesn't show at twelve-fifteen. The cold and the wet and the itches and the bladder and the fly and the radio become almost unbearable. By twelve-forty-five you're on the verge of explosion. One o'clock and no brother, but more rain, more discomfort.

At just about one-thirty you hear footfalls. Brother walks in, puts his hand on your shoulder, and says: "I was caught in a traffic jam. I'm sorry I'm late."

Now let the reader seriously ask himself these questions:
1. Just how would you *feel* about your brother at this moment?
2. What do you think you would *do* to your brother at this moment?
Your answers probably fall into one of these major categories: (1) I would feel angry and resentful. (2) I would feel extemely relieved; extremely grateful that he had finally arrived. (3) I would feel mixed up: angry and resentful, on the one hand, and relieved and grateful, on the other.

To the action question, answers range from: (1) I would sock him on the nose to (2) I would throw my arms around him and kiss him.

Each of these answers is appropriate and understandable. Together they represent the necessary conflict of feelings that derive from the complete dependency of one individual on another. The person who says he would feel angry and hostile will probably be ready to admit that those would be predominant but not exclusive feelings. While he feels angry, he may at the same time feel affectionate and grateful. The man who says he will feel grateful and relieved will probably admit that he is also angry and irritated. Some admixture of these almost polar feelings will probably be present in everyone. This is the peculiar phenomenon of *ambivalence,* of the simultaneous existence of opposite feelings in the same place at the same time.

Similarly, at the action level, the man who says, "I would sock my brother on the nose," might be willing to add, "But I might feel awfully sorry afterward." And the man who says, "I would throw my arms around him," might add that his embrace would include a touch of a bear hug.

Suppose further that this sort of incident happened often, for month after month. Might you then develop an increasing wish for independence from your brother? Might you also seek ways of controlling your brother, of "getting something on him," so that you would not have to count impotently on his good will? And suppose he was a particularly bad brother who didn't care much for you? Wouldn't that intensify your wishes for independence from him or power over him?

Extreme dependency thus serves as a lever for initiating other kinds of needs. To the extent that dependency yields ready satisfaction of existing needs that one cannot satisfy independently—to that extent one's feelings are likely to be positive, friendly, affectionate, protective, grateful, and one is likely to develop strong *social* needs. To the extent that dependency does not satisfy, but rather frustrates—to that extent one is likely to develop feelings of anger and hostility and to wish more strongly for independence and autonomy, to develop strong *egoistic* needs. [Dr. Leavitt goes on with examples of infant/parent dependence.]

*   *   *   *   *

DEPENDENCY IN INDUSTRY

The things people learn in this first and most important dependency relationship probably also have a good deal to do with the way they face and deal with the less extreme dependency relationships of later life—like the relationship one has with his superiors in industrial organizations.

In fact, if we want to put this story in managerial terms, we need only to go over the last few pages and change a few labels. We can read "manager" for "parent," and "employee" for "child." And then we go on to tone down all the consequences a few notches. The employee, a "used" model of a child, enters a less extreme dependency relationship when he goes to work, and he enters with already existent social and egoistic as well as physical needs. If people in the company are "good brothers," the probability that the employee will learn to feel trustful and affiliative is pretty good—if he is already reasonably trustful of people with power. If people in the company are "bad brothers," his predominant local feelings (superimposed in a complicated way on the general feelings he brought in) are more likely to be hostile and competitive.

It is important to point out here that this view about early dependency may conflict with some widespread beliefs about training both children and employees. For example, this position suggests that strong discipline for the infant will probably lead to hostility and fear and to active power and independence seeking. It suggests further that a history of frustration probably makes later frustrations *more* difficult to take rather than easier. And, in a situation in which great psychological pressure is to be put on a man, holders of this position would place their money on the man who had *not* gone through an infantile school of hard psychological knocks. They would pick the man whose parental relationships and preferably his later ones had been comfortable and relatively free from psychological want. (Incidentally, the evidence from studies of successful executives is consonant with this view. Successful executives tend to come from harmonious, higher-income homes and to have liked their families and teachers.) For the first year or two, the best way to "spoil" a child would therefore seem to be to deny him what he wants. The best way not to "spoil" him is to help him get everything he wants. And, if one considers the new employee instead of the new baby, the same conclusions might hold. . . .

THE HIERARCHY OF NEEDS

One outstanding psychologist has pointed out that certain needs take operational precedence over others if both are unsatisfied at the same time. The ambitious man who is lost in the desert pays attention to his thirst, not his ambition. In general, the ordering of needs seems to be from the physical needs, which take first place when unsatisfied, to the social needs, to the egoistic needs, and, within what we have called the egoistic group, to those needs involving "self-fulfilment"—that is, to needs for knowledge or understanding or the successful completion of tasks.

Suppose that such a hierarchy does operate; suppose we begin to get interested in social relationships after our bellies are filled, and in achievement after our social relationship are secure. What implications does the hierarchy have for management? One implication is that when management tries to reward or punish, it had better reward or punish the needs that are operational and not those above or below that operational level. . . .

From: A. H. Maslow

*"A THEORY OF HUMAN MOTIVATION"** *

[EDITORS' NOTE: The author is Professor of Psychology at Brandeis University.]

THE BASIC NEEDS

THE PHYSIOLOGICAL NEEDS

The needs that are usually taken as the starting point for motivation theory are the so-called physiological drives. Two recent lines of research make it necessary to revise our customary notions about these needs: first, the development of the concept of homeostasis, and second, the finding that appetites (preferential choices among foods) are a fairly efficient indication of actual needs or lacks in the body.

---

* By permission from *Motivation and Personality*, 2d ed., by A. H. Maslow (New York: Harper & Bros., 1954). (Excerpts from pp. 80–94.)

Homeostasis refers to the body's automatic efforts to maintain a constant, normal state of the blood stream. Cannon . . . has described this process for (1) the water content of the blood, (2) salt content, (3) sugar content, (4) protein content, (5) fat content, (6) calcium content, (7) oxygen content, (8) constant hydrogen-ion level (acid-base balance), and (9) constant temperature of the blood. Obviously this list can be extended to include other minerals, the hormones, vitamins, etc.

Young . . . has summarized the work on appetite in its relation to body needs. If the body lacks some chemical, the individual will tend (in an imperfect way) to develop a specific appetite or partial hunger for that food element.

Thus it seems impossible as well as useless to make any list of fundamental physiological needs, for they can come to almost any number one might wish, depending on the degree of specificity of description. We cannot identify all physiological needs as homeostatic. That sexual desire, sleepiness, sheer activity, and maternal behavior in animals are homeostatic has not yet been demonstrated. Furthermore, this list would not include the various sensory pleasure (tastes, smells, tickling, stroking), which are probably physiological and which may become the goals of motivated behavior.

*   *   *   *   *

Undoubtedly these physiological needs are the most prepotent of all needs. What this means specifically is that in the human being who is missing everything in life in an extreme fashion, it is most likely that the major motivation would be the physiological needs rather than any others. A person who is lacking food, safety, love, and esteem would most probably hunger for good more strongly than for anything else.

If all the needs are unsatisfied, and the organism is then dominated by the physiological needs, all other needs may become simply nonexistent or be pushed into the background. It is then fair to characterize the whole organism by saying simply that it is hungry, for consciousness is almost completely preëmpted by hunger. All capacities are put into the service of hunger-satisfaction, and the organization of these capacities is almost entirely determined by the one purpose of satisfying hunger. The receptors and effectors, the intelligence, memory, habits, all may now be defined simply as hunger-gratifying tools. Capacities that are not useful for this purpose lie dormant, or are pushed into the background. The urge to write poetry, the desire to acquire an automobile, the interest in American history, the desire for a new pair of shoes are, in the extreme case, forgotten or become of secondary importance. . . .

Another peculiar characteristic of the human organism when it is dominated by a certain need is that the whole philosophy of the future tends also to change. For our chronically and extremely hungry man, Utopia can be defined simply as a place where there is plenty of food. He tends to think that, if only he is guaranteed food for the rest of his life, he will be perfectly happy and will never want anything more. Life itself tends to be defined in terms of eating. Anything else will be defined as unimportant. Freedom, love, community feeling, respect, philosophy, may all be waved aside as fripperies that are useless, since they fail to fill the stomach. Such a man may fairly be said to live by bread alone.

. . . It is quite true that man lives by bread alone—when there is no bread. But what happens to man's desires when there *is* plenty of bread and when his belly is chronically filled?

At once other (and higher) needs emerge and these, rather than physiological hungers, dominate the organism. And when these in turn are satisfied, again new (and still higher) needs emerge, and so on. This is what we mean by saying that the basic human needs are organized into a hierarchy of relative prepotency.

One main implication of this phrasing is that gratification becomes as important a concept as deprivation in motivation theory, for it releases the organism from the domination of a relatively more physiological need, permitting thereby the emergence of other more social goals. The physiological needs, along with their partial goals, when chronically gratified cease to exist as active determinants or organizers of behavior. They now exist only in a potential fashion in the sense that they may emerge again to dominate the organism if they are thwarted. But a want that is satisfied is no longer a want. The organism is dominated and its behavior organized only by unsatisfied needs. If hunger is satisfied, it becomes unimportant in the current dynamics of the individual.

This statement is somewhat qualified by a hypothesis to be discussed more fully later, namely, that it is precisely those individuals in whom a certain need has always been satisfied who are best equipped to tolerate deprivation of that need in the future, and that furthermore, those who have been deprived in the past will react differently to current satisfactions than the one who has never been deprived.

THE SAFETY NEEDS

If the physiological needs are relatively well gratified, there then emerges a new set of needs, which we may categorize roughly as the safety needs. All that has been said of the physiological needs is equally true, although in less degree, of these desires. The organism may equally well be wholly dominated by them. They may serve as the almost exclusive organizers of behavior, recruiting all the capacities of the organism in their service, and we may then fairly describe the whole organism as a safety-seeking mechanism. Again we may say of the receptors, the effectors, of the intellect, and of the other capacities that they are primarily safety-seeking tools. Again, as in the hungry man, we find that the dominating goal is a strong determinant not only of his current world outlook and philosophy but also of his philosophy of the future. Practically everything looks less important than safety (even sometimes the physiological needs, which being satisfied are now underestimated). A man in this state, if it is extreme enough and chronic enough, may be characterized as living almost for safety alone.

* * * * *

Another indication of the child's need for safety is his preference for some kind of undisrupted routine or rhythm. He seems to want a predictable, orderly world. For instance, injustice, unfairness, or inconsistency in the parents seems to make a child feel anxious and unsafe. This attitude may be not so much because of the injustice *per se* or any particular pains involved, but rather because this treatment threatens to make the world look unreliable, or unsafe, or unpredictable. Young children seem to thrive better under a system that has at least a skeletal outline of rigidity, in which there is a schedule of a kind, some sort of routine, something that can be counted upon, not only for the present but also far into the future. Child psychologists, teachers, and psychotherapists have found that permissiveness within limits, rather than unrestricted permissiveness is preferred as well as *needed* by children. Perhaps one could express this more accurately by saying that the child needs an organized world rather than an unorganized or unstructured one.

* * * * *

Confronting the average child with new, unfamiliar, strange, unmanageable stimuli or situations will too frequently elicit the danger or terror reaction, as for example, getting lost or even being separated from the parents for a short time, being confronted with new faces, new situations, or new tasks, the sight of strange, unfamiliar, or uncontrollable objects, illness, or death. Particularly at such times, the child's frantic clinging to his parents is eloquent testimony to their role as protectors (quite apart from their roles as food givers and love givers).

From these and similar observations, we may generalize and say that the average child in our society generally prefers a safe, orderly, predictable, organized world, which he can count on, and in which unexpected, unmanageable, or other dangerous things do not happen, and in which, in any case, he has all-powerful parents who protect and shield him from harm. . . .

That these reactions may so easily be observed in children is in a way a proof of the fact that children in our society feel too unsafe (or, in a word, are badly brought up). Children who are reared in an unthreatening, loving family do *not* ordinarily react as we have described above. In such children the danger reactions are apt to come mostly to objects or situations that adults too would consider dangerous.

The healthy, normal, fortunate adult in our culture is largely satisfied in his safety needs. The peaceful, smoothly running, good society ordinarily makes its members feel safe enough from wild animals, extremes of temperature, criminal assault, murder, tyranny, etc. Therefore, in a very real sense, he no longer has any safety needs as active motivators. Just as a sated man no longer feels hungry, a safe man no longer feels endangered. . . .

*   *   *   *   *

The Belongingness and Love Needs

If both the physiological and the safety needs are fairly well gratified, there will emerge the love and affection and belongingness needs, and the whole cycle already described will repeat itself with this new center. Now the person will feel keenly, as never before, the absence of friends, or a sweetheart, or a wife, or children. He will hunger for affectionate relations with people in general, namely, for a place in his group, and he will strive with great intensity to achieve this goal. He will want to attain such a place more than anything else in the world and may even forget that once, when he was hungry, he sneered at love as unreal or unnecessary or unimportant.

In our society the thwarting of these needs is the most commonly found core in cases of maladjustment and more severe psychopathology. Love and affection, as well as their possible expression in sexuality, are generally looked upon with ambivalence and are customarily hedged about with many restrictions and inhibitions. Practically all theorists of psychopathology have stressed thwarting of the love needs as basic in the picture of maladjustment. Many clinical studies have therefore been made of this need, and we know more about it perhaps than any of the other needs except the physiological ones. Suttie . . . has written an excellent analysis of our "taboo on tenderness."

One thing that must be stressed at this point is that love is not synonymous with sex. Sex may be studied as a purely physiological need. Ordinarily sexual behavior is multidetermined, that is to say, determined not only by sexual but also by other needs, chief among which are the love and affection needs. Also not to be overlooked is the fact that the love needs involve both giving *and* receiving love. . . .

The Esteem Needs

All people in our society (with a few pathological exceptions) have a need or desire for a stable, firmly based, usually high evaluation of themselves, for self-respect, or self-esteem, and for the esteem of others. These needs may therefore be classified into two subsidiary sets. These are, first, the desire for strength, for achievement, for adequacy, for mastery and competence, for confidence in the face of the world, and for independence and freedom.* Second, we have what we may call the desire for reputation or prestige (defining it as respect or esteem from other people), status, dominance, recognition, attention, importance, or appreciation. These needs have been relatively stressed by Alfred Adler and his followers, and have been relatively neglected by Freud. More and more today, however, there is appearing widespread appreciation of their central importance, among psychoanalysts as well as among clinical psychologists.

Satisfaction of the self-esteem need leads to feelings of self-confidence, worth, strength, capability, and adequacy, of being useful and necessary in the world. But thwarting of these needs produces feelings of inferiority, of weakness, and of helplessness. These feelings in turn give rise to either basic discouragement or else compensatory or neurotic trends. An appreciation of the necessity of basic self-confidence and an understanding of how helpless people are without it can be easily gained from a study of severe traumatic neurosis . . .

From the theologians' discussion of pride and *hubris,* from the Frommian theories about the self-perception of untruth to one's own nature, from the Rogerian work with self, from essayists like Ayn Rand . . ., and from other sources as well, we have been learning more and more of the dangers of basing self-esteem on the opinions of others rather than on real capacity, competence, and adequacy to the task. The most stable and therefore most healthy self-esteem is based on *deserved* respect from others rather than on external fame or celebrity and unwarranted adulation.

THE NEED FOR SELF-ACTUALIZATION

Even if all these needs are satisfied, we may still often (if not always) expect that a new discontent and restlessness will soon develop, unless the individual is doing what he is fitted for. A musician must make music, an artist must paint, a poet must write, if he is to be ultimately at peace with himself. What a man *can* be, he *must* be. This need we may call self-actualization. . . .

This term, first coined by Kurt Goldstein . . ., is being used in this book in a much more specific and limited fashion. It refers to man's desire for self-fulfillment, namely, to the tendency for him to become actualized in what he is potentially. This tendency might be phrased as the desire to become more and more what one is, to become everything that one is capable of becoming.

The specific form that these needs will take will of course vary greatly from person to person. In one individual it may take the form of the desire to be an ideal mother, in another it may be expressed athletically, and in still another it may be expressed in painting pictures or in inventions.†

The clear emergence of these needs usually rests upon prior satisfaction of the physiological, safety, love, and esteem needs.

---

* Whether or not this particular desire is universal we do not know. The crucial question, especially important today, is, Will men who are enslaved and dominated inevitably feel dissatisfied and rebellious? We may assume on the basis of commonly known clinical data that a man who has known true freedom (not paid for by giving up safety and security but rather built on the basis of adequate safety and security) will not willingly or easily allow his freedom to be taken away from him. But we do not know that this is true for the person born into slavery.

† Clearly creative behavior, like painting, is like any other behavior in having multiple determinants. It may be seen in innately creative people whether they are satisfied or not, happy or unhappy, hungry or sated. Also it is clear that creative activity may be compensatory, ameliorative, or purely economic. It is my impression (from informal experiments) that it is possible to distinguish the artistic and intellectual

THE PRECONDITIONS FOR THE BASIC NEED SATISFACTIONS

There are certain conditions that are immediate prerequisites for the basic need satisfactions. Danger to these is reacted to as if it were direct danger to the basic needs themselves. Such conditions as freedom to speak, freedom to do what one wishes so long as no harm is done to others, freedom to express oneself, freedom to investigate and seek for information, freedom to defend oneself, justice, fairness, honesty, orderliness in the group are examples of such preconditions for basic need satisfactions. Thwarting in these freedoms will be reacted to with a threat or emergency response. These conditions are not ends in themselves but they are *almost* so since they are so closely related to the basic needs, which are apparently the only ends in themselves. These conditions are defended because without them the basic satisfactions are quite impossible, or at least, severely endangered.

If we remember that the cognitive capacities (perceptual, intellectual, learning) are a set of adjustive tools, which have, among other functions, that of satisfaction of our basic needs, then it is clear that any danger to them, any deprivation or blocking of their free use, must also be indirectly threatening to the basic needs themselves. Such a statement is a partial solution of the general problems of curiosity, the search for knowledge, truth, and wisdom, and the ever-persistent urge to solve the cosmic mysteries.

We must therefore introduce another hypothesis and speak of degrees of closeness to the basic needs, for we have already pointed out that *any* conscious desires (partial goals) are more or less important as they are more or less close to the basic needs. The same statement may be made for various behavior acts. An act is psychologically important if it contributes directly to satisfaction of basic needs. The less directly it so contributes, or the weaker this contribution is, the less important this act must be conceived to be from the point of view of dynamic psychology. A similar statement may be made for the various defense or coping mechanisms. Some are directly related to the protection or attainment of the basic needs, others are only weakly and distantly related. Indeed, if we wished, we could speak of more basic and less basic defense mechanisms, and then affirm that danger to the more basic defenses is more threatening than danger to less basic defenses (always remembering that this is so only because of their relationship to the basic needs) .

THE DESIRES TO KNOW AND TO UNDERSTAND

The main reason we know little about the cognitive impulses, their dynamics, or their pathology, is that they are not important in the clinic, and certainly not in the clinic dominated by the medical-therapeutic tradition, i.e., getting rid of disease. The florid, exciting, and mysterious symptoms found in the classical neuroses are lacking here. Cognitive psychopathology is pale, subtle, and easily overlooked, or defined as normal. It does not cry for help. As a consequence we find nothing on the subject in the writings of the great inventors of psychotherapy and psychodynamics, Freud, Adler, Jung, etc. Nor has anyone yet made any systematic attempts at constructing cognitive psychotherapies.

Schilder is the only psychoanalyst I know in whose writings curiosity and understanding are seen dynamically. Among the academic psychologists Murphy, Wertheimer, and Asch . . . have treated the problem. So far, we have mentioned the cognitive needs only in passing. Acquiring knowledge and sys-

products of basically satisfied people from those of basically unsatisfied people by inspection alone. In any case, here too we must distinguish, in a dynamic fashion, the overt behavior itself from its various motivations or purposes.

tematizing the universe have been considered as, in part, techniques for the achievement of basic safety in the world, or for the intelligent man, expressions of self-actualization. Also freedom of inquiry and expression have been discussed as preconditions of satisfactions of the basic needs. Useful though these formulations may be, they do not constitute definitive answers to the questions as to the motivational role of curiosity, learning, philosophizing, experimenting, etc. They are at best no more than partial answers. . . .

CASE MATERIALS:

Complex Cases

NATIONAL MOTOR PARTS COMPANY

I Case Introduction

Synopsis

The corporate director of industrial engineering of National Motor Parts Company proposes a general audit and research study of jobs to insure that changes over time have not reduced accuracy of standards of output for workers. The audit is approved by the executive vice president. The proposal is explained to division managers of industrial engineering, who in turn present it to division general managers for approval.

In the Metal Parts Division, the manager of industrial engineering explains the project to plant supervisors of industrial engineering, who present it to plant managers for approval. At one plant, a study of the lock pin job operation results in a new standard for the position, and for Sullivan, the incumbent in the job. The plant manager instructs Bauer, Sullivan's foreman, to relay the new standard to Sullivan.

Sullivan files a grievance with Andrews, his union steward. Leach, the plant manager, prepares to take action with Ed Lillian, head of the local union.

Why This Case Is Included

This case offers opportunity to see how rational planning of objectives and jobs in the company, based on technology and economics, conflicts with the desires of individual workers, and with the power structure of the union.

The relationship of scientific planning, in the form of quantification and research, done by specialists, to both the process of influence and to the authority process in the company can be studied.

Finally, the issues of management rights in United States society, versus the functions and rights of labor unions, stands out as a prominent issue.

Diagnostic and Predictive Questions

In answering the following diagnostic and predictive questions, remember that these questions apply theories and conceptual ideas from certain disciplines. Such theories are valuable to understand basic forces at work in the policy system (diagnosis) and to predict what will happen in the system in the future (prediction). Since each reading abstracts from the total policy system certain factors or variables into the closed or partial viewpoint of one theory or discipline, no one reading gives answers to the practical policy problems of the case.

In diagnosis and prediction, the parts of the problem are studied with "other things being equal."

Following each question are listed readings which will be helpful in answering the question. The readings included with this case are marked (*). By referring to the author index at the end of this book, you may locate the other readings listed.

1. From the viewpoint of technology and economics, why did King propose the general audit? Why did the industrial engineers at two lower levels approve it? Why did management approve it?

Read: *Martin's Memorandum, "Standards on Lock Pin Operation, Exhibit 2 in case. *Galbraith, *The Affluent Society*, pp. 121–24, 126. *Towne, "Foreword to *Shop management*."
(Optional, not in this volume: J. D. Black and A. G. Black, *Production Organization* [New York: Henry Holt & Co., Inc., 1939]. This is an advanced reading in economic theory. Or, one may simply think of the inputs of physical resources, including man-hours, in relation to the output of products. This is the physical or technological relationship. The relationship of cost of inputs to value of output is the economic equivalent.)

2. From the viewpoint of science and decision theory, why did management propose the audit in the form of a quantitative, industrial engineering, approach?

Read: *Moroney, *Facts from Figures*, pp. 460–63. *Howell and Teichroew, *Mathematical Analysis for Business Decisions*, pp. 281–84, 287–88. Anderson, *An Organization Appraisal*, pp. 1–2. *Barber, *Science and the Social Order*, pp. 7–8, 12–13, 18, 21. *Beard, *Public Policy and the General Welfare*, pp. 148 et seq. Veblen, *The Engineers and the Price System*, chap. v.

3. From the viewpoint of political science and management theory, why did the industrial engineers at each level do the intellectual investigation of the decision and then recommend it to the line executives (try drawing a diagram of who did what in this decision process). Later, why did Carter, the division manager, Leach, the plant manager, and Bauer, the foreman, accept the proposals and carry out the audit?

Read: Hobbes, *Leviathan*, chap. x. O'Donnell, "The Source of Managerial Authority." Fayol, *General and Industrial Management*, pp. 24–25, 68–70. Locke, *Concerning Civil Government*, chap. ix. Lippmann, *The Method of Freedom*, pp. 100–2.

4. From the viewpoint of sociology, answer the same questions as immediately above.

Read: *Thompson, *Modern Organization*, pp. 4–6, 12–13, 19–21, 61, 63–65, 77–78. Lasswell and Kaplan, *Power and Society*, pp. 157–59. Simon et al., *Public Administration*, pp. 182, 189–200. Drucker, *The Future of Industrial Man*, pp. 32–38.

5. Why do you think Glen Carter, general manager of the division, raised the issue of the right of a plant manager to manage the plant?

Read: Citations for Question 3. O'Donnell, "The Source of Managerial Authority."
(Optional, not in this volume: Montesquieu, *The Spirit of Laws*, Book I, Sec. 2, "Of the Laws of Nature," Sec. 3, "Of Positive Laws.")

6. Considering the question of management rights (Question 5), what "rights" does the union seem to possess in the National Motor Parts Company? What is its function in the bargaining process?

Read: Selekman, *A Moral Philosophy for Management,* pp. 174–77.
(Optional, not in this volume: J. T. Dunlop, *Industrial Relations Systems* [New York: Henry Holt & Co., Inc., 1958], chaps. i and x.)

Policy Questions for This Specific Case

In answering the following policy questions, the results of diagnosis and pre-diction are used to reduce the amount of guesswork, or judgment, in designing action solutions. However, since certain parts of the total case situation cannot be reduced to science, and since "other things are not equal," judgment must still be used to fill in the factors not accounted for by readings. You will also need a second kind of judgment as you put value weights on different scientific pre-dictions, since different theories may point to conflicting solutions.

7. Are the concepts of "pluralism," "constructive conflict," or "participation" applicable in this situation? Why might they work (or not work)?

Read: Newman and Summer, *The Process of Management: Concepts, Be-havior, and Practice,* pp. 439–48. McGregor, *The Human Side of Enterprise,* pp. 124–31, 172–75.
(Optional: Eells and Walton, *Conceptual foundations of Business,* pp. 361–63. Follett, "Constructive Conflict.")

8. If you were the plant manager, what line of action would you pursue with the head of the local union, Ed Lillian? Outline the steps you would take, and list carefully your reasons.

Major Policy Issues: Tentative Generalizations about Any Policy System

In arriving at conclusions for the following questions, generalize from the facts in the case and use your own ideas to (*a*) confirm, (*b*) modify, or (*c*) test the workability of the concepts and theories from readings. As an executive or professional, use wisdom to merge theory, on the one hand, with "brute facts" and practice, on the other.

9. What relative importance do technology and economics, on the one hand, and the desires of individual workers, on the other, assume in questions of *rules for action?* In other words, which factors receive the greatest weight in United States companies? In society in general?

10. To what extent is science, especially quantification of problems, important to the corporation? To society?

11. To what extent should specialists in engineering and operations research establish policies? To what extent should general executives? To what extent should labor unions?

12. Is private property the basis for freedom? What are its benefits and limita-tions as an institution of our society?

Questions for Original Student Work in Analysis and Policy

The methods of viewing this case as represented by the authors' questions and selection of readings are not exhaustive. There are other relevant ideas for diag-nosis and prediction. Furthermore, there are other ways of stating policy ques-tions. More powerful analyses and wiser solutions will result by drawing on your own training and experience for (*a*) relevant concepts and theories, and (*b*) creative ways of asking policy questions. The following questions are designed to help you acquire this skill.

13. While reflecting on case facts, what additional theories from prior education give you insights as to "what is going on" in National Motor Parts Company? As to what might be predicted to happen in the future?

14. Other than the policy questions asked by the authors, what pragmatic ways can you think of to state the practical problems faced by executives in the case?

II National Motor Parts Company*

The National Motor Parts Company is one of the five largest firms in the basic auto parts industry. It has nine operating divisions and a total work force of over 80,000 employees. Its extensive staff organization provides specialized skills at the corporate, divisional, and plant level. At each of these levels, the cost accounting and industrial engineering groups exert a considerable amount of interest over the development and execution of corporate policy. Though individual divisions are operationally autonomous, division officials generally follow the policy suggestions made by the cost accounting and industrial engineering staffs. A partial organization chart is shown in Exhibit 1.

One program recently advocated by Phil King, corporate director of industrial engineering, was a review of work standards on all jobs which had not been checked or audited within the previous two years. King's request arose from the fact that he had seen several instances of what appeared to him to be goldbricking during a tour of plants in several of National's operating divisions. Upon his return to the central office, Mr. King met with two of his staff engineers, and after careful deliberation, an audit plan was drawn up. This plan was subsequently approved by the executive vice president in charge of manufacturing operations.

The basic plan suggested by King used a technique known as work sampling to check on the idle time present in individual job standards. In essence, the approach taken relied on the fact that a series of short, random observations, if taken often enough over an appropriate time period, could give an accurate picture of the operations performed in each job. The work sampling results would be used to determine which jobs were not requiring the employees to work for an entire day to meet their stated output standards. By the same token, those jobs which were demanding a full day's work to meet existing standards would also be recognized. Though work sampling was to be used to identify standards which

* Copyright 1968 by the Graduate School of Business, Columbia University.

Exhibit 1

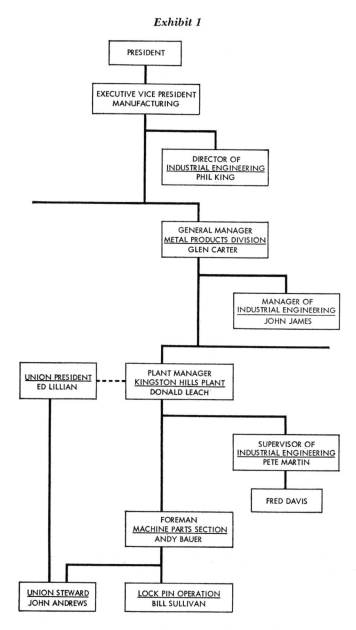

were loose (i.e., standards which did not require a full day's work to meet standard output requirements for that day), King's proposal included the further suggestion that looseness, when detected, should be checked in detail by the use of stopwatch time study and a thorough motion study of the job in question.

To launch his program, Mr. King held a series of meetings with the heads of divisional industrial engineering groups. Though objections were raised about the cost and time considerations inherent in the proposal, the division engineering managers agreed that the plan was technically sound and agreed to put it into effect as soon as possible.

One of the more receptive listeners to Mr. King's standards audit procedure was John James, manager of industrial engineering in National's Metal Products Division. This division employs 21,000 people in five plants. James, who holds degrees in both industrial engineering and mathematics, thought that King's plan was both technically sound and eminently practical. He returned to division headquarters in Kingston, Michigan, and drew up procedures to utilize the plan in the Metal Products Division's five plants.

Within a month after the corporate staff meeting, James offered his own version of the audit plan to Glenn Carter, the division manager. Carter, who had come to respect James' technical ability and practical know-how, accepted the plan readily and agreed to present it at the next weekly meeting of his plant managers. Carter suggested that he should merely outline the plan to his plant managers and that James should be available to fill in details and to answer questions.

In the subsequent meeting, each of the plant managers agreed that such an audit was sound, and each, in turn, suggested that James contact the heads of their plant industrial engineering departments to explain the details of his plan. Three plant managers who had formerly been in charge of industrial engineering groups in the National hierarchy offered to provide additional clerical and engineering help on a temporary basis in order to get the program moving quickly.

After gaining the support of Mr. Carter and the five plant managers, James met with the heads of industrial engineering in each of the division's five plants. Though the familiar objections were raised about the time and cost of such a program, all five men stated that the audit procedure was practical and they agreed to put it into effect immediately. Within this group, the plan was embraced most enthusiastically by Pete Martin, the industrial engineer in charge of the Kingston Hills plant.

The Kingston Hills plant shared the same plot of land as the headquarters of the Metal Products Division. It employed more than 5,000 workers and was generally considered to be the most modern and most efficient of the division's plants. Donald Leach, the plant manager, was one of the three men in the division who rose to his present position from a supervisory job in the industrial engineering hierarchy. Leach's plant was equipped with the latest advances in automated equipment, and it was, according to division records, the most profitable plant in the division. Leach prided himself on his ability to attract and retain good managerial talent and he was particularly proud of the work done by Pete Martin in developing new methods of work and in adapting mathematical techniques and procedures to fit the needs of the operations at the Kingston Hills plant. Thus, when Martin suggested the adoption of an audit program, Leach agreed readily and offered Martin additional clerical help to work on the details of setting up the program.

Pete Martin went to work on the program immediately, and within a week the first audit reports were completed. After one month, audits had been completed on seventeen operations. Sixteen of these audits indicated that very little idle time was evident in the operations studied, but the audit performed on one job, the production of a tiny metal lock pin used in automatic transmission units, seemed to show an unusual amount of idle time. The job in question was performed by Bill Sullivan, an experienced long-service employee. Sullivan set up, tended, and performed certain minor maintenance tasks on an automatic screw machine. Because the products he worked on were varied, the original standards had been measured quite carefully.[1] Since the time when the original standards were set, changes had occurred which caused the standards to become loose. Materials changes, changes in tolerance limits on the various machined parts, the time and methods used to set up the various runs, the actual length of machine runs, and the adoption of a more standardized parts line had all occurred in recent years; and since several of these changes had apparently not been reflected in adjustments in the affected output standards, it was a rare day when Sullivan failed to obtain his expected or standard output.

The looseness of Sullivan's standards was no revelation to several of his immediate co-workers. One worker, for example, when conversing with Pete Martin about the audit, stated, "If your audit doesn't pick up that soft touch Sullivan's got, you'd better toss the whole thing down the drain." Few of the workers were bitter about Sullivan's "gravy train" job, however, since the looseness of his standards give him no wage advantages over his fellow workers. In other National plants where payment was tied directly to output through the use of incentive payment plans, the relative looseness of standards had frequently caused bitter disputes because of the wage inequities it generated. In the Kingston Hills Plant, the failure of management to detect a loose standard meant that workers accrued leisure time benefits, not higher wages. Though workers objected to such "unfair" work loads, no grievance had ever been filed to ask management to correct such inequities.

The second phase of the audit procedure entailed a review of Sullivan's job by Fred Davis, one of Martin's most competent engineers. In this study, Davis compared the previously set standard (Table 1 in Martin's memo) with the newly calculated time required to perform the operation under changed conditions (Table 2 in the memo). This, in turn, showed

---

[1] Sullivan's standard at this time was .33734 minutes per piece, or approximately 180 units of output per hour. This is shown in Table 1 in Martin's memo (Exhibit 2).

a tentative idle time of four hours per shift.[2] Davis's stopwatch time study of the screw machine operation confirmed the results of the initial audit, and a detailed methods study of the job turned up substantial changes in the original working conditions including changes in materials and methods of operation. Mr. Leach, when confronted with this information by Martin and Davis, ordered them to take steps to correct what he believed was an inequity in the basic work load structure.

After several weeks of study, Davis devised a plan where, with certain layout changes and some methods improvements, Sullivan would operate not one, but two machines. Davis's methods study showed that the time allowances were adequate enough to allow Sullivan to complete the requirements of the revised job if he worked a full eight-hour day. Davis showed his plan to Pete Martin, and together they presented it to Mr. Leach. Leach approved the plan and directed the purchasing department to acquire another automatic screw machine. He thereupon called in Andy Bauer, Sullivan's immediate supervisor, and informed him that Sullivan should be told of the impending change.[3] Bauer, who had worked with Mr. Davis on the methods study, agreed to tell Sullivan that management intended to exercise its contractual right "to make changes in methods, equipment, materials, and conditions of work in order to obtain greater efficiency and to adjust existing work standards to reflect such changes." The labor contract further stated that "in case of such methods change only those elements of the standard will be changed which are affected by the change in methods, etc." One other section of the contract spelled out the fact that "standards will be set on the basis of fairness and equity and that they shall be consistent with the quality of workmanship, efficiency of operation, and reasonable working capacities of normal operations." In the National Motors contract, as in most others in the basic auto industry, the resolution of work standards disputes can be solved only by dealings between management and the labor union. Arbitration is specifically prohibited as a means of settling disputes over work standards.

Two months later, the new machine was installed at the workplace along with several minor changes in layout and work flow. Foreman Bauer instructed Sullivan in his new duties, and Sullivan, though he was unhappy about the new layout, started to work with the two machines. During the day, John Andrews, the union steward, stopped by to check on the new job.[4] Sullivan complained violently that he was the victim of

---

2 Though a four-hour idle time may seem to be so high as to be almost unbelievable, engineering studies performed elsewhere in National Motors uncovered similar looseness. Experts in the industrial engineering field concede that this situation can arise in even the best-managed plants.

3 The new standard called for a time of .1664 minutes per piece, or approximately 360 units per hour.

4 One of the main duties of a union steward is to represent the worker in presenting grievances to management. He is usually elected to this office by fellow workers. Stewards

a "speedup." Andrews, after listening to the details of the shift from one to two machines, suggested that Sullivan file a grievance.

That evening Sullivan wrote a grievance and, shortly before starting work the next morning, turned it over to John Andrews. Andrews, following the normal procedure for processing such grievances, presented it to Andy Bauer for discussion and possible solution. Because of the technical nature of the grievance, Bauer called upon Pete Martin and Fred Davis to explain the nature of the change to Andrews. When Martin and Davis showed their detailed methods studies to Andrews, he stated, "What your guys have done here is to blow up a big smoke screen to hide the fact that you're pulling a speedup on Sullivan's job." The net result of the meeting was that the grievance, still unsettled, moved to the second step in grievance procedure. This step involved discussion between the head of the local union, Ed Lillian, and Donald Leach, the plant manager.

Mr. Leach, when presented with Bill Sullivan's grievance, immediately called Pete Martin into his office to discuss the problem. Together they reviewed the methods study and the subsequent standards revisions. The approaches and the figures shown by Martin seemed correct and reasonable to Mr. Leach, and he believed that the contractual clause allowing him to "make changes in methods equipment, materials, and conditions of work in order to obtain greater efficiency and to adjust existing work standards to reflect such changes" justified the introduction of the second machine. He stated, "It's my duty to my work force to maintain an efficient operation so that the job security of all the workers will be protected." Leach also said, "The only way we can continue to grow and prosper and provide steady employment for our workers is to push for more efficiency in all of our plant activities." In his upcoming meeting with Ed Lillian, Leach planned to use this reasoning as the basis for his insistence on the introduction of the second machine. He also intended to allow Lillian to review any and all of the data used as the basis for changes made on the disputed job.

Ed Lillian, on the other hand, expected to rely heavily on John Andrews to present the union side of the dispute. Lillian told Andrews that he would support him fully if the company's actions were in violation of the labor contract.

The feelings of the parties prior to the grievance meeting are summarized below:

BILL SULLIVAN: All of a sudden I'm expected to turn out three thousand pieces per day where I used to have to do fourteen hundred.[5] If this isn't a

---

hold regular jobs in the plants where they perform their duties, and they receive no extra pay for their union activities.

[5] In actuality Sullivan was required to turn out 1,440 pieces per day before the audit. After the methods change and subsequent standards revision, Sullivan's quota rose to 2,880 (Exhibit 2).

speedup I don't know what the hell it is. I've got rights and I expect the union to protect them.

JOHN ANDREWS: The company hasn't done a thing to change methods here. They've just come in and made changes to correct their mistakes from the past. Their actions violate the fairness and equity clauses relating to revisions of work standards which exist in the labor contract.

PETE MARTIN: We've made good studies of Sullivan's job and we know that the lock pin standard is loose. It's not unfair to ask him to put in a fair day's work in order to earn a fair day's pay.

ED LILLIAN: Even though Don Leach is sometimes tough in his dealings with us, he's been fair and consistent. On this issue, however, I'm not sure he's really right.

DONALD LEACH: I believe that I'm both contractually and economically correct when I take the stand that the second machine should be maintained on this operation. After all, if we don't have efficiency in this plant the workers won't have any job security.

GLENN CARTER: The real issue here is whether or not managers have the right to run their own plants. If we have to subsidize inefficiency in our operations we won't be in business very long.

The grievance meeting scheduled to resolve this dispute was affected by at least two other factors:

1. Strikes over production standards are legal during the life of the labor contract. Though other issues (wages, hours, working conditions, etc.) could be grieved, no strikes could be called legally on these matters until the existing contract expired.

2. Though one more step remained in the division's grievance procedure, Mr. Carter had written a note to Ed Lillian which stated that he "would not, under any circumstances, alter the stand taken by Mr. Leach in the plant level negotiations." Since the dispute cannot be arbitrated, the parties are faced with the problem of devising some other strategy to solve (or to "win") the disagreement.

In a front-page editorial on the day before the grievance meeting, the local *Kingston Daily Record* asks the disputants to act with "caution and care." The *Record's* editorial recalls that "the steel industry in 1959 and 1960 became embroiled in a similar issue which evolved into a strike lasting six months."

Exhibit 2

To: Andy Bauer, Foreman, Machined Parts Section
FROM: Peter Martin, Plant Industrial Engineer
SUBJECT: Standards on lock pin operation performed by William Sullivan, Clock No. 45716.

In response to your request during our recent standards grievance meeting with Bill Sullivan and John Andrews, I have described both the general procedure for setting machine standards and the specific calculations performed to set a standard on Sullivan's lock pin operation. Though you may feel that

Exhibit 2—Continued

some parts of the explanation are overly detailed, I have included them so that your records on this matter will be complete and accurate.

A production standard for a machine operation is determined by measuring two things: (1) the time used by the operator to complete a unit of output, and (2) the machine time needed to produce each unit. The operator's time might consist of the following items: setting up the necessary tooling, jigs, and fixtures to produce the part, feeding materials into the machine, inspection activities, some minor maintenance activities such as oiling the machine and keeping it clean, and other factors which could vary widely depending upon the nature of the job and/or the equipment in use. Machine time represents the time when the machine is performing some operation on the unit being produced.

A simple addition of the operator's time and the machine time rarely produces an accurate work standard, however, since workers can perform certain of their activities during the run time of the machine. It is also true that machines don't always operate perfectly, so it may be necessary to determine an allowance to compensate for such a contingency (commonly called a "downtime allowance") in the final standard. Such complicating factors make a rather knotty problem out of what seems to be at first glance nothing more than a simple job of measurement.

Take for example the standard on Bill Sullivan's job at National Motors. Sullivan was, prior to the industrial engineering audit, operating one machine. When a machine is operated by one man, a good deal of overlap generally occurs between operator time and machine run time. In order to illustrate the setting of a work standard on this operation, we would first determine which of the operator's activities can be performed during the machine's run time. We would then have to adjust the total elapsed time observed during our study of the lock pin operation to reflect such overlap. If we can grasp the relationship between operator time and machine time on a one machine job, we can, if we so desire, expand the concept to illustrate the methods used to measure standards on more complicated multimachine operations.

The first step in setting a standard is to identify the unit by which we intend to measure output. Sullivan's machine is turning out a metal part called a lock pin. The lock pin then is the unit of output which our standard is based.

The next task we face is to thoroughly analyze the job, to determine a standard method of performing the job, and to measure the various elements of this standard operating method. One procedure used to determine the most efficient way to do the job involves the use of a flow chart. Flow charts trace the path of materials and men as they relate to the machines needed to make the product under observation. Another attack uses detailed studies of the motions made by the operator in setting up and running a machine. This latter approach may be performed in very detailed fashion and may even utilize motion pictures of the operation to enable the industrial engineer to study the most refined and intricate motion patterns practiced by the operator.

Though a number of methods are used to set work standards, stopwatch time study is used most widely. In time study a trained observer records the time taken to manufacture (say) a lock pin. He then rates these observed times to reflect a so-called "normal" output expectation on the job. A normal or average rating is generally assigned a value of 100%. A below-average performance or less-than-normal performance is given a less than 100% rating, while a better-than-average operator would be rated in excess of the 100% (normal) rating. The rating factor multiplied by the observed time yields the normal time for performing the portion of the job under observation.

Exhibit 2—Continued

If, for example, a rating of 110% was given to a time value of .2000 (two tenths of a minute), the "normal" time to perform this task would be .2200 (1.10 × .2000). This shows us how a faster than normal man's time (.2000) would be adjusted to reflect the pace expected of an average operator (.2200). If a rating of 90% was placed on an observed time of .2444 for the same task, the normal time for the operation would be (still) .22 (.90 × .2444). It is no accident that both of these normal (.22) times are identical. If the rating process is done correctly, the observed times multiplied by the rating *will always yield an identical normal time.* Since human errors invariably crop up in the rating procedure, there is always some variance in so-called normal times. Skilled industrial engineers, however, claim that such variance will not exceed the "true normal" by more than ± 5%. Though the veracity of this claim is often disputed, the rating process is still the most common method of evaluating the elapsed times recorded during a stopwatch time study.

Once the times are recorded and rated, adjustments must be made to reflect the number of times each element occurs during the production of one lock pin. Setup time, for example, occurs only once per production run, but each run may result in thousands of lock pins. The setup time must then be spread out or prorated over the total production of lock pins. This adjustment occurs in the final standard as a setup time per unit allowance. Similar adjustments are made for all other items which occur more or less frequently than the cycle needed to produce one lock pin.

As a final step in the standard setting procedure, allowances are added for personal time, delay beyond the control of the operator, and, in some cases, for fatigue. Where particularly unusual job conditions exist, other allowances are sometimes added to the standard. As you know, many of the allowances in use in our plant are set by collective bargaining rather than by work measurement.

The actual calculations of the original standard on the basic lock pin portion of Bill Sullivan's job appear in Table 1. The .33734 minutes per unit figure means that the standard time allowed to produce one lock pin is approximately one third of a minute. Thus a standard output of three lock pins per minute, or one hundred eighty lock pins per hour, is expected. If we could assume an eight-hour workday for Sullivan, his daily output quota on this standard would be 1,440 units.

To illustrate how standards can become loose, we can take Bill Sullivan's job as a prime example. Let us first assume that the setup operation became easier for Bill as he developed skill. Then, longer production runs were planned and changes were made in the materials used to manufacture the lock pin. Now let us assume that Bill performs his inspection operations during the run time of the machine and also manages to cut his oiling and cleanup time in half.

The big item to consider is the machine run time. Suppose now that the new materials allow a more rapid machining cycle and that the machines on the job, after an initial break in period, operate faster and with less down time than the same machines measured in the original job time study.

The new time study by Fred Davis detected the changes described above, and the time study summary sheet in Table 2 shows the results of Davis's study.

The .1664 minutes per unit figure means that the standard time allowed to produce one lock pin is approximately one sixth of a minute. This rate of six per minute calls for an hourly quota of 360 units. Again assuming an eight-hour day, Sullivan's new standard output requirement would be 2,880 units per day.

The problems of undetected methods changes are quite common, although they are usually not as obvious as they appear to be in this case. Though the

Table 1

Column 1	Column 2 Average Time*	Column 3 Rating	(Col. 3 × Col. 2) Column 4 Leveled Time	Column 5 Occurrence per Cycle	Column 6 External Time	(Col. 4 × Col. 5) Column 7 Internal Time
1. Set up machine to run lock nuts†	12.00	100 (1.00)	12.00	1/2000	.00600	
2. Feed first metal bar into machine, run initial pieces, inspect, adjust tooling‡	10.00	90 (.90)	9.00	1/2000	.00450	
3. Remove old bar end, feed new bar	4.00	90 (.90)	3.60	1/270	.01333	
4. Inspection. Sampling basis at end of each run‖	12.00	80 (.80)	9.60	1/2000	.00480	
5. Oiling and machine cleaning	31.90	100 (1.00)	31.90	1/6000	.00532	
6. Get metal bar into position to feed into machine as needed	1.35	100 (1.00)	1.35	1/270		.00500
7. Clear chips from machine	5.50	80 (.80)	4.40	1/135		.03259
8. Remove pieces from drop pans, place in slots in special tray holder	20.25	100 (1.00)	20.25	1/135		.15000
9. Sharpen spare tools for next run	20.00	100 (1.00)	20.00	1/2000		.01000
Total normal time (manual) per unit					.03395	.19759
Add allowances (10% allowance for rest and delay taken from local labor contract)					.00339	.01976
Total standard time (manual) per unit					.03734	.21735
Machine Time (actual) per unit §					.30000	
Standard Cycle time per unit					.33734	

* All times recorded in decimal minutes, i.e., 20 is two tenths of a minute.
† Average production run per setup—2,000 units.
‡ Standard metal bars of a particular hardness are specified for this product by the general foreman.
§ Based on average run time for varying grades of materials utilized. Also contains allowances for unavoidable down time.
‖ Based on tolerances specified by general foreman acting under the direction of the statistical quality control group.

Table 2

Column 1	Column 2 Average Time	Column 3 Rating	Column 4 (Col. 3 × Col. 2) Leveled Time	Column 5 Occurrence per Cycle	Column 6 (Col. 4 × Col. 5) External Time	Column 7 (Col. 4 × Col. 5) Internal Time
1. Set up machine to run lock nuts*	10.00	100	10.00	1/6000	.00167	
2. Feed first metal bar into machine, run initial pieces, inspect, adjust tooling†	10.00	80	8.00	1/6000	.00133	
3. Remove old bar end, feed new bar	2.50	100	2.50	1/270	.00926	
4. Inspection. Sampling basis during each run§	1.35	100	1.35	1/270		.00500
5. Oiling and machine cleaning	15.90	100	15.90	1/6000	.00265	
6. Get metal bar into position to feed into machine as needed	1.35	100	1.35	1/270		.00500
7. Clear chips from machine	4.05	100	4.05	1/135		.03000
8. Remove pieces from drop pans and dump into metal tote boxes	1.35	100	1.35	1/270		.00500
9. Sharpen spare tools	10.00	100	10.00	1/2000		.00500
Total normal time (manual) per unit					.01491	.05000
Add allowances (10% allowance for rest and delay taken from local labor contract)					.00149	.00500
Total standard time (manual) per unit					.01640	.05500
Machine Time (actual) per unit‡					.15000	
Standard Cycle time per unit					.16640	

* Average production run per setup—6,000 units.
† Standard metal bars of a particular hardness are specified for this product by the general foreman.
‡ Based on average run time for varying grades of materials utilized. Also contains unavoidable down time allowances.
§ Based on tolerances and procedures specified by the statistical quality control group.

Exhibit 2—Continued

numerical calculations shown above are quite simple, the problems they illustrate are not.

I hope that this memo answers the questions you raised last week. If I can be of any further help, do not hesitate to call me. By the way, I am now in 408 Engineering but my extension number is still 4193.

P.M.

III Selected Readings

From: John Kenneth Galbraith
*THE AFFLUENT SOCIETY**

THE PARAMOUNT POSITION OF PRODUCTION

In the autumn of 1954, during the Congressional elections of that year, the Republicans replied to Democratic attacks on their stewardship by arguing that this was the second best year in history. It was not, in all respects, a happy defense. Many promptly said that second best was not good enough—certainly not for Americans. But no person in either party showed the slightest disposition to challenge the standard by which it is decided that one year is better than another. Nor was it felt that any explanation was required. No one would be so eccentric as to suppose that second best meant second best in the progress of the arts and the sciences. No one would assume that it referred to health, education, or the battle against juvenile delinquency. There was no suggestion that a better or poorer year was one in which the chances for survival amidst the radioactive furniture of the world had increased or diminished. Despite a marked and somewhat ostensible preoccupation with religious observances at the time, no one was moved to suppose that 1954 was the second best year as measured by the number of people who had found enduring spiritual solace.

Second best could mean only one thing—that the production of goods was the second highest in history. There had been a year in which production was higher and which hence was better. In fact in 1954 the Gross National Product was $360.5 billion; the year before it had been $364.5. This measure of achievement was acceptable to all. It is a relief on occasion to find a conclusion that is above faction, indeed above debate. On the importance of production there is no difference between Republicans and Democrats, right and left, white or colored, Catholic or Protestant. It is common ground for the general secretary of the Communist Party, the Chairman of Americans for Democratic Action, the President of the United States Chamber of Commerce, and the President of the National Association of Manufacturers.

. . . It is an index of the prestige of production in our national attitudes that it is identified with the sensible and the practical. And no greater compliment

---

* Reprinted by permission of Houghton Mifflin Co., Boston, Massachusetts, 1958 (chap. ix, pp. 121–24, 126).

can be paid to the forthright intelligence of any businessman than to say that he understands production. Scientists are not without prestige in our day, but to be really useful we still assume that they should be under the direction of a production man. . . .

*   *   *   *   *

. . . Yet production remains central to our thoughts. There is no tendency to take it, like sun and water, for granted; on the contrary, it continues to measure the quality and progress of our civilization.

Our preoccupation with production is, in fact, the culminating consequence of powerful historical and phychological forces—forces which only by an act of will we can hope to escape. Productivity, as we have seen, has enabled us to avoid or finesse the tensions anciently associated with inequality and its inconvenient remedies. It has become central to our strivings to reduce insecurity. And as we shall observe in the next chapters its importance is buttressed by a highly dubious but widely accepted psychology of want; by an equally dubious but equally accepted interpretation of national interest; and by powerful vested interest. . . .

*   *   *   *   *

Thus even in the conventional wisdom no one questions the importance of technological advance for increasing the production (and also multiplying the products) from the available resources. These gains are regularly viewed with great and even extravagant pride. Improvements in technology do not come by accident. They are the result of investment in highly organized scientific and engineering knowledge and skills. Yet we do very little to increase the volume of this investment, except perhaps where some objective of military urgency is involved. Rather we accept whatever investment is currently being made and applaud the outcome.

The investment almost certainly could be much greater and far more rational. Even on the most superficial view, the scientific and engineering resources by which modern technology is advanced are most unevenly distributed between industries. In industries where firms are few and comparatively large—oil, metallurgy, automobiles, chemicals, rubber, heavy engineering—the investment in technological advance is considerable. The research and developmental work on which this advance depends is well financed and comprehensive. But in many industries where the firms are numerous and small—coal mining, home construction, clothing manufacture, the natural-fiber textile industry, the service industries—the investment in innovation is negligible. No firm is large enough to afford it on an appreciable scale; there is real question as to whether it is worth while for such firms. . . .

From: Henry R. Towne
*"FOREWORD TO SHOP MANAGEMENT"**

[EDITORS' NOTE: Col. Towne was President of the American Society of Mechanical Engineers, and President of Yale and Towne Manufacturing Company. His active career spanned the period from the 1880's to the first decade of this century.]

The monogram of our national initials, which is the symbol for our monetary unit, the dollar, is almost as frequently conjoined to the figures of an engineer's calculations as are the symbols indicating feet, minutes, pounds, or gallons. The final issue of his work, in probably a majority of cases, resolves itself into a question of dollars and cents, of relative or absolute values. . . . To ensure the best results, the organization of productive labor must be directed and controlled by persons having not only good executive ability, and possessing the practical familiarity of a mechanic or engineer, with the goods produced and the processes employed, but having also, and equally, a practical knowledge of how to observe, record, analyze, and compare essential facts in relation to wages, supplies, expense accounts, and all else that enters into or affects the economy of production and the cost of the product.

As pertinent to the subject of industrial engineering, I will also quote the following from an address delivered by me, in February, 1905, to the graduating students of Purdue University:

"The *dollar* is the final term in almost every equation which arises in the practice of engineering in any or all of its branches, except qualifiedly as to military and naval engineering, where in some cases cost may be ignored. In other words, the true function of the engineer is, or should be, not only to determine how physical problems may be solved, but also how they may be solved most economically. For example, a railroad may have to be carried over a gorge or arroyo. Obviously it does not need an engineer to point out that this may be done by filling the chasm with earth, but only a bridge engineer is competent to determine whether it is cheaper to do this or to bridge it, and to design the bridge which will safely and most cheaply serve, the cost of which should be compared with that of an earth fill. Therefore, the engineer is, by the nature of his vocation, an economist. His function is not only to design, but also so to design as to ensure the best economical result. He who designs an unsafe structure or an in-operative machine is a bad engineer; he who designs them so that they are safe and operative, but needlessly expensive, is a poor engineer, and, it may be remarked, usually earns poor pay; he who designs good work, which can be executed at a fair cost, is a sound and usually a successful engineer; he who does the best work at the lowest cost sooner or later stands at the top of his profession, and usually has the reward which this implies."

I avail of these quotations to emphasize the fact that industrial engineering, of which shop management is an integral and vital part, implies not merely the

---

making of a given product, but the making of that product at the *lowest cost* consistent with the maintenance of the intended standard of quality. The attainment of this result is the object which Dr. Taylor has had in view during the many years through which he has pursued his studies and investigations.

*   *   *   *   *

The conclusions embodied in Dr. Taylor's "Shop Management" constitute in effect the foundations for a new science—"The Science of Industrial Management." As in the case of constructive work the ideal engineer is he who does the best work at the lowest cost, so also, in the case of industrial operations, the best manager is he who so organizes the forces under his control that each individual shall work at his best efficiency and shall be compensated accordingly. Dr. Taylor has demonstrated conclusively that, to accomplish this, it is essential to segregate the *planning* of work from its *execution;* to employ for the former trained experts possessing the right mental equipment, and for the latter men having the right physical equipment for their respective tasks and being receptive of expert guidance in their performance. Under Dr. Taylor's leadership the combination of these elements has produced, in numberless cases, astonishing increments of output and of earnings per employee.

We are proud of the fact that the United States has led all other nations in the development of labor-saving machinery in almost every field of industry. Dr. Taylor has shown us methods whereby we can duplicate this achievement by vastly increasing the efficiency of human labor, and of accomplishing thereby a large increase in the wage-earning capacity of the workman, and a still larger decrease in the labor cost of his product.

The records of experience, and the principles deduced therefrom, set forth by Dr. Taylor in this book, should interest and appeal to all workers in the industrial field, employer and employee alike, for they point the way to increased efficiency and earning power for both. We are justly proud of the high wage rates which prevail throughout our country, and jealous of any interference with them by the products of the cheaper labor of other countries. To maintain this condition, to strengthen our control of home markets, and, above all, to broaden our opportunities in foreign markets where we must compete with the products of other industrial nations, we should welcome and encourage every influence tending to increase the efficiency of our productive processes.

From: M. J. Moroney

*FACTS FROM FIGURES**

[EDITORS' NOTE: The author is a Fellow of the Association of Incorporated Statisticians, and of the Royal Statistical Society.]

A very little consideration shows that there is scarcely a hole or corner of modern life which could not find some application, however simple, for statistical theory and show a profit as a result. It has something to offer the man who specializes in any of the branches of management in industry. It offers assistance

* Reprinted by permission of Penguin Books, Ltd., Baltimore, Maryland, 1953 (pp. 460–63).

to the man responsible for purchasing and goods inward inspection. In the hands of the cost accountant or the time and motion study man it acts as a hone to sharpen traditional tools. . . .

Consider, for a moment, some of the fields where the techniques may be applied. There is scope and often real necessity for them in leather tanning, in the paper-making mill, and in the preparation of pharmaceutical products. It is applied in glass technology, in rubber technology, and in the manifold branches of applied chemistry and metallurgy on which we so much depend for the comforts of modern civilization. We find it in steel works, in agricultural research, and in the textiles industry. . . . Mathematical principles spread out in ever widening circles of practical application; diverse techniques developed in varying fields by practical men are unified and strengthened by the mathematicians.

At bottom it boils down to this: wherever anything is measured numerically, wherever there is an attempt, however rough, to assess anything in the form of numbers, even by the simple process of counting, then there begins to arise the necessity for making judgements as to the significance of the data and the necessity for traffic rules by which the flow of information may proceed smoothly and purposefully. In a word, there is the need for statistics. The application of scientific method to every phase of industry (which is a phenomenon of rapidly growing proportions) inevitably has brought about an increase in measurement of every kind. It is widely accepted now that, even if in the present state of knowledge and in the hurlyburly of production we are able to measure what we are dealing with only roughly, it is far better to make some rough measurement than no measurement at all. . . .

*   *   *   *   *

If you are young, then I say: Learn something about statistics as soon as you can. Don't dismiss it through ignorance or because it calls for thought. Don't pass into eternity without having examined these techniques and thought about the possibility of application in your field of work, because very likely you will find it an excellent substitute for your lack of experience in some directions. It will curb your over-enthusiasm. If you are older and already crowned with the laurels of success, see to it that those under your wing who look to you for advice are encouraged to look into this subject. . . .

From: James E. Howell and Daniel Teichroew

*MATHEMATICAL ANALYSIS FOR BUSINESS DECISIONS**

[EDITORS' NOTE: The authors are Associate Professor of Economics and Professor of Management, Graduate School of Business, Stanford University.]

. . . [I]t is appropriate to ask just how practical the application of mathematics to business problems really is. The chapter has been titled "Management Science Models" because the words "management science" are coming to be

---

* Reprinted by permission of Richard D. Irwin, Inc., Homewood, Illinois, 1963 (pp. 281–84, 287–88).

associated with the practical application of mathematics and quantitative techniques to business problems.

The application of mathematics to business problems can be termed successful if it aids the manager in his tasks of decision making, planning, and administering, or if it aids in the development of a body of knowledge and techniques which reduces formerly unsolvable problems to solvable ones.

*   *   *   *   *

THE MANAGEMENT SCIENCE APPROACH

Management science models have their origins in certain qualitative and para-quantitative decision-making methods which have long been used by managers. These methods are based primarily on intuition and experience. The decision maker by accumulating experience has acquired, perhaps subconsciously, the ability to make a "good" or "the best" decision.

A further improvement in decision making usually occurs when the decision maker explicitly formulates his alternatives and the qualitative effect of his proposed decision. For example, suppose a decision maker is concerned with the economic order quantity. . . . He has presumably been using some order quantity in the past, say x_0, which he is considering increasing. He might prepare, or have in mind, a table such as the following:

Desirable Consequences	*Undesirable Consequences*
1. If the order quantity is increased, there will have to be fewer orders in in any given time period, and hence the clerical cost of ordering will be decreased.	1. If the order quantity is increased, the average inventory will be increased, and hence more money will be tied up in carrying the inventory.
2. If the price should rise, the firm would have received a larger number of units at the old price.	2. Because of the larger inventory there is more danger that the item will become obsolete, and hence a loss will be suffered.

As a refinement of this approach, the decision maker can attach subjective weights to the several effects and then determine whether or not the order quantity should be increased. Since the method is still essentially qualitative, no information is given about the amount of change in the order quantity.

The procedure can be made more quantitative by specifying the objectives more explicitly and by assigning numerical weights to each according to its importance. This is an *index-number* approach. In the example, the decision maker might decide that he has two major objectives—to reduce clerical cost and to guard against obsolescence—and that the first objective is twice as important as the second. He might then determine that doubling the quantity ordered would reduce clerical costs by $100 and increase the potential cost of obsolescence by an amount equivalent to $50. The value of doubling the quantity ordered is then

$$100 - 50 = 50$$

Since this is positive, he would probably want to double the order quantity. The calculation would be carried out for other plausible changes in the quantity ordered and a decision made.

. . . Management science models as they are known today are simply formal, logical extensions of the earlier, less systematic decision processes. The following is a description of the elements in the development of these more formal and more quantitative models.

Quantitative analysis of business problems has several important characteristics. First, the problem is encountered in a "real-world setting," in an "environment." After identifying it in qualitative terms, the problem must be translated into quantitative terms; that is, the problem must be abstracted from its environment. This step, probably a large part of the whole analytical process, means building a model which is an abstract representation of the situation being analyzed. This step of abstracting to a formal model is a very difficult one and requires a degree of skill which rests in large part on experience and judgment.

The model will not, and should not, be an exact equivalent of the situation as the analyst encounters it; the whole approach is based on the premise that the problem as encountered is too complex, too "environmentally rich," to be solved by direct attack. If this is not true, then, of course, no formal analytical apparatus is necessary.

The verbal descriptions of problems are actually verbal models of particular situations. The following is a typical political model:

"The right wing of the French electorate is sufficiently aroused by the inept handling of overseas affairs that if the Communist vote lines up with them, as is possible due to the Communist opposition to Monsieur X, the government will fall."

This verbal economic model purports to explain the 1957–58 recession:

"The recession could have been stopped had the defense spending cutback been delayed, had the money rates been eased sooner and business confidence restored before unemployment had passed three million."

The inadequacy of words becomes apparent when a model is presented quantitatively. It is in the attempt to present relationships with precision, as well as quantitatively, that the use of mathematics is growing in model development. The vagueness, the ambiguity, the lack of clear and specific definitions of the character of a situation described verbally are faults which can be avoided by formalized mathematical presentation of problems. This objective is not always achieved. In the minds of many, formalized models take on an aura of authenticity and accuracy which can lead to misapplication. . . .

*　　*　　*　　*　　*

LIMITATIONS AND EXTENSIONS OF THE MANAGEMENT SCIENCE APPROACH

The reactions of a manager to the management science approach may be that the procedure is fine for hypothetical problems, but that it cannot be applied because the assumptions are never satisfied in real life. . . .

Consider the practical objection that the variables or factors which affect decision-making problems cannot be quantified. It is true that many of the factors which enter into business decision problems are presently thought of as being qualitative variables and, therefore, incapable of being expressed quantitatively. However, the history of science can be stated in terms of the sequence of situations whereby variables which were thought of as being qualitative came to be treated quantitatively. . . .

A second objection . . . is that there will be so many variables and the relationships among them will be so complex that it will be impossible to include them all in a quantitative model. This complexity, of course, is the very reason why a human being needs some help as a decision maker, and this help can come only from an objective and abstract treatment of the problem.

Most business problems become extremely complicated if one attempts to consider all the possible factors that might affect the problem. A basic premise made throughout this text is that problems can be simplified by neglecting some factors and simplifying some relationships without necessarily invalidating the subsequent results. It is, of course, possible to oversimplify a problem; the real art is to determine how much a problem should be simplified. . . .

Relationships can be approximated to any desired degree of accuracy by increasing the effort spent in determining the relationships and by making use of the power and complexity of mathematics. The mathematical techniques tend to become complicated as the relationships become more complex. A number of the techniques covered in this text illustrate how the relationships and the mathematics become more difficult as the models become more realistic. . . .

From: Bernard Barber

SCIENCE AND THE SOCIAL ORDER*

[EDITORS' NOTE: The author is Professor of Sociology in Barnard College, Columbia University.]

THE NATURE OF SCIENCE: THE PLACE OF RATIONALITY IN HUMAN SOCIETY

Man has always dreamed of, but never actually lived in a Garden of Eden. It is of the essence of the human condition that man lives not in a compliant but in a resistant environment, an environment which he must constantly make an effort to control, if he cannot wholly master it. Man's physical and social situations are ever setting tasks for him in which he must somehow efficiently adapt means to ends. For if it is inherent in man's situation to have to expend "effort" to cope with the environment, it is also in his nature to have a limited amount of energy for this general effort. Man everywhere and at all times, therefore, has had to make at least some of this effort efficiently and economically.

In his need to economize energy, in his need to adapt means to ends efficiently, man has always had the indispensable aid of his power of rationality and of some knowledge about his environment. . . . Here it is enough to recognize the universality of human rationality, to examine its characteristics somewhat more closely, and to show its connection with science. For this is the essential point from which our whole investigation starts: that the germ of science in human society lies in man's aboriginal and unceasing attempt to understand and control the world in which he lives by the use of rational thought and activity. I take it that Professor Percy Bridgman, the Nobel Prize physicist, was making much the same point when he said, "I like to say there is no scientific method as such, but rather only the free and utmost use of intelligence." We shall see, of course, how rationality and intelligence must be disciplined before they become the highly developed science we are familiar with, but it is essential to understand first this prime human source of science.

*   *   *   *   *

* Reprinted with permission of the publisher from *Science and the Social Order* by Bernard Barber. Copyright 1952 by The Free Press, A Corporation. (Excerpts from pp. 7–8, 12–13, 18, 21.)

President Conant of Harvard, who is himself a chemist, has recently described the essential functions for all science of those highly generalized and systematic sets of ideas which . . . are the heart of highly developed modern science. He calls these ideas "conceptual schemes." It is with the nature of conceptual schemes and their relations with such matters as experimentation, mathematics, and "common sense" that we now wish to deal.

*   *   *   *   *

. . . Modern science has been remarkably successful in defining and isolating "concrete" systems of phenomena which correspond precisely to the abstract systems of ideas which compose its conceptual schemes. As Professor H. Levy has indicated, this isolation of systems is highly important for science. Once a system is isolated, by controlled variation of one part, the effect on other parts of the system can be ascertained. In this fashion, experimentation, as we call this procedure of controlled variation which compares like and unlike cases, discloses the effect of the several variables in the conceptual scheme.

*   *   *   *   *

Perhaps we can now see very clearly the sense in which highly developed science based on conceptual schemes of great generality is essentially a dynamic enterprise. The endless making of improved conceptual schemes introduces a dynamic element into the very center of scientific activity. In this way, human rationality takes on the unending power to move heaven and earth, for sooner or later changes in conceptual schemes issue in changes in everyday life and everyday technology. Veblen has said that "the outcome of any serious research can only be to make two questions grow where one question grew before." This is a characteristic of science, this is a dynamic quality it has, that modern man must not only learn about, but learn to live with. For this is the source of the unending social consequences of science. . . .

From: Charles A. Beard

*PUBLIC POLICY AND THE GENERAL WELFARE**

[EDITORS' NOTE: Mr. Beard is a prominent historian of the twentieth century.]

"Every enterprise in the Great Society itself, as well as the Great Society itself, rests upon administration. Industry on a large scale depends upon organization—upon the management of large numbers of employees of different crafts and arts and the disposition of material goods. In some industries, the administrative organization is national and even international in its range. Thousands, hundreds of thousands, of men and women must be brought together and distributed among various departments of production. They must be graded in

---

* Beard, Charles A., *Public Policy and the General Welfare,* copyright © 1941, Holt, Rinehart & Winston, Incorporated. Reprinted by permission. (Excerpts from pp. 148 *et seq.*)

a vast economic hierarchy, with skilled engineers and managers at the top and
the simple day laborers at the bottom. They must be assigned specific and appropriate tasks in the operation of the organization. They must be directed,
controlled."

"The state in the Great Society, like the private corporation, also rests upon
administration."

From: Victor A. Thompson
*MODERN ORGANIZATION**

[EDITORS' NOTE: The author is Professor and Chairman of the Department of Political and Social Science, Illinois Institute of Technology.]

As the bureaucratic form has developed, associated at it is with the advance
of specialization, the most stubborn problem has proved to be the securing of
cooperation among individual specialists. . . .

*   *   *   *   *

Modern bureaucracy is an adaptation of older organizational forms, altered
to meet the needs of specialization. Modern specialization is grafted onto it, but
old traces of the past remain. Along with technological specialiation we find sur-
vivals of Genghis Khan and aboriginal war chiefs. We find the latest in science
and technology associated with the autocratic, monistic, hierarchical organization
of a simpler time. We find, in short, specialization and hierarchy together.

*   *   *   *   *

. . . [M]odern bureaucracy attempts to fit specialization into the older hierarchical framework. The fitting is more and more difficult. There is a growing
gap between the right to decide, which is authority, and the power to do, which
is specialized ability. This gap is growing because technological change, with
resulting increase in specialization, occurs at a faster rate than the change in
cultural definitions of hierarchical roles. This situation produces tensions and
strains the willingness to cooperate. Much bureaucratic behavior can be understood as a reaction to these tensions. In short, *the most symptomatic characteristic of modern bureaucracy is the growing imbalance between ability and
authority.* . . .

*   *   *   *   *

. . . In an earlier period organizations could depend much more on the "line
of command." The superior could tell others what to do because he could master
the knowledge and techniques necessary to do so intelligently. As science and
technology developed, the superior lost to experts the *ability* to command in
one field after another, but he retained the *right* as part of his role.

*   *   *   *   *

* Reprinted from *Modern Organization* by Victor A. Thompson, by permission of
Alfred A. Knopf, Inc. Copyright 1961. (Excerpts from pp. 4–6, 12–13, 19–21, 61, 63–65,
77–78.)

Internally, the bureaucratic organization is a complex structure of technical interdependence superimposed upon a strict hierarchy of authority. The entire structure is characterized by a *preoccupation with the monistic ideal.* The hierarchical institution is monocratic. It is a system of superior and subordinate role-relationships in which the superior is the *only* source of legitimate influence upon the subordinate. Everyone in the organization finds himself in such a relationship. Since this was the original organizational relationship, it has dominated organizational theory and practice and still does so. This exclusive emphasis on hierarchy has produced our prevailing organizational theory and informed management practice. We shall refer to this theory as the monistic or monocratic conception of organization. Although conditions are undoubtedly changing, it is our prevailing organizational ideal. . . .

* * * * *

Under the influence of the primitive monistic ideal, modern organizations are modeled more on the parent-child relationship than on the adult relationships of specialist equals and colleagues. Attempts to maintain the legitimacy of the ideal leads to a great deal of hypocrisy and pretence and to the creation of myths, such as "the ignorance of the masses," "the indispensability of leadership," and "the magical power of fear."[1] Since a monocratic institution cannot admit the legitimacy of conflicts, the legitimacy of divergent goals and interests, much effort is spent securing the appearance of consensus and agreement—securing a "smooth-running organization." The modern organization wants converts as much as it wants workers. It is concerned with the thoughts of its members as well as their actions, and with the thoughts of its public about the thoughts and actions of its members. Consequently, it is concerned with its members' total lives, with what they think and do away from work as well as at work.

Preoccupation with hierarchy governs the distribution of rewards by modern organizations. Ranks of deference correspond to ranks of authority, and deference is manifested by the bestowal of good things. Success within our society means, for the most part, progression up an organizational hierarchy. Modern organizations, consequently, face a growing problem of rewarding specialists. To be socially regarded as successful, specialists must give up their technical fields and enter a hierarchy. Many do, leaving us with growing shortages of many kinds of technically trained people. . . .

* * * * *

Hierarchical relations overemphasize the veto and underemphasize approval of innovation. Since there is no appeal from the superior's decision, a veto usually ends the matter. However, an approval will often have to go to the next higher level where it is again subject to a veto. A hierarchical system, therefore, always favors the status quo. . . .

* * * * *

The superior has the right to deference from his subordinates. What makes this right significant is that it is one-way. The superior has a right to be somewhat insensitive as to subordinates' personal needs.[2] The ranking of roles with

---

[1] Peter Blau, *The Dynamics of Bureaucracy* (Chicago: University of Chicago Press; 1955), p. 219.

[2] Wilbert E. Moore, *Industrial Relations and the Social Order,* rev. ed. (New York: The Macmillan Company, 1951), pp. 183–184. He says this insentivity of superiors to the needs of subordinates is the cause of much trouble in organizations. Harold Leavitt says superiors generally resist the introduction of objective performance stand-

regard to the amount of deference due them is what we mean by the "status system."[3] Although specialties are also status ranked, by far the most visible and virile ranking in organization is ranking according to hierarchical position. . . .

*   *   *   *   *

These roles and the corresponding status system are simply incompatible with democratic egalitarianism. People are always grateful when a person in a superordinate position exercises his rights with humanitarian restraint. "He's a regular guy." They do not feel that they have a right to expect this.

*   *   *   *   *

The monistic concepts is unable to account for specialization. More specifically, it cannot account for the delegation of nonhierarchical authority. The existence of such authority is consequently denied or hidden by fictions, such as, for example, "The staff only advises; it does not command." Furthermore, the monistic concept asserts that *hierarchical authority* is created by delegation from above. . . . Only nonhierarchical authority is created by delegation from above.

The monistic concept, since it is based entirely upon the institution of hierarchy and completely ignores the fact of specialization, naturally confuses rights with abilities: for example, the right to make decisions with the ability to do so. This confusion of rights with abilities results in the popular journalistic presentation of the actions of organizations, including states, as the actions of their top officials. It also encourages elitist interpretations of society, one of the latest of which is *The Power Elite,* by C. Wright Mills.[4]

Hierarchical roles began to develop at times and under conditions when it was credible to think of the chief as the most capable person. Under these circumstances, vast rights became associated with the role. Belief in the unusual powers, or charisma, of persons who perform such roles has continued in the form of the status system. Although specialization has enormously changed the circumstances of organized action, modern organization theory and, to a considerable extent, practice is fixated on the system of hierarchical roles.[5] The fact and implications of specialization are hardly recognized in organization theory. The forcing of specialization into the hierarchical framework gives us our characteristic form of organization, bureaucracy. As we shall see in the following chapters, much of the behavior within bureaucracy derives from tensions generated by the conflict between specialization and hierarchy. The cultural definitions which comprise hierarchy change much more slowly than do the facts of specialization. This resistance to further rationalization of organized activity performs no particular instrumental function.[6] It is more in the nature of a

---

ards because they interfere with the superiors' right to dominate the situation, to command respect, to rule the roost. (Harold J. Leavitt, *Managerial Psychology*, Chicago: University of Chicago Press, 1958, p. 261.)

[3] The term "status system" is not entirely adequate. "Status" is a social position. Positions are ranked according to the amount of deference due them—according to their prestige. Here we are really concerned with the "prestige system"; however, the term "status system" has been used so much in place of such terms as "prestige system" that we feel it will communicate more.

[4] New York: Oxford University Press, Inc., 1957. [Mills'] "elite" consists, by definition, of the top two or three persons in big-business, political, and military hierarchies. He says that if the line were lowered, the "elite" could be defined away (p. 18).

[5] Even the departmentalists, the "Gulick school," were concerned only with arranging jobs for purposes of supervision. The jobs—specialization—were taken for granted.

[6] Among those who have argued that the extreme deference ranking (status) aspect of these roles performs no organizational function are Moore: *op. cit.,* p. 138; Carl

"cultural lag." This lag in modification of the roles is undoubtedly reinforced by vested interests in the old role definitions because of their intimate relation to the distributive system. The lag is also reinforced by mechanisms supportive of the status system. Incompatibilities between hierarchical claims to dominance, on the one hand, and on the other, the cultural norms of autonomy, independence, and equality may be softened by charismatic overevaluations of superordinates and by the other mechanisms discussed above. Romanticism comes to the rescue of an unsatisfactory reality.

Dreyfuss: *Occupation and Ideology of the Salaried Employee*, trans. Ernst E. Warbling (New York: Columbia University Press; 1938), pp. 1–18; Henri De Man: *Joy in Work*, trans. Eden and Cedar Paul (London: George Allen and Unwin, Ltd., 1929), pp. 200–204. Barnard argues that *status* aids in communication, but he really means *positions* and *roles* rather than prestige ranking. His point that status, as the principal motivation in organizations, is an extremely important part of the incentive system, while true, proves too much. If status is to function as an incentive, it must be available to all. The skewed distribution of status causes it to act as an anti-incentive; it reduces solidarity, hence motivation to cooperate. Barnard himself points this out. (Chester Barnard, "Functions and Pathology of Status Systems in Formal Organizations," in William Foote Whyte, ed. *Industry and Society*, New York: McGraw-Hill Book Company, 1946). See also, Moore, *op. cit.*, p. 184; Peter Drucker: *The New Society: The Anatomy of the Industrial Order* (New York: Harper & Brothers, 1950), pp. 92–95.

FABRICATED STEEL PRODUCTS

I Case Introduction

Synopsis

Fabricated Steel Products manufactures and sells $80 million in three lines of high-quality steel products. Only the last two of the past five years have been profitable for the company. The largest share of the doubling in sales volume since 1963 came in the last year. With the huge sales expansion have come concerns for increased overtime, growing in-process inventories, and finished goods stockouts. The marketing department expresses displeasure at the mounting late orders. The production department retorts with the claim that the volume of customized items sold by marketing causes bottlenecks on the production floor. The production department also finds difficulty working with the computer-based production planning, scheduling, and control system "housed" in the controller's office. The controller insists that the production people act without regard for the computer system and that the mathematical bugs that may be in the system won't be uncovered unless the production people do exactly what the system directs them to do. The general manager wants a consultant to help him get his people to work together as a system.

Why This Case Is Included

The Fabricated Steel Products case poses an instance of the classical conflict between marketing and production. There is opportunity to examine the application of management science to inventory control in a computerized planning, scheduling, and control system. The case portrays another dimension of conflict in the relationship of men and computerized control systems. The reader can explore the reasons for the failure of the computerized system to produce the expected results.

Diagnostic and Predictive Questions

In answering the following diagnostic and predictive questions, remember that these questions apply theories and conceptual ideas from certain disciplines. Such theories are valuable to understand basic forces at work in the policy system (diagnosis) and to predict what will happen in the system in the future (prediction). Since each reading abstracts from the total policy system certain factors or variables into the closed or partial viewpoint of one theory or discipline, no one reading gives answers to the practical policy problems of the case.

In diagnosis and prediction, the parts of the problem are studied with "other things being equal."

Following each question are listed readings which will be helpful in answering the question. The readings included with this case are marked (*). By referring to the author index at the end of this book, you may locate the other readings listed.

1. Given the facts concerning FSP as a producing system, use the concepts from managerial economics to understand more clearly the history of losses, the present profits, and the prospects for the future.

Read: *Spencer and Siegelman, *Managerial Economics: Decision Making and Forward Planning*, pp. 202–12, 242–48.

2. What are the assumptions built into the inventory model which is the heart of the planning, scheduling, and control system? Are the assumptions valid in this particular case?

Read: *Buffa, *Production-Inventory Systems: Planning and Control*, pp. 49–58; Buffa, *Modern Production Management*, pp. 442–43, 450–51, 471.

3. Why have the production manager and his production employees not accepted the planning, scheduling, and control system? Even if there were no technical "bugs" in the system as designed by the controller's office, would the system have been accepted from the specialists by the functional managers?

Read: *Ackoff, "Management Misinformation Systems"; *O'Connell, "Beyond Economics: Coordinomics," Part II.

4. By logically using case facts specify the conflict between the marketing strategy and the production process. Why does the conflict arise?

Read: Miller and Starr, *Executive Decisions and Operations Research*, pp. 38–42, 45–47, 50; Buffa, *Modern Production Management*, pp. 442–43, 450–51, 471.

5. What would be the advantages to the scientific approach proposed by the controller—provided it was technically sound—over the judgment or traditional rules of thumb seemingly used in scheduling by the production department?

Read: Lieber and Lieber, *The Education of T. C. Mits*, pp. 44–49; Taylor, "Principles of Scientific Management"; Barber, *Science and the Social Order*, pp. 7–8, 12–13, 18, 21.

6. Picture the impact of a machine operator ignoring the computer-issued EOQ for shelving, producing the traditional lot size, and then disregarding the exception report from the production control department. Trace the impact through the FSP Production Control System in Exhibit C in the case.

7. What do you think would happen if the production people in FSP immediately began acting in a stereotypical bureaucratic style in response to the present planning, scheduling, and control system—that is, blindly obeying the orders from the computer so as to sanctify these means into ends?

Read: Merton, "Bureaucratic Structure and Personality."

Policy Questions for This Specific Case

In answering the following policy questions, the results of diagnosis and prediction are used to reduce the amount of guesswork, or judgment, in designing action solutions. However, since certain parts of the total case situation cannot be reduced to science, and since "other things are not equal," judgment must still be used to fill in the factors not accounted for by readings. You will also need a second kind of judgment as you put value weights on different scientific predictions, since different theories may point to conflicting solutions.

8. What changes, if any, would you make in the design of the planning, scheduling, and control system? (See Questions 2 and 3 with their assigned readings.)

9. What would you do to manage the conflict between the marketing strategy and the production process? (See Question 4 and its assigned readings.)

10. If you were the consultant, Mr. Owens, what would you recommend to the general manager as a plan of action? Specify the sequence of specific steps to be done by specific individuals. (See Question 3 and its assigned reading.)

11. Would you make any change in the FSP organization structure in order to improve the relationship between the production department and the controller's department?

Major Policy Issues: Tentative Generalizations about Any Policy System

In arriving at conclusions for the following questions, generalize from the facts in the case and use your own ideas to (a) confirm, (b) modify, or (c) test the workability of the concepts and theories from readings. As an executive or professional, use wisdom to merge theory, on the one hand, with "brute facts" and practice, on the other.

12. Does the installation of an integrated, computer-based planning and control system necessarily alter the balance of power among the functional departments? Under what conditions is it truly possible for functional managers to control the system instead of being controlled by it? (See the Ackoff reading assigned in Question 3.)

13. It is often said that interpersonal conflict in organizations is dysfunctional and should be resolved but that technical conflict (competition for resources, tension over market demands and production economies, etc.) may well be functional if well managed. Do the events in the FSP case suggest that the distinction obscures reality and suggests too simplistic an approach? Are there indeed types of conflict we not only tolerate but foster in organizations?

Questions for Original Student Work in Analysis and Policy

The methods of viewing this case as represented by the authors' questions and selection of readings are not exhaustive. There are other relevant ideas for diagnosis and prediction. Furthermore, there are other ways of stating policy questions. More powerful analyses and wiser solutions will result by drawing on your own training and experience for (a) relevant concepts and theories and (b) creative ways of asking policy questions. The following questions are designed to help you acquire this skill.

14. While reflecting on case facts, what additional theories from prior education give you insights as to "what is going on" in Fabricated Steel Products? As to what might be predicted to happen in the future?

15. Other than the policy questions asked by the authors, what pragmatic ways can you think of to state the practical problems faced by executives in the case?

II Fabricated Steel Products*

Fabricated Steel Products (FSP) is a medium-sized manufacturer of steel products whose yearly sales are approximately $80 million. (See Exhibit A, page 290.)

Although profits have increased markedly from 1963 to 1967, the company has had serious difficulties in scheduling production and meeting delivery commitments. FSP has three lines of products that are sold through separate sales organizations. The 1967 sales breakdown among the product lines is as follows:

Acme .... $30 million
Bell .... 20 million
Zenith .... 30 million

The Bell line is a set of products manufactured for use by governmental agencies, schools, and the like. It is a new line (introduced in mid-1965) and accounts for a large proportion of the recent sales increase.

The Zenith line has been known as the "Cadillac" of the industry. The products are built of heavy gauge steel and have the reputation of being so strong that "they can support an elephant." The line consists of 2,500 different items, although many of the items differ only in color or size of various components. The general manager of FSP is concerned about the increasing number of late orders filled for Zenith products and about a continual state of emergency that exists in the plant. With a 40% sales increase in one year, overtime has increased, in-process inventories consume most of the available storage space and the number of stockouts of finished goods is increasing.

Mr. George Owens was called in by the general manager as a consultant. His assignment was to try to determine the major causes of FSP's difficulties and to recommend a plan to overcome them. The general manager suggested that he talk to any appropriate people in the organization. (See Exhibit B.) Because the sales department bore the brunt of customer complaints, Mr. Owens decided to start with the sales manager:

Look, five years ago another consultant came in here and told us to cut the product line. But we know it can't be done because in this business you need a full line in order to sell anything. We sell to distributors who will buy our competitors' products if we cut our line. There is something rotten in our production department. They ought to be able to schedule our products but they can't. Look, six months ago we averaged 300 late orders per week. Our production people said that they needed to get away from the customer so we

---

* Case written by Richard J. Swersey, Assistant Professor of Industry and Operations Research, Wharton School of Finance and Commerce, University of Pennsylvania.

instituted a four-week delivery policy. We were the last company in the industry to give instantaneous service, and we gave up the policy. And for what? We now average 360 late orders per week. I am tired of customers complaining to the general manager about late orders.

It seemed to Mr. Owens that the sales manager made some good points about modern industrial practice. Many companies handled extensive product lines without serious difficulty and they shipped on time. Since it seemed that the difficulty lay with the production department, he went to see the production manager:

Those clowns in sales are going to drive us into the ground. We have a modern plant, a highly automated process, and yet all of these newfangled special products keep us behind the eight ball. Why, just last week we got an order for a pink bench with a 63-inch wooden top. A pink bench!! Ninety-eight per cent of our products are grey or green, and we have automated paint lines. Do you know what it costs to hand spray something? And another thing, they sell bench tops by the lineal inch. I have to take a 72-inch top and throw away 9 inches to make a 63-inch top. No wonder we can't fill our orders on time. I have too many men tied up making things like 63-inch pink benches!

Mr. Owens ventured the feeling that maybe some help was needed in scheduling:

Five years ago the systems people designed and installed a production planning, scheduling, and control system. I told them it wouldn't work because it required too much paper work from the machine operators. The computer is supposed to tell us when to produce things and the economic quantities to produce. Hell, the numbers we've been getting lately are ridiculous. For years we've always run shelves in batches of 10,000. Everyone understood that. In the last six months that computer told us to run anywhere from 6,364 to 13,459 per batch. That just had to be wrong, so we stuck to our normal pattern of 10,000.

I can see that look in your eyes that says he doesn't understand inventory and production models. I know those numbers came from a lot-size formula, but no one has ever explained to me where they get the data for that formula or that it is properly applied here. We'd be better off without that damn system. I get a weekly printout of control exceptions that I don't understand. No one from that systems outfit has ever explained the principles of the system and what the potential savings are if we worry about some of these control exceptions like inventory shortages, machine bottlenecks, etc.

If those aren't enough headaches, I have in-process inventories coming out of my ears, and it's the fault of those clowns in production control. We used to have a clean manufacturing system. We'd start from steel and run a product straight through either to finished goods inventory or to a truck for a delivery. I'll admit we had baskets of parts lying around waiting to be used, but this was necessary in order to schedule our machines efficiently. Three years ago we got a new hotshot production controller fresh out of an MBA program. He was really going to set the world right. First thing he did was insist we put a fence around the in-process inventory. So we put in a controlled access storage area, bought some forklift trucks, hired 20 people for materials handling and paperwork, and what do you think happened? The last consultant we hired told us to stock those in-process parts on a regular basis because of possible economies in linking fabrication and assembly. Now, 75 per cent of our storage is in these parts. No wonder we can't stock enough finished goods to ship on time.

Mr. Owens was sure he was on the right track now. All fingers pointed to the production control system and the computer, so he went to see the controller:

Our production control system was beautifully designed. [See Exhibit C.] It is easy to understand and easy to work with. The trouble with it is the lack of implementation by the production people. We asked for two of their best people when we designed the system, and we got no cooperation from those people. All they do is fight the system. Our idea of control is based on some fundamental principles. We let the computer do the routine calculations of quantities and timing of production and the routine paper work processing for bills of materials and methods sheets. The rest of the system is keyed to the computerized information. If a machine operator varies from the quantity requested, or if the amount logged into the storage area varies from the quantity requested, or from the operator's count, the computer rings a bell. Production control gets a daily exception report so that we can track down the errors. Our machine operators are too used to loose control. They produce the same batch sizes that they've always produced without regard to what anyone else knows is correct. We have a weekly meeting with production control and the foremen to discuss these exceptions. All we ever get are excuses or lost memories as to what happened. I'll admit that there may be some mathematical bugs in our system, but we'll never know what's wrong unless the production people carry out exactly what the system directs them to do. This is the only way to improve or debug the system.

Mr. Owens then had a long discussion with the systems people concerning the mathematical model in the system. The model was a standard *EOQ* with Safety Stock, and the same model was used for in-process parts and finished goods. The calculations were as follows:

$$EOQ_i = \sqrt{\frac{2A_i r_i(t)}{h_i}}$$

Safety Stock$_i = 3 \times LT_i \times$ Mean Absolute Deviation of Demand$_i$

where

$r_i(t) =$ Forecasted monthly demand in month t for product i.
$A_i =$ Setup cost per run for product i.
$h_i =$ Carrying cost per item per month h for product i.
$LT_i =$ Average production lead time for product i.

and demand was forecasted by,

$$r_i(t) = 0.2 \text{ actual demand in month } t - 1 + 0.8\, r_i(t-1)$$

The model was designed to allow only one stockout in 20 times. The constants in the forecasting equation had been adopted as being the best practice for these products. Setup costs were determined by the engineering department as each new product had been designed. They were adjusted annually for changes in wage rates. The company's policy was to change 25% of standard cost as yearly inventory carrying cost.

Mr. Owens then reported briefly to the general manager that he had enough information to recommend a plan to deal with the major issues of the study.

Exhibit A

FSP SALES AND PROFITS
(In Millions of Dollars)

	Sales	Profits
1963	$40	$ −2,500,000
1964	45	−2,000,000
1965	50	−3,000,000
1966	57	500,000
1967	80	3,200,000

Exhibit B

FSP ORGANIZATION CHART

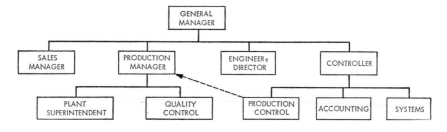

Exhibit C

FSP PRODUCTION CONTROL SYSTEM

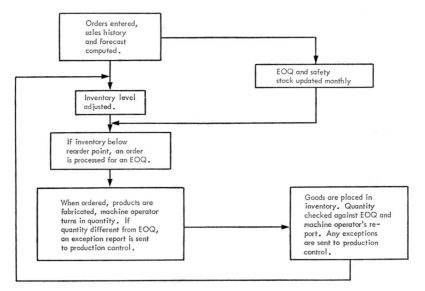

He did inquire, however, why the general manager allowed this situation to deteriorate:

This plant and equipment is modern enough to support a sales level of $120 million. When I took over in 1966, we had just suffered our third straight year of net loss. My staff consists of people who are competent in their jobs. I will admit they lack the skills to work together as a system. Complaints come in from all size-class of customers and about almost every product. This, in light of our reputation, which equates custom and standard products, is intolerable. I know very well that the computer is the lightning rod for staff complaints. What I want you to do is to show us how to work as a system and if you don't do anything else around here, I want you to train my staff so that we can have at least one staff meeting where I don't hear the computer being blamed for our ills.

III Selected Readings

From: Milton H. Spencer and Louis Siegelman
*MANAGERIAL ECONOMICS: DECISION MAKING AND FORWARD PLANNING**

[EDITORS' NOTE: Dr. Spencer is Professor of Business Administration at Wayne State University. Dr. Siegelman is an economist with the First National Bank of Chicago.]

COST-OUTPUT FUNCTIONS

*   *   *   *   *

Short-Run Costs. In production economics the *short run* is defined as a period long enough to vary output by altering the combination of variable to fixed factors. The short run thus refers to a cost structure and time period in which some of the productive factors (e.g., plant, basic equipment, management) are fixed in quantity and form. A firm with a given arrangement of productive factors will experience one short-run cost situation, while another firm twice as large with twice as many resources available will have a different short-run cost curve. The *long run* refers to the cost structure of a firm over a period of time long enough so that no factors need be considered as fixed, or in other words a period of time long enough so that all of the firm's costs are variable. . . .

The level of the various cost curves—fixed, variable, total, and marginal—will be affected by factor prices, but the exact nature (curvature) of the curves will depend on the nature of the underlying production function. . . . The fundamental starting point in the development of cost theory is that a unique functional relationship exists between cost and the rate of output for a firm. Admittedly, there may be independent variables other than output that will

---

* Reprinted by permission of Richard D. Irwin, Inc., Homewood, Illinois, 1959 (pp. 202–12, 242–48) .

affect cost (e.g., lot size, factor prices, etc.), but these are assumed to remain constant in constructing the cost curves. The curves thus derived are static or timeless in nature, meaning that they show only the various costs that will prevail under alternative output levels. . . . At the present our interest turns to the nature of the theoretical cost curves as determined by their underlying production functions.

Figure 7–1 illustrates three kinds of short-run total cost curves under condi-

FIGURE 7–1

THREE KINDS OF SHORT-RUN TOTAL COST FUNCTIONS

A, Constant Productivity; B, Decreasing Productivity; C. Increasing Productivity

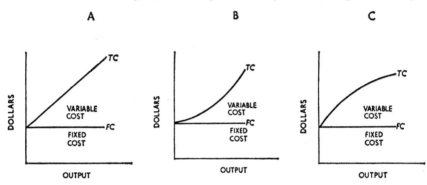

tions of constant, decreasing, and increasing productivity, with output scaled horizontally and dollar costs vertically. In Figure 7–1A the TC curve is linear, thus indicating a constant price per unit of variable input purchased, and hence the fact that each unit of input as well as each unit of output adds the same amount to total cost. This type of linear cost function exists over a range of output when, assuming constant price levels and technology, the fixed factors are readily divisible so that the fixed and variable resources can be mixed at minimum-cost proportions for each output level. . . . At zero output, fixed cost (cash rent, taxes, insurance, and depreciation as a function of time and obsolescence) equals total cost, while at higher output levels the difference is represented by variable costs. The total cost curve, it may be noted, would turn sharply upward for output levels beyond the physical capacity of the equipment.

Figure 7–1B shows a total cost function where the factor-product relationship is one of diminishing marginal productivity throughout the entire range of output. The reason for this is that even if each unit of the variable factor costs as much as any previous unit, each additional unit of the input adds less to total output than the previous unit. (The elasticity of the production function is less than 1 throughout.) This illustration of diminishing returns throughout the entire output range occurs when the fixed factor is limited and not divisible. The shape or curvature of the TC curve is due solely to the technical nature of the input-output relationship and not to market conditions or factor prices.

Figure 7–1C shows the total cost curve for a production process under conditions of increasing returns throughout the entire output range. This means that each unit of output adds less to total cost than the previous unit, and this in turn is due to the fact that each unit of input in the underlying production function (whose elasticity is greater than 1 throughout) adds more output than does the previous unit of input. Actually, the possibility of an enterprise experiencing increasing returns for all output levels is unlikely; at best, it may perhaps be found at the lower levels of production where the fixed factors are excessive relative to the variable, and before the stage of diminishing productivity sets in. Incidentally, it should be noted, as must be evident by now, that the curvature of the production function and the total cost curve is always reversed in that when one is concave, the other is convex and vice versa, except with a linear relationship.

The most common cost functions are those that combine the phases of both increasing and decreasing returns. Most cost functions that appear to be of a constant or increasing returns nature are more likely to be only segments of curves and, if they could be extrapolated, would eventually exhibit a phase of decreasing returns. Figure 7–2 illustrates this generalized type of cost function

FIGURE 7–2

GENERALIZED SHORT-RUN TOTAL COST FUNCTION

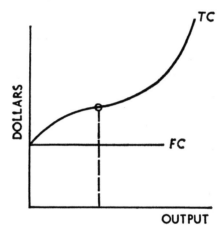

with increasing returns resulting at all levels of output to the left of the vertical dashed line (because total cost rises at a decreasing rate) and decreasing returns to the right of the dashed line (because total cost is rising at an increasing rate). The curve as shown is the type commonly encountered in economics textbooks and is based on the classic production function of increasing-decreasing returns. . . .

To improve comprehension of a firm's cost structure as well as serve as a better basis for various kinds of decision problems confronting management, the average and marginal cost curves are necessary. For most purposes these include average total cost (ATC), average variable cost (AVC) and marginal cost (MC). All of these can be derived from the total cost data. Thus, $ATC = TC \div$ output; $AVC = TVC \div$ output; $MC = \triangle TC \div \triangle$ output. Numerous other methods can be employed in deriving these curves from given output and total cost data, since $TC = FC + VC$ is the basic relationship, and the quantities can be algebraically transposed as desired. In Figure 7–3 the ATC, AVC, and MC curves corresponding to the generalized total cost curve of Figure 7–2 are presented. Note that the MC curve passes through the minimum ATC and AVG points in accordance with the rule of the "average-marginal relationship" . . . as with the total cost curve, the shape (curvature) of the average and marginal

FIGURE 7–3

GENERALIZED SHORT-RUN AVERAGE AND MARGINAL COST FUNCTIONS

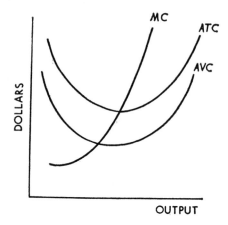

curves is conditioned by the technical nature of the underlying production function and not by factor prices. A change in the latter will shift the curves up or down but will not affect the slopes as such.

Long-Run Costs.   The analysis of short-run costs reveals how a firm's costs will vary in response to output changes within the limits of a time period short enough so that the size of the plant may be regarded as fixed. By extending the logic one step further, it is possible to develop a *long-run cost curve* or function which, correspondingly, is one that shows the variation of cost with output for a period long enough so that all productive factors, including plant and equipment, are freely variable in amount. The knowledge of such a long-run cost curve, or "planning curve" as it is also called, can be of use to management in determining output rates over periods long enough so that assets acquired for use during the period can be fully amortized, and in establishing rational policies as to optimum plant size, location, and operational standards in general.

The formal nature of the relationship between long-run costs, short-run costs, and size of plant may be established conceptually in this way. At the planning stage when management is considering the erection of a plant, it is faced with the problem of selecting one of many alternative combinations of fixed and variable factors. But at the planning stage all factors are variable, and only for each "output level" will there be a given production function and cost structure. Assuming that production costs and the nature of market demand were known for each particular layout, the appropriate layout could be determined. The long-run average cost curve, *LAC* in Figure 7–4, would then show for each possible output level, the lowest cost of producing that output, assuming plant size and intensity of utilization are covaried to obtain the best results. The following principles are thus evident or can be deduced.

1. There will exist a different short-run average cost curve, *SAC*, for each possible plant size or for each technique of production (production function). There is thus an entire family of short-run cost curves, each corresponding to a particular point on the long-run average cost curve. That is, although only five *SAC* curves are shown, infinitely more could be drawn, depending on the divisibility of productive units and their technical nature.

2. The *LAC* curve generalizes the entire family of *SAC* curves by enveloping them together. The U shape of the long-run curve implies at first lower and

FIGURE 7–4

SHORT- AND LONG-RUN AVERAGE COST FUNCTIONS

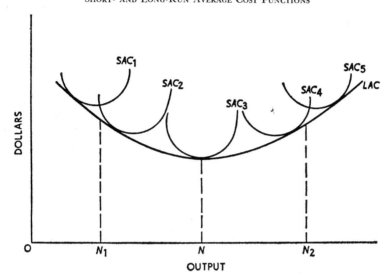

lower average costs until the "optimum" scale of plant shown by SAC_3 is reached, and thereafter successively higher average costs with larger plants.

3. The LAC curve is tangent to only one point on each SAC curve as in Figure 7–4. The tangency point occurs (*a*) to the left of the minimum-cost point on all short-run curves, which in turn are to the left of the optimum curve SAC_3, and (*b*) to the right of the lowest cost point on all short-run curves that are to the right of the optimum curve. For the optimum curve, however, the tangency occurs at the minimum point on that curve, i.e., at the lowest point on SAC_3. Therefore, for outputs less than ON for which the optimum scale is SAC_3, it is more economical to "underuse" a slightly larger plant operating at less than its minimum-cost output than to "overuse" a smaller plant. For example, it would be cheaper to produce output ON_1 with a plant designated by SAC_2 than with one represented by SAC_1. Conversely, at outputs beyond the optimum level ON, it is more economical to "overuse" a slightly smaller plant than to "underuse" a slightly larger one. Thus, it is cheaper to produce ON_2 units with plant SAC_4 than with SAC_5.

5. Finally, the tendency for long-run average costs to fall as the firm expands its scale of operations is a reflection of cost economies that are frequently encountered with increasing size, while the ultimate rise in the long-run curve is due largely to the eventual setting in of diseconomies of large-scale management. . . . [A]s the firm becomes larger and decision making more complex, the burden of administration becomes disproportionately great and "diminishing returns" to management set in.

[EDITORS' NOTE: As the authors have pointed out, the shape of the cost curves depends on the underlying production function, i.e., the relationship between inputs (men, capital, and machines) and outputs (units of production and service). The abstract below shows how the addition of a unit of input may, under certain circumstances, result in a proportionate increase in output, a greater than proportionate increase in output, a lesser than proportionate increase in output, or a decrease in output. While the authors speak of these relationships in the context of a firm's production, the same line of reasoning applies to a department, an industry, or even a country.]

*   *   *   *   *

PRODUCTION FUNCTIONS: SIMPLE RELATIONS

Taking as synonymous the terms "resources" and "factors of production" to represent the inputs (men, machines, materials, etc.) required in production, the procedure followed below is to set forth the basic relationships between resources and products in a production process. By "production process" is meant the *transformation* of inputs into output. Such transformations of factors into product may occur within a single time period such as a year, or they may occur over several time periods, or they may never occur completely. The transformation (production) period thus varies between resources and thereby complicates the problems confronting the decision maker. . . . [R]esources (representing investments over the years) must be analyzed for their effect upon output in terms of both fixed and variable costs. . . .

The economics of production management takes as its starting point the study of the entire group of possible factor combinations that could be used to produce a certain output, within a given state of technology. The heading under which this type of analysis goes is that of the *production function*. A production function is an expression of the dependent or functional relationship that exists between the inputs (factors) of a production process and the output (product) that results. Hence it is also sometimes called the "input-output" relation. Like a demand function, a production function can also be expressed in the form of a schedule or a graph as shown subsequently, or algebraically by an equation such as $Y = f(X)$.

Realistically, the output of a product can never be ascribed to a single factor of production but is rather the result of combining several factors. A more accurate expression of the production function, therefore, would be $Y = f(X_1, X_2, X_3 \ldots X_n)$, where Y refers to the specific output as a function of the various input factors specified and unspecified. The only real requirement is that each of the letters represent a specific homogeneous class of factors. . . .

The most elementary form of production analysis and the one which provides the basis for more complex consideration in production management is the single factor–product relationship. It is concerned with the transformation of a single input into a single output and hence for estimational purposes may be expressed conceptually by writing it in the form $Y = f(X)$. However, since the product Y will be the result of combining the input factor X (e.g., labor) with other factors (such as capital, land, management, etc.), the functional relationship may more appropriately be written $Y = f(X_1 \mid X_2, X_3 \ldots X_n)$. The vertical bar indicates that the input factors to the right are regarded as fixed in the production process under analysis, the factor to the left being varied. The fundamental problem in the study of the production function is to discover the probable nature of this input-output relationship. . . .

AUTO LAUNDRY STUDY

Figure 6–1, derived from Table 6–1, illustrates the results of a production function study for a small Detroit auto laundry.[1] The regression equation was a

---

[1] The study was financed by a firm interested in marketing a new type of mechanical washing system. A select group of auto laundries was chosen as a basis for the analysis.

polynomial of the second degree fitted by the method of least squares; it took the form

$$Y = -0.8 + 4.5X - .3X^2$$

where Y represents total output in cars washed per hour and X is number of men. The study was based on 22 observations over a one-month period during which time the number of workers varied from a minimum of 3 to a maximum of 10. Given the equation, the total product data in column 2 of the table can be found simply by substituting values of X from 1 to 10 in the equation and computing the corresponding values of Y. The remaining columns can then be derived directly from this information and the three curves plotted as in the chart. Since no figures were available for less than three men, the curves were extrapolated as shown by the dashed portions and by the data in parentheses in Table 6–1. Incidentally, it should also be noted that the marginal product values

TABLE 6–1

PRODUCTION FUNCTION FOR AN AUTO LAUNDRY

Regression Equation: $Y = -.80 + 4.5X - .3X^2$

(1) Variable Input (No. of Men) X	(2) Total Product (Cars Washed per Hour) Y	(3) Average Product AP AP = Y/X	(4) Marginal Product MP MP = $\Delta Y / \Delta X$
(1)	(3.4)	(3.4)	
(2)	(7.0)	(3.5)	(3.6)
3	10.0	3.3	3.0
4	12.4	3.1	2.4
5	14.2	2.8	1.8
6	15.4	2.6	1.2
7	16.0	2.3	0.6
8	16.0	2.0	0.0
9	15.4	1.7	−0.6
10	14.2	1.4	−1.2

Source: See footnote 1.

in column 4 of the table are written midway between the X values in the table and plotted midway between the X values in the chart, since they represent the *change* in total output divided by the *change* in variable input ($\Delta Y/\Delta X$). A scale break (shown on the vertical axis) is also necessary to allow for greater readability of the average and marginal product curves.

Table 6–1 and Figure 6–1, especially the latter, reveal all the characteristics of the production function as they are typically expressed in standard works on economic theory. Hence, the important features of the chart, integrating both theory and measurement, may be summarized briefly as follows.

First, the chart as a whole reveals the operation of the *Law of Variable Proportions* or the *Law of Diminishing Returns*. It shows that in a given state of technology, the addition of a variable factor of production, keeping other productive services constant, will yield increasing returns per unit of variable factor added, until a point is reached beyond which further additions of the variable factor yield diminishing returns per unit of variable factor added. This is the nature of the law as it is usually expressed in economics textbooks. It encompasses virtually all types of production functions from agriculture and automobile production through retailing and textile operations to the manufacture of zinc and zippers. It is thus a law of enormous significance as well as generality, as will become clearer from the discussion below.

Second, the chart reveals what may be called the *total-marginal relationship*. The marginal productivity curve expresses the change in total product resulting from a unit change in input. Since total product is plotted on the Y axis and input on the X axis, marginal productivity is $MP = \triangle Y / \triangle X$. As long as this ratio $\triangle Y / \triangle X$ is increasing, i.e., the MP curve is rising, the total product curve is increasing at an increasing rate and is *convex* to the X axis. The point at which the TP curve changes its curvature is the point of inflection and corresponds vertically with the peak of the MP curve as shown by the broken line in the

FIGURE 6–1

PHYSICAL PRODUCTION FUNCTION FOR AN AUTO LAUNDRY

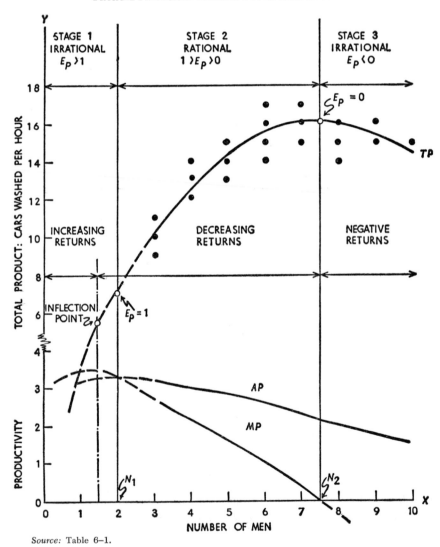

Source: Table 6–1.

diagram. In the Law of Diminishing Returns stated above, it is the peak of the marginal product curve that is referred to as the point of diminishing (marginal) returns—the point prior to which there are increasing returns to the variable factor and beyond which there are decreasing returns. (The peak of the average product curve represents the point of diminishing average returns.) When the total product curve reaches the maximum, at that point it is neither rising nor falling and hence its slope is zero. Since the ratio $\triangle Y / \triangle X$ also defines the slope of the total product curve, it follows that at that point the marginal product is zero. Beyond that point the total product is declining and hence must have a negative slope; the marginal product, therefore, is also negative, i.e., goes below the X axis. Increasing returns to the variable factor exist, therefore, when MP is positive and rising; decreasing returns occur when MP is positive and falling; and negative returns are realized when MP is negative and falling.[2]

Third, the chart reveals what may be called the *average-marginal relationship.* This is such that as long as the marginal product exceeds the average product, the average productivity of the variable factor increases; when the marginal product is less than the average product, the latter decreases; and when the average product is constant or a maximum, the marginal product is equal to it. A simple example illustrates this point. If to a class of students there is added a student whose age is above the average age of the class, the average age is increased; if his age is below the average age, the average decreases; if his age is equal to the average, the average remains the same. It should be noted from the diagram that even when the marginal productivity of the input turns down from its maximum point, the average productivity of the factor is still rising as long as its marginal productivity is greater than the average.

Fourth, economists customarily divide a production function of the type shown into what is known as the *three stages of production,* as illustrated in the chart. Stage 1 extends from zero input of the variable factor to where the average productivity of that factor is a maximum; stage 2 extends from the end of stage 1 to where the marginal product of the variable factor is zero (or to where total product is a maximum) ; stage 3 occurs where marginal product is negative (or total product is falling) . Stages 1 and 3 are defined as *irrational* in that management, if it is to maximize profits, will never knowingly apply the variable to the fixed factors in any combination that will yield a total product falling in either of these two stages. The explanation is that stages 1 and 3 are completely symmetrical and hence the reasoning is as follows. In stage 1 the fixed factors are excessive relative to the variable factor and output can always be increased by increasing the variable relative to the fixed (or by reducing the "fixed" relative to the "variable"). In a large department store understaffed with clerks, for example, sales can be increased by employing more clerks (the variable factor) relative to counters, floor space, etc. (the fixed factors) , or by closing off sections of the store relative to the number of clerks. In stage 3 the variable factor is excessive relative to the fixed, and total output can be increased by reducing the variable relative to the fixed (or increasing the "fixed" relative to the "variable") . In the case of the department store again, if it were so overstaffed with clerks that they hampered each other or perhaps even kept customers from

---

[2] It should be evident by now, at least to the reader familiar with elementary calculus, that the equation for any marginal curve can be derived by taking the derivative of the equation for the total curve. Thus, marginal profit is the derivative of total profit, marginal revenue is the derivative of total revenue, marginal product is the derivative of total product and, as will be seen in the next chapter, marginal cost is the derivative of total cost. In general, for any marginal value M,

$$M = \frac{dY}{dX} = \mathop{L}_{\triangle X \to 0} \frac{\triangle Y}{\triangle X}$$

getting into the store and hence sales were declining, sales could be increased by reducing the number of clerks (or by increasing the size of the store). Stage 2 is the only *rational* stage of production, i.e., the only area within which profits can be maximized. Accordingly, management will seek to operate in the second stage because then neither input is being used in such excessive quantity as to reduce total output. Hence, the decision maker will employ a quantity of variable factor somewhere between N_1 and N_2 to maximize the economic returns of the firm.[3]

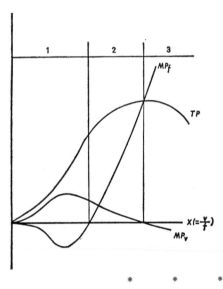

The fundamental concepts underlying the three production stages can be further developed from Figure A in which are plotted total product (*TP*), the marginal product of the variable factor (MP_v), and the deduced marginal product of the fixed factor (MP_f). The diagram illustrates the symmetry of the relations. In stage 1 the marginal product of the variable factor is positive while that of the fixed factor is negative; in stage 3 the reverse is true. Only in stage 2 are both marginal productivity curves positive. If the variable factor is available free, the manager will go to the end of the second stage; if the fixed service is free, he will stop at the beginning of the second stage. The former principle is indicative of agricultural practices where labor is abundant relative to land, as in parts of the Far East; the latter helps to explain the lavish use of land by the colonists in early American history.

*   *   *   *   *

Fifth and finally, the chart reveals the elasticity of productivity (E_p) which measures the percentage change in output resulting from a 1 per cent change in variable input, and hence helps to explain the three stages of production outlined above.[4] In stage 1 the E_p coefficient is greater than unity (written $E_p > 1$) which means that a 1 per cent change in variable input brings a more than 1 per cent change in output. In stage 2 the percentage change in output is less than proportional to the percentage change in input but greater than zero (written $1 > E_p > 0$). In stage 3 where total product is falling, the percentage change in output is negative with respect to any percentage increase in variable input.

PRODUCTION FUNCTIONS: MULTIPLE RELATIONS

*   *   *   *   *

An important law . . . is the "Law of Returns to Scale." That is, instead of varying only one input and noting the effect on output as was done previously, we can consider the possibility of varying all inputs and measuring the change in

---

[3] The *precise* amount of factor hire will depend upon its price and the price of the product. The ratio of the two is the economic choice indicator which, when equated to the marginal product ratio, determines the maximum profit position.

[4] The point elasticity formula is:

$$E_p = (\Delta Y/Y) / (\Delta X/X) = (X\Delta Y) / (Y\Delta X) \overset{>}{\underset{<}{=}} 1,$$

and can be used to measure the elasticity at any point on the *TP* curve either graphically or from the data in Table 6–1.

output. For example, suppose that all of the factors in a production process could be varied in the same proportion, say doubled or trebled. It seems that the consequent change in total output would also be altered in the same proportion, being doubled if all inputs were doubled and trebled if all imputs were trebled. A relation of this type, where the percentage change in output is exactly proportional to the percentage change in all inputs as a whole (so that $E_p = 1$) is known as constant returns to scale, and a production function that exhibits this characteristic is said to be *linear and homogeneous*. In reality, conditions are rarely if ever encountered in which a production function is characterized by constant returns to scale over the full range of inputs, despite the fact that it might seem very plausible for constant returns to scale to be the rule rather than the exception. Actually, a production function would almost always exhibit alternating stages of both increasing $(E_p > 1)$ and decreasing $(E_p > 1)$ returns to scale due to two categories of phenomena explained below.

1. *Indivisibility of Productive Services.* The first condition which tends to prevent the occurrence of constant returns to scale over the full range of inputs is the indivisibility of productive services. Rarely is it possible to increase all of the productive factors in the same proportion; as a consequence, some of the factors are always being underworked or overworked relative to others at most levels of output, and this results in alternations of increasing and decreasing returns. For example, doubling the rate of output of an assembly line may still require only one final inspector instead of two; one locomotive may have sufficient horsepower to pull forty freight cars as adequately as twenty; a salesman may be able to take on a full line of goods instead of a single item at no significant increase in costs; and to a bank, the expense of investigating and managing a loan does not increase in proportion to the size of the loan. These examples from the fields of production, marketing, finance, etc., serve to illustrate that the advantage of size may result in economies that yield increasing returns to scale. That of decreasing returns to scale is illustrated in the following passage from a classic work on the subject:

"There is a story of a man who thought of getting the economy of large scale production in plowing, and built a plow three times as long, three times as wide, and three times as deep as the ordinary plow and harnessed six horses to pull it, instead of two. To his surprise, the plow refused to budge, and to his greater surprise it finally took fifty horses to move the refractory machine. In this case, the resistance, which is the thing he did not want, increased faster than the surface area of the earth plowed, which was the thing he did want. Furthermore, when he increased his power to overcome this resistance, he multiplied the number of his power units instead of their size, which eliminated all chance of saving there, and since his units were horses, the fifty could not pull together as well as two."[5]

2. *Decision-Making Role of Management.* The second factor tending to upset the plausibility of constant returns to scale lies in the decision-making role of management. In its function as coordinator, management may be able to delegate authority, but ultimately decisions must emanate from a final center if there is to be uniformity in performance and policy. As the firm grows, increasingly heavy burdens are placed on management so that eventually this class as a factor of production is overworked relative to others, and "diminishing returns to management" set in. Thus it is the growing difficulty of coordination that eventually stops the growth of any firm. As pointed out in Chapter 1, the development of sequential decision making as a science may have the effect of (*a*) reducing the time necessary to make a given number of correct decisions, or (*b*) increasing the number of correct decisions that can be made in a given time period. However, this would only tend to prolong the realization of decreasing

---

[5] J. M. Clark, *Studies in the Economics of Overhead Costs*, p. 116.

returns to scale rather than eliminate it. Further, even if sequential-decision science could eventually overcome the limitational factor due to management, there is still the indivisibility consideration discussed previously that serves as a major factor preventing constant returns to scale.

From: Elwood S. Buffa
BASIC INVENTORY MODELS*

Earlier we classified pure inventory systems as being a special case of continuous production-inventory systems, that is, systems which are producing for stock. Recall that we stated that the pure inventory system was really a truncated system where it was logical to abstract just the inventory portion from the system as a whole because direct managerial control was restricted. Though if one views the overall system it is difficult to envision a pure inventory system which has no interaction at all with the rest of the distribution system and with the production system. However, there are some values in looking at just inventories. First, as we have noted, some systems are in fact truncated, and the operations phase of the activity is dominated by the inventory problem. These are largely wholesaling, retailing, and some government and military supply situations. A second value, however, is the fact that especially in the postwar period a great deal of effort has been poured into the study of inventory problems by practitioners and operations researchers. We know more about the behavior of the inventory system than we do about the more complex systems. The result is that in studying a broad range of production-inventory systems it may be of value to start with the simpler pure inventory situation.

Recall from our discussion of the functions of inventories in Chapter 1 that we isolated five basic functions: inventories to fill the transit pipelines, cycle inventories, buffer inventories, seasonal inventories, and the decoupling function. The fact that inventories serve these functions indicates immediately that they have a basic set of values for management. They are not to be minimized; rather we are seeking their correct levels in the context of the requirements of the particular system we may be analyzing or designing. We are seeking a balance between one set of costs which increase with inventories and another set of costs which decrease with inventories. In more complex systems we will be seeking a trade off between inventories and labor costs, or inventories and customer service, or inventories and community relations and public image.

RELEVANT COSTS

Our ability to quantify and develop rigorous models of most managerial problems is dependent on the determination of the behavior of relevant costs. The practical application of such models is also dependent on our ability to obtain the cost data as we have defined it. Most cost accounting data is related to "responsibility centers," and cost data usually represent average product costs or period costs. The process is normally one of grouping individual component costs, which may represent the average of the appropriate variable costs, and by

---

* Reprinted from Elwood S. Buffa, *Production-Inventory Systems: Planning and Control* (Homewood, Ill.: Richard D. Irwin, Inc., 1968) , pp. 49–58.

adding in an allocation for joint costs. The result is that in many instances the relevant cost behavior for model-building purposes must be determined by special studies. The following types of incremental or out-of-pocket cost items are commonly relevant: costs which depend on lot sizes, production costs, handling and storage costs, shortage costs, and capital costs.

Costs Depending on Lot Sizes. There are certain costs which remain the same regardless of the size of the lot purchased or requisitioned. This would be true for the retailer ordering from the distributor, for the distributor ordering from a factory warehouse, for the factory warehouse ordering a new production run from the factory, and for the factory ordering raw materials from vendors. We call these kinds of costs "preparation" or "setup" costs. If we are ordering to replenish supplies at one stock point from another stock point, our interest is in the incremental clerical costs of preparing orders, following up these orders, expediting them when necessary, etc. We must take care, however, to be sure that we obtain a true incremental cost of order preparation. It is not correct to derive the figure by simply dividing the total cost of the ordering operation by the average number of orders processed. A large segment of the total costs of the ordering function are fixed, regardless of the number of orders issued. There is, however, a variable component, and this is the pertinent figure for our use. Even then it may be difficult to determine satisfactorily the incremental cost which results from placing one more order. Quantity discounts and handling and shipping costs are other factors which vary with lot sizes.

When the order to be placed is on the factory, then the equivalent decision is in determining the size of the production run. In this instance the preparation costs are the incremental costs of planning production, writing production orders, setting up machines, and controlling the flow of orders through the factory. Material handling costs in the plant have an effect on production lot sizes in much the same way that freight costs may affect purchase lot sizes.

Production Costs. We have already discussed, in the previous paragraph, the preparation costs of production. There are some other production costs which can have a direct bearing on inventory models, however. These are overtime premiums and the incremental costs of changing production levels, such as hiring, training, and separation costs.

Handling and Storage Costs. Some incremental costs vary directly with the size of inventories. There are handling costs required to place materials in inventory and to issue them from inventory and costs associated with storage, such as insurance, taxes, rent, obsolescence, spoilage, and capital costs. If average inventories increase, these costs will also increase and vice versa.

Shortage Costs. What costs occur if we run out of stock? It would be difficult to find such an item in accounting records. Nevertheless, a part shortage can be the cause of idle labor on a production line and be the cause of incremental labor cost to perform operations out of sequence. What is the magnitude of the opportunity cost we must absorb if business is lost because of stock shortages?

Capital Costs. If average inventories increase, then the capital invested in inventory increases proportionately, and we must assign an opportunity cost. This cost does not appear in the accounting records. In general, the appropriate interest rate to use should reflect the opportunities for investment of comparable funds within the organization. The cost of our borrowed funds would represent the lower limit.

THE CLASSICAL INVENTORY MODEL

The earliest derivation of a classical inventory model is due to F. W. Harris. Incongruously, however, this formula is often referred to in the literature as the "Wilson formula." Wilson was a consultant and used such a formula in many company applications. In 1931, F. E. Raymond . . . published the first book-

length work on inventory control and attempted to show how the classical
inventory model could be extended to account for a wide variety of conditions
in industry.

The objective of the classical inventory model is to determine the lot size (Q)
under highly idealized conditions. Figure 1 shows the assumed structure of

FIGURE 1

IDEALIZED STRUCTURE OF INVENTORY LEVELS IN RELATION TO TIME
IN THE CLASSICAL INVENTORY MODEL

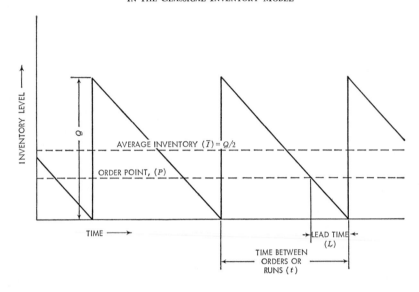

inventory level in relation to time. Q units are ordered when the inventory level
has declined to the reorder point (P). The order is placed precisely at the point
such that demand over the procurement lead time (L) will draw the inventory
down to zero. The previous order for Q units is timed to be received exactly at
that point which raises the inventory level to Q and the cycle repeats itself. Let us
establish the following list of symbols:

TIC = total incremental cost.
TIC_o = total incremental cost of an optimal solution.
Q = lot size.
Q_o = optimal lot size [economic order quantity (EOQ)].
R = annual requirements in units.
c_H = inventory holding cost per unit per year.
c_P = preparation costs per order.
P = order point.
L = lead time.
B = buffer stock.
I = inventory level.
S = sales rate.

Objective Function. The incremental costs for this simple system are those
associated with holding inventory and those associated with the preparation costs
of an order of size Q. Therefore, the cost function which we wish to minimize is:

$$TIC = \text{inventory holding costs} + \text{preparation costs.}$$

The lot size Q is the variable which is under managerial control. We can see from Figure 1 that if Q is increased the average inventory level, $Q/2$, will increase proportionately. If the inventory holding cost per unit per year is c_H, the annual incremental costs associated with inventory are:

$$c_H \frac{Q}{2}$$

If we now take a specific example where the inventory holding cost $c_H = \$0.50$ per unit per year, then the inventory holding cost function reduces to 0.50 $(Q/2) = Q/4$. The graph of the inventory holding cost function appears in Figure 2 (a).

FIGURE 2a

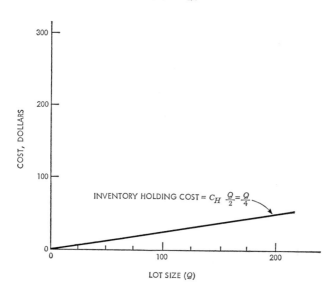

LOT SIZE (Q)

In a similar way we can make a general statement about the annual preparation cost. These costs depend on the number of times that orders are placed each year and the incremental cost of placing an order. The number of orders written to supply an annual requirement of R will depend on the lot size Q of each order, or R/Q. If the preparation cost is c_P for each order, then the annual preparation costs may be expressed as:

$$c_P \frac{R}{Q}$$

In our example let us assume that $R = 250$ units per year and $c_P = \$10$ per order. The annual preparation cost function then reduces to 250 $(10/Q) = 2,500/Q$. The graph for this function is shown in Figure 2 (b).

The two components of cost shown in Figure 2 (a) and (b) are simply added algebraically to form the total incremental cost (TIC) curve shown in Figure 2 (c). In Table 1 we have shown the computed points for all three curves for specified values of lot size. We can see that the minimum cost lot size is $Q_o = 100$ units by inspection of either Figure 2 (c) or Table 1. The lot size of 100 units is,

FIGURE 2*b*

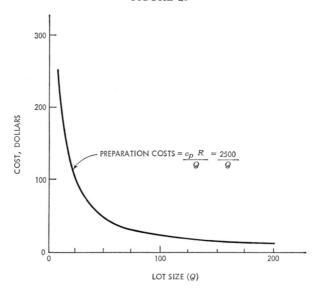

LOT SIZE (Q)

FIGURE 2*c*

CLASSICAL INVENTORY MODEL. $R = 250$ UNITS PER YEAR, $c_H = \$0.50$
PER UNIT PER YEAR, AND $c_p = \$10$ PER ORDER

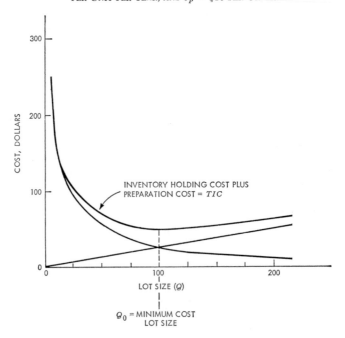

LOT SIZE (Q)

Q_0 = MINIMUM COST
LOT SIZE

of course, associated with the total incremental cost of $50 in column (4). What we want is a general solution for all problems of this type.

TABLE 1

INCREMENTAL COSTS FOR HOLDING INVENTORY, PREPARATION, AND TOTAL COSTS FOR CURVES OF FIGURE 2 (c). $R = 250$ UNITS PER YEAR, $c_H = \$0.50$ PER UNIT PER YEAR, AND $c_p = \$10$ PER ORDER

(1) Lot Size, Q	(2) Inventory Holding Cost = Q/4	(3) Preparation Costs = 2,500/Q	(4) Total Incremental Cost = Col. (2) + Col. (3)
25	$ 6.25	$100.00	$106.25
50	12.50	50.00	62.50
75	18.75	33.33	52.08
100 = Q_o	25.00	25.00	50.00
125	31.25	20.00	51.25
150	37.50	16.67	54.17
175	43.75	14.30	58.05
200	50.00	12.50	62.50

Derivation of Minimum Cost Formulas. In order to develop formulas for easy computation which are applicable to any set of data we will start with the general expression for total incremental cost which we have already developed.

$$TIC = \frac{c_H Q}{2} + \frac{c_p R}{Q} \tag{1}$$

This is an equation for the total incremental cost curve, and we wish to determine a general expression for Q_o, the lot size associated with this, the minimum of the total incremental cost curve. Mathematically, this may be done by finding the value of Q for which the slope of the total incremental cost curve is zero. Using the elements of simple differential calculus, the first derivative of equation (1) with respect to Q is:

$$\frac{d(TIC)}{dQ} = \frac{c_H}{2} - \frac{c_p R}{Q^2} \tag{2}$$

The value of equation (2) is the slope of the line tangent to the total incremental cost curve. We wish to know the value of Q when this slope is zero, therefore, we set equation (2) equal to zero and solve for Q:

$$\frac{c_H}{2} - \frac{c_p R}{Q_o^2} = 0 \tag{3}$$

$$Q_o = \sqrt{2c_p R / c_H}$$

The cost of an optimal solution computed by equation (3) may be derived by substituting the value of Q_o in equation (1):

$$TIC_o = \sqrt{2c_p c_H R} \tag{4}$$

The optimal number of orders or manufacturing runs per year N_o and the time between orders or manufacturing runs t_o for an optimal solution follow:

$$N_o = R / Q_o \tag{5}$$

$$t_o = Q_o/R = 1/N_o \tag{6}$$

Equations (3, 4, 5, and 6) are the ones of possible value in computations. If we substitute the values for R, c_H, and c_P used in our specific example we obtain:

$$Q_o = \sqrt{\frac{2 \times 250 \times 10}{0.50}} = \sqrt{10,000} = 100 \text{ units}$$

$$TIC_o = \sqrt{2 \times 10 \times 0.50 \times 250} = \sqrt{2500} = \$50$$

$$N_o = \frac{250}{100} = 2.5 \text{ orders per year}$$

$$t_o = \frac{1}{2.5} = 0.4 \text{ years between orders}$$

Some simple extensions of the classical inventory model are useful in relaxing some of the assumptions of the model. For example, the classical model assumes that all demand is satisfied on time. We can, however, allow back orders to occur through the provision for shortage costs in the model. The classical model assumes price or value to be fixed, whereas we know that quantity discounts are a common practice. The assumption that the entire order is received in inventory all at one time is often not appropriate, particularly in production lots where the finished items may be placed in inventory over a period of time as they are produced. We will discuss these extensions in the balance of this chapter and reserve the discussion of the removal of the assumption of constant demand and lead time for the following chapter, where we will consider inventory management systems.

*   *   *   *   *

From: Russell L. Ackoff

MANAGEMENT MISINFORMATION SYSTEMS*

INTRODUCTION

The growing preoccupation of operations researchers and management scientists with Management Information Systems (MIS's) is apparent. In fact, for some the design of such systems has almost become synonymous with operations research or management science. Enthusiasm for such systems is understandable: it involves the researcher in a romantic relationship with the most glamorous instrument of our time, the computer. Such enthusiasm is understandable but, nevertheless, some of the excesses to which it has led are not excusable.

Contrary to the impression produced by the growing literature few computerized management information systems have been put into operation. Of those I've seen that have implemented, most have not matched expectations and some have been outright failures. I believe that these near- and far-

* Reprinted from *Management Science*, Vol. XIV, No. 4 (December 1967), pp. B147–B156.

misses could have been avoided if certain false (and usually implicit) assumptions on which many such systems have been erected had not been made.

There seems to be five common and erroneous assumptions underlying the design of most MIS's each of which I will consider. After doing so I will outline an MIS design procedure which avoids these assumptions.

GIVE THEM MORE

Most MIS's are designed on the assumption that the critical deficiency under which most managers operate is the *lack of relevant information*. I do not deny that most managers lack a good deal of information that they should have, but I do deny that this is the most important informational deficiency from which they suffer. It seems to me that they suffer more from an *overabundance of irrelevant information*.

This is not a play on words. The consequences of changing the emphasis of the MIS from supplying relevant information to eliminating irrelevant information is considerable. If one is preoccupied with supplying relevant information, attention is almost exclusively given to the generation, storage, and retrieval of information: hence emphasis is placed on constructing data banks, coding, indexing, updating files, access languages, and so on. The ideal which has emerged from this orientation is an infinite pool of data into which a manager can reach to pull out any information he wants. If, on the other hand, one sees the manager's information problem primarily, but not exclusively, as one that arises out of an overabundance of irrelevant information, most of which was not asked for, then the two most important functions of an information system become *filtration* (or evaluation) and *condensation*. The literature on MIS's seldom refers to these functions let alone considers how to carry them out.

My experience indicates that most managers receive much more data (if not information) than they can possibly absorb even if they spend all of their time trying to do so. Hence they already suffer from an information overload. They must spend a great deal of time separating the relevant from the irrelevant and searching for the kernels in the relevant documents. For example, I have found that I receive an average of forty-three hours of unsolicited reading material each week. The solicited material is usually half again this amount.

I have seen a daily stock status report that consists of approximately six hundred pages of computer print-out. The report is circulated daily across managers' desks. I've also seen requests for major capital expenditures that come in book size, several of which are distributed to managers each week. It is not uncommon for many managers to receive an average of one journal a day or more. One could go on and on.

Unless the information overload to which managers are subjected is reduced, any additional information made available by an MIS cannot be expected to be used effectively.

Even relevant documents have too much redundancy. Most documents can be considerably condensed without loss of content. My point here is best made, perhaps, by describing briefly an experiment that a few of my colleagues and I conducted on the OR literature several years ago. By using a panel of well-known experts we identified four OR articles that all members of the panel considered to be "above average," and four articles that were considered to be "below average." The authors of the eight articles were asked to prepare "objective" examinations (duration thirty minutes) plus answers for graduate students who were to be assigned the articles for reading. (The authors were not informed about the experiment.) Then several experienced writers were asked to reduce each article to 2/3 and 1/3 of its original length only by eliminating words. They also prepared a brief abstract of each article. Those who did the condensing did not see the examinations to be given to the students.

A group of graduate students who had not previously read the articles were then selected. Each one was given a random selection of four articles each of which was in one of its four versions: 100%, 67%, 33%, or abstract. Each version of each article was read by two students. All were given the same examinations. The average scores on the examinations were then compared.

For the above-average articles there was no significant difference between average test scores for the 100%, 67%, and 33% versions, but there was a significant decrease in average test scores for those who had read only the abstract. For the below-average articles there was no difference in average test scores among those who had read the 100%, 67% and 33% versions, but there was a significant *increase* in average test scores of those who had read only the abstract.

The sample used was obviously too small for general conclusions, but the results strongly indicate the extent to which even good writing can be condensed without loss of information. I refrain from drawing the obvious conclusion about bad writing.

It seems clear that condensation as well as filtration performed mechanically or otherwise, should be an essential part of an MIS, and that such a system should be capable of handling much, if not all of the unsolicited as well as solicited information that a manager receives.

THE MANAGER NEEDS THE INFORMATION
THAT HE WANTS

Most MIS designers "determine" what information is needed by asking managers what information they would like to have. This is based on the assumption that managers know what information they need and want it.

For a manager to know what information he needs he must be aware of each type of decision he should make (as well as does) and he must have an adequate model of each. These conditions are seldom satisfied. Most managers have some conception of at least some of the types of decision they must make. Their conceptions, however, are likely to be deficient in a very critical way, a way that follows from an important principle of scientific economy: the less we understand a phenomenon, the more variables we require to explain it. Hence, the manager who does not understand the phenomenon he controls plays it "safe" and with respect to information, wants "everything." The MIS designer, who has even less understanding of the relevant phenomenon than the manager, tries to provide even more than everything. He thereby increases what is already an overload of irrelevant information.

For example, market researchers in a major oil company once asked their marketing managers what variables they thought were relevant in estimating the sales volume of future service stations. Almost seventy variables were identified. The market researchers then added about half again this many variables and performed a large multiple linear regression analysis of sales of existing stations against these variables and found about thirty-five to be statistically significant. A forecasting equation was based on this analysis. An OR team subsequently constructed a model based on only one of these variables, traffic flow, which predicted sales better than the thirty-five-variable regression equation. The team went on to *explain* sales at service stations in terms of the customers' preception of the amount of time lost by stopping for service. The relevance of all but a few of the variables used by the market researchers could be explained by their effect on such perception.

The moral is simple: one cannot specify what information is required for decision making until an explanatory model of the decision process and the system involved has been constructed and tested. Information systems are subsystems of control systems. They cannot be designed adequately without taking control in account. Furthermore, whatever else regression analyses can yield, they cannot yield understanding and explanation of phenomena. They describe and, at best, predict.

GIVE A MANAGER WHAT INFORMATION HE NEEDS AND HIS DECISION MAKING WILL IMPROVE

It is frequently assumed that if a manager is provided with what information he needs, then he has no problem in using it effectively. The history of OR stands to the contrary. For example, give most managers an initial tableau of a typical "real" mathematical programming, sequencing, or network problem and see how close they come to an optimal solution. If their experience and judgment have any value they may not do badly, but they will seldom do very well. In most management problems there are too many possibilities to expect experience, judgment, or intuition to provide good guesses, even with perfect information.

Furthermore, when several probabilities are involved in a problem the unguided mind of even a manager has difficulty in aggregating them in a valid way. We all know many simple problems in probability in which untutored intuition usually does very badly (e.g., What are the correct odds that 2 of 25 people selected at random will have their birthdays on the same day of the year?). For example, very few of the results obtained by queuing theory, when arrivals and service and probabilistic, are obvious to managers; nor are the results of risk analysis where the managers' own subjective estimates of probabilities are used.

The moral: it is necessary to determine how well managers can use needed information. When, because of the complexity of the decision process, they can't use it well, then they should be provided with either decision rules or performance feedback so that they can identify and learn from their mistakes. More on this point later.

MORE COMMUNICATION MEANS BETTER PERFORMANCE

One characteristic of most MIS's which I have seen is that they provide managers with better current information about what other managers and their departments and divisions are doing. Underlying this provision is the belief that better interdepartmental communication enables managers to coordinate their decisions more effectively and hence improves the organization's overall performance. Not only is this not necessarily so, but it seldom is so. One would hardly expect two competing companies to become more cooperative because the information each acquires about the other is improved. This analogy is not as farfetched as one might first suppose. For example, consider the following very much simplified version of a situation I once ran into. The simplification of the case does not affect any of its essential characteristics.

A department store has two "line" operations: buying and selling. Each function is performed by a separate department. The Purchasing Department primarily controls one variable: how much of each item is bought. The Merchandising Department controls the price at which it is sold. Typically, the measure of performance applied to the Purchasing Department was the turnover rate of inventory. The measure applied to the Merchandising Department was gross sales; this department sought to maximize the number of items sold times their price.

Now by examining a single item let us consider what happens in this system. The merchandising manager, using his knowledge of competition and consumption, set a price which he judged would maximize gross sales. In doing so he utilized price-demand curves for each type of item. For each price the curves show the expected sales and values on an upper and lower confidence band as well. (See Figure 1.) When instructing the Purchasing Department how many items to make available the merchandising manager quite naturally used the value on the upper confidence curve. This minimized the chances of his running short which, if it occurred, would hurt his performance. It also maximized the chances of being over-stocked but this was not his concern, only the purchasing manager's. Say, therefore, that the merchandising manager initially selected price P_1 and requested that amount Q_1 be made available by the Purchasing Department.

In this company the purchasing manager also had access to the price-demand curves. He knew the merchandising manager always ordered optimistically. Therefore, using the same curve he read over from Q_1 to the upper limit and down to the expected value from which he obtained Q_2, the quantity he actually intended to make available. He did not intend to pay for the merchandising manager's optimism. If merchandising ran out of stock, it was not his worry. Now the merchandising manager was informed about what the purchasing manager had done so he adjusted his price to P_2. The purchasing manager in turn was told that the merchandising manager had made this readjustment so he planned to make only Q_3 available. If this process—made possible only by perfect communication between departments—had been allowed to continue, nothing would have been bought and nothing would have been sold. This outcome was avoided by prohibiting communication between the two departments and forcing them to guess what the other was doing.

I have obviously caricatured the situation in order to make the point clear: when organizational units have inappropriate measures of performance which

FIGURE 1

PRICE-DEMAND CURVE

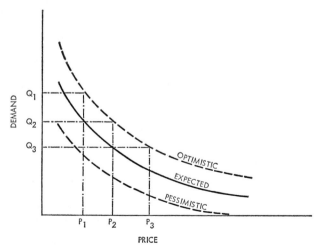

put them in conflict with each other, as is often the case, communication between them may hurt organizational performance, not help it. Organizational structure and performance measurement must be taken into account before opening the floodgates and permitting the free flow of information between parts of the organization. (A more rigorous discussion or organizational structure and the relationship of communication to it can be found in [1]) .

A MANAGER DOES NOT HAVE TO UNDERSTAND
HOW AN INFORMATION SYSTEM WORKS,
ONLY HOW TO USE IT

Most MIS designers seek to make their systems as innocuous and unobtrusive as possible to managers lest they are frightened. The designers try to provide managers with very easy access to the system and assure them that they need to know nothing more about it. The designers usually succeed in keeping managers ignorant in this regard. This leaves managers unable to evaluate the MIS as a whole. It often makes them afraid to even try to do so lest they display their ignorance publicly. In failing to evaluate their MIS, managers delegate much of the control of the organization to the system's designers and operators, who may have many virtues, but managerial competence is seldom among them.

Let me cite a case in point. A Chairman of a Board of a medium size company asked for help on the following problem. One of his larger (decentralized) divisions had installed a computerized production-inventory control and manufacturing-manager information system about a year earlier. It had acquired about $2,000,000 worth of equipment to do so. The Board Chairman had just received a request from the Division for permission to replace the original equipment with newly announced equipment the cost of which was several times that of the original. An extensive "justification" for so doing was provided with the request. The Chairman wanted to know whether the request was really justified. He admitted to complete incompetence in this connection.

A meeting was arranged at the Division at which I was subjected to an extended and detailed briefing. The system was large but relatively simple. At the heart of it was a reorder point for each item and a maximum allowable stock level. Reorder quantities took lead-time as well as the allowable maximum into account. The computer kept track of stock, ordered items when required and generated numerous reports on both the state of the system it controlled and its own "actions."

When the briefing was over I was asked if I had any questions. I did. First I asked if, when the system had been installed, there had been many parts whose stock level exceeded the maximum amount possible under the new system. I was told there were many. I asked for a list of about thirty and for some graph paper. Both were provided. With the help of the system designer and volumes of old daily reports I began to plot the stock level of the first listed item over time. When this item reached the maximum "allowable" stock level it had been reordered. The system designer was surprised and said that by sheer "luck" I had found one of the few errors made by the system. Continued plotting showed that because of repeated premature reordering the item had never gone much below the maximum stock level. Clearly the program was confusing the maximum allowable stock level and the reorder point. This turned out to be the case in more than half of the items on the list.

Next I asked if they had many paired parts, ones that were only used with each other; for example, matched nuts and bolts. They had many. A list was produced and we began checking the previous day's withdrawals. For more than half of the pairs the differences in the numbers recorded as withdrawn were very large. No explanation was provided.

Before the day was out it was possible to show by some quick and dirty calculations that the new computerized system was costing the company almost $150,000 per month more than the hand system which it had replaced, most of this in excess inventories.

The recommendation was that the system be redesigned as quickly as possible and that the new equipment not be authorized for the time being.

The questions asked of the system had been obvious and simple ones. Managers should have been able to ask them but—and this is the point—they felt themselves to be incompetent to do so. They would not have allowed a hand-operated system to get so far out of their control.

No MIS should ever be installed unless the managers for whom it is intended are trained to evaluate and hence control it rather than be controlled by it.

A SUGGESTED PROCEDURE FOR DESIGNING AN MIS

The erroneous assumptions I have tried to reveal in the preceding discussion can, I believe, be avoided by an appropriate design procedure. One is briefly outlined here.

1. *Analysis of the Decision System.* Each (or at least each important) type of managerial decision required by the organization under study should be identified and the relationships between them should be determined and flow-charted. Note that this is *not* necessarily the same thing as determining what decisions *are* made. For example, in one company I found that make-or-buy decisions concerning parts were made only at the time when a part was introduced into stock and was never subsequently reviewed. For some items this decision had gone unreviewed for as many as twenty years. Obviously, such decisions should be made more often; in some cases, every time an order is placed, in order to take account of current shop loading, underused shifts, delivery times from suppliers, and so on.

Decision-flow analyses are usually self-justifying. They often reveal important decisions that are being made by default (e.g., the make-buy decision referred to above), and they disclose interdependent decisions that are being made independently. Decision-flow charts frequently suggest changes in managerial responsibility, organizational structure, and measure of performance which can correct the types of deficiencies cited.

Decision analyses can be conducted with varying degrees of detail, that is, they may be anywhere from coarse to find grained. How much detail one should become involved with depends on the amount of time and resources that are available for the analysis. Although practical considerations frequently restrict initial analyses to a particular organizational function, it is preferable to perform a coarse analysis of all of an organization's managerial functions than a fine analysis of one or a subset of functions. It is easier to introduce finer information into an integrated information system than it is to combine fine subsystems into one integrated system.

2. *An Analysis of Information Requirements.* Managerial decisions can be classified into three types:

(a) Decisions for which adequate models are available or can be constructed and from which optimal (or near optimal) solutions can be derived. In such cases the decision process itself should be incorporated into the information system thereby cnverting it (at least partially) to a control system. A decision model identifies what information is required and hence what information is relevant.

(*b*) Decisions for which adequate models can be constructed but from which optimal solutions cannot be extracted. Here some kind of heuristic or search procedure should be provided even if it consists of no more than computerized trial and error. A simulation of the model will, as a minimum, permit comparison of proposed alternative solutions. Here too the model specifies what information is required.

(*c*) Decisions for which adequate models cannot be constructed. Research is required here to determine what information is relevant. If decision making cannot be delayed for the completion of such research or the decision's effect is not large enough to justify the cost of research, then judgment must be used to "guess" what information is relevant. It may be possible to make explicit the implicit model used by the decision maker and treat it as a model of type (*b*).

In each of these three types of situation it is necessary to provide feedback by comparing actual decision outcomes with those predicted by the model or decision maker. Each decision that is made, along with its predicted outcome, should be an essential input to a management control system. I shall return to this point below.

3. *Aggregation of Decisions.* Decisions with the same or largely overlapping informational requirements should be grouped together as a single manager's task. So doing will reduce the information a manager requires to do his job and is likely to increase his understanding of it. This may require a reorganization of the system. Even if such a reorganization cannot be implemented completely what can be done is likely to improve performance significantly and reduce the information loaded on managers.

4. *Design of Information Processing.* Now the procedure for collecting, storing, retrieving, and treating information can be designed. Since there is a voluminous literature on this subject I leave it at this except for one point. Such a system must not only be able to answer questions addressed to it, it should also be able to answer questions that have not been asked by reporting any deviations from expectations. An extensive exception-reporting system is required.

5. *Design of Control of the Control System.* It must be assumed that the system that is being designed will be deficient in many and significant ways. Therefore it is necessary to identify the ways in which it may be deficient, to design procedures for detecting its deficiencies, and for correcting the system so as to remove or reduce them. Hence the system should be designed to be flexible and adaptive. This is little more than a platitude, but it has a not-so-obvious implication. No completely computerized system can be as flexible and adaptive as can a man-machine system. This is illustrated by a concluding example of a system that is being developed and is partially in operation. (See Figure 2.)

The company involved has its market divided into approximately two hundred marketing areas. A model for each has been constructed and is "in" the computer. On the basis of competitive intelligence supplied to the service marketing manager by marketing researchers and information specialists he and his staff make policy decisions for each area each month. Their tentative decisions are fed into the computer, which yields a forecast of expected performance. Changes are made until the expectations match what is desired. In this way they arrive at "final" decisions. At the end of the month the computer compares the actual performance of each area with what was predicted. If a deviation exceeds what could be expected by chance, the company's OR Group then seeks the reason for the deviation, performing as much research as is required to find it. If the cause is found to be permanent the computerized model is adjusted appropriately. The result is an adaptive man-machine system whose precision and generality is continuously increasing with use.

Finally, it should be noted that in carrying out of the design steps enumerated above, three groups should collaborate: information systems special-

FIGURE 2

SIMPLIFIED DIAGRAM OF A MARKET-AREA CONTROL SYSTEM

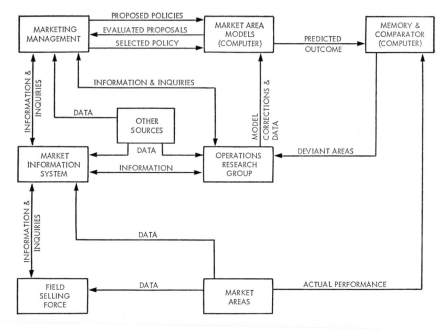

ists, operations researchers, *and managers.* The participation of managers in the design of a system that is to serve them assures their ability to evaluate its performance by comparing its output with what was predicted. Managers who are not willing to invest some of their time in this process are not likely to use a management control system well, and their system, in turn, is likely to abuse them.

Reference

1. SENGUPTA, S. S., and ACKOFF, R. L. "Systems Theory from an Operations Research Point of View," *IEEE Transactions on Systems Science and Cybernetics,* Vol. I (November 1965), pp. 9–13.

From: Jeremiah J. O'Connell
*"BEYOND ECONOMICS: COORDINOMICS"**
(PART II)

BRIDGING CREATIVITY AND INNOVATION

Now, with the third generation of computers, we have the capacity to really build integrated planning and control systems to get the full benefit from coordination. Knowing *what* to do in such system design isn't the problem; it's knowing *how* to do it—that is, knowing how to install the system and implement the change. Recently I heard an expert tell of the design for the most complete planning and control system I have seen. It was large, fully integrated, sophisticated, and based on a 360 system. The company for which it was designed was dragging its feet and effectively blocking the installation of the system even though it had paid for its design. The chief architect for the system knew he had developed a real piece of creativity, but as Levitt said in a *Harvard Business Review* article: "Creativity Is Not Enough!" Creativity is the production of an idea or concept; innovation is the production of change. I would wager that it's the bridging of creativity and innovation that haunts and frustrates those engaged in systems work.

WHY THE GAP BETWEEN SYSTEMS CREATIVITY AND SYSTEMS INNOVATION?

It's very common for systems men to carp about the incompetence, or blindness, or narrowness of the functional specialists who stand in the way of the implementation of systems creativity. There are academicians who observe this static in organizations and come away with the conviction that there is a growing gap between authority and ability in organizations. The people who sit on top of functionally specialized departments have the authority to make the decisions which should produce efficiency and greater productivity within the corporation. Within their functional specialties it is hard to deny that they do have ability based on analysis. It is the ability based on synthesis which is really scarce among the ranks of those who have the right to make decisions affecting corporate efficiency. The static between line management in functional departments and staff experts in systems is in large measure explained by the threat posed by synthesis skills. I can picture a frustrated systems man saying what a cynical former colleague of mine used to say on his way to teach class: "Here I go to cast synthetic pearls before real swine!" The systems man who has a balance of depth and breadth can bring to bear powerful tools and techniques to produce coordination efficiencies from an organization. He may have to ignore sanctified functional boundaries and specialized empires in the process. . . .

---

* From the Keynote Address of the Eighth Annual Systems Conference of the Southwest, Dallas, Texas, May 9, 1966.

INNOVATION IN A SOCIO-TECHNICAL SYSTEM

I hope it's not unfair to say to people in the systems field that there is some self-delusion in the comfortable diagnosis which blames the lack of ability of operating people for the frustrating, still-born, miscarriages for so many of your creative systems designs. Recall that I said earlier synthesis skill depended on a balance of breadth and depth in one's job. Part of the breadth is an appreciation of the organization as an interdependent system. The inter-dependencies, though, are not all technical—work flow, information flow, and so forth. There are also social inter-dependencies. The system is really a socio-technical system. The complexities of the technical system are so engrossing that the danger is one loses sight of the human side of enterprise. Can a fuller appreciation of the present-day plight of those in the organization who seem to stand in the way of systems innovation help the systems man in designing implementation programs sensitive to the human side of enterprise? Wasn't it an old Indian saying that you should walk a mile in a man's moccasins before you criticize him? Knowing what is on the mind of the functional line manager will hopefully help in bridging the gap between creative systems designs and innovative systems changes.

The Functional Line Manager Is Hearing a Dour Forecast

Who would not be threatened by such a black litany as the following? The middle manager will disappear. There will be more centralization and less autonomy in lower levels of the organization. Historical lines of the functional departments like marketing, production, finance, and so forth, will tend to disappear. Expect a blurring of the demarcation between line and staff positions. The concept of unity of command—that one man report to one boss—is becoming outmoded. In this era of the knowledge explosion and the geometrically pyramiding technological advances no man can avoid obsolescence without retreading his knowledge and skills three times in his career. To achieve richness in personal development and enjoy a fullness of comraderie, a man will have to look toward professional or para-professional groups outside the organization rather than to intra-organizational affiliations.

A Strange Congerie of Changes in the Functional Line Manager's Environment

The predictions the line manager hears are reinforced by changes already taking place all around the functional line manager. He sees a raft of cross-functional project teams on which functional allegiance is subservient to the project's objectives. The organization chart—if drawn to reflect reality—now very often looks like a matrix of horizontal and vertical relationships. In the Weapons System Division of RCA, for instance, the men in the several engineering departments at once report to their engineering department supervisor as well as to several weapons programs' managers. Such is also the case for the salesman in a branch office of Dow Chemical who reports to his office manager but has a complex relationship with a number of product managers. A similar organization even appears in the Pension Department of a large New York bank where a securities specialist in a particular industry reports to his immediate superior but also has responsibility to several pension portfolio managers. Imagine the graphic maze we would have if we showed each of the dotted line—functional authority—relationships that make up the cobweb of real-life organizational interactions. As if the structural changes were not enough, the functional line manager sees an elite corps forming whose status is ostensibly based on an esoteric language of bits, micro seconds, FORTRAN, binary code, integrated circuits, random access, real time, time sharing, and so forth. He somehow gets the feeling that his eight-year-old son could more easily join this elite corps because he at least is familiar with the new math lingo.

The functional line manager may find himself in the novel situation in which his immediate superior and even higher superiors get operational reports before he gets them. Some of the real-time control systems and new data display facilities deprive some managers of the protection they had in their superior's organizational distance and in the time lag of the reporting procedures.

Especially in these days of a healthy economy, the functional line manager has been pinched, patted, and kissed by more and more social scientists who are eager to improve his "inter-personal compentence." He is desperately trying to keep up with the changing technology of his job. He is told to prepare to manage the man-machine interface, and yet he is sent off to participate in one of the fads in industry—sensitivity training, managerial grid training, etc.

The harassed functional line manager, who has a chance to look over his shoulder, sees labor contracts with the blue-collar worker which protect this worker from technological unemployment and offer him a whole host of other guarantees. Our white-collar manager, without formal contract, looks at his own payroll card for such guarantees for himself and all he reads is: "Guaranteed not to rip, tear, wrinkle, shrink, or fade." Many such managers have a growing and uneasy awareness that of all employees they have the least protection, in terms of due process, against arbitrary behavior of superiors.

THE ENEMY: UNCERTAINTY, NOT CHANGE

The functional line manager, living under the pressures listed above, is accused of resisting change. There is no such thing as natural resistance to change. A man doesn't resist a raise or a promotion. He resists uncertainty. The functional line manager is understandably dragging his feet. He is facing a buzzing world of confusion. We might just as well recognize it—changes in the technical system have ramifications in the social system or in the human side of enterprise. It is a point of wisdom to recognize that there are trade-offs between these two phases of the organization. The technical system will have to give a little lest the human system come to a grinding halt.

There is a clear message in all this for the systems man. In using the skill of synthesis to achieve the benefits of coordination, the systems man should spend at least as much time in designing the program of implementation as in designing the system itself. The implementation will have to take account of the constraints in the social system. Even when much time is spent in trying to reduce the uncertainty which is so much feared in change, there will still remain some basic conflicts in values. But it is better to take a stand on these critical value issues than in trying to nail down a commitment from men who are running from ghostly shadows on the wall.

*   *   *   *   *

TRANS WORLD AIRLINES

I Case Introduction

Synopsis

The coming of the jet age brought a technological leap forward for the airline industry. Fear of a cutback on job opportunities for flight crews and concern for air safety—both rooted in the technological change—triggered a triangular conflict among the separate unions representing the pilots and flight engineers and the individual airlines. Powerful by virtue of large membership, the pilot's union has taken the initiative in responding to technological change.

This case focuses on one litigation which reflects most of the facets of the five-year dispute. The flight engineers strongly object to what they view as management policies conciliatory to the pilots. Arguments of the three parties are presented as the flight engineers seek redress in court.

Why This Case Is Included

In this case there is opportunity to examine the economic causes of technological change as well as the economic consequences of such change. Human reaction to change can be viewed in terms of the psychology of the resistance to change. It will be helpful also to draw on concepts from political science to analyze the behavior of the parties in their attempts at conflict resolution in the presence of legally structured interaction patterns and unbalanced power centers. The psychology of perception and semantics throws some light on why the parties believe as they do and why they say what they say. Finally, the case raises the knotty issue of featherbedding and management rights.

Diagnostic and Predictive Questions

In answering the following diagnostic and predictive questions, remember that these questions apply theories and conceptual ideas from certain disciplines. Such theories are valuable to understand basic forces at work in the policy system (diagnosis) and to predict what will happen in the system in the future (prediction). Since each reading abstracts from the total policy system certain factors or variables into the closed or partial viewpoint of one theory or discipline, no one reading gives answers to the practical policy problems of the case. In diagnosis and prediction, the parts of the problem are studied with "other things being equal."

Following each question are listed readings which will be helpful in answering the question. The readings included with this case are marked (*). By referring to the author index at the end of this book, you may locate the other readings listed.

1. From the viewpoint of economics, why has Trans World Airlines switched from conventionel craft to jets?

Read: Spencer and Siegelman, *Managerial Economics: Decision Making and Forward Planning,* pp. 242–48, 202–12. Bright, "Are We Falling Behind in Mechanization?" Cordiner, "Automation in the Manufacturing Industries."

2. Does economic theory help in predicting the effect on the pilots and engineers of the technological leap forward from piston engines to jets?

Read: *Heilbroner, "The Impact of Technology: The Historic Debate."

3. Would psychological theories about resistance to change have helped predict how the pilots and engineers would react to the transition to jets?

Read: *Selekman, *Labor Relations and Human Relations,* pp. 111–37. (Additional reading, not in this volume: W. G. Bennis, K. D. Benne, R. Chin, *The Planning of Change* [New York: Holt, Rinehart & Winston, 1962]. This is an excellent source for comprehensive coverage of the dynamics of the change process.)

4. The engineers and pilots are in what may be called a power struggle. From the facts of this case, is this form of human relations inevitable? Why? Or, why not? Would some other form of human relations based on communication and understanding be possible? Why? Or, why not? To phrase the question differently: From the viewpoint of the psychology of human interaction, why do you think this case ended up in court and was not worked out by the parties themselves?

Read: Follett, "Constructive Conflict." Eells and Walton, *Conceptual Foundations of Business,* pp. 361–63.

5. Has the very structure of American unions (in this case, ALPA and FEIA representing different crafts) been conducive, or inimical, to labor peace between pilots and engineers?

Read: *Killingsworth, "Organized Labor in a Free Enterprise Economy."

6. The pilots, the engineers, the airline management, and government officials have all supported their separate positions by citing safety advantages.

a) Drawing on the psychology of perception, how can we explain the differing interpretations of the "facts" about "safety"?

Read: Krech and Crutchfield, *Theory and Problems of Social Psychology,* pp. 81–83, 87–89, 94–96, 98, 102–3. Boulding, *The Image,* pp. 11–14. Leavitt, *Managerial Psychology,* pp. 27–33.

b) Does the science of semantics help explain why the word "safety" was used as a cogent symbol in discussions among the contending parties?

Read: Hayakawa, *Language in Thought and Actions,* pp. 100–102. (Additional reading, not in this volume: Bell Sondel, *The Humanity of Words* [Cleveland, N.Y.: World Publishing Co., 1958]. See especially pp. 31 ff.)

7. What are the real issues in this dispute from the viewpoint of the pilots, the engineers, Trans World Airlines management, John Q. Public? Review the case facts and read the following abstracts:

Read: *Jacobs, *Dead Horse and the Featherbird,* pp. 56, 58, 60 (the latter part of this volume will give a good historical perspective for those who wish to do further research). *Dahl and Lindblom, *Politics, Economics, and Welfare,* pp. 28–29, 31–33, 38–41, 45–46, 49–53.

8. Both the pilots and engineers have been accused of featherbedding in this case. Do you find evidence of featherbedding? If so, who is responsible?

> Read: *Kuhn and Berg, "The Trouble with Labor Is Featherbedding."
> *Selekman, *A Moral Philosophy for Management*, pp. 174–77, 195–96.

9. Trans World Airlines management contends that it has the prerogative of determining flight crew composition and the training appropriate for all employees. On what might this prerogative be based? (The contract in force between Trans World Airlines and FEIA contained a "management's rights" clause, reserving to Trans World Airlines all rights not otherwise included in the contractual relationship.)

> Read: *"Arbitration Decisions on Management Rights." Lippmann, *The Method of Freedom*, pp. 100–102. O'Donnell, "The Source of Managerial Authority."

10. If you had to take a look five years into the future, which of the contending parties would you predict would have decisive power? Has the exercise of this power been legitimate or illegitimate to date?

> Read: Drucker, *The Future of Industrial Man*, pp. 32–38. Lasswell and Kaplan, *Power and Society*, pp. 157–59.
> (Additional reading, not in this volume: Murray Edelman, "Concepts of Power," *Labor Law Journal*, September 1958, pp. 623–28.)

Policy Questions for This Specific Case

In answering the following policy questions, the results of diagnosis and prediction are used to reduce the amount of guesswork, or judgment, in designing action solutions. However, since certain parts of the total case situation cannot be reduced to science, and since "other things are not equal," judgment must still be used to fill in the factors not accounted for by readings. You will also need a second kind of judgment as you put value weights on different scientific predictions, since different theories may point to conflicting solutions.

11. Could Trans World Airlines management have done anything earlier to avoid the present impasse? (See Questions 2, 3, 4, 5, 6, 7, and 8.)

12. What should Trans World Airlines management do now?

Major Policy Issues: Tentative Generalizations about Any Policy System

In arriving at conclusions for the following questions, generalize from the facts in the case and use your own ideas to (a) confirm, (b) modify, or (c) test the workability of the concepts and theories from readings. As an executive or professional, use wisdom to merge theory, on the one hand, with "brute facts" and practice, on the other.

13. J. M. Clark has pointed out: "When labor is laid off its cost does not disappear; it changes its form, and a very appreciable part of it comes back to plague the same industry which started the vicious circle by laying off its workers." (*Economics of Overhead Costs* [Chicago: University of Chicago Press, 1943], pp. 371–72.)

In what sense is technological unemployment a source of danger to the Gross National Product? To the autonomy of "free" corporations? To social welfare?

> Read: Cordiner, "Automation in the Manufacturing Industries." Heilbroner, *The Future as History*, pp. 158–59. (See also Question 2 and its attached readings.)

(Additional reading, not in this volume: John T. Dunlop, *Automation and Technological Change* [Englewood Cliffs, N.J.: Prentice-Hall, Inc., 1962]. The ten authors in this volume provide a multi-faceted commentary on this subject.)

14. What should be the function (if any) of corporate managers in coping with these effects of technological advance? (See Question 13.)

Questions for Original Student Work in Analysis and Policy

The methods of viewing this case as represented by the authors' questions and selection of readings are not exhaustive. There are other relevant ideas for diagnosis and prediction. Furthermore, there are other ways of stating policy questions. More powerful analyses and wiser solutions will result by drawing on your own training and experience for (a) relevant concepts and theories, and (b) creative ways of asking policy questions. The following questions are designed to help you acquire this skill.

15. While reflecting on case facts, what additional theories from prior education give you insights as to "what is going on" in Trans World Airlines? As to what might be predicted to happen in the future?

16. Other than the policy questions asked by the authors, what pragmatic ways can you think of to state the practical problems faced by executives in the case?

II Trans World Airlines*

On February 23, 1962 the Flight Engineers union sought an injunction to stop Trans World Airlines from providing flight engineer training for pilots. The two employee groups are represented by different unions, both affiliated with the AFL-CIO—the flight engineers by the Flight Engineers International Association and the pilots by the Air Line Pilots Association. The engineers feared that the arrangement, worked out between TWA and ALPA, for the training of the pilots in flight engineering jeopardized the jobs of the FEIA members. Neither labor union wanted its members to suffer because of the personnel cutbacks consequent on the airlines' adoption of the larger, faster jet aircraft.

Trans World Airlines

Trans World Airlines ranks among the giants in both domestic and international passenger and air freight service. By asset size TWA, with some $450,000,000, is fourth among the United States airlines. TWA's 1.1% return on equity (five-year average) places it in seventh place behind

---

Northwest (11.2%), American (10.6%), United (8.5%), Eastern (7.3%), Delta (6.5%), and Pan American (6.2%).

Year	Operating Revenue	Net Income
1956	$244,468,000	$2,346,000d
1957	268,065,672	1,575,384d
1958	286,417,817	1,793,485d
1959	329,762,019	9,440,514
1960	361,874,705	6,481,413
1961		

d = Deficit.
Source: Moody's.

Air Line Pilots Association

Approximately 14,000, or virtually all, of the commercial airline pilots in the United States belong to the Air Line Pilots Association. Their salary range—$11,000 to $32,000—and contract benefits are generally thought to rank the pilots as a class very close to the top of the union ladder nationally.

The TWA Chapter of ALPA serves as bargaining representative for the 1,400 pilots employed by TWA.

Flight Engineers International Association

FEIA represents about 3,500, or 90%, of the 4,000 certified flight engineers employed as such by the airlines in the United States. The AFL chartered FEIA in 1948 after the Civil Aeronautics Board ordered flight engineers on the larger planes. Previously the flight engineers sought affiliation with ALPA and were refused. The National Mediation Board had recognized the flight engineers as a "separate class or craft" for representation and bargaining purposes in 1945. In 1953 and again in 1957 ALPA tried to have the AF of L (and later the AFL-CIO) turn over control of FEIA. The late William Green of AF of L blocked the first move and George Meany turned back the second attempt.

TWA's 600 flight engineers are represented by the TWA Chapter of FEIA. In contrast to the ALPA members the flight engineers' salary range is $6,000 to $14,000, with some higher-paid men on the international flights.

Technological Roots of the Dispute

Among the rules instituted in 1948 by the Civil Aeronautics Administration was the following (40.263):

An airman holding a valid flight engineer certificate shall be required on all airplanes certificated for more than 80,000 pounds maximum certificated take off weight. Such airmen shall also be required on all four engine airplanes certificated for more than 30,000 pounds maximum certificated take off weight where the Administrator finds that the design of the airplane used or the type of operation is such as to require engineer personnel for the safe operation of the airplane.

Civil air regulations also provide:

On flights requiring a flight engineer, at least one other crew member shall be sufficiently qualified, so that in the event of illness or other incapacity, emergency coverage can be provided for that function for the safe completion of the flight. A pilot need not hold a flight engineer certificate to function in the capacity of a flight engineer for such emergency coverage.

Finally, civil air regulations place upon the pilot in command full responsibility for the safety of the persons and goods carried and for the conduct and safety of the crew members. This responsibility is ultimate and nondelegable, covering all aspects of the proposed flight or the flight while in progress.

Though the equipment used by the airlines has changed drastically in the postwar years, there have been no rules prescribed by federal regulatory agencies superseding or essentially modifying the above rules. Official safety regulations about the number and competence of the crew complement and the functions to be performed have not changed as the equipment evolved from the small, piston engine, DC-3 type of aircraft to the larger turbo prop and turbo jet craft.

The actual functions to be performed by the various crew members have been appreciably altered. Because of the technological changes, the equipment is vastly more complex and, at the same time, much more automatic. The producers of the new jet craft intended both the pilot and the flight engineer functions be performed. See the photograph of the DC-8 cockpit in Exhibit 1. The minimum standards of competence for those performing the two functions are maintained by the federal agencies who examine and issue certificates to prospective pilots and flight engineers. The airlines themselves sometimes prescribe additional qualifications for those who perform the two functions.

Technological change caused significant repercussions in the employment picture of the airlines industry. The introduction of the turbo jets in late 1958 began to reduce the total number of crew personnel needed to service air passenger demand. The giant jets can carry up to three times the passenger load that the older craft carried. Cruising speed in the jets in many cases is double what the piston airliners could do. As a consequence of this greater carrying capacity and the shorter turn around time, one jet can replace three to three and a half of the conventional craft in meeting the airline schedules. Every new jet on every airline means about twenty-four fewer airline personnel, the majority of whom are pilots. The decline in the rate of increase in passenger miles at this time added to the woes of everyone concerned with the airline industry.

ALPA'S RESPONSE TO TECHNOLOGICAL CHANGE

In 1954, at its thirteenth convention, the Air Line Pilots Association passed the resolution: "Be it resolved, that the Air Line Pilots adopt the policy henceforth this date, that the primary requirement of any aircraft operating crew member shall be to possess a Commercial Pilot's Certificate."

In 1955 United Airlines acceded to the pilots and required all of its crew members to receive Commercial Pilot's Certificates.

At the ALPA's fourteenth convention in 1956 it was resolved "that it shall be the policy that all members of the operating crew shall be pilot qualified. Be it further resolved that it shall not be inconsistent with the implementation of this policy for the association to provide job protection for currently employed non-pilot crew members. . . ."

The Eastern Case

On November 18, 1957, ALPA submitted a proposal to Eastern Air lines calling for all crew members to be on the pilots' seniority list and serving in the employ of the company as pilots. ALPA struck Eastern to achieve its purposes and received support from an emergency board appointed by President Eisenhower.

(See Exhibit 2 for ALPA's testimony before the Emergency Board and Exhibit 3 for the Report of the Emergency Board.) Flight Engineer objection blocked any final settlement for a year. On November 12, 1958, ALPA and Eastern Airlines agreed on having a third pilot in the cockpit. However, not until January 1, 1959 was it finally agreed that the third pilot would be a fourth man in the cockpit and not a pilot-trained flight engineer. Twenty-one days later American Airlines signed a similar agreement with ALPA. Pan American, Continental, and TWA followed before June 1, and Western and Northwestern soon after.

ALPA's Fifteenth Convention

In its fifteenth convention, on November 3, 1958, ALPA examined its position. The Wage and Working Conditions Committee reported as follows:

We have more job security than many other workers in the country today. Seniority is a fundamental protective device. . . . We have furlough pay, technical unemployment furlough sections, pilot third crew members, travel pay and credit. . . .

One domestic airline seems to be the "ringleader" in the race to jet equipment. This is an indication that its managers will equip with jets as rapidly as possible. Rapid transition of this sort increases the problems of pilots manyfold. Nevertheless, these problems can be measured and overcome by the pilots. This particular line has twin engine equipment which will be replaced by Electras. The Electras will require three crew members. Some additional third crew members will have to be hired. It does not make sense that new employees should be hired for these jobs while pilots are on furlough. Arrangements must be made to prevent this happening. These examples are not predictions and should not be used out of context to prove or disprove anything. They are merely to illustrate how uncertain the situation really is.

Continental Case

ALPA's negotiations with Continental Airlines initially paralleled the United pattern. The flight engineers' contract on October 31, 1958 required the flight engineers on turbo jet powered equipment to have commercial pilots rating and an instrument rating. FEIA members were assured, however, that all flight engineers on turbo jet craft would be taken from FEIA's seniority lists. But (as Continental Airlines officials put it) "under great economic pressure" from ALPA, Continental agreed to carry a third pilot on jet crews. Moreover, Continental agreed to operate a flight engineer's school to enable all pilots to obtain flight engineer's certificates. Continental was to begin carrying the third pilot on April 1, 1960. The FEIA contract expired on May 1, 1960. From then on, flight engineer–trained pilots from ALPA's seniority lists assumed the flight engineer duties on Continental's jets. ALPA was the sole union representative and collective bargaining agent for the whole operating crew.

United Case

At United Airlines the same result was accomplished but in a different way. Since early 1955 all of the flight crew, including the engineers, were pilot-trained, though pilots and engineers had different union representation. In early 1961 ALPA called for a vote of all "flight deck personnel" to choose a bargaining agent. When the vote was taken on February 6, 1961, United employed 1,566 pilots and 624 flight engineers. The vote of the "flight deck personnel" was 1,682 in favor of ALPA as union representative to 58 for FEIA. On July 17, 1961 the National Mediation Board, looking at the crew as a unit by virtue of its common pilot training, ruled through its chairman, J. Glenn Donaldson, that the vote should stand—ALPA was the exclusive bargaining representative of the "flight deck personnel." (See Exhibit 4 for the findings of the National Mediation Board.)

TWA Case

ALPA's negotiations with TWA closely resembled the relations with Continental. As early as May 22, 1958 the pilots began bargaining for flight engineering training for pilots. Exactly one year later the "third-pilot" agreement was signed and provision made for flight engineer training for the pilots. ALPA found it necessary to institute legal action against TWA to actually have the training section of the agreement fulfilled adequately. It was not until November 20, 1961 that the flight engineer training of pilots began. It is the unilateral action of ALPA in securing this training arrangement and TWA's actual supplying of this training which provide the issue for the court action which concerns us in this case.

The Pilots' Argument

Basically, ALPA points to the increased safety demands of the new aircraft to support its efforts at getting all pilot crews (see Exhibit 2). The pilots received support successively from the reports of the Presidential Emergency Board in June 1958 (Exhibit 3), the National Mediation Board in February 1961 (Exhibit 4), and the Feinsinger Commission in October 1961 (Exhibit 5).

ALPA's efforts to insure safety through the all-pilot crew have produced three different types of results. First, in the United pattern, the three-man all-pilot crew was achieved by having the airline require pilot training of the flight engineers and then voting for exclusive representation of the crew by ALPA. Second, in the Continental pattern, ALPA secured the "third-pilot" agreement and flight engineer training for pilots. The airline then, to avoid the burdensome expense of having a four-man crew, refused to renew the flight engineers' contract, leaving the three-man crew for exclusive representation by ALPA. Third, in the Eastern, American, Pan American pattern, ALPA secured the "third-pilot" agreement, but the airlines assumed the additional expense of the four-man crew, retaining the flight engineer represented by FEIA.

The TWA situation is midway between the second and third patterns. At present TWA has four-man crews, but the pilots have a contract binding TWA to offer the opportunity for ALPA members to get flight engineer certificates.

TWA's Argument

TWA is caught in the middle between the unions. Finding itself as co-defendant with ALPA over the issue of providing flight engineer training to pilots, TWA uses the defense of its management rights. David J. Crombie, TWA's vice president of industrial relations, says:

> TWA is entirely free to train any member of its flight crews in the manner TWA deems most advisable for the proper operation of its aircraft and that no union may dictate to TWA the nature of the training TWA desires to afford its employees, whatever class or craft may be involved. The training of a pilot to enable him to provide relief of all flight crew positions within meaning of the Second Officer's Agreement cannot be deemed in violation of the Railway Labor Act.

TWA finds itself in a knotty position. Back in early 1958 company officials stated publicly (in company with American Airlines and Pan American) that TWA would retain flight engineer specialists on its turbo jet operations in the interest of safety. The reported $70,000 a year expense of having the fourth man in the cockpit puts TWA at a competitive disadvantage with those airlines who have three-man crews. Obviously, TWA would prefer to cut to a three-man crew. The question of on whose seniority list, ALPA's or FEIA's, the occupant of the third crew chair appears is a knotty one. The company would much prefer to look upon the entire matter as a jurisdictional dispute in the union ranks, but bargaining agreements made with either one often give the other cause for grievance, court action, or strike.

FEIA REACTION TO TECHNOLOGICAL CHANGE

Since the coming of the jet age did not put as much pressure on the flight engineers, FEIA embarked on no special program in response to technological change. FEIA did, however, get deeply involved in strike threats, strikes, court, mediation board, and emergency board proceedings—all in response to moves by one or the other of the parties involved in the triangular dispute. In a word, the engineers insist that safety dictates the presence of a flight engineer specialist on jet craft—notwithstanding the various reports of four emergency boards—and that a pilot certificate for a third man in the cockpit as well as a flight engineering certificate for any of the pilots are superfluous. In support of their stand they cite the existing safety rules of the federal agencies who have the competence and commission to regulate air safety. FEIA draws attention to a statement made by the Federal Aviation Agency on May 16, 1960: "The duties of a Flight Engineer aboard an aircraft are related directly to the mechanical operation of the aircraft. These duties differ substantially from those of the pilot." Mr. H. S. Dietrick, president of the TWA Chapter of FEIA, puts the engineers' case this way:

The public has a large stake in having a fully qualified and devoted member of the flight engineer's craft sitting in the flight engineer's seat. The flight engineer does not view his job as a stepping stone to a co-pilot or captain status. It is not a passing fancy for him. He is devoted to his job and spends considerable time keeping up with the latest technical developments, in an effort to guarantee the quality of his skill and the competent performance of his duties. In this age of modernization of mechanical equipment it is all he can do to keep abreast of the latest developments in systems and engines and in the various devices that are constantly being appended to the modern aircraft. If the flight engineer's seat is viewed as merely a halfway house on the road to becoming a pilot, the travelling public will have lost the security of knowing that a highly skilled, devoted technician (a flight "engineer") sits in the cockpit—his full attention and experience concentrated on the mastery of his occupation. [See also the statement issued by FEIA in its *Fact Kit* in Exhibit 6.]

The Four-Man Crew Issue

The flight engineers have labeled the third-pilot drive of the ALPA which forced many major airlines into a four-man jet crew a featherbedding maneuver in the face of technological unemployment. The engineers find support in their insistence that the third pilot is superfluous from Floyd D. Hall, executive vice president of TWA:

> I can only advise that TWA has not changed its position with respect to the necessity for a second officer (third pilot) in the Boeing 707 or the Convair 880 from that maintained before and during the negotiations, which resulted in the May 22, 1959 working agreement. The aircraft aforementioned were never designed to carry a second officer and we did not then, and do not now, feel that such an officer is necessary for either a safe or an efficient operation of the aircraft. The record with the 707 during 6 months of operation of the Boeing confirms the validity of this position.

The opinion of C. R. Smith, American's president, reflects similar sentiments:

> . . . The point at issue is whether or not the Flight Engineer, in addition to proving his competency according to the standards of CAB should also be required to have the ability to fly the airplane. If the Flight Engineer must be a pilot, in addition to the other duties of his profession, then the obvious end result of that requirement would be to increase job opportunities for pilots, with a reduction in job opportunities for Flight Engineers who are not pilots. To that requirement and to that end result the Flight Engineers have objected. The facts of the situation are that there is need for the services of a Flight Engineer and there is no need for the services of a third pilot. There are two competent qualified pilots on the airline planes and that number has been found sufficient by the CAB, by airline experience and by the judgment of airline management. . . .
>
> . . . It is the opinion of the management of American Airlines, Inc., that the highest standards of operating safety will accrue if the different members of the flight crew are required to have proven competency in their own professional field. It is in our opinion, preferable, as contributing most to safety, that the Flight Engineer prove and maintain his competency in his own field, that of Flight Engineer. . . . [From a Press Release issued by C. R. Smith, July 28, 1958.]

Support came from a third source at the Symposium on Pilot Training during the technical conference of the International Air Transportation Association in May 1959. A Pan American pilot, Captain Fleming, said:

> In the question of crew complement my opinion is that a crew of three should be the basic crew in a jet aircraft; a fourth man may be required for navigation and similar supplementary duties. It is my belief that any form of featherbedding is thoroughly undesirable from the point of view of efficient cockpit management.

At the same conference A. M. "Tex" Johnston, the chief test pilot for Boeing, repeated the skepticism over the third-pilot agreements:

> I should like to state in the first place that the airplane can be operated by a crew consisting of a pilot, a first officer and a Flight Engineer, quite adequately and very safely. The 707 cockpit has been laid out to accommodate

these personnel. If you are going to put another member in the crew the cockpit should be designed to help him. The only thing you do by just putting a third pilot in the crew without this action is to muddy up things.

. . . The pilot must know the systems he has control over and have full knowledge of the action necessary to effect safety. Malfunctioning in a system can have spreading effects. The Flight Engineer must put everything down that is likely to interest maintenance. This is one of the reasons why I do not agree with three pilots in the cockpit.

. . . I have no objection to Labor Unions, but they are undoubtedly a very dangerous factor from one standpoint, i.e., the case of the problem pilot. It is very important that the objectives of the pilot's union are realistic and governed by due integrity. I think that pilots' unions should insist on a very high degree of proficiency in the members, and not degenerate into a protective agency to protect its less efficient members. Unions should give due consideration to the economies of operating an airline. They should fight for efficiency and economy rather than enforcing featherbedding and the carriage of a fourth crew member in the form of a third pilot. . . .

FEIA and the TWA Case

The court action taken by the TWA Chapter of FEIA against TWA and ALPA is only the most recent effort of the flight engineers to preserve their status as a "separate class or craft." In this case specifically FEIA contends that the execution of the "Second Officers Agreement" between ALPA and TWA breaches the statutory command to the carrier to treat only with the certified bargaining representative of the class or craft of employees involved. The pilots bargained for and received flight engineer training from TWA without FEIA's participation in the bargaining. FEIA's members' functions in the flight crew were subject to bargaining in the absence of the proper bargaining representative. H. S. Dietrick, president of the TWA Chapter of FEIA, forthrightly says: "The training of pilots in engineer's duties is just a phase in the elimination of the flight engineer as a distinct category of employee on the nations air carriers—witness the experience of the FEIA in the recent dealing with Continental Airlines."

In its suit before the U.S. District Court in New York City, FEIA calls the action of TWA and ALPA "predatory appropriation without prior notice or negotiation of FEIA's interests, job security, and exclusive bargaining status." It finds its grievance aggravated by the fact that, though the training was to be given the pilots on their "own time," TWA was granting the pilots a 60-hour guarantee plus all expenses, training pay credit, and 60 cents an hour expense allowance while receiving the flight engineer training. TWA also bears the training cost of $1,500 per man. (See Exhibit 7 for FEIA's impression of the pilots' preparation for the certification as flight engineers compared to the required education.) On these grounds the 600 engineers at TWA seek an injunction to prevent the airline from providing the 1,400 pilots with flight engineer training.

Exhibit 1

The cockpit, or flight deck, of the Douglas DC-8 Jet. To the right is the flight engineer's seat and instrument panel.

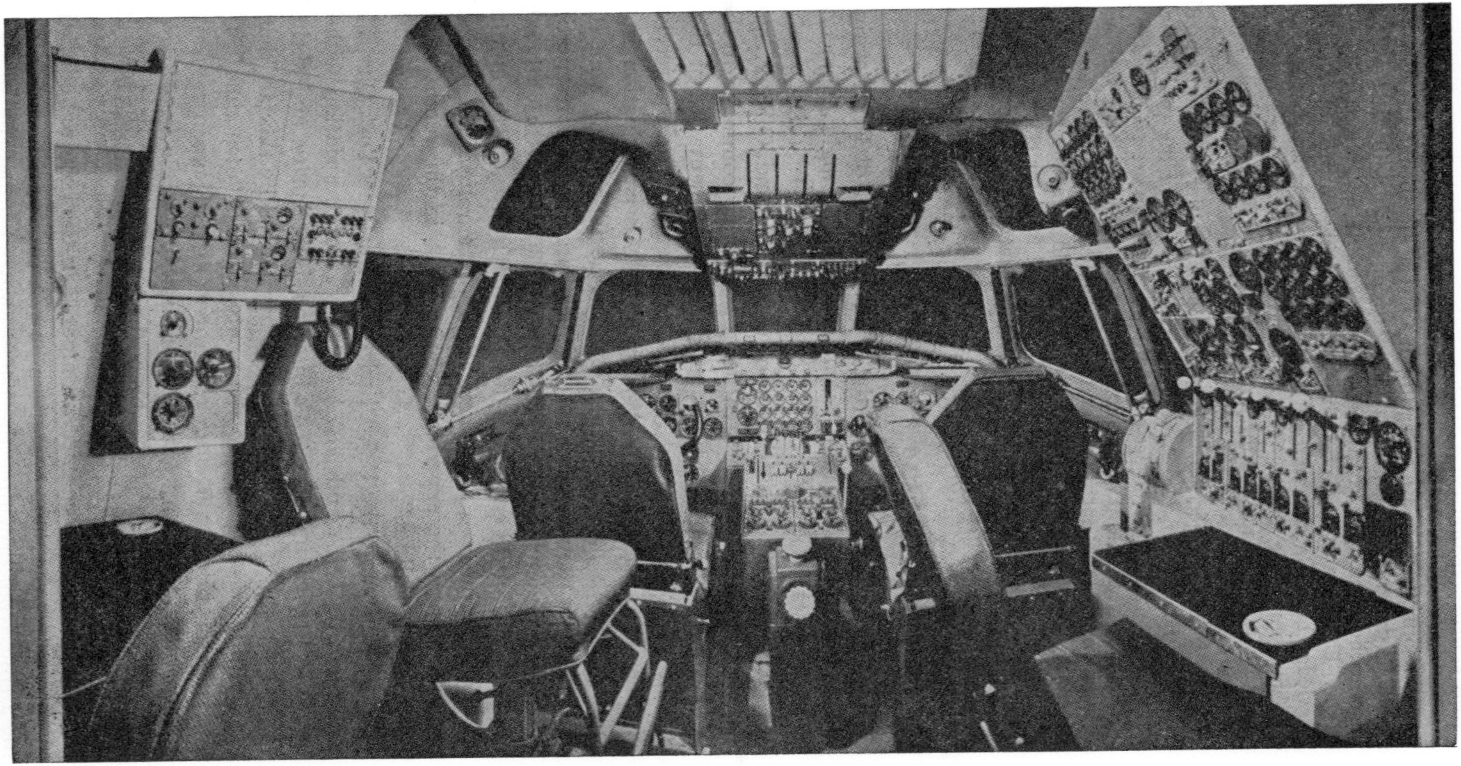

Exhibit 2

EXCERPTS FROM A STATEMENT BY CLARENCE N. SAYEN, PRESIDENT
OF ALPA, BEFORE PRESIDENTIAL EMERGENCY BOARD—APRIL 3, 1958

. . . The Association has concluded that this compromise (or crew complement) cannot be tolerated any longer, with the changing technology of these
turbine aircraft.

The sharply decreased mechanical aspect on these airplanes, coupled with
the sharply increased requirements in the field of communications, navigation,
air traffic control, the more stringent operational requirements with lessened
tolerances for error, make it imperative that the third crew member on these airplanes be Pilot qualified. The present so-called specialist engineer on a turbine
powered aircraft will simply not be qualified to assume the responsibilities of
the third crew member on the turbine aircraft.

. . . The third crew member was established by statute in 1948. In enacting
the statute, there was a failure to specify what kind of an individual would do
the job. Some airlines immediately established a fully qualified crew with three
pilots. Some airlines chose to employ miscellaneous people for this work. The
ten years' experience we have had has seen a great technological change. The
changes have emphasized the growth of the operational work load. Those airlines who chose to put miscellaneous, non-pilot personnel in the job now have
personnel who cannot provide help in the area of greatest growth of job content.

*   *   *   *   *

Now, future airplanes will aggravate all of the work load orientation that
I have just described. Emergency decisions will need to be made faster, requiring a similar background and similar training in all crew members for coordinated action. There simply is no time to stop and consult with the specialist.
He has to possess the qualifications and be able to think in the same terms as
the rest of the crew.

I'd like to talk a minute about what we call the fail-safe crew complement. . . .

. . . Under the present specialist crew concept and present regulations, if
something should happen to the Pilot in command that incapacitates him, you
will have no guarantee that the Co-Pilot is qualified to fly that particular airplane, or that the third crew member can fly at all.

We have just finished a series of studies on incapacitation, and we've been
amazed at the frequencies with which crew members become incapacitated—
not from serious problems like heart failures or breakdowns, but from simple
problems like diarrhea, food poisoning, and so forth. You have noticed in the
newspapers about ten days ago, a case of food poisoning of both Pilots.

My Association feels very strongly that we must provide a fail-safe crew concept if we are going to fulfill our responsibility to the travelling public. . . .

Exhibit 3

EXCERPTS FROM THE REPORT OF THE PRESIDENTIAL
EMERGENCY BOARD—JUNE 1958

We recommend: as to the crew complement issue . . . that flight engineers
who will serve on turbojet equipment be required to have pilot qualifications to
the extent of a commercial license and instrument rating and the ability to fly
and land the airplane in case of emergency. . . .

*   *   *   *   *

Exhibit 3—Continued

Our principal reasons for arriving at these conclusions are:

a) Safety is paramount, and it is wiser to employ too much caution than too little.

b) The introduction into air traffic of these very large, fast, high-flying, and rapidly climbing and descending airplanes, will aggravate the already critical problems of traffic density and control, and will materially increase the burdens of the pilots.

c) A number of items within the control of the flight engineer on piston aircraft will either be eliminated or transferred to the pilots' panel, and in addition most of the systems will be much more automatic and in case of malfunction will have alternates available.

d) Under the job description of flight engineers on Eastern Air Lines there is no duty which calls for the A or E license, and it will be even less likely that turbojet flight engineers will have any functions which will call for such qualifications.

e) The uncertainties associated with airplanes which will fly at altitudes of 25.000 to 40,000 feet, at speeds well in excess of 500 miles per hour, and which will consume their fuel at a greatly accelerated rate at the lower levels induce one to believe that the entire flight crew should be pilot-oriented and coordinated so that necessary action can be swiftly taken and the pilots engaged in active flying duties may be relieved of some of their related tasks, as, e.g., communications, navigation, paper work, flight planning and replanning, as well as that there be available a third crew member capable of flying and landing the airplane in an emergency.

f) The Air Force operates its modern, large jet aircraft without mechanic flight engineers, although they were used on prior models; the KC-135 tanker, which is the prototype of the Boeing 707 passenger air transport, is also operated by the Air Force without a mechanic flight engineer.

g) While other airlines differ as to the desirability of pilot or mechanic flight engineers, depending apparently on the practices they have followed in their piston-operations and their particular problems, some requiring pilot qualifications and others. mechanic qualifications, two domestic trunk airlines which formerly used the mechanic type are now transferring to pilot flight engineers.

Exhibit 4

EXCERPTS FROM THE FINDINGS OF THE NATIONAL MEDIATION BOARD IN THE UNITED AIRLINES DISPUTE—FEBRUARY 6, 1961

. . . Through selection, training and use during the intervening decade, his (the flight engineer's) resemblance is more accurately that to a pilot than to a mechanic. In today's jets, in-flight repair or trouble shooting is virtually impossible. Any repairs needed are a ground force mechanical function. The pilots on United are trained and capable of taking over and performing all of the functions of the Flight Engineer. . . . The crew in essence is a single operating unit, each member with certain primary responsibilities but still a single unit engaged in flying an airplane.

Obviously the two jobs, pilot and flight engineer, must be performed in close cooperation. Perhaps the only situation in which need of teamwork is comparable is that of the chief surgeon, the assistant surgeon and the anesthetist in conducting a major operation. Each complements the specialized skill of the others; each could, in the case of emergency, relieve the others.

Exhibit 5

EXCERPTS FROM THE REPORTS OF THE PRESIDENTIAL FACT-FINDING
FEINSINGER COMMISSION—MAY–OCTOBER 1961

FEIA charges that this pattern (three-pilot crew) is simply an historical accident, brought about by the power tactics of ALPA, and that the presence in the cockpit of an engineer specialist performing no pilot duties, whether two or three pilots be carried, is essential to safe and efficient operations. The FAA, however, has advised the Commission, on the basis of experience, that an all-pilot crew is equally safe. There is no evidence that it is less efficient. . . .

There is reliable opinion that a three-pilot crew has advantages from the point of view of efficiency, interchangeability and job security.

. . . In the considered opinion of the Commission, neither peace nor safety on the airlines will be fully assured as long as there are two unions in the cockpit.

*　　*　　*　　*　　*

The Commission recommended as a first step the establishment of a Joint Committee in Interunion Cooperation on each airline. As a permanent solution, the Commission strongly endorsed the voluntary merger of FEIA and ALPA into a single union.* . . .

* In a letter to the chairman of the Commission dated June 13, 1961, acknowledging receipt of a copy of the Commission's May 24 report, AFL-CIO President George Meany stated: "As you know, the AFL-CIO has devoted a great deal of time and energy, in recent years, to the effort to resolve the controversy between the FEIA and the ALPA in a fair and equitable manner. We arrived some time ago at the conclusion that a voluntary merger between the two groups would be the only effective and durable solution and have so recommended. I am pleased to note that the Commission's report lends further support to that conclusion."

Exhibit 6

FEIA FACT KIT

What the Flight Engineer Means to Your Safety

The Air Line Pilots Association wants eventually to replace all the Professional Flight Engineers on jets with junior co-pilots. That, in a nutshell is what it boils down to. There are less jobs in the jet age and the ALPA wants what's left.

Exhibit 7

Flight Engineer Howard Mann of Great River, N.Y., holds a 64-page "Study Guide" prepared by the Air Line Pilots Association to help its members secure flight engineer licenses. To his right is a portion of the texts and manuals the professional engineer must be thoroughly familiar with to successfully complete the FAA test for flight engineers. The "Study Guide" was prepared by the ALPA to enable its men to memorize answers for the flight engineer test and thus pass the written part of the exam. Once the license is secured the ALPA members are then legally equipped to fill the flight engineer's seat—regardless of whether they are actually mentally prepared or not. It has been necessary to change the government tests twice in the past because of the similarity between the "Study Guide" and the actual exam.

III Selected Readings

From: Robert L. Heilbroner
*"THE IMPACT OF TECHNOLOGY: THE HISTORIC DEBATE"**

[EDITORS' NOTE: Mr. Heilbroner is an economic historian, especially well known for his book, *The Worldly Philosophers.*]

. . . [T]he curve of the technological revolution continues to rise nearly vertically beneath our feet. With each year its impact—on work and play, on mind and body—becomes more unmistakable, more inescapable.

. . . What have the economists, the sociologists, the philosophers of the past 200 years to say about the revolution which already in their day was irreversibly altering the condition of human existence?

                    *   *   *   *   *

ADAM SMITH: THE DEBATE OPENS

. . . Smith conceives of technical improvement and advance as a means of extending the market, not only by cheapening goods, but by augmenting the demand for labor itself: "The number of workmen in every branch of business generally increases with the division of labor in that branch, or rather it is the increase in their number which enables them to class and subdivide themselves in this manner." In other words, the growing market makes possible the introduction of a labor-specializing technology, and this technology, by *attracting* labor, in turn helps the market to grow. And to give yet another impetus to this reciprocal mechanism, "as the operations of each workman are gradually reduced to a greater degree of simplicity, a variety of *new* machines come to be invented for facilitating and abridging these operations."

Thus technological advance is not only conceived as a basic source of economic progress, but one which is continually refreshed and replenished by the consequences of progress itself. As both cause and effect of economic growth, a dynamic conception of technology was located by Smith at the very core of the economic process; and the *economic* repercussions of technologial change were demonstrated to be wholly salutary.

RICARDO AND MILL: THE OTHER SIDE OF THE DEBATE

                    *   *   *   *   *

David Ricardo, the outstanding economist of the times, had at first shared the prevailing optimistic view of technology. . . . Now suddenly, in the 3rd edition

---

* "The Impact of Technology: The Historic Debate," Robert L. Heilbroner, in *Automation and Technological Change,* The American Assembly. © 1962 by Prentice-Hall, Inc., Englewood Cliffs, New Jersey (pp. 8–16).

of his famous *Principles,* published in 1821, Ricardo himself executed a startling turn-about. In a newly-inserted chapter *On Machinery* appeared the unexpected declaration that ". . . the opinion expressed by the labouring class, that the employment of machinery is frequently detrimental to their interests, is not founded on prejudice and error, but is conformable to the correct principles of political economy."

*   *   *   *   *

Ricardo did not deny—and the point is an important one—that this increase in the capitalists' earning might not initiate a general expansion of trade. Neither did he deny that the dismissed workmen might not be reemployed if capitalists spent their enhanced revenues on menials (somewhat like the "transfer payments" of a welfare state). His argument rather was that this process of reemployment was a second and *entirely separate* step from the original substitution of machinery for labor. What was lacking was an automatic mechanism of compensation set into motion by the process of substitution itself.

*   *   *   *   *

. . . It was John Stuart Mill who pointed to a missing link in the argument of the "increased purchasing power" school. . . . To be sure, the shift in income consequent upon a technological improvement augmented the real purchasing power of those *who were still engaged in the economic process.* But this was counterbalanced by the loss of purchasing power of those who had been displaced by the mechanical abridgment of labor. . . .

KARL MARX: TECHNOLOGY AND UNDERCONSUMPTION

Yet, as with Ricardo, Mill could not be said to view technology pessimistically. At worst, the problem seemed to concern nothing more than a hitch in the market mechanism—an obstacle in the way of a smooth frictionless adjustment. Even more than Ricardo, Mill would have acquiesced in the contention of the optimists—that in the long run, the progressive introduction of machinery, by creating new industries and by cheapening costs, acted as a spur to economic development, and by implication, to social cohesion and contentment.

It was against this general consensus that Karl Marx launched his powerful—albeit slow-acting—theoretical dissent. Here, for the first time, the long-run effects of technology were viewed as disruptive for the system as a whole.

*   *   *   *   *

. . . [T]he Marxian analysis proceeds in its characteristic inexorability. (1) Capitalists, pitted against one another in a competitive struggle, are forced to introduce cost-cutting (labor-saving) machinery. Note that this integrates the process of innovation into the process of production, making the quest for technological superiority an inherent feature of capitalist competition. (2) As capitalists introduce technological change, they substitute machinery for labor, or in the Marxian terminology, constant capital for variable capital. Consequently, once the transient profits of innovation have been competed away, all capitalists are left with . . . less labor input per unit of output than before. (3) Since profit springs exclusively from labor, the *rate* of profit must therefore fall *pari passu* with the proportionate decline in labor input.

But worse follows. Thus far, technology has temporarily stimulated the accumulation process, only to depress it still more profoundly. Now technology brings the process to a total halt. . . . [J]obs depend on the presence of equipment, such as lathes or looms or whatever. Hence to employ the technologically displaced labor force, more equipment must be provided. But how, asks Marx, are capitalists to become persuaded to produce more equipment in the face of the sagging consumption brought about by the displacement of labor? Thus, far from stimulating long-run expansion, technology brings the system to the crisis of an underconsumption collapse.

THE MARGINALISTS: A COUNTERATTACK

*   *   *   *   *

. . . [T]his school held that the wage of labor . . . was determined by the marginal contribution which it made to the value of output—that is, by its marginal productivity. Therefore, if there was a technological advance this meant only that new marginal productivities had been established, and that the ratios in which it was profitable to combine men and machines would have to be altered accordingly. But this was no reason, argued the marginalists, why unemployment should ensue. For at some lower wage, it would again be profitable for the employer to use labor instead of machinery, and at that wage all would find work.

. . . But were they right? In large part, the answer depends on the shape of the productivity curve—that is, on the actual changes in output associated with varying the input of labor applied to a fixed capital stock. For certain kinds of capital equipment—let us say for a fishing boat—the addition of extra hands will clearly be practicable and profitable as wages fall. But with other kinds of equipment—as for instance a modern high-speed printing press—the addition of extra hands *at any wage* will not significantly increase output. . . .

*   *   *   *   *

TECHNOCRACY: THE ECONOMICS OF DEPRESSION

*   *   *   *   *

. . . With the advent of the Great Depression a new "school" of economic thought rose to overnight prominence. . . .

*   *   *   *   *

. . . The technocratic movement blamed the machine for our ills, and then prescribed for the antidote a monetary unit based on an invariant standard of value, the erg. . . .

TECHNOLOGY AND ECONOMIC GROWTH

Technocracy passed, leaving little imprint on academic thought. But the crushing problem of depression nonetheless refocussed professional attention on the problem of technology from an unexpected angle. It was no longer the quiet erosion of technological job displacement which now attracted the primary interest of investigators. Rather, it was the question with which Adam Smith himself had been originally concerned—that is, the role of technology in widening the market and thus promoting capitalist growth.

. . . To Josef Schumpeter, for instance, the entire trajectory of capitalist development was essentially set into motion by the fruitful combination of pioneering entrepreneurs and technological innovations. . . .

Hence, as the Depression deepened, the question presented itself as to whether it might not be a dearth of these investment outlets—again including those of a technological nature—which lay at the heart of the trouble. . . .

. . . [T]he Second World War burst upon the American scene. . . . With the rush of war investment came not only an unparalleled economic boom, but a hitherto unimagined—and indeed, unimaginable—horizon of technological advance.

On the momentum of this scientific floodtide we have ridden down to the present day. The doubts concerning the adequacy of technological opportunities have been stilled. But now, curiously, we find ourselves confronting an old issue in new guise. For as the problems of automation rise to engage our attention, we re-enter the debate, so to speak, at the stage of the 1830's. Today, once again, we must concern ourselves not with the volume of *investment* inherent in technological advance, but with the volume of *employment* which a technologically dynamic economy can offer.

From: Benjamin M. Selekman
LABOR RELATIONS AND HUMAN RELATIONS*

[EDITORS' NOTE: Professor Selekman taught (at Harvard University) and wrote in the field of industrial relations. Before his death in 1962 he became a respected authority in business ethics.]

. . . [A]dministrators when planning new methods of work fail to make allowance for the emotions and sentiments that will be evoked in the workers who must accept the changes.

The problem of what to do about these feelings constitutes the heart of the task in adapting shop change into the structure of shop relations. In terms of the diagnosis here offered, two areas for action suggest themselves: (1) The *negative* feelings must be brought to conscious recognition and given acceptance as a normal response to a situation of change; moreover, reassurance must be provided against whatever prospect of injury seems to be felt by those involved. (2) The responses stimulated by these negative feelings must be turned into *positive*, constructive channels by utilizing such affirmative values as the change may possess.

Mitigating Negative Emotions. What concrete measures offer promise for mitigating negative emotions? Perhaps the first is *prior consultation*. . . . It is the imposed change that constitutes the feared change; consultation offers an antidote against the sense of imposition.

. . . Instead of concentrating upon talking men out of their fears, suspicions, or resentments by decrying them, instead of emphasizing the lack of logical basis for their fears, management must accept these emotions as the entirely normal and human response most men give in such situations.

. . . [T]alking things over relaxes tensions and dispels suspicions. Anxieties that are ventilated, accepted, and frankly discussed are likely to be relieved.

Introducing Changes Gradually. The proper *timing* of change constitutes a second important ingredient for reducing resistance. . . . [A]s soon as we understand the emotional mechanisms that underlie the response to change, it is not hard to realize why the rate of change becomes an important component in conditioning response. The appearance of new demands and new threats before earlier ones have been met multiplies fears and hostilities and so intensifies resistance. Thus it is important to allow enough time for assimilation and adaptation.

An integral part of such considerations regarding the rate and timing of change, what we might term the "rhythm of change" requires the most alert attention. On the whole, management has acted as if changes are to be introduced whenever the time seems technically right for them, however whimsical and erratic the underlying decision may appear to the men who must assimilate the new methods. Yet unless shop change bears some manifestly planned relation to prior shop practice, including prior shop changes, shop operations bog down somewhere. . . .

Establishing Adequate Grievance Machinery. Just because change disrupts going habits of work, a well-understood *grievance machinery* fortifies against the sense of threat and danger. Systematic procedures represent a continuing and stable element in the midst of impending changes. . . .

Evoking Positive Feelings. . . . [P]ositive values, too, must be focused upon the three elements that the worker feels are threatened by innovations: earnings, skills, and personal relationships.

Earnings. . . . The management that finds ways of sharing gains with its workers through an opportunity for higher earnings and better conditions obtains thereby a very real incentive for the acceptance of the change. Certain changes, of course, inevitably entail drastic consequences for the workers immediately affected. In such instances it is futile to look for any positive values. But, at the least, adequate offsetting measures should be provided. . . .

Skills. . . . By its very nature, the engineering that advances efficiency erodes craftsmanship. . . . When this is admitted, how can the sense of workmanship afford a means of promoting positive support for new methods that are continually being developed? . . . . We must somehow recapture for workers their feeling of identification with the whole product their combined labor turns out.

Interpersonal Relationships. This simply means that in modern industry, with its division of labor, the satisfactions inherent in workmanship must be consciously tied in with those of good interpersonal relationships. The team as a whole, the working unit, alone can transmit to most workers the full creative satisfactions of work well done and of communal significance. Management must therefore give serious attention to discovering means for making each worker feel himself a part of the team.

CONCLUDING REMARKS

. . . Because they know that their ultimate objectives are right, the men who define their goal as the production of ever more goods at ever lower costs resent the interference of other men. Resentment, of course, is itself an emotion; it makes human resistance to shop changes seem like sheer human cussedness. The administrator then becomes hortatory and moralistic when he needs above all an open-minded willingness to approach human interference precisely as he does technical difficulties—as a problem to be studied and solved in terms of its causative factors. Resistance does have its causes; it stems from individual emotions and social interrelationships. The emotions are powerful, but they also are entirely normal. They must be accepted as the typical response of men faced with situations that seem to threaten their customary security systems. . . .

From: Charles C. Killingsworth

"ORGANIZED LABOR IN A FREE ENTERPRISE ECONOMY"*

[EDITORS' NOTE: The author is Professor and head of the Department of Economics, Michigan State College; formerly chairman, U.S. Wage Stabilization Board.]

Samuel Gompers, who became the leading spokesman for the A.F.L. viewpoint, argued that—given this outstanding characteristic of the American environment—a labor movement could survive only by appealing to the "job consciousness" of the workers. . . .

When the labor organizer decides to appeal to job consciousness, certain consequences ensue. Obviously, the appeal to job consciousness will be most effective if workers are organized according to job lines—that is, in job groups—because the job problems and interests of teamsters will differ from those of teachers, those of steel workers will differ from those of retail clerks, and so on. Today, therefore, instead of workers being organized along geographical or political lines, they are organized according to function. Such organization creates a difficulty of drawing and maintaining boundaries, because products, processes, and materials are constantly changing. One result is jurisdictional disputes, which have plagued the American labor movement from its beginning. Another important consequence of the appeal to job consciousness is the doctrine of craft or trade autonomy, under which each job group is given complete freedom to formulate its own policies and demands without any central direction or control from within the labor movement. This is done on the theory that no one can know the desires and interests of a particular job group better than the workers in that group. The result is a type of particularistic bargaining that has sometimes been criticized. In view of this criticism it is important to emphasize the vital connection between craft or trade autonomy and the fundamental concept of job consciousness.

A further consequence of the appeal to job consciousness is a deliberate refusal to set up long range goals. Gompers and his associates observed that many of the early labor organizations in this country had been wrecked by doctrinaire debates on the details of the blueprint for the future. Such high-flown debates too often interfered with what Gompers considered the real task of a labor movement: the immediate improvement of the lot of the working man. Take care of today and tomorrow will take care of itself, he thought.

---

* Reprinted with permission of The Macmillan Company from *The Structure of American Industry* by Walter Adams. Copyright 1954. (Excerpts from pp. 550–51.)

From: Paul Jacobs

*DEAD HORSE AND THE FEATHERBIRD**

[EDITORS' NOTE: The author is on the staff of the Institute of Industrial Relations of the University of California at Berkeley.]

Probably no labor dispute in the United States has been more complex and confusing than the one over who shall occupy the third seat of the jets. And probably in no other labor dispute have the real issues been so well hidden as in this one where all the parties so frequently invoke "safety" as an explanation for their actions. Surely, few words have been more overworked and misused. By now, it has been emptied of any real meaning; by now, it is impossible for the public to decide when a proposal made in the name of safety, as all of them are, is or isn't a cover-up, even when unconscious, for gaining some economic advantage.

*   *   *   *   *

Who is to blame for the "featherbird" in the cockpit? Again, the responsibility must be shared. The Air Line Pilots Association has used its economic power, in the name of safety, to demand three pilots in the cockpit; the flight engineers have been equally adamant, again in the name of safety, that jets must have only two pilots and a mechanic flight engineer; the managements of the seven airlines who bought themselves a little labor peace, also in the name of safety, cannot adopt the pose of innocent victims; and, finally, the government must assume its share of the responsibility because of the vagueness of its 1948 ruling.

More than anything else, however, the reason for "unwork" is the workers' fear of permanent job loss or temporary layoff. If an employee is given a choice between doing "unwork" or not working at all, he will choose the "unwork." Once having been trapped into doing something he hates, he seeks justification for it. He must rationalize that what he does is not only acceptable but necessary. If he does not do this, he cannot face himself or a society in which work is so important. Soon, his stake in "unwork" becomes as important to him as the economic benefits he may derive from it.

*   *   *   *   *

All of the measures to relieve the burdens that come with unemployment are necessary because of an unchallenged assumption that management has an absolute right to automate its production system at all times. The newspapers attack union leaders who resist automation. "Management's right to manage must be preserved and as part of that right the unhindered, unqualified introduction of automation," a *New York Times* editorialist wrote. But who gave management its "right" to the "unhindered, unqualified introduction of automation"? If management's right to automate its property is an absolute one, then does not

---

* A report for the Center for the Study of Democratic Institutions, Santa Barbara, California, 1962 (pp. 56, 58, 60).

the union have an equally absolute right to resist automation in order to protect the workers' property—their jobs?

In fact, what fixed and absolute management or union rights are there outside newspaper editorials? Once, management insisted it had the "right" unilaterally to discharge an employee; now that right is considerably limited by public law and private contract. Once, management insisted it had the fixed and absolute right to move its plant where it pleased; now that right is becoming more and more limited by unions and the courts. Once, unions were free to keep out Negroes, but that kind of "freedom" is disappearing under the moral and legal pressures of the community. Ultimately, technology may force America to adopt a different set of axioms, based on an understanding that the acceptance of technology does not mean an unquestioning acceptance of its uses, products, and results.

From: Robert A. Dahl and Charles E. Lindblom
*POLITICS, ECONOMICS, AND WELFARE**

[EDITORS' NOTE: Both authors teach at Yale University.]

SEVEN BASIC ENDS FOR SOCIAL ACTION

The important prime goals of human beings in Western societies include existence or survival, physiological gratifications (through food, sex, sleep, and comfort), love and affection, respect, self-respect, power or control, skill, enlightenment, prestige, aesthetic satisfaction, excitement, novelty, and many others. These are the ultimate criteria by which we would like to test alternative politico-economic devices. But to use criteria of this kind would force one to a level of specificity that would require an encyclopedia of particular techniques.

On the other hand, there are seven goals that govern both the degree to which these prime goals of individuals are attained and the manner of deciding who is to attain his goals when individuals conflict in their goal seeking. . . . These seven instrumental goals are freedom, rationality, democracy, subjective equality, security, progress, and appropriate inclusion.

FREEDOM

*   *   *   *   *

. . . it seems useful to define freedom as the absence of obstacles to the realization of desires. Subjective freedom is detected by an absence of frustration; or, if frustrations are present, by the individual's expectation that he can make

---

* From *Politics, Economics, and Welfare* by Robert A. Dahl and Charles E. Lindblom. Copyright 1953 by Robert A. Dahl and Charles E. Lindblom. Reprinted with permission of Harper & Row, Publishers, Incorporated. (Excerpts from pp. 28–29, 31–33, 38–41, 45–46, 49–53.)

choices that will eliminate his frustrations. Objective freedom is tested by an observer's judgment as to whether an individual, when he is faced with choice situations which the observer expects to arise, will in fact make choices that will attain his desires.

Three Limits on Freedom. Given this definition, it is clear that no one is ever "absolutely free," certainly not in the objective sense. For no one ever attains all his desires. More than that, in all probability no one can be entirely free in any predictable future. Individuals can only be relatively less free or relatively more free; it is this difference in degree that is relevant to appraisal, not the difference between relative and absolute freedom.

One set of limits on freedom is imposed by natural impossibilities, physical, physiological, technological, psychological. . . .

Second, there are usually conflicts among one's own goals. Thus optimum goal achievement requires one to give up some goals to attain others. . . .

A special conflict among goals is imposed by time. One cannot do everything at once. . . .

From a social and political point of view, however, the third and most important limit on freedom is imposed by the activities of others. . . .

RATIONALITY

Meaning and Measurement of Rationality. To maximize freedom one must remove obstacles to desires, or adjust desires or both. These actions frequently require rational calculation and control. . . .

. . . An action is rational to the extent that it is "correctly" designed to maximize goal achievement, given the goal in question and the real world as it exists. Given more than one goal (the usual human situation), an action is rational to the extent that it is correctly designed to maximize *net* goal achievement. . . .

*   *   *   *   *

. . . To agree whether one action is more rational than another, observers must agree on the goals involved, their assumptions about reality, and the consequence for goal achievement of certain alternative courses of action given the assumed reality. . . .

Efficiency. The more rational action is also the more efficient action. . . . [E]fficiency is the ratio between valued input and valued output. . . . [A]n action is "correctly" designed to maximize goal satisfaction to the extent that it is efficient, or in other words to the extent that goal satisfaction exceeds goal cost.

*   *   *   *   *

DEMOCRACY

. . . [S]uppose your freedom conflicts with the freedom of someone else? . . . Democracy is a principle and a method of adjudicating such conflicts.

The democratic goal is twofold. It consists of a condition to be attained and a principle guiding the procedure for attaining it. The condition is political equality, which we define as follows: *Control over governmental decisions is shared so that the preferences of no one citizen are weighted more heavily than the preferences of any other one citizen.* The principle is majority rule, which we define as follows: *Governmental decisions should be controlled by the greater number expressing their preferences in the "last say."*

*   *   *   *   *

SUBJECTIVE EQUALITY

*   *   *   *   *

. . . The condition of subjective equality exists wherever, in any specific situation in which more people rather than less can have the opportunity to achieve their goals, the decision is for the greater number rather than for any lesser number.

*   *   *   *   *

SECURITY

. . . Subjectively, one is secure to the extent that he has a high or confident expectation that he will continue to have opportunities to achieve his goals. To an observer, one is objectively secure if, in the observer's view, one's confident expectation is based on a correct view of reality. To the extent that one feels fear and anxiety, he is insecure. . . .

. . . [S]ecurity is merely an aspect of freedom. A free individual is secure, and a secure individual is free. . . .

. . . [S]ecurity is merely an aspect or mode of freedom. It is a useful word to employ in discussing the likelihood that the freedoms of some individual or group will persist over some period of time.

*   *   *   *   *

. . . [T]he desire to be secure about some goals may conflict with the desire to be secure about others. . . .

. . . [P]robably most people do not really want "absolute" security . . . "optimum" security would probably still leave an area of challenge, risk, doubt, danger, hazard, and anxiety. . . .

And short-run security may conflict with long-run security; therefore one must choose. . . .

Finally, subjective security is often at war, not with freedom, but with objective security. A certain minimum level of subjective insecurity may be necessary to induce individuals and groups to take precautions against the future.

. . . [G]reat security feelings in the present tend to bring about policies that promise tremendous insecurity for the future.

PROGRESS

. . . One progresses to the extent that his opportunities for net goal achievement increase. Hence, like security, progress is a mode of freedom; for progress is an increase of freedom.

Progress, then, is always relative to some conception of goal achievement. . . . To one who places a high value on physical output and a low value on communal life, the modern city represents progress; to one with the opposite preferences, "conurbation" is a step towards a barbarization as ugly as the word itself. . . .

APPROPRIATE INCLUSION

*   *   *   *   *

. . . The problem of inclusiveness is a problem of adjusting margins. What are the likely consequences for the goal in question if we include this group or exclude that one? In any case, how likely is any particular line of exclusion-inclusion? Are there some convenient cultural, institutional, historical grounds of exclusion and inclusion?

The democratic goal raises the question of inclusion in its most practical form. For it would be one thing to want "everyone" to live in a democracy; but it would be quite another to want "everyone" to live in the *same* democracy.

For the purposes of this volume, the United States is the territorial nation-state within which we wish to maximize democracy. But the boundaries of the United States provide no fixed and eternal basis of inclusion-exclusion. The most that can be said is that the United States offers a sufficiently practical organization to furnish us with the conceptual basis necessary to a discussion of techniques for achieving the goals we have discussed.

For however loudly the super-patriots may insist on the territorial nation-state as an almost divinely approved design for inclusion and exclusion, it seems clear that exclusion-inclusion on the basis of the territorial nation-state, or on any other basis, is entirely a pragmatic question. If as a practical matter one needs to operate with more or less stable assumptions about the answers, nonetheless any answer must be tentative. For the answer would vary with the particular goals involved and their bearing on other goals, the availability of social techniques to achieve the goals, ease of identification, historical and geographical factors, and many other circumstances.

From: James Kuhn and Ivar Berg
*"THE TROUBLE WITH LABOR IS FEATHERBEDDING"**

[EDITORS' NOTE: The authors teach at the Graduate School of Business, Columbia University.]

The current railroad dispute over notorious "make-work" practices by railroad employees threatens another national emergency—and shows no more promise of shedding light on featherbedding. But clearly, the public need not understand what featherbedding is in order to invest its sympathies and uncritical enthusiasm in a crusade against it, against alleged wasteful work practices, obsolete work rules, and loafing.

*　　*　　*　　*　　*

Now, work rules are formal and informal arrangements in the shop, sanctioned by custom, tradition, and bargains. They are the oral and written regulations that govern work activities, crew sizes, and job assignments. Work rules set the amount, quality, and manner of work a man must do. They establish the standards by which one can tell how fast is fast, how fair is fair, and how reasonable is reasonable. Most are mutually beneficial. They allow foremen and

---

*Reprinted by permission of the *Columbia University Forum*, Spring, 1960, pp. 22–26.

workers a necessary and useful degree of flexibility in meeting unforeseen, unpredictable daily work difficulties.

Since most work rules are established through give and take, they can be changed in the same way. Having bargained for work rules, and thus created an "investment" of rights and benefits, workers are but prudent managers of their capital. Work rules are the coin of the bargaining realm; a coin that both managers and workers try to use profitably.

To be sure, some rules do serve only one party and become a source of legitimate concern to the other. When painters refuse to allow the use of sprayguns and tie building contractors to outmoded, expensive handwork, they featherbed. . . .

That unions should defend, and that management should have to fight to eliminate, such work rules is unthinkable to many Americans. A worker who featherbeds is one who "lays down on his job"; he is unjustifiably making the job softer and easier or demanding pay for useless, wasteful, work. With our atavistic Puritan streak, we rebel at featherbedding; like sin, it is something everyone must be against. . . .

*   *   *   *   *

Managers are *not* always interested in avoiding featherbedding. Under the coercive pressures of the head office to get production out, to meet contract deadlines, and to keep up in a seller's market, practices develop and flourish that would be undesirable in less frenzied—and less profitable—times.

*   *   *   *   *

Most work rules develop gradually, almost imperceptibly, from day to day and month to month. They allow an escape from the impersonality of machine and organization. They reduce the grinding frictions of the industrial process for managers as well as workers, and allow adjustments to the tensions and pressures of daily shop life. Once developed, however, rules tend to remain, protecting workers' rights and shop practices.

When managers believe that slack sales and foreign competition have cut profits, cost reduction is uppermost in their minds. At such a time, they attack the incrustation of work rules in the shop with no little indignation: according to economics, work rules clearly infringe on their rights to manage and their need to deploy workers efficiently. A successful attack should result in greater efficiency and larger earnings with which a firm may finance new labor-saving investments. In this way, workers lose their work rules in exchange for the dubious privilege of financing their own displacement. That they resist management's attacks on work rules is not surprising.

While managers may resent their workers' resistance to changes in work rules aimed at cutting costs, they could well heed the words of Dr. George Taylor, chairman of the Presidential fact-finding board in the steel dispute. He warned that, while "obsolete" rules that permit featherbedding should be done away with, "jobs are involved here . . . [Management should not] assert the right overnight to change practices that have been in here for years." And Mr. Sylvester Garrett, prominent arbitrator between United States Steel and the Steelworkers, told both parties during their recent dispute that work rules have been "accepted in the sense of being regarded by the men involved as the normal and proper response to the underlying circumstances presented." He reminded management and the union that in changing work rules they should carefully consider the benefits of stability, as well as the dangers of stagnation.

The matter is, of course, complicated. Work rules protect human rights, but they may also guarantee pay for phantom work. Work rules that contribute to safety can also restrict work; work rules once reasonable may become unreasonable as circumstances change. . . .

Management does not approach lesser work rules in the shop with as much consistency. Managers may feel that they simply cannot at all times settle for the benefits of *stability*. Work rules and shop practices quite acceptable at one time—indeed proposed or encouraged by management—become featherbedding at another time. . . .

Work practices encouraged and tolerated by management through years of high employment, easy markets, and cost-plus contracts, can hardly be eliminated at whim without severe social consequences. To redesign the worker's methods of work or to cut out a part of the worker's job disturbs the worker's very life and emotions. However rational, however sensible the change may be, no man can quickly or easily reorganize his habits or junk a part of his labor. . . .

American labor leaders have not adamantly refused to change work rules or to investigate alleged abuses. Guy L. Brown, head of the Locomotive Engineers, has declared that "the working rules need to be revised . . . [but] this must be a two-way street." . . .

*   *   *   *   *

. . . The loss of a job in middle or late working life means a loss of dignity, a desperate search for a new job. Unlike the manager (or even the union leader), the worker in the shop may not be able to afford much objectivity in defending his protective work rules; he may see union approval of changes in work rules, not as statesmanship, but as a "sweetheart" arrangement with management.

If workers at times seek private gains through featherbedding, to management's loss and society's, we need to remember that all too often management and society—the rest of us—have sought gain through technological change to the loss of the immediately affected workers. Unless management, the union, and the public speak plainly about and assume full responsibility for the deeper conflicts underlying "featherbedding," wasteful and inefficient practices will continue and spread from industry to industry, as workers seek to escape what Elton Mayo called the inevitable experience of change, "a sense of void and emptiness."

From: Benjamin M. Selekman

*A MORAL PHILOSOPHY FOR MANAGEMENT**

[EDITORS' NOTE: The author was Professor of Labor Relations, Graduate School of Business Administration, Harvard University.]

. . . [N]ot all unions are alike any more than all corporations are alike. They differ a great deal. . . . But, allowing for differences, what are their common characteristics? Perhaps the best way to approach this question is to see what a union is not:

---

* By permission from *A Moral Philosophy for Management,* by Benjamin Selekman. Copyright 1959. McGraw-Hill Book Company, Inc. (Excerpts from pp. 174–77, 195–96.)

1. A union though perhaps idealistic in origin, is a practical, usually hard-boiled organization with its eye on securing material gains for its members and, at the same time, enhancing the prestige and power of its leaders.

*   *   *   *   *

3. A union is not a public-service organization. It is primarily interested in its own members and in its own leadership. Of course, like all economic and political groups, a union may well argue that to the extent it serves its members it also serves the public. Nevertheless, it is essentially a self-interest organization; its primary aim is to get the very best wages, hours, and working conditions for its members.

*   *   *   *   *

5. Trade unions are not polite or well mannered or even diplomatic in their dealings with corporation executives, or even with government officials. Indeed, they usually adopt a posture of hostility, at least publicly, as they organize pressure to attain their objectives.

*   *   *   *   *

All of these negative aspects stem from the fundamental nature of unions. A union is a power organization. Its positive role is to mobilize economic, political, and moral power to win objectives for members and leaders. . . .

*   *   *   *   *

It is from the perspective of a power system that one can best understand the nature and function of trade unions. First and primarily, a union is a combination of a political and business organization. From the business point of view a union is primarily a marketing agency. Every union is essentially a collectivity for selling labor as a unit in the form of various skills. All its other activities are directed to making this selling function as effective as possible.

*   *   *   *   *

If, however, we keep in mind the function of a union as a marketing agency, we see that what looks like political propaganda is in reality part of a merchandising campaign particularly suited to its purpose of exacting the price desired as wages for its membership. . . .

*   *   *   *   *

It is all to the good that management has become by sheer logic of events the "government of the day"; for, in truth, the very nature of its function makes it the dynamic agency with major responsibility for the production of wealth. It mobilizes capital, builds factories, assembles machinery, engages labor, and establishes marketing and distribution channels. The test of profitability operating in a competitive market puts the burden of efficiency on the managerial apparatus—to produce wealth, that is, goods and services, at the lowest possible cost.
. . . The union's primary function then becomes the equitable *distribution* of the wealth created in terms of wages, fringe benefits, and conditions of work.
A moment's reflection will show that such a distribution of function is consistent with the organization and the specialization characteristic of our American society. Management is judged by the professional criteria of good performance in turning out products and services at a price which the consumer will pay. The labor leader is judged by the effectiveness with which he advances the welfare of his members. Since management has to be productive, competitive, and profitable, limits are set as to what the labor leader and his members may obtain. In this sense, management again, by the very nature of its function,

indirectly represents the other groups in the community—stockholders and consumers in particular.

Thus this voluntary constitutional system becomes a combined operation of management and union officials to keep the productive mechanism at the highest possible efficiency and with a maximum degree of practical justice for the largest number of people. In addition, the constitutional system protects employees from possible abuse as a result of management's preoccupation with efficiency. For union leaders not only market labor at the best possible bargain in terms of wages and working conditions, but they also see to it that civil rights as spelled out in the agreement are observed in the shop. In this sense, the grievance and arbitration machinery operates as a protective device to ensure that workers are not subject to capricious and intolerable treatment as their skills are mobilized in the drive for production.

From:

"ARBITRATION DECISIONS ON MANAGEMENT RIGHTS"*

"Implicit in every collective agreement is the right of management to conduct normal business operations and make normal management decisions and the right of the union to have a voice in such decisions of management as would impose arbitary changes in working conditions previously established. When these rights are not explicitly defined, a contract may properly be construed to protect for each party the rights set forth above." (4 LA 655)

"By an overwhelming weight of authority, it is well established that, prior to the designation of a collective bargaining representative or execution of a collective bargaining agreement, an employer had a full and complete right to establish all working conditions and rates of pay. A collective bargaining agreement operates as a limitation upon such right, but that right still exists as to all conditions not established by such collective bargaining agreement." (6 LA 283)

"It is a well recognized rule of contract construction, that the parties to a Collective Bargaining Agreement are bound only to perform it according to its terms. Neither party is obligated to perform acts which it has not contracted to perform, and the failure of any party to perform acts not bargained for or agreed upon, obviously cannot constitute the breach of a labor contract. It is an equally well recognized principle of law, that every person may control his own property as he pleases, and improve it or not as he chooses, subject only to his obligation with respect thereto, to perform the duties which he owes the State, and the duties which he has contracted with his fellowmen to discharge. One of the basic concepts upon which the American system of private enterprise rests is, that an employer has an original and generic right to control, manage, direct, and operate his business establishment as he sees fit, except insofar as such original or generic right has been diluted by statute, or surrendered and restricted through the signing of a Collective Bargaining Agreement. . . ." (16 LA 83)

---

* Published in *Labor Arbitration Reports,* Bureau of National Affairs, 1959.

"It is a fundamental principle in the interpretation of labor contracts that Management retains all rights and prerogatives with respect to plant operations, direction of working forces, assignment of duties, product produced, hours of work, and the right to make reasonable rules and regulations concerning the conduct of its business and employees, unless abridged by language in the Agreement or practices to the contrary." (28 LA 429)

NORMAN MANUFACTURING COMPANY

I Case Introduction

Synopsis

The Norman Manufacturing Company, originally a family-owned company in the capital goods industry, has sold stock to the public and acquired a smaller company that produces sporting goods. Top management sets objectives for profit and market share for the new company, but there are problems in achieving these objectives—both technical problems from the standpoint of finance, and human problems in the form of disagreement.

Why This Case Is Included

The Norman case offers opportunity to look at the philosophy and accounting facets of decentralization, as well as the human motivations and communications patterns connected with it. Various types of authority, and the phenomena of role conflict, are studied in relation to the operation of the company system. Since the executives in the case have actually designed a decision-making procedure, this can be critically examined to see the kinds of networks that produce a workable method for deciding financial objectives, and that produce accurate appraisal of operating results.

Diagnostic and Predictive Questions

In answering the following diagnostic and predictive questions, remember that these questions apply theories and conceptual ideas from certain disciplines. Such theories are valuable to understand basic forces at work in the policy system (diagnosis) and to predict what will happen in the system in the future (prediction). Since each reading abstracts from the total policy system certain factors or variables into the closed or partial viewpoint of one theory or discipline, no one reading gives answers to the practical policy problems of the case. In diagnosis and prediction, the parts of the problem are studied with "other things being equal."

Following each question are listed readings which will be helpful in answering the question. The readings included with this case are marked (*). By referring to the author index at the end of this book, you may locate the other readings listed.

1. What were L. D. Norman's overall objectives, and what motivated him

to adopt them from (a) the viewpoint of economics, (b) the viewpoint of psychology, and (c) the viewpoint of organizational philosophy?

Read: Odiorne, *How Managers Make Things Happen,* pp. 4–11, 37–38, 52–53. Schumpeter, *The Theory of Economic Development,* pp. 84–94. *Curtice, "General Motors Organization Philosophy and Structure."

2. Were these objectives in accord with the prevailing cultural beliefs about what corporations and executives *ought* to strive to attain?

Read: Schumpeter, *The Theory of Economic Development,* pp. 84–94. Galbraith, *The Affluent Society,* pp. 121–24, 126. *Roosevelt, "The Life of Strenuous Endeavor." Towne, "Foreword to *Shop Management.*" Taylor, "Principles of Scientific Management."

3. Given Norman's broad philosophical objectives, what did he fail to see in the way of the economic and financial details (balance) of putting them into effect?

Read: *Shillinglaw, *Cost Accounting,* pp. 680–84, 688–89. Drucker, *The Practice of Management,* pp. 62–131.

4. Given Norman's broad philosophical objectives, what did he fail to see in the way of the psychological and sociological realities of putting them into effect?

Read: Argyris, *Personality and Organization,* pp. 27–31, 33–51, 66–67, 77–90, 95, 103–4, 123–25, 130, 137–39, 150, 153–55. Etzioni, "Authority Structure and Organizational Effectiveness." Abrahams, "Status, Role and Conflict." *Newman and Summer, *The Process of Management: Concepts, Behavior, and Practice,* pp. 605–10.

5. What motivations, including those in Question 4, seem to be causing Gibbs' actions in the case? Be specific—list various of his actions throughout, and relate to various causes of behavior.

Read: Selections from Question 4. *Simon *et al., Public Administration,* pp. 182, 189–200. Etzioni, *A Comparative Analysis of Complex Organizations,* pp. 31–39, 80–82.

6. From the viewpoint of economic philosophy, what must Gibbs realize about conditions for "freedom" or "autonomy" in an organization?

Read: Clark, *Alternative to Serfdom,* pp. 4–7.

7. From the viewpoints of decision theory—suboptimization—why might not "the good of the whole Norman company" be the same as "the good of Lange division"?

Read: Miller and Starr, *Executive Decisions and Operations Research,* pp. 38–42, 45–47, 50. *Rapoport and Drews, "Mathematical Approach to Long-Range Planning."

8. What was Gibbs "ignorant" of in the case? What was Langford "ignorant" of? What implications does this have for a solution to the problem? Who, if anyone, is competent to state the "true" objectives of the Lange Division? What psychological laws cause Norman, Langford, or Gibbs to suboptimize?

Read: *Krech and Crutchfield, *Theory and Problems of Social Psychology,* pp. 81–83, 87–89, 94–96, 98, 102–3. Merton, "Bureaucratic Structure and Personality."

9. Remembering that (profit = revenues − cost) and (rate of return on investment = revenue − cost/investment), why did Gibbs want to charge advertising and research outlays to investment? What were his ultimate goals? What were Langford's ultimate goals in wanting to charge the outlays to expense?

Policy Questions for This Specific Case

In answering the following policy questions, the results of diagnosis and prediction are used to reduce the amount of guesswork, or judgment, in designing action solutions. However, since certain parts of the total case situation cannot be reduced to science, and since "other things are not equal," judgment must still be used to fill in the factors not accounted for by readings. You will also need a second kind of judgment as you put value weights on different scientific predictions, since different theories may point to conflicting solutions.

10. What would be the characteristics of a decision-making process which would arrive at the most accurate decisions on the objectives of the division and the most accurate way to enter outlays for advertising and research?

Read: Follett, "Constructive Conflict." Newman and Summer, *The Process of Management: Concepts, Behavior, and Practice,* pp. 439–48. *Enell and Haas, *Setting Standards for Executive Performance,* pp. 16–18, 31–32.

11. What specific process can you design for the people in this company to "apply" the insights from Question 9 to solution of their problem? Who will do what and when? (Name times, places, and people.)

12. If you were Norman and had studied the questions in this case, what would you do to put the process into action? That is, what ground rules, or insights, would you give at the first meeting with the parties concerned?

Major Policy Issues: Tentative Generalizations about Any Policy System

In arriving at conclusions for the following questions, generalize from the facts in the case and use your own ideas to (a) confirm, (b) modify, or (c) test the workability of the concepts and theories from readings. As an executive or professional, use wisdom to merge theory, on the one hand, with "brute facts" and practice, on the other.

13. For an organization, are there such things as a balance of objectives which can be applied as a formula to give the answers to specific projects and actions? Give comments and reasoning behind your answer. Consider the economic-financial implications first, and then the behavioral implications.

14. What are the characteristics of a system in which objectives can be used to secure the necessary degree of central planning and direction, and yet provide the dynamic and motivational advantages of autonomy?

Questions for Original Student Work in Analysis and Policy

The methods of viewing this case as represented by the authors' questions and selection of readings are not exhaustive. There are other relevant ideas for diagnosis and prediction. Furthermore, there are other ways of stating policy questions. More powerful analyses and wiser solutions will result by drawing on your own training and experience for (a) relevant concepts and theories, and (b) creative ways of asking policy questions. The following questions are designed to help you acquire this skill.

15. While reflecting on case facts, what additional theories from prior education give you insights as to "what is going on" in Norman Manufacturing Company? As to what might be predicted to happen in the future?

16. Other than the policy questions asked by the authors, what pragmatic ways can you think of to state the practical problems faced by executives in the case?

II Norman Manufacturing Company*

The Norman Manufacturing Company produces a variety of industrial machinery and equipment, including electrical switches and relay boxes; the smaller items of coal-mining equipment; and chains, hoists, conveyers and other materials-handling products. In addition to these lines, the company has expanded, through acquisition in the past ten years, into two lines less closely connected with its original product line: the manufacture of sporting goods and of furnishings (hardware, plumbing, furniture) for pleasure yachts. At the present time, the company employs 1,650 people, and its annual sales have averaged $40 million for the past three years.

Norman Manufacturing Company originated 30 years ago as a family-owned company that specialized in manufacturing and selling chains and hoists, with a plant located in Bridgeport, Connecticut. The company has experienced rapid growth through the years. Products allied to heavy industry have been added during the past 15 years. Company headquarters were moved from Bridgeport to New York City seven years ago.

Regarding the objectives of the Company, L. D. Norman, Jr., the President, states:

Since my father's death 13 years ago, we have endeavored to stress even more strongly the objective of growth over the years. The public now owns 63 per cent of our stock, but they, as well as our family and our management, have certain principal accomplishments in mind: to have this company grow in assets, market coverage, profitability, and prestige over the years; and to have it gain a national reputation for quality and service to our customers. This is the reason why we have taken on two new divisions that are not connected with our past experience. We feel that the company has a future in many product lines. Technology and consumer tastes mean you can't stand still with your same traditional products and ways of doing things.

The Lange Division

Seven years ago, the Norman Company purchased the Lange Sporting Goods Company and established it as the Lange Division of NMC. The research bulletin of a New York investment firm, at that time, carried the following statement:

---

* Copyright 1960 by the Graduate School of Business, Columbia University.

The Lange Company, with a good stable line of products, has suffered in recent years from a lack of vitality in keeping its products, production methods, and advertising up to the "zip" displayed by its competitors. We believe that Norman's record of capable and aggressive management should enable this company to show good growth over the intermediate term future.

The management of Lange had been in the hands of four members of the Lange family, all of whom retired at the time of the merger. L. D. Norman, Jr., immediately replaced them with Fred K. Gibbs as general manager of the Lange Division, and with two Norman middle management executives as controller and production superintendent respectively.

Fred Gibbs, 42, had been executive vice president of a competing sporting goods manufacturing company. After graduation from Stanford University, he held positions as production-scheduling trainee, salesman, sales manager, and marketing vice president for that company. Reference checks at the time of his employment with Norman Manufacturing Company indicated that he was well liked by his fellow executives, possessed an unusual degree of energy and drive, and had initiated many of the ideas that later, in the form of company policies, led to sales increases and the growth of his company.

L. Donald Norman, Jr., has been president of the Norman Manufacturing Company for 13 years. At age 50, he has worked for the Company 26 years, first in the plants, then as a salesman, and for 10 years as a staff man to his father, designing and supervising procedures to coordinate production, sales, shipping, and inventories. As president he has spent most of his time planning new customer strategy and sales incentive programs, and projecting financial statements to plan increases in plant investment. Together with T. M. Farish, executive vice president, and C. A. Langford, treasurer, he sits on the executive committee. This committee meets three times a week to discuss all important matters in sales, production, and finance.

At the time the Lange Division was established, the executive committee minutes show, Farish and Langford were somewhat apprehensive about the ability of Norman Company management "to take hold of this new venture and manage it successfully, since we do not have experience in consumer products."

Mr. Norman, the minutes also show, gave the committee a summary of the study he had been making of decentralization. He pointed out that such companies as General Motors and du Pont were able to grow by creating independent divisions, selecting capable men to run them, and retaining only very broad measures of performance. In this way, he said, the Norman Company could delegate virtually the entire management task "to Fred Gibbs and his team. We do not have to know much about the details of the division, so long as we establish broad controls."

In the five months after the acquisition, the three top Norman officials drew up the following control points. They were careful to make clear,

Norman says, that Gibbs' own performance would be measured only in terms of these controls. "Everything else—all of the details of running the division—would be left to Fred."

Rate of return on investment: Lange was earning an average of 14% (before taxes) on book value, and it was agreed to raise the target to 19% within five years.

Sales as a percentage of industry sales: Norman judged that the Lange Company had been performing as indicated below, and new targets were set for Lange's three principal products:

Product	Present	Five-Year Target
Tennis equipment	11%	15%
Golf bags	8	12
Gym clothing	10	25

Of the total dollar sales volume of Lange, averaged over the five-year period prior to acquisition, tennis equipment accounted for 40%, gym clothing for 45%, and golf bags for 15%.

In setting these figures, all three executives agreed that there was no accurate way to be "scientific" about what percentages could be reached. All recognized that the Lange Company had been, in the words of Norman, "conservative, lacking in morale, and complacent." It therefore seemed reasonable that "with a hard-hitting management and some new ideas, the targets are neither over- nor understated—they are realistic."

Gibbs at first expressed the idea that the gym clothing sales target was too high. But Langford and Norman showed him the results of their study of profits in this line compared to others. The profitability of selling gym clothing, particularly to institutions, was much higher than the other items. Gibbs, too, agreed that his target was a wise one.

Operating Results: First Six Years of Operation

At the time this case is written, Lange Division has been in operation for six fiscal years. Rates of return on investment and percentages of industry sales appear in Exhibits 1 and 2, respectively.

During the first four years, the executive committee of the Norman Company had a verbal agreement, of which they frequently reminded themselves, that none of Norman's management should initiate inquiries about *specific* operations in Lange. Langford reports, for instance, that when he noticed, on the expense statements furnished for the first year, that telephone and telegraph expenses of Lange were, in his opinion, far out of line with the rest of the company, he felt that he should not use these statements as detailed controls.

The committee also agreed that Norman should make fairly frequent (perhaps bimonthly) visits to Lange headquarters in Providence for the purpose of inquiring about overall sales improvement. He should also encourage Gibbs to come to New York whenever *"he* feels the need to discuss any matter, broad, detailed, or otherwise."

As a matter of practice, Norman, Gibbs, and Langford did meet about three times a month, at which times (*a*) they discussed overall sales results for 10 to 20 minutes, and (*b*) they discussed and approved lump-sum amounts of money requested by Gibbs to be budgeted for both capital expenditures and current expenses.

At the end of the fourth year, Langford, who had been raising questions with Norman all along about the wisdom of Gibbs' expenditures, suggested that investment return and sales targets were

far less than satisfactory. We have been holding off telling him how to manage various phases of his budget too long. There is little doubt but that he has gone too fast and too far in increasing expenditures for advertising, salesmen's bonuses, and salesmen's expense accounts. Furthermore, his expenditures for employee-recreation facilities and increases in factory salaries have been unwise when we are trying to increase return on investment. The former increased the investment side of the ratio, and the latter decreased the income side.

Langford, incidentally, received expense summaries regularly—as he says, "not as control reports, but for the purpose of consolidating the figures with the rest of the company divisions for the profit and loss statement." These summaries contained 35 account captions (for excerpts of five captions, see Exhibit 3).

After reviewing Langford's cost statements, the executive committee agreed that "Gibbs needs some helpful guidance." Since Langford knew more about the details of expense and capital budgets, they also agreed that he should visit Gibbs once a month to go over the 35 expense accounts and see how each progresses during the year.

Gibbs recalls that early in his fifth year at Lange, when Langford first came to Providence and told him what the executive committee had decided,

I was surprised. I guess it scared me a little right off the bat, since I had no idea they were thinking like that. The targets weren't being met, but I thought that surely they must know that things were going quite well, considering all of the things which must be done to put this division on a solid footing for the future. After my initial anxiousness and surprise, I got downright mad for a few days.

Gibbs also states that

early in the fifth year, I began to cut back on some of the spending inaugurated in the beginning. I got the salesmen together on four occasions and gave them a talk about the necessity of cutting their expense-account expenditures, and the fact that we would have to stop making some of the purely promotional calls, and concentrate on those customers that looked more like immediate prospects. I also cut the number of direct-mail promotional brochures from 12 mailings a year to six, and decided to let one man go whom we had hired as a merchandising man. He had helped, in the four years he had been with us, in designing the products for eye appeal, in creating point-of-sale displays, and in improving the eye appeal of our packages. I did not cut down on the number of salesmen employed, however.

The Question of Advertising and Research Costs

As early as February of the second year, Gibbs objected—in his words, "mildly"—to Norman "because of the way Langford entered on certain financial statements the money spent for advertising, the market research department, and the product research department." When the first year statement of return was prepared by Lange's own controller, Gibbs and he felt that the total of $340,000 represented an investment rather than a current operating expense. They reasoned that the increase in new products and the increase in good will or consumer acceptance would not begin to pay off for two or three years. Since return on investment is the ratio of income to investment, charging these three items to investment showed a higher performance (14% in the first year) than the same statement prepared by Langford (12% in the same year). It seemed to Gibbs that by subtracting the $340,000 from profits "was a real injustice—Tom Farish and Norman family stockholders have pretty much stayed out of my end of the business, but I don't want them to get the wrong impression. They will, from that kind of misleading figure."

Gibbs and Langford both feel that, in spite of this disagreement, the relationship of the Norman management group to Gibbs is "a pretty good one." Gibbs states that as of now,

I pretty much go along with their guidance, though it one time looked like interference. The only thing I'm still darn mad about is this way of figuring return. Norman overruled me when Langford and I had it out in front of him one time, but it's still such a hot subject that Langford and I won't bring it up any more. Why, just look at the figures for the whole period that the division has been in existence! [See Exhibit 1.]

Exhibit 1

RATIO OF PROFIT (BEFORE TAX) TO
INVESTMENT IN THE LANGE DIVISION

Year	Method 1*	Method 2†
First	14%	12%
Second	14	11
Third	15	13
Fourth	15	13
Fifth	17	16
Sixth	17	16
Present‡	17	16

 ° Used by Lange Division controller, charging advertising and research to capital investment, the lower half of the ratio.

 † Used by Norman Company management, charging advertising and research to current expense, thus decreasing the top of the ratio.

 ‡ First quarter adjusted.

Exhibit 2

SALES AS A PERCENTAGE OF TOTAL INDUSTRY SALES

Year	Tennis Equipment	Golf Bags	Gym Clothing
First	11%	9%	10%
Second	12	10	15
Third	12	9	21
Fourth	13	11	22
Fifth	12	10	23
Sixth	12	10	22
Present (1st quarter)	12	10	21

Exhibit 3

SELECTED EXPENSE CAPTIONS AND AMOUNTS FROM LANGE DIVISION EXPENSE TABULATION

Expense Caption	Fourth Year	Year Prior to Merger
Advertising	$280,000	$ 47,000
Salesmen Bonuses	210,000	23,000
Salesmen Expense	145,000	68,000
Factory salaries	665,000	550,000*
Employee Service	80,000	2,010

* Average salary per employee in the year prior to merger was $6,540. If this is adjusted for cost-of-living increase from that time to the fourth year, it comes out to an equivalent of $7,185. Average actual salary paid by Lange in the fourth year was $7,540.

III Selected Readings

From: Harlow H. Curtice

*"GENERAL MOTORS ORGANIZATION PHILOSOPHY AND STRUCTURE"**

[EDITORS' NOTE: Mr. Curtice is former President of General Motors Corporation.]

May I first make the point that the growth of General Motors has taken place principally over the past 35 years. This period coincides with that in which the policies and business of the corporation have functioned under the existing management organization.

---

* Reprinted by permission. From a Statement before the Subcommittee on Anti-Trust and Monopoly of the United States Senate Committee on the Judiciary, December 2, 1955 (pp. 5–12) "The Development and Growth of General Motors."

In my opinion there are four principal reasons for our success. These are, first, the dynamic growth of our country; second, the even more rapid growth of the automobile industry; third, our management structure; and, fourth, our approach to problems.

*   *   *   *   *

General Motors has grown faster than has the automobile industry as a whole. Quite obviously, we have made things that people wanted, and people in increasing numbers have bought them. . . .

General Motors has been able to offer greater dollar values in its products, and at the same time it has been able to operate efficiently to provide dividends for its shareholders and substantial sums for reinvestment in the business.

But, one may well ask why and how; and this brings me to what to my mind are the two fundamental reasons for the success of General Motors.

Both fall under the heading of what might be termed management philosophy. When this General Motors philosophy was formulated in the early 1920's—and I might add that the credit for its formulation largely goes to one man, Alfred P. Sloan, Jr.—it was unique as applied to industry. That it is no longer unique is in itself evidence of its soundness.

The first element of this philosophy has to do with organizational structure, the second with our approach to problems. Both, of course, concern people—in fact, can only be put into practice by people.

*   *   *   *   *

To fully appreciate the revolutionary nature of the organizational structure developed by Mr. Sloan in the early 1920's, it is necessary to appraise it in the light of conditions as they existed at that time. The business enterprise which the present management took charge of in 1921 had been put together, beginning in 1908, by W. C. Durant, and it largely bore the stamp of his personality. Durant had genius as a creator and super-salesman. He was not an administrator and did not develop an effective organization. Twice under his administration the Corporation was in serious financial difficulties—first in 1910 and again in 1920.

Prior to 1921 there existed no real concept of sound management in General Motors. Operations were neither integrated nor coordinated. There was no consistent policy with respect to product programs. Frequently poor judgment was exercised in making capital expenditures and establishing production schedules. The Corporation did not have a properly developed research and engineering staff nor any sound concept of budgetary control. The central administration did not exercise adequate control over the operations of the individual divisions. There were wide variations in the competence of divisional managements. In short, the Corporation was unorganized and the individual units largely out of control.

It is not surprising, therefore, that this [Vehicle sales for 1921: G.M., 11.79%; Ford, 55.45%; all others, 32.76%] was the competitive picture in 1921 when the management changed and Mr. Sloan began to put into effect the policies with respect to organizational structure which I will now outline.

Even before the crisis of 1920 materialized, Mr. Sloan was very conscious of the need in General Motors for a new and clearly defined concept of management philosophy. He had observed that much time was being consumed in solving detailed administrative problems and in meeting the critical situations which were constantly arising. He recognized that too great a concentration of problems upon a small number of executives limited initiative, caused delay, increased expense, reduced efficiency and retarded development.

Chart I

GENERAL MOTORS PER CENT OF INDUSTRY VEHICLE SALES
FOR THE YEAR 1921

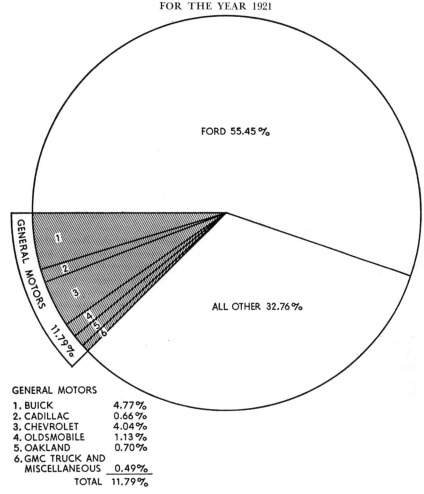

GENERAL MOTORS
1. BUICK	4.77%	
2. CADILLAC	0.66%	
3. CHEVROLET	4.04%	
4. OLDSMOBILE	1.13%	
5. OAKLAND	0.70%	
6. GMC TRUCK AND MISCELLANEOUS	0.49%	
TOTAL	11.79%	

Source: F.T.C. "Report on Motor Vehicle Industry," page 27.

He realized that centralization, properly established, makes possible directional control, coordination, specialization, and resulting economies. He also realized that decentralization, properly established, develops initiative and responsibility; it makes possible a proper distribution of decisions at all levels of management, including the foreman—with resulting flexibility and cooperative effort, so necessary to a large-scale enterprise. His objective was to obtain the proper balance between these two apparently conflicting principles of centralization and decentralization in order to obtain the best elements of each in the combination. He concluded that, to achieve this balance so necessary for flexibility of operation, General Motors management should be established on a foundation of centralized policy and decentralized administration.

Mr. Sloan's concept of the management of a great industrial organization, expressed in his own words as he finally evolved it, is "to divide it into as many parts as consistently as can be done, place in charge of each part the most capable executive that can be found, develop a system of coordination so that each part may strengthen and support each other part; thus not only welding all parts together in the common interests of a joint enterprise, but importantly developing ability and initiative through the intrumentalities of responsibility and ambition—developing men and giving them an opportunity to exercise their talents, both in their own interests as well as in that of the business."

In pursuance of that plan each of the various operations was established as an integral unit under a General Manager. Then, those operations which had a common relationship were grouped under a Group Executive for coordinating purposes. These Group Executives reported to the President who was the Chief Executive Officer.

To perform those functional activities that could be accomplished more effectively by one activity in the interest of the whole and to coordinate similar functional activities of the different operating units and promote their effectiveness, a General Staff, and in addition, Financial and Legal Staffs, were established to operate on a functional basis.

     *   *   *   *   *

Today, General Motors has two principal committees of the Board of Directors—the Financial Policy Committee, which is concerned with the financial and legal affairs of the Corporation, and the Operations Policy Committee, which deals primarily with the operating affairs of the business.

There are two additional committees of the Board of Directors, namely, an Audit Committee and a Bonus and Salary Committee, consisting of directors who are not members of management.

     *   *   *   *   *

The balance between decentralized operations, on the one hand, and coordinated control, on the other, varies according to areas. It also varies according to the temperaments and talents of executives, and the way in which they work. While the relationships of physical things are inherent in the business, it is men who establish and govern these relationships. The relationship between the Central Office Staff and the Divisional line operations may vary according to conditions and circumstances.

In summary, the organization of General Motors Corporation under the Board of Directors consists of the Financial Policy Committee and the Operations Policy Committee, supported by other committees and policy groups; staff operations; component product divisions; end product divisions; and service operations; all headed up by staff executives or general line officers who report to the Chief Executive Officer, except for the executives in charge of the financial and legal activities who report to the Chairman of the Financial Policy Committee.

     *   *   *   *   *

Such a management concept provides a continuous flow of ideas and information upward and downward through the management organization, by means of reports, meetings and conferences of both staff executives and line executives at all appropriate levels. This results in mutual education and understanding with respect to the authority, responsibility, objectives and purposes of management at all levels from the foreman to the Chief Executive Officer. It provides interpretation and understanding of policy and procedure as it is or may be established or changed. It produces an upward flow of information with respect to situations arising in operations, full knowledge of which is necessary if appropriate changes in policy or procedure are to be accomplished intelligently and promptly. It provides maximum initiative at every managerial level and at every point requiring administrative judgment, by the men closest to all the facts of the situation having full responsibility for their decisions. Finally, it makes possible accurate and prompt appraisal and evaluation of the contribution of the individual executive at every level of management, and of the contribution as well of every divisional organization and staff operation.

Although for many years this form of decentralized industrial management was identified primarily with General Motors, in more recent years decentralized management has been adopted by other large industrial companies.

The success of General Motors is the proof of the soundness of this management philosophy and its effectiveness in its application to a large industrial organization. Testifying to this has been a growing consumer preference expressed in the purchase of General Motors products.

From: Theodore Roosevelt
"THE LIFE OF STRENUOUS ENDEAVOR"

Our country calls not for the life of ease, but for the life of strenuous endeavor. The twentieth century looms before us big with the fate of many nations. If we stand idly by, if we seek merely swollen, slothful ease and ignoble peace, if we shrink from the hard contests where men must win at the hazard of their lives and the risk of all they hold dear, then the bolder and stronger peoples will pass us by and will win for themselves the domination of the world.

From: Gordon Shillinglaw
*COST ACCOUNTING**

[EDITORS' NOTE: The author is Associate Professor in the Graduate School of Business, Columbia University.]

A company is *divisionalized* whenever certain related activities are grouped together for administrative direction and control by high-level executives. Whenever this is accompanied by the delegation to division managers of the responsibility for a segment of the company's profits, then the company is

* Reprinted by permission of Richard D. Irwin, Inc., Homewood, Illinois, 1961 (pp. 680–84, 688–89).

said to be *decentralized*. The hallmark of the decentralized company is its subdivision into a number of smaller, relatively self-contained entities that are equipped to operate in substantially the same manner as independent firms dependent on their own profit performance for economic survival. The creation of these semiautonomous units, often referred to as *profit centers,* has three major objectives: . . .

Perhaps the most important of these is to overcome the sheer weight of the decision-making responsibility in a large corporation. With operations spread over a vast geographical area and encompassing hundreds of products and thousands of customers, central management cannot hope to be completely and continuously in direct personal contact with every segment of the company's business. To provide flexibility and adaptability to changing conditions, it has become increasingly necessary to delegate substantial powers to executives who can maintain a closer, more detailed familiarity with individual products or markets. In other words, decentralization aims to recreate in the large organization the conditions that give life and flexibility to the small company without sacrificing the advantages of size—diversification of risk, centralized financing, and specialization in the planning and advisory functions of management.

A second objective of decentralization is to bring subordinate executives into more direct contact with the ultimate profit objectives of the firm. A strictly manufacturing executive sees all problems as production problems with a cost overlay. A marketing executive focuses his attention on sales volume and distribution cost. In a centralized organization these viewpoints come together only at the top of the pyramid. Decentralization is one way of attempting to bring them together at lower levels.

Closely related to this is a third objective of decentralization, namely, to provide a more comprehensive training ground for the top managers of the future. The ranks of the top executives are continually being thinned by death and retirement, and there is a need for replacements who have been schooled in various aspects of business management and are thereby better prepared to face the major problems that can be resolved only at the top-management level. This kind of experience is best obtained at lower levels where the inevitable mistakes are likely to be smaller.

*   *   *   *   *

. . . The ideal basis for profit decentralization exists whenever a division can be relatively self-contained, with its own manufacturing and distributive facilities and relatively few transfers of product internally among divisions. In other words, decentralization is at its best whenever a division's operations come closest in scope and depth to those of separate independent companies. In these cirmumstances, the profit reported by each division is largely independent of operating performance in other divisions of the company, thus facilitating the interpretation of reported profits.

Unfortunately, these ideal conditions are often unattainable. Organization structure cannot be determined solely by the need for profit separability. Other factors, such as economies of common use of sales forces or facilities, may override the desirability of separating profit centers from each other. In these circumstances, the problem is to seek means of measurement and evaluation that will achieve a satisfactory compromise between conflicting objectives. Management has the task of deciding whether departures from the ideal are sufficiently serious to make profit decentralization unworkable. . . .

*   *   *   *   *

. . . No matter how it is defined, decentralization never represents a complete delegation of authority. Even in the most decentralized companies, top management retains some vestige of authority, particularly over financing and capital expenditures. In any case, divisional autonomy is limited by the need to conform to over-all company policies and by the need for co-ordination. . . .

Both at the corporate level and within each profit center there are units that are not organized on a profit responsibility basis. These are called *service centers* or *budget centers* to distinguish them from profit centers. . . . In each of these the executive in charge is responsible for costs but not for profits. . . . Within each product division there are also staff departments, such as divisional accounting or marketing research, which act in an advisory capacity to the division managers. The managers of these departments are also responsible for costs, but they generally have no direct profit responsibilities.

* * * * *

. . . Three criteria that divisional profit measures must meet stand out as especially important:

1. Divisional profit should not be increased by any action that reduces total company profit.
2. Each division's profit should be as independent as possible of performance efficiency and managerial decisions elsewhere in the company.
3. Each division's profit should reflect all items that are subject to any substantial degree of control by the division manager or his subordinates.

Four alternative concepts may be examined to see how well they fit these criteria:

1. *Variable profit,* or total revenues less total variable costs to make and sell.
2. *Controllable profit,* or variable profit less all the division's controllable fixed costs.
3. *Contribution margin,* or controllable profit less all other costs directly traceable to the division.
4. *Net profits,* or contribution margin less some share of general management and service center costs.

Exhibit 21–5

FOUR PROFIT CONCEPTS ILLUSTRATED

Sales	$760,000
Less:	
Variable costs of goods sold	$270,000
Variable divisional selling and administrative expense	30,000
Variable profit	$460,000
Less: Controllable divisional overhead	200,000
Controllable Profit	$260,000
Less: Fixed, noncontrollable divisional overhead	150,000
Contribution margin	$110,000
Less: Allocation of extradivisional fixed expenses—noncontrollable ...	50,000
Net Profit before Taxes	$ 60,000

From: William H. Newman and Charles E. Summer, Jr.

THE PROCESS OF MANAGEMENT: CONCEPTS, BEHAVIOR, AND PRACTICE*

[EDITORS' NOTE: The authors are on the faculty of the Graduate School of Business, Columbia University.]

The responses of people to standards, measurements, reports and other control devices depend, of course, on each total situation. The way a man feels toward his boss, whether he likes his work, his opportunities for self-expression, and similar factors influence his responses to controls as to other managerial actions. In the following discussion we are concerned with a narrower issue. What is there about controls per se that makes them objectionable to so many people? Why do we so often hear people say, "This is a good place to work. But I sure don't like those damn controls."

*   *   *   *   *

One reason why people may not like a control is that they have no genuine interest in accomplishing the objective behind the control. . . .

Each of us has only a limited amount of energy, but many things he would like to do. A control, by its very nature, prods us to expend more energy in particular directions. If those directions are not so appealing to us as other things we might do, we resent the prod.

*   *   *   *   *

To put this matter in terms of personal "needs,". . . if a person fails to accept certain objectives and so to include them among his needs, he is likely to find any control mechanism that pushes him toward those objectives a distinct annoyance.

*   *   *   *   *

Often a person may agree with an objective but dislike a control because he thinks the standard of performance is set too high. . . .

*   *   *   *   *

Whether a standard is considered reasonable also depends on how it is administered. Circumstances beyond the influence of a person who is being controlled may affect his actual results. Or a standard may be so tight that it can be met only half the time. . . .

A person's feeling about the unreasonableness of controls is also influenced by the total number of different controls that bear on him. Most people expect, and even welcome, some control over their activities, but as more and more

* *The Process of Management: Concepts, Behavior, and Practice,* William H. Newman and Charles E. Summer, Jr., © 1961 by Prentice-Hall, Inc., Englewood Cliffs, New Jersey (pp. 605–10).

aspects of their work become subject to standards, inspection, and reports, a feeling of being pressed on arises. . . .

*　　*　　*　　*　　*

Controls may increase the squabbles between departments when the people involved lack confidence in the measurements. . . .

*　　*　　*　　*　　*

Another fundamental reason why controls are unpopular is that from time to time control reports bear bad news. A person who is loath to face unpleasant facts almost always wishes the control system would vanish.

Each of us has his own personal aspirations about our work. These include both hopes and expectations. They reflect the kind of a person and the quality of worker each of us thinks he is. Now, control reports are one means of learning whether we have lived up to our own expectations. Often, we fail, and a realist accordingly adjusts the balance between expectations and facts; he may even readjust his hopes. Other persons, however, find it difficult to accept the facts of life, and so develop a sense of frustration. And since a frustrated person needs some relief, it is only natural for him to put part of the blame on the mechanism that tells him he isn't as good as he thinks he ought to be.

Furthermore, control reports may put us in an unfavorable light before our associates. To the extent that control systems measure desirable action, reports can make us appear strong or weak. . . .

The fear of unpleasant consequences can add to our aversion to controls. If an unfavorable report may lead to demotion, a cut in pay, or a bawling-out, we aren't going to feel very kindly toward the control system.

*　　*　　*　　*　　*

The response to controls depends, in part, on who tries to do the controlling. . . .

Once the social structure of a business has been established, people become sensitive about what kind of action is "legitimate.". . . Fairly strong opposition can be generated if the control pressure comes from sources employees believe are illegitimate.

*　　*　　*　　*　　*

. . . [S]ocial pressure applies to control as well as to other managerial action; . . .

*　　*　　*　　*　　*

. . . The attitudes that really count are those of associates whose friendship and respect a man wants to keep. If these persons feel that a control standard and its measurement are fair and that cooperating with management is the right thing to do, they will constitute a social force supporting that standard. Thus, there will porbably be strong social support for a control over stealing money, whereas control over wasting money through unnecessary expenses will receive support only if employees feel that management administers the control reasonably and fairly. . . .

. . . [G]roup pressure becomes significant only if it is difficult to meet both company and group objectives. . . .

From: Herbert A. Simon, Donald W. Smithburg, and Victor A. Thompson
PUBLIC ADMINISTRATION*

[EDITORS' NOTE: Dr. Simon is Professor of Administration at Carnegie Institute of Technology; Drs. Smithburg and Thompson are Professors of Political Science at Illinois Institute of Technology.]

From a psychological standpoint the exercise of authority involves a relationship between two or more persons. On the one side we have a person who makes proposals for the action of others. On the other side we have a person who accepts the proposals—who "obeys" them. Now a person may accept another's proposals under three different sets of circumstances:

(1) He may examine the merits of the proposal, and, on the basis of its merits become convinced that he should carry it out. We shall exclude such instances of acceptance from our notion of authority, although some writers on administration have called this the "authority of ideas."

(2) He may carry out the proposals without being fully, or even partially, convinced of its merits. In fact he may not examine the merits of the proposal at all.

(3) He may carry out the proposal even though he is convinced it is wrong—wrong either in terms of personal values or of organizational values or both.

We will treat both the second and third cases as instances of the acceptance of authority. Of course in any actual instance all three of the "pure types" of acceptance listed above may be combined in various proportions. In actual practice authority is almost always liberally admixed with persuasion. . . .

    *   *   *   *   *

Because the person who accepts proposals may do so for a variety of motives, there will be seen in any organization a number of different types of authority relationship, corresponding to these different motives for acceptance. . . .

People accept the proposals of persons in whom they have great confidence. In any organization there are some individuals who, because of past performance, general reputation, or other factors, have great influence or authority. Their proposals will often be accepted without analysis as to their wisdom. Even when the suggestions of such a person are not accepted, they will be rejected reluctantly and only because a stronger authority contradicts them.

The authority of confidence may be limited to a special area of competence in which a person has acquired a reputation. . . .

    *   *   *   *   *

. . . The willingness to accept authority on the basis of confidence, both within and outside organizations, goes even one step further. Not only is the

---

layman generally unable to judge the quality of the advice he is getting from the specialist, but he often is in no position to judge the competence of the specialist, except on the basis of certain superficial and formal criteria that give the specialist his *status*.

. . . [T]here are at least two kinds of status, which may be called *functional status* and *hierarchical status*. It is with functional status that we are concerned at the moment. A person has functional status in a particular area of knowledge when his decisions and recommendations in that area are accepted as more or less authoritative.

In the established professions, status is generally conferred on the basis of standards developed by the profession itself. The M.D. degree is conferred on the young doctor by the medical profession (acting through an "accredited" medical school). Law and engineering degrees and the certificate of the public accountant are awarded in much the same way. In other cases, job experience in a particular field confers functional status in that field. A person with long experience in a professional position in the Interstate Commerce Commission may acquire status as a transportation economist.

* * * * *

. . . Confidence can be a powerful support for hierarchical as well as for nonhierarchical authority. A subordinate will much more readily obey a command of a superior if he has confidence in the intelligence and judgment of that superior or if he believes that the superior has knowledge of the situation not available to himself.

In particular, where a problem requiring decision affects the work of several units in an organization, the superior who has hierarchical authority in the formal organization plan over all the units involved is often accepted as the person best located—because he has the "whole picture"—to make the decision. Hence, the coordinating functions that are commonly performed by those in hierarchical authority are based, in part at least, upon the authority of confidence—upon the belief of subordinates that the superior is the best informed about the situation as a whole.

* * * * *

The most generally recognized weapon of the superior is the sanction—the ability of the superior to attach pleasant or unpleasant consequences to the actions of the subordinate. . . .

* * * * *

. . . The relationship of the authority of sanctions with the organizational hierarchy can be viewed from a more general standpoint. When a person joins an organization he is accepting a system of relationships that restricts his individuality or his freedom of action. He is willing to do so because he feels that, in spite of the organizational restraints, being a member of the organization is preferable to other alternatives available to him. To continue as a member of the organization, he must continue, to some extent, to abide by the complex of procedures which constitutes the organization. Although, increasingly, the power to discharge an employee is not lodged in any specific superior (because of merit systems, central personnel offices, labor unions, etc.), nevertheless, this power resides somewhere in the organization, being, in fact, one of its working procedures. The sanctions discussed in this section are increasingly *organization* sanctions, brought into play through the working procedures of the organization, and not the special prerogatives or powers of *individual superiors*. . . .

. . . For the most part the authority of sanction rests on the behavior responses that are induced by the *possibility* that a sanction may be applied. An organization member is seldom presented with an ultimatum "to do so and so or suffer the consequences." Rather, he anticipates the consequences of continual insubordination or failure to please the person or persons who have the ability to apply sanctions to him, and this anticipation acts as a constant motivation without expressed threats from any person. . . .

*   *   *   *   *

There is another reason why employees accept the proposals of other organization members—a reason less rationalistic but probably more important than the desire to avoid the organization sanctions discussed above. People accept "legitimate" authority because they feel that they *ought* to go along with the "rules of the game."

. . . [T]hroughout their development to maturity and after, people are educated in the beliefs, values, or mores of society. They learn what they ought to do and what they ought not to do. One of the values with which they are indoctrinated is that a person should play according to the rules of the game. This ethic is acquired very early. When a child enters a ball game in the sand lot he does not expect the game to be altered at various points to suit his convenience. Rather he expects to adjust his behavior to the rules of the game. Although there may be disputes as to what the rule is on some point, once this is established, the proposition that he should abide by the rule is unquestioned.

Likewise, when people enter organizations most of them feel that they ought to abide by the rules of the game—the working procedures of the organization. These working procedures define how the work will be done; how working problems will be solved when they arise; how conflicts will be settled. They prescribe that on such and such matters the individual will accept the suggestions of this or that person or organization; secure the advice of such and such unit; clear his work with so and so; work on matters that come to him in such and such a way; etc.

The working procedures of an organization prescribe that the individual member will accept the proposals of other members in matters assigned to them. This acceptance is one of the rules of the game which he feels he should abide by. Thus, individuals in organizations also accept the authority of other persons because they think they *ought* to accept it.

*   *   *   *   *

. . . The working relationships in an organization designated by the term "hierarchy" constitute a particular organization procedure for handling the authority of legitimacy. Acceptance of the working procedures of an organization by a member includes acceptance of the obligation to go along with the proposals of an hierarchical superior, at least within a limit of toleration—the "area of acceptance." Thus, whether the other reasons for obedience are operating or not (confidence, identification, or sanctions), organization members will feel that they ought to obey their superiors. Legitimacy is one of the most important sources of the authority of the hierarchical superior.

The feeling that hierarchical authority is legitimate is immensely strengthened by previous social conditioning. Hierarchical behavior is an institutionalized behavior that all organization members bring to the organization with them. Like the players in the Oberammergau Passion Play who begin to learn their roles in early childhood, "inferiors" obey "superiors" because they have been taught to do so from infancy, beginning with the parent-child relationship and running through almost constant experience with social and organizational hierarchies until death brings graduation from this particular social schooling. Hierarchical behavior involves an inferior-superior role-taking of persons well versed in their roles. "Inferiors" feel that they ought to obey "superiors"; "superiors" feel that they ought to be obeyed.

Our society is extremely hierarchical. Success is generally interpreted in terms of hierarchical preferment. Social position and financial rewards are closely related to hierarchical preferment, as also are education and even perhaps romantic attainment. Advancement up a hierarchy is generally considered a sign of moral worth, of good character, of good stewardship, of social responsibility, and of the possession of superior intellectual qualities.

Hierarchy receives a tremendous emphasis in nearly all organizations. This is so because hierarchy is a procedure that requires no training, no indoctrination, no special inducements. It rests almost entirely on "pre-entry" training—a training so thorough that few other organization procedures can ever compete with it. Furthermore, hierarchy is a great simplification. . . .

From: Leo A. Rapoport and William P. Drews
"MATHEMATICAL APPROACH TO LONG-RANGE PLANNING"*

[EDITORS' NOTE: The authors are Research Associates with Esso Research and Engineering Company.]

Almost everybody will agree that over-all optimization is desirable. At the same time, however, there still is a widespread belief that the best plan for an integrated business will be obtained by letting each of the component activities improve its own efficiency as much as possible. Another common view is that for purposes of optimal planning it suffices to evaluate and screen projects or budget proposals on the basis of their individual profitability. These are serious misconceptions.

Mathematically it can be demonstrated that the maximum of a composite function generally does not correspond to the values of variables which maximize the individual components of that function. A simple graphical illustration of this situation in the context of economics appeared in a recent article by Edward G. Bennion.[1] The optimization principle has also been stated in clear terms by Peter F. Drucker:

". . . If there is one fundamental insight underlying all management science, it is that the business enterprise is a *system* of the highest order. . . .

"The whole of [such] a system is not necessarily improved if one particular function or part is improved or made more efficient. In fact, the system may well be damaged thereby, or even destroyed. In some cases the best way to strengthen

---

* Reprinted by permission of the *Harvard Business Review*, May–June 1962, pp. 77–78.

1 "Econometrics for Management," *Harvard Business Review*, March–April 1961, p. 100.

the system may be to *weaken* a part—to make it *less* precise or *less* efficient. For what matters in any system is the performance of the whole. . . .

"Primary emphasis on the efficiency of parts in management science is therefore bound to do damage. It is bound to optimize precision of the tool at the expense of the health and performance of the whole.

"This is hardly a hypothetical danger. The literature abounds in actual examples—inventory controls that improve production runs and cut down working capital but fail to consider the delivery expectations of the customer and the market risks of the business; machine-loading schedules that overlook the impact of the operations of one department on the rest of the plant; forecasts that assume the company's competitors will just stand still; and so on."[2]

Admittedly, the above statements are somewhat general and, therefore, might appear as unfounded abstractions to the hardened skeptic. A simple example, however, might help to illustrate their practical importance:

In the case of our hypothetical oil company in Exhibit I, suppose that one of the refineries should find it most profitable to install a particular processing unit of Type T in order to utilize a certain low-price crude, C_t. The installation of this unit would be justified *from the refiner's viewpoint* by showing an attractive return on incremental investment. This "conventional" approach, however, may overlook the aspects of functional interdependence.

Bear in mind that the installation and efficient utilization of a processing unit of Type T would commit the producing function to a continued supply of crude, C_t. This crude, although low priced (on the outside market), may not, in fact, be the least costly to produce, nor would it necessarily remain the least costly as greater amounts of it become required in the future. Accordingly, from an over-all viewpoint, it could prove more desirable to install a different processing unit of Type S. This other unit might be more expensive to install or to operate than Type T. In compensation, however, it would permit utilization of some other crude, C_s, which in the long run might be less costly to produce than crude, C_t.

Under such conditions, it is apparent that over-all company economics could actually be improved by *weakening* the economics of one of the refineries.

DANGER OF SUBOPTIMIZATION

The preceding example, oversimplified as it is, highlights one of the basic shortcomings of the conventional methods of economic analysis. This shortcoming amounts to excessive "suboptimization" from the viewpoint of investment planning. . . .

---

2 "Thinking Ahead: Potentials of Management Science," *Harvard Business Review,* January–February 1959, p. 26.

From: David Krech and Richard S. Crutchfield

THEORY AND PROBLEMS OF SOCIAL PSYCHOLOGY*

[EDITORS' NOTE: The authors are Professors at the University of California and Swarthmore College. In the passages below, the authors are discussing the mental process of *perception*. In prior pages of the chapter, they point out that the meaning a human mind derives from an event or stimuli is determined by two things: structural factors (what is "out there" in the world) and functional factors (what is "in the head" of the individual, stored in the form of needs, moods, memories of past experiences, etc.). The abstract below deals only with functional factors—how decision making is affected by the past experiences, moods, needs, attitudes, of the individual.]

TWO MAJOR DETERMINANTS OF PERCEPTION

*   *   *   *   *

Structural Factors. By *structural* factors are meant those factors deriving solely from the nature of the physical stimuli and the neural effects they evoke in the nervous system of the individual.[1] Thus, for the Gestalt psychologist, perceptual organizations are determined primarily by the physiological events occurring in the nervous system of the individual in direct reaction to the stimulation by the physical objects. Though not denying the influence, under certain conditions, of motivation and mental set, they emphasize that the sensory factors are primary in accounting for the "look of things."

To use a very simple and common example, the Gestalt psychologist would point out that our perception of the dots in Fig. 1a is perforce a perception of two horizontal groupings and not, say, an ungrouped collection of dots or of

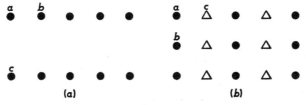

(a)   (b)

FIG. 1

---

* By permission from *Theory and Problems of Social Psychology*, by David Krech and Richard S. Crutchfield. Copyright 1948. McGraw-Hill Book Company, Inc. (Excerpts from pp. 81–83, 87–89, 94–96, 98, 102–3.)

[1] The term *autochthonous* is frequently used by the Gestalt psychologist when referring to these factors.

five vertical groupings, etc. Furthermore, they would insist that the factors which force this organization derive from the spatial relationships among the physical dots themselves as faithfully projected in the sensory region of the brain and are relatively independent of our reasoning, needs, moods, past learning, etc. To repeat: Those sensory factors which are independent of the perceiving individual's needs and personality and which force certain organizations in his cognitive field are referred to as "structural factors of perception." The isolation of these factors, their careful description, and the laws of their operation have led to the formulation of the "laws of organization."

Functional Factors. The *functional* factors of perceptual organization, on the other hand, are those which derive primarily from the needs, moods, past experience, and memory of the individual.[2] Thus, for example, in an experiment performed by Bruner and Goodman (1947), two groups of children (one a poor group from a settlement house in one of Boston's slum areas and the other a rich group from a "progressive school in the Boston area, catering to the sons and daughters of prosperous business and professional people") were asked to judge the size of various coins. The differences in the perceptions of the two groups of children were striking, with the poor group overestimating the size of the coins considerably more than did the rich group. The experimenters suggest that these results indicate the effect of need upon perception, and they formulate the following two hypotheses as possible general laws:

1. *The greater the social value of an object, the more will it be susceptible to organization by behavioral determinants.*
2. *The greater the individual need for a socially valued object, the more marked will be the operation of behavioral determinants.*

Another illustration of the operation of functional factors is found in an experiment by Levine, Chein, and Murphy (1942). In that experiment, ambiguous drawings, when presented behind a ground-glass screen to hungry college students, were more frequently perceived as food objects (ham sandwiches, salads, etc.) than when presented to college students who had just finished eating. The different perceptions of the hungry and not-hungry students could not be due to "structural" factors, since the same pictures were presented to both groups but could be due only to the differences in need or motivation of the members of the two groups.

While quantitative laws of how these "functional" factors actually operate in perception are lacking, a great deal of experimental work is available that demonstrates their pervasive influence in perception.

*   *   *   *   *

PERCEPTION IS FUNCTIONALLY SELECTIVE

No one perceives everything that there is "out there" to be perceived. Our mental apparatus is not an indifferent organizing machine ready to accord equal importance to all stimuli that impinge upon our sense organs. The factors that determine the specific organization of our cognitive field and select out only

---

[2] The term *functional* as applied to these factors was first suggested by Meunzinger (1942). In their treatment of these same factors, Bruner and Goodman (1947) suggest the term "behavioral determinants" which they define as ". . . those active, adaptive functions of the organism which lead to the governance and control of all higher-level functions including perception. . . . "

certain stimuli to integrate into that field are frequently at work even before we are exposed to the physical stimuli. Typically, only certain physical stimuli are "used" in making up the organized perception, while other stimuli are either not used at all or are given a very minor role. This is what is meant by saying that perception is "selective.". . . this selectivity is functional. The objects that play the major role in the organized perception, the objects that are *accentuated, are usually those objects which serve some immediate purpose of the perceiving individual.* . . .

. . . Let us take the simple example of two men seated at a lunchroom counter surveying the posted menu on the wall. One is very hungry; the other, only thirsty. Both are exposed to the same physical objects, yet the first will notice the hamburger and tomato-and-lettuce sandwiches, while the "tea, coffee, beer, pepsi-cola" items will be neglected or relatively so. The second man will react in the opposite manner. Ask both men to tell you what they "saw" on the menu, and the first will respond with a list of food items "and other stuff"; the second will enumerate the drink items "and other things." In one case the food items have been clearly and specifically perceived and organized against a background of nondifferentiated "other stuff"; in the second case the figure-ground relationships have been reversed.

Mental Set. . . . We see hundreds of men, every day, wearing different suits of clothing—suits that differ in cut, material, color, styling, number of buttons, etc. But usually all we perceive is that they are wearing clothes, and our resulting perceptual organization is not a very clear cut and differentiated one. What is the mental picture you have, for example, of the suit you saw your friend wear yesterday? But if we are on the way to a store to buy a suit, our perceptions of the clothes worn by friends and even strangers change rather remarkably. . . .

*   *   *   *   *

THE PERCEPTUAL AND COGNITIVE PROPERTIES OF A SUBSTRUCTURE ARE DETERMINED IN LARGE MEASURE BY THE PROPERTIES OF THE STRUCTURE OF WHICH IT IS A PART

. . . Our mental world is a structured or organized one, and it can also be seen as broken down into hierarchies of structures. Our cognitive field does not consist of completely independent organized structures; each of our perceptions is not an experience that "lives a life of its own," as it were. Every perception is embedded in an organization of other percepts—the whole going to make up a specific "cognitive structure." . . . [W]hen we perceive a politician, our perception of that particular politician is influenced by all our other percepts involving politicians. But the major structure, politicians, may have substructures: Democratic politicians, Republican politicians, honest politicians, etc. . . .

Illustrations from Simple Visual Perception. Figure 2 is usually perceived as a simple figure of three lines meeting at a center point *O*. Each angle made by any two adjacent lines, say angle *AOC,* can be described as a substructure of the figure. That is, the perception of that angle is of an organized figure "in its own right," but it is also perceived as a part of a larger figure—the whole of Fig. 2. Each of these angles is usually perceived as an obtuse angle, *i.e.,* larger than a right angle. What would happen to our perception of angle *AOC* if we added a few lines so as to induce a change in our perception of the *whole* structure without, in any way changing the lines that make up angle *AOC?* The answer is immediately given if we look at Fig. 3. Now we perceive the substructure, angle *AOC,* as a right angle! Although we have not done anything phys-

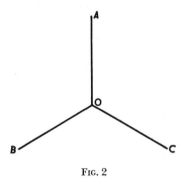

FIG. 2

ically to angle *AOC*, it "looks" different. It looks different because the *whole* figure, of which angle *AOC* is a part, looks different.

*   *   *   *   *

Now suppose that all you could see were angle *AOC* of Fig. 2 or only the single dot in our last illustration and you were told that a given person insisted that he perceived angle *AOC* as a right angle or that another individual perceived the dot as light gray. Would it not appear to you either that these people had defective vision or that they were inaccurate in their descriptions of their own perceptions? This would be a logical deduction if you could not see the whole of Fig. 2 of which angle *AOC* was a part. . . . We cannot understand an indi-

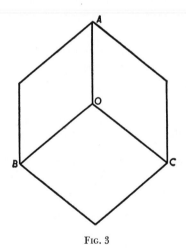

FIG. 3

vidual's perception, or interpretation of an event that is part of a larger organization for *him*, unless we also know what that larger organization is. . . .

*   *   *   *   *

. . . This general whole-part principle has so many ramifications in our cognitive and social life that it might be useful to reformulate it in still another way. Frequently we are forced to pay attention to new facts, facts that seem not to fit in with our existing structures or that even contradict them. At times, this results in a fairly radical reorganization of the existing major structures of our cognitive field, but frequently such a reorganization does not take place despite our perception of contradictory facts. For example, if we have a very strongly structured field in which the Jew is always penurious, we will not easily see any single Jew as a philanthropist, no matter how philanthropic his activities may be. In some way or other this disturbing Jew is "assimilated" into our rigidly structured organization. However, close analysis will reveal that such facts as these are encompassed by our original generalization. To comprehend what frequently happens when "contradictory" perceptions occur, it is useful to reformulate Proposition III in the following way: *Other things being equal, a change introduced into the psychological field will be absorbed in such a way as to produce the smallest effect on a strong structucre.*

* * * * *

Objects or Events That Are Close to Each Other in Space or Time or Resemble Each Other Tend to Be Apprehended as Parts of a Common Structure

If we are to know just why certain perceptions are organized together with other perceptions to make one cognitive structure, we must have some general understanding of what determines why an individual will organize the perceptions of object A with that of object B into one common structure rather than the perception of object A with that of object C. Why, for example, do some people have a cognitive structure in which socialism and Christianity are organized together, while other people have a cognitive structure in which socialism and atheism are found together? Proposition IV attempts to indicate the major factors that determine the contents of a single strucure.

Proximity and Similarity. In visual perception, experimental literature is replete with demonstrations that proximity and similarity are important organizing factors. Fig. 1a, which was used to illustrate the structural factors in perception, can serve to illustrate that in simple perception those objects which are close to each other in space (proximity) tend to be organized together in perception. Dot A is perceived as belonging to dot B rather than to dot C simply because A is closer to B than it is to C. A simple measurement of the physical distances among the different dots, everything else being equal, would permit us to predict, with a high degree of accuracy, which dots would be organized with which other dots. Similarly, Fig. 1b can be used to illustrate the principle of similarity. Here, dot A will be organized with dot B rather than with dot C because A is more similar (in shape) to B than it is to C.

From: John W. Enell and George H. Haas

SETTING STANDARDS FOR EXECUTIVE PERFORMANCE*

[EDITORS' NOTE: The authors are research associate, and director of Information Service and Surveys, both of the American Management Association. In 1960 the A.M.A. conducted a seminar on setting standards for executive performance. Fifteen corporations were represented. The abstracts below summarize certain important ideas from a 793-page transcript of the seminar proceedings.]

During the seminar, it was noted by many of the panelists that the very process of formulating standards of performance can itself be of great benefit. In almost all the companies represented in this study, supervisor and subordinate work together in drawing up standards for the subordinate's job, sometimes in conference with a staff man from the personnel department. Standards developed in this manner are usually taken seriously by the executives who have had a part in their formulation; a give-and-take discussion results in a better understanding of the nature of the job expected and also of the priorities of its various segments. This formulation-by-conference method can help, too, by giving the supervisor a better understanding of the real conditions present in the subordinate's work. The seminar participants reported that, when standards were first tried in their firms, instances were found where a supervisor and his subordinate were at the outset completely at variance in their understanding of the nature of the job under consideration. This sort of misunderstanding apparently arises at every level of management. The process of correcting these conflicting views and hammering out agreement on the nature and quality of results expected on the job is an important phase of management development.

*   *   *   *   *

Almost all the participants agreed that the executive and the subordinate must come together at some point in the process and candidly bring up—and iron out—any differences that arise. Even Robert Grover of Snap-On Tools took this point of view, despite the fact that his firm's chief standard of performance is a very detailed company-wide and departmental system of budgets. Mr. Grover remarked that the subordinate is given an opportunity to express himself when the budget for his unit is in the discussion stage. If he feels that he cannot live within his budget or produce the amount of income required of him (provided that he is in an income-producing area), he has an adequate opportunity to make his point of view clear. Once he has agreed to his budget, he must comply with it.

. . . Mr. Daffern cited one instance in which the subordinate declared that the discussion during which standards were worked out was the only time in a long work history when he had had any really frank discussion with his boss about his responsibilities and their fulfillment. . . .

* Reprinted by permission of the American Management Association, New York, Research Study No. 42, 1960 (pp. 16–18, 31–32).

LAKELAND FOOD PRODUCTS COMPANY, INC.

I Case Introduction

Synopsis

The president of this company asks the vice president for marketing to interview a younger man, William Proctor, for an important job in the Marketing Division, that of market planning director. Both president and vice president are instrumental in his taking the position. During the first year of Proctor's tenure, the case describes his actions and beliefs, as well as his technical competence. These competences, beliefs, and actions are contrasted with those of other executives in the Marketing Division. The vice president for marketing resigns, giving as his reasons the improvement of his career and a desire to satisfy certain family obligations.

Why This Case Is Included

Lakeland Food Products offers an opportunity to see two types of leadership patterns contrasted, together with the practical reasons each executive uses for behaving in his own way. Thus, insights may be gained into the important question, "What motivates an executive?" In the sense that the two executive styles are conflicting, one can also see both the advantages and disadvantages of the two styles. At certain points in the case, we can observe the feelings and attitudes of subordinates as they develop in response to different leader styles. Finally, the difference between overt behavior or "game playing" on the one hand, and true inner feelings, comes to light in the behavior of both individual top executives and a group of lower executives.

Diagnostic and Predictive Questions

In answering the following diagnostic and predictive questions, remember that these questions apply theories and conceptual ideas from certain disciplines. Such theories are valuable to understand basic forces at work in the policy system (diagnosis and to predict what will happen in the system in the future (prediction). Since each reading abstracts from the total policy system certain factors or variables into the closed or partial viewpoint of one theory or discipline, no one reading gives answers to the practical policy problems of the case. In diagnosis and prediction, the parts of the problem are studied with "other things being equal."

Following each question are listed readings which will be helpful in answering the question. The readings included with this case are marked (*). By referring to the author index at the end of this book, you may locate the other readings listed.

1. Why did Paul Brown "just shut up" when Proctor presented his plan to the first meeting? Why did attendance at staff meetings drop off later? Why, when Saunders asked about the value of staff meetings, did some managers seem indifferent as to advantages and disadvantages? Why did Brown and Davidson at one of the later meetings look at the floor or out the window?

> Read: Argyris, *Personality and Organization*, pp. 27–157 (sections on Defense Mechanisms and Individual Adaptation). McGregor, *The Human Side of Enterprise*, pp. 124–31, 172–75. *Gardner, *Self-Renewal*, pp. 54–61, 101–2.

2. Summarize Saunders' system for staff meetings as he describes it in the case—who does what and why. Add a summary of his theory of executive behavior or leadership style. Why did he believe in this theory of management or leadership?

> Read: *Gellerman, *Motivation and Productivity*, pp. 109–18 (section on The Affiliation Motive). McGregor, *The Human Side of Enterprise*, pp. 3–54. Also utilize the readings from Question 1.

3. What two motivations might have caused Saunders to feel conflicted or frustrated (*a*) when he "felt uncomfortable at having Proctor start work in this position," (*b*) when he "felt uneasy passing Proctor's office in the first two weeks," and (*c*) when he "felt awkward in starting the meeting" on a different agenda than the important problem raised by Proctor? Why *didn't* Proctor feel frustrated when he "had to speak up and let Brown know he was wrong?"

> Read: *Gellerman, *Motivation and Productivity*, pp. 109–18 (sections on The Power Motive and The Affiliation Motive). *Gardner, *Self-Renewal*, pp. 54–61, 101–2.

4. Why did Proctor think about the advertising plan over the weekend and call Saunders on Sunday afternoon?

> Read: Hampton, Summer, and Webber, *Organizational Behavior and the Practice of Management*, Chap. X. (Select which parts of the reading apply to this question.) *John Wiley & Sons, Advertisement for *Science in Marketing*, 1965.

5. Summarize Proctor's system of staff meetings—who does what and when. Why did he believe in this system of group action and this form of executive behavior? Summarize Williams' system for division-wide meetings—who does what and why. Why did he believe in this system of group action and this form of executive behavior?

> Read: Utilize readings for Question 4. Smith, *The Wealth of Nations*, pp. 4–15. *Carr *et al.*, *American Democracy in Theory and Practice*, pp. 214–19. *Cartwright. *Public Opinion Polls and Democratic Leadership*, pp. 23–32.

6. As one reason for division meetings, Williams believes that the salesmen and sales managers would "feel important as an individual by being personally invited to company headquarters." Cite reasoning as to why this might be true. Then cite reasoning why this might be false.

> Preparation: Use your own analytical ability here. Or, if you are familiar with status motivation versus motivation through acting out one's own talents and abilities (personal motivation), you may want to use a more technical basis for answering.

7. Describe in factual terms any difference you see in the way in which Saunders behaves with his subordinates and the way in which he behaves with his superior, Williams. Explain the apparent contradiction.

Preparation: Think deeply about what the most fundamental difference in his two action patterns were. If you watched him, what differences could you *see?* Then ask *why*, in terms of his attitudes, feelings, or other motivations, he differed. You might also separate these motivations into (*a*) those "from within" Saunders and (*b*) those "out there in the situation."

8. Why did Williams interpret Saunders' resignation in the way he did?

Read: *Leavitt, *Managerial Psychology*, pp. 27–33. Readings from Questions 4 and 5 will help make the Leavitt reading more practically applicable to the case.

Policy Questions for This Specific Case

In answering the following policy questions, the results of diagnosis and prediction are used to reduce the amount of guesswork, or judgment, in designing action solutions. However, since certain parts of the total case situation cannot be reduced to science, and since "other things are not equal," judgment must still be used to fill in the factors not accounted for by readings. You will also need a second kind of judgment as you put value weights on different scientific predictions, since different theories may point to conflicting solutions.

9. If you were the president of Lakeland, and had diagnosed the basic factors in the situation (Questions 1–8), how would you have handled Saunders and Proctor to keep this problem from occurring?

Read: *Newman and Summer, *The Process of Management*, pp. 439–48.
*Mary Parker Follett, "Constructive Conflict."

10. (Role-Playing Question). One student who understands the motivations of Saunders should assume his role and play it as much like the Saunders in the case as possible. Another student who believes he understands the problem should assume the role of an "enlightened" Williams—that is, a Williams who *formerly* acted exactly as in the case, but who now understands the kinds of basic insights developed in the readings, individual reflection on these, and class discussion of the diagnosis.

The setting is in Williams' office, on Monday morning after Saunders has resigned the previous Friday. Williams has called Saunders in to ask him to reconsider.

Even though the role-play is short, the rest of the class should act as observers. Williams might give the class a short explanation of *what specifically* he expects to achieve with Saunders (Saunders should leave the room during this explanation). Then, after the instructor cuts off the role-play, the class might discuss how Williams performed. In this discussion, stick to objective reporting. Ask yourselves, "What did Williams *do* and *say*, and what effect did this have on Saunders?

If time allows, Saunders should be held "constant" (the same student plays Saunders) while two or more Williams players try additional role-plays.

Major Policy Issues: Tentative Generalizations about Any Policy System

In arriving at conclusions for the following questions, generalize from the facts in the case and use your own ideas to (*a*) confirm, (*b*) modify, or (*c*) test the workability of the concepts and theories from readings. As an executive or professional, use wisdom to merge theory, on the one hand, with "brute facts" and practice, on the other.

11. Is there an inevitable conflict between the requirements of economics and technology (specialization and authority), on the one hand, and positive human motivations (generally using one's mind in social participation with others), on the other?

Questions for Original Student Work in Analysis and Policy

The methods of viewing this case as represented by the authors' questions and selection of readings are not exhaustive. There are other relevant ideas for diagnosis and prediction. Furthermore, there are other ways of stating policy questions. More powerful analyses and wiser solutions will result by drawing on your own training and experience for (a) relevant concepts and theories, and (b) creative ways of asking policy questions. The following questions are designed to help you acquire this skill.

12. While reflecting on case facts, what additional theories from prior education give you insights as to "what is going on" in the Lakeland Food Products Company, Inc.? As to what might be predicted to happen in the future?

13. Other than the policy questions asked by the authors, what pragmatic ways can you think of to state the practical problems faced by executives in the case?

II Lakeland Food Products Company, Inc.*

Lakeland Food Products Company, Inc., produces and markets a broad variety of food products for ultimate sale through smaller grocery stores and large regional chain food stores. With net profits of $18 million in the latest year, the company is considerably smaller than the largest companies in the industry, such as General Foods Corporation, but it has been able to achieve a continuous growth rate by specializing in certain product lines such as spices, mayonnaise and salad dressings, frozen vegetables, and frozen meats. Furthermore, the company management has deliberately limited its market to one large region of the United States. In this way, according to A. F. Williams, Lakeland's president:

We can more thoroughly saturate the area with direct sales effort, and concentrate our advertising and sales promotion. I have often been asked how we can compete successfully with the giants. The answer is specialty products—we don't try to cover the whole field—and a relatively limited market, in which our brand name can become known, and in which our large sales force can work much more closely with wholesalers and large regional chain operations.

A partial organization chart of Lakeland Company appears as Exhibit 1. Reporting to A. F. Williams, the president, are five principal officers of

---

* Copyright 1968 by the Graduate School of Business, Columbia University.

Exhibit 1

ORGANIZATION CHART

LAKELAND FOOD PRODUCTS COMPANY, INC.

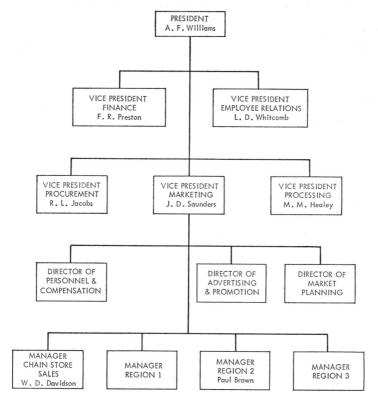

the company: R. L. Jacobs, vice president for procurement; M. M. Healey, vice president for manufacturing and processing: J. D. Saunders, sales vice president; F. R. Preston, financial vice president; and L. D. Whitcomb, vice president for employee and public relations.

This case concerns a situation which Mr. Williams describes as one of the most pressing problems confronting him at the present time. As Williams puts it,

I am extremely concerned about a conversation I had with Jim Saunders, our vice president for sales. Saunders came into my office about a week ago and in a very pleasant way informed me that he thought he owed it to himself to try to improve his own career and horizons and that he had accepted a job with a large regional food chain in California. He said that there were some personal problems involved, in the way of aged parents in California, who needed caring for.

He also said that Bill Proctor, his director of market planning, was fully capable of taking over the leadership of our marketing division.

I just can't account for Saunders' rather sudden decision, other than the fact that some men do have family problems, and I guess some people also make rather sudden and major decisions about their careers. He and I have always had a close and rather personal working relationship, but this decision was a bolt out of the blue.

Saunders has been with the company for 23 years, having joined us when he first got out of college. He started as a salesman, went through a usual training period under one of the regional managers, and achieved a really excellent record. I can remember getting to know him about five years after he joined the company, when I was assistant to the vice president for procurement. I had some contact with him over the years, and, of course, as we both got promoted up the ladder I had more and more contact. He eventually became manager of Region One, general sales manager for the whole company, and 10 years ago, I appointed him, with board approval, to be vice president for sales. In my opinion, Jim Saunders today knows more about the problems of field selling, and more details of who our customers are and why they buy from us, than anyone else in the company. He is a virtual storehouse of information—and he has the attitude of a salesman. That is, he is always asking, "What does this mean to the *customer*—what does he want, and how can we best get our story over to him?"

The remainder of this case describes the relationships between Williams, Saunders, and Proctor, starting at a point of time 12 months ago when Proctor was made director of market planning.

W. D. (Bill) Proctor joined Lakeland eight years ago, at the age of 28. He had received his Bachelor's degree in engineering at M.I.T., spent three years as a junior staff officer in planning and logistics in the military, and then obtained an M.B.A. degree from the Columbia University Graduate School of Business.

Proctor's first job had been assistant to R. L. Jacobs, vice president of the Procurement Division. Although most of Proctor's time with the company has been spent in Procurement, he has, from time to time, and before joining the sales department, spent time on leave with the manager of chain store sales and the vice president for finance. In both instances, these executives had heard of his applications of systems analysis to procurement and asked to have him assigned to them on temporary leave. Over these years, Saunders had seen Proctor frequently in the office, at company functions, and in other casual encounters, but he did not know him well. He appeared to Saunders to be a very capable young executive, always on the move.

Twelve months ago, Williams called Saunders and asked him to talk with Proctor. "I want to know what you think of him, as it occurred to me that he might be a good man for that opening we have in market planning." Saunders later told Williams, "I judge Bill Proctor to be very bright, and probably very competent. He seems to have some good ideas about market planning, even though he does not know too much about what we are doing. He also seems to know procurement well, and one specialized aspect of our planning of chain store volume."

Williams seemed to Saunders to be pleased with this reply, answering, "We have had excellent results with his work in procurement and even in helping to plan the product lines in chain store sales. Of course, we have had some joking around the office about his 'McNamara System,' but it has paid off."

Saunders later told the case writer that, at the time of the above conversation, he actually felt a little uncomfortable at the thought of having Proctor start work in the capacity of market planning director. Nevertheless, he decided that the Marketing Division certainly could use a person with talent, and he therefore agreed to his having the position.

As an indoctrination period, Proctor asked for two weeks to read the files of market planning which existed at the time he took the position. Particularly, he wanted to study the way in which sales territories, quotas for territories by product, and advertising were correlated in company policies in all three areas. He also wanted to read the salesmen's reports on market demand predictions.

During these two weeks, Saunders states that he felt rather uneasy as he passed Proctor's office each day. At the end of the period, he asked Proctor if he thought that the reports gave a clear picture of the Marketing Division's activities. "The files and reports are really excellent," Proctor answered with obvious sincerity. Saunders recalls that he was surprised that he felt relief at this point and that he felt almost jovial when he said goodnight to Proctor that evening.

The following Sunday, Proctor called Saunders at his home. He said that he had been studying the sales figures for each of 20 important products in Region Three, together with advertising expenditures for these products. He further seemed to Saunders to be

. . . very enthusiastic about his conclusions, if not downright excited. I could tell that he felt very much like telling me about a discovery that he thought was important. I remember thinking that he must be oblivious to the fact that I might be engaged in a relaxing time with the family by the pool. As he talked rather quickly about what he was doing, I exhibited some interest and told him that we could discuss it at our biweekly staff meeting on Wednesday, which is attended by our three regional sales managers, the manager of chain sales, and the three staff directors of personnel, advertising, and market planning.

Saunders takes much pride in the way these meetings are conducted and the way major marketing policies are made in Lakeland. He believes that each of his line managers, as well as his three staff directors, has much to contribute in the way of creativity and experience, but that one man usually should take the lead in developing facts, data and a recommendation. According to Saunders:

In this way, the man with the most interest in a subject gets a crack at developing the original recommendation in a clear, timesaving format, for our discussions. At the same time, the whole group gets a crack at creatively bringing to bear their experience regarding alternative ways to solve the policy problem. After talking it through, if any one or more men have serious reservations, the originator of the recommendation should take the initiative to work with the dissenting persons after the meeting, until either both men agree on the original recommendation, or until both agree on a change or modification. In this way, the group of top sales executives always reach a consensus which is best for the company—each man understands the decision, and is prepared to carry it out.

The following Wednesday, Saunders started the meeting by bringing up a matter of change in the company's sales compensation policy. He felt somewhat awkward because he knew "that Proctor was champing at the bit to start with his own proposal, and because . . . well . . . I wanted to let him know he wasn't running the show."

Although all executives at the meeting believed that the sales force had high morale—"favorable attitudes toward the company, its products, and top managers"—all were aware that some competing companies in the food business had recently changed their compensation methods. This resulted in some suggestions from a number of salesmen to the effect that Lakeland is out-of-date, but an apparently sincere attitude on their part that they know the company will make a new policy if they supply the facts. Prior to the meeting, Ivar Sorensen, director of personnel and compensation, and the man most interested in this problem, presented a plan which he believed would be perceived as fair to the salesmen, yet which would direct their attention to the most profitable product lines and cost the company less than any alternative plan that would attain the same objectives.

At the Wednesday meeting, two of the regional managers began by saying that their reservations to Sorensen's original plan had been thoroughly discussed and that they were now prepared to make the final consensus to the plan. As Paul Brown, the manager of Region Two, put it,

. . . to try to arrive at a balance between cost to the company in salaries, maximum motivation of salesmen to spend time on the most profitable items (while not ignoring other items completely) , and the general feeling of fairness in the minds of salesmen, is a tough proposition. I don't think anyone at the meeting here believes we have the ideal Utopian plan, but it is the best policy we can formulate. This present recommendation is *it* as far as I'm concerned.

Other members of management followed with similar statements, except for Proctor:

Although I had never studied this plan, I knew from statistics on product line mix, volume by territory, and a variety of compensation methods I've picked up in business school and in marketing journals, that this plan Sorensen recommended was just plain mediocre. I just couldn't sit there and see a bunch of men accept it when Paul Brown said it's the best they could do, without letting him know that he was wrong.

Proctor asked Saunders if he might get up to an easel in the room and list some of the important statistics and factors that bear on Lakeland's compensation policy. First, he took Sorensen's proposed policy and asked for clarification on the reasoning behind it. Most members of the meeting entered into this discussion in rather lively fashion but, according to Paul Brown,

After about 20 minutes, it seemed to most of us that Bill was not trying to understand our proposal at all—he seemed as if he were disagreeing with it. When this happened, I for one just shut up. I felt that we were being cross-examined. Never in our staff meetings have we had to feel that way, since everyone from Jim Saunders on down uses an offhand, calm tone of voice in asking questions of each other—it's just by intuition that we know that the other man's purpose is to *understand* what we are proposing, before he equally calmly points out deficiencies. Certainly, no one jumps fast to another tactic, that of proposing a competitive decision, until all of us have understood what we're talking about. Bill Proctor, however, was different. His tone and demeanor told us otherwise—it came through loud and clear that he was attacking Sorensen's proposal and my conclusion of consensus. And then, he moved on to present his own plan, after we all shut up.

Regarding Proctor's participation in the meeting, Jim Saunders had this to say:

I could hardly believe my ears. In spite of the fact that Bill Proctor could not possibly have prepared before the meeting on this particular subject, it was almost as if he had written out and memorized a carefully worded analysis of sales compensation. After questioning the other managers about Sorensen's proposal, he first presented a five-point proposal for a new compensation policy. Then he said he wanted to take up each of these subproposals and cite facts to prove that they were the most logical route for the company to follow. Although my stomach was beginning to get upset, I forced myself to listen—I kept feeling embarrassed at having him lecture Brown, Sorensen, and the other managers, each of whom have had great success in their work with the company. To my utter astonishment, he turned out to have a proposal that I admired and which, sure enough, was superior to Sorensen's. I suggested that we take his proposal under advisement, with each manager studying it after the meeting. All agree that he has the answer. At the next meeting, at least Bill will have the satisfaction of hearing me (and Paul Brown) report a consensus.

Saunders reports that in ensuing meetings over a period of eight months, the subject of biweekly staff meetings was brought up by W. D. Davidson, manager of chain store sales. Davidson noted that attendance was becoming lax, "because many of us are under such heavy pressure of work—training of new salesmen, emergency calls from very important customers, or sudden demands for new advertising strategies." (These were reasons which were submitted by managers in memos to Davidson, as secretary of the meetings.) In a discussion on this point, other managers seemed to Saunders rather indifferent, without much to say about the advantages or disadvantages of holding these meetings. Proctor was very clear on this point. He stated that meetings are very expensive and time-consuming if one multiplies the salaries of the eight top marketing managers of Lakeland times the one-half day of conferences.

This represents 8 man-days a month or 96 man-days a year. But there is a logic to the meetings. *If* they are done right, we can accomplish an awful lot. I am in favor of meetings if their purpose is to inform each other of the progress we are making on our individual projects. In giving a half day, we can accomplish twice as much if reports are clearly stated, with declarative sentence headings stating the problem and the recommendations. Then, under each heading there should be various subheadings, equally clear, with facts under them to show the logic. In this way, the whole report adds up to a logical argument with precision and

clarity. I remember learning in one of my case-writing courses back in business
school that this is a practical, staff-report type of application of Aristotelian
logic. I didn't appreciate it at the time, but I've discovered that there is no other
way to so clearly convey a complex problem: The Problem and its Causes, Facts
Which Bear on the Problem, Alternative Solutions, and Final Recommendations. Incidentally, it is necessary that one think of all possible alternative
solutions, but it is a waste of time to write this in the report. When we have a
roomful of busy executives, they don't have time to study through all of the
alternatives that we *aren't* going to use—their time should be spent only on the
one that we *are* going to make use of.

Saunders also noted that during Proctor's presentations at meetings
over the next few months, Paul Brown and Davidson would often look at
the floor, fidget, look out of the window, or even sometimes give out a
nervous "ha-ha" when Proctor was making a particularly strong point.

Five weeks ago, A. F. Williams suggested a special meeting, at company headquarters, for all sales personnel from the whole company, in
order to give them a sense of feeling a part of one large organization and
to bring them up-to-date on some of the recent things the company is
doing in the way of studies of consumer motivation, changes in sales
compensation policies, systems analysis for the flow of products to the
various markets, and linear programming as used to plan new warehouse
facilities, capital investment, and location. In past years, it had been
Williams' firm belief that such meetings, held about once a year for each
of the three major company divisions, would have a very good effect on
employee performance. He felt that their effect was threefold: employees
at all levels would (*a*) get a better understanding of the facts of company
operations, including what the policies are and why they were decided
that way, (*b*) feel a part of the total organization, with an *esprit de corps*
based on knowledge that if all worked together as a team, the organization could achieve a degree of excellence through its men and leadership,
and (*c*) feel important as an individual, by being invited personally to
company headquarters.

At this particular meeting, Williams explained to Saunders:

The theme should be exposition of what the company is doing in forward-
looking management terms, such as the application of systems analysis, mathematical programming, and advertising research. In view of the nature of the
subjects, and from what I can see of Proctor's sharp and clear presentations on
his feet, I think that you are really fortunate in having, this year, Bill Proctor to
give the results of his work. The morale of people in the field will be raised
considerably when they see what a really fine job the company is doing to insure
that we are as good as anybody—including the national chains—when it comes to
a hard-hitting management team and a streamlined method of carrying out our
operations.

When this suggestion was made, according to Saunders:

I felt just about like that first staff meeting Bill attended. I know for sure that
Williams is right, and that some of our headquarters personnel *are* doing
impressive things, including Bill Proctor. But at the same time, I'm dead sure in
my own mind that Bill is having a really bad effect on the teamwork among

managers in the Marketing Division, and that this is going to have adverse effects on major marketing policy decisions in the long run. I also wonder how long those regional managers are going to sit there and carry out policies with the old hard-hitting spirit that the company has now.

III Selected Readings

From: John W. Gardner
*SELF-RENEWAL**

[EDITORS' NOTE: The author is Secretary of Health, Education, and Welfare in President Johnson's Cabinet; and formerly, was President of the Carnegie Corporation.]

TYRANNY WITHOUT A TYRANT

THE TYRANNY OF THE FORMULA

The tides of change that move society on to new solutions or catastrophes run deeper than the swirling events of the day. In relation to these great tidal movements, the trends we observe in our lifetimes are surface currents and the crises of the morning newspaper the merest whitecaps.

One of the deep tidal currents—perhaps the most fateful—is the movement over recent centuries toward the creation of ever larger, more complex and more highly organized social groupings.

It is a trend that we must examine here because it threatens the freedom and integrity of the individual; and the capacity of society for continuous renewal depends ultimately upon the individual. He is the seedbed of change, the inventor and innovator, the critic of old ways and mapper of new paths. John Stuart Mill wrote, "A state which dwarfs its men . . . will find that with small men no great thing can be accomplished." We need only add that no *new* thing can be accomplished, no renewing thing, no revitalizing thing.

. . . every thoughtful man today worries about the novel and subtle restraints placed on the individual by modern large-scale organization—and fears that we may triumph over the old evils only to find ourselves enmeshed in a new and streamlined tyranny.

It is futile to hope that the movement toward more intricate and inclusive social organization will reverse itself. A modern society is—and must be—characterized by complex organization. It is not a matter of choice. We must cope as best we can with the pressures that modern large-scale organization places on the individual. These pressures have been a favorite theme of social critics and it is not necessary to describe them here. But it may be useful to clear up some of the confusions that have surrounded the subject.

---

* From *Self-Renewal: The Individual and the Innovative Society* by John W. Gardner. Copyright 1963 by John W. Gardner. Reprinted with permission of Harper & Row, Publishers, Incorporated. (Excerpts from pp. 54–61, 101–2.)

One shortcoming in current writing on this subject has been the tendency to seek a villain. An essential feature of the individual's predicament today is that there is no villain. It is not a question of one social class dominating another; nor of believers in one dogma oppressing believers in another dogma. It is not a tyrant who subjugates the individual. It is not even that tired old bogeyman, Madison Avenue. Nor that fanciful new bobgeyman—The Establishment. What is oppressing the individual is the very nature of modern society.

Yet the search for a villain continues. Clearly, it fills some emotional need on the part of the searchers.

There are oppressors on the scene, of course, and we may learn something by observing them closely. We still think of the typical dictator as one who flouts the wishes of the people, but outright tyranny without concern for the appearance of popular consent is the most old-fashioned of political maneuvers today. The truly modern dictator achieves his goals *through* the people, not in spite of them. He rides their aspirations to power. He manipulates their hopes and fears and is ushered into office with their joyous shouts. He may then construct, with the consent of the people, precisely the same machinery of control that he would otherwise have had to construct over their opposition. The process may be observed in some nations today, in some communities and in some labor unions.

If we understand how these things can happen, then we are in a position to understand that people can construct their own tyrannies. If one's freedom must be invaded, it is perhaps comforting to find the invasion accomplished democratically. But loss of freedom is loss of freedom.

*   *   *   *   *

Still another error is to assert, as many do, that the "inhuman" aspects of modern social organization are the fault of science and technology. This view has deep emotional roots and there is not much point in arguing with those who hold it. They would rather stay mad.

But the truth is that workers in the grimmest moments of modern industrialism were no more miserable than, let us say, the Egyptian slaves who built the pyramids. It is not advanced technology that causes the trouble. The root of the difficulty is an attitude of mind that has never really died out in the world, nor perhaps even diminished greatly since the days of the Pharaohs—a willingness to sacrifice human values to other objectives.

Modern technology *need not* destroy aesthetic, spiritual and social values, but it will most certainly do so unless the individuals who manage our technology are firmly committed to the preservation of such values.

The tyranny of mass society is not a matter of one man's foot on another man's neck. It is a tyranny of the formula. Mass society searches for common denominators. Sheer numbers make it impossible to take account of individual identity. Serving the mass market requires standardization. Popular culture becomes homogenized. Even political campaigns are planned by the market researcher.

The exacting requirements of a highly organized society lead to the development of ingenious and powerful management techniques—in communications, information processing, cost accounting, personnel and public relations. Such techniques are rarely designed by men who harbor conscious tyrannical purposes. But in the hands of men insensitive to the needs of the individual such techniques do all too often result in the "processing" of human beings.

The pressures that produce conformity are often misunderstood. The precisely interlocked processes of a complex modern society require a high degree of predictability of individual behavior. The individual conforms because it seems like the sensible way to keep the organization running smoothly. Eccentric convictions, unpopular views, unique styles of behavior get in the way.

Personnel directors look for the man who will fit in. Parents say, "You want to be popular, don't you?" The Image Managers encourage the individual to fashion himself into a smooth coin, negotiable in any market. An occasional Kierkegaard may insist that "the crowd is untruth," but the man in the street takes a more practical view.

The long-run hazard for a society that needs independent and creative men and women to ensure its continued vitality is clear. The very subtlety and blandness of the process adds to the danger.

Another difficulty (which we have already explored) is that the complex processes of modern society tend to force the individual into an excessively specialized role. To the extent that they do they deprive him of the wholeness, versatility and generalized competence that he should preserve at all costs. Not only does it become increasingly difficult for him to comprehend his relationship to the world about him, he has less time (or inclination) to explore this relationship as he whittles himself down to fit a slot in the intricate pattern.

One of the clearest dangers in modern society is that men and women will lose the experience of participating in meaningful decisions concerning their own life and work, that they will become cogs in the machine because they *feel like* cogs in the machine. All too often today they are inert components of the group, not participating in any significant way but simply being carried along like grains of sand in a bucket.

Malcolm Cowley, speaking of the Lost Generation, wrote:

> But the decay of society was psychologically equivalent to its progress: both were automatic processes that we ourselves could neither hasten nor retard. Society was something alien, which our own lives and writings could never affect; it was a sort of parlor car in which we rode, over smooth tracks, toward a destination we should never have chosen for ourselves.

The disastrous consequences of such attitudes for the morale of a society are obvious. Without some grasp of the meaning of his relationship to the whole, it is not easy for the individual to retain a vivid sense of his own capacity to act as an individual, a sure sense of his own dignity and an awareness of his roles and responsibilities. He tends to accept the spectator role and to sink into passivity.

It is not easy for a modern, complex society to prevent such an outcome. The individual is fixed in a network of abstractions. Instead of working for a known boss, he is employed by a corporation. Instead of coping with a rival across the street, he copes with forces of the market. Instead of fashioning a product with his own hands, he shuffles papers, juggles figures or pushes buttons. He receives orders from people he has never met and makes recommendations without knowing those who will be affected by them. A well-known government official offered a poignant vignette of modern organizational life when he said: "What we sign we haven't written, and what we write someone else signs."

*　　　*　　　*　　　*

This is in some measure an inevitable consequence of large-scale modern organization. Economies of scale can be achieved by centralizing decisions, and the complex modern society has been incredibly ingenious in accomplishing such centralization. Countless schemes and devices, from prepared cake mixes to electronic computers, relieve the individual of the burden of decision. No wonder critics ask whether modern man will become a sodden, immobile consumer of predigested offerings and a mindless performer of pre-programmed tasks.

But then the individual, with some obscure instinct for his own survival, takes up a hobby in which decisions are still possible. The do-it-yourself movement deserves comment. When a manufacturer markets high-fidelity sound equipment that is designed to be sold in an unassembled state so that the customer can have the fun of assembling it, he is going counter to some of the most powerful currents of our time. Over the past century, industrial society has devoted untold ingenuity and skill to the objective of placing a foolproof, prefabricated device in the hands of a supposedly passive and moronic consumer. Now a respectable fraction of those consumers turn out to have vagrant impulses that are not served by ingenuities of prefabrication. They want to exercise their hands and minds on concrete tasks. They want to puzzle over something, shape something, contribute their sweat to something. We have hardly begun to absorb the implications of that fact.

*   *   *   *   *

HUNGER FOR MEANING

Man is in his very nature a seeker of meanings. He cannot help being so any more than he can help breathing or maintaining a certain body temperature. It is the way his central nervous system works.

In most societies and most ages, however primitive they may have been technologically, man's hunger for meaning was amply served. Though some of the religions, mythologies, and tribal superstitions with which the hunger for meaning was fed were crude and impoverished, they did purport to describe a larger framework in terms of which events might be interpreted.

With the arrival of the modern age many misguided souls conceived the notion that man could do without such nourishment. And for a breath-taking moment it did seem possible in view of the glittering promises which modern life offered. Under the banner of a beneficial modernity, the individual was to have security, money, power, sensual gratification and status as high as any man. He would be a solvent and eupeptic Walter Mitty in a rich and meaningless world.

But even (or especially) those who came close to achieving the dream never got over the nagging hunger for meaning.

At one level, man's search for meanings is objectively intellectual. He strives to organize what he knows into coherent patterns. Studies of perception have demonstrated that this tendency to organize experience is not an afterthought or the result of conscious impulse but an integral feature of the perceptual process. At the level of ideas, his tendency to organize meaningful wholes out of his experience is equally demonstrable. He tries to reduce the stream of experience to orderly sequences and patterns. He produces legends, theories, philosophies.

To an impressive degree, the theories of nature and the universe which man has developed are impersonal in the sense that they take no special account of man's own aspirations and status (though they are strictly dependent on his conceptualizing power and rarely wholly divorced from his values). Out of this impersonal search for meaning has come modern science.

But man has never been satisfied to let it go at that. He has throughout history shown a compelling need to arrive at conceptions of the universe *in terms of which he could regard his own life as meaningful.* He wants to know where *he* fits into the scheme of things. He wants to understand how the great facts of the objective world relate to *him* and what they imply for his behavior. He wants to know what significance may be found in his own existence, the succeeding generations of his kind and the vivid events of his inner life. He seeks some kind of meaningful framework in which to understand (or at least to reconcile himself to) the indignities of chance and circumstance and the fact of death. A number of philosophers and scientists have told him sternly that he must not expect answers to that sort of question, but he pays little heed. He wants, in the words of Kierkegaard, "a truth which is true for me." He seeks conceptions of the universe that give dignity, purpose and sense to his own existence. . . .

From: Saul W. Gellerman
*MOTIVATION AND PRODUCTIVITY**

[EDITORS' NOTE: The author is a Staff Specialist in Behavioral Sciences for International Business Machines Corporation.]

THE CLASSICAL THEORIES

* * * * *

Alfred Adler, a one-time collaborator of Freud's who later broke with him to establish his own school of thought, has also had an important influence on our understanding of work motivation. Adler is not as well known as Freud, even among professionals; in fact, many of his ideas have become accepted today without having his name attached to them. Unlike Freud, who stressed the pleasure-seeking and life-sustaining motives, Adler placed a great deal of emphasis on the power motive. By "power" he meant the ability to require others to behave in ways that suited one's purposes. An infant actually has a great deal of power over others. As any parent can testify, a baby can cause a considerable commotion among all the adults within earshot with the merest yelp.

According to Adler, this ability to manipulate other people is inherently pleasurable. Not only does the child have a hard time unlearning it, but he may also spend a good deal of his adult life trying to recapture that blissful condition of having other people do as he wills. However, Adler did not consider the child to be merely a miniature dictator. He recognized, first of all, that power was not sought for its own sake so much as it was a refuge from the utter helplessness of childhood. Adults are the child's lifeline, and it is a life-and-death matter to the child that the adults in his world be reliable; therefore, the power motive acquires an urgency which it never quite loses even though it eventually becomes unnecessary. It is especially strong in an older child or in an adult who feels handicapped in some way in his ability to win the respect and attention of others. Such people may go to considerable lengths to command attention, thereby overcoming whatever real or imagined weakness it was that had disturbed them in the first place. In describing this process, Adler introduced two well-known terms to psychology: inferiority complex (underlying fears of inadequacy or handicap which need not necessarily have a basis in fact) and *compensation* (the tendency to exert extreme efforts to achieve the goals which the "inferiority" would ordinarily deny).

Second, Adler recognized that power was not the only way to solve the problem of helplessness. In time the growing child realizes that cooperativeness wins a more permanent assurance of safety for him than power ever could, and at considerably less cost in terms of watchfulness and fear of retaliation. If the child's development proceeds normally and does not encounter too much tension, the power motive gradually transforms itself into a desire to perfect his relationships with others—that is, to make these relationships more confident, open, and helpful. Thus the mature adult would be able to move among others freely, without fear or suspicion. On the other hand, if the process were stunted

---

* Reprinted by permission of the American Management Association, New York. Copyright 1963. (Excerpts from pp. 109–18.)

somewhere along the line, perhaps by too many disappointing contacts with untrustworthy adults, the power motive would not only persist but would actually become stronger. The adult who had grown up in this way would be on guard, rarely willing to reveal very much of his plans or feelings and continually on the lookout for an advantage that would secure his position in what seemed a treacherous world.

*　　　*　　　*　　　*　　　*

THE COMPETENCE MOTIVE: ROBERT W. WHITE*

*　　　*　　　*　　　*　　　*

. . . White notes that the original Freudian theory, for all its complexity, is still a little too simple to account for all the facets of human behavior. Specifically, the individual is more than just a vehicle for a set of instincts; he is also an active observer and sharer of his environment. For White, one of the mainsprings of human motivation is an interest in getting to know what the world is like and in learning to get what one wants from it. Whereas Freud stressed the life-preserving and comfort-seeking instincts and Adler, going a step further, stressed the drive for power over others, White notes that people also want to understand and manipulate their physical environment (and, later on, their social environment too). In the broadest sense, they like to be able to make things happen—to create events rather than merely to await them passively.

White calls this desire for mastery "the competence motive." It can be seen even in very young infants, he believes, in the form of random fingering of objects, poking around, and feeling whatever is in reach. Later on it takes the form of exploring, tinkering, taking things apart, putting them together, and the like. As a result of years of learning his way around his own small world, learning what its possibilities are and how to exploit them, the young boy develops a certain assurance that he can handle himself equally well in the larger world he will enter as an adult. Whether his sense of competence is strong or weak depends on the balance of successes and failures the boy has experienced in his pint-sized forays into the world around him. If successes have predominated, he will probably come to regard life as a fairly promising venture where a little common sense and persistence can take him a long way. On the other hand, if the failures have outweighed the successes, the boy may regard life as a hazardous game at best, one in which running risks is likely to lead to nothing but another fiasco, so that it makes more sense simply to wait for circumstances to come along and have their will with him than to try to influence them.

Because the individual can hardly avoid some kind of transactions with his environment every day, the ledger of successes and failures is altered constantly. Consequently, one's fate is never entirely sealed. There is always the possibility that a particularly fortunate set of experiences will come along to bolster a timid ego, or contrariwise an unfortunate set may knock the props out from under an overly confident one. While the emerging personality may be pretty well jelled in a number of important respects by age five, this is not true of the sense of competence: It can get off to a bad start and still develop strongly as the result of later successes.

But there is, alas, a limit to this. After a time the sense of competence is also likely to reach a sort of plateau from which it may vary somewhat but not (ordinarily) a great deal. This is because after a while the sense of competence begins to affect the likelihood of a given experience's turning into a success or a failure. The more venturesome spirits will be out trying to win things or change things, and by brushing aside obstacles and persisting toward their goals they tip the scales of chance in their favor. Meeker individuals will venture less and

---

* *Ibid.*, chap. x.

therefore gain less and will perhaps shrink a little too readily from obstacles. Thus the sense of competence gradually becomes a sort of self-fulfilling prophecy: The individual seldom achieves more than he expects because he does not try to achieve more than he thinks he can.

*   *   *   *   *

In adults the competence motive is very likely to express itself as a desire for job mastery and professional growth. It may therefore have a great deal to do with Herzberg's finding that the most lasting satisfactions of accountants and engineers are derived from solving difficult technical problems. The need for a suitable outlet for this motive, in a civilized society that has had most of the elemental challenges engineered out of it, may even underlie the growing tendency for people to identify themselves with their professions rather than with a particular employer or the region or group in which they were born and raised.

The job can be one of the few remaining arenas in which a man can match his skills against the environment in a contest that is neither absurdly easy nor prohibitively difficult. Where such a contest is possible, the competence motive may be exercised and considerable rewards may be enjoyed. But, where it is impossible, as in most routinized or oversupervised jobs, a strong competence motive leads only to frustration, while a weak one merely encourages resignation and dependency.

Further, the sense of competence probably plays a key role in effecting job success, especially in those jobs where initiative or innovation is essential. A man who trusts his own ability to influence his environment will actually try to influence it more often and more boldly than someone who is inclined to let the environment influence him. Can it be, then, that the games and horseplay of seven- and eight-year-olds have something to do with events in the executive suite thirty years later? White's theory suggests that they may. . . .

THE AFFILIATION MOTIVE: STANLEY SCHACHTER*

Psychologists have been attacking the problem of human motivation from more than one angle. In addition to studying the ways in which assurance and daring evolve out of a basic sense of competence, they have turned their attention to the question of what makes some people such strikingly social creatures and why others seem to be able to spend most of their time quite happily by themselves. That most people like to be in other people's company is obvious enough, but it also seems to be true that this liking is stronger in some than in others and stronger under certain kinds of circumstances.

A promising beginning toward understanding this urge to be sociable has been made by Stanley Schachter of the University of Minnesota. . . .

*   *   *   *   *

The importance of affiliative needs is clear. . . . Yet the existence of an affiliation motive has been more or less taken for granted, so that when Schachter first began to direct serious scientific attention to it, he could find little in the way of previous research or even theorizing to guide him. It was generally assumed that affiliation could be either a means to an end or an end in itself. That is, people might seek the company of others in order to gain some kind of impersonal reward which the others meted out, such as money, favors, or protection. Or they might socialize simply because they enjoyed it. It was with this latter kind of affiliation that Schachter concerned himself: the desire to be with other people regardless of whether anything but company was apparently gained thereby.

---
* *Ibid.*, chap. xi.

Some previous research had touched on the question in a way. Psychologists had found that when something happens which contradicts a strongly held belief, the "believers" will tend to seek each other out with great urgency. They then go through an excited process of comparing notes, speculating about the event, and seeking explanations. Eventually some sort of consensus emerges from all this discussion, and most of the people will quickly associate themselves with it. Whether the new ideas fit the facts any better than the old ones did, or indeed whether they are very different from the old ones at all, does not seem to matter particularly. What *does* seem to matter is that one's beliefs are squared with everyone else's. There seems, in other words, to be a great deal of relief when one's thinking is shared by many others, almost as if this agreement confirmed the "rightness" and therefore the safety of one's own ideas.

       *   *   *   *   *

For Schachter, the most important element in the pattern was the reassuring effect of sharing an opinion. Apparently this kind of sharing provided a feeling that the world was understood and that therefore life was not really so dangerous after all. Evidently something more than just company was being provided by this particular form of affiliation. Socializing, in this instance, served to make life *seem* a little more manageable, a little less inexplicable, even though the shared ideas themselves might be utterly without foundation. (This probably helps to explain the unpopularity of most new ideas: They suddenly make the world seem unfamiliar!) If the pattern is not particularly rational, that does not make it any less human.

So one motive for affiliation can be the opportunity to have one's beliefs confirmed. But Schachter found himself wondering whether the discomfort of uncertainty was the only form of discomfort that would lead to affiliation or whether it was just a special case of a broader class of anxieties that would make people want to get together. To answer the question he devised an ingenious, though somewhat diabolical, series of experiments. The subjects in these experiments were those unsung heroes (heroines in this case) of most psychological research: the college sophomores who, in return for volunteering to be subjects for an experiment, are excused from a lab report.

Schachter's technique was to produce a mild state of fright by implying that his subjects would have to endure a certain amount of pain during the experiment. They endured nothing of the kind, of course; Schachter was deliberately trying to create a rather upset frame of mind. Once he had gotten his subjects sufficiently perturbed, Schachter told them that they would have to wait for further developments and gave them an opportunity to do so either alone or together. Most of them chose togetherness, despite the fact that they were strangers. At this point Schachter confessed his trick, apologized, and explained the experiment to his much-relieved subjects. He had proved his point: Misery definitely does love company.

       *   *   *   *   *

The informal work group is a way of adapting to a humiliating lack of competence in the face of a mechanized organization. The group provides some degree of reassurance: Everyone else is equally "beaten" by the system; therefore, it is less of a reflection on each individual to be beaten. Viewed in this light, the informal work group is not necessarily due to "natural" gregariousness; it may also be a defensive reaction and a symptom of deep distress.

       *   *   *   *   *

Affiliation, then, can be a simple expression of good fellowship or the symptom of a drastic loss of self-respect. (It can also be many other things: a voluntary stratagem for increasing the likelihood of obtaining certain advantages, for example.) . . .

From: John Wiley & Sons, Inc.

ADVERTISEMENT FOR

SCIENCE IN MARKETING (*1965*)

This new text offers their objective and lucid appraisals of . .

SCIENCE IN MARKETING *

Edited by GEORGE SCHWARTZ, *Assistant Professor of Marketing, College of Business Administration, University of Rochester.*

Nineteen authorities on marketing science are represented in this fascinating analysis of what is known and what still needs to be learned about marketing. It will give your students an understanding of what is meant by the *realistic assessment of information* — and will show them how to determine whether or not such information constitutes *knowledge.*

SCIENCE IN MARKETING begins with a general consideration of the nature, goals, and usefulness of marketing science. Next, students are given a close look at specific aspects of marketing. The discussion of such topics as pricing, personal selling, and product development is organized around two questions: 1) What empirically validated descriptive, predictive, and control knowledge is currently available? and 2) What research studies should be undertaken to secure new knowledge?

An entire chapter is devoted to the evaluation of the utility and limitations of operations research in marketing, and another to the strengths and weaknesses of stochastic brand switching models.

SCIENCE IN MARKETING also includes an examination of the relationship of ethics to marketing science. The text concludes with an overview assessment of the state of marketing knowledge and suggestions for future research.

This is a volume in the Wiley Marketing Series, *Advisory Editor:* WILLIAM LAZER, Michigan State University.

The Contents...

Nature and Goals of Marketing Science.
Marketing Science: Significance to the Professor of Marketing.
Marketing Science: Usefulness to the Consumer.
Development of Marketing Thought: A Brief History.
The Marketing Concept.
Consumer Behavior: Some Psychological Aspects.
Consumer Behavior: Disbursements and Welfare.
Product Development.
Research in Personal Selling.
Pricing. Trading Areas.
Marketing Channels: Analytical Systems and Approaches.
The Concept of the Marketing Mix.
Comparative Marketing and Economic Development.
Operations Research and Marketing Science.
Stochastic Models of Brand Switching.
Ethics and Science in Marketing.
Marketing Science: Past, Present, and Future Development. Index.

The Contributors...

JULES BACKMAN, New York University.
ROBERT BARTELS, The Ohio State University.
WARREN J. BILKEY, University of Notre Dame.
NEIL H. BORDEN, Harvard University.
JAC L. GOLDSTUCKER, De Paul University.
JOHN U. FARLEY, Carnegie Institute of Technology.
DAVID HAMILTON, University of New Mexico.
JAMES G. HAUK, Syracuse University.
EUGENE J. KELLEY, The Pennsylvania State University.
ROBERT LEROY KING, University of South Carolina.
ALFRED A. KUEHN, Carnegie Institute of Technology.
WILLIAM LAZER, Michigan State University.
ROBERT W. LITTLE, University of Washington.
BERT C. McCAMMON, Jr., Indiana University.
JOSEPH W. NEWMAN, Stanford University.
ROBERT W. PRATT, Jr., General Electric Company.
GEORGE SCHWARTZ, University of Rochester.
STANLEY J. SHAPIRO, formerly of the University of Pennsylvania;
    currently with Canadian Advertising Agency, Ltd., Montreal.
JOHN B. STEWART, University of Richmond.

1965.   **512 pages**   **$9.95.**

From: Robert Carr, Marver Bernstein, and Donald Morrison

AMERICAN DEMOCRACY IN THEORY AND PRACTICE*

[EDITORS' NOTE: Mr. Carr is President of Oberlin College; Mr. Bernstein is a Professor of Politics at Princeton University; and Mr. Morrison was formerly Provost and Professor of Government at Dartmouth College.]

The highly technological character of American civilization makes it possible through the mass-circulation newspaper and magazine and the magic of radio and television, to bring essential information concerning social problems to every citizen and thereby to encourage the formation of intelligent public opinion. At the same time, it renders the problems themselves so complex and difficult that there arises a question concerning the ability of even an educated and informed citizenry to think about these problems intelligently and rationally. For example, two of the greatest issues of our time—finding satisfactory systems for the social control of atomic energy and space weapons and satellites—are made almost impossibly difficult. . . . The machine age is placing a strain upon the democratic process in this respect. It is clear that if the democratic system is to survive, increasing attention must be paid to such a basic point as bringing essential information concerning the social problems of a technological age to the people so that the process of forming public opinion may be carried forward.

         *   *   *   *   *

Mention of dissemination of information by the government raises the issue whether public officers in a democracy should try to influence public opinion or should only be influenced by it. Public officers in a democracy must show a high sensitivity to public opinion. But it is also clear that they must often provide strong leadership as public opinion takes shape on a difficult issue. For example, where the President possesses expert information concerning such matters as the international situation or economic trends within the country, which information in his judgment seems to necessitate the following of particular policies, he must do his best to shape a favorable public opinion in support of these policies.

---

* Robert Carr, Marver Bernstein, Donald Morrison, *American Democracy in Theory and Practice,* copyright © 1960 (Third Edition), Holt, Rinehart & Winston, Incorporated. Reprinted by permission. (Excerpts from pp. 214–19.)

From: Dorwin Cartwright

"PUBLIC OPINION POLLS AND DEMOCRATIC LEADERSHIP"*

[EDITORS' NOTE: The author is Research Coordinator, Research Center for Group Dynamics, University of Michigan.]

The great potentialities of sample surveys in serving both the legislative and administrative branches of the Government are now well established. Through an extremely rapid growth of the science of sampling it has become possible to obtain relatively quickly and with moderate expense an accurate miniature of the total population. . . .

The Founding Fathers, not knowing of the science of sampling, could, of course, make no provision for public opinion research in the democratic process of government. Their method for keeping control in the hands of the people was that of assuring free elections in which *leaders* were chosen to represent the people. . . . The democratic control, and the very essence of democracy, lay in the fact that elected leaders would have to stand before the people periodically for re-election: In the years that have followed, this control has proved to be quite limited; on many issues the will of the people has been but weakly exercised.

. . . Had the founders of our government foreseen the tremendous growth of bureaucracy which has taken place since their day and had they been able to imagine the intimate way in which the executive agencies would come to touch the lives of all our citizens, it is possible that they would have devised some more direct method of control over this branch of government. Had they known of public opinion research, they might have made provision in the Constitution for its regular use.

Pressure groups constitute a most impressive symptom of the illness of our democratic functioning. . . . Techniques of lobbying have become so highly developed that persons with a professional reputation in the field are avidly sought by groups able to pay well to have their wishes felt in Washington.

Against such a barrage the conscientious public servant has little defense. . . .

Looking at the government through the eyes of those who shape policies, there is need to keep in touch with the public for yet another reason. It is not enough to know whether or not the public is in favor of some broadly defined program; let us say, inflation control. Even though its objectives receive overwhelming approval, a program may fail because its detailed operation does not correctly take into account the "human element" inherent in any public action. . . .

*   *   *   *   *

What do we want of our leaders in a democracy? What should they do for us? Certainly they should represent the will of the majority; . . . But they should do more. We want men who will lead as well as follow the public will; we want

* Reprinted by permission of the *Journal of Social Issues*, Vol. II, No. 2 (1946), pp. 23–32.

experts who know more about the subject than anyone else; we want men of vision who can invent new solutions to our problems. No doubt a poll of the American people would reveal support of each of these propositions. If the public really accepts these functions of the leader, however, it then follows that leaders should by no means always abide by the results of the polls. There are certain circumstances under which they are obligated to disregard them.

PUBLIC INFORMATION AND THE EXPERT

Although the educational level of this country is high and media of information reach every segment of the population daily, popular knowledge of public affairs is meager. . . . For instance, at the height of discussion of the Little Steel Formula, April, 1945, only 52 per cent of those approached by Gallup interviewers asserted that they had heard of it, and only 30 per cent could give a reasonably accurate indication of what it was intended to do. It has been found on several occasions that less than half of the population can give correctly such items of information as the number of years for which a member of the House of Representatives is elected. Perhaps more revealing is the finding of the *Fortune* poll in August, 1944, that 46 per cent of the population thought that John L. Lewis was president of the C.I.O. while nearly one per cent mentioned Eric Johnston and another Beardsley Ruml. . . .

. . . The kind of government established by our Constitution did not envision going to the public for the solution of the thousands of problems which arise each year. It was intended that these problems would be solved by leaders and experts selected by the people. Public opinion polls which go to the people and ask them to choose among specific proposals for the solution of these detailed problems actually force many people to make pronouncements upon matters about which they know little. To expect government leaders to follow these choices as a mandate from the people is to substitute mediocrity for expertness.

*   *   *   *   *

. . . Modern government has become so extensive and so complicated that even experts must specialize on certain types of problems. The danger of applying public opinion polls to these areas lies in the fact that people can be induced to express an opinion in a poll on matters about which they know little. . . .

*   *   *   *   *

Social progress, like technological progress, depends upon the widespread adoption of new procedures which have been developed by a relatively small number of people. As much as we might wish it, the average man is neither an inventor nor an innovator. . . .

In another way the inventor differs from the rest of us. He is a restless soul who is never satisfied with the present condition of things. He is constantly looking for improvements, for better procedures. But only when our needs are seriously thwarted do we common mortals search out new practices. If the horse will get us where we want to go, we are happy—until the automobile leaves us in its dust. We are quick to adopt a new and better creation after we have seen it work, but we are slow to perceive its need and to invent it.

*   *   *   *   *

. . . In the guise of being democratic and of giving the average man a greater voice in social affairs, public opinion research can be used to impede progress through misplacing the function of invention in our society. By asking the public to invent solutions to social problems and by interpreting the absence of new solutions as a desire for the *status quo,* public opinion polls are sometimes employed to bring pressure to bear against innovation and change.

* * * * *

From this discussion it would be incorrect to conclude that public opinion research can make no contribution to invention and progress in government. On the contrary, it is just this area of public life where it can be of the greatest assistance. Properly designed and executed research on public needs can give social inventors goals to aim at. . . . Sample surveys can be very useful in determining whether a program that is sound from an economics point-of-view will be at all satisfactory when the "human element" is considered.

* * * * *

From: Harold J. Leavitt
MANAGERIAL PSYCHOLOGY*

[EDITORS' NOTE: The author is Professor of Psychology at Stanford University.]

THE PERCEPTUAL WORLD

Most of us recognize that the world-as-we-see-it is not necessarily the same as the world-as-it-"really"-is. Our answer depends on what we heard, not on what was really said. The housewife buys what she likes best, not what is best. Whether we feel hot or cold depends on us, not on the thermometer. The same job may look like a good job to one of us and a sloppy job to another.

To specify the problem, consider the line drawing in Figure 2. This is a picture of a woman. Here are some questions about it: (1) How old is the woman at the time of the picture? (2) Does she have any outstanding physical characteristics? (3) Is she "reasonably attractive" or "downright ugly"?

Show the picture to ten other people. Do they all see the same thing? If some think she looks between twenty and thirty, does anyone think she's over fifty? If some think she's over fifty, does anyone think she's between twenty and thirty? How does one account for the conflicts? Are the differences simply differences in taste? Or in standards of beauty? Or is each person distorting the "real" world in a different way?

This old psychology-textbook picture is intentionally ambiguous. It can be seen either as an ugly old hag with a long and crooked nose and toothless mouth or as a reasonably attractive young girl with head turned away so that one can barely see one eyelash and part of a nose. More importantly, the picture will be based on the "facts" as they are seen by the viewer, which may be different from the "facts" seen by another viewer.

Incidentally, if the reader still sees only one of the two figures, he is getting a good feeling of what a "need" is. The tension or discomfort that one feels when he thinks he is missing something others can see or when he feels he hasn't quite

* Reprinted from *Managerial Psychology* by Harold J. Leavitt, by permission of The University of Chicago Press. Copyright 1958. (Excerpts from pp. 27–33.)

Fig. 2—Wife or mother-in-law?

closed a gap in his knowledge—that is a need. And it will probably be difficult to concentrate on reading further until he satisfies that unsatisfied need by finding the second face in the picture.

THE INFLUENCE OF OUR NEEDS ON OUR PERCEPTIONS

The hag picture is another demonstration of a commonplace observation, i.e., that people see things differently, that the world is what we make it, that everyone wears his own rose-colored glasses. But consider some additional questions: Whence the rose-colored glasses? Are the glasses always rose-colored? That is, does one always see what he wants to see, or does he see what he is afraid he will see, or both?

These questions are important because the primary issue of "human relations" is to consider ways in which individuals can affect the behavior of other individuals. If it is true that people behave on the basis of the perceived world, then changing behavior in a predetermined direction can be made easier by understanding the individual's present perception of the world. For if there is any common human-relations mistake made by industrial superiors in their relations with subordinates, it is the mistake of assuming that the "real" world is all that counts, that everyone works for the same goals, that the facts speak for themselves.

But if people do act on their perceptions, different people perceive things differently. How, then, is the manager, for example, to know what to expect? What determines how particular people will perceive particular things?

The answer has already been given in the preceding chapters. People's perceptions are determined by their needs. Like the mirrors at amusement parks, we distort the world in relation to our own tensions. Children from poorer homes, when asked to draw a quarter, draw a bigger than actual one. Industrial employees, when asked to describe the people they work with, talk more about their bosses (the people more important to their needs) than about their peers or subordinates, and so on.

But the problem is more complicated than that. People may perceive what is important to their needs, but does this mean people see what they want to see, or what they are afraid to see? Both wishes and fears are important to one's needs. The answer seems to be that we perceive both, but according to certain rules. We magnify a compliment from higher up in the organization but we also magnify a word of disapproval. We dream of blondes, but we also have night-mares. And sometimes we just don't pay attention at all to things that are quite relevant. We forget dentist's appointments; we oversleep when we have exami-nations coming up; we manage to forget to clean the basement or to call on this particular customer.

SELECTIVE PERCEPTION

What, then, are the rules of selective perception? The best answer we can give is this one: If one re-examines his memories of the past, he may find that his recall of positive, satisfying things is better than his recall of negative, un-pleasant things. He may find it easier to wake early to go fishing than to get to a dentist's appointment. He may look forward, in fact, to doing pleasant, satisfying jobs but may evade mildly disturbing and unpleasant jobs. One senior executive recently commented to the author that the biggest problem he encounters with young management people is their tendency to avoid the little unpleasant decisions—like disciplining people or digging through boring and repetitive records or writing unpleasant letters. This executive felt that his younger men would be far more effective if they could learn to deal as promptly with these uncomfortable little decisions as they did with the big ones.

But we can see some sense in this selective remembering if we look for it. There are some advantages to a person in being blind to unpleasantness, even if such blindness cuts down his working effectiveness. Ignoring the unpleasant may represent more than "laziness." It may be a sensible defensive device, psycho-logically speaking. Thus, most people are able to ignore soft background con-versation while working. In effect they are psychologically deaf to a potentially distracting part of the real world. And this defense helps them to concentrate on their work. Similarly, most people manage to ignore the threat of the hydrogen bomb and to go on eating and sleeping as though this dangerous part of the real world were not here. It can even be shown experimentally that words with unpleasant connotations tend to be recognized more slowly when exposed for very brief intervals than words with pleasant connotations.

The strange part of this defensive process, however, is that in order *not* to hear the distracting music or *not* to see the unpleasant words one must first hear and see them. One has to see the word, recognize that it is unpleasant, and reject it almost simultaneously, so that one can say, "No. I didn't see what that word was." Hence the label "defense" attached to this phenomenon—defense against the entry of preselected things mildly disturbing to one's equilibrium. So two of our rules of selective perception become: (1) see what promises to help satisfy needs, and (2) ignore mildly disturbing things.

Suppose, though, that while one is successfully ignoring background talk someone back there starts to shout; or, while one is successfully ignoring the H-bomb, an H-bomb falls on London. At those points, when the unpleasantness becomes intense and dangerous, people stop defending and begin attacking.

They stop ignoring the irritation and start directing all their attention to it. This reversal seems to happen suddenly, at some specific threshold. The distant irritation increases to a point at which it becomes so real, so imminent, and so threatening that we reverse our course, discard the blindfold, and preoccupy ourselves completely with the thing previously ignored.

This is the third rule: Pay attention to things that are really dangerous. The whole picture now begins to look like this: *People perceive what they think will help satisfy needs; ignore what is disturbing; and again perceive disturbances that persist and increase.*

There is yet a fourth step in this process. What can happen when perceived threats become even more intense and imminent? When the soldier in combat watches his buddies die around him? That one we shall consider later, in the chapter on conflict.

This process may not seem entirely logical to an outside observer, but it is quite reasonable psychologically. For this kind of self-imposed psychological blindness helps the person to maintain his equilibrium while moving toward his objectives. An organism lacking this ability to fend off minor threats might well find itself torn apart in its attempt to deal simultaneously with all of them. Or, at least, an individual unable to ignore unpleasant realities might spend so much of his energy dealing with them that he would make little progress toward his major goals. For once a person has learned to perceive a multitude of threats and dangers in his world he needs a system of defense against them. One should add, however, that some individuals may see relatively few things as dangerous and therefore have little need for defense, while for others the world holds dangers at every turn.

In the preceding chapter we suggested that a person who has encountered a relatively helpful world is likely to perceive more of his environment as potentially helpful. If, however, the world has been mostly frustrating, then more of it, and especially new things in it, will be seen as potentially dangerous. Being dangerous, they must be fended off. But, paradoxically, to be fended off they must first be seen. So to protect himself from more insecurity, the insecure person must first see the things that will provoke insecurity and then manage to deny to himself that he has seen them.

From: William H. Newman and Charles E. Summer, Jr.

*THE PROCESS OF MANAGEMENT: CONCEPTS, BEHAVIOR, AND PRACTICE**

[EDITORS' NOTE: The authors are on the Faculty of the Graduate School of Business, Columbia University.]

"Participation in decision-making," however, usually has a specific meaning: that when formulating a plan, a manager draws on the ideas of his subordinates and others who will be affected by the plan. . . . Normally, there is a face-to-

* William H. Newman and Charles E. Summer, Jr., *The Process of Management: Concepts, Behavior, and Practice.* © 1961. Reprinted by permission of Prentice-Hall, Inc., Englewood Cliffs, New Jersey. (Excerpts from pp. 439–48.)

face discussion of a problem so that a free exchange of ideas can take place. This kind of participation requires, of course, that all participants—manager and subordinates—share a belief that the final plan will be better because the ideas of two or more persons are integrated into the decision.

*　　　*　　　*　　　*　　　*

DEGREES OF PARTICIPATION

A manager does not simply choose to use, or not to use, participation. In practice, we find varying degrees of influence by subordinates on decisions. Participation on a specific problem may fall anywhere between two extremes: complete delegation of the problem to a subordinate or complete centralization of decision-making, whereby the manager merely announces his conclusion and tries to get subordinates to carry out the plan. The degree of participation depends on (a) who initiates ideas; (b) how completely a subordinate carries out each phase of decision-making—diagnosing, finding alternatives, estimating consequences, and making the choice; and (c) how much weight an executive attaches to the ideas he receives. . . .

*　　　*　　　*　　　*　　　*

When more than one person participates in making a decision, we often obtain these advantages: diverse knowledge, different viewpoints and biases, and complementary decision-making skills.

*　　　*　　　*　　　*　　　*

RECOGNIZING WHEN PARTICIPATION IS FEASIBLE

Participation is effective only when a manager is skillful in selecting problems that call for it and when he determines the degree of participation that is appropriate for the people who will be involved. No simple rule will tell him just when to utilize this potentially powerful technique, but we can identify several factors that will be helpful guides.

TIME AVAILABLE FOR DECISION

Participation requires a suggestion by one person (say, Frank), consideration of the idea by a second person (John), and John's verbal reaction to Frank. This sequence will probably be followed by a discussion of John's ideas, further consideration by Frank, and so on. Such *interaction* takes *time*.

Time can be costly in two ways: It *may* result in a decision that comes too late for strategic effectiveness and it *always* involves an expenditure of human energies. If a crude oil pipeline breaks down, the man in charge of maintaining a flow of raw materials to the refinery served by the pipeline must act fast to arrange alternative sources of supply. At most, he has only brief consultations with other people, and he must brush aside a detailed examination of the best possible sources in making sure that the refinery can continue to operate without interruption. Participation would mean costly delays. In the following example, too, time for joint action would have meant money lost. The president of a U.S. manufacturing concern discovered on a visit to Australia that the company's sales agent was so ineffective that its reputation was suffering and new competitors were likely to enter the field. He immediately set up a new distribution arrangement while he was on the local scene without waiting to consult with his associates back home. Some toes were stepped on in the process, but everyone recognized that decisive action was more valuable in this circumstance than joint participation that would have delayed a reorganization for at least several months.

Even when there is no emergency pressure, the time required for participation may be a serious obstacle to its use. . . .

*   *   *   *   *

AVOIDING MOTIVATIONAL DEADLOCKS

A manager should think about the interests of each person he consults on a problem. The president of a chemical company, for example, was trying to decide whether the company should stop producing its own wooden boxes to pack chemicals for shipment. The Package Division of this company was large, employing 600 people—it comprised a box factory and a logging operation that cut trees to produce the boxes. In this case, the vice president in charge of the division had no experience in chemical manufacture, nor did his age and qualifications fit him for an executive position other than managing timber operations and the production of boxes and barrels. Because of the vice president's motivations and capacities, it would have been unreasonable for the president to say sincerely to this man, in effect, "Harold, we are thinking of closing up your division. I'd be greatly interested in your helping us gather facts and marshal reasons about whether this ought to be done."

Such a conflict between personal interests and company interests often arises in long-range planning. When a man has devoted his entire career to a particular product or function and has deep convictions about the importance of the activity, it may be impossible for him to think objectively and logically about a drastic curtailment of the activity or about merging it into a completely new organization structure. Once a decision has been made to move in a general direction, and a man affected by the decision has been able to reconcile himself with the inevitable, he may become a valuable participant in planning the transition. . . .

CAPACITY AND WILLINGNESS TO CONTRIBUTE

A third criterion we should pay attention to when we decide whether participation is desirable deals with the characteristics of potential participants. For instance, high *mental ability* is desirable. A participant need not be exceptional in all respects, but he needs strength in at least one of the following intellectual qualities: originality, penetrating analysis, good memory, or balanced judgment. Participation for unintelligent subordinates clearly must be restricted to limited phases of simple problems.

We have already noted that some people face new problems realistically, whereas others have a habit of withdrawing from problems, dreaming rosy dreams, becoming unduly pessimistic, failing to face facts, or resorting to other defensive mechanisms. The more *realistic* a person is, the more likely he is to be a helpful participant.

Self-confidence also helps make a good participant. A man with confidence in his own ideas feels freer to express them to his boss and other senior officials, even though his views may not be in harmony with what already has been said. In contrast, a highly dependent person who typically looks to others for help in solving problems is unlikely to provide fresh ideas. Moreover, such a dependent person often gets trapped by a feeling that opposition to views of a supervisor is a sign of disloyalty. Yes-men are of little help in the process of participation.

A particular problem may be so far removed from chief interests of subordinates that they are not *willing to devote effort* to participating in its solution. . . .

*   *   *   *   *

ECONOMIC REALITIES

The economic facts of life may dictate a course of action, and for a manager to invite his subordinates to consider whether that action should be taken would be near chicanery. Much research is being devoted to devising electronic machines that will sort and post checks in a bank; if a machine is developed that will cut costs of these operations in half, we should not ask the clerks now performing the operation to help us decide whether to install the new equipment. We might well seek their advice on a program of transition from the existing method to the new one, but for them the adoption of a new method should simply be treated as a given premise.

*   *   *   *   *

AID TO VOLUNTARY COOPERATION

Certainly in thinking about when to use participation we should also consider how much it will develop voluntary cooperation among those who actively share in the decision-making process. The participants will have an opportunity for self-expression, an increased sense of security, and the satisfaction of being an important part of a group. Such feelings foster cooperation.

Voluntary cooperation, however, should be regarded simply as a by-product. If participation cannot be justified in terms of wiser decisions, we do not recommend its use. When participation is used merely as a motivational device, employees are led to believe that their ideas are being solicited sincerely, but in fact the soliciting executive has little or no real interest in their suggestions. Such an executive will at most half-heartedly make use of the ideas. Sooner or later, the employees will sense that what is being done under the guise of participation is an attempt to maneuver them to support management's ideas and decisions. . . .

From: Mary Parker Follett
*"CONSTRUCTIVE CONFLICT"**

. . . I wish to consider in this paper the most fruitful way of dealing with conflict. At the outset, I should like to ask you to agree for the moment to think of conflict as neither good nor bad; to consider it without ethical pre-judgment; to think of it not as warfare, but as the appearance of difference, difference of opinions, of interests. For that is what conflict means—difference. We shall not consider merely the differences between employer and employee, but those between managers, between the directors at the Board meetings, or wherever difference appears.

As conflict—difference—is here in the world, as we cannot avoid it, we should,

---

* From *Dynamic Administration: The Collected Papers of Mary Parker Follett* by H. C. Metcalf and L. Urwick. Copyright © 1942. Reprinted by permission of Harper & Row, Publishers, Incorporated. (Excerpts from pp. 30–49.)

I think, use it. Instead of condemning it, we should set it to work for us. Why not? What does the mechanical engineer do with friction? Of course his chief job is to eliminate friction, but it is true that he also capitalizes friction. The transmission of power by belts depends on friction between the belt and the pulley. The friction between the driving wheel of the locomotive and the track is necessary to haul the train. All polishing is done by friction. The music of the violin we get by friction. We left the savage state when we discovered fire by friction. We talk of the friction of mind on mind as a good thing. So in business, too, we have to know when to try to eliminate friction and when to try to capitalize it, when to see what work we can make it do. That is what I wish to consider here, whether we can set conflict to work and make it *do* something for us.

*   *   *   *   *

There are three main ways of dealing with conflict: domination, compromise, and integration. Domination, obviously, is a victory of one side over the other. This is the easiest way of dealing with conflict, the easiest for the moment but not usually successful in the long run, as we can see from what has happened since the War.

The second way of dealing with conflict, that of compromise, we understand well, for it is the way we settle most of our controversies; each side gives up a little in order to have peace, or, to speak more accurately in order that the activity which has been interrupted by the conflict may go on. Compromise is the basis of trade union tactics. In collective bargaining, the trade unionist asks for more than he expects to get, allows for what is going to be lopped off in the conference. Thus we often do not know what he really thinks he should have, and this ignorance is a great barrier to dealing with conflict fruitfully. . . .

But I certainly ought not to imply that compromise is peculiarly a trade union method. It is the accepted, the approved, way of ending controversy. Yet no one really wants to compromise, because that means a giving up of something. Is there then any other method of ending conflict? There is a way beginning now to be recognized at least, and even occasionally followed: when two desires are *integrated,* that means that a solution has been found in which both desires have found a place, that neither side has had to sacrifice anything. Let us take some very simple illustration. In the Harvard Library one day, in one of the smaller rooms, someone wanted the window open, I wanted it shut. We opened the window in the next room, where no one was sitting. This was not a compromise because there was no curtailing of desire; we both got what we really wanted. For I did not want a closed room, I simply did not want the north wind to blow directly on me; likewise the other occupant did not want that particular window open, he merely wanted more air in the room.

. . . A Dairymen's Cooperative League almost went to pieces last year on the question of precedence in unloading cans at a creamery platform. The men who came down the hill (the creamery was on a down grade) thought they should have precedence; the men who came up the hill thought they should unload first. The thinking of both sides in the controversy was thus confined within the walls of these two possibilities, and this prevented their even trying to find a way of settling the dispute which would avoid these alternatives. The solution was obviously to change the position of the platform so that both up-hillers and down-hillers could unload at the same time. But this solution was not found until they had asked the advice of a more or less professional integrator. When, however, it was pointed out to them, they were quite ready to accept it. Integration involves invention, and the clever thing is to recognize this, and not to let one's thinking stay within the boundaries of two alternatives which are mutually exclusive.

*   *   *   *   *

Some people tell me that they like what I have written on integration, but say that I am talking of what ought to be instead of what is. But indeed I am not; I am talking neither of what is, to any great extent, or of what ought to be merely, but of what perhaps may be. This we can discover only by experiment. That is all I am urging, that we try experiments in methods of resolving differences. . . .

The key-word of psychology today is desire. If we wish to speak of conflict in the language of contemporary psychology, we might call it a moment in the interacting of desires. Thus we take from it any connotation of good or bad. Thus we shall not be afraid of conflict, but shall recognize that there is a destructive way of dealing with such moments and a constructive way. Conflict as the moment of the appearing and focusing of difference may be a sign of health, a prophecy of progress. If the Dairymen's League had not fought over the question of precedence, the improved method of unloading would not have been thought of. The conflict in this case was constructive. And this was because, instead of compromising, they sought a way of integrating. Compromise does not create, it deals with what already exists; integration creates something new, in this case a different way of unloading. And because this not only settled the controversy but was actually better technique, saved time for both the farmers and the creamery, I call this: setting friction to work, making it *do* something.

. . . What I think we should do in business organization is to try to find the machinery best suited for the normal appearing and uniting of diversity so that the difference does not stay too long crystallized, so that the pathological stage shall not be reached.

One advantage of integration over compromise I have not yet mentioned. If we get only compromise, the conflict will come up again and again in some other form, for in compromise we give up part of our desire, and because we shall not be content to rest there, sometime we shall try to get the whole of our desire. Watch industrial controversy, watch international controversy, and see how often this occurs. Only integration really stabilizes. But by stabilization I do not mean anything stationary. Nothing ever stays put. I mean only that that particular conflict is settled and the next occurs on a higher level.

*   *   *   *   *

Having suggested integration as perhaps the way by which we can deal most fruitfully with conflict, with difference, we should now consider the method by which integration can be obtained. But before we do that I want to say definitely that I do not think integration is possible in all cases. When two men want to marry the same woman, there can be no integration; when two sons both want the old family home, there can usually be no integration. And there are many such cases, some of little, some of great seriousness. I do not say that there is no tragedy in life. All that I say is that if we were alive to its advantages, we could often integrate instead of compromising. . . .

*   *   *   *   *

If, then, we do not think that differing necessarily means fighting, even when two desires both claim right of way, if we think that integration is more profitable than conquering or compromising, the first step toward this consummation is *to bring the differences into the open*. We cannot hope to integrate our differences unless we know what they are. I will give some illustrations of the opposite method—evading or suppressing the issue.

I know a factory where, after the War, the employees asked for a five per cent increase in wages, but it was not clear to either side whether this meant a five per cent raise over present wages or over pre-War wages. Moreover, it was seen that neither side wished to know! The employees naturally preferred to think the former, the managers the latter. It was some time before both sides were willing to face the exact issue; each, unconsciously, hoped to win by keeping the whole problem hazy.

*   *   *   *   *

Wherever you have the fight-set, you are in danger of obscurities, conscious or unconscious. As long as trade unionism is a defensive movement, as long as employers' associations are defensive movements, we shall have obscurities. As long as internationalism is what it is, evasion will go on. Of course not to *appear* to evade is part of good diplomacy, for you don't want the other side to think you are trying to "get by" on anything. But we shall continue to evade or suppress as long as our real aim is not agreement, but domination. Lord Shaw, chairman of the Coal Commission, put it as one of the essentials in arbitration that both sides should genuinely desire agreement. Here we get a very direct lesson from psychology.

The psychiatrist tells his patient that he cannot help him unless he is honest in wanting his conflict to end. The "uncovering" which every book on psychology has rubbed into us for some years now as a process of the utmost importance for solving the conflicts which the individual has within himself is equally important for the relations between individuals, or between groups, classes, races, nations. In business, the employer, in dealing either with his associates or his employees, has to get underneath all the camouflage, has to find the real demand as against the demand put forward, distinguish declared motive from real motive, alleged cause from real cause, and to remember that sometimes the underlying motive is deliberately concealed and that sometimes it exists unconsciously.

The first rule, then, for obtaining integration is to put your cards on the table, face the real issue, uncover the conflict, bring the whole thing into the open.

One of the most important reasons for bringing the desires of each side to a place where they can be clearly examined and valued is that evaluation often leads to *revaluation*. We progress by a revaluation of desire, but usually we do not stop to examine a desire until another is disputing right of way with it. Watch the evolution of your desires from childhood, through youth, etc. The baby has many infantile desires which are not compatible with his wish for approbation; therefore he revalues his desires. We see this all through our life. We want to do so-and-so, but we do not estimate how much this really means to us until it comes into conflict with another desire. Revaluation is the flower of comparison.

This conception of the revaluation of desire is necessary to keep in the foreground of our thinking in dealing with conflict, for neither side ever "gives in" really, it is hopeless to expect it, but there often comes a moment when there is a simultaneous revaluation of interests on both sides and unity precipitates itself. This, I think, happened in Europe at the London Conference last summer, or rather it happened before that and led to the Conference. Integration is often more a spontaneous flowing together of desire than one might think from what I have said; the revaluing of interests on both sides may lead the interests to fit into each other, so that all find some place in the final solution.

*   *   *   *   *

It will be understood, of course, that all this applies to ourselves as well as to the other side; we have to uncover our subarticulate egoisms, and then, when we see them in relation to other facts and desires, we may estimate them differently. . . .

*   *   *   *   *

. . . If the first step is to uncover the real conflict, the next is to take the demands of both sides and break them up into their constituent parts. Contemporary psychology shows how fatal it is to try to deal with conglomerates. I know a boy who wanted a college education. His father died and he had to go to work at once to support his mother. Had he then to give up his desire? No, for on analysis he found that what he wanted was not a college education, but an education, and there were still ways of his getting that. You remember the southern girl who said, "Why, I always thought damned Yankee was one word until I came north."

*   *   *   *   *

You will notice that to break up a problem into its various parts involves the *examination of symbols,* involves, that is, the careful scrutiny of the language used to see what it really means. A friend of mine wanted to go to Europe, but also she did not want to spend the money it would cost. Was there any integration? Yes, she found one. In order to understand it, let us use the method I am advocating; let us ask, what did "going to Europe" symbolize to her? In order to do that, we have to break up this whole, "going to Europe." What does "going to Europe" stand for to different people? A sea voyage, seeing beautiful places, meeting new people, a rest or change from daily duties, and a dozen other things. Now, this woman had taught for a few years after leaving college and then had gone away and led a somewhat secluded life for a good many years. "Going to Europe" was to her a symbol, not of snow mountains, or cathedrals, or pictures, but of meeting people—that was what she wanted. When she was asked to teach in a summer school of young men and women where she would meet a rather interesting staff of teachers and a rather interesting group of students, she immediately accepted. This was her integration. This was not a substitution for her wish, it was her *real* wish fulfilled.

*   *   *   *   *

It is, of course, unavoidable to use symbols; all language is symbolic; but we should be always on our guard as to what is symbolized. For instance, the marketing cooperatives say that they want their members to keep their pledges. That statement is a symbol for what they really want, which is to get enough of the commodity to control the market. Every day we use many more not-understood symbols, many more whole-words, unanalyzed words, than we ought to. . . .

We have been considering the breaking up of the whole-demand. On the other hand, one often has to do just the opposite; find the whole-demand, the real demand, which is being obscured by miscellaneous minor claims or by ineffective presentation. The man with a genius for leadership is the one who can make articulate the whole-demand, unless it is a matter of tactics deliberately to conceal it. I shall not stop to give instances of this, as I wish to have time for some consideration of a point which seems to me very important for business, both in dealings with employees and with competing firms, and that is the anticipation of demands, of difference, of conflict.

*   *   *   *   *

. . . There is circular as well as *linear* response, and the exposition of that is I think the most interesting contribution of contemporary psychology to the social sciences. A good example of circular response is a game of tennis. A serves. The way B returns the ball depends partly on the way it was served to him. A's next play will depend on his own original serve plus the return of B, and so on and so on. We see this in discussion. We see this in most activity between one and another. Mischievous or idle boys say, "Let's start something"; we must remember that whenever we act we have always "started something," behavior precipitates behavior in others. Every employer should remember this. One of the managers in a factory expressed it to me thus: "I am in command of a situation until I behave; when I act I have lost control of the situation." This does not mean that we should not act! It is, however, something to which it is very important that we give full consideration.

Circular response seems a simple matter, quite obvious, something we must all accept. Yet every day we try to evade it, every day we act and hope to avoid the inescapable response. As someone has said in another connection, "We feed Cerberus raw meat and hope that when we lie between his paws, he will turn out to be a vegetarian."

The conception of circular behavior throws much light on conflict, for I now realize that I can never fight you, I am always fighting you plus me. I have put it this way: that response is always to a relation. I respond, not only to you, but to the relation between you and me. Employees do not respond only to their employers, but to the relation between themselves and their employer. Trade unionism is responding, not only to capitalism, but to the relation between itself and capitalism. The Dawes plan, the London Conference, were obviously moments in circular behavior. Circular behavior as the basis of integration gives us the key to constructive conflict.

*   *   *   *   *

Finally, let us consider the chief *obtacles to integration*. It requires a high order of intelligence, keen perception and discrimination, more than all, a brilliant inventiveness; it is easier for the trade union to fight than to suggest a better way of running the factory. . . .

Another obstacle to integration is that our way of life has habituated many of us to enjoy domination. Integration seems to many a tamer affair; it leaves no "thrills" of conquest. I knew a dispute within a trade union where, by the skillful action of the chairman, a true integration was discovered and accepted, but instead of the satisfaction one might have expected from such a happy result, the evening seemed to end rather dully, flatly; there was no climax, there was no side left swelling its chest, no one had conquered, no one had "won out." It is even true that to some people defeat, as well as conquest, is more interesting than integration. That is, the person with decided fight habits feels more at home, happier, in the fight movement. Moreover, it leaves the door open for further fighting, with the possibility of conquest the next time.

Another obstacle to integration is that the matter in dispute is often theorized over instead of being taken up as a proposed activity. I think this important in business administration. Intellectual agreement does not alone bring full integration. I know one factory which deliberately provides for this by the many activities of its many sub-committees, some of which seem rather trivial unless one sees just how these activities are a contribution to that functional unity which we shall consider in a later paper.

*   *   *   *   *

A serious obstacle to integration which every businessman should consider is the language used. We have noted the necessity of making preparation in the other man, and in ourselves too, for the attitude most favorable to reconciliation. A trade unionist said to me, "Our representatives didn't manage it right. If instead of a 15 per cent increase they had asked for an adjustment of wages, the management would have been more willing to listen to us; it would have put them in a different frame of mind." I don't quite see why we are not more careful about our language in business, for in most delicate situations we quite consciously choose that which will not arouse antagonism. You say to your wife at breakfast, "Let's reconsider that decision we came to last night." You do not say, "I wish to give you my criticism of the decision you made last night."

I cannot refrain from mentioning a personal experience. I went into the

Edison Electric Light Company and said to a young woman at a counter, "Where shall I go to speak about my bill?" "Room D for complaints," she replied. "But I don't wish to make a complaint," I said. "I thought there was a mistake in your bill." "I think there is," I said, "but I don't wish to complain about it; it was a very natural mistake." The girl looked nonplussed, and as she was obviously speechless a man came out from behind a desk and said: "You would prefer to ask for an adjustment, wouldn't you?" and we had a chat about it.

*   *   *   *   *

I have left untouched one of the chief obstacles to integration—namely, the undue influence of leaders—the manipulation of the unscrupulous on the one hand and the suggestibility of the crowd on the other. Moreover, even when the power of suggestion is not used deliberately, it exists in all meetings between people; the whole emotional field of human intercourse has to be taken fully into account in dealing with methods of reconciliation. I am deliberately omitting the consideration of this, not because I do not feel its importance as keenly as anyone, but because in these few papers we cannot cover everything.

Finally, perhaps the greatest of all obstacles to integration is our lack of training for it. In our college debates we try always to beat the other side. . . . Managers need it just as much. I have found, in the case of the wage boards which I have been on, that many employers . . . came to these joint conferences of employers and employees with little notion of conferring, but to push through, to force through, plans *previously* arrived at, based on *preconceived* ideas of what employees are like. It seems as if the methods of genuine conference have yet to be learned. Even if there were not the barriers of an unenlightened self-interest, of prejudice, rigidity, dogmatism, routine, there would still be required training and practice for us to master the technique of integration. A friend of mine said to me, "Open-mindedness is the whole thing, isn't it?" No, it isn't; it needs just as great a respect for your own view as for that of others, and a firm upholding of it until you are convinced. Mushy people are no more good at this than stubborn people.

As an indirect summing up of this discussion, I should like to emphasize our responsibility for integration. We saw in our consideration of circular response that my behavior helps create the situation to which I am responding. That implies (what we have daily to take into account) that my behavior is helping to *develop* the situation to which I am responding. . . . This conception of the developing situation is of the utmost importance for business administration. It makes it impossible to construct a map of the future, yet all our maxims of foresight hold good; every business should reconcile these two statements. We should work always with the evolving situation, and note what part our own activities have in that evolving situation.

This is the most important word, not only for business relations, but for all human relations: not to adapt ourselves to a situation—we are all more necessary to the world than that; neither to mould a situation to *our* liking—we are all, or rather each, of too little importance to the world for that; but to take account of that reciprocal adjustment, that interactive behavior between the situation and ourselves which means a change in both the situation and ourselves. One test of business administration should be: is the organization such that both employers and employees, or co-managers, co-directors, are stimulated to a reciprocal activity which will give more than mere adjustment, more than an equilibrium? Our outlook kis narrowed, our activity is restricted, our chances of business success largely diminished when our thinking is constrained within the limits of what has been called an either-or situation. We should never allow ourselves to be bullied by an "either-or." There is often the possibility of something better than either of two given alternatives. . . .

STANDARD OIL COMPANY (NEW JERSEY)

I Case Introduction

Synopsis

A stockholder of Standard Oil Company objects to management's policy of annually granting the equivalent of $1\frac{1}{2}$ cents a share to philanthropic and educational institutions. At the annual meeting a shareholder attempts to force management to commit corporate earnings only to those projects which *directly* further the company's quest for profits or to distribute the earnings to the owners.

Why This Case Is Included

The stockholder challenge raises the question: Who are the legitimate claimants on the corporation? In this context one can bring to bear the conflicting views of economic philosophers concerning the objectives of the corporation and the theories of political philosophers concerning the role of voluntary organizations in society. The stated motivations of the corporate managers can be examined to see how they jibe with these conceptual schemes. There is opportunity, too, to see how the very composition of the board of directors may affect corporate policy. Finally, corporate philanthropy raises the issue of the legitimacy of power among subgovernmental units of society.

Diagnostic and Predictive Questions

In answering the following diagnostic and predictive questions, remember that these questions apply theories and conceptual ideas from certain disciplines. Such theories are valuable to understand basic forces at work in the policy system (diagnosis) and to predict what will happen in the system in the future (prediction). Since each reading abstracts from the total policy system certain factors or variables into the closed or partial viewpoint of one theory or discipline, no one reading gives answers to the practical policy problems of the case. In diagnosis and prediction, the parts of the problem are studied with "other things being equal."

Following each question are listed readings which will be helpful in answering the question. The readings included with this case are marked (*). By referring to the author index at the end of this book, you may locate the other readings listed.

1. Where did the $8.3 million, which Standard Oil allocated in the past five years to educational aid, come from? Where might these funds have been allocated had they not been donated to educational institutions?

Read: Anthony, *Management Accounting*, pp. 290–92, 306.

2. Mrs. Alice V. Gordon, the stockholder challenging Standard Oil's philanthropy, contended: "Your company is supposedly run solely for the stockholders' benefit." What is Mr. Rathbone's (Standard Oil president) view on this point? From the standpoint of economic philosophy, should the corporation be run *solely* for the stockholder's benefit?

    Read: Eells and Walton, *Conceptual Foundations of Business,* pp. 185–87, 149–67, 458–75. *Rostow, "To Whom and For What Ends Is Corporate Management Responsible?" Hayek, "The Corporation in a Democratic Society: In Whose Interest Ought It and Will It Be Run" *Berle, *The 20th Century Capitalistic Revolution,* pp. 164–69, 171–73, 182–88.

3. Concentrating now on the motivations involved in the allocation of $8.3 million, recall that Mrs. Gordon said: "It (Standard Oil) is not an *eleemosynary* institution. Many stockholders undoubtedly feel that *charity* begins at home." (Emphasis added.) What was the motivation for Standard Oil's gifts to education? Was it charity, as Mrs. Gordon implied? Was it economic self-interest—the hope of a monetary return usually expected of corporate investments? Was it compliance with an informally imposed "tax" obligation (". . . the public has come to expect it of corporations")? Some other motivation, or some mixture of motivations?

    Read: *A. P. Smith Manufacturing Company* v. *Barlow et al.* *Glover, *The Attack on Big Business,* pp. 328, 330–35. Smith, *Wealth of Nations,* pp. 423, 508.

4. From the viewpoint of political philosophy what is the role of the corporation in the social system? Do you find a consciousness of this role definition in the statements of Standard Oil's directors and president, Mr. Rathbone? In what way, if any, should this role definition affect corporate policy?

    Read: *Clark, *Alternative to Serfdom,* pp. 4–7. *O'Connell, "Social Overhead Capital and the Principle of Subsidiarity." Eells and Walton, *Conceptual Foundations of Business,* pp. 360–63.

5. In matters like the one presently before the annual meeting, what are the advantages and disadvantages of having all full-time, inside directors? Recall that such is the composition of Standard Oil's board. Answer the question from the viewpoint of corporate management, the individual shareholder, and the public.

    Read: *Brown and Smith, *The Director Looks at His Job,* pp. 38–39, 77–78, 81–83, 85–86, 89, 91–93.

             (Additional reading, not in this volume: Peter F. Drucker, *The Practice of Management* [New York: Harper & Bros., 1954], pp. 161–81.)

6. "Allowing corporations to give one fifth of all voluntary support to higher education is putting further power into the hands of corporate managers, who are in effect responsible to no one, instead of into the hands of a duly elected (and controlled) representative body." Comment. Do corporations in fact gain power through their philanthropy? If so, is this legitimate power?

    Read: Drucker, *The Future of Industrial Man,* pp. 32–38.

Policy Questions for This Specific Case

In answering the following policy questions, the results of diagnosis and prediction are used to reduce the amount of guesswork, or judgment, in designing action solutions. However, since certain parts of the total case situation cannot be reduced to science, and since "other things are not equal," judgment must still be used to fill in the factors not accounted for by readings. You will also need a second kind of judgment as you put value weights on different scientific predictions, since different theories may point to conflicting solutions.

7. If you were Mr. Rathbone, Standard Oil's president, how would you justify corporate gifts to education to the stockholders? (See Questions 2, 3, 4, and their attached readings.)

8. Again, as Standard Oil's president, what steps, if any, would you take to allay the fears of those who suspect that control will follow contribution—that the party holding the purse strings will manipulate educational institutions or stifle academic freedom? (See Question 6.)

9. If you were a director of Standard Oil, would you vote to continue the educational aid? Do you think it would make a difference in your opinion if you were an outside instead of an inside director? (See Question 5.)

10. If you were a stockholder, how would you have voted on Mrs. Gordon's proposal at the annual meeting?

Major Policy Issues: Tentative Generalizations about Any Policy System

In arriving at conclusions for the following questions, generalize from the facts in the case and use your own ideas to (a) confirm, (b) modify, or (c) test the workability of the concepts and theories from readings. As an executive or professional, use wisdom to merge theory, on the one hand, with "brute facts" and practice, on the other.

11. Is self-interest and profits maximization in conflict with the contribution expected of the corporation to social welfare? (See Questions 2, 3, and 4 and their attached readings.)

12. What should be the motivation for corporate donations? May corporate management act out of unmixed altruism (charity) as an individual philanthropist often does? (See Question 3 and the attached readings.)

13. To what extent is Standard Oil not the father of its own child? Is the corporate policy on gifts to education more the product of forces external to the corporation than self-directed management action?

Questions for Original Student Work in Analysis and Policy

The methods of viewing this case as represented by the authors' questions and selection of readings are not exhaustive. There are other relevant ideas for diagnosis and prediction. Furthermore, there are other ways of stating policy questions. More powerful analyses and wiser solutions will result by drawing on your own training and experience for (a) relevant concepts and theories, and (b) creative ways of asking policy questions. The following questions are designed to help you acquire this skill.

14. While reflecting on case facts, what additional theories from prior education give you insights as to "what is going on" in the Standard Oil Company? As to what might be predicted to happen in the future?

15. Other than the policy questions asked by the authors, what pragmatic ways can you think of to state the practical problems faced by executives in the case?

II The Standard Oil Company (New Jersey)*

As the Standard Oil Company (New Jersey) prepared for its annual meeting on May 24, 1961, Mrs. Alice V. Gordon, a stockholder, challenged management's policy on philanthropic and educational contributions. Mrs. Gordon proposed an amendment to the corporation bylaws: "No corporate funds of this corporation shall be given away to any charitable, educational, or similar organization except for purposes in direct furtherance of the business interests of this corporation." The proxy statement of April 4, 1961 appraised all the stockholders of the proposed resolution which was to be discussed and voted on in the forthcoming annual meeting.

Company Profile

The Standard Oil Company of New Jersey is a holding company for a worldwide complex of affiliates engaged in the exploration, production, refining, transportation, and marketing of petroleum products. The parent and affiliate companies, which together employ some 145,000 people, generate about 35% of the consolidated earnings in the United States. Almost 60% of the remainder is earned in other Western Hemisphere operations. In terms of assets—almost $10 billion—Standard Oil of New Jersey ranks first in the industry, almost triple the size of the next largest integrated petroleum company. The company's 680,000 shareholders have recently been receiving an annual per share cash dividend of $2.25.

Year	Gross Operating Income	Net Income
1955	6,272,440,655	709,309,992
1956	7,126,855,410	808,534,919
1957	7,830,250,000	805,178,000
1958	7,543,571,000	562,475,000
1959	7,910,659,000	629,778,000
1960	8,034,735,000	688,573,000
1961	8,437,722,000	758,083,000

Source: Moodys.

Contributions by Standard Oil Company

Mr. M. J. Rathbone, president of Standard Oil, states that the annual after-tax cost of the philanthropic and educational contributions made by the entire company since 1955 amount to $1\frac{1}{2}$ cents per share. By far the largest proportion of this amount is directed toward education.

---

* Copyright 1964 by the Graduate School of Business, Columbia University.

In 1955 Standard Oil of New Jersey created the ESSO Education Foundation to coordinate and administer grants to education made by the parent company and its domestic affiliates. Some 429 private colleges have benefited from the Foundation's program since 1955.

ESSO EDUCATION FOUNDATION STATEMENT OF GRANTS

	1956–61	*Number of Grants*
Unrestricted	$3,783,500	1,390
National Fund for Medical Education	415,000	5
United Negro College Fund	225,000	5
Total Unrestricted	$4,423,500	1,400
Capital	1,159,000	139
Scientific research	828,715	129
Miscellaneous	495,044	61
Subtotal	$6,906,259	1,729
Special three-year science program	1,464,568	210
Total	$8,370,827	1,939

Source: Standard Oil public statements.

Stockholder Opposition to Company Contributions

Mrs. Alice V. Gordon felt that corporate contributions were inimical to her stockholder rights unless such gifts directly furthered the business interests of the Standard Oil Company. She presented her reasons in the April 4 proxy statement as follows:

Your directors are giving millions of dollars of your corporation's money to charity. This seems wrong. Your company is supposedly run solely for the stockholders' benefit. It is not an eleemosynary institution. Many stockholders undoubtedly feel that charity begins at home. Others who can afford donations are certainly entitled to choose their own beneficiaries. The current practice is especially reprehensible when as here nearly ten million have been given since 1955 to educational institutions many of which now teach socialism and ridicule business men, savers and investors, as recently explained in the well-documented best-seller "Keynes at Harvard."

Corporate Directors' Defense of Contributions Policy

In the same proxy statement Standard Oil's directors appealed to the stockholders to vote against Mrs. Gordon's proposal. They defended the long-standing corporate policy on contributions in the following words:

By requiring that a "direct" benefit be shown in order to validate a particular philanthropic or educational contribution, this proposed by-law would unduly restrict the management in the normal discharge of its responsibilities and deprive it of an effective tool in furthering corporate and shareholder interests.

As a responsible corporate citizen, any company of Jersey's stature must give financial support to philanthropic and educational institutions that rely on private sources for support. Such participation has become an integral part of the discharge of a corporation's business and civic responsibilities and, as such, has been encouraged by our tax laws, sustained by our courts and legislatures, and widely endorsed by the public at large. In the directors' judgment, such contributions further the interests of the shareholders and are extremely important if the Company is to enjoy and retain the good will of the public which is so essential to the Company's prosperity. Quite clearly, the benefits arising from such contributions, although of real and substantial value, cannot be measured in dollars and cents.

Corporate contributions are as much the responsibility of management, and receive the same careful consideration from management, as any other legitimate and necessary business expenditure. The amount of such contributions by Jersey is believed by the directors to be reasonable by any standard. In each of the last five years, the total after-tax cost to the Company and its domestic and foreign affiliates of supporting educational and philanthropic objectives has amounted to about 1½ cents per share. In management's opinion, the benefits derived and to be derived, although not necessarily "direct," fully justify this expenditure.

Discussion at the Annual Meeting

At the annual meeting of the Standard Oil Company in Boston, Massachusetts, on May 24, 1961, Mr. Watson Washburn represented Mrs. Alice V. Gordon. Before the assembled shareholders Mr. Washburn expanded on the arguments supporting the proposed amendment to the corporation bylaws.

. . . undoubtedly the directors are tremendously busy running the affairs of this gigantic enterprise we're all interested in. They apparently don't have enough time—and I'm very glad of it for the sake of the profits of the company— to spend their energies investigating hundreds of charities to see whether they are charities to which you stockholders would want to have your money given, assuming that the directors should give your money away to anyone over the objection of even a single stockholder.

Actually your company has made unrestricted grants to 429 different educational institutions in this country in the last five years. By merely inspecting the list one could say that some of them were not the kind of college where they encourage companies like ours and stockholders like ours. For example, among the men's colleges Harvard, Yale, and Princeton have been the beneficiaries of the company's donations; and among the women's colleges, Smith, Vassar, and Sarah Lawrence. Those are just examples of places where, on the whole, left-wing doctrines are taught in the economics departments.

[To support his point about economic doctrines, Mr. Washburn then read from and commented critically on the writings of Stuart Chase, with specific reference to an article by Mr. Chase which appeared in the Spring 1961 issue of *The Lamp,* a Standard Oil Company magazine.]

Mr. M. J. Rathbone, Standard Oil's president, answered Mr. Washburn, giving the company's rationale for its contributions and the selection of beneficiaries:

When you're a good corporate citizen, it is often necessary to give support to private institutions from which you expect no direct dollars-and-cents benefit— hospitals, community service organizations, the Red Cross, colleges, universities, and so on. If good citizens, corporate and individual alike, did not support these institutions, they would have to turn to the government for support—and that, certainly, is not the way to advance the cause of free enterprise.

As to the merits of giving to one institution, or one type of institution, over another, the possibilities for discussion are infinite. As we normally do in such a situation, we call upon a competent staff to gather information, to study the various facets of the problem, to appraise and analyze the facts, to evaluate the direct and indirect benefit to the company and its shareholders, and to make recommendations to the board. Your directors are then in a position to make a sound decision, and I assure you that in every instance the shareholders' interests are paramount.

Certainly I take no exception with Mr. Washburn or his principal, Mrs. Gordon, with respect to the undesirability of supporting anything unsound and improper. We try not to do that. We know that the group of our people studying these matters is capable, competent, and objective. I would be the first to agree that there is hardly a college or a university in the United States in which some of the faculty do not hold and express views which are contrary to what we, sitting as your board, might think was right and proper.

And yet this goes to the heart of the Bill of Rights. We have freedom in this country which few other countries have to the same extent, and these freedoms must be protected. If we reserve judgment to any small group of people as to what's right and what's wrong, without the ability of expression, we have lost something we can't afford to lose. In effect, we have to take a bit of the bitter with the sweet.

An exchange of questions and comments followed between Mr. Rathbone and stockholders for and against Mrs. Gordon's proposal. The chairman then declared voting on the resolution in order. Ballots were distributed; voting proceeded.

III Selected Readings

From: Eugene V. Rostow

"TO WHOM AND FOR WHAT ENDS IS CORPORATE MANAGEMENT RESPONSIBLE?"*

[EDITORS' NOTE: E. V. Rostow is Dean of the Law School, Yale University.]

From the point of view of legal and economic orthodoxy, the New Capitalism is all bewildering balderdash. The law books have always said that the board of directors owes a single-minded duty of unswerving loyalty to the stockholders,

---

* Reprinted by permission of Harvard University Press, Cambridge, Massachusetts, 1960 (in Edward S. Mason, *The Corporation in Modern Society*, pp. 63–65, 68–71).

and only to the stockholders. The economist has demonstrated with all the apparent precision of plane geometry and the calculus that the quest for maximum revenue in a competitive market leads to a system of prices, and an allocation of resources and rewards, superior to any alternative, in its contributions to the economic welfare of the community as a whole. To the orthodox mind, it is therefore unsettling, to say the least, to have the respected head of the Standard Oil Company of New Jersey equating the management's duty to stockholders with its obligation to employees, customers, suppliers, and the public at large.

*   *   *   *   *

. . . [W]hat does the "new" concept of corporate responsibility imply? Does it mean that the management of a great corporation should not bargain very hard in negotiations over wages or the prices paid to suppliers? Does it mean that a statesman-like and well-run company should charge less for its product than the market would bear, less than the prices which would maximize its short-term revenues, or what it conceives to be its long-term profits? Should it regard its residual profits, not as "belonging to" its stockholders in some ultimate sense, but as a pool of funds to be devoted in considerable part to the public interest, as the directors conceive it—to hospitals, parks, and charities in the neighborhood of its plants; to the local symphony or the art museum; to scholarships for the children of employees, or to other forms of support for the educational system of the nation at large? If what is good for the country is good for General Motors, as is indeed the case, does this view of managerial responsibility set any limit upon the directors' discretion in spending corporate funds for what they decide is the public good?

*   *   *   *   *

If, as is widely thought, the essence of corporate statesmanship is to seek less than maximum profits, postwar experience is eloquent evidence that such statesmanship leads to serious malfunctioning of the economy as a whole. . . .

*   *   *   *   *

This kind of policy, in either of its aspects, records a failure of the market as the chief instrument for guiding the allocation of capital and labor. If long continued, policies of self-restraint may result in a serious distortion in the pattern of resource use. . . .

*   *   *   *   *

The political and legal aspects of corporate statesmanship present vistas which are quite as disturbing as its economics. The endocratic corporations are accepted as powerful and effective instruments for carrying on the business of society. If their directors begin to act as if they really were general trustees for the public at large, they may well imperil their present freedom. Corporations are not accepted in public opinion as institutions through which society makes its educational policy, its foreign policy, or its political policy. Programs which would give reality to the idea of spending corporate funds to advance the general welfare, as the directors visualize it, will sooner or later invite the critical attention of legislators, governors, and presidents, who consider that they have been elected by the people to advance the general welfare, and know more about it than the directors of endocratic corporations. As Professor Ben W. Lewis has recently said, commenting on the thesis that "the corporation, almost against its will, has been compelled to assume in appreciable part the role of conscience-carrier of twentieth century American society":

"It is not going to happen; if it did happen it would not work; and if it did work it would still be intolerable to free men. I am willing to dream, perhaps selfishly, of a society of selfless men. Certainly, if those who direct our corporate concentrates are to be free from regulation either by competition or government, I can only hope that they will be conscientious, responsible, and kindly men; and I am prepared to be grateful if this proves to be the case. But, I shall still be uneasy and a little ashamed, with others who are ashamed, to be living my economic life within the limits set by the gracious bounty of the precious few. If we are to have rulers, let them be men of good will; but above all, let us join in choosing our rulers—and in ruling them."[1]

The responsibility of corporate directors requires redefinition. It may give us a warm and comfortable feeling to say that the director is a trustee for the community, rather than for his stockholders; that he is a semipublic official, or a quasi-public official, or some other kind of hyphenated public officer. It would be more constructive, however, to seek redefinition in another sense: to restate the law of corporate trusteeship in terms which take full account of the social advances of this century, but which direct the directors more sharply to concentrate their efforts on discharging their historic economic duties to their stockholders. The economic job of directors and management is quite difficult enough to absorb the full time of first-rate minds, in an economy of changing technology, significant general instability, and considerable competition, both from rival firms in the same industry and from those which steadily offer rival products.

*   *   *   *   *

. . . Is "the long-run economic interest of stockholders" any more meaningful as a standard to guide the deliberation of directors, or the decisions of courts or other public bodies reviewing what the directors have done, than "the interests of the enterprise as a whole," or "the interests of the community?" . . .

*   *   *   *   *

. . . As an abstract statement of the social duty of business enterprise in the middle of the twentieth century, I believe the "rule" I have suggested—that of long-term profit maximization—conforms more concretely than any alternative both to the image of preferred reality for business behavior in public opinion, at this state in the evolution of our legal and economic order, and to the ends business enterprise is expected to fulfill as part of the nation's system of law for governing the economy.

*   *   *   *   *

. . . [A] clear acceptance of profit maximization as a legal principle might well do something, perhaps a good deal, to order the pattern of corporate policy. Legal rules are not always fully self-enforcing, of course. But they do exert an influence, even though procedures of enforcement are not comprehensive. Adequate means for surveillance and accounting can and should be developed, to minimize abuses of corporate power. The more important problem, however, is the orientation of legitimate business policy: should it be essentially economic in purpose, or should it become an ambiguous amalgam of economic and noneconomic themes? I, for one, conclude that a clear-cut economic directive should help directors to discriminate more effectively among competing claims upon them, in carrying out their public trusteeship for the economic system as a whole.

---

[1] "Economics by Admonition," *American Economic Review*, Supplement, 49: 384, 395 (1959).

From: Adolf A. Berle

*THE 20TH CENTURY CAPITALISTIC REVOLUTION**

[EDITORS' NOTE: The author is Professor Emeritus of Law at Columbia Law School, a corporate lawyer, corporate director, and government official.]

Now planning all or any fragment of an economy has enormous implications. This is why any "planned economy" has been feared in America; why economy planned by the state has usually been bitterly fought; why emergence of planning power immediately raises doubts and wonders in the minds of the constituency affected. Naturally, any plan (if it is not a naked power-grab) must be a plan for something, and affects or limits people. Planning, however limited in scope, means planning for some kind of a community, or at least some aspect of a community, deemed by some group to be desirable. Capacity to plan, united with power to give effect to the plan, is perhaps the highest trust granted to statesmen. Its devolution has forced into the hands of many businessmen a complex of problems far beyond their chosen fields, problems of overpassing those of producing oil or electrical supplies, of manufacturing steel or motor cars, as the case may be. It may have been naive public relations for an officer of General Motors, proposed for confirmation as Secretary of Defense in the Cabinet of the United States, to say that what was good for General Motors was good for the country, and what was good for the country was good for General Motors; but he could have adduced an impressive array of statistical fact to back up his statement.

For the fact seems to be that the really great corporation managements have reached a position for the first time in their history in which they must consciously take account of philosophical considerations. They must consider the kind of a community in which they have faith, and which they will serve, and which they intend to help to construct and maintain. In a word, they must consider at least in its more elementary phases the ancient problem of the "good life," and how their operations in the community can be adapted to affording or fostering it. They may endeavor to give their views exact statement, or they may merely proceed on undisclosed premises; but, explicitly or implicitly, the premises are there.

Businessmen charged with commercial enterprise are not accustomed to this sort of thinking. As a rule, they reject the idea that this is part of their function. Most corporation executives are acutely aware of the fact that foresight is extremely difficult. Many believe quite frankly, and not without justification, that community welfare is as likely to be developed soundly by hazard as by plan.

The greatest leaders in the corporate field take a contrary view. They forcefully argue that corporations are always citizens of the community in which they operate, while large ones necessarily play a mighty part in the life of their time. It is not possible for them, these men state, to carry on great corporate businesses apart from the main context of American life. If private business and businessmen do not assume community responsibilities, government must step in and American life will become increasingly statist. In consequence, they have urged that corporations must share the burdens of supporting the non-govern-mental philanthropic and educational institutions which have played so stately a role in the development of twentieth-century America. Mr. Irving Olds, at the time Chairman of the Board of Directors of U.S. Steel Company, made a brilliant and moving address at Yale University, insisting that corporations must contribute to the general educational facilities of the country, such as universities and graduate schools, and that the duties of big business overpass their tradi-tional power to make gifts to those minor or local charities incident to plant and sales operations. He was forcefully supported by Mr. Frank Abrams, Chairman of the Board of Standard Oil Company of New Jersey. Both corporations gave emphatic proof of assent by voting substantial gifts to liberal arts colleges. Twenty-nine states have already passed statutes authorizing corporations, both presently existing and subsequently organized, to make contributions to philan-thropy and education. . . . For practical purposes, the state has authorized cor-porations to withhold from their shareholders a portion of their profits, chan-neling it to schools, colleges, hospitals, research, and other good causes.

Twenty years ago, the writer had a controversy with the late Professor E. Merrick Dodd, of Harvard Law School, the writer holding that corporate powers were powers in trust for shareholders while Professor Dodd argued that these powers were held in trust for the entire community. The argument has been settled (at least for the time being) squarely in favor of Professor Dodd's contention.

*   *   *   *   *

Growing consciousness of the power thus achieved and its implications has excited a very considerable discussion in the corporate world. Directors, espe-cially those of the largest and most responsible companies, are acutely aware of the problems thus raised. A division of opinion is reported in these circles. One group believes it necessary to pick up the load and tackle the immense responsi-bilities foreshadowed as did Mr. Olds and Mr. Abrams. Another group take the view that this is not their affair, that they are not equipped to meet it, and that they should find ways of avoiding so great a burden. After all, a board of direc-tors is chosen primarily for its ability in running a particular business. It cannot properly or effectively enter into a whole series of extraneous problems extending all the way from methods of administering individual justice to community development, community organization and community values. This school of thought believes that teachers, scholars, philosophers, and possibly politicians and governments, have to wrestle with these questions: boards of directors can-not. Both views are expressed with honesty and great sincerity.

Corporations still have, perhaps, some range of choice: they can either take an extended view of their responsibility, or a limited one. Yet the choice is probably less free than would appear. Power has laws of its own. One of them is that when one group having power declines or abdicates it, some other direct-ing group immediately picks it up; and this appears constant throughout history. The choice of corporate managements is not whether so great a power shall cease to exist; they can merely determine whether they will serve as the nuclei of its organization or pass it over to someone else, probably the modern state. The present current of thinking and insistence that private rather than governmental decisions are soundest for the community are clearly forcing the largest corporations toward a greater rather than a lesser acceptance of the responsibility that goes with power.

Men squarely facing this problem, in small or in large application, now find themselves, with some surprise, in the realm of philosophy. They have not, it is true, been assigned the job of sketching an Utopia; they only have to take— indeed, can only take—one step at a time. But they can hardly avoid determining the direction of the steps, and the aggregate of their steps in the second half of the twentieth century must necessarily go far toward determining the framework of the American community of the twenty-first. Some sort of hypothesis, however hazy, as to what that community should be, should do, and should look like, seems implicit in this situation.

*   *   *   *   *

. . . [T]he corporation, almost against its will, has been compelled to assume in appreciable part the role of conscience-carrier of twentieth-century American society. Unlike other great groups which have attempted a major part in this task, the modern corporation has done so without intent to dominate and without clearly defined doctrine. . . .

. . . [O]ut of the common denominator of the decision-making machinery, some sort of consensus of mind is emerging, by compulsion as it were, which for good or ill is acting surprisingly like a collective soul. Great organizations energizing this sort of causative apparatus have their frightening side. When Mary Wollstonecraft Shelley's hero, Frankenstein, endowed his synthetic robot with a human heart, the monster which before had been a useful mechanical servant suddenly became an uncontrollable force. Our ancestors feared that corporations had no conscience. We are treated to the colder, more modern fear that, perhaps, they do.

Certain safeguards do exist. Perhaps during the next hitch in this twentieth-century drama they will be sufficient. The great difference between the American corporate system and any socialist system lies in the fact that in America there are a few hundred powerful units, each of which has a limited capacity to disagree with its fellow giants and to do something different. . . .

. . . The reality—a "conscience" in business organizations which do control many men—need be neither impractical nor dangerous once the business community has learned to honor difference and deviation as well as agreement and conformity. Happily in America there have always been the men who will not "go along." We have reason to hope there will be enough disagreement so that the nuclei of power and of social organization will not only agree, but differ as well.

There is also still another and greater hope. Even within the pressures which organizations exact—even in spite of the necessity that men in great enterprises shall work as a team—the individuals themselves are invariably influenced by certain great philosophical premises. These, in our system, are not derived from within business organization. They come from schools and from teachers; from universities and philosophers; from men of deep human instinct who are, by occasional miracle, saints. . . .

*   *   *   *   *

. . . There is fair historical ground to anticipate that moral and intellectual leadership will appear capable of balancing our Frankenstein creations. Men working in that range are measurably steeled to resist normal pressures and often free from normal fears. They frequently have a rough time on the way. It is no accident that some of the greatest saints in the Christian Calendar were non-conformist deviants in their time; but they still grasp the future with their conceptions.

These, I think, are the real builders of any "City of God" Americans would come to accept. Corporations cannot make them. But they may protect and maintain them. Corporate managements, like others, knowingly or unknowingly, are constrained to work within a frame of surrounding conceptions which in time impose themselves. The price of failure to understand and observe them is decay of the corporation itself. . . .

From:

A. P. SMITH MANUFACTURING COMPANY
V. BARLOW ET AL.*

[EDITORS' NOTE: A. P. Smith Manufacturing Company appropriated $1,500 as a gift to Princeton University. Stockholders objected on the grounds that such gift-giving was an *ultra vires* act—outside the chartered powers of the company. Below are excerpts from statements made in the case by business executives, a college President, and one of the Supreme Court judges.]

Mr. Hubert F. O'Brien, the president of the company, testified that he considered the contribution to be a sound investment, that the public expects corporations to aid philanthropic and benevolent institutions, that they obtain good will in the community by so doing, and that their charitable donations create favorable environment for their business operations. In addition, he expressed the thought that in contributing to liberal arts institutions, corporations were furthering their self-interest in assuring the free flow of properly trained personnel for administrative and other corporate employment. Mr. Frank W. Abrams, chairman of the board of the Standard Oil Company of New Jersey, testified that corporations are expected to acknowledge their public responsibilities in support of the essential elements of our free enterprise system. He indicated that it was not "good business" to disappoint "this reasonable and justified public expectation," nor was it good business for corporations "to take substantial benefits from their membership in the economic community while avoiding the normally accepted obligations of citizenship in the social community." Mr. Irving S. Olds, former chairman of the board of the United States Steel Corporation, pointed out that corporations have a self-interest in the maintenance of liberal education as the bulwark of good government. He stated that "Capitalism and free enterprise owe their survival in no small degree to the existence of our private, independent universities" and that if American business does not aid in their maintenance, it is not "properly protecting the long-range interest of its stockholders, its employees and its customers." Similarly, Dr. Harold W. Dodds, President of Princeton University, suggested that if private institutions of higher learning were replaced by governmental institutions our

---

* Reprinted from 98 *Atlantic Reporter,* 2nd Series, New Jersey Supreme Court 1953 (pp. 582–83, 586, 590).

society would be vastly different and private enterprise in other fields would fade out rather promptly. Further on he stated that "democratic society will not long endure if it does not nourish within itself strong centers of non-governmental fountains of knowledge, opinions of all sorts not governmentally or politically originated. If the time comes when all these centers are absorbed into government, then freedom as we know it, I submit, is at an end."

* * * * *

[Judge Jacobs:]

* * * * *

During the first world war corporations loaned their personnel and contributed substantial corporate funds in order to insure survival; during the depression of the '30's they made contributions to alleviate the desperate hardships of the millions of unemployed; and during the second world war they again contributed to insure survival. They now recognize that we are faced with other, though nonetheless vicious, threats from abroad which must be withstood without impairing the vigor of our democratic institutions at home and that otherwise victory will be pyrrhic indeed. More and more they have come to recognize that their salvation rests upon sound economic and social environment which in turn rests in no insignificant part upon free and vigorous nongovernmental institutions of learning. It seems to us that just as the conditions prevailing when corporations were originally created required that they serve public as well as private interests, modern conditions require that corporations acknowledge and discharge social as well as private responsibilities as members of the communities within which they operate. Within this broad concept there is no difficulty in sustaining, as incidental to their proper objects and in aid of the public welfare, the power of corporations to contribute corporate funds within reasonable limits in support of academic institutions. But even if we confine ourselves to the terms of the common-law rule in its application to current conditions, such expenditures may likewise readily be justified as being for the benefit of the corporation; indeed, if need be the matter may be viewed strictly in terms of actual survival of the corporation in a free enterprise system. The genius of our common law has been its capacity for growth and its adaptability to the needs of the times. Generally courts have accomplished the desired result indirectly through the molding of old forms. Occasionally they have done it directly through frank rejection of the old and recognition of the new. But whichever path the common law has taken it has not been found wanting as the proper tool for the advancement of the general good. . . .

* * * * *

. . . [T]here is now widespread belief throughout the nation that free and vigorous non-governmental institutions of learning are vital to our democracy and the system of free enterprise and that withdrawal of corporate authority to make such contributions within reasonable limits would seriously threaten their continuance. Corporations have come to recognize this and with their enlightenment have sought in varying measures, as has the plaintiff by its contribution, to insure and strengthen the society which gives them existence and the means of aiding themselves and their fellow citizens. Clearly then, the appellants, as individual stockholders whose private interests rest entirely upon the well-being of the plaintiff corporation, ought not be permitted to close their eyes to present-day realities and thwart the long-visioned corporate action in recognizing and voluntarily discharging its high obligations as a constituent of our modern social structure.

From: John Desmond Glover

THE ATTACK ON BIG BUSINESS*

[EDITORS' NOTE: The author is Professor of Business Administration, Graduate School of Business Administration, Harvard University.]

. . . It is surprising and ironical, that, to judge by what businessmen often *say*, one would think that they, too, agree that the nature of business corporations is exactly and precisely what critics say it is; namely, that the corporation has no other purpose, and recognizes no other criterion of decision except profits, and that it pursues these profits just as single-mindedly and irresponsibly as it can.

*   *   *   *   *

For one thing, it is probable that some objectives of corporate policy and some of the considerations which actually enter decisions are so much *taken for granted* that, in all its dealing with suppliers, customers, employees, and others, "the company" will endeavor to be generous, honest, sincere, and responsible. Yet it sometimes seems difficult for people to talk about things like this—to concede, for instance, that one of the major objectives of the company *is* to be a *good* company. Perhaps it is because that is entirely taken for granted. Perhaps it is because, in our culture, people are sometimes "ashamed" or embarrassed to talk of such things. . . .

Another factor which may account for the curiously narrow concept of the purposes and values of the large corporation that often seems to come through to the public may be that business enterprise has, as yet, no systematic rationalization that takes into account these other "taken-for-granted" factors. The only systematic rationalization we have is that which stemmed out of a materialistic, mechanistic philosophy. Possibly, these ideas have buried themselves so deeply in our thinking that many people, when they come to rationalize about business, have only these traditional concepts with which to think and to talk about it. . . .

. . . [I]t is probable that these two considerations account for the fact that in their talk and in their rationalizations, businessmen sometimes do *sound* just like the stereotype cast up for them by the critics. Some businessmen seem emotionally as well as intellectually unable to admit that they do govern their actions by something more than economic expediency and that they are, in fact, at least no less responsible and less good citizens than others in the community. . . .

. . . For many purposes of the law, the business corporation is conceived to be the very same bloodless, heartless, opportunistic, selfishly calculating entity depicted by its critics. . . .

This stark concept of the corporation shows up nowhere more clearly than in decisions in suits concerning the power of corporations to make contributions and in decisions as to what are "ordinary and necessary" business expenses.

---

* Reprinted by permission of the Graduate School of Business Administration, Harvard University, Division of Research, Cambridge, Massachusetts, 1954 (pp. 328, 330–35).

A leading case in this field is the English case of *Hutton* v. *West Cork Railway Company*. In this case, a company *in liquidation* had voluntarily made additional severance payments to employees who were being discharged and who had been paid their regular wages in full. In the stockholders' suit over this matter, the judge accepted the argument that the stockholders of the company could receive no benefit in return from these additional payments. That is, they could receive no pecuniary return. He therefore ruled that the directors exceeded their powers in making such terminal payments.

Revealing the concept of the corporation as a chilled entity quite unresponsive to feelings of warmth, obligation, or responsibility, the judge held that the directors exceeded their powers in making these payments, because they were not *businesslike*, but *charitable*. He laid down the rule that, "Charity has no business to sit at boards of directors *qua* charity."

*   *   *   *   *

The judge, if he had had a different concept of business and of the corporation, might have viewed these payments simply as a warm act flowing from a feeling of obligation—the kind of act that people individually and in corporate bodies engage in every day in the normal carrying on of business. Had he had such a concept, the judge might well have held that making such payments was well "within the ordinary scope of the company's business." He did accept the idea, however, that since there was no pecuniary return to the stockholders, the act was not an act of *business*, but—and the categorical contrast is a deeply invidious one—an act of "charity."

*   *   *   *   *

. . . [A] seemingly charitable act can be justified if it can be shown that it was *really* motivated only by the ulterior intent of furthering the corporation's own interest in a calculated way. For that *is* in accord with the assumed nature of the corporation, which is to direct all its actions to furthering its own interests.

*   *   *   *   *

In other words, the test of an act, as to whether it is the sort of thing a corporation might ordinarily and necessarily do in carrying on its business, is whether the motivation is *purely mercenary*.

In the inverted morality of corporations—as laid down for them by the law—any act in which there enters a thought of charity or philanthropy, or any imponderable feelings of business responsibility and obligation, is not the kind of thing corporations can be expected ordinarily to do. The reason, of course, is that the corporation is conceived to be single-purposed and irresponsible. The norm of corporate behavior is what such an entity as this might do—not what a normal group of people might do.

This concept of the business corporation in law, and the rule which flows from it, results in corporation lawyers cooking up, for formal resolutions to be adopted by boards of directors, the most far-fetched kinds of reasons to rationalize as calculating acts for gain what were simply normal acts of people trying to exercise ordinary judgment. In fact, the rule *drives* lawyers to insist upon the invention of elaborate ulterior reasons for decisions which are actually made on the basis of ordinary, common-sense judgments. Corporations are compelled, for the record, to malign their own motives.

From: John Maurice Clark
*ALTERNATIVE TO SERFDOM**

[EDITORS' NOTE: J. M. Clark is former Professor of Economics in Columbia University. This articulate spokesman of the free enterprise system sounds a clarion of warning to self-interest—"the price of freedom is its responsible exercise." He scores exclusive reliance on the market mechanism to equitably maintain the balance within our social system. Mutuality of interest demands a new dimension of intelligent interaction.]

So, if this series of talks has a single keynote, it is the principle that the price of freedom is its responsible exercise. This has always been true; irresponsible self-interest would have wrecked our system long ago if it had been pushed to the utmost limits that some theories contemplated. But today the need is vastly greater and more immediate. New and greater private powers call for new and greater responsibilities, and the disaster that waits on failure is more immediate and more complete.

The responsibility in question works in two directions. Whenever man acts as an individual, he is responsible to his group or his community; and when he acts on behalf of his group, he is responsible to the members of the group he represents; and on behalf of the group he is responsible to his community—to the whole society or to some larger constituent group of which the first group is a member. This two-way relationship extends from the smallest groups to the largest one of which we are accustomed to thinking—the nation. The nation is recognizing long-neglected responsibilities to its individual members, and in addition is wrestling with its responsibilities to the world community that is struggling to be born, and that must be born if the world is to go on living.

Groups are numerous and varied, and every individual is a member of many. Our job of social salvation lies in reworking the relations of these groups and of the individuals within them. And there is much to be done. The democratic state has not found its place, nor how to do its job, in the new world. Instead of being the organ of a unified society, with its functions and powers arising rather naturally from the constitution of the society it represents, it is groping desperately, precisely because it has no organized society back of it in respect of most things—only when the country is attacked overtly, by force of arms and by a foreign power. More dangerous threats to our social constitution, from within, do not unify, but divide us.

Economically, we are not a community. The market has had such marvelous organizing powers that it has deluded many of us, for some hundred and seventy years, into thinking that it could do all that was needed to organize an economic community on a basis of consent as embodied in the act of free exchange. But it has been growingly evident for many years that this was expecting from it something beyond its powers, great as these were. We have gradually discovered—

though many have not admitted it—that markets can organize material interests only, and not all of these, and that this is not enough to constitute a society. Some of us learned this many years ago, from Charles H. Cooley; today the lesson is being driven home again, with freshly urgent emphasis, by Karl Polanyi. Things the market pseudo-society has wrecked are hopefully turned over to the state, a too vast and impersonal mechanism whose constitution does not correspond too well to the economic realities.

Between the individual and government, or markets, stand great organized groups; farm federations, business corporations, and labor unions. And these are the crux of the present dilemma. In a simple economy without such groups, irresponsible self-interest is—almost—a possible organizing principle in the strictly material realm. It would merely mean the exploitation of the weak by the strong, the incapable by the capable. But organize society into groups, and irresponsible self-interest can both corrupt the groups and shatter the society.

Why does a state need an organized community back of it, to the constitution of which its own constitution corresponds? Because otherwise the alternative is coercion or chaos. If the community is itself well knit, it can call on the state to do various things that the state can best do; but coercion will be needed only to keep recalcitrant minorities within bounds. But if within the society there is a "state of nature" that approximates a state of war, then the state either will fail to maintain tolerable order, or will do it at the cost of general and indiscriminate coercion, and either way personal liberty is lost.

And at present the economic groups into which we are organized are too near this condition, bringing the alternative of coercion or chaos too close for either comfort or safety. These groups are too large, to sophisticated, too consciously and rationally purposeful, to organize themselves into a community of the "natural" sort of which anthropologists tell us, as found, for example, in the South Sea Islands before white civilization submerged them. The organizing of these warring groups must be done by the most deliberate kind of action associated with the theory of the "social contract." In fact, we seem to be in a stage of human development to which some form of "social contract" theory may, for the first time, be applicable on the scale of a "great society." But not for the whole job of organizing a community. There must be an underlying feeling of a common bond, if only the danger of mutual annihilation, to furnish a basis for a willingness to recognize mutual rights and responsibilities. And so we come back to our central theme.

This calls for an adventure in reconstruction, for which no happy outcome can be guaranteed. The world is in the grip of a mighty struggle. On one side are forces driving toward chaos and anarchy, political, social, economic, and moral. On the other side are forces of centralized control. Between them stand the forces and men who are trying desperately to salvage a workable basis for a humane and ordered community, in which some effective degree of freedom and democracy may be kept alive, without wrecking society by their undisciplined exercise and disruptive excesses. There is no point in asking, in the Year of Atomic Energy II, for a world safe for freedom and democracy. Society is condemned to live dangerously—of that much we can be sure. Our fighting chance depends on developing the capacity for generous and constructive thinking and acting, beneath the sword of Damocles.

From: J. J. O'Connell

"SOCIAL OVERHEAD CAPITAL AND THE PRINCIPLE OF SUBSIDIARITY"*

Colleges and universities face a 100% increase in enrollment in the next decade. We are on the verge of tearing down the "distance curtain" with a satellite communications system to simultaneously unite all men with sight and sound. Expanded life expectancy and shorter work hours open vistas of the "good life" for millions and hold out vast leisure time markets if we can overcome the choking effects of megapolis and provide recreational and cultural facilities. Cancer, heart diseases, and the common cold have yet to be conquered by medical science.

In all these and in innumerable other areas our nation faces the challenges of growth and progress. Who foots the bill? Who should invest in these basic areas? Can we step back and get guides to policy by examining some conceptual schemes from economics and political philosophy?

Our title borrows one concept from economics and one from political philosophy. The first is descriptive (what is) of one part of our economic system. The second is prescriptive (what should be) about one phase of our political system. Neither system exists by itself, so we put the two concepts together to throw some light on policy-making in the politico-economic system.

Jargon need not prevent us from getting a handle on an illusive segment of economic reality and on a powerful conceptualization of political experience. We first examine these two ideas separately and then combine them to see if they help us understand better how our politico-economic system does (or should) work.

SOCIAL OVERHEAD CAPITAL

The concept of social overhead capital (hereafter abbreviated SOC) is used mostly by economists who deal with economic development. Broadly speaking, SOC is the substrate of assets and institutions necessary for growth and stability—the underpinnings of a country. The "assets" share the nature of fixed assets in that they are not consumed in use (in less than a year, by convention) nor does their form change in use (though they may depreciate)—a dam, for instance. The "institutions" are formalized and relatively permanent behavior patterns—the jury system, for example. Obviously, a nation's stock of SOC grows and changes in composition at different stages of development. The SOC of U.S.A.—1963 is vastly different from the SOC of U.S.A.—1776, and just as different from the SOC of present-day Haiti. It is not easy to define the concept so that it will include the stock of both the mature and the underdeveloped nations. We will build on the attempts at definition made by economists speaking in the context of emerging nations in order to clarify our notion of the stock of SOC of U.S.A.—1963.

---

* Copyright 1963. Jeremiah J. O'Connell. Unpublished manuscript.

One author[1] defines SOC "as comprising those basic services without which primary, secondary, and tertiary productive activities cannot function." While we find Hirshman's definition too confining, his list of distinguishing characteristics is more meaningful, especially when supplemented by W. W. Rostow's similar list.[2] Generally speaking, SOC includes those assets and institutions which (1) support a wide range of economic activities and (2) cannot be imported in the normal sense. The investments called for by such assets and institutions (3) tend to be sizable, indivisible, lump sums, and (4) the payoff period is usually very long. (5) The capital-output ratio (dollars invested divided by dollars realized) is generally large, and (6) the returns more likely benefit the community at large directly than the investors. Pedantically rigid application of these criteria would serve no purpose. We find sufficient reason to include the following in the fund of SOC of the U.S.A.—1963: physical assets like harbors, airports, highways, railroads, dams, munitions and armaments, national forests, satellites, air raid sirens, gas transmission lines, reservoirs, etc.; assets representing institutions (figuratively, the part for the whole) like police revolvers, postal trucks, judges' gavels, legislators' benches, blackboards, etc.; intangible assets like (a) the accumulated knowledge and skill of doctors, managers, scientists, lathe operators, generals, teachers, composers, judges, etc., (b) the physical and mental health of the population, (c) the mobility, and (d) even the sense of security and wellbeing of the citizenry. Are these not the underpinnings of our growing and stable country?

Our listing prompts three observations. First, not all SOC is government owned nor the product of government investment alone. Second, some items of SOC seem difficult to express in our customary dollar terms. However, reduction to dollar valuation may not be impossible if we follow the logic of the corporation and value the asset in terms of the money outlay necessary to secure it. Note that some costs will have to be opportunity costs (the foregone earnings of a doctor during medical school, for instance). Note, too, that there is danger of double counting in valuing something like a fund of knowledge of an individual and in registering the cost of a school building. Such quantification is hazardous and far from perfection.

Third, the quantification of returns generated by SOC raises even more difficulties than the quantification of the costs of such assets. Each case has its peculiar difficulties, so a general treatment here is impossible. We can give an example, though, which indicates economists are making progress in this complex area. Men like Professors Gary S. Becker and Jacob Mincer of Columbia University have been working on projects to figure the rate of return on educational investments. In one study Professor Mincer determined a 12.7% return on the total cost of medical specialization by measuring the returns in dollar income differentials of specialists and general practitioners.[3] Of course, such estimates do not include any quantification of what the incremental education did for the man himself or of what societal satisfactions were derived from the extra education. These attempts may be crude but it is hard to deny that they are steps in the right direction.

Our final point about SOC concerns the investors in such assets. A considera-

---

[1] Hirshman, Albert O., *The Strategy of Economic Development*, New Haven: The University Press, 1958, p. 83.

[2] Rostow, W. W., *The Stages of Economic Growth*, Cambridge: The University Press, 1961, pp. 24–25.

[3] Mincer, Jacob, "On-the-Job Training: Costs, Returns, and Some Implications," *Journal of Political Economy*, Oct., 1962, p. 65. (This entire *Journal* Supplement is pertinent to our subject.)

tion of the examples we have cited will reveal that, while government is the largest investor, groups and individuals too invest in SOC. The policy question of prime importance is: who *should* invest in SOC? Approaches to an answer must wait until we discuss the principle of subsidiarity.

PRINCIPLE OF SUBSIDIARITY

Stated simply, the principle of subsidiarity prescribes that in any system each function be performed by the lowest competent and willing level in the system's hierarchy. In speaking of the structure of the state, political philosophers reason that a higher level does not exist to swallow up or supersede the lower level but to supplement and extend it. Such reasoning is based on a view of man with rights pre-existing the state. Man as a person transcends the state, yet the individual needs the state. Living in an organized society is natural to man. Such a concept of man and the state dictates that the relationship of the parts, or the building blocks, of society be viewed as an organic unity. The individual, the family, voluntary organizations, and the state form a hierarchical arrangement that is organic—in the moral sense. That is, a necessary mutuality of purpose binds the building blocks together without causing the parts to lose independent identity as cells do in a biological entity. On the other side, the organic unity avoids the trap of the atomistic view of society which exaggerates the independence of the parts so that all that remains is a mere juxtaposition of self-serving units.[4]

Given the organic unity in society, the ends of society are best achieved when the individuals, the families, voluntary organizations, and the state severally contribute a pyramid of efforts toward the common good. The principle of subsidiarity offers a guide to order these contributions so that the system as a whole maintains its balanced existence. To repeat: in any system each function should be performed by the lowest competent and willing level in the system's hierarchy.

We have sketched elliptically how the principle is deductively derived—reasoning from premise to conclusion. History shouts empirical verification in every era. Economic statism is lampooned in Adam Smith's diatribe against 18th century mercantilism. Hitler Germany provides dramatic evidence of a system's deterioration because of state usurpation of virtually all societal functions. Witness the parody of proper order in company unions and industrial paternalism. Agricultural difficulties in China are commentary enough on a communal system which does violence to the family. We should not forget either that the lower level can usurp a higher level's function, as when churches over-stepped their competence and entered the political sphere.

WHO SHOULD INVEST IN SOCIAL OVERHEAD CAPITAL?

Because of the nature of SOC (described best by the six characteristics listed above) we tend to start and end with the question: who *can* invest in SOC? We reduce the issue to a financial question, jerk a thumb skyward, and say: "Let George do it!" By juxtaposing SOC with the principle of subsidiarity, the burden of our message is that a concern for the perversion of societal order should be added to the financial criteria in feasibility studies on SOC projects. A prior consideration of who *should* invest in SOC will hopefully affect the decision about who *can* invest in SOC by adding some cogency to the development of creative approaches by subgovernmental units.

---

4 Fagothey, Austin, *Right and Reason,* St. Louis: C. V. Mosby, 1959, pp. 379-95.

A social critic inclined to sounding jeremiads might prophesy that units of society, whose functions are passed to the next higher level by default, will atrophy so that they no longer can do what they once could do, should have done, but did not do.

From: Courtney C. Brown and E. Everett Smith (eds.)
*THE DIRECTOR LOOKS AT HIS JOB**

[EDITORS' NOTE: Courtney C. Brown is Dean of the Graduate School of Business, Columbia University. E. Everett Smith is Director, McKinsey and Company. The material in this abstract is drawn from a symposium in which the participants were directors of leading American corporations.]

A director may be either "inside," in the sense of having come up through the company and of being identified with its management, or "outside," in the sense of a person who has been unconnected with the business and has no operating familiarity with it. Directors may also be part-time or full-time, depending on whether they devote the whole of their attention to their director's job or only some portion of their time.

* * * * *

The Inside Full-Time Director. Such a person is exemplified in the board of Standard Oil Company (New Jersey) and by the executive committee of the du Pont board. In these and other such cases men who have spent years in the service of the company, having occupied responsible operating positions, have been made directors. But, in contrast to the inside part-time director, they have been released from all operating responsibilities. . . .

* * * * *

—The board in a sense is legally conceived, isn't it, to protect the stockholders' interest? It is a representative of the stockholder, if you will.
—Yes.
—There's the implication there that there might be a difference between the interest of the management and that of the stockholder, and the board is there to see that it's properly cared for. The implication of the inside board . . . is that there is no distinction between the interest of the management and that of the stockholder.
—I don't follow your conclusion that there is no difference in interest; obviously there is an adverse interest any way you look at it—by adverse I don't mean hostile interest.
—No.
—The more management takes for itself the less there is available for stockholders. So there is that basic conflict of interest.

* * * * *

---

* Reproduced by permission of Columbia University Press, New York, 1957 (pp. 38–39, 77–78, 81–83, 85–86, 89, 91–93).

—Is the inside full-time board as likely to be as perceptive to the political requirements of a corporation as some of the outside people might?

*   *   *   *   *

—. . . [T]he reason we have outside auditors is because even honest and capable accounting executives recognize the need for an independent check on their judgment; and isn't there a need for some kind of external check, and isn't it likely to be welcomed even by capable people?
  —Well, are you going to get that through an outside part-time director?
  —As one possibility, not the only one.
  —I think that you'd get it a lot better through education of full-time directors.

*   *   *   *   *

—As between the strong board, which is a full-time payroll board concerned only with this company, and the board of the kind I described for our company, we prefer the latter on the premise of the danger of getting ingrown—it seems to us to be too real the other way, the danger of overcentralizing too great the other way. Men who have come to a full-time board position through talent and ability as strong executives inside the company carry that symbolism in front of the people in the organization into their new full-time directorate job; they are executives inside the company. We do not think that brings the independence on their part, or the capacity for taking an objective view on their part, or the relationship with the people still in the executive and operating setup, on the other hand, that you can and should get.

*   *   *   *   *

—. . . I don't think there's the slightest doubt in my mind that a great many shareholders have a feeling of satisfaction when they see the names of some very prominent people on their board of directors. I have a feeling also that they place a great deal more confidence in the contribution the big name people make to the company than is justified. But they certainly have a feeling of satisfaction about it; they would like to see, oh, President Eisenhower on the board. It just makes them feel good to have those kinds of people.
  —I think the general run of stockholders rather favor outside part-time boards of directors. Not only because they're used to it but I think they're more comfortable about the operation of the company. . . .

*   *   *   *   *

-. . . Let's assume that there is a gradual diminution in the share of the market which a company is getting, or a part of a company. It goes on for let's say five years. Now how do you, with an internal board, a full-time board, measure that decline in participation of market, and how quickly can an inside board do something about it, rather than an outside board?
  —I think I can answer that with a great deal of assurance. I think that our board would be much more sensitive to the development of that kind of a situation than the outside or part-time director would be. I'm positive of that, because we look at the thing all the time, we live with it all the time.
  I'm also sure that we would be able to evaluate the basic factors, the reasons that are behind that decline, much more quickly and much more readily than part-time directors would, and institute some kind of action, if action is indicated, much more readily than a person who is not close to the business.

*   *   *   *   *

—. . . I think one of the things that might be argued in favor of getting, in this case, outside directors into the picture, rather than those that are being brought up through the ranks of the company, is the fact that you will put on the board a completely new viewpoint, because they haven't got a heritage or any background of tradition or preceptorship that has been drilled into them through many years of association with the organization.

So I think that is one of the arguments for at least a leavening of that type of addition to a full-time board.

* * * * *

In summary, the philosophy behind the advocacy of the full-time director is that the meaningful discharge of a director's responsibilities requires a more extensive knowledge of corporate operations than can be acquired through part-time contact. Especially in the large corporation, some of the panel felt, directing is a full-time job, requiring substantial work on the part of individual directors between board meetings, to understand the full range of the business' affairs. Moreover, if the one overriding function of the board is to select the management and to continue to evaluate it, this requires a more continuous contact with management than is possible through even monthly board meetings. Appraisal of management must include more than simple inspection of results as they appear in certain operating statements, if costly mistakes are to be avoided.

The responsibility of the board is a group responsibility, and it is difficult to make this operationally meaningful when the members of the board assemble only briefly and at intervals. Moreover, the danger of a board's becoming ingrown through too much reliance on home-grown talent is reduced when its members can be released from all operational responsibilities, even if they come from the inside (that is, have been brought up through the ranks). Finally, the fear that inside board members will subordinate independent judgment to the will of the chief executive is partly removed since any who have come up through the ranks shed their administrative or executive functions upon assuming the directorial function. Their job specifications change in a more complete and thorough way than is possible when they continue to serve dual functions.

There are, however, serious practical problems in the full-time arrangement. The questions of cost and availability of personnel were raised. . . .

. . . The inside-outside blueprint had evoked a favorable response because it emphasized the independent character of the board and appeared to sharpen the distinction between the functions of the board and those of management. At the same time, the conception of a full-time board had the attractive quality of providing a knowledgeable group in whose judgment management might have greater confidence, on whom it might rely to a greater extent because of its familiarity with the firm's operations, even though the actual organizational arrangements might tend to blur somewhat the lines dividing directorial from management functions.

KING SCALE COMPANY

I Case Introduction

Synopsis

The management of King Scale Company must select its pricing strategy for the coming year. Particular attention must be given to the pricing of its Model 190B, a specialty scale which has enjoyed top-market acceptance for nearly thirty years. The pricing decision is complicated by the fact that Ohio Scale Company is aggressively challenging the 190B's market dominance, now that King Scale's patents have expired. Traditionally, Ohio has waited until King published new list prices before pegging its own price, usually $10 below King's. King Scale's management is uncertain whether this pattern will continue.

A second uncertainty complicates this year's pricing decision. King Scale management has to consider the effect of a threatened strike on its manufacturing costs. King's marketing manager proposes to "get around" the uncertainties by using mathematical decision-making techniques to arrive at the best pricing decision. Other members of the pricing committee express skepticism over these techniques because of unrealistic built-in assumptions and/or the omission of relevant factors.

Why This Case Is Included

This case gives ample opportunity to see how economic theory informs policy decisions. Projected cash needs are related to pricing decisions through cash flow analysis. Relevant concepts can be drawn from what economists have generalized about the impact of price changes on consumer demand, about the competitive maneuvers of oligopolists, and about the relationships between unit costs and volume of output. There is cause, also, to inquire into the place of patents in competitive strategies and product management.

In this case management struggles with the advantages and disadvantages of quantification in decision making and with the applicability of specific decision-making rules to their pricing problem. Some voices are raised in favor of science; others in favor of "judgment."

Finally, there is opportunity to use the psychology of perception to come to grips with the differing points of view of the members of the management team. The very presence of disagreement raises the issue of the role of conflict in the quest for truth or for workable solutions to managerial problems.

Diagnostic and Predictive Questions

In answering the following diagnostic and predictive questions, remember that these questions apply theories and conceptual ideas from certain disciplines. Such theories are valuable to understand basic forces at work in the policy system (diagnosis) and to predict what will happen in the system in the future (prediction). Since each reading abstracts from the total policy system certain factors or variables into the closed or partial viewpoint of one theory or discipline, no one reading gives answers to the practical policy problems of the case. In diagnosis and prediction, the parts of the problem are studied with "other things being equal."

Following each question are listed readings which will be helpful in answering the question. The readings included with this case are marked (*). By referring to the author index at the end of this book, you may locate the other readings listed.

1. In the economic and financial sense, why is the King Scale management so concerned about this year's price and the union demand for a cafeteria? Relate the sales revenue (volume × price) to the possible $150,000 outlay for the cafeteria and to the possible increased manufacturing costs due to a strike. Note the interdependence of the sources and uses of funds.

   Read: *Anthony, *Management Accounting*, pp. 290–92, 306.

2. What are the assumptions about customer behavior built into the sales volume forecast in Exhibit 1 of the case? Do you think the assumptions fit this situation?

   Read: *Davis, *Marketing Management*, pp. 214–16.

3. Does the economic theory of oligopolistic competition help predict what pricing policy Ohio will follow? How do the prospects of higher costs for manufacturing at King Scale affect the predictions under oligopoly theory?

   Read: Dean, *Managerial Economics*, pp. 329–35. Spencer and Siegelman, *Managerial Economics: Decision Making and Forward Planning*, pp. 242–48, 202–12.

4. Why is Ohio Scale now able to compete aggressively against King Scale? Can King Scale's management draw any lessons concerning product management from the competitive experience with 190B?

   Read: *Clark, *Competition as a Dynamic Process*, pp. 203–8.

5. Now that King Scale's patents on 190B have expired, the management is stressing pricing in its competitive strategy. Drawing on the economic theory of competition and on concepts in marketing management, can you see any other competitive technique King Scale might consider?

   Read: *Harriss, *The American Economy*, pp. 400–3.
            (Additional reading, not in this volume: Kenneth R. Davis, *Marketing Management* [New York: Ronald Press, 1961])

6. In what way does microeconomic analysis explain why Carson, the vice president of manufacturing, estimates different costs for different volumes of production?

   Read: Spencer and Siegelman, *Managerial Economics: Decision Making and Forward Planning*, pp. 242–48, 202–12.

7. Do you consider Carson's complaint that the payoff matrix omitted some of the relevant costs is a valid objection to the use of Spector's decision-making techniques?

   Read: *Lindblom, "The Science of 'Muddling Through'." *Miller and Starr, *Executive Decisions and Operations Research*, pp. 38–42, 45–

47, 50. Rapoport and Drews, "Mathematical Approach to Long-Range Planning."

8. Has Jerry Spector, the marketing manager, offered a useful way of dealing with the uncertainties of the pricing decision? Discuss the applicability of each approach ([a] four techniques for dealing with uncertainty, [b] the introduction of subjective probabilities to change the decision from one under uncertainty to one under risk, [c] a game theory technique to cope with a conflict situation) for this specific decision.

Read: *O'Connell, "Decision Making Rules and Computational Techniques."

9. Why did Spector seem so set on using scientific procedures despite Robinson's comment that King Scale might come up with a better pricing decision, "if we just played it by hunch and by feel"?

Read: Bross, Design for Decision, pp. 29, 38–41, 85–87, 92–94, 102–106, 108–109, 128–29, 255–57. Lieber and Lieber, The Education of T. C. Mits, pp. 44–49. Barber, Science and the Social Order, pp. 7–8, 12–13, 18, 21.

10. Does Robinson make a reasonable point when he asks: "Won't we be better off tackling these issues one at a time as they arise?" Must the pricing problem and the strike threat be part of the same decision?

Read: *Barnard, The Functions of the Executive, pp. 193–94.

11. Obviously the executives in this case see things quite differently, although each is exposed to the same facts and forecasts. Can you explain this phenomenon? Do you think their disagreements are good or bad for the organization?

Read: Leavitt, Managerial Psychology, pp. 27–33. Boulding, The Image, pp. 11–14. Follett, "Constructive Conflict."

Policy Questions for This Specific Case

In answering the following policy questions, the results of diagnosis and prediction are used to reduce the amount of guesswork, or judgment, in designing action solutions. However, since certain parts of the total case situation cannot be reduced to science, and since "other things are not equal," judgment must still be used to fill in the factors not accounted for by readings. You will also need a second kind of judgment as you put value weights on different scientific predictions, since different theories may point to conflicting solutions.

12. (a) Assuming complete uncertainty of the probabilities of Ohio's pricing reactions and the union's decision on a strike, determine the best price for the 190B under the four rules for decisions under uncertainty. (See the O'Connell reading cited in Question 8.) Assign your own coefficient of optimism for King's management.

(b) Based on the views expressed by King's management, assign what you feel are the most reasonable subjective probabilities to the projected outcomes and find the best price, using the rule for decision under risk.

(c) Can you determine a best price, using the rule for decisions under conflict?

(d) What would be the maximum amount that Phillips could offer in the way of cafeteria facilities to the union to insure King against a strike?

13. Taking into account the various reservations expressed by members of management (see Questions 7 and 8), would you use the mathematical decision-making techniques? If yes, which one? Why? If no, why not? What other approach would you use?

14. Would you treat the pricing and the union questions as a compound decision problem or would you rather face the issues in sequence as they arise? Why? (See Question 10.)

15. Would you favor nonprice competitive strategies? Which one(s)? Why?

16. Outline your recommendations to Robinson on the following:
   a) The price of 190B for 1964.
   b) A program of product management and a marketing program for 190B.
   c) A guide to Phillips in negotiating the labor contract renewal.

Major Policy Issues: Tentative Generalizations about Any Policy System

In arriving at conclusions for the following questions, generalize from the facts in the case and use your own ideas to (a) confirm, (b) modify, or (c) test the workability of the concepts and theories from readings. As an executive or professional, use wisdom to merge theory, on the one hand, with "brute facts" and practice, on the other.

17. What role does the union play in the pricing of King Scale's products? If we start back with the classical economists of Ricardo's day and move forward to the time of King Scale's pricing decision, we can see how the pricing policy system has expanded. Based on Say's law assumptions, the early emphasis was on the costs of producing a single product—the supply side. Then, multiple product firms required a consideration of the balance of production costs—still the supply side. Somewhat later, demand came to be seen as a codeterminant (with supply) of product prices. The concepts of imperfect competition and duopoly introduced competitive suppliers into the system. Government—hardly ever fully outside the system—became entrenched with the advent of antitrust legislation. Must the union now be included in the system? Should the union have an active place in the pricing policy system?

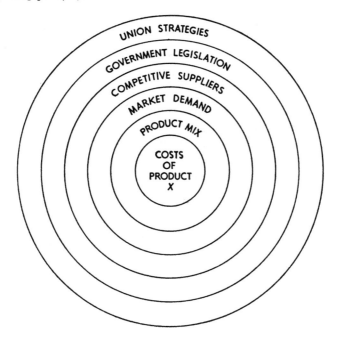

(See the following reading, not in this volume: Thomas L. Berg, "Union Inroads in Marketing Decisions," *Harvard Business Review*, July–August 1962, pp. 67–73.)

18. What is the impact of patent protection on competition, on price, and on technological change? In answering this question assume the role of King Scale management, Ohio Scale management, the purchasers of industrial scales, and J. Q. Public. (See Questions 4 and 5 and the attached readings.)

(Additional reading, not in this volume: Walton Hamilton, *The Politics of Industry* [New York: Alfred A. Knopf, Inc., 1957], pp. 68–92.)

Questions for Original Student Work in Analysis and Policy

The methods of viewing this case as represented by the authors' questions and selection of readings are not exhaustive. There are other relevant ideas for diagnosis and prediction. Furthermore, there are other ways of stating policy questions. More powerful analyses and wiser solutions will result by drawing on your own training and experience for (a) relevant concepts and theories, and (b) creative ways of asking policy questions. The following questions are designed to help you acquire this skill.

19. While reflecting on case facts, what additional theories from prior education give you insights as to "what is going on" in King Scale Company? As to what might be predicted to happen in the future?

20. Other than the policy questions asked by the authors, what pragmatic ways can you think of to state the practical problems faced by executives in the case?

II King Scale Company*

The Company and Its Product

The King Scale Company, Inc., is one of the leading and best-known producers of industrial scales and related products. Its home office and largest plant are located on the outskirts of Chicago. It also has plants in Camden, New Jersey, and Belvedere, Ohio. The Belvedere plant, the smallest of the three, concentrates its entire capacity on the production of a special-purpose scale—the King Model 190B.

The 190B was originally developed by King's own engineers, and all its distinctive features were tightly protected by patents. During the life of the patents several near-imitations of the 190B were placed on the market by a number of competitors. None of these was successful in duplicating all of King's features, and consequently none gained the market acceptance enjoyed by the 190B. As Ben Robinson, King's presi-

---

* Copyright 1964 by the Graduate School of Business, Columbia University.

dent, put it, "Our 190B was always known as *the* scale, the 'standard' in the industry. We've been fortunate in holding this position for so many years that our customers have been thoroughly educated to regard the 190B as the Cadillac of scales."

Some four years ago the protective patents on the 190B ran out, and a number of competitors started adopting its special features. One competitor in particular, the Ohio Scale Company, introduced a model almost identical to King's 190B and has been competing aggressively for its share of the market for the past four years. Ohio's model has also undergone a number of improvements during this period to the point where King's engineers believe that its current scale is fully comparable to the 190B.

Competitive Pricing Practices

Pricing of the King line is done by a pricing committee, consisting of King's president, as chairman, the vice presidents of sales and manufacturing, and the marketing manager. Traditionally, the price list is announced in early January, and barring any major changes in product and /or competition, these prices remain in effect for a year. Most of King's specialty competitors, including Ohio Scale, have in the past waited for King to publish its price list before announcing their own price schedules. Mr. Robinson placed great value on the prestige of being the price leader. "It's part of our leader image, and enforces our customers' belief in the superiority of our specialty products. I'd hate to have our customers see us waiting for Ohio to announce its prices in response to theirs. In a model like the 190B this would be equivalent to telling our customers that we consider Ohio's scale a comparable product and a potential threat. This is something we've got to avoid at all cost."

In 1963 King's price for the 190B was $210, while Ohio's competitive model was priced at $200. This was typical of the pricing pattern in the past four years when Ohio—apparently feeling that it still had King's reputation to overcome—had always set its price at $10 to $15 below the 190B. Henry Pierce, vice president–sales, is not at all certain as to what Ohio's price strategy may be for 1964. While Ohio might continue to price $10 below the 190B, they might also decide that this was the year to take the bull by the horns and match King's price for the first time. He personally feels such a move would be premature and, hence, not too likely. He is certain that Ohio would not even consider setting a price *higher* than the 190B, but does consider the possibility of Ohio's widening the price gap by setting its price more than $10 below King's. He reasons that Ohio may wish to demonstrate the comparability of its scale to the 190B by greater market penetration in the coming year. This, he believes, would be more likely if King should decide to raise its price for the 190B thus increasing the margin between revenue and cost.

Sales Forecasts for 1964

Based on Pierce's projections, reports from salesmen in the field, and King's 1962 cost data, the pricing committee is considering pricing the 190B at either $200, $210, or $220. Jerry Spector, the marketing manager, has been assigned the task of forecasting 1964 sales volume at each of the above prices, taking into account the most likely prices Ohio is expected to set on its competitive model. His forecast is summarized in Exhibit 1.

Exhibit 1

1964 SALES FORECAST FOR KING MODEL 190B

King Price	Ohio Price	Forecast of 190B Sales Volume
$200	$190	5,000 units
200	200	7,000
210	190	2,000
210	200	5,000
210	210	6,000
220	200	2,000
220	210	4,000

Unit Costs for 1964

David Carsen, vice president–manufacturing, upon completing a survey of costs and capacities for the coming year, reported that at maximum capacity King could turn out 10,000 units of the 190B, and that an increase in average unit cost would result if production fell below 3,000 units. His total unit cost estimates for 1964 were:

$175 per unit, if production is 3,000–10,000 scales.
$200 per unit, if production is less than 3,000 scales.

At this point, however, the pricing committee's work was complicated by a new issue which could have an important effect on the 190B unit cost.

Harry Phillips, director of industrial relations, reported to the president that he could see the possibility of a strike being called at the Belvedere plant. Phillips is currently engaged in preliminary discussions with the union, preparing the ground work for formal contract renewal talks, scheduled for March 1964. One of the issues which Phillips believes will be pushed hard by the union will be the establishment of an employees' cafeteria at the Belvedere plant. The King plants in Camden and Chicago both have such cafeterias, and the union has rejected Phillips' argument that the Belvedere plant does not require the same facilities because public eating facilities are available within easy reach. The union was demanding a fully equipped cafeteria, which King's engineers estimate would involve an expenditure of roughly $150,000, and seemed quite cool to the suggestion that a less elaborate coffee shop would serve as well. Phillips explained that King would be expected to provide the cafeteria space and equipment, but would not be involved in any of its operating expenses. The arrangement would be similar to the other King plants where commercial caterers operated the cafeterias on a long-term lease, self-supporting basis.

"At this point," Phillips stated, "it's too early for me to guess how likely the union is to strike if we don't go for the cafeteria, or how much less than a full cafeteria setup they'd settle for. If they do go out on strike I'm convinced it'd be a relatively short one, although Dave tells me that even a short strike would increase our manufacturing costs significantly. That's why I thought you should be aware of the situation while you're fixing next year's 190B prices."

Carsen was asked for an estimate of total unit costs in the event of a short strike materializing in 1964. His best estimate was:

$205 per unit for an output of 3,000 to 9,000 scales.
$230 per unit for outputs below 3,000 scales.

With this added information, Spector prepared a summary of anticipated 1964 profits on the 190B under various combinations of King and Ohio prices, with or without a strike at the Belvedere plant. This data is presented in Exhibit 2.

Exhibit 2

1964 PROFIT FORECAST FOR KING MODEL 190B

	King Price	Ohio Price	King Cost	King Unit Profit	King* Volume (Units)	King Anticipated 1963 Profit
If No	$200	$190	$175	$25	5,000	$125,000
Strike	200	200	175	25	7,000	175,000
Occurs						
	210	190	200	10	2,000	20,000
	210	200	175	35	5,000	175,000
	210	210	175	35	6,000	210,000
	220	200	200	20	2,000	40,000
	220	210	175	45	4,000	180,000
If	$200	$190	$205	$−5	5,000	$−25,000
Strike	200	200	205	−5	7,000	−35,000
Occurs						
	210	190	230	−20	2,000	−40,000
	210	200	205	+5	5,000	25,000
	210	210	205	+5	6,000	30,000
	220	200	230	−10		−20,000
	220	210	205	+15		60,000

* From Exhibit 1.

Setting Up a Profit Matrix

Pierce observed that Exhibit 2 presented a rather terrifying range of profit potentials. "It's bad enough to have to outguess Ohio's price strategy, but when the lower half of your table comes up with a rash of red figures [negative values in last column of Exhibit 2] for the same price combinations, this thing really gets out of hand." Spector suggested that a clearer picture of the decision problem could be obtained by rearranging the profit data of Exhibit 2 in the form of a payoff matrix. He accordingly presented the pricing committee with the matrix shown in Exhibit 3.

Exhibit 3

ESTIMATED 1964 PROFITS UNDER VARYING CONDITIONS

King Price	If Strike Occurs and—			If Strike Does Not Occur and—		
	Ohio Price $190	Ohio Price $200	Ohio Price $210	Ohio Price $190	Ohio Price $200	Ohio Price $210
$200	$−25,000	$−35,000	....	$+125,000	$+175,000	....
210	−40,000	+25,000	$+30,000	+20,000	+175,000	$+210,000
220	....	−20,000	+60,000	....	+40,000	+180,000

"This matrix," Spector explained, "clearly sets up our problem. We can select any one of three prices for our 190B, and there are 18 possible combinations of external conditions which would determine what our 1964 profit—or payoff—would look like. Four of these 18 combinations we apparently consider so remote that we assign them a zero probability of occurrence; for example, the probability of Ohio pricing at $190 if we go for $220. In this form of presentation we can clearly see that if we price the 190B at $200 our profit could be as high as $175,000 or as low as a $35,000 loss. If we go for $210 the range would be +$210,000 to −$40,000, and so on."

In response to Robinson's question of whether there is some "scientific" way for selecting the best strategy, Spector replied: "As the matrix now stands, and if we assume that we have absolutely no knowledge of which external condition will prevail, there are several techniques for picking a price strategy which you could describe as scientific. Unfortunately, they'll probably give you different answers, since they depend on the criterion by which you define your 'best' strategy. There are some fancy names for the various techniques used such as Maximin, Regret, Laplace, and Coefficient of Optimism. As the last name implies, these criteria primarily reflect your inherent optimism or pessimism. This is assuming complete uncertainty about Ohio's pricing intents and the possibility of a strike. I personally feel that it's very rare for anybody to feel *that* uncertain about the future. Just listening to Henry describe Ohio's possible reaction to our prices, you can see that he thinks one type of response is more likely than another. Now if you can translate these feelings into probabilities, expressed as decimals [i.e., absolute certainty = a probability of 1.0; a fifty-fifty chance = a probability of .5], then we have a much more 'scientific' method for picking our best strategy. This method is based on calculating the 'expected value' of each strategy, and then selecting the one that shows the highest expected value. In this way we're, in effect, betting on the odds or playing the percentages."

Pierce commented that he might be able to assign probabilities to various Ohio responses, and that Phillips—if pushed hard enough—could probably guess at the probability of a strike. "But how do you figure the probabilities of any combination of the two happening together?" Spector responded that combined probabilities presented no problem. "You simply multiply the probability of one event happening by the probability of the other event happening and you get the probability of *both* events happening." After a minute's thought he added that this procedure assumes that the two events are independent. "This means that we're assuming that Ohio's pricing strategy will not depend on whether we have a strike or not, and conversely, that our union will strike or not strike regardless of Ohio's pricing strategy. Both these seem pretty reasonable to me. Ohio will come out with their price lists well before our contract expiration date, and I honestly doubt that our union would ever consider consulting Ohio's price lists before deciding whether to strike or not."

Robinson was not sure Spector's assumptions are quite so watertight as he would like to have them. "Ohio may announce its prices before March, but they know darned well that we're being pushed by the union, and you can bet your life they're busy figuring what a possible strike would do to us. By the same token there are some pretty sharp boys in the union office and they'll have a pretty good idea how Ohio's prices are going to affect our profits and how hard they can push us. That's one of the troubles with this scientific pricing business, we're not the only hot-shot mathematicians. If Ohio and the union both have their own Jerry Spectors, then we're playing poker with everybody else looking over our shoulder and seeing every card in our hand, and that's playing poker the hard way."

"If you're right, Ben," Pierce added, "then you could almost say that the union participates in our price-setting. Not just indirectly, in the old sense that labor costs have always had to be taken into consideration, but in a new and very direct sense. They could almost be sitting here with us deciding what our price strategy has got to be. Anything in the Taft-Hartley Act about that?"

"Well, I think you're a little far out," Spector responded, "but I do know that Harry [Phillips] asked me if I could give him some idea of how far he could go with a scaled-down cafeteria as a counter offer. In fact, based on the expected value calculations I described to you, we can very easily work out whether preventing the strike is worth the full $150,000 they're asking, or only $100,000 or maybe only $5,000. This is the kind of dollar-and-cents guidance to bargaining that you couldn't get without these mathematical procedures you're knocking."

At this point Carsen questioned the real value of this guide to bargaining. "Don't forget Ben's poker analogy, Jerry. If the union makes the same calculations you do, they're sitting there opposite you knowing exactly how much you're prepared to give. This immediately gives them a 'floor' below which they won't even listen to you. Kind of one-sided bargaining I'd say."

Spector started to explain that if the company believed that the union had full access to all the information available to management, then "game theory" techniques should be used in determining strategy. But Carsen continued with what he considered a more basic objection to the numerical presentations. "It seems to me that Jerry, by taking the two sets of cost figures I gave him, is implying that these figures can give us a dollar-and-cent-price tag to pin on a possible strike. I was just talking to George Stern [Belvedere plant manager] yesterday, and he thinks we should make every effort to avoid a strike down there. Aside from any direct increase in costs that we figured, he's very concerned about the morale and productivity of his people. He's spent years getting their co-operation and doesn't want to see it all shot by a single strike, even if it's only a short one. That's all part of the cost of a strike even if it doesn't show up in our accounting reports."

"I'm also concerned by the fact that with this complete fascination with Jerry's figures we haven't heard anything about other ways of beating Ohio's competition. You're a pretty hot salesman, Henry, and I'm sure you can push the 190B regardless of Ohio's price as compared to ours. You know I'm not an anti-mathematics crank. I keep my own slide rule pretty busy, but let's not get mesmerized by tables of figures that can be worked out to three-decimal places."

As the discussion continued, and expanded, Robinson observed, "I honestly don't know if we're better off with or without this mathematical stuff. Do you think, Jerry, that by formalizing and tabulating our problem, and trying to quantify probabilities, we're going to come up with a better pricing decision than if we just played it by hunch and by feel? Don't forget we've done pretty well with the 190B for over 20 years and we didn't know a thing about payoff matrixes. I'm not even sure we should be complicating our pricing problem by introducing the strike issue at this time. Won't we be better off tackling these issues one at a time as they arise?"

III Selected Readings

From: Robert N. Anthony
*MANAGEMENT ACCOUNTING**

[EDITORS' NOTE: The author is Professor of Business Administration, Graduate School of Business Administration, Harvard University.]

. . . As goods are purchased or manufactured, inventory is increased; as they are sold, inventory is decreased, accounts receivables are increased, and income is earned; as the receivables are collected, cash is increased; and the cycle is completed with the use of cash to pay off the payables created when purchases were made or costs incurred. Because this cycle occurs over and over again in the course of normal operations, current assets and current liabilities are often referred to collectively as *circulating capital.*

Part of the funds tied up in current assets is supplied by vendors (accounts payable) and other short-term creditors. The remainder, which is the difference between current assets and current liabilities, and which is called working capital, must come from other, more permanent sources. These other sources must also supply the funds that are tied up in the noncurrent assets. Funds supplied for these purposes are called *permanent capital.* Changes in the sources of permanent capital and the uses to which it is put are likely to be of more than ordinary interest both to management and to outsiders since they reflect the results of the important financial decisions that have significant long-run consequences. In order to focus on these changes, we shall not bother with the recurring movement of funds among the separate current asset and current liability accounts. The necessity for tracing these separate flows can be avoided by combining all these accounts into the single item, working capital.

Basic Relationships

A balance sheet shows the net effect of funds transactions from the beginning of the business to the balance sheet date. The equities side shows the sources from which funds have been obtained, and the assets side shows the way in which these funds have been used. The balance sheet in Illustration 12–1 shows that as of the end of 1957, long-term creditors have furnished $145,000 of capital, and stockholders have furnished $394,000. Of the latter, $211,000 represents their original contribution and $183,000 represents earnings that they have permitted the company to retain in the business. The total amount of funds provided is therefore $539,000, of which $125,000 is used for working capital and $414,000 is in fixed assets.

If all earnings were paid out in dividends and if replacements of fixed assets

---

* Reprinted by permission of Richard D. Irwin, Inc., Homewood, Illinois, 1960 (pp. 290–92, 306).

Illustration 12–1

CONDENSED BALANCE SHEET
DECEMBER 31, 1957

ASSETS		EQUITIES	
Working capital	$125,000	Long-term debt	$145,000
		Capital stock	211,000
Fixed assets	414,000	Retained earnings	183,000
Total Assets	$539,000	Total Equities	$539,000

exactly equaled the annual depreciation charge, the amounts shown on Illustration 12–1 could remain unchanged indefinitely. Despite the fact that there would be numerous changes in the several current asset and current liability accounts, these could offset one another so that the total working capital could remain constant. Under these circumstances, the business would not need additional financing. But of course the balance sheet items do change; additional funds are provided, and these are put to use.

Consider the possible ways in which the company could obtain additional funds. For example, if it wished to buy a new plant: it could borrow, thus increasing long-term debt; it could sell more stock, thus increasing the Capital Stock account; it could wait until operations had generated funds, which would show up as an increase in Retained Earnings; it could use available cash, thus decreasing working capital; or it could sell some of its existing fixed assets, thus decreasing Fixed Assets. It follows, therefore, that *sources of funds are indicated by increases in equities and decreases in assets.*

Looking at the other side of the coin, what uses could the company make of additional funds that it acquired? It could add new fixed assets, it could add to working capital, it could pay off existing debt, or it could pay dividends to the stockholders, which decreases Retained Earnings. From these possibilities, it follows that *uses of funds are indicated by increases in assets and decreases in equities.*

In accordance with the dual-aspect principle, total sources of funds must equal total uses of funds. The following relationships therefore exist:

1. SOURCES = USES
2. INCREASES IN EQUITIES + DECREASES IN ASSETS =
           INCREASES IN ASSETS + DECREASES IN EQUITIES

These same relationships can be explained in terms of debit and credit. Increases in equities and decreases in assets are both credits; increases in assets and decreases in equities are both debits. Thus, the above equation follows from the fact that changes in debits must equal changes in credits.

*   *   *   *   *

DIAGRAMMATIC REPRESENTATION OF CASH FLOW

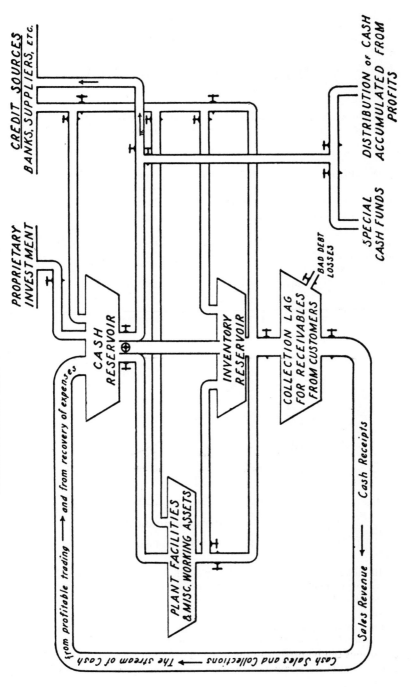

From: Kenneth R. Davis

MARKETING MANAGEMENT*

[EDITORS' NOTE: The author is Professor of Marketing at the Amos Tuck School of Business Administration, Dartmouth College.]

. . . Price is the most obvious determinant of demand for a product. Other things being equal (namely, the other three factors—prices of other products, incomes, and consumer preference), the higher the price of a product, the less will be sold. In economic analysis, a *demand schedule*, Table 5–1, is used to represent the amounts of a particular product that will be sold at different prices. But a graph or *demand curve*, Fig. 5–1, is usually used, for it aids in visualizing relationships.

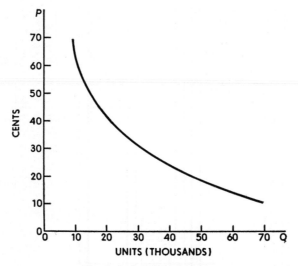

Fig. 5–1. A demand curve.

In describing demand schedules, economists make use of the term "price elasticity of demand." Thus, they refer to the demand for a product as being *elastic* if the total revenue increases as the price is cut. Conversely, the demand is considered *inelastic* if total revenue decreases with a price cut. If there is no change in the total revenue with a change in price, the situation is considered one of *unitary elasticity*. As can be seen from Table 5–1, any one of these three conditions can be present in the demand schedule for a product.

To facilitate the analysis of the price elasticity of a product, it is desirable

---

* From Kenneth R. Davis, *Marketing Management*. Copyright © 1961, The Ronald Press Company. (Excerpts from pp. 214–16.)

Table 5–1

A DEMAND SCHEDULE

Price (P)	Quantity Demanded (Q)	Revenue (R = P × Q)
$0.70	10,000	$ 7,000
0.60	11,000	6,600
0.50	13,200	6,600
0.40	20,000	8,000
0.30	30,000	9,000
0.20	50,000	10,000
0.10	70,000	7,000

to put the concept of price elasticity into some quantifiable terms. This is easily accomplished through the following formula:

$$\text{Price elasticity} = \frac{\text{Percentage change in the sales of a product}}{\text{Percentage change in price}}$$

An example of the application of this formula is illustrated below:

Example of Price Elasticity

Old Conditions
 Price of butter .... 60¢
 Quantity sold .... 1,000 lb.

New Conditions
 Price of butter is cut 6¢, or 10 per cent
 Quantity sold .... 1,200 lb.

Price Elasticity
$$E = \frac{20\%}{10\%} = 2$$

We should not let this simple example mislead us. The computation of the price elasticity of demand for a product is a very difficult task. You will recall that in order to develop the concept of price elasticity, it was necessary to assume that other things be kept constant. Unfortunately, this is not likely to be the case. Because of these complexities, however, it does not follow that we cannot use the concept of price elasticity, or that we cannot develop somewhat precise mathematical measures of price elasticity. . . .

One useful generalization that can be made in relation to the price elasticity of demand is that it usually is greater the longer the period that the price has prevailed. Immediately after a price reduction one might conclude, on the basis of the added volume, that demand was inelastic. But eventually sales may increase and the opposite conclusion can be drawn—demand is elastic. Why? We should recognize three possible explanations. First, the product may be a complement of some other products; and, if the latter are expensive and postponable purchases, the increases in volume will not come about until the consumer has bought these complementary products. A drop in the price of a complement such as electricity will not be reflected completely until some users of gas ranges convert to electric ranges. A second more pervasive factor leading to a higher long-run price elasticity is the lack of knowledge on the part of buyers. It takes time to publicize price reductions, especially when the product is one that is purchased infrequently. Finally, a third factor is the tendency for habit to discourage consumers from immediately taking advantage of a price reduction. Consumer inertia may be reflected in an unwillingness to go through the process of revising purchasing behavior. Usually such deterrents to price reductions are present only when the cut is small. But it is important to recognize that when we are talking about the price elasticity of demand for a product, we are thinking in terms of a relatively slight change from the prevailing price.

From: John Maurice Clark

COMPETITION AS A DYNAMIC PROCESS*

[EDITORS' NOTE: The author is former Professor of Economics in Columbia University.]

The most general conclusion is that from the standpoint both of enabling factors and inducements to innovation, the optimum condition calls for adjusting a variety of requirements. It may include some very large firms, whose volume of production permits large gains to be made; but other considerations require that they be surrounded by the largest number of competing firms that is compatible with these smaller firms being strong and large enough to command the necessary enabling resources for effective innovation.[1] This might include firms that concentrate in specialized sectors of the industry, provided market conditions are such that their limited coverage does not expose them to competitive tactics that would reduce them to the status of dependent satellites. In most industries this need not mean that the actively innovating firms must be very numerous: the essential thing is that they should set a pace that competitors are under defensive pressure to follow, because their competitive standing depends on their relative success in keeping up with, or close to, the advancing "state of the art" as led by the active innovators. The industry might include a number of firms that avoid the costs of initiatory pioneering and, by acting as ready followers, maintain a competitive position and help to keep the more active innovators on their mettle. But for the purpose in hand—competitive stimulus to innovation—the total number in any given market could be moderate: far smaller than the number called for by the atomistic competition of theory.

Lastly, as an inducement to innovation, comes the prospect of an interval of time during which the innovator can enjoy an advantage and recover his costs of pioneering before his advantage is dissipated. This dissipation may occur by imitation, by the development of equivalent alternatives, or by new innovations that render the first one obsolete. In either way, the generally available "state of the arts" approaches or catches up with the innovations and sets a new competitive level, the benefit of which is diffused over the economy. Then the first

---

* Copyright by The Brookings Institution, Washington, D.C., 1961, and reprinted by permission (pp. 203–8).

[1] Cf. Willard D. Arant, "Competition of the Few Among the Many," *Quarterly Journal of Economics* (August 1956), pp. 327–45.

innovator is challenged in turn to renew his advantage—if he can—as the only way to go on earning the liberal profits that successful innovation brings. This completes the cycle of "creative destruction" stressed by Schumpeter and continues the "race between innovation and imputation."

The principle involved has well-nigh universal application; but it takes a variety of forms, and the time interval within which the innovator can keep his advantage and reap his reward varies greatly, so also does the amount of uncertainty involved. The outcome varies according to the nature of the innovator's advantage, the methods he uses to realize his gains from it, the extent to which competitors are equipped with defensive preparedness to enable them to respond promptly and effectively, and the kinds of countermoves they employ. As to the durability of the advantage in process or product, it goes almost without saying that it is increased if protected by patent rights—almost but not quite, since patents involve disclosure, and this invites imitations or substitutes that attempt to stop short of legal infringement. . . .

As for the effect of competitors' research and preparedness, it is obvious in general that it must tend to shorten the time they would need to meet a rival's innovation. As to specific defensive responses they might make to his improvement, it may teach them something that they could put to use more promptly because of the "know-how" gained from their own research. Or it may put pressure on them to put into earlier use something on which they are working and which they would otherwise have subjected to more deliberate and thorough testing. If a competitor has a thoroughly tested improvement available, of a sort that may widen profit margins or increase sales volume, it is not often that he will hold it in reserve, waiting for someone else to make the first move. To do so habitually would stultify his research department. The chief circumstance in which something like this might be expected to happen would be if the improvement called for considerable capital, and especially if several firms were known to have similar improvements ready to introduce. . . .

. . . What may be called the "innovational interval" is threefold: the interval before the innovator's gains are felt by his competitors and put pressure on them, the interval before the competitor makes an effective response, and the interval before the response wipes out the competitive aftermath of the gains made by the first innovator during the first two intervals, when he held an advantage. One test of an adequate innovational interval might be whether an efficient and progressive firm can hope to make a fresh step ahead before the competitive advantage of the last one has been completely eroded, so that it may hope to go on earning something more than the minimum competitive return. The converse is that a laggard firm will cease to earn even this the minimum rate.

If major innovations are intermittent, there may be intervening periods in an industry in which imitation is followed by intervals of approximate equilibrium. But the more usual trend involves a fairly continuous series of minor innovations intervening between major ones. If a firm follows a major innovation with a series of minor improvements, this helps it to keep a step or two ahead of imitators, and so prolong its advantage. This raises obvious problems whether the diffusion of the benefits of the original innovation is being unduly delayed, and the spread between the best available and the generally available made unduly wide. Such problems play a large part in connection with patents.

GENERAL ROLE OF PATENTS

The patent system is a public policy, adopted to promote the interests the public has in invention and its utilization, in the setting of a system of primarily private business enterprise. It plays a major part in four distinguishable functions: the stimulation (and rewarding) of invention and its utilization, the selection of inventions for adoption and for receipt of rewards, the determination of the amount and character of rewards to individual inventors and to industrial developers, and the ultimate general diffusion of the resulting benefits. Needless to say, this final function is crucial. From one standpoint, the method followed may be regarded as a grant to the inventor of property rights in the thing he has created, with a recognition that in such cases the thing created is not only a physical object but—since it is unique and novel—the whole class of objects following this model. This means that in such cases property—the essence of which is rights to exclude others from one's property—implies monopoly. But since monopoly is an exception to the general property system, it does not carry, in this case, all the rights regularly attached to physical property "in fee simple." It is, in essence, property qualified by a public interest of a rather special sort, conditioned on the fulfillment of the four functions just mentioned.

. . . The possession of a patent—if it operates as it is supposed to do—means that during its term the rewards of the innovator are determined by the competitive superiority of his innovation to existing practice, not by such superiority, if any, as he may be able to maintain in a free-for-all scramble with imitators. This second level of competition is, in theory, deferred until the expiration of the patent, and this deferment increases the inducement of the innovator to incur the expenses and risks of development.

Actually, an innovation that has proved its value will normally give rise to near imitations or substitute devices, and will have to meet their competition, even if it is protected against literal infringements. The growing practice of licensing proved patents may reduce the incentive to this kind of counter-innovation. But in theory and intent, a patent formalizes the "innovational interval" at seventeen years, thus increasing the inducement to innovate and allowing the innovator to meet competition in two stages, the first confined to his competition with existing practice and the second a free-for-all. In this sense it involves the maximum reliance on competition consistent with allowing the rewards of innovation to be determined by its proved economic value. The many defects of the system in operation do not extinguish this basic feature, for which any radically different system would have to find a substitute of a less automatic sort.

If inventions were not patentable, would competition be increased? It is an interesting subject for speculation. It might make little difference in cases in which patents are already freely interchanged. In other cases it might mean that the inventor or his assignee could not get a return by charging royalties to competing users, but only from his own direct use of the innovation. This might increase the incentive to attempt to establish a monopoly. Also, as already suggested, the public disclosure required as a condition of a patent might be replaced by attempted secrecy, leading to considerable misdirected effort and doing no good to the morale of industry. It is far from clear that the abolishing of patents would increase effective competition.

From: C. Lowell Harriss
THE AMERICAN ECONOMY*

[EDITORS' NOTE: The author is Professor of Economics at Columbia University.]

Nonprice Competition

Both the ivory tower economist and the child begging its mother to buy the cereal with the box top needed for the supersonic magic code ring know that businesses compete in ways other than price. They devote effort to selling. They change the product; in a sense, they create different products, using that term broadly as the total "package" of goods and services offered the buyer. They can make prices different, in fact, although perhaps not in the nominal quotation. Rivalry of this sort seems to become increasingly important. It appears under both oligopoly and monopolistic competition.

More or Less Disguised Price Reductions. Most of us are familiar with discounts. Among businesses, small discounts for cash payments are common; and when competition increases, regular discounts are increased (uniformly or for special customers). Differences in credit terms and in charges for installment purchases, and financial aid of other forms, provide ways of adjusting the buyer's net cost a little. Closely related to discounts are variations in the allowance for "trade-ins." Manufacturers compete for dealers' favors by varying such things as the portion of the cost of local advertising assumed and charges for containers, thus altering the net charge. "Extras" of various types may be "thrown in"; a retailer may be given premiums, samples, or containers to distribute to his customers. The seller may provide demonstrators (the beautiful girl showing how to use the marvelous new cosmetic) or counter displays to save the retailer selling expense.

Some manufacturers will guarantee the retailer against loss from their price reductions or give generous allowance for return of merchandise. The services provided with the article can vary widely. Is the guarantee for three months or three years? Who pays for installation? What are the terms for reconditioning? Who pays for delivery?

Other adjustments include such things as entertainment, gifts to a special charity, splitting of commissions and fees, reversing the telephone bill, settling old debts on favored terms, letting a buyer out of an onerous contract, or sending more or a better quality than had been agreed upon. The variety of possible adjustment is huge. What suits one case will not apply in another—the seller of a new house who adds in some landscaping, the bank that prints the depositor's name on the checks, the store that accepts returns without question, the chain of gasoline stations whose rest rooms are always clean, and the apartment owner who gives a "concession" of a month's rent.

These "price" variations may work both ways, of course, sometimes to the

---

* Reprinted by permission of Richard D. Irwin, Inc., Homewood, Illinois, 1959 (pp. 400–403).

benefit of the buyer, sometimes the seller. During World War II, when prices were "fixed," businesses found many ways to adjust upward their effective charges.

Product Improvement. Product differentiation is at the base of monopolistic competition and may be important in oligopoly. The seller tries to distinguish his product from that of others. Having something that belongs to him alone, he can profitably spend effort on making it better. Rather than cutting price to sell more of the item in its present form, he may prepare to increase sales by improving the quality. He may, for example, feel certain that if he cuts his price, others will follow. But if he can develop an improvement, patent it, and get a head start in manufacturing and selling, he may benefit, for a time more or less securely. If he does not make such product innovations, he is likely to suffer as someone else gets ahead. One result is a powerful impetus to technological research. Outside of technical areas, there are also improvements. Life insurance companies develop new forms of policies. Banks improve their small loan services. Magazines try for more appealing articles and illustrations, colleges for better faculties.

Product improvement, incidentally, is a form of progress we could not expect from firms in a purely competitive market. They would probably be too small to finance many kinds of research and to develop new products. Moreover, they might have little incentive because they could not count upon exclusive use of the results. In agriculture, for example, the major research has been done not by farmers but by government agencies, notably agricultural colleges, and larger businesses such as seed companies and manufacturers of chemicals and machinery.

Product Variation. The seller may vary the product or service. He may give better or poorer service, depending on what he thinks buyers want. "Cash and carry" permits price reductions for those who will take the less expensive service. Changing the size of a 10-cent candy bar, or the years between redecorating an apartment, or the quality of a suit in a particular "price line" offers a form of competition—to get ahead of rivals, or to take advantage of the consumer. Enlarging or contracting the line of goods—for example, the number of choices offered by a restaurant—alters the firm's service. Sometimes the variations increase the net benefit to the public, even allowing for the extra costs that may be involved. Other product differences may do little more than use up skilled design talent, require scrapping of still good productive equipment, and add to the consumer's problem of choice, perhaps deceiving him and diverting his attention from features which he might consider more important. As products vary, comparison and learning from experience become more difficult; maintenance, especially getting replacement parts, tends to grow more costly.

Selling Effort. The firm whose product is different has a chance to try to create a demand. Selling effort may then pay. The firm uses resources to try to raise the demand schedule for its product. Yet such action, notably advertising expense, may be largely a gamble; so it is strategically different from the use of resources to lower production costs and thus get a definite, concrete saving. The gamble in using resources to help sell, results from the fact that both (1) consumer response and (2) the reaction of rivals are uncertain.

Perhaps rivals will meekly let one firm take away customers by advertising and other more aggressive selling. More likely other firms will follow suit, and selling expense then becomes like competitive armaments. Protection demands as much as the "enemy" has. The whole process has a self-defeating aspect. Yet as rivals boost advertising expense to keep from losing out to each other, they may increase the demand for the whole industry. Colgate may challenge Pepsodent, but together their efforts may make us spend more on toothpaste. Hotels explain their own individual merits while extolling the charms of their resort.

Selling takes many forms. Advertising itself uses many media—newspapers, magazines, billboards, radio, premiums, and direct mail. The firm may use more salesmen, or pay its present salesmen more. It may allow greater discounts to dealers, or provide them with selling aids such as one sees in profusion in a drugstore. . . . Packaging, delivery, or other selling services may be made more appealing. Staying open at night may add customers—husbands snared to "OK" buying of expensive items or lug home big grocery purchases. A larger parking lot or a playground appeals to some buyers. Free engineering service helps sell industrial equipment. Hotels finance conventions. Each industry has its own special devices for stimulating sales, and some of America's most fertile brains concentrate on adding to what is already a long list of ways to sell.

From: Charles E. Lindblom
*"THE SCIENCE OF 'MUDDLING THROUGH'"**

Suppose an administrator is given responsibility for formulating policy with respect to inflation. He might start by trying to list all related values in order of importance, e.g., full employment, reasonable business profit, protection of small savings, prevention of a stock market crash. Then all possible policy outcomes could be rated as more or less efficient in attaining a maximum of these values. This would of course require a prodigious inquiry into values held by members of society and an equally prodigious set of calculations on how much of each value is equal to how much of each other value. He could then proceed to outline all possible policy alternatives. In a third step, he would undertake systematic comparison of his multitude of alternatives to determine which attains the greatest amount of values.

In comparing policies, he would take advantage of any theory available that generalized about classes of policies. In considering inflation, for example, he would compare all policies in the light of the theory of prices. Since no alternatives are beyond his investigation, he would consider strict central control and the abolition of all prices and markets on the one hand and elimination of all public controls with reliance completely on the free market on the other, both in the light of whatever theoretical generalizations he could find on such hypothetical economies.

Finally, he would try to make the choice that would in fact maximize his values.

An alternative line of attack would be to set as his principal objective, either explicitly or without conscious thought, the relatively simple goal of keeping prices level. This objective might be compromised or complicated by only a few other goals, such as full employment. He would in fact disregard most other social values as beyond his present interest, and he would for the moment not even attempt to rank the few values that he regarded as immediately relevant.

* Reprinted by permission of *Public Administration Review*, Vol. XIX, No. 2 (Spring 1959), quarterly journal of the *American Society for Public Administration*, 6042 Kimbark Avenue, Chicago 37, Illinois.

Were he pressed, he would quickly admit that he was ignoring many related values and many possible important consequences of his policies.

As a second step, he would outline those relatively few policy alternatives that occurred to him. He would then compare them. In comparing his limited number of alternatives, most of them familiar from past controversies, he would not ordinarily find a body of theory precise enough to carry him through a comparison of their respective consequences. Instead he would rely heavily on the record of past experience with small policy steps to predict the consequences of similar steps extended into the future.

Moreover, he would find that the policy alternatives combined objectives or values in different ways. For example, one policy might offer price level stability at the cost of some risk of unemployment; another might offer less price stability but also less risk of unemployment. Hence, the next step in his approach—the final selection—would combine into one the choice among values and the choice among instruments for reaching values. It would not, as in the first method of policy-making, approximate a more mechanical process of choosing the means that best satisfied goals that were previously clarified and ranked. Because practitioners of the second approach expect to achieve their goals only partially, they would expect to repeat endlessly the sequence just described, as conditions and aspirations changed and as accuracy of prediction improved.

BY ROOT OR BY BRANCH

For complex problems, the first of these two approaches is of course impossible. Although such an approach can be described, it cannot be practiced except for relatively simple problems and even then only in a somewhat modified form. It assumes intellectual capacities and sources of information that men simply do not possess, and it is even more absurd as an approach to policy when the time and money that can be allocated to a policy problem is limited, as is always the case. . . .

Curiously, however, the literatures of decision-making, policy formulation, planning, and public administration formalize the first approach rather than the second, leaving public administrators who handle complex decisions in the position of practicing what few preach. For emphasis I run some risk of overstatement. True enough, the literature is well aware of limits on man's capacities and of the inevitability that policies will be approached in some such style as the second. But attempts to formalize rational policy formulation—to lay out explicitly the necessary steps in the process—usually describe the first approach and not the second.[1]

The common tendency to describe policy formulation even for complex problems as though it followed the first approach has been strengthened by the attention given to, and successes enjoyed by, operations research, statistical decision theory, and systems analysis. The hallmarks of these procedures, typical of the first approach, are clarity of objective, explicitness of evaluation, a high degree of comprehensiveness of overview, and, wherever possible, quantification of values for mathematical analysis. But these advanced procedures remain largely the appropriate techniques of relatively small-scale problem-solving where the total number of variables to be considered is small and value problems restricted. Charles Hitch, head of the Economics Division of RAND Corporation, one of the leading centers for application of these techniques, has written:

---

[1] James G. March and Herbert A. Simon similarly characterize the literature. They also take some important steps, as have Simon's recent articles, to describe a less heroic model of policy-making. See *Organizations* (John Wiley and Sons, 1958), p. 137.

"I would make the empirical generalization from my experience at RAND and elsewhere that operations research is the art of sub-optimizing, i.e., of solving some lower-level problems, and that difficulties increase and our special competence diminishes by an order of magnitude with every level of decision making we attempt to ascend. The sort of simple explicit model which operations researchers are so proficient in using can certainly reflect most of the significant factors influencing traffic control on the George Washington Bridge, but the proportion of the relevant reality which we can represent by any such model or models in studying, say, a major foreign-policy decision, appears to be almost trivial."[2]

Accordingly, I propose in this paper to clarify and formalize the second method, much neglected in the literature. This might be described as the method of *successive limited comparisons*. I will contrast it with the first approach, which might be called the rational-comprehensive method.[3] More impressionistically and briefly—and therefore generally used in this article—they could be characterized as the branch method and root method, the former continually building out from the current situation, step-by-step and by small degrees; the latter starting from fundamentals anew each time, building on the past only as experience is embodied in a theory, and always prepared to start completely from the ground up.

Let us put the characteristics of the two methods side by side in simplest terms.

Rational-Comprehensive (Root)	Successive Limited Comparisons (Branch)
1a. Clarification of values or objectives distinct from and usually prerequisite to empirical analysis of alternative policies.	1b. Selection of value goals and empirical analysis of the needed action are not distinct from one another but are closely intertwined.
2a. Policy-formulation is therefore approached through means-end analysis: First the ends are isolated, then the means to achieve them are sought.	2b. Since means and ends are not distinct, means-end analysis is often inappropriate or limited.
3a. The test of a "good" policy is that it can be shown to be the most appropriate means to desired ends.	3b. The test of a "good" policy is typically that various analysts find themselves directly agreeing on a policy (without their agreeing that it is the most appropriate means to an agreed objective).

---

[2] "Operations Research and National Planning—A Dissent," 5 *Operations Research* 718 (October, 1957). Hitch's dissent is from particular points made in the article to which his paper is a reply; his claim that operations research is for low-level problems is widely accepted.

For examples of the kind of problems to which operations research is applied, see C. W. Churchman, R. L. Ackoff and E. L. Arnoff, *Introduction to Operations Research* (John Wiley and Sons, 1957); and J. F. McCloskey and J. M. Coppinger (eds.), *Operations Research for Management*, Vol. II (The Johns Hopkins Press, 1956).

[3] I am assuming that administrators often make policy and advise in the making of policy and am treating decision-making and policy-making as synonymous for purposes of this paper.

4a. Analysis is comprehensive; every important relevant factor is taken into account.	4b. Analysis is drastically limited:

4b. Analysis is drastically limited:
  i) Important possible outcomes are neglected.
  ii) Important alternative poten- tial policies are neglected.
  iii) Imported affected values are neglected.

5a. Theory is often heavily relied upon.	5b. A succession of comparisons greatly reduces or eliminates reliance on theory.

Assuming that the root method is familiar and understandable, we proceed directly to clarification of its alternative by contrast. In explaining the second, we shall be describing how most administrators do in fact approach complex questions, for the root method, the "best" way as a blueprint or model, is in fact not workable for complex policy questions, and administrators are forced to use the method of successive limited comparisons.

INTERTWINING EVALUATION AND EMPIRICAL ANALYSIS (1B)

The quickest way to understand how values are handled in the method of successive limited comparisons is to see how the root method often breaks down in *its* handling of values or objectives. The idea that values should be clarified, and in advance of the examination of alternative policies, is appealing. But what happens when we attempt it for complex social problems? The first difficulty is that on many critical values or objectives, citizens disagree, congressmen disagree, and public administrators disagree. Even where a fairly specific objective is pre- scribed for the administrator, there remains considerable room for disagreement on sub-objectives. . . .

Administrators cannot escape these conflicts by ascertaining the majority's preference, for preferences have not been registered on most issues; indeed, there often *are* no preferences in the absence of public discussion sufficient to bring an issue to the attention of the electorate. Furthermore, there is a question of whether intensity of feeling should be considered as well as the number of persons preferring each alternative. By the impossibility of doing otherwise, administrators often are reduced to deciding policy without clarifying objectives first.

Even when an administrator resolves to follow his own values as a criterion for decisions, he often will not know how to rank them when they conflict with one another, as they usually do. Suppose, for example, that an administrator must relocate tenants, living in tenements scheduled for destruction. One objective is to empty the buildings fairly promptly, another is to find suitable accommoda- tion for persons displaced, another is to avoid friction with residents in other areas in which a large influx would be unwelcome, another is to deal with all concerned through persuasion if possible, and so on.

How does one state even to himself the relative importance of these partially conflicting values? A simple ranking of them is not enough; one needs ideally to know how much of one value is worth sacrificing for some of another value. The answer is that typically the administrator chooses—and must choose—directly among policies in which these values are combined in different ways. He cannot first clarify his values and then choose among policies.

A more subtle third point underlies both the first two. Social objectives do not always have the same relative values. One objective may be highly prized in one circumstance, another in another circumstance. If, for example, an administrator values highly both the dispatch with which his agency can carry through its projects *and* good public relations, it matters little which of the two possibly conflicting values he favors in some abstract or general sense. Policy questions arise in forms which put to administrators such a question as: Given the degree to which we are or are not already achieving the values of dispatch and the values of good public relations, is it worth sacrificing a little speed for a happier clientele, or is it better to risk offending the clientele so that we can get on with our work? The answer to such a question varies with circumstances.

The value problem is, as the example shows, always a problem of adjustments at a margin. But there is no practicable way to state marginal objectives or values except in terms of particular policies. That one value is preferred to another in one decision situation does not mean that it will be preferred in another decision situation in which it can be had only at great sacrifice of another value. Attempts to rank or order values in general and abstract terms so that they do not shift from decision to decision end up by ignoring the relevant marginal preferences. The significance of this third point thus goes very far. Even if all administrators had at hand an agreed set of values, objectives, and constraints, and an agreed ranking of these values, objectives, and constraints, their marginal values in actual choice situations would be impossible to formulate.

Unable consequently to formulate the relevant values first and then choose among policies to achieve them, administrators must choose directly among alternative policies that offer different marginal combinations of values. Somewhat paradoxically, the only practicable way to disclose one's relevant marginal values even to oneself is to describe the policy one chooses to achieve them. Except roughly and vaguely, I know of no way to describe—or even to understand— what my relative evaluations are for, say, freedom and security, speed and accuracy in governmental decisions, or low taxes and better schools than to describe my preferences among specific policy choices that might be made between the alternatives in each of the pairs.

In summary, two aspects of the process by which values are actually handled can be distinguished. The first is clear: evaluation and empirical analysis are intertwined; that is, one chooses among values and among policies at one and the same time. Put a little more elaborately, one simultaneously chooses a policy to attain certain objectives and chooses the objectives themselves. The second aspect is related but distinct: the administrator focuses his attention on marginal or incremental values. Whether he is aware of it or not, he does not find general formulations of objectives very helpful and in fact makes specific marginal or incremental comparisons. Two policies, X and Y, confront him. Both promise the same degree of attainment of objectives a, b, c, d, and e. But X promises him somewhat more of f than does Y, while Y promises him somewhat more of g than does X. In choosing between them, he is in fact offered the alternative of a marginal or incremental amount of f at the expense of a marginal or incremental amount of g. The only values that are relevant to his choice are these increments by which the two policies differ; and, when he finally chooses between the two marginal values, he does so by making a choice between policies.[4]

As to whether the attempt to clarify objectives in advance of policy selection is more or less rational than the close intertwining of marginal evaluation and empirical analysis, the principal difference established is that for complex problems the first is impossible and irrelevant, and the second is both possible and

---

[4] The line of argument is, of course, an extension of the theory of market choice, especially the theory of consumer choice, to public policy choices.

relevant. The second is possible because the administrator need not try to analyze any values except the values by which alternative policies differ and need not be concerned with them except as they differ marginally. His need for information on values or objectives is drastically reduced as compared with the root method; and his capacity for grasping, comprehending, and relating values to one another is not strained beyond the breaking point.

[EDITORS' NOTE: Article proceeds to discuss the remaining four points 2b–5b listed above.]

From: David W. Miller and Martin K. Starr

EXECUTIVE DECISIONS AND OPERATIONS RESEARCH*

[EDITORS' NOTE: The authors are professors at the Columbia University Graduate School of Business.]

GOALS OF THE ROLE

People play many roles. Each role can be associated with its own objectives. Individuals simplify their decision problems by establishing for themselves these multiple objectives instead of just one basic objective. Most people, for example, will establish some kind of objective for themselves in the area of their professional activities. They will usually have other objectives relating to their interpersonal relationships; e.g., father, husband, son. They will also have objectives regarding their relationship to society as a whole, e.g., political activity or public-spirited work. They will often have some objectives regarding their leisure activities. And, of course, we can continue and obtain quite a catalogue of the different areas in which people are likely to set themselves some kind of objectives. It appears that most people handle their decision problems in a particular field of activity by ignoring the objectives of other fields of activity. Thus, a business executive will solve his decision problems in business—for example, what position he will accept—in terms of his professional objective.

Even within a single field of activity an individual has many different roles. An executive reports to his boss and in turn has people reporting to him. His position in the organization determines the extent of his responsibility and the importance of decisions he must make. The goal of the executive is strongly tied to the complex image he has of his role. Although no two executives have the same situations, the similarity of goals which they share as a group causes us to speak about executive goals. However, similarity should not blind us to the differences. In the same way, for convenience, we group employee goals, ownership goals, salesmen's goals, and so on. There is a certain relevant pattern of

* *Executive Decisions and Operations Research*, David W. Miller and Martin K. Starr © 1961 by Prentice-Hall, Inc., Englewood Cliffs, New Jersey (pp. 38–42, 45–47, 50).

goal-seeking within each of these groups. It is hardly necessary to expand on what these might be. On the other hand, it is an observable fact that sometimes there is a conflict between the objectives of several groups to which the individual belongs.

SUBOPTIMIZATION

. . . Whenever there is no conflict between objectives, the individual can proceed to solve his decision problems separately. As long as the action taken to achieve either objective is independent of the other, he can do this. However, when objectives are dependent, the optimization of one can result in a lower degree of attainment for all the others. This condition is known as *suboptimization*. For example, an executive may decide to take a new position on the basis of his professional objectives. The new job, however, entails extremely long hours and much traveling. Assume that the new job is optimal in terms of the executive's professional objective. The fact that the time he can now spend with his family is sharply reduced may have such adverse effects that he will find that his optimization in terms of one objective has produced a result which is very much less than optimal in terms of all his objectives.

This same notion of suboptimization is involved in the effects on the decision problem of the fact that we lead our lives through time and that we have only very imperfect ability to foresee the future. This means that any decision problem can be solved only in terms of the knowledge and situation obtaining currently. But the action chosen may, and probably will, have effects on the decision-maker's situation for a considerable period in the future. An optimal action at one time may, therefore, turn out to have been a very inferior suboptimization in terms of a longer period of time.

* * * * *

It is quite clear that we can never really achieve optimization. Over time, unexpected events can change what had appeared to be an optimal decision into an inferior decision. There is almost no reversibility in decision systems. Generally speaking, by the time we find out that a decision was not a good one, we cannot return to the state which prevailed before the decision had been made. Consequently, decision systems should provide the best possible predictions of future expectations. And in addition, decision systems should not commit us to irrevocable action for very long periods of time. And so we reach the conclusion that a *sequential decision process* permits maximum flexibility with respect to both objectives and actions.

BOUNDED RATIONALITY

. . . We have been using the word "optimum," and some other forms of the same word, rather loosely. In fact, it is important to note that people rarely make a prolonged effort to achieve the optimum action in any realistic decision problem facing them. To paraphrase John Maurice Clark, people simply don't have such an irrational passion for dispassionate rationality. Furthermore, there are good reasons why they shouldn't. All of the reasons have reference to the exorbitant complexity of any realistic decision problem. Three main aspects of this complexity should be noted.

First, consider the point just made, that an optimum decision made at one point in time is only suboptimum in terms of subsequent times. . . .

. . . Second, there are an enormous number of possible choices of action (strategies, as we have called them) and any attempt to obtain information on all of them would be self-defeating.

. . . Third, there are virtually innumerable factors outside the control of the decision-maker (we call them states of nature) which may affect the outcome of his decision.

. . . The net effect of these limitations on human decision-making procedures has been observed and neatly summarized by Herbert Simon in his "principle of bounded rationality." According to this principle human beings seldom make any effort to find the optimum action in a decision problem. Instead, they select a number of possible outcomes of their available strategies which would be good enough. Then they select a strategy (choose an action) that is likely to achieve one of the good-enough outcomes. Thus, the executive looking for a new job makes no effort to discover all possible jobs from which he can then select the best (optimum) one. Instead, he decides what he wants from a job in terms of his various objectives. Then he searches for a job that will provide him with the things he wants, e.g., a certain income, satisfactory working conditions, chances for advancement. He does not try to find that one job somewhere in the world which might give him the optimum. The principle of bounded rationality is a neat way to describe the actual procedure of human beings involved in the decision problems of life, and it succinctly reminds us not to assume any irrational extremes of rationality.

*   *   *   *   *

ORGANIZATIONAL PROBLEMS OF SUBOPTIMIZATION

. . . Under what conditions does suboptimization arise in business? Of course we can answer that it arises whenever an action has an effect on several different objectives simultaneously. But this is merely to state the same thing in different words. In fact, there is no general answer to this question. The best that can be done in any specific decision problem is to utilize intuition, experience, and all available methodology to endeavor to see whether actions intended for one purpose have any probable effects on other objectives. If they do then it follows that the problem is one that involves a possible conflict of objectives and it must be handled with this fact in mind.

It should be explicitly noted that no genuine problem of a conflict of objectives can be reconciled by expressing all the possible outcomes in terms of the utility measure for one of the objectives. Now, it is fortunate that many decision problems of business can be framed in terms such that the possible outcomes can be measured in dollars. But it is by no means the case that all business objectives can be expressed in dollars. If, to take an instance, workers' attitudes could be measured in dollars, then it would follow that all possible outcomes in the area of workers' attitudes could be expressed in dollars. The total objective need only be stated as the maximization of profit. We would not require a special description of workers' attitudes. No such easy solution to the problem of conflicting objectives is usually available. . . .

Looking at the bright side, there are a great number of important decision problems that do not involve any conflict of objectives. For any one of these we can attempt to optimize with no fear of difficulties arising from suboptimization. In particular, we can state that, at the minimum, a business must attempt to optimize its situation with regard to each specific objective as long as it does not affect adversely its situation with regard to any other objective. This construction is a variant of an idea introduced in a different context by the Italian economist and sociologist, Vilfredo Pareto. Pareto was concerned with the problem of what should govern the actions of society if it is assumed that the utilities of the various individuals composing the society cannot be compared. By utility we mean the subjective value that each individual subscribes for the various goods and services available. Under these circumstances society cannot act to achieve the greatest total utility because this idea has no meaning for the stated conditions. Pareto suggested that society should then try to achieve at least an optimum such that each individual had the maximum utility possible without subtracting anything from anyone else's utility. In other words, if society can act so as to increase one individual's total utility without taking anything away from anyone else, then it should do so. A condition where this has been accomplished is known as *Paretian optimality*.

The problem with which Pareto was dealing arises because there is no common standard of measure of value between individuals. And this is precisely analogous to the problem of multiple objectives with which we are dealing. Our problem arises because there is no common measure of value for the various objectives. If there were one common measure we could formulate one objective rather than several. Therefore we can state, along with Pareto, that any business should always attempt to achieve a condition of Paretian optimality with regard to its various objectives.

*　　*　　*　　*　　*

Business organizations are subject to still another kind of suboptimization problem. Whereas a real person is a unit that is more or less indecomposable, the fictitious person of the business corporation is usually made up of a number of different departments or divisions. The successful functioning of the business demands the integration of the efforts of the various departments that compose it. The achievement of any of the business objectives requires that the various departments should each achieve some departmental objectives. But, by the very nature of things, departments are likely to have considerable autonomy and it can happen that the objectives they set are not in accord with the over-all business objectives. It can also happen that the actions of one department have an effect on the situation of other departments such that an optimal strategy for one department in terms of its own objectives deleteriously affects other departments and, hence, the entire business. Both of these kinds of situations represent other variants of the suboptimization problem.

*　　*　　*　　*　　*

. . . We can now look at illustrations of suboptimization where two parts of the company are in conflict with each other. For example, a division's objective of achieving the best possible profitability record may lead it to purchase parts from competitors rather than from another division of the same company. This may lower the profitability of the division that normally supplies parts. As another aspect of the inventory problem, a sales manager's objective of getting the largest possible sales may lead him to want a large inventory so that all orders can be promptly filled. This might be in conflict with the controller's objective of tying up a minimum of capital in inventory. Which one is in the best interests of the business? As a final example, a production department uses less steel by cutting down on the upper limit of the tolerances to which it machines a part. This results in a higher number of rejects of the finished assembly and an eventual complete redesign of the product with no appreciable gain in quality.

All of these examples serve to demonstrate the crucial importance of the suboptimization problem. Once again we could raise the question: When does this kind of problem arise? And once again, there is no general answer. Being aware of the problem we must rely on common and uncommon sense to help us to discover which particular decision may exemplify it. Fortunately, the majority of the forms of this kind of suboptimization problem involve objectives that can be expressed in quantitative form, so many of these problems can be re-solved by methods which we will be discussing at length below. Thus, for example, the problem of inventory size and the conflicting interests of the sales manager and the controller can generally be resolved by expressing all the costs in dollars and solving the decision problem in terms of the over-all business objective of minimizing costs. This simple statement may make it seem easy. It isn't, as we know from the problem of the small-plant manager. How can we express the loss of dignity which he experiences as a result of being out of stock more often than he would like? Similarly, how do we represent the loss of customer goodwill that results from being out of inventory on an item that the customer wants immediately? Nonetheless, despite some difficulties, these kinds of problems can often be satisfactorily resolved.

From: J. J. O'Connell

"DECISION MAKING RULES AND COMPUTATIONAL TECHNIQUES"*

Certain rules and techniques have becomes standardized for making decisions under conditions of uncertainty, risk, and conflict. The following is a brief synthesis of those rules and techniques. No effort is made to: (a) define all terms, (b) explain the complete reasoning of the steps, (c) point out the underlying assumptions, or (d) enumerate the benefits and limitations of each application. The reader will profit by attempting to infer these points from our cookbook presentation of the techniques. Help in this task and more advanced treatments can be found in the sources cited in each section below.

I. DECISION MAKING UNDER UNCERTAINTY

I.1. *Maximin*

Situation: A will get various profit amounts depending on what strategy he uses (A_1 or A_2) and depending on which state of nature (B_1 or B_2) exists when A acts. A has no idea whether he will face B_1 or B_2.
Technique: Identify the minimum payoff for each of A's strategies (in each row). Pick the maximum of these minima.

Payoff Matrix		Minimum Payoffs	Maximum of Minima	Choose
	B_1 B_2			
A_1	23 35	23		
A_2	34 26	26	26	26 (i.e., Strategy A_2)

Rule: A should choose the strategy in which he gets the higher of the minimum payoffs open to him.

* Unpublished manuscript, 1963.

I.2. *Coefficient of Optimism*

Situation: Same as I.1.

Technique: Identify the maximum payoff for each of A's strategies. Identify the minimum payoff for each of A's strategies. Weight the maxima and minima by coefficients which express how optimistic you are (expect the best) relative to your pessimism (expect the worst). Sum the products in each row to get the expected value in each row.

Payoff Matrix		*Maximum Payoffs*	*Minimum Payoffs*	*Coefficient of Optimism*
	B_1 B_2			
A_1	23 35	35	23	Inclined to
A_2	34 26	34	26	expect maximum payoff 6 times out of 10.

Expected Value Table	*Choose*
$35 \times .6 + 23 \times .4 = 30.2$	
$34 \times .6 + 26 \times .4 = 30.8$	30.8 (i.e., Strategy A_2)

Rule: A should choose the strategy with the highest expected value.

I.3. *Minimax (Regret)*

Situation: Same as I.1.

Technique: Subtract the highest payoff given each possible outcome from each other payoff for that outcome (subtract the highest number in each column from each number in that column). Identify the maximum "regret" for each of A's strategies. Pick the minimum of these maxima.

Payoff Matrix		*Regret Matrix*		*Maximum Regrets*	*Minimum of Maxima*	*Choose*
	B_1 B_2		B_1 B_2			
A_1	23 35	A_1	11 0	11		
A_2	34 26	A_2	0 9	9	9	Strategy A_2

Rule: A should choose the strategy in which he suffers the lesser of the maximum "regrets" he faces.

I.4. *Laplace Criterion*

Situation: Same as I.1.

Technique: Assign equal probabilities to each state of nature, thereby weighting each payoff equally. Sum the products in each row to get the expected values of each row.

Payoff Matrix		*Probabilities*	(.5) (.5)	
	B_1 B_2		B_1 B_2	
A_1	23 35	That B_1 will occur $= .5$	A_1	23 35
A_2	34 26	That B_2 will occur $= .5$	A_2	34 26

Expected Value Table	*Choose*
$23 \times .5 + 35 \times .5 = 29.0$	
$34 \times .5 + 26 \times .5 = 30.0$	30.0 (i.e., Strategy A_2)

Rule: A should choose the strategy with the highest expected value.

[EDITORS' NOTE: See David W. Miller and Martin K. Starr, *Executive Decisions and Operations Research* (Englewood Cliffs, N.J.: Prentice-Hall, Inc., 1960), pp. 85–94; William J. Baumol, *Economic Theory and Operations Analysis* (Englewood Cliffs, N.J.: Prentice-Hall, Inc., 1961), pp. 368–75.]

II. DECISION MAKING UNDER RISK

Situation: A will get various profit amounts depending on what strategy he uses and depending on what state of nature exists when he acts. Using additional information A has about himself and about the possible states of nature, A can make some estimate how likely B_1 is to occur compared to the chances of B_2's occurring.

Technique: Assign probabilities to each state of nature which represent A's judgment about the chances of B_1 or B_2 happening. The probabilities serve as weights for the payoffs in each column. Sum the products in each row to get the expected payoff for each row.

Payoff Matrix			Subjective Probabilities	(.4)	(.6)
	B_1	B_2		B_1	B_2
A_1	23	35	That B_1 will occur $= .4$	A_1 23	35
A_2	34	26	That B_2 will occur $= .6$	A_2 34	26

Expected Value Table	Choose
$23 \times .4 + 35 \times .6 = 30.2$	30.2 (i.e., Strategy A_1)
$34 \times .4 + 26 \times .6 = 29.2$	

Rule: A should choose the strategy with the highest expected value.

[EDITORS' NOTE: See Miller and Starr, *op. cit.*, pp. 82–85; Morris, *Management Science in Action* (see author index).]

III. DECISION MAKING UNDER CONFLICT (GAME THEORY)

Situation: A will get various profit amounts depending on what strategy he uses and depending on what strategy B uses. In this situation, the profit A gains will be a loss for B—a two-person, zero sum game. In contrast to the above situations, A here has an intelligent adversary for the first time.

Technique: Identify the minimum payoff for each of A's strategies. Pick the maximum of these minima.

Identify the maximum loss for each of B's alternatives. Pick the minimum of these maxima.

Payoff Matrix			A's Minimum Payoffs	Maximum of Minima	A Will Choose
	B_1	B_2			
A_1	23	35	23		
A_2	34	26	26	26	26 (i.e., Strategy A_2)

B's Maximum Losses		Minimum of Maxima	B Will Choose
B_1	34	34	34 (i.e., Strategy B_1)
B_2	35		

Rule: A should choose the strategy in which he gets the higher of the minimum payoffs open to him. B should choose the strategy in which he suffers the lower of the maximum losses facing him.

Note: B can figure out that A's most rational strategy is A_2. If B were 100% certain A would use strategy A_2, B then would himself prefer strategy B_2, so that he would lose 26 instead of 34.

A can figure out that B's most rational strategy is B_1. If A were 100% certain B would use strategy B_1, A would stick with his most rational strategy, A_2. Of course, if A thought B would switch to strategy B_2, then A might be tempted to switch to strategy A_1, so that he would gain 35 instead of 34.

A could certainly "ride" with his most rational strategy, A_2, which assures him at least the better of the minimum profits, 26. On the other hand, A could use what is called a "mixed strategy."

Situation: Both opponents have figured their own most rational strategies (and each is aware of the other's) but the "game" is still indeterminate— further gamesmanship could benefit either party.

Technique: A could judge that he might outsmart B by employing a random strategy. He could use a method which made it equally probable that he would employ A_1 or A_2.[1] To see if this is a better strategy than the "most rational" one figured above, A would set equal weights to each payoff in each of his strategies. He then can determine the expected value in the two cases: B uses B_1, B uses B_2.

Apply the appropriate weights to the payoffs in each column. In each case, sum the products to get the expected value of each column.

Payoff Matrix				*Expected Value Table*	
	B_1	B_2		B_1	B_2
A_1	23	35		23 × .50	35 × .50
A_2	34	26		34 × .50	26 × .50
				28.5	30.5

Rule: Since both 28.5 and 30.5 are better than the 26 which A is willing to settle for in his most rational strategy, it will "pay" A to do some gambling. A should flip a coin. If heads, strategy A_1; if tails, strategy A_2.

[EDITORS' NOTE: See Miller and Starr, *op. cit.*, pp. 94–98; Baumol, *op. cit.*, pp. 348–66; John McDonald, *Strategy in Poker, Business and War* (New York: W. W. Norton & Co., Inc., 1950), especially pp. 50–83.]

From: Chester I. Barnard

THE FUNCTIONS OF THE EXECUTIVE*

[EDITORS' NOTE: The author was President of the New Jersey Bell Telephone Company and later President of the Rockefeller Foundation.]

. . . [T]he decision may be not to decide. This is a most frequent decision, and from some points of view probably the most important. For every alert executive continually raises in his own mind questions for determination. As a

---

1 Techniques are available for determining the probabilities from the values in the payoff matrix. (See the Baumol reference cited below.)

* Reprinted by permission of the Harvard University Press, Cambridge, Massachusetts, 1954 (pp. 193–94).

result of his consideration he may determine that the question is not pertinent. He may determine that it is not now pertinent. He may determine that it is pertinent now, but that there are lacking adequate data upon which to base a final decision. He may determine that it is pertinent for decision now, but that it should or must be decided by someone else on the latter's initiative. He may determine that the question is pertinent, can be decided, will not be decided except by himself, and yet it would be better that it be not decided because his competence is insufficient.

The fine art of executive decision consists in not deciding questions that are not now pertinent, in not deciding prematurely, in not making decisions that cannot be made effective, and in not making decisions that others should make. Not to decide questions that are not pertinent at the time is uncommon good sense, though to raise them may be uncommon perspicacity. Not to decide questions prematurely is to refuse commitment of attitude or the development of prejudice. Not to make decisions that cannot be made effective is to refrain from destroying authority. Not to make decisions that others should make is to preserve morale, to develop competence, to fix responsibility, and to preserve authority.

From this it may be seen that decisions fall into two major classes, positive decisions—to do something, to direct action, to cease action, to prevent action; and negative decisions, which are decisions not to decide. Both are inescapable; but the negative decisions are often largely unconscious, relatively non-logical, "instinctive," "good sense." It is because of the rejections that the selection is good. The best of moves may be offset by a false move. . . .

CASE MATERIALS:

More Complex Cases

ELECTRONICS INTERNATIONAL CORPORATION

I Case Introduction

Synopsis

The United States Department of Defense plans a radar system to track all objects orbiting in space. In an effort to win the developmental contract for this system Electronics International Corporation attempts to influence the military to incorporate EIC concepts into the specifications for the proposed system. The Army does incorporate some EIC ideas into the specifications, but other defense contractors also appear in relatively good positions in the upcoming formal competition. Under time pressure a cross-functional task force in EIC responds to the Army Request for Quotation. Costs are estimated, the technical proposal written, and the management proposal written. Top management pares the estimated costs and decides to submit a fixed-price bid.

Why This Case Is Included

This case describes program management in action. There is opportunity to observe the interaction between the *ad hoc* program management organization and the standard, functionally departmented, organization. The *ad hoc* organizational arrangement seems to challenge the conventional wisdoms about the structural relationships and the management processes of the usual staff-line organization. The normative models of how organizations should operate may be tested against the description of how an organization does operate. The psychology of human needs and perception may be used to understand and explain the various displays of cooperative and uncooperative, defensive and aggressive, behavior of executives. This typical case of government-business—buyer-seller—relationship reveals the dynamics of this growing form of enterprise activity with its rather unique marketing practices, contract features, etc.

Diagnostic and Predictive Questions

In answering the following diagnostic and predictive questions, remember that these questions apply theories and conceptual ideas from certain disciplines. Such theories are valuable to understand basic forces at work in the policy system (diagnosis) and to predict what will happen in the system in the future (prediction). Since each reading abstracts from the total policy system certain factors or variables into the closed or partial viewpoint of one theory or discipline, no one reading gives answers to the practical policy problems of the case. In diagnosis and prediction, the parts of the problem are studied with "other things being equal."

Following each question are listed readings which will be helpful in answering the question. The readings included with this case are marked (*). By referring to the author index at the end of this book, you may locate the other readings listed.

1. How important is the Ortrack contract to EIC and the Weapons Systems Division? By sifting case facts identify the *economic* motivation for winning the sealed bid competition.

2. How does the *de facto* organization in WSD for preparing the response to the RFQ compare to what has come to be called the "matrix" organization?

Read: *Mee "Matrix Organization"; *Cleland, "Why Project Management?" *Cleland, "Understanding Project Authority."

3. What benefits does "project management" or the matrix organization form offer in comparison with the traditional functional organization? Does the actual performance of the proposal team in WSD give evidence of these purported benefits?

Read: The readings assigned in Question 2.

4. Explain the behavior of Travers as he attempts to bring together the proposal team. Why did he appeal to Young to get cooperation from Ives?

Read: The readings assigned in Question 2.

5. Explain the behavior of Ives in the following incidents: (*a*) refusing to commit his men to the proposal team before receiving the RFQ; (*b*) removing Ransom from the proposal team; (*c*) telling Svendon not to use Ted Forbes' name in the proposed ORTRACK organization.

Read: The readings assigned in Question 2.

6. Do the management practices implied in program management jibe with the "principles" espoused and/or debated in the management literature—especially the principle of unity of command?

Read: Fayol, *General and Industrial Management*, pp. 24–25, 68–70; Taylor, "Shop Management," pp. 92–96, 98–100.

7. How can the behavior of Magnus during the cost-cutting session on October 11 be explained? What makes a man like Magnus behave differently from his colleagues? Do the various theories of human needs aid in the diagnosis?

Read: *Jennings, "Business Needs Mature Autocrats"; *Odiorne, *How Managers Make Things Happen*, pp. 5–53; *Barnard, *Organizations and Management*, pp. 48, 85–87, 89–90, 94; Gellerman, *Motivation and Productivity*, pp. 109–18; Maslow, *Motivation and Personality*, pp. 80–94; Hampton, Summer, Webber, *Organizational Behavior and the Practice of Management*, chap. x.

8. Do the psychological theories of perception help explain why Magnus' behavior left some of his colleagues "concerned"?

Read: *Boulding, *The Image*, pp. 11–14; Leavitt. *Managerial Psychology*. pp. 27–33; Krech and Crutchfield, *Theory and Problems of Social Psychology*, pp. 81–83, 87–89, 94–96, 98, 102–3.

9. How do you explain the successive levels of "padding" in the cost estimates made in the engineering departments?

Read: Argyris, "Human Problems with Budgets."

Policy Questions for This Specific Case

In answering the following policy questions, the results of diagnosis and prediction are used to reduce the amount of guesswork, or judgment, in designing action solutions. However, since certain parts of the total case situation cannot be reduced to science, and since "other things are not equal," judgment must still be used to fill in the factors not accounted for by readings. You will also need a second kind of judgment as you put value weights on different scientific predictions, since different theories may point to conflicting solutions.

10. Would you make any changes in the structural arrangements in the Weapons System Division for responding to future RFQ's?
Read: The readings assigned in Questions 2 and 6.

11. Would you make any changes in the manner of cost estimation procedures in drawing up future proposals? (See Question 9 and its attached readings.)

12. Would you have bid fixed price on the ORTRACK contract?
Read: Appendix 2 attached to the case and review the case facts.

13. Would the logic of decision-making techniques for risk or conflict situations be of any help in deciding between a fixed-price and a CPIF bid? (Hint: set up a two by two matrix so that both EIC and their chief competitor, Universal Electrodynamics, have a choice of strategies—FP or CPIF. Push the logic of the techniques as far as case facts will allow.)
Read: O'Connell, "Decision-Making Rules and Computational Techniques."

14. If it were your decision as an EIC executive how would you react to the extension of the proposal formulation period? Would you use the extra time to do more on the proposal? If so, what would you do? If not, why not?

Major Policy Issues: Tentative Generalizations about Any Policy System

In arriving at conclusions for the following questions, generalize from the facts in the case and use your own ideas to (a) confirm, (b) modify, or (c) test the workability of the concepts and theories from readings. As an executive or professional, use wisdom to merge theory, on the one hand, with "brute facts" and practice, on the other.

15. Is education for management truly preparing men for the realities of organizational life? Are prospective managers developing invalid expectations concerning the "neatness" of job definitions and departmentation and concerning the sanctity of unity of command?

16. Is the government-contract, competitive-bid environment as evidenced in this typical case conducive to the effective use and development of company manpower, overall corporate efficiency, and national efficiency.

Questions for Original Student Work in Analysis and Policy

The methods of viewing this case as represented by the authors' questions and selection of readings are not exhaustive. There are other relevant ideas for diagnosis and prediction. Furthermore, there are other ways of stating policy questions. More powerful analyses and wiser solutions will result by drawing on your own training and experience for (a) relevant concepts and theories, and (b) creative ways of asking policy questions. The following questions are designed to help you acquire this skill.

17. While reflecting on the case facts, what additional theories from prior education give you insights as to "what is going on" in the Electronics International Corporation? As to what might be predicted to happen in the future?

18. Other than the policy questions asked by the authors, what pragmatic ways can think of to state the practical problems faced by executives in the case?

II Electronics International Corporation*

Electronics International Corporation is one of several defense contractors interested in developing an orbital tracking radar system (OR TRACK) for the Department of Defense. During much of 1963, the Weapons Systems Division of EIC is preparing for, and responding to, a Request for Quotation (RFQ) on the ORTRACK system.

Electronics International Corporation is a major, internationally known company, located mainly on the east coast of the United States, but with divisions in 12 states and six foreign countries. Annual sales are about $850 million, of which $300 million are in defense sales by the Defense Products Department. The line operation of the company reports to the president through three group executive vice presidents responsible for the Consumer Products, Industrial Products, and the Defense Products Departments (see Exhibit 1). The Defense Products Department consists of three major divisions. The Weapons System Division (WSD) is the one we are concerned with here. The Communications Division furnishes communication services to both the military and the public by radio and by cable in a worldwide network; they also build military microwave and VHF communications equipment, and mobile sets such as walkie-talkies, back-pack command sets, etc. The Aeronautical Division builds airborne equipment primarily, although in recent years they have become heavily involved in the extensive ground support equipment required for aeronautical and space flights. Each of these three major divisions of DPD is headed by a vice president and general manager.

The WSD Organization

Exhibit 2 shows a simplified chart of the Weapons System Division. This division consists of 2,800 people located in the Baltimore, Maryland, metropolitan area. The organization is typical of a medium-sized defense plant doing custom R.&D. and advanced techniques work, with rather limited production. This particular division has specialized in the con-

---

* Case written by Mr. Avrel Mason.

Exhibit 1

ORGANIZATION OF ELECTRONICS INTERNATIONAL CORPORATION

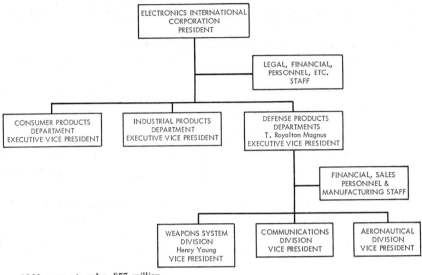

1963 corporate sales—857 million.
1963 DPD sales—301 million.
1963 DPD employment—12,000.

ception, development, and integration of complete weapons systems. Many of these have been "passive" systems whose purpose is to provide only information to be used as a basis for taking action with offensive weapons designed and developed by others. Examples of typical systems that WSD has built are a very large, multisite early warning system to detect enemy ballistic missile launchings, and a large-range radar installation that scans communist countries' air space and reports automatically the movements and positions of all aircraft and missiles. The sales

Exhibit 2

ORGANIZATION OF WEAPONS SYSTEM DIVISION OF E.I.C.

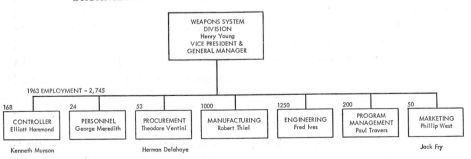

Numbers indicate size of organizational groups.

of these types of systems tend to be somewhat restricted, and it is unusual when more than several copies of any one item are produced.

The *controller's* function is a typical one in that he is responsible for the financial accounting of all activities that go on within the WSD. He is responsible for establishing the rates to be quoted for various labor grades, etc.; for determining overhead rates; and for allocation of overhead to the various operating departments. He is responsible for a centralized automated accounting system, which by use of a computer publishes detailed financial reports on each program within a week after the end of each month. The controller is responsible for establishing divisional financial planning, profit forecasting, and status determination. He is also responsible for a group called Business Administration, which has the responsibility for assisting engineering and particularly program management, in keeping track of the cost and schedule status of all the WSD programs.

The *personnel* department needs no comment. The *manufacturing* organization fluctuates widely depending upon load. During the time of this case, a number of medium-sized jobs were going through the plant, and the outlook was poor for sufficient load to keep the thousand-man work force active over the next year.

Inasmuch as highly engineered weapons systems are the product of this division, the burden of responsibility for divisional success falls essentially on the *program management* and *engineering* departments. The company is really selling engineering more than it is selling production. Accordingly, the chief engineer's position is looked upon as second only to that of the vice president/general manager, and the engineering organization reporting to him is the largest of any in the division. The program management department is separated from the engineering department so that it can objectively represent, and report directly to, the general manager and give an independent viewpoint of the status of all programs going on within WSD and its subcontractors.

The program management department can be thought of as a group of general contractors who are responsible for a project, and who get the work done by contracting it out to the engineering department and to such other corporate divisions and subcontractors as are needed to complete a total job. It had been found from a number of unpleasant experiences that it was undesirable for program management to report to the chief engineer, and a year before this study, the group was separated from engineering to report to the general manager, in order to obtain more total management and less engineering-oriented perspective and evaluation of program status and problems. This was also appealing to the customer, who liked to think that his particular program was receiving attention directly from the general manager, and not through successive layers of supervision. Personnel comprising the program management group were generally very senior men with broad interests and

Exhibit 3

ENGINEERING DEPARTMENT ORGANIZATION

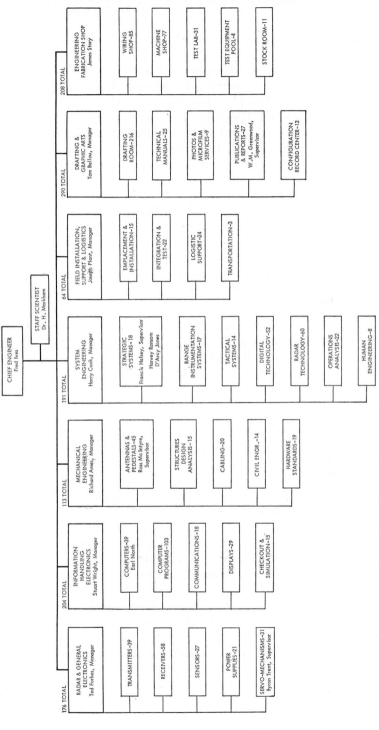

Note: Names given only for those concerned with ORTRACK Program. Numbers indicate number of personnel in each activity (1250 Total).

backgrounds, keen organizational sense, and a demonstrated capability to get things done through other people.

The marketing group had responsibility for actually bringing in the order, for customer contracts, and in general, handling all long-term forecasting and product planning. However, since engineering is the real product in most research and development work, marketing was virtually helpless without the detailed advice and support of both the engineering and program management departments. The marketing men tended to act as intelligence agents and door openers, operating as a catalyst between the customer and the engineers, who did virtually all the conceptual work and technical selling.

Exhibit 3 shows the organization of the engineering department. The figure shows, in some detail, the organizational structure of this department of 1,251 total personnel. This total includes drafting, technicians, and model shop personnel as noted. About 700 of these 1,200 are professional people, having college degrees. Within the Systems and Design sections about 40% of the engineers have master's degrees and 5% doctorates.[1]

ORGANIZATIONAL RELATIONSHIPS—BEFORE AND DURING A PROPOSAL

Exhibit 4 shows the other key organizations of the Weapons Systems Division involved in this case. This case is especially concerned with the interactions between the marketing, program management, and engineering departments. The names of personnel involved in the study are shown in their proper organizational location. The *modus operandi* of accomplishing a proposal typically tends to be that a carefully chosen appropriate-level team of engineers is assigned to work with a market representative. The market representative is supposed to know the customer, is supposed to set up meetings with him, and to gain entree and access to all proper levels. He must become familiar with the customer's procurement personnel as well as the technical members of the customer's organization, and is supposed to be knowledgeable in, and help influence, all decisions in all parts of the military and government, regardless of activity or location, that might affect the subject program.

The ORTRACK program, being a large one and of worldwide significance, is unique in that it involved many government agencies and all military services, either because they had an intelligence need for the information furnished by ORTRACK, or who were going to use OR-TRACK outputs as automatic inputs to certain antisatellite defensive operations, in event of a national emergency. It can well be imagined that the knowledge of existing satellite orbits, the unheralded arrival of

---

[1] See Appendix 1 (of this case) for detail on the functions of each of the engineering sections.

Exhibit 4

MARKETING & PROGRAM MANAGEMENT
ORGANIZATIONS OF WSD

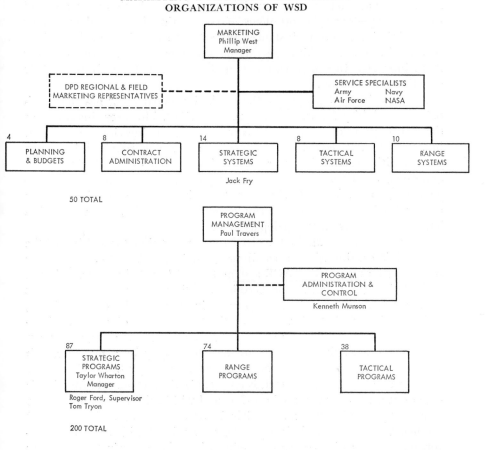

new satellites, the disappearance of known satellites, changes in course of existing satellites, change in apparent size, changes in transmitting frequencies, etc., were all of vital importance from the standpoint of intelligence, deployment of ground and naval defenses, and the civilian defense agencies.

Note that both the marketing and program management organizations, as illustrated above in Exhibit 4, have common groups associated with strategic, range instrumentation, and tactical programs. Division of all products made by the Weapons System Division into these three categories has proved to be an excellent way of focusing attention on the three different types of markets and also in coordinating the activities as required between the engineering, program management, and marketing departments in the quest for new business. Although this was a recent change in organization, it was already generally agreed by those participating that it permitted an unprecedented focusing of attention on proposing and getting new business, and inasmuch as usually only the more senior and mature personnel from each organization were assigned to the large efforts, the problems of cooperation between departments were minimized. In some instances, indeed, the supervisors of the various personnel who are working together on a program, accused them of being more interested in the program than they were in the welfare of their own line organization.

In the writing of proposals, the marketing department has the nominal responsibility for the entire proposal effort. However, inasmuch as the vast majority of the proposal is based on its engineering content, and inasmuch as the degree of engineering knowledge required is incompatible with the knowledge usually available from the marketing representatives, in effect the engineering department and program management groups are forced to shoulder the main burden of getting out the proposal, with only customer-oriented guidance, advice, and supervision imposed from the marketing department.

Over the years, WSD had evolved the concept that the writing of the proposal is considered as a small program in itself. Indeed, for larger systems such as the ORTRACK system, the writing of the proposal in the limited time period available becomes a rather major challenge and is considered as a job requiring the utmost in energy, technical knowledge, and organizational ability. Because the preparation of a proposal requires inputs from virtually all activities, especially for a large program like ORTRACK, the programs are headed usually by a manager with broad capabilities, selected from program management. He then pulls together a team which, in effect, is an organization whose sole function is to get out a winning proposal on time and within the funds allotted. To successfully handle the many difficult organizational and procedural problems, as well as technical problems, associated with such an endeavor, particularly with regard to dealing with other organizations, such as other divisions, subcontractors, and remote parts of the engineering department, only very senior people with previous program management experience are assigned to run a proposal. The proposal manager is the real boss of the proposal effort, although nominally in doing this, he is working for the marketing department.

The proposal team is generally dissolved as soon as the proposal is submitted. The people named in the proposal to perform the program, should it be won, are often those who helped in the proposal effort. This fact provides excellent motivation for people to do their best on the proposals, because in general, both supervisory and working level groups in WSD feel that a job on a new program is a desirable thing and furnishes an opportunity to face new creative and organizational challenges, etc., as well as allow an opportunity for promotion.

The proposal team invariably runs out of time toward the end of the effort, and over the years, it has been observed that it seemed a virtual impossibility to avoid a frantic last minute rush, despite the most careful efforts to schedule ample time for final reviews, re-editing, etc.

Proposals are usually financed by allocation of WSD funds. Generally, where other divisions of the corporation participate, an agreement is written allocating suitable parts of the program to them. In the event that the job is won, participating divisions win a *pro rata* share of the profit associated with their share in the program. In dealing with subcontractors, a team relationship is typically confirmed by a letter of understanding between the Electronics International Corporation and the potential subcontractor, stating their (EIC's) intent to give certain areas of work to the subcontractor should the proposal be won.

In return, when desirable, the subcontractor is asked to write an agreement that he will not "team" with any other company than EIC. This exchange of mutual agreements is not used when a subcontractor has already completed the item needed and in effect has them in stock as "shelf items." In such cases, there is no need for "teaming" and the subcontractor really becomes a "vendor of standard equipment" that he will quote to anyone interested.

CHRONOLOGY LEADING UP TO THE DATE OF RECEIPT OF RFQ

The Weapons System Division of Electronics International Corporation had, for a number of years, been associated with the design and development of systems utilizing high-power radars. These instruments had become more and more popular, and indeed, EIC had achieved a national reputation for precision work in the tracking of guided missiles, and later, satellites. They were used for range instrumentation work to determine reentry trajectories of missile nose cones, launch orbits from Cape Kennedy, ICBM tests, etc. WSD had built many types of precision and high-power radar, ranging from small, self-contained units capable of being placed on the roof of a small van with the electronics inside, making a highly mobile instrumentation facility, to giant 84-foot-diameter early warning radars with several thousand mile range, capable of detecting incoming enemy intercontinental ballistic missiles. WSD had participated rather lightly in the construction of actual defense weapons. Rather, their role seemed to be, when a warhead carrying weapon was required, to team with a major airframe manufacturer who would design and develop, either as a joint teammate or on a subcontracting basis, the required missile. A number of the larger efforts of the Weapons System Division did not involve missile-type weapons, as they were used either to provide range information or intelligence information from which further action by other offensive weapons systems could be initiated.

Origins of ORTRACK

WSD had recognized, several years before, the eventual need for a system such as ORTRACK. In 1957, when the Russians first launched "Sputnik," the possibilities of placing in orbit satellites containing bombs which could be dropped out upon command from the ground became immediately evident. WSD was extremely interested in this, and indeed, Harry Cook, present manager of systems engineering, wrote in 1959 a now famous technical paper outlining the possibility of detection of such satellites in orbit by a combination of high-power radars, communication and data processing links, and control centers, such that all space traffic could be detected by a number of sites placed at strategic locations around the world.

Harry Cook had approached both the Air Force and the Army with this concept and together with Jack Fry, of marketing, had made many visits to try to sell successively more refined concepts to the military customers. It was perhaps as a direct result of their effort that the military gathered their requirements together and focused them into a new system to be procured to be called ORTRACK, OR for "orbital" TRACK for "tracking." The name ORTRACK thus became the acronym for a system which would perform obrital tracking of *all* space objects, their changes in orbit, and orbital population additions and subtractions, and which would permit a virtually instantaneous determination of changes in threat to the USA from changes in the orbital population.

The procurement was held up for a long time by jurisdictional problems between the Army, the Air Force, and the Navy. Cook and Fry had barely touched the Navy because they felt the heavy equipment required to detect satellites at the long ranges required to get early warning precluded their use on shipboard. The Army felt that its role of defense against incoming weapons, ICBM's, etc., gave them the need for having an ORTRACK system. The Air Force felt that its role of offense was such that it had to have the ORTRACK system to tell its ICBM's and planned satellite interceptors when to "go." Considerable pushing and pulling between the two latter services over a period of three years finally resulted in a clear pronouncement from the Secretary of Defense that the Army would have responsibility for the ORTRACK mission; that the outputs from the ORTRACK system would be displayed at the required command and control centers of the Army, Air Force, and Navy, in order that all could get immediate access to the information coming out of the system and take their own action as befitted their individual roles.

This compromise, although it added considerably to the complexity of the system, was satisfactory to the services, and it became evident in the fall of 1962 that a procurement of the system could be expected in 1963. The Weapons System Division, in the fall of 1962, delivered to the Army an unsolicited proposal, outlining in some detail, a system concept involving seven radar sensing stations, three in the United States and four in strategic locations outside of the United States, utilizing coaxial cable, RF, and tropospheric scatter communications back to a central command point for the Army in the United States, and with microwave relay stations to carry the information from there as required to Air Force NORAD command and control centers at Colorado Springs; the Pentagon, and the Strategic Air Force Headquarters at Omaha, Nebraska; and also to Navy CINCCOM Headquarters in the Pentagon.

WSD Alerted to Expect RFQ

All indications from the Army were that in the spring of 1963 a Request for Proposal would be issued to competing companies, upon which an award for a research program would be based, which would lead to prototype development of a sensing station data processing and control center; that this phase would then be followed after extensive prototype testing by an extension of the contract for production, installation test, and test of the seven operating sites. In April 1963, Fry sounded an alarm within WSD at a marketing staff meeting, stating that indeed money had been approved for ORTRACK by the Department of Defense for fiscal year 1964–65; and that it looked as though an RFQ would be forthcoming within a month or two, judging from a sudden spurt of activity, special meetings, etc., that were being held at Army Headquarters to develop a specification for the system upon which the procurement would be based.

Phillip West, head of marketing, personally looked into this, discussed it with Harry Cook, and decided that Fry was right; and at Mr. Young's staff meeting the last week in April, West pointed out that WSD should immediately form a proposal team, get started on an outline, and start aligning a subcontractor team. It was apparent that much system analysis work remained to be done and that time was indeed running out. West got approval from the general manager, Henry Young, to treat this oncoming procurement as the highest priority program within the division, and requested that a tentative proposal team be established and reported on at Young's next staff meeting. At the next staff meeting, Fry reported that he could not get Paul Travers to name anyone from program management to manage the proposal effort. Travers replied that he fully recognized the importance of this program and that he had an excellent man named Roger Ford working in the strategic weapons group under Taylor Wharton, who should be free within another month, but right now was already involved over his head in getting acceptance of late delivery by the customer on a piece of equipment which had been particularly troublesome and on which the company was losing money. A penalty clause on delivery of this item made it imperative that the program not be disturbed until delivery was completed. Then, Roger Ford would be made available. Travers ended the meeting by indicating he wanted to see immediate action in formation of a proposal team. He asked Wharton to make an estimate of the cost of the proposal and report on this at Young's next staff meeting.

On May 15, at Young's staff meeting, Wharton gave a short presentation to Young's staff on an organization, a schedule, and a proposed budget for accomplishing the ORTRACK proposal. The budget was approximately $200,000 but could be less if a major subcontractor could be chosen to share the load of designing and developing the major structural parts of the pedestal and antennas for the large search radars that would be required.

The controller, Elliot Hammond, questioned the wisdom of proceeding with the proposal effort at that time, in view of not having a definite indication as to when the RFQ would be issued by the Army. He pointed out the expensive gamble that was being taken by going ahead with detailed plans, without knowing fully what the RFQ would specify. The group called in Harry Cook to express his feelings concerning what possible unforeseen requirements might be in store for them when the RFQ came in.

Cook stated that, based on contracts both he and Fry had had recently, there was every indication that the earlier unsolicited proposal that Electronics International had submitted was being used as a basis for the specification preparation and that in all likelihood, the RFQ, when issued, would have their own words, specifications, and numbers in it. He stated that it was difficult to determine this accurately because, at this point in a procurement, the services "always clamp up tight" and are under strict instructions not to talk to prospective competitors, in order not to give one unfair advantage over the other, etc.

Fry was called in, and agreed completely with Cook that their years of doing their "homework" were paying off; that no other contractor had done nearly as much ORTRACK-oriented work as Electronics International had; and that he was virtually certain that the specifications in the RFQ would be very similar to what they had proposed earlier.

Young asked him about his certainty of dates on the RFQ, and Fry quoted Col. Bernhardt of Army Headquarters as saying that the Army "simply had to have it done and out by June, in order that competitive responses could be received, the evaluation of the competitors made, a winner chosen, and the program 'go-ahead' authorized by October of '64." Since Col. Bernhardt was to become the senior officer in charge of ORTRACK for the Army, certainly a key position with regard to the whole procurement, it was agreed that Wharton should go ahead with the proposal program, bringing Ford on board as soon as he could get free; that Fry would retain marketing responsibility for the job; and that Hammond was to set up a shop order that the proposal team could charge to, in the amount of $150,000. Young said the division could not afford $200,000 for the proposal—that all their budgeting and profit forecasting was based on a $150,000 cost and that WSD would have to do it for that. Hammond objected violently to authorizing $150,000, stating that he felt a much more detailed estimate than the rough $200,000 that Wharton had prepared was desirable for an effort of this size. Before committing a full $150,000, Young requested permission to fund only $30,000, which would suffice till a more detailed cost estimate could be made. This was agreed to by all concerned. Young's staff meeting was adjourned with the understanding that a detailed cost proposal would be available the next week.

RFQ Delayed

At Young's May 31 staff meeting, Phillip West reported that Fry had called him from Washington that morning, stating that apparently there was going to be a delay in the RFQ; that the Army internal review cycles were taking longer than had been anticipated. Col. Bernhardt had assured him that in all probability, the slippage would be only two weeks; however, to be conservative, it might be wise to plan for up to a month. Paul Travers reported that this was indeed fortunate, as Taylor Wharton had reported to him that he was finding it extremely difficult to man the prop team. Virtually all the senior personnel were already engaged on important jobs, both within the program management and within Fred Ives engineering department. He stated he got lots of sympathy but no action, in getting people assigned to the job. He had approached Harry Cook, manager of systems engineering, with the request that Francis Halsey personally supervise the technical aspects of the proposal from the position of systems engineering manager of the proposal. Halsey had done a lot on the original unsolicited proposal. Cook said this would be impossible due to his existing commitments on several programs. He suggested Harvey Ransom for the job who, although not as experienced as Halsey himself, was a likely and capable man to head up the systems engineering.

Ransom was coming off a job and was available immediately, so he was signed up by Wharton and given the assignment of manning the systems group who would work underneath him. Ransom was known as a very brilliant systems engineer with a great depth of knowledge in many technical disciplines. He was somewhat mercurial in disposition, however. He had been known to actually walk off the job on one occasion. However, he had also been known to work 18 hours a day, without being asked, for weeks on end, if it was necessary in order to meet a goal in which he felt a strong personal interest. He had been a key participant in the submission of the unsolicited proposal which reputedly was the basis for the Army specification in the RFQ and was agreeable to serve in this role, although he suggested that he would much rather spend his time on technical problems rather than the management problems involved in organizing and running a high-pressure proposal team.

Travers said that due to lack of manpower he had not been able to get the detailed cost estimate that Hammond had asked for in the earlier staff meeting. However, he would have it by the next meeting and urged everyone, particularly Fred Ives, to get good people freed up to support the requirement. He showed an organization chart of the proposed proposal team to the staff. Everyone concurred on the organizational concept but did not see how approximately 50 senior engineers and scientists could be divorced from their present activities in order to spend the two months estimated required to turn out the proposal.

At his June 7 staff meeting, Young asked about progress on the RFQ. West had just heard from Fry. Fry had heard nothing about any further delay and said that he still expected the RFQ in from one to two weeks. He stated that he knew that final copies of the specification were resting on the desk of the Director of Procurement, Lt. Col. Youngquest. He presumed that these were there for final review, attaching of "boiler plate" terms, etc., prior to mailing. Despite numerous attempts at contacts by Fry and Cook, as well as exploiting the full resources of the regional sales offices both at Washington and Army Headquarters, no new information could be brought to bear on either the nature of the specification or time at which the RFQ would be issued.

On June 15, West reported no new information on the proposal. Indeed, he was getting skeptical that the RFQ would be out as soon as Col. Bernhardt had said, and he said the delay was fortunate, because WSD still had not been able to organize effectively to do the proposal. Hammond said it was fortunate that they had not organized to do the proposal, or they would have already spent a good deal of the $150,000 originally estimated, and that, indeed, before WSD proceeded any further with any expenditures, they should get a firmer indication of when the RFQ would be out. He suggested curtailment of all activity.

This was protested violently by both West and Travers on the basis that all work done in the preproposal period gave them that much more of a chance to do a better job when the RFQ came out; they would have more homework done and would be able for once to avoid the desperate last minute climax usually associated with proposal efforts. Young agreed that effort should continue but at a very low level. Travers pointed out that Wharton, despite continuing efforts over the past weeks, had been unable to get commitments for manning the proposal from Fred Ives's engineering organization; that except for Harvey Ransom there was not a single, solitary commitment; that in general, Ives and his organization seemed to be taking the attitude that they would face up to the reality of manning the proposal team when, and if, the RFQ was issued; and that, meanwhile, all the cries of "wolf" had proven to be false alarms, and they were getting tired of it.

Further Delay on RFQ Virtually Halts ORTRACK Program Activity

On June 15, Fry called in from Washington saying that he had heard that the RFQ was going to be delayed another month as a result of the Department of Defense (Office of the Secretary for Research and Engineering) disagreement with the estimation of the orbital threat. There seemed to be dissension between the services and DOD as to what the satellite population would be in subsequent years and wat percentage of the satellite population might possibly contain weapons. DOD also questioned the ability of the system to give usable information in view of possible course changes which could be made by sophisticated, self-maneuvering satellites. DOD also felt that it would be cheaper and would be more effective to have a larger number of smaller stations equipped with smaller, lower-powered radars, deployed over a larger number of locations for picking up early additions, omissions, and changes in the satellite orbit population.

Harry Cook was quizzed on this and pointed out that if one looked at the economics of a large number of small stations compared to the cost of the seven large, high-power ones that WSD had proposed, the odds were greatly in favor of the large stations. He pointed out that the Department of Defense was increasingly concerned over the cost of operating detection and warning sites and that concentrating the support services in several large stations represented a genuine economy. He felt that air space orbital coverage would be about the same in either case.

With the interests in Washington strongly centered on cost effectiveness, it was agreed that this probably would be the eventual concept. Fry was ordered to keep an ear to the ground. Meanwhile, all detailed work on the preproposal effort came to a halt. Ransom was reassigned to a job in trouble, with the commitment to make himself immediately available to the ORTRACK proposal once the RFQ came in. By this time Roger Ford became available from his previous job and was spending time studying the earlier unsolicited proposal, early marketing reports, etc., and in general, trying to get ready for the RFQ.

Fry, West, Ford, Wharton, and Travers all kept a close eye on what was going on with regard to the RFQ down at Army Headquarters. By this time they had briefed all personnel and all marketing activities, both within the Weapons System Division and elsewhere, to be on the alert for information with regard to RFQ issue, and in particular with regard to any intelligence which might bear upon the DOD objections to the system and any possible changes that might be forthcoming. Isolated reports were sent in from the field offices, which contributed essentially nothing to what was already known, and it was concluded by Fry and West that, indeed, they were closest to the situation of anyone and that they could count on little outside help in getting information.

Col. Bernhardt was extremely embarrassed at the RFQ not having been issued. Although he felt unable to discuss the issue, he did state that he felt he owed it to the various contractors not to keep them on the hook unnecessarily and that it was possible it might be another month before the RFQ was issued. He stated that there was still considerable discussion going on in the procurement circles, in parallel with the technical discussions with DOD, as to what type of contract should be issued for this work. The procurement people felt that a fixed-price proposal was desirable in that it would limit the liability of the government. Bernhardt said he was not sure just what he was in favor of, that he was concerned about the rigidity of a fixed-price contract situation in view of the "researchy" nature of the development, particularly on the prototype phases. He stated that the manner of contracting might be left up to the competitors as part of their proposal. He said that in any event a cost-plus-fixed-fee contract would be out of the question, but a cost-plus-incentive-free type of contract with realistic incentives should certainly be considered.

Fry kept following progress by weekly contacts at Col. Bernhardt's office in Army Headquarters. In early August, Col. Bernhardt was called on a special assignment to the West Coast, to be gone for three months. Fry was extremely concerned about this, as Bernhardt was the spark plug for the whole program, and with him gone, Fry doubted if much action would take place until the requirement for budgeting next year's funds came up, at which time a decision would have to be made as to whether to go ahead and utilize the funds already budgeted this year for the program or to tide them over to the next year.

By this time the word ORTRACK had become a dirty word back at WSD. Indeed, the word was used to denote something that was scheduled to happen which really never quite did. Roger Ford stayed on the job but had no assistants, and he largely spent his time refining his concepts of the proposal team and laying out schedules for the proposal based on various contingencies. He had worked out a detailed proposal schedule in the event that a two-month response time, a six-week response time, or a one-month response time were given. He had discussions with the Communications Divisions of DPD with regard to their role in participating in the proposal, and had a tentative agreement from their marketing manager that they would participate in, and take responsibility for, all communications aspects of the job, including the handling of any communications subcontractors who might be required.

Ford also approached a number of heavy mechanical construction organizations with the objective of selecting a teammate for the large radar pedestal assembly construction, which was too large and heavy a type of work to be performed at the Weapons System Division electronic plant. As a result of these efforts, he had established a good rapport with the Parker Mechanisms Company, the major manufacturer of servo-driven pedestals for instrumentation radars. They indicated an interest in teaming up with Electronics International, and a letter of understanding had been received stating that it was their desire to participate at their own cost in the proposal effort, with the understanding that if the job were won by EIC they would become subcontractors for the mechanical elements of the antenna and pedestal. EIC confirmed this relationship.

Ford discussed optimum proposal organizations with West, Fry, Wharton, Travers, Ives, Cook, Markham, Forbes, and Ames. After several rounds of refinement, an organization was evolved which was considered novel, but a genuine improvement over the one Travers had presented at Young's May 31 staff meeting. Ford was unable, though, to get any commitments for manning this organization except for himself and Ransom.

THE ORTRACK PROGRAM

August 28

Fry received a telegram from Col. Bernhardt's headquarters stating that the three copies of the ORTRACK Request for Quotation (RFQ) would be issued on August 31 to each competitor. Fry alerted all management personnel involved in ORTRACK and told them he would go to Washington to personally pick up the three copies on August 31, with a view toward having himself, Ransom, and Roger Ford review the RFQ over the weekend so that on Monday, September 1, they would have completed an analysis of wherein the RFQ differed from what they had expected.

August 31

Fry picked up the three copies from Lt. Col. Youngquist at 3 P.M. He personally delivered copies that evening to Ransom and Ford at their homes. All three spent the weekend studying the RFQ.

September 1

At 8:15 Monday morning, Ransom, Ford, and Fry reviewed their separate analyses of the RFQ. All had been shocked and extremely distressed to see that a system consisting of a large number of small low-powered radar stations was specified quite clearly. It was apparent that the Department of Defense influence had made itself felt and that EIC's earlier analyses of the economics of the configuration were either wrong or failed to include some apparently important considerations.

Ransom guessed that it would take approximately 16 separate stations to get the required air space coverage, using the radars with the size and power that the RFQ specified. This meant that the radar for ORTRACK would resemble hardly at all the giant 80-foot dish radars that WSD had been building for missile early warning applications, upon which they had had extensive prior technical, schedule, and cost knowledge, and from experience with which they had hoped to borrow heavily, so that the ORTRACK radar would be only a slightly modified copy of a radar they had built earlier; and for which Parker Mechanisms, Inc., had supplied the pedestal and antenna dish.

A second distressing fact related to the smaller radars was that a number of radars developed by other firms already existed which were potentially of the right size and power to accomplish the ORTRACK mission. One competitor in particular, probably the most formidable of the five to whom RFQ's had been sent, was the Universal Electro-dynamics Corporation, an industry giant which had long been working in the radar field in competition with WSD. Universal Electrodynamics had, in 1962, won a competition, in which WSD participated, for developing a small experimental, high-precision, high-frequency radar designed to exploit new technologies in signal processing, range, and velocity resolu-tion. Ransom stated that it appeared that the ORTRACK specification could be filled almost perfectly by that radar now completed and under test at Universal Electrodynamics.

Most of the requirements for communications, displays, command, and control centers, etc., were similar to what had been specified in the early unsolicited WSD proposal.

The RFQ called for submission of separate technical, management, and cost proposals on October 15, which worked out to be exactly 45 calendar days from the date of publication. Since Ford had developed his schedule for essentially a six weeks' program, he at least felt he had the working basis for planning the proposal. A page limitation was stressed, allowing only 100 pages for the technical proposal and 75 for the management section. Detailed formats were provided for submission of cost data in the cost section.

After lunch, a meeting was called in the general manager's office with all concerned department heads, and others as required, to brief them on the content of the FRQ. Harry Cook was absolutely stunned at the news of the small-radar requirement. He stated he would stake his professional reputation on the fact that the number of radars called for in the RFQ would cost 50 per cent more than the large ones WSD had quoted earlier; that the operational cost would be virtually twice as much; and that, indeed, it should be completely obvious to the government that the cost of the system would be far more than the amount that had earlier been budgeted for the system for fiscal year 1964 to 1967 budgets.

Phillip West felt that they must have missed something in their evalu-ation of what the customer wanted; that marketing would do its best to find out what had happened; but that meanwhile, the job must proceed, and everyone should start working.

Fred Ives, who had remained on the fringes of all the previous ORTRACK planning, stated that based on what he had heard that morning, he felt it would be wiser for WSD not to bid ORTRACK, since the radars represented over half of the cost of the system, and since WSD was caught without an existing design of its own and would have to develop a brand new one, whereas Universal Electrodynamics Corporation already had a suitable design paid for by another project. He felt WSD was virtually out of the running from a cost standpoint even before it started. Ives was overruled on this suggestion by virtually everyone present. ORTRACK was exactly the type of business that WSD had made its reputation in; it was the major procurement of the year; and no other large ones were in sight for some time. Although WSD was indeed in an undesirable radar development position, WSD still was generally superior in the radar field to Universal Electrodynamics. In other areas WSD felt quite confident that it was superior to them and, indeed, might even have usable existing designs for displays, consoles, etc., that Universal Electrodynamics did not have, which would tend to offset their radar advantage. Travers pointed out that Parker Mechanisms had built smaller radars before; that they were already on the WSD team; and that they could be of great assistance to WSD as far as the mechanical aspects of the newer, smaller radars would be concerned.

The meeting continued until 5:30, whereupon it broke up with full agreement that WSD should proceed full speed ahead with the OR-TRACK proposal effort. Ford was requested to pull together his "prop" team and have a full staff working by the end of the week, with the really key people assigned by the following day.

As Ransom left the meeting, he told Ford that he would not be able to start work on ORTRACK until the 5th, since he was leaving that night for Eglin Field, Florida, to brief an irate customer, General W. V. LeComte, on the performance to be expected from a small data display system that Ransom had conceived over a year ago and which was two months late on its delivery schedule. He stated that under the circumstances it would be unheard of to cancel such a briefing, and that Ford should look to Harry Cook to get things started in his absence.

Ford gave a copy of the RFQ to Bill Greenwood, who had been waiting all day to take it to a local vendor to get 50 copies made so that all key personnel on the proposal would have their own copy for reference, etc.

September 4

At 9 A.M. Ford called a kickoff meeting for all who would be concerned with the ORTRACK job. This meeting included those whom he wanted assigned to the prop team, as well as most of the supervisors of the engineering department, whose people would, in one way or another, participate during the proposal effort, either as members of the proposal team or within the department working on preliminary design, costing, and scheduling of hardware items for the proposal team.

At the meeting, Fry pointed out the importance of this job to WSD. Ford outlined the job in detail, going through its early history, pointing out what had to be done and what the organizational concept was for getting it done, and asked for support from all concerned for what he knew would be a very busy six weeks. People left the meeting feeling generally very good about the program and believing that somehow they would overcome the handicap resulting from the change in radar concept. They felt that with Ford running it, a good job would probably get done.

September 7

Travers asked Ford how the proposal was going. Ford showed him the schedule shown in Exhibit 5. He pointed out that by this date the team was to have been selected and all assignments made. However, because of Ransom's absence, and because a number of people on whom he had counted could not break free immediately from their other jobs, the proposal was only half manned at the time. He stated he was spending virtually all of his time trying to get people assigned to the job. The 50 copies of the RFQ had been delivered on the 6th and were just waiting for people to come and use them.

Travers was greatly concerned at the unmanned state of the proposal organization. He called Henry Young, requesting his urgent assistance in getting support for the ORTRACK proposal team. Young called Fred Ives, mentioning the names of some people whom Ford had told him were needed immediately on this job. Ives knew the existing assignments of several of these people and pointed out to Young that their present assignments had been planned from months back; that it simply was not reasonable to expect them to drop their efforts in midstream, so to speak, to change to another job. He stated that in some cases it would take several days to phase in a substitute and that a hurried phase-in of replacement engineers would without question cause delays and increase the costs of existing programs. He said that Harvey Ransom had reported back from his briefing of General LeComte that the General was furious at WSD's delay in delivering his display system as promised and had said that if WSD couldn't demonstrate a working system within the next two weeks, he would institute cancellation proceedings.

In order to preserve WSD's reputation, Ives stated that it was obviously necessary for Ransom to stay on his present job of investigating apparent incompatibilities between key elements of the system. He stated that, in fact, he felt that two weeks was not going to see the end of the problems; that they thought they could convince General LeComte to stick with them a little longer, since it was not costing the General anything, the equipment being on a fixed-price contract. Ives stated that

Exhibit 5

SCHEDULE FOR ORTRACK PROPOSAL ESTABLISHED
AUGUST 15 BY RODGER FORD

A schedule/Gantt chart with calendar dates for SEPTEMBER and OCTOBER, and "DAYS AFTER RFQ RECEIPT" (1 2 3 4 5 6 7 8 9 10 11 12 13 14 15 16 17 18 19 20 21 22 23 24 25 26 27 28 29 30 31 32 33 34 35 36 37 38 39 40 41 42 43 44 45).

MANAGEMENT PROPOSAL
- RFQ REPRODUCED AND DISTRIBUTED — S
- KICK OFF MEETING — A
- PROPOSAL TEAM SELECTED — T
- ORGANIZATION CHART COMPLETE — U (ALL ASSIGNMENTS TO TEAM MADE) (INDIVIDUALS NAMED FOR KEY POSITIONS – RESPONSIBILITY AND AUTHORITY ESTABLISHED)
- SHOP ORDER STRUCTURE ESTABLISHED — R,S
- MGMT. INFO. & CONTROL SECTION COMPLETE — D,U — S
- FACILITY INVENTORY SECTION COMPLETE — A,N — A
- EXPERIENCE BACKGROUND SECTION COMPLETE — Y,D — T,S
- INDIVIDUAL RESUMES COMPLETE — A — U,U
- EDITING AND REWRITE — Y — R,N
- CRITICAL REVIEW — D,D
- TOP MANAGEMENT REVIEW — A,A
- PRINTING — Y–Y

TECHNICAL PROPOSAL
- RFQ REPRODUCED AND DISTRIBUTED
- KICK OFF MEETING
- PROPOSAL TEAM SELECTED — (ALL ASSIGNMENTS TO TEAM MADE)
- SYSTEM BLOCK DIAGRAM COMPLETE — (ROUGH SUBSYSTEM SPECIFICATIONS AVAILABLE)
- FINAL SUBSYSTEM SPECS AVAILABLE
- RECEIPT OF TECHNICAL DRAFTS
- EDITING AND REWRITE
- CRITICAL REVIEW
- TOP MANAGEMENT REVIEW
- PRINTING

COST PROPOSAL
- COST ESTIMATE REQUESTS SENT TO:
- MFG. AND ENG. DEPARTMENTS
- SUBCONTRACTORS & VENDORS
- ALL ESTIMATES RECEIVED
- PROJECT MANAGEMENT REVIEW
- V.P. COST REVIEW
- EXEC. V.P. REVIEW
- PRINTING

DELIVERY OF TOTAL PROPOSAL

although Ransom should be available in from three to four weeks, that this was so late into the prop effort that it would be undesirable to wait for him, and he suggested D'Arcy Jones as a substitute.

Young told Ives to get in touch with Ford and to please do whatever he could to support Ford, who had a very difficult job to do, and it appeared, he was getting a slow start despite energetic effort. Ives agreed to do everything he could and called Ford about Jones. Ford asked Jones to study the system over the weekend so that on Monday the 10th, he would be able to take over the systems engineering prop team.

Ford's problems on the technical side of the proposal were somewhat offset by good news on the management prop progress. He had been fortunate in getting Lars Svendon, another of Taylor Wharton's program management men, assigned to head up the management proposal. Svendon had written many management proposals, and this one appeared to be fairly straightforward. He had already sat down with those members who had been assigned to the team and outlined what he expected from each for the management proposal. He had reviewed the schedule shown in Exhibit 5 that Ford had prepared earlier, and concurred in it. He had Kenneth Munson get together all of the major proposals that had been written in the past two years, with a view toward selecting techniques and/or excerpts from the best features of each. He wanted particularly to convey to the military the unique management control concept that had evolved at WSD. This concept represented an integration of financial, cost, and schedule reporting with the majority of operations being performed automatically by computers and tabulating machines. Svendon had been instrumental in getting this system accepted at WSD and had achieved a certain recognition in the American Management Society for his contributions to this field. He was able to report to Ford that he was on schedule with the management prop and foresaw no difficulties, provided the inputs which depended on the technical proposal did not slip.

September 11

Ford reported to Travers, West, and Young that he had completed forming his prop team and that work was well underway. The prop team is shown in Exhibit 6 (to assist the reader, the major roles of each group of the prop team are described). Ford felt that although this was not the caliber group he had hoped for, it still represented a very talented group, and he felt that they could do a good job.

September 12

Ford asked D'Arcy Jones if the systems block diagram would be completed on schedule on the 14th.

The systems block diagram is a schematic method of representing all of

Exhibit 6

THE "ORTRACK" PROPOSAL TEAM

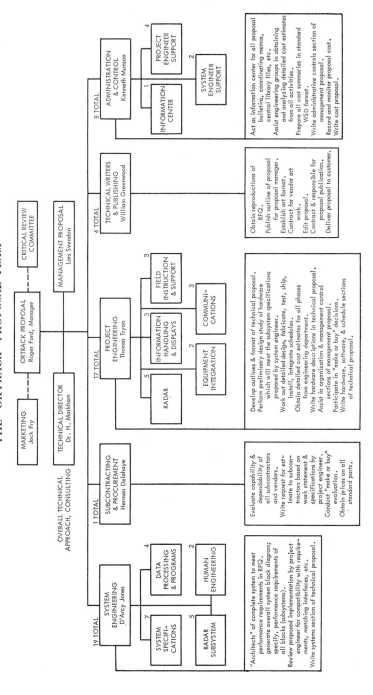

the major interactions between all of the major components of any system. For a complex system such as ORTRACK, it usually takes a sheet of paper about 3×4 feet filled fairly solidly with 2-inch-square blocks, each labeled for a different component in the system. All of the signal or information flow going out of, and coming into, each block is noted along appropriately coded lines drawn between blocks. It resembles a giant electrical wiring diagram for a radio. This diagram having established the performance requirements for each block, a specification can be written for the contents of the block, which can vary from a single electronic chassis anywhere up to whole rows of cabinets full of electronic gear.

These specifications are then carefully checked so that the input and output to each and every block is compatible with the output and input of related blocks throughout the whole diagram. Once the block diagram and equipment specifications have been written and checked, the major conceptual effort is concerned with further refinements, more sophisticated analysis of system performance for off-design conditions, and so on.

Jones replied that due to the late start, he would be unable to complete the diagram by the 14th. Indeed, he wasn't even sure he could get it out by the 18th. Ford, upon investigation, found that Jones was right, and that the whole effort was going to be slowed up by the late availability of the block diagram. He called Harry Cook to urge him to assist Jones in any way possible, as a real bottleneck was apparent in this area. Cook authorized Jones's entire group to work over the weekend, but despite that extra time, he doubted that the block diagram would be ready by the 18th.

Ford asked Svendon whether the organizational chart that would be shown in the management proposal for the proposed implementation of ORTRACK would be completed on schedule. Svendon pointed out that he had till Saturday, according to the schedule, to complete it. However, he was having a difficult time getting permission from their supervisors to show individuals whom he considered essential as committed to the proposed implementation organization. Previously, he and Ford had decided it would be wise to show the same people in the implementation organization chart who worked on the proposal. Many additional, of course, would be required. It was felt that the customer would react favorably to the idea of having the people who had demonstrated their knowledgeability of ORTRACK in writing the proposal assigned to the job when it was won.

Some of the line managers objected strenuously to committing their people, stating that ORTRACK was trying to gobble up the best men in every area and that the division could not afford this. For instance, Svendon wanted to show Ted Forbes as full-time manager of ORTRACK radar development; similarly Daniel Troast as full-time manager of communications, and Ross MacIntyre as manager of antennas and pedestals. Ives pointed out that with these key men spending full time on ORTRACK, their unique and senior talents would be lost to the rest of the developments in their functional areas, and he was very much against this. He stated the job could be done by lower-level supervision, and nonsupervisors, that they would have the full benefits of working under senior personnel such as had been requested, and that this approach would not penalize all the other programs who were depending on the same level of talent.

September 17

Tom Tryon told Ford that the situation was becoming critical with regards to getting detailed design and cost estimates done on time. These depended on the availability of specifications. The system block diagram would only be in rough form by the 18th, and the specifications were barely started. Tryon and Kenneth Munson joined in saying that they had already allowed systems engineering all the time they possibly could; that because of this, less than two weeks had been allowed for sending out RFQ's to vendors and subcontractors and for getting quotes back. This was somewhat faster than the fastest they had ever succeeded in doing this before. Tryon pointed out that in lieu of having a system block diagram, they had been in close contact with Parker Mechanisms Company and the Communications Division of DPD, as well as with Fred Ives's functional department, but by now all preliminary groundwork and estimating that could be done had been done; and that further work was useless until usable specifications were published that could be the basis of cost estimates from the various vendors, subcontractors, and so on.

September 20

Herman Delahaye received a telegram from Parker Mechanisms saying that they had not received their RFQ yet, and that because of press of other work, they would have to take their people off the ORTRACK proposal until the RFQ arrived; that it would take them two weeks from receipt of RFQ (with specifications) to deliver firm cost estimates. They requested guidance as to whether the estimates would be expected on a CPFF, CPIF, or fixed-price basis.[2] The Army RFQ left it open to the bidders as to what contract type was proposed. Parker Mechanisms said they would prefer to quote CPIF, as the new radar, although very similar in size to one they had developed before, the dynamic servo requirements were considerably greater, even to the point of being a considerable technical risk. Hence they felt it unwise to quote on a fixed-price basis.

Svendon told Ford that he had essentially completed the organiza-

---

2 See Appendix 2 (to this case) for an explanation of the types of government contracts and Appendix 3 (to this case) for a perspective on the patterns of defense contracting after World War II.

tional chart to be shown in the proposal, but he didn't have full approval of all the names. The one he was worried about most was Ted Forbes, his proposed radar manager. He and Ford decided not to try further to obtain Ives approval on this, since he was almost bound to say no. They sincerely felt that the best use of Forbes for the welfare of WSD was in this role, and left it for higher-level management to change, should they see fit, during the final review period. Svendon had completed a tentative shop order structure for all the hardware, by working with the project engineering people under Tryon and in Kenneth Munson's group. This was done on the basis of a very rough system black diagram available on the 18th. Since it was merely an administrative control structure, it would probably not change, even though the system structure changed appreciably.

September 21

The system block diagram was published with suitable specifications attached. The project organization under Tryon pounced on these, incorporated them into cost estimate requests, etc., that had already been written but were awaiting the specification to be referenced in the request.

Ford called a meeting with Young, West, Fry, Ives, Hammond, and Jones to discuss how to bid, CPIF or fixed price. Ford outlined the background WSD had in building roughly similar equipments under CPFF contracts. All but one of nine contracts in the last three years had overrun, an average of 23 per cent.

Ives protested, saying that WSD was much more mature now, was down to a fighting team, and would not overrun anymore in jobs such as ORTRACK. He felt that WSD should bid CPIF to demonstrate its sincerity in meeting a target price.

West rejoined that WSD "hadn't a Chinaman's chance in hell" of winning ORTRACK on a CPIF basis. He said the customer, based on WSD's past performance, could only conclude that WSD would overrun again and that the thought of losing perhaps 20 per cent of their profit wasn't going to make WSD meet its cost arget. West stated that the only price the customer would believe was a fixed price. He stated that this would give WSD a big advantage over other competitors who usually overran also.

Ives claimed that other competitors, and in particular Universal Elec- trodynamics, had overrun contracts much more than WSD did and that the customer would believe a WSD CPIF price much more than the other's CPFF or CPIF prices. He said to quote fixed price would require the addition of such large contingencies that WSD would price itself out of the competition.

Young asked why we were so unsure of ourselves that we have to add large contingencies to our price? He pointed out that WSD had built

ORTRACK type equipment for many years and that if WSD couldn't price it accurately by now "we'd better give up."

Ives protested again, but West won the point by asking Ives if he thought that the customer would award WSD the contract if WSD bid CPIF, but Universal Electrodynamics bid fixed price *without* a large contingency? There was a reluctant agreement finally that the job should be bid fixed price. Ford asked Munson to notify Parker Mechanisms and the Communications Division that fixed-price responses to WSD RFQ's were mandatory.

September 24

By working through Saturday and Sunday, the 22nd and 23rd, Tryon's and Munson's team were able to get the cost estimate requests out to both internal and external groups.

Upon finding that all of the cost estimate requests had been finished over the weekend, Ford was delighted, and called Munson's boss Elliot Hammond to commend Munson for his energy and diligence. He also commended Tryon's people in a brief status meeting which was designed to bring all up to date on latest progress. At the status meeting, Fry brought in some new intelligence. He had been talking with some officers from the Air Force Electronic Systems Command, who had been concerned with ballistic missile warning systems, etc. They pointed out that they had been having a good deal of trouble with natural electromagnetic radiation (aurora borealis or Northern Lights) in their northern sites, which tended to blind the radar system so that it could not see target missiles. They had sponsored a research program on means of combating this problem, which had shown that a much higher-frequency radar gave over 100 times better penetration through the electromagnetic radiation than their normal operating frequency. They stated that for future early warning work, they were going to specify higher-frequency radars. They pointed out that an additional bonus was better accuracy in distance (range) measurements and that by utilizing new low-noise signal-processing techniques, they were able to obtain the same effective missile detection capability with small, lower-powered radars than they achieved before, with the giant low-frequency radars.

D'Arcy Jones, upon hearing this, stated that this could explain the change from low- to high-frequency radars in the RFQ. He pointed out that in the original WSD unsolicited proposal, the seven site locations which had been selected had been placed in such a manner that they never directly faced northward into the electromagnetic radiation zones. Accordingly, the electromagnetic radiation problem was avoided in the system as proposed. He pointed out that with 16 stations of a generally shorter range, the stations had to be dispersed over a larger area and that undoubtedly a number of the 16 were going to be forced to work against the electromagnetic environment. With this being the case, it would not make sense to have both small, high-frequency and large, low-frequency radars in the same system, due to logistics support problems, etc., as well as the cost of two developments instead of one, etc. He pointed out that with the smaller, higher-frequency radar, utilizing techniques that had become known since the unsolicited proposal had been submitted, even the range would be considerably better than they had earlier imagined.

It was pointed out that at the higher frequency, a smaller antenna dish is desirable in order not to focus the beam to a too narrow, pencil-type beam. He stated the antenna dish size specified for the higher operating frequency resulted in a narrower radar beam than that of the large WSD radars that had been built, and that this could be the reason for the higher dynamic requirements in pedestal servo performance for the smaller radar, since the smaller beams must be moved around faster through space to cover the same volume of air as a wider beam. No one disagreed with Jones on this hypothesis.

Svendon reported that the management prop was on schedule. He had completed the facility inventory, summary of appropriate WSD experience background, and had collected résumés from previous props for all who were going to be named in the implementation organization. These were to be updated to include the individual's latest experience. He stated he felt they had done a beautiful job on the section on the Management Information and Control System and that the section would be applicable to all future management props as well. He stated that his main problem was that it appeared that too much had been written and that there was going to have to be an appreciable condensation in order to fit within the 75-page limit specified by the RFQ.

Ford asked Jones how he was making out with the technical prop length, which was limited to 100 pages. Jones stated that there was a great deal of analytical background that had to go into the prop, and it was going to be extremely difficult to keep the size down. He stated that he felt that the systems engineering section alone would need approximately 45 pages out of the 100 to define the systems block diagram and the analytical background behind it. Tryon, present at the meeting, stated that he had been counting on systems not taking more than 25 pages; that indeed it would take him at least 80 pages to describe the hardware and the various phases of the implementation program, together with schedule considerations, test programs, government-furnished equipment requirements, etc. He stated, based on draft material he had seen, that it might well total 100 pages, and he would have to edit it heavily.

September 26

At Greenwood's suggestion, Ford published a bulletin showing the exact page count allotted to every section of both the management and technical proposals. Systems engineering ended up with 35 of the 100 pages in the technical prop. Svendon was horrified to find that the Management Information and Control System section, of which he had been so proud, had only been allowed 10 pages. He protested that this was the real "meat" of the management prop and that at least 25 pages should be allotted to it. He reviewed with Ford the contribution of each paragraph and figure, using rough drafts. Ford agreed it was a beautiful treatment but that since WSD was bidding fixed price, "the government won't really care how we manage it, since it is our own money we are losing if we manage it poorly." Svendon disagreed, saying that the government was very concerned about management because poor management resulted in delays which in turn caused upsets in their own plans, causing additional expense. He still felt that 25 pages should be utilized for this section. Ford overruled him, said it had to be 10 pages and patiently pointed out why he felt that way. It was obvious from Svendon's attitude that he felt very bitter about this "emasculation" of his favorite subject. Ford made a mental note to check on page content at the end of the week, to see how people were doing against the new targets.

Paul Travers had succeeded in lining up a Critical Review Team consisting of eight very senior and experienced program management and engineering personnel, including two from the Communications Division. They were to receive copies of the draft material when it was submitted October 2, and were to have their criticism submitted back to Ford by October 5, in time for their comments to be incorporated in the inevitable rewrite cycle.

Henry Young, WSD general manager, received a phone call from the president and general manager of Parker Mechanisms, Baxter Thorndyke. He protested the requirement to bid fixed price on the pedestal and antenna. He said that the dynamic servo requirements appeared too risky to them to bid fixed price; that in order to protect themselves against loss if they bid fixed price, they would have to add a large contingency to their estimate. Young told him that he expected the same professional performance from Parker Mechanisms that he expected from his own people; that WSD was going to bid fixed price without large contingencies; that if they submitted prices to the customer inflated with contingencies, they didn't stand much chance of winning the job. Young stated that his own engineers had reviewed the servo requirement and that although rigorous, they were within the state of existing technical art and shouldn't cause much uncertainty.

Thorndyke stated that they had felt at first glance that they could meet the servo requirements alright, but that the dynamic stresses put on the antenna by high-performance servos had resulted in a requirement for much heavier antenna construction than was previously foreseen; that this heavy construction in turn, made more of a load for the servos to move, so that the servo problem became increasingly harder, etc., etc. He stated that no one, to his knowledge had ever built such a fast response servo system for a radar set of similar size. Young asked him to do his best on price, saying that it was absolutely essential that WSD bid fixed price and that Parker Mechanisms bid their part fixed price also. Thorndyke agreed to comply with Young's request.

September 28

Tryon reported to Ford that he was getting all kinds of static from virtually everybody who had received an internal ORTRACK RFQ, and in particular from members of Fred Ives's department. Ives's people claimed that the specifications were not detailed enough for the basis of a fixed-price bid. Indeed, it was true that the specifications left a number of questions unanswered. Amendments to the specifications were being issued as these areas were discovered. Tryon reported that the engineering department groups performing the detailed estimates were doing reasonably well in the data processing and display areas, but that they seemed to be floundering rather badly in the radar area. Ford attributed this to the newness of this particular type of radar compared to others that WSD had built before, whereas the command and control, data processing and display equipment was more conventional, based on their past experience.

Tryon estimated that they would have all costs back from both vendors and the engineering department and the Communications Division by October 5. Anything earlier than that appeared totally out of the question. Both Tryon and Ford realized the schedule implications of this with regard to what still had to take place: negotiating each estimate with its originator and conducting the successive management reviews required for approval prior to delivery of the proposal. Ford and Tryon together with Munson, personally visited key areas in Ives's activity to determine the status of the estimating. They were distressed at the general lack of progress that had been made. In talking it over with Ives, Ives stated that he was also disappointed at the lack of progress; that the men simply were not used to bidding fixed price and were very much afraid of making serious estimating errors that could cost the company its entire profit. He pointed out that he had trained his technical people to be conservative in their planning and that this conservatism was probably going to show up in the size of their estimate.

Tryon immediately proposed having the project engineering prop team establish target prices for each component, which Ives's people could use as a guide in performing the detailed estimating. Tryon felt that the prop team had maturity and experience enough to quickly establish very close to the true price for all of the hardware and software. He felt that if a reasonable target price for each component were placed in front of the cognizant engineers, the whole process of estimating would be speeded up. Ives objected violently to this proposal, stating that the engineers had to come up with prices on their own, otherwise they could not be held responsible for the work. He doubted the ability of the prop team to establish reasonable targets, particularly in view of the new nature of the radar that was being quoted. He reminded Tryon and Ford that this particular estimating authority/responsibility controversy had gone on for years; that time-honored methods had worked out the best, namely, having a man who was going to be responsible for executing a job do the pricing of it.

Since this was in truth both an established WSD practice and procedure, Ford and Tryon agreed to leave Ives's people alone in finishing their estimates. They reemphasized to Ives the urgency of getting the estimates in by October 5, pointing out that this was already 5 days behind their original schedule with only 10 days remaining for all the many final tasks required. Ives replied he could not be expected to make up the time that the prop team had lost by late issuance of the component specifications.

Ford reviewed the plans for work over the weekend. Virtually the entire proposal team would be working right on through Saturday and Sunday, the 29th and 30th. By this time most of the prop team effort was associated with the actual writing of the proposal, and it appeared that the October 2 deadline for the first draft would be met. An increasing irritability of all team members was evident. However, many of them had been through this experience enough times before that it was an expected phenomenon, and everyone discounted the other fellow's sensitivity to criticism.

October 2

All draft material for both management and technical props was submitted as scheduled. However, it became immediately evident that virtually everyone had exceeded his allotted page limitation. The technical proposal looked like about 140 pages; the management proposal around 95. Considerable duplication was also found, and the structural treatment varied excessively from section to section, depending upon who had written it. The Critical Review Team asked for eight copies of the draft. Ford was reluctant to have them spend any time on what was so obviously in need of major surgery. However, recognizing the need to receive Critical Review Team comments in time to be incorporated with other rewrites, he authorized Greenwood to make the copies. Greenwood rushed the drafts to an outside vendor for reproduction on a high-speed machine that was not available with WSD. Considerable consternation arose when it was realized that Greenwood had the sole master copy and that until he got back from the vendor, little review work could be accomplished on the text itself.

October 3

Draft copies were made available to the Critical Review Team and extra copies were distributed among key proposal team personnel. In a brief staff meeting Ford chastized all concerned for their excess verbosity. He stated that a lot of thought had gone into establishing the allocation of pages for each section and that he wanted the allocation complied with, without further discussion; and that it was absolutely essential that the draft material be cut down to proper length before the 5th. He stated he expected those concerned to work as many hours as required to meet this deadline.

Thorndyke, president of Parker Mechanisms, called Henry Young and said that after a truly sincere effort at estimating the radar pedestal and antenna on a fixed-price basis per Young's earlier request, they found they simply could not do this without what appeared to be an unreasonable padding of 40 per cent of engineering costs and 10 per cent material cost. This amounted to almost a 50 per cent increase over their CPIF price. Thorndyke pointed out that CPIF pricing could apply only for the first prototype model; that once they had gotten that development experience under their belts, they would later be glad to quote fixed price on the 16 production units. Young pointed out that WSD would not have a chance to come in later with separate quotes for the 16 production units and that the entire bid must be done *now* on a fixed-price basis. Thorndyke replied that their only recourse then was to put in their high fixed-price bid. Before hanging up, Young asked them to quote both ways, so that WSD would have the option at the last minute of deciding which bid to use. Thorndyke was agreeable to this, as they had been working on both methods, and they expected to be able to submit the two estimates by October 5.

When told of this call, Tryon, Munson, and Ford asked Ives to perform a quick one-day investigation of the risks involved in the servo system and structure of the pedestal and antenna that Parker Mechanisms was bidding on. Ives's servomechanisms section had done some excellent servo work and in fact, probably had more total servo experience (although it was of a more varied nature) than the servo people at Parker Mechanisms. Tryon felt that the opinion of Ives's group, particularly that of Byron Trent, should be the basis of WSD's decision as to whether to use Parker Mechanisms' fixed price or the CPIF quote. Trent was alerted by Ives to the problem and proceded immediately with three of his people to dig into all known aspects of it.

October 5

By Friday afternoon, Munson had received most of the detailed equipment estimates from the engineering groups under Ives. He also had a Communications Division estimate and was promised that the Parker

Mechanisms' quote, delayed one day, would be telegraphed in on Saturday morning, the 6th. The quote from the Communications Division surprised everyone by appearing quite reasonable. However, the engineering department quotes appeared astronomical. It was indeed apparent that fear of fixed-price contracting had resulted in considerable padding of the estimates. Whether it had been done consciously or unconsciously, Ford did not know, but he determined to find out. He made an appointment to meet with Ives on Saturday morning to discuss the cost estimate. Until late Friday night, Ford, Tryon, Munson, and their key hardware people worked on their own estimate of what the items to be developed by Ives's department should cost. Ford was sorry this hadn't been done before and that he hadn't insisted on establishing component cost targets for Ives's personnel.

By researching costs from other props, from their own records, plus considerable intuition, they arrived at what they thought was a reasonable figure for Ives's scope of work. Their figure was 35 per cent lower for engineering and other labor than the estimates Ives's group had submitted. Purchased material turned out to be only slightly lower. They agreed to put the maximum possible pressure on Ives the following morning, to get him to rework his estimate.

October 6

Ford, Tryon, and Munson met with Ives, Forbes, Wright, and Ames. The latter came armed with large stacks of estimate notes and appeared to have been well briefed beforehand to defend their estimates. After an hour of caustic opinions being expressed as to the validity of each other's estimates, it became apparent to Ford what had happened. Successive layers of supervision had reviewed and approved the equipment estimates within Ives's engineering department. Each level of reviewers, knowing that they would be responsible for performing the work should the job be won, in order to protect themselves against the unfamiliar fixed-price risks they knew could be expected, had padded the estimates. The designers working at the subassembly level had apparently applied a 10 per cent contingency to their work. The first layer of supervision, in gathering subassembly quotes into a component quote had added another contingency to cover themselves, "just in case."

At Ives's staff review level, Forbes and Wright admitted that due to the uncertainty of the radar area in particular, which embraced both Forbes's and Ames's organizations, they had added a 5 per cent contingency prior to submitting the data to Ives for approval, which was required prior to sending it on to Munson. Ford suggested they spot-check the estimates from other areas for the same phenomenon. Ives protested this, but finally went through Ames's notes in front of the group. Indeed, in Ames's organization, too, contingencies had been added at each level of review. Ives himself, upon ascertaining on Friday that "cushions" had been added, decided not to add any of his own.

After this detailed look, it became apparent even to Ives, that although they might well have protected themselves by this type of estimating, they would undoubtedly lose the job from too high a bid, and he agreed to go back and meet with his people first thing Monday morning, to eliminate all "fat" from the estimate. He in turn requested that Tryon and Munson specify more clearly the documentation, field installation, and test requirements. He had been told that each equipment designer had put in an allowance for configuration control, microfilm reproduction, and handbook rough draft writing, but that the specification invoked on the drafting and graphic arts group also requested costs for handbook writing, microfilming, and configuration control services, etc.

Ives also said that the specifications were not clear with regard to cabling responsibility and that each engineer had put in an allowance for cabling as well as Ames's cabling group, which had been requested to quote the cabling required for the entire system. Ives felt that more care should have been taken earlier in clarifying and eliminating duplication from the specifications. He requested this be done by Ford Monday morning, so that with one reestimating cycle, they could eliminate the duplication and the "fat" at the same time.

Ives stated that it would be impossible at this late date, to call all his people to work for the remainder of the weekend. Ford had not been home before midnight for the past two and one-half weeks and decided to take off for the rest of the day Saturday and all day Sunday. He made sure however, that the rewrite of the technical and management props texts proceeded over the weekend. He had established a new date of the 9th to have a final draft written for top-management's review, including consideration of Critical Review Team comments. He pointed out to all concerned that this was the date the props were originally scheduled to go to the printers and that, indeed, they were skating on thin ice to let it go that long.

October 8

An intense check early in the morning did uncover some areas of overlap in the RFQ's that had been sent out from the prop team to Ives's organization. Ives had been right about the field installation and tests. The field installation and logistic group had quoted on manning the entire site integration test phase, including site management, whereas this duplicated design and development engineering work that had been requested for this phase from Fred Ives's group. This information was passed on to Ives, who was now heavily involved personally in expediting the recosting cycle within engineering.

In the morning mail was a letter from Parker Mechanisms, furnishing both fixed-price and CPIF quotes as previously agreed to. They had neglected to telegraph their quote on the 6th as promised. Ford called Byron Trent to see what conclusion he had reached with regard to the risk inherent in quoting the radar pedestal fixed price. Trent stated it really looked like a 50–50 proposition; that there was indeed some risk involved. However, some quick checks he had run, using rule-of-thumb performance criteria, and assuming a performance from presently available servo components, led him to believe that he could design a servo system that would meet the dynamic requirements. He stated that it should be possible to install pressure unloading valves in the hydraulic drives, which would prevent the buildup of high mechanical accelerations caused by peak pressure transients in the drive system. This feature would decrease very measurably the dynamic loadings and stresses on the antenna structure. This, in turn, would permit a lighter structure, which would in turn minimize the servo, power, and response requirements that had bothered Parker Mechanisms.

When asked what he recommended that WSD do, Trent said he didn't feel he should be asked to make a management decision of how Parker Mechanisms should bid. He would be willing to develop such a servomechanism himself and deliver it to Parker Mechanisms. Ford pressed Forbes, Trent's boss for a management recommendation. Forbes felt very uncomfortable about having to make a quick decision and stated that the matter really required considerably more investigation before an intelligent decision could be made.

Time was running out, and Ford realized that if a decision were going to be made, he would have to make it personally, at the risk of rather severe criticism from the controller, Elliot Hammond, who would take a very dim view, indeed, of WSD's bidding fixed price on something that their own subcontractor only dared bid CPIF. Ford was convinced enough of the need for a fixed-price quote from WSD, and had faith enough in Trent, that he was willing to take the risk of servo troubles with Parker Mechanisms, and he instructed Munson to incorporate the CPIF quote as written from Parker Mechanisms into the overall WSD quote.

The afternoon and evening were spent in frantic snatches of reviewing the rewritten pieces of the proposal; in reviewing individual sections of the cost estimates (now coming back considerably lower from Ives's group). By midnight, October 9th, the complete cost estimate was totaled and put into the standard WSD format. This is shown in column 1, Table 1. The assumptions included manufacturing a prototype radar equipment in the model shop and then manufacturing the 16 production models in the factory. The labor rates used, obtained from Hammond's office, were standard rates updated quarterly, used in quoting all new jobs. The overhead rates applied were also standard rates.

The Communications Division quotation was left untouched, and the Parker Mechanisms cost shown at the CPIF quoted value. Midnight of

October 9th also saw a completion of the final draft of the proposal which had incorporated comments of the Critical Review Board delivered on October 8th. Ford and his staff went home exhausted but with a feeling of genuine accomplishment. All the creative processes had been completed. From here on, it was a matter of review, formating, editing, obtaining approvals, and expediting publication.

October 10

Henry Young dropped into Ford's office asking when he would be able to review the prop and particularly the prop cost. Ford set up a meeting at 1 o'clock and requested that Young make arrangements with T. Royalton Magnus for a top-executive review on the 11th.

In midmorning, H. Markham, the prop technical director, who had contributed very little on the job to date, stopped in Ford's office. Markham stated that he had been working for the past week and a half on a new idea which had turned out to appear very practical, and which should save around $2 million on each radar set. Ford called in Harry Cook, Ted Forbes, and Stewart Wright to hear what Markham had to say. It turned out, indeed, that Markham had a brilliant concept. His idea was to take the raw radar return signal from the target and to digitize it as soon as received; then form the data into standard digital computer language; then utilize a standard commercial type digital computer to do all the data processing. Digital-to-analogue converters in the pedestal would permit the digital computer to command the pedestal directly from the computer output for aiming at a target. This immediate digitizing and direct link to and from the computer would save about 12 expensive cabinets full of electronic gear on each radar set and would eliminate some of the most complex and risky electronic circuits in the entire radar system. The idea seemed so simple that it was remarkable that no one had thought of it before. Stewart Wright remembered reading about a research program which the Air Force had conducted which was aimed at accomplishing this same sort of thing, although as he remembered it, there was still considerable interfacing between the computer and the radar-received signal.

Forbes and Wright were extremely enthusiastic and wanted to immediately revise their cost estimate to incorporate the new system. Tryon asked how they could do this when no block diagram of the new system was in existence nor was a specification available. Forbes and Wright said they really didn't need the diagram or specification; that they felt they had enough intuitive experience and practical knowledge of the type of equipment that would be involved to come up with a fairly good target quote without detailed estimates from their own lower levels. Ford, very reluctantly, said that it was too late, that within a half hour he had to brief the general manager on the costs and get his approval, that one day later he was going to have to brief the executive vice president, and that this simply didn't allow enough time to thoroughly check out the scheme to determine what was really required and what unknown difficulties if any, a more thorough look might uncover.

Markham was somewhat incensed at this decision, saying that he had worked very hard on this concept and saw no reason why it should be dropped just because it involved some extra work at the last minute. Ford pointed out that the Army RFQ specifically called for signal processing equipment which would be thrown out under the "Markham" concept and that the new "Markham" approach would be, therefore, non-responsive to the RFQ. He felt that with adequate time and explanation the idea could certainly be "sold" to the Army, but that they had no time left to write it into the technical prop and that they would just have to keep it as an "ace" up their sleeve for the future. Ford secretly doubted that $2 million per set could be saved, although he felt it probably would save at least $1 million per set.

Ford had lunch with Henry Young, bringing him up to date on the Markham concept, and requested that Young's review not be held until late that afternoon as some loose ends had turned up in the estimate that needed further resolution. Young said that he felt very uncomfortable about the lateness of this review and that he didn't particularly enjoy asking his own boss, the executive vice president, to review the prop on a schedule which allowed no time for coming back with answers to suggestions or questions that he might raise. Ford stated that he did not dare put in a prop for review at either Young's or Magnus' level that wasn't thoroughly substantiated with reasonable estimates; that once before he had been caught in a review with Magnus without adequate backup material, and had been "almost crucified" by Magnus. They agreed to review the prop at 5 o'clock.

A large number of individual reviews had been held with members of the proposal team and the detailed estimators in Ives's organization. As a result of these reviews, further overlaps were discovered, and adjustments downward were made in the estimates. Engineering labor was cut from $71,312,000 down to $64,396,000 at cost level. Also, the prop team convinced Ives's people that they had allowed for procurement of too many spare parts for the test period. They found as high as 10 per cent of the procurement dollar going for spares for this period, and got engineering to agree to a uniform 5 per cent for spares allowance. This cut over $4 million from the purchased material estimate.

At 5 o'clock that day, Ford met with Henry Young and presented the figures shown in column 2 of Table 1. Young inquired in detail as to how the estimate had been formed, what the history of the numbers were, and what risks were involved. Elliot Hammond protested violently (as expected) the idea of using the Parker Mechanisms' CPIF figure in the WSD fixed-price bid. He stated that Parker was more expert in the radar pedestal field than WSD, and that if they felt that a 40 per cent contingency might be required to bid fixed price, that "we'd better pay attention to them, and not gamble." This whole subject was reviewed at length, and Young finally agreed to keeping the estimate the way it had been proposed. He pointed out that the risks associated with the Parker Mechanisms CPIF bid tended to be offset by the potential savings of incorporating Dr. Markham's concept, should it be permitted later by the customer.

Hammond reviewed all the markups and agreed that they were satisfactory. For the first time in anyone's knowledge, a proposal passed the vice president's review with no changes. They were scheduled to meet Mr. Magnus in his office at 1 P.M. on the 11th.

October 11

Ford found that the day before had been spent in improving the figures and artwork for both the management and technical props and that consequently the material hadn't reached the printers until that morning. Bill Greenwood seemed on top of the situation, though, and stated that he felt there would be no problem in getting the volumes printed by the 14th provided he was allowed to authorize overtime for the printer. He stated that the printer would probably have to work over the weekend. Approval was obtained. Ford asked Greenwood to send final draft copies of the management and technical prop down to Young's office so he could see them before Magnus did.

Ford, Munson, Young, and Hammond met with Executive Vice President Magnus and his financial staff at 1 P.M. Magnus had many years of experience in defense contracting and was noted for his memory of critical statistics and control ratios and miscellaneous numerical operating data. Magnus inquired as to the history of the prop, how the numbers had evolved, and asked what confidence Young and Ford had in them. Hammond replied that they looked all right except for Parker Mechanisms quote and described briefly that particular situation. Ford pointed out that the Markham concept could offset this possible liability with Parker Mechanisms.

Magnus pursued the Markham concept in some detail with regard to possible savings, etc., and sureness of success using this concept. No one in the room could really talk knowledgeably in technical terms about the concept. However, Ford said he would guarantee that there would be at least $1 million saved per set using the concept, and that some more optimistic individuals might feel that $2 million were possible. Magnus said if this were so, then the estimate should be reduced by the $1 million per set in order to be able to quote a lower price. He pointed out that some other company might have come up with the idea and had time to explore it; their quote would be less by that amount, and therefore, WSD would be jeopardizing its competitive position very substantially by not anticipating the approval and eventual use of the Markham concept.

Hammond pointed out that if this were done, it would leave no cushion to offset the liability of the Parker Mechanisms CPIF quote. Magnus cut him off curtly with a statement that WSD's staff had better learn that in order to live, you have to have a job, and that in order to have a job, you have to win a low bid occasionally. He stated that he felt the entire estimate was priced too high, and likened this job to others that have been done previously within the Defense Products Department. He ordered Young to take $1 million per radar set out of the proposal and after that was done, to take 5 per cent off all remaining engineering labor, 10 per cent off manufacturing labor, and 5 per cent off purchased materials. He ordered that the material handling expense (MHX) and all profit be omitted on the subcontractors, both Parker Mechanisms, and the Communications Division. He stated that with these changes, he felt WSD had a good bid and that he was "sure Henry Young and his boys could do the job at the stated 10 per cent profit if it were won."

The group left Magnus' office in various stages of relief and concern. Hammond grumbled that he didn't know how he could eliminate the materials handling expense on the subcontractors, since there were a number of CPFF contracts active in WSD; and that a uniform application of MHX was a prerequisite to substantiating cost reimbursement for the MHX of those CPFF contracts. He stated that Magnus' order had put him in an impossible position. If he eliminated the MHX for the ORTRACK job, the auditors would certainly notice it and would insist that he eliminate it on all the CPFF contracts within the division. This would cause an equivalent of 4 per cent loss of profit. If he did apply the 4 per cent in spite of Magnus' instructions, it might cause WSD to lose the competition, in which case, he would probably be fired.

Ford said that unless Young told him otherwise, he was going to follow Magnus' instructions. Ford asked Munson to sit with Ted Forbes, Stewart Wright, and Dick Ames to get the three of them "back into" a $1 million reduction per radar set from the earlier figure. Since this involved virtually every type of labor and all related subsystems in software, it involved a rewrite of almost every area's cost.

The afternoon was spent largely in revising the cost estimate to include the Markham concept and incorporate Magnus' changes. It was not until late that afernoon that the new totals were determined and the numbers frozen. In the course of the afternoon's work, they had come across a number of numerical errors made in the haste of getting ready for management reviews. These totaled $1.6 million that should have been included in both labor and materials, but had been omitted in the prop numbers. Ford checked with Hammond with regard to his position on the $1.6 million. He and Hammond agreed that in view of the uncertainty of cost saving of the Markham concept, the $1.6 million was really a smaller figure than the accuracy they could expect of their estimate, and that therefore they would not correct the estimate for the omission. They remembered the Magnus' memory retention for figures and knew that an addition of $1.6 million would be spotted by him and would raise all sorts of unpleasant questions. They decided there was no point in involving Young with this, and the totals were left uncorrected by this amount. The fixed-cost figures are shown in column 3 of Table 1.

Table 1

ENGINEERING DIVISION PROPOSITION SHEET

Date:

EQUIPMENT: ORTRACK SYSTEM	1 Prototype Radar Comm. Links — 16 Delivery Radar 4 Display Centers		Proposition No:

CUSTOMER: U. S. ARMY   Sheet *1* of 2

All Figures in $1,000's	Column 1 Original Submission	Column 2 After Project Management Review	Column 3 After Exec. V.P. Review
ENGINEERING—OVERHEAD APPLIED *105%*			
Electrical	43,638	38,838	36,437
Mechanical	26,443	24,327	22,938
Other	1,231	1,231	1,169
Total	71,312	64,396	60,544
SUPPORT LABOR—OVERHEAD APPLIED *105%*			
Technician	382	382	363
Drafting	3,138	3,538	3,152
Other	1,481	1,480	1,406
Total	5,001	5,400	4,921
MODEL SHOP—OVERHEAD APPLIED *105%* MHX APPLIED *4.0%*			
Purchased Material	9,561	9,616	9,016
Labor	1,978	1,988	1,708
Spec. T&T	78	83	83
Total	11,617	11,687	10,807
MANUFACTURING (PRODUCTION) —OVERHEAD APPLIED *120%* MHX APPLIED *4.0%*			
Purchased Material	98,656	94,576	80,727
Labor	22,940	21,640	15,444
Spec. T&T	649	649	649
Mfg. Engineering	1,032	1,232	974
Total	123,277	118,097	97,794
SUBCONTRACTORS—MHX APPLIED *4.0%*			**MHX ELIMINATED**
Parker Mechanisms	38,780	38,780	37,229
Communications Division	18,345	18,345	17,611
Total	57,125	57,125	54,840
OTHER COSTS			
Premium Labor	160	160	158
Travel and Living	1,480	1,280	1,277
Computer Usage	985	985	985
Total	2,625	2,425	2,420
TOTAL PROPOSITION	270,957	259,130	231,326

Table 1 *(Continued)*

			Date:
			Proposition No:
			Sheet 2 of 2

All Figures in $1,000's	Column 1 Original Submission	Column 2 After Project Management Review	Column 3 After Exec. V.P. Review
COST LEVEL ESTIMATE	270,957	259,130	
APPLIED RESEARCH & DEVEL. @ 2.5%	6,774	6,478	
SUB TOTAL	277,731	265,608	
GENERAL and ADMINISTRATIVE EXPENSE @ 6.8%	18,886	18,061	
SUB TOTAL	296,617	283,669	
PROFIT @ 10%	29,662	28,367	
TOTAL SALES PRICE	326,279	312,036	
COST LEVEL ESTIMATE			231,326
LESS: SUBCONTRACTS			54,840
SUB TOTAL			176,486
APPLIED RESEARCH & DEVEL. @ 2.5%			4,412
SUB TOTAL			180,898
GENERAL and ADMINISTRATIVE EXPENSE @ 6.8%			12,301
SUB TOTAL			193,199
PROFIT @ 10%			19,320
SUB TOTAL			212,519
PLUS SUBCONTRACTS			54,840
TOTAL SALES PRICE			267,359

Munson now had the job of putting the cost figures into the format required by the Army RFQ. This involved about 15 pages of detailed cost breakdowns. A small army of administrative people was assigned, each with a few columns to correlate. The process proved more difficult than had been anticipated because the Army breakdown did not correlate the same quantities as the WSD engineering proposition sheet. The extreme detail of the Army format seemed a waste of time when one realized the manner in which some of the figures had been derived, such as the nominal $1 million cut for the Markham concept. However, there was no alternative to being responsive. This "reformating" continued late into the night but still was not finished. Before going home, Ford called Greenwood, who was at the printers, and who stated that the management and technical props were coming along well. He requested that the key project engineering staff go directly to the printers the next morning to proofread their various sections. He thought most proof copies would be done before noon.

October 12

Munson continued his cost reformating. This was finished by noon and the pages rushed to the printer. The project engineering staff reviewed most of the draft at the printers. Jones insisted on substituting seven new pages to describe the dynamic requirements of the radar and to point out briefly the possible advantages of the Markham concept. (The prop text was still written about the original method of signal processing.) The Markham concept was mentioned simply as something that should be looked into in the future as an alternate method of accomplishing the signal processing job with fewer parts and, therefore, with greater system reliability. No mention was made, of course, of the fact that the WSD price was based on the approval of the Markham concept.

The printer was upset at "having all these engineers crawling all around the place," but he accepted the revised text and promised delivery to Greenwood of all three volumes by noon of the 14th. Greenwood and his assistants stayed with the job over the weekend and delivered the required number of 40 copies to Jack Fry at his home Sunday afternoon.

October 15

Fry drove the proposals down to Army Headquarters in his own car. He delivered them to Lt. Col. Youngquist, who stated that it was good to see one company, at least, do something on time. He explained that all five other competitors had requested a one- or two-week's extension for proposal submission, and that he had written a letter to all including WSD on Thursday, the 11th, granting a one-week extension. (The letter either was not delivered on time, or else it was apparently stuck in the WSD mail room.) He asked Fry if he wanted to take the volumes back for further work for the extra week.

APPENDIX I

DETAIL OF THE FUNCTION OF THE VARIOUS SECTIONS OF THE ENGINEERING DEPARTMENT OF THE WEAPONS SYSTEMS DIVISION

The Radar and General Electronics, Information Handling Electronics, Mechanical Engineering, and Systems Engineering sections are considered the heart of the department. The radar group designs and builds transmitters which power the radar sets; builds receivers and signal processors which receive the reflected signal back from whatever target is illuminated by a radar beam.

The power supply group develops power sources which give the various required voltages, either AC or DC, at whatever frequency is required, to all the various electrical and electronic equipments requiring them in all parts of the system. This group is a central design group which supplies power supplies as well for the Information Handling and any other sections requiring them.

The servomechanisms group performs the theoretical design of servomechanisms; the closed loop analysis, optimization of performance, etc., in conjunction with the various equipment designs conceived by other activities.

The Information Handling Electronics Section works very largely in the digital field and has responsibility for computer design and development (for those computers that are nonstandard). (The corporation has a product line of scientific computers made by the Industrial Products Department. See Exhibit 1, page 481.) They also have a large group doing the programming of the computers, consisting of both engineers doing the mathematical specifications and the programmers (who tend to be of less than professional level) to do the actual detailed program coding.

The communications group represents a new effort to design special communications gear associated with the Weapon Systems Division equipment. It had been found earlier that it was difficult for WSD to get assistance and help from the Communications Division, and this was a trial at seeing whether they could handle their own communications problems without resorting to an outside division.

The displays group were specialists in the manufacture of consoles, complete with knobs, handles, and pushbutton controls, colored lights, etc., to indicate status of equipment and provide operating information to the human operators of the systems and to control the system. These displays generally represent a very great deal of "human engineering" effort, the study of optimizing the man-machine combination based on what can be expected of an operator, depending on his physical and mental capacity to react, and the limitations of his speed of response, ability to exercise logical judgement, etc., in various tactical situations.

The checkout and simulation group performs systems-wide work in which synthetic signals are inserted into the system; these signals are traced through the system and compared with acceptable standards at each stage, so that the satisfactory performance of any part of a complex system can be determined without actually having an enemy target, for instance, to operate against.

The Mechanical Engineering Section performs all the heavy mechanical design, establishes the basis for the mechanical standardization of cabinets, racks, and detailed packaging of the hardware, etc. It also performs mechanical structural analysis of all types as a service to other groups.

A small civil engineering group has the capability of designing custom buildings and integrating them with system requirements so that the buildings become an organic part of the total system.

The Systems Engineering Section is the conceptual fountainhead and the "long hair" seat of technical knowledge. There are three program-oriented groups in this section: the strategic, range instrumentation, and tactical groups, each of which has people with a broad systems knowledge in those specialties, capable of establishing requirements for all parts of such systems. Two technology groups support these with detailed knowledge of what can be accomplished with digital and radar techniques at the component rather than the entire system level. The operational analysis group works on assignment from various programs as a service. Inasmuch as the human engineering group has been found to play a vital role in establishment of any system concept involving humans as part of the control or intelligence link, they are located in the Systems Section to perform that role during the conceptual stages of any program.

The Field Installation Section is concerned exclusively with problems of installing and testing equipment at sites located remote from the plant. These could be in other parts of the United States and other divisions, or in foreign countries. They are concerned with getting the equipment transported, putting it in the proper places inside the buildings, and planning and executing the step-by-step test and assembly of the whole system at the site.

The Drafting and Graphic Art Section includes, besides the conventional drafting rooms, groups associated with the writing and editing of technical manuals and handbooks which are shipped with the equipment in order to enable service personnel to install, operate, repair, and maintain the equipment. It includes a photo services group which, besides making photographs, does microfilm work and movie production for special presentations, etc. The publications and reports group consists of professional engineering writers who are assigned to various programs to handle scheduled reports, special reports, and also, on assignment, participate actively in proposal efforts. These people are also responsible for getting the proposal volumes published by a printing contractor at the end of a proposal effort.

The Configuration Records Center is a master file of drawings and specifications, block diagrams and schematics, sufficient to totally define any system being built.

The Engineering Fabrication Shop is a special, highly skilled shop, which reports to engineering in order to avoid the formalities of dealing with a large, separate factory organization. The skill level of this shop is such that its workmen can work from rough, hand-written sketches made by engineers, etc., rather than the precise formal drawings normally required by the factory. In working with the Engineering Fabrication Shop, an engineer actually goes down to the shop and works on an as-required basis with the wiremen, machinists, test technicians, etc., to get his product built and tested. The Test Equipment Pool contains large quantities of highly specialized and expensive electronic and mechanical test equipment which is signed out to individual engineers for use in testing their assembled equipment. The stock room consists of raw material from which the equipment will be constructed. It also includes an "accumulation" room where all parts ordered for each program are segregated in separate areas for easy identification and accountability.

APPENDIX II

Types of Government Contracts

There are essentially three common types of government contracts used for research and development work. They are the cost-plus-fixed-fee (CPFF) contract, the fixed-price (FP) contract, and the cost-plus-incentive-fee (CPIF) contract. We will discuss these in that order.

Cost Plus Fixed Fee

The CPFF contract was a very common type of contract for research and development effort during World War II and in the years immediately following. In this type of contract, the company performing the contract is permitted to charge all allowable costs associated with that work against the contract price. The allowable costs are determined by a very complex series of Armed Forces Procurement Regulations called ASPRS, backed up by a government audit of the operating costs in the plant, such that a government is able to substantiate the reasonableness of all charges assigned against the contract. In the CPFF procedure, the estimated costs against a contract are budgeted in the bid proposal, are reported on by the company in financial program reports, and are later audited against actual corporate records by government auditors. The complete operation is, therefore, an open book to government auditors, and this creates a check on the degree to which this freedom can be exploited. The early uses of the CPFF contract, however, particularly during the war, resulted in a number of abuses.

During World War II, interest was mainly in achieving the greatest production possible in the shortest amount of time, with cost a minor consideration. In the years subsequent to World War II, the CPFF contract was used as a vehicle for financing new research and development programs. The concept was that in any endeavor into new technology, where high technical risk was inherent, it was almost impossible to estimate costs accurately, or to estimate schedules (which have a direct effect on cost) accurately. The saying was that "you cannot schedule creativeness, etc." Accordingly, it seemed logical that allowable proper costs should be accumulated as long as they were under control, and the company performing research and development should not be penalized for not being able to estimate the inestimable in an accurate manner.

The fixed-fee portion of the contract was the government's way of saying "no matter how high your costs run, we will not give you more than this fixed amount of profit." The fixed fee was usually negotiated separately with each contract and by commercial business standards was generally low, varying from approximately 4 to 8 per cent, depending on the amount of company investment, facilities, and proprietary technology, etc., required to do the job, and also depending upon the degree of skill required to do the job. Generally speaking, research programs requiring a high percentage of Ph.D.'s and advanced engineering analytical talents, etc., commanded a high percentage fee compared to straight production runs, where over half the contract expense was in purchasing parts from suppliers.

It is obvious that underbidding a CPFF job results in cost overruns which, although they may be allowable costs under the contract, because of the fixed fee, do not permit one to profit further from the additional costs. One can look at it from the standpoint that the percentage of *profit on sales* diminishes below the negotiated amount as one overruns the basic estimated contract price. Another way of looking at it, is that any overrun involves tying up of corporate assets in terms of work in progress, key personnel, and facilities, to a degree greater than originally anticipated. Therefore, with the fee being fixed, the *return on assets* for the job are less than planned, and therefore, are undesirable.

The fixed-free contract played a very useful role. However, the CPFF vehicle began to present problems as research and development programs became more complex, lengthy, and costly, and eventually the abuses of the CPFF contract by industry and by government both, resulted in a search for a better vehicle. The problems associated with the CPFF job were that there was no sound way of determining from among competitive bids for a job, which company would in the long run have the lowest cost. Over the years, the selection of low bidder on a CPFF basis came to be a rather meaningless ritual.

Former Defense Secretary McNamara recently said that over the past 10 years, research and development contracts of a CPFF nature had average overruns of between 100 and 200 per cent, often running as high as 300 per cent.

Unscrupulous corporations have been known to intentionally understate their costs in order to win a job, being in a position of desperation for work load to carry them until better times came along, etc. Or inexperienced firms are overly optimistic, submitting bids far below what it really takes to perform the contract work, etc., and not the least important by far, is that there simply isn't the pressure to estimate accurately when one knows he will get reimbursed for his costs no matter how far off he is in his estimate.

The inability of the CPFF contract vehicle to provide a fair basis for competition, and the grossly practiced uncertainty of the cost outcome of any given job, result in the fact that almost no jobs are now let on a CPFF basis.

Fixed Price

The fixed-price contract is a simple vehicle, and when submitted in response to a very clear-cut specification and requirement, is an excellent vehicle from the government's standpoint. It also permits a larger profit from the business standpoint, since the government recognizes the added risk a corporation takes in bidding a job fixed price. Profits up to 20 per cent are considerable allowable under fixed-price contracting, whereas the legal limit for CPFF or CPIF type contracting is 15 per cent with special approvals required by the Secretary of Defense's office for anything over 10 per cent. Fixed-price research and development work requires a very, very careful planning of expenditures, the utmost foresight into all possible contingencies, and the ability to knowledgeably price these into the job. The fact that procurements are competitive, however, means that great care must be taken not to overprice the job by overprotecting against contingencies, overloading the job with high-priced talent, etc.

One can liken a fixed-price research and development job to the job that a general contractor does in bidding to the detailed architect's specifications for a new building. Usually, the contractor has never built that particular size or shape of building before; it generally has different specifications from ones he has worked on previously; and this will be a one-of-a-kind job. The contractor relies on his past experience, his knowledge of the problems he is likely to run into, and a good bit of rule-of-thumb estimating, etc., in order to come up with a fixed price.

For research into new technical areas which extend the known state-of-the-art in many disciplines, the problem of writing highly precise specifications is a very difficult one. The danger to the government of a fixed-price job is that unless the specifications and requirements are crystal clear, the person bidding the job can interpret them widely and perhaps deliver substandard equipment or achieve minimum performance, which is not to the best interest of the government. The government is somewhat at the mercy of the contractor who has been selected and is already at work on the job, if the government asks for any changes in specifications, etc. In such a case, there is really no practical alternative to dealing with the contractor on virtually his own terms, although he must substantiate the price he charges for making the change.

Competition is so strong that a contractor may bid his fixed-price contract at zero or a very low profit margin, with the hope that the government will later ask for numerous changes, and he will make his profit back by charging highly for the changes. This, of course, is not in the best interest of fair competition and does not necessarily result in the lowest final cost to the government. However, the problems associated with changes are well recognized, and the government has taken steps to avoid this problem by setting up formalized programs, leading to thoroughly studied, detailed specifications before contracts are left.

Cost Plus Incentive Fee

The CPIF type of contract represents a compromise between CPFF and fixed-price contracting. It is designed to reward the contractor for good performance and to penalize him for bad performance, in order to circumvent some of the abuses of the CPFF environment noted above and yet, at the same time, permit industry to bid on comparatively risky and indeterminate jobs without the full attendant risks of a fixed-price contract. The CPIF contract is quite a difficult one to handle, as the schemes for establishing and measuring the incentives that affect the size of the fee can become very cumbersome, impractical, and in some cases, impossible to implement. Accordingly, very great care has to be taken in setting up incentives in order that a meaningful contract may evolve.

The concept of the incentive fee can be applied to numerous aspects of performance. For instance, a contractor might receive a higher than normal on-target fee if he completed a contract for less cost than the original target cost estimate; or a lower fee than the target fee for completing the contract at a greater cost. Similarly, a contractor can be rewarded for higher performance, for instance, in a missile system, than the target design performance or be penalized for a lesser performance. Or he could be rewarded by a higher fee if his equipment has lower maintenance requirements that the target value; or be penalized for greater than normal maintenance requirements, etc. The incentive can also be used in terms of schedule performance. It may be in the interests of the government to obtain certain critical weapon components or systems earlier than what seems like a reasonable target date. Accordingly, the higher fee can be given for earlier delivery, and a penalty be associated with a late delivery. This combination of cost, schedule, and performance incentives can get very complex and, actually, requires rather careful study of what can happen in order to be able to tell exactly what the profit picture might be for various combinations of end circumstances. A real possibility exists that engineers, while designing to better the performance and thus be rewarded with a higher fee, may in practice add extra costs into the equipment and therefore lose out on the cost incentive reward, etc., etc.

The procedure in setting up an incentive fee generally involves studying the possible deviations from what appear to be reasonable cost, schedule, and performance targets. These can, in effect, be the basic specification targets outlined by the government in their Request for Quotation. The establishment and negotiation of incentives with the government becomes quite a challenging game. The government is interested in establishing heavy penalties for not meeting the target specification, cost, and schedule. The contractor, of course, is interested in very little penalty and wants high incentives for beating target performance schedules and costs. Government, procurement, and particularly civil service personnel tend to be embarrassed in having to give to a contractor high fees, even for good performance. This push and pull can result in some interesting distortions of what appear to be reasonable patterns.

Discussion of the finances of performance either above or below the target value is often discussed in terms of "fee sharing" or "sharing slopes." For instance, a 10 per cent sharing slope means that for every $10 you complete the job for under the basic target cost, you get $1 extra profit. This is called "90–10" sharing with the government. Conversely, if you overrun, for every $10 you go over the target, you lose $1 profit.

Considerable diversity can be negotiated in sharing slopes. Some contracts are established with a plateau in the middle, wherein for plus or minus 5 per cent about the target value there is no sharing. From that point on, the slope can take off both upward and downward, typically at a 90 or 80 per cent sharing slope. Generally, a maximum sharing is established at perhaps 75 or 85 per cent of target cost. This is to prevent "exhorbitant" profits.

There is always the requirement in bidding defense contracts of having to substantiate your costs to the government in order that it may determine, before a contract is let, what your likely profit will be, what labor rates, etc., are going to be charged, and what all the key financial costs associated with your plant are.

It should be pointed out that from the government's standpoint, the easiest decision in picking a bidder is associated with fixed-price competition. Here there is no question about what the right decision is, provided each bidder is fully responsive to all the specifications outlined in the Request for Quotation and provided the specifications are spelled out so clearly that there is no wide margin for interpretation, etc., in different manners by each of the bidders. In practice, as noted earlier, these problems are extremely difficult, particularly for complex new defense systems wherein the state of technology and the problems of specifications are often limited by contemporary knowledge; in these cases, interpretation of specifications can lead to very great differences in bids by companies having essentially the same cost base and with approximately the same level of talent and capability. Not the least of the procurement problems in the pressure from congressmen to get contracts into their home district; or political pressures to award work to distressed labor areas; or the desire to keep a company in business because its capability would be needed in time of emergency.

One thing is certain, that the problem of fairly procuring complicated research and development equipment under any kind of contract is a very difficult one, and a great deal of high-level attention has been paid to the subject.

The recent implementation of incentive and fixed-price contracting will go a long way toward eliminating the previous abuses of CPFF. They will permit the government to have more precise knowledge of what the total cost of a job will be, and will tend to conserve the taxpayers' dollar and to make realistic budgeting possible.

APPENDIX III

Patterns of Defense Contracting after World War II

World War II demonstrated, through such achievements as the atom bomb development and the extensive development and use of radar, the tremendous strides that could be made by methodical research and development in weaponry. Immediately following World War II, great interest existed in exploiting ideas for new weapons systems, etc., through research and development techniques.

A whole flood of new missile systems, new sensor systems, warning systems, attack systems, defense systems, etc., blossomed into being in the form of a large number of CPFF-type contracts. There was relatively little coordination between the three military services, and in many cases, duplicate developments were initiated by competing services. The individual roles of the Air Force, Army, and Navy in missilery, for instance, had not been defined. Who was responsible for defending the field army from air attack, for example, was not established.

Through the late 1940's and early 1950's, some major weapons systems and a gradual definition and settling down of the military roles and missions and the attendant contracting processes took place. The increasing strength of the position of Secretary of Defense brought about greater coordination in contracting procedures and practice and eliminated much overlap between competing services. These years also saw the beginning of the end of large-scale use of CPFF contracts, as large overruns became more and more commonplace, with the result that it was virtually impossible for the military to budget the proper amount of money more than a year ahead of time for any one project.

Former Secretary McNamara recently made a statement that the history of the last decade's worth of CPFF contracts shows an average overrun of between 100 to 200 per cent. Obviously, this had to be remedied, and increasing attention to sound contracting procedure, sound budgeting, and enforced heavy coordination between services followed. The net result of this trend was the McNamara position wherein the staff exerts virtually undisputed control on expenditure of all military funds, and military budget forecasts for five years ahead have real meaning.

With the use of incentive and fixed-price contracts and the exclusion of CPFF contracts, Mr. McNamara succeeded to a large extent in putting defense work on a businesslike basis. This has been done perhaps at the expense of the authority and responsibility of the various military staffs; the centralized control of funds from the Secretary of Defense's office can, and often has, resulted in important programs being completely stalemated for a period of over a year. In fairness, however, it must be said that McNamara brought a sense of business and order to the previously chaotic area of defense contracting.

How It All Gets Started

During the decade of the 1950's, a typical pattern emerged of how a defense contract came into being and how it was performed and terminated. There is remarkably little difference in this pattern, despite the tremendous spectrum of development-type contracts. Some contracts end simply with "breadboard" prototypes proving the technical feasibility of the development. Others, of course, go on into high production. (The pattern discussed below is not applicable to pure research work, such as is carried on in purely research laboratories.)

The pattern goes something like this:

A company may have an idea for a new weapons system, or perhaps for a very small component, such as a rifle, or a new computer. The company, using its own funds, usually writes what is called an "unsolicited proposal" and submits it to the service most concerned with that potential product. This "unsolicited proposal" is studied by the military, and if it meets a need, a contract may be negotiated with the firm on a sole source basis to develop the idea. Or, if the idea fits a broad requirement and does not represent a unique contribution of the company's proprietary efforts, it can result in the service establishing what is called a "requirement." Many noncompetitive awards on the basis of unsolicited proposals were common in the late 1940's and 1950's. Today they are quite rare because of the pressure to hold a competition no matter how small or insignificant the item to be competed.

The development of a requirement within the service, which is to be the basis of a competition, generally takes over a year and in some cases, several years. During this time, numerous contractors will have gotten wind of the idea and the requirement through their military marketing contracts or through their own industrial intelligence systems; or perhaps through creative efforts of their own people, they may by coincidence simultaneously come up with the same idea. Defense contractors are in constant touch with the military and aid them, generally at their own expense, in the development of the requirement, and advise them as to what is practical and what is not practical, etc.

Industry invests considerable amounts to pay for these efforts and looks upon early participation in the development and definition of the requirement as a necessary preliminary to good sales opportunities and assurance of a share in the future market. When a requirement is well established, the military development agency gets in touch with the military procurement agency, and the process of going about selecting bidders is initiated.

Some types of contracts are open to anybody who wants to bid on them. Generally, the larger development-type contracts are restricted to those whom the government feels are capable of handling the job, both from an investment, facility, and capability standpoint. It is typical to have from five to seven nationally known, major corporations bidding on a fair-sized defense contract. Usually, all of these concerns will know a good deal about the requirement before it is written, will have helped formulate and influence it, and also will have a fair idea of when it will be issued as a Request for Quotation (RFQ) , which is the formal request from a service for industry to submit its bid for the job.

When the RFQ is issued, the competitors are generally poised, ready to pounce on it and get to work. Many may try to second-guess what is in the requirement from their own previous knowledge and contacts and start detailed work answering the RFQ long before it is issued. Unfortunately, although the process of evolving the requirement within the military sometimes takes years, answers are expected back from industry in an extremely short time. This is possible for those who have become thoroughly familiar with what they think the content of the RFQ will be. However, for those who have not done their homework ahead of time, and for whom the RFQ contents are not famliar, the job of writing an effective and winning proposal is almost impossible. The trend nowadays is to allow shorter and shorter response times, even for very major proposals. A response time of 30 days for a complicated system contract which will involve several years of development, and cost in the hundreds of millions of dollars, is not unusual. Response times of more than eight weeks are now unusual.

The Request for Quotation

The Request for Quotation consists of many pages of "boiler plate" defining the service's role in the procurement, procurement regulations, and the terms proposed for the contract. It includes a "work statement" specifically describing the work that is expected to be performed and often the expected schedule for such work. It includes a list of required delivery items; it references all military specifications that are applicable to the product. In many cases, it provides information with regard to equipment which the government will furnish from other contracts, or which it plans to buy separately on its own, in order to avoid a prime contractor's markup on subcontracts, or which it makes itself, such as atomic warheads, etc. The typical RFQ for a large development contract will be a volume about 2 inches thick and will reference specifications that will make a stack approximately 2 feet high.

The modern RFQ is very specific in its requirements. It will often provide a very precise outline which the contractor must follow in writing his proposal. It is particularly rigid with respect to the format of cost breakdowns. Breakdowns are required in great detail under headings of hardware, software, documentation, etc., and with cross plots of labor, technicians, drafting, shop labor, test labor, etc. Facilities requirements have to be very carefully handled, and use of any government facilities or equipment in the execution of a contract are clearly stated.

It has been found, over the years, that a page limitation must be placed on the size of the contractor's response; otherwise there would not be enough people in the services to read the thousands of pages they would receive in their proposals. By this technique of clearly specifying in the RFQ, the format type and size of response desired, the contractors are put on a common basis for evaluation purposes, and a true competition is maintained despite the relative size and ability of contractors to supply beautiful pictures, foldouts, etc. The page limitation in a proposal invariably represents problems to those writing the proposal, and excruciating surgery on the choice words of proud contributing authors is one of the most painful jobs a proposal editor has to face.

Problems in Getting Started with the Proposal

The 30- to 60-day activity associated with a proposal is generally a frantic one despite the fact that a company is well prepared, has expected its arrival, and had done a lot of preplanning to get ready for it. It is very difficult, for instance, to obtain commitments ahead of time for the services of key people who must contribute to the proposal, when the extent of their contribution and the days on which it will be required cannot be known for sure. One particular problem in preplanning is that the RFQ's never come out when the military promises they will. Delays of from two to four months are not atypical, and after a number of experiences of this type, no mature manager is willing to commit his people for proposal work, away from their presently assigned jobs, for some indeterminate starting date and period. Accordingly, the practical problem of assembling a proposal organization is a very real one, even under the best of circumstances.

Generally, the preparation of a proposal is regarded as a whole little program within itself. It is thought of as a development program with the end product being a written document reflecting the total knowledge and capability of the company bidding. It has been found by long experience that the proposal must be managed by a "proposal manager" and that he must be supported by a team which in general resembles the team which would go ahead and do the job should they win. In fact, it is usually pointed out in the proposals that the people who worked on the various sections will be the ones assigned to the job, so that the military is assured of getting as great a combination of talent as went into the writing of the proposal.

Various means of conducting proposals have been developed, but the pattern generally seems to be that the proposal team does its best to shorten communications between members, to communicate frequently, and to keep updated. A rather sophisticated information system is usually established, wherein a numbered series of bulletins is issued, with automatic distribution to all participants. In these bulletins every significant change, every significant plan, and every significant accomplishment by all participating groups is documented, so that each group is apprised of the progress of the others, and the problems of the others. The impact of any change which one group makes can be measured for its effects on equipment of other groups.

"Make or Buy" and "Teaming"

A major problem in bidding is the decision of whether to make something in your own company or to buy it from someone else who already manufactures it. This is a very simple decision in cases where you have no capability and another company has a great capability, or he has a shelf item already in production, whereas you would have to develop one. In large, diversified companies, it frequently happens that the proposal manager faces the problem of having a component made by another of his corporate divisions versus having it made by a subcontractor. This type of thinking is called "make or buy" thinking, and "make or buy" decisions are an everyday part of the proposal manager's life.

Sometimes proposals represent the joint efforts of a "team" of contractors. For instance, a computer manufacturer might team up with a radar manufacturer, who might team up with a missile manufacturer to submit a proposal on a missile defense system. The famous TFX fighter, for instance, was bid by a team of Convair (doing the Army version) and Grumman (doing the Navy version). Usually, joint proposals describe the team relationship and include a statement that in the event of award, the lesser ones will become subcontractors to the prime.

Another approach might be to state that any award would be done as a "joint venture" under a special corporation set up to perform just this job. The advantage of this to the military is that one contractor does not put a markup on the product of another, thus affecting a saving and permitting a lower bid price. A disadvantage of this approach, and a strong one, is that control and responsibility tend to be decentralized, with consequent opportunity for errors and costly mistakes and resultant overruns. The "joint-venture" type of contractor team, which experienced a brief period of popularity a few years ago, is now seldom used except in the construction industry.

Intelligence Gathering

During the RFQ period, the sales, or as it is usually called in government contracting circles, the "marketing," organization is busy doing its best to find out how the customer feels about the various competitors. Who will be on the evaluation board which the military will assemble to evaluate the various proposals? What is the other fellow bidding, both technically and costwise, etc., etc.? One prime piece of information which is extremely helpful to the bidding company is knowing how much has been allotted in the service's annual budget for this particular program. Usually, it is possible to uncover an approximation of this number; this is often used as a basis for setting a cost target somewhat lower for your own system. Faulty information of this nature can be disastrous, so great care is paid to determining the authenticity, etc., of these "facts." The full resources of large corporations are marshaled to obtain this type of information; regional marketing representatives, all engineers having customer contacts, divisional marketing personnel, and high-level corporate officials are all briefed and organized to obtain pertinent information from all possible sources.

Pricing Policy and Procedure

The procedures used for pricing developments by different companies vary considerably. This is one of the most difficult and, of course, is one of the key aspects of the proposal preparation. In the competitive, fixed-price, or incentive contract environment now prevalent, the best technical proposal seldom wins the job unless it also has the lowest price. Recent procurement philosophy in the government tends to be similar to that of industry: that any proposal which is capable of meeting the government's requirements is considered technically *acceptable*. Therefore, the one with the lowest price is virtualy automatically the winner, even though perhaps a more costly bid would be a "better buy" from broader consideration. The military people are fully aware that this policy does not necessarily mean that they get the best value when they pick the low bidder. For instance, in a defense system, one competitor might propose a system which required only two men to operate one set of equipment. Their price might be somewhat higher than the company that proposes a system which would do the same job but which required four men to operate it. If the long-term cost to the service were figured in terms of manning requirements, additional cooks, bottle washers, etc., required to support the additional operators, for a five-year period for instance, it would often show that the higher-priced system would be cheaper in the long run.

Generally, however, procurement personnel are not inclined to risk their professional reputations by selecting a bidder at other than the lowest cost, and it takes a fairly significant difference in costs such as mentioned above to have any bearing on selecting other than the lowest bidder. The procurement people point out that a properly written RFQ will include specifications on acceptable levels of manning, support manpower allowances, serviceable maintenance levels, etc., and that this should be the proper way to assure that the government gets the "best buy."

The pricing of development work tends to be difficult largely from the standpoint that almost invariably developments involve a substantial proportion of creative and experimental work never done before. Even fairly common articles of equipment, such as electronic power supplies, amplifiers, etc., become genuine technical challenges when optimized for unusual applications, etc. Accordingly, it is seldom possible to look up in a file what a similar power supply cost in a previous program. Not only was the previous one considerably different, but the chances are the cost records were accumulated on a different overhead base, etc., and you couldn't trust the information anyway.

The net result of this unhappy situation is that pricing of equipment yet to be developed becomes something of an art, and no attempts to make it a science have not really been successful, although one suspects industry in general should do much better in this respect and will indeed be forced to do much better, now that we are in an era of fixed-price contracting where it is possible for one bad pricing mistake on a large job to nullify a million dollars of corporate profit.

Contractor Option in Type of Contract

In some RFQ's an option is given as to whether the contractor bids CPIF or fixed price. This is a matter for considerable thought and strategizing. When quoting fixed price, of course, you assume a high risk unless you add a substantial contingency allowance to the price. You can lose heavily as a result of an error in pricing. In CPIF you cannot actually lose money, but it is easy for your profit to approach zero under a bad overrun condition.

If you are in a competition where this option is offered, you would like very much to know what the other competitors are bidding. If a company bids fixed price at a low figure, close to those of other competitors who are bidding CPIF, the one bidding fixed price has an advantage because the representatives of the government know (if the company is a reputable one) that it will stand behind its price, and they can count on there not being any overrun. The government purchasers also know, however, that the slightest change on their part will be cause for price readjustment, and depending on the attitude and integrity of the contractor, as determined from past contract experience with him, that he might be unreasonable about pricing changes. They might therefore rather have a CPIF contract with someone who might not be so "difficult" about changes. As discussed in Appendix 1, the fixed-price bidder will sometimes bid with the desperate hope that he can make most of his profit on unforeseen changes. If a company has a record of previous CPFF contract overruns, it would do well to bid fixed price. This would allay the customer's fears that the company would repeat its usual overrun performance if it won the job.

Management Participation—Proposal Finance

Usually, in any big proposal, the top company officials concerned are briefed by the proposal team when the RFQ is received, if not before. The issues are presented and guidance sought as to what approach should be taken with regard to sales strategy, emphasis within the proposal, team arrangements, making available funds to cover proposal costs, etc. These same people are called upon to review the rough draft of the proposal as soon as it appears. Some companies have established as a standard procedure, the use of a "Critical Review Team." A group of experts, not participating in the proposal, selected when the RFQ came in, review the rough draft of the proposal, note its compliance with RFQ requirements, the quality and coverage of its content, etc., and then give an objective evaluation to the proposal team. This is a sophisticated way of bringing additional, objective, constructive criticism to the proposal at a time when changes can still be incorporated.

Each company has different regulations for management approval of proposal content and cost. A proposal in the multimillion dollar range will usually require approvals of all levels up through group executive vice presidents of the major national corporations. Review and approval meetings are generally held after the cost is established. It is at these reviews that final management judgment gets exerted and where pricing strategy at the highest level is applied to outguess the competition and win the job.

Very often at these meetings, drastic cuts of estimates fully approved by lower levels are made by top management, on the basis of previous experience, intuition, and overall desire to get the job. Sometimes increases are ordered in areas they feel are risky; very often standard corporate policy is "stretched" with regard to eliminating markups of subcontracted work, or eliminating even the administrative and material handling markups associated with work subcontracted to other corporate divisions.

The government in recent years has shown increasing disinclination to allow normal markups, or in some cases even any markups, on the work done by subcontractors.

The final cost review by top management is usually performed during the final days of the proposal, and generally there is no time to check back on the significance of the changes made with those people who made the original estimate and who will have to execute the work if the job is won.

Evaluation Period

After a proposal has been submitted to the government, an evaluation period follows. This can take anywhere from one to three months, but the latter is typical of the more complex proposals. The procuring office calls together experts from all of the service activities who will be concerned with the program. They utilize consultants from nonprofit corporations and consultants from government laboratories. Very often extremely high-quality talent is applied to the evaluation of the proposals. Previous to the evaluation period, the procurement office will have developed a formal weighted rating scheme, which will consider such things as reliability, maintainability, technical excellence, etc. The evaluation of cost and technical aspects is performed by completely separate terms. This is the reason for separating the cost volume from the management and technical volumes. Very often, separate teams are used to evaluate the technical and management sections of the proposals, which are sometimes submitted in separate volumes.

The technical evaluation is checked against the cost evaluation by procurement personnel so that it can be determined that each competitor has bid the same quantity, etc., and therefore, that costs are put on a common basis for comparison purposes.

The evaluation board then sends its recommendations to what is called a Source Selection Board. This consists of perhaps two or three top military officials, who will then pick one of the two or three sources usually recommended. It will not necessarily pick the most highly recommended. McNamara's reversal of the Evaluation Board's recommendations of the TFX fighter is a famous case of this. Contracts can be influenced and awarded to other than the low bidder for many reasons other than the content and cost of the proposal. One bidder's plant might be in a more "distressed labor area" than the others; previous political connections, personal friendships, and many other such factors which may not seem fair or reasonable, invariably end up influencing the overall judgment. The importance of these factors in influencing the decisions of Source Selection Boards has increased greatly during the past few years, and unfortunately, offsets the tremendous improvement in objective competitive evaluation techniques developed in this same period at working procurement levels.

III Selected Readings

From: John F. Mee
*MATRIX ORGANIZATION**

[EDITORS' NOTE: The author is Mead Johnson Professor of Management, Indiana University.]

A matrix organizational design has evolved in the flow of aerospace technology; changing conditions have caused managers to create new relationships of established organizational concepts and principles. A matrix organization is used to establish a flexible and adaptable system of resources and procedures to achieve a series of project objectives. The accompanying figure is a conceptual framework for a matrix type of organization. It illustrates the coordinated or matrix system of relationships among the functions essential to market, finance, and produce highly specialized goods or services.

From a divisionalized organization structure has emerged a new way of thinking and working to create products dependent upon advanced research and urgency for completion. Time and technology factors forced a more efficient utilization of human talents and facilitating resources.

The traditional divisional type of organization permits a flow of work to progress among autonomous functional units of a specific division. A division manager is responsible for total programs of work involving the products of his division. In a matrix organization, the divisional manager has the same responsibility, authority, and accountability for results. Differences occur in the division of work performed as well as in the allocation of authority, responsibility, and accountability for the completion of work projects.

       *   *   *   *   *

Unless managers and operating personnel are educated and trained to work in the developing organizational designs, they can suffer frustrations, emotional disturbances, and loss of motivation. Working in an environment characterized by change as projects are started and completed is not as comfortable and secure as performing a continuing function in a more stable standardized work flow situation.

       *   *   *   *   *

---

* Reprinted from *Business Horizons,* Summer 1964.

MATRIX ORGANIZATION (AEROSPACE DIVISION)

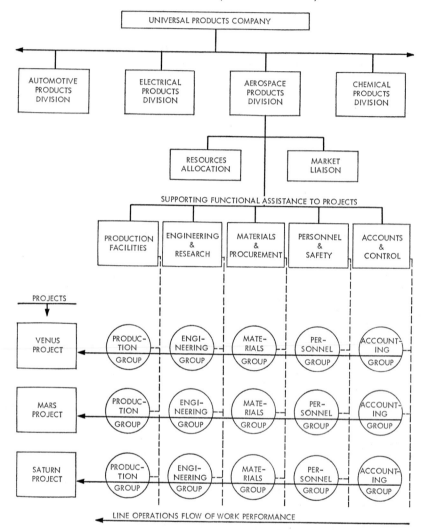

From: David I. Cleland
WHY PROJECT MANAGEMENT?*

[EDITORS' NOTE: Lt. Col. Cleland is Associate Professor of Management, Department of Systems Management, Air Force Institute of Technology, Air University, Wright-Patterson Air Force Base, Ohio.]

The advancement of technology in all phases of industrial management since World War II has no precedent; radical changes occurring in the design and marketing of products have forced innovation in management theories and techniques. Because new products and marketing strategy often do not fit the purely functional type of organization, attention is being given to molding the organization around the task. The need for a new type of managerial surveillance is apparent as terms such as "systems management" and "project management" are heard with increasing frequency.

Traditional business organizations function mostly on a vertical basis and depend almost exclusively on a strong, inviolate superior-subordinate relationship to ensure a unified effort. Individual managers tend to identify boundaries of responsibilities and specialization. When organizations were relatively small this presented no problem since the functional manager could maintain lateral staff contact to ensure mutual support and understanding of interfunctional goals.

*   *   *   *   *

The pure functional approach cannot be applied when the task involves the coordinated effort of hundreds of organizations and people. Unique management relationships evolve in the development of a large single-purpose project that cuts across interior organizational flows of authority and responsibility, and radiates outside to independent organizations.

The traditional management theory of Henri Fayol and Fredrick Taylor is not suitable for managing large, single projects, such as those in the construction industry, or in manufacturing when a costly product requires the coordinated involvement of several organizations. A combat aircraft, for example, is developed and produced through the coordinated efforts of dozens of industrial and Department of Defense organizations.

These new purposes require a management philosophy that has no organizational or functional constraints. Project management provides this philosophy—a way of thinking that allows for radical changes in organizational theory and in the management of activities. . . .

THE PROJECT MANAGER

In a sense project management is compatible with the traditional and functional approach to management, yet it has provided a way of thinking about management of highly technical and costly products whose development and

---

* Reprinted from *Business Horizons,* Winter 1964.

acquisition spread across several large autonomous organizations. The project manager crosses functional lines to bring together the management activities required to accomplish project objectives. The project manager has certain characteristics that differentiate him from the traditional manager.

1. As a manager he is concerned with accomplishing specific projects that require participation by organizations and agencies outside his direct control.

2. Since the project manager's authority cuts through superior-subordinate lines of authority, he conflicts with the functional managers who must share authority in their functional areas for the particular project.

3. As a focal point for project activities, the project manager enters into on an exception basis those matters necessary for the successful accomplishmment of the project. He determines the *when* and *what* of the project activities; the functional manager, who supports many different projects in the organization, determines *how* the support will be given.

4. The project manager's task is finite; after the project is completed, the personnel directly supporting the project can be assigned to other activities.

5. The project manager oversees a high proportion of professionals; consequently he must use different management techniques than in the simple superior-subordinate relationship. His attitude regarding the traditional functions of management must necessarily be tempered by increased motivation, persuasion, and control techniques. For many professionals his leadership consists of explanations of the rationale of the effort, as well as the more obvious functions of planning, organizing, directing, and controlling.

6. His diverse and extraorganizational activities require unification and integration directed toward the objective of the project. As a unifying agent for the total management function he has no line authority to act but depends on other manifestations of authority to attain the objective. Thus the directing function is somewhat less important from the perspective of the project manager. What direction he does accomplish is through the functional managers supporting him.

7. The project manager does not normally possess any traditional line authority over the line organizations involved in creating the goods or services.

FOCAL POSITION

The project manager acts as a focal point for the concentration of attention on the major problems of the project. This concentration forces the channeling of major program considerations through an individual who has the proper perspective to integrate relative matters of cost, time, technology, and total product compatibility. The project manager is personally involved in critical project decisions concerning organizational policy including: cost and cost estimating; schedules; product performance (quality, reliability) ; commitment of organizational resources; project tasking; trade-offs involving time, money, and performance; contract performance; and total product integration.

The above description of the project manager's role is not meant to downgrade the interfunctional lines of communications or the necessary and frequent lateral staff contacts between the functional organizations involved in the project. Rather, a focal point must be established where critical decisions, policy making, and key managerial prerogatives relating to the specific project are synthesized for all functional and organizational elements. Such a position enables the timely resolution of interfunctional and interorganizational conflicts of purpose arising during the course of the project. Such an organizational relationship prevents any one functional manager from overemphasizing his area of interest in the project to the neglect of the over-all project goals.

EVOLUTION

One major difficulty of management in adjusting to the concept of project management is their failure to understand it. The concept of project management is still evolving; it has already gone through stages in which different titles and degrees of responsibility have been associated with the position. The construction industry early recognized the need for a management process that permitted a unifying agent in the *ad hoc* activities involved in the construction of single, costly projects such as dams, turnpikes, and large factories and buildings.

A new method of management developed during World War II that integrated the many diverse activities involved in the development and production of large numbers of aircraft. In the military establishment, evidence of the project manager appears in such endeavors as the Manhattan Project, the ballistic missile program, and in the management of the Polaris program.

The need for a unifying agent in these large projects motivated the development of a project type organization superimposed on the traditional and functional organizational structure. This idea of a unifying agent reflects contemporary thinking about project management. Forerunners of the project manager were designated as "project expediters"; they did not perform line functions but rather informally motivated those persons doing the work. The project expediter was mainly concerned with schedules and depended upon his personal diplomacy and persuasive abilities to remove bottlenecks in the management process. He was perhaps the earliest kind of project manager; ranked slightly above him in terms of time and responsibility was the "project coordinator" who had a more formal role in the organization and was concerned with the synchronization of organizational activities directed toward a specific objective in the over-all functional activities. His limited independence was reflected in his freedom to make decisions within the framework of the over-all project objectives; he did not actively enter into the management functions outside of his particular organization. The project coordinator had specific functional authority in certain areas such as budgeting, release of funds, and release of authority to act as in the dispatching function in the production control environment.

Today's project manager is in every sense a manager; he actively participates in the organic functions of planning, organizing, directing, and controlling the organization of the specific project. The project manager accomplishes the management process through other managers. Many of the people who feel the force of his leadership are in departments or organizations separate from the project manager's parent unit. Since these people are not subject to his operating supervision and owe their fidelity to a superior line manager, a unique set of conflicts of purpose and tenure arise. The project manager has real and explicit authority, but only over major considerations involved in the project plan. One of the project manager's biggest problems is how to get full support when the functional people are responsible to someone else for pay raises, promotion, and the other expected line superior-subordinate relationships.

AUTHORITY AND RESPONSIBILITY

Since the project manager acts as the focal point for major decisions and considerations, he must be given a special kind of recognition with respect to his authority and responsibility in his relationships with other managers in the organization. Authority is the legal or rightful power to command, to act, and to direct. Ultimate authority derives from the society in which the organized effort exists; authority is *de jure* in the sense that it exists by rightful title. Specific delineations of the authority of an organizational position are contained in the unit's documentation, such as policy and procedure, job descriptions, and organizational charters. Not to be neglected is the *de facto* authority that can be exercised by the project manager. This authority is implied in his organizational position; it is the intrinsic and necessary power to fully discharge responsibilities inherent in the task or job. Thus an organization receiving public funds has *de facto* authority to create administrative policy stipulating how the funds will be maintained, to appoint a custodian who will assume responsibility for the safe-guarding and legal obligation of the monies, and to take other measures neces-sary for adequate control of the expenditure of funds within the specific conditions of authority under the grant. Other aspects of the *de facto* authority include the project manager's persuasive ability, his rapport with extraorganiza-tional units, and his reputation in resolving opposing viewpoints intra- and extraorganizationally. Other factors influencing the degree of authority available to the project manager are:

1. Influence inherent in his rank, organizational position, or specialized knowledge

2. His status or prestige within the informal organizational relationships

3. The priority and obligation existing within the organization for the timely and efficient accomplishment of the project goals

4. The existence of a bilateral agreement with a contracting party for the completion of the project within the terms of the contract in such areas as cost, performance (quality, reliability, and technology) , and schedule

5. The integrative requirements of the project manager's job in the sense that he has the sole responsibility within the organization to pull together the separate functional activities and direct them to a coordinated project goal.

The project manager's authority and responsibility flows horizontally across the vertical superior-subordinate relationships existing within the functional organizational elements. Within this environment the authority of the project manager may often come under serious questioning, particularly in cases involving the allocation of scarce resources for several projects. Generally, the project manager has no explicit authority to resolve interfunctional disputes by issuing orders to functional groups outside his office. However, since the project manager is the central point through which program information flows, and by which total project executive control is effected, he often exercises additional authority over and above that which has been specifically delegated. His superior knowledge of the relative roles and functions of the individual parts of the project places him in a logical position to become intimately involved in the major organizational decisions that might affect the outcome of his project. As the centralized and focal point through which major project decisions flow, the project manager's contribution to the decision process cannot be ignored or disparaged. The unique position of the project manager gives him superior knowledge of any subsystem or subactivity. (This superior knowledge does not exist as the single authority within the total organization, but only as the single authority with respect to a particular project.)

Organizational rank carries both explicit and implicit authority. The project manager should have sufficient executive rank to enable him to exercise a subtle and pervasive authority by virtue of his office. He should have sufficient rank (through evidence of seniority, title, status, prestige, and so on) to provide general administrative leverage in dealing with other line officials, with supporting staff personnel, and with authorities external to the parent unit. This implies a correlation between the rank of the project manager and the cost and complexity of his project. The more costly the project, the greater the degree of risk, and the more complex the internal and external organizational structures, the higher the rank of the project manager should be. Within the military services there has been a tendency to increase the authority of a project manager's position by assigning higher ranking officers to these positions. A brigadier general would be exepcted to exercise more influence (and thus authority) over his subordinates, his peers, and extraorganizational elements than would a lower-ranking officer.

Management literature has neglected any real definition or discussion of the authority of the project manager; this is to be expected because the functional approach to management education and practice is nearly universal. Until contemporary management thinking has fully conceptualized the unique nature of the project manager's role, extraordinary manifestations of authority will be required. It will be an uphill struggle because of the threat that project management poses to ingrained functional management practices and thinking.

The project manager requires a clear delineation of authority and responsibility so that he can properly balance the considerations involved in the development and successful conclusion of the project. He is frequently faced with major and minor "trade-offs" involving cost, schedule, and performance of the product. Many times these trade-offs lack clear lines of demarcation and foster internal and extraorganizational conflicts of purpose. Referral of the problem for resolution to the functional managers may not serve the best interests of the project, since the functional manager tends to be parochial (and rightly so) in his view and concerned with providing the services of the particular function for all projects.

The creation of the position of project manager in an organization requires careful planning to prepare existing management groups. Certain criteria are offered for delineating the authority and responsibility of project managers:

1. *The charter of the project manager should be broad enough to enable his active participation in major managerial and technical activities.* He should be given sufficient policy-making authority to integrate the functional contributions to the project goals.

2. The project manager must have the *necessary executive rank* to insure responsiveness in the parent company to his requirements and acceptance as its unquestioned agent in dealing with contractors and others.

3. His staff should be qualified to provide personal administrative and technical support. He should have sufficient authority to increase or decrease his staff as necessary throughout the life of the project. This authorization should include selective augmentation for varying periods of time from the supporting functional agencies.

4. He should participate in making technical, engineering, and functional decisions within the bounds of his project.

5. The project manager must have sufficient authority and capability to control funds, budgeting, and scheduling for the project.

*   *   *   *   *

From: David I. Cleland*
UNDERSTANDING PROJECT AUTHORITY†

That today's manager must be able to deal with change is nowhere more evident than in the development and acquisition of major military and industrial products. Project management—molding the organization around a specific task or project—is the concept that has been developed to deal with situations where production and marketing strategy for new products do not fit into a purely functional type of organization.[1] The concept of the project manager is relatively new, and his authority is, as yet, unclear. Contemporary literature, which is incomplete in its study of the project manager's *modus operandi,* defines the manager's role but contains little information concerning the authority patterns in project management. It is the purpose of this article to examine the authority of the project manager, particularly in contrast to that of the traditional bureaucratic manager.

WHY PROJECT MANAGEMENT

The need for project management is illustrated by the organizational activities of the engineering aspect of a research and development department. This is the area where the original effort on a project is made; yet, with many projects on hand, it is extremely difficult for the functional manager of engineering to cover both the project and the other efforts. One individual, therefore, is appointed to achieve management unity for each of the projects. Thus, two complementary management organizations exist within the operation: the *vertical* traditional organization and the *horizontal* project organization. Eventually, a matrix structure will extend across such functions as manufacturing, finance, contract management, engineering, and procurement.[2] The resulting organization will not consist of a single matrix and a single functional organization but rather of many matrices, even of a hierarchy of matrices. Such a structure reflects the impact of technological change on the corporate structure and its functions. Moreover, it points up the need to provide a management structure around a specific task with commensurate lateral and horizontal relationships.

WHAT IS AUTHORITY?

Authority is required to accomplish the work of the manager. No philosophy of authority, however, can tell the manager how to proceed in specific cases, but it can give him a conceptual framework on which to base his thinking. Although

---

* Lt. Col. Cleland is an associate professor of management, department of systems management, Air Force Institute of Technology, Wright-Patterson Air Force Base. The views expressed herein are those of the author and do not necessarily reflect the views of the Air Force or the Department of Defense.
† Reprinted from *Business Horizons,* Spring 1967.
1 See David Cleland, "Why Project Management," *Business Horizons* (Winter 1964), pp. 81–88
2 For a discussion of this concept see John F. Mee, "Matrix Organization," *Business Horizons* (Summer 1964), pp. 70–72.

most commentators agree that the authority patterns in an organization serve as both a motivating and a tempering influence, they are divided in the emphasis placed on a given authority concept. In general, the concept of authority is in a period of transformation, changing from the bureaucratic hierarchal model to a participative and persuasive one. While early theories of management regarded authority as a gravitational force that flowed from the top down, recent theories view it as a force to be accepted voluntarily, and which moves both vertically and horizontally. The elements of participation and persuasion in the authority relationship are products of modern organizations and reflect the influence of the democratic and scientific revolution in contemporary society.

Although authority is the key to the management process, it is not always used in the same way. The standard definition of authority is a "legal or rightful power, a right to command or to act." As applied to the manager, authority is the power to command others to act or not to act. It provides the cohesive force for any group and is created because of the group effort. In the traditional theory of management, authority is a right granted from a superior to a subordinate. But where does this right originate? Every manager obtains his formal authority as a delegation from the next higher level. The ultimate source of formal authority (as contrasted to other types of authority) lies in the right to private property[3] in our society, or in the charismatic power of a hierarchal role.[4] In theory, authority is still concentrated at the top of the organization and is delegated in the scalar chain to subordinate organizational elements. It is used in resolving intraorganizational disputes, in making basic strategic decisions affecting the whole organization, and in establishing overall policy for the organization. Barnard tempers this traditional view by recognizing the rights of the contributors (members) of the organization to accept or reject an order given by a higher official in a formal organization.[5]

Traditional theory has never considered that the sources and uses of authority are ever manifested outside the boundaries of the parent organization. This viewpoint, therefore, ignores the authority patterns that exist between managers and technicians in different organizations. Nor does the traditional view recognize the impact of the reciprocal authority relationships existing between peers and associates. With the exception of functional authority, the traditional view presupposes some superordinate-subordinate relationship in the organizational arrangement.

POWER

Power is a concept frequently associated with authority. It is defined as the ability to unilaterally determine the behavior of others, regardless of the basis for that ability.[6] Authority provides power that is legitimately attached to the organizational position; it is delegated by job descriptions, organizational titles, standard operating procedures, and related policies.

INFLUENCE

Influence, on the other hand, is authority assumed without the legitimacy of an organizational position. An individual may exercise influence in his environ-

---

3 Ralph C. Davis, *The Fundamentals of Top Management* (New York: Harper & Bros., 1951), pp. 281–322.

4 Victor A. Thompson, *Modern Organization* (New York: Alfred A. Knopf, Inc., 1961), p. 77.

5 Chester I. Barnard, *The Functions of the Executive* (Cambridge, Mass.: Harvard University Press, 1938), p. 163.

6 For example, see James D. Thompson, "Authority and Power in 'Identical' Organizations," *American Journal of Sociology*, Vol. LX (November 1956).

ment simply because he has knowledge and expertise. There is little doubt that a duly appointed superior has power over his subordinates in matters involving pay, promotion, and effectiveness reports, and that this delegated power functions unilaterally, from the top down. A manager's authority, however, is a result of his power and his influence combined so that subordinates, peers, and associates alike willingly accept his judgment. This combination of power and influence emphasizes both the project manager's legal rights and the personal effectiveness of his organizational position. Fayol uses this approach in defining the manager's authority as follows:

> Authority is the right to give orders and the power to exact obedience. Distinction must be made between a manager's official authority deriving from office and personal authority, compounded of intelligence, experience, moral worth, ability to lead, past services, etc. . . . personal authority is the indispensable complement of official authority.[7]

PROJECT AUTHORITY

To understand the concept of project authority, one must first understand the framework of the project environment, which points up the salient differences between the role of the project manager and the traditional functional manager. (See Figure 1.) While these differences are possibly more theoretical than actual, they do exist and they affect the manager's *modus operandi* and philosophy. Such comparison highlights a singular characteristic of the project manager—his role in managing activities that include extensive participation by organizations and agencies not under his direct (line) control.

The exercise of authority in the day-to-day conduct of a project is far removed from the organic power of the chief executive. Decisions are made constantly and their success depends upon the integration of delegated and assumed authority by the functional and project managers. In the project environment, the real basis of a man's authority (or perhaps better, his influence) is his professional reputation among his peers and associates. A man gains this type of authority only through recognition of his accomplishment by the other members of his environment, not by policy documentation, however extensive.

A significant measure of the project manager's authority springs from his function and the style with which he performs it. Thus the project manager's authority is a combination of *de jure* and *de facto* elements in the total project environment. In this context, his authority has no organizational or functional constraints, but diffuses throughout and beyond the organization, seeking out the ideas and the people it needs to influence and control.

In its total sense, project authority is the legal and personal influence that the project manager exercises over the schedule, cost, and technical considerations of the project. Project authority exists within the legitimacy of the project; it extends horizontally, diagonally, and vertically within the parent organization and radiates to outside participating organizations. Traditional line-staff relationships are modified in the project enditional bureaucratic organization, authority relationships are based on the vertical hierarchy. The project manager, on the other hand, is concerned with the flow of work in horizontal and diagonal relationships. The problems of motivation that exist for the traditional vertical manager are compounded for the project manager because the traditional leverages of hierarchal authority are not his to use. For example, the people working on a given project may be paid and promoted by the functional

---

[7] Henri Fayol, *General and Industrial Management* (London: Sir Isaac Pitman & Sons, Ltd., 1949) , p. 21.

FIGURE 1

COMPARISON OF FUNCTIONAL AND PROJECT VIEWPOINTS

Phenomenon	*Project Viewpoint*	*Functional Viewpoint*
Line-staff organizational dichotomy	Vestiges of the hierarchal model remain, but line functions are placed in a support position. A web of authority and responsibility relationships exists.	Line functions have direct responsibility for accomplishing the objectives; the line commands, staff advises.
Scalar principle	Elements of the vertical chain exist, but prime emphasis is placed on horizontal and diagonal work flow. Important business is conducted as the legitimacy of the task requires.	The chain of authority relationships is from superior to subordinate throughout the organization. Central, crucial, and important business is conducted up and down the vertical hierarchy.
Superior-subordinate relationship	Peer to peer, manager to technical expert, associate to associate relationships are used to conduct much of the salient business.	This is the most important relationship; if kept healthy, success will follow. All important business is conducted through a pyramiding structure of superiors-subordinates.
Organizational objectives	Management of a project becomes a joint venture of many relatively independent organizations. Thus, the objective becomes multilateral.	Organizational objectives are sought by the parent unit (an assembly of suborganizations) working within its environment. The objective is unilateral.
Unity of direction	The project manager manages across functional and organizational lines to accomplish a common interorganizational objective.	The general manager acts as the head for a group of activities having the same plan.
Parity of authority and responsibility	Considerable opportunity exists for the project manager's responsibility to exceed his authority. Support people are often responsible to other managers (functional) for pay, performance reports, promotions, and so forth.	Consistent with functional management; the integrity of the superior-subordinate relationship is maintained through functional authority and advisory staff services.
Time duration	The project (and hence the organization) is finite in duration.	Tends to perpetuate itself to provide continuing facilitative support.

manager, not their supervisor on the project. However, if the project manager must act as the focal point for major project decisions and considerations, he must be given adequate authority to accomplish these objectives.

Several authors have commented on the efficacy of the project manager's authority. Peck and Scherer claim he has no legal basis to resolve interfunctional disagreements.[9] Ramo adds that project managers do not have substantial, well-

---

[9] Merton J. Peck and Frederic M. Scherer, *The Weapons Acquisition Process* (Cambridge, Mass.: Harvard University Press, 1962).

FIGURE 2

A MODEL OF PROJECT AUTHORITY

De jure (legal)
Organizational charter
Organizational position
Position description
Executive rank
Policy documents
Superior's right to command
Delegated power
The hierarchal flow
De facto (real)
Technical knowledge
Maintenance of rapport
Negotiation with peers, associates,
  and so forth
Building and maintaining alliances
Project manager's focal position
The informal organization
The deliberate conflict
The resolution of conflict

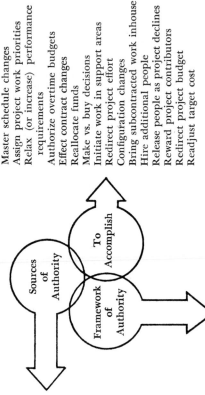

Sources
of
Authority

To
Accomplish

Framework
of
Authority

Master schedule changes
Assign project work priorities
Relax (or increase) performance
  requirements
Authorize overtime budgets
Effect contract changes
Reallocate funds
Make vs. buy decisions
Initiate work in support areas
Redirect project effort
Configuration changes
Bring subcontracted work inhouse
Hire additional people
Release people as project declines
Reward project contributors
Redirect project budget
Readjust target cost

Determine project requirements
Provide organizational and functional mobility
Participate in major management and
  technical decisions
Collaborate in staffing the project
Participate in budgeting, funding,
  and scheduling
Select the project team
Maintain project team integrity
Create project plans
Prescribe project information system
Select project organizational form
Serve as prime customer liaison

delegated, clearly defined responsibilities nor commensurate authority.[10] These views, while only a sample, reflect the consensus about the project manager's authority. They are not an accurate reflection of the project manager's authority, however, since they consider only the legal aspect, which is, admittedly, important, but not complete. His other source of authority, the *de facto* source, is equally or even more important.

The project manager, it appears, must be a distinct type of specialist, a man with a broad perspective of the total organizational system, who can also unify the many activities involved in his project. Thus, he must have the authority to decide to abandon the hierarchal model of management completely and to establish closely coordinated and integrated teams or task forces to circumvent chains of command; these teams may contain within themselves personnel with a complete heterogeneous collection of skills. The project environment is indeed a radical departure from Max Weber's bureaucracy, where business was carried out "according to calculable rules and 'without regard for persons.' "

But rearranging the compartments and shifting the lines on the organizational charts do not create adequate authority to accomplish project objectives. Participants in the project organization at all levels must modify, negate, add to, and reinforce the legal authority that emanates from a given arrangement of positions. The project manager accomplishes his objectives by working with personnel who are largely professional. Consequently, his use of authority must be different from what one would expect to find in a simple superior-subordinate relationship. For professional people, project leadership must include explanations of the rationale of the effort as well as the more obvious functions of planning, organizing, directing, and controlling.

Authority in project decisions may be indifferent to the hierarchal order of affairs. In many cases, the decisions that executives in the higher echelons reserve for themselves amount to nothing more than approving the proposals made by the project manager. The role played by these line-and-staff managers can easily deteriorate to one of delay, debate, investigation, coordination, and veto.

Upper-echelon executives may be in a more precarious position than they realize. The folklore of functional management includes the image of the powerful executive who sits at the head of a highly organized, tightly run, organizational pyramid, and runs things from the top down. In project management, the vertical organization still plays an important role, but this role is largely to facilitate project affairs and ensure that the proper environment is provided for those participating in the project.

Project management proves that "simply being in an executive hierarchy does not mean that one can freely direct those below him."[11] High-level officials in an organization are more dependent on their subordinates and peers than traditional theory will admit. So many complex decisions are made in the course of a large project that one individual, acting unilaterally, cannot hope to have sufficient time to make a thorough analysis of all the factors involved. The decision maker in project management must depend on many others to provide analysis, alternatives, and a recommended course of action.

In sum, project authority depends heavily on the personality of the project manager and how he sees his role in relation to the project environment. His authority is not necessarily weak because it is not thoroughly documented and because it functions outside the parent organization and between the participating organizations. The project manager is in a focal position in the project

---

[10] Simon Ramo, "Management of Government Programs," *Harvard Business Review* (July-August 1965).

[11] Herbert A. Simon, Donald W. Smithburg, and Victor A. Thompson, *Public Administration* (New York: Alfred A. Knopf, Inc., 1950), p. 404.

endeavors, which allows him to control the flow of information and to have superior knowledge of the project. The scope of power and control exercised by the project manager may be virtually independent of his legal authority.

*   *   *   *   *

From: Eugene E. Jennings
"BUSINESS NEEDS MATURE AUTOCRATS"*

[EDITORS' NOTE: The author is a clinical psychologist and Professor in the School of Business and Public Service, Michigan State University.]

The democratic approach to business administration and leadership seems to have reached its apex. To some people its future is subject to much doubt. What these critics refer to as its veneer has been cracking for at least five years.

Substantial research has been devoted to seeking a pattern of management which will yield the highest production and morale. So far as the research data are concerned, evidence today is insufficient to warrant the assumption that there is a single approach to better performance. Why then, after enjoying for some 30 years a gradual and somewhat unexpected increase in acceptance, especially verbal, should the democratic approach now be subject to doubts? What kind of executives do we now need and want?

The social scientists can wait for answers to these questions but businessmen cannot. If the commonly held assumption that democratic executive procedures are most effective is being challenged, business needs to know the nature of the challenge and what kind of procedures are suggested as substitutes.

One of the most difficult things to understand is the meaning of democracy, especially in terms of the business system. A common technique is to define the opposite approach, that is, the autocratic, and base the definition of the democratic on that.

The autocratic approach means that group members are dependent on a single person. That person—called leader, executive, supervisor, etc.—so behaves that he makes himself the key to all group action and eventually becomes indispensable. His need to dominate is expressed by keeping the group acting as individuals and on a personal basis with him. This means usually that communication is kept to the minimum of administrative necessity except insofar as it is through him and focused upon him. Because he becomes and remains the focus of group attention, he is a firm believer in the indispensability of a good leader, such as he tries to be.

The democratic approach in many respects is the direct opposite. The individuals in the group, including the leader, are so closely knit that cohesion sometimes disguises who actually is running things. The leader seeks to evoke maximum participation and involvement of every member in determining group activities and objectives. He so leads the group that the result of the joint effort is not ascribable to his own virtues and superiority.

In short, the autocrat recognizes the superiority of the individual over the

---

* Reprinted by permission of *Nation's Business*, Chamber of Commerce of the United States, Washington, D.C., September 1958.

group, whereas the democrat recognizes the superiority of the group over himself.

There are differences of view in other regards as to how the democrat and the autocrat behave, but these definitions are generally acceptable. My own research could not find evidence that the autocratic type or democratic was superior; but criticism of the democratic, sometimes called human relations, approach which began five years ago is gaining in strength.

In 1953 Douglas McGregor of M.I.T., then president of Antioch College, warned that business was confused about human relations. He described as a major error of management the assumption that personnel administration consisted largely in dealing with human relations problems. He said that this was looking at the subject as a repair job, instead of a way to prevent the need for repairs. Since then other writers and observers have continued the attack on human relations as being essentially a tool by which management manipulates people into the desired patterns of productivity and conformity. These writers see considerable moral and intellectual degradation and degeneration as a result of the human relations exploitation approach.

Since the human relations approach has had such lofty ideals and high verbal acceptance, it is to be expected that these critics will find numerous and severe opponents. Already a defense seems to have taken shape. Some defenders, believing that the many advocates of human relations have failed to make clear just what they are talking about, have tried to relieve the misunderstanding and confusion by suggesting that the underlying theme of the human relations approach is an attempt to understand people as they really are and to accept them as such. The theme is that better understanding of the problems of people at work, of discovering ways for making work a more rewarding experience, will likely create positive benefits for all concerned.

This implies that management should so manage that the workers' purposes and the firm's purpose are mutual and complementary. Translated in the language of the critics of the manipulation-conformity thesis, this means that the unique strengths of the democratic work process can be used as positive forces for accomplishing the objective aims of the large organization: that is, making a profit.

In theory this might be logical, desirable and perhaps even necessary, but it covers up an underlying problem that may turn out to be an insurmountable contradiction. This problem is how to include in an autocratic system the democratic urges of the subordinate and inferior members of that system.

There are opposing drives here that go far deeper than changing manifest behavior to accommodate and compromise forces that are in conflict with each other.

One may question whether executives are psychologically able to allow the group to participate in decisions affecting both them and the larger organization. I have found that by and large the typical executive does not have the psychological capacity to integrate to this extent even if he wanted to.

Even appearing to give lip service and some degree of credence to the democratic approach in such things as decision-making and policy formulation is almost beyond the psychological capacity of most executives.

The difficulty becomes plain once we recognize what the typical executive is really like. Robert McMurry, senior partner of McMurry, Hamstra & Co., a Chicago-based personnel consulting firm, has supplied a good description. He says that most executives are likely to be hard-driving, egocentric entrepreneurs who came up in careers where they have had to keep the power in their hands. They may be veterans and victors in the give-and-take, no-quarter, in-fighting for position of power within the business. Instead of participative management, Mr. McMurry describes business as a "benevolent autocracy" wherein the top man stresses the desirability of humanistic management but remains undeniably the strong man. This diagnosis would suggest that the democratic approach is basically a result of some kind of external pressure and not a manifestation of inner conviction on the part of executives. The possibility is that the democratic approach will from here on be attacked more openly by executives themselves and repudiated by a regression to a firmer autocratic approach.

*   *   *   *   *

. . . [M]ore democracy was bound to be urged upon executives if for no other reason than that a democratic society, believing in certain dignities of the individual, will constantly exert a force to have these dignities accepted in the most inaccessible crevices. This external pressure upon management, plus the demands of large-scale organization for group decision-making, caused some degree of acceptance of the human relations approach.

Even so, this surge to group decision-making came relatively quickly. When some 69 executives of leading firms were interviewed by this writer, the general reaction was that they use group decision-making for getting acceptance of their decisions—not necessarily for getting better decisions. This reaction is in part a result of the failure of social scientists to come up with an adequate definition of what the new executive, who is bending somewhat to this pressure of democratic participation, should be.

In overthrowing previous authoritarian concepts of leadership the social scientists have failed to offer a new management pattern that is 1, commonly agreed upon by them, 2, commonly understood by executives, and, 3, sufficiently motivating to these executives.

*   *   *   *   *

Consultants who are to some extent both observers and practitioners must offer rather arbitrary advice even though they know science will not yet affirm it. When I am placed in this role my answer has been that the type of executive needed is the polished autocrat. That is to say, the business system seems to be perfectly set up today for the individual who wants to run with the ball but who at the same time makes the team feel needed. He makes decisions, he controls and dominates individually and with emphasis on personal influence but he does not arouse animosity. Historians often call him . . . a man who walks with a firm, but quiet step.

*   *   *   *   *

In presenting this model of leadership to businessmen I have had considerable concurrence that the firm but quiet type is becoming increasingly necessary. Some of the most eminent businessmen have this attribute about them.

Whether the polished, mature autocrat has replaced the crude type is still an academic question because our idealistic eyes sometimes indicate that more executives are less autocratic today than yesterday. What is a good bit of insight, although not yet supported by research, is that there must be dominance of the majority by a few and that these few must make decisions on behalf of themselves or the majority, or both, and that consultation with the majority is seldom feasible.

What is feasible is that the few appear to be humanitarian, conscientious and open minded. They generate not necessarily love or hate, but respect and a little, but not too much, fear.

They do not, however, consult any more than necessary to get acceptance. When they do it is with other power individuals who, when allied with them, will bring the advantages of their leadership.

That these polished autocrats are useful and necessary to society is attested to by the fact that they are numerously found in some of our most democratic institutions. I have found them in religious, social work agencies, and charitable organizations.

They are in educational, political, and economic organizations. They represent at best the attempt to respond as administratively as possible to the democratic urges of a mass culture.

But such a response is only possible to a degree. That degree, I believe, qualifies them to be called Mature Autocrats.

From: George S. Odiorne
*HOW MANAGERS MAKE THINGS HAPPEN**

[EDITORS' NOTE: The author is Professor of Industrial Relations in the University of Michigan, School of Business Administration.]

MANAGEMENT IS NOT A PASSIVE ART

*   *   *   *   *

A manager is more than a problem solver. He's a goal setter. Without waiting for others to ask him, he envisions things that should happen, and thinks through some possible paths by which the goal can be reached. At this stage he has few, if any, people who would agree with him that the goal is possible. Because he's active in deed as well as thought, however, he converts them into action in his plan, and enlists their talents toward reaching the goal which he dreamed up. Before long he has a full scale movement afoot and people become ego-involved in his goal just as if they themselves had thought of it.

*   *   *   *   *

MAKING GROWTH A COMPANY GOAL

. . . [A] few dominant trends seem to emerge. One of these is that *company growth* is one present day goal which seems to spur executive action and make things happen. This has some important implications for the company which wants to grow. It also has a great deal of relevance to the budding manager—or the one who's arrived—who has talents for making things happen and seeks ample opportunity to demonstrate his prowess along these lines.

Studies by the Stanford Research Institute of several hundred companies with records of growth show that there are several traits which are common to most of them. . . .

*   *   *   *   *

Stanford's studies also showed that those companies which have growth patterns have been led by management of great moral courage in making decisions in favor of growth and sticking with them to make the growth occur. . . .

---

* *How Managers Make Things Happen,* George S. Odiorne. © 1961 by Prentice-Hall, Englewood Cliffs, New Jersey (pp. 4–11, 37–38, 52–53) .

. . . [The manager has] the heavy responsiblity for spurring others to overcome their own inertia. . . . He's got to be able to move projects and people off dead center and get them rolling toward his goals. He's got to generate enthusiasm for these goals so that people adopt them as their own, with the result that they generate enthusiasm on their own part for getting there. He must further instill a desire to excel and do the job fully and without mistakes or altering. To do this demands several traits in the action-getting manager which he must assiduously cultivate at the risk of failure.

1. He's going to have to maintain optimism if he's going to overcome inertia. Most managers who make things happen have ego drives that push them on personally, and unbounded optimism and confidence that others will ultimately see his vision of what's to be accomplished despite repeated defeats and failures.

2. He needs a sound knowledge of people to impel them to produce and create. He needs to know what incentives are required to get action from others, and to have some artistry in using them.

3. He needs a certain callousness in demanding high standards of performance from others who are helping him. The manager with an overdeveloped sense of sympathy and understanding of failure will usually "usurp all of the dirty jobs for himself while others stand about and marvel at his performance," as David Moore puts it.

*   *   *   *   *

Profit Requires Action

Being a successful manager in a commercial and industrial enterprise means a profit-minded one. Conversely, it's the profit-minded manager at any level who stands the best chance of moving upward. This is more than simple avarice, or single minded love of money for itself. It's largely because profit is a universal standard for measurement that is easily grasped by managers and quite clearly understood by those who judge his performance.

It's entirely possible that someday a more commonly held standard will come along, for example—service; but it must always meet the standard which profit has become—immediate, easy to calculate, universally accepted. Profit, for all the criticisms leveled against it, is the best available instrument and standard of managerial success and organizational performance. With adaptations it applies to any organization, even in Soviet Russia.

We hear a great deal of pious foolishness written and said about profit. At the annual congress of industry of the NAM each winter, solemn and quite pompous words are uttered in defense of this mysterious lubricant which causes the wheels of industry to turn. To some it becomes a divinely inspired instrument which it becomes sacrilegious to damn. This of course is not the point here.

*   *   *   *   *

Profit, then, is more than an accounting term. It's a positive creation and stand-ard of measuring effectiveness of management action and decision making.

*   *   *   *   *

. . . Profit is the result almost wholly of the *actions of managers* who exercise initiative and leadership of a dynamic nature, and of the people who respond to this leadership to carry through toward the goals of the organization.

There is probably no company in business today which couldn't be out of business through lack of profit inside of ten years if its management attempted to conduct its affairs simply through mechanical application of administrative practice, at the expense of the more vital, personal, and human application of individual leadership.

*   *   *   *   *

. . . The most pernicious trait a manager can have when faced with obstacles is indecisiveness. Very often this is explained away as a need for mature consideration of the situation, but actually indecision is the result of the mind slipping away into inappropriate or trivial matters. He may find that ordering a new desk or settling a squabble between two secretaries is much more intriguing than writing the order, or picking up the telephone to announce the decision. The obstacle hurdler makes his decision when he can—and the sooner the better.

*   *   *   *   *

Equally vital among the qualities of the obstacle breaker is that of using people without becoming sentimentally overinvolved with their successes or failures. A survey of fifty company presidents by two graduate students at the School of Business at Michigan showed that such things as fraternal connections and other sentimental ties rated last among these executives' considerations when picking men for positions of leadership.

*   *   *   *   *

Despite his concern with meeting the needs of others and meeting the basic needs of people, the action-getter has developed a tough-mindedness. For one thing, as Chris Argyris, management researcher of Yale, has put it, he has "a high tolerance for frustration." He can plug through all sorts of red tape without blowing his top when he has to. He frequently endures the delays and run-arounds of committees and clearances with spartan endurance. He is patient where such patience is the only possible way of getting the final payoff that he seeks.

This patience isn't submissiveness, however, and when the time for patience is past and more direct action is called for, the action-minded manager is willing to be ruthless. When the choice is between maintaining old relationships and getting the job done he is always ready to decide in favor of the job. Stepping on people's corns isn't his first choice, but he does it firmly if the occasion demands.

*   *   *   *   *

The action-minded manager is probably tough-minded in his relations with people, too. He's willing to stick by his people through their honest mistakes—or to chop off heads as the need arises. He assumes that men are made of tough stuff and will work hard and take heavy blows as a price of making a living and contributing to the success of the business.

He will urge on a man who is working at less than his best abilities.

He is liberal with recognition for good work, and equally liberal with a reverse kind of recognition for the people who aren't performing up to their capacities. People over their heads in their jobs find this action-minded man a fearsome figure, one who will certainly drive them to perform things they hadn't thought possible, or face up to the fact that they have no great future in the organization until they do.

He's tough-minded, too, in being willing to pay the prices for personal success. Long hours, hard work, and man-killing travel schedules are the way of life for him. He concentrates on his job with a fury and singleness of purpose that reduces other things to a lesser role. This doesn't mean he's inhuman or a dull grind. . . .

From: Chester I. Barnard
ORGANIZATION AND MANAGEMENT*

[EDITORS' NOTE: Mr. Barnard was former President of New Jersey Bell Telephone Company.]

. . . [M]atters of urgent speed, of highly technical character, of profound intellectual content, or of very complex conscious coordination, must in practice be exluded from the democratic process except in most general terms.

Moreover, a considerable capacity for abstract thought, that is, for reading, writing, and speaking is necessary. Excepting for small organizations, where decision is very closely related to concrete conditions, the democratic method is not suitable for the illiterate; but marked diversity of education and of intellectual intelligence is also not conducive to the use of this method. Wide expansion of the degrees of education, the minute specialization of knowledge and of function are unfavorable conditions.

Again, there must be such restrictions of the fields of decision or of their details that the number of decisions to be taken democratically is not large. The tediousness and slowness of the process are notorious, the difficulty of maintaining interest nearly obvious, its costliness apparent. I think it likely to be generally conceived at some later time that there is an optimum proportion of decisions in a given organization that can be made by democratic methods, or conversely by other methods. . . .

*   *   *   *   *

. . . Leaders lead. This implies activity, and suggests the obvious question "What is it that they have to do?" Now, I must confess that heretofore on the few occasions when I have been asked: "What do you do?" I have been unable to reply intelligibly. Yet I shall attempt here to say generally what leaders do, dividing their work under four topics, which for present purposes will be sufficient. The topics I shall use are: The Determination of Objectives; The Manipulation of Means; The Control of the Instrumentality of Action; and The Stimulation of Coordinated Action.

*   *   *   *   *

. . . An obvious function of a leader is to know and say what to do, what not to do, where to go, and when to stop, with reference to the general purpose or objective of the undertaking in which he is engaged. Such a statement appears to exhaust the ideas of many individuals as to a leader's *raison d'être*. But if they are able to observe the operations closely, it often disconcerts them to note that many things a leader tells others to do were suggested to him by the very people he leads. Unless he is very dynamic—too dynamic, full of his own ideas—or pompous or Napoleonic, this sometimes gives the impression that he is a rather stupid fellow, an arbitrary functionary, a mere channel of communication, and a filcher of ideas. In a measure this is correct. He has to be stupid enough to listen a great deal, he certainly must arbitrate to maintain order, and he has to be at

* Reprinted by permission of Harvard University Press, Cambridge, Massachusetts, 1956 (pp. 48, 85–87, 89–90, 94).

times a mere center of communication. If he used only his own ideas he would be somewhat like a one-man orchestra, rather than a good conductor, who is a very high type of leader.

However, one thing should make us cautious about drawing false conclusions from this description. It is that experience has shown it to be difficult to secure leaders who are able to be properly stupid, to function arbitrarily, to be effective channels of communication, and to steal the right ideas, in such ways that they still retain followers. . . .

*   *   *   *   *

. . . [O]n the whole we may regard leadership without technical competence as increasingly exceptional, unless for the most general work. Usually leaders, even though not extraordinarily expert, appear to have an understanding of the technological or technical work which they guide, particularly in its relation to the activities and situations with which they deal. In fact, we usually assume that a leader will have considerable knowledge and experience in the specifically technical aspects of the work he directs. . . .

*   *   *   *   *

. . . *An organization is the instrumentality of action so far as leaders are concerned, and it is the indispensable instrumentality.* . . .

The primary efforts of leaders need to be directed to the maintenance and guidance of organizations as whole systems of activities. I believe this to be the most distinctive and characteristic sector of leadership behavior, but it is the least obvious and least understood. . . . [A]ny act done in such a way as to disrupt cooperation destroys the capacity of organization. Thus the leader has to guide all in such a way as to preserve organization as the instrumentality of action.

*   *   *   *   *

. . . [O]ne important kind of thing that leaders do is to induce people to convert abilities into coordinated effort, thereby maintaining an organization while simultaneously getting its work done. . . . In a broad sense this is the business of persuasion. Nor need I say that the sorts of acts or behavior by which executives "persuade" to coordinated action are innumerable. They vary from providing the example in "going over the top," or calm poise inspiring confidence, or quiet commands in tense moments, to fervid oratory, or flattery, or promises to reward in money, prestige, position, glory, or to threats and coercion. Why do they vary? Some obvious differences of combination in leaders, in followers, in organizations, in technology, in objectives, in conditions, will occur to you. . . .

*   *   *   *   *

. . . Ability to make decisions is the characteristic of leaders I think most to be noted. It depends upon a propensity or willingness to decide and a capacity to do so. . . .

*   *   *   *   *

. . . [D]ecisiveness needs to be considered in both its positive and negative aspects. Positively, decision is necessary to get the right things done at the right time and to prevent erroneous action. Negatively, failure to decide undoubtedly creates an exceedingly destructive condition in organized effort. . . .

From: Kenneth E. Boulding
THE IMAGE*

[EDITORS' NOTE: Professor Boulding teaches economics at the University of Michigan.]

The subjective knowledge structure or image of any individual or organization consists not only of images of "fact" but also images of "value." . . .

. . . [I]t is clear that there is a certain difference between the image which I have of physical objects in space and time and the valuations which I put on these objects or on the events which concern them. It is clear that there is a certain difference between, shall we say, my image of Stanford University existing at a certain point in space and time, and my image of the value of Stanford University. If I say "Stanford University is in California," this is rather different from the statement "Stanford University is a good university, or is a better university than X, or a worse university than Y." The latter statements concern my image of values, and although I shall argue that the process by which we obtain an image of values is not very different from the process whereby we obtain an image of fact, there is clearly a certain difference between them.

The image of value is concerned with the *rating* of the various parts of our image of the world, according to some scale of betterness or worseness. We, all of us, possess one or more of these scales. It is what the economists call a welfare function. It does not extend over the whole universe. We do not now, for instance, generally regard Jupiter as a better planet than Saturn. Over that part of the universe which is closest to ourselves, however, we all erect these scales of valuation. Moreover, we change these scales of valuation in response to messages received much as we change our image of the world around us. It is almost certain that most people possess not merely one scale of valuation but many scales for different purposes. For instance, we may say A is better than B for me but worse for the country, or it is better for the country but worse for the world at large. The notion of a hierarchy of scales is very important in determining the effect of messages on the scales themselves.

One of the most important propositions of this theory is that the value scales of any individual or organization are perhaps the most important single element determining the effect of the messages it receives on its image of the world. If a message is perceived that is neither good nor bad it may have little or no effect on the image. If it is perceived as bad or hostile to the image which is held, there will be resistance to accepting it. . . .

On the other hand, messages which are favorable to the existing image of the world are received easily and even though they may make minor modifications of the knowledge structure, there will not be any fundamental reorganization. Such messages either will make no impact on the knowledge structure or their impact will be one of rather simple addition or accretion. Such messages may also have the effect of increasing the stability, that is to say, the resistance to unfavorable messages, which the knowledge structure or image possesses.

The stability or resistance to change of a knowledge structure also depends on its internal consistency and arrangement. There seems to be some kind of principle of minimization of internal strain at work which makes some images stable and others unstable for purely internal reasons. In the same way, some crystals or molecules are more stable than others because of the minimization of internal strain. It must be emphasized that it is not merely logical consistency which gives rise to internal cohesiveness of a knowledge structure, although this is an important element. There are important qualities of a nonlogical nature which also give rise to stability. The structure may, for instance, have certain aesthetic relationships among the parts. It may represent or justify a way of life or have certain consequences which are highly regarded in the value system, and so on. Even in mathematics, which is of all knowledge structures the one whose internal consistency is most due to logic, is not devoid of these nonlogical elements. In the acceptance of mathematical arguments by mathematicians there are important criteria of elegance, beauty, and simplicity which contribute toward the stability of these structures.

Even at the level of simple or supposedly simple sense perception we are increasingly discovering that the message which comes through the senses is itself mediated through a value system. We do not perceive our sense data raw; they are mediated through a highly learned process of interpretation and acceptance. When an object apparently increases in size on the retina of the eye, we interpret this not as an increase in size but as movement. Indeed, we only get along in the world because we consistently and persistently disbelieve the plain evidence of our senses. The stick in water is not bent; the movie is not a succession of still pictures; and so on.

What this means is that for any individual organism or organization, there are no such things as "facts." There are only messages filtered through a changeable value system. This statement may sound rather startling. It is inherent, however, in the view which I have been propounding. This does not mean, however, that the image of the world possessed by an individual is a purely private matter or that all knowledge is simply subjective knowledge, in the sense in which I have used the word. Part of our image of the world is the belief that this image is shared by other people like ourselves who also are part of our image of the world. In common daily intercourse we all behave as if we possess roughly the same image of the world. If a group of people are in a room together, their behavior clearly shows that they all think they are in the same room. It is this shared image which is "public" knowledge as opposed to "private" knowledge. . . .

MIDWEST HARDWARE
MANUFACTURING COMPANY

I Case Introduction

Synopsis

In the spring of 1961, Midwest Hardware Manufacturing Company was in the midst of a substantial expansion program designed to increase its capacity to meet the steadily increasing demand for its products. Midwest's management was determined to finance the expansion with internally generated funds, and was therefore seeking all possible means to maximize its allocation of the cash available. A survey of current inventory control practices indicates that a large amount of funds can be released from the inventory account for more productive allocation elsewhere. Also, a revamped method of ordering component parts for assembly would bring significant savings in operating expenses. A mathematical model is used to compute optimum inventory levels and optimum purchase lot sizes.

The new inventory control system was adopted and implemented during the summer of 1961. In October, when the new system is evaluated by Midwest's management, results appear quite disappointing. Predicted benefits have not been realized, and some unforeseen problems have arisen. Management must decide whether the new system should be continued, modified, or abandoned.

Why This Case Is Included

Midwest's concern over the short supply of working capital—concentrating on internally generated cash as the source of funds—and the best use of such funds—allocation to inventory, receivables, fixed assets, etc.—highlights the influence of economic and financial matters on policy making. Not only does the adequacy of the sources of funds set parameters, or boundaries, around the alternatives open to management, but the same factor also acts as a stimulant and pressure to plan carefully and design effective policies for the allocation of funds.

Analyzing the use of the mathematical model for inventory control has value of itself, but this case raises the larger issue of the benefits and limitations of scientific rationality (operations research techniques) in business policy formulation. Science is pitted against "judgment." The utilization of techniques of scientific rationality affects the relationships among people and even alters organization structure. The unshared expertise of the specialist further complicates the traditional line-staff conflicts. The issue of the desirability and feasibility of subordinate participation in management decisions and action is also raised. Finally, the case offers the opportunity to examine the economic theory relating to the use of overhead departments in various size enterprises (here considering the new inventory system comparable to the introduction of a service department or overhead unit).

Diagnostic and Predictive Questions

In answering the following diagnostic and predictive questions, remember that these questions apply theories and conceptual ideas from certain disciplines. Such theories are valuable to understand basic forces at work in the policy system (diagnosis) and to predict what will happen in the system in the future (prediction). Since each reading abstracts from the total policy system certain factors or variables into the closed or partial viewpoint of one theory or discipline, no one reading gives answers to the practical policy problems of the case. In diagnosis and prediction, the parts of the problem are studied with "other things being equal."

Following each question are listed readings which will be helpful in answering the question. The readings included with this case are marked (*). By referring to the author index at the end of this book, you may locate the other readings listed.

1. In what way has the short supply of funds affected the policy making of Midwest's management? Recall from the case that Mr. Gilbert, the president, pointed to the strain on working capital caused by recent expansion moves. Relate this concern to Maxon's comment: "I've always felt that we have far too much cash tied up in inventories of components awaiting assembly."

Read: Anthony, *Management Accounting,* pp. 290–92, 306.

2. Why did Maxon have more confidence in "hard thinking and close calculating" than in "flying by the seat of our pants"?

Read: *Lieber and Lieber, *The Education of T. C. Mits,* pp. 44–49.

3. What are the advantages of Maxon's "science" as compared to Iverson's "judgment"?

Read: *Taylor, "Principles of Scientific Management." Barber, *Science and the Social Order,* pp. 7–8, 12–13, 18, 21.

4. What assumptions are inherent in the inventory control model adopted by Maxon? Are all such assumptions justified by conditions in Midwest's plant? How closely would you expect Maxon's model to predict the savings to be achieved by the new system?

(A close examination of the data and formulae in the exhibits should permit an evaluation of Maxon's use of the inventory control model. More detailed discussion of the techniques used by Maxon, if required, may be found in: David Miller and M. K. Starr, *Executive Decisions and Operations Research* [Englewood Cliffs, N.J.: Prentice-Hall, Inc., 1960], chap. x.)

5. Was Hennessey right in claiming that operations research techniques are only feasible for use in large corporations?

Read: *Marshall, *Principles of Economics,* pp. 283–85. Summer, "Economies of Scale and Organization Structure."

6. In modifying its inventory controls the management of Midwest went through at least six phases: (*a*) search for ways of increasing the available working capital, (*b*) investigation of the Iverson inventory control system, (*c*) computation of optimum stock levels and reorder quantities, (*d*) explanation of the new system and training of personnel, (*e*) implementation and administration of the new system during shakedown period, (*f*) evaluation of results. To what extent did all the interested parties participate in this process as a whole? What advantages—if any—could be gained by having subordinate participation in each phase of the process? Are there reasons which would make participation impossible or undesirable in specific phases?

>   Read: McGregor, *Human Side of Enterprise*, pp. 124–30. Newman and
>   Summer, *The Process of Management: Concepts, Behavior, and Prac-
>   tice*, pp. 439–48. Odiorne, *How Managers Make Things Happen*,
>   pp. 5–11, 37–38, 52–53. Jennings, "Business Needs Mature Autocrats."
>   *Taylor, "Testimony before the Special House Committee Investigat-
>   ing the Taylor and Other Systems," pp. 211–13, 215–17.

7. Was Maxon's role in the entire process one of a line manager or a staff specialist? What should his role have been? It has been said that knowledge is power. (Francis Bacon, 1561–1626, *Religious Meditations—Of Heresies:* "Nam et ipsa scientia potestas est." Knowledge itself is power.) Does this in any way dictate what role Maxon, as an expert in operations research, will necessarily play in the organization?

>   Read: *Hobbes, *Leviathan.* *Lasswell and Kaplan, *Power and Society*,
>   pp. 157–59. Thompson, *Modern Organization*, pp. 4–6, 12–13, 19–21,
>   61, 63–65, 77–78. Carr *et al.*, *American Democracy in Theory and
>   Practice*, pp. 214–19. Etzioni, "Authority Structure and Organiza-
>   tional Effectiveness."

8. In setting objective and fixed standards for inventory ordering and evaluating compliance with the new procedures, should Maxon have expected Iverson to welcome the new system or resist it?

>   Read: *Argyris, "Human Problems with Budgets." Newman and Sum-
>   mer, *Process of Management: Concepts, Behavior, and Practice*,
>   pp. 605–10.

9. As the implementation of the new system evolved, should Mr. Gilbert have been able to predict that Iverson would feel he was "the guy in the middle" between Hennessey and Maxon? If so, should he have insisted that Iverson take orders from one superior only?

>   Read: Fayol, *General and Industrial Management*, pp. 24–25, 68–70. Tay-
>   lor, "Shop Management," pp. 92–96, 98–100. McGregor, *The Hu-
>   man Side of Enterprise*, pp. 124–31, 172–75.

10. Reasoning from the logic of the scientific inventory method and its use in Midwest, why didn't Maxon's new system produce the results hoped for? Recall that at the executive committee's last meeting Hennessey stated he could see many practical difficulties which Maxon's figures did not show (e.g., low morale, quality deterioration, component C stamping costs, etc.).

>   Read: *Buffa, *Modern Production Management*, pp. 442–43, 450–51, 471.
>   Miller and Starr, *Executive Decisions and Operations Research*, pp.
>   38–42, 45–47, 50. Lindblom, "The Science of 'Muddling Through'."

11. In studying the formalization, rationalization, or bureaucratization of organizations, sociologists have developed the notion of the dysfunctions of bureaucracy—unforeseen and undesirable consequences resulting from efforts to formalize procedures, rules, structure, etc. Would a knowledge of this notion have helped Gilbert anticipate such things as the hoarding of parts by the foremen and the interdepartment "wars"? Would it have helped him to design preventive policies?

Read: Merton, "Bureaucratic Structure and Personality."

Policy Questions for This Specific Case

In answering the following policy questions, the results of diagnosis and prediction are used to reduce the amount of guesswork, or judgment, in designing action solutions. However, since certain parts of the total case situation cannot be reduced to science, and since "other things are not equal," judgment must still be used to fill in the factors not accounted for by readings. You will also need a second kind of judgment as you put value weights on different scientific predictions, since different theories may point to conflicting solutions.

12. Knowing Midwest's need for more working capital, what other ways seem feasible for dealing with the problem—other than Maxon's effort to release cash from inventories and cut operating costs? (See Question 1 and its readings.)

13. Could you have done anything with the operations research technique itself to make the Maxon inventory model conform better to the concrete circumstances of the Midwest situation? (See Questions 4 and 10 with their attached readings.)

14. If you had been Gilbert, the president, would you have directed Maxon's efforts any differently? Why? Or, why not? (See Questions 6, 7, 8, 9, and 11 with their attached readings.) As president, would you have encouraged more participation of subordinates in the design and implementation of the new system? In which—if any—of the six phases of the process (identified in Question 6) would you have desired more participation?

15. Had you been Maxon, would you have handled your relationship with Iverson any differently? Why? Or, why not? (See Questions 6 and 8 and their attached readings.)

16. What should Gilbert do now about the inventory control system?

Major Policy Issues: Tentative Generalizations about Any Policy System

In arriving at conclusions for the following questions, generalize from the facts in the case and use your own ideas to (a) confirm, (b) modify, or (c) test the workability of the concepts and theories from readings. As an executive or professional, use wisdom to merge theory, on the one hand, with "brute facts" and practice, on the other.

17. Do the esoteric knowledge and skills of the expert, like Maxon, alter the traditional role of the staff personnel vis-à-vis the line personnel?

Read: (See the readings under Question 7, especially Thompson.)

18. Discuss the applicability and limitations of mathematical or operations research techniques to the solution of business problems. (See the Miller and Starr, and Lindblom readings as cited in Question 10; also the readings under Question 8.)

Questions for Original Student Work in Analysis and Policy

The methods of viewing this case as represented by the authors' questions and selection of readings are not exhaustive. There are other relevant ideas for diagnosis and prediction. Furthermore, there are other ways of stating policy questions. More powerful analyses and wiser solutions will result by drawing on your own training and experience for (a) relevant concepts and theories, and (b) creative ways of asking policy questions. The following questions are designed to help you acquire this skill.

19. While reflecting on case facts, what additional theories from prior education give you insights as to "what is going on" in Midwest Hardware Manufacturing Company? As to what might be predicted to happen in the future?

20. Other than the policy questions asked by the authors, what pragmatic ways can you think of to state the practical problems faced by executives in the case?

II Midwest Hardware Manufacturing Company*

The Company and Its Products

Midwest Hardware is an old-line, well-known manufacturer of hardware, plumbing supplies, spigots, valves, and other construction accessories for residential and industrial use. The assembly, finishing, and testing of its products comprise the bulk of the company's manufacturing operations. Only a small portion of the components are manufactured by Midwest itself, the majority being purchased from a relatively few near-by suppliers, most of whom are located in the same city as Midwest's plant. Almost every supplier of components had been doing business with Midwest for many years, and relations have generally been close and satisfactory between the company and its suppliers.

Annual sales volume has been fairly stable at around $28 million for the past seven years, and the work force has averaged some 300 employees. Thomas Gilbert, Jr., Midwest's president, believes that, although the company has not grown much in the past few years, it has established an outstanding reputation for quality and dependability of its products. To support his claim that the company is among the leaders in its field, he cites the fact that Midwest currently has a full year's backlog of orders on many of its products. Mr. Gilbert has recently initiated an expansion program, designed to increase manufacturing capacity by additions to plant space, machinery, and equipment. This expansion program was spurred by a rising level of regional construction activity and by market surveys forecasting a doubling of the demand for Midwest's products within the next eight years.

At the monthly meeting of the executive committee in April, Mr. Gilbert reviewed the progress of the expansion program to date, and concluded with the comment that growth was indeed exciting and satisfying, but its resultant strain on working capital was becoming evident. The balance of the meeting was devoted to discussion of working capital needs and conservation. John Wm. Maxon, the company's controller, emphasized the importance of conserving internally generated cash funds by minimizing the use of scarce cash on nonessentials. "As a prime example of what I mean," Maxon stated, "I've always felt that we have far too much cash tied up in inventories of components awaiting assembly. A whole battery of new techniques have been developed in so-called Operations Research, designed to minimize inventory costs; yet we're still flying by the seat of our pants when it comes to our inventories. I firmly believe that some hard thinking and close calculating can yield pretty impressive savings in this area."

Joseph Hennessey, vice president–production, agreed that some savings might be achievable, but pointed out that production personnel had neither the time nor the mathematical backgrounds to apply O. R. methods to inventory problems. It was then agreed that Maxon would undertake an investigation of Midwest's present inventory controls and then present any recommendations he may have at the next meeting.

Present Method of Component Inventory Controls

All component inventories in the plant are under the control of Peter Iverson, head foreman in charge of assembly, manufacturing, and receiving. Iverson initiates all orders for components—whether manufactured in the plant or purchased outside—and has been doing so for many years. He relies primarily on frequent inspections of inventories on hand, observations of "how things stood in each department," and periodic checks with his foremen and their requirements. Whenever Iverson judges the time is ripe, he enters a buy or make order for the needed component. Over the years Iverson has established a standard order size, in terms of number of units, for each component used.

Thus order quantities are held constant for each item, while the frequency of placing orders will vary with the rate at which components are taken into production. Since output rates and product mixes have historically been quite stable, there has been a high degree of constancy in the frequency of orders for each major component. The ordering procedure followed by Iverson is, in effect, a variant of the traditional "two-bin" system, under which inventories are physically divided between two separate bins or storage areas. As one bin is exhausted, a standard-size lot order is placed, while withdrawals are continued from the second bin. Iverson believes that operating results confirm the soundness of his inventory control system: "There may be some talk about me playing it extra-safe, but Mr. Hennessey or anybody else will tell you that we've *never* been out of stock on any part we needed in all the years I've been in charge of the inventory."

Analysis of Present Control System

At the May meeting of the executive committee (consisting of the president and all the department heads), Maxon was ready to present the findings of his investigation of Iverson's present component inventory controls. He reported that he had a detailed analysis of the components needed for a typical Midwest product—a gas furnace control unit—referred to as "GFC-5" on the company's product line lists.

The GFC-5 unit is assembled from five components (labeled A through E in all exhibits), of which four were purchased, and one was manufactured by Midwest. Exhibit 1 presents a simplified product flow chart for the GFC-5 superimposed on an organization chart identifying relevant supervisory personnel. Also shown is the monthly requirement of each component for meeting current output levels of 5,000 GFC-5 units per month (see Exhibit 2).

Maxon distributed copies of his analysis sheets to all participants in the meeting (reproduced in Exhibits 3 and 4).

Referring to Exhibit 3, the analysis of Iverson's present practices, Maxon explained that he had calculated—from accounting records—the average value of inventories Iverson had been carrying for each GFC-5 component. (These are presented in Column 6.) He next computed the average value of the "circulating" inventory (Column 5), based on the assumptions graphed in Exhibit 4. Maxon explained that circulating inventory was derived by dividing the order lot size typically used by Iverson (Column 3) by two, thereby getting the average inventory of each component needed to meet the monthly requirements of the assembly operation. He then multiplied these units of circulating inventory by the component price to get the average value of circulating inventory (Column 5). By subtracting average circulating inventory from total inventory, he then arrived at the average value of "safety stocks" presently being carried (Column 7).

"Exhibit 3 tells us," said Maxon, "that we've had an average of $33,450 (Column 6) tied up in components for the GFC-5, and that of this amount an average of $13,155 (Column 7) was never circulated into production, but was tied up permanently as a safety cushion against a possible runout. Safety stocks are in effect equivalent to an insurance premium against runouts, and it's my contention that we're paying a high premium to cover an almost negligible risk. Quantitative analysis tells us that in setting up levels of safety stocks we must balance the cost of carrying this stock against the *cost* and *probability* of a runout on any component. The cost of running out of any component is usually tough to estimate, since it requires placing a value on the cost of missed sales and production downtime. In our case, I think it's reasonable to place this cost at close to zero. With a year's backlog of orders we're not liable to lose *any* sales, and with our flexible assembly schedules there's no reason for any downtime due to missing parts. We can easily switch assembly to other products until the missing parts come in. Furthermore the *probability* of running out, in our case, is just about negligible. Our suppliers are highly reliable; they are very close to us and will do their darndest to deliver right on time. We could, theoretically, get by with no safety stocks whatsoever, but I'd say a stock of one or two days' production would be ample."

Proposed Control System

Maxon proceeded to outline the proposed inventory control system he had developed, as tabulated in Exhibit 5. By comparing Exhibits 3 and 5, he pointed out that his analytical approach to the problem achieved significant reductions in the levels of both "circulating" (Column 5 versus Column 12) and "safety" (Column 7 versus Column 13) stocks, so that the total component inventory for the GFC-5, carried by Midwest, was reduced in value from an average of $33,450 to $19,291 (Column 6 versus Column 14).

Safety stocks were reduced to a level representing one to two days' production for the reasons cited by Maxon in criticizing the present system. Circulating inventories were reduced by the application of a computing technique which establishes optimum order lot sizes for each component. By balancing the cost of placing and receiving an order against the cost of carrying the parts in inventory, this technique establishes the size of lots to be ordered so as to minimize total inventory costs.

"After quite a bit of digging around," said Maxon, "we've calculated that it costs us $11 to place a purchase order, inspect, receive, and store it in place. In the illustration worked out in Exhibit 5 we have used the symbol C_1 to indicate these ordering costs. On the other hand, we figure that it costs us 19 cents a year for every dollar we have tied up in inventory—this is based on our cost of capital of 12%, plus an additional 7% representing insurance, space charges, loss, waste, etc. In the illustration worked out in Exhibit 5 we have used the symbol C_2 to indicate these carrying costs. We use both these values, for the C_1 and C_2 factors, in the equations we set up to determine optimum lot size. Any of you who are interested in the methods used can follow the example in Exhibit 5.

"Now, let me show you that the proposed inventory control system will yield a number of significant benefits, both immediate and long-run.

"Initially, we should have a significant amount of cash released from inventory to help us in our problems with working capital. Just by reducing the average value of the GFC-5 inventories from the present $33,450 (Column 6) to the proposed $19,291 level (Column 14), we will immediately release some $14,000 of sorely needed cash. This is about 42% of the cash we now have tied up in GFC-5 components. If a like percentage can be drawn out of *all* our inventories, I would guess we're talking about something in the order of $100,000 added to our working capital. That ain't hay in any league.

"We can also put dollar and cents signs on savings on ordering and carrying costs. The proposed system will allow us to cut our operating expenses. First, Exhibit 6 compares the order and carrying costs of the *circulating component inventories* under the present system run by Iverson and our proposed system. Again, we use the GFC-5 components as our example. Monthly savings in costs of this type amount to $71.27 (Column 21). Second, Exhibit 7 compares the carrying costs of the *safety stocks* under the present Iverson system and our proposed system. Annual savings here amount to $1,018.10 (Column 26). Exhibit 8 summarizes these two aspects of the savings on operating expenses. Notice that the total annual saving is in excess of $1,900 for the GFC-5 components alone (Column 29). Assuming comparable results in all our other products, I'd guess at annual savings of over $15,000—certainly an attractive piece of change to pick up without any extra work, effort or investment on our part. It's simply a by-product of using scientific methods to determine the proper inventory levels and reorder quantities."

In response to Mr. Gilbert's concern that suppliers may raise their unit prices as a result of the reduced order sizes, Maxon replied that he had already checked out several of the key suppliers. "They'll go along with us, and will hold their prices even on smaller individual orders as long as our annual purchases run at about the same volume we've been giving them. They're just as anxious as we are to see us expand our sales volume, and just as quickly as possible."

Maxon's proposals were discussed at some length, and it was unanimously agreed that he should proceed to implement his suggestions as rapidly as possible. Hennessey again questioned the competence of his production personnel and their ability to devote the necessary time needed to install the new system. He did not foresee any problems, however, in their operating with the system once installed. "That means, John," said Hennessey to Maxon, "that it'll be up to you to get the thing going and do all the necessary missionary work. I'll certainly tell my boys to cooperate with you fully." Maxon was quite agreeable to undertaking the task and stated he would proceed as rapidly as possible.

Implementation of New System

By early June, Maxon had completed his calculations for all major components used by Midwest, and had prepared a set of procedure outlines and guide sheets for implementation of the new ordering system.

On June 4 he called a meeting of all foremen and inventory clerks at which Joe Hennessey was also present. Maxon outlined Midwest's urgent need for working capital in its current expansion program. He then proceeded to explain the importance of establishing optimum order lot sizes and minimal safety stock levels. Maxon distributed the same exhibit sheets he had used in his presentation at the executive committee meetings, although his explanations were given on a more elementary level. "Don't worry too much about the formulas and tables," he suggested, "the most important thing you should note is the savings the company is going to get out of this new system. I know it'll mean writing up more orders per month than you've been doing so far, but the cost of this extra work is all allowed for in the calculations we've made and, as you see, we come out well ahead of the game."

Hennessey initiated the discussion of Maxon's presentation by stating that he too was anxious to achieve any possible savings, and that as far as he could see Maxon's ideas appeared to make good sense. "You fellows will be dealing with this new system, and you're familiar with our inventory problems," he told the group, "so let's hear your reactions to Mr. Maxon's proposals." In the discussion that followed most foremen felt they were not qualified to evaluate the mathematical computations involved and, with various degrees of reservation, agreed that the new system deserved a trial. Pointing out that Iverson would be in charge of the system, when installed, Hennessey asked for any suggestions he might have. "For a guy who had trouble with high school math" Iverson replied, "I can't claim that I understand all the figures. It doesn't seem to me that I've been loading up too heavy on parts, but I guess I could've been. I guess I was just naturally more concerned with the smooth running of the shop than with the theoretical costs involved." Iverson, after pointing out that he couldn't really tell how things would work out from just looking at tables of figures, agreed he would do his best to adapt to the new system.

Maxon spent the next two weeks distributing lists of proposed inventory levels and reorder lot sizes for all major components to the foremen and clerks involved. He devoted as much time as he could to explaining the lists and procedures to Iverson, and overseeing the ordering of any specific components which happened to come up during his visits with Iverson. While Maxon was devoting much of his time to the inventory system installation, he found that some of his other duties were being unavoidably neglected. He was, therefore, quite relieved when, towards the end of June, he felt that Iverson and the other foremen were acquiring the necessary familiarity and competence in the new system and could be safely left to their own devices. Before returning to full-time pursuit of his controller's duties, Maxon set up a monthly summary form to be maintained by Iverson's chief clerk. The form was designed to show monthly average inventory levels and reorder quantities, by components, from which Maxon could compute actual reductions and savings for comparison with the newly set standards. Maxon felt that it would probably take three to four months for the new procedures to "shake down." Accordingly, he informed Mr. Gilbert that he would be ready to present the results of his drive on component inventories at the October meeting of the executive committee.

During the "shakedown" period, Maxon made it his business to pay Iverson a visit or two a month and to ask how things were coming along. Iverson reported that he was doing his best to follow the new inventory procedures whenever his day-to-day production problems permitted it. He made a few attempts to point out some of those production problems, which seemed to be increasing in recent weeks. Maxon, conscious of his limited competence in production problems, and careful not to overstep his functional authority, suggested that Iverson discuss his manufacturing problems with Hennessey, "one of the best production men in our industry." After one of Maxon's visits, Iverson turned to his stamping foreman and said: "Boy, am I the guy in the middle! Hennessey tells me my troubles all come from this inventory system and to see Maxon, and Maxon tells me to go see Hennessey. One way or another I'm as busy as a one-armed paperhanger."

The New System Reviewed

At the October meeting of the executive committee Mr. Gilbert called on John Maxon to present his scheduled evaluation of the new inventory procedures installed in June. Maxon reported that he was most disappointed in the results to date. His summary records showed that some reduction in inventory levels was indeed achieved, but that it was a long way from the goals he had established. Using the GFC-5 components again as a typical example, Maxon reported that average inventory levels were reduced by only about $5,000, as against the goal of $14,000 computed in his original presentations. Monthly total costs of ordering and carrying inventories showed an almost negligible reduction, well below the $1,900 annual rate predicted. The reasons for this disappointing performance, Maxon pointed out, were quite self-evident from his summary records. Iverson had only cut back his "safety stocks" by some $3,500 (instead of the proposed $5,690), and had adopted the recommended optimum order lot size in only 40% of his reordering. "The solution is as obvious as the cause of the failure," claimed Maxon. "Iverson is just not competent to be in charge of a system which requires some understanding of mathematical techniques, and at least some appreciation of costs. Sure, Iverson can understand a price-tag of $9.50 on each 'A' component he orders, but he just has no idea of how much it costs us to have it lying around. If we're ever going to succeed in putting some of the modern mathematical techniques to work for us, we've got to have people who understand what it's all about. It is my recommendation that we pull

Iverson off the inventory control job and put in some bright kid who's had some accounting or record-keeping experience. This inventory thing isn't the only modernization in plant methods that we're going to have, so we might as well face the issue and put in some people who can move with the times."

Hennessey strongly objected to Maxon's analysis of the situation. Iverson, he pointed out, was a top-notch foreman who knew his job and had demonstrated his ability to perform it for many years. The fault was not in Iverson's handling of the system, but in the system itself. "Now that we've had a few month's experience with it," Hennessey stated, "I can see many practical problems which John's figures didn't show."

"In the first place, since John's system was put in we've had several runouts on components needed for assembly. Now I know that we can theoretically switch assembly jobs around so as not to run into any downtime, but in practice my people aren't used to being shifted around without notice. They just didn't expect runouts, and as a result this switching around gets them upset and rattled. I've even noticed some secret hoarding of parts by foremen—something we've never had before. In addition every time we get hit by a runout, I find myself in the middle of interdepartmental wars. The assembly department blames ordering and receiving for disrupting their work schedules, ordering blames assembly for late requisitioning, and the shipping room—with the sales department on their neck—scream blue murder at everybody in the place when they have no finished units to ship. These frictions and hassles are really knocking down morale.

"Now in the past few weeks I've also had Jack Werner (quality control supervisor) almost constantly on my back. He's complaining bitterly about a tremendous increase in the per cent rejects we're turning out. Even though I know Jack's a real nut on quality, his figures really shook me up. I started checking up and I can see the reason for these figures. Aside from the effect of the disturbances on my people, I find that Iverson just isn't giving sufficient supervision to his departments. He's constantly chasing around with his inventory and ordering problems, putting out brush fires and trying to keep the peace; so he just isn't there when he's needed.

"Another thing that's causing trouble is John's lot size for Component 'C' which we turn out in our own stamping department. We used to order 5,000 units at a time, which meant scheduling about two runs of it a month. (Actually an average of 2.18 per month, see Exhibit 3, Column 4.) Now John wants it ordered in 2,900-unit lots. This means we've got to set up the job four times a month—twice as often as before—and that's double the trouble and expense. Maybe we're saving some money in 'C' inventories under the new system, but we're sure throwing it away in the stamping department.

"As far as I'm concerned, this whole trial run convinces me that we're saving pennies and throwing away dollars. I can't show you any neat figures of how much runouts, frictions, quality troubles, and disruptions are costing us in dollars and cents, but I'm convinced it's well over any-thing John can save us in inventory costs. I'm for going to some simpler and more practical inventory ordering system. The fancy stuff is prob-ably good for the real big companies, with their computers and experts, but just doesn't work in an outfit our size."

Mr. Gilbert believed that the arguments presented should be studied in detail by him before making a decision on the inventory procedures to be followed. He did not feel it was worthwhile to take up the entire executive committee's time with further discussion of the issue, and ac-cordingly set up a meeting with Maxon and Hennessey at his office for the following day. He suggested they give the matter further thought and bring whatever additional data they could develop in support of their position.

Turning to Maxon, the president remarked with a smile, "Just don't show me too much with high-level differential equations which you know I can't handle."

Upon returning to his office, Hennessey told Iverson, who was waiting for him, "I really let them have it, Pete. Maxon was trying to nail you with it, but I wasn't having any. You know, after this whole hassle, I believe there's something to cleaning up and formalizing our inventory systems. We don't need any fancy accounting stuff, but I think we can improve on what we had. Let's you and I get together Monday to work something out."

Exhibit 1

MIDWEST HARDWARE MANUFACTURING COMPANY

PRODUCT FLOW AND RELEVANT ORGANIZATION CHART

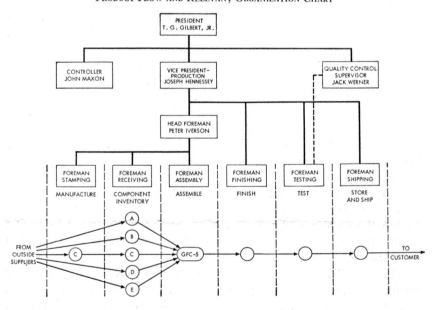

Exhibit 2

MIDWEST HARDWARE MANUFACTURING COMPANY

MONTHLY COMPONENT REQUIREMENT FOR 5,000 UNITS OF GFC-5 PER MONTH

Component	Number Needed for Each GFC-5	Net Monthly Requirement	Monthly Requirement Including Allowance for Rejects, Waste	Unit Cost	Make or Buy
A	1	5,000	5,000	$9.50	B
B	1	5,000	5,000	4.00	B
C	2	10,000	10,900	1.75	M
D	4	20,000	22,000	.23	B
E	1	5,000	5,000	.95	B

Exhibit 3

MIDWEST HARDWARE MANUFACTURING COMPANY

COMPONENTS FOR GFC-5

Present Inventory Levels and Ordering Practices

Component	(1) Monthly Requirement in Units (D)	(2) Unit Cost (P)	(3) Order Lot Size in Units (Z)	(4) Number of Orders per Month $\left(\dfrac{D}{Z}\right)$	(5) Average Value of Circulating Inventory $\left(\dfrac{Z}{2} \times P\right)$	(6) Average Value of Inventory Actually Carried from Accounting Records	(7) Average Value of "Safety Stock" (Col. 6 − Col. 5)
A	5,000	$9.50	1,900	2.63	$ 9,025	$14,728	$ 5,703
B	5,000	4.00	1,800	2.78	3,600	6,802	3,202
C	10,900	1.75	5,000	2.18	4,375	6,985	2,610
D	22,000	.23	8,000	2.75	920	1,612	692
E	5,000	.95	5,000	1.00	2,375	3,323	948
					$20,295	$33,450	$13,155

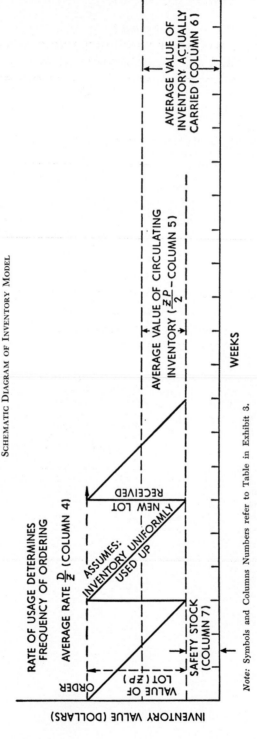

Exhibit 4

MIDWEST HARDWARE MANUFACTURING COMPANY

SCHEMATIC DIAGRAM OF INVENTORY MODEL

RATE OF USAGE DETERMINES
FREQUENCY OF ORDERING

AVERAGE RATE $\frac{D}{2}$ (COLUMN 4)

ASSUMES:
INVENTORY UNIFORMLY
USED UP

NEW LOT
RECEIVED

ORDER

VALUE OF
LOT (ZP)

SAFETY STOCK
(COLUMN 7)

INVENTORY VALUE (DOLLARS)

AVERAGE VALUE OF CIRCULATING
INVENTORY ($\frac{ZP}{2}$ – COLUMN 5)

AVERAGE VALUE OF
INVENTORY ACTUALLY
CARRIED (COLUMN 6)

WEEKS

Note: Symbols and Columns Numbers refer to Table in Exhibit 3.

Exhibit 5

MIDWEST HARDWARE MANUFACTURING COMPANY

COMPONENTS FOR GFC-5

Optimal Inventory Levels and Lot Sizes—as Proposed by Controller's Office

Components	(8) Monthly Requirement in Units (D)	(9) Unit Cost (P)	(10) Optimal Order Lot Size in Units (Z)	(11) Number of Orders per Month $\left(\dfrac{D}{Z}\right)$	(12) Average Value of Circulating Inventory $\left(\dfrac{Z}{2} \times P\right)$	(13) Average Value of "Safety Stock" (1–2 Day's Production)	(14) Average Value of Inventory to Be Carried (Col. 12 + Col. 13)
A	5,000	$9.50	860*	5.81	$ 4,085	$3,800	$ 7,885
B	5,000	4.00	1,300	3.85	2,600	1,600	4,200
C	10,900	1.75	2,900	3.76	2,537	1,225	3,762
D	22,000	.23	11,500	1.91	1,322	460	1,782
E	5,000	.95	2,700	1.85	1,282	380	1,662
					$11,826	$7,465	$19,291

ILLUSTRATION OF METHOD OF DETERMINING OPTIMAL ORDER LOT SIZE*

Component A

$$\text{Optimum Lot Size } Z = \sqrt{\frac{2DC_1}{PC_2}}$$

where: $C_1 = $ cost of ordering, receiving, inspecting, etc. $= \$11.00$ per order;
$C_2 = .016$ since cost of carrying inventory $= 19\%$ of its value per year, or

$$\frac{.19}{12} = .016 \text{ per month.}$$

For Component A:

$$Z_A = \sqrt{\frac{2 \times 5.000 \times 11}{9.50 \times .016}} = \sqrt{723,684} = 851 \text{ units}$$

Rounding off: $Z_A = 860$ *units*—inserted in Row A, Column 10, above. In similar fashion, optimal lot sizes are calculated for components B, C, D, and E.

Exhibit 6

MIDWEST HARDWARE MANUFACTURING COMPANY

COMPARISON OF ORDER AND CARRYING COSTS OF "CIRCULATING" COMPONENT

Inventories—Present and Proposed Methods

$$\text{Total inventory costs, } TC = \underbrace{\frac{DC_1}{Z}}_{\substack{\text{Total ordering} \\ \text{cost per month}}} + \underbrace{\frac{Z\,C_2}{2}}_{\substack{\text{Total carrying} \\ \text{cost per month}}}$$

where $\left.\begin{array}{l} C_1 = \$11.00 \\ C_2 = .016 \end{array}\right\}$ see Exhibit 5

Exhibit 6—Continued

Com-ponent	Present Method			Proposed Method			
	(15) Order Cost $\frac{D}{Z} \times 11.00$ (Col. 4) × (C$_1$)	(16) Carrying Cost $\frac{ZP}{2} \times .016$ (Col. 5) × (C$_2$)	(17) Total Cost (per Month) (15 + 16)	(18) Order Cost $\frac{D}{Z} \times 11.00$ (Col. 11) × (C$_1$)	(19) Carrying Cost $\frac{ZP}{2} \times .016$ (Col. 12) × (C$_2$)	(20) Total Cost (per Month) (18 + 19)	(21) Savings in Total Cost (per Month) (17 − 20)
A	$ 28.93	$144.40	$173.33	$ 63.91	$ 65.36	$129.27	$44.06
B	30.58	57.60	88.18	42.35	41.60	83.95	4.23
C	23.98	70.00	93.98	41.36	40.59	81.95	12.03
D	30.25	14.72	44.97	21.01	21.15	42.16	2.81
E	11.00	38.00	49.00	20.35	20.51	40.86	8.14
	$124.74	$324.72	$449.46	$188.98	$189.21	$378.19	$71.27

Exhibit 7

MIDWEST HARDWARE MANUFACTURING COMPANY

COMPARISON OF CARRYING COSTS OF "SAFETY STOCKS"

Present and Proposed Methods

Present Method		Proposed Method		
(22) Average Value of "Safety Stock" (See Col. 7)	(23) Annual Carrying Cost of "Safety Stock" (13,155 × C$_2$)	(24) Average Value of "Safety Stock" (See Col. 13)	(25) Annual Carrying Cost of "Safety Stock" (7,465 × C$_2$)	(26) Annual Savings (23 − 25)
$13,155	$2,499.45	$7,465	$1,418.35	$1,081.10

Exhibit 8

MIDWEST HARDWARE MANUFACTURING COMPANY

SUMMARY OF ANNUAL SAVINGS IN OPERATING COSTS BY USING THE PROPOSED SYSTEM INSTEAD OF THE PRESENT SYSTEM

(27) Annual Savings in Ordering and Carrying Costs of the Circulating Component Inventories (Col. 21 × 12 Months)	(28) Annual Savings in Carrying Costs of "Safety Stocks" (Col. 26)	(29) Total Annual Savings in Operating Costs under Proposed System (Col. 27 + Col. 28)
$855.24	$1,081.10	$1,936.34

III Selected Readings

From: Hugh Gray Lieber and Lillian R. Lieber
THE EDUCATION OF T. C. MITS*

. . . Algebra is more GENERAL
than Arithmetic.
But perhaps you will say that
this is not much of a difference—
since in Arithmetic
we also have general rules,
but they are given in WORDS,
instead of in LETTERS as in (1).
Thus in Arithmetic we would say:
"To find the area of any rectangle
 multiply its altitude by its base,"
whereas in Algebra we say:
$$A = ab,$$
but, after all, you may feel that
this is merely a matter of
a convenient shorthand
rather than anything radically new.

Now the fact is that
it is not merely a question of
a convenient shorthand,
but
by writing formulas in this
very convenient symbolism—
especially when a formula is
much more complicated than
the one given above—
we are able to tell
AT A GLANCE
many interesting facts
which would be very difficult to
dig out from a complicated
statement in words.
And, furthermore,
when we learn to handle
the formulas,
we find that

we are able to solve problems
almost automatically
which would otherwise require
a great deal of hard thinking.
Just as,
when we learn to drive a car
we are able to "go places"
easily and pleasantly
instead of walking to them
with a great deal of effort.
And so you will see that
the more Mathematics we know
the EASIER life becomes,
for it is a TOOL with which
we can accomplish things
that we could not do at all
with our bare hands.
Thus Mathematics helps
our brains and hands and feet,
and can make
a race of supermen out of us.
Perhaps you will say:
"But I like to walk,
  I don't want to ride all the time.
  and I like to talk,
  I don't want to use
  abstract symbols all the time."
To which the answer is:
By all means enjoy yourself by
walking and talking,
but when you have a hard job to do,
be sure to avail yourself
of all possible tools,
for otherwise
you may find it impossible
to do it at all.

       *   *   *   *   *

In fact
the trouble with the world today
is not that
we have too much Mathematics,
but that we do not yet have enough. . . .

       *   *   *   *   *

No doubt someone will say:
"But the war-makers
  DO use modern machinery which
  IS based on Mathematics.
  Science is really to blame for
  the success of Hitler,
  and therefore
  it cannot possibly guide us to
  the good life."

Now we hope to show here
that this is not so—
that Science and Mathematics can
not only protect us from
floods and lightning and disease
and other physical dangers,
but have within them
a PHILOSOPHY which
can protect us from
the errors of our own
loose thinking.
And thus they can be
a veritable defense against
ALL evil— . . .
The Moral: Streamline your mind
with
Mathematics.

From: Frederick Winslow Taylor
*"PRINCIPLES OF SCIENTIFIC MANAGEMENT"**

[EDITORS' NOTE: The author was an engineer at Bethlehem Steel and became consultant for many leading industries.]

President Roosevelt, in his address to the Governors at the White House, prophetically remarked that "The conservation of our national resources is only preliminary to the larger question of national efficiency."

The whole country at once recognized the importance of conserving our material resources and a large movement has been started which will be effective in accomplishing this object. As yet, however, we have but vaguely appreciated the importance of the "larger question of increasing our national efficiency."

We can see our forests vanishing, our water-powers going to waste, our soil being carried by floods into the sea; and the end of our coal and our iron is in sight. But our larger wastes of human effort, which go on every day through such of our acts as are blundering, ill-directed, or inefficient, and which Mr. Roosevelt refers to as a lack of "national efficiency," are less visible, less tangible, and are but vaguely appreciated.

We can see and feel the waste of material things. Awkward, inefficient, or ill-directed movements of men, however, leave nothing visible or tangible behind them. Their appreciation calls for an act of memory, an effort of the imagination. And for this reason, even though our daily loss from this source is greater than from our waste of material things, the one has stirred us deeply, while the other has moved us but little.

As yet there has been no public agitation for "greater national efficiency," no meetings have been called to consider how this is to be brought about. And still there are signs that the need for greater efficiency is widely felt.

The search for better, for more competent men, from the presidents of our great companies down to our household servants, was never more vigorous than it is now. And more than ever before is the demand for competent men in excess of the supply.

*   *   *   *   *

In the past the man has been first; in the future the system must be first. This in no sense, however, implies that great men are not needed. On the contrary, the first object of any good system must be that of developing first-class men; and under systematic management the best man rises to the top more certainly and more rapidly than ever before.

This paper has been written:

First. To point out, through a series of simple illustrations, the great loss which the whole country is suffering through inefficiency in almost all of our daily acts.

Second. To try to convince the reader that the remedy for this inefficiency lies in systematic management, rather than in searching for some unusual or extraordinary man.

Third. To prove that the best management is a true science, resting upon clearly defined laws, rules, and principles, as a foundation. And further to show that the fundamental principles of scientific management are applicable to all kinds of human activities, from our simplest individual acts to the work of our great corporations, which call for the most elaborate cooperation. And, briefly, through a series of illustrations, to convince the reader that whenever these principles are correctly applied, results must follow which are truly astounding.

This paper was originally prepared for presentation to The American Society of Mechanical Engineers. The illustrations chosen are such as, it is believed, will especially appeal to engineers and to managers of industrial and manufacturing establishments, and also quite as much to all of the men who are working in these establishments. It is hoped, however, that it will be clear to other readers that the same principles can be applied with equal force to all social activities: to the management of our homes; the management of our farms; the management of the business of our tradesmen, large and small; of our churches, our philanthropic institutions, our universities, and our governmental departments.

*   *   *   *   *

The first illustration is that of handling pig iron, and this work is chosen because it is typical of perhaps the crudest and most elementary form of labor which is performed by man. The work is done by men with no other implements than their hands. The pig iron handler stoops down, picks up a pig weighing about 92 lbs., walks for a few feet or yards and then drops it on to the ground or upon a pile. This work is so crude and elementary in its nature that the writer firmly believes that it would be possible to train an intelligent gorilla so as to become a more efficient pig-iron handler than any man can be. Yet it will be shown that the science of handling pig iron is so great and amounts to so much that it is impossible for the man who is best suited to this type of work to understand the principles of this science, or even to work in accordance with these principles without the aid of a man better educated than he is. And the further illustrations to be given will make it clear that in almost all of the mechanic arts the science which underlies each workman's act is so great and amounts to so much that the workman who is best suited actually to do the work is incapable (either through lack of education or through insufficient mental capacity) of understanding this science. This is announced as a general principle. . . .

From: Alfred Marshall
*PRINCIPLES OF ECONOMICS**

[EDITORS' NOTE: The author was Professor of Economics at Cambridge University. This book was first published in 1890.]

§ 3. Next, with regard to the economy of skill. Everything that has been said with regard to the advantages which a large establishment has in being able to afford highly specialized machinery applies equally with regard to highly specialized skill. It can contrive to keep each of its employees constantly engaged in the most difficult work of which he is capable, and yet so to narrow the range of his work that he can attain that facility and excellence which come from long-continued practice. But enough has already been said on the advantage of division of labour: and we may pass to an important though indirect advantage which a manufacturer derives from having a great many men in his employment.

> IV, XI, 3.
> Advantages of a large factory as regards specialized skill,

The large manufacturer has a much better chance than a small one has, of getting hold of men with exceptional natural abilities, to do the most difficult part of his work—that on which the reputation of his establishment chiefly depends. This is occasionally important as regards mere handiwork in trades which require much taste and originality, as for instance that of a house decorator, and in those which require exceptionally fine workmanship, as for instance that of a manufacturer of delicate mechanism.[1] But in most businesses its chief importance lies in the facilities which it gives to the employer for the selection of able and tried men, men whom he trusts and who trust him, to be his foremen and heads of departments. We are thus brought to the central problem of the modern organization of indus-

> the selection of leading men, etc.

---

* Reprinted with permission of The Macmillan Company from *Principles of Economics* by Alfred Marshall. Copyright The Royal Economic Society 1961. (Excerpts from pp. 283–85.)

1 Thus Boulton writing in 1770 when he had 700 or 800 persons employed as metallic artists and workers in tortoiseshell, stones, glass, and enamel, says:—"I have trained up many, and am training up more, plain country lads into good workmen; and wherever I find indications of skill and ability, I encourage them. I have likewise established correspondence with almost every mercantile town in Europe, and am thus regularly supplied with orders for the grosser articles in common demand, by which I am enabled to employ such a number of hands as to provide me with an ample choice of artists for the finer branches of work: and I am thus encouraged to erect and employ a more extensive apparatus than it would be prudent to employ for the production of the finer articles only." Smiles' *Life of Boulton*, p. 128.

try, viz. that which relates to the advantages and disadvantages of the subdivision of the work of business management.

IV, xi, 4.

The sub-
division
of the
work of
business
manage-
ment:
advantages
of the large
manu-
facturer;

§ 4. The head of a large business can reserve all his strength for the broadest and most fundamental problems of his trade: he must indeed assure himself that his managers, clerks and foremen are the right men for their work, and are doing their work well; but beyond this he need not trouble himself much about details. He can keep his mind fresh and clear for thinking out the most difficult and vital problems of his business; for studying the broader movements of the markets, the yet undeveloped results of current events at home and abroad; and for contriving how to improve the organization of the internal and external relations of his business.

For much of this work the small employer has not the time if he has the ability; he cannot take so broad a survey of his trade, or look so far ahead; he must often be content to follow the lead of others. And he must spend much of his time on work that is below him; for if he is to succeed at all, his mind must be in some respects of a high quality, and must have a good deal of originating and organizing force; and yet he must do much routine work.

On the other hand the small employer has advantages of his own. The master's eye is everywhere; there is no shirking by his foremen or workmen, no divided responsibility, no sending half-understood messages backwards and forwards from one department to another. He saves much of the book-keeping, and nearly all of the cumbrous system of checks that are necessary in the business of a large firm; and the gain from this source is of very great importance in trades which use the more valuable metals and other expensive materials.

And though he must always remain at a great disadvantage in getting information and in making experiments, yet in this matter the general course of progress is on his side. For External economies are constantly growing in importance relatively to Internal in all matters of Trade-knowledge: newspapers, and trade and technical publications of all kinds are perpetually scouting for him and bringing him much of the knowledge he wants—knowledge which a little while ago would have been beyond the reach of anyone who could not

afford to have well-paid agents in many distant places. Again, it is to his interest also that the secrecy of business is on the whole diminishing, and that the most important improvements in method seldom remain secret for long after they have passed from the experimental stage. It is to his advantage that changes in manufacture depend less on mere rules of thumb and more on broad developments of scientific principle; and that many of these are made by students in the pursuit of knowledge for its own sake, and are promptly published in the general interest. Although therefore the small manufacturer can seldom be in the front of the race of progress, he need not be far from it, if he has the time and the ability for availing himself of the modern facilities for obtaining knowledge. But it is true that he must be exceptionally strong if he can do this without neglecting the minor but necessary details of the business. . . .

From: Frederick Winslow Taylor

*"TESTIMONY BEFORE THE SPECIAL HOUSE COMMITTEE INVESTIGATING THE TAYLOR AND OTHER SYSTEMS"**

[EDITORS' NOTE: The author was an engineer at Bethlehem Steel and became consultant for many leading industries.]

The Chairman. Is it not the purpose of all production to add to the comfort and well-being of mankind?

Mr. Taylor. It is.

The Chairman. If by any system of production you increase the discomfort of mankind, have you not thereby destroyed the very purposes of your production?

Mr. Taylor. That depends entirely upon the amount of discomfort which the workman had before. If a man had not been working faithfully, if he had spent one-half of his time in idleness, I do not look upon it as anything of a misfortune to that man that he is brought to spend his working time in useful effort instead of in useless exertion.

The Chairman. Do you think that the comparatively small number of employees should have the power to determine absolutely for the comparatively large number of employees what constitutes comfort for them?

Mr. Taylor. I certainly do not think it ought to be in the power of any outside man to say what shall constitute the comfort of his fellow man. Every person should be free to decide what is for his own comfort, and I think in this country, so far as I know, that is true.

The Chairman. Would not the fact that industry is to be directed by scientific management—by one central intelligence—and that the question of whether the workmen are comfortable or uncomfortable is to be determined by that central intelligence, place in the hands of the employers the power to determine what constitutes comfort for the employees?

Mr. Taylor. Mr. Chairman, I must again state that under scientific management those men who are in the management, such as, for instance, the superintendent, the foremen, the president of the company, have far, far less arbitrary power than is now possessed by the corresponding men who are occupying those positions in the older types of management. I must again state that under scientific management the officers of the company, those on the management side, are quite as much subject to the same laws as are the workmen. As I have again and again stated, our great difficulty in the introduction of scientific management has been to get those on the management side to obey these laws and to do the share which it becomes their duty to do in the actual work of the establishment in cooperating with the workmen, so that I hope that I may be able to

---

* From *Scientific Management* by Frederick Winslow Taylor. Copyright © 1947. Reprinted by permission of Harper & Row, Publishers, Inc. (Excerpts from pp. 211–13, 215–17.)

make myself clear that under scientific management arbitrary power, arbitrary dictation, ceases; and that every single subject, large and small, becomes the question for scientific investigation, for reduction to law, and that the workmen have quite as large a share in the development of these laws and in subsequently carrying them out as the management have.

The Chairman. Is not the management the final arbiter in the determining of those questions under scientific management?

Mr. Taylor. In most cases the laws and the formulas and the facts of scientific management, which are vital both to the workmen and the management, have been developed during years preceding the one on which the work is going on. And that being the case, neither the management nor the workmen have any final arbitrary dictum as to those laws. The laws of scientific management are somewhat analogous to the laws of this country. We are all working under certain laws that were not enacted by the present Congress or the present President of the United States, and which have not been interpreted by the present courts, and yet the President of the United States and all the citizens of the United States are alike working under those laws. Now, under scientific management there have gradually grown up a code of laws which are accepted by both as just and fair. What I want to make clear is that the old arbitrary way of having a dictator, who was at the head of the company, decide everything with his dictum, and having his word final, has ceased to exist.

*   *   *   *   *

The Chairman. When your scientific management has gathered together its information, its formulas, and formulated its rules and regulations, systematized its work, etc., giving its direction to the workman, and the workman fails to obey these formulas that are laid down for him, is there any method in scientific management to discipline the workman?

Mr. Taylor. There certainly is, Mr. Chairman; and any system of whatever nature under which there is no such thing as discipline is, I think I can say, pretty nearly worthless. Under scientific management the discipline is at the very minimum, but out of kindness to the workman, out of personal kindness to him, in my judgment, it is the duty of those who are in the management to use all the arts of persuasion first to get the workman to conform to the rules, and after that has been done, then to gradually increase the severity of the language until, practically, before you are through, the powers of the English language have been exhausted in an effort to make the man do what he ought to do. And if that fails, then in the interest of the workman some more severe type of discipline should be resorted to.

The Chairman. Having gathered together all your information, and built up your formulas and introduced your scientific management, if the management violates its formulas, what method is there in scientific management to discipline the management for its violation of its principles?

Mr. Taylor. I am very glad that you asked that question. Just the moment that any of our men in the planning room does not attend to his end of the business, just the moment one of the teachers or one of the functional foremen does not attend to his duties, or do whatever he ought to do in the way of serving the workmen—I say serving advisedly, because if there is anything that is characteristic of scientific management it is the fact that the men who were formerly called bosses under the old type of management, under scientific management become the servants of the workmen. It is their duty to wait on the workmen and help them in all kinds of ways, and just let a boss fall down in any one thing and not do his duty, and a howl goes right straight up. The workman comes to the planning room and raises a great big howl because the foreman has not done his duty. I tell you that those in the management are disciplined quite as severely as the workmen are. Scientific management is a true democracy.

The Chairman. Suppose that it is the man higher up that violates these formulas? As I understand your testimony before this committee, no scientific management can exist until there has been an entire change of mind on the part of the management as well as on the part of the workmen?

Mr. Taylor. Yes, sir.

The Chairman. And that this change must take place in the point of view, in the mind of the employer and the employee.

Mr. Taylor. Yes, sir.

From: Thomas Hobbes

LEVIATHAN (CHAPTER X, "OF POWER, WORTH, DIGNITY, HONOUR, AND WORTHINESS")

[EDITORS' NOTE: Thomas Hobbes, 1588–1679, made significant contributions to political science through *Leviathan*, his major work.]

The power of a man, to take it universally, is his present means to obtain some future apparent good, and is either original or instrumental.

Natural power is the eminence of the faculties of body, or mind; as extraordinary strength, form, prudence, arts, eloquence, liberality, nobility. *Instrumental* are those powers which, acquired by these, or by fortune, are means and instruments to acquire more; as riches, reputation, friends, and the secret working of God, which men call good luck. For the nature of power is, in this point, like to fame, increasing as it proceeds; or like the motion of heavy bodies, which, the further they go, make still the more haste.

The greatest of human powers is that which is compounded of the powers of most men, united by consent, in one person, natural or civil, that has the use of all their powers depending on his will; such as is the power of a Commonwealth: or depending on the wills of each particular; such as is the power of a faction, or of diverse factions leagued. Therefore to have servants is power; to have friends is power: for they are strengths united.

Also, riches joined with liberality is power; because it procureth friends and servants: without liberality, not so; because in this case they defend not, but expose men to envy, as a prey.

Reputation of power is power; because it draweth with it the adherence of those that need protection.

So is reputation of love of a man's country, called *popularity*, for the same reason.

Also, what quality soever maketh a man beloved or feared of many, or the reputation of such quality, is power; because it is a means to have the assistance and service of many.

Good success is power; because it maketh reputation of wisdom or good fortune, which makes men either fear him or rely on him.

Affability of men already in power is increase of power; because it gaineth love.

Reputation of prudence in the conduct of peace or war is power; because to prudent men we commit the government of ourselves more willingly than to others.

Nobility is power, not in all places, but only in those Commonwealths where it has privileges; for in such privileges consisteth their power.

Eloquence is power; because it is seeming prudence.

Form is power; because being a promise of good, it recommendeth men to the favour of women and strangers.

The sciences are small powers; because not eminent, and therefore, not acknowledged in any man; nor are at all, but in a few, and in them, but of a few things. For science is of that nature, as none can understand it to be, but such as in a good measure have attained it.

Arts of public use, as fortification, making of engines, and other instruments of war, because they confer to defence and victory, are power; and though the true mother of them be science, namely, the mathematics; yet, because they are brought into the light by the hand of the artificer, they be esteemed (the midwife passing with the vulgar for the mother) as his issue.

From: Harold D. Lasswell and Abraham Kaplan
*POWER AND SOCIETY**

[EDITORS' NOTE: Harold D. Lasswell is Professor of Law and Political Science, Yale Law School. Abraham Kaplan, philosopher, teaches at the University of California in Los Angeles.]

. . . The circulation of a leadership varies inversely with the disparity between its skills and those of the rank and file.

This is one of Michels' basic theses, elaborated throughout his study of *Political Parties:* "the leader's principal source of power is found in his indispensability." Every organization rests on a division of labor, and hence specialization. And to the degree that distinctive skills are involved the specialist becomes indispensable. The leader is such a specialist.

"The leaders cannot be replaced at a moment's notice, since all the other members of the party [or other group] are absorbed in their everyday occupations and are strangers to the bureaucratic mechanism. This special competence, this expert knowledge, which the leader acquires in matters inaccessible, or almost inaccessible to the mass, gives him a security of tenure . . . (1915, 84)."

What is fundamental is that the possession of certain values is a requisite of leadership, and that these values are nontransferable. (Leadership resting on a transferable value could be replaced by effecting the transfer.) Skill is the most

---

* Reprinted by permission of the Yale University Press, New Haven, Connecticut, 1950 (pp. 157–59).

striking of the nontransferable values; but there are others as well. Thus prestige is an important requisite of leadership not readily transferable. Hence stability of leadership will also vary with the disparity in the respect accorded the leaders and the rank and file. And the same will be true with regard to personal characteristics (for instance, prowess) on which leadership in a given case might be based.

As a consequence, the major threat to the leadership is provided, not by the rank and file itself, but by potential rivals for leadership with the requisite skills and other qualities.

"Whenever the power of the leaders is seriously threatened, it is in most cases because a new leader or a new group of leaders is on the point of becoming dominant, and is inculcating views opposed to those of the old rulers of the party. . . . It is not the masses which have devoured the leaders: the chiefs have devoured one another with the aid of the masses (1915, 164–5)."

As a further consequence of the skill conditions, a leadership is rarely completely replaced by its rivals. In criticism of Pareto's "theory of the circulation of elites" Michels points out that "in most cases there is not a simple replacement of one group of élites by another, but a continuous process of intermixture, the old elements incessantly attracting, absorbing, and assimilating the new" (1915, 378). The rival leaderships are indispensable to one another as well as to the group. The new leadership cannot dispense altogether with the skills and experience of the old, nor can the old better maintain its favorable power position than by extending to rivals a restricted share in their own power. Hence

"very rarely does the struggle between the old leaders and the new end in the complete defeat of the former. The result of the process is not so much a 'circulation des élites' as a 'reunion des élites,' an amalgam, that is to say, of the two elements (1915, 177)."

Throughout even the most revolutionary changes a stable administration core remains, which is the more prominent the more specialized are the skills it possesses.

From: Chris Argyris

*"HUMAN PROBLEMS WITH BUDGETS"**

[EDITORS' NOTE: The author is Professor of Industrial Administration and Research Project Director, Labor and Management Center, Yale University.

Professor Argyris speaks here specifically about financial budgets, but his remarks are applicable to operations research control techniques.]

Budgets are accounting techniques designed to control costs through *people*. As such their impact is felt by everyone in the organization. They are continuously being brought into the picture when anyone is trying to determine, plan, and implement an organizational policy or practice. Moreover, budgets fre-

* Reprinted by permission of *Harvard Business Review*, Vol. XXXI, No. 1 (January–February 1953), pp. 97–110.

quently serve as a basis for rewarding and penalizing those in the organization. Failure to meet the budget in many plants invites much punishment; success, much reward.

*   *   *   *   *

One of the most common of the factory supervisors' assumptions about budgets is that they can be used as a pressure device to increase production efficiency. Finance people also admit to the attitude that budgets help "keep employees on the ball" by raising their goals and increasing their motivation. The problem of the effects of pressure applied through budgets seems to be at the core of the budget problem.

*   *   *   *   *

. . . Being concrete, . . . budgets seem to serve as a medium through which the total effects of management pressure are best expressed. . . .

*   *   *   *   *

It is not difficult to see what happens. Tension begins to mount. People become uneasy and suspicious. They increase the informal pressure to keep production at the new level. . . .

*   *   *   *   *

. . . We know, from psychological research, that people can stand only a certain amount of pressure. After this point is passed, it becomes intolerable to an individual. We also know that one method people use to reduce the effect of the pressure (assuming that the employees cannot reduce the pressure itself) is to join groups, which help absorb much of the pressure and thus relieve the individual personally.

*   *   *   *   *

Gradually, therefore, the individuals become a group because in so doing they are able to satisfy their need to (a) reduce the pressure on each individual; (b) get rid of tension; (c) feel more secure by belonging to a group which can counteract the pressure. . . .

*   *   *   *   *

But what about the supervisor, particularly the front-line supervisor or foreman? Strong pressures also converge upon him. How does he protect himself from these pressures?

He cannot join a group against management, as his work force does. For one thing, he probably has at least partially identified himself with management. For another, he may be trying to advance in the hierarchy. Naturally, he would not help his chances for advancement if he joined an antimanagement group.

The evidence obtained from our study seems to indicate that the line supervisor cannot pass all the pressure he feels along to his workers. Time and time again factory supervisors stated that passing the pressure down would only create conflict and trouble, which in turn would lead to a decrease in production.

The question thus arises: Where does the pressure go? How do the supervisors relieve themselves of at least some of it? There is evidence to suggest at least three ways in which pressure is handled by the supervisors:

1. *Interdepartmental strife*—Some foremen seek release from pressure by continuously trying to blame others for the troubles that exist. . . .

2. *Staff versus factory strife*—Foremen also try to diminish pressure by blaming the budget people, production-control people, and salesmen for their problems.

3. *"Internalizing" pressure*—Many supervisors who do not complain about the pressure have in reality "internalized" it, and, in a sense, made it a part of

themselves. Such damming up of pressure can affect supervisors in at least two different ways:

a. Supervisor A is quiet, relatively nonemotional, seldom expresses his negative feelings to anyone, but at the same time he works excessively. He can be found at his desk long after the others have gone home. He often draws the comment, "That guy works himself to death."

b. Supervisor B is nervous, always running around "checking up" on all his employees. He usually talks fast, gives one the impression that he is "selling" himself and his job when interviewed. He is forever picking up the phone, barking commands, and requesting prompt action.

*   *   *   *   *

. . . Constant tension leads to frustration. A person who has become frustrated no longer operates as effectively as he used to. He finds that he tends to forget things he used to remember. Work that he once did with pleasure he now delegates to someone else. He is not able to make decisions as fast as previously. Now he finds he has to take a walk or get a cup of coffee—anything to "get away from it all."

*   *   *   *   *

. . . Extreme application to work or extreme aggression become "natural" —part of the "human nature" of the supervisor. His consequent attempts to alleviate some of the factors causing the tension may lead to quick, ill-conceived, confused, or violent action.

Withdrawal, apathy, indifference are other results of such stresses and strains. Rumors begin to fly; mistrust, suspicion, and intolerance grow fast. In short, conflict, tension, and unhappiness become the key characteristics of the supervisor's life.

*   *   *   *   *

Our interviewers suggested that the budget people perceive their role as being "the watchdog of the company." They are always trying to improve the situation in the plant. As one finance supervisor said, *"Always* there is room to make it better." . . .

In other words, the success of the finance men derives from finding errors, weaknesses, and faults that exist in the plant. But when they discover such conditions, in effect they also are singling out a "guilty party" and implicitly, at least, placing him in failure. Naturally, any comment that "things aren't going along as well as they could in your department" tends to make the particular foreman feel he is deficient.

*   *   *   *   *

The way in which foremen's shortcomings are reported also is important.

Let us assume that a finance man discovers an error in a particular foreman's department. How is this error reported? Does the finance man go directly to the factory foreman? In the plants studied the answer, usually, is no.

The finance man cannot take the "shortest" route between the foreman and himself. For one reason, it may be a violation of policy for staff personnel to go directly to line personnel. Even more important (from a human point of view), the finance man achieves his success when *his boss* knows he is finding errors. But his boss would never know how good a job he is doing unless he brought attention to it. . . .

*   *   *   *   *

But how about factory people? The answer seems evident. In such a situation, the foreman experiences the negative feelings not only of being wrong but also of knowing that his superiors know it, and that he has placed them in an undesirable position.

Finally, to add insult to injury, the entire incident is made permanent and exhibited to the plant officials by being placed in some budget report which is to be, or has been, circulated through many top channels.

From: Elwood S. Buffa

*MODERN PRODUCTION MANAGEMENT**

[EDITORS' NOTE: The author is Associate Professor of Production Management, University of California, Los Angeles.]

In a sense, inventories make possible a rational production system. Without them we could not achieve smooth production flow, obtain reasonable utilization of machines, reasonable material handling costs, or expect to give reasonable service to customers on hundreds of items regarded as "stock" items. At each stage of both manufacturing and distribution, inventories serve the vital function of *decoupling* the various operations in the sequence beginning with raw materials, extending through all of the manufacturing operations and into finished goods storage, and thence to warehouses and retail stores. Between each pair of activities in this sequence, inventories make the required operations enough independent of each other that low cost operations can be carried out. Thus, when raw materials are ordered, a supply is ordered that is large enough to justify the out-of-pocket cost of putting through the order and transporting it to the plant. When production orders to manufacture parts and products are released, we try to make them big enough to justify the cost of writing the orders and setting up machines to perform the required operations. Otherwise, order writing and setup costs could easily become prohibitive. Running parts through the system in lots also tends to reduce handling costs because parts can be handled in groups. . . .

*   *   *   *   *

Unfortunately, the inventory question is not a one-sided one, which is precisely why inventories are a problem in the operation of a production system. If there were not an optimal level to shoot for, there would be no problem. Anyone could follow the simple rule: "Make inventories as big as possible." Inventories require that invested capital be tied up, and, therefore, there is an appropriate opportunity cost associated with their value. Not only that, they require valuable space and absorb insurance and taxation charges. . . .

Thus, we have one set of costs that are fixed by the purchase or production order size and another set of costs which increase with the level of inventory. The first set of costs exert a pressure toward large purchase and production lots to reduce unit order writing and setup costs to a reasonable level. The second

_____
* Reprinted by permission of John M. Wiley, New York, 1961 (pp. 442–43, 450–51, 471).

set of costs exerts a pressure toward small lots in order to maintain inventory costs at reasonable levels. . . .

*   *   *   *   *

We have been discussing inventory controls as if they could be set up independently of the production system, inferring criteria, or measures of effectiveness, that do not reflect the effect of inventories on production programs and on the control of general levels of production. This independence is unrealistic because there are interactions between these problems. Inventory policy must fit in with schedules to produce a *combined* minimum cost of operation rather than a minimum for inventories alone. . . .

*   *   *   *   *

Production and inventory control are one subject, because any partitioning of the problems in this area that does not consider both will likely result in a suboptimum solution. The development of economic lot sizes is a good example of this. This concept holds in the narrower sense, but when interactions with production fluctuations are taken into account, other basic schemes of control may exhibit superior overall cost characteristics. There may be other interactions. For example, how does the length of a production run affect learning time and, therefore, labor cost? Perhaps this effect is insignificant for some situations, but it is known to be important in many others. Do lot size formulations account for this effect? What other interactions are not accounted for? We are witnessing some of the difficulties in attempting mathematical solutions to problems of restricted definition.

APEX WIRE AND CABLE COMPANY

I Case Introduction

Synopsis

An exhaustive three-year investigation of Apex' Charleston plant showed that the buildings, location, and expansion potential so severely handicap the company in its cost control and growth programs that re- location is economically necessary. A majority of the Charleston em- ployees accept the Apex offer and follow their jobs to the new plant. Negotiations on the new union contract, however, break down, and a strike ensues.

Why This Case Is Included

This case provides an excellent opportunity for analyzing the forces at work in a plant relocation decision and implementation, the demands of economics and technology, the concern for employee needs, the human reaction to change, the force of incentives, the union relationships, etc. Beyond giving occasion to (a) apply the conceptual schemes of economics, political science, and psychology, and (b) vicariously experience the diffi- culty of making a complex decision, the case is interesting for another reason. In the Apex case the need for a multilevel analysis stands out— focusing on the irate worker, the recalcitrant union membership, the multiplant corporation complex, the economically distressed community, and the national economy.

Diagnostic and Predictive Questions

In answering the following diagnostic and predictive questions, remember that these questions apply theories and conceptual ideas from certain disci- plines. Such theories are valuable to understand basic forces at work in the policy system (diagnosis) and to predict what will happen in the system in the future (prediction). Since each reading abstracts from the total policy system certain factors or variables into the closed or partial viewpoint of one theory or discipline, no one reading gives answers to the practical policy problems of the case. In diagnosis and prediction, the parts of the problem are studied with "other things being equal."

Following each question are listed readings which will be helpful in answering the question. The readings included with this case are marked (*). By referring to the author index at the end of this book, you may locate the other readings listed.

1. Putting aside for the moment the fact that Apex faces another plant relocation shortly, identify the basic problem (s) faced at the end of the case by Apex management. (Make your problem statement a snapshot of the log (s) responsible for the log jam—the roadblock to be hurdled in getting from the present to the desired situation.) Write your problem statement before going on to the more formal diagnoses below.

2. Using economic reasoning, why did Apex decide to relocate the Charleston plant?

Read: Spencer and Siegelman, *Managerial Economics: Decision Making and Forward Planning,* pp. 242–48, 202–12. Anthony, *Management Accounting,* pp. 290–92, 306.

3. Did management give consideration to any decision-making criteria other than the exigencies of economics and technology in choosing to move from Charleston to Mansfield? Was anything other than profit maximization weighed in the decision process?

Read: *Veblen, *The Engineers and the Price System,* chap. v. Berle, "The Corporation in a Democratic Society." *Eells and Walton, *Conceptual Foundations of Business,* pp. 185–87, 149–67, 458–75. Heilbroner, *The Future as History,* pp. 158–59.

4. Using the concepts of national income accounting, what will be the probable effect of the plant relocation on the Gross *Municipal* Product and the *Municipal* Income of Charleston? The effect on Mansfield? What is the probable effect of the Gross *National* Product and *National* Income?

Read: *Harriss, *The American Economy,* p. 281. *Twentieth Century Fund, *USA in New Dimensions,* p. 15. Berle, "The Corporation in a Democratic Society." (The diagrams in the first two readings are reproduced together in Harriss' book. Those who seek additional understanding of national income accounting will find Chapter 1 in Harriss' book helpful.)

5. Building on your answer to Question 4, but now taking the point of view of social values, do you think the residents of Charleston agreed or disagreed with management's decision to relocate? Would you think the nation as a whole would be favorable or unfavorable to the decision?

Read: Galbraith, *The Affluent Society,* pp. 121–24, 126. Dahl and Lindblom, *Politics, Economics and Welfare,* pp. 28–29, 31–33, 38–41, 45–46, 49–53.

6. From the viewpoint of the psychology of human needs, why are the workers on strike? Why are the workers holding out for monetary benefits beyond what they were used to and beyond what the "going rate" is in the Mansfield location and in the wire and cable industry? Why are many employees commuting the 100 miles from Charleston to Mansfield instead of moving to the new locale?

Read: *Brown, *The Social Psychology of Industry,* pp. 186–87, 199–203. Selekman, *Labor Relations and Human Relations,* pp. 111–37. *McMurray, "Conflicts in Human Values."

7. How would you explain the phenomenon of the workers at Mansfield seemingly forming a new "informal group," ostensibly under the leadership of the four workers discharged in Charleston?

Read: Argyris, *Personality and Organization*, pp. 27–31, 33–51, 66–67, 77–90, 95, 103–4, 123–25, 130, 137–39, 150, 153–55, 157.

8. How has the union's democratic process for membership ratification of the contract bargained by Apex management and the union's representatives affected efforts of reaching an agreement? Is this a necessary result of the democratic process? Why has such been the case in this situation?

Read: *Berg, "The Nice Kind of Union Democracy."

9. Having gone through some formal diagnosis, make another effort at an accurate statement of the basic problem(s) facing the Apex management at the end of the case. Does this second statement differ from the one you wrote in Question 1?

Policy Questions for This Specific Case

In answering the following policy questions, the results of diagnosis and prediction are used to reduce the amount of guesswork, or judgment, in designing action solutions. However, since certain parts of the total case situation cannot be reduced to science, and since "other things are not equal," judgment must still be used to fill in the factors not accounted for by readings. You will also need a second kind of judgment as you put value weights on different scientific predictions, since different theories may point to conflicting solutions.

10. If you were the Apex president, would you have made the move? If your answer is "no," why not? If yes, why? If yes, would you have planned to move any differently? (See Questions 2, 3, 4, 5, 6, and 7 and their attached readings.)

11. What would you, as Apex president, do now? Set up priorities and a time table for handling the issues. Justify each step of your program and the sequencing of steps. (See Question 9.)

12. Design a detailed program for handling the Ferndale plant relocation.

Major Policy Issues: Tentative Generalizations about Any Policy System

In arriving at conclusions for the following questions, generalize from the facts in the case and use your own ideas to (a) confirm, (b) modify, or (c) test the workability of the concepts and theories from readings. As an executive or professional, use wisdom to merge theory, on the one hand, with "brute facts" and practice, on the other.

13. Whose responsibility is it to assist a town or locality in adjusting to the loss of a major employer? (See the readings cited in Question 3.)

14. To what extent does the right of private property allow management to act autonomously? To what extent do workers have rights to be party to company decisions? (See the Eells and Walton reading cited in Question 3.)

Read: *Petro, *The Labor Policy of a Free Society*, pp. 37–42. *Lippmann, *The Method of Freedom*, pp. 100–102. "Arbitration Decisions on Management Rights."

15. Does the effort for technological efficiency conflict with needs of the human person and the desires for autonomy? Or, can these things be reconciled without compromise? (See the Dahl and Lindblom, Argyris, Heilbroner, and McMurray readings cited above.)

16. How important is it—if at all—that an administrator have a composite of knowledge about, skill in handling, and attitudes toward man's intellectual and

volitional make-up, his needs and his defense mechanisms, in order to effectively administer a policy system? Compare the need here with the administrator's need to know about the economic system's structure and dynamics or the construction and workings of a plant or key machine (the computer, for example). (See the readings cited under Questions 6 and 7.) (Additional reading, not in this volume: Charles E. Summer, Jr., *Factors in Effective Administration* [New York: Columbia University Press, 1956], Parts I through V.)

Questions for Original Student Work in Analysis and Policy

The methods of viewing this case as represented by the authors' questions and selections of readings are not exhaustive. There are other relevant ideas for diagnosis and prediction. Furthermore, there are other ways of stating policy questions. More powerful analyses and wiser solutions will result by drawing on your own training and experience for (a) relevant concepts and theories, and (b) creative ways of asking policy questions. The following questions are designed to help you acquire this skill.

17. While reflecting on case facts, what additional theories from prior education give you insights as to "what is going on" in Apex Wire and Cable Company? As to what might be predicted to happen in the future?

18. Other than the policy questions asked by the authors, what pragmatic ways can you think of to state the practical problems faced by executives in the case?

II Apex Wire & Cable Company*

History of the Company

Eighty years ago the Apex Wire & Cable Company began its operations in Ferndale, Michigan. With the growing market for wire and cable, Apex expanded its facilities to include two more plants, one in Dearborn and the other in Charleston, West Virginia.

Today Apex is one of the leaders in its field, meeting competition in the production of heavy wire and cable primarily for public utilities and the armed forces. Sales have increased from $3 million in 1920 to $53 million last year.

Robert Douglas, manager of industrial relations, states that employee satisfaction at Apex's three plants seems evidenced by the relatively large number of two-generation teams on the company's payroll. In Ferndale there are 28 fathers and sons or daughters; and in several cases three and even four members of the family working in the plant. At the Dearborn plant, a smaller operation, there are 12 such teams, and at Charleston, 18.

---

* Copyright 1964 by the Graduate School of Business, Columbia University.

Employee benefits have been instituted, but, in the words of Mr. Leif, president of Apex, "Few have been forced on the company by employees or unions; Apex has, in almost every instance, taken the lead in both the industry and the area. In addition to a widely recognized liberal insurance plan, Apex maintains premium pension plans and high wages, thus attracting a high class of workmen."

The company's newspaper keeps employees in the offices and factory abreast of all new developments within the company, the area, and the industry. Apex has interested itself also in the support of various educational activities in the area extending from night school classes to those on a college level.

Strikes have been few and far between. Two of the plants are organized under the leadership of the United Rubber Workers and the International Brotherhood of Electrical Workers; the third is represented by an independent union which has repeatedly rejected overtures from national and international unions. Even when a strike has been called, none of the kinds of demonstrations which make front-page news were staged; as a rule, only two or three pickets at a time came to the site, and caused no trouble to those of the office staff who continued to report for work.

A two-way communication program of the company continues to stress personal contact techniques, aided by written communications such as plant and company-wide newspapers, employees' handbooks, incentive plan booklets, reading racks, suggestions systems, product displays, letters to employees, and bulletin board presentations.

The Charleston Plant

Six years ago, upon a close and thorough examination of the relative productivity of the three plants, the management at Apex began to doubt the justification of the Charleston, West Virginia, factory.

From a purely financial aspect, it was proved that, except for the war years, it actually lost money. Over the years, past earnings of the Charleston plant had been unsatisfactory and spotty. Total net earnings for the past 16 years have been less than $460,000. For a company whose net sales for the current year were over $53 million, this figure for the Charleston plant accounts for very little of the company's profits.

Top management and the board of directors recently visited Charleston to see for themselves. After a prolonged investigation by this committee, and with the aid of industrial and production engineers, it was decided that the Charleston factory is in a poor position to meet the demands of competition. Buildings and the space arrangements impose serious handicaps to efficient, low-cost production. Its location is too far from a main rail center, thus making transportation difficult and expensive. Only a very limited gain can be made through machinery improvement, but not enough to make the investment worthwhile. There is no room to permit the adequate building up of stocks of finished products. Finally, improvement of this factory to make it a modern, single-story, properly laid-out plant is deemed practically impossible at any reasonable cost.

The heavy construction market, upon which Apex principally depends for business, has maintained its impetus. Although sales are increasing for the company as a whole, "they do not reflect," in the minds of top management and the board of directors, "the volume which might have been achieved had the Charleston plant not been in the position of a high cost operation." Not only is production costly and difficult at Charleston, but markets, too, are often inaccessible or unable to be exploited as a result of limited manufacturing facilities. And because of its location and delivery schedules, a very important part of the competition in the wire and cable industry, were difficult to meet.

A long-range forecast by the economics and marketing staff departments indicates that in five years there will be a 45% increase in the need for the types of cable which Apex produces. But with the condition of the Charleston plant, Apex probably will be able to increase its sales by only 30 to 35%.

The only feasible solution which is acceptable to all segments of management, directors and engineers, is relocation. The company's obligation to the community at large and to its workers in particular was questioned by some; and Roger S. Leif, the president, suggested that insofar as possible, an invitation be extended to all present employees at Charleston, giving them the option of moving with the company or remaining in Charleston on their own.

Arrangements for Moving the Charleston Plant

On March 1 of last year, Mr. Leif issued a mimeographed letter to all of the employees of Apex. It stated in part:

> I am writing to you and all our personnel because of a recent development in the company's plans which has to do with the future location of part of our operations.
>
> We realize, as you probably do, that the facilities at our Charleston and Ferndale plants are inadequate from the standpoint both of efficient operation and potential growth. This has become more and more evident with the growth of business. What we need are up-to-date plants.

The letter went on in accurate detail about the intensive, three-year investigation which Apex had conducted in connection with plant locations and that the company had finally decided upon buying a new but recently vacated automobile plant a little less than one hundred miles from Charleston. This, the president went on to say, more nearly fulfilled all the requirements which Apex was looking for—modern factory, good location, room for expansion, etc. He also went into detail regarding the costs of the move, the potential savings, and the greater share of the expanding market which would be more readily available to Apex. These facts, he stressed, were the results of research by a team of competent specialists in engineering, marketing, and economics:

> Over the next several years, a number of our Ferndale operations may similarly be transferred to the new site. It is difficult to say now whether five years from now will see the Ferndale operations all located at the new site, or whether it will be more economical to keep certain operations at the present Ferndale plant on an expanded basis.
>
> Insofar as possible, jobs at the new location will be filled by present employees who are available and willing to make the move. As to those employees whose jobs are displaced and who are not in a position to take employment at the new site, we will cooperate in their attempt to find employment elsewhere.

The cost of the new plant at Mansfield, exclusive of the new equipment and requisite construction of a 16,000-foot addition, was estimated at $6,000,000. The company arranged a long-term loan for $4,000,000 with its insurance company to pay for the purchase of the new plant. An additional $2,700,000 was spent from past savings to pay for new equipment. To make ready for the new increase in sales and output, the sales force was enlarged by 15%.

On April 4 the president sent another letter to the employees of Apex:

> Your future, as well as that of your family, is a matter of concern to the company, and we want to work together with you in helping to determine what steps we both will have to make in the next few months.
>
> As you were told in our letter of March 1st, we are anxious to find out from you whether you would consider moving to Mansfield and sharing in the company's future, or whether you feel you will be compelled to remain in the Charleston area.
>
> Next week we will interview you to find out what you think about moving. Won't you please discuss this with your family over the weekend and be prepared to help us in our plans for the future.

Soon after, a survey was taken to find out how many employees would make the move to Mansfield and what problems were uppermost in their minds. The questionnaire avoided controversial subjects such as seniority, rates, pensions, and vacations, since the company had no answers to these questions as yet. Six hundred employees were interviewed at the factory or at their homes. The results were as follows on one question:

Would you move to Mansfield	YES	498	82%
and work at your present job	NO	49	8%
there?	?	57	10%

Some Factors in Relocating the Plant

Even before the time of the survey, work had progressed at Mansfield. Engineers and crews were working to place the new plant into operation.

Robert Douglas, manager of industrial relations, expressed some concern, at this stage. At a meeting called by the president, Douglas stated that "a plant move is one of the saddest things that can occur in the life of an employee who has spent almost his entire life in the same work location and living area. His family, his church, friends, and living habits have all been attuned to the particular job and work. A large portion of the workers are foreign-born, and these have settled in the same vicinity, retaining many of the customs of their native land."

A question arose as to what should be done about four employees. All four of the men, it was ascertained from their records, presented absenteeism problems to the company; all of them were difficult to get along with according to their foreman; none of them had good production records; and one was found to have owed considerable amounts of money to the company which he admitted not intending to pay back. It was decided to wait for further developments to see whether or not the company should extend an invitation to these four in question to join in the move to Mansfield.

At the same meeting, Mr. Douglas reported on a survey taken of the real estate situation in the Mansfield area. The report indicated (1) a dearth of homes in the $10,000–$20,000 category, (2) substantial downpayments which were exacted in the area (usually one third), and (3) a large number of people moving in from the surrounding areas.

The president issued another letter to employees on June 11. It read, in part, as follows:

The company is now selecting a real estate coordinator familiar with the Mansfield area who will be able to assist our employees in locating housing facilities. The August issue of the company newspaper will be devoted to a discussion of real estate, housing, schools, taxes, churches, and other social, recreational and economic aspects of the communities surrounding the Mansfield area.

A few weeks later the paper was issued with a good coverage of the area in question. Moreover, long letters were sent to the employees, entitled "Moving Day," giving complete summaries and hints as to what should be done to move a family.

Policies Governing Relocation of Employees

On August 9 the industrial relations department and the public relations department recommended to top management:

That a moving allowance of $250 to each family that applies for a job at Mansfield be provided. In addition, it is recommended that an additional $25 be allotted for each child under 18, up to an addition of $100.

The advantages of this recommendation were, in the minds of the department heads: (1) that a good personnel climate would be established, (2) it would provide an inducement to move, (3) it would help to reduce the training problem, (4) it would lessen both the union and personal antagonism to the move, (5) and it would create community good will. The recommendations were accepted and later put into effect.

As time for moving to Mansfield neared, a policy was drawn up affecting those eligible to move. Those employees subject to layoff in a particular department would be advised as to the availability of employment in other departments at Mansfield, and invited to fill out applications for such jobs. Applications would be considered by the company on the basis of seniority at Charleston as well as employment records there. A letter was again sent to the Charleston employees indicating this policy. In the same letter, it was noted that Charleston was becoming an area of relatively severe depression economically, and that area wages in Mansfield would be higher than those being paid in Charleston.

Conditions Surrounding the Actual Move

In late fall of last year, Apex began the actual moving of equipment from the Charleston plant to the new site at Mansfield. Departments were moved piecemeal so that production would not cease altogether. As one department moved, its workers either went to Mansfield or remained in Charleston and looked for new employment. When the last bit of machinery had been relocated and the Charleston plant entirely closed down, as of July of this year, almost 72% of the old work force had made the move.

The assumption made by management that employees would sell their houses in Charleston and purchase in Mansfield did not materialize. Even those who rented in Charleston had not yet brought their families with them. This meant that the men remained for five or six days without their families in the new location, and then commuted home for the weekend.

General discontent prevailed at Mansfield and at Charleston. During the workweek, a number of machine operators frequented bars after work, getting into fights, spending their weekly wages, and feeling that the company was responsible for their problem. Rooming houses were crowded, and the new group from Charleston did not find a warm reception or low prices. Those who were ready to sell their homes in Charleston found that, due to the general economic depression in the area, they were unable to obtain reasonable prices for them, and thus were unwilling to sell.

The four workers mentioned earlier (who requested to make the move) were refused by the company. Company management states that "in an effort to retaliate, they traveled to Mansfield on their own and (successfully) attempted to stir up trouble for the company. It was found by on-the-spot inspection by company representatives that these four men were speaking out against the company, that they were present when fights occurred, and that they jeered at workers as they entered the plant."

Union Relations Subsequent to the Move

Early in July, after production was at full capacity, negotiations opened for the signing of a new contract. A committee was elected and met with management over the collective bargaining table. The contract, prepared in advance by management, was submitted to the committee for its approval. Because it was entirely new, the workers called in their national and international representatives for assistance. After ten days of negotiations, with only a few minor changes to the original contract, the committee accepted the contract and appealed to the membership to do the same.

The meeting of the membership that night was attended by the four former employees who were not invited to move. The result was that the committee was instructed by the membership to decline the company's offer, but was given no reason nor any alternative measures to those offered by management.

Negotiations continued for several more weeks, and the same pattern persisted: agreements were made by management and the union committee, but declined by the membership. Each time, the union committee stressed that the offers were fair. The national and international officers went to the membership meetings and appealed to the workers, but to no avail. A strike was called, and the factory was picketed.

On August 7, the president sent a letter (Exhibit 1) to all the employees at Mansfield, explaining the cause of the trouble, and appealing to the employees for clear thinking.

In an interview between the case writer and a member of top management, the latter stated:

I believe that this will be a costly strike for the company, and for employees. On our part, we will lose well over a million dollars in overhead and depreciation expenses, to say nothing of the loss in future sales due to customers changing to competitive products.

Considering the area and the industry, the contract proposals were fair—even the union committee and national union officers agreed. I don't know whether to blame the strike on pent-up enmity toward the company, or to sheeplike following by the rank and file—following of those four trouble makers. Personally, I think that nothing the company might have done, save not moving at all, would have prevented the strike. . . . It seems that we did all that was humanly possible to take care of our people.

I am particularly concerned because, in spite of all objections, it seems that we will have to relocate the Ferndale plant also—possibly as an extension of the new Mansfield installation. Cost savings on combining these two have been estimated at about $600,000 per year by our own engineers and a reliable team of accountants. There are twice as many employees at Ferndale than there were at Charleston. We could certainly use some advice about what to do in this situation.

Exhibit 1

LETTER FROM PRESIDENT OF APEX TO
ALL EMPLOYEES AT MANSFIELD

Since this looks like a long, costly, pay-losing strike, we want all concerned to have the facts as to what happened prior to the strike.

*   *   *   *   * . .   . .

Your union committee and national representatives expressed the opinion that the company's offer was fair and that they would recommend its adoption by the membership without reservation. The Federal Mediator also indicated that, in his opinion, the company's offer was fair and worthy of acceptance by the membership.

The membership rejected the proposal and sent the committee back with an ultimatum that a strike would be called within 24 hours unless

1. The company agreed to additional fringe-benefit items costing more than 4 cents an hour.
2. The length of the contract be reduced.

During the entire contract negotiations, the company emphasized the point that our Mansfield plant must be operated competitively with other cable manufacturers in the area. This means being competitive in regard to labor cost as well as length of the contract. We are willing to offer a substantial increase the first year, only with the understanding that a long-term contract would be agreed to. General Cable, Circle, Hudson, Anaconda, and Phelps-Dodge who manufacture the same products in almost the same areas all have three-year contracts without wage reopeners or cost-of-living clauses. We are only asking for equal treatment.

Over $9,000,000 was spent in moving from Charleston to Mansfield, with the single purpose in mind to place us in a competitive position. After spending so much money, it would not be logical to start off with higher labor cost than our competitors. This would undo the very thing which prompted the action to move.

We were prepared to assume a labor cost equal to the two competitive plants in the immediate area. Our offer meets that policy—a statement which has gone unchallenged and can readily be checked. In fact, we offered the General Cable cost items as a substitute to our proposal, but your committee rejected them as they were not as good as our offer.

It was the company's desire that our employees accept the transfer to Mansfield, and we were pleased when more than 70% made the move voluntarily. Prior to the move we gave an increase averaging 5½ cents an hour. We gave a moving allowance to those bringing their families; we offered an improved pension plan.

We are attaching a comparison of your rates at Charleston with the rates offered at Mansfield and an outline of the highlights of the company's proposals.

We have proven beyond doubt that the company wanted you at Mansfield, but evidently a small vocal group within your membership does not wish to move and has led you out on a useless strike. This group is against everyone—you, the union, and the company.

There is a good job waiting for you at Mansfield, paying a fair wage. It is up to you whether or not you want the job.

III Selected Readings

From: Thorstein Veblen
THE ENGINEERS AND THE PRICE SYSTEM*

[EDITORS' NOTE: The author was a prominent Professor of Economics at Chicago, California, and Columbia Universities, writing in the early decades of the twentieth century.]

. . . [T]he country's industrial system . . . is a comprehensive and balanced scheme of technological administration. Industry of this modern sort—mechanical, specialised, standardised, running to quantity production, drawn on a large scale—is highly productive; provided always that the necessary conditions of its working are met in some passable fashion. These necessary conditions of productive industry are of a well-defined technical character, and they are growing more and more exacting with every farther advance in the industrial arts. . . . [T]he mechanical technology is impersonal and dispassionate, and its end is very simply to serve human needs, without fear or favor or respect of persons, prerogatives, or politics. It makes up an industrial system of an unexampled character—a mechanically balanced and interlocking system of work to be done, the prime requisite of whose working is a painstaking and intelligent co-ordination of the processes at work, and an equally painstaking allocation of mechanical power and materials. The foundation and driving force of it all is a massive body of technological knowledge, of a highly impersonal and altogether unbusinesslike nature, running in close contact with the material sciences, on which it draws freely at every turn—exactingly specialised, endlessly detailed, reaching out into all domains of empirical fact.

Such is the system of productive work which has grown out of the Industrial Revolution, and on the full and free run of which the material welfare of all of the civilised peoples now depends from day to day. Any defect or hindrance in its technical administration, any intrusion or nontechnical considerations, any failure or obstruction at any point, unavoidably results in a disproportionate set-back to the balanced whole and brings a disproportionate burden of privation on all these peoples whose productive industry has come within the sweep of the system.

It follows that those gifted, trained, and experienced technicians who now are in possession of the requisite technological information and experience are the first and instantly indispensable factor in the everyday work of carrying on the country's productive industry. They now constitute the General Staff of the industrial system, in fact; whatever law and custom may formally say in protest. The "captains of industry" may still vaingloriously claim that distinction, and law and custom still countenance their claim; but the captains have no technological value, in fact.

---

* Reprinted from Thorstein Veblen, *The Engineers and the Price System* (New York: The Viking Press, 1921), chap. V.

From: Richard Eells and Clarence Walton

CONCEPTUAL FOUNDATIONS OF BUSINESS*

[EDITORS' NOTE: Richard Eells heads Richard Eells and Associates, Inc., and Clarence Walton is Dean, School of General Studies, Columbia University.]

"Property" is the word we use to describe land, tangible objects, and certain intangible legal rights, with specific reference to the ownership thereof. "Private property" is property the ownership of which is vested, more or less, in individuals or groups other than public governments. The commonest form of group ownership today is the business corporation.

Historically, "ownership" has meant possession *and* the right, enforceable by legal process, to possess, control, and use the particular item of property and its products. . . . One of the great law teachers of the early part of this century defined property as follows: "A true property may, therefore, be shortly defined as possession coupled with the unlimited right of possession. If these two elements are vested in different persons there is a divided ownership."[1]

*   *   *   *   *

, . . It is easy to demonstrate that property, especially that which is productive, has rarely if ever in our Western civilization been entirely free from the claims of the polity.

*   *   *   *   *

The varieties of claimants on the corporation—and hence upon the resources controlled by managerial decision makers—can best be understood in another way: through a study of the art of governance within the corporate constellation and through a consideration of the roles of *direct* and *indirect* claimants and contributors to the wealth and welfare of the organization.

DIRECT CLAIMANTS ON THE CORPORATION

SECURITY HOLDERS

Those who supply the capital represented by the capital stock, the corporate bonds, and the notes with maturities in excess of a year are potent contributors to the corporate enterprise. The contributors of capital thus fall into several categories of senior and junior security holders. Their respective "stakes" in the venture are variously defined by law and custom, and their claims on the corporate usufruct vary accordingly.

*   *   *   *   *

The property of a corporation is owned by the *persona ficta* and not, either in law or in fact, by the "share owners." The corporate "person" acts through

---

* Reprinted by permission of Richard D. Irwin, Inc., Homewood, Illinois, 1961 (pp. 185–87, 149–67, 458, 468–75).

1 James Barr Ames, "The Disseisin of Chattels," in Association of American Law Schools (ed.), *Select Essays in Anglo-American Legal History* (Boston: Little, Brown & Co., 1909), Vol. III, p. 563.

its board of directors, as a collective body, and it is they alone who may determine how the property is used, how earnings are calculated, and how net earnings are distributed. Although they must act within the boundaries of legally set norms, their diescretionary area for decision making is wide. . . .

* * * * *

If, as the more adamant traditionalists[2] argue, the common stockholders alone have a legitimate claim on the earnings of a company, it is obvious that the structure of authority in most corporations does not guarantee such a result. On the contrary, what we have is a business institution in which the directors tend to act as "trustees for the institution and not merely as attorneys for the stockholder" and in which "the management of large corporations is largely unaccountable to the stockholders.[3] This is not to say that management bears no responsibility to stockholders, but that the line of accountability does not run to the "ultimate owners" directly. And it is often said that managerial responsibility ought not to run either directly *or* indirectly to the share owners *alone.*

* * * * *

The contrary view is that this amounts to establishing an authoritarian status for a managerial elite "who from their *own* ethical standards will 'assign' income shares."[4] It is one thing to say that the risk-bearing stockholder has little function; it is quite another to say that he deserves little respect. When the demands of other claimants are given equal weight, it is argued, the nature of corporate enterprise is radically altered and the foundations of capitalism are threatened.

The issue thus joined is certain to become one of the most difficult for strategic decision makers of the future, in the fields both of business and of public policy.

EMPLOYEES

Employees as a group are clearly direct claimants on the corporate enterprise because they are direct contributors to it and are contractually related to the firm. Like the contributors of risk capital, they invest something they own. Their investment is comparable in that they expect a return on it from the fruits of the venture.

Dividends have been called "the wages of capital." . . . In much the same way, people invest the best part of their lives in some established and promising companies at a rate of return—in the form of wages and salaries—that may seem modest enough at the start but is acceptable in anticipation of other benefits.

Nor are these benefits only the expected wage and salary benefits and advances over the years; the anticipated income includes those "fringe benefits" that increasingly go along with the job, plus some benefits that nowhere appear in the formal employment contracts. Association with certain companies yields "psychic income." Prestige, a sense of security, the feeling that one works for a "good corporate citizen" in a laudable field of endeavor, satisfaction in

---

2 Louis O. Kelso and Mortimer J. Adler, *The Capitalist Manifesto* (New York: Random House, 1958). See Eells, *The Meaning of Modern Business*, pp. 77–94.

3 George B. Hurff, *Social Aspects of Enterprise in the Large Corporation* (Philadelphia: University of Pennsylvania Press, 1950), pp. 96 ff.

4 David McCord Wright, "The Modern Corporation—Twenty Years After," *University of Chicago Law Review,* Vol. XIX (Summer, 1952), pp. 663 ff.

work that contributes to one's skills and enlightenment about some aspect of nature or society—these are some of the considerations that attract the necessary human resources to the organization, just as the anticipated growth and earnings prospects of a company attract capital resources.

* * * * *

There is . . . a competition for the loyalty and solidarity of employees between firm and union. Insofar as an employee's loyalties are polarized toward the outside organization, his place in the constellation of corporate interests moves toward the periphery of that constellation.

The corporate executive of the future will have to recast the theory of the firm to account for this trend. The implications are many. One, or course, has to do with the whole area of "human relations," or the restoration of organic unity in the enterprise as a human association, and not merely an aggregation of capital in the accounting sense of that term. . . .

* * * * *

CUSTOMERS

According to Peter F. Drucker, "there is only one valid definition of business purpose: to create a customer." It follows that "any business enterprise has two—and only two—basic functions: marketing and innovation." This is in line with the doctrine of customer sovereignty: "King Customer" must be placed above all.

Here some distinctions are in order. Does one mean that the general public is the legitimate determiner of corporate policy? Or is something else meant —for example, the meeting and creating of "demands" for salable products and services, regardless of the "public interest" as expressed by representatives of the general public? Obviously not all products of profitable enterprise are "good" products, and some salable services are proscribed by law and morals. Customers and consumers are not necessarily identical groups, nor can either be designated, without careful qualification, as a direct contributor-claimant in any corporate constellation of interests.

A corporation's customers are the main source of its business income; but it is one thing to center the goals of the business on supplying demand and quite another to proliferate corporate objectives so as to meet all the ideal requirements of a hypothetical consumer public.

* * * * *

SUPPLIERS

The sources of supply for the large corporation as a going concern are extremely diverse. In the widest sense, suppliers include all contributors of material, financial, and human resources. Supply refers also to certain social costs, that are not accounted for in the entrepreneurial outlays but instead are shifted to and borne by third persons and the community as a whole.[5]

---

[5] K. William Kapp, *The Social Costs of Private Enterprise* (Cambridge: Harvard University Press, 1950). He includes costs resulting from the impairment of the human factor of production; depletion and destruction of animal resources; depletion of energy resources; soil erosion, soil depletion, and deforestation; and social costs of air and water pollution, of technological change, of unemployment and idle resources, and of distribution and transportation.

Here we are concerned with those direct contributor-claimant suppliers outside the firm whose goods and services are reflected directly in entrepreneurial outlays, except for taxes. . . .

* * * * *

INDIRECT CLAIMANTS ON THE CORPORATION

* * * * *

COMPETITORS

A competitive firm has no obligation, strictly speaking, toward competitors; its obligation, if any, is to the competitive system and to the norms that organized society establishes for competitive conduct. All responsible business executives recognize that, quite aside from their legal obligations to obey antitrust laws, there is a moral obligation to competitors that arises independently of the rules of law. Some of this nonlegal obligation has its roots in "enlightened self-interest" to the extent that competition is regarded as "the life of trade," or as a stimulant to innovation and *esprit de corps* in the organization, and so on. . . .

* * * * *

LOCAL COMMUNITIES

The most immediate peripheral group of interests that vitally concern a corporation is the local community—or rather the numerous local communities—in which it operates as a going concern. The contributions of these communities are many, and so are their claims on the businesses located there.

* * * * *

The claimant community specifies its own requirements: regular employment, good working conditions, fair play, satisfying work, local purchase of a reasonable part of the firm's supply of goods and services, the maintenance of a plant worthy of a good neighbor, and interest in and support of the local government and of local charitable and cultural projects.

THE GENERAL PUBLIC AND GOVERNMENTS

The contributions of the general public have been alluded to earlier with reference to the "social costs of private enterprise." As a taxpayer, the corporation is clearly a direct contributor to public governments as claimants on the fruits of the enterprise. . . .

* * * * *

"SOCIAL RESPONSIBILITIES"

* * * * *

But what are the major or minor types of responsibility? As to the ultimate owners, is it a "fair return" on their investment or all the net profits in any year? As to customers, is it a "fair" price for products or all that the traffic will bear? (Or is it a "good" product and constant innovation to provide more and better new products?) As to employees, is it a "fair" wage and good working conditions or status, with all the overtones of security and the dimensions of the good life? As to others in the business community—competitors, suppliers— is it the minimal standard of conduct in a hard and competitive drive for profits or behavior in accordance with some ideal code? As to the public and governments, is it a shrewd avoidance of infractions of the law and the building of stout barriers against any encroachment of government on business, or a common pursuit of the general welfare through some form of mixed economy?

The question of the "social responsibilities" of the modern corporation thus turns out to be no simple issue but a large bundle of issues. It cannot be reduced to the single relationship between corporation and society, for the referents in these ambiguous terms are unclear. . . .

*   *   *   *   *

Interrelationships and the Balancing of Interests

If we concede that there is an accountability that goes with wealth and power, then the logic of responsibility for those who hold it is easy to establish. The corporation is a center of wealth and power, and it has, therefore, responsibilities to those most dependent upon it. These are its stockholders, its employees, and its customers. But its employees, its customers, and its stockholders are also the community. Therefore, it has a social as well as an economic responsibility.

To assess the nature of this responsibility is one of the functions of management. . . .

*   *   *   *   *

THEORETICAL BASIS OF OPPOSITION TO CORPORATE SOCIAL RESPONSIBILITY

The root of the conflict over social responsibility lies in the irreconcilability of two equally untenable theories of the corporation—the theory of the *traditional* corporation, on the one hand, and, on the other, the theory of what might be called the *metrocorporation*.[6]

The Traditional Theory

The *traditional corporation* is the instrumentality of a single group—the shareholders. It has one clear-cut purpose: the conduct of business for their maximal profit.

Managerial austerity is the governing principle of the traditional corporation. There is no "balancing" of interests by management in distributing the corporate usufruct. The prior claim of stockholders on earnings after taxes is unquestioned.

The traditional corporation has nothing to give away. Its managers must always insist on the *quid pro quo* in every market. The traditional corporation recognizes no public responsibilities except for clear legal obligations. Labor unions and corporations, the traditionalists would say, are by function the stewards of special interests. Each must look out for his own.

---

6 These two terms, along with the term "well-tempered corporation," come from Richard Eells's *The Meaning of Modern Business* (New York: Columbia University Press, 1960), which introduced and developed both terms and models.

This position, which leaves the public interest to the care of the state or to the automatic operations of the market, has been attacked as shortsighted and ultimately destructive of the foundations of a free society. De Jouvenel, for instance, has warned that the body politic as a whole will not be well served by "the untrammelled clash of special interests within it."[7] He urges further that concern for the public interest is not the business of public officials alone but of everyone and, not least, of the large and powerful organizations in the private sector.

If the internal governments of corporations are to be designed with no concern whatever for representation of the public interest, that interest will inevitably be expressed by other private and public sectors. According to the critics, the probable result of corporate traditionalism will be the progressive encroachment of the authority of these other sectors upon business. The corporation might then have to retreat into a relatively uninfluential position in the management of our economy.

THE METROCORPORATE THEORY

In contrast to the model of the *traditional* corporation stands the model—again a purely heuristic one—of the *metrocorporation* with limitless social obligations. A major social institution with comprehensive aims, it is far removed from the strictly limited-function organization of traditional corporation.

The metrocorporation does not confine its activities to business purposes in any narrowly defined sense. It is a species of society in its own right, and its managers hold themselves accountable to many different sectors of society. The metrocorporation emphasizes its rights and duties as a "citizen" in its relationships. But these relationships are far more complicated than are those of the traditional corporation; the metrocorporation has a pervasive concern for the "good life."

The dangers inherent in this model are many, as the antagonists of corporate social responsibility have been quick to point out: undue power for corporations and corporate managers and the consequent risk of a coming neofeudalism; the prospect of a quasi-public corporate polity, which might be forced by reason of its character to conform to democratic principles in the government of its internal affairs; perversion of corporate economic goals and functions. Eventually there might be no aspect in the private life of an individual that the metrocorporation would concede to be beyond its province. As a paternalistic donor, it might become a meddling intruder in the affairs of its beneficiaries. As a watchful protector of the manifold interests of its great brood, the metrocorporation could make the "organization man" of today look like an uncontrollable maverick.

SPECIFIC ARGUMENTS FROM THE OPPOSITION

*   *   *   *   *

The "social responsibility syndrome," says Levitt, clashes with the sound principles that "the business of business is profits," and: "In the end business has only two responsibilities—to obey the elementary canons of everyday face-to-face civility (honesty, good faith, and so on) and to seek material gain." This is bad enough, since the "social responsibility syndrome" diverts the energy of businessmen into peripheral activities. Far worse is the specter of "a new

---

[7] Bertrand de Jouvenel, "Wage Restraint," *The Economist*, August 10, 1957.

feudalism" with the corporation investing itself "with all-embracing duties, obligations, and finally powers—ministering to the whole man and molding him and society into the image of the corporation's narrow ambitions and its essentially anti-social needs."[8]

Levitt is not alone in arguing this. Friedman has declared, in the same vein, that "if anything is certain to destroy our free society, to undermine its very foundations, it would be a widespread acceptance by management of some social responsibilities in some sense other than to make as much money as possible."[9] The so-called corporate social responsibilities, Friedman says, are public and not business functions, and "it is intolerable that public functions be performed by self-designated private officials." The voluntary assumption of public functions by private business opens the door to further public control of business. Friedman is also extremely critical of corporate giving, which, he believes, prevents the stockholder from deciding for himself how he should dispose of his funds—the corporation being the instrument of the stockholder who owns it.

*   *   *   *   *

THE MIDDLE GROUND

The large business corporation is here to stay. It is an indispensable instrument for getting done some of the things that people want done. It is neither the exclusive instrument of one class of interests nor an indiscriminate roster of "social" interests. Like other large organizations, the corporation must be tempered to the times, and as a viable instrument it must adapt to the changing requirements of our free, complex, and interdependent society.

The impossibility of direct owner management of large-scale private enterprise calls for professional management by persons whose relationship to the owners is difficult to define. Is it a fiduciary relationship, one of agency, or perhaps one of representation?

*   *   *   *   *

To resist the many new claims made on the corporation is to assume an eminently respectable traditional position grounded on the logic of property. But to be rational is not necessarily to be reasonable. Reasonable regard for the interests of society is a practical necessity.

---

8 Theodore Levitt, "The Dangers of Social Responsibility," *Harvard Business Review*, Vol. XXXVI (September–October, 1958), pp. 41–60 *passim*.

9 Milton Friedman, *Three Major Factors in Business Management: Leadership, Decision-Making, and Social Responsibility* (reprinted from *Social Science Reporter's* Eighth Social Science Seminar) (San Francisco, March 19, 1958), pp. 4–5.

From: C. Lowell Harriss
THE AMERICAN ECONOMY†

[EDITORS' NOTE: The author is Professor of Economics at Columbia University.]

National Product and Income Measures: Relation of Concepts*
(Billions)

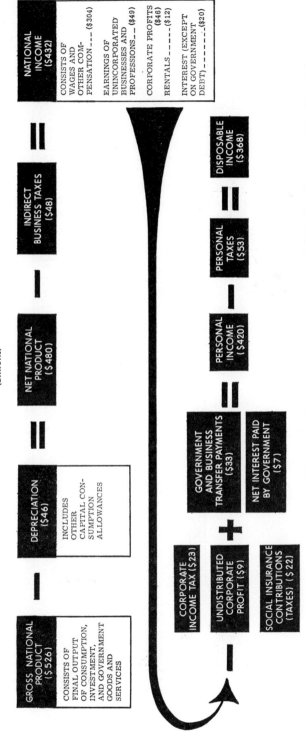

* Certain minor items are not shown. Amounts are annual rates in third quarter of 1961. Because of rounding, details will not necessarily add to totals.

† Reprinted by permission of Richard D. Irwin, Inc., Homewood, Illinois, 1962 (p. 281).

From: Twentieth Century Fund
*USA IN NEW DIMENSIONS**

National Income Measures: Flow of Income and Expenditures

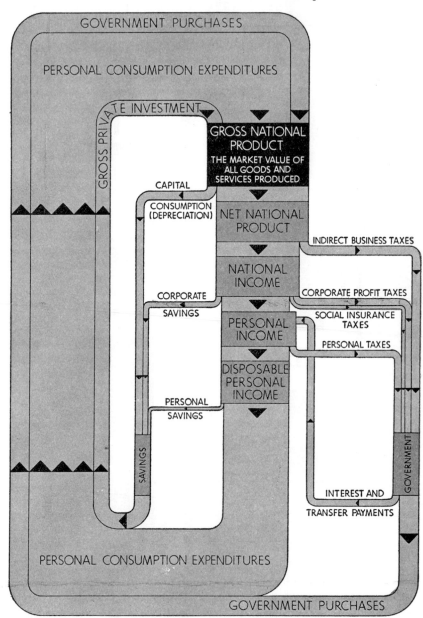

* Reprinted by permission of Twentieth Century Fund, *USA in New Dimensions*, 1957 (p. 15). (Reproduced in C. Lowell Hariss, *The American Economy* [Homewood, Illinois: Richard D. Irwin, Inc., 1962], p. 283.)

From: James A. C. Brown

*THE SOCIAL PSYCHOLOGY OF INDUSTRY**

[EDITORS' NOTE: The author is a practicing psychiatrist. This book is the product of seven years of research in a large industrial firm in England.]

. . . Regarding the *nature* of work, the orthodox view accepts the Old Testament belief that physical labour is a curse imposed on man as a punishment for his sins and that the sensible man labours solely in order to keep himself and his family alive, or, if he is fortunate, in order to make a sufficient surplus to enable him to do the things he really likes.[1] Regarding the *conditions* of work, it is assumed that improving the conditions of the job will cause the worker's natural dislike of it to be somewhat mitigated, and, in addition, will keep him physically healthy and therefore more efficient in the mechanistic sense. Finally, regarding the *motivation* of work, the carrot and stick hypothesis asserts that the main positive incentive is money, the main negative one fear of unemployment. . . .

Now modern research has shown that these views are incorrect, . . . the following statements are nearer the truth, and should, therefore, form the basis of any new approach to industrial problems:

1. Work is an essential part of a man's life since it is that aspect of his life which gives him status and binds him to society. . . . [W]ork is a *social* activity.
2. The morale of the worker (i.e., whether or not he works willingly) has no *direct* relationship whatsoever to the material conditions of the job. . . .
3. There are many incentives, of which, under normal conditions, money is one of the least important. Unemployment is a powerful negative incentive, precisely because (1) is true. That is to say, unemployment is feared because it cuts man off from his society.

* * * * *

An incentive is an objective goal which is capable of satisfying what we are aware of subjectively as a need, drive, or desire. Some needs, as we have seen elsewhere, are innate, but the vast majority are acquired in the process of social interaction and from everyday experience. . . . What is clear is that acquired needs are, for the most part, culturally defined. . . . [C]ertain needs, . . . are virtually universal since they derive, not from the peculiarities of any single culture, but from certain features which are universal to all societies everywhere.

---

* Reprinted by permission of Penguin Books Ltd., Baltimore, Maryland, 1954 (pp. 186–87, 199–203).

1 "No society can long continue in health by merely paying for work which it cannot make satisfying. Because the Victorians regarded work in industry as necessarily hard and disagreeable, they made little effort to introduce tolerable conditions into mines, and mills, and foundries, and were content to think of industry itself as an economic necessity instead of as an element in society," Christopher Salmon, in a B.B.C. lecture.

Such needs as the desire for status, for appreciation, or for emotional security come into this category. . . . Acquired needs may be just as real and intense to the person experiencing them as his innate drives, and, since they are derived from experience, it follows that people define their needs in terms of the time and place in which they live. This statement may seem to be a truism, but it is quite obviously not understood by those who express the opinion that, since the workers of today are much better off than their counterparts of a century ago, they should be satisfied with their lot and stop grumbling. . . . Frustration is not wholly related to the objective circumstances of the individual but rather to what he feels himself entitled to. An important point which those whose idea of "welfare" is giving people free gifts fail to notice is that such gifts never continue to give the same degree of satisfaction—the object which was a source of delight when it was first received soon comes to be regarded either as a commonplace necessity or a useless piece of bric-a-brac. Trying to satisfy people with material gifts is, in the long run, like trying to fill a bottomless pit. When certain psychological needs are satisfied, however, they continue to give pleasure: emotional security, a status which gives the holder self-respect, satisfying relationships at work and at home, pride of craftsmanship, and appreciation from seniors, are all satisfactions of this nature. It follows, then, that workers who are placed in a comfortable and attractive new workshop may like it at first, but this attitude will soon give way to acceptance, to the feeling that such surroundings are "natural," and even a slight lowering in the standard of the surroundings will cause more grumbling than if they had never been experienced. When their emotional needs are satisfied, this "law of diminishing returns" does not apply. . . . [T]he attempt to keep people quiet with gifts, fussing, and unnecessary "improvements" while ignoring their self-respect and other psychological needs leads to a situation rather like that of the traveller pursued by wolves who has to cut loose one of the horses drawing his sledge every now and then in order momentarily to satisfy the wolves and gain himself some respite from the chase.

. . . Concerning incentives in general, the following facts are significant:

1. There is no one ideal incentive. Incentives vary from one culture to another, from one firm to another, and from one individual to another. . . .

2. The law of diminishing returns applies to all material incentives—that is to say, as the reward increased the desire for further reward decreases until it reaches the vanishing point. . . .

3. Incentives may conflict with other motives (e.g., a worker may ignore financial incentives if he fears that his rate may be cut or that he may work himself out of a job.

4. . . . Except under conditions when wages are very low or during periods of inflation, money is one of the least powerful incentives.

5. On the other hand, we must remember that in our own culture, as Taylor has noted, motives tend to become "monetized." "People have been taught that money is the key to satisfaction, so when they feel that something is wrong with their lives they naturally ask for more money. A demand for money undoubtedly indicates that they want *something*, but it does not tell us what." Professor Viteles similarly observes that *"if money is all that a man gets for his work,* he will take any means possible to get all that he can." Constant demands for more money (when wages are already adequate) indicate either that the workers feel vague dissatisfaction without quite knowing why, and think of money as the obvious solution, or else that they are aware of the causes of their discontent and are taking the attitude "If you won't give us what we really need, you must pay us in the only way you seem to understand." . . .

From: Robert N. McMurry
*"CONFLICTS IN HUMAN VALUES"**

[EDITORS' NOTE: The author is the head of the McMurry Company, consultants in personnel, industrial relations and market research.]

One of man's most prized possessions is his intellect. Of all his attributes, it is probably his *reason* in which he takes the greatest pride. He even describes himself as "Homo sapiens," the thinking man. Yet much of his behavior, if observed impartially by a visitor from Mars, might better be characterized as "unreasoned," rather than "reasoned."

*   *   *   *   *

. . . Why is there so much "unreason" in interpersonal relations in industry? The tendency these days seems to be to blame the failure on poor communications, conflicts of interest, lack of knowledge, or inadequate management control. I readily agree that such matters are frequently factors in the picture— but not always the most important ones. In case after case with which I am familiar the real cause of breakdowns is conflicting *values*. This diagnosis throws many key management problems in an entirely different light and suggests radically different prescriptions for action.

*   *   *   *   *

HOW VALUES ALTER BEHAVIOR

. . . While it is commonly recognized that values differ widely from person to person and from culture to culture, their influence on people's thinking, acting, and behavior tends to be seriously underestimated. Their influence on the individual is powerful because:

(1) They principally determine what he regards as right, good, worthy, beautiful, ethical, and so forth. . . .

(2) They also provide the standards and norms by which he guides his day-to-day behavior. (In this sense they constitute an integral part of his conscience.)

(3) They chiefly determine his attitudes toward the causes and issues (political, economic, social, and industrial) with which he comes into contact daily.

(4) They exert a powerful influence on the kinds and types of persons with whom he can be personally compatible and the kinds of social activities in which he can engage.

(5) They largely determine which ideas, principles, and concepts he can accept, assimilate, remember, and transmit without distortion.

(6) They provide him with an almost unlimited number and variety of moral principles which can be employed to rationalize and justify any action he has taken or is contemplating. . . .

* Reprinted by permission of *The Harvard Business Review*, May–June 1963, pp. 130–35, 145.

CONFLICTS AND INCONSISTENCIES

Human values . . . tend to create internal and external conflict, to show internal inconsistency, and to deny reality. Few, if any, of a person's values are the products of ratiocination. Instead, they reflect faithfully the mores and ideologies of the cultures in which the individual has lived. . . .

*   *   *   *   *

Everyone's values have had a wide variety of sources and have been acquired over a long period of time; hence, in the aggregate a person's value system may be riddled with inconsistencies. . . .

These internalized value conflicts are often both painful and anxiety-provoking. Not knowing which set of values to use as a guide, the individual resolves the problem as he does others by repressing . . . those values which are in conflict. . . .[1]

Normally he is conscious of only one set of values at a time—those that are appropriate to the circumstances which happen fortuitously to prevail. At the same time, he also has a wide variety of values from which to draw in rationalizing and defending his beliefs and actions. . . .

*   *   *   *   *

If management is to cope successfully with its people problems, it must take into greater account than it usually does the roles played by values, with all of their inconsistencies, conflicts, and unrealities. And it should attack the problems discriminately, without attaching value labels to whole groups.

*   *   *   *   *

Conflicts of values between labor and management cause strife more often than is usually recognized. Economic factors are often of lesser importance than are value conflicts. Each party naturally regards its goals, standards, and shibboleths—especially insofar as these can be identified with values—as indisputably the right ones; each side is intolerant of the values of the other. Each contestant supports his position by appeals to logic, by moral arguments, and by reference to the principles on which he stands; but the basic problem lies in conflicts of values. . . .

*   *   *   *   *

There is no simple, inexpensive, sovereign remedy for conflicts of this nature. Improved communication, for instance, is no answer. The roots of conflict are too deep and complex, and the values of both parties are too bitterly opposed. The important thing to face is the fact that when the causes of strife are primarily value-oriented, the arguments are more emotional than rational. They are not only manifestations of unreason, frequently by both parties, but, by the same token, largely proof against logic. In fact, the application of logic often succeeds only in *exacerbating* the difficulty.

However, it is realistic to try to lessen the bitterness of the strife. To that end, the following principles and steps are valuable:

Initiative.   Management must realize that it must take the initiative in seeking remedial action. . . .

Recognition of Union's Role.   Management must also recognize the fact that the typical union member's value system is so constituted that he *must* prove to his employer, to the world, and to himself that he fears no one; and that he is a

---

[1] For a fuller explanation of the theory behind various aspects of psychology, see Harry Levinson's article, "What Killed Bob Lyons?" HBR January–February 1963, p. 127.

wholly autonomous, independent individual who should have as influential a voice in what he does on the job as does the company. . . . This emotional need to prove his "manhood" frequently leads to the eruption of violence.

Self-Review. Management should openly, honestly, and candidly review its own values, particularly as they impinge on the lives, duties, and responsibilities of its employees. . . .

Evaluation of Situation. Executives should ascertain by means of a joint analysis of (a) union policies and demands and (b) the results of employee information and opinion polls, the content and goals of prevailing worker ideologies. . . .

* * * * *

Value Comparison. Management must compare, as objectively as possible, *its* values with those of its employees, within the broad frame of reference of conditions which prevail within the company, its industry, and the economy. The aim of this study is to find *common goals and values,* i.e., to seek to integrate conflicting desires. . . .

* * * * *

The best approach to the problem of dealing with inconsistent, conflicting, or unrealistic values is a relatively simple one. It is based on the recognition that, as already stated, *nearly everyone has more than one set of values which relate to a given topic.* Often these values are of a totally opposed character. Instead of questioning expressed values, the individual or the group must either be researched thoroughly, using sophisticated interviewing techniques, or encouraged to "talk the problem out" at length. By this means, alternative and, hopefully, more appropriate values which are already a part of their ideological systems (though not always clearly appreciated) may often be discovered. These can then be seized on by management and strongly advocated. Since they already were held by the persons or groups whom it desired to influence, their advocacy by management will constitute no affront to the employees' self-respect and create few resentments.

Obviously, most such solutions are in the nature of compromises; hence few are perfect. Nevertheless, their consequences are often far superior to the results obtained by direct, frontal attacks on aberrant values.

From: Ivar Berg

*"THE NICE KIND OF UNION DEMOCRACY"**

[EDITORS' NOTE: The author is Associate Professor of Business Administration at the Graduate School of Business, Columbia University.]

Not since wartime, when workers walked out on wildcat strikes in defiance of their union leaders, has the press become as excited as it was last summer over the rash of "revolts" by workers against labor officials. . . .

* Reprinted by permission of *The Columbia University Forum,* New York, Spring 1962 (pp. 18–23).

. . . Increasingly we are given to see by a number of editorialists that the private interests of intractable union members are trivial compared with the interests of the defenseless public; equally clear is the obligation of unions to confine disputes affecting the public to disputes with employers and to keep these, in turn, to a minimum. Unions are to have a sense of "public responsibility" and come to negotiations with demands to which employers may confidently address themselves; when agreement is reached between negotiating teams, there is to be no costly interference with the public's convenience brought on by recalcitrant members. Above all, it has now become a part of the conventional wisdom that "strikes are extremely costly, and the fewer we have the better."

All of these are the lessons which pundits, editorialists and reporters are teaching us in the 1960's: our society is, after all, confronted with so many threats and wracked by such uncertainty that we cannot afford irresponsible interference with orderly economic recovery and growth. . . .

But then there is the principle of union democracy to be considered. Thus, when milk deliverers in Cincinnati voted themselves out of the Teamsters this past summer, there was no little joy in the press. Dissident drivers were interviewed and their actions reported as hopeful signs that even Hoffa could not violate minimum democratic requirements forever without paying a price. Yet when some of Walter Reuther's striking auto workers voted down a hard-won settlement at Kenosha, a number of newspapers inveighed against prolongation of a strike that seriously and needlessly hampered the manufacture and sales of The Automobile.

Democracy and a healthy economy, we are informed, have major social value. Both must be served—and they were by the milk deliverers but were not by the auto workers. . . .

*   *   *   *   *

. . . There is a pharisaical quality in commitments to the democratic faith which are accompanied by reservations of convenience and ease. Restricting use of the term "democracy" to cases in which constituents of private governments weaken their leaders but offend not the "public interest" is suggestive of hypocrisy. . . .

*   *   *   *   *

. . . [T]hose of us who fear "bossism" in unions will have to hope that Reuther's hitherto abiding faith in democracy is not as thoroughly shattered as that of the editorialists has so often been lately. "Who's In Charge In The UAW?" cries one. The paper, a champion of democracy for the man in overalls when it does not like a union leader or a union's policies, reversed its piety, never mind its logic, and pointed out to its readers that

"One of the disturbing questions raised by the Ford Motor Company strike is whether Walter P. Reuther of the UAW is losing his grip."

It went on, taking dim views and noting with alarm, that

"The country whose future depends on growth, work, productivity has been standing still. Reuther knows that. The Ford strike goes on."

The menacing implication was clear: Reuther had better take hold of things. We are for democracy, the editors seemed to say, when it is free, but let us not permit our ideals to stand in the way of order. Editorial misgivings over the loose "grip" of union leaders on their members will surprise those of us who think democracy is more than simply a method; the same misgivings will provide both aid and comfort to Jimmy Hoffa, Dave Beck and others who have doubts whether an organization can be both democratic and efficient.

*   *   *   *   *

. . . What moralizing editors fail to make clear to reasonable minds is why efforts to keep strikers *on* the picket line are coercive, while perhaps similar efforts to have them get *off* it are merely persuasive.

*   *   *   *   *

. . . Few of Dave Beck's and Jimmy Hoffa's counterparts in management have let their high principles concerning democracy obstruct their search for strike-free and "predictable" relations with labor groups. One simply wonders how many Americans there are who are so completely committed to democracy as to be unequivocally willing to take a chance on the vagaries and whims that are so often a part of a democratic process. We are, I am afraid, unhappy with democracy when we have it—and unhappy when we do not.

*   *   *   *   *

. . . When popular discussions of unions appear in the press and on television they tend to focus on union democracy, union corruption and strikes. Lack of the first is generally taken to be a cause of the second; but rarely, as we have seen, is the first "blamed" for the occurrence of the third. Since we find democracy praiseworthy but strikes deplorable, we hesitate to consider any relationship between the two. Similarly, since corruption, by definition, is bad and democracy, by postulation, is good, we deny, *a priori,* any association between democracy and corruption.

*   *   *   *   *

. . . Democracy, Plato argued, tends to perish by excess of its own basic principle.

Sophisticated students of labor have shaken their heads over the typical American response to Plato, perhaps best summarized in a 1933 speech by Al Smith: "All the ills of democracy," he said, "can be cured by more democracy." . . .

. . . [W]e will, in America, probably continue to maintain the inconsistency of fear over "too much democracy" and righteous indignation over "not enough democracy," as though democracy were an object with quantitative attributes instead of a method and a substantive philosophy, good or bad only to the degree that it facilitates the building of the good society. . . .

In our thoughtless ambivalence, we will please dictators abroad and autocratic union leaders at home. For we do our ideals a disservice when we borrow the logic of aristocrats and tyrants to criticize the *outcome* of democratic processes instead of working harder *at* democracy when it leads, now and again, to inconvenience, conflict and a temporary idling of the economic machine. . . .

If democracy is worth fighting for, worth dying for, then, it may be suggested, it is at least occasionally worth paying for.

From: Sylvester Petro

*THE LABOR POLICY OF THE FREE SOCIETY**

[EDITORS' NOTE: The author is Professor of Law, New York University Law School.]

If personal freedom is the basic institution of the free society, then the principles of private property and freedom of contract must be the vital instruments of the free society; for personal freedom cannot even be conceived outside the environment provided by property and contract rights. And since all rights are meaningful only to the degree that they are secured against invasion, it follows that the role of the state . . . is a critical one. . . .

The founding fathers . . . knew what they were doing . . . when they took the "life, liberty and pursuit of happiness" of the Declaration of Independence, and substituted for it, in the Constitution, the phrase "life, liberty, and *property.*"

A secured freedom to act in the pursuit of personal ends prevails only in a social environment based on private property and freedom of contract. Anyone inclined to doubt this proposition must try to visualize . . . a community where these are not secured rights. . . . In (their) absence . . . persons own and control nothing . . . the very food they eat_____when and if they eat_____ is not, properly speaking, *theirs.* . . .

It is currently fashionable to pose a strong contrast between "human rights" and "property rights." One also frequently hears it said that property and contract rights necessarily conflict with social goals. Such statements reflect a misunderstanding of the principles . . . for these principles by their very nature relate to human, personal right. . . .

Individual and social goals are, in fact, unified *only* by property and contract rights. . . . Keep a man from exercising his mind, his body, his faculties in the pursuit of his own wishes and delights, keep him from enjoying the fruits of his efforts—and you have done everything evil to him that you can. The greatest desire of each person, in short, is to be free to get the most he can out of life. There is no other way objectively to define social goals than to call them the sum of those individual goals which can be harmonized in society.

. . . Each member of society (children and other legal incompetents excepted) must be in control of his own person. All must be afforded protection against attempts by others to invade the integrity of their person. A property right in this sense means that everyone has a legally protected interest in his person, the invasion of which is interdicted by society.

The principle of private property involves more than personal autonomy and the exclusive right to the enjoyment of the fruits of one's personal efforts; it includes also the ultimate control of one's productions. If a man is entitled, in the legal phrase, to the quiet enjoyment of a machine he has made, he is necessarily entitled to use the machine, to control it, to give it or sell it to someone, or merely to sit and worship it.

. . . Freedom of contract is . . . conceptually implicit in the right of private

---

property. . . . [L]awyers often refer to freedom of contract as a "property right." And it has been habitual among jurists to say that the free access of workers to employment opportunities is a property right. When they express themselves in this way, they mean that employers and workers have mutual property rights to make employment contracts with each other.

From: Walter Lippmann
*THE METHOD OF FREEDOM**

[EDITORS' NOTE: The author is one of the leading political commentators and philosophers of the twentieth century.]

It has been the fashion to speak of the conflict between human rights and property rights, and from this it has come to be widely believed that the cause of private property is tainted with evil. . . . In so far as these ideas refer to plutocratic property, to great impersonal corporate properties, they make sense. These are not in reality private properties. They are public properties privately controlled and they have either to be reduced to genuinely private properties or to be publicly controlled. But the issue between the giant corporation and the public should not be allowed to obscure the truth that the only dependable foundation of personal liberty is the personal economic security of private property.

. . . It was in the medieval doctrine that to kings belong authority but to private persons, property, that the way was discovered to limit the authority of the king and to promote the liberties of the subject. Private property was the original source of freedom. It is still its main bulwark. . . . Where men have yielded without serious resistance to the tyranny of new dictators, it is because . . . resistance meant destitution. The lack of a strong middle class in Russia, the impoverishment of the middle class in Italy, the ruin of the middle class in Germany, are the real reasons, much more than the ruthlessness of the Black Shirts, the Brown Shirts, and the Red Army. . . . What maintains liberty in France, in Scandinavia, and in the English-speaking countries is more than any other thing the great mass of people who are independent because they have, as Aristotle said, "a moderate and sufficient property." . . . An official, a teacher, a scholar, a minister, a journalist, all those whose business is to make articulate and to lead opinion will act the part of free men if they can resign or be discharged without subjecting their wives, their children, and themselves to misery and squalor.

For we must not expect to find in ordinary men the stuff of martyrs, and we must, therefore, secure their freedom by their normal motives. There is no surer way to give men the courage to be free than to insure them a competence upon which they can rely. Men cannot be made free by laws unless they are in fact free because no man can buy and no man can coerce them. That is why the Englishman's belief that his home is his castle and that the king cannot enter it, like the American's conviction that he must be able to look any man in the eye and tell him to go to hell, are the very essence of the free man's way of life.

---

* Reprinted by permission of George Allen & Unwin, Ltd., London, 1934 (pp. 100–102).

MISSISSIPPI VALLEY EQUIPMENT CORPORATION

I Case Introduction

Synopsis

A group of St. Louis bankers, who own the Valley Corporation, merge the company with another to form Mississippi Valley Equipment Corporation. J. D. Skinner, president of Mississippi Valley Equipment Corporation, takes certain actions in building the organization structure of the company and in the formulation of company-wide policies. There are problems of inventory control, sales training, finance, and personnel management—both in the corporate staff and in the Kansas City branch. T. J. Duncan, manager at Kansas City, and various staff personnel disagree on the establishment of policies in these areas.

Why This Case Is Included

The Mississippi Valley Equipment Corporation situation offers opportunity to study the rational plan of decentralization, as well as certain counter tendencies to central planning. The informal organization in the company can be studied as it relates to the formal plan. One can also see how these two types of organization influence the behavior of people, and how they may either reinforce or conflict with one another.

The technological and economic influences on organization (design and custom) can be studied along with the human influences. The case also throws light on the question as to whether there is an inherent conflict between technology and economics of organization, on the one hand, and human needs, on the other.

Finally, the case shows the place of science and rational planning in the corporate affairs of this company.

Diagnostic and Predictive Questions

In answering the following diagnostic and predictive questions, remember that these questions apply theories and conceptual ideas from certain disciplines. Such theories are valuable to understand basic forces at work in the policy system (diagnosis) and to predict what will happen in the system in the future (prediction). Since each reading abstracts from the total policy system certain factors or variables into the closed or partial viewpoint of one theory or discipline, no one reading gives answers to the practical policy problems of the case. In diagnosis and prediction, the parts of the problem are studied with "other things being equal."

Following each question are listed readings which will be helpful in answering the question. The readings included with this case are marked (*). By referring to the author index at the end of this book, you may locate the other readings listed.

1. From the viewpoints of economic theory and psychological theory, what are the goals of the Mississippi Valley Equipment Corporation? Who set them? Why did they set these particular goals?

> Read: Smith, *The Wealth of Nations*, pp. 423, 508. Hayek, "The Corporation in a Democratic Society: In Whose Interest Ought It and Will It Be Run?" Odiorne, *How Managers Make Things Happen*, pp. 4–11, 37–38, 52–53. Schumpeter, *The Theory of Economic Development*, pp. 84–94.

2. Contrast the goals of the Mississippi Supply Company prior to the merger, with those of the Mississippi Valley Equipment Corporation. What, explicitly, were goals of the former? Who set them? Why did these persons set these particular goals?

Note: There is no reading in the literature of economics or management which adequately covers this question. The reader may draw his own conclusions, and in doing so will be drawing original hypotheses about corporate goals, what they are, who sets them, and for what reasons.

3. What changes do you see in the old means by which top management is managing the company? From the standpoint of economic theory, why are these changes coming about?

> Read: *Summer, "Economies of Scale and Organization Structure." Marshall, *Principles of Economics*, pp. 283–85. Smith, *The Wealth of Nations*, pp. 4–15.

4. From the standpoint of increasing "scientific" planning of operations, why is the organization structure and leadership pattern in Mississippi Valley Equipment Corporation changing?

> Read: Taylor, "Principles of Scientific Management." Lieber and Lieber, *The Education of T. C. Mits*, pp. 44–49. Barber, *Science and the Social Order*, pp. 7–8, 12–13, 18, 21. *Anderson, *An Organization Appraisal*, pp. 1–2.

5. From the viewpoint of political sociology, why is the organization structure and leadership pattern in the Mississippi Valley Equipment Corporation changing?

> Read: Cartwright, "Public Opinion Polls and Democratic Leadership." Carr, *American Democracy in Theory and Practice*, pp. 214–19. Locke, *Concerning Civil Government*, chap. ix. Hobbes, *Leviathan*, chap. x. Lasswell and Kaplan, *Power and Society*, pp. 157–59. *Dubin, "Imperatives Affecting Industrial Relations Decisions."

6. From the viewpoint of certain concpets in sociology and psychology, what problems do technology and economics (e.g., Questions 1–5) create in the coordination of the human organization?

> Read: Argyris, *Personality and Organization*, pp. 27–31, 33–51, 66–67, 77–90, 95, 103–4, 123–25, 130, 137–39, 150, 153–55, 157. *Abrahams,

"Status, Role and Conflict." Either Krech and Crutchfield, *Theory and Problems of Social Psychology,* pp. 81–83, 87–89, 94–96, 98, 102–3 (an advanced reading); or Leavitt, *Managerial Psychology,* pp. 27–33 (a less complicated reading). Etzioni, "Authority Structure and Organizational Effectiveness."

7. What is the "rationally planned organization structure" pattern in the Mississippi Valley Equipment Corporation? What is the "informal, or natural, organization"? Describe in detail, using facts from the case, any conflict you see between the two. Which organization pattern or structure is the most powerful and enduring?

Read: Beard, *Public Policy and the General Welfare,* p. 148. *Summer, "Leadership Action and the Informal Organization." Curtice, "General Motors Organization Philosophy and Structure." *Friedman, *Law in a Changing Society,* pp. 3–6, 22–23.
(Optional, not in this volume: Auguste Comte, *The Positive Philosophy,* Vol. II, Book VI, chap. iii. Herbert Spencer, *Principles of Sociology,* Vol. II, Book II, sections 212–17. Alvin Gouldner, "Organizational Analysis," in Robert Merton *et al., Sociology Today* [New York: Basic Books, Inc., 1959], pp. 400–428.)

Policy Questions for This Specific Case

In answering the following policy questions, the results of diagnosis and prediction are used to reduce the amount of guesswork, or judgment, in designing action solutions. However, since certain parts of the total case situation cannot be reduced to science, and since "other things are not equal," judgment must still be used to fill in the factors not accounted for by readings. You will also need a second kind of judgment as you put value weights on different scientific predictions, since different theories may point to conflicting solutions.

8. What should Skinner do about establishing the staff positions at company headquarters? Why? What, if anything, should he do in clarifying Dugan's and Cooper's position descriptions?

9. What kind of leadership pattern would be best for the president to use in the long run? In the short run?

10. In the long run, how should the informal organization in the Mississippi Valley Equipment Corporation be reconciled with the rationally planned organization? Which of these two should be changed to fit the other, or, should both be changed? Be specific about what changes should be made, in some detail.

Major Policy Issues: Tentative Generalizations about Any Policy System

In arriving at conclusions for the following question, generalize from the facts in the case and use your own ideas to (*a*) confirm, (*b*) modify, or (*c*) test the workability of the concepts and theories from readings. As an executive or professional, use wisdom to merge theory, on the one hand, with "brute facts" and practice, on the other.

11. Is there inevitable conflict between technology and economic forces in organization and human needs? Do central planning and freedom conflict? How can such conflicts be reconciled or minimized?

Read: Follett, "Constructive Conflict." Eells and Walton, *Conceptual Foundations of Business,* pp. 361–63. McGregor, *The Human Side* of Enterprise, pp. 124–31, 172–75. Enell and Haas, *Setting Standards for Executive Performance*, pp. 16–18, 31–32. Readings with Question 7.

Questions for Original Student Work in Analysis and Policy

The methods of viewing this case as represented by the authors' questions and selection of readings are not exhaustive. There are other relevant ideas for diagnosis and prediction. Furthermore, there are other ways of stating policy questions. More powerful analyses and wiser solutions will result by drawing on your own training and experience for (a) relevant concepts and theories, and (b) creative ways of asking policy questions. The following questions are designed to help you acquire this skill.

12. While reflecting on case facts, what additional theories from prior education give you insights as to "what is going on" in the Mississippi Valley Equipment Corporation? As to what might be predicted to happen in the future?

13. Other than the policy questions asked by the authors, what pragmatic ways can you think of to state the practical problems faced by executives in the case?

II *Mississippi Valley Equipment Corporation**

Background of the Company

The Mississippi Valley Equipment Corporation, with headquarters in St. Louis, engages in the distribution of heavy equipment, machinery, and industrial hardware. Although it is not a "giant" corporation if measured by manufacturing company standards, its sales this year are expected by the management to exceed $17 million, thus qualifying the company as one of the largest of its kind in the nation. The present firm was formed two years ago when the owners of the Valley Corporation purchased 80% of the stock of Mississippi Supply Company. At that time the corporate name was changed. Today, all letterheads and nameplates on company property show the company's trademark, MVEC, enclosed in a diamond-shaped symbol.

The company acts as manufacturer's agent in the sale of approximately 11,400 items in its product line, and it purchases for its own account approximately 6,000 items. Products range in value from nuts and bolts that sell for a few cents to air and gas compressors that sell for $12,000 to $15,000 each.

Storage and sale of equipment are carried out through six branches: two in St. Louis, and one each in Houston, New Orleans, Kansas City, and Cincinnati. At every location, the company maintains extensive warehouse facilities and a sales force to call on industrial concerns that use company products.

At the time of the merger, Mississippi Supply Company, which was founded by M. J. Wheeler at the age of 28, had sales of $2 million at its St. Louis and Kansas City locations. During the last ten years of its existence, MSC increased its sales approximately 5%, while there was an 80% increase in the industry, as estimated by a trade association economist, during the same period. Mr. Wheeler states that his wife and three children all agreed that it would be wise to sell the company, since the heirs had no interest in actively entering the field. Now 70, he also says:

I will be rather frank and say that I had my hands completely full operating the St. Louis and Kansas City businesses, could not have worked any harder, and consciously made the decision not to try to grow to be a giant and to set the world on fire. My company has always made a good profit, and I am proud of its record. We had sales of $2 million at the time the company was sold, and our employees were well cared for. That ought to be evident by the fact that over half of the 102 people had been with me for more than 20 years.

James D. Skinner, President of MVEC, states that:

The purchase was equally good for the Valley and for Mr. Wheeler. My board employed me as president of Valley eight years ago with the specific belief that we can grow large and profitable. In its two locations, MSC sold essentially the same kinds of products as we did, but we all recognized that it had become accustomed to selling the same items to the same customers, and to carrying out its operations in warehousing, financing and shipping in the same way it always had. We knew that its sales could be increased substantially and its operating methods streamlined.

Mr. Skinner, now 49, has seen sales of the Valley Corporation increase from $6 million to $12 million in eight years before the purchase, and the combined sales of the MVEC increase from $14 million to $17 million in the two years since the merger. The owners of MVEC, five prominent St. Louis businessmen engaged in banking and real estate, believe that James Skinner is an extremely capable man for the job, and as one of them put it,

His principal qualifications are that he knows how to get the thing organized and then let it run while he sees new opportunities for sales or cost cutting. He also knows how to pick good men as lieutenants. That's all it takes.

The Kansas City Branch

The Kansas City Branch has been headed by T. J. (Jack) Duncan for the past 12 months. Duncan, 45 years old, had worked as operating manager of the Valley branch in St. Louis for a period of 11 years. Shortly after he became president, Mr. Skinner recognized Duncan as a good executive, and felt that he would be ideal as the man to "take hold of the Kansas City operation and make something of it."

Before the purchase, Kansas City had increased its sales approximately 5% in ten years. It sold industrial equipment, machinery, and construction materials to local hardware stores, builders, institutions such as office buildings and schools, and to the State Highway Department. Its profit had been "moderately good" according to Duncan.

At the time that Duncan became manager at Kansas City, Mr. Skinner spent a day in drawing up a job description (Exhibit 1) for the new position of general manager at Kansas City. He had been to Kansas City on numerous trouble-shooting trips, had spent two months there after he became president of MVEC, and appears to have considerable knowledge of operations there. Along with this he says that he knows "very much about operations in St. Louis, and these are almost identical with Kansas City."

Mr. Skinner feels that there are still some "rough spots to be worked out in Kansas City."

For example, the purchasing and personnel functions have never been clearly defined. Both Duncan and I will get around to it one of these days. He has been working on a set of recommendations, but we disagree slightly on purchasing. He wants to be able to purchase all of his own merchandise out there except (1) items which cost over $3,000 individually, or (2) volume items in which he purchases less than maximum quantity discount. That is, when Kansas City orders bolts in sufficient quantity to get the discount they would not submit through here. I'm afraid that will tend to make them carry too much inventory out there and tie up too much money; also it cuts down on MVEC prestige with vendors not to have our large orders handled centrally. As a matter of fact, one of Duncan's weak spots is his inventory management—on my bimonthly visits to Kansas City I go over the levels of inventory with his accountant for each of 400 busy items. I don't have any exact standards to prove this, but I judge that he is either ordering in too large quantities, or he is being too conservative on his lead times—ordering too far ahead. I mention this each time to Jack but so far he only wants the two policies I mentioned a minute ago. We will have to do some long planning on this one, especially since close control of inventory is one of the ways you make money in this business. His inventory ratio to sales is less satisfactory than that of New Orleans or Cincinnati.

Specific Activities at Kansas City

Within the last two weeks, Mr. Skinner received from J. F. Dugan, Inventory and Purchasing Manager for MVEC, a list of proposed controls that Dugan thinks should be instituted to insure that all branches keep investment and risk in inventory to a minimum. This proposal is summarized in Exhibit 2. Mr. Dugan's formal education was in mathematics and, later, in engineering. Within the last year he has attended two short courses in Operations Research and has studied the subject of mathematical techniques of inventory control in books and journals. He declares that "linear programming and other techniques will be of great help to MVEC, though it will be five years before we can hope to apply these in our company."

In the area of personnel management, MVEC has employed two executives to plan policies and practices for the whole company. It is felt that this will give MVEC a significant lead over its competitors through greater cooperation of employees with less turnover and less damage of stock in receiving and storage. It has confidentially been predicted that this will reduce waste and pilferage. Oliver Cooper, manager of personnel, has submitted a proposed policy manual containing approximately 45 policies and procedures, one of which states that the central office should send a personnel man to each branch once a year "for the purpose of determining, jointly with the branch manager, the salary ranges for all positions in the branch."

The selling effort at Kansas City appears to be successful. The four salesmen seem to have taken a new interest in their work with the formation of MVEC, and their sales have increased about 12% over the previous year since Duncan came to Kansas City. Just why this has happened, nobody is certain. Skinner is interested in finding out since he hopes to be able to apply the same incentive at other branches.

Jack Duncan gives most of the credit to Mr. Skinner.

I have a good knowledge of sales, but I've always been in operations—when I was operations manager of the Valley in St. Louis, and before that when I worked in operations both in the St. Louis Branch and in Cincinnati. I sit down with these salesmen once a month and look at their plans for the next month—new customers, routes, number of calls, items to be pushed, and so on. Mr. Skinner not only worked out the present compensation plan (which I suspect is one of our reasons for success in selling), but he also visits with salesmen here once a month and helps them go over their plans that I see two weeks later. I've gathered that "going over" is sometimes a mild way of putting it, since Mr. Skinner proceeds to lay out routes for them when he isn't satisfied with the number of customers served or the amount of territory covered. He also tells them whether salesmen in other branches are outselling them and what techniques they use. At any rate, the salesmen seem to be happy, sales are increasing, and I simply couldn't do without help in the sales area. He sometimes brings along Dick Boling, whom I knew when he was such a hot salesman in St. Louis. There's been a rumor in St. Louis that Dick will take over a new job as sales manager for the whole company and continue the kind of thing Mr. Skinner is doing.

Apparently, the salesmen are evenly divided on the value of advice from Mr. Skinner. Two indicated that Skinner was most helpful, though they had also found Duncan to be helpful. Two others said that Skinner did not know very much about territories in Missouri, Kansas, Oklahoma, and Nebraska, and that he was unreasonable because he lacked knowledge of the obstacles and hardships in certain parts of the region. "It all looked the same to him on a map."

Mr. Skinner says that, "I am wholeheartedly in favor of the decentralization idea. There is nothing that so relieves a president, and at the same time encourages people to work hard and efficiently."

At Kansas City the decentralization idea is carried out particularly in the four operating sections—receiving, handling, storing, and shipping. Duncan drew up his own job descriptions for the foremen in each section. When on visits to Kansas City, nobody from St. Louis ever sees any reason to discuss the work of these men. Duncan makes the rounds of the warehouses at least once a week in order to make suggestions for storing specific items ("We need a lower bin nearer the door for those nipples—they're a heavy moving item"), and he makes his own storage rules ("Never keep inflammable items in the east end of the building"). "Of course," says Duncan, "St. Louis specifies such things as type of equipment to be used in operations, and a methods-study man drew up handling methods for each warehouseman's job." These are provided to Duncan in manuals, but he reports that nobody from St. Louis checks to see whether the manuals are being obeyed. Duncan follows some of these instructions and ignores others. Skinner has said privately that as soon as other phases of the merger are working smoothly, it will be necessary for his office to have a man check all branches to see that there is uniformity in certain job methods, otherwise branch managers won't have the benefit of really low-cost operations based on expert study of methods.

Expense and Capital Budgets

The only serious disagreement that Duncan has had with St. Louis is about the budget. Skinner has insisted on a procedure whereby all branch managers (except those in Houston and the St. Louis Marine branch) should submit a budget based on a certain breakdown form, supplied by St. Louis, that lists, under approximately 40 headings, all expense items in the branch. Twice a year, St. Louis furnishes the branches with a forecast of total industry sales in each territory. Each manager is supposed to adjust this forecast according to his guess about the percentage of industry sales MVEC will get. With this target in mind, the branch manager then submits an estimate of the amounts of money necessary for each of the 40 expense captions (newspaper advertising, salesmen's salaries, receiving platform personnel salaries, and so on) to reach the target. In addition, there are six captions (including inventory, other working capital, and building) that show what capital investment is needed. For any capital items other than working capital, each project must be listed regardless of size.

Duncan has objected forcefully to having to present 40 expense captions every six months. He has frequently said that so long as his profits, as a percentage of sales and as a percentage of investments, are adequate, St. Louis should not even be concerned with the "numerators and denominators of this ratio—that is, if the percentages are good, why worry about whether it is as a result of increased sales, cost savings, or what?"

Skinner, on the other hand, has found three or four instances where branch managers requested either capital amounts for projects that did not pay off or expense amounts that were not needed to operate the branch. He says:

We've got to have some control beyond the profit figure, otherwise these admittedly good executives sometimes just get carried away with their own operation and can't be objective—the idea, for instance, of Duncan's requesting an extra relief man on the shipping platform is nonsense. He is under such pressure from the men that he *thinks* he sees the need for such. If we weren't backing him up on a number of these things he'd have to give in for sure. So we ought either to turn it down in the budget or make a rule about the use of relief men. Sure, Duncan would buck these actions, but they are for his good in the long run.

A Problem in Personnel Policy

The remainder of this case reports on a problem which arose between St. Louis management and Duncan regarding the personnel policy manual submitted by Oliver Cooper. A series of events, extending over a period of about two years, illustrates the problem.

Immediately after he was employed, Cooper was instructed to draw up a set of objectives for the personnel department and its function. He talked many hours with Skinner about this, and the two of them jointly agreed on the statement of objectives shown in Exhibit 3.

Cooper was then given six weeks in which to travel to all the branches, spending one week at each branch. Mr. Skinner wrote to branch managers about this visit in a memorandum (Exhibit 4).

At the completion of his trips to all branches, Cooper spent two months in St. Louis drawing up the personnel policy manual. He had collected about 200 pages of notes on what he saw happening in the branches, and had concluded that, although some branch managers did better than others in applying prudent practices, at no branch did anyone seem to give any special attention "to a balanced and systematic plan to promote better employee relations." He also did further research in publications of the Industrial Relations Research Association and of the National Industrial Conference Board. From these two sources, from information gathered at the branches, and from other research on industry practices, he isolated 45 actions he felt the branch managers should carry out. These he grouped into six categories, which constituted the chief headings of the manual:

> Employment Standards and Procedures
> Compensation Practices
> Employee Benefits
> Disciplinary Procedures
> Termination Procedures
> Training Policies and Procedures.

Cooper's First Visit

Seven months after Skinner approved the manual and mailed it to all branches, Cooper discovered, on a trip to Kansas City, that two policies were apparently not being carried out there. These were:

1. All branch managers should hold a meeting of foremen and supervisors once a week, for the purpose of training and informing them on problems of mutual interest.
2. The branch manager should hold a meeting of all employees in the branch once each three months to explain company employee benefits and other personnel policies.

Cooper reports as follows about what took place when he called Duncan's attention to these two policies:

Jack told me that he was glad that the subject of these two policies had come up, because he was somewhat perplexed about operating under the whole policy manual. He said that he was in close touch with his foremen and supervisors and that everyone knew enough about what was going on so that a weekly information meeting was a waste of time. He also said that a meeting of all employees every three months seemed to be a waste of time because he and his foremen could keep people informed in day-to-day conversations as problems arose. I then explained to him as best I could that, if we didn't have some system, represented by these and the other balanced policies, big and growing branches would one day let employee relations get lost in the shuffle. That seemed to make an impression on him, because at least he said it sounded reasonable.

Cooper's Second Visit

Six months after this visit, Cooper again visited Kansas City to observe what progress was being made in instituting the personnel policies suggested by headquarters. When he found that the two policies in question earlier still were not implemented, he was quite surprised. This time he spent about three hours with Duncan "during which I explained in great detail how practice in other branches pointed to the necessity of these training sessions, how recognized research in industrial relations proved that they would be valuable to him, and that Mr. Skinner would be upset when he found out that the policies weren't being followed."

On returning to St. Louis, Cooper reported to Skinner his earlier conversation with Duncan about the training matters. He told Skinner that he had spent considerable time in presenting the reasoning behind the policies and that he had, in effect, given Duncan two chances to institute them before he brought the matter up with the president.

Cooper's Third Conversation with Duncan

Since Jack Duncan was scheduled to be in St. Louis on a routine trip three weeks after Cooper's last visit to Kansas City, Cooper requested

Mr. Skinner to have a talk with Duncan about the training situation at this time. Skinner agreed, but added that it would be a good idea if he and Cooper talked jointly to Duncan.

On the appointed morning, Skinner, Cooper, and Duncan met in Skinner's office. Skinner opened the conversation.

SKINNER: Jack, I've asked Oliver and you to come in because we have a problem in getting our personnel policies into operation. Now, I'm not criticizing you personally by any means. It's just that you and I and all managers have so many urgent things on our minds that we don't have time to study and understand these policies, and to recognize the importance of putting them into effect.

DUNCAN: I surely know what you mean by that, Mr. Skinner. We've got our hands full meeting competition and generating sales. I'm glad, however, to take time out here to discuss more about personnel matters.

SKINNER: That's right, Jack. And I do want to commend you on your sales performance out there. It's really important to us here in St. Louis. But I'm concerned because those two training policies still aren't being carried out in your branch. These things are important, too.

DUNCAN: I agree. Oliver and I discussed them, and close relations between management and employees is absolutely vital. Out there in Kansas City, I spend many hours a week talking not only with foremen and supervisors, but with employees, too. We have such good and frequent contacts among management that those meetings would take unnecessary time, and might even make our contacts kind of stuffy and formal.

SKINNER: I would compliment you on this, too, Jack. The directors can feel fortunate in having someone like yourself out there who is capable of keeping good contact with personnel. But we believe that such things as employee benefits and work rules and various personnel practices will be ignored in the pressure of other activities. I know you must agree that when employees are aware of the benefits we give, their loyalty increases. And if they know the policies and rules, they are more likely to follow them and be good employees. What I'm really doing is proposing something that is good for you *and* the company. You'll find that it is going to pay off for you in the long run if you have some systematic coverage of these things in regular, periodic meetings, when there is a specific time set aside from other pressures on you and your men, a time to consider and discuss these things. Oliver, you know more about this than most of us, what do you think?

COOPER: Jack, I've seen in other companies, as they grow and become more complex, a neglect of training time and time again. Recent industry sudies also show that few employees in American business are knowledgeable on just how great their employee benefits are—how much they are worth to them in dollars and cents. This isn't because there is anything wrong with management, but simply because there is no forceful and periodic indoctrination on these matters. Now I'm not trying to tell you how to run your branch out there, but only giving you information on why these policies are important. Wouldn't you agree on this?

DUNCAN: Yes, I agree. I certainly think, Oliver, that it's important to get this kind of message over to the employees, regardless of the specific method that we use to go about it.

SKINNER: Good. I was certain that this matter didn't represent any real disagreement. We're all after the same thing—good, profitable operations and good relations with employees. Oliver, you continue to work with Jack on whatever aid you can give him out there in Kansas City with personnel problems. Either of you can call on me any time, you know, if I can be of help. Jack, we've got several other important things to cover here—sales estimates, your request for a new loading platform, and so on. With the personnel matter out of the way, let's move right ahead on sales. Oliver, did you have anything else?

COOPER: No, Mr. Skinner. Jack is going great guns on all other matters I know of. Glad I had the opportunity to get in a visit with you this time, Jack, even if it was a brief one.

DUNCAN: Same here, Oliver. Come on out and see us when you can let go things here in St. Louis long enough.

Formulation of a New Training Policy

Five months after the conversation in St. Louis, Oliver Cooper spent a day in Kansas City for the purpose of talking to Duncan about a new set of salary scales for the entire work force. This was a rather complicated project, according to both Cooper and Duncan. It involved many changes in the salary ranges for salesmen, warehousemen, clerks, foremen, and others. It was Cooper's intention to use the information he obtained from Duncan in the final preparation of ranges when he returned to St. Louis.

During this visit, the subject of training was mentioned, and Cooper found that Duncan still had not held any formal training sessions, nor did he apparently have a schedule for doing so in the future. Although Cooper was surprised, he felt that he should not pursue this matter further "in view of its past history and the fact that Jack and I had much to cover about salary ranges."

On returning to St. Louis, Cooper decided to write a new policy to be placed in the training section of the manual. This policy was approved by Mr. Skinner and was mailed out the following week to all branch managers, with instructions to insert it in the manual:

Each branch manager will submit a report to the manager of personnel each three months that shows the number of training sessions held in the branch during that quarter and a brief summary of the subjects discussed at each meeting.

Duncan later had this to say about the new policy:

Of course I'm going to follow it. Within the next three weeks we will have our first training session. I'm convinced that this isn't the way to do it, and I'm sure the sessions will be dull and unproductive. I must say that Cooper is getting pretty had to get along with, and even Mr. Skinner is losing some of his good ways of working with branch managers. But of course this isn't a major gripe; I can get along with staff men and the president, too. But I'll tell you one thing. I'm going to let them run it—if they want a speech at a meeting I'll make it. I'm going to follow the rule book from now on. I'll have to spend more of my time setting up meetings and keeping abreast of the directives from St. Louis, and less time wandering around the plant talking to foremen and workers individually.

Exhibit 1

POSITION DESCRIPTION OF GENERAL MANAGER, KANSAS CITY BRANCH

1. The general manager is responsible for all work performed at the Kansas City Branch. As such, he has authority to request all personnel to perform their specified duties.
2. The general manager will plan his sales, expenses, and investment needs two times a year so that he can control his branch operations in order to make a profit.
3. The general manager will give personal attention to the two principal functions that make a profit for MVEC: sales and operations. He will draw up such policies and procedures as are required to produce effective selling and operating performance. He will then personally oversee both functions to see that his policies and procedures are being followed.
4. The general manager will, subject to the broad limits indicated by company-wide policy, establish jobs, policies, and procedures in the functions of purchasing, personnel, and inventory control.
5. The general manager will select, hire, and compensate all personnel who work in the branch.
6. The general manager will cooperate with representatives from the St. Louis office when they visit the branch seeking data and information for company decisions and policies.

Exhibit 2

PROPOSED INVENTORY CONTROL, MISSISSIPPI VALLEY EQUIPMENT CORPORATION

The purpose of inventory control in MVEC is to keep storage, insurance, and interests costs lower than our competitors', and to reduce the risk of damage and obsolescence.

At intervals of six months (or one year, if branches react unfavorably to more frequent checks), the branch should submit a list of all items whose value (price × quantity on hand) exceeds $250. Of the 5,000 to 6,000 items carried by the average branch, about 1,500 fall in this category. For each of these items the following information should be given:

NAME OF ITEM	CODE	QUANTITY ON HAND	QUANTITY SOLD IN LAST 12 MONTHS	LEAD TIME: FOR PURCH.

Exhibit 3

OBJECTIVES OF THE PERSONNEL DEPARTMENT

1. To draw up standard policies, procedures, and methods which will increase the efficiency of employees throughout the company.
2. To draw up policies that will increase the morale of employees in the branches, thus creating a more loyal work force and making MVEC a better place to work.
3. To instruct branch managers in the use of the policies and procedures so that they will be effective in carrying them out.
4. To keep the president informed of personnel practices that need improvement in specific branches.

Exhibit 4

MEMORANDUM FROM SKINNER TO DUNCAN

To: T. J. Duncan
From: James D. Skinner
Subject: Visit of Oliver Cooper to Kansas City

DEAR JACK:

The purpose of this memo is to inform you of something that I imagine you will be glad to hear. As you know, the company is going great guns in tooling up for growth and for meeting the problems of a bigger and more progressive business.

We've succeeded in getting a good man, Oliver Cooper, to help us with personnel practices. Our branch managers are all good at managing their men, but as you probably know, the bigger we get, the more we can learn about how to deal with employees to make them more responsible and more efficient. Oliver has had a lot of experience and training in personnel, and he will bring to our company an expertness that none of us have.

I've arranged for Oliver to be in Kansas City for a week as part of an orientation program in all branches. He'll spend about three days looking around, talking to you and your men. Then he'll need about two days to collect his ideas and notes.

I know you'll do all you can to make his stay productive.

(s) James D. Skinner

III Selected Readings

From: Charles E. Summer, Jr.
"ECONOMIES OF SCALE AND ORGANIZATION STRUCTURE"*

[EDITORS' NOTE: The author is Associate Professor of Management, Graduate School of Business, Columbia University.]

ECONOMIES OF SCALE IN ECONOMIC THEORY

Economic theory has traditionally discussed economies of larger scale firms in terms of physical efficiency (higher output with the same inputs of land, labor and capital equipment, or the same output with less inputs of land, labor and capital equipment). This theory also has discussed economies of scale in terms of monetary efficiency (higher revenue with the same costs or a given revenue with lower costs of input factors).

Using the mathematics of cost curves, or break even analyses, the principle of economies of scale stands out: with a large market to allow mass production, large and efficient machines and plants can be added (capital equipment inputs), the costs of which are spread over many units of output—thus fixed costs per unit of production become less. The long run average unit cost curve slopes downward as the *scale* (output of product units) increases. The bigger the plants added, and the larger the total company production facilities, the more efficient (less costly) is each unit of production. Presumably, the costs become less and less until the cost of coordinating the complex organization begins to rise.[1]

It has also been pointed out that the degree to which economies of scale can actually be realized in practice, is dependent on two other factors: the existence of a mass market, large enough to warrant large plants and machines; and the fact that input units of capital equipment frequently are indivisible.

In regard to the last factor, take the case of an aircraft company that wishes to install a wind tunnel to test aircraft. These tunnels, which must be large

---

* Excerpts from unpublished manuscript, copyright 1963, Charles E. Summer, Jr.

[1] This is usually assumed away by economists, simply by stating that the cost of coordinating plants begins to rise. We know from other disciplines that this phenomena may be caused by such dysfunctions as distortion of communications, or an increase in cost of passing information between many staff departments, line executives, and operating plants, in the decision-making process. Today, we would also say that, eventually, increasing costs set in because of the adverse effect of large organizations on the psychological self-actualization of individuals. This may reduce the energy and creativity released in the organization. All of these causes of increasing costs are valid, but beyond the scope of the present paper. Herein, we are interested in *economic* principles of economies of scale, as applied to organization structure, in the decreasing part of the long run cost curve.

enough to hold a complete airplane mock up, obviously will require a large capital expenditure. Suppose, hypothetically, that a small aircraft manufacturer entering the industry needs such a test device. A wind tunnel is not indivisible—the president of the XYZ company cannot say, "we are small, and our output isn't large enough to purchase a whole tunnel. So we will purchase ⅓ of a wind tunnel." He must, of course, go "whole hog or none." He may purchase the tunnel, and spread the $.5 million cost of it over a few airplanes, thus raising the fixed cost going into each unit of output, and probably pricing himself out of the market in competition with large companies, whose economies of scale are greater (fixed cost per unit are less). Or, he may decide not to enter the aircraft industry, but to produce smaller parts for large companies—in other words, he sees the laws of economies of scale as economic handwriting on the wall.[2] Only aircraft companies which have resources, and markets, to install large, complex capital equipment, can achieve a competitive long run average cost curve position which is competitive.

Economists have also concerned themselves with *size* of companies. Whole plants, rather than machines, have been viewed as the basic input units of capital equipment. Similar reasoning to the wind tunnel example, where a machine was used as the input unit, has been used to show economies of scale and its relation to size of the firm.

ECONOMIES OF SCALE IN ORGANIZATION THEORY: STAFF AND AUXILIARY DEPARTMENTS

Unfortunately, no literature exists which translates these principles into any realistic guides for management, when faced with the problem of adding staff and auxiliary service units to the company, or to a department of the company. It is my purpose simply to indicate along what lines such reasoning might proceed.

First, the staff or auxiliary service department should be viewed in much the same way as a machine or a plant—that is, as an input of fixed capital. If a firm's president is thinking about adding a personnel department at company headquarters, or an electronic computer service department, he is faced with the same factors as above. The market for the firm's products must be large enough to utilize the department, and spread its output over a large number of units of product. A small bank may not be able to afford a personnel manager, or an electronic computer in bookkeeping and mailing. Additionally, though there are many combinations of service and machines that might be designed for a personnel department or data processing unit, there is a limit to which the company can buy "one half of a personnel manager," or "⅔ of a memory storage unit."

There is one difference between plant scale, and staff department scale, which should be pointed out. In the case of plants, the "market size" is the number of units or final product produced for customers—because the machines and plants are producing directly for shipment or service to customers. But in the case of staff and auxiliary service departments, the output of the department is an input to other *internal* company departments, instead of an input to organiza-

---

2 In one interesting technological sense, he thereby becomes an "auxiliary department" of the larger company to which he sells. If the larger customer company gives the sub-contractor advice on operations, this arrangement is similar to the decentralized company structure of General Electric, mentioned later. The difference is that in the latter case, departments of General Electric are divisions of a *legal* entity as well as a *technological* entity.

tions and customers *external* to the firm. In other words, the "market" or "customers" for a personnel department output are the manufacturing department, the sales department, and the central office clerical and accounting office, inside the company.

This difference has important effects on the logic which management uses to decide when to install staff and auxiliary service departments. First, it is the size of the primary operating departments (plants, sales offices, branch offices, etc.) which determines when a company can afford a staff department or auxiliary service department. Second, with the advance in specializations (in all fields from biochemistry to market research to data processing), this kind of "market," and these kinds of "economies of scale" are becoming more and more important in determining which firms survive, and what a growing company *must do,* technologically (here the word technology refers to specializations of human brains, as well as to advance in machinery).

The length of time which it takes to train and install, as a working part of the organization, a biochemist, or a corps of data systems planners and computer programmers, suggests that this kind of fixed input is even more crucial, at times, than the acquisition of plants and machines. Long run costs are not only thoroughly committed, but they are committed in large amounts to relatively fixed blocks of input resources.

The same viewpoint can be applied at lower levels in a large firm. If management of the St. Louis sales office wishes to install a personnel clerk, or the Esso Research Laboratories in Linden, New Jersey, wishes to install a training director, or a group of patent attorneys, the basic factors are the same.

ECONOMIES OF SCALE IN ORGANIZATION THEORY: LINE DEPARTMENTS

There is no clear-cut way to distinguish "line" and "staff" in organizations. Rather than get into details of a controversy, we can simply use the concept of "specialist" to denote the staff and auxiliary person, and the "general manager" notion as the line department.

Though Alfred Marshall made brief reference to the advantages of large firms in employing skilled general management,[3] he did not foresee the kind of developments in company organization which we have in the second half of the 20th century.

The same factors are relevant to economies of scale vis-à-vis line executives. A large unit today has a vast upward hierarchy of "coordinators," who devote time to planning and innovation, and whose marginal contribution to the firm's efficiency is spread over large volumes of output.

The most notable example is a company like General Electric, with 101 product divisions, each with a general manager, surrounded by staff and auxiliary service personnel—clerks, personnel people, training aids, etc. When the principle of indivisibility of people and machine prevents the duplication of a given service department at the division level, there are group executives with their helpers at the next level up. When indivisibility sets in even at the group vice president level, then the latest in fixed human resources (executive compensation specialists, organization planners, operations research personnel, and other "departments") are available at the corporate headquarters.

Each of these levels represents a pool composed of a general executive, with whatever staff assistance is allowed by the principle of "market" size and the principle of indivisibility.

---

[3] Alfred Marshall, *Principles of Economics,* Eighth edition, New York: The Macmillan Company, 1952, pp. 283–85.

There is no doubt but that these principles become more and more important 1) in determining the future organization and destiny of growing firms, and 2) determining the gross national product which issues forth from the manufacturing companies, banks, and hospitals of the nation. Advance in science, and in information processing will assure this.

LIMITATIONS IN PRACTICE

In order to calculate when to add a staff or auxiliary service department, or when to add another level in the general management hierarchy, one would have to calculate the marginal productivity that the executive or specialist group provides to the line operating departments of the company. The marginal costs and revenues of the line departments, occasioned by adding a personnel department to advise them, would have to be calculated.

As most economics books point out, this is not possible in most situations. The data is not clearly available, nor can the marginal productivity and profits be clearly attributable to variations in the inputs of people and facilities. In spite of these limitations on quantification, and proof, the principles of market size (using the concept of market in this paper), indivisibility, and decreasing costs to scale, are, all three, useful logical tools of analysis in an age of rapidly advancing technology, and in an age of more complex organizations.

From: Richard C. Anderson
*AN ORGANIZATION APPRAISAL**

Science tells us that every living organism has within it the seeds of its own destruction. Organisms survive not alone by the strength of their parts but by a balance among those parts. The planned organization structure becomes the means for achieving this balance in the business enterprise.

The organization appraisal provides a means to measure organization efficiency and to give a picture of how well an organization unit has provided for required functions; described the relationship among those functions; and how well it has informed each individual about his job, about what is expected of him, and about how his job relates to others. At the same time, it provides the basic information upon which to build (or rebuild) an organization structure. In the shifting tides of products and markets, the balance so essential for continued success requires that the business enterprise continually adjust its organization to meet new competitive conditions.

As product research attempts to improve the company's product line and market research to improve the company's competitive position, so organization appraisal attempts to improve the company's management capability through providing members with the most favorable working environment. Also, as in the cases of product or market research, changing conditions both inside and outside the company require continuing attention to the relationship of necessary functions and to organization structure.

---

* Reprinted by permission of Richard C. Anderson (in collaboration with C. W. Barkdull), 1962 (pp. 1–2).

The planning of organization structure is not a luxury of the giant enter-prise—it is a necessity for continued profitability in all business organizations. Every manager is responsible for organization structure just as he is for budgeting, hiring of employees, maintaining financial accountability, repre-senting the company to the public, etc. There comes a time, however, when continuing and concentrated attention should be given to organization matters just as it is given to Budgeting, Personnel, Public Relations, etc. Most com-panies, of course, are limited in how many specialists they can afford to em-ploy for product research, industrial engineering, personnel recruitment, or such a new speciality as organization appraisal. At the same time, however, there is also a point beyond which the company can not afford to go in neglecting such specialized activities.

From: Robert Dubin

"IMPERATIVES AFFECTING INDUSTRIAL RELATIONS DECISIONS"*

GOVERNING BY RULES

In a large company with multiple plant operations the most obvious single consideration affecting labor relations decisions is the need for standardization and uniformity. Unquestionably, the administration of a work force of several hundred thousand, or fifty thousand, or even five thousand is a staggering job. It would be totally impracticable to attempt individualized treatment of so many workers. The almost nostalgic plea for the "clinical" approach, that is, for the setting-forth of "all the facts" in every employee problem, is hardly possible in the large-scale enterprise. This is not to say that it would not be desirable or humane to treat each worker as an individual. The emphasis is rather on the fact that administration in the big firm necessitates standardiza-tion through rules and uniform procedures as a basis for prediction of future events. Management must be in a position to predict what will be the out-come, granting a given personnel situation. Similarly, employees are provided with a basis for predicting the effect of their own action or that of management representatives in the light of the rules governing their relationship to each other.

The "reign of rules" is the administrative answer to the problems of governing in large-scale organizations. This rule-making habit is all-pervading. It takes its most obvious form in shop rules governing personal conduct and in the union agreement which sets forth the mutual rights and obligations of the contracting parties and their constituents. But job descriptions, production standards, stand-ard procedures, wage-rate structures, and policy manuals are rule-making, too. Even a casual examination of the manuals of procedures, operating codes, stand-ards, and specifications to be found in most any industrial or commercial firm

* Reprinted by permission of the *American Journal of Sociology* (from "Decision-Making by Management in Industrial Relations"), 54:292–96 (January 1949), University of Chicago Press.

should be convincing evidence that rule-making and enforcing for the class rather than decision-making in the individual case plays an increasing role in the functions of the executive.

There is an interesting paradox involved in the growth of governing by rule in large businesses. The goal of standardization and hence of predictability is certainly achieved. But making the rule for the class rather than the individual does two things to the individual worker. He becomes aware of his personal inability to make an individual "deal" for himself outside the company rules and procedures, except under the circumstances of a "lucky break." He tends also to view himself as part of a group of similarly situated fellow-employees who are defined by the rules as being like each other. In addition, uniform rule-making and administration of the rules makes unionism easier and, in a sense, inevitable.

From: Fred Abrahams

"STATUS, ROLE AND CONFLICT"*

[EDITORS' NOTE: Mr. Abrahams is on the Senior Research Staff of the Bureau of Applied Social Research, Columbia University.]

STATUS AND ROLE ARE THEORETICAL CONCEPTS RATHER THAN REAL ENTITIES

Status and role are terms frequently encountered in contemporary sociological writings. They are the basic buildings blocks of many sociological theories; just as the electron, proton, neutron, and other subatomic particles are the basic building blocks of theories of the physical universe. In both of these cases the building blocks are mentally constructed abstractions, rather than directly observable entities. When we observe a group or collectivity of individuals behaving certain ways, we do not "see" statuses and roles as such. Rather we *infer* the statuses people occupy and the roles they perform from our observations or suppositions of what they do and how they behave. It may be asked why, then, do we bother with categorizing social relations and behavior into statuses and roles at all? The point is that such abstract categorization vastly simplifies (and simultaneously distorts) our picture of the social world, and allows us to systematically attempt to account for different patterns of social relations. In brief such theoretical abstractions are necessary prerequisites for our intellectually coming to grips with the world; which in turn serves as the basis for rational decision-making in practical situations.

STATUS AND ROLE REFER TO THE "APPROPRIATE" BEHAVIOR OF CERTAIN TYPES OF PEOPLE IN PARTICULAR SITUATIONS

A cardinal assumption of the social sciences is that human behavior is largely not random or idiosyncratic. Rather, such behavior exhibits regularly predictable patterns. The basis of such regularities lies in the fact that in their development

* Reprinted by permission of the author. (From an unpublished article, 1963.)

human beings *learn* the supposedly "appropriate" behavior that is *expected* of themselves and others in particular situations. These social expectations—or social norms—are not to be found in any "rule book," but rather are inferences we informally pick up. Sociologists find it useful to focus on those expectations that relate to the "appropriate" behavior expected when "pairs" of generalized "types" of people (or actors) come together. A "type" of actor refers to such generalized categories as teacher, student, manager, supervisor, foreman, worker, etc. Thus, an industrial sociologist might focus on workers, and analyze their patterned expectations concerning what is "appropriate" behavior when in the presence of, say, fellow workers, as contrasted to foremen. These relatively stable expectations between pairs of "types" of actors are known as *roles*. It is important to realize that these expectations concerning "appropriate" behavior are mutual affairs—*i.e.,* each "type" of person in his dealings with another "type" can legitimately expect this other "type" to behave towards him in certain prescribed ways (rights) ; while on the other hand, this other "type" can justifiably expect our initial "type" to exhibit certain appropriate behaviors (obligations) . Sociologists use the term *status* to refer to "types" of actors; each "type" being a different status. Thus, an "office manager" can be regarded as a status position, embodying all the roles such a person could reasonably be expected to be involved in—*e.g.,* his involvement with his superiors, fellow managers, clerks, and secretary.

The Importance of Status and Role in Organizational Control and Planning

Why are roles important in any organization? Primarily the answer lies in the fact that they are crucial in two major aspects of organizational life: namely, control and planning. Basically, there are two ways to control the action of others: applying some form of *external* force (coercion, persuasion, remuneration) to encourage some acts or discourage others; or recruit persons who have *internalized* certain desired patterns of behavior, and therefore act as "self regulators." Roles are things that are internalized, and consequently facilitate this latter form of control. Thus, when workers accept a job in a plant they *themselves* expect management to lay down certain directives and they feel that management has a legitimate right to act in that fashion.

Planning would be impossible if we were limited to dealing with organizational members as *specific unique individuals*. Instead we deal with particular generalized statuses such as foreman, supervisor, etc., and with their role relationships. In other words, organizational planning is only possible if we can think of the organization in skeleton form, staffed by actors occupying various statuses and performing certain roles. In business, these are sometimes called job descriptions or positions. Such planning is built on our expectations that *regardless* what person fills such statuses he will act "appropriately" despite his unique personal characteristics. Attempts at organizational planning and control would break down in a chaotic mire of individual idiosyncratic behavior if executives did not think roughly in terms of statuses and roles (although these executives usually are not aware of statuses and roles as such) , and if people did not act, *to some degree,* in conformity to the expectations embodied in the statuses they occupy and the roles they perform.

The Importance of Status and Role in Motivation

Socially acceptable roles also explain, in many instances, why people obey authority—why they act in accord with the decisions made by someone else. We obey a "policeman" (this word is a symbol for expected duties, rights on his part, and certain obligations on ours; his uniform is a symbol of these things also) because we expect that he has a right to direct traffic. And we obey the "boss" because he is a "vice president," a "foreman," a "director of research." Or, we listen to lectures because "students" and "professors" are expected to behave in certain ways. This is the right, or legitimate, thing to do.

STATUS AND ROLE CONFLICT: THE DILEMMA OF INCONSISTENT EXPECTATIONS

Organizations are set up to achieve certain goals through coordinated efforts of numerous people. To utilize human resources most efficiently, the tasks performed by members of the organization are divided into specialized types. This forms the basis of the division of labor. And the division of labor delineates the distinct separate statuses found in organizational settings. Unfortunately, at times, leaders of organizational enterprises work on the assumption that all people in a particular status will act strictly in accord with what they feel are the prescribed "appropriate" behaviors for that status position. However, in reality, each person occupies several different statuses whose expectations may be in conflict. Furthermore, what management sees as the expectations binding on the occupant of a particular status may not correspond to what others view as the appropriate expectations for that status. Thus, management may see the status of foreman as involving expectations of being management's representative to the work force, while the workers expect the occupant of the same status to serve as an intermediary between them and management. The foreman in such a situation is experiencing role conflict since he cannot be all things to all men.

In a similar vein, the management may overlook the obvious fact that our foreman occupies several statuses which may well be in conflict with one another. Thus the foreman is most likely a member of a friendship "clique," where the expectations placed on him are quite different than those expected of him as a foreman.

In any case, when an individual belongs to a group he has a certain expected behavior (role-responsibility). If this is not performed as expected, the group usually has sanctions or penalties available. These sanctions underlie a person's conflict. Nobody relishes the thought that he will be punished by some group whichever way he moves.

THE RESOLUTION OF STATUS AND ROLE CONFLICTS

If status and role conflicts frequently occur in organizational settings, how are they resolved? There are four logical resolutions that can occur. Namely, if a set of expectations "A" are in conflict with a set of expectations "B," then an individual can either: (1) conform to "A"; (2) conform to "B"; (3) reach a compromise position between "A" and "B"; or (4) reject or avoid conforming to either "A" or "B." Gross, Mason, and McEachern, in their study of school superintendents entitled *Explorations in Role Analysis,* maintain that there are three factors which influence which of these four resolutions will most likely occur in a given situation. The first factor concerns the extent to which the occupant of a given status perceives the set of "A" expectations as more legitimate than the set of "B" expectations. This they label the moral dimension. The second factor pivots about the degree of perceived sanctions the occupant of a given status feels will result as a consequence of not conforming to the set of "A" expectations rather than the set of "B" expectations. This is the expediency dimension. Lastly, what resolution of conflict occurs depends on the extent to which for each individual moral considerations are more important than expedient ones, or vice versa.

In our example of the foreman's dilemma the following factors would have to be taken into account: Which of the two potential "reference groups" (management or workers) does our foreman feel has a more legitimate set of expectations concerning his "appropriate" behavior? In this context, "reference groups" refers to the *source* of status or role expectations. Second, which "reference group's" sanctions does our foreman fear the most? Finally, which of these two factors (legitimacy and sanctions) is our foreman most concerned with?

THE CONSEQUENCES OF STATUS AND ROLE CONFLICTS

Gross, Bason, and McEachern attempt to discern what are the major consequences of status and role conflicts. In brief they conclude that such conflicts usually result in reducing the gratification a person receives from occupying particular statuses. Moreover, the research showed that persons who themselves were aware of such conflict, apparently were less gratified with their statuses than were those who were subjectively ignorant of the existence of conflict. Thus, school superintendents who expressed an awareness of role conflicts were less likely to be satisfied with their jobs, or their careers, and were more likely to worry about their occupational situation. The authors attempted to interject psychological as well as sociological factors by pointing out that the greater the level of anxiety an individual had, the more pronounced were the consequences of role conflict.

From: Charles E. Summer, Jr.
"LEADERSHIP ACTION AND THE INFORMAL ORGANIZATION"*

In any company, there are at least two organizations which influence the behavior of people. The formal organization, often pictured in the organization manual, is a series of job descriptions showing the rational plan of how management expects people to behave. Such a manual assigns "jobs" (in management terms) or formal "roles" (in sociological terms). There is no doubt that such a formal assignment, drawing on motivations of authority (unconscious compliance based on habit, or conscious compliance based on legitimacy and reason) and power, has an important influence on what a person in the organization does.

On the other hand, there is the informal organization, based on customs that arise during the day-to-day dynamic actions of people. This organization does not come into being by a rational planning act. It rises through the reactions of people as they face day-to-day problems. In short, it evolves naturally.

---

* Copyright 1963, Charles E. Summer, Jr. Abstracts from unpublished manuscript. Examples are taken from W. H. Newman and C. E. Summer, Jr., *The Process of Management: Concepts, Behavior, and Practice* (Englewood Cliffs, N.J.: Prentice-Hall, Inc., 1960).

It is the purpose of this paper to show how the actions of formally appointed executives give rise to the informal organization. This, of course, is a special case (superior-subordinate interaction) of the more generic concept of informal organization.

*   *   *   *   *

Almost every single action of the executive in some way influences the future actions of his subordinates. It is quite easy to see that a manager, when he writes job descriptions in the formal organization structure, expects them to influence subordinates' actions. The job description, as well as policies and other plans, are formulated to, in effect, "tell" the subordinate "this is what you are supposed to do."

However, it is not so easy to see that each little action during the day on the part of the superior is probably a more powerful determinant of employees' actions than are the written plans and organization charts.

It may be that the reason why it is difficult to see this phenomenon is that it is so obvious and simple. The executive is likely more or less unconsciously to take it for granted. It may be one of those things which is so "plain as the nose on your face" that the manager *behaves,* and acts on the spur of the moment, without being conscious of what effect each little action has on the future behavior pattern of subordinates.

*   *   *   *   *

As a first example, let us illustrate how a seemingly casual action on the part of the executive might contribute toward employee attitudes or beliefs. We know that these are in turn *one* of *the* important determinants of behavior.

C. T. Crane is manager of the Buffalo Plant of Union Paper Company, the headquarters of which is in New York. He has an organization chart which states that "the plant manager has authority over all operations and personnel in the plant." M. J. Palmer, Production Vice-President in New York, not only drew up and approved the job description for Plant Managers, but he states that he is wholeheartedly in favor of decentralizing and of autonomy at the plant level. Palmer and Crane have been working together in their present positions in a harmonious fashion for about eight years.

Because of a rather strict cost-cutting campaign instituted by the President over the past six months, Palmer recently sent one of his staff men to Buffalo "to investigate the production scheduling system." While staff men from headquarters had visited Buffalo on other subjects in the past, none had ever delved into the production scheduling system.

The visit was viewed as routine, run-of-the-mill operations by both Crane and Palmer. The production scheduling system was duly modified on recommendation of the staff man. About four months later, Palmer again asked the staff man to "go to Buffalo and see how the scheduling system is working and if there are any further changes that ought to be made."

This time, according to an interview with Crane, the latter felt "a little annoyed that New York is sending a man to make changes." Nevertheless, Crane said that little annoyances come up all the time, and it didn't make too much difference anyway.

In this actual case example (names and places have been disguised), the actions of Palmer in sending the staff man was simply one of ordinary day-to-day operating expediency. Neither man viewed the action of particular importance, yet Crane's attitudes and beliefs about both "New York headquarters" and, probably, his attitude toward Palmer, was affected in a small way. Attitudes and beliefs, after all, can be developed slowly and by small piecemeal experiences. This one little incident contributes to such attitudes and belief development.

A Series of Leadership Actions May Produce a New Job Description

Continuing the case, a study of the relationship of Palmer and Crane over the two years after that event showed that both continued to get along with one another on a friendly basis. The production control staff man in time came regularly to visit Buffalo and to work out details on the scheduling *procedures*. This also happened in two other operating problems—shipping invoices procedures, and the filing system for employee service (historical) files.

Now, we do not know whether these things are correct or incorrect. The point to be made is that, by gradual *actions* on the part of Palmer, he was changing the job description of Crane (who no longer decided on these procedures). He was also changing the *real* authority relationships. Even though Crane still, according to his job description, "had authority over all operations," Palmer's looking to the staff man for deciding on these various procedures meant that all three parties more or less unconsciously knew that he (the staff man) now has the real say-so about them.

"Personal Actions" Need Not Be Face-to-Face Verbal Communications

Leadership is a personal process which usually involves the way an executive personally communicates and behaves with subordinates. While this is essentially true, we should at least modify that concept to include actions which a superior takes that change his subordinates' behavior without verbal communication.

In another incident which was studied in the same company as above, Crane had a minor disagreement with the New York sales manager over the level of inventories to be stored in the plant warehouse. Heretofore, Crane had carried 800,000 sheets of #2 grade book stock, but the sales manager requested him to increase this to 900,000. Both men knew that the sales manager discussed the problem with Palmer in an effort to get him to tell Crane to increase the inventory. About a year passed and Crane got no word from Palmer on this matter. The sales manager again brought up the subject with Palmer, and Palmer again did not act.

In interviewing the three parties concerned, it turned out in this case that both the sales manager and Crane *interpreted* the actions (or lack of action) by Palmer to mean that Crane was in charge of deciding on plant level inventories. All three also interpreted the sales manager's actions (or lack of action) in not appealing to the President to mean that he (the sales manager) acknowledged the authority of Palmer and Crane over plant level inventories. It is important to notice that the sales manager never *said* to the others that he knew that they had authority, nor did Palmer say to Crane that he was delegating this authority to the plant level. All that took place was a disagreement and a raising of the problem. Nobody ever enunciated a verbal solution, yet each "sensed" the communications from the sales manager and Palmer regarding the solution.

The guide to be drawn from this incident is that, granted that a superior's own behavior can change his subordinates' behavior (our first guide, above), we now see that the *superior's behavior need not even be a verbal exchange between the superior and subordinate.*

RESULTING BEHAVIOR MAY EITHER REINFORCE OR CONFLICT WITH FORMAL
MANAGEMENT STRUCTURES

* * * * *

In the last example cited, the President of Union Paper and his staff had actually written a policy three years before the event that all finished goods inventories, both in plant warehouses and in sales warehouses across the country, should be determined by the Product and Inventory Manager, Mr. Warren (a staff man assigned at the top or presidential level). The *policy* was supported by a *job description* for Warren, and *procedures* for both Crane and the sales manager to report data and information to Warren. Nevertheless, in this case, day-to-day behavior was setting up a *pattern* of customary relationships which, though not written down and official, were nevertheless part of the work structures of the company. Importantly, these new and informal policies, jobs and procedures conflicted with the rational structures on paper.

* * * * *

DYNAMIC INTERACTION: A FURTHER CLARIFICATION

Many of us have heard the proverb from a once popular song: "It takes two to tango." Social scientists have coined the word "interaction" to denote the phenomenon of two people whose activities and communications each affect the other at the same time. This is an important concept because it shows us that leadership is not a one-way passing of orders from an executive to his subordinate. The Union Paper case above showed that when Mr. Palmer initiated some action Mr. Crane's *response* also determined whether or not leadership was actually exercised. If Crane had acted in a different way, perhaps telephoning Palmer and selling him on the idea of not sending the production control expert, there may have been a different outcome. In other words, both Palmer's and Crane's behavior *jointly* and *at the same time* determined the pattern of behavior.

The principle to be derived from these examples is that it is the *combined and concurrent day-to-day behavior of both manager and subordinate that constitutes a leadership pattern.*

LEADERSHIP AS BUILDING THE SOCIAL SYSTEM: A FURTHER CLARIFICATION

In the same way that Crane, Palmer and Warren were working out a pattern (habit, structure) of behavior in the Union Paper Company—there are hundreds of other people in a large company—bosses and subordinates as well as "peers" on the same level—who are *by their day-to-day actions* forming habits of behavior and more or less stable attitudes. Out of all of this comes a vast and complex network of habits which may not be written down in organization charts, procedures and policies, but which nevertheless is a *social structure that,* after it is formed, causes people to behave according to its customary "norms." A *norm,* to the sociologist, is simply an enduring (repetitive) action or an enduring belief or attitude which causes repetitive behavior. Both this social structure and the official management structures (jobs, relationships of authority and influence, standing plans such as policies) are at work as forces playing on employees and acting as determining factors in their daily action.

From one viewpoint, therefore, leadership is a process of building an informal social system through day-to-day action.

From: W. Friedman

*LAW IN A CHANGING SOCIETY**

[EDITORS' NOTE: The author is Professor of Law in Columbia University.]

The controversy between those who believe that law should essentially follow, not lead, and that it should do so slowly, in response to clearly formulated
social sentiment—and those who believe that the law should be a determined
agent in the creation of new norms, is one of the recurrent themes of the history
of legal thought. It is tellingly illustrated by the conflicting approaches of
Savingy and Bentham.

For Savingy, a bitter opponent of the rationalizing and law-making tendencies, spurred by the French Revolution, law was "found," not "made." Only
when popular custom in part articulated by lawyers, had fully evolved, could
and should the legislature take action. Savingy particularly deprecated the trend
towards the codification of law, inaugurated by the Napoleonic Codes, and
spreading rapidly over the civilized world.

By contrast, Bentham, a fervent believer in the efficacy of rationally constructed reforming laws, devoted a great part of his life to the drafting of codes
for a large number of countries, from Czarist Russia to the newly emergent
republics of Latin America. While most of these efforts were not immediately
successful, notably in his own country, whether in the field of civil law, criminal
law, evidence or poor law, his philosophy became increasingly influential as the
nineteenth century progressed. It was Bentham's philosophy, and that of his
disciples, which turned the British Parliament—and similar institutions in other
countries,—into active legislative instruments, effecting social reforms, partly in
response to, and partly in stimulation of, felt social needs. It is essentially the
judge-made law that, in the countries of the common law world, has still in
large measure resisted legislative—as distinct from judicial—reform, although
even in the traditional fields of the common law, legislative activity is steadily
increasing. In most other fields—of which electoral reform, social welfare legislation in the broadest sense, tax law and the reform of the machinery of justice
are examples—the Bentham philosophy triumphed in the practice of States, as
the urbanisation and industrialisation of nineteenth-century Western society
proceeded, and long before political and social cataclysms of the twentieth
century posed a series of new challenges. . . .

A highly urbanised and mechanized society, in which great numbers of peoples live close together and are ever more dependent upon each other's actions
and the supply of necessities outside their own sphere of control, has led to an
increasingly active and creative role of the conscious law-making instrumentali-
ties of the State.

The traditional view is not without its modern defenders, especially among
laissez-faire economists who oppose the growing role of the State in the planning
and regulation of contemporary social life. Thus, Professor Hayek has restated
a distinction similar to that drawn by Ehrlich by opposing the planned State to

* Reprinted by permission of Stevens & Sons, Ltd., London, 1959 (pp. 3–6, 22–23).

the rule of law and asserting that the former "commands people which road to take, whereas the latter only provides signposts." Even if we accept this as an adequate parable of the problem of the function of law in modern society, we need only to point to the vast number of one-way streets in modern cities to illustrate the superficiality of this distinction. No sane person would advocate the abolition of one-way streets in cities with heavy motor traffic so as to restore a measure of individual freedom of decision, with the inevitable consequence of a vastly increased rate of accidents to life and property. Such a measure would make sense only if the volume of traffic, in particular the use of motor-cars, were severely restricted, in other words, if individual freedom of property and movement were far more drastically curtailed. This might become a necessary and acceptable measure to advocate for those who accept the planning function of the law, but not for the advocates of unrestricted individual freedom.

However, the traffic problem hardly touches the core of the matter, for it may well be accepted even by the most outspoken individualists as a typical police function, and therefore properly within the regulatory function of government. The shift in public opinion and in the legislative policy of all major parties and of contemporary governments has gone much further. Conservatives and Liberals, Democrats and Republicans, Socialists and individualists, all hold the State responsible for ensuring conditions of stable and full employment through public works and relief schemes, tax policies and other instruments of public policy; it is expected by the community to provide minimum standards of living, housing, labor conditions and social insurance. While there is controversy on the degree of public controls and the socialisation of industries and public utilities, some degree of public operation or control of business is recognized by all major parties as necessary, and practiced in all modern States. In Britain, as in Australia, France, Sweden or India, not to speak of the Soviet Union, a number of important public utilities, such as electricity, forestry and transport, are run by the government or by State-controlled corporations. The Federal Government and other public authorities in the United States control a vast proportion of the generation of electric power, harbour facilities and other public utilities. Public housing programmes and social insurance schemes, farm support and other subsidy schemes have been enacted to an increasing extent.

Technical facts and a gradual change in the public philosophy thus combine to effect a drastic and organic change in the relation between lawmaking and social evolution. . . .

Public opinion on vital social issues constantly expresses itself not only through the elected representatives in the legislative assemblies, but through public discussion in press, radio, public lectures, pressure groups and, on a more sophisticated level, through scientific and professional associations, universities and a multitude of other channels.

Because of this constant interaction between the articulation of public opinion and the legislative process, the tension between the legal and the social norm can seldom be too great. It is not possible in a democratic system to impose a law on an utterly hostile community. But, a strong social ground-swell sooner or later compels legal action. Between these two extremes there is a great variety of the patterns of challenge and response. On the one hand, the law may at length, and tardily, respond to an irresistible tide of social habit or opinion. Such is the case with the gradual enlargement of divorce grounds in the great majority of non-Catholic Western countries—either through the addition of new divorce grounds (cruelty, incompatibility, etc.) or the judicial extension of existing grounds for divorce or annulment (e.g., annulment for fraud in the State of New York). The extension of legitimate divorce is a response to the increasing freedom of the movement of married women in modern Western society, a loosening of religious ties and social taboos, and the development of social habits which lead to the dissolution of a vastly increased number of marriages, with or without the sanction of law. Here the alternative for the legislator is to permit an increasing gap between legal theory and social practice to develop, or to respond to an overwhelming change in the social facts of life. . . .

We have seen that, in a democratic system of State organization, there is a great variety of interactions between social evolution and legal change. The stimulus may come from a variety of sources, some of which have been briefly surveyed. There may be the slowly growing pressure of changed patterns and norms of social life, creating an increasing gap between the facts of life and the law, to which the latter must eventually respond. There may be the sudden imperious demand of a national emergency, for a redistribution of natural resources or a new standard of social justice. There may be a far-sighted initiative of a small group of individuals, slowly moulding official opinion until the time is ripe for action. There may be a technical injustice or inconsistency of the law demanding correction. There may be a new scientific development calling for new forms of legal evidence (such as acceptance of blood-group tests for the negative proof of paternity).

The Law responds in various ways, too. The speed and manner of its response is usually proportionate to the degree of social pressure. It is also influenced by the constitutional structure. But circumstances and personalities may hasten or retard the response. In the sphere of "political law" or where a new status is created, legislative action is required. In other fields, there is a give and take between legislative and judicial remedial action in part determined by the subject-matter but in part by the changing and diverse attitudes of legislators and judges.

UNITED STATES STEEL CORPORATION

I Case Introduction

Synopsis

The management of the United States Steel Corporation announced a general price increase and stressed that the change will serve both the company and public interest. The President of the United States and various government officials cite reasons why such an increase is not beneficial to the society as a whole. Some competitive steel producers break industry tradition and do not "follow the leader." United States Steel rescinds its price increase amid conflicting arguments by the contending parties and by interested observers from union executives to university economists.

Why This Case Is Included

The U.S. Steel case offers the opportunity to explore the interrelationship between the forces of technology (plants and equipment), finance (profits and cash flow), and marketing (prices and sales volume). Involved also is the interplay between these internal technological and economic forces and external variables in the government sector (laws and government attitudes), in the macroeconomic sphere (international trade and inflation), and in the social system (public beliefs about government-business relations under free enterprise and public attitude toward the use of economic and political power).

Furthermore, this case offers the opportunity to work with much of the same data which serves as the basis for the factual arguments of the opposing parties. Not only is it possible to examine the validity of factual reasoning, but it is also possible to see how value judgments affect the perception of facts and weigh individual facts differentially in the arguments of the interested parties.

Finally, the issue is raised about the nature of corporate goals in the free enterprise system at this point in history. The case captures what may be a significant phase of the evolution of values and mores in society.

Diagnostic and Predictive Questions

In answering the following diagnostic and predictive questions, remember that these questions apply theories and conceptual ideas from certain disciplines. Such theories are valuable to understand basic forces at work in the policy system (diagnosis) and to predict what will happen in the system in the future (prediction). Since each reading abstracts from the total policy system certain factors or variables into the closed or partial viewpoint of one theory or discipline, no one reading gives answers to the practical policy problems of the case. In diagnosis and prediction, the parts of the problem are studied with "other things being equal."

Following each question are listed readings which will be helpful in answering the question. The readings included with this case are marked (*). By referring to the author index at the end of this book, you may locate the other readings listed.

1. From the standpoint of cash flow, what was the U.S. Steel management concerned about? Comment on the adequacy of internally generated funds for U.S. Steel's capital needs. Why does neither Mr. Blough nor Mr. Worthington speak of the feasibility of seeking funds from the capital markets?

> Read: *Summer, "Profit, Flow of Funds, and Depreciation." Anthony, *Management Accounting*, 290–92, 306.

2. Some competitors are making a better utilization of capacity than U.S. Steel and therefore should have lower average cost curves. How does this fact affect U.S. Steel's competitive position?

> Read: Spencer and Siegelman, *Managerial Economics*, pp. 242–48, 202–12. *Bright, "Are We Falling Behind in Mechanization?"

3. Judging from the theory of oligopoly, what predictions should the U.S. Steel management have made concerning the other steel producers' competitive reaction to the general price increase?

> Read: *Dean, *Managerial Economics*, pp. 429–31, 433–35.

4. Discuss the use made of productivity data by both Mr. Blough and the Kennedy Administration. What is the relationship among wages, productivity, and inflation?

> Read: *Clark, *Competition as a Dynamic Process*, pp. 442–54. *Sirkin, *Introduction to Macroeconomic Theory*, pp. 169–72.

5. Comment on the legitimacy of the power used in this case. It may be helpful to examine the ways in which the Kennedy Administration used power to influence the decision of U.S. Steel management and to think over why the President of the United States did not directly order U.S. Steel not to raise prices.

> Read: *Drucker, *The Future of Industrial Man*, pp. 32–38. Clark, *Alternative to Serfdom*, pp. 4–7. Simon *et al.*, *Public Administration*, pp. 182, 189–200. O'Donnell, "The Source of Managerial Authority."

6. What does Mr. Blough (or Mr. Worthington) view as the major goals of the United States Steel Corporation? What does President Kennedy view as the major goals of the corporation? Do the actions of each coincide with the above positions? Is there a gap between the Blough-Worthington position and the Kennedy position?

> Read: *Hayek, "The Corporation in a Democratic Society: In Whose Interest Ought It and Will It Be Run?" Berle, *The 20th Century Capitalistic Revolution*, pp. 164–69, 171–73, 182–88. Smith, *The Wealth of Nations*, pp. 423, 508. Eells and Walton, *Conceptual Foundations of Business*, pp. 185–87, 149–69, 458–75.

Policy Questions for This Specific Case

In answering the following policy questions, the results of diagnosis and prediction are used to reduce the amount of guesswork, or judgment, in designing action solutions. However, since certain parts of the total case situation cannot be reduced to science, and since "other things are not equal," judgment must still be used to fill in the factors not accounted for by readings. You will also need a second kind of judgment as you put value weights on different scientific predictions, since different theories may point to conflicting solutions.

7. Assess the alternative(s) U.S. Steel had for increasing its cash flow or gaining capital for modernization. As a member of U.S. Steel's top management, would you have favored an alternative method? Why? Or, why not?

8. Make a list of the factors you would have weighed in making the decision about prices had you been Mr. Blough. As the U.S. Steel chief executive, can you simultaneously meet all these decision criteria?

Read: Miller and Starr, *Executive Decisions and Operations Research*, pp. 38–42, 45–47, 50.

9. Given reasonable predictions (from Question 3 above) of the behavior of interested parties outside U.S. Steel, based on your analysis of the case facts, what strategies would you have used as the chief corporate executive to prepare the way for a general price increase?

Major Policy Issues: Tentative Generalizations about Any Policy System

In arriving at conclusions for the following questions, generalize from the facts in the case and use your own ideas to (a) confirm, (b) modify, or (c) test the workability of the concepts and theories from readings. As an executive or professional, use wisdom to merge theory, on the one hand, with "brute facts" and practice, on the other.

10. Judging from the actions and reactions in the U.S. Steel case, do you see the emergence of a new adjustive mechanism in those areas of government-business relations where specific laws are lacking and rights are ill-defined and/or in conflict? Do you attach any special significance to the prompt action of both parties in projecting the conflict into the public forum and their alleged attempts at "managing" public opinion? "The Kennedy Administration has formed, not followed public opinion." Comment.

Read: *Boulding, *The Image*, pp. 102–4, 109. *Hayakawa, *Language in Thought and Action*, pp. 78–79.

11. In what sense is it true that "the corporation is an instrument of national foreign policy"? Is there something more than an economic pressure on U.S. Steel for technological modernization because the United States is engaged in an international struggle of economic systems? (Recall from the case facts that the international position of American steel producers is deteriorating compared to some low cost foreign producers.) Do corporate goals take on any different character because of this international situation?

Read: *Bright citation from Question 2, and from Question 6 citations by Hayek, Berle, and Eells and Walton.

Questions for Original Student Work in Analysis and Policy

The methods of viewing this case as represented by the authors' questions and selection of readings are not exhaustive. There are other relevant ideas for diagnosis and prediction. Furthermore, there are other ways of stating policy questions. More powerful analyses and wiser solutions will result by drawing on your own training and experience for (a) relevant concepts and theories, and (b) creative ways of asking policy questions. The following questions are designed to help you acquire this skill.

12. While reflection on case facts, what additional theories from prior education give you insights as to "what is going on" in United States Steel? As to what might be predicted to happen in the future?

13. Other than the policy questions asked by the authors, what pragmatic ways can you think of to state the practical problems faced by executives in the case?

II United States Steel Corporation*

On Tuesday, April 10, 1962, Leslie Worthington, president of United States Steel Corporation, announced an increase of 3.5%, or $6.00 a ton, for finished steel (Exhibit 1). The corporation's chairman, Roger Blough, called at the White House that same afternoon to report this to the President of the United States. During the following three days, there were strong reactions from officials of the United States government, and a statement from another steel company, Inland, that it would not raise its price. Subsequently, on Friday, April 13, U.S. Steel rescinded the increase. This case deals with the details of actions and arguments on both sides of the issue.

Position of United States Steel in the Industry

The steel industry in the United States is made up of 22 integrated steelmakers, 60 semi-integrated producers, and over 150 nonintegrated producers. The top 15 companies rank as follows in terms of steel ingot capacity:

	Percent
U.S. Steel	28.4
Bethlehem	15.6
Republic	8.6
Jones & Laughlin	5.5
National	4.7
Youngstown	4.6
Armco	4.6
Inland	4.4
Colorado Fuel & Iron	2.0
Kaiser	2.0
McLouth	1.7
Wheeling	1.6
Sharon	1.3
Pittsburgh	1.1
Granite City	1.1

* Copyright 1964 by the Graduate School of Business, Columbia University.

These producers own approximately 85% of the iron ore reserves, 88% of the blast furnace capacity, 84% of the ingot and "steel for casting" capacity, and 81% of the finished hot-rolled capacity.

U.S. Steel's share in the industry has declined since 1900. Early in the century U.S. Steel accounted for about 65% of the steel output, in the late twenties about 40%, and in 1962 about 26%.

The steel industry's significance in the United States economy can be gauged from its direct employment of 569,000 people in producing one quarter of the world's output—a 14 billion dollar annual sales volume.

Historically, the steel industry has followed the lead of U.S. Steel in adjusting prices. That is, when U.S. Steel raised or lowered its price, all other companies usually followed suit. While some economists and others believed this to be oligopoly, or even unreasonable restraint of trade, the companies have defended their actions on the ground that such behavior is really highly competitive—that in order to compete for volume and profit no company could go against the major industry leaders.

Historical Review of Wages, Prices, and Profits

For some years, United States Steel Corporation has bargained with the United Steel Workers in labor contract sessions which, in fact, has resulted in increasing wages for steelworkers. Further, the company has increased the price of finished steel. Particularly since World War II, the price of steel has risen steadily and so have average hourly wage rates (Exhibit 2).

In increasing the price of steel, company management has cited as major reasons the profit squeeze, occasioned by increasing costs of labor and materials, on the one hand, and the given revenues level (price × volume) at the time of the increase in cost of resource inputs.

Steel executives, labor leaders, and government officials have all gone on record that inflation is bad for the stability and growth of the national economy. They disagree, however, as to whether (1) price increases (inflation) are caused by increasing wage demands (labor causes inflation); or (2) whether price increases by large industries necessitate increased wages to maintain purchasing power (corporations' profits cause inflation); or (3) whether this is a "chicken and egg" agrument—both cause each other.

The succession of union contracts since 1940 produced an average annual increase in hourly employment costs of about 8%. That pattern was broken with the settlement after the 1959 strike, which provided for a 3.5% to 3.75% increase. The contract signed on April 6, 1962 calls for slightly less than a 3% increase.

Privately, executives in the steel industry have stated opinions that the national government has put more pressure on steel companies to absorb added labor costs than it put on labor unions to forego added wages.

Spokesmen for American Industry have also pointed out that the government "sides with the unions because of the number of votes they have, and their political influence, rather than letting free economic laws of supply and demand set prices and wages." The union response to this has been that the government can see the facts—that steel company profits are large enough to sustain increased wages without raising prices.

In 1961, government officials again showed interest in the pricing of steel. The 1960 contract between U.S. Steel and the United Steel Workers called for a final increase in wages, to be granted in October, 1961. On September 6, the President of the United States wrote a letter to leading steel executives formally requesting them to forego any price increase. Mr. Blough, speaking for U.S. Steel, replied on September 13 (Exhibit 3).

In January 1962 the Council of Economic Advisors (to the President of the United States) made public certain "guideposts" which the Administration advocated for wage and price increases in the economy. These guides have been explained arithmetically as follows:

Take for example a company with sales—that is, income—of $100,000 a year. Say that 70 per cent, or $70,000 of it goes to pay labor—cash wages and fringe benefits. If the company raises its productivity by 3 per cent, by adopting more efficient methods or by installing more efficient machinery, the same number of hours will produce 3 per cent more—$103,000, or an increase of $3,000. A 3 per cent increase in the workers' compensation would be $2,100—that is, 3 per cent of $70,000. The $2,100 is only part, albeit the major part, of the full $3,000 realized from the increased productivity. The other $900 is a 3 per cent for the non-labor slice of the company's income. Both slices, labor and non-labor, have realized a 3 per cent gain with no increase in prices. Their relative share of the whole pie—70 per cent and 30 per cent—remains the same.[1]

Even though the government and the steel industry have used different base years from which to compare data, and support their arguments, Exhibits 2 and 4 to 8 summarize all data. Any person studying this case may, therefore, draw his own conclusions about how the various arguments relate to the financial and operating "facts."

Company Reaction to Productivity Guideposts

Mr. Robert C. Tyson, chairman of the finance committee of U.S. Steel, spoke for the corporation about tying wage increases to productivity (output per man-hour) in the corporation's annual report for 1961. He criticized such a formula on three counts:

First, "dependable productivity measurements for firms and industries are unavailable." Second, too often people "use and abuse output per man hour data on the pretense that they are productivity measurements. A firm may purchase costly equipment and thereby secure more output per man hour. But

---

[1] Richard E. Mooney, "Productivity Key to U.S. Formula," *New York Times,* May 7, 1962.

to call it a true productivity increase is erroneous, for the calculation leaves out the man hours required to build the equipment and the costs of acquiring and having it. True productivity increases are thus virtually always much less than output per man hour increases." Third, "one can pick a recent short period of high level operations and compare the output per man hour with one in a prior period of low level operations, as in 1958, for example. In that fashion a big increase in productivity can, however falsely, be claimed. An honest indication of the trend in output per man hour—but not true productivity—can be obtained by fitting a trend line to the data for a substantial number of years. Such a trend line fitted to the steel industry data has an increase from 1940 to 1961 equivalent to 1.7 per cent per annum compounded."

Although productivity was the key to the "guidepost" doctrine espoused by the government for noninflationary wage-price policies, U.S. Steel did not officially reject government overtures to bring management and labor together for an early, noninflationary agreement in the public interest. When, in January 1962, the Council of Economic Advisors published the "guidepost" doctrine, it was the union leadership rather than U.S. Steel who objected to its applicability to the union contract negotiations.

Union-Management Negotiations and Settlement

On February 6, 1962 the Secretary of Labor, Mr. Goldberg, urged the United Steel Workers and the steel companies to start negotiations as soon as possible for a new contract to be effective July 1. Negotiations began on February 14, broke down on March 3, and resumed again on March 14 due to heavy influence (and implicit threat of more direct intervention) on the part of the government. On April 6, U.S. Steel signed an agreement with the union for a 10 cents per hour increase in fringe benefits. The President of the United States described the contract as "noninflationary" and urged that both sides use restraint in wages and prices so that the economy would remain stable, and competitive with foreign companies who produce and sell steel cheaper than American companies. By Tuesday, April 10, the last of the major steel companies had signed labor contracts, comparable in fringe benefit increase (10 cents) to U.S. Steel.

The Price Increase

In mid-afternoon on April 10, President Kennedy learned that Mr. Blough had asked for a 5:45 appointment that day because he had something "important" to say about the steel industry. At the White House, he stated that the executive committee of U.S. Steel had unanimously voted to raise the price of steel. He handed the President the announcement shown as Exhibit 1, which was simultaneously being released to the press by the corporation.

Inadequate Depreciation Allowance

Between 1939 and 1956 U.S. Steel incurred a depreciation deficiency of $904 million. That is, by using depreciation methods allowable within the existing Internal Revenue Code, U.S. Steel had to expand almost a billion dollars more on plant and equipment than it recovered from depreciation allowances. U.S. Steel insists that inflated prices in capital equipment and construction make it unrealistic to base depreciation allowances on original cost. Steel spokemen point to the policy on inventory accounting which allows a consideration for price inflation. In the 1961 annual report, Roger M. Blough, Steel's chairman, said: "The $326.8 million of property expenditures compares with wear and exhaustion of $210.5 million for the year. (See Exhibit 6.) This latter amount was inadequate to recover the buying power originally expended for facilities used up during the year."

Competitive Pressures

Some of the smaller domestic producers like Inland and Kaiser have about the same profit margin on sales as U.S. Steel, but they enjoy higher returns on equity chiefly because they have newer facilities and their capital commitment to backward integration is not as great as U.S. Steel's. Substitute products like plastic, glass, cement, and nonferrous metals continue to make a strong bid for steel markets. Foreign competition, too, has been stiffening. Since 1958 the United States has been a net importer on a quantity (ton) basis (see Exhibit 7). The United States exports chiefly high-quality steel, so on a dollar value basis we remain a net exporter.

The competitive pressures served as a two-edged sword for U.S. Steel. Such pressures stimulated the need for modern competitive machinery and plants, and hence contributed to the motivation for the price increase. However, management states that domestic and foreign competition prevented U.S. Steel from making a price adjustment comparable to the 6% cost increase from 1958 to 1962. The controversial price increase was held to 3.5%.

Need for Investment Capital

Given the profit squeeze between rising production costs, the steady price, and the deficiency of depreciation allowances, U.S. Steel found cause for the $6.00 a ton price increase. The internal generation of funds was proving inadequate for maintenance of competitive facilities. "Behind our inability to meet low wage competition from other lands through the advanced technology and improved productive efficiency which was once our course of action lies a dwindling supply of investment capital. And behind that lies the squeeze on profits." In reporting the earnings for the first quarter of 1962, U.S. Steel officials indicated that income equaled the declared dividend and a pro rata share of the year's debt repayment, leaving no margin for reinvestment in the business.

Responsibility to Shareholders

U.S. Steel also pointed to its responsibility to those who had invested in the company, some 325,000 shareholders. While the dividend had not been changed for five years, the employees' position had been bettered seven times by wage or fringe-benefit increases since 1957.

"Cost Push" Rather Than "Profit Pull" Inflation

The Administration viewed the steel industry as the bellwether of the economy. It feared psychological as well as direct inflationary pressures from a steel price increase. U.S. Steel countered with: ". . . where inflation is concerned, the price of steel is a symptom of the problem and not a bellwether cause. Simon Whitney, the Director of the Bureau of Economics, Federal Trade Commission, said in 1959: 'Over the long run any psychological impact attached to steel will hardly give it more weight in the gross national product than the dollar figures show. I believe that there is as much or more truth in viewing steel wages as the pace setter for other industries.' " The historic inflationary influence of steel prices remains an academically moot point after two studies independently made in 1959–60. One report by Otto Eckstein and Garry Fromm maintained: "The impact of the increase of steel prices on other industrial prices is large. If steel prices had behaved like other industrial prices, the rise in the total wholesale price index would have been 40 per cent less over the past decade. . . ." (See Exhibit 4.) The second report by E. Robert Livernash says: ". . . the independent influence of steel prices on inflation has been modest in the post-war period. . . . The price behavior of steel-using industries seems to have been dominated more by the demand for particular final products than the rise in steel prices by themselves."

No Broken Promises

U.S. Steel's chief concern with the matter of timing was the "misunderstanding" that U.S. Steel had made any hold-the-line commitments in the contract negotiations which ended on April 6. "No assurances were asked and none were given regarding price action. . . ."

Government Reactions

Within an hour after Mr. Blough's visit on Tuesday, President Kennedy had assembled in his office: Secretary of Labor Goldberg, Economic Advisors Walter Heller and Kermit Gordon, White House Special Counsel, Theodore Sorensen, Assistant Press Secretary, Andrew Hatcher, and

Appointment Secretary Kenneth O'Donnell. A remark was made by the President and gave the tenor to the activity to follow: "My father always told me that all businessmen were sons of bitches but I never believed it till now." Initial plans took two courses. First, the economists together with the Labor Department were to analyze the economic justification for the price increase. Second, a formal response was to be prepared for the President's scheduled press conference at 3:30 P.M. Wednesday. Early in the evening, the President discussed U.S. Steel's action by phone with Attorney General Robert Kennedy, Secretary of Defense Robert Mc-Namara, Secretary of the Treasury Douglas Dillon, and Senator Estes Kefauver, chairman of the Senate Anti-trust Subcommittee.

During an hour and forty-five-minute breakfast Wednesday morning, advisors briefed the President about the results of the night's work. Key among the conclusions was the following from the Bureau of Labor Statistics: "While employment costs per hour of all wage and salaried employees in the basic iron and steel industry rose from 1958 to 1961, there was an equivalent increase in output per man-hour. As a result, employment costs per unit of steel output in 1961 was essentially the same as in 1958." During the morning the President phoned Secretary Dillon to discuss the Treasury's work on tax write-offs on expenditures for new plant and equipment in the light of Steel's action. A phone call from the President to Commerce Secretary Luther Hodges prompted the latter to spend most of the day in phone conversations with businessmen throughout the nation. To the utterances of "unjustified," "shocking," "arrogant," "irresponsible," "an affront to the President," made by Sena-tors Mike Mansfield and Hubert Humphrey and House Speaker John McCormack, Senator Albert Gore added the suggestion that a law be enacted to empower the courts to prohibit price increases in basic in-dustries such as steel until there had been "a cooling-off period." Both the House and the Senate Anti-trust Subcommittees scheduled broad investigations of the steel industry.

Action by Other Steel Companies

As the President prepared for his 3:30 press conference, members of the steel industry's big twelve began to follow the pricing pattern set by U.S. Steel just hours before. Bethlehem Steel announced its increase be-fore noon, and Republic, Jones & Laughlin, Youngstown, and Wheeling soon followed. In what has been called a scathing rebuke to the industry, President Kennedy said: "The simultaneous and identical actions of U.S. Steel and other leading corporations increasing steel prices by some $6.00 a ton constitute a wholly unjustifiable and irresponsible defiance of the public interest. . . . Some time ago I asked each American what he would do for his country and I asked the steel companies. In the last 24 hours we had their answer."

Further Government Response to the Steel Industry Action

By late Wednesday afternoon the governmental activity was channeled in three additional areas. First, besides the antitrust investigations promised by both the House and Senate, the Federal Trade Commission and the Justice Department started into action. The former, through its chairman, Paul Rand Dixon, announced at 6:00 P.M. that it was informally investigating to determine whether the steel companies had violated a consent decree of June 15, 1951, which bound the industry to refrain from collusive price fixing or maintaining identical delivered prices. At the same time that evening, the Justice Department ordered the Federal Bureau of Investigation to determine if a statement attributed to Edmund Martin, Bethlehem Steel's president, was an accurate quotation. The statement, supposedly made at a stockholders' meeting on the morning of the previous day, indicated that Mr. Martin opposed a price increase. If such were the case, the government planned to use the statement as evidence to the undue influnce of U.S. Steel over industry pricing.

The second avenue of governmental activity was an attempt to arrest the dynamics of U.S. Steel's price leadership. Influenced by the Council of Economic Advisors, the President directed an effort at keeping some of the holdouts (Armco, Inland, Kaiser, Colorado Fuel and Iron, McLouth, and Allegheny-Ludlum) from joining in the price hike. These companies represented some 15% of the industry capacity. Inland Steel was singled out for special contact because it was a highly efficient producer and it had a long history of public service. Significantly, Inland was operating at about 80% of capacity—variously estimated to be 10% to 25% better than U.S. Steel's position. Three calls were made on Wednesday from Washington officials to Inland executives: Under-Secretary of Commerce Edward Gudeman to Inland's Vice-Chairman Philip D. Block, Jr.; Under-Secretary of the Treasury Henry Fowler to Inland's President, John F. Smith, Jr.; Secretary Goldberg to Inland's Vice-President for Purchasing, Leigh B. Block. Calls also went out to Armco, Kaiser, and Allegheny-Ludlum officials from friends and former associates in the Kennedy Administration. The President himself called Edgar Kaiser, chairman of Kaiser Steel.

The third form of government activity was directed at producing pressure on the steel companies from local governmental officials and from influential business figures. The Democratic National Committee called many Democratic governors to elicit public statements supporting the President and to ask them to request steel producers in their states to hold the line. Under-Secretary of the Treasury Robert V. Rocca had a telephone discussion with Henry Alexander, chairman of Morgan Guaranty Trust in New York. (Morgan's senior vice-president sits on the board of U.S. Steel.)

Thursday, April 12

In predawn calls and visits, the F.B.I. attempted to get the facts on the statement attributed to Bethlehem's president. The investigators roused and questioned reporters who had covered the stockholders' meeting on Tuesday. The inquiries supported Mr. Martin's earlier claim that he had been misquoted.

At an early White House session it was decided that Commerce Secretary Hodges should rebut Mr. Roger Blough's planned news conference that afternoon. Mr. Blough was to address the T.V. audience at 3:30 and Mr. Hodges at 5:00. Before the news conference, U.S. Steel gained support when two other corporations, National Steel and Pittsburgh Steel—fifth and fourteenth producers in terms of size—raised their price $6.00 a ton.

In his televised remarks, Mr. Blough reaffirmed the justification outlined above. In answer to a question about what would happen if the hold-the-line companies persisted, Mr. Blough said: "It would definitely affect us and I don't know how much longer we could maintain our position."

Secretary Hodges' televised rebuttal began with a sharp criticism of Mr. Blough's defense of the price increase. Mr. Blough, he said, mentioned the rise in labor costs over the last few years, ". . . but did not mention the corresponding rise in productivity." Mr. Hodges continued: "I do not enjoy criticizing a major American industry. I am a confirmed supporter of our free enterprise system. I do not want to see any encroachment by government on private decision making which can be avoided. But I think there is clear responsibility for the Federal Government to speak out when private actions are taken which may well jeopardize the continuation of a healthy free enterprise system. This goes for irresponsible action which may be taken by labor, by industry, or by any other segment.

"Despite the provocation by the leading steel companies I call upon American industry generally to do everything possible to hold the price level. Our economic recovery requires it; our international balance of payment situation requires it; our future economic growth and prosperity require it."

Mr. Hodges said that although he was sure that both President Kennedy and Mr. Blough were completely accurate in saying that no promise not to raise prices had been asked or given during the steel-labor union negotiations, he felt that one was implied. "I believe the President felt that the price line would be held if wage costs did not rise," he said. The public also had that impression, he said.

Mr. Hodges added a final note about some of the companies who joined U.S. Steel in the price increase. He pointed out that profits cited by U.S. Steel do not apply to several of the smaller companies.

The day was not over yet. Mr. Blough received a telegram from two

Pennsylvania Republicans—Representative William Scranton, candidate for Governor, and James VanZandt, candidate for Senator. Republican sentiment up to this time had been relatively noncommittal. The wire read: "The increase at this time is wrong—wrong for Pennsylvania, wrong for America, wrong for the free world. The increase surely will set off another round of inflation. It will hurt people most who can least afford to be hurt."

The government's final actions of the day were to subpoena documents concerning the price increase from the headquarters of U.S. Steel and the other companies who had followed suit and to announce that the Justice Department had ordered a Grand Jury investigation of the price increase.

Friday the 13th

Unknown to the government and the rest of the business community, Inland Steel officials had decided on Thursday afternoon to hold the line. A board meeting had been called for Friday morning to ratify the decision. First word of the hold-the-line policy came from Inland's board chairman who was traveling in Japan: "We do not feel that an advance in steel prices at this time would be in the national interest." Washington got the official word shortly after 10:00 A.M., but activity continued on four fronts.

First, Solicitor General Archibald Cox met with Mr. Sorensen and representatives of the Treasury, Commerce, and Labor Departments, the Budget Bureau, and the Council of Economic Advisors to discuss emergency wage-price legislation. Second, Secretary McNamara announced at 11:45 A.M. that the Defense Department had ordered defense contractors to shift steel purchases to companies that had not raised prices. (Later in the day, Lukens Steel, a holdout producer, received a 5 million dollar contract for special armor plate for Polaris-missile submarines.) Secretary McNamara also said: "I have noted that while iron and steel prices have increased by 90% since 1947, the prices of non-ferrous metals have increased by only 40%. Therefore we are particularly studying the possibility for replacement of steel by other materials including the potential of increased research and development in this area." Third, at 12:15 President Kennedy and those who advised him on the steel issue met to assess the situation. Inland had announced. Armco had decided to hold out but not announce. Kaiser's announcement to hold the line came while the meeting was on. It was estimated that some 16% of the industry's capacity was holding the line. Further personal contact with the holdouts was ordered as lists of directors were distributed to the officials present. Fourth, behind-the-scenes negotiations between government representatives and U.S. Steel executives stepped up as Secretary Goldberg flew to New York, with a Washington lawyer, Clark Clifford, acting as intermediary, for a secret meeting with Mr. Blough. At 3:30 that afternoon both Mr. Blough and Mr. Goldberg received the same news from separate phone calls—Bethlehem Steel had rescinded its price increase! Government officials surmised that competitive pressure especially from the firm positions of Inland and Kaiser prompted Bethlehem's action. Certainly, the Administration centered no special effort on moving Bethlehem's officers or directors.

Scarcely two hours later, without calling together the executive committee which had made the original decision, U.S. Steel's officers rescinded the price increase. In announcing the decision, U.S. Steel President Leslie Worthington said: "The price decision was made in the light of the competitive developments today and all other current circumstances in the removal of a serious obstacle to proper relations between Government and business." The rest of the price-rise followers quickly followed suit.

Union Reaction

David McDonald, head of the United Steel Workers reacted quite moderately. "I am surprised, troubled and concerned by the announcement of U.S. Steel that steel prices are being increased by $6.00 per ton. The Steel Workers Union has never bargained with the steel companies about prices and it did not do so this year. The decision of U.S. Steel is its own, not ours. . . . I am troubled by U.S. Steel's attempt to place the blame for this price increase upon the settlements which have been made in the past by the United Steel Workers. The fact is that since 1958, the date of the industry's last price increase, the labor cost of producing a ton of steel has gone down, not up, despite the increase in wages and other benefits. . . ."

Walter Reuther, president of the United Auto Workers, characterized the price increase as "a sneak attack on price stability." In a letter to President Kennedy he proposed "an administered price board" to which price leaders in major industries would be required to give advance notice of proposed rises. They would have to produce all pertinent facts and records at a public hearing at which a consumer counsel represented the public. Once the hearings had been held and the findings of fact made public, the companies could pursue their course of action freely. Mr. Reuther also proposed that the union be required to defend its economic collective bargaining demands in the same public hearings if a corporation held that the demands would require a price increase.

The Stock Market

There were statements that the Administration's action depressed the stock market by "raising the specter of administered pricing and putting in doubt the future of the free enterprise system." The stock market had been trending lower for some time before the price increase attempt. However, when a definite break appeared on May 28, and over $20 billion in values were wiped out, many businessmen assigned much of the blame to the Administration's action in the Steel dispute. On the following day a *New York World Telegram & Sun* editorial said: "If the stock market reflects anything, it reflects volatile human emotions—the desire for gain, the fear of loss. Both are conducive to bandwagon psychology—and that seems to be what we are witnessing now. The two most common explanations are (1) that it's a basic correction of long-bloated valuations and (2) that President Kennedy started the downturn by causing the steel price rollback and 'making profit a dirty word.' These two explanations seem the opposite sides of the same coin. If investors, especially those in quest of a quick profit, feel that the inflationary picnic is about over, that could produce a wave of selling—and, like most reactions, it would end up by going too far. . . ."

Reaction from Other Quarters

The government victory left it unclear what mechanism business should use in seeking a price adjustment and how to submit proposals or appeal government vetoes. One letter to the *New York Times* stated:

. . . In a constitutional democracy even "the greatest good for the greatest number" does not justify the use of governmental power to achieve political and economic ends of a president if those aims are attained at a price which surrenders political freedoms for elusive economic freedoms. President Kennedy should not forget that millions of our citizens have serious doubts as to the means which the Government used to attain what might otherwise be a desirable end.

The following remark of Yale Law Professor, Charles A. Reich, in *New Republic* is similar:

Such use of power, whether its objectives are good or bad, is dangerous.

In a letter to the *New York Times* by H. B. Malmgren, an Economics Professor at Cornell, provides a commentary on some of the economic issues raised in the Steel dispute:

One of the arguments used by the steel companies to justify the need for higher prices was that higher profits were needed for capital improvement and modernization. Many newspapers and broadcasters took up this argument without criticism. Indeed, in one case a newspaper editorial suggested that if consumers were prepared to pay the higher price, this was the "true market test."

It ought to be clear that this is an invalid argument to anyone who takes the position that competition is the most efficient kind of arrangement in a market economy. The conventional attitude is that the "true market test" is borrowing from the capital market.

Self financing through undistributed profits is definitely a means of avoiding the market test. If the capital market is too expensive, or the capital is not forthcoming to a particular firm, this has always been taken as a sign that the prospects in that firm were not as attractive as in other firms, or that capital expansion has proceeded too far to justify further investment.

While we may perhaps feel that self-financing is important for other reasons, we cannot, nor can the steel companies, suggest that this is a competitive measure which is subject to a "market test." In fact, many economists would take it as a sign of monopoly power.

The range of public sentiment is also indicated in the following excerpts from editorials in the *New York Times* and the *Wall Street Journal:*

The forces of our democracy scored a dramatic triumph last week when the major steel companies bowed to the storm of both governmental and public protest and rescinded the price increases they had decreed. The industry's turn-about is a spectacular victory for President Kennedy. In words reminiscent of other fighting Presidents, he denounced a "tiny handful of steel executives" for what he called "irresponsible defiance of public interest" and set the governmental machinery in motion to bring them to terms. But the turn-about is also a victory of the self-regulatory forces of our free enterprise system. United States Steel acknowledged that "competitive developments" were not as potent in compelling the reversal as a desire for "removal of a serious obstacle to proper relations between Government and Business."

. . . Lack of adequate capital investment is the main reason why our economic growth rate lags behind that of most European countries. But capital investment depends on industrial profits that alone can enable industry to raise the money for new equipment. If profits are squeezed to death between higher wages and taxes and low prices, industry languishes and unemployment is the result.[2]

What was really at issue here, and still is, is whether the price of steel is to be determined by the constant bargaining in the market place between the makers and buyers of steel; you may be sure that if the makers guessed wrong the market would promptly change their decision. Or whether the price of steel is to be decided and then enforced by the Government. In short, the issue is whether we have a free market system or whether we do not. That, and nothing more.

Thus the true "crime" of this company was that it did not get permission from the Government and that its attempted asking price did not suit the ideas of a tiny handful of men around the White House.

It was for this that last week we saw the President of the United States in a fury, a public pillorying of an industry, threatened reprisals against all business, the spectacle of a private citizen helplessly trying to defend himself against unnamed accusations, the knock of policemen on the midnight door. And there was hardly a voice heard rising above the clamor to ask what it was all about.

If we had not seen it with our eyes and heard it with our own ears, we would not have been able to believe that in America it actually happened.[3]

Later Reaction by U. S. Steel

Just as U.S. Steel's president, Leslie Worthington, had done in announcing that his company was rescinding the price increase, Chairman Roger Blough insisted that the reversal was brought about by competitive pressures, not the action of the Administration.

At U.S. Steel's annual stockholders' meeting on May 7, Mr. Blough appealed for better mutual understanding by business and government of

---

[2] *New York Times,* April 15, 1962.

[3] *Wall Street Journal,* April 16, 1962.

each other's needs in the national interest. He defended the price increase in the following words: ". . . it would appear that a rise of 3.5 per cent . . . in the price of steel somehow constitutes an intolerable threat to the security and economic welfare of this nation with all the strength and vigor it possesses. This concept is as incomprehensible to me as the belief that government can ever serve the national interest in peacetime by seeking to control prices in competitive American business, directly or indirectly, through force of law or otherwise."

On June 4, Mr. Blough said: ". . . the Administration's uncertain attitude toward profits is a cause of grave concern. . . . There may be some justification for guidelines as a part of our mutual process of education but if they are preludes to direct controls, how can they be justified?"

Later Reaction by the Administration

At a press conference on April 18 President Kennedy insisted: "The Administration is not setting wages or prices." Two weeks later in addressing the Chamber of Commerce he disclaimed any appetite for "the added burden of determining individual prices." On May 9, in speaking to the U.A.W. convention, the President repeated: "This Administration has not undertaken and will not undertake to fix prices and wages in this economy."

On this same occasion the President commented on the current concern over the profit squeeze:

When they talk about the profit squeeze, it has been because we've been operating in basic industries at 60, 70, or 75 per cent of capacity—in the steel industry as low as 38 to 40 per cent. No wonder there has been under those conditions a squeeze on employment . . . and on the ability to build up capital for reinvestment. And there can be no increase in sales abroad and at home unless our prices and costs are competitive as a result of plant investment and modernization and increased productivity in a prosperous economy leading towards full employment. [See Exhibit 8.]

Exhibit 1

UNITED STATES STEEL CORPORATION

PUBLIC RELATIONS DEPARTMENT
71 BROADWAY, NEW YORK 6, N.Y.

TELEPHONE
DI 4–9000

NIGHT TELEPHONE
DI 4–9054

FOR A.M. PAPERS
WEDNESDAY, APRIL 11, 1962

Pittsburgh, Pa., April 10—For the first time in nearly four years, United States Steel today announced an increase in the general level of its steel prices. This "catch-up" adjustment, effective at 12:01 A.M. tomorrow, will raise the price of

Exhibit 1—Continued

the company's steel products by an average of about 3.5 per cent—or three-tenths of a cent per pound.*

In announcing the new prices Leslie B. Worthington, President, said:

"Since our last over-all adjustment in the summer of 1958, the level of steel prices has not been increased but, if anything, has declined somewhat. This situation, in the face of steadily mounting production costs which have included four increases in steel worker wages and benefits prior to the end of last year, has been due to the competitive pressures from domestic producers and from imports of foreign-made steel as well as from other materials which are used as substitutes for steel.

"The severity of these competitive pressures has not diminished; and to their influence may be attributed the fact that the partial catch-up adjustment announced today is substantially less than the cost increases which have already occurred since 1958, without taking into consideration the additional costs which will result from the new labor agreements which become effective next July 1.

"Nevertheless, taking into account all the competitive factors affecting the market for steel, we have reluctantly concluded that a modest price adjustment can no longer be avoided in the light of the production cost increases that have made it necessary.

* * * * *

"In the three years since the end of 1958, United States Steel has spent $1 billion 185 millions for modernization and replacement of facilities and for the development of new sources of raw materials. Internally, there were only two sources from which this money could come: depreciation and reinvested profit. Depreciation in these years amounted to $610 millions; and reinvested profit, $187 millions—or, together, only about two-thirds of the total sum required. So after using all the income available from operations, we had to make up the difference of $388 millions out of borrowings from the public. In fact, during the period 1958–1961, we have actually borrowed a total of $800 millions to provide for present and future needs. And this must be repaid out of profits that have not yet been earned, and will not be earned for some years to come.

"During these three years, moreover, U.S. Steel's profits have dropped to the lowest levels since 1952; while reinvested profit—which is all the profit there is to be plowed back into the business after payment of dividends—has declined from $115 millions in 1958 to less than $3 millions last year. Yet the dividend rate has not been increased in more than five years, although there have been seven general increases in employment costs during this interval.

"This squeeze which has thus dried up a major source of the funds necessary to improve the competitive efficiency of our plants and facilities, has resulted inevitably from the continual rise in costs over a period of almost four years, with no offsetting improvement in prices.

"Since the last general price adjustment in 1958, there have been a number of increases in the cost of products and services purchased by the Corporation, in state and local taxes, and in other expenses including interest on the money we have had to borrow—an item which has jumped from $11½ millions in 1958 to nearly $30 millions in 1961.

"And from 1958 through 1961, there have been industry-wide increases in steelworker wages and benefits on four occasions amounting to about 40 cents an hour, and also increases in employment costs for other employees. These

---

* On Thursday, April 12, U.S. Steel clarified the general price increase by announcing that the new prices applied only to the domestic market and not to exports.

Exhibit 1—Continued

persistent increases have added several hundred million dollars to the employment costs of U.S. Steel, without regard to future costs resulting from the new labor agreement just negotiated.

"In all, we have experienced a net increase of about 6 per cent in our costs over this period despite cost reductions which have been effected through the use of new, more efficient facilities, improved techniques and better raw materials. Compared with this net increase of 6 per cent, the price increase of 3½ per cent announced today clearly falls considerably short of the amount needed to restore even the cost-price relationship in the low production year of 1958.

"In reaching this conclusion, we have given full consideration, of course, to the fact that any price increase which comes, as this does, at a time when foreign-made steels are already underselling ours in a number of product lines, will add —temporarily, at least—to the competitive difficulties which we are now experiencing. But the present price level cannot be maintained any longer when our problems are viewed in long-range perspective. For the long pull a strong, profitable company is the only insurance that formidable competition can be met and that the necessary lower costs to meet that competition will be assured.

"Only through profits can a company improve its competitive potential through better equipment and through expanded research. On this latter phase we are constantly developing lighter, stronger steels which—ton for ton—will do more work and go much farther than the steels that were previously available on the market. They thus give the customer considerably more value per dollar of cost. As more and more of these new steels come from our laboratories, therefore, our ability to compete should steadily improve. But the development of new steels can only be supported by profits or the hope of profits.

"The financial resources supporting continuous research and resultant new products as well as those supporting new equipment, are therefore vital in this competitive situation—vital not alone to the company and its employees, but to our international balance of payments, the value of our dollar, and to the strength and security of the nation as well."

Exhibit 2

TOTAL EMPLOYMENT, COSTS, AND STEEL PRICES

U.S. STEEL INDUSTRY, 1940–61

Years	Average Number* Wage Earners	Average Hours† per Week	Average Hourly‡* Wage Costs	Index§ Output Man-Hour	Price Index‖ Total Steel Mill Products
1961	405,924	36.6	3.501	138.7**	101.7
1960	449,888	35.7	3.349	136.7	102.1
1959	399,738	36.9	3.417	141.9	102.2
1958	411,565	35.2	3.181	126.6	100.6
1957	508,434	37.2	2.917	128.9	97.2
1956	509,231	38.6	2.700	130.4	88.7
1955	519,145	39.2	2.509	129.4	81.8
1954	478,030	36.1	2.333	115.9	78.2
1953	544,325	39.4	2.267	118.8	74.7
1952	519,265	35.8	2.148	117.6	69.3
1951	540,365	40.2	1.945	113.0	67.8
1950	503,309	39.0	1.746	111.9	62.9
1949	491,615	34.5	1.703	102.8	59.7
1948	503,351	39.1	1.629	100.4	55.1

Exhibit 2—Continued

Years	Average Number* Wage Earners	Average Hours† per Week	Average Hourly‡* Wage Costs	Index§ Output Man-Hour	Price Index‖ Total Steel Mill Products
1947	489,138	38.6	1.513	100.0	48.2
1946	458,259	35.0	1.354	NA	41.2
1945	438,825	44.1	1.257	NA	37.9
1944	456,682	46.6	1.228	NA	37.0
1943	487,187	42.9	1.140	NA	37.0
1942	511,414	38.9	1.063	NA	36.9
1941	507,306	38.5	.962	87.2	36.9
1940	453,990	36.1	.855	82.3	36.7

° Wage employees engaged in production and sale of iron and steel products. Source: Iron and Steel Institute.
† Production worker hours paid. Source: Department of Labor.
‡ Does not include other employment costs such as social security, pensions, and insurance.
§ Index (1947 = 100). Basic Steel Industry. Source: Department of Labor.
‖ Index (1957–59 = 100). Source: U.S. Department of Commerce.
°° Not completely comparable with series because of change in industry definition. Discrepancy is, however, slight.
NA = not available.

Exhibit 3

TEXT OF BLOUGH'S LETTER TO THE PRESIDENT

DEAR MR. PRESIDENT:

May I respectfully acknowledge receipt of your letter of Sept. 6 in which you express concern regarding inflation and steel wage and price movements.

I am certain, Mr. President, that your concern regarding inflation is shared by every thinking American who has experienced its serious effects during the past twenty years. And although we in United States Steel cannot forecast the future trend of prices in any segment of the steel industry and have no definite conclusions regarding our own course during the foreseeable future, nevertheless it should be useful to put some of the information referred to in your letter in proper cause-and-effect perspective. Moreover, your letter does raise questions of such serious import, including the future of freedom in marketing, that I feel impelled to include a word on that score also, for whatever value it may be.

First, let me assure you that if you seek the cause of inflation in the United States, past, present or future, you will not find them in the levels of steel prices or steel profits.

The facts, as developed by the American Iron and Steel Institute, are that from 1940 through 1960 steel prices rose 174 per cent, but the industry's hourly employment costs rose 322 per cent, or nearly twice as much. I use 1940 as a starting point rather than 1947 because during the war-affected years of 1940 through 1944 steel wages rose substantially as did the level of wholesale prices; but steel prices increased not at all. Any comparison of these trends which starts with post-war 1947 as a base, therefore, obscures, rather than reveals the realities which the steel companies have had to face through this entire period of inflation.

RISE IN COSTS CITED

In dollars and cents, wage-earner employment costs per hour worked increased from 90½ cents in 1940 to $3.82 in 1960 and far exceeded any produc-

Exhibit 3—Continued

tivity gains that could be achieved, even though some $15,000,000,000 was invested in new and more efficient plant and equipment during this period. Shipments of steel per man hour worked (a measurement which overstates the gain in true productivity) improved by less than 40 per cent, in contrast to the 322 per cent rise in employment cost. Prices at higher competitive levels were the inevitable result.

Your letter speaks on the uncertainty in the amount of the employment cost increases which will occur at the end of this month, and which have sometimes been inaccurately reported elsewhere as being about 8 cents. While these costs will obviously vary somewhat among the several companies in the steel industry, the fact is that they will increase by about 13 cents per hour for wage earners; and beyond this the companies face the added cost of adjusting the pay of many thousands of their salaried employees. In the aggregate, therefore, industry employment costs alone will rise by more than $200,000,000 a year on Oct. 1.

So far as profits are concerned, your advisers have chosen to measure them in terms of the return on reported net worth; and again I am afraid that this does more to confuse than to clarify the issue in the light of the eroding effects of inflation on investments in steel-making facilities over the past twenty years. If we compare the 50-cent profit dollars of today to the 100-cent dollars that were invested in our business twenty years ago, the resulting profit ratio can hardly be said to have any validity.

To be meaningful, therefore, any such comparison must naturally be adjusted for the effects of inflation, and when this is done it will be found that in the case of United States Steel (the adjusted data for the industry are not available) the return on investment over the past ten years has averaged about 3 per cent and at its highest point was 5.1 per cent.

PERCENTAGE OF SALES

The most useful measurement of the profit trend in a single industry, over an inflationary period, is of course profit as a percentage of sales. On this basis, it will be noted . . . that profits in the steel industry have only once in the past twenty years equaled the 8 per cent level at which they stood in 1940, and have averaged only 6½ per cent in the past five years, thus demonstrating clearly that steel price increases during this period have not fully covered the rapid rise in total steel-making costs.

In this connection, it is interesting to note that following the steel strike which ended last year an official Government report was prepared for the Department of Labor by Prof. [Edward R.] Livernash of Harvard University. In this report, which analyzes the cost-price relationship in steel at length, Dr. Livernash concludes:

"Obviously, while price policy can be debated in the short run, in the long run all cost increases must be met. Steel has done no more than this."

Another point of caution which should be noted in any discussion of profits on an industry-wide basis is that the industry's profit rate is merely an average—and averages can be dangerously misleading. Some companies will earn more than the average, while some may be suffering losses which they cannot sustain indefinitely. So it was in 1960 that among the thirty largest steel companies the profit rate as a percentage of sales ranged from a plus 9.3 per cent to a loss of 5.2 per cent.

Whatever figures your advisers may elect to use, however, the simple fact is that the profit left in any company, after it pays all costs, is all that there is out of which to make up for the serious inadequacy in depreciation, to repay bor-

Exhibit 3—Continued

rowings, to pay dividends and to provide for added equipment. If the profit is not good enough to do these things, they cannot and will not be done; and that would not be in the national interest.

So reviewing the whole picture, I cannot quite see how steel profits could be responsible for inflation—especially when their portion of the sales dollar over the last twenty years has never exceeded 8 cents and is lower than that today.

HAZARDOUS TASK

As for the admittedly hazardous task which your economic advisers have undertaken in forecasting steel industry profits at varying rates of operation, let me respectfully underline the word hazardous. Moreover, it might reasonably appear to some—as, frankly, it does to me—that they seem to be assuming the role of informal price-setters for steel—psychological or otherwise. But if for steel, what then for automobiles, or rubber, or machinery or electrical products, or food, or paper, or chemicals—or a thousand other products? Do we thus head into unworkable, stifling peace-time controls of prices? Do we do this when the causes of inflation—in a highly competitive economy with ample industrial capacity such as ours—are clearly associated with the fiscal, monetary, labor and other policies of Government?

*   *   *   *   *

. . . [Y]our letter mentions foreign competition in steel and that, of course, is of serious concern to producers in our industry. Between 1952 and 1959, for a composite of eight nations which are our principal competitors in steel, the average hourly employment cost rose about 35 cents, compared with a rise of $1.48 in the United States. Overcoming this growing cost disadvantage is far from simple. Moreover, these employment costs at the end of 1959 averaged less than $1 per hour in those same nations, compared with $3.80 for us. These facts go a long way toward explaining why we are less competitive abroad than we were.

LETTER IS QUOTED

I am glad your letter, along with emphasizing steel prices, says: I do not wish to minimize the urgency of preventing inflationary movements in steel wages. I recognize, too, that the steel industry, by absorbing increases in employment costs since 1958, has demonstrated a will to halt the price-wage spiral in steel.

That will to do what we could to halt the wage-price spiral of steel involved thousands of employees and many companies in the serious human and financial costs of a 116-day strike in 1959. The subsequent settlement resulted in a 3½ to 3¾ per cent annual increase in our employment costs, and while this represented a substantial improvement from the corresponding 8 per cent average annual increase that had occurred throughout the period since 1940, it was still nearly twice as great as the average long-range improvement in steel shipments per man hour, which amounted to only 2 per cent. So I am afraid there is little justification for the belief that improving productivity will offset the cost of the Oct. 1 wage increase during any reasonable period of time.

*   *   *   *   *

1940–1944 RECALLED

. . . [T]here was no increase whatever in steel prices during the years 1940 through 1944; but this did not prevent a substantial inflation in wholesale prices generally during the same period. Conversely, from 1951 to 1956 there was

Exhibit 3—Continued

virtually no net change in the wholesale price level, despite the fact that steel prices advanced by about 30 per cent.

Again there is little support for the theory that a steel price rise consistently pyramids. Dr. Whitney has pointed out that between 1953 and 1958:

"The average steel-using item advanced only a tiny fraction of the amount that the rest of the (Bureau of Labor Statistics [consumer] price) index advanced."

*　　*　　*　　*　　*

Each industrial unit and every individual in it does bear, as your letter infers, a serious responsibility in maintaining the economic freedom of the country. I assure you that so far as our own corporation is concerned, we have in the past made every effort to maintain the economic freedom in the light of that responsibility and our purpose is to do so in the future.

Respectfully yours,
ROGER M. BLOUGH

Exhibit 4

PRICE INDEXES, 1940–61
(1957–59 = 100)

Years	Total Steel Mill Products	Scrap Iron and Steel	Nonferrous Metals*	Wholesale Price Index
1961	101.7	84.7	101.8	100.3
1960	102.1	79.9	103.6	100.7
1959	102.2	96.7	100.3	100.6
1958	100.6	90.5	95.0	100.4
1957	97.2	112.9	104.6	99.0
1956	88.7	127.8	120.9	96.2
1955	81.8	101.0	111.5	93.2
1954	78.2	77.0	97.9	92.9
1953	74.7	99.5	97.0	92.7
1952	69.3	110.2	107.3	94.0
1951	67.8	114.7	112.3	96.7
1950	62.9	101.0	90.1	86.8
1949	59.7	78.0	73.8	83.5
1948	55.1	118.1	79.1	87.9
1947	48.2	93.5	71.5	81.2
1946	41.2	NA	52.0	66.1
1945	37.9	NA	45.1	57.9
1944	37.0	NA	45.1	56.9
1943	37.0	NA	45.2	56.5
1942	36.9	NA	45.0	54.0
1941	36.9	NA	44.3	47.8
1940	36.7	NA	42.6	43.0

* 1940 through 1949 data are for series code 10–2. 1950 through 1961 data are for series code 10–22.

Source: U.S. Department of Commerce.

Exhibit 5

PRODUCTION, SHIPMENTS, OPERATING RATE,
AND MARGIN ON SALES
FOR U.S. STEEL CORPORATION, 1940–61

Years	Ingots and Castings Total Production*	% Capacity Operated	Steel Products Shipped*	Income % of Sales
1961	25.2	NA	16.8	5.7
1960	27.3	65.1	18.7	8.2
1959	24.4	58.3	18.1	7.0
1958	23.8	59.2	17.0	8.7
1957	33.7	85.2	23.4	9.5
1956	33.4	85.2	23.9	8.2
1955	35.3	90.8	25.5	9.0
1954	28.4	73.2	20.2	6.0
1953	35.8	98.4	25.1	5.8
1952	29.4	85.0	21.1	4.6
1951	34.3	101.3	24.6	5.2
1950	31.5	98.2	22.6	7.3
1949	28.5	82.5	18.2	7.2
1948	29.3	93.8	20.7	5.2
1947	28.6	96.7	20.2	6.0
1946	21.3	72.9	15.2	5.9
1945	26.5	82.0	18.4	3.3
1944	30.8	94.7	21.1	2.9
1943	30.5	97.8	20.1	3.2
1942	30.0	98.1	20.6	3.8
1941	29.0	96.8	20.4	7.2
1940	22.9	82.5	15.0	9.5

* Net tons in millions.

Source: Public statements, United States Steel Corporation.

Exhibit 6

UNITED STATES STEEL CORPORATION FINANCIAL SUMMARY, 1946–61

Year	Additions				For Plant and Equipment		Deductions — For Long-Term Debt		Dividends Declared on Stocks	Miscellaneous Other Deductions	Securities Set Aside for Plant and Equipment	Plant and Equipment Less Depreciation	Long-Term Debt Due after One Year	Reserves for Insurance Contingencies and Other Expenses	Ownership (Stocks and Income Reinvested)	Reinvested in Business
	Income as Reported	Wear and Exhaustion of Facilities	Sale of Securities	Miscellaneous Other Additions	Total Expenditures	Securities Set Aside	Total Repayment	Added to Current Debt								
1946	88.6	68.7		48.6	201.0	110.0	5.2	7.8	60.0	29.2	140.0	826.9	81.2	142.2	1,454.6	28.6
1947	127.1	114.0		5.4	206.6	15.0	4.6	.6	70.9	30.5	155.0	914.2	77.2	132.0	1,510.8	56.2
1948	129.6	146.0		12.6	275.2	—	5.5	.1	77.4	9.1	155.0	1,300.8	71.6	125.5	1,833.0	52.2
1949	165.9	119.7		4.2	179.1	—	5.6	—	81.3	9.5	155.0	1,356.0	66.0	117.5	1,917.6	84.6
1950	215.5	143.9		6.4	179.3	95.0	6.0	1.8	117.9	11.4	250.0	1,386.6	61.8	114.7	2,015.2	97.6
1951	184.3	162.1		9.5	352.4	—	8.5	1.6	103.5	—	250.0	1,571.4	54.9	112.0	2,096.0	80.8
1952	143.6	176.9		12.0	469.2	231.0	6.8	.7	103.5	5.2	19.0	1,851.6	61.0	107.2	2,136.1	40.1
1953	222.1	236.6		6.4	361.4	19.0	5.0	1.5	103.5	3.3	—	1,970.0	64.5	100.0	2,254.7	118.6
1954	195.4	261.8	309.5	17.8	227.4	—	5.1	35.3	110.7		—	1,925.7	324.1	101.9	2,348.7	84.7
1955	370.1	285.2	13.7	6.7	239.8	300.0	44.8	6.8	148.1	6.7	300.0	1,873.7	286.1	103.7	2,582.6	222.0
1956	348.1	277.6	4.8	29.8	311.8	225.0	42.7	1.6	170.1	3.7	525.0	1,878.0	245.0	105.1	2,764.0	178.0
1957	419.4	276.0	2.1	7.3	514.9	110.0	33.2	4.7	186.5	9.0	415.0	2,109.6	216.5	106.3	2,997.8	232.9
1958	301.5	204.9	302.6	7.6	448.1	115.0	27.2	1.8	186.6	21.2	530.0	2,345.1	487.5	108.5	3,114.0	114.9
1959	254.5	189.9	6.5	19.4	366.1	35.0	28.9	4.1	187.0	—	495.0	2,511.9	454.5	112.7	3,183.7	67.5
1960	304.2	208.4	2.9	8.3	492.4	195.0	32.8	1.1	187.2	14.9	300.0	2,787.6	422.8	114.4	3,301.9	117.0
1961	190.2	210.5	499.2	4.4	326.8	—	28.6	.8	187.5	21.2	300.0	2,899.5	893.4	117.1	3,305.9	2.7

Source: Public statement, United States Steel Corporation.

Exhibit 7

EXPORTS AND IMPORTS OF TOTAL STEEL PRODUCTS, 1946–61

(Net Tons)

Years	Exports	Imports
1961	2,227,763	3,322,526
1960	3,224,125	3,578,019
1959	1,982,781	4,628,320
1958	3,237,378	1,831,080
1957	5,954,535	1,304,070
1956	4,768,685	1,480,890
1955	4,410,316	1,075,194
1954	3,086,317	377,437
1953	3,328,722	1,741,890
1952	4,395,945	1,230,181
1951	3,453,024	2,283,714
1950	3,109,052	1,095,709
1949	5,006,213	300,908
1948	4,642,798	155,869
1947	6,837,800	34,834
1946	4,928,471	25,780

Source: U.S. Department of Commerce.

Exhibit 8

STEEL—RELATIONSHIP BETWEEN OPERATING RATE AND RATE OF RETURN ON NET WORTH AFTER TAXES

Year	Steel Industry Operating Rate	Rate of Return	United States Steel Operating Rate	Rate of Return	Year	Steel Industry Operating Rate	Rate of Return	United States Steel Operating Rate	Rate of Return
1920 ..	76.7	12.1	86.2	11.5	1936 ..	68.4	4.8	63.4	3.8
1921 ..	34.9	2.2	48.3	4.3	1937 ..	72.5	7.2	71.9	7.0
1922 ..	61.7	3.8	70.9	4.6	1938 ..	39.6	.3	36.4	—.6
1923 ..	77.3	9.4	89.1	10.9	1939 ..	64.5	4.2	61.0	3.1
1924 ..	64.6	6.5	72.2	8.4	1940 ..	82.1	8.2	82.5	7.5
1925 ..	75.4	7.6	81.7	8.6	1947 ..	93.0	11.4	96.7	10.0
1926 ..	84.1	9.3	89.1	10.1	1948 ..	94.1	14.0	93.8	10.5
1927 ..	75.4	6.6	79.8	7.4	1949 ..	81.1	11.7	82.5	9.4
1928 ..	84.6	8.4	84.6	9.0	1950 ..	96.9	15.0	98.2	11.8
1929 ..	88.7	12.1	90.4	12.6	1953 ..	94.9	11.2	98.4	9.9
1930 ..	62.8	5.1	67.2	5.8	1954 ..	71.0	9.4	73.2	8.3
1931 ..	38.0	—.3	37.5	.7	1955 ..	93.0	14.7	90.8	14.8
1932 ..	19.7	—4.5	17.7	—4.1	1956 ..	89.8	13.2	85.2	12.8
1933 ..	33.5	—2.2	29.4	—2.2	1957 ..	84.5	12.5	85.2	14.3
1934 ..	37.4	—.7	31.7	—1.3	1958 ..	61.0	8.5	59.2	9.8
1935 ..	48.7	1.4	40.7	.1					

Source: Congressional Record, June 30, 1959, p. 11165.

III Selected Readings

From: Charles E. Summer, Jr.
"PROFIT, FLOW OF FUNDS, AND DEPRECIATION"*

[EDITORS' NOTE: The author is Associate Professor of Management in Columbia University.]

In studying accounting and finance, we are told that two of the most important instruments for making a wide range of management decisions are the income (profit and loss) statement, and the statement of flow of funds.

INCOME, DEFERRED COSTS, AND PROFIT

In simple terms, the profit statement shows a list (and total) of all income received during a year, and a list (and total) of all costs incurred during that year, and the difference between the two: profit.

In a manufacturing company, the most important source of income is revenue from sales, arrived at by multiplying the (volume, or units sold) times the (price per unit).

On the cost side, total costs include actual costs paid out in cash during the year (say, checks issued for wages) *plus* certain costs for resources which were paid for in cash during a previous year, but not used until the current year. For example, suppose a company paid $1 million for a plant four years ago. This is a long-term or fixed cost, which is used up slowly during the life of the plant. If the plant is to be theoretically "used up" in ten years, and the company uses a "straight line" formula for figuring how much of the $1 million capital investment cost is to be used each year, then the annual depreciation cost is $100,000. Here would be a simplified income statement for the company in the fourth year after the plant was built and paid for:

Income	
1 million units sold at $1 each	$1,000,000
Costs	
Wages paid out in cash	800,000
Depreciation cost	100,000
Profit	$ 100,000

Thus the concept "profit" is important in figuring the difference between the input of resources (labor, plants) for a given operating period, and the output of products to consumers or other manufacturers.

The accounting entries which keep track of deferred costs such as depreciation

---

* Copyright 1963 by the author.

can be simply stated. At the time the plant is built, $1 million is debited to the asset account "plants and equipment," and credited (subtracted) from the cash account, or credited (added) to the debts payable accounts. At the end of the first year of operation of the plant, the cost account "depreciation" is debited, and the account "reserve for depreciation" is credited, for the $100,000 applicable to that period. Thus, each year, over the life of the plant, a cost account is closed to the profit statement for $100,000, and the reserve account builds up, or accumulates, $100,000 more. After 10 years the "reserve for depreciation" account will have increased to $1 million and, theoretically, the company has recovered the initial investment and is able to build a new plant.

EFFECT OF CHANGES IN THE PRICE LEVEL, OR TECHNOLOGY

The word "theoretically" was used above because this concept of depreciation accounting assumes that a new plant, of exactly the type of the old one, a) will be needed, and b) can be constructed for the same cost. Also, the depreciation reserve account on the asset side of the balance sheet does not mean that the designated amount is actually on hand at the balance sheet date for reinvestment. Normally the depreciation is part of the company's cash flow during the life of the asset and does not accumulate as a savings account, for instance.

Two variables, however, may upset the theory. In the first place, there may be advances in technology. The maker of anti-freeze, for example, may find that his own scientists, or those of competitors, have discovered a new process of producing ethylene glycol which is more efficient, but involves a more technologically elaborate plant. Or, even if the same kind of plant is technologically feasible, the business cycle may mean that prices of the machinery and construction labor are higher. In either case, the depreciation reserve of $1 million is not enough.

THE FLOW OF FUNDS STATEMENT

In the first example, our simplified income statement showed a profit of $100,000. However, the input-output of resources (costs-revenues) *does not equal the input-output of cash*. Study the statement and you will see that the net inflow of cash was $200,000—$1 million in sales less $800,000 paid out in wages.

In financial circles, the statement that "depreciation liberates cash" is used to refer to the fact that a cash amount equal to the annual depreciation cost, remains in the business as available for spending on current operating costs or new investment costs.

Other items which make the cash flow (input-output) different from the revenue-cost flow (profit) are such items as changes in debts, accounts receivable, or changes in the amount of money paid in, or paid out, to stockholders. For example:

—bonds issued for $1 million bring in a like amount of cash, but are not a revenue from sales, therefore do not affect profits. Likewise, bonds paid off result in a cash outflow, but not a cost of doing business

—increase of $50,000 in accounts receivable from customers results in a like amount of increased revenue (sales), and therefore an increase in profit, but does not change or increase the amount of cash inflow

—dividends paid to stockholders result in cash outflow but not a decrease in profits

—stock sold to stockholders increases cash inflow but does not result in increased income (revenue) from operations.

In planning how much to borrow from banks, how much debt can be paid off, how much the company can afford to pay out for new plant and equipment, and in many other important decisions, it is the flow of funds statement which tells whether the company "has the money"—not the profit statement.

From: James R. Bright
*"ARE WE FALLING BEHIND IN MECHANIZATION?"**

[EDITORS' NOTE: The author is Professor of Business Administration at the Harvard Business School.]

For many years the United States has had one strength that seemed un-assailable—leadership in mass production. Few would deny that this country has been pre-eminent in making a great variety of goods of fair to excellent quality—with a speed, in quantities, and at prices that the rest of the world could hardly match. In the broadest sense, this leadership in production technology has been a major contribution in two wars; it has been substantially responsible for our standard of living; it has been the foundation of our economic and military potential.

The source of manufacturing leadership lies in advanced production systems justified and made feasible by mass marketing. The basis of production excellence is extensive and ingenious mechanization, surrounded and directed by effective industrial organization.

LOST LEADERSHIP

It is disturbing and alarming to find that this traditional resource—our edge in production skill—is now shrinking. True, we still surpass most nations in many production technologies, and the scale of our manufacturing systems is generally larger. Nevertheless, there are many indications that we are becoming significantly vulnerable to production competition from abroad. Our position of world leadership in production is being assaulted—sporadically, perhaps, but seriously nonetheless . . . our competitive strength will be diminished to a truly serious degree unless American management develops a far more aggressive program of mechanization throughout every phase of economic activity.

Consider any given industry and ask: Where is the most advanced production system or concept to be found? Where is the most advanced machinery to be seen? What is the origin of these advanced equipment ideas? All too often the answer is: *abroad*. Although we generally have superiority in pure physical capacity, this is not as true of concepts. In many cases we are the followers, not

* Reprinted by permission of *The Harvard Business Review*, November–December 1960, pp. 93–95, 105–6.

the leaders, in manufacturing advances. Even where we are leading, our lead has been reduced. . . .

Three years ago, the *American Machinist* described a highly automated Russian ball-bearing plant.[1] According to observers sent abroad by our government, this was the most advanced automatic production system of its kind. Apparently nettled by the claims for Russian superiority, the Timken Roller Bearing Company shortly thereafter released to *American Machinist* a complete description of its new bearing factory at Bucyrus, Ohio. The evidence presented in that article indicated that the Timken plant was distinctly superior to the Russian factory in degree of automaticity, flexibility, and capacity.[2] Productivity per man-hour appeared to be about 6 to 1 in favor of Timken.

It is encouraging to know that we were not behind in this instance, but is it not suggestive that our official observers and the editors of a leading metalworking journal, both of whom closely follow our industrial progress, in effect recognized that this Russian plant was well in advance of our *general* practices?

*   *   *   *   *

I do not mean to imply that the United States is widely outclassed in total production skill or in every production operation. My point is that we do not have as great an edge in production imagination and capacity as we once had; and accordingly that we had better rouse ourselves to new efforts.

Nor do I mean we are no longer contributing any new mechanization concepts. The computer, for example, is undoubtedly the most promising and powerful mechanization accomplishment since the development of the assembly line, and it is substantially American in conception and application. Similarly, numerically controlled machine tools are our innovation (initiated, significantly, by the government, not by private industry).

What I do want to emphasize is that, on the whole, *our production leadership is shrinking.* Conditions abroad are now more favorable than ever to foreign mechanization progress. We can expect increasing competition from Europe and other countries like Japan as mass production brought about by rising living standards and larger international markets enables them to achieve economies that formerly were exclusively ours.[3] This competition will be sharpened as their new production systems challenge ours in technical advances.

What shall be the answer of American industry? Restrictive tariffs are the immediate response of some; yet every thoughtful businessman knows that these tariffs have multiple effects that are not totally happy, nor is protection assured. We must face up to the fact that it is impossible to live in a world of technical isolation. . . .

Another answer proposed by some is that our leadership must be retained through marketing concepts and skill. Marketing strength, however, can go only so far in compensating for higher costs or inferior products.

International production competition, the accelerating rate of technological change, and the dynamics of domestic competition, all point to the same conclusion: it is *vital* that American management develop and lead an aggressive program of mechanization. A simple, one-time effort at equipment replacement is not enough. Mechanization must be recognized as the primary tool for maintaining a competitive production strength. This means that most firms will have

---

[1] Peter Trippe, "Report on Russia, Part 4, 'Automatic Factory,'" *American Machinist,* January 14, 1957, pp. 147–55.

[2] Anderson Ashburn, "America's 'Automatic Factory,'" *American Machinist,* September 23, 1957, pp. 153–60.

[3] See Hodgson and Michaelis, "Planning for Profits in World Business," page 135, this issue.—*The Editors*

to develop programs for *continuous* technological advancement in manufacturing processes and equipment, as well as in materials and product design. A philosophy of perpetual dissatisfaction with the status quo must become a part of corporate policy.

[EDITORS' NOTE: After outlining the major trends in technological modernization, Professor Bright turns to the overall implications for management.]

*   *   *   *   *

Let us begin with the more specific, measurable, precise effects of advanced mechanization. Perhaps these are the most significant:

❰ In one way or another all of these trends will reduce operating costs, including every kind of labor cost per unit of output (except possibly maintenance cost).

❰ Most of the trends probably will increase capital investment in equipment. I suspect equipment complexity and volume in any machinery system will increase its first cost by 20% to 100%. At the same time, however, they will achieve more capacity in less physical space; hence they *may* reduce building investment. Therefore, the net cost of a new facility *may* not be substantially larger than at present.

*   *   *   *   *

The new age has the effect of forcing management to assume the role—conceptually—of a "machine designer." This master machine of business must fit an environment that has three dimensions: technical, economic, and social. What is more, intelligent "design" requires the integration of manufacturing, marketing, distribution, procurement, product design, and administrative activities. A team approach therefore is essential, and sophisticated techniques like simulation are necessary to explore complex relationships in planning and scheduling.

REGAINING LEADERSHIP

Technological change in business is proceeding very rapidly. Techniques that were advanced five years ago are commonplace today. Difficulties are disposed of more rapidly than we might expect. We have probably been too readily inclined to technological skepticism. While some companies may be relatively invulnerable to these advances in mechanization, and while not all industries are equally affected, I believe that most managements will have to follow mechanization progress closely and continuously in order to hold their own in competition, both foreign and domestic.

Most foreign countries have an important edge in the cost of labor. But we still have advantages in the form of larger markets, better distribution methods, greater capital resources, and, hopefully, greater willingness to change. What we need now is management sensitivity, imagination, and aggressiveness in the role that mechanization can play in retaining our production leadership. How many managers today can say: "Yes, we have a vigorous and imaginative program on mechanization progress"? Yet it is apparent, from the survey in this article of what our leading mechanization experts are doing or could do, that the competitive tools *are available*.

Management must recognize what is happening and wholeheartedly set out to establish continuous progress in mechanization. Three steps are especially important:

1. A program for machinery review, planned replacement, and significant technological advances must be established.

2. Tax structure and depreciation laws, hampering though they may be, must not be allowed to hold back major mechanization advances.

3. All Americans, on every level of the business, must be made aware of the critical nature of our production position.

We have the imagination, the intellect, the capital, and the markets. Now we need determination and action by management to regain undisputed production leadership of the world.

From: Joel Dean
*MANAGERIAL ECONOMICS**

[EDITORS' NOTE: The author is Professor of Economics at Columbia University.]

THE PRICING PROBLEM OF OLIGOPOLY

In industries where a few competitors dominate the supply of relatively uniform products, periods of low demand and excess capacity create serious competitive problems. This is particularly so in industries with heavy plant investments, and high barriers to entry. Each manufacturer is acutely aware of the disastrous effects that an announced reduction of his own price would have on the prices charged by competitors. As a result, these companies have by painful experience developed a pronounced aversion for attempting to gain market share by open and announced price cutting. The main conditions that cause this aversion may be summarized thus:

1. The seller knows that price cuts will be met promptly (either precisely or with differentials that are likely to preserve competitors' market shares). This reaction virtually destroys the effectiveness of overt price cuts as a means of extending a firm's market share.

2. Price reductions are not easily reversible. Once industry prices are cut, it is usually difficult to get them back up again until the cost and demand situation again commands higher prices.

3. Open price competition often degenerates into an uncontrolled price war,[1] particularly where marginal cost is considerably below average cost over the relevant range of output.

---

* *Managerial Economics*, Joel Dean. © 1951 by Prentice-Hill, Inc., Englewood Cliffs, New Jersey (pp. 429–31, 433–35).

[1] The distinction between price war and price competition is frequently impossible to make on objective grounds, particularly in "sick" industries where demand is falling secularly. The only indisputable evidence of war is prices below marginal costs. The existence of warfare depends ultimately on the attitudes and plans of competitors about the situation, and in fact there are as many degrees of price warfare as there are of military war, where aggression ranges from diplomacy, through guerrilla tactics and fifth columns, to open battle.

4. Sellers doubt that a lower price throughout the industry will expand total sales enough to offset the reduction in unit revenue. They usually believe that industry demand is highly inelastic.

Under these circumstances, substantial uniformity of published price is to be expected and market share is largely determined by secret price concessions and by non-price competition.

Under conditions of "pure" oligopoly, there is no such thing as a demand function for the individual firm. What the firm can sell at a given price and with a given amount of selling activity depends upon rivals' reaction to the firm's market policy. To draw a demand curve, some stable pattern of market shares acceptable to all sellers must be established automatically for each price the firm might set.

To analyze this problem of interdependence, economic theorists have set up various assumptions about the chain of reactions to rivals' prices. These assumptions suggest the adventures of Dick Tracy, and give about equally convincing results. But the fact that the "equilibrium" price is by logical analysis indeterminate does not mean that it is so in practice. Actually, the seller in many industries has, from his knowledge of rivals' cost and demand situations and personal traits, and from industry experience, a very good idea of the probable reaction of major rivals to his price or other market actions.[2] When, as is quite common, price makes little difference in the industry's total sales (even though small price disparities shift business quickly), then the pattern of rivals' reactions to a price cut can be quite clearly foreseen.

What determines the likelihood that rivals will meet an announced price change? It depends on whether the change is compatible with the dynamic setting, i.e., with changes in demand, costs, and substitute prices. During a business decline, when demand is drying up, rivals' excess capacity and low marginal costs typically cause informal price concessions that undermine the official prices. Under the circumstances an announced rise in price is unlikely to be followed but an announced cut in price will be followed immediately. On the other hand, when demand is booming and when costs and substitutes' prices are rising, price reductions are less likely to be followed than price advances.

When the dynamic changes in demand and cost conditions that prompted a given price change are viewed in much the same way by all rivals, they do not cause serious uncertainties concerning rivals' reactions. But these uncertainties do become serious: (a) when rivals are quite differently affected by the same general changes in conditions, (b) when rivals differ in their estimates concerning the future conditions for which they are pricing, and (c) when rivals have drastically different notions about the industry elasticity of demand with respect to price.[3]

Since these disruptive influences are continually at work to some degree in many industries, a critical problem of oligopoly is to devise industry practices that can reconcile the need for adjustments to changing industry demand with the need to maintain the precarious price structure that has been established.

*　　*　　*　　*　　*

---

[2] For example, any major oil company selling a well accepted house brand of gasoline knows that an open reduction in its price in a market in which the brand's share is substantial will be met promptly and precisely by house brands of major companies, by other brands, and by lesser rivals, with a fairly predictable pattern of differentials.

[3] Many industries have had, at one time or another, a discordant personality, such as Firestone or Carnegie, whose heterodox views disrupt the whole pattern of reasonable oligopoly behavior.

PRICE LEADERSHIP

The institution of price leadership is [a] way for oligopoly competitors to achieve the delicate adjustment to changing cost and demand conditions without precipitating a price war. One firm takes the initiating role in all price changes, and the other firms follow along, matching the leader's price exactly, or with established differentials. Price leadership in action may be seen most clearly in a mature and stable industry with a highly standardized product, such as steel, oil, cement, or building materials. But it plays an important part in many industries that have considerable product differentiations.

REQUIREMENTS FOR LEADERSHIP PRICING

Price leadership is, in essence, a tacit concurrence by major firms in the industry with the wisdom of the leader's pricing decision.[4] It greatly reduces the number of possible reactions of a price change, and thus gives a modicum of certainty to the pricing aspects of market forecasting. It does not, of course, involve agreements that would explicitly violate the Sherman Act. The origins of leadership in any one industry are often too intricate and obscure to be analyzed. Round-table conferences are not needed to set it up. All that is needed is one firm whose price policy is consistently acceptable to most of the industry. The leader may take responsibility for setting prices that followers will accept independently without starting a price war, but in more sophisticated industries, where members have better *rapport,* followers, too, accept responsibility for behaving in the best interests of the group. Indeed, "leadership" can function with all degrees of group action, up to a cartelized market-quota system. The form it actually takes depends on the size structure of the industry's firms, on disparities in their cost function, product differentiation, and geographical distribution, and on the pattern and stability of demand.

QUALIFICATIONS OF PRICE LEADER

What are the requisites for being a price leader? (1) A substantial share of the market. Typically, although not necessarily, the largest firm becomes the leader, because this firm is presumed to have the greatest stake in "industry welfare"; to be able to "enforce" followership (although it rarely can or does); and to be best informed about industry demand and supply conditions, and hence best equipped to determine industry price policy. (2) A reputation for sound pricing decisions, based on better information and more experienced judgment than the other firms have. (3) Initiative. Often the company that first develops a product or area retains the price leadership, whether or not it retains the largest market. Often a company may take leadership by default by developing aggressive pricing. Thus the company that believes that lower prices will penetrate large and profitable markets wrests leadership from more conservative rivals whether or not its decision appeals to followers.

---

4 A distinction should be made between "followers," in a positive sense, and merely the "rest of the industry." Some firms are price leaders because they control most of the industry's output, and set their prices with little regard to the marginal producers. There is little leader-follower relation in such industries. Much more important are the industries in which the leader's market share is not dominating and where successful leadership requires reasonably loyal followers. There are always marginal firms who follow no one, but these can be neglected if prices are stabilized on the bulk of production.

In some industries the price leadership shifts among major firms. But more commonly, one firm remains the leader for long periods.

Leadership structure is sometimes segmented. Geographical and product segmentation are common. Thus, in gasoline pricing, different companies are market leaders in different areas. Broad-line chemical manufacturers are typically price leaders for some chemicals and followers for others.

PROBLEMS OF THE PRICE LEADER

Broadly conceived, the problem of the price leader is a problem of industrial statesmanship; the leader makes (within the willingness of his followers) decisions for the entire industry. Narrowly conceived, the leader's problem is a compromise between the price solution that is best for the leader and the price solution that is best for certain other members of the industry.

The price leader's problems of industrial statesmanship are serious, particularly when industry conditions are changing rapidly. If he fails to reconcile his own and the industry's interests with those of the followers, he may easily impair his own position in leadership and market share.[5]

In many industries, price leadership has been fairly responsive to changes in cost and in demand, but generally it has managed to dampen the amplitude of cyclical fluctuations. Under leadership, prices have not gone as high in boom periods or as low in depressions. Since a price change for the industry may have a wide range of unpredictable effects on individual firms, the leader is usually reluctant to stir up the market with frequent price adjustments to meet changed demand and costs perfectly. Continuous change would undermine the loyalty of hard-hit firms and give an appearance of vacillation by the leader. Price leadership usually produces few, but large and dramatic, price changes in the industry over the cycle. After World War II, a few leaders, notably International Harvester and General Electric, tried lowering prices in an attempt to curb inflation, but they were too far out of line with market conditions to be followed. They subsequently raised their prices again.

Even in normal conditions, however, the leader usually leads only in price rises. On downslides the leader actually becomes a follower.

---

[5] The stable price policy of U.S. Steel in the deflation of 1920–1922 caused unhappiness among some of the independents. They reacted by disrupting the market to such an extent that Bethlehem Steel, acting in a quasi-leadership role, acquired them and thus stabilized the industry again. As a result, Bethlehem's market share was substantially increased. (TNEC Monograph 13, p. 106.)

From: John Maurice Clark

COMPETITION AS A DYNAMIC PROCESS*

[EDITORS' NOTE: The author is a Professor Emeritus of Economics at Columbia University.]

. . . A procedure more in accord with prevailing mores is for the gains made in leading industries to be wholly or largely shared between wages and profits in these industries. If these same industries hold on to their position of leadership, this would build up for them the status of a favored group. The workers in this group would get their share in the shape of wages higher than those of workers of equal grade and quality in relatively lagging industries. Property income would get its share in terms of a larger aggregate return on the larger investment per worker which has been necessary to the increased productivity, without (in most cases) any notable increase or decrease in the percentage rate of return. The improvements take effect in finding ways in which increased capital per worker can be used without the drastic and precipitous decline in its "marginal productivity" which would result from such massive increases in capital per worker in the absence of such improvements. This is the chief enduring form in which "capital" gets its share and does not ordinarily require an increase in its fraction of the product. "Enterprise," as distinct from capital, may get an increased profit, which competition (where it is effective) tends to limit to the period before the improved processes become standard practice, available to the "representative firms" whose costs determine prices.

This favored status of enterprise and capital in "leading" industries may be ironed out by competition, but the favored status of labor in these industries tends to be, not ironed out, but partially and laggingly offset in a different way: by increases in the wages demanded and secured by unions in the lagging industries; in other words, wage increases in excess of increases of productivity in these latter industries. Such wage increases raise wage costs of production, and, since the presumption is that profits in these industries would not have much capacity to absorb increased wage costs, this means that their prices will rise. Some of this increase may flow back in the shape of increased money costs on purchases made by the leading industries; but its chief impact is in increased cost of living, for which workers throughout the economy will seek offsetting wage increases so far as their bargaining strength permits. As a result, the cumulative effects include price increases in the original leading industries, which we assumed did not initially raise their prices.

Of course, if the unions in these leading industries are able to exact wage increases in excess of their above-average increases in productivity, thus raising *their* wage costs of production, the rise in prices follows a fortiori: these industries are virtually sure to raise prices to offset their increased costs and restore their former profit margins if possible. There will be controversy whether the price increases were needed, or whether the wage increases could and should have been absorbed; but this is not likely to deter the employers if market conditions are such as to make the restoration of profits feasible. The cumulative effect is further increased if the leading industries anticipate the flow back and raise prices further to offset some part of it in advance—as U.S. Steel has apparently sometimes done, in a policy that has exposed it to widespread criticism.[1]

Characteristic behavior in twelve industries or industrial groups is exhibited very revealingly in the following table, in which the twelve groups are arranged in the order of their rates of increase in productivity (measured in terms of total employees), and this is correlated with changes in wages and in prices. Even if one has reservations about the precise accuracy of the figures, certain relationships stand out with surprising clearness. Changes in productivity differ widely; changes in wages differ by only a fraction as much, though higher wages accompany higher increases in productivity with remarkable, if rough, consistency. Iron and steel is the outstanding departure from type, being seventh in increased productivity and first in increased wages. In every industry but one, wages increased faster than productivity, indicating an increase in wage costs per unit; and these discrepancies were naturally greatest where the increase in productivity was least. With some exceptions, the six industries showing greatest increase in productivity (and in wages), showed the least increase in prices, and the converse was true with a single exception for the six industries showing the least increase in productivity (and in wages). The excess of increased wages

Table 1[a]

PERCENTAGE CHANGES IN PRODUCTIVITY, OUTPUT, WAGES, AND PRICES FOR TWELVE MANUFACTURING INDUSTRIES, FIRST QUARTER 1955 TO FIRST QUARTER 1959

Industry	Productivity	Output	Wages	Prices
Tobacco	30.2	18.1	23.0	8.7
Nonferrous metals	22.9	0.6	26.4	1.9
Chemicals	20.0	24.8	22.2	2.7
Petroleum and products	17.8	9.8	24.8	6.7
Paper and allied products	14.7	17.7	21.2	13.0
Food and kindred products	14.0	10.2	20.8	4.8
Iron and steel	11.3	11.6	34.8	26.5
Rubber	9.7	7.6	20.0	5.6
All manufacturing	9.3	12.0	20.2	10.6
Nonelectrical machinery	8.9	9.6	20.6	23.2
Fabricated metal products	8.2	17.7	19.5	13.8
Electrical machinery	0.0	5.4	19.5	20.7
Motor vehicles	−1.7	−25.1	17.7	17.7

[a] From exhibits of T. A. Anderson, in *Employment, Growth, and Price Levels*, Hearings before the Joint Economic Committee, 86 Cong. 1 sess. (1959), Pt. 7, p. 2156. The data are identical with those of Mr. Anderson's Table I, merely rearranged in the order indicated, the better to bring out the relationships that hinge on differences in the rate of increase in productivity. Anderson's table also shows changes in profits: all downward (presumably cyclically) except for tobacco, food, etc., and the iron and steel group, these three all being among the upper seven in terms of increase in productivity.

---

[1] See Gardiner C. Means, *Administrative Inflation and Public Policy* (1959), pp. 26–31, referring to U.S. Steel's price increase of July 1957 and citing Roger Blough's testimony, in *Administered Prices,* Hearings before the Senate Committee on the Judiciary, 85 Cong. 1 sess. (1957), Pt. 2, pp. 211, 244.

over increased productivity—signifying increased wage cost per unit—was least where both increased productivity and increased wages were greatest, and vice versa.

* * * * *

REQUIREMENTS OF A NONINFLATIONARY MODEL

If the method of adjustment we have been examining is inflationary, what method would be consistent with general stability of the price-level? The basic condition is that the sum of realized claims to income should increase at the same rate at which real product increases, and that the more rapid increase of productivity in the "leading" industries should not accrue to either wages or profits in these industries as differential, favored-group incomes, to such an extent that other groups would be bound to take action in an attempt to catch up. As we have seen, even if they do not succeed in catching up, the pursuit raises unit costs. The conditioning factor here is that differences in rates of increase in productivity, and of immediate bargaining power, are much greater than differences of income in which the market will acquiesce without moving to reduce them.

A noninflationary adjustment requires, then, that income in the leading industries shall absorb only a fraction of their increased productivity: in fact, assuming that they will be able to secure gains exceeding the economy-wide average, their differential, compared to others which are below the average, must be not only limited to a size that will be tenable market-wise but one that will not lead to countervailing movements. A 41 per cent differential in favor of strong industries may be tenable, but only in the sense of ability to keep that far ahead in an inflationary pursuit race. A noninflationary differential must not start a pursuit race. How big a differential is noninflationary? Available evidence cannot answer, but it seems amply certain that it is much smaller than the differentials that actually exist.

The simplest model, which can be taken as nothing more than a point of departure, would be one in which wages rise at the rate at which product per worker or per man-hour increases in the economy as a whole, while the over-all proportion going to profits does not increase. In some respects this model is not too unrealistic. It seems fairly probable that wages and profits in the lagging industries as a group will not fall much further behind those of the leading industries than they have already fallen; though there will, of course, be departures from any norm in particular instances. These departures may furnish useful incentives to mobility or to acceptance of improvements, or may remedy particular inequities—or may create fresh inequities. The bulk of such departures from norm are bound to be upward. As to the relative division between wages and profits, it may shift in particular industries, one reason being unequal changes in the amount of capital per worker.

In manufacturing as a whole, the relative division has shifted in favor of labor in recent years. This may have been facilitated in part by the fact that real product has increased faster than real investment. (This has not been true in all periods.) This could mean that if capital received its former share of product, the percentage return on investment could rise; or the former percentage return could be maintained with a slightly smaller share of value added. This may not apply to other sectors of the economy than manufacturing; and it is not safe to count on it as an important continuing feature of our system. As far as it goes, it affords a margin out of which special departures from the overall wage formula could be met without raising prices. But it appears virtually certain that this margin would not suffice to finance any major part of the special departures that would be successfully bargained for.

The basic rate of increase, which we are estimating as less than 2 per cent per year per worker, or 2.3 per cent per weighted man-hour, may seem skimpy to workers who have been making nominal gains, in money terms, at something like twice that rate, and then have felt they had a grievance because inflation robbed them of the excess—as it was bound to do. For the increase in real product sets the limit on the economically possible increase of real wages (except for such small and nonprogressive gains as may be made at the expense of the proportion going to profits). That is approximately what labor as a whole had been getting as a long-run trend. The reason was that, with the minor qualifications just mentioned, this was all there was available in the economy which labor could get. Moreover 2 per cent per year, if sustained, is far from a skimpy rate of increase. It doubles the original amount in thirty-five years, just as inflation at 2 per cent per year halves the real value of fixed money incomes in thirty-five years. The one is a notable gain, the other a formidable loss.

If money wages rise at something like the economy-wide rate of increase in productivity, this reduces wage costs per unit of product in what we are calling the leading industries, and increases them in the lagging ones. Prices must rise in the lagging industries, and if the price-level is to remain stable, prices must fall in the leading industries, which must pass their reduced wage costs on to their customers. These conditions of price-level stability appear, to say the least, highly unlikely to come to pass. The industries in question include too many with restricted downward price flexibility, facing competitive forces that act too sluggishly to compel the prompt reductions of prices which, at this strategic point in the economy, are demonstrably necessary to a stabilized price level by the inescapable logic of arithmetic.

As for unions, there are some competitive forces tending to set limits on the wages they can obtain; but where unions are strong, their most powerful competitive forces tend to raise wages: namely, the competition of leaders with potential rivals, or of unions with rival unions, in offering gains to their members. This is competition in making the most of monopolistic bargaining power. In the light of this power, which is at its strongest in leading or highly concentrated industries, and in the light of the pressures exerted on union leaders by their strategic situation, it seems well-nigh inevitable that wage adjustments should be based on the ability of these leading industries to pay wage increases above the average. This would mean that the employers' wage costs might not be reduced, so that there might not appear to be any occasion for them to reduce their prices. Then the noninflationary model would have failed to be realized; and the most that could be hoped for would be that the progress of education in the economics of this brand of inflation would result in some kind of compromise, which would stop short of the full inflationary effect that results when the various participants in the leading industries succeed in absorbing as their own property or perquisite the above-average gains that accrue in these industries.

The relation between wages and the introduction of improvements which increase man-hour productivity is a two-way one. Where wages rise enough to raise wage costs of production, they afford the employer an incentive to adopt more labor-saving equipment, in order to economize the expensive labor and raise its productivity. Or he may develop improvements in order to be able to increase productivity enough to pay the wage increases which experience tells him are coming And if he installs an improvement, its success may hinge on having the willing acceptance and cooperation of the workers affected, and this may be promoted by a wage increase that shares some part of the gains with these workers. This is clearly a rational basis for departing from the strict average-productivity standard, but appears capable of being harmonized with it if the incentive premium is moderate enough to be acquiesced in without starting an inflationary pursuit race, or is allowed to remain unchanged long enough for others to catch up by the normal, gradual increase of productivity. This calls for restraint on the part of the recipients of the premium, whose natural tendency would be to regard it as establishing a higher relative place in the country's scale of differential wages, to be made permanent if possible, by keeping that far ahead of others who might be trying to catch up.

In competitive industry, it is sound economics that improvements are a source of special differential gains only until they have become standard practice, available to those "representative firms" whose costs set prices in the industry; after which the improvement is in the public domain and not a source of differential gain to the user. What is here suggested is that the same principle is equally sound with respect to any differential gain that may accrue to workers from incentive payments made in connection with any particular innovation; but with whatever differences are called for by the acceptance of the principle that the labor of a human being should not be subject to the same competitive forces that apply to commodities. In that light it is suggested that in general such innovational premiums should be retained, but their differential character ironed out gradually by the rise in the general level of wages.

*   *   *   *   *

To revert to the more general picture, the conclusion to which it points is that, existing economic forces being what they are, some inflationary trend is well-nigh inevitable in the course of the adjustments to different rates of increase in productivity. One can understand the position of S. H. Slichter and others, that the best we can hope to do is to hold the trend down to a creep—say, less than 2 per cent per year. Incidentally, a 2 per cent annual inflation, superimposed on a 2 per cent annual increase in real income per worker, would mean that money incomes are increasing twice as fast as real incomes do or can increase; also that anyone whose money income is not increasing at that rate is falling behind the procession in relative terms. In the above discussion, the tendencies leading to this kind of result have been analyzed in a way that attempts to show the parts played by the behavior of "administered prices" and by the bargaining power of strongly organized labor, both of which are involved, and both share in causal responsibility, but in different ways.

THE TOUGH PROBLEM OF CAUSAL RESPONSIBILITY

Thus the noninflationary model makes a contribution to the identifying of causal relations: in a direct sense any behavior that departs from the requirements of the model is a proximate cause of inflation. But for the student the question does not end there; it moves on to the underlying causes of the proximate behavior and, with remedies in mind, inquires how far they are modifiable. Meanwhile parties at interest dispute over whose behavior is to blame. Here a key question is whether certain inflationary behavior was voluntarily initiated or was a response to the behavior of others; and in the latter case, whether the response was necessary. And since there are discretionary margins of policy in these cases, the question of the necessity of a particular response is endlessly arguable. When the issue is thus joined, the reasons for failure to agree are not mysterious.

Spokesmen for business naturally identify increased wage costs as the main causal factor and affirm that offsetting increases of prices are an unavoidable necessity, commonly including the controversial item of capital expansion out of plowed-back earnings. In this connection they sometimes add that the necessity of raising prices to cover increased costs holds for the weaker firms in an industry, if not for the strongest ones; and that if the strongest firms reduced their profit margins to absorb increased costs, too many weaker firms would be extinguished, and the resulting increased concentration would invite antitrust action.

This argument raises a problem of economic differentiation, for the investigation of which the necessary data are not available in the general statistics of industries. Insofar as this argument is valid, it points toward the probable existence of undesirably large differences of economic strength among firms in concentrated industries. It appears inescapable that a progressive increase in wage costs, at the rates we have been recently experiencing, if absorbed out of profit margins—already a minority share—would in less than a decade reduce these margins below the minimum necessary to the function they perform in our kind of economy, whatever allowances may be made for the imprecise character of that minimum. The greater size of the wage share ensures this result.

On the other side, spokesmen for organized labor, including its able staff economists, and other economists whose sympathies lie with that side, go far toward placing the entire causal responsibility on "administered" prices, citing detailed statistical analyses in support of this position. A few theoretical economists, whose predilections favor neither side as such, but are strongly on the side of a competitively ruled economy, have decided that the most strongly intrenched monopoly power in the country is that of labor unions, and are ranking this, along with anticompetitive business conditions and practices, as twin problems to be at least mitigated if we hope to avoid the replacement of private bargaining by direct public controls.[2] Specific remedies generally remain insufficiently defined. It is earnestly to be hoped that the issues involved can somehow be dealt with on the basis of the requirements of a properly operating ecomomy, rather than on the basis of the relative political power of organized pressure groups, or the issue-obscuring epithets and generalities that prevail in too much public discussion.

As indicated, the question of causal responsibility is often entangled with the normative question of the reasonableness of the share which each side is trying to protect or to increase, or whether a given wage increase warrants a proportionate price increase or only one that is equal in dollar terms. In the case of the steel price increase of July 1957, following a wage increase in 1956, Gardiner C. Means argued that the price increase greatly exceeded any increase in wage cost of production traceable to the wage contract, and was therefore an independent inflationary move in an industry of a "bellwether" character.[3] The argument includes some telling points of statistical interpretation. But after an able and at least partially successful attempt to deflate the company's figures on increased wage cost of production, Means is left with a finding that the contract did increase wage costs somewhat. And if the preceding analysis is correct, any increase in wage costs in an industry with a more-than-average rate of increase in pro-

2 Cf. E. H. Chamberlin, *The Economic Analysis of Labor Union Power* (January 1958); also "Can Union Power Be Curbed?" *Atlantic Monthly* (June 1959), pp. 46–50; also Fritz Machlup, *Monopolistic Wage Determination as a Part of the General Problem of Monopoly* (1947); also papers by various writers in *The Impact of the Union*, D. McCord Wright, Ed. (1951); and *The Public Stake in Union Power*, Philip D. Bradley, Ed. (1958).

3 *Op. cit.,* pp. 28–29.

ductivity is inconsistent with the requirements of a noninflationary adjustment. It is inflationary, though the price increase that followed it may have been inflationary also, beyond what the wage increase necessitated.

The attempt may be made to assign causal responsibility to one share or the other according to which increased first, or which increased the most, in each case from some selected starting point. There is even some reason in assigning greater causal importance to the larger share, merely because it is larger. The argument from priority of movement is the basis of a disclaimer of causal responsibility by one group on the ground that they are merely catching up with an initial disequilibrating movement originating elsewhere. Here the nature of the starting point is crucial, and it is too temptingly easy to select a starting point which contains some initial inflationary disequilibrium, favorable to one group. Then the first move after this starting-point is likely to be one that reduces this disequilibrium: that is, one that impairs this group's former favorable position. Then this group will try to catch up with its former position, quite sincerely unconscious that this means restoring an inflationary imbalance.

The same thing is true, whether it is a case of a business corporation raising its prices to restore its former profit margin and catch up with the effect of a wage increase, or whether it is a case of a union whose 4 per cent annual wage increase has been cut in two by a 2 per cent annual rise in the cost of living, and which demands further wage increases, to catch up with the rise in the cost of living and restore the (inflationary) 4 per cent increase, figured in dollars of stable buying power. The fact that one party is catching up is meaningless until the observer not only knows what this party is catching up with, but knows enough about it to be in a position to judge whether the catching up is in the interest of balance or the opposite. Attributing causal responsibility on the basis of priority of movement has much in common with the problem of priority between the chicken and the egg. As qualifying this negative view, there appears to be some truth in the "bellwether" theory of the strategic importance of particular industries, notably steel.

*   *   *   *   *

If priority of movement is an uncertain guide to causal importance, relative extent of movement might furnish more meaningful evidence, if either share had increased notably at the other's expense; but neither has, to a convincing extent. If anything, wages have gained on profits in recent years, but, as already noted, the increase of product per unit of capital has made room for a small shift of this sort. In itself, it does not prove that either share is responsible for inflation. The over-all picture is at least consistent with the analysis given above, which assigned some causal responsibility to each share.

From: Gerald Sirkin

*INTRODUCTION TO MACROECONOMIC THEORY**

THREE TYPES OF INFLATION

"EXCESS-DEMAND" INFLATION

The simplest kind of inflation to describe is the one that arises from excess demand for current output. In an earlier chapter, we referred to excess demand as an "inflationary gap." In Figure 38, where Y_f is the full-potential level of real gross national product and Y_e is the equilibrium gross national product, output will be at full potential, and aggregate demand (AY_f) will exceed output (BY_f) by the inflationary gap, AB. The excess demand for output, which implies also excess demand for inputs, will, through the competitive bidding of buyers, raise the prices of outputs and inputs, provided prices are free to rise. The system must continue in disequilibrium until either (a) growth of the economy raises Y_f to the level of Y_e; or (b) some autonomous change lowers the aggregate demand function in real terms, bringing Y_e down to the level of Y_f; or (c) the process of rising prices, through certain induced effects, lowers the aggregate demand function and reduces Y_e to equality with Y_f.

If prices are prevented from rising by governmental controls, "open" inflation may be prevented, but "suppressed" inflation is present. The symptoms are

AN INFLATIONARY GAP

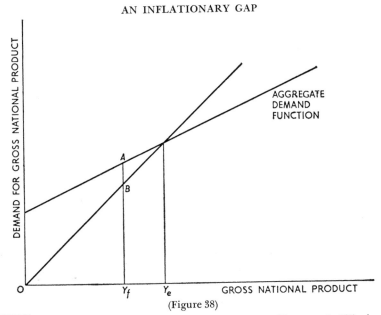

(Figure 38)

* Reprinted by permission of Richard D. Irwin, Inc., Homewood, Illinois, 1961 (pp. 169–72).

altered, rising prices being replaced by queuing and other forms of nonprice rationing, but the economy continues to be afflicted with an inflationary problem. Indeed, the affliction may be even greater under suppressed than under open inflation since (a) the equilibrating effects of rising prices (to be described shortly) are eliminated in suppressed inflation and (b) expectations of future shortages are more likely than are expectations of rising prices to increase excess demand.

"Cost-Push" or "Profit-Push" Inflation

Economic analysts have become increasingly aware, in recent years, of the possibility of a generally rising price level even in the absence of excess demand. A number of different mechanisms which might operate to inflate prices without excess demand have been described. Of these, the most frequently mentioned is the "wage-push" process, in which wage increases, obtained through the bargaining power of labor unions, raise costs of production and thereby cause producers to raise prices. However, wages are not the only costs that can play this part; it is possible that overhead costs (selling, administration, research and development costs) rising independently of wages can provide an upward thrust to the price level.

Recent discussions have given considerably more attention to "wage-push" origins of inflation than to "profit push," in which monopolistic or oligopolistic firms seek to increase profits by increasing their markups over cost. In theory, profit push is as possible as wage push. If a profit-push mechanism is ignored, it is largely because of a presumption that, while labor organizations behave in a way that can generate persistent wage-push inflation, the behavior of monopolists and oligopolists does not conform to the requirements of a profit-push model. The reasoning is roughly this: unions press periodically for wage increases with no "maximization" objective in mind and without regard to the demand curve for labor, either because they consider the demand curve to be perfectly inelastic within a range which includes the proposed wage level or because they are more concerned with the wage rate than with the amount of employment in the industry. With such behavior, no equilibrium wage rate can be defined. On the other hand, monopolistic and oligopolistic entrepreneurs are considered to be aiming at the maximization of profits and, with given cost and demand data, will arrive at equilibrium prices of output. Product prices move toward an equilibrium; they are induced rather than autonomous variables. Wage rates have no equilibrium; they are autonomous forces in the system. From this view of wage and price determination it follows that wages initiate the upward push while prices trail after, in search of a new equilibrium.

It is difficult to sustain this clear distinction between the behavior of labor organizations and entrepreneurs with monopoly power. Entrepreneurs are prone to think of the demand for their industry's product as being highly inelastic with respect to price. Further, there is evidence that monopolies or the price leaders of oligopolies aim, not at profit maximization, but at some "target" rate of return on investment. A decision to increase the target rate, combined with belief in the inelasticity of demand, will lead to autonomous increases of product prices. The possibility of profit-push inflation cannot be ruled out on a priori grounds.

"Ratchet" Inflation

A third inflation mechanism, which I will call "ratchet" inflation, is a blend of the previous two. The ratchet-inflation hypothesis holds that though demand may not be excessive in the aggregate, it may be so distributed as to be excessive in some sectors of the economy and inadequate in others. In an economy with flexible prices, prices would increase in the sectors with excess demand and fall in the others, with no increase in the general price level. But when prices are "administered" by labor unions and by firms in imperfect competition, there is a pronounced downward rigidity of prices. Prices in sectors with excess demand rise but prices in the sectors with inadequate demand do not fall. The net effect is a rise in the over-all price level. Excess demand provides the upward thrust; administered prices provide the ratchet which prevents the compensating drop of prices elsewhere.

From: Peter F. Drucker

THE FUTURE OF INDUSTRIAL MAN*

[EDITORS' NOTE: The author is Professor of Management at New York University.]

Legitimate power stems from the same basic belief of society regarding man's nature and fulfillment on which the individual's social status and function rest. Indeed, legitimate power can be defined as rulership which finds its justification in the basic ethos of the society. In every society there are many powers which have nothing to do with such a basic principle and institutions which in no way are either designed or devoted to its fulfillment. In other words, there are always a great many "unfree" institutions in a free society, a great many inequalities in an equal society, and a great many sinners among the saints. But as long as that decisive social power which we call rulership is based upon the claim of freedom, equality or saintliness, and is exercised through institutions which are designed toward the fulfillment of these ideal purposes, society can function as a free, equal or saintly society. For its institutional structure is one of legitimate power.

This does not mean that it is immaterial whether non-decisive powers and institutions of a society are in contradiction to its basic principles. On the contrary, the most serious problems of politics arise from such conflicts. And a society may well feel that a non-decisive institution or power relationship is in such blatant contrast to its basic beliefs as to endanger social life in spite of its non-decisive character. The best case in point is that of the American Civil War when the chattel-slavery of the South was felt to endanger the whole structure of a free society. Yet the decisive power of ante-bellum America was undoubtedly legitimate power deriving its claim from the principle of freedom, and exercised through institutions designed and devoted to the realization of freedom. American society did thus function as a free society. It was indeed only because it functioned as such that it felt slavery as a threat.

What is the decisive power, and the decisive institutional organization in any society cannot be determined by statistical analysis.

Nothing could be more futile than to measure a society by counting noses, quoting tax receipts or comparing income levels. Decisive is a political, and that means a purely qualitative, term. The English landed gentry comprised never more than a small fraction of the population; furthermore, after the rise of the merchants and manufacturers it had only a very modest share of the national wealth and income. Nevertheless, down to our times it held the decisive social power. Its institutions were the decisive institutions of English society. Its beliefs were the basis for social life; its standards the representative standards; its way of life the social pattern. And its personality ideal, the gentleman, remained the ideal type of all society. Its power was not only decisive; it was legitimate power.

Equally, laws and constitutions will rarely, if ever, tell us where the decisive power lies. In other words, rulership is not identical with political government. Rulership is a social, political government largely a legal category. The Prussian Army between 1870 and 1914 was, for instance, hardly as much as mentioned in the Imperial German Constitution; yet it undoubtedly held decisive power and probably legitimately. The government was actually subordinated to the army, in spite of a civilian and usually antimilitaristic Parliament.

*   *   *   *   *

Finally, it should be understood that legitimacy is a purely functional concept. There is no absolute legitimacy. Power can be legitimate only in relation to a basic social belief. What constitutes "legitimacy" is a question that must be answered in terms of a given society and its given political beliefs. Legitimate is a power when it is justified by an ethical or metaphysical principle that has been accepted by the society. Whether this principle is good or bad ethically, true or false metaphysically, has nothing to with legitimacy which is as indifferent ethically and metaphysically as any other formal criterion. Legitimate power is socially functioning power; but why it functions and to what purpose is a question entirely outside and before legitimacy.

Failure to understand this was responsible for the confusion which made "legitimism" the name of a political creed in the early nineteenth century. The European reactionaries of 1815 were, of course, absolutely within their rights when they taught that no society could be *good* except under an absolute monarch; to have an opinion on what is desirable or just as basis of a society is not only a right, it is a duty, of man. But they were simply confusing ethical choice with functional analysis, when they said that no society could *function* unless it had an absolute monarch. And they were probably wrong when they proclaimed the dogma that only absolute monarchy was *legitimate*. . . .

The functional analysis as to what is legitimate power does not in any way prejudge the ethical question of the individual's right or duty to resist what he considers pernicious power. Whether it is better that society perish than that justice perish is a question outside and before functional analysis. The same man who maintains most vigorously that society can function only under a legitimate power may well decide that society is less of a value than certain individual rights or beliefs. But he cannot decide, as the Legitimists did, that his values and beliefs *are* the socially accepted values and beliefs because they *ought* to be.

Illegitimate power is a power which does not derive its claim from the basic beliefs of the society. Accordingly, there is no possibility to decide whether the ruler wielding the power is exercising it in conformity with the purpose of power or not; for there is no social purpose. Illegitimate power cannot be controlled; it is by its nature uncontrollable. It cannot be made responsible since there is no criterion of responsibility, no socially accepted final authority for its justification. And what is unjustifiable cannot be responsible.

For the same reason, it cannot be limited. To limit the exercise of power is to fix the lines beyond which power ceases to be legitimate; that is, ceases to realize the basic social purpose. And if power is not legitimate to begin with, there are no limits beyond which it ceases to be legitimate.

No illegitimate ruler can possibly be a good or wise ruler. Illegitimate power invariably corrupts; for it can be only "might," never authority. It cannot be a controlled, limited, responsible, or rationally determinable power. And it has been an axiom of politics—ever since Tacitus in his history of the Roman emperors gave us one case study after another—that no human being, however good, wise or judicious, can wield uncontrolled, irresponsible, unlimited or rationally not determinable power without becoming very soon arbitrary, cruel, inhuman and capricious—in other words, a tyrant.

For all these reasons a society in which the socially decisive power is illegitimate power cannot function as a society. It can only be held together by sheer brute force—tyranny, slavery, civil war. Of course, force is the ultimate safeguard of every power; but in a functioning society it is not more than a desperate remedy for exceptional and rare diseases. In a functioning society power is exercised as authority, and *authority is the rule of right over might*. But only a legitimate power can have authority and can expect and command that social self-discipline which alone makes organized institutional life possible. Illegitimate power, even if wielded by the best and the wisest, can never depend upon anything but the submission to force. On that basis a functioning, institutional organization of social life cannot be built. Even the best tyrant is still a tyrant.

From: Kenneth E. Boulding
*THE IMAGE**

[EDITORS' NOTE: Professor Boulding teaches economics at the University of Michigan.]

The view of the political process which I have outlined above, which regards it as a process of mutual modification of images through the processes of feedback and communication, is in marked contrast to certain conventional views of the democratic process. In the conventional view, the democratic process is regarded as a summation, indexing, or resolution of individual preferences. This view leads to the so-called "voting paradoxes" and the "Arrow dilemma." This is the view put forth by Kenneth Arrow: that it is impossible to construct a social welfare function, that is, an ordering of possible alternatives by any process of the summation of the individual preference functions of the members of the society—impossible, that is to say, except under certain very unlikely or undesirable conditions. This seems to be a completely unreal model of the nature of

* Reprinted from *The Image* by Kenneth E. Boulding by permission of The University of Michigan Press. Copyright 1956. (Excerpts from pp. 102–4, 109.)

the political process, which is not that of the summation of fixed individual preferences but is the process of the mutual modification of images both relational and evaluational in the course of mutual communication, discussion, and discourse. The course of the discussion is punctuated by decisions which are essentially temporary in nature in the sense that they do not close the discussion, although they do, of course, have the effect of modifying it. In one sense, in a successful political process all decisions are interim. We live in a perpetual state of unresolved conflict. A decision is a partial resolution of conflict. It should never be a complete resolution. The majority does not rule; a majority decision is simply a setting of the terms under which the minority continues the discussion—a discussion which presumably goes on forever or at least for the lifetime of the organization. We need careful study of the way in which the communication networks of organizations affect not only the distribution of images of the role but also affect the value structures of the individuals concerned. Only thus will we come to a real understanding of the decision-making process.

The dynamics of political life can be interpreted largely in terms of the interaction of two processes. The first is the process whereby political images are created and distributed among the individuals of a society. The second is the process whereby specialized skills and knowledge are distributed among the people of the society. The political image is essentially an image of roles. Consider, for instance, the picture that we have of the American presidency. This is a role image which originated in the minds of the founding fathers and in the course of the long political and constitutional discussions which preceded the founding of this republic. It is an image which is partly enshrined in the transcript of the Constitution. It is an image, however, which has been changing slowly in the course of history and which is derived in part from the recorded experience of the occupants of the role. The role is the center of a complex network of communications both in and out, part of which each occupant of the role inherits and a part of which he creates for himself. It is an essential part of the image of the role that the occupant should be selected by a national election and that he should terminate the role at a stated date, unless, of course, he is re-elected. The occupant of the role is expected to be affable and accessible; he is expected to shake hands with innumerable people; he is expected to sign his name to innumerable documents; he is expected to make public pronouncements on important occasions; and he has large numbers of rights and duties prescribed to him both by the formal and informal constitution. An image of this role is present in the minds of millions of Americans in greater or less degree of clarity. It is not only present, it is accepted, that is, it is placed high on the value scale. The image, both in its behavioral aspects and in its value aspects, is perpetuated from generation to generation partly through the agencies of formal instruction, even more perhaps through the informal face-to-face communication between parents and child or among peers. The image of the role is so strong that it has a profound influence on its occupants. . . .

*   *   *   *   *

. . . There is a very real dilemma of power in society in that the images which are useful in gaining power are seldom useful in exercising it wisely or in keeping it. In formal democracies the ability to get elected is not identical with the ability to govern wisely. We are still far from solving the problem of devising a political institution which will at the same time permit extensive discussion and optimum feedbacks and minimize coercion on the one hand, and yet will also insure that the skills which lead to the attainment of the leadership roles are also identical with the skills required in performing these roles.

From: S. I. Hayakawa

*LANGUAGE IN THOUGHT AND ACTION**

[EDITORS' NOTE: The author is a noted semanticist, currently teaching at San Jose State College in California.]

THE LANGUAGE OF SOCIAL CONTROL

The effect of a parade of sonorous phrases upon human conduct has never been adequately studied.

THURMAN W. ARNOLD

MAKING THINGS HAPPEN

The most interesting and perhaps least understood of the relations between words and things is the relation between words and future events. When we say, for example, "Come here!" we are not describing the extensional world about us, nor are we merely expressing our feelings; we are trying to *make something happen*. What we call "commands," "pleas," "requests," and "orders" are the simplest ways we have of making things happen by means of words. There are, however, more roundabout ways. When we say, for example, "Our candidate is a Great American," we are of course making an enthusiastic purr about him, but we may also be influencing other people to vote for him. Again, when we say, "Our war against the enemy is God's war. God wills that we must triumph," we are saying something that is incapable of scientific verification; nevertheless, it may influence others to help in the prosecution of the war. Or if we merely state as a fact, "Milk contains vitamins," we may be influencing others to buy milk.

Consider, too, such a statement as "I'll meet you tomorrow at two o'clock in front of the Palace Theater." Such a statement about *future* events can only be made, it will be observed, in a system in which symbols are independent of things symbolized. The future, like the recorded past, is a specifically human dimension. To a dog, the expression "hamburger *tomorrow*" is meaningless—he will look at you expectantly, hoping for the extensional meaning of the word "hamburger" to be produced *now*. Squirrels, to be sure, store food for "next winter," but the fact that they store food regardless of whether or not their needs are adequately provided for demonstrates that such behavior (usually called "instinctive") is governed neither by symbols nor by other interpreted stimuli. Human beings are unique in their ability to react meaningfully to such expressions as "next Saturday," "on our next wedding anniversary," "twenty years after date I promise to pay," "some day, perhaps five hundred years from now." That is to say, maps can be made, in spite of the fact that the territories they stand for are not yet an actuality. Guiding ourselves by means of such maps of territories-to-be, we can impose a certain predictability upon future events.

With words, therefore, we influence and to an enormous extent *control future events*. It is for this reason that writers write; preachers preach; employers, parents, and teachers scold; propagandists send out news releases; statesmen give addresses. All of them, for various reasons, are trying to influence our conduct—sometimes for our good, sometimes for their own. These attempts to control, direct, or influence the future actions of fellow human beings with words may be termed *directive uses of language*.

Now it is obvious that if directive language is going to direct, it cannot be dull or uninteresting. If it is to influence our conduct, it *must* make use of every affective element in language: dramatic variations in tone of voice, rhyme and rhythm, purring and snarling, words with strong affective connotations, endless repetition. If meaningless noises will move the audience, meaningless noises must be made; if facts move them, facts must be given; if noble ideals move them, we must make our proposals appear noble; if they will respond only to fear, we must scare them stiff.

The nature of the affective means used in directive language is limited, of course, by the nature of our aims. If we are trying to direct people to be more kindly toward each other, we obviously do not want to arouse feelings of cruelty or hate. If we are trying to direct people to think and act more intelligently, we obviously should not use subrational appeals. If we are trying to direct people to lead better lives, we use affective appeals that arouse their finest feelings. . . .

From: Friedrich A. Hayek

"THE CORPORATION IN A DEMOCRATIC SOCIETY: IN WHOSE INTEREST OUGHT IT AND WILL IT BE RUN?"*

[EDITORS' NOTE: The author is Professor of Economics at the University of Chicago.]

My thesis will be that if we want effectively to limit the powers of corporations to where they are beneficial, we shall have to confine them much more than we have yet done to one specific goal, that of the profitable use of the capital entrusted to the management by the stockholders. I shall argue that it is precisely the tendency to allow and even to impel the corporations to use their resources for specific ends other than those of a long-run maximization of the return on the capital placed under their control which tends to confer upon them undesirable and socially dangerous powers and that the fashionable doctrine that their policy should be guided by "social considerations" is likely to produce most undesirable results.

*   *   *   *   *

* By permission from *Management and Corporations 1985*, by Melvin Anshen and George L. Bach. Copyright 1960. McGraw-Hill Book Company, Incorporated. (Excerpts from pp. 100–101, 104–7, 116–17.

Power, in the objectionable sense of the word, is the capacity to direct the energy and resources of others to the service of values which those others do not share. The corporation that has the sole task of putting assets to the most profitable use has no power to choose between values: It administers resources in the service of the values of others. It is perhaps only natural that management should desire to be able to pursue values which they think are important and that they need little encouragement from public opinion to indulge in these "idealistic" aims. But it is just in this that the danger rests of their acquiring real and uncontrollable power. . . . I shall maintain, therefore, that the old-fashioned conception, which regards management as the trustee of the stockholders and leaves to the individual stockholder the decision whether any of the proceeds of the activities of the corporation are to be used in the service of higher values, is the most important safeguard against the acquisition of arbitrary and politically dangerous powers by corporations.

*　　*　　*　　*　　*

There remain, then, as possible claimants for the position of the dominating interest in whose service the individual corporation ought to be conducted the owners of the equity and the public at large. . . . The traditional reconciliation of those two interests rested on the assumption that the general rules of law can be given such form that an enterprise, by aiming at long-run maximum return, will also serve the public interest best. . . .

Apart from these special instances, the general case for free enterprise and the division of labor rests on a recognition of the fact that, so long as each item of resources gets into the control of the enterprise willing to pay the highest price for it, it will, on the whole, also be used where it will make the largest contribution to the aggregate product of society. This contention is based on the assumption that each firm will in its decisions consider only such effects as will influence, directly or indirectly, the value of its assets and that it will not directly concern itself with the question of whether a particular use is "socially beneficial." I believe this is both necessary and right under a regime based on the division of labor and that the aggregation of assets brought together for the specific purpose of putting them to the most productive use is not a proper source for expenditure which is thought to be generally socially desirable. Such expenditure should be defrayed either by the voluntary payment of individuals out of their income or capital or out of funds raised by taxation.

*　　*　　*　　*　　*

. . . [T]he only argument I can discover in favor of allowing corporations to devote their funds to such purposes as higher education and research—not in instances where this is likely to make it a profitable investment for their stockholders, but because this is regarded as a generally desirable purpose—is that in existing circumstances this seems to be the easiest way to raise adequate funds for what many influential people regard as important ends. This, however, seems to me not to be an adequate argument when we consider the consequences that would follow if it were to become generally recognized that managements have such power. If the large aggregations of capital which the corporations represent could, at the discretion of the management, be used for any purpose approved as morally or socially good, if the opinion of the management that a certain end was intellectually or esthetically, scientifically or artistically desirable, were to justify expenditure by the corporation for such purposes, this would turn corporations from institutions serving the expressed needs of individual men into institutions determining which ends the efforts of individual men should serve. To allow the management to be guided in the use of funds, entrusted to them for the purpose of putting them to the materially most productive use, by what they regard as their social responsibility, would create centers of uncontrollable power never intended by those who provided the capital. It seems to me, therefore, clearly not desirable that general higher education or research should be regarded as legitimate purposes of corporation expenditure because this would not only vest powers over cultural decisions in men selected for capacities in an entirely different field, but would also establish a principle which, if generally applied, would enormously enhance the actual powers of corporations.

*   *   *   *   *

. . . Unless we believe that the corporations serve the public interest best by devoting their resources to the single aim of securing the largest return in terms of long-run profits, the case for free enterprise breaks down.

I cannot better sum up what I have been trying to say than by quoting a brief statement in which my colleague Professor Milton Friedman expressed the chief contention two years ago: "If anything is certain to destroy our free society, to undermine its very foundations, it would be a wide-spread acceptance by management of social responsibilities in some sense other than to make as much money as possible. This is a fundamentally subversive doctrine."

CONTINENTAL ELECTRIC COMPANY

I Case Introduction

Synopsis

The Continental Electric Company is organized by relatively autonomous product divisions for the manufacture and sale of a diverse number of electrical products. Top company management has a set of goals on which the performance of division managers is evaluated. There is a difference of opinion between top management and Mr. North, manager of the Electric Motor Division, as to whether the division has performed up to standard in the past. At the same time, Mr. North and his technical staff are faced with a choice between three investments in new technological innovation. He must recommend one of these to meet performance standards in the future. Various opinions and technical data are used to try to choose which capital investment to make.

Why This Case Is Included

This case offers opportunity to look at the philosophy of the decentralized form of organization—what advantages it *should* have for both technological excellence and human motivation. However, the details of making decentralization work, both from a financial and a human standpoint, are not so simple as the philosophy indicates.

Particularly important are conflicts between objectives at any one time, conflicts of long- versus short-run objectives, the perceptions of human beings of the "facts" they see in attaining objectives, and the problem of generalist executives who balance objectives but who also must obtain highly technical information from staff specialists.

The case offers opportunity to understand some concepts of financial management—the relation of profits, cash flows, and time—and the relation of long-term to short-run profits.

Finally, as an advanced project, this case provides opportunity to test the place of "management science" or quantification in the coordination (concurrence, governance, agreement, etc.) of human beings in organizations. To what extent does quantification produce agreement? To what extent does it result in the *authority of fact* as opposed to the *authority of sentiment, authority of personal judgment,* or *authority of power?*

Diagnostic and Predictive Questions

In answering the following diagnostic and predictive questions, remember that these questions apply theories and conceptual ideas from certain disciplines.

Such theories are valuable to understand basic forces at work in the policy system (diagnosis) and to predict what will happen in the system in the future (prediction). Since each reading abstracts from the total policy system certain factors or variables into the closed or partial viewpoint of one theory or discipline, no one reading gives answers to the practical policy problems of the case. In diagnosis and prediction, the parts of the problem are studied with "other things being equal."

Following each question are listed readings which will be helpful in answering the question. The readings included with this case are marked (*). By referring to the author index at the end of this book, you may locate the other readings listed.

1. What has the top management tried to achieve by organizing the company by product divisions rather than by functional divisions (manufacturing, sales, etc.)? Illustrate with facts from the case as to how management expects this organization will (should) affect the actions of North and his staff, as well as the economic and technical performance of the Electric Motor Division.

    Read: Curtice, "General Motors Organization Philosophy and Structure." Shillinglaw, *Cost Accounting,* pp. 680–89.

2. From the viewpoint of setting economic and financial objectives, why do Richardson and Grundy view North's performance as unsatisfactory, while North views his own performance as realistic?

    Read: *Drucker, *The Practice of Management,* pp. 62–64, 66, 84–87, 121, 128–31.

3. From the two concepts of "cash flow" and "rate of return," why might Linz and Donat disagree on whether to charge the cost of the patent to current expenses or to charge it to investment?

    Read: Linz' explanation of cash flow, Exhibit 3. Summer, "Profit, Flow of Funds, and Depreciation." Anthony, *Management Accounting,* pp. 290–92, 306. Also relate to Drucker, Question 2.

4. From the viewpoint of psychology—concepts of structural and functional factors in perception—what is causing the viewpoint of top management to differ from that of North in judging the quality of performance of the Motor Division?

    Read: Krech and Crutchfield, *Theory and Problems of Social Psychology,* pp. 81–83, 87–89, 94–96, 98, 102–3.

5. From the viewpoint of sociology—personalities of line and technical executives, and sources of authority in organizations—what might cause friction between North and Glass if the latter's project is not accepted? If we view North as a specialist on motors and Richardson as a generalist over all products, is this also true between these two "line" executives?

    Read: Thompson, *Modern Organization,* pp. 4–6, 12–13, 19–21, 61, 63–65, 77–78. *Etzioni, "Authority Structure and Organizational Effectiveness."

6. Suppose the only criterion for selecting investment projects were the total profit to the company generated over the life of the project. What advantage would this have? What limitations? Which project would be selected?

7. Suppose that the only criterion for capital investment were the *average* rate of return per year from the project. What advantage would this have over the total dollar return (Question 6)? What does average rate have to do with the payback period from each project? Which project would be selected?

    Study: The method for determining total profit, and average return, Exhibits 2, 4, 5.

8. Actually, Dr. Glass objected to the average rate of return as a selection criterion for investment projects. Examine his project, particularly the method

of figuring the average. If you were in his shoes, why would you object? What factor does it leave out?

Read: This question has to do with the limitations of an *average* as representing a series of numbers. Look at the series of yearly profits in Exhibit 5, and see why the average figure may be misleading. For those interested, review the use of the average as a statistical measure in any introductory statistics text.

Policy Questions for This Specific Case

In answering the following policy questions, the results of diagnosis and prediction are used to reduce the amount of guesswork, or judgment, in designing action solutions. However, since certain parts of the total case situation cannot be reduced to science, and since "other things are not equal," judgment must still be used to fill in the factors not accounted for by readings. You will also need a second kind of judgment as you put value weights on different scientific predictions, since different theories may point to conflicting solutions.

9. Which project is the best for long-run profits of Continental? Which project is best for shorter-run profits?

10. Suppose you want a criterion for selecting investment projects which would measure the worth of a project—that would select between the three taking into consideration both payback period *and* amounts. What would you use, and which project would be best?

Read: This question is related to Question 8. A measure may be devised creatively by the student, or for those who wish a more sophisticated method consider the following: Robert N. Anthony, *Management Accounting*, pp. 531–35. This deals with the discounted cash flow method of arriving at "worth" of an investment. It is not included in this book. A verbal summary is included from *Lewis, *Financial Controls for Management*, pp. 82–83.

11. If you were North, which project would you recommend? Would this be based on (*a*) what is best for the company as a whole? (*b*) What is best for the Motor Division? (*c*) What is best for you as an employed executive in the company? How do these differ? (Think of case facts, plus the readings in Questions 1–5.

12. From the viewpoint of both accuracy in the decision (deciding on what is best for the technology and finance of the company) and from the viewpoint of human motivation (the morale and learning of North, his staff, and top management), what methods are available for setting the financial criteria for investments, and for selecting the right project? How would these work in this case?

Read: Newman and Summer, *The Process of Management: Concepts, Behavior, and Practice*, pp. 439–48. *McGregor, *The Human Side of Enterprise*, pp. 124–31, 172–75. Enell and Haas, *Setting Standards for Executive Performance*, pp. 16–18, 31–32.

Major Policy Issues: Tentative Generalizations about Any Policy System

In arriving at conclusions for the following questions, generalize from the facts in the case and use your own ideas to (*a*) confirm, (*b*) modify, or (*c*) test the workability of the concepts and theories from readings. As an executive or professional, use wisdom to merge theory, on the one hand, with "brute facts" and practice, on the other.

13. What are the technological and human advantages of a decentralized organization structure? What are its limitations?

(Readings from Question 1, plus study of Richardson-Grundy-North actions, and the actions of the Military Products divisions will throw light on this issue.)

14. Can acceptable detailed rules or criteria be worked out which will make the philosophy of decentralization work in practice? What happens if the goals of top executives shift in emphasis over time, putting higher weight on certain goals at certain times than on others? What happens if the goals of lower executives or employees do likewise?

15. Will the processes of pluralism, constructive conflict, and participation in decision processes work *in reality* when matters of technology and economics (finance) are at stake between people in *parts* (versus the *whole*) of an organization? If so, under what conditions or modifications?

Read:　　Follett, "Constructive Conflict."

16. (Optional.) Can the use of "science" and "quantification" (e.g., use of the discounted cash flow) result in less friction between people? Why can measurements eliminate judgment and perceptual distortion? What is the "authority of fact" as contrasted with "the authority of command or of personal opinion"?

Read:　　Review Questions 8 and 10. Summer, "The Managerial Mind."
Lieber and Lieber, *The Education of T. C. Mits,* pp. 44–49. J. W. N. Sullivan, *The Limitations of Science,* chaps. 6, 7 (not reproduced herein). A. N. Whitehead, *Science in the Modern World,* chaps. 1, 2 (not reproduced herein).

Questions for Original Student Work in Analysis and Policy

The methods of viewing this case as represented by the authors' questions and selection of readings are not exhaustive. There are other relevant ideas for diagnosis and prediction. Furthermore, there are other ways of stating policy questions. More powerful analyses and wiser solutions will result by drawing on your own training and experience for (a) relevant concepts and theories, and (b) creative ways of asking policy questions. The following questions are designed to help you acquire this skill.

17. While reflecting on case facts, what additional theories from prior education give you insights as to "what is going on" in Continental Electric Company? As to what might be predicted to happen in the future?

18. Other than the policy questions asked by the authors, what pragmatic ways can you think of to state the practical problems faced by executives in the case?

II Continental Electric Company*

Company Background and Organization

Continental Electric Company is a leading producer of a wide variety of electrical products. Organizationally, it is divided into three major

---

product groups specializing in (1) consumer products—television sets, radios, kitchen appliances, etc.; (2) industrial products—generators, motors, transformers, etc.; and (3) military products—radar and communications equipment, missile parts, etc.

Each of these major product groups, headed by a vice president, is in turn divided into a number of related product divisions. For example, within the consumer product group there is a lighting division which produces a wide range of lamps and bulbs. There are sixteen such product divisions in the company, and each is headed by a division general manager.

Since 1950, when this organization structure was adopted, the corporate management of Continental has sought to make each of the sixteen divisions a semiautonomous business.

Edward M. Richardson, company president, described the philosophy of his organization's structure as follows:

> Along with the many benefits which come with long-scale business operation one of the most serious drawbacks can be the loss of entrepreneurial drive. . . . The organization structure of Continental Electric is designed to divide our big business into sixteen little businesses. Each of my sixteen general managers thinks of himself as the president of a small business. . . .
> Each is responsible for the long-run success of his business.

*   *   *   *   *

> We guide the divisions by defining their broad responsibilities, or missions, in terms of total corporate goals. Within these broad guidelines they are on their own. To be sure, division performance is evaluated regularly in terms of short- and long-range criteria.
> These criteria are:
> 1. Profitability:
>   a) Net profit before taxes: Each division computes this for corporate review just as the company as a whole computes its income statement for stockholders' review.
>   b) Rate of return: Net income as a percent of division assets. Again top corporate management receives the same kind of figures from the divisions as the corporation must present to its stockholders.
> 2. Market Share: The division's percent of total industry sales.
> 3. Product Leadership: The degree to which the division maintains and increases the company's reputation as a technological leader in the electrical products industry.
> 4. Utilization of Human Resources: A series of measures are used to determine the morale and effective utilization of the division's work force.
> 5. Corporate Citizenship: A series of measures are used to determine whether the division is meeting its responsibilities in terms of local, state, and national needs.

Mr. Richardson went on to explain that the divisions are reviewed formally by their respective group vice presidents on a quarterly basis and annually by the corporate review board. Chaired by Richardson, the review board is made up of the company's executive vice president, F. L.

Taylor, the vice president of finance, George M. Rettenbush, and the vice president of corporate staff, Paul D. Faust. The secretary of the board is William Lavanger who is also chief counsel.

In addition to reviewing division performance, the review board also has final say on budget requests. In accord with the philosophy of decentralization, each division sets its own sales targets and develops its requests for operating funds and capital needed for more permanent divisional investments. In addition to a detailed one-year budget, the divisions also prepare three-year sales and profit forecasts which serve as a backdrop to the annual plan.

Sales targets and budget requests are reviewed by the division's respective group vice presidents. The group vice president does not have the authority to change the division's proposals but since he does have the authority to change divisional personnel he can exert some informal pressure if he feels that sales goals or cash requirements are out of line. However, since the success or failure of top division management is closely correlated to divisional performance, the group vice presidents tend to interfere as little as possible with division plans as long as performance is good and expectations promising.

As one group vice president put it, "The proof of who's right and who's wrong is profits. We try to let the divisions run their own show and then they stand or fall on their own decisions."

Electric Motor Division

The Electric Motor Division produces a variety of small fractional and one-horsepower motors. Roughly 40% of the division's output is sold to other divisions of Continental which use small motors in their products. The remaining 60% is sold to outside companies some of which use the motors in products competing with Continental products.

The "sales" within the company are made at a price based on manufacturing cost plus 8% markup. By way of contrast, the division's profit margin on sales to outside customers has been between 12% and 14% over full cost (manufacturing plus selling and corporate overhead).

The general manager of the Electric Motor Division, William North, is 46 years old. He has been with the company for 14 years and has been manager of the Electric Motor Division for the past five years. His performance after three years in this post was regarded by Richardson as excellent.

"We were really pleased with the way Bill improved a division that had many problems in the past," Richardson said, "and we felt at that time that in a few years Bill was slated for even bigger responsibilities. Unfortunately his last two years as divisional manager have not been as successful."

In 1961 the division fell short of realizing its estimated profit level by 18%. Total sales were estimated at $12 million, and the profit forecast was for $1,250,000. Actual sales came to $11,860,000, but profit was only $1,025,000.

On the basis of third-quarter results it is almost certain that the Electric Motor Division sales will rise in 1962 to the $12,300,000 level which was forecast in the profit plan for 1962. In addition, it seems equally likely that the profit objective of $1,250,000 will be met. However, Thomas Grundy, group vice president of industrial products, is not overly pleased with the division's anticipated performance in 1962.

Grundy stated, "When Bill North took over the Electric Motor Division, we all saw bigger things in store for him. His performance from 1958–60 confirmed our confidence in him. However, in 1961 things seemed to turn sour, and this year it looks as though he will meet his profit forecast only by virtue of having reduced division expectations below what they should have been. While his sales and profits goals are higher than last year's results, they are not high enough. I warned him when he submitted his 1962 plan that I thought he should set his sights higher, but the bad year in 1961 must have scared him.

"Therefore, I can't get very excited about his 1962 results for even if he reaches his objectives, I feel they were too conservative to begin with. I hope Bill is willing to present a more optimistic profit outlook for his division in 1963. If he sets his goals high enough and reaches them, he may find himself promoted in 1964. If he plays it too conservatively or fails to show a better profit picture, we'll be forced to reconsider his future with Continental."

When asked whether he had informed North about his feelings, Grundy replied, "I think Bill knows where he stands. Of course, I can't promise him anything if he does a good job nor do I want to unnerve him with threats. However, if he is the kind of executive we hope he is, he should understand his position."

When questioned about his division's performance over the past two years, North made the following observations:

Our sales and profit forecasts for 1961 reflected an anticipation on our part of wide acceptance of a new half-horsepower motor designed especially for use in lawn mowers. Doug Glass, division director of research, and Ralph Hulnick, director of engineering, did a wonderful job on the design and development of the motor. Unfortunately, in order to reach projected sales targets we had to spend more than anticipated to get market acceptance. This, along with a three-week work stoppage due to a wildcat strike, pushed our operating costs above our estimates and accounted for most of the 18% discrepancy between projected and actual profits.

I explained this to the review board and indicated that the increased marketing expenditures would pay off in future years sales and that the stoppage was a result of a labor problem I had inherited from the previous general manager. They seemed to accept my position, but Mr. Richardson also reminded me that "you can't run a business on tomorrow's profits or yesterday's mistakes." Somehow I don't think I got through to them.

Our 1962 profit forecast may have been lower than Tom Grundy would have liked, but I think results showed our estimates to be realistic.

Division Plans for 1963

In developing the 1963 profit plan for the Electric Motor Division, Mr. North is faced with a decision on three proposals for substantial capital investment put to him by his staff. Because of the size of the outlays, North feels he cannot propose more than one of these projects to corporate management.

Proposal No. 1: Purchase of a Patent on Component Part. The first proposal under consideration is one of several submitted by Ralph Hulnick, divisional director of engineering. All of Hulnick's proposals at this time have been included in the operating budget except this one, which will involve an outlay of $210,000 to acquire patent rights on a new component part. Hulnick estimates that this new component part, which would be used in the assembly of motors, would reduce manufacturing costs about $110,000 a year.

Unfortunately, the inventors of the part have tried for many years to find a way of producing it at a cost low enough to make its use economically feasible; as a result, Continental's legal department estimates that the patents have but three years of protection remaining. The inventors have recently solved the production problems, but lack the capital needed to take advantage of their discovery. They are, therefore, willing to sell their rights to Continental for $210,000.

Based on engineering estimates of cost savings, Hulnick and the division controller, Amos Linz, have prepared the figures summarized in Exhibit 2.

In submitting these estimates, Linz told Mr. North that he did not think it would be wise to propose this project to corporate management even though it showed a good rate of return.

"There is a slight chance," Linz stated, "that Donat (the corporate controller) will make us treat the $210,000 paid for the patent as a period expense thus forcing us to absorb the cost in one year. This would help the company's cash position by reducing taxable income and taxes paid next year, but it'll really knock our reported profit down for 1963."

North requested Linz to expand on this point. Linz prepared a set of tables, accompanied by explanatory notes, showing what would happen to cash flows and reported profits if the patent purchase price was treated either as a capital investment or an operating expense. These are presented in Exhibit 3.

"As you can see," Linz explained, "as long as overall corporate profits are good enough to keep the stockholders happy, Donat is probably going to insist that we expense the $210,000, since it'll almost double the available cash flow for next year. But we're not going to see a penny of this cash until we come in with our 1964 budget. By then it's not *our* cash, but just part of the entire company's cash account, and we're but one of sixteen divisions trying to get our hands on some of it."

"In a nutshell, Bill," Linz concluded, "if we propose the patent purchase we may end up having to work just that much harder to show a good profit picture. Certainly, if they treat the $210,000 as an expense, our profits in 1964 and 1965 will be even better. But, remember Richardson's comment about not being able to run a business on next year's profits. It's the 1963 results they're going to judge us by."

North questioned this reasoning by asking, "Look Amos, don't you think that if they request us to expense the $210,000 outlay at the start of the year, they'll remember at the end of the year why our profits are a little lower?"

Linz' reply was: "Don't count on it, Bill. Don't forget this is only one of many many factors that is going to influence our divisional profits. And if we show lower profit forecasts because we expect them to treat the $210,000 as an expense, then Grundy [group vice president] will be all over us for not being more aggressive. If we come up with a more optimistic forecast and don't make it, the review board will treat any explanations on our part—as far as the $210,000 expense is concerned—as simply an alibi. If I were you I wouldn't take the chance on this one and put my money on Kirkpatrick's request."

Proposal No. 2: Purchase of New Wiring Equipment. North stated that he was not completely convinced by Amos Linz' reasoning but that he had a great deal of respect for Linz' judgment particularly in financial matters such as this. In addition, Linz has been with the company for 41 years and knows as much about company politics as anyone in the firm. Having started with the company in the accounting department as a clerk after graduation from high school, he worked his way up from the bottom. Linz is well regarded in the company, and his opinion is often sought by younger executives like North.

The project Linz advised North to include in the budget was made by Owen Kirkpatrick, director of manufacturing. Kirkpatrick has seen a piece of equipment known as the Margot-Toledo Wirer demonstrated and feels "that it could be used to automate the attachment of wire coils in the one-horsepower motors. Such automatic attachment would permit a more efficient assembly line operation, and should reduce manufacturing costs between $80,000 and $100,000 a year."

The cost of purchasing the Margot-Toledo equipment is estimated at $250,000, but Kirkpatrick stated that "even in the face of rapid changes in such automated equipment and technology, I am sure that this equipment will have at least a five-year economic life.

"I'd love to see us get that patent Ralph Hulnick's after, but if what

Linz says is right and in light of my proposal's five-year life compared to the three-year life of Ralph's patent, I think we ought to put our money in the new equipment."

Working with Linz, Kirkpatrick submitted a summary of the financial estimates to North (Exhibit 4).

Proposal No. 3: Research on Insulation Materials. A third proposal under consideration has been put forth by Dr. Douglas Glass, division director of research. Dr. Glass who is 42, joined the company three years ago. After having taught electrical engineering at a major eastern university for ten years, he joined the research staff of one of Continental's principal competitors where he worked for two years.

North states that he was quite happy to get Glass to join the company three years ago but soon recognized that while he had acquired the talents of a brilliant research engineer he had also taken on a strong-minded and impatient individual.

Glass explained his reasons for accepting Continental's offer as follows: "I took this job because the people I worked with on my former job should be managing a rocking chair company. They are painfully conservative, scared stiff by corporate management, and haven't listened to a new idea in ten years. I can't work in an environment like that. Things change too swiftly to sit around milking yesterday's good ideas."

Dr. Glass' largest proposal for this year's budget is the third project being considered by North. It involves embarking upon a research program designed to develop a new insulation material for use under extremely high and low temperature conditions. Success in this venture would give the division a motor which would find wide use in industry.

Dr. Glass has requested that $75,000 a year be allocated for this project for the next three years. Then if all goes well, an investment of about $100,000 will be necessary in the fourth year to begin production.

Mr. North has consulted with the group vice president of military products and the general managers of several divisions within his own group, and they are all very enthusiastic about such a breakthrough. However, none are willing to contribute to the cost of the project.

"After all," said the general manager of one division, "your division has the responsibility for updating technology in small motors. This is one of the five major criteria by which any division performance is evaluated. As much as we would like to see you come through on this project we can't see why we should subsidize you on it."

Dr. Glass, however, has taken a very strong stand for the research project.

"These other proposals are nothing but short-run cost cutting solutions to a profit problem which has long-run implications. As a division, we are dead, competitively, if we don't start moving ahead into new products and new technologies. This research cost is peanuts compared to its potential value to the company," he said, "and don't forget that product leadership is one of the goals set for us by top management."

Dr. Glass and his staff, however, are the only ones who support the project within the division. As Linz points out, "this project would take almost six years before we begin to get into the black on it. It's fine for Glass to talk about the long-run, but none of us are going to be here in the long run if we don't do something about our short-term profit picture."

Based on Glass' estimates, Linz has summarized the financial outlook for the research project in Exhibit 5.

Dr. Glass feels that the benefits from his project should go well beyond eight years, but Mr. Linz is unwilling to develop financial forecasts beyond that period. In addition, Dr. Glass feels that the use of averages to compute rate of return when comparing projects such as these is deceptive. He told North in the midst of a stormy budget meeting, "I'm no financial expert but I'm sure that all these figures Amos throws around are not true measure of these projects' value."

When Amos Linz suggested that Glass stick to his research business and not meddle with financial analysis, Glass stated that "this is the same kind of ostrich thinking" he had been forced to deal with when working for Continental's competition.

A heated exchange followed, and North thought it best to call a halt to the meeting. As Linz left he turned to North and said, "Young man, you've got a real future in this company if you use your head. Every warning I gave you about the patent proposal goes double on this research project.

"Backing the research project means sacrificing between $15,000 and $25,000 of extra profits by passing up the savings on new equipment. In addition, it sticks us with a $37,500 loss per year for the next three years. I cannot see why anyone striving for a better profit picture should want to start off by throwing away roughly $60,000 in profits a year for three years."

A summary of the financial projections for the three projects prepared by Linz for North is shown below:

COMPARATIVE FINANCIAL PROJECTIONS
FOR THREE PROPOSALS

Project	*Payback Period**	*Total Profit after Taxes*	*Average Rate of Return*
No. 1 Patent	2 years, 4 months	$ 60,000	19.00%
No. 2 New equipment	3 years, 7 months	100,000	16.00
No. 3 Research project	6 years, 4 months	187,500	14.42

* Using cash flow (after tax income + depreciation), this is the length of time it takes to recover the cash outlays.

Exhibit 1

CONTINENTAL ELECTRIC COMPANY
Relevant Portion of Organization Chart

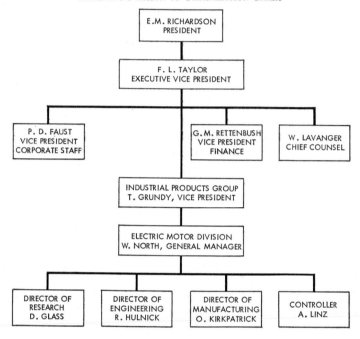

Exhibit 2

FINANCIAL PROJECTIONS FOR INVESTMENT IN PATENT
(PROJECT NO. 1)

Year	Cost Savings before Taxes	Deprecia- tion*	Additional Taxable Income	Taxes†	Additional after Tax Income
1963	$110,000	$70,000	$40,000	$20,000	$20,000
1964	110,000	70,000	40,000	20,000	20,000
1965	110,000	70,000	40,000	20,000	20,000
					$60,000

* If the $210,000 payment for the patent is treated as a capital investment and depreciated over three years, the annual depreciation would be $70,000 ($210,000 ÷ 3 = $70,000).
† Using a 50% tax rate to simplify estimates.

Profit Summary

Total profit over life of patent = $ 60,000
Average annual profit   =   20,000
Average investment   =   105,000*

* Average capital tied up in 1963 (with annual depreciation of $70,000) = $175,000
Average capital tied up in 1964 (with annual depreciation of $70,000) =   105,000
Average capital tied up in 1965 (with annual depreciation of $70,000) =   35,000

Average capital tied up during project life   = $315,000

Average capital tied up per year, $315,000 ÷ 3 = $105,000

$$\text{Average rate of return} = \frac{\$ \ 20,000}{\$105,000} = 19.00\%$$

Exhibit 3

PURCHASE OF PATENTS (PROJECT NO. 1)

IMPLICATIONS OF TREATING PURCHASE PRICE AS INVESTMENT OR CURRENT EXPENSE
ALTERNATIVE 1—CAPITALIZING THE $210,000 EXPENDITURE

(Assumes the Company Treats the Outlay as a Capital Expenditure and
Thus "Writes It Off" over Three Years)

Year	(1) Extra Cost Savings before Taxes and Depreciation	(2) Depreciation	(3) Taxable Income	(4) Taxes (at 50% Rate)	(5) After Tax Profit	Cash Flow; Increase or Decrease in Cash Available Col. (1) — Col. (4)
0	$ 0	$ 0	$ 0	$ 0	$ 0	$ —210,000*
0–1	110,000	70,000	40,000	20,000	20,000	+ 90,000†
1–2	110,000	70,000	40,000	20,000	20,000	+ 90,000
2–3	110,000	70,000	40,000	20,000	20,000	+ 90,000
						$ + 60,000

* At point in time zero when the $210,000 is paid out, the only impact is $210,000 less in the "cash box."

† From point zero to one (calendar year 1963), an extra $110,000 is saved. The $70,000 in Col. (2) is not an actual outflow since depreciation is merely a partial delayed tax credit for the $210,000 that actually left the "cash box" earlier. Thus the company actually has an extra $110,000 it saves, minus the $20,000 in taxes it pays, or a net cash increase of $90,000 ($110,000 — $20,000 = $90,000).

ALTERNATIVE 2—EXPENSING THE $210,000 EXPENDITURE

(Assumes Entire $210,000 Is Charged Off in 1963, and That Taxable Income from Other Division Operations Will Be Sufficient to Offset Losses Reported from This Project)

Year	Extra Cost Savings before Taxes	Expense to Purchase Patent	Taxable Income	Extra Taxes Saved or Paid	After Tax Profit	Cash Flow (Increase or Decrease in Cash Available)
0	$ 0	$ 0	$ 0	$ 0	$ 0	$ —210,000*
0–1	110,000	210,000	—100,000	—50,000	—50,000	+160,000†
1–2	110,000	0	+110,000	+55,000	+55,000	+ 55,000‡
2–3	110,000	0	+110,000	+55,000	+55,000	+ 55,000
						$ + 60,000

* As in *Alternative Treatment 1*, at point in time zero when the $210,000 is paid out the only impact is $210,000 less in the "cash box."

† From zero to one (calendar year 1963), an extra $110,000 is saved, but if the $210,000 is treated as an expense, the division has $210,000 worth of tax credit, $110,000 of this credit is used to offset the extra income so the division "pays" no taxes on it and all $110,000 stays in the cash box.

In addition the division has $100,000 ($210,000 — $110,000 = $100,000) worth of tax credit left to apply to other division income. Thus (using a 50% tax rate) the division "pays" $50,000 less taxes on its other income and has an extra $50,000 left in the "cash box." The total effect of this first year is to have an extra $160,000 in the cash box:

$110,000 extra income
50,000 taxes saved
$160,000

‡ In years two and three, $110,000 is saved each year. There is no deduction for depreciation so $55,000 is "paid out" in extra taxes, and the division ends each year with an extra $55,000 in cash having been generated.

Exhibit 3—Continued

COMPARISON OF ALTERNATIVES 1 AND 2

Note: At the end of the three years (December 31, 1965), no matter which alternative is used, the company has a calculated net gain of $60,000.

In First Year (1963): Alternative 1 shows higher profit but lower cash available for other company uses than Alternative 2.

In Second and Third Years (1964, 1965): Alternative 1 shows lower profit, higher available cash than Alternative 2.

SUMMARIZING RESULTS FOR END OF 1963

Alternative Treatment of the Expenditure	(1963) Net Profit after Taxes	1963 Cash Flow Available for Reinvestment
1. ($210,000 treated as investment)	$ +20,000	$ +90,000
2. ($210,000 treated as an expense)	$ −50,000	$ +160,000

Note: Under Alternative 2, the company will have an extra $70,000 ($160,000 − $90,000 = $70,000) working for it for a full year, which it would not have under Alternative 1. While it is true the company will recoup this $70,000 during 1964 and 1965, at least one year's income on $70,000 will be lost to the company.

Exhibit 4

FINANCIAL PROJECTIONS FOR INVESTMENT IN NEW EQUIPMENT (PROJECT NO. 2)

Year	Cost Savings before Taxes	Depre-ciation*	Additional Taxable Income	Taxes†	Additional after Tax Income
1	$ 80,000	$50,000	$30,000	$15,000	$ 15,000
2	90,000	50,000	40,000	20,000	20,000
3	100,000	50,000	50,000	25,000	25,000
4	90,000	50,000	40,000	20,000	20,000
5	90,000	50,000	40,000	20,000	20,000
					$100,000

* Assuming the equipment will have a five-year economic life, depreciation will be $50,000 per year ($250,000 ÷ 5 = $50,000).
† Using a 50% tax rate to simplify estimates.

PROFIT SUMMARY

Total profit	$100,000
Average profit	20,000
Average investment	125,000
Average rate of return	$\dfrac{20,000}{125,000} = 16.00\%$

Exhibit 5

FINANCIAL PROJECTIONS FOR RESEARCH PROGRAM (PROJECT NO. 3)

Year	Added Income before Taxes	Research Cost*	Depre- ciation†	Addi- tional Taxable Income	Taxes Paid‡	Addi- tional after Tax Income
1	$ 0	$75,000	$ 0	$ −75,000	$ −37,500	$ −37,500
2	0	75,000	0	−75,000	−37,500	−37,500
3	0	75,000	0	−75,000	−37,500	−37,500
4	50,000	0	20,000	30,000	15,000	15,000
5	75,000	0	20,000	55,000	27,500	27,500
6	175,000	0	20,000	155,000	77,500	77,500
7	200,000	0	20,000	180,000	90,000	90,000
8	200,000	0	20,000	180,000	90,000	90,000
						$187,500

* Assuming research cost will have to be treated as an expense and charged to period income.
† Assuming the $100,000 investment in the fourth years has a five-year economic life, depreciation will be $20,000 per year ($100,000 ÷ 5 = $20,000).
‡ Using 50% tax rate to simplify estimates and assuming other taxable earnings will be offset.

PROFIT SUMMARY

Total profit $187,500
Average profit .... $ 23,438 ($187,500 ÷ 8 = $23,438)
Average Investment .... $162,500 ($225,000 + $100,000 = $325,000
$325,000 ÷ 2 = $162,500)

Average rate of return .... $\dfrac{\$23,438}{\$162,500} = 14.42\%$

III Selected Readings

From: Peter F. Drucker

THE PRACTICE OF MANAGEMENT*

[EDITORS' NOTE: The author is Professor in the Graduate School of Business, New York University.]

Most of today's lively discussion of management by objectives is concerned with the search for the one right objective. This search is not only likely to be as

---

* From *The Practice of Management* by Peter F. Drucker. Copyright 1954 by Peter F. Drucker. Reprinted with permission of Harper & Row, Publishers, Incorporated. (Excerpts from pp. 62–64, 66, 84–87, 121, 128–31.)

unproductive as the quest for the philosopher's stone; it is certain to do harm and to misdirect.

To emphasize only profit, for instance, misdirects managers to the point where they may endanger the survival of the business. To obtain profit today they tend to undermine the future. They may push the most easily saleable product lines and slight those that are the market of tomorrow. They tend to short-change research, promotion and the other postponable investments. Above all, they shy away from any capital expenditure that may increase the invested-capital base against which profits are measured; and the result is dangerous obsolescence of equipment. In other words, they are directed into the worst practices of management.

To manage a business is to balance a variety of needs and goals. This requires judgment. The search for the one objective is essentially a search for a magic formula that will make judgment unnecessary. But the attempt to replace judgment by formula is always irrational; all that can be done is to make judgment possible by narrowing its range and the available alternatives, giving it clear focus, a sound foundation in facts and reliable measurements of the effects and validity of actions and decisions. And this, by the very nature of business enterprise, requires multiple objectives.

What should these objectives be, then? There is only one answer: *Objectives are needed in every area where performance and results directly and vitally affect the survival and prosperity of the business.* These are the areas which are affected by every management decision and which therefore have to be considered in every management decision. They decide what it means concretely to manage the business. They spell out what results the business must aim at and what is needed to work effectively toward these targets.

*   *   *   *   *

There are eight areas in which objectives of performance and results have to be set:

Market standing; innovation; productivity; physical and financial resources; profitability; manager performance and development; worker performance and attitude; public responsibility.

*   *   *   *   *

Yet, even if managing were merely the application of economics, we would have to include these three areas and would have to demand that objectives be set for them. They belong in the most purely formal economic theory of the business enterprise. For neglect of manager performance and development, worker performance and public responsibility soon results in the most practical and tangible loss of market standing, technological leadership, productivity and profit—and ultimately in the loss of business life. That they look so different from anything the economist—especially the modern economic analyst—is wont to deal with, that they do not readily submit to quantification and mathematical treatment, is the economist's bad luck; but it is no argument against their consideration.

The very reason for which economist and accountant consider these areas impractical—that they deal with principles and values rather than solely with dollars and cents—makes them central to the management of the enterprise, as tangible, as practical—and indeed as measurable—as dollars and cents.

*   *   *   *   *

"We don't care what share of the market we have, as long as our sales go up," is a fairly common comment. It sounds plausible enough; but it does not stand up under analysis. By itself, volume of sales tells little about performance, results or the future of the business. A company's sales may go up—and the company may actually be headed for rapid collapse. A company's sales may go down—and the reason may not be that its marketing is poor but that it is in a dying field and had better change fast.

A maker of oil refinery equipment reported rising sales year after year. Actually new refineries and their equipment were being supplied by the company's competitors. But because the equipment it had supplied in the past was getting old and needed repairs, sales spurted; for replacement parts for equipment of this kind have usually to be bought from the original supplier. Sooner or later, however, the original customers were going to put in new and efficient equipment rather than patch up the old and obsolescent stuff. Then almost certainly they were going to go to the competitors designing and building the new equipment. The company was thus threatened with going out of business—which is what actually happened.

*   *   *   *   *

THE TIME-SPAN OF OBJECTIVES

For what time-span should objectives be set? How far ahead should we set our targets?

The nature of the business clearly has a bearing here. In certain parts of the garment business next week's clearance sale is "long-range future." It may take four years to build a big steam turbine and two more to install it; in the turbine business six years may be "immediate present" therefore. And Crown Zellerbach is forced to plant today the trees it will harvest fifty years hence.

Different areas require different time-spans. To build a marketing organization takes at least five years. Innovations in engineering and chemistry made today are unlikely to show up in marketing results and profits for five years or longer. On the other hand a sales campaign, veteran sales managers believe, must show results within six weeks or less; "Sure, there are sleepers," one of these veterans once said, "but most of them never wake up."

This means that in getting objectives management has to balance the immediate future—the next few years—against the long range: five years or longer. This balance can best be found through a "managed-expenditures budget." For practically all the decisions that affect the balance are made as decisions on what the accountant calls "managed expenditures"—those expenditures that are determined by current management decision rather than by past and irrevocable decisions (like capital charges), or by the requirements of current business (like labor and raw material costs). Today's managed expenditures are tomorrow's profit; but they may also be today's loss.

Every second-year accountancy student knows that almost any "profit" figure can be turned into a "loss" by changing the basis of depreciation charges; and the new basis can usually be made to appear as rational as the old. But few managements—including their accountants—realize how many such expenditures there are that are based, knowingly or not, on an assessment of short-range versus long-range needs, and that vitally affect both. Here is a partial list:

Depreciation charges; maintenance budgets; capital replacement, modernization and expansion costs; research budgets; expenditures on product development and design; expenditures on the management group, its compensation and rewards, its size, and on developing tomorrow's managers; cost of building and maintining a marketing organzation; promotion and advertising budgets; cost of service to the customer; personnel management, especially training expenditures.

Almost any one of these expenditures can be cut back sharply, if not eliminated; and for some time, perhaps for a long time, there will be no adverse effect. Any one of these expenditures can be increased sharply and for good reasons, with no resulting benefits visible for a long time. By cutting these expenditures immediate results can always be made to look better. By raising them immediate results can always be made to look worse.

*   *   *   *   *

BALANCING THE OBJECTIVES

In addition to balancing the immediate and the long-range future, management also has to balance objectives. What is more important: an expansion in markets and sales volume, or a higher rate of return? How much time, effort and energy should be expended on improving manufacturing productivity? Would the same amount of effort or money bring greater returns if invested in new-product design?

There are few things that distinguish competent from incompetent management quite as sharply as the performance in balancing objectives. Yet, there is no formula for doing the job. Each business requires its own balance—and it may require a different balance at different times. . . .

*   *   *   *   *

Any business enterprise must build a true team and weld individual efforts into a common effort. Each member of the enterprise contributes something different, but they must all contribute toward a common goal. Their efforts must all pull in the same direction, and their contributions must fit together to produce a whole—without gaps, without friction, without unnecessary duplication of effort.

Business performance therefore requires that each job be directed toward the objectives of the whole business. And in particular each manager's job must be focused on the success of the whole. . . .

*   *   *   *   *

By definition, a manager is responsible for the contribution that his component makes to the larger unit above him and eventually to the enterprise. His performance aims upward rather than downward. This means that the goals of each manager's job must be defined by the contribution he has to make to the success of the larger unit of which he is a part. The objectives of the district sales manager's job should be defined by the contribution he and his district sales force have to make to the sales department. . . .

*   *   *   *   *

This requires each manager to develop and set the objectives of his unit himself. Higher management must, of course, reserve the power to approve or disapprove these objectives. But their development is part of a manager's responsibility; indeed, it is his first responsibility. It means, too, that every manager should responsibly participate in the development of the objectives of the higher unit of which his is a part. . . . He must know and understand the ultimate business goals, what is expected of him and why, what he will be measured against and how. There must be a "meeting of minds" within the entire management of each unit. This can be achieved only when each of the contributing managers is expected to think through what the unit objectives are, is led, in others words, to participate actively and responsibly in the work of defining them. And only if his lower managers participate in this way can the higher manager know what to expect of them and can make exacting demands.

*   *   *   *   *

SELF-CONTROL THROUGH MEASUREMENTS

The greatest advantage of management by objectives is perhaps that it makes it possible for a manager to control his own performance. Self-control means stronger motivation: a desire to do the best rather than just enough to get by. It means higher performance goals and broader vision. Even if management by objectives were not necessary to give the enterprise the unity of direction and effort of a management team, it would be necessary to make possible management by self-control.

So far in this book I have not talked of "control" at all; I have talked of "measurements." This was intentional. For "control" is an ambiguous word. It means the ability to direct oneself and one's work. It can also mean domination of one person by another. Objectives are the basis of "control" in the first sense; but they must never become the basis of "control" in the second, for this would defeat their purpose. Indeed, one of the major contributions of management by objectives is that it enables us to substitute management by self-control for management by domination. . . .

From: Amitai Etzioni

"AUTHORITY STRUCTURE AND ORGANIZATIONAL EFFECTIVENESS"*

[EDITORS' NOTE: Dr. Etzioni is Associate Professor of Sociology in Columbia University.]

. . . Managers are generally considered as those who have the major (line) authority because they direct the major goal activity. Experts deal only with means, with secondary activities. Therefore it is functional for them to have none, or only limited (staff), authority.

. . . Managers and experts may be differentiated from four points of view: (a) role structure, (b) personality, (c) background, mainly in terms of educational and occupational experience, and (d) normative orientations.

The *role* of the expert is to create and institutionalize knowledge. The role of the manager is to integrate (create or maintain) organizational systems or sub-

* Reprinted by permission of The Graduate School of Business and Public Administration, Cornell University, Ithaca, New York (*Administrative Science Quarterly*, June 1959, pp. 45–47).

systems from the point of view of the institutional goals and needs.[1] The expert typically deals with symbols and materials (although there are many who disagree with this point of view).[2] The manager deals with people. The two role types require different *personality* types. The expert who has intensive knowledge in a limited area, tends to have a restricted perspective. The manager has extensive, though limited, knowledge of many areas, and the resulting broad perspective is essential for his role. Experts are committed to abstract ideas and therefore tend to be unrealistic, whereas managers are more practical. Managers are skilled in human relations; experts are temperamental.[3]

Managers and experts differ in *background*. Experts usually have higher educations than managers and tend to enter their first job at a later age and at higher initial salaries. They often start at relatively high positions in the hierarchy but are limited in the range of their mobility. Managers enter their first job at a younger age, with less education, and at lower positions, but they move upward faster than the experts and some of them eventually get higher than any expert.[4] Whereas many experts remain more or less restricted to the same organizational functions, the typical manager is assigned to a large variety of tasks in what is called the process of broadening.

Managers' *orientations* differ considerably from those of experts. Managers are more committed or loyal to their specific organization than are experts.[5] Experts are often primarily oriented toward their professional reference and membership groups. While managers are often committed to the organization's particular goals, experts are committed to the scientific and professional ethos regardless of the particular needs and goals of their institution.[6]

Obviously though there is a high correlation among these four variables, they are not inevitably associated. Two major mechanisms explain how the correlation is maintained. First of all there is *selective recruitment*. People with managerial personalities and background are recruited to managerial roles, and those with the personalities and education of experts tend to enter staff positions. The second mechanism is *role adaptation*. People who enter roles which are initially incompatible with their personalities often adjust to their new roles. . . .

---

[1] The roles of managers will be discussed here only with regard to the internal functions of the organization. Their roles with regard to environment will be disregarded because of space limitations.

[2] Experts can be arranged in a continuum from the less to the more skilled in human relations. Chemists, for instance, are on the average less skilled from this point of view than are labor relations experts. See L. E. Danielson, Management's Relations with Engineers and Scientists, *Proceedings of Industrial Relations Research Association*, Tenth Annual Meeting, 1957, pp. 314–321.

[3] See Robert Dubin, *Human Relations in Administration* (New York, 1951), pp. 113–138.

[4] For a comparison, see M. Dalton, Conflicts between Staff and Line Managerial Officers, *American Sociological Review*, 15 (1950), 342–351; and C. A. Myers and J. G. Turnbull, Line and Staff in Industrial Relations, *Harvard Business Review*, 34 (July–Aug. 1956), 113–124.

[5] For a case study which brings out this point, see A. H. Stanton and M. S. Schwartz, *The Mental Hospital* (New York, 1954).

[6] A. W. Gouldner, Cosmopolitans and Locals: Toward an Analysis of Latent Social Roles, *Administrative Science Quarterly*, 2 (1957), 444–480.

From: Ralph B. Lewis
*FINANCIAL CONTROLS FOR MANAGEMENT**

THE THEORY OF INVESTMENT AND RETURN

From the standpoint of pure theory, there is only one true method (for determining rate of return on an investment). This is the investor's method. It is also called the discount method, or present value method. All the money that is to be laid out prior to the start of operations is measured. This includes payments for plant, property and equipment and working capital as well as expenditures for research and development and other preparatory expenses. On the other hand, all of the money to be returned as profit or depreciation, i.e., cash throw-off, is likewise projected, perhaps for as long as fifteen or twenty years. The date for the start of operations is the significant key to the calculation, because this is the date used in computing present value. A number of probable rates are selected. Then using a financial table one converts all of the outlays and returns into present values: And that interest rate at which the present value of the outlays offsets the present value of the return is the true rate of return.

* *Financial Controls for Management* by Ralph B. Lewis, © by Prentice-Hall, Inc., Englewood Cliffs, New Jersey, 1961 (pp. 82–83).

From: Douglas McGregor
*THE HUMAN SIDE OF ENTERPRISE**

[EDITORS' NOTE: The author was Professor in the School of Industrial Management at the Massachusetts Institute of Technology.]

Participation is one of the most misunderstood ideas that have emerged from the field of human relations. It is praised by some, condemned by others, and used with considerable success by still others. The differences in point of view between its proponents and its critics are about as great as those between the leaders of Iron Curtain countries and those of the Free World when they use the term "democracy."

Some proponents of participation give the impression that it is a magic for-

* By permission from *The Human Side of Enterprise*, by McGregor, Douglas. Copyright 1960. McGraw-Hill Book Company, Incorporated. (Excerpts from 124–31, 172–75.)

mula which will eliminate conflict and disagreement and come pretty close to solving all of management's problems. These enthusiasts appear to believe that people yearn to participate, much as children of a generation or two ago yearned for Castoria. They give the impression that it is a formula which can be applied by any manager regardless of his skill, that virtually no preparation is necessary for its use, and that it can spring full-blown into existence and transform industrial relationships overnight.

Some critics of participation, on the other hand, see it as a form of managerial abdication. It is a dangerous idea that will undermine management prerogatives and almost certainly get out of control. It is a concept which for them fits the pattern of "soft" management exclusively. It wastes time, lowers efficiency, and weakens management's effectiveness.

A third group of managers view participation as a useful item in their bag of managerial tricks. It is for them a manipulative device for getting people to do what they want, under conditions which delude the "participators" into thinking that they have had a voice in decision making. The idea is to handle them so skillfully that they come up with the answer which the manager had in the first place, but believing it was their own. This is a way of "making people feel important" which these managers are quick to emphasize as a significant motivational tool of management. (It is important to note the distinction between making people *feel* important and *making* people important.)

Naturally, there are severe critics of this manipulative approach to participation, and they tend to conceive of all participation as taking this form.

A fourth group of managers makes successful use of participation, but they don't think of it as a panacea or magic formula. They do not share either the unrestrained enthusiasm of the faddists or the fears of the critics. They would flatly refuse to employ participation as a manipulative sales device.

Among all of these groups is a rather general but tacit agreement—incorrect, I believe—that participation applies to groups and not to individuals. None of them appears to view it as having any relationship to delegation. After all, it has a different name! Many of the strong proponents of delegation have no use whatever for participation.

In the light of all this it is not surprising that a fair number of thoughtful managers view this whole subject with some skepticism.

The effective use of participation is a consequence of a managerial point of view which includes confidence in the potentialities of subordinates, awareness of management's dependency downwards, and a desire to avoid some of the negative consequences of emphasis on personal authority. . . .

It is perhaps most useful to consider participation in terms of a range of managerial actions. At one end of the range the exercise of authority in the decision-making process is almost complete and participation is negligible. At the other end of the range the exercise of authority is relatively small and participation is maximum. There is no implication that more participation is better than less. The degree of participation which will be suitable depends upon a variety of factors, including the problem or issue, the attitudes and past experience of the subordinates, the manager's skill, and the point of view alluded to above.

*   *   *   *   *

. . . Participation is not confined to the relationship between a first-line supervisor and his workers. It can occur between a president and his executive committee. Moreover, since there are many managerial decisions which affect a single subordinate, it is equally applicable to the individual or to the group.

The kind of participation which will be utilized will vary depending upon the level of the organization as well as upon the other factors mentioned above.

* * * * *

Since one of the major purposes of the use of participation is to encourage the growth of subordinates and their ability to accept responsibility, the superior will be concerned to pick appropriate problems or issues for discussion and decision. These will be matters of some significance to subordinates; otherwise they will see little point in their involvement. . . .

Of course, there are some risks connected with the use of participation. All significant managerial activities involve risk, and this is no exception. The usual fear is that if employees are given an opportunity to influence decisions affecting them, they will soon want to participate in matters which should be none of their concern. Managements who express this fear most acutely tend to have a very narrow conception of the issues which should concern employees. If management's concern is with the growth of employees and their increasing ability to undertake responsibility, there will of course be an expectation that employees will become involved in an increasing range of decision-making activities.

* * * * *

In any event, there are now so many instances of the successful use of participation which has not in any discernible way weakened management's ability to manage that I can see little basis for anxiety over the issue of management prerogatives. The only conclusion I would draw is that the managements who are primarily concerned to protect their power and authority had better leave the whole matter alone.

. . . In view of the interdependence characteristic of industrial organizations there is reason for modifying the typical unilateral nature of the decision-making process. Participation, used judiciously, and in many different ways, depending upon the circumstances, offers help along these lines. It is a process which differs very little from delegation in its essential character. In fact, participation is a special case of delegation in which the subordinate gains greater control, greater freedom of choice, with respect to his own responsibility. The term participation is usually applied to the subordinate's greater influence over matters within the sphere of his superior's responsibilities. When these matters affect him and his job—when interdependence is involved—it seems reasonable that he should have the opportunity to exert some influence. . . .

Participation . . . offers substantial opportunities for ego satisfaction for the subordinate and thus can affect motivation toward organizational objectives. It is an aid to achieving integration. In the first place, the subordinate can discover the satisfaction that comes from tackling problems and finding successful solutions for them. This is by no means a minor form of satisfaction. It is one of the reasons that the whole do-it-yourself movement has grown to such proportions in recent years. Beyond this there is a greater sense of independence and of achieving some control over one's destiny. Finally, there are the satisfactions that come by way of recognition from peers and superiors for having made a worth-while contribution to the solution of an organizational problem. At lower levels of the organization, where the opportunities for satisfactions like these are distinctly limited, participation in departmental problem solving may have considerable significance in demonstrating to people how they can satisfy their own needs best by working toward organizational objectives.

Viewed thus, participation is not a panacea, a manipulative device, a gimmick, or a threat. Used wisely, and with understanding, it is a natural concomitant of management by integration and self-control.

* * * * *

In order to create a climate of mutual confidence surrounding staff-line relationships within which collaboration in achieving organizational objectives will become possible, several requirements must be met:

1. The inadequacy of the conventional principles of unity of command and of equality of authority and responsibility must be recognized. Not only are these principles unrealistic in the modern industrial corporation, they are the source of many of the difficulties we are trying to correct. . . .

2. The primary task of any staff group is that of providing specialized help to *all levels* of management, not just to the level at which the group reports.

3. The proper role of the staff member is that of the professional vis-à-vis his clients. The genuinely competent professional recognizes (*a*) that help is always defined by the recipient and (*b*) that he can neither fulfill his responsibilities to the organization nor maintain proper ethical standards of conduct if he is placed in a position which involves conflicting obligations to his managerial "clients."

4. The central principle of managerial control is the principle of self-control. This principle severely limits *both* staff and line use of data and information collected for control purposes as well as the so-called coordinative activities of staff groups. If the principle of self-control is violated, the staff inevitably becomes involved in conflicting obligations, and in addition is required to occupy the incompatible roles of professional helper and policeman.

It may seem impractical to attempt to create a climate of staff-line relationships within the organization similar to that which characterizes effective professional-client relationships in private practice, yet this is essentially what is required. . . .

We are now in a position to consider a couple of interesting questions about the staff-line relationship. First, where is the issue of who exercises authority over whom?

With the approach suggested above, the traditional principles which define the role of staff evaporate. The professional-client relationship is an interdependent one in which neither typically exercises authority over the other although there is influence in both directions. The managerial client is dependent on the specialized knowledge and skill of the professional, but if he attempts to get the help he needs by authoritative methods he will defeat his purposes. It is not possible to obtain by command the imaginative, creative effort which distinguishes the competent professional from the glorified clerk. The manager who perceives staff members as flunkies to carry out his orders will never obtain *professional* staff help. On the other hand, the manager who perceives himself as a client utilizing the knowledge and skill of professional specialists will not attempt to achieve this purpose by relying on his authority over them.

The professional, in turn, is dependent upon his clients. Unless they accept and use his help, he has no value to the organization and therefore there is no reason for employing him. If, however, he attempts to impose "help" authoritatively (whether directly or by accepting assignments of control and coordinative responsibilities from his superiors), he places himself in the role of policeman, which is completely incompatible with the professional role.

There is, in fact, no solution to the problem of staff-line relationships in authoritative terms which will achieve organizational objectives adequately. Waste of human resources, friction and antagonism, elaborate and costly protective mechanisms, and lowered commitment to organizational objectives are the inescapable consequences of the traditional conception of the relationship.

Second, what has happened to the distinction between line and staff? It has become evident as a result of our examination of line management's task in the preceding chapters of this volume that the most appropriate roles of the manager vis-à-vis his subordinates are those of teacher, professional helper, colleague, consultant. Only to a limited degree will he assume the role of authoritative boss. The line manager who seeks to operate within the context of Theory Y will establish relationships with his subordinates, his superiors, and his colleagues which are much like those of the professional vis-à-vis his clients. He will become more like a professional staff member (although in general rather than specialized ways) and less like a traditional line manager.

The various functions within the organization differ in many ways (in the number of other functions with which they are related, for example), but not particularly in terms of the traditional line-staff distinction. All managers, whether line or staff, have responsibilities for collaborating with other members of the organization in achieving organizational objectives. Each is concerned with (1) making his own resources of knowledge, skill, and experience available to others; (2) obtaining help from others in fulfilling his own responsibilities; and (3) controlling his own job. Each has *both* line and staff responsibilities.

One consequence of this approach is the greater significance which the managerial *team* acquires at each level of organization. Much of the manager's work—be he line or staff—requires his collaboration with other managers in a relationship where personal authority and power must be subordinated to the requirements of the *task* if the organizational objectives are to be achieved. Effective collaboration of this kind is hindered, not helped, by the traditional distinctions between line and staff. The goal is to utilize the contributions of all the available human resources in reaching the best decisions or problem solutions or action strategies.

The modern industrial organization is a vast complex of interdependent relationships, up, down, across, and even "diagonally." In fact, the interdependence is so great that only collaborative team efforts can make the system work effectively. It is probable that one day we shall begin to draw organization charts as a series of linked groups rather than as a hierarchical structure of individual "reporting" relationships. . . .

GENERAL AMERICAN STEEL COMPANY

I Case Introduction

Synopsis

This steel company is showing unfavorable profits compared with its principal competitors, and the steel industry as a whole is operating at considerably less than 100% of capacity. W. J. Grand, president, issues a statement to officers and employees citing the reasons why a cost-cutting campaign is to the benefit of all concerned.

The case deals more specifically with a typing pool at Rushton works —its organization structure, the leadership pattern of the supervisor, and the feelings and actions of employees.

Why This Case Is Included

This case provides opportunity to examine the technological and economic principles which influence the way work is organized, and some of the psychological principles which sometimes give conflicting prescriptions for organizing work. It also points up the connection between lower-level organization structure and leadership patterns, and the overall profits of the company as viewed by top management.

Other important issues in the case revolve around (a) the way organization structure affects the leadership style of executives and the motivation of employees; (b) the relation of organization structure to pay systems and the place of pay in employee motivation; (c) the causes of the formation of labor unions; and (d) the role conflict of lower supervisors.

Diagnostic and Predictive Questions

In answering the following diagnostic and predictive questions, remember that these questions apply theories and conceptual ideas from certain disciplines. Such theories are valuable to understand basic forces at work in the policy system (diagnosis) and to predict what will happen in the system in the future (prediction). Since each reading abstracts from the total policy system certain factors or variables into the closed or partial viewpoint of one theory or discipline, no on reading gives answers to the practical policy problems of the case. In diagnosis and prediction, the parts of the problem are studied with "other things being equal."

Following each question are listed readings which will be helpful in answering the question. The readings included with this case are marked (*). By referring to the author index at the end of this book, you may locate the other readings listed.

1. From the viewpoint of technology and economics, what is motivating the behavior of the top management of the General American Steel Company? Why, for example, do they communicate to the employees that the steel industry is operating at less than 100% of capacity, and that GASCO's ratio of net income to book value of assets is 6.5%, compared to a range of 6.9% to 9.6%?

Read: Anderson, *An Organization Appraisal*, pp. 1–2. Bright, "Are We Falling Behind in Mechanization?" Veblen, *The Engineers and the Price System*, chap. v. Taylor, "Testimony before the Special House Committee Investigating the Taylor and Other Systems." Taylor, "Principles of Scientific Management."

2. Assume for the moment that the research done by the headquarters director of work measurement is valid and true. What economic relationships exist between top management's concern (Question 1) and the way the headquarters staff organized the work "at the bottom"—in the General Services Department? What sociological relationships exist?

Read: Smith, *The Wealth of Nations*, pp. 4–15. Veblen, *The Engineers and the Price System*, chap. 5.
(Optional, advanced: Spencer and Siegelman, *Managerial Economics: Decision Making and Forward Planning*, pp. 242–48, 202–12. This deals with the efficiency ratio of output/input, and stresses the efficiency generated by varying the input of both fixed costs and variable costs [e.g., the relation of fixed plant cost, and variable labor cost] for different levels of output.)

3. In contrast to the technological-economic factors which determined the way the work in the General Services Department was organized (Question 1), what implication does each of the alternative organization structures have on the motivations and actions of the girls in the department? What implications do these alternatives have for the complaint of the plant executives that the girls are not competently trained? What implication do they have for the amount of energy each girl would exert for each hour worked? (Note: One alternative is to have each girl specialize by type of document and by proofreading; another would be to have each girl type all forms of documents, and perhaps do her own proofreading. This latter alternative is known as "job enlargement.")

Read: *Smith, *The Wealth of Nations*, pp 734–35. Brown, *The Social Psychology of Industry*, pp. 186–87, 199–203. *Roethlisberger, *Management and Morale*, pp. 36–37.
(Optional, not in this volume: C. R. Walker and R. H. Guest, "The Man on the Assembly Line," *Harvard Business Review*, May–June 1952.)

4. What economic reasons prompted Mr. Neal to conduct the meeting the way he did—to use this particular leadership pattern? Read his statements to the girls in the meeting carefully. What approach is he taking to try to motivate them? What unintended consequences might this have in terms of loyalty and morale of the girls? In terms of productivity of the girls per hour worked?

Read: Items for Question 1 and 2. *Argyris, *Personality and Organization*, pp. 27–31, 33–51, 66–67, 77–90, 95, 103–4, 123–25, 130, 137–39, 150, 153–55, 157. *McGregor, *The Human Side of Enterprise*, pp. 3–10, 47–48, 53–54. Etzioni, *A Comparative Analysis of Complex Organizations*, pp. 31–39, 80–82.

5. Did the way the work was organized in the General Service Department have anything to do with the girls' request for a salary increase?

Read: Brown, *The Social Psychology of Industry*, pp. 186–87, 199–203.

6. Why did Marjorie Kramer run for union steward? Why do you think there is a union in the plant to represent the office workers?

Read: * Argyris, *Personality and Organization* (pages listed above).

7. In some research on human behavior, foreman and first-line supervisors are known as "the men in the middle." In what sense in this particular case is Mr. Neal the man in the middle? In what sense is he *not* the man in the middle?

Read: *Etzioni, "Human Relations and the Foreman."

Policy Questions for This Specific Case

In answering the following policy questions, the results of diagnosis and prediction are used to reduce the amount of guesswork, or judgment, in designing action solutions. However, since certain parts of the total case situation cannot be reduced to science, and since "other things are not equal," judgment must still be used to fill in the factors not accounted for by readings. You will also need a second kind of judgment as you put value weights on different scientific predictions, since different theories may point to conflicting solutions.

8. If you were a stockholder of the General American Steel Company, how would you want the work organized in the General Service Department? How would you want Mr. Neal to deal with the girls when he called the meeting?

9. If you were in Mr. Neal's place, would you recommend that the typists be organized (*a*) by special kinds of typing and proofreading, or (*b*) under "job enlargement," where each girl would do all forms of typing and proofread her own documents? Consider both the research of the headquarters staff and the readings with this case—then form an independent judgment of your own.

10. Would your answer to Question 8 determine how you would communicate, or otherwise deal with the girls on a face-to-face basis, in order to develop incentive to produce?

Read: Follett, "Constructive Conflict." Odiorne, *How Managers Make Things Happen,* pp. 4–11, 37–38, 52–53.

Major Policy Issues: Tentative Generalizations about Any Policy System

In arriving at conclusions for the following questions, generalize from the facts in the case and use your own ideas to (*a*) confirm, (*b*) modify, or (*c*) test the workability of the concepts and theories from readings. As an executive or professional, use wisdom to merge theory, on the one hand, with "brute facts" and practice, on the other.

11. In a choice between creating "specialists" jobs and "generalists" jobs, is the increment of efficiency occasioned by the economic law of specialization and hierarchical control greater than or less than the increment of efficiency generated by the psychological law of self-actualization?

12. If these two increments *are* different—(specialization-hierarchical control) versus (job enlargement-participation)—what *should* the executive do? What value weights should he put on these two factors when faced with practical organization structure decisions; the choice between specialization or job enlargement?

Questions for Original Student Work in Analysis and Policy

The methods of viewing this case as represented by the authors' questions and selection of readings are not exhaustive. There are other relevant ideas for diagnosis and prediction. Furthermore, there are other ways of stating policy questions. More powerful analyses and wiser solutions will result by drawing on your own training and experience for (a) relevant concepts and theories, and (b) creative ways of asking policy questions. The following questions are designed to help you acquire this skill.

13. While reflecting on case facts, what additional theories from prior education give you insights as to "what is going on" in General American Steel Company? As to what might be predicted to happen in the future?

14. Other than the policy questions asked by the authors, what pragmatic ways can you think of to state the practical problems faced by executives in the case?

II General American Steel Company*

General American Steel Company is a leading company in the domestic steel industry. With its subsidiaries and affiliates, the company employs 22,000 people, and it operates as an integrated unit for the manufacture and sale of a diversified line of iron and steel products. Having an ingot capacity of six million tons, GASCO produces and sells hot and cold sheet, tinplate, blackplate, steel strip, pipes and tubing, and hot and cold rolled plate.

As one of the 22 integrated companies in the industry, GASCO appears to have shown slightly unfavorable operating results compared to the seven other integrated companies. Its profit margin in the last year has been 16.2 per cent, compared with the margins of other companies that range from 17.1 per cent to 24.5 per cent. The ratio of net income after taxes to book value of assets in the past year has been 6.5 per cent for GASCO, compared with a range of 6.9 per cent to 9.6 per cent for its major competitors.

As a result of these comparisons, and because the president and some of his advisors (financial vice president, sales vice president) predict a further decline in sales for the company in the next 12 months, a cost-cutting campaign has been instituted. Mr. W. J. Grand, President, issued the following statement addressed to all officers and employees of the company:

---

* William H. Newman and Charles E. Summer, Jr., *The Process of Management: Concepts, Behavior, and Practice.* © 1961. Reprinted by permission of Prentice-Hall, Inc., Englewood Cliffs, New Jersey.

The steel industry has operated at considerably less than 100 per cent capacity during the previous year, and our company has shown operating results on the lower side of the industry average. . . . Every indication points to the prospect that next year will bring further declines.

Mr. Grand's statement went on to point out that, unless the cost of the company's products could be decreased, investors might prefer to put their money in other steel companies than GASCO. This, in turn, would seriously hamper the company's ability to raise capital and to continue scientific research on new products. Thus, Mr. Grand pointed out, cost-cutting can determine whether in the long run the company serves society with good products, and whether it continues to grow and make profits for the sake of both generous dividends for stockholders and high wage levels for employees.

This case deals with some problems in the General Services Department of Rushton Works, one of the company's principal mills for producing hot and cold rolled steel. The plant employs 4,100 people and has an open-hearth capacity of three million tons of ingots.

The office building for Rushton Works is a four-story building of modern brick-and-glass construction situated at the left of the main thoroughfare inside the main gate of the mill. An office force of 385 people is organized in departments such as cost accounting, order processing, materials accounting, payroll accounting, personnel records, production scheduling, and so on.

The General Services Department

The General Services Department has as its over-all function the typing of documents, letters, and statistical tables for other departments in the office. It employs 14 women, all between the ages of 19 and 35. According to J. E. Neil, supervisor of the department, not many girls like to type exclusively—and the work that comes into the GSD (as it is called by most employees) falls into this category. The pay rate for typists ranges from $70 to $80 per week, next to the lowest for clerical workers except office boys and file clerks. Nevertheless, this rate is slightly above the going wage for this type of work in the city, according to data collected in the personnel research department. Most girls like to "bid out" of the department as soon as their seniority is sufficient, and move on to be secretaries ($75–$105) and then executive secretaries ($98–$140).

The department is divided into four groups. Three girls do statistical typing—for instance, each morning the cost accounting department sends Mr. Neil about nine legal-sized sheets of identical statements (but including the new figures from the previous day's production in the plant) that must be typed in neat columns; proper headings and extreme accuracy are required. It has been the opinion of the central office-methods group (located at company headquarters) that a small number of girls can accomplish all the work if in each of the company's plants some girls specialize in statistical work, others in letter-writing, and still others in narrative document copy work. Therefore, at Rushton, three girls do only narrative document copy, five write letters, four do statistical statements, and two girls do proofreading.

R. L. Stringer, director of work measurement at Company headquarters, states:

We have done an intensive research study of clerical work, under controlled experimental conditions. For example, at one plant we had a clerical department in which girls did all four types of work—statistical, document, letter, and proofreading (of their own work). We compared the total output of this department with a department at another plant in which girls specialized by type of work. Then we also compared it with the same department, after a change from the "generalist" principle to the "specialist" principle. In all cases, when we divided the total output by the number of girls, we found that productivity was greater under a specialized system. In a department with a given volume of typing work to be done, for example, fourteen girls organized by specialties could do work that it took sixteen to do if each girl performed all four functions.

Mr. Neil says that the company has taken many steps to provide good working conditions for the girls:

We have a ladies' lounge with modern furniture, we have purchased the most comfortable desks and chairs, the office is air-conditioned, and concealed loudspeakers play soft music continuously during working hours. We found that the girls like this music, and that output in number of pages has increased about four per cent since it was installed. The company spends about $14 million a year on group insurance, pensions, payments into industry welfare funds, social security, and other nonsalary benefits for its people.

Some Problems in the Department

Mr. Neil, supervisor of the General Services Department, feels that the department "is, on the whole, running smoothly. We have a number of small things that bother us, as in any organization. Nevertheless, the work gets out with reasonably good efficiency."

He did, however, mention a problem that has been brought to his attention on two occasions by Mr. Haley, the controller, to whom he (Neil) reports on the organization chart. Mr. Haley reported that he had had a number of complaints from plant executives about the competence of secretaries who are promoted from the GSD to higher secretarial positions. According to the plant seniority system, all secretaries are chosen from among the GSD girls, and all new girls are hired into the plant for positions in GSD. According to Haley, most of the complaints are that although the girls seem competent in doing what they are told, they show little individual judgment and creativity in helping their bosses "by figuring out little things to do that they aren't told." For example, Ed Jenkins (Training Director) gets a set of forms from foremen throughout the plant once a month, and he has trained Ethyl Cary to summarize these for him to send in to the Industrial Relations Department at company headquarters. While Ed was on vacation, a group of the foremen sent in a special report, not on the monthly schedule, that was very important. Ethyl, Jenkins states, ought to have known that Industrial Relations would think this report was important, and would want it right away, but she just typed the routine stuff he left for her, and that report lay on his desk for three weeks. The foremen later complained that the company doesn't pay much attention to the hard work they do trying to improve training practices.

A second problem, which Mr. Neil feels is more or less routine, has to do with the satisfaction and morale of the girls. About a year ago, four of the girls came to him and said they were wondering if something couldn't be done about salary scales for typists. Two girls, Marjorie Kramer and Laura Nichols, who appeared to be spokesmen for the group, argued that the cost of living had gone up, city bus fare had just been increased, and in short, they thought a company as big as GASCO could certainly afford to pay more. Neil says:

We would *all* like to make more money, and I'd like to give them all they want (it would make life easier for me). But I told them that the company already paid more than the city average—I got out a study of area salaries and showed them the figures, and pointed out to them what Mr. Grand had said about the welfare of the whole company.

Eight months ago, the same four girls came to Mr. Neil, but this time there were three others with them in the group. Marjorie Kramer and Laura Nichols spoke more often than the others this time, too. Mr. Neil noticed that this was the same group he often saw having coffee together in the cafeteria. This time, the girls wondered "if there is anything the company can do to have department heads send more interesting work." Mr. Neil told them that this was a matter beyond his control.

Neil says that the pensions, insurance, salaries, and working conditions at GASCO are sufficient to attract and hold good help. There are a couple of cases each year of girls who leave the company to take jobs with law offices, advertising agencies, and other employers in the downtown area of the city, "because they find that location suits them better than the plant, which is on the outskirts of the city." He says that there is also a perennial problem of girls coming in late to work occasionally and staying out too long to lunch. In each instance, he gives them "a short and courteous disciplinary lecture, and this seems to hold the line all right."

Interviews with Two Employees

Marjorie Kramer has been in the department for 19 months. Following are some of the comments she made about her job:

Sure, secretaries downtown don't have to punch a time clock, can go shopping at lunch, and even go out for a Coke. Here, there is always a stack of typing to do, it isn't too much for a day, or too little, just keeps you busy all of the time. I'm on letters, which isn't as bad as the statistical girls, but even with letters, after you've done them two months, you don't have to think of what you're doing. All of us think at first that we're going to pay attention to the meaning, because you want to learn something about the company. However, you soon see that it isn't interesting, and it won't do you any good to know whether that coke oven is a better place to spend money than this blast furnace.

Laura Nichols, who has been in the department two years, made these remarks about her job:

Statistical typing, which I do, takes more skill than the rest. Mr. Neil and the company know this. But when you get the hang of it, you really feel just like part of the typewriter. Numbers, columns, rows, and all just reel off while I listen to the music, think about going shopping on Saturday, and about new clothes. Mr. Neil once said that girls make more mistakes if they're too conscious of what they're typing or how they're using the machine, and I think he's right. Of course, Mr. Neil sits there watching us all of the time, and if you slow down a couple of days you can bet he'll know it.

The Question of Coffee Breaks and "Office Talk"

Mr. Neil, supervisor of the General Services Department, says that for about seven months he has had a problem with girls who go either to the plant cafeteria or to the ladies' lounge to drink coffee and remain away from their work too long. "I have also mentioned to the girls once or twice every two months that they are spending too much time talking among themselves in idle chit-chat in the office. As in previous instances, Laura Nichols and Marjorie Kramer have been offenders in these two practices."

Five months ago, Mr. Neil decided that something must be done to improve both *esprit de corps* and discipline in the department. So one day, he asked all the girls to help him arrange chairs around his desk so that he could "discuss some common problems that you and I must face together." Following is his account of the meeting, which lasted from nine to nine-thirty one morning.

I opened the meeting by explaining to them the profit margins of our company and our return on investment, compared to those of competitive companies. The only way we can stay in business, and—very importantly from their viewpoint—the only way we can continue to provide good salaries and many other employee benefits, is to make a profit. We cannot make a profit if investors don't see the results of efficient operations, because they will cease to put money in our company. Therefore, I made the point very strongly that it is to the employees' benefit as well as the company's that each person and each department do what they can to maintain efficient operations.

In a way, I told them, our situation is like that of a country at war—except that the common enemies of both employees and management, are other competitive steel companies. And if all of us—managers and typists and the rest—don't work together, we won't succeed. Thus, I could truthfully and sincerely say to them that we (the girls and I) both want the same thing—good work and a well-run, efficient company.

I then enumerated the many things the company provides that cost money—air-conditioning, comfortable lounges, the most healthful design of desks and equipment, group insurance, pensions, vacations, and security. I asked them to remember that these things can only be paid for if we all do our part to produce and sell products with little waste of time and a high degree of efficiency.

After I saw that the girls were being attentive, I pointed out the relationship between what was happening in our office on the one hand, and the general subject of good work, efficiency, and company profits on the other. I explained that the practice of staying out too long for coffee meant a higher input of work time for a given output of typing. I said I would be more than glad to see individual people take extra time when they really wanted to, but I called their attention to the fact that we have 14 people in the department, 4,100 in the plant, and 22,000 in the company, and that if coffee-break time starts to be extended, it will get out of hand. I even said that I would be glad to let my department have more liberal amounts of time than the rest of the plant, if we could get away with it—but that the bosses higher up would surely catch me on that score.

Then I got around to the matter of talking in the office. Here is about what I said: "I'm sure you all have been disturbed at certain times by noisy conversations going on at adjoining desks. All of you have slipped into the practice of walking around the office to talk to one another. Now, don't get me wrong; there's certainly nothing wrong with good conversations about home, shopping, dates, new cars, and so on. But the office is simply not the place for too much of this. It's not that I personally mind—I can certainly carry on my work with the talk. But there are two reasons why we can't do this. First, I'm thinking about you—I've often seen a girl disturbed by the noise and thoughtless chatter of others near her desk, and I've had a complaint or two from girls that certain people talk too much. Second, I'm thinking about complaints I've had from certain plant officials up the line who have commented on the talking in our department. I'm sure you all know that these men can do nice things for the department in the future to make things easier for us, or they can deny us our requests for improvements. So look, girls, please try to save your social visiting for breaks out of the office, or for lunch-time, or for evenings at home."

Mr. Neil reports that he ended the meeting by asking whether there were any questions about what he had said. After a rather long silence, he then asked the girls whether what he had said made sense and sounded reasonable to them as people working for the company. Several girls nodded their heads and others answered that it did. He then thanked them for their attentiveness and said that he was sure that he could count on them to improve in these two matters.

Subsequent Events

Following the meeting, for about two weeks, Mr. Neil noticed a marked improvement in both promptness in returning from breaks and in the elimination of conversation in the office. In about a month, however, he became aware of an increasing incidence of lateness in returning from lunch, and, for some reason, an increase in petty arguments among girls, many of which were brought to him for settlement. In view of the cooperation he had received at the meeting, Mr. Neil was surprised. Laura Nichols and Marjorie Kramer, in particular, were turning in work with too many errors and were openly returning from coffee breaks appreciably later than they ever had been before. Mr. Neil also discovered that some of the girls were visiting the ladies' room "entirely too frequently" and were engaging in long conversations there.

After thinking at length about what to do about this, Mr. Neil decided that the time had come for forthright action. He further decided on four things: (1) He limited all breaks to 15 minutes, (2) he personally sampled each girl's work for errors each day, (3) he kept a record of how often each girl got into arguments (at least arguments that were reported to him) in order to identify possible trouble-makers, and (4) he kept watch from his desk on the number of times each typist reported back over two minutes late from lunch or breaks, and reprimanded offenders at the end of each two weeks.

These measures seemed to Neil to restore the smooth functioning of the department, since lateness decreased, the desired level of accuracy was restored, and girls did not come to him with petty differences among themselves. Although Mr. Neil must spend a great deal of time supervising the work group, he nevertheless feels that the supervision is necessary for over-all departmental results.

Marjorie Kramer, Again

A few months after all the problems had apparently been ironed out, Mr. Neil was somewhat surprised to hear from Mr. Haley that Marjorie Kramer had announced her intention to run for steward in the union that represents the office workers, and that the GSD girls were taking an active part in union meetings and in backing Marjorie for the job. He was surprised because none of the department personnel had ever before taken even moderate interest in union affairs. When he mentioned the subject to Marjorie, she said she felt she could do her fellow workers a great deal of good by seeing that the contract was carried out properly in the Rushton Works office, by striving for improved pay and benefits for the work force, and by placing grievances before the proper authorities when any employee was not treated according to the spirit of the union contract. She said she wanted Mr. Neil to understand that there was certainly no apparent unreasonable treatment of employees in the General Services Department and that she could think of no particular official grievances that needed to be reported about his department at the present time.

III Selected Readings

From: Adam Smith

*THE WEALTH OF NATIONS**

[Editors' Note: Adam Smith, writing in the latter part of the eighteenth century, is considered the founder of the field of economics.]

In the progress of the division of labour, the employment of the far greater part of those who live by labour, that is, of the great body of people, comes to be confined to a few very simple operations, frequently to one or two. But the understandings of the greater part of men are necessarily formed by their ordinary employments. The man whose whole life is spent in performing a few simple operations, of which the effects too are, perhaps, always the same or very nearly the same, has no occasion to exert his understanding, or to exercise his invention in finding out expedients for removing difficulties which never occur. He naturally loses, therefore, the habit of such exertion, and generally becomes as stupid and ignorant as it is possible for a human creature to become. The torpor of his mind renders him, not only incapable of relishing or bearing a part in any rational conversation, but of conceiving any generous, noble, or tender sentiment, and consequently of forming any just judgement concerning many even of the ordinary duties of private life. Of the great and extensive interests of his country he is altogether incapable of judging; and unless very particular pains have been taken to render him otherwise, he is equally incapable of defending his country in war. The uniformity of his stationary life naturally corrupts the courage of his mind, and makes him regard with abhorrence the irregular, uncertain, and adventurous life of a soldier. It corrupts even the activity of his body, and renders him incapable of exerting his strength with vigour and perseverance, in any other employment than that to which he has been bred. His dexterity at his own particular trade seems, in this manner, to be acquired at the expense of his intellectual, social and martial virtues. But in every improved and civilized society this is the state into which the labouring poor, that is, the great body of the people, must necessarily fall, unless the government takes some pains to prevent it.

---

* Published by Random House, Inc., in the Modern Library Series, 1937 (pp. 734–35). This citation is taken from the 1789 edition of the book.

From: F. J. Roethlisberger
*MANAGEMENT AND MORALE**

Perhaps the chief characteristic of the technologist group of persons is that they are experimentally minded. They think in terms of the logic of efficiency, and they scrutinize everything that comes within their scope in these terms. This group is constantly striving to make improvements in machines, mechanical processes, and products. Sometimes they devise ingenious ways of bringing the worker's actions in line with the logic of efficiency. If the assumptions on which such plans are based be granted, they are perfectly sound. . . .

Now it happens frequently that these logical plans to promote efficiency and collaboration do not work out as intended. From the point of view of sentiments, they involve consequences which sometimes defeat the logical purposes of the plan as conceived. Let me point out some of these possible nonlogical consequences. When skill is divorced from the job at the work level and put in the hands of a group of technologists, a situation is created whereby the worker is put in a position of having to accommodate himself continually to changes which he does not initiate. . . . [A]lso many of these changes deprive him of those very things which give meaning and significance to his work. In the language of the sentiments, it is as if the worker were told that his own individual skills, his acquired routines of work, his cultural traditions of craftsmanship, his personal interrelations, had absolutely no value. Now, such nonlogical consequences have devastating effects on the individual. They make him feel insecure, frustrated, or exasperated. . . .

Among physicists, chemists, mechanical, civil, chemical engineers, and so on, certain characteristics are evident. Most of them are concerned with a particular, limited class of phenomena. . . . Within this area their judgments are likely to be sound. Outside it their judgments are more questionable. Some of them recognize quite clearly this limitation. They do not want to be concerned with the human factor; they want to design the best tool, the best machine to accomplish certain technical purposes. Whether or not the introduction of this tool or machine will involve the layoff of certain employees, quite rightly, is not their concern as engineers. Their contribution, in terms of the skill they practice, is to improve from a technical standpoint the performance or utility of a machine, a tool, or a product.

These men are invaluable to the administrator in any industrial organization. . . . To them we owe the new and powerful technology of modern industry. To criticize them for failing to take into account the social consequences of their own discipline is absurd. . . . Bringing into cooperative relation their particular skills with other skills is not their function; it is a quite different function performed by other groups in the organization.

---
* Reprinted by permission of Harvard University Press, Cambridge, Massachusetts, 1947 (pp. 36–37).

From: Chris Argyris
PERSONALITY AND ORGANIZATION*

[EDITORS' NOTE: Dr. Argyris is Professor of Industrial Administration at Yale University.]

THE HUMAN PERSONALITY

THE SOURCE OF PSYCHOLOGICAL ENERGY IS IN THE NEEDS

The energy that most researchers postulate is pictured as being located in the need systems of the personality.

People behave. They love, hate, eat, cry, fight, work, strike, study, shop, go to the movies, play bridge, bring up children, go to church. The psychological energy to behave in all these ways comes from the need systems that exist in our personalities. . . .

The energy in every need system is always ready to release itself, to bubble over. But so long as the boundary of the need system is strong enough, the energy will not release itself. When the energy bubbles over, the need system is in action. Need systems that are quiet and not in action are inert needs or potential active needs. This is similar to the pressure in a boiler. So long as the pressure does not become too great, the boiler will not burst.

*   *   *   *   *

Let us ask, "So what?"

What is the advantage of saying that people have needs in tension in relation to goals? Why go all through this fuss? To answer the question let us imagine that there are two foremen. Mr. A is hard-working, does an exceptional job, and is up for promotion. Mr. B., on the other hand, is slow, is lax on the job, has many problems which he does not seem to care about, and is being considered for a demotion.

Common sense answers to why these two foremen behave the way they do usually go like this:

"Well, that's human nature."

"I guess Mr. B. just doesn't give a damn."

"Mr. A. is really loyal to our company. Looks like Mr. B. isn't."

"Mr. A.'s attitudes are better; that's why he works harder."

"Maybe B. has been having some 'off days.' "

Tackling the same question by using the scheme above, we would have to say:

"Mr. A. has a need in tension which is directed at certain goals. He needs to be hard-working."

"Mr. B. had a need in tension which is also directed at a certain goal. He needs to be slow."

Examining both sets of answers, we note that the practical set jumps immediately to such vague, high-sounding conclusions as "human nature," "doesn't give a damn," "loyalty." None of these conclusions provides a jumping-off point for constructive action. Every one of them immediately implies there is something wrong with Mr. B.

The second list, on the other hand, jumps to questions. It forces the person to find out more facts. For example, "What need is in tension?" "At what goal is it directed?" "Why does Mr. A. have a certain need and why does Mr. B. have a different need in action?" The second list points out one of the most important rules in trying to understand human behavior. The real causes of human behavior are rarely found in the observable behavior. It is important to ask, "What is behind this behavior that we see?"

The second list does not immediately classify someone as "bad" and someone as "good." . . . Therefore, the second list is more useful, in that it does not automatically condemn Mr. B., or praise Mr. A. . . . Probably one of the greatest weaknesses in trying to understand others is the immediate attempt at labeling them "good" or "bad." Once this is done, it is impossible to think objectively about a person.

*　　*　　*　　*　　*

PERSONALITY HAS ABILITIES

Bordering the needs, and in most cases evolving from them, are the abilities. Abilities are the tools, so to speak, with which a person expresses and fulfills his needs. Abilities are the communications systems for the needs to express themselves. Once the energy bubbles over from the needs, it goes "through" the appropriate ability designed to express the need. . . .

Interests are usually a product of a fusion of several needs. This fusion usually comes about at an early age and is unconscious. Interests, therefore, are indicators of the kinds of needs people have. For example, a person with a strong need to be independent, to achieve, and to know things, might make a good scientist.

The skills that are given to us by inheritance are such skills as finger dexterity and other manual and manipulative skills. Few abilities are inherited. The majority of the more important abilities are learned and developed in interaction with others. This is especially true for such abilities as leadership. There are no born leaders. The personality of a leader is developed, probably during early home life and by the situations in which this personality finds appropriate expression.

Abilities, in summary, function between needs and the environment, thus providing the line of communication for needs. . . .

PERSONALITY ORGANIZATION IS CONCEPTUALIZED AS "THE SELF"

It has been found convenient to label the unique personality whole created by the specific inter-relationships of the parts, the self. To put it another way, the basic parts of the personality are the same (needs and abilities). However, the way these parts are organized may differ for each individual and even within the same individual as he develops. The self is a concept used by the scientists to focus on the unique integration of the parts of the personality for any given individual.

To introduce this concept, let us consider the growing infant. As soon as he discovers his physical body (his hands, feet, face), he turns to the task of discovering who he is, i.e., his self. He becomes aware that there is a "me" that exists. From the day this awareness begins, the child will throughout his life be discovering and rediscovering, changing, and adding new parts to the picture he has of himself. This marks the beginning of awareness of the self.

The self is more than just the physical body. It includes the child's unique organization, conscious and unconscious, of his needs, goals, abilities, and the resulting feelings, values, and prejudices. It includes how he evaluates his abilities (e.g., the confidence he has in them). Finally, it includes his sensitivity for understanding himself and others. This sensitivity is called "empathy." A person who has empathy usually has a lot of insight (understanding) into people's feelings.

The self is seldom built up by the person by merely reflecting about himself. It is built through his social contacts (interaction) with others. We cannot become "whole" by ourselves. We need contact with others.

Once the picture of the self is formed, it serves as a frame-work or a guide with which to make sense out of experience. All future experiences are either (1) accepted and integrated with the picture one already has of the self, (2) ignored because the experiences do not make sense to the person in terms of his self concept, and (3) denied or distorted because the experience is inconsistent with the picture of the self. Those ways of behaving are adopted that are consistent with, or in agreement with, the self picture. Because individuals tend to see only that which agrees with their concept of self, it is difficult to be a truly objective observer. There is in fact no objective world for the individual; rather, it is always his picture of the objective world. It is always his "private world."

DEFENSE MECHANISMS MAINTAIN SELF AGAINST THREAT

Generally speaking, there are at least two ways to reduce feelings of threat. One is to change the self so that it becomes congruent with whatever is causing the difficulty. This involves "accepting" the fact that one is "wrong." It involves admitting the limitations associated with the difficulty will not arise again. The second approach is to defend the self by somehow denying or destroying (consciously or unconsciously) what is threatening and clinging to the present self concept. This behavior is called a defense reaction. A defense reaction, therefore, is any sequence of behavior in response to a threat whose goal is to maintain the present state of the self against threat.

A defensive reaction may create difficulty if it happens that the individual instead of the situation in the environment, is "wrong." A defense reaction reduces the awareness of threat but never affects that which is causing the threat. For example, let us say that supervisor A is threatened because he "knows" his boss does not think that he (supervisor A) is doing a good job. Let us assume that he defends his self by placing the blame on the boss. This will not in any way stop the boss from feeling the way he does about supervisor A. Soon the supervisor will have to justify his defensive reactions to himself. He may do this by saying that the boss is "out to get him." Each of these defenses is a distortion which in turn will require further justification and further defense. After some time supervisor A has built up deep layers of defense, all of which will have to be uncovered if he is to understand the cause. . . .

Defense mechanisms are therefore developed to be used any time that the self feels threatened. All individuals have a set of defenses. This set of defenses is not to be viewed as necessarily being "bad" or "good." It is best to view them as simply the individual's way of defending himself from threat. The four most frequently threatening experiences are anxiety, conflict, frustration, and failure.

Since defense mechanisms are primarily related to experiences of anxiety, conflict, frustration, and failure, it may be wise to define these experiences before the defense mechanisms are listed.

Anxiety. Anxiety is an emotional state that resembles fear and anger in that it is aroused by something that is threatening to the individual. Anxiety is a response to nothing particular in the environment, while fear is always a response to a genuine threat, which clearly requires some sort of escape or attack. When we are in a state of fear, we have something before us that we can see, that we can try to remove, or that we can run away from. We can point to it and say, "This is what makes me fearful." Anxiety, on the other hand, "attacks from behind." We experience it but we cannot figure out where it is coming from or what causes it. Thus, we do not know whether to run or to attack.

Some specific symptoms of anxiety are: . . . sleeplessness, stage fright, headaches, stubbornness, stomach upsets, and prejudice. Anxiety usually appears as a symptom, that is to say, it makes itself as some specific form of behavior, using that word in its broadest sense; but in its "pure" form it usually appears as a vague sort of uneasiness; a feeling of panic, discomfort, or helplessness; or an awareness of tension with no identifiable cause. . . .

Conflict. Conflict, generally speaking, refers to the event which occurs when a person is not able to act in a specific situation. All conflict involves opposite needs being in action (tension) at the same time. The conflict may be due to indecision over doing something, or it may be due to wanting to do two things simultaneously which cannot be done simultaneously.

Behavioral scientists have analyzed four types of conflict.

Conflict will tend to exist when the person desires to do two things which he likes equally well but it is possible to do only one. A child tries to decide whether to buy a vanilla cone or a candy bar, both of which he likes equally well.

Conflict will tend to exist when a person has the choice of doing two things, each of which he dislikes equally. It is being, so to speak, "between the devil and the deep blue sea." For example, there is the person who hates his job but has not found another one and therefore risks unemployment if he quits.

Conflict will tend to exist when the person has the choice of doing something he likes, but runs the risk of punishment or loss. For some people, gambling provides this conflict.

Conflict will tend to exist when the person has the alternative choices of doing something he likes but running the risk of some loss or punishment. For example, there is the investor who has before him three or four equally good investment possibilities, each with an equal possibility of failure.

Many people have been brought up to think that conflict is bad. This is not necessarily so. True, conflict can be uncomfortable, but it is even more true that conflict harms a person's personality when the personality uses incorrect ways of dealing with the conflict. Conflict dealt with correctly, is an experience of growth for the personality. In fact, without conflict (psychologists suggest) there would be little need for us to develop new ways of behaving. The old ways would merely be sharpened up a bit, but there would be little reason to try something new. Odd but true, conflict can be used to help build the personality as well as to distort and even destroy it.

Frustration. Coupled with, and perhaps a special case of, conflict is the problem of not being able to overcome some barrier in order to arrive at a goal. If the goal is not reached, the person will become emotional, uneasy, antagonistic—he will show signs of being frustrated. The person under frustration does release emotions, whether he shows these emotions in his observable behavior or not. These emotions act like a sleeping pill, so to speak, on the person's whole personality (especially his abilities) and reduce his efficiency.

For example, if prior to frustration the person's efficiency is said to equal ten, under frustration it is usually reduced (e.g., to five) without the person's realizing it (i.e., unconsciously). The person therefore cannot figure out what is wrong with himself. "Why can't I overcome these barriers? I was certain I could. What's wrong with me?" All these are typical questions. This worry only increases the emotional imbalance, which increases the action of the emotions on the efficiency of the personality, and down goes the efficiency some more. It is like quicksand; the more he struggles the deeper he sinks. The thing that makes frustration most destructive is that a person may not know why he is less efficient.

The reduction of psychological efficiency is called regression. Regression means that the personality has returned to a more primitive, childlike state, where efficiency is much lower. The important property of regression is that while the person becomes more like a child, he is not a child; he is still an adult.

Every person has developed his own tolerance against frustration. Some people have little tolerance and become easily frustrated. Others have developed a high resistance and therefore it takes quite a bit to frustrate them. The individual's ability to withstand frustration is known as frustration tolerance. The higher the frustration tolerance, up to a point, the more adaptive life will be. We emphasize "up to a point" because a person who never becomes frustrated, no matter how difficult the situation, is not necessarily a healthy personality.

Failure. Perhaps the easiest way to explain psychological failure is to define what is not failure. Psychological success, the opposite of failure, occurs when the individual is able to direct his energy toward a goal that he defines, whose achievement will fulfill his inner needs, and which cannot be reached without overcoming a barrier strong enough to make him "put up a fight" but just weak enough to be overcome. (In other words, the individual has a realistic level of aspiration.)

Failure occurs when an individual lives in a world in which he is not able to define his own goals in relation to his inner needs and whose barriers are either too great to overcome or so small that no success is derived in overcoming them.

DEFENSE MECHANISMS

1. Aggression. One of the common results of regression is aggression. Aggression means trying to injure or hurt the person, group, object that is acting as the barrier or as the cause of conflict. By the words "injure" and "hurt" we include all types of injuries, including social and psychological injury, such as name-calling insults, and cheating.

2. Guilt. If the "block" is due to the limitations of one's own personality, (e.g., the individual who desires to become a supervisor but does not have a good enough record), then the aggression can be turned toward the self. The person usually feels guilt, criticizes himself, or may even go so far as to hurt himself. Guilt is, therefore, aggression from ourselves to ourselves.

3. Continuation. Sometimes the conflict is not resolved but the person continues to live by making another choice which is "second best." For example, a student who becomes a businessman but still wishes he could have gone to medical school is in a sense continuing his conflict.

4. Discriminatory Decision. At times, a conflict is resolved by sitting down and writing the reasons for and the reasons against doing something. We try to make a list of the reasons and then pick out (discriminate) the best one. This mechanism almost always occurs on a conscious level. In general, it may be used

when the personality is healthy and the conflict is not strong. For example, an executive, in order to choose between foreman A and foreman B for a new promotion, may sit down, list the "goods" and "bads" of each foreman, and then pick (discriminate) one.

5. Denial. An easy course to follow when threatened is simply to remain unaware of the facts which could create one side of a conflict. An example that is particularly annoying to supervisors occurs when employees apparently do not seem to hear instructions concerning a new regulation or a forthcoming change. Although the supervisor may speak clearly and concisely, the employees will insist "they didn't quite hear what he said" or "they had difficulty in understanding what he said." Actually, what happens under denial is that the employees do not allow what has just been said to penetrate into their consciousness. (Denial, it should be pointed out, is a different thing from deliberate pretense, in which the individual knows something but decides to make believe that he does not.)

6. Repression. When the threat is due to factors active within ourselves, we often forbid ourselves to recognize them. Repression is thus forcing down into the unconscious that part of a threat which we do not like. Repression almost always occurs unconsciously. It is usually a response to an inner threat. For example, a patient once complained of a great fear of running water. She could not go near a drinking fountain. A careful analysis brought out the fact that as a young child she fell in a lake near a waterfall and nearly drowned. The incident had been repressed, all except the noise of running water. Once the patient was able to recognize and accept the fact, progress could be made in therapy.

7. Suppression. Suppression is somewhat like repression. Whereas in repression we push things into the unconscious without realizing it, in suppression we push things into the unconscious and generally know it. Suppression is hardly ever permanent, while repression is usually permanent.

8. Inhibition. Inhibition is like repression but it most often occurs on a conscious level. In inhibition the person purposely and knowingly refrains from doing something. For instance, an inhibited person would be one who never speaks up in a conference because he fears he may say something wrong or he fears what he has to say is not important.

9. Conversion. Conversion occurs when a person fears he will not be capable of meeting an unusual situation and converts this fear into some bodily trouble. An example would be the child who because he fears to take an examination in school, suddenly develops some kind of illness. Or the newly elected foreman feeling inadequate, becomes "run down" after the first week in his new job. Finally, the foreman, who is afraid to see the boss in the boss's office suddenly becomes ill (e.g., gets a splitting headache) and has the meeting postponed. He may actually be converting his difficulty into a physical problem (i.e., headache).

10. Overcompensation. Sometimes a person resolves his fear of not being able to do something by working so hard that he accomplishes his goal and usually goes way beyond it. The person who thinks that he is incapable of doing something tries to make up for his limitations and in fact makes up too much or overcompensates for these limitations. A typical example is the hard-working executive who accomplishes his goal, does better than expected, but never seems to relax once the goal is achieved.

11. Rationalization. Rationalization occurs when we knowingly invent some acceptable excuse (acceptable to our own personality) to cover up a failure or to cover up an inability to accept something. Rationalization occurs when an alibi is created for otherwise untenable behavior. For example, a person might walk to the drug store to buy some cigarettes. On arriving at the drug store, he

finds it is closed and remarks, "Oh well, I did not want to smoke anyway." Or the employee who, upon finding out he did not become a foreman (although he was hoping he would be) remarks, "Who wants all that responsibility anyway?" Rationalization can also occur unconsciously, for example, some multimillionaires who feel guilty about their wealth try to cover up these feelings by giving away huge fortunes to charity.

12. Identification. Identification refers to the desire to be like someone else or to identify with other people's experiences. We have identified with someone when we act in a situation as we feel that person would act. Top management men usually have some subordinates who tend to identify with them.

13. Projection. The concept of projection has two meanings. Colloquially, it is usually used to mean any attempt we make to avoid blame for, or to ascribe to others, ways of behaving, feeling and thinking which we really have ourselves. Some employees, for example, continually "get into trouble" and, despite all evidence to the contrary, really believe the other fellow is always to blame.

In the true psychological sense, projection is a mechanism whereby we "see" in other people a quality which would embarrass us greatly if we were to admit it is our own. For example, a person might be watching someone go up to a stage to make a speech and remark, "I bet he (the speaker) is scared." Actually, it is the person watching the potential speaker who is frightened. Another example is the well-behaved employee who continually "squeals" on the other employees who break the rules. The employee is actually pointing to something happening outside of him (e.g., the other employees breaking the rules) as a way of denying his own desire to break the rules. The employee who does this is usually sincere and does not feel he is a hypocrite.

14. Vacillation. At one time people in conflict may decide in favor of solution A, then a minute later reject it and accept solution B. This constant rejection and acceptance and never coming to a conclusion is called vacillation.

15. Ambivalence. People attempt to resolve some conflict situations by hating and liking the same person who is the focus of the threat. For example, a foreman working for an autocratic boss once said, "The s.o.b. I hate his guts, but you know, I really admire him. He's a pretty good egg." This contradictory statement is hardly ever seen as contradictory by the person who makes it. In this case, the ambivalence is probably due to the fact that an autocrat never permits real freedom, but is always quick to do personal favors to keep the subordinates happy, and thereby keep them dependent on him. . . .

One resultant of defense mechanisms is that they make it difficult to differentiate between an individual's underlying motivations and the skin-surface ones. We observe Mr. A. and Mr. B. while we interview them for a job. Mr. A. talks so much that we cannot speak. Mr. B hardly says a word. These two bits of behavior at the immediately observed "manifest" level seem to be different. But on the "latent" or deeper level—the level to which we must learn to go—both people may really have the same self-concept and, as a result, may feel insecure and fear unknown situations. But they make up for their fear in different ways. Mr. B. adapts by doing little talking. Mr. A. adapts by talking so much that no one else is able to say a word.

Or it may be that the personalities of supervisor A., who "works himself to death," and supervisor B. who "hardly lifts a finger," are basically similar. Both may feel they are not competent. One works hard and overcompensates for limitations he senses in himself. The other does very little for fear of doing something wrong.

The practical implications are that a clear distinction between "manifest" and "latent" must be made if we want to predict how individual supervisors, for example, will react to frustration, conflict, and anxiety. The same is true if changes are to be made.

If the changes made satisfy only manifest behavior, then the underlying latent reasons will not be satisfied. We can predict that the complaining will continue but probably shift to another area. It is similar to taking an aspirin to relieve migraine headaches. The headache will be relieved but not cured.

Ball parks, athletic teams, company picnics, and company lectures are programs that fulfill the skin-surface or manifest needs of the workers. Company newspapers, slogan schemes, and pep talks are also in the same category. If so, increased benefit and communications programs will not tend to decrease the company's human problems. Moreover, since these programs tend to focus on skin-surface needs, they tend to leave the employees' important needs unfilled (e.g., the need to be led by effective leaders). The employees, not truly satisfied and therefore still requiring need fulfillment, ask for more. Soon management begins to feel that the quality of the employees is going down. "All the employees want is more. How much do they expect us to give them?" According to this analysis, the management trains the workers to focus on material satisfactions (e.g., ball teams, pictures in the newspaper, and so on), and then complains when the workers want more. . . .

* * * * *

GROWTH MEANS AN INCREASE IN PARTS AND IN OUR "PRIVATE WORLD"

Most personality theories are in agreement that as the individual matures, he not only acquires more parts (i.e., more needs, abilities), but he also deepens many of them. As these parts are acquired, they are also integrated with the already existing parts of the personality. Every part which is added must be added so that the balance (organization) is not upset. Simultaneously with the personality growth of the individual is the expansion of the individual's private world or environment. Every time a new part is created "in" his personality, a new part is also experienced in his own private world. The world of experience is called "private" because it can never include the total objective world. It is impossible for the individual to experience everything, no matter how long he lives. . . .

Most personality theories state that the personality becomes complete, organized, and integrated only when it interacts with other people, ideas, and social organizations. Growth cannot occur if the person exists alone. He must interact with others in order to understand himself and thereby develop. Thus, we cannot understand ourselves unless we understand others, and we cannot understand others unless we understand ourselves.

To summarize man, in his need-fulfilling, goal directed behavior is to some extent: "like all other men, like some other men, like no other men."

He is like all other men because some of his personality is derived from common biological roots. He is like all other men because he always lives in a culture and must adjust to the traditionally defined expectations of the culture. He is like all other men because he has to use other men to develop. Finally, he is like all other men in that he experiences both gratification and deprivations. These experiences accumulate and become a storehouse of learning which, in turn, he uses to adapt to the continual occurrence of new problems and situations.

Man is like some other men in that he shares common experiences with his own work group, social class, sporting club, or other cultural organization. . . .

BASIC SELF–ACTUALIZATION TRENDS OF THE HUMAN PERSONALITY

Since the human personality is a developing organism, one way to become more precise is to define the basic growth or development trends "inherent" in it (so long as it remains in the same culture). One can then logically assume that, at any given moment in time, the human personality is a developing organism, one will be predisposed to find expression for these developmental trends. Such an assumption implies another, namely, that there are basic development trends characteristic of a relatively large majority of the population being considered. . . .

It is assumed that human beings in our culture:

1. Tend to develop from a state of passivity as infants to a state of increasing activity as adults. . . .

2. Tend to develop from a state of dependence upon others as infants to a state of relative independence as adults. Relative independence is the ability to "stand on one's own two feet" and simultaneously to acknowledge healthy dependencies. . . .

3. Tend to develop from being capable of behaving only in a few ways as an infant to being capable of behaving in many different ways as an adult.

4. Tend to develop from having erratic, casual, shallow, quickly-dropped interests as an infant to having deeper interests as an adult. The mature state is characterized by an endless series of challenges, where the reward comes from doing something for its own sake. The tendency is to analyze and study phenomena in their full-blown wholeness, complexity, and depth.

5. Tend to develop from having a short time perspective (i.e., the present largely determines behavior) as an infant to a much longer time perspective as an adult (i.e., where the behavior is more affected by the past and the future). . . .

6. Tend to develop from being in a subordinate position in the family and society as an infant to aspiring to occupy an equal and/or superordinate position relative to their peers.

7. Tend to develop from a lack of awareness of self as an infant to an awareness of and control over self as an adult. The adult who tends to experience adequate and successful control over his own behavior tends to develop a sense of integrity (Erikson) and feelings of self-worth. Bakke shows that one of the most important needs of workers is to enlarge those areas of their lives in which their own decisions determine the outcome of their efforts.

*   *   *   *   *

THE FORMAL ORGANIZATION

BASIC INCONGRUENCY BETWEEN THE NEEDS OF A MATURE PERSONALITY AND THE REQUIREMENTS OF FORMAL ORGANIZATION

Bringing together the evidence regarding the impact of the formal organizational principles upon the individual, it is concluded that there are some basic *incongruencies between the growth trends of a healthy personality and the requirements of the formal organization.* If the principles of formal organization are used as ideally defined, employees will tend to work in an environment where (1) they are provided minimal control over their workaday world, (2) they are expected to be passive, dependent, and subordinate, (3) they are expected to have a short time perspective, (4) they are induced to perfect and value the frequent use of a few skin-surface shallow abilities and, (5) they are expected to produce under conditions leading to psychological failure.

All these characteristics are incongruent to the ones human beings are postulated to desire. They are much more congruent with the needs of infants in our culture. *In effect, therefore, organizations are willing to pay high wages and provide adequate seniority if mature adults will, for eight hours a day, behave in a less than mature manner!*

If the analysis is correct, this inevitable incongruency increases as (1) the employees are of increasing maturity, (2) as the formal structure (based upon the above principles) is made more clear-cut and logically tight for maximum formal organizational effectiveness, (3) as one goes down the line of command, and (4) as the jobs become more and more mechanized (i.e., take on assembly line characteristics). . . .

It is not difficult to see why some students of organization suggest that immature and even mentally retarded individuals would probably make excellent employees.

* * * * *

INDIVIDUAL AND GROUP ADAPTATION

The Individual Adapts

If the formal organization is defined by the use of such "organization" principles as task specialization, unity of direction, chain of command, and span of control, and if these principles are used correctly, the employees will work in situations in which they tend to be dependent, subordinate, and passive toward the leader. They will tend to use few of their abilities (probably none of which are important ones for the individual anyway). The degree of passivity, dependence, and submissiveness tends to increase for those employees as one goes down the line of command and as the work takes on more of the mass production characteristics. As a result, it is hypothesized that the formal organization creates in a healthy individual feelings of failure and frustration, short time perspective, and conflict. . . .

An employee experiencing frustration, failure, conflict and short time perspective may behave in any one or a combination of the following ways:

a. He may leave the organization. (But where else can he go? Most other companies are organized in the same way.)

b. He may work hard to climb the ladder and become the president. (But how many can become presidents?)

c. He may defend his self-concept and adapt through the use of defense mechanisms.

d. He may "pressure" himself to stay and, in spite of the conflict simultaneously adapt as much as possible by lowering his work standards and becoming apathetic and uninterested.

e. This apathy and disinterest may lead him to place more value on material rewards and to depreciate the value of human or nonmaterial rewards.

f. Although not directly inferable from the above, the employee may teach his children not to expect satisfaction on the job: to expect rather to earn good wages and "live" outside the plant (the same lesson the formal organizational experts are teaching him). This hypothesis is based on the known property of human beings of evaluating life in terms of their own self-concept . . . If the employee's self-concept includes as "good" activities, goldbricking, learning the ropes, and quota restricting, then these will tend to be passed on to his children through the process of acculturation. . . .

The Use of Defense Mechanisms. The third mode of adaptation, the use of defense mechanisms, is perhaps the least explored. As we have seen . . . in a defense reaction the individual distorts or denies the "facts" in order that he may live in some sort of equilibrium with himself and his environment. Systematic research is so meager in this area that our illustrations are mostly abstracted anecdotal accounts obtained from field research. We present a few:

a. To rationalize the fact that they are not accomplishing what they know the company requires. For example (one operator to another) "Take it easy—don't work too hard; this outfit has plenty of dough. They don't need whatever you give them by breaking your ass." Or, "I know the company doesn't want me to work too fast; I can get all worn out." (typist-secretary). Or (piece rate employee), "Well, they don't need those extra pieces until Monday anyway. Why should I knock myself out?"

b. To project their feelings upon others. They may blame them and ignore their own part in the problem.

For example (foreman), "it's those goddamned budgets. If I didn't have those on my neck, I'd have no problem—absolutely none." Or (an order department clerk), "Have you ever tried to keep the sales orders straight with the self-centered thickheads we have for salesmen? All they think of is themselves." Or (a production manager), "The basic problem we have is that everything we produce is custom-made. We ain't got no long runs like most other plants. We have to be careful of every order." Or (a piece-rate worker), "To hell with it," he said, "let the day man run 'em. He likes 'em. He turned in nine dollars today."

"You've got time to make another dollar yourself," I said. "To hell with that job!" Gus exclaimed. "I'm not going to bust my neck any more on it. Let the day man run it."

Another example is found in a recent study of a hospital which reports that the nurses partially adapt to their own inability to be what they believe is an effective administrator by projecting their limitations upon the administrative staff of the hospital. As one nurse describes it: "If you ask me, administration doesn't even know we exist. If they did, they would get busy and solve the many annoying administrative difficulties we have. Just take scheduling. They haven't been able to solve that at O.R. (Operating room) or X-ray or the chemical laboratories. If you want to help us nurses, please go upstairs and make administrators out of them."

Finally workers may defend their resistance to increased mechanization or to the way management is handling the change by blaming increased technology for unemployment. Centers find that blaming technology for unemployment increases as one goes toward the lower levels of the organization.

c. To be ambivalent. "I cannot make up my mind. I like the job—yet I don't. I like the company—yet I'd leave. I don't know what it is, except I know it ain't the boss or the pay" (a clerk-typist). "I run hot and cold about this outfit."

"I can't seem to make up my mind if I should stay or ask for a transfer" (tool and die maker).

Researcher: "What kinds of things do you like and dislike about the company?" Worker: "I like the pay; I like the management—I think they're trying to be fair. But I don't like not being my own boss. I want to be my own boss, I guess. Here you got to be on a schedule. You're always working under pressure for someone else."

d. To escape from reality. An increasingly used defense against nonsatisfying work is for the individual to detach himself from his work. For example, a group of adolescent girls learned to use certain semi-automatic bookkeeping equipment. "Without advance notice," as one girl put it, "you suddenly realize you can work and at the same time think of a million other things. You know what I mean, daydream. You feel free."

e. To develop psychosomatic illnesses. Another type of defensive mechanism which has hardly been studied is the one by which the individual transforms a psychological problem into a physiological one. On the top management level, ulcers is a well-known psychosomatic disease. On the employee level, there is increasing evidence that employees are developing dubious backaches, headaches, and run-down feelings, to adapt to anxieties they tend to experience on the job.

Individual Apathy and Noninvolvement. Apathy, lack of interest, and non-involvement are types of defense mechanisms that may be becoming so popular that they require special emphasis. The basis of these defenses, we have pointed out, is the continuous frustration, conflict and failure an employee experiences.

Let us picture an employee whom we may call Dick. He works on an assembly line and finds that he cannot obtain minimal personality expression on his job. He is frustrated. From the studies of frustration it is hypothesized that Dick will tend to regress to a more childlike state. He will not be as "mature" as he was before he was frustrated. This "primitivation" (regression) of his personality may cause him (1) to leave the situation, (2) to try to change the work situation constructively or destructively, (3) to accept (internalize) the tension and "hand on," i.e., keep working.

If Dick accepts the third possible course, he places himself in a difficult situation. On the one hand, his predisposition for health and maturity puts pressure on him to leave.

He feels his own pressure to leave. On the other hand, if he decides to stay, he must create new self-pressures to overcomome the ones caused by his own desire to leave and to remain healthy. Dick is surrounded by his own pressures. He may blame managment for creating the assembly line world but he also knows they are not forcing him to stay. He is forcing himself to stay. If he blames anyone for being where he is, he blames himself. The tension that builds up tends to increase his human ineffectiveness. Recent research suggests quite clearly that such tension leads to a decrease in self-confidence, and increase in aggression, and regression.

One way for Dick to defend himself is to reduce the psychological importance of the work situation. He may say (unconsciously) in effect, "To hell with it: I am not going to permit myself to become involved. Why should I pressure myself to leave and to stay? Why should all this mean so much to me? I'll do just enough to get by. I'll block up my need for self-actualization until I get out of work. Then I will live!"

GROUP ADAPTATION

The individual adapts to the impact of the organization by any one or some combination of: (1) leaving the organization, (2) climbing the organizational ladder, (3) using defensive mechanisms, and (4) becoming apathetic and disinterested. These are all adaptive mechanisms and therefore need fulfilling. People will want to maintain these adaptive behaviors.

In order to guarantee their existence, the individual seeks group sanctions. The informal work groups are "organized" to perpetuate these adaptive processes (to reward those employees who follow the informal codes and to penalize those who do not). The individual adaptive acts now become sanctioned by the group, and therefore feed back to reinforce the continuance of the individual need-fulfilling adaptive behavior. . . .

*   *   *   *   *

FORMALIZING SMALL GROUPS (TRADE UNIONS)

Up to now we note that the individual adapts on the psychological level and on the small informal group level. The latter are initially created to sanction and therefore perpetuate those activities that the work group on any level of the organization finds need-fulfilling.

However, if the company decides to disband the informal activities, in the final analysis they could be defended by the employees only by threatening to do harm to the productive process (e.g., strike, slow down). Such measures are not easily used and the psychological and financial costs on both sides are high.

Management's formal power is basically derived by making the employees dependent on management for their rewards, directions, positions, and so forth. It follows logically from the above that one way for the employees to reduce their dependence is to take away some of the management's formal authority and place it within their own control. According to Coleman this is an important basis for the rise of trade unions. As McGregor states, "And to the extent to which unions have attempted to place restrictions upon management's authority reflects not only a desire for power, but a conscious attempt to reduce the dependence of the workers upon their bosses." . . .

In order to create trade unions, the employees must reach outside the organization into the political world, where their power and managements (due to our political system) is, man for man, equal. Once trade unions come to existence, the employees can sanction many of their informal activities through the formal power residing in the union as an organization.

The employees now live between two sets of dependencies. They depend upon both management and the trade union leaders. Theoretically, the critical difference is that the former dependence is mandatory while the latter is voluntary. In actual practice, however, it is common knowledge that trade unions are becoming increasingly formalized and routinized. Many have already reached the stage where a primary objective is to maintain themselves internally and adapt to their external environment.

In order to do this, the unions tend to organize themselves by creating a formal organization whose structure is based upon the principles of chain of command, unity of direction, task specialization and span of control. The moment this occurs, they become, in administrative make-up (not necessarily in philosophy) similar to other industrial organizations. The members become dependent, passive, and subordinate to their trade union officers.

*   *   *   *   *

MANAGEMENT'S REACTION AND ITS IMPACT UPON THE EMPLOYEES

We have been primarily concerned with the employees' adaptation to the formal organizational structure, such as decreases in production and identification with the organization; increases in waste, errors, absenteeism, sickness, apathy, disinterest in work, and increase in importance of material (financial) aspects of work. These are all understandable and predictable ways for relatively healthy employees to adapt to the conflict, frustration, and failure they experience as a result of the formal organization. . . .

MANAGEMENT'S DOMINANT ASSUMPTIONS

The top administrators, however, tend to diagnose the problems in another way. They observe their employees while at work and they conclude: (1) The employees are lazy. (2) The employees are uninterested and apathetic. (3) The employees are money crazy. (4) The employees create errors and waste.

Management blames the employees and "sees" the disloyalty, disinterest, and goldbricking as being "in" and caused by the employees. It follows logically for management, that if any changes are to occur the employees must be changed. Thus management initiates programs to "change peoples' attitudes," to "sell them free enterprise," to "make people more interested in the company."

The basic action policy that management tends to define to solve the above "problems" actually stems from the logics of the formal organization and formal leadership already discussed . . .

For example, the logics of the formal organization tend to influence management to assume that: (1) The only relations that matter between people in organizations are those defined by organization charts and manuals. (2) The behavior of people in organizations is governed by explicit logical thinking. (3) The subordinates will do what the purpose and circumstances of the organization require only under logical incentives and clear communications. (4) The administrator is responsible to solve the problem. He knows best what should be done. (5) The way to get things done is through authority of the leader's position. He can apply persuasion and compulsion if necessary. (6) The employees at the bottom would behave differently if they understood the economic problems of the business.

There are three fundamental policy decisions running through these six policy assumptions. The first is the importance of strong, "dynamic," loyal leadership. Second, is the importance of a logical and systematic control over the employees' behavior. Finally, is the importance of communicating to the employees management's thinking related to their organization and its economic problems. Let us examine each of these to see what action management takes to implement these policy decisions and then to analyze the impact of management's actions on the employees and the organization.

STRONGER "DYNAMIC" LEADERSHIP AND ITS IMPACT UPON THE EMPLOYEES

An important pillar of most management policy is to develop competent executives who among other things: (1) are able to "needle," "drive," "sell," "push," "pressure," "persuade," "urge," "coerce," "win" employees to increase productivity, loyalty, and interest for the organization and for their job; (2) are able to get all the facts, weigh them correctly, and make effective decisions; (3) know clearly management's objectives, policies, and practices; (4) communicate these policies and practices clearly to the employees; and (5) evaluate the performance of the employee strictly and honestly according to these policies and practices.

There is ample evidence to illustrate management's use of pressure-oriented leadership.

Summarizing the characteristics found in most of the research, one may conclude that the autocratic, directive leader places the followers in a situation where they tend to be (1) passive, dependent, subordinate, and submissive; (2) centered toward the organization's and the leader's needs rather than the needs of all the followers; (3) competing with each other for the leader's favor; (4)

confronted with a short time perspective; and (5) experiencing psychological failure.

We must conclude that the *impact of directive leadership upon the subordinates is similar to that which the formal* organization *has upon the subordinate. Pressure-oriented directive* leadership *"compounds the felony" that the formal organization* commits every *minute every hour of the day and every day of the year.* Authoritarian leadership *reinforces and perpetuates* the "damage" created *by the organizational structure.* The adaptive activities . . . are also caused by directive leadership. Directive leadership helps to reinforce, in the employees' minds, the necessity for the same adaptive activities that this leadership is originally designed to decrease.

TIGHTER MANAGEMENT CONTROLS AND THEIR IMPACT UPON THE EMPLOYEES

The second policy decision made by many managers to combat reduced productivity is careful definition, inspection, and evaluation of the quality and quantity of every employee's performance. This leads us to the field of management controls.

Management controls are becoming increasingly important in the eyes of top management. Management control is seen as a fundamental process in all organization. . . .

*   *   *   *   *

Management controls are not only necessary and inevitable if the traditional formal organizational structure is to be maintained, but they also become increasingly important as the formal organization becomes larger and more decentralized. Management decision making would suffer if management controls were abandoned.

*   *   *   *   *

As a result of the pressure, tension, and general mistrust of management controls, employees tend to unite against management.

Psychological research shows that people can stand only a certain amount of pressure and tension, after which it becomes intolerable. One method people use to reduce the effect of the pressure (assuming that the employees cannot reduce the pressure itself) is to join groups, which help absorb much of the pressure and thus relieve the individual personally. Gradually, therefore, the individuals become a group because in so doing they are able to satisfy their need to (1) reduce the pressure on each individual; (2) get rid of tension; (3) feel more secure by belonging to a group which can counteract the pressure. In short, new cohesive groups developed to *combat* management pressure. In a sense, the people had learned that they could be happier if they combined against it. This result is predicted . . . [above] as a "natural" consequence of the employees' adapting to the dependence and submissiveness that they experience.

To summarize up to this point, management controls like budgets tend to make the employees feel dependent, passive, and subordinate to management. As a result of budgets, they experience pressure, interdepartmental strife, psychological failure, lack of control over their work environment, barriers to communication between the budget people and the line people, pressure to be department-centered rather than organization centered.

The impact of management controls is similar to that which the formal organization and directive leadership have upon the subordinates. Management controls feed back upon and give support to directive leadership as both "com-

*pound the felony" committed by the formal organization every hour of the day
and every day of the year. . . .*

THE "HUMAN RELATIONS FAD" AND ITS IMPACT UPON THE EMPLOYEES

The third response by management to the problems of inadequate productivity and employee apathy is the let's-be-human approach. If directive leadership and tight management controls do not succeed, perhaps helping the workers
to identify with their jobs and the company might succeed.

How did the human relations fad begin? The growth of trade unionism
brought to light much of the discontent the employees had been feeling for
years, and placed much of the blame on poor management. A second important
stimulus was the research by Mayo, Roethlisberger and Dickson, who presented
concrete evidence showing that productivity and human relations were intimately tied up. Poor human relations, wrote the authors, creates low production (e.g., rate-setting and goldbricking which leads to worse human relations
which in turn leads to lower production. A key to the solution, Mayo suggests,
is to help the employees feel that they belong to a small primary work group. If
people could be helped to feel they belong, he suggested, human relations would
be better. Both of these events had a strong impact upon management, many of
whom still did not fully accept trade unionism. Third, many executives were
beginning to develop a sense of social responsibility.

A difficulty with Mayo and other "human realtors" is that they observed employees goldbricking, rate-setting, expressing low feelings of identification,
apathy, and disinterest and they conclude, like management, that this is "bad."
It may be bad from management's point of view, but as our analysis suggests, it
may also be adaptive as long as relatively mature workers are working in a
difficult work situation.

Management picked up the message and for the next fifteen to twenty years
there existed a great interest in human relations.

*   *   *   *   *

To summarize, research shows that under democratic conditions people do
tend to feel that they are part of a team and respected. However, this does not
mean this will tend to be the case if a supervisor tries to be pseudo democratic
or democratic under autocratic conditions. We must not forget that the formal
structure of most organizations and the management controls are fundamentally
autocratic. The small groups experiments from which the use of "democratic
leadership" seems to have arisen never coped with these two factors.

*   *   *   *   *

Communications programs, benefits, suggestion programs, better working conditions, cafeterias, clean locker rooms, uniforms become part of "good" human
relations. In an analysis of thirty communication programs, for example, management "communicates" frequently the following topics: (1) "Make the worker
feel he's part of the company." (2) "Tell him how important his job is to the
whole picture." (3) "Show him that management is truly interested in the employees." (4) "Keep him informed of costs, errors, and the financial progress of
the company." (5) "Sell him on the importance of free enterprise system." (6)
"Emphasize the possibilities of opportunity for advancement."

With the possible exception of aspects of 4 and 6, topics like these represent
management's worries more than they do employees' needs. Communication programs have become an excellent medium for management to express and try
to do something about its own worries.

Research suggests that telling a worker he is an important part of the company, when through actual experience he sees he is a very minor part (thanks to task specialization) with little responsibility (thanks to chain of command, directive leadership, and management controls) may only increase the employees' dissatisfaction with management. As one worker concluded, "Who are they kidding, us or themselves?" To emphasize to an assembly line worker that he should feel proud of the four bolts that he puts into the right rear end of a car may be viewed as an insult by the worker who is a "whole" human being (although it allays management's anxieties about employee apathy). As one employee remarked, "It's ironic—damn. It hurts to know that four bolts are important. What a hell of a life." . . .

These "fads" assume it is possible to make human relations better, not by attacking the causes (formal organization, directive leadership, and management controls) but in effect by making the activities outside the actual work situation more pleasant for the worker (e.g., new toilets, new cafeterias, sports, picnics, newspapers), or by sugar-coating the work situation. In the case of the former, management is in effect paying the worker to live in the tension-producing life of the plant. Thus employees find their predisposition for more materialistic things reinforced by management's own behavior. In the case of the latter, they are simply ignoring the problem and maybe teaching the employees, by their behavior, that it is acceptable to sugar-coat problems.

*   *   *   *   *

There are more problems. Our analysis . . . states that employees are adapting to their work-a-day world by such ways as apathy, disinterest, goldbricking, and rate-setting. Management dislikes this and tries to solve or alleviate the problems. One important method is to increase communication. They communicate to the worker that he should feel "important," "loyal," "part of the company," "interested." But this is not necessarily how the employees actually feel. It follows, therefore, that to the extent the employees behave in a way they know is antagonistic to management's values, and to the extent that they want to remain in the organization with a minimum of employee-management friction, the employees must not communicate to management these antagonistic activities. Thus, the program management originally defined to increase communication may have the opposite effect in the area where the employees know they are doing something "illegal." This is precisely the area management would want to know of and to correct! It is not long before the manager becomes isolated from the realities that exist "down in the shop," "out on the floor" along the flow of work.

From: Douglas McGregor

THE HUMAN SIDE OF ENTERPRISE*

[EDITORS' NOTE: The author was a Professor in the School of Industrial Management at the Massachusetts Institute of Technology. In the abstract below, he is stating some fundamental principles of human motivation.

In other chapters, McGregor points out that in the practice of management, many executives believe that many employees inherently dislike to work, that they therefore must be controlled and directed by reward and punishment to get them to put forth efforts for the organization, and that they prefer to be directed, because they have relatively little ambition.

From a psychological standpoint, however, McGregor says that employment, wages, working conditions and benefits, which control people by the "carrot and stick" method, are really the causes of indolence, passivity, and unwillingness to accept responsibility. Thus it is not the natural motivations of employees but management methods which cause these reactions.

There is thus a vicious circle: management believes people are behaving in a certain way; then management "manages" in a certain way; people in fact act to confirm the original misconception.

As a way out, McGregor suggests creation of jobs and work which satisfy social needs ("the need for the fairest possible break"; ". . . needs for belonging, association, friendship . . . for self esteem, autonomy, competence . . . recognition, respect of one's fellows . . . and for self fulfillment, that is, for realizing one's own potential for continued self-development").

This abstract gives in the author's own words the kinds of motivations that would be produced if the management and the work organization provide these things.]

There are some other reasons why management has been relatively slow to utilize social science knowledge. Two of these are specially important. The first is that every manager quite naturally considers himself his own social scientist. His personal experience with people from childhood on has been so rich that he feels little real need to turn elsewhere for knowledge of human behavior. . . .

*   *   *   *   *

Every managerial act rests on assumptions, generalizations, and hypotheses —that is to say, on theory. Our assumptions are frequently implicit, sometimes quite unconscious, often conflicting; nevertheless, they determine our predictions that if we do *a*, *b* will occur. Theory and practice are inseparable.

*   *   *   *   *

It is possible to have more or less adequate theoretical assumptions; it is not possible to reach a managerial decision or take a managerial action uninfluenced by assumptions, whether adequate or not. The insistence on being practical really means, "Let's accept *my* theoretical assumptions without argument or test." The common practice of proceeding without explicit examination of theoretical assumptions leads, at times, to remarkable inconsistencies in managerial behavior.

*   *   *   *   *

Another common way of denying the importance of theory to managerial behavior is to insist that management is an art. This also precludes critical examination of the theoretical assumptions underlying managerial actions by placing reliance on intuitions and feelings, which are by definition not subject to question. The issue is not whether management is a science. It is not. Its purposes are different. Science is concerned with the advancement of knowledge; management, like any profession, is concerned with the achievement of practical objectives. The issue is whether management can utilize scientific knowledge in the achievement of those objectives. To insist that management is an art is frequently no more than a denial of the relevance of systematic, tested knowledge to practice. So long as the manager fails to question the validity of his personal assumptions, he is unlikely to avail himself of what is available in science. . . .

An equally important reason for management's failure to make effective use of current social science knowledge has to do with a misconception concerning the nature of control in the field of human behavior. In engineering, control consists in adjustment to natural law. It does not mean making nature do our bidding. We do not, for example, dig channels in the expectation that water will flow uphill; we do not use kerosene to put out a fire. In designing an internal combustion engine we recognize and adjust to the fact that gases expand when heated; we do not attempt to make them behave otherwise. With respect to physical phenomena, control involves the selection of means which are *appropriate* to the nature of the phenomena with which we are concerned.

In the human field the situation is the same, but we often dig channels to make water flow uphill. Many of our attempts to control behavior, far from representing selective adaptations, are in direct violation of human nature. They consist in trying to make people behave as we wish without concern for natural law. . . .

*   *   *   *   *

Another fallacy is often revealed in managerial attempts to control human behavior. When we fail to achieve the results we desire, we tend to seek the cause everywhere but where it usually lies: in our choice of inappropriate methods of control. The engineer does not blame water for flowing downhill rather than up, nor gases for expanding rather than contracting when heated. However, when people respond to managerial decisions in undesired ways, the normal response is to blame them. . . .

*   *   *   *   *

There have been few dramatic break-throughs in social science theory like those which have occurred in the physical sciences during the past half century. Nevertheless, the accumulation of knowledge about human behavior in many specialized fields has made possible the formulation of a number of generalizations. . . . Some of these assumptions . . . are as follows:

1. *The expenditure of physical and mental effort in work is as natural as play or rest.* The average human being does not inherently dislike work. Depending upon controllable conditions, work may be a source of satisfaction (and will be voluntarily performed) or a source of punishment (and will be avoided if possible).

2. *External control and the threat of punishment are not the only means for bringing about effort toward organizational objectives. Man will exercise self-direction and self-control in the service of objectives to which he is committed.*

3. *Commitment to objectives is a function of the rewards associated with their achievement.* The most significant of such rewards, e.g., the satisfaction of ego and self-actualization needs, can be direct products of effort directed toward organizational objectives.

4. *The average human being learns, under proper conditions, not only to accept but to seek responsibility.* Avoidance of responsibility, lack of ambition, and emphasis on security are generally consequences of experience, not inherent human characteristics.

5. *The capacity to exercise a relatively high degree of imagination, ingenuity, and creativity in the solution of organizational problems is widely, not narrowly, distributed in the population.*

6. *Under the conditions of modern industrial life, the intellectual potentialities of the average human being are only partially utilized.*

*　　*　　*　　*　　*

In the physical sciences there are many theoretical phenomena which cannot be achieved in practice. Absolute zero and a perfect vacuum are examples. Others, such as nuclear power, jet aircraft, and human space flight, are recognized theoretically to be possible long before they become feasible. This fact does not make theory less useful. . . .

Similarly, in the management of the human resources of industry, the assumptions and theories about human nature at any given time limit innovation. . . . Assumptions like those [above] open up a range of possibilities for new managerial policies and practices. . . .

From: Amitai Etzioni

*"HUMAN RELATIONS AND THE FOREMAN"**

[EDITORS' NOTE: Dr. Etzioni is Associate Professor of Sociology at Columbia University.]

. . . The human relations approach . . . has several levels of application. On the most superficial level it means talking in a "nice," "human," considerate way to subordinates instead of using the more authoritative forms of speech. Seen in a deeper way and in more psychological terms, it means being sensitive to the other's psychological needs and expressions, understanding the other, and taking his feelings into account. Basically, it means a democratic rather than authoritarian way of leading people, a minimum of coercion, a maximum of persuasion, two way communication, direct or representative participation in decision-making, and a sharing of responsibility. . . . It was long believed, and many still do, that supervision applying these standard techniques will achieve

* Reprinted by permission of *The Pacific Sociological Review*, Eugene, Oregon, Vol. 1, No. 1 (Spring, 1958), pp. 34–37.

higher quality and quantity of production as well as higher satisfaction of the workers. Participation is considered an important way for achieving both.[1] There seems to be an implicit cultural assumption behind these beliefs. . . . It is over-looked that this may be a consequence of being raised in a democratic family. . . . This gives rise to a question seldom raised and only rarely studied: What about the worker who has been raised in a different society . . . being used to an authoritarian way of leadership? There is some material which indicates that workers . . . in the so-called traditional societies, will tend to be most effective and most satisfied under paternalistic-authoritarian supervision.[2] For these workers any other type of leadership, including democratic leadership, may be quite disruptive and disturbing. . . . There are no conclusive data about the supervisor-worker relationship. Although it seems quite plausible that those raised under one type of leadership will prefer it to any other type, whatever the other type may be, there is at least one significant alternative hypothesis which must be considered.

The basic assumption of the human relations philosophy is that the human relations approach is better tuned to the basic psychological needs of the human being than any other approach. This *may* be so even though workers raised in a traditional or totalitarian society will *temporarily* prefer authori-tarian supervision because they are used to it from childhood, since every change, even to an improved state from the point of view of psychological equilibrium, involves strains and tensions and therefore some resistance. The alternative hypothesis suggests that, even in the long run, after the workers have been thoroughly exposed to the human relations approach, they will not prefer it. Sociologists cannot answer this question by pointing out the virtues of democracy and the vices of authoritarian leadership. The hypothesis has to be empirically tested. It is hard to overestimate the significance of this test. The findings will be relevant for those interested in the possibilities of introducing political democracy into newly developed countries, as well as contributing in-sight to the age old controversy about the relative determining power of child-hood experience and early socialization (which would mean in this context that democratic leadership would be relatively unsuccessful for people raised in a non-democratic society) versus the relative significance of situational factors in molding behavior (which would mean here that people can, at least after a period of adjustment, be brought to prefer democratic leadership even if raised in a non-democratic society).

*   *   *   *   *

The foreman has often been described as the "man in the middle," a marginal man, a victim of industrialization.[3] He has lost functions (e.g., train-ing, inspection),[4] authority (e.g., the right to hire and fire), power (because of

---

[1] Kurt Lewin, "Group Decision and Social Change," in Guy E. Swanson, Theo-dore M. Newcomb and Eugene L. Hartley (eds.) *Readings in Social Psychology*, rev. ed., New York: Henry Holt & Co., 1952, pp. 459–73; Lester Coch and John R. P. French, Jr., "Overcoming Resistance to Change," *Human Relations*, I (1948), pp. 512–23. On the relationship between the Mayo school and the Kurt Lewin group see C. M. Arensberg and G. Tootell, "Plant Sociology: Real Discoveries and New Problems," in Mirra Komarovsky (ed.), *Common Frontiers of the Social Sciences*, Glencoe: The Free Press, 1957.

[2] Keo-Heng Shin, *China Enters the Machine Age*, Cambridge: Harvard University Press, 1944, especially pp. 179–95.

[3] See Donald W. Wray, "Marginal Men of Industry: The Foreman," *American Journal of Sociology*, 49 (January, 1944), pp. 298–301.

[4] Reinhard Bendix, *Work and Authority in Industry*, New York: Wiley & Sons, 1956, pp. 213, 215.

unionization), chances for mobility (because of lack of higher education), and much of his means of control over the worker (because of decline in his influence over distribution of rewards like pay, bonus, over-hours, allocation of vacation, promotion, transfers).[5]

*   *   *   *   *

A foreman may view his role as *management representative*. In this case he will be inclined to see the human relations techniques as just another tool in achieving the objectives dictated by management through the authority line. Personally he may feel quite uncomfortable over the need to cultivate personal relations with the workers. . . . The workers may respect his clear position on the management side, but tend to be constantly aware of the separating line between management (including the foreman) and the workers, which means that they will be strongly interest-oriented, calculative and uncommitted. In this situation, not only may alienation and unionization be higher, but the workers often will have their own informal leaders.[6] . . .

The second type of foreman puts extra stress on his relationship with the *workers*. His first loyalty is to them. . . . He will tend to forget, distort, delay and water, down, any orders which put strain on his relations with his friends, the workers. In his communication with management he will tend to play up the workers' demands and the difficulties in executing certain tasks and orders. . . .

The third type of foreman tries to keep both sides happy and is caught in a dilemma of *dual loyalty*.[7] To the management he conveys the idea of a loyal subordinate eagerly reporting about opinions, activities and moods of the workers. He tries to avoid transmitting workers' requests and demands in order not to be considered as identifying with the workers. He will tend to promise high performance and to put the blame on the workers for failure to keep these promises. To the workers he conveys loyalty and understanding; he attenuates management's orders and demands; and he promises to transfer their requests and demands upwards and to "raise hell" if they are not accepted. He tries not to be identified with management. Playing on the "conspiracy psychology" of the workers (as he does on that of the management), he claims the demands have not been fulfilled because management is uncooperative and hardhearted. He is not only an "expert of double talk,"[8] but also an expert on double behavior.

---

5 See C. Wright Mills, *White Collar*, New York: Oxford University Press, 1956, pp. 87–91; Scott A. Greer, *Social Organization*, New York: Doubleday & Co., 1955, pp. 1–4; W. F. Whyte and B. Gardner, "The Man in the Middle," *Applied Anthropology*, 4 (Spring, 1945), pp. 1–28.

6 Daniel Katz, Nathan Maccoby, Gerald Gurin, Lucretia G. Floor, *Productivity, Supervision and Morale Among Railroad Workers*, Ann Arbor: Institute for Social Research, University of Michigan, 1951, p. 15.

7 On the relationship between human relations approach and organizational change see Alex Bavelas, "Some Problems of Organizational Change," *Journal of Social Issues*, IV (Summer, 1948), pp. 48–52.

8 Fritz J. Roethlisberger, "The Foreman: Master and Victim of Double Talk," *Harvard Business Review*, 23 (Spring, 1945), pp. 285–94.

LINCOLN ROCHESTER TRUST COMPANY

I Case Introduction

Synopsis

Six upstate New York commercial banks approach Morgan Guaranty Trust Company of New York City with a proposal to form a bank holding company. In this formalized pooling of efforts, the bankers seek to achieve the size necessary to satisfy the expanding need for ever larger credit and for highly specialized services. Investigation by the Superintendent of Banks of New York State brings favorable backing, but the detailed testimony (much of it is reproduced here) pointing to improved banking services, contribution to the public interest, and preservation of competition brings a negative response from the Federal Reserve Board. Faced with this refusal, the bankers are trying to determine their next step.

Why This Case Is Included

The evaluation of the merger proposal draws together the views of all the interested parties on a complex problem. Economies of scale, the benefits of specialization, and stimulation to balanced regional economic growth are weighed against concern for size, concentration, and the preservation of competition. On the human side, there is opportunity to test conceptual schemes in reconciling individualism, organizational demands, personality needs, and efficiency in a large, rationally planned, system.

Diagnostic and Predictive Questions

In answering the following diagnostic and predictive questions, remember that these questions apply theories and conceptual ideas from certain disciplines. Such theories are valuable to understand basic forces at work in the policy system (diagnosis) and to predict what will happen in the system in the future (prediction). Since each reading abstracts from the total policy system certain factors or variables into the closed or partial viewpoint of one theory or discipline, no one reading gives answers to the practical policy problems of the case. In diagnosis and prediction, the parts of the problem are studied with "other things being equal."

Following each question are listed readings which will be helpful in answering the question. The readings included with this case are marked (*). By referring to the author index at the end of this book, you may locate the other readings listed.

1. From the standpoint of classical economic theory what were the six upstate bankers seeking in their proposed holding company relationship with the Morgan Guaranty Trust Company?

Read: Summer, "Economies of Scale and Organization Structure." Spencer and Siegelman, *Managerial Economics: Decision Making and Forward Planning*, pp. 242–48, 202–12. McGuire, *Interdisciplinary Studies in Business Behavior*, pp. 3–6. Marshall, *Principles of Economics*, pp. 283–85. Smith, *The Wealth of Nations*, pp. 4–15.

2. Why do the public officials quoted in Exhibit 15 favor the formation of the Morgan New York State Corporation? Is it reasonable for these men to predict a boost for the Gross *Regional* Product and the *Regional* Income as a result of the formation of the holding company? How, in fact, might such economic benefits be generated?

Read: Twentieth Century Fund, *USA in New Dimensions*, p. 15. Harriss, *The American Economy*, p. 212. (See Chapter 11 of Harriss' book for an explanation of the national—and, by analogy, the regional—accounting system.)

3. Using the categories developed by classical economists, how would you characterize the form, or forms, of banking competition in upstate New York prior to the proposed holding company? (It might be helpful to think of some of the specific "products" offered the public: credit, consulting and underwriting services, trust and investment counsel, etc.) Would the existence of the Morgan New York State Corporation change any of the competitive patterns? (Examine the statements of the executives of competing banks for insights into this situation—Exhibits 12, 13, 14.) Comment on the before and after competitive picture in terms of the single criterion of efficiency (the best banking services for the most people at the lowest cost). Sift carefully and distinguish "fact" from "opinion" in the case and exhibits.

Read: Stonier and Hague, *A Textbook of Economic Theory*, pp. 123–26, 162–64, 182–83, 189, 197–99, 201, 204–5, 208.

4. In terms of public policy toward business and social values, distinguish the concept of "size" from the concept of "concentration" and apply each to the proposed holding company in this case. Must "size" always go hand in hand with "concentration" and vice versa?

Read: *Kaysen, "The Corporation, How Much Power? What Scope?" *Clark, *Competition as a Dynamic Process*, pp. 141–43. (See also the remarks of Mr. Jennings and Congressman Celler in Exhibits 16 and 17.)

5. Considering the expanding needs of upstate New York—as attested to by bankers, businessmen, academicians, and public officials in the case—is there need for a statewide financial institution just to insure a balanced growth of all economic sectors? Note the evidence in the case of instances like the farmers' cooperative (Exhibit 6) which is indeed headquartered in one location but whose operations honeycomb the system. From the viewpoint of executives of such enterprises, does it make more economic sense to deal with autonomous and geographically dispersed decision centers or to deal with one central decision locus through several interrelated channels?

Read: *Galbraith, *The Affluent Society*, pp. 253–54. Veblen, *The Engineers and the Price System*, chap. v. (While Galbraith and Veblen touch on the issue of balanced growth, this concept of "line balancing" in economic systems—and, in fact, in any system—simply has not received attention in the literature. Draw your own conclusions about this issue using analogies of physical growth processes, your knowledge of the evolution of social institutions, and the case facts.)

6. Certain theories would seem to look with disfavor on the action of the six upstate bank presidents in abandoning their autonomous positions as chief executives for subordinate roles in a larger organization. Classical economic philosophy lauds the enterprising individual and hinges economic well-being on his self-serving efforts. Other theories—especially from psychology, sociology, and political science—seem to predict that the motivation, initiative, and freedom of the individual bank presidents would be lessened in their subordinate positions of the holding company. This in turn would seem to have harmful effects on the offices of the local banks, their motivation, and the efficiency of the system as a whole. In terms of a careful analysis of the facts of the case:

a) Do you predict the harmful effects to the individuals, the local offices, and the entire system?

b) Why didn't the presidents of the local banks object to the merger? (Recall that they, in fact, initiated the move.)

Read: *National Association of Manufacturers, "Principles of Freedom of Action." *Hazlitt, "Private Enterprise Regained." *Schumpeter, *The Theory of Economic Development*, pp. 84–94. *Nisbet, *Community and Power*, pp. 224–29, 235–40. Argyris, *Personality and Organization*, pp. 27–31, 33–51, 66–67, 77–90, 103–4, 123–25, 130, 137–39, 150, 153–55, 157. Merton, "Bureaucratic Structure and Personality." Locke, *Concerning Civil Government.*

7. Does the sociological conceptual scheme concerning status and role help you in predicting some of the adjustments that each of the six upstate bank presidents will have to make in the transition from being a "big fish in a small pond" to bring "a small fish in a big pond"?

Read: Abrahams, "Status, Role, and Conflict." (Additional reading, abridged on pages 75–79 of this volume. Daniel Levinson, "Role, Personality, and Social Structure in the Organizational Setting," *Journal of Abnormal Psychology*, Vol. 58 [1959]) .

Policy Questions for This Specific Case

In answering the following policy questions, the results of diagnosis and prediction are used to reduce the amount of guesswork, or judgment, in designing action solutions. However, since certain parts of the total case situation cannot be reduced to science, and since "other things are not equal," judgment must still be used to fill in the factors not accounted for by readings. You will also need a second kind of judgment as you put value weights on different scientific predictions, since different theories may point to conflicting solutions.

8. Which of the three remaining courses of action should the bankers involved in the proposed Morgan New York State Corporation take: (*a*) ask the board to reconsider, (*b*) drop the merger plan, or (*c*) go to the federal courts to try to prove their case? Cite your reasoning—pro and con—for each alternative.

9. Having decided what to do, draw up directions for planning and implementing your program of action. (Synthesize the various "pieces" from your diagnosis in Questions 1 through 5.)

Major Policy Issues: Tentative Generalizations about Any Policy System

In arriving at conclusions for the following questions, generalize from the facts in the case and use your own ideas to (*a*) confirm, (*b*) modify, or (*c*) test the workability of the concepts and theories from readings. As an executive or professional, use wisdom to merge theory, on the one hand, with "brute facts" and practice, on the other.

10. Is there a conflict between the social value of progress (or productive efficiency) and the social concern over size (voiced by Congressman Celler in Exhibit 17)? Can the two values be reconciled? Does corporate management have a role in this reconciliation? (Refer back to Questions 1 through 5 and their attached readings.)

> Read: Galbraith, *The Affluent Society*, pp. 121–24, 126. Dahl and Lindblom, *Politics, Economics, and Welfare*, pp. 28–29, 31–33, 38–41, 45–46, 49–53.

11. Common observation reveals quite a predictable growth process in nature. "Built-in" laws dictate that a child's growth be proportional—at any one time the two legs match, the ears match, the stomach is large enough to process the required amount of food. Yet, even in such a well-balanced system, we find it necessary to monitor the growth process to avoid overweight or undernourishment. In the economic system we classically rely on the laws of the market to assure proportional development of all segments. Do you see any need for a monitor—or "line balancer"—in the economic system comparable to the monitoring function in the human system? If such a monitory function is necessary, what role, if any, should corporate management serve in supplementing the laws of the market with rational "line-balancing"? (See Question 5.)

12. In what way, if any, is the policy maker affected by the academic dispute about the conflict between the demands of organization structure and the needs of the human personality? Can the social value of individualism—fostered by classical economic philosophy—be integrated with the social need for cooperative effort? (See Question 6 and the readings assigned there.)

Questions for Original Student Work in Analysis and Policy

The methods of viewing this case as represented by the authors' questions and selection of readings are not exhaustive. There are other relevant ideas for diagnosis and prediction. Furthermore, there are other ways of stating policy questions. More powerful analyses and wiser solutions will result by drawing on your own training and experience for (*a*) relevant concepts and theories, and (*b*) creative ways of asking policy questions. The following questions are designed to help you acquire this skill.

13. While reflecting on case facts, what additional theories from prior education give you insights as to "what is going on" in the Lincoln Rochester Trust Company? As to what might be predicted to happen in the future?

14. Other than the policy questions asked by the authors, what pragmatic ways can you think of to state the practical problems faced by executives in the case?

II Lincoln Rochester Trust Company*

Over a period of about seven years prior to the writing of this case, Mr. John W. Remington, chairman of the board of the Lincoln Rochester Trust Company, had held conversations with officers of six other banks in New York State concerning the possibility of forming a bank holding company. A brief description of such a holding company is included in Exhibit 1. Exhibit 2 is an excerpt from the Bank Holding Company Act of 1956, and Exhibit 3 provides data on the proposed Morgan New York State Corporation.

At first Messrs. Harriman and Newburn, officers of the Manufacturers and Traders Bank of Buffalo, had initiated the idea with Mr. Remington. Later, Mr. Remington spoke with Mr. Wynkoop, president of the First Trust and Deposit Company of Syracuse. Then, this group of officers from three banks decided to invite to an exploratory meeting the presidents of National Commercial Bank and Trust Company (Albany), Oneida National Bank and Trust Company (Utica), and First-City National Bank (Binghamton). After an exchange of information among banks, a second meeting was held at which the officers of the six banks decided "that it was important to have allied with us a strong bank located in New York City," and "that Morgan Guaranty Trust Company should be approached" (statements of Mr. Remington). Accordingly, since Mr. Remington was scheduled to attend a meeting in Washington at which Henry Alexander, chairman of Morgan Guaranty, would be present, it was decided that Remington should present the idea to Alexander.

At the Washington meeting, Henry Alexander told Remington that this proposal came as a complete surprise to him, but that he would talk the matter over with his fellow officers at Morgan Guaranty. A few days later, he telephoned Remington in Rochester, saying that he would like to pursue discussions further, within the framework of four factors of high importance in the decision:

1. The retention of a strong local autonomy by upstate banks.
2. The need for the holding company to have 100% stock ownership of all affiliated banks.
3. A well-considered opinion that the proposed company had an excellent chance to obtain approval from regulatory authorities.
4. That the basis of exchange (of stock) could be worked out in a manner fair to all banks and their stockholders. Also, to make the decision process more orderly, he suggested that discussion of exchange ratios be deferred until other matters (advantages and disadvantages of the combination) were resolved in joint meetings.

---

* Copyright 1964 by the Graduate School of Business, Columbia University.

History of Growth of Separate Banks

Each of the separate banks had, at the time of their proposal, grown through merger with other banks over the years. A history of these mergers is shown in Exhibit 4. A review of the literature on bank mergers in this period shows that the managements of the banks believe that greater efficiency of operations, as well as better service to the public, results from merger. The reasons advanced as to why this occurs are similar to those summarized in the exhibits to this case, as applicable to the seven banks' formation of Morgan New York State Corporation.

The Decision to Apply for Consolidation: The Public Interest as a Factor

Under provisions of the Bank Holding Company Act, banks which wish to consolidate in this form of organization structure are required to show that it is in the public interest to consolidate. Applications must be approved by the Federal Reserve Board. This is why Mr. Alexander listed as his third point that, during the discussions, and in making the decision to apply for permission to consolidate, the officers of the banks should investigate all reasons, pro and con, why this would (or would not) be in the public interest. In the research, all possible information was to be gathered on the effects of the merger on competition, on customer services, and other matters. For $8\frac{1}{2}$ months prior to filing the application to consolidate with the Federal Reserve Board, officers, and other personnel (accountants, lawyers) of the seven banks engaged in much research and information gathering on the effects of the new corporation on the public.

In their own testimony before the Federal Reserve Board, the officials of the banks themselves cited case histories and reasons why the affiliated system would provide better banking service to customers (Exhibits 5 through 11).

In the research leading up to the decision, the banks also consulted various public officials (Exhibit 15) for their opinions regarding the effects of the new company on their local economies. That is, how the new corporation might affect the "gross regional product," employment, and income in the parts of New York State which it would serve. Competitor banks, including small banks, were consulted (Exhibits 12 through 14).

In addition, the banks employed outside consultants, including an economist, Lewellyn A. Jennings, to render an expert opinion as to whether the new bank would be consistent with (1) adequate and sound banking services to customers, (2) the public interest, and (3) the preservation of competition in the field of banking. Mr. Jennings' research findings were in the affirmative on all three counts, as shown in his testimony (Exhibit 16). In addition, in the opinion of Mr. Thompson, president of a small competitor bank, the new company would meet the need for better banking services, as outlined in a study by Dr. Marcus Nadler, prominent economist and banking scholar, of New York University. Dr. Nadler, in a study for the American Bankers Association in 1956, concluded that the holding company is a sound device because it combines the advantages of local management, at the same time providing central supervision, and centralized services, not available in smaller independent banks.

After all of this investigation, the officers of the six banks took the facts, and then exercised their judgment, concluding that the new institution, the Morgan New York Corporation, would not only provide additional and better service to customers, but that it would provide various advantages to the communities served. They judged that it would not have enough adverse effect (if any) on competition to outweigh the first two benefits. Therefore, they reasoned that the State Superintendent of Banks would approve it, and, later, that it had, as Mr. Alexander had put it, "an excellent chance to obtain approval from regulatory authorities."

Competition

The statements of smaller competitor bank officials (Exhibits 12 through 14), and Congressman Celler's testimony (Exhibit 17) contain certain information on the effects of the Morgan New York State Corporation on existing banks in New York State. One point, however, needs clarifying.

There is, in New York, one statewide bank holding company in existence—the Marine Midland Corporation. It controls eleven banks, operating 180 branches, in 105 communities in the state. The proposed consolidation would have 156 branches, based on the number operated by each of the seven banks. While the new company would have resources (loans receivable, investments) of roughly $6 billion, the Marine Midland has resources of roughly $3 billion. After the merger, if approved, the bank would still not be as large, in resources, as the Bank of America in California, or the Chase-Manhattan, both of which have resulted from numerous mergers. The Marine Midland, incidentally, has an application before the Federal Reserve Board to acquire the Security National Bank of Long Island, which owns an additional 28 offices.

The Decision to Apply: Costs, Revenues, Profits, and Growth

In addition to the public interest factors in the decision to apply for the consolidated bank, the officers of the seven banks were concerned with short-term and long-term profits of the new institution, as compared with these factors for separate institutions. In a way, this was a question of whether the new institution would produce more profit than the sum of profits of seven separate institutions.

In the statements provided by public officials and member-bank officers, many reasons are given which would affect both revenues (volume and size of loans to customers) and costs.

In the final judgment of the officials of these banks, the holding company would be beneficial in terms of profit and growth for stockholders.

Statements of Customers of the Bank regarding Efficiency of a Larger Bank

A number of customers of the separate banks believe that the new bank would improve the service they get, or lower the cost of services, or both. In short, they believe that the new institution's services would result in more efficiency of their own organizations.

Robert Stevens, president of Stevens and Thompson Paper Mills, states that he would obtain more expert advice and service on loan problems. To efficiently compete with large companies such as Scott and Kimberly-Clark, he must innovate through new products and packages, and in this process he must sometimes act quickly. While he can obtain capital through pooling of a loan through several local banks, one larger institution would provide larger amounts of capital without the time-consuming negotiations among a group of smaller banks. Also, the information and advice he could get from staff departments of the larger bank regarding export operations was also important to him in competing with large companies who can readily obtain such advice.

W. V. Daugherty, chairman of American Emblem Company of Oneida, states that, with the growth of his company, his loan requirements have become larger than can be supplied by one bank—the Oneida National—alone. He cited two cases when the company needed working capital and approached the Chase and Hanover Banks in New York City to pool the loan with the Oneida National Bank. After negotiations, the loan was not approved. Thereupon, he opened new negotiations with banks in Albany and New York and obtained funds. He stated that the holding company could provide such funds, shifting quickly from other parts of the system, without time-consuming negotiations.

Joseph C. Wilson, president of Xerox Corporation of Rochester, states that his company increased in sales from $6.5 million in 1946 to $60 million. In this growth, he has had to borrow money in nine out of fifteen years, in amounts growing steadily larger, from $1 million to $15 million in 1961. "At first, we borrowed only from Lincoln Rochester and Security Trust of Rochester. In 1961 we were borrowing from nine banks, four in Rochester and five outside, since all of the Rochester Banks together could not supply our needs." He also pointed out that at the time his company formed a British company, local banks could not supply the advice on international finance required; and that local banks could not supply the expert talent and specialists in some fields required by his company—for example, the profit-sharing retirement plan. "We need a thoroughly sophisticated, competent investment counsel from a staff

which is widely specialized if we are to get the most retirement benefits
for our dollars of contribution . . . [a] holding company with a central
core of distinguished analysts will provide this."

Mervin H. Baker, president of National Gypsum Company (Buffalo);
Charles Durkin, president of Leaseway Transportation Company; and
Raymond Hebert, president of Filtration Equipment Company all made
similar statements to the above.

Action on the Application: Stockholders and Regulatory Authorities

Before the application was made to state and federal authorities, the
officers of all seven banks submitted the proposal to their stockholders,
summarizing the reasons why the larger bank was believed to be in their
interests. In a short period of time, the stockholders approved the consolidation, in which they would receive shares in the new Morgan New
York State Corporation, in exchange, for example, for their stock in The
Lincoln Rochester Trust Company. Stockholders who exercised their
ownership rights, therefore, judged it themselves to be in their best
interests.

Application was duly made to the New York State Banking Board,
which approved the holding company. Oren Root, State Banking Superintendent, judged that it is necessary "to the kind of expanding economy
which is so essential to the welfare of the state and the country."

The Federal Reserve Board then held hearings after the above approvals, and denied the application. Members of the board stated that the
company "might contribute to banking convenience of upstate customers," and could "to some extent" help economic expansion of the area.
But they said that these "are outweighed by concern for preserving competition."

The board, in its decision, said the application wasn't turned down
simply because of size; "size alone is not a controlling consideration," it
said. But the board did contend that the new concern would tend to over-
concentrate banking power that currently is "strategically located throughout the State of New York."

The board added: "This is not to suggest that the economic power of
the proposed holding company would be abused or improperly exercised;
the Board's conclusion is based upon its belief that the trend toward
concentration that would result from the proposed transaction would be
inconsistent with the intent of Congress. . . ."

Future Action of the Banks

The banks concerned have the benefit of their own factual investigations and judgments, and the judgments of a wide range of customers,
competitors, and the (public) banking department of New York State.

They have alternative courses of action: (1) ask the board to reconsider,

(2) drop the merger plan, or (3) go to the federal courts to try to prove their case. The courts, as one banker put it, "have the final say in whether actions of corporations are right or wrong, according to the laws of the nation."

Exhibit 1

SUMMARY DESCRIPTION OF A BANK HOLDING COMPANY*

The major purpose of the Bank Holding Company Act of 1956 is to define bank holding companies, control their future expansion, and require divestment of their non-banking interests. Section 2(a) of the Act defines a bank holding company as any company (1) which directly or indirectly owns, controls, or holds with power to vote 25 per cent or more of the voting shares of each of two or more banks or of a company which is or becomes a bank holding company, or (2) which controls the election of the majority of the board of directors of each of two or more banks.

A bank holding company is prohibited from acquiring a bank outside its home state, unless the laws of the outside state expressly permit such acquisitions by out-of-state holding companies.

Without prior approval of the Board of Governors of the Federal Reserve Board no bank holding company may acquire direct or indirect ownership or control of any voting shares of any bank if, after such acquisition, such company will directly or indirectly own or control more than 5 per cent of the voting shares of such bank; no bank holding company or subsidiary thereof, other than a bank, may acquire all or substantially all of the assets of a bank; no bank holding company may merge or consolidate with any other bank holding company.

In determining whether or not to approve any acquisition, merger, or consolidation the Board must consider the factors listed in Section 3(c) of the Act: (1) the financial history and condition of the company or companies and the banks concerned; (2) their prospects; (3) the character of their management; (4) the convenience, needs and welfare of the communities and the area concerned; and (5) whether or not the effect of such acquisition or merger or consolidation would be to expand the size or extent of the bank holding company system involved beyond limits consistent with adequate and sound banking, the public interest, and the preservation of competition in the field of banking.

Holding companies have grown apparently because they fill an economic need. A holding company has many of the advantages of the branch banking system and avoids some of the disadvantages. It has central guidance and policy but at the same time permits the operations of each bank to be independent. The subsidiary banks have their own local boards of directors and their own chief executives.

Bank holding companies appear to possess a number of advantages from the standpoint of the public, the employees, and the stockholders. They are in a better position than an individual bank to provide general services and also specialized services such as trust work, investment advice, and foreign departments. They can draw on trained personnel from one unit and make it available to others, and hence broaden the opportunities for employees. They are better able to raise new capital when necessary.

---

* Benjamin J. Klebaner, "The Bank Holding Company Act of 1956," *Southern Economic Journal*, January, 1958, pp. 313–26. For further reading see Marcus Nadler, *The Banking Situation in New York State*, 1956, pp. 106–27; Gerald C. Fischer, *Bank Holding Companies* (New York: Columbia University Press, 1961), pp. 69–85.

Exhibit 2

FROM: BANK HOLDING COMPANY ACT OF 1956*

In determining whether or not to approve any acquisition or merger or consolidation under this section, the Board shall take into consideration the following factors: (1) the financial history and condition of the company or companies and the banks concerned; (2) their prospects; (3) the character of their management; (4) the convenience, needs, and welfare of the communities and the area concerned; and (5) whether or not the effect of such acquisition or merger or consolidation would be to expand the size or extent of the bank holding company system involved beyond limits consistent with adequate and sound banking, the public interest, and the preservation of competition in the field of banking.

Exhibit 3

THE MORGAN NEW YORK STATE CORPORATION

The following information regarding the Morgan New York State Corporation has been abstracted from a report prepared by the First Boston Corporation for the benefit of its investor clients:

The constituent banks, at December 31, 1960, had aggregate capital funds of over $680 million, total resources of over $6 billion, and total deposits exceeding $5 billion of which $1.5 billion were those of the six upstate banks. In consolidated resources, compared with existing institutions, Morgan New York State Corporation would rank third among banking entities in New York State and fourth among those in the United States. The banking operations of the constituent banks are carried on in 144 offices in upstate New York, 5 in New York City, and 4 overseas.

The important corporate relationships and the extensive fiduciary and foreign connections of Morgan Guaranty would be strongly complemented within the holding company structure by the addition of the six upstate banks. The operations of the latter have reflected a materially greater deposit growth (18.5% for the period of 1955–1960 as compared with 0.5% for Morgan Guaranty) and an emphasis on "retail" banking services such as instalment lending to individual customers. Some of the advantages of the proposed bank holding company operation would be:

a. Greater territorial coverage, resulting in enhanced deposit growth potential, and broader diversification of banking services and sources of income,
b. Greater flexibility in the allocation of capital resources among, and in providing new capital for, the constituent banks,
c. A pooling of managerial skills, while retaining the identity and distinctive local character of the constituent banks,
d. The provision of centralized services in specialized fields, such as trust and portfolio management and international banking, for the common use of the constituent banks,
e. Greater marketability for the shares of the holding company than exists for the shares of the individual banks.

Morgan Guaranty reported net operating earnings for 1960 of $52,118,000, or $6.91 per share. Its $4.00 dividend represented a payout rate of 57.9% of such earnings. The combined net operating earnings for 1960 of the constituent banks totaled $65,461,000. After deducting estimated holding company expenses and taxes of $3,000,000, net operating earnings would have been $62,461,000, or

---

* Public Law 511, Chap. 240, 84th Cong., 2d sess., H.R. 6227.

Exhibit 3—Continued

approximately $2.59 per share, on the shares of the holding company to be outstanding. If an annual dividend rate for the holding company shares of $1.64 per share is assumed, as it is understood it was in the development of the proposal, the aggregate dividend requirement would be approximately $39,608,000, or 63.4% of adjusted 1960 net operating earnings.

Under the above dividend assumption, the shareholders of each participating bank would receive an increase in dividend income. Morgan Guaranty shareholders would receive the equivalent of $4.10 per present share instead of $4.00. Shareholders of the other banks would receive larger percentage increases in dividend income. Such increases in dividend income would be made possible in part by reason of the unusually strong capital position of the combined constituent banks.

Exhibit 4

HISTORY OF MERGERS OF SEVEN NEW YORK BANKS, 1945–61

Bank Acquired or Merged

MORGAN GUARANTY TRUST COMPANY:

J. P. Morgan & Co., Incorporated	Morgan & Cie. Incorporated

MANUFACTURERS AND TRADERS BANK OF BUFFALO:

First National Bank of Kenmore	First National Bank of Buffalo
Citizens National Bank of Lancaster	Bank of Clarence
American Bank of Lackawanna	Adam, Meldrum & Anderson State Bank
Farmers Bank of Springville	Genessee Trust Company
Merchants National Bank of Dunkirk	Citizens Trust Company
Bank of Corfu	First National Bank of Silver Creek
Ebenezer State Bank	Bank of Ellicottville
Lockport Exchange Trust Company	Bank of Blasdell

LINCOLN ROCHESTER TRUST COMPANY:

Rochester Trust & Safe Deposit Company	Ontario County Trust Company
	Bank of Hammondsport
Corning Trust Company	Citizens Bank of Penn Yan

NATIONAL COMMERCIAL BANK AND TRUST COMPANY (ALBANY):

Rensselaer County Bank	State Bank of Ellenburg
Hudson River Trust Company	First National Bank
Plattsburgh National Bank	Bank of Waterford
Athens National Bank	Hartwick National Bank
Merchants National Bank	Farmers National Bank
Peoples First National Bank	Fultonville National Bank
Second National Bank	First National Bank of Amsterdam

FIRST TRUST AND DEPOSIT COMPANY OF SYRACUSE:

First National Bank of Canastota	First National Bank of Weedsport
Liverpool Bank	Cazenovia National Bank
State Bank of Parish	First National Bank of Morrisville
First National Bank & Trust Company	National Bank & Trust Co. of Skaneateles
First National Bank of Marcellus	DeRuyter State Bank
Bank of East Syracuse	

Exhibit 4—Continued

ONEIDA NATIONAL BANK AND TRUST COMPANY (UTICA):

First National Bank of Holland Patent   First National Bank of Camden
First National Bank of New Hartford   Rome Trust Company
First National Bank of Old Forge   Manufacturers National Bank of Ilion
West Winfield National Bank

FIRST-CITY NATIONAL BANK (BINGHAMTON):

City National Bank   First National Bank, Owego
First National Bank, Whitney Point

Exhibit 5

STATEMENT OF WILMOT R. CRAIG

I am Wilmot R. Craig of Rochester, New York. Since June 16, 1961, I have been President and Chief Executive Officer of Lincoln Rochester Trust Company where I have been employed for over 25 years.

In this statement I will discuss the major reasons why Lincoln Rochester believes that its joining the proposed holding company is important to its future and of the region served by it. . . .

I should like to comment briefly about each of these in the order given:

1. *The formation of the European Common Market and economic recovery in other foreign countries*

These have resulted in heightened interest on the part of many business organizations in the establishment of productive and other facilities in one or more of the countries forming the common market to avoid exclusion from the important market area represented therein and to participate in the growing markets of other countries. A need has developed for advice and know-how in connection with the plan and functioning of the European Common Market and in connection with doing business in other foreign countries. A need exists also for advice and assistance in determining the implications involved in the establishment of facilities abroad in terms of foreign exchange problems, foreign banking connections, credit information, and other advisory contacts and affiliations which could be of assistance. Continuing service is required following the establishment of facilities abroad to facilitate the transfer of funds in either direction, to provide a flow of credit information and intelligence as to internal developments which may affect foreign exchange and related matters.

Among the companies located in our area which are engaged in foreign business and are expanding such business in foreign countries and Canada are:

> Ritter Co., Inc.
> General Railway Signal Company
> Gleason Works
> Eastman Kodak Company
> Bausch & Lomb Incorporated
> Xerox, Inc.
> Taylor Instrument Companies
> R. T. French Company
> Pfaudler Permutit, Inc.

In addition to these larger companies a growing number of small and medium-sized companies in our banking area are expanding their interest in foreign markets or are contemplating doing so. Their needs exceed those of larger companies because it is more difficult for them to establish the required contacts

Exhibit 5—Continued

and sources of advice and information. The following smaller and medium-sized companies are among those in our banking area which have needs of this nature:

Company*	Type of Business
Company A	Beauty preparations and schools
Company B	Laboratory supplies
Company C	Zinc die casting
Company D	Metalworking and assemblies
Company E	Automotive accessories
Company F	Printed circuits
Company G	Optical products
Company H	Electric motors
Company I	Bowling halls
Company J	Photographic products and processing
Company K	Optical products
Company L	Magneto parts
Company M	Minerals

*Identified by code name because plans may not have been announced publicly.

Although we have had a Foreign Department in our bank for many years, its activities have consisted largely of issuing Commercial and Individual Letters of Credit, handling remittances and acceptances, dealing in limited amounts of foreign exchange and issuing travelers checks. We do not possess the experience, knowledge or foreign connections required to provide the extensive and sophisticated services required under existing conditions. If we were successful in equipping ourselves to meet these needs the cost would far exceed the volume of business that we could acquire from our banking area.

2. *Broader ownership of corporate securities and growth in size and number of pension, profit-sharing and other employee benefit funds*

These have brought about a need by a growing number of individuals and businesses for investment management services provided through our Trust and Investment Departments.

To provide the type and quality of investment management and service increasingly needed and required by many Trust Department customers under the complex conditions affecting investments that exist today necessitates a depth and breadth of research capacities and highly specialized staff which are difficult for us to provide at a cost which is not prohibitive. Because trust services are so personal in nature and extend beyond the investment aspects of the services, the service needs are provided best through the local institution aided by the expertness in investment matters of an affiliate possessing the necessary staff and skills which can be consulted frequently and is located in the nation's financial center.

3. *Expansion of business and industrial companies*

This expansion has occurred through normal growth in an expanding economy accelerated by research and new products, through the opening of new facilities over a wider area of this country and abroad, and through acquisitions.

The expansion, however caused, has been accompanied by increased needs for banking services. This is true of large, medium-sized and smaller businesses of all types. In addition to the needs for special skills in Foreign Department services and in Trust Investment services, previously mentioned, expansion and growth have required greater availability of credit, both in quantity and form. Projected continued growth and expansion in our area will continue and accelerate this need.

Exhibit 5—Continued

. . . There is little room for further expansion of loans consistent with sound banking practices except through a higher rate of growth in deposits and through increased capital. Affiliation with Morgan New York State Corporation can give us an ability to contribute in fuller fashion to the growth and varied needs of our customers. They, in turn, should then be in a position to increase their deposits which are so necessary to sustain an advancing economy. This affiliation will enable us to accumulate a higher proportion of our earnings or otherwise acquire capital needed to meet the increasing credit requirements of our customers. . . .

4. *Improvements in transportation and communication locally, domestically and world-wide*

Such developments in transportation as the New York State Thruway, the St. Lawrence Seaway and jet air services have had and will have increasing influence on the need for added banking services. These developments will tend to remove our banking and trade area from a position of relative remoteness from other banking and trade areas to a position of relative proximity to each of the others in the state, the country and the world.

This makes increasingly important provision for banking services through a state-wide organization of local banks, each thoroughly familiar with its own area, affiliated through common ownership in Morgan New York State Corporation. Through such an organization there would be afforded a choice of source of state-wide banking services now available only through Marine Midland Corporation.

*   *   *   *   *

6. *Growth in population particularly in those of school age*

The "population explosion" has many implications to banking in terms of present and future needs to be met. The large increase in the school population at various levels has required and will continue to require substantial investment in new school buildings and related capital equipment. To finance these investments school districts and municipalities must "go to the market" with bonds to sell. They require counsel and competitive bids in order to be able to obtain the most favorable terms for their issues. Ability to provide helpful counsel to financial officers of school districts and municipalities requires specialists in this field aided by the "on the ground" services and knowledge of the local bank. Aid to school districts and municipalities in the form of bidding competitively for their issues requires specialized knowledge of the municipal market and adequate distribution facilities. At the present time Lincoln Rochester is able to do little in this field. Affiliation of our bank with Morgan New York State Corporation which can provide the specialized services of the Municipal Bond Department of Morgan Guaranty Trust Company would enable us to meet these growing needs.

7. *Recognition by civic authorities of the need for urban renewal and redevelopment*

Sparked by the example of a few cities, such as my own, which have provided leadership in urban renewal and redevelopment, and encouraged by action of Federal and State governments vast sums of money are going to be required to rebuild our cities and towns. To carry out planned projects in our own area will necessitate very substantial sums of credit in various forms. Through our affiliation with Morgan New York State Corporation we could expect to receive the supplemental credit that will be required for us to carry our proportionate share of the responsibility for providing worthy credit for these activities.

Exhibit 6

STATEMENT OF GEORGE A. NEWBURY

My name is George A. Newbury. I am President of the Manufacturers and Traders Trust Company, Buffalo, New York.

I . . . have engaged in the discussions leading up to the formation of Morgan New York State Corporation. My reason for doing so was a growing conviction, based on experience, that a substantial and rapidly growing segment of business could no longer be served adequately on a regional basis. Typical of these experiences were the following:

Company One: Company is a farmers co-operative. Banking relationship began January 15, 1932. It still continues and we extend a line of credit in the amount of $1,000,000. In 1954 and 1955 company was promoting a change in milk handling methods by farmers involving the installation of cooling tanks by farmers costing $1,000 and upwards each. We were unable to get this business despite our long relationship because we could not provide a state-wide financing service for the farmers.

Company Two: Banking relationship began August 9, 1937. On May 14, 1957 the relationship was terminated and we were told that although our service was satisfactory they felt the many contacts that could be made through a state-wide banking connection would be of immense help to their sales department.

Company Three: Banking relationship began April 14, 1933 and continued to April 15, 1960. Over that period we were the principal, if not the only banking connection of the company. During a period of financial stress we stood by the company, making it loans which were classified by the supervisory authorities and against which we set up reserves. In 1960 the company was sold to a concern that did business with a state-wide banking group and the banking connection with us was wholly terminated.

Instances such as these where a firmly established banking connection was broken because its service was limited to a single trade area can be multiplied many times. Instances where endeavors to get new business failed for the same reason are even more numerous.

Banking services that were satisfactory a generation ago no longer can serve adequately in a dynamic economy that is witnessing an evolution in business methods little short of revolutionary. Business today is not anchored to a single establishment and a neighborhood market. Express highways link operations in communities scores and even hundreds of miles apart, reducing operating costs and improving profit potentials through better utilization of warehouse facilities, inventories and head office facilities.

*   *   *   *   *

Business today uses a bank in a multitude of ways in addition to those of serving as a depository for its funds and a source of credit—Lock Boxes, Freight Payment Plans, Account Reconciliation, Agent for receiving payment of utility bills, Insurance, Blue Cross and Blue Shield payments, In Plant Banking, Night Transit Service and many others. The greater the area a bank covers the more effective these services become. Many companies look to a bank for introductions and other assistance in developing sales, for credit information and services of that character. Here again the more far reaching organization the greater the service it can render.

*   *   *   *   *

Of the one hundred (100) largest corporations in America twenty-five (25) have an operation in the Buffalo-Niagara industrial district, and of the top five hundred (500) approximately seventy (70) have an operation here.

Exhibit 7

STATEMENT OF W. NIVER WYNKOOP

My name is W. Niver Wynkoop, President of First Trust & Deposit Company of Syracuse, New York.

After graduating from Hamilton College in 1921, I entered the Bank as a messenger and worked in various departments, and in 1953 was elected a Director and Executive Vice President. I held that title until 1956 when I was elected President.

As a result of [certain factors], capital has not kept pace with the growth of deposits. The Bank now finds itself in a capital position that will limit the ability of the Bank to provide the community with the increasing needs of bank services, especially credit.

The affiliation with Morgan New York State Corporation will, in my opinion, supply the capital which will allow First Trust to better serve the needs of this rapidly expanding area.

As an outgrowth of the unique history of First Trust the managerial resources have been affected, especially in the age bracket of 40–55 years of age. This is being partially corrected by the training of younger men for these positions who have been obtained through an aggressive recruitment program. However, the training and experience of these younger men that will be provided by such an association of banks will assist us, as it would any bank, in attracting young men and in broadening management's views and so help them do a much better job in providing service to the community.

Foreign services are so complex and highly specialized that we have not had trained personnel to offer a full range of these services to our customers. Through our affiliation with the Holding Company, we will have the facilities of Morgan Guaranty which will provide customers in our community with all the expert advice and services that are available to the businesses in large metropolitan areas.

First Trust has close contact with the municipalities in the area it serves and holds many of the obligations of these political bodies. We have not been able to offer the consulting and underwriting services that Marine Midland offers through its Municipal Service Department of their Buffalo affiliate.

With the growth of these municipalities there will be increasing demands for financing capital improvements. First Trust could offer through the Holding Company all the services and the wide range of markets that are available to the Morgan Guaranty Trust Company.

Our Bank is rapidly approaching the 100 million dollar mark in trust assets.

With Morgan Guaranty's highly qualified staff of specialists, we can be certain that the best trust and investment advice available will be supplied to us immediately and continuously. Our customers could benefit from services now offered by all large metropolitan banks.

Exhibit 8

STATEMENT OF CHARLES W. HALL, PRESIDENT, ONEIDA NATIONAL BANK

Over the past few years the increasing tempo of general business has brought about a real challenge to us as we serve the Oneida-Herkimer County area encompassing approximately 3,500 square miles in the heart of the Empire State. . . . These requirements have centered in all phases of the needs of the people—

Exhibit 8—Continued

commercial and industrial loans, consumer and personal credit loans, mortgages for new homes, mortgages for industrial building construction and increased loans for the serving of our large farm area.

In serving our approximately 50,000 customers, it has been necessary for us on many occasions to attempt to participate loans to bankers in other parts of the state. On these occasions we have been required to canvass banks of New York State to find out whether or not they would have an interest in a participation and, if so, whether their commitments would permit them to participate. We have had many delays and in some instances considerable disappointment from correspondent bank contacts.

An important example of such a delay and disappointment occurred shortly after an account was opened with us when the company received a very substantial order for the manufacture of blades for airplane engines. We went to our New York correspondent and asked them to share the loan with us, which was then a $500,000 loan. We were to take $200,000 and they were to take $300,000. After considerable study they made the commitment. However, the company, having moved into a new area of business, had an immediate requirement for more financing. New contracts were being offered to the company so that it had seven orders totaling $3,250,000 and had to increase its bank borrowings. We worked out a commitment under a V Loan arrangement pursuant to which the company ultimately borrowed $3,000,000. It was at this point of increasing need that our New York correspondent bank indicated to us that the ratios were not such that they cared to follow as a participant in the loan and we were required to seek other banking assistance. Sixty days later, and I might say an embarrassing sixty days, we were able to develop a contact outside New York City who said that they would share this loan with us in the ratio that would come within our legal limits. If we had been a part of a holding company, we would have been much better able to serve this customer than in the manner in which we had to serve.

*   *   *   *   *

Another very important consideration which has been forced on us is our inability to serve our customers at more distant points in the way that Marine Midland Trust Company of the Mohawk Valley can do. Over the past several years we have lost important business to that competitor, not by reason of the quality of our service locally but because of the service given to our customer at a distant point by Marine Midland affiliates. For example, we have been the banker to an independent gas station owner who, having started from one station handling a well-known brand of gas, had with our banking help acquired a series of stations that made him one of our largest distributors of gasoline. He was invited to sell his business to the Gulf Oil Company and they immediately closed our banking relation, giving all of the business to our competitor for the reason that the Buffalo office of this company had made some special banking accommodation available to them.

Another important consideration, and once again we have in mind the interests of our customer, is the need for a counselling service in matters of capital financing. We are the depositor for a majority of the central school districts located in Oneida and Herkimer Counties. Each of these school districts has been moving through the experience of population growth requiring additional facilities. . . . Our competitor, however, with its holding company affiliation, has offered these districts a counselling service that looks to the permanent funding of their needs. It is not practicable for a bank of our size to have a depart-

Exhibit 8—Continued

ment to offer this kind of service; for the sums to be underwritten and the programs required are much beyond commitments possible for us to make. A holding company makes it possible for us to call on our associates to offer the same kind of advice and thus to provide our customers with an alternative source for such advice.

Exhibit 9

STATEMENT OF EDGAR W. COUPER

First City National Bank, Binghamton, New York

The directors of our Bank have voted to join the proposed Morgan New York State Corporation because they believe it offers an opportunity to serve better the community in which we are located and to compete more effectively with our chief rival, the Marine Midland Trust Company of Southern New York.

*   *   *   *   *

The holding company will help us rise to this needed new level of banking service. For example, it will help us provide:

*   *   *   *   *

3. More complete automation than our individual bank can afford through combining such facilities with other members of the holding company. This should help hold down the price of bank services.

*   *   *   *   *

We do not compete with any of the other proposed members of the Morgan New York State Corporation. The nearest bank to us is the First Trust and Deposit Company of Syracuse, whose headquarters are 75 miles away, and whose nearest branch is some 40 miles from our most northern branch.

Exhibit 10

STATEMENT OF F. W. McCABE

President, National Commercial Bank, Albany, New York

Three times in the past six years we have increased our capital funds by selling additional shares to our stockholders. Many other attractive avenues of investment are open to these ladies and gentlemen and institutions. It was apparent to us that the last offering was far less cheerfully received than the first had been. The pitcher was going too often to the well! The ample capital resources of Morgan New York State Corporation, either now in hand or easily obtainable by the issuance of new senior or equity securities, can be a vital factor in the present and future growth of Northeastern New York State.

*   *   *   *   *

[If this application is approved] when we learn that an industry may need a new location for expansion in the Northeast, the National Division of Morgan Guaranty Trust Company will be available through the Area Development Department of the proposed Holding Company to aid us in persuasively presenting the advantages of a location in our territory. No correspondent bank can assist us to this extent because it will have other banks in different areas, for which it is also correspondent, competing with us to persuade the industry to locate in other areas. Quite clearly under such circumstances our correspondent cannot favor us at the expense of the other banks.

Exhibit 11

STATEMENT OF HENRY CLAY ALEXANDER

My name is Henry Clay Alexander. I am Chairman of the Board of Directors of Morgan New York State Corporation and also of the Board of Directors of Morgan Guaranty Trust Company of New York. I appear here to urge the granting of the application being discussed before you today.

* * * * *

. . . Approval has been given, without dissent, by the Banking Board of the State of New York on the strong and unqualified recommendations of the New York Superintendent of Banks. . . . The Superintendent's conclusions were made after a thorough and painstaking examination conducted by the expert and long-experienced staff of the New York State Banking Department. The statutory factors applied by the Superintendent under the New York banking law are in essence the same as those set forth in the Bank Holding Company Act of 1956. In order to make sure that some of the findings of the Superintendent are clearly in the minds of the members of the Board of Governors, I would like to quote a few excerpts from the Superintendent's recommendations:

Regarding the lessening of competition, the Superintendent found:

"The evidence compels the conclusion that there would be no significant lessening of competition among the seven banks involved in the application."

Regarding the encouragement of competition, the Superintendent found:

"Approval of the application would, in my judgment, tend to encourage healthy competition between the banks to be owned by the applicant and the other large banks with which the applicant's banks would be competing, including those affiliated with the existing statewide bank holding company system of the Marine Midland Corporation."

Regarding the impact on smaller banks, the Superintendent found:

"The possibility is remote that formation of the proposed holding company would create, in so far as the smaller upstate banks are concerned, an unsound or destructive competitive climate."

Regarding the public interest, needs and convenience, the Superintendent found:

"I have concluded that the public interest will best be served by approval of the application, and I so recommend.

"In arriving at this conclusion, I have been influenced primarily by the conviction that the contemplated bank holding company would materially expand the opportunities for the economic growth of that part of the State of New York which lies outside of the City of New York and its suburbs, and will thus contribute to the accelerated economic expansion which is the cornerstone of both state and national policy. Whatever negative considerations there may be are heavily outweighed, in my judgment, by this important circumstance."

The Board of Governors may wonder why Morgan Guaranty, with its background and tradition of "wholesale" banking, became interested to be a member of a holding company such as is proposed. The answer is that it believes the

Exhibit 11—Continued

proposal will be beneficial to its stockholders and, at the same time, bring stronger, wider and more efficient banking to the people of the State of New York.

Our interest centered around the fact that Morgan Guaranty is, and its predecessors were, engaged in the "wholesale" banking business. We were aware that, generally speaking, our competitors with large branch systems catering to the consumer were enjoying much greater growth in deposits. Demands from our clients for loans and credits appeared to be growing faster than our deposits. The ratio of loans to deposits has run rather consistently higher in Morgan Guaranty than in banks generally throughout the country or in our large and strong competitors in New York City. We have had only limited experience in branch banking, and New York City with some 550 banking offices has for some time appeared to us to be rather fully covered with banking services.

A holding company seemed to us to provide a means whereby our bank could have an affiliation with six growing upstate banks primarily engaged in "retail" banking in six different and separate trading areas of the state.

. . . Morgan Guaranty's present ability to extend additional bank credit is limited principally because its deposits have declined over the last 15 or 20 years. Its capital resources, however, are sufficient to support additional loans. On the other hand the upstate banks' present ability to extend such credit is limited because of their capital position. Their deposits have been growing steadily and are expected to continue to do so. If, however, Morgan Guaranty and the upstate banks were affiliated through the proposed holding company their resources would complement each other with the result that the affiliating banks as a group could extend greater bank credit than the member banks could do if unaffiliated.

*   *   *   *   *

All that the holding company itself would provide, aside from the corporate form into which the seven investment interests would be blended, would be a service organization consisting of a relatively small staff designed to facilitate both the quality and the quantity of services which the seven member banks will be able to render to their customers throughout the State of New York.

. . . The commercial banking business is a service business and should be so structured as to serve most efficiently and effectively the many and different economic units that contribute toward our economic growth; otherwise, growth will surely be hampered.

Exhibit 12

STATEMENT OF ROGER B. PRESCOTT, JR.

I am the President of Keeseville National Bank, Keeseville, New York, established by my ancestors in 1870.

Keeseville National Bank has always been a small independent family banking institution and I am the fourth generation of my family to assume its presidency. Its banking area has been primarily the northern section of Essex County and the southern areas of Clinton County, both in the Fourth Banking District of New York State.

Keeseville National Bank has only one office, located in Keeseville, New York, a one-industry town with a population of about three thousand and situated approximately eighteen miles from Plattsburgh, N.Y.

Exhibit 12—Continued

From 1870 to 1950 growth was very slow and its assets in October 1951 aggregated only $2,600,000.

In the ten-year period since October 1951 growth has been much more rapid. Its assets have increased to $6,500,000 and its deposits have increased by one hundred and forty percent. . . .

*   *   *   *   *

The establishment by the National Commercial Bank & Trust Co. of a branch bank adjacent to the Air Base not only provided the banking service badly needed by the Air Force, but relieved us of business which we could not easily handle. On one occasion the purchase of $100,000 Air Force installment paper from our bank without recourse by National Commercial relieved us in respect to requirements for money in our immediate community.

A small bank such as Keeseville National is not in a position to attract new industry to the district. Larger banks are, and increased industrial activity in the vicinity means increased activity for our bank, not necessarily directly but the small bank will always attract accounts desiring more personalized service than the larger banks offer. They may be banking "crumbs" but we can operate profitably and grow on crumbs.

. . . I see no reason to believe that the National Commercial Bank & Trust Co. becoming a member of the banking group to be known as the Morgan New York State Corporation would mean a change from fair to unfair competition. . . .

*   *   *   *   *

We have never had a Trust Department and would be happy to see trust services of a high caliber available to our customers.

Exhibit 13

STATEMENT OF ROBERT A. LOVETT

My name is Robert A. Lovett. I am a general partner of the firm of Brown Brothers Harriman & Co., a commercial bank licensed as private bankers and subject to examination and regulation by the Superintendent of Banks of the State of New York. Except for intervals of Government service [Mr. Lovett was Secretary of the Army], I have been engaged in banking in New York City since 1921, starting as a clerk with the National Bank of Commerce of New York. I have been a partner in Brown Brothers Harriman & Co. since 1926.

My firm is a moderate-sized bank, with total assets of about $275 million and deposits of about $235 million—and, with its predecessor, Brown Brothers & Co., it has conducted a general banking business in copartnership form continuously for 143 years. . . .

*   *   *   *   *

Granting of the application of Morgan New York State Corporation is, I believe, clearly in the public interest and designed to meet its needs and convenience. . . .

In the first place, the contemplated step seems to me a natural and evolutionary response to developments in this country. Under the forced draft of two wars in the past 20 years, industry and production have grown enormously and have become geographically dispersed in a national sense. The population explosion, occurring at the same time, has caused cities to burst their former boundaries

Exhibit 13—Continued

and people have poured out to the suburbs and to even more distant areas. Development of arterial highways has improved transportation and communication to the point where business has followed the pattern of the movement to the country. We now find continuous, elongated communities and industrial developments bordering arterial highways connecting two formerly separate centers of population.

If adequate banking service of high quality is to be provided the ever-widening geographical area caused by a combination of explosive growth of population and industry coinciding with their migration away from congested centers, it seems to me inevitable that some such organization as that envisaged here should be developed. If the doctrine of competition is to be maintained, a second Holding Company is both necessary and desirable for New York State.

*   *   *   *   *

. . . We have not found that our giant neighbors have acted in any way adverse to the interests of the small or moderate-sized independent banks but, on the contrary, have provided the necessary machinery for handling the enormous volume of routine banking services now demanded and, in addition, have consistently cooperated with us in making available to us, as depositors, their clearing and other services.

Exhibit 14

STATEMENTS OF OTHER COMPETITOR BANKS

In addition to the statements in Exhibits 10–12, the statements of other officers of smaller competitor banks were filed.

Mr. James R. Hughes, trustee of the Savings Bank of Utica, a 122-year-old bank, pointed out that his bank competed vigorously with the Oneida National, and that this competition has been good for the public interest. He stated that the Marine Midland Trust Company affiliate in his community, for the past seven years, has not prevented his bank from increasing its deposits 53%. He also pointed to the Bank of Utica, a small commercial bank which had increased its deposits from three to twelve million in the period 1950–60. He also said the Morgan Corporation would "provide better management information, such as investment advice from highly skilled research staffs; technical know-how in the changing area of bank operations (clerical systems, bookkeeping machines, computers, etc.) could be provided to a degree that no moderate-sized bank by itself could afford."

Schuyler L. Baum, chairman of two small banks near Syracuse (Minoa and Waterloo), each of which have as nearby competitors either the Marine Midland, or a branch of one of the applicant banks. Mr. Baum stated that the Morgan Corporation would have "little, if any, effect on either of my banks. I say this because there are Marine branches near Minoa, and we have never been bothered with their competition. (They) have been a help, because there are some bank customers who like to do business with an independent bank, and (others who prefer chain banks)."

James K. Albright, president of the State Bank of Ontario, testified that his bank would view the Morgan Company as a help to the community, and therefore to his own bank, for similar reasons.

Albert A. McMullen, president of the State Bank of Kenmore, with deposits of $15 million, made similar statements.

Exhibit 15

REASONING OF PUBLIC OFFICIALS IN SUPPORT OF THE MERGER

1. Congressman O'Brien testified that the new company would assist his district (Albany, Troy, Schenectady) in coping with a serious unemployment problem—because its larger capital and staff services could attract new industry and allow present industry to grow.

2. Donald Kramer, a lawyer for 30 years in Binghamton, who also is "active in commercial and political life," stated that large urban rehabilitation projects (housing, etc.) and industrial growth in his city would be aided by the merger. Financing of schools was another factor he stressed. He feels also that, since Marine Midland has a bank in his city, healthy competition between large banks would be beneficial.

3. Vincent Corrou, executive vice president of the Utica Chamber of Commerce, points out that the new bank would help eliminate unemployment and provide higher income in his city through attracting new industry, providing commercial air service, and a number of other vital enterprises to his city.

4. Hon. Peter Barry, mayor of Rochester, stated that his city is "one of the foremost growth areas of the country" which "means extensive financing both for private organizations and the city itself. We are completing a two thousand car underground garage, and . . . a fifty million dollar Civic Center. The holding company could loan more, and participate more extensively in underwriting and distributing municipal bonds. . . . Our industry has greatly increased its emphasis on foreign sales. . . . Only Marine Midland can offer the services of the type which could be offered by the holding company."

5. Austin Murphy, dean of the Business School at Canisius College in Buffalo, stated that the holding company "recognizes the basic compatibility and interdependence of major cities in their financial capacities" and the interdependence of needs of corporations with many branches.

6. William P. Tolley, chancellor of Syracuse University, stated that the holding company is desirable because "there is a clear need for commensurate sized banking institutions" to develop the university's large growth: $9 million earmarked for new dormitories, $2 million for a new fieldhouse, $4.5 million for classrooms, and $16 million total construction plans over ten years. He also pointed to working capital needs such as an annual salary payroll of $10 million (the university is the fourth largest employer in Syracuse).

Exhibit 16

STATEMENT OF LEWELLYN A. JENNINGS

(Economist, Consultant to the Banks of the Proposed Morgan New York
State Corporation)

. . . [T]he formation of Morgan New York State Corp. will not result in an increase of concentration of resources in the separate banking districts because . . . there is only negligible competition between the affiliated banks. If we measure concentration of resources on a state-wide basis and add the resources of the six proposed upstate affiliates to those of Morgan Guaranty Trust Company, the proposed holding company will have 7.43% of the deposits of all banks in New York State, 7.46% of the loans and 7.23% of the offices. The addition of resources to those already possessed by Morgan Guaranty amount to only 2.31% for deposits, 2.14% for loans and 6.99% for offices. These figures reveal only a small increase in the concentration of resources on a state-wide basis.

Exhibit 16—Continued

The competitive effect of the proposed bank holding company on other banking institutions in upstate New York will not be in direct proportion to the concentration of resources and deposits held by the seven affiliated banks. On the contrary, from the standpoint of upstate banks the competitive effect of the size of the concentration loses meaning when such concentration goes beyond a point necessary to permit the affiliating banks to provide an improved or enlarged capacity to meet the requirements of customers and render greater service. A concentration of resources and deposits such as that enjoyed by Marine Midland Corporation is fully as effective for competitive purposes in upstate New York as that of the proposed Morgan New York State Corp. . . .

*   *   *   *   *

Moreover, concentration of banking resources cannot be compared to concentration in industry. Banking resources consist primarily of deposits which are not owned by the bank—like assets are owned by industry—but represent amounts which the bank owes. If a bank does not render adequate service its deposits will disappear.

*   *   *   *   *

The 1960 annual report of the Federal Deposit Insurance Corp. reveals that at the end of 1958 the largest bank or bank group in each of 34 states held in excess of 11% of the commercial banking deposits of the state. This 11% is approximately the same percentage which the Morgan New York State Corp. would enjoy in the commercial banking field in New York State. This report shows that the largest commercial bank in New York State held 16.3% of the State's commercial bank deposits. In 13 states, the largest bank or bank group held 20% or more of the commercial banking deposits. The latter include states such as Michigan, Massachusetts, North Carolina, South Carolina, Delaware, Oregon, Washington and California. Banking competition is healthy in each of these states. The public interest is being well served.

Exhibit 17

TESTIMONY BY REPRESENTATIVE EMANUEL CELLER

CHAIRMAN OF THE COMMITTEE ON THE JUDICIARY, U.S. HOUSE OF REPRESENTATIVES

Either we maintain our traditional way of competition or we change our direction and travel the way of cartelization. Industrial and business mergers never were more expansive than today. Concentration of economic power has become inordinate. Leading the field are financial entities.

*   *   *   *   *

The number of banks has shrunk from 28,921 in 1929 to 13,971 in 1960.

Monolithic banks like Morgan Guaranty have emerged as a result of merger after merger and, as this application illustrates, continue to seek ever greater power through mergers.

The vise-like grip of an oligopoly of banks dominates the banking interests in all large cities. The five largest commercial banks in every large metropolitan area save two held more than 50 percent of the commercial bank deposits in 1960. In the majority of such areas they held over 75 percent of such deposits. In 26 of such areas the five largest commercial banks held over 90 percent of all commercial deposits. In most of the metropolitan areas three commercial banks held from 65 to 96.9 percent of all commercial deposits. . . .

*   *   *   *   *

Exhibit 17—Continued

If the application is approved, the new bank holding company would be the largest in the nation. Its resources of nearly $6 billion would aggregate about $1 billion more than Western Bancorporation, which is now the largest.

Morgan New York State Corporation would be one of the largest banking institutions in the United States.

Against the background of some 13,000 commercial banks in this country, this merger would combine three out of the largest 100 of such banks, two out of the largest 200, one out of the largest 300, and one with deposits of over $86 million.

The applicant would control 11 percent of the commercial banking assets and 8 percent of the commercial offices in New York State. Eliminating New York City, it would combine 16 percent of the State's commercial banking assets and 13 percent of the commercial banking offices. . . .

* * * * *

There has been a very sharp decline in the number of banking institutions in this country. While it is said that a large number vanished during the major depression of the early '30s, it is a fact that there has been no upsurge in the number of banks since that time despite a burgeoning population and economy.

Thus, at the end of 1941, there were almost 15,000 banks in the United States. By the end of 1960, there were less than 14,000. Even more pertinent, in 1940 there were 14,385 commercial banks; in 1950, 14,054; in 1955, 13,656; in 1960, 13,472. It is apparent that the rate of disappearance has been greater in the last decade than in the prior decade.

* * * * *

In 1958 the ten largest commercial banks had 19.9 percent of the deposits of all the commercial banks in this country. In 1959 they had 20.2 percent. As of December 31, 1960, the ten largest commercial banks held 20.3 percent of all commercial bank deposits. . . .

* * * * *

Size, because of the power of control it embodies, and because of the deterrence by its existence to an incentive to enter the field or to compete on the part of smaller banks, is a most relevant consideration. . . .

III Selected Readings

From: Carl Kaysen

"THE CORPORATION: HOW MUCH POWER? WHAT SCOPE?"*

[EDITORS' NOTE: The author is Professor of Economics, Harvard University.

The author relates size and concentration to corporate power. Size is an absolute measure expressed in terms of assets, sales, number of employees, etc. Concentration is a relative measure expressed in terms of the percentage of industry sales accounted for by one corporation (market share), or the percentage of assets, or percentage of employees. Professor Kaysen gives his own definition of power (his concept refers to social and political power as well as economic power) which is helpful in analyzing competition in various industries.]

The power of any actor on the social stage I define as the scope of significant choice open to him. Accordingly, his power over others is the scope of his choices which affect them significantly. Our fundamental proposition thus asserts that a few large corporations exert significant power over others; indeed, as we shall see, over the whole of society with respect to many choices, and over large segments of it with respect to others. It is worth noting that this sense of "power" is not that in which we speak of the "power" of a waterfall or a fusion reaction, or any other transformation in a fully deterministic system; rather it is appropriate to a social system in which we see human actors, individually or in organized groups, as facing alternative courses of action, the choice among which is not fully determined without reference to the actors themselves.

        *   *   *   *   *

Disproportionate share alone, however, is not a valid basis for inferring power as I have defined it. In addition, we must consider the range of choice with respect to significant decisions open to the managers of the large corporation. The disproportionate share of the sun in the total mass of our solar system would not justify the ascription to it of "power" over the planets, since in the fully-determinate gravitational system the sun has no choice among alternative paths of motion which would change the configuration of the whole system. Though the relative weight of the sun is great, its range of choice is nil, and it is the product of the two, so to speak, which measures "power." It is to an examination of the managers' range of choice that we now turn.

---

* Reprinted by permission of Harvard University Press, Cambridge, Massachusetts; from Edward S. Mason, *The Corporation in Modern Society,* 1959 (pp. 85, 88).

From: John Maurice Clark

*COMPETITION AS A DYNAMIC PROCESS**

[EDITORS' NOTE: The author is Professor Emeritus of Economics in Columbia University.]

. . . Long-run economies of scale . . . may lead to "natural monopoly." . . . More often they tend to natural oligopoly. . . .

. . . [E]conomies of scale have something to do with advantages derived from combining related processes in physical juxtaposition (in a "plant") or in administrative correlation, or both. In some processes, very large units are highly economical (subject to the need for flexibility); and where complementary processes are as well or better handled by small units, the number of these may be multiplied without loss of efficiency. Where the economy of the large units is of dominant importance, and where these different processes naturally go together within the bounds of a single plant, the economy of the large units may dictate the optimum scale for the whole, resulting in a tendency to large plants. Where small-unit processes are of a sort that can be independently carried on without loss of efficiency (through cost of transport, need for larger inventories, or other causes), the firm may have the option of farming out such processes to small-scale specialists. But if it tries to farm out too much, it will reduce the scale of its large-unit processes, as well as impair its operational coordination. Where the large-unit processes can be economically segregated in distinct physical units (*e.g.,* research, finance, and important features of selling), and where they go beyond the optimum scale of single plants, they tend to multiplant firms. There may be some qualified tendency in such cases for the processes with the largest optimum scale to govern the optimum scale of the whole firm; but fortunately this is no absolute law and is subject to counteracting influences, otherwise concentration would be even greater than it is.[1]

In general, it appears very rare that the economies of scale in a single plant continue to the point of "natural monopoly," with qualification for the element of limited local monopoly characterizing a plant whose only competition comes from a distance, as already mentioned. . . . Negatively, there is no clear evidence that cost increases with extreme size of single plants or of firms. Perhaps this means no more than that size has not been pushed past the point at which substantial diseconomies would be incurred. . . .

The indicated typical curve seems to be one in which the smallest size group shows high costs due to small size, after which the curve flattens out until it shows no clear and material economies traceable to size within the largest size group. One fact that appears clearly in the "envelope" form of cost curve is that

---

* Copyright by The Brookings Institution, Washington, D.C., 1961, and reprinted by permission (pp. 141–43).

1 E. A. G. Robinson gives a very good treatment of this problem: see *The Structure of Competitive Industry* (1932). It seems possible that in the United States, the largest-scale processes may have more tendency to govern the scale of the whole than under English conditions, which afford the setting for Robinson's study.

the long-run economies of scale are less than the short-run economies of full utilization of a plant of any given scale. In other words, the long-run curve is flatter than the short-run curves to which it is depicted as tangent in the envelope cost curve. If there is an exception to this, it occurs at very small sizes of plants and is likely to occur where such obstacles as the cost or difficulty of reaching an adequate market or limited access to capital cause plants to be built of a size so small as to incur high costs.

. . . Thus the firm . . . might face a choice between the high operating cost of a small plant and the comparably high operating cost of a larger plant operated too far below capacity. Since the larger plant would incur a heavier capital cost, this would tend to decide the choice against it.

*   *   *   *   *

. . . [T]hat is not the same thing as saying that the one large firm would make a larger contribution to the technique of the industry than two smaller firms which between them spend the same amount (e.g.) on research. Here the advantage of competitive diversity enters in, with multiple independent formulation of problems to work on; and the general judgment appears to be that the competitive system is likely to be more fruitful of results, always assuming that it is not too seriously handicapped by limited financial resources available to the competing units. Where this is the case, cooperative, governmental, or academic research are likely to step in. Otherwise, where the importance of research is great, the accompanying economies of scale appear to tend, not to natural monopoly, but to natural oligopoly.

From: John Kenneth Galbraith

THE AFFLUENT SOCIETY*

[EDITORS' NOTE: The author has taught economics at Harvard and been advisor to the Kennedy Administration as well as ambassador to India.]

In the production of goods within the private economy it has long been recognized that a tolerably close relationship must be maintained between the production of various kinds of products. The output of steel and oil and machine tools is related to the production of automobiles. Investment in transportation must keep abreast of the output of goods to be transported. The supply of power must be abreast of the growth of industries requiring it. The existence of these relationships—coefficients to the economist—has made possible the construction of the input-output table which shows how changes in the production in one industry will increase or diminish the demands on other industries. To this table, and more especially to its ingenious author, Professor Wassily Leontief, the world is indebted for one of its most important of modern insights into economic relationships. If expansion in one part of the economy were not

* Reprinted by permission of Houghton Mifflin Company, Boston, Massachusetts, 1958 (pp. 253–54).

matched by the requisite expansion in other parts—were the need for balance not respected—then bottlenecks and shortages, speculative hoarding of scarce supplies, and sharply increasing costs would ensue. . . .

From: National Association of Manufacturers

"PRINCIPLES OF FREEDOM OF ACTION"*

Adopted December 5, 1950
Revised, April 21, 1959

Freedom of action is our way of life. Our progress has been founded on individual initiative, ingenuity, and freedom of action. A free competitive economy is based on individual ambition which is the most universal, reliable and powerful of human motives.

The principles of freedom of action recognize that individuals know their own wants best and that human dignity requires that free men should not have their wants dictated by others. Freedom of action is based, therefore, on individual decisions and voluntary agreements and not on commands and obedience. It recognizes that the individual producer is best qualified to make sound decisions concerning his business problems, and that the aggregate of such decisions as tested in the free market results in wiser solutions of the economic problems of society than would decisions imposed by any outside agency.

Nevertheless a Government of law is necessary to guarantee freedom of action, to encourage individual initiative and to settle conflicts. It is an essential condition of freedom of action that the methods of competition must be peaceful and honest.

We stand for a nation of free people, free to act, work and choose. We are opposed to monopoly in the fields of production and distribution, whether it be a monopoly of capital, of labor, or of government. A free society within a dynamic economy where the welfare of each citizen depends primarily upon his own ability, industry and thrift has been shown by experience to be the best way to create large real national income and to promote social, material and technological progress. A society built on these principles is eminently able to make adequate provisions for those of its citizens who through no fault of their own are unable to provide for themselves, in such a way as not to diminish the individual's sense of responsibility for his own welfare. This is the fundamental philosophy upon which our way of life was founded and adherence to its precepts constitutes our best guarantee for the future.

---

* Reprinted by permission of the National Association of Manufacturers, *Industry Believes* (New York: National Association of Manufacturers, 1963), p. vi.

From: Henry Hazlitt
*"PRIVATE ENTERPRISE REGAINED"**

I am indebted to Betty Knowles Hunt for sending me a column she contributed to The New Hampshire Morning Union quoting from Governor Bradford's own history of the Plymouth Bay Colony over which he presided. It is a story that deserves to be far better known, particularly in an age that has acquired a mania for socialism and Communism, regards them as peculiarly "progressive" and entirely new, and is sure that they represent "the wave of the future."

Most of us have forgotten that when the Pilgrim Fathers landed on the shores of Massachusetts they established a Communist system. Out of their common product and storehouse they set up a system of rationing, though it came to "but a quarter of a pound of bread a day to each person." Even when harvest came, "it arose to but a little." A vicious circle seemed to set in. The people complained that they were too weak from want of food to tend the crops as they should. Deeply religious though they were, they took to stealing from each other. "So as it well appeared," writes Governor Bradford, "that famine must still insue the next year allso, if not some way prevented."

So the colonists, he continues, "begane to think how they might raise as much corne as they could, and obtaine a beter crope than they had done, that they might not still thus languish in miserie. At length [in 1623] after much debate of things, the Gov. (with the advise of the cheefest amongst them) gave way that they should set corne every man for his owne perticuler, and in that regard trust to them selves . . . And so assigned to every family a parcell of land . . .

"This had very good success; for it made all hands very industrious, so as much more corne was planted than other waise would have bene by any means the Gov. or any other could use, and saved him a great deall of trouble, and gave farr better contente.

"The women now wente willingly into the feild, and tooke their litle-ons with them to set corne, which before would aledg weakness, and inabilitie; whom to have compelled would have bene thought great tiranie and oppression.

"The experience that was had in this commone course and condition, tried sundrie years and that amongst godly and sober men, may well evince the vanitie of that conceite of Platos and other ancients, applauded by some of later times;—that the taking away of propertie, and bringing in communitie into a comone wealth, would make them happy and flourishing; as if they were wiser than God. For this communitie (so farr as it was) was found to breed much confusion and discontent, and retard much imployment that would have been to their benefite and comforte.

"For the yong-men that were most able and fitte for labour and service did repine that they should spend their time and streingth to worke for other mens wives and children, with out any recompense. The strong, or man of

---

* Reprinted by permission of The Foundation for Economic Education, Irvington-on-Hudson, New York, 1952. From *Essays on Liberty*. This essay first appeared in *Newsweek,* June 27, 1949.

parts, had no more in devission of victails and cloaths, than he that was weake and not able to doe a quarter the other could; this was thought injuestice . . .

"And for men's wives to be commanded to doe servise for other men, as dressing their meate, washing their cloaths, etc., they deemed it a kind of slaverie, neither could many husbands well brooke it . . .

"By this time harvest was come, and instead of famine, now God gave them plentie, and the face of things was changed, to the rejoysing of the harts of many, for which they blessed God. And the effect of their particuler [private] planting was well seene, for all had, one way and other, pretty well to bring the year aboute, and some of the abler sorte and more industrous had to spare, and sell to others, so as any generall wante or famine hath not been amongest them since to this day."

The moral is too obvious to need elaboration.

From: Joseph A. Schumpeter

THE THEORY OF ECONOMIC DEVELOPMENT*

[EDITORS' NOTE: Schumpeter is Late Professor of Economics in Harvard University.

In the passages below, Schumpeter describes the function of an "executive" or "manager" in society—whether he be the owner-entrepreneur, or an "employee manager." Schumpeter's book, which is considered by many a milestone in economic theory, took as its task to study *economic development* or *change* in the economy, as opposed to traditional equilibrium analysis. By "development," he means new combinations of resources—introduction of new goods, new methods of production, opening of new markets, conquest of new supplies of materials, or carrying out of the new organization of any industry.

One of his main theses is that "it is the producer who as a rule initiates economic change, and consumers (and presumably employees) are educated by him if necessary." This is in direct contrast to the study of equilibrium, where theories hold that it is the consumer wants which are the moving force, and executives respond to these forces, acting as a mechanical computer of supply and demand.

One of the prime and fundamental causes of change, to Schumpeter, are the actions of the "relatively few" men of action—executives—whose motivations are still deeper causes. Thus the argument: If change and innovations occur, it is the executive who produces them, not the "followers," or the "customers," or the "employees."]

This is so because all knowledge and habit once acquired becomes as firmly rooted in ourselves as a railway embankment in the earth. It does not require to be continually renewed and consciously reproduced. . . . It is normally trans-

* Reprinted by permission of Harvard University Press, Cambridge, Massachusetts, 1934 (Vol. XLVI, Harvard Economic Studies), pp. 84–94.

mitted almost without friction by inheritance, teaching, upbringing, pressure of environment. Everything we think, feel, or do often enough becomes automatic and our conscious life is unburdened of it. . . . And from this it follows also for economic life that every step outside the boundary of routine has difficulties and involves a new element. It is this element that constitutes the phenomenon of leadership.

. . . First, outside these accustomed channels the individual is without those data for his decisions and those rules of conduct which are usually very accurately known to him within them. Of course he must still foresee and estimate on the basis of his experience. But many things must remain uncertain, still others are only ascertainable within wide limits, some can perhaps only be "guessed." In particular this is true of those data which the individual strives to alter and of those which he wants to create. . . . Carrying out a new plan and acting according to a customary one are things as different as making a road and walking along it.

. . . As military action must be taken in a given strategic position even if all the data potentially procurable are not available, so also in economic life action must be taken without working out all the details of what is to be done. Here the success of everything depends upon intuition, the capacity of seeing things in a way which afterwards proves to be true. . . . The more accurately, however, we learn to know the natural and social world, the more perfect our control of facts becomes; and the greater the extent, with time and progressive rationalisation, within which things can be simply calculated, and indeed quickly and reliably calculated, the more the significance of this function decreases. Therefore the importance of the entrepreneur type must diminish just as the importance of the military commander has already diminished. . . .

. . . [T]he second lies in the psyche of the businessman himself. It is not only objectively more difficult to do something new than what is familiar and tested by experience, but the individual feels reluctance to it and would do so even if the objective difficulties did not exist. . . . In the breast of one who wishes to do something new, the forces of habit rise up and bear witness against the embryonic project. A new and another kind of effort of will is therefore necessary. . . . This mental freedom presupposes a great surplus force over the everyday demand and is something peculiar and by nature rare.

The third point consists in the reaction of the social environment against one who wishes to do something new. This reaction may manifest itself first of all in the existence of legal or political impediments. But neglecting this, any deviating conduct by a member of a social group is condemned, though in greatly varying degrees according as the social group is used to such conduct or not. Even a deviation from social custom in such things as dress or manners arouses opposition, and of course all the more so in the graver cases. . . . Even mere astonishment at the deviation, even merely noticing it, exercises a pressure on the individual. . . .

There is leadership *only* for these reasons—leadership, that is, as a special kind of function and in contrast to a mere difference in rank. . . . The facts alluded to create a boundary beyond which the majority of people do not function promptly by themselves and require help from a minority. If social life had in all respects the relative immutability of, for example, the astronomical world, or if mutable this mutability were yet incapable of being influenced by human action, or finally if capable of being so influenced this type of action were yet equally open to everyone, then there would be no special function of leadership as distinguished from routine work.

. . . Our three points characterise the nature of the *function* as well as the *conduct* or behavior which constitutes the leader type. It is no part of his function to "find" or to "create" new possibilities. They are always present, abundantly accumulated by all sorts of people. Often they are also generally known and being discussed by scientific or literary writers. In other cases, there is nothing to discover about them, because they are quite obvious. To take an example from political life, it was not at all difficult to see how the social and political conditions of France at the time of Louis XVI could have been improved so as to avoid a breakdown of the *ancien régime.* Plenty of people as a matter of fact did see it. But nobody was in a position to *do* it. Now, it is this "doing the thing," without which possibilities are dead, of which the leader's function consists. . . . It is, therefore, more by will than by intellect that the leaders fulfil their function, more by "authority," "personal weight," and so forth than by original ideas.

*   *   *   *   *

The entrepreneurial kind of leadership . . . consists in fulfilling a very special task which only in rare cases appeals to the imagination of the public. . . . "Personal weight" is, to be sure, not without importance. Yet the personality of the capitalistic entrepreneur need not, and generally does not, answer to the idea most of us have of what a "leader" looks like, so much so that there is some difficulty in realizing that he comes within the sociological category of leader at all. He "leads" the means of production into new channels. But this he does, not by convincing people of the desirability of carrying out his plan or by creating confidence in his leading in the manner of a political leader—the only man he has to convince or to impress is the banker who is to finance him—but by buying them or their services, and then using them as he sees fit. He also leads in the sense that he draws other producers in his branch after him. But as they are his competitors, who first reduce and then annihilate his profit, this is, as it were, leadership against one's own will. Finally, he renders a service, the full appreciation of which takes a specialist's knowledge of the case. It is not so easily understood by the public at large as a politician's successful speech or a general's victory in the field, not to insist on the fact that he seems to act—and often harshly—in his individual interest alone. . . .

We shall finally try to round off our picture of the entrepreneur in the same manner in which we always . . . try to understand human behavior, viz. by analysing the characteristic motives of his conduct. . . .

*   *   *   *   *

First of all, there is the dream and the will to found a private kingdom, usually, though not necessarily, also a dynasty. The modern world really does not know any such positions, but what may be attained by industrial or commercial success is still the nearest approach to medieval lordship possible to modern man. Its fascination is specially strong for people who have no other chance of achieving social distinction. The sensation of power and independence loses nothing by the fact that both are largely illusions. . . .

Then there is the will to conquer: the impulse to fight, to prove oneself superior to others, to succeed for the sake, not of the fruits of success, but of success itself. From this aspect, economic action becomes akin to sport—there are financial races, or rather boxing-matches. . . .

Finally, there is the joy of creating, of getting things done, or simply of exercising one's energy and ingenuity. This is akin to a ubiquitous motive, but nowhere else does it stand out as an independent factor of behavior with anything like the clearness with which it obtrudes itself in our case. Our type seeks out difficulties, changes in order to change, delights in ventures. This group of motives is the most distinctly antihedonist of the three.

Only with the first groups of motives is private property as the result of entrepreneurial activity an essential factor in making it operative. With the other two it is not. . . .

From: Robert A. Nisbet

*COMMUNITY AND POWER**

[EDITORS' NOTE: The author is Professor of Sociology and Dean of Letters and Science at the University of California, Riverside.]

. . . The philosophy of individualism is based on a belief, Ramsay Muir has written, "in the value of the human personality and a conviction that the source of all progress lies in the free exercise of individual energy."

. . . A conception of freedom that does not center upon the ethical primacy of the person is either naive or malevolent. . . .

But from the unquestioned ethical centrality of the person it does not follow that the philosophy of individualism, as we have inherited it from the eighteenth and nineteenth centuries, is equally valid. For individualism is more than an ethic, historically; it is also a psychology and an implied theory of the relation between man and his institutions. And most of our difficulties with the philosophy of individualism at the present time come from our unconscious efforts to make the ethical aspect of individualism remain evocative when we have ceased to hold to the psychological and sociological premises of this philosophy.

* * * * *

When the basic principles of modern liberalism were being formulated by such men as Locke, Montesquieu, Adam Smith, and Jefferson . . . [m]an, abstract man, was deemed to be inherently self-sufficing, equipped by nature with both the instincts and the reason that could make him autonomous.

. . . [T]he founders of liberalism abstracted certain moral and psychological attributes from a *social organization* and considered these the timeless, natural, qualities of the *individual,* who was regarded as independent of the influences of any historically developed social organization. . . .

. . . The philosophy of individualism, in short, began with the Christian-Judaic stress upon the ethical primacy of the person; but from that point it became a rationalist psychology devoted to the ends of the release of man from the old and a sociology based upon the view that groups and institutions are at best mere reflections of the solid and ineffaceable fact of the individual.

* * * * *

. . . Order in society would be the product of a natural equilibrium of economic and political forces. Freedom would arise from the individual's release from all the inherited personal interdependences of traditional community, and from his existence in an impersonal, natural, economic order.

* * * * *

. . . What is significant here is that when the philosophical individualists were dealing with the assumed nature of man, they were dealing in large part with a hypothetical being created by their political imaginations.

. . . Freedom was held to lie in emancipation from association, not within association.

Thus in what is perhaps the noblest of individualistic testaments of freedom in the nineteenth century, John Stuart Mill's essay *On Liberty,* there is the clear implication that membership in any kind of association or community represents an unfortunate limitation upon the creative powers of the individual. . . .

* * * * *

What we have learned under the guidance of studies in modern social psychology . . . is that the rationalist image of man is theoretically inadequate and practically intolerable. . . . We know no conception of individuality is adequate that does not take into consideration the myriad ties which normally bind the individual to others from birth to death.

* * * * *

Neither personal freedom nor personal achievement can ever be separated from the contexts of community. These are the contexts not of mechanical restraint but of the incentive and values that men wish to express in enduring works and to defend against wanton external aggression. This is not to deny the role of the individual, nor the reality of personal differences. It is assuredly not to accept the argument of crude social determinism—which asserts that creative works of individuals are but the reflection of group interests and group demands. It is merely to insist on the fundamental fact that the perspectives and incentives of the free creative mind arise out of communities of purpose. . . .

* * * * *

Nor does economic freedom rest upon the lone individual. . . . Society was envisaged by the classical economist as being, naturally, an aggregate of socially and culturally emancipated individuals, each free to respond to the drives that lay buried within his nature. Economic freedom would be the result, it was declared, of the same conditions that produced economic equilibrium: masses of autonomous, separated individuals, a minimum of social constraint of any kind, and a reliance upon the automatic workings of the free market.

But here too we are in the presence of the typical failure of the rationalist to recognize the social memberships of men in society and the dependence of human motivations upon these memberships. . . .

There is indeed a sense in which the so-called free market never existed at all save in the imaginations of the rationalists. What has so often been called the natural economic order of the nineteenth century turns out to be, when carefully examined, a special set of political controls and immunities existing on the foundations of institutions, most notably the family and local community, which had nothing whatsoever to do with the essence of capitalism. Freedom of contract, the fluidity of capital, the mobility of labor, and the whole factory system were able to thrive and to give the appearance of internal stability only because of the continued existence of institutional and cultural allegiances which were, in every sense, precapitalist. Despite the rationalist faith in natural economic harmonies, the real roots of economic stability lay in groups and associations that were not essentially economic at all.

Most of the relative stability of nineteenth-century capitalism arose from the fact of the very *incompleteness* of the capitalist revolution. . . . Through ingenious processes of rationalization this institutional stability was converted by the economic rationalist into an imaginary equilibrium of the market place. The struggle of man against man, the individual striving for gain and success, the conversion of real property into shares of industrial wealth, unrestrained competition, and complete freedom of contract—all of this, it was imagined, had in it the materials of stability as well as freedom.

But there has never been a time when a successful economic system has rested upon purely individualistic drives or upon the impersonal relationships so prized by the rationalists. There are always, in fact, associations and incentives nourished by the noneconomic processes of kinship, religion, and various other forms of social relationships.

*   *   *   *   *

. . . To divorce economic ends from the contexts of social association within which allegiance to these ends can be nourished is fatal. . . .

. . . Incentives to economic freedom, like those of economic production, are the product not of instincts but of social relationships and of tangible norms and institutions.

*   *   *   *   *

Economic freedom cannot rest upon moral atomism or upon large-scale impersonalities. It never has. Economic freedom has prospered, and continues to prosper, only in areas and spheres where it has been joined to a flourishing associational life. . . .

CASE MATERIALS:
Cases for Original Analysis

DAYTON METAL WORKS*

The Dayton Metal Works is owned and managed by Mr. James E. Foote. Mr. Foote went to work for one of the automobile companies in Detroit immediately after graduating from high school at the age of 18. He began as an apprentice helper working on a punch press, and, over a period of years, progressed to jobs of machinist, master mechanic, and finally, foreman of one of the company's largest machine shop installations. He had experience on almost all of the various machines in a large shop (single-purpose, multi-purpose, and fully automatic), and he had experience for six years in managing the entire shop operation. Although he had never served in the so-called staff positions of the shop (inspection, scheduling, routing, inventory control, and so on), he became acquainted with these functions while he was foreman.

After 20 years in Detroit, Mr. Foote received an offer from his father-in-law, P. M. Brown, of part-ownership in the Dayton Metal Works, a small machine shop in Dayton, Ohio, with the stipulation that the latter would retire in three years and sell the remaining part of the business to Foote.

When Mr. Foote took over the business from Mr. Brown eight years ago, he continued to operate it very much as his father-in-law had. The company's products were fairly simple—stamped metal parts for cans and containers (bodies, screw caps, ends), and custom-made valves for liquid and steam pipelines. In addition, the company did a fairly large business in repairing valves from steam generating companies and chemical manufacturers.

The machine shop consisted of 12 single-purpose machines—grinding, cutting, milling, and threading machines, punch presses, and so on. Plant space come to a total of 11,000 square feet, with machines spaced in two lines on either side of a 30-foot middle aisle. Eighteen machinists and helpers were employed, all of whom had been with the company over ten years—a fact that Foote recognized as remarkable for a small firm located among larger companies such as Frigidaire and National Cash Register. This loyalty he attributed to the company's high wage policy, and to Brown's habit of spending a good deal of time with the machinists on the job, not only in watching and advising on their work, but also in helping them to learn and in rotating them among jobs. Foote says that

* William H. Newman and Charles E. Summer, Jr., *The Process of Management: Concepts, Behavior, and Practice.* © 1961. Reprinted by permission of Prentice-Hall, Inc., Englewood Cliffs, New Jersey.

each employee was not only expert in his present job, but that he knew a great deal about all others in the shop. Although customers ordered job lots, Dayton Metal Works had supplied all the customers for a number of years, so each time an order came in the company had considerable experience in producing the item. The Ohio Paint Company, for instance, ordered certain sizes of cans, with the same screw caps and the same stamped bottoms, two or three times annually. And each month the Dayton Power Company sent over large batches of valves of the same type to be ground and repaired.

During his first two years in charge, Foote continued to deal with the customers developed by Mr. Brown. He visited their engineers and talked frequently to customers on the telephone. Gross sales remained approximately the same level over this period, at about $190,000.

Expansion Over a Six-Year Period

After his first two years with DMW, Foote began to travel to other cities to seek business for the company—Cleveland and Pittsburgh yielded a good bit of business both in the valve line and the metal container line, and he added customers from Columbus and, later, as far away as Indianapolis.

Of considerable importance in the growth of the business was a developing demand for metal cans ranging in sizes from four ounces to one pint. These were not only cut and stamped, but also soldered and assembled into finished products. Foote found that after producing these in large quantity for one account, he could sell them to one or two other customers. Eventually, demand rose to the point where the company now carries an inventory and mass-produces them. Volume has also necessitated renting another Dayton shop of 8,000 square feet with seven machines, eight machinists, and seven helpers, plus two combination service-maintenance men. One salesman is employed exclusively in this product, known in the company as "the stock can line." The can shop is located eight blocks from the main shop.

Quite by accident, at a meeting of the National Association of Manufacturers, Foote became interested in the possibility of securing government contracts for Dayton Metal Works. Through an attorney whom he retained, and some hard work on his own, he succeeded in obtaining a government contract for small hydraulic valves in very large quantity. These are high quality precision valves used in aircraft. In fact, this contract alone has yielded $650,000 in sales annually and is expected to continue for at least five more years.

Foote himself has handled all negotiations with the government, with the aid of a lawyer and outside accountant who provide technical facts and information on cost allowances, government procurement regulations, price redetermination, and so on. He has rented an old warehouse next door and set up a special production line for hydraulic valves. This facility contains six machines in an area of 6,000 square feet. Twenty-two employees are currently engaged in the production of hydraulic valves, in two shifts.

At the present time, eight years after Foote took over, the company has an annual gross sales of $1,400,000. This represents an increase of $1,200,000 in six years.

Profit Picture

The company was unusually profitable, by percentage, under Mr. Brown and during the first two years of Foote's ownership. Net profit to sales averaged 19 per cent. During the last six years, profits have increased to $168,000 on the average, but have decreased to 12 per cent of sales. Although general business conditions have been partly responsible, both Foote and his auditor recognize that part of the decrease has resulted from an increase in the overhead burden. Overhead costs have climbed from 13 per cent of total costs to 20 per cent. This has been especially disappointing to Foote in view of the remarkable increase in sales.

Problems in Government Contracts

The government contract business is judged by Mr. Foote to be well worth the efforts of himself and his other personnel, even though there has been a lower profit ratio in this line, and even though government work has caused a large number of troubles.

First, there have been financial troubles. Two years ago, John M. Freeman, a C.P.A., was employed to head the accounting and clerical function of the business. Freeman is 36, had four years with a public accounting firm and ten years' experience with a larger machine shop in Columbus. Since Freeman has a wide knowledge of machine shop operation and substantial experience in government contracts and taxation, Foote feels fortunate in hiring him. A graduate of Ohio State, Freeman has qualities of technical competence as well as a personality that all the men seem to like.

Government work calls for accurate accounting records, especially set up for proving to the government which expenses were allocable to the contract. The company has also been subject to price redetermination by the General Accounting Office. On two contracts, the GAO has disallowed certain expenses, amounting to a total of $8,000. Foote is sure that these expenses were recorded improperly by Freeman's department at the time the money was paid out, and that profit on the contract would have been shown as lower had they not been. Furthermore, when prices were redetermined on the basis of the profit (figured without these expenses), the company was penalized by having the price and, therefore, its revenue cut.

Mr. Foote reports that since he has had more dealings with the government than anyone else, and since he has studied procurement regulations and been exposed to more "education" by his lawyer and outside accountant, he spends about six hours each week reviewing expense allocation accounts from the controller's department. He also spends about six to eight days each quarter attending meetings of industry groups in order to learn more about government procurement regulations. He has also studied a great deal, and he makes two or three trips to New York to consult with the Eastern Air Procurement District headquarters.

Freeman says that he welcomes the frequent advice he receives from his boss, especially since the subject is so complicated and since there is a fairly high degree of risk in case a mistake is made.

Besides the financial problems, there has also been some trouble in quality control of the hydraulic valves produced for the Air Force. Threading has been the greatest cause of rejection at receiving points. When returned, these valves have been suitable for reworking, but Freeman compiled figures to show that they have cost the company approximately $9,000 in the last four months. This is in addition to a $7,800 loss due to other defects in the same period.

A. M. Fowler, foreman of the general (main) shop, is responsible for inspection and quality control at both the main shop and the hydraulic shop. Since new customers have increasingly ordered custom-made parts, he has spent most of his inspection efforts in the main shop, for the many and varied items produced there are especially susceptible to deviations in quality. Actually, quality standards for finished hydraulic valves were set by Foote and Fowler jointly, according to government specifications. All personnel understand them clearly. No systematic check points in the production process itself (until valves are finished) have been set up. Both men feel that a system is unnecessary since Fowler makes continuous rounds of informal observation. On all days that he is in the plant, Foote also drops in to the hydraulic shop and makes checks of work just finished on various machines.

In view of this seemingly effective arrangement, Foote is puzzled by just what the cause of quality deviations might be. He has confidence in his master machinist on the dual buffing machine, Clyde Noble. Noble not only functions as machinist on the key machine operation, which is the end of the hydraulic production line, but also serves as foreman of the hydraulic shop. Because of the repetitiveness of this process and the small number of personnel, Noble is able to shift work to his helper and also to care for the training and supervision of other personnel in the shop.

There has been some friction between Noble and Fowler, particularly when Fowler makes suggestions to Noble about maintaining machines or utilizing personnel in the hydraulic shop. Another conflict occurs periodically over the shipping operation. The cartmen, who transport finished parts from both production lines to the shipping room and loading platform, report to Fowler. At times, when there is a peak load to work in the main shop, Fowler removes the cartman from the hydraulic shop in order to keep up with movements in the main shop. This results in a congestion at the end of the hydraulic line and has actually stopped production there on several occasions. Foote must spend a great deal of time in settling these disputes. But he feels that both men are so valuable that he must live with this kind of trouble. He once attempted to straighten the shipping problem out by writing a procedure for handling carting loads in the main shop, but Fowler objected forcefully to having his operation "strapped down" when he needed the flexibility of calling on cartmen when he needs them. Foote has noted that Fowler also resents having him (Foote) come in and ask that the cartman be restored to the hydraulic shop in order to remove congestion there. At one point Foote discovered that a rule specifying that the hydraulic cartman could be reassigned for a maximum of two hours on any one day would prevent actual stoppages on the hydraulic line. It would also allow Fowler flexibility in the main shop. Noble agreed to this, but Fowler again made it clear that he would resent this intrusion on his prerogative of managing his men.

Personnel Matters

Mr. Foote says that he is the only person in the company who has had extensive experience in supervising, hiring, and training a large number of men. In addition, he has studied a great deal about labor relations, training programs, how to interview job applicants, and setting wage rates. This study has been accomplished "on my own, with a lot of hard night work," and "in some pretty good training programs conducted by the company while I was in Detroit."

Hiring. Foote has employed an assistant, Herbert Rowzee, who is in charge of personnel problems and who also spends about one-half of his time in Freeman's department keeping the books on maintenance cost and equipment depreciation. Rowzee is primarily an accountant, but he formerly had experience in hiring and training office personnel. Generally, Rowzee is the point where all requests for jobs are channeled. He interviews applicants, and, if they look likely, arranges for them to see the boss. Foote has had such a good record of success in picking good men that he judges it a waste of company time, and a creation of needless red tape for those under him, to hire someone to draw up forms, standards for selection, or procedures for hiring. This custom has also been most acceptable to his foremen, who do not want undue procedures. Fowler, however, has, in his own words, "had a rough time getting along with two of the people Mr. Foote hired."

Employee Regulations. The company has never had a "book of rules." Mr. Foote has said that "this is one competitive advantage we have over

National Cash and other big companies that we compete with in the labor market. People like to work in a place where they get treated separately; foremen don't like to be told how to run their shows either." Employees are granted days off for personal business as they need it, and Christmas bonuses are granted on the merits and needs of the individual man, not on specific wage scales. Next to scheduling, Foote spends more time in dealing with his men than in any other task. There are occasional charges that he has not been fair—for example, Will Jarvis, a machinist in the can plant, told his foreman that Foote didn't give him as much paid time off when his son was born as he gave to Chapman in the Hydraulic shop. Once Foote wrote up a principle to be applied to time off, so that he could point to it and explain to men that for everybody's good he had to have a rule. He abandoned this for several reasons. "First, I can, if I listen patiently and make just decisions, settle things for the good of everybody. Everybody's good can also be served by deciding each case on its merits. We have customs and can treat everyone fairly over the long haul. Secondly, when I asked the foreman about this, not only Fowler but, on this point, Noble and Richards also, pleaded not to start laying down rules." Richards said, "We just can't do our job, Mr. Foote, if we get balled up in rules. You yourself have told me many times about how we have a better shop here than them big shops in Detroit."

These examples give some picture of the entire range of employer relations. While there are some difficulties, a personnel man from a larger company advised Foote that he had far fewer problems than most companies. The only rules that exist and are known by everyone are the base rates paid on each job. Thus, there is no question but that a helper will get $2.05 an hour—not that anybody has put it in writing, but it is well known Foote pays the wage to everyone. Consequently, no one complains that rules are being made or that one person is getting more than another.

James Foote's Personal Status

James Foote appears to be, at 48, in robust health and extremely interested in his work. Although owning his own business has been troublesome in many respects, he declares that he has never regretted leaving the automobile company. Two business associates mentioned that Foote is known in Dayton as a man who is respected by other businessmen and by his employees. In a conversation with a partner in the auditing firm retained by his company, Foote said:

Actually, I get a little worried at times about the way things are going. I'm not particularly "old," but I surely haven't got the energy I used to have. The Washington trips take time, and there is an endless bunch of problems with customers. Men at the shop think we have a fine place to work, but there are times when petty differences get out of hand. What happens is either I go nuts listening and worrying about problems, or I make quick judgments and settle them—sometimes wrong, and sometimes making people mad.

Then my wife has been compaining that I spend too much time at the plant. We have always intended that I would slow down when I got to be over 45. I want to, but I just can't. Why, I know of many close calls that the business has had even with my staying as many hours as I do.

Mr. Foote says that production scheduling can be described quite simply:

It means taking the customer orders that we receive, seeing which of our products has to be produced, translating the finished product into the various machining operations it has to go through in process, figuring how much time must be spent on each machine for the particular volume requested by the customer, assigning machines that are available, then sending this information to the foremen.

In order to help with this process, two clerks were employed by Mr. Brown, the previous president. One of these men has been with the company ten years now, the other twelve years. Since the company used to produce a more or less stable, repetitive group of products for essentially the same customers, these clerks were familiar, from long experience of doing the same task over and over, with the customers, the products they usually ordered, and the appropriate machines on which each order should be run.

The clerks drew up simple work orders to instruct machinists on which operations to perform on each customer order. Routing sheets from machinists to machinist were simple—they showed the various machines that raw metal had to be processed on for each customer order. Both clerks and machinists knew approximately the time that would be required on each machine. The clerks looked at the size of the order, estimated the time, fitted the whole shop each Monday morning into what they called the "jigsaw." Foote studied this on Monday, and, since he had an intimate knowledge of about how long each operation would take, he sometimes made adjustments of time spent on each machine and the schedule from machine to machine. He says that by applying his more expert planning ability, he could eliminate some of the time "padding" that the clerks left in the schedule. The result of this padding is that machines and men sometimes remain idle.

One of the clerks maintained a perpetual inventory of materials such as tin plate and castings for valve parts. He knew from experience that the 12 or 13 major materials items had to be kept at certain levels, and he adjusted these levels for the number of sales orders he saw come in. Tool control was no problem since 30 to 40 tools were all that were required. Foote inspected these tools fairly frequently to see if new ones should be ordered.

Frequently during the recent years of company growth, Foote reveals, certain orders have been delayed because the clerks either got mixed up and scheduled the same machine for two different products or customer orders, or because some machines were left idle when there was a heavy backlog of work to be done.

Foote has found that one of the schedulers works all right as long as he is scheduling orders for the same kinds of valves that he has always worked with. But he takes an unusually long time to schedule machine times, work routings, and materials requisitions on products that are slightly different from the usual, or on those for new customers that require unusual specifications. Foote has spoken to this scheduler "for six months, but when that did not work, I began to watch his work even more carefully. He gets along with the machinists fine, but he has created more bottlenecks than the other two schedulers put together."

A third scheduler has been added, and all three work closely with Foote. Also, certain changes have been made in procedures. Typically, now, all orders for each product in a week are totaled by a clerk in accounting and forwarded to Foote on Friday. Foote looks at each product and makes out a routing sheet (the men call it a "machine list") that shows which operations—grinding, cutting, threading, polishing—must be performed on raw metal in order to produce the finished product. Foote then passes on this routing sheet to any one of the schedulers who doesn't seem to have a full week's work ahead of him. The scheduler looks at the volume of the order, figures out the times that need to be spent on each machine, and assigns specific machines. Here is where machinists, schedulers, and Foote have all complained about the present system.

The problem is to consider all available machines in the plant and find a time when each order can be run, without either leaving machines idle or having two orders that call for punch presses arrive at the punch press machines at the same time. For example, one order for 20 large gate valves required a sequence of grinding (ten hours), threading (six hours), and drilling (five hours). A second order, for another type of valve, which was processed by another clerk, required grinding (eight hours), threading (eight hours) and polishing (five hours). Since there are only two grinding machines of sufficient size to handle both orders, the first order would take five hours to run on grinding, and the second four hours. The mistake on these orders was that order #1 arrived at the grinding machines at 11 A.M. Monday, and #2 arrived at the same machines at 1 P.M. the same day. The latter order was put aside while the first was run, with the result that the threading machines stood idle Tuesday morning because order #2 did not arrive for the threading operation until late Tuesday afternoon. This order had been scheduled to arrive at the polishing machines early Tuesday morning.

These problems are supposed to be settled by informal communications among the schedulers. Watching the three of them at work, one sees them frequently asking among themselves, for instance, "Does anybody have punch press No. 2 busy on Thursday morning?" or "I've got both threading machines tied up all day Wednesday." In addition, Foote catches about two or three mistakes every Monday when he goes over the "jigsaw."

Foote complains that the men make entirely too many mistakes, and that entirely too much of his time is taken up in checking on this every Monday and in going out on the plant floor to make on-the-spot arrangements when there is an actual bottleneck. The schedulers, on the other hand, complain that Foote himself has made some mistakes when he readjusted their scheduling. "After all, he is so busy that he just tears through our schedule, making adjustments."

One scheduler also complains that the other two are not so careful about listening to what he says and taking it into account in their own work. For instance, "The jam that occurred on the gate valves the other day wouldn't have occurred if Jack had remembered that I told him that I was tying up the large grinders starting at 11 on Monday. Besides, that jam was partly Foote's fault, since he is the one whose job it is to catch the errors we're naturally bound to make operating this way."

GENERAL MOTORS CORPORATION*

On August 20, 1964, British Commercial Property Investments, Ltd., a subsidiary of a large London investment trust, announced that one of its properties, the Savoy Plaza Hotel, on Fifth Avenue and 59th Street in New York City, would be razed to make way for a 40-story office building. It was later announced that British Commercial had formed a subsidiary corporation, the Savoy Fifth Avenue Corporation, with General Motors Corporation. Each parent company owns 50% of Savoy Fifth Avenue. The latter company's principal business is to own the land and construct a new building on the hotel site. General Motors will also be the principal tenant, occupying about 750,000 square feet out of a total floor space of 1.5 million square feet. The new building will be named the General Motors Building.

According to *The New York Times,* no estimate of the cost of the new building was given by any of the principals. However, one official of the London company said that it would probably be comparable in cost to the recently constructed Pan American Building. That building, the *Times* went on, is generally regarded as having a total cost of $100 million.

In an interview with the case writer at the time this case was being written (March 1965), an executive of one of the largest real estate firms in New York stated:

A prime, 80,000-square-foot block similar to the Savoy location would sell at a price somewhere between $33 million and $40 million. These are prices for blocks termed "best available," of which there are no more than three in the city, one of which GM bought. After all, Fifth and Park Avenues are prime, with Madison and Lexington Avenues a close second, in terms of prestige desirability. GM is simply willing to pay much more in investment and in rental for this prestige location. I estimate that the space in the new building will rent between $6.50 and $8.50 a square foot, whereas rent in the area of their old building would be somewhere around $4.50 a square foot.

General Motors' net income for 1964 amounted to $1.7 billion.

The Grand Army Plaza Area

One of the unique features of Manhattan Island is that a walk of a few blocks can transport a person from one entirely different atmosphere to another. The 10-minute walk from the present General Motors Building at Broadway and 57th Street, to the Grand Army Plaza at Fifth Avenue

---

and 59th Street is an example. The first location is characterized by heavy, fast-moving traffic, many trucks, automobile dealer displays, and neon advertisements. On the other hand, the second location is vastly different. No commercial trucks are allowed on Fifth Avenue. The pedestrians are expensively dressed, and the buildings house either luxury hotels (the Plaza, the St. Regis, the Pierre) or New York's most sophisticated stores (Bergdorf Goodman, Bonwit Teller, Van Cleef & Arpels, Tiffany & Co., and Cartier). Limousines line the side streets, waiting for owners to return from shopping, or from lunch in elegant hotels or restaurants.

Across the Grand Army Plaza from the Plaza Hotel is the 1000-room Savoy Plaza Hotel. The two photographs in Exhibit 1 show the front of the Savoy as viewed looking east across Fifth Avenue, through the trees and past the Pulitzer Fountain located in Grand Army Plaza. The hotel was built in the 1920's from plans by the architects McKim, Mead, and White, generally accepted as the leading firm of the era. Particularly well known and one of the best known architects in the nation was Stanford White, who was later murdered while dining at the roof restaurant of Madison Square Garden.

Various Reactions to the Move

Shortly after the announcement of the building in August, there was considerable attention given to the project from a number of different people and groups.

The Fifth Avenue Association, composed of executives of stores and hotels located on Fifth Avenue, immediately retained a panel of architects who, it was hoped, would be given a voice in the plans for the building. Walter Hoving, chairman of Tiffany and Company, said that the project could not help hurting the area, while Andrew Goodman, chairman of Bergdorf Goodman, said, "It will bring a lot of purchasing power into the area and should increase the value of our property. These views are presented in Exhibit 2.

The New York Times itself, in an editorial, expressed "fear of a dismaying new plunge . . . toward architectural mediocrity," and held that "the tragedy, of course, is that New York, unlike Paris or Washington, has no review rights on its main avenues or plazas" (Exhibit 3). Arnold D. Kates, vice president of the Park Association of New York, responded in a letter to the editor that he was pleased with the editorial, that he hoped that the parties concerned would heed its admonitions, and that, if not, "this will arouse the Park Association of New York and the civic agencies with which it cooperates."

Later on, in January and February of 1965, a group of socially prominent New York women formed a committee which threatened a boycott of General Motors products unless the building project was abandoned. The activities of this committee are reported in Exhibits 4 and 5.

Prominent architects of the current era also joined in the public controversy. On September 2, Robert Weinberg warned that "if the area's solid core of hotel, restaurant, and distinguished shopping character is breached, the resulting change in the nature of the open space we call the Plaza may affect New York's prestige more than the facade of a single building." Mr. Weinberg went on to say that the selection of a "name" architect is not enough to insure good design—that unless the *owners* "adopt a publicly announced policy" of esthetics, and unless the architect is "backed up by the owners," there is danger of damage to the area (Exhibit 6). Joseph Watterson, editor of the *Journal of the American Institute of Architects,* went one step further. He wrote the *Times* on October 3 that government review or control is necessary if the esthetic values of the city are to be maintained (Exhibit 7).

One architect, William Lescaze, wrote to the *Times* on September 17 in support of the new building:

. . . since when do we not welcome new and fresh sources of investment, and fresh adventures in building and design? I fail to see why the Fifth Avenue Association should become so disturbed that a new and modern building would be built on that site. In my opinion, this may very well be good not only for our Fifth Avenue, but also for our whole city. We cannot assume that the British-Canadian sponsors are motivated solely by the revenue and profit factors.

Throughout this period, the General Motors Corporation offered no public comment on its reasons for moving the headquarters to this site, or on the opposition appearing in the press. Statements were made, however, by Mrs. Cecilia Benatter, secretary-treasurer of the Savoy Fifth Avenue Corporation, wholly owned subsidiary of British Commercial (Canada), Ltd. Mrs. Benattar stated in the August 21 *Times* that no architect had been engaged but that "we are going to build a really beautiful building. The whole aim of ourselves and of General Motors is to achieve excellence."

On December 16, however, the public relations firm of Wolcott & Associates, representing Savoy Fifth Avenue Corporation, released an announcement stating that Edward Stone and Emery Roth & Sons had been appointed architects for the building. This release, commenting on Mr. Stone's qualifications, appears as Exhibit 8. On January 27, the *Times* reported that General Motors had filed plans with the New York City Department of Buildings for permission to build the building under existing zoning laws. Sometime after, Wolcott & Associates released the preliminary sketch of the building appearing as Exhibit 9.

On February 4, the officers and Architectural Committee members of the Fifth Avenue Association were invited to view preliminary designs and models of the building in the office of Edward Durell Stone, one of the principal architects. These officers and committee members gave their endorsement to the building, stating that they had not previously known of the unique way in which architect Stone was to design the plaza in front of the building. "[This plaza] will provide a delightful promenade for sightseers and shoppers."

Exhibit 1

SAVOY PLAZA HOTEL

Looking north on Fifth Avenue. To the left is entrance to Bergdorf Goodman.

View of entrance taken from front door of Plaza Hotel at lunchtime. Fountain at right is in the Grand Army Plaza (park).

Apparently concerned about the "tougher job of preserving landmarks in big cities as realty values climb," *The Wall Street Journal* surveyed the national situation (Exhibit 10). "Unless the landmarks advocates can find new uses for old buildings, the wrecking is likely to continue. Already about 2,500 of the 10,000 structures (in the United States) recorded since the 1930's in the Government's Historic American Buildings survey have been torn down."

Exhibit 2

MERCHANTS SCAN SAVOY PLAZA PLAN

Panel of Architects Named
to Urge that New Building
Uphold 5th Ave. Dignity

By Thomas Buckley

The Fifth Avenue Association urged yesterday that the 40-story office building that will replace the Savoy Plaza Hotel "conform to the character and dignity" of the area.

Frank E. Conant, president of the association, appointed a committee of three architects to confer with the company that plans to build the skyscraper and with the General Motors Corporation which will be the principal tenant.

* * * * *

Although an official of the Canadian concern said that "a really beautiful building" would be erected on the site, real estate leaders here said they doubted that it would be economically possible to construct a showplace such as the Seagram Building or Lever House.

However, at least one leading merchant, Andrew Goodman, chairman of Bergdorf Goodman, said he favored the project.

"It will bring a lot of purchasing power into the area," he said, "and should increase the value of our own property."

Walter Hoving, the chairman of Tiffany & Co., said demolition of the Savoy Plaza could not help hurting the area, which for many years has been noted for fine shops and hotels, and he expressed doubt that it would increase trade.

"I view with a certain amount of sadness the reduction of high-grade residential facilities," he said.

* * * * *

Looking across the street at the 33-story gray-brick and limestone Savoy Plaza, a Good Humor man tending his wagon at the edge of Central Park said, "I can think of at least 1,000 buildings they could tear down before they tear down that one."

Paul Wilson, driver of one of the carriages that stand along the plaza, said: "It'll spoil the area. This whole section is strictly like the Riviera, cities in Europe, where you've got fine hotels and stores, but no office buildings."

Mr. Wilson, a slender, elegant figure with a hairline mustache, neatly brushed topper and black silk jacket, went on: "Now you've got shops in the Savoy. It's a pleasure. Jewels, perfume, flowers at Max Schling's. So along comes an office building and what've you got? A bank on the street floor?"

Source: From *The New York Times*, August 22, 1964.

Exhibit 3

DOWN WITH THE SAVOY PLAZA

The news that New York is to have another blockbuster like the Pan Am Building and that it is to be built on the city's most urbane and gracious midtown plaza stirs fear of a dismaying new plunge in the city's unrelenting postwar movement toward architectural mediocrity.

A large British investment trust plans to raze the Savoy Plaza Hotel and erect a metropolitan headquarters for General Motors on the site. "It promises to be," in the trust's words, "one of the most important construction projects of its kind in the world." It also promises to be a concrete threat to one of the city's few genuine claims to urban elegance—the handsome open square at Fifty-ninth Street and Fifth Avenue, at the foot of Central Park, where General Sherman rides confidently toward the tasteful luxuries of Bergdorf Goodman and the last of the grand hotels surround a landscaped fountain offering the waters of Abundance to grateful New Yorkers.

Not that the new building can't be a good one, or a suitable one in its setting. Seagram has proved that corporate palaces may be splendid additions to the city's theme. General Motors, when it built for itself in Michigan, had the late Eero Saarinen design a commercial complex acclaimed as an "industrial Versailles."

On this critical, central New York site anything but the best will spell catastrophe. This will be the first sizeable breach by large commercial construction of a rare area of Old World style and distinction; there is too much danger it could be the beginning of the end.

The tragedy, of course, is that New York, unlike Paris or Washington, has no review rights on its main avenues or plazas. It is now up to the conscience, capabilities and sense of public responsibility of a group of private investors with no direct ties to New York to make or mar the city's face. New York needs no more cut-rate monuments like Pan Am. If the results of this gigantic undertaking are of less than landmark quality it will be an urban disaster.

Source: An Editorial from *The New York Times*, August 24, 1964.

Exhibit 4

WOMEN SCORE G.M. ON BUILDING PLAN

Group Threatens a Boycott if
'Tombstone' Is Erected on
Site of Savoy Plaza
Landmark Ruin Feared
Fannie Hurst and Daughter
of Alfred E. Smith among
Supporters of Move

By Thomas W. Ennis

A group of socially prominent New York women are threatening to organize a nationwide boycott of General Motors cars and home appliances.

They say they would do so if the company proceeded with plans to participate in the construction of a 48-story skyscraper on the site of the Savoy Plaza Hotel. The hotel occupies the blockfront on Fifth Avenue between 58th and 59th Streets opposite the Grand Army Plaza at Central Park.

Some of the women own General Motors stock and it is understood that they

Exhibit 4—Continued

will put pressure on other women shareholders in the giant industrial concern to join the boycott.

The women have formed a committee called Save our Landmarks!—Save the Plaza Square. The committee, which is still in formation, has about 32 members. Several men have joined it.

Fannie Hurst, the novelist, is honorary chairman of the committee. The chairman and spokesman is Mrs. Helen M. Clark, a lawyer active in New York civic affairs. Among the committee members listed in the Social Register is Mrs. John A. Warner, the former Emily Smith, daughter of the late Gov. Alfred E. Smith.

*   *   *   *   *

In an interview yesterday Mrs. Clark, a middle-aged woman with soft, cultivated, yet firm, voice, said if General Motors was "only interested in the dollar sign at the expense of ruining our landmarks . . . we are not interested in buying their cars." The boycott, she declared, would be concentrated on General Motors automobiles, the company's principal product, but would include its several lines of home appliances.

"We don't care," Mrs. Clark said, "if General Motors wants to put up another tombstone; that's all right, but don't build on the Grand Army Plaza."

*   *   *   *   *

"The Plaza Square," she declared, "is an internationally known landmark, and is the only part of New York where visitors, particularly from abroad, wish to stay." Other luxury hotels in the vicinity of the Savoy Plaza are the Pierre, the Sherry-Netherland and the Plaza.

*   *   *   *   *

Her indignation increased when she recalled that the Federal Government had contributed $12 million to the United Arab Republic last October to help save the 3,000-year-old Abu Simbel temples in Egypt. The temples, on the banks of the Nile, were threatened by the construction on the Aswan High Dam.

*   *   *   *   *

A General Motors spokesman said yesterday the company's officials would refrain from comment "at this time." A spokesman for Savoy Fifth Avenue seemed surprised at the committee's opposition, remarking that the Savoy Plaza was not an "architectural gem" and that the company did not know the committee was in existence.

*   *   *   *   *

One member of the committee that proposes a General Motors boycott is Mrs. Frederick E. C. Roelker, secretary of the group. She said the committee was formed because its members "got tired of seeing office buildings going up one after the other, every pretty spot in the city deteriorate and the human element disappear."

Mrs. Roelker is the wife of a retired lawyer.

Other members of the committee are Miss Rosalie Armistead Higgins, Mrs. Raymond Seabrook, Mrs. Albert Bostwick, Mrs. Louis J. de G. de Milhau, Mrs. C. Hendry Mellon, Mrs. Cutting Wilmerding, Mrs. James McVickar, Mrs. George Harris, Mrs. Harold T. Pulsifer, Mrs. R. B. Montgomery, Mrs. George Mc-Murtry, Mrs. Nathaniel Hill, Miss Jane Ashley, Mrs. William Morris and Mrs. Edward Wineapple.

Source: From The New York Times, January 20, 1965.

Exhibit 5

STAUNCH DEFENDERS OF THE SAVOY PLAZA

By Ann Geracimos

The battle to prevent General Motors from putting up an office building on the site of the Savoy Plaza Hotel continues over telephones and behind locked doors.

The chief protagonist is a stocky, gray-haired lawyer named Mrs. Helen M. Clark, chairman of Save Our Landmarks!—Save the Plaza Square committee. She vows a struggle to the death before one of the world's largest corporations begins demolition of the hotel—scheduled the day after the World's Fair closes.

Committee members, she says, number in "the hundreds" and come from all parts of the country. Petitions are now in circulation, and boycotts and picketing are planned.

Like David before Goliath, Mrs. Clark is undaunted by the size of her foe. She has fought giants before. "Anything can be stopped," she says.

"I hear they are quite worried," she confided to well-wishers last week. G.M. hired a public relations agency specially to handle her group, she said.

GM OWNS HALF

The public relations man in question, Harry Carlson, of Wolcott & Associates, said he was hired by the Savoy Fifth Avenue Corp. last August, five months before Mrs. Clark's committee formed. G.M. owns 50 per cent of the Savoy Fifth Avenue Corp., which is putting up the 48-story building designed by Edward Durell Stone, in co-operation with Emery Roth & Sons, on Fifth Ave., between 58th and 59th Sts., opposite the Plaza Hotel. The officers and architectural committee of the Fifth Ave. Assn., to which Mr. Stone belongs, have heartily endorsed the preliminary design.

Mrs. Clark wouldn't qualify her strength or say what is the largest number of shares owned by any one member. (The boycott plan includes giving up G.M. stock.) The petitions read: "We, the Undersigned, Support the Preservation of Our Landmarks." Nowhere is mention made of General Motors.

Neither side has spoken directly to the other. G.M. recently issued a statement from Mr. Stone pleading for "patience and forebearance."

"Fifth Avenue has always been a nostalgic, esthetic battleground," the statement reads. "When the old gothic Vanderbilt Mansions between 57th and 58th gave way to commercial structures, when the old Waldorf-Astoria was replaced by the Empire State Building, and when Rockefeller Center went up, the hue and cry was heard across the land."

TO BE PREPARED

The statement was prepared "just to be ready for any inquiry," according to Mr. Carlson. "There's no reason to get people stirred up. There always are a handful of cranky shareholders who write in and ask when something happens." General Motors has nearly 1.2 million shares outstanding. Recently announced the largest profits ever made by a U.S. company in a year.

Mrs. Clark doesn't intend to argue the building's design, only its location on the Grand Army Plaza.

"The area is more or less a residential center for people from all over the world," she said. "Now they're trying to make it commercial. I don't care if they want to put it some place else." She suggested a site on 110th St. and Fifth Ave.

Exhibit 5—Continued

Mr. Carlson, who refers to the committee as "Fannie Hurst's group," said he would consider inviting them to view a seven-foot model when it is ready, in about a month's time. Miss Hurst is honorary chairman of the committee.

Miss Hurst, who says she is "utterly free of the delights of General Motors ownership," admits their effort is like "attempting to fight the Grand Canyon."

But, "if we let such things go on, we will have no past," she tells interview audiences. "I don't consider the Savoy Plaza the most beautiful building, but it is a lively and healthy monument of what we have been."

It appears there are people from as far away as California and Quebec whose stomachs turn upside down at the thought of a general office building with a ground-floor automobile showroom, replacing the elegant Savoy, the somber Madison Hotel, Lanvin perfume displays, Mayflower Coffee House and a host of little businesses.

A woman in Orlando, Fla., said she would sell her 400 shares of G.M. stock because she doesn't approve of "greedy buildings." An owner of three automobile outlets in California pledged to stop selling G.M. cars. A woman with 200 shares said she would sell these and cancel the family's order for a G.M. car.

Mrs. Clark's office is a third-floor suite in the Greybar Building, at 420 Lexington Ave., with rooms for a receptionist, secretary and the lawyers who work for her.

Prominent on the coffee table in the large conference room was a copy of FACT magazine headlined, "American Cars Are Deathtraps." A tiny room with a portable bar contained a carton of paperback books about the Krebiozen drug case. She is a counsel for cancer patients in the government's case against Dr. Andrew Ivy, the inventor of Krebiozen.

Source: From the *New York Herald-Tribune,* February 17, 1965.

Exhibit 6

LETTER FROM ROBERT C. WEINBERG TO *THE NEW YORK TIMES* SEPTEMBER 2, 1964

To the Editor:

There are two things to be added to the excellent editorial that appeared in *The Times* of Aug. 24 regarding the proposal to replace the Savoy Plaza by an office building.

First, if such a building must be built, the selection of a "name" architect is not enough to insure good design. The owners must adopt a publicly announced policy program which would establish that the design will measure up esthetically to the standards so well set forth by *The Times,* and the architect will be backed up by the owner when he produces such a design. With these assurances of quality no "name" architect is necessary.

Secondly, an important consideration which *The Times*'s editorial did not cover: if the area's solid core of hotel, restaurant and distinguished shopping character is breached, the resulting change in the nature of the open space we call the Plaza may affect New York's prestige more than the facade of a single building.

The Plaza as a space has for generations been the city's most famous center of fashion and glamour, like the Place Vendome in Paris. Its nature stems from the people who use it and what goes on there as much as from the design of the structures that surround it. Populating its sidewalks with thousands of office workers will obliterate the atmosphere that has made it, during the past century, New York's true center of swank.

Exhibit 6—Continued

Unfortunately, neither the Planning Commission nor the Landmarks Commission—the latter not yet officially with powers—is in a position to take action in such a matter, much less enforce any decision. Without official restraining powers in New York, esthetic controls of open spaces as well as of buildings rest in the pressure of public opinion.

The future of the Plaza area may be favorably affected by convincing the new owners they should adopt a combination of the two considerations I have outlined. They must be persuaded not to retain a name architect as a mere empty gesture, and also to announce at the outset that, to maintain the present characteristic usage of the great open space on which their building will face, no ground floor space will be leased to—much less designed for—banks, airlines or other occupancies creating dead sidewalk activity, especially at night.

Frontage on the Plaza must be specifically developed for restaurants, cafes and specialty shops, perhaps with arcaded sidewalks. Ultraluxury hotel suites could occupy certain parts of the new building, entering from Fifth Avenue, while access to the office spaces would be firmly restricted to Madison Avenue or the side streets. In this way New Yorkers and the building investors could actually have their cake and eat it, too.

Exhibit 7

LETTER FROM JOSEPH WATTERSON,
EDITOR OF THE *JOURNAL OF THE
F.A.I.A.* TO *THE NEW YORK TIMES,*
OCTOBER 3, 1964

TO THE EDITOR:

Robert C. Weinberg in his letter published Sept. 21 made some important points regarding the disaster that is threatening the Plaza area.

He is right when he says that a "name" architect is not necessary to insure good design for the building proposed for the site of the Savoy Plaza. However, the architect must be a "good" architect—whatever that means.

I can tell you what it means to me: It means an architect, big name or unknown, who is sensitive to the spirit of the place.

The Plaza has a very special character which stands alone now in the entire area of New York City, and Mr. Weinberg defines it very well. The Plaza is the one spot in the city where elan and true sophistication have survived, and the unsophisticated love it! The new building must preserve the flavor that now exists in this little enclave.

When the building housing Bergdorf Goodman's was built years ago, many of us groaned, for surely it could not equal the quality of the great French Renaissance mansion which stood on the site. It didn't, but in scale and character it turned out all right. When the Savoy Plaza was built, we groaned again—despite its name architects. But it too turned out all right. Now what? It must turn out all right!

Quality, character, scale, atmosphere—these are the most important attributes of urban architecture. Their adherence to prevailing standards of "good design" is secondary. The quality of urban neighborhoods depends more upon the neighborly sympathy and harmony of its buildings than upon their pronouncement of a new breakthrough in architectural design. Possibly we've had enough of that for a while.

There is one great step that must be taken by all cities sooner or later, and the sooner they face it the less damage they will have to undo later. This idea is not my own, for it is put forth in "Pittsburgh Perceived," a study of the visual

Exhibit 7—Continued

possibilities of that city prepared last year by Patrick Horsbrugh, at the behest of the City Planning Commission.

This is it: Within certain areas—all the downtown portion of the city, at least—no building permit should be issued until the owner and the architect of the property involved have appeared with their designs before a responsible commission and convinced them that the proposed building would be an asset to and an enhancement of its environment, not just economically, but visually.

New York, and all cities, have taken too many steps backward because any building newer than the one it replaced was considered better.

It is inescapable that old buildings must be torn down, sometimes. But it is inexcusable that what replaces them should be poorer architecture. If a new building is not better in every way than the one it is replacing it has no justification whatever.

So the improvement of the neighborhood should be demonstrated before the building permit is granted. The future amenity of New York and all cities will depend upon control over the quality of the design of its buildings and the spaces which they enclose.

Exhibit 8

FROM: Wolcott & Associates, Inc.
           777 Third Avenue
           New York, New York 10017

           Contact: Harry Carlson
                    PLaza 5–5530

FOR: SAVOY FIFTH AVENUE CORPORATION

FOR RELEASE
Wednesday, Dec. 16, 1964

NEW YORK, Dec. 16—The appointment of Edward Durell Stone and Emery Roth & Sons as associated architects for the 48-story Fifth Avenue office building in which General Motors Corporation will be a major tenant was announced today by Savoy Fifth Avenue Corporation.

The new General Motors Building will occupy the entire city block from Fifth to Madison Avenues and between 58th and 59th Streets. It will contain in excess of 1,500,000 square feet of space.

The site is now occupied by the 33-story Savoy Plaza Hotel, the 15-story Madison Hotel and the four-story Emmet Arcade Building. Demolition is scheduled to begin the latter part of 1965. Construction of the new building is expected to be completed in 1968.

The white tower of the new structure, which will rise from a low, landscaped podium, will be placed almost 100 feet back from the Fifth Avenue building line, the architects revealed in releasing design plans for the building.

"In effect, this will create additional park-like space, with sunken courtyards and gardens," they said. "Naturally, we wish to bring more beauty, not less, to the neighborhood."

Mr. Stone, considered by many as the foremost living American architect, said he has set out "to create a building that will salute the skyline and enhance one of New York's finest neighborhoods."

"We have sought the quality of permanence and have designed for the future as well as the present and the past. That is to say, we have also considered that

Exhibit 8—Continued

in its particular location, this building should harmonize with the neighboring buildings which are primarily built of masonry."

A typical office floor in the new building will contain approximately 32,000 square feet. The main landscaped plaza on Fifth Avenue plus one facing Madison Avenue will cover an area in excess of one-half acre.

Shops will be located in arcades around the perimeter of the sunken plaza and at street level along portions of the 58th and 59th Street frontages.

Parking facilities for tenants will be provided in an underground garage.

Mr. Stone has designed buildings of architectural distinction throughout the world, including the United States Embassy in New Delhi and the United States Pavilion at the Brussels World's Fair. In the United States, his designs include those for the Stanford Medical Center in Palo Alto, California, the State University of New York in Albany, the National Geographic Building and the John Fitzgerald Kennedy Center for the Performing Arts, both in Washington, D.C.

In New York City, he has designed the Museum of Modern Art, the Huntington Hartford Gallery of Modern Art, and is one of the architects on the proposed Civic Center in lower Manhattan.

Emery Roth & Sons is headed by brothers Richard and Julian Roth, sons of the firm's founder. Since World War II their firm has been very active in Manhattan and has been responsible for numerous office buildings, including The Chemical New York Trust Company Building, The Burroughs Building, and The Sperry Rand Building. They were recently awarded the Fifth Avenue Association prize for The Bankers Trust Company Building and the Regency Hotel.

Completion of the new building will enable General Motors to consolidate all of its present operations in New York City in a single location. It is expected that General Motors will occupy about one-half of the new building.

General Motors currently employs approximately 3,300 persons headquartered in midtown Manhattan, most of whom are in the 25-story General Motors Building at 1775 Broadway.

Exhibit 9

PHOTOGRAPH OF SKETCH OF PROPOSED GENERAL MOTORS BUILDING

Exhibit 10

PRESERVING LANDMARKS

It Becomes Tougher Job in Big Cities as Realty Values Climb
By LAURENCE G. O'DONNELL

NEW YORK—How can American cities preserve historically important buildings in the face of mounting economic pressures for optimum usage of land and space?

Here in the nation's largest city, an emotionally charged campaign to save worthy old buildings seems on the verge of a significant victory: The chances are New York soon will become the 70th city in the nation to pass legislation aimed at preserving its landmarks. Yet talk to proponents of such legislation and they give the impression of being at the door of defeat. The difficulties they cite are common to most other cities and point up the problem of saving old buildings even when nearly everyone agrees it's a good idea.

No one expects the New York City bill to totally halt the wrecking boom that is removing many of Manhattan's landmarks. Advocates of preservation already are fretting privately that the bill, like those in most other cities, will have "no teeth"—that is, it probably won't empower a city landmarks commission to buy buildings it deems worthy of saving or to prevent permanently their destruction.

At best, leaders of the preservation movement hope the New York bill will do what most others do: Buy time by delaying demolition or alteration while city officials or others work behind the scenes to save the landmarks with private funds.

ECONOMIC JUSTIFICATIONS

In fact, there is a growing awareness among experts in the field of saving old buildings that victories are scored only when arguments of economics, not aesthetics, are brought to bear. "In areas where preservation has been spectacular, it has been done by private money," mainly putting deteriorating residential property back into use, says an official of the National Trust for Historic Preservation, a Washington, D.C., clearinghouse for such movements.

In cities such as Charleston, S.C., New Orleans and San Juan, restoration efforts have received a push from business interests eager to promote historic districts as tourist attractions. "In a sense," says one landmarks authority, "for the drive to be successful there has to be an economic justification. Aesthetic reasons unfortunately aren't enough."

But in many major cities, and here in New York City in particular, the economic justifications are becoming increasingly hard to come by. In Manhattan, skyscraper builders long since have used up all the prime sites so they've triggered a wrecking boom in their search for new places to build. A few weeks ago, the Bowery Savings Bank paid $5 million an acre for an old bus terminal site on which it plans to place a 48-story skyscraper.

"Now anything under 12 stories in the center of Manhattan is going to be torn down because of the value of the real estate under it," enthuses one wrecker. "In other words, taller buildings are replacing smaller ones because of the land value."

For the last year and a half, architects, historians and other citizens have been protesting that increasingly these smaller buildings include structures the city ought to save. When wreckers arrived at Pennsylvania Station in mid-1963, they were greeted by pickets who argued the 54-year-old superstructure with its ornate, high-ceiling waiting room and columned facade should be preserved.

Exhibit 10—Continued

The pickets lost the Penn Station battle. Many of its columns now lie discarded in a New Jersey swamp. And wreckers are busy preparing the site for a sports arena and office building slated to rise over the underground tracks and waiting rooms.

But the Penn Station defeat fueled a campaign that has been on the front pages of New York newspapers ever since. The movement has gained wide support. During a seven-hour public hearing recently on proposed landmarks legislation, 84 speakers argued in favor while only five, mainly representing real estate and building interests, opposed the bill.

Yet many advocates realize that despite lopsided support for the bill city councilmen were paying careful attention to the objections of builders and property owners. A spokesman for one industry group was asked to submit suggested legislation that would meet these objections.

As in many other cities, New York counts heavily on real estate taxes to pay the mounting costs of the services its taxpayers demand. Bigger buildings raise assessments and produce increased revenues, so the city has a vital stake in continuing the building boom.

In a city like New York where prime building sites are scarce, the cost squeeze on the city raises the question of whether the city can afford to save its landmarks. "I certainly think this is something we have to consider," says David Ross, majority leader on New York's City Council. He believes the city could be hurt by a landmarks bill that stifles improvements and shrinks the amount of building sites.

"We would assume most people agree landmarks ought to be preserved," says Mr. Ross. "The problem is how you do it. We will have to see to it that the bill is good and sound, considering aesthetics, economics and city finances."

The city council's special committee on codes is now at work hammering out a bill. Some officials are already bristling about the pressure to produce some sort of bill that the landmarks campaign has engendered.

OFF THE TAX ROLLS

They also view as a mixed blessing one result the campaign recently brought about. Two Park Avenue mansions, considered to be "among the finest in the country of their period and type," were saved from demolition after wreckers had already started their work. A granddaughter of John D. Rockefeller, Jr., paid an estimated $2 million to buy the buildings and now reportedly plans to give them to the city for cultural use. One city official observes the proposed gift, besides giving the city two buildings it hadn't sought, will remove valuable property from the tax rolls.

Advocates of preservation are sensitive to such criticism. Recently one group of socially prominent New York women decided to take their fight to the doorstep of the builder rather than to city hall. The builder happened to be General Motors Corp.

The women said they would organize a campaign to boycott General Motors products—including presumably its Cadillacs—if the auto giant and its British partner went ahead with plans to tear down the stately 33-story Savoy Plaza hotel and replace it with a 48-story "tombstone," housing General Motors headquarters here. The skyscraper, they suggested, would besmirch the quaint plaza onto which the hotel now faces.

Whether such tactics will dent the auto giant's plans seems doubtful. In fact, unless landmarks advocates can find new uses for old buildings, the wrecking boom is likely to continue unabated. Already about 2,500 of the 10,000 structures

Exhibit 10—Continued

recorded since the 1930s in the Government's Historic American Buildings Survey have been torn down, mainly to make way for new buildings.

Ironically, as cities get older, and passing time produces more landmarks, the pressures will increase to remove them. Growing slums, the cost of city services and spiraling urban land costs—all these factors are conspiring against preserving buildings that help new generations retain their ties with the past.

"Our best chance," according to one veteran in the landmarks field, "is by making these buildings useful and continuing them on the tax rolls. Buildings saved as museums are the hardest to justify." Despite the trend toward more landmarks legislation, he adds, the job of actually saving old buildings is getting tougher.

Source: From *The Wall Street Journal*, March 11, 1965.

THE GLIDDEN COMPANY *

The Glidden Company, incorporated in Ohio in 1917, annually sells over $200 million in paint (45%), food (40%), chemicals-pigments-metals (10%), and organic chemicals (5%). The company employs over 6,000 people in 20 principal plants in 15 states. It has foreign subsidiaries and affiliates in Canada, Venezuela, Japan, Colombia, and Ecuador.

Glidden has owned and operated the Durkee Famous Foods Plant in Elmhurst, Long Island, since 1929. Approximately 100 salaried and 250 wage employees have been involved in the refining of vegetable oils and the processing of condiments, coconut, and spices.

Operations Discontinued at Elmhurst

In 1953 the Glidden board of directors instituted a program to review all its operations in detail, with the view to improving operations and profitability in all divisions. Certain operations were sold outright, consolidated with other operations, or closed down because they did not fit into the company's long-range growth and modernization plans. These reviews, in the opinion of the Glidden management, revealed that the Elmhurst plant was a comparatively marginal operation. In support of this conclusion, management pointed out that the equipment in the plant was old and outdated. Also, because of the Elmhurst plant's geographical location, Glidden was forced to pay certain freight penalties for the shipment of oils to and from the vegetable oil refinery there. It was prohibitively expensive, management believed, to attempt to modernize the old plant. Because it had four floors and a basement, production lines could not be arranged for more efficient operations.

In October 1956 Glidden took its first step in a two-stage operations improvement plan. The vegetable oil refining operations were moved from the Elmhurst plant to Glidden's large vegetable oil refinery in Louisville, Kentucky.

The second stage began on May 16, 1957 when Glidden notified the Elmhurst employees that the condiment, coconut, and spice operations would be discontinued at the Elmhurst plant and initiated in a new plant in Bethlehem, Pennsylvania, during the fall of 1957.

The new Bethlehem plant is a modern 1½-floor building which allows greatly improved work flow layout and does away with the costly elevator movements of goods. Modern equipment supplements and in some cases replaces the Elmhurst equipment. The managers of the new plant

---

* Copyright 1964 by the Graduate School of Business, Columbia University.

estimate that the change in production procedures and the installation of the additional equipment have resulted in an overall increase of production of approximately 30 to 40% with 25% fewer employees.

Personnel Policy

In anticipation of the discontinuation of all operations at the Elmhurst plant, Glidden—

1. Notified all employees six months in advance.
2. Offered to consider the applications of Elmhurst employees as *new* employees if they applied at the Bethlehem plant. (Two wage employees who did apply at Bethlehem received job offers—without seniority—and one accepted. Twenty salaried employees from Elmhurst followed the operations to Bethlehem.)
3. Found 120 job openings at comparable wage rates in the Greater New York area for which the Elmhurst employees could apply.
4. Brought in representatives of the New York State Employment Service to conduct employment interviews.
5. Gave employees reasonable time off to look for other jobs.
6. Attempted to sell the Elmhurst plant to other food processors or a similar operation.
7. Met and discussed the best arrangement for handling the rights accrued to Elmhurst employees in terms of vacations, pensions, and insurance.

The Union and Its Contract

Since December 1, 1949 the General Warehousemen's Union, Local 852, of the International Brotherhood of Teamsters, Chauffeurs, and Warehousemen represented the 250 Elmhurst plant employees. On December 1, 1955, the company management and the union agreed on a contract which was to last until November 30, 1957 and from year to year thereafter unless either party notified the other not less than 60 days prior to the expiration of the agreement. (See Exhibit 1.)

Union Reaction to Proposed Discontinuance of Operations

On September 16, 1957 the company formally notified the union of its intention to terminate the contract on November 30, 1957, its expiration date. Shortly thereafter, the union served the company with a notice to arbitrate six issues in connection with closing the Elmhurst plant. Local 852 acted to protect the property rights of its members which, it insisted, were violated when the company closed the Elmhurst plant without first offering each employee continued employment with full seniority rights. The collective bargaining agreement provided for (1) a welfare plan, (2) a pension plan, and (3) a group insurance plan, all of which created property rights for employees. Local 852 also maintained that (4) closing the Elmhurst plant without offering each employee continued employment with full seniority was a breach of contract, and that (5) the closing was done to evade the agreement and prevent collective bargaining, in violation of the law, and finally that (6) the employees were discriminated against because of their union membership by being barred from continued employment with full seniority, or denied severance pay as an alternative.

The Court Rules in Glidden's Favor

Glidden promptly obtained from the New York State Supreme Court a stay of arbitration on the grounds that Glidden was not depriving the employees of any property rights, and that the charges were not subject to arbitration. In its ruling of February 10, 1958 the court said that Glidden had lived up to every item of its agreement with the union in regard to welfare, pension, and group insurance plans. The judge referred to the contract's wording under "Dispute Settlement" (see Exhibit 1) and said: "No one is under duty to resort to arbitration unless by clear language he has so agreed." The issues raised by the union did not arise out of, or involve, an interpretation and application of the "specific terms" of the contract, so it "follows . . . that Glidden's motion to stay arbitration must be granted, whatever other remedies the union may have with respect to the alleged disputes."

Action Taken by Plant Employees Individually

Five employees of the Elmhurst plant ranging in age from 43 to 60, and ranging in length of service from 10 to 25 years, filed suit against the company for breach of contract. The employment of four of the five had been terminated on November 1, 1957, and the fifth on November 18, 1957. (One hundred and twenty-two other Elmhurst wage employees later filed similar suits.) The former employees saw new workers in the Bethlehem plant carrying on essentially the same tasks they had performed for years in Elmhurst. Had the operations continued in Elmhurst, the former employees reasoned that their jobs would have been protected by their seniority rights as described in the contract (see Exhibit 1). They argued that their seniority rights should also protect their jobs at the new location.

Victory for the Glidden Company in the U.S. District Court Case

On May 23, 1960, in the United States District Court in New York, the former employees (supported by the general warehousemen's union) maintained that the seniority rights created by the contract survived the termination date of the contract. Therefore, the company was required to offer them jobs at Bethlehem with full seniority rights acquired at Elmhurst. They insisted that the company's failure to do this deprived them of continued employment, as well as benefits from the company's pension plan, group insurance plans, and the union's welfare plan.

Counsel for the Glidden Company argued that seniority rights and the benefits of seniority rights flowed from a specific contract—a contract expressly confined in scope and application to the plant in Elmhurst. When the contract was legally terminated and the operations in the plant ceased, the employment and seniority rights ceased to exist. In short, said the company's counsel, the company and the union never bargained for transferable seniority rights, and there is simply no foundation to the implication that seniority rights could outlive the plant or contract.

Judge Palmieri concentrated on the geographical extension of employee's rights as the critical point at issue and ruled in favor of Glidden.

Former Employees Appeal to the U.S. Court of Appeals

The five former employees (again with union support) presented their appeal on February 8, 1961. The employees argued as follows: "The defendant's refusal to re-employ plaintiffs with seniority at its Bethlehem plant constitutes a breach of contract enforceable by plaintiffs. The subsequent expiration of the contract period did not deprive plaintiffs of their seniority rights established and accrued under the agreement, nor were these rights confined to the defendant's Elmhurst plant." The employees also distinguished between terminating business operations and transferring business operations, holding the latter to be the case here.

In support of their case the former employees cited precedent to show that "seniority provisions enure directly to the benefit of employees and may be enforced by them. . . . Once seniority rights have been gained by an employee, they belong solely to him. Their existence certainly does not depend on their being represented by a union."

The employees also appealed to a legal authority on the subject of seniority rights:

Aware that our legal concept of property rights has broadened with changes in our economic and industrial system, the courts have recognized that the "right to work . . . is as much property as the more obvious forms of goods and merchandise, stocks, and bonds. . . .

Seniority represents in the highest degree the right to work. By seniority the oldest man in point of service (ability and fitness for the job being sufficient) is given the choice of jobs, is first promoted within the range of jobs subject to seniority, and is the last laid off. It proceeds so on down the line to the youngest in point of service. Seniority is more than merely the right to work; it is the best kind of unemployment insurance. It assures the man that the longer he works the more certain it is that he will retain his job at a wage greater than the small amount available as unemployment compensation. Seniority is no less a property right and entitles to equitable protection because it is subject to modification by changing the craft agreement by which it was created or because the employee is subject to discharge and is not required by the craft agreement to continue to work for the employer.

Finally, commenting on the reasoning of the lower court the employees said: "We particularly cannot accept the view of the district court that all rights ended with the closing of the Elmhurst plant where the continued operation of the plant was prevented, as here, by act of the defendant itself. In such instance, there is applicable the proposition that every agreement carries within it the implied condition that no party to it shall do any act which will impede performance of the agreement or render its performance impossible."

Glidden Company's Response in the Court of Appeals

The Glidden company countered with arguments on the following points. First, the five employees were not "layed off." Rather their employment was "terminated." Hence, the provisions of the contract concerning seniority rights are not applicable. Second, "an employer has the right to discontinue and terminate his business or to discontinue and terminate a section or department of his business without necessity of explanation or excuse to anyone." ". . . This right of an employer may be exercised during the term of a collective bargaining agreement unless there are provisions in the collective bargaining agreement providing otherwise." Third, "plaintiffs individually are not entitled to enforce any rights which they claim arise under the collective bargaining agreement containing provision for arbitration of disputes. . . ." "The plaintiffs . . . are without any remedy other than that to be pursued on their behalf by Local 852, at the option of Local 852."

Appeals Court Favors the Employees

The court decided in favor of the former employees. At the nub of the court's reasoning was the following:

These rights to retired pay, though their realization will extent far into the future, and though they arise solely and only out of the terms of the union agreement with the defendant, have been treated as "vested" rights and are being voluntarily honored by the defendant. This was, we suppose, because the employees had earned these rights by compliance with the terms of the contract, and the fact that the contract was not renewed, and that other workmen in the future might not have the opportunity to earn similar rights, was irrelevant. We think the plaintiff employees had, by the same token, "earned" their valuable unemployment insurance, and that their rights to it were "vested" and could not be unilaterally annulled. [See Exhibit 2 for Judge Madden's majority opinion and Judge Lumbard's minority opinion.]

Reaction to the Appeals Court Decision

Judge Madden's opinion came as a blow to the Glidden Company. Glidden immediately appealed to the Supreme Court of the United States. (At the writing of this case—July 1962—the appeal was still pending before that court.) Industrial relations people and union leaders sensed the implications of the decision which, in the words of the Glidden management, "could change the entire complexion of many vital aspects of labor-management relations." The unions hailed the decision as the death nell to "plant pirating practices."

Within the year Zdanok versus Glidden established a precedent for similar suits involving Gemmer Company, Consolidated Electronic Industries Corporation, Selb Manufacturing Company, Blades Manufacturing Company, Hoover Ball and Bearing Company, and Trabon Engineering Corporation. The major automobile manufacturing companies have felt it necessary to provide for technological relocation pay in their recently negotiated contracts. Armour and Swift recently wrote into their contracts provisions for technological adjustment pay based on seniority. The last six months of 1961 saw the "vested" rights dispute as the issue in several strikes.

In part to satisfy the many requests from industrial relations and personnel people throughout the country for information about the case, Glidden's manager of personnel relations, Jack B. Bredt, spoke to an American Management Association Conference in Chicago on February 15, 1962. He summarized Glidden's view of the ramifications of the case as follows:

> Unless our case is reversed, based on existing decisions, the federal courts will have developed doctrines that:
> A. There is a property right in employment
> B. The property right arises from the seniority provisions of a collective bargaining agreement
> C. Seniority becomes "vested" when earned, regardless of whether or not this is specified in the contract
> D. Seniority continues beyond the termination of the collective bargaining agreement at the location where the work was performed but, in addition, it follows the work to any other place in the United States even though the contract has expired
> E. It, therefore, appears that an employee acquires greater property rights than his union
> . . . The emphasis has been placed upon moral and social responsibility rather than an agreement negotiated between the parties.

Widespread national concern is in large part reflected in an article by Arthur Krock in the *New York Times* of August 18, 1961:

> The issues raised in this decision include: the right of management to close or geographically transfer a plant in pursuance of its judgment that the health of the business requires the action; the right of the employees who are not carried to the new location, or who decline to transfer there, to collect damages from the company; the right of a company to execute a bilateral agreement with a community to move its plant and recruit its employees locally in exchange for tax and other incentives; and the power of the Federal judiciary to rewrite management-labor contracts reached in collective bargaining. . . .

Exhibit 1

EXCERPTS FROM THE AGREEMENT BETWEEN DURKEE FAMOUS FOODS, DIVISION OF THE GLIDDEN COMPANY—NO. 23—ELMHURST, NEW YORK, AND GENERAL WAREHOUSEMEN'S UNION, LOCAL 852. DECEMBER 1, 1955 TO NOVEMBER 30, 1957.

AGREEMENT

This agreement made and entered into at New York, New York, by and between the Glidden Company, Durkee Famous Foods Division, for and on behalf of its plant facilities located at Corona Avenue and 94th Street, Elmhurst, Long Island, New York, herein after referred to as "the Company," and the General Warehousemen's Union, Local 852 affiliated with the International Brotherhood of Teamsters, Chauffeurs, Warehousemen and Helpers of America, AFL-CIO, hereinafter referred to as "the Union."

* * * * *

ARTICLE XI—SENIORITY.

1. New employees shall be employed on a probationary basis for thirty (30) working days, and if retained beyond that period their seniority shall accrue from the date of their employment.

2. The Company shall prepare a seniority list showing the names and hiring dates of all employees with the most senior employee at the head of the list and all other employees ranked by hiring date in order thereafter, down to the last senior employee. A copy of this list shall be furnished to the Union upon request.

3. For the purposes of layoff and recall only, Union representatives, not exceeding ten (10) in number for the entire plant, shall head the seniority lists in their respective Departments as long as retained in such office.

4. When a curtailment of production is required, the following procedure shall apply:

(a) ALL DEPARTMENTS: Employees without seniority shall be laid off first.

(b) MECHANICAL DEPARTMENT: Employees shall be laid off in the reverse order of their seniority in the crafts affected. Laid off employees shall be given other work for which they are qualified on the basis of plant seniority.

(c) REFINERY: Employees shall be laid off in the reverse order of their plant seniority in the operations affected. Such employees shall be given other work for which they are qualified on the basis of plant seniority.

(d) ALL OTHER DEPARTMENTS: Employees shall be laid off in the reverse order of their plant seniority.

(e) Employees shall be recalled to work in the reverse order of their layoff.

(f) Employees on layoff shall notify the Company in writing of any change of address.

5. The provisions of this Article are based on the ability of each employee to do the work required. Promotions to vacancies or to new positions of a non-supervisory character shall be upon the basis of departmental seniority. If there is no one in a Department available for such promotion, then the position shall be awarded on the same terms on the basis of plant seniorty after notice has been on the bulletin board for three (3) working days. Such position may be filled temporarily pending the selection of a permanent employee.

6. (a) Seniority shall be terminated for the following reasons:

(1) An employee quits voluntarily.

(2) An employee is discharged for cause.

Exhibit 1—Continued

(3) An employee fails to acknowledge within two (2) days a notice to report to work.

(4) An employee fails to return to work within three (3) days after being notified to report to work.

(b) In instances of continuous layoff, seniority shall be terminated after:

(1) An employee with less than five (5) years' continuous employment at the time his layoff began is on a continuous layoff of two (2) years; or

(2) An employee with more than five (5) years' continuous employment at the time his layoff began is on a continuous layoff of three (3) years.

(c) Employees whose seniority is terminated due to continuous layoff shall receive first preference for employment before new employees are hired.

* * * * *

ARTICLE XII—MANAGEMENT.

1. The supervision and control of all operations and the direction of all employees is vested solely in the Company. The Union, upon request, shall be informed fully concerning the reasons for layoffs, demotions and discharges and may submit same for review in the manner provided for the submission of grievances.

* * * * *

ARTICLE XIV—WELFARE PLAN.

1. The Company shall continue to pay into the Union Welfare Fund the amount of four and one-half (4½) cents per paid hour for each employee who has completed sixty (60) days employment with the Company. Such payments are limited in any one work week to a maximum of forty (40) hours or $1.80 per employee.

2. Effective December 1, 1956, the Company shall pay into the Union Welfare Fund an additional amount of four and five one-hundredths (4.05) cents per paid hour, making a total of eight and fifty-five one-hundredths (8.55) cents per paid hour for each employee who has completed sixty (60) days employment with the Company. Such payments shall be limited in any one work week to a maximum of forty (40) hours, or $3.42, per employee.

3. The Company shall forward contributions to the Fund to the Union on or before the 15th of each month, following a completed monthly payroll period.

4. The Union agrees to maintain Blue Cross hospitalization and Group Health surgical and medical coverage for all employees and their dependents up to eighteen (18) years of age after the completion of sixty (60) days employment.

5. The Disability Benefit Plan which has been approved by the State of New York shall be continued in effect according to its terms.

6. All future assessments made by the State of New York to maintain the fund for providing disability benefits for unemployed persons shall be paid by the Company.

7. Employees with less than one full year of continuous employment with the Company shall have all permanent contributions required by law deducted from their wages. Such amounts deducted shall be applied to provide Disability Benefits for those workers under the approved Plan.

* * * * *

Exhibit 1—Continued

ARTICLE XVI—PENSION PLAN.

Effective January 1, 1956, all eligible employees shall be covered by Company Retirement Plan for Hourly Employees, as amended January 1, 1956.

* * * * *

ARTICLE XX—DISPUTE SETTLEMENT.

* * * * *

(e) Any question, grievance or dispute arising out of and involving the interpretation and application of the specific terms of this Agreement over which the Director of Personnel Relations of the Company and a Representative of the Union are unable to reach a satisfactory settlement shall, at the request of either party, be referred to the New York State Mediation Board for arbitration. The Arbitrator shall have no power to add to, subtract from, or modify any of the terms of this Agreement or any other agreement supplementary hereto, and his decision shall be binding on the parties.

* * * * *

ARTICLE XXII—DURATION OF AGREEMENT.

1. This Agreement expresses the full and complete understanding and obligations of the parties on the subject of wages, method of payment, hours of employment, working conditions, and other conditions of employment including welfare, fringe and retirement benefits, and was freely arrived at through the processes of collective bargaining.

2. This Agreement shall become effective on, and all adjustments agreed upon shall be retroactive to, December 1, 1955, unless otherwise specifically provided herein. This Agreement shall remain in full force and effect until November 30, 1957, and from year to year thereafter until either party hereto notifies the other party not less than sixty (60) days prior to the expiration of this Agreement or any extension hereof, that such party elects to terminate or modify his Agreement on its expiration date.

Exhibit 2

EXCERPTS FROM OPINION AND JUDGMENT OF JUDGE MADDEN AND DISSENTING OPINION OF JUDGE LUMBARD

U.S. COURT OF APPEALS

Zdanok v. *Glidden*
March 28, 1961

The plaintiffs contend that they were, as beneficiaries of the contract between their union and the defendant, entitled to the jobs which were created by the opening of the plant at Bethlehem. They say that they were laid off because of the removal of the machinery and the cessation of operations at Elmhurst, and that as work was opened up at Bethlehem they were entitled, by reason of their seniority and the contract provisions relating to it, to go to work at Bethlehem with the seniority which they had acquired at Elmhurst.

* * * * *

The defendant . . . contends that because the collective bargaining agreements contained provisions for the arbitration of disputes, the plaintiffs are not entitled to individually enforce their rights under the agreement. The defendant

Exhibit 2—Continued

relies heavily upon *Parker* v. *Borock* . . . as support for its contention that the plaintiffs individually are not entitled to enforce the rights which they claim here. In the *Parker* case, . . . the Court of Appeals said, . . . that the plaintiff, who was also "bound by and limited to the provisions of the agreement," had "entrusted his rights to his union representative," who alone could have sought arbitration of the plaintiff's discharge. . . . The court noted that the plaintiff's only remedy would be against the union for failing to fulfill its duties under the agreement.

The *Parker* case is, therefore, significantly different from the instant case. In *Parker,* the question which the plaintiff sought to litigate had been entrusted by him, under the collective agreement, to the arbitration process. That was the interpretation which the New York Court of Appeals placed upon the contract there before it. In the instant case, as we have seen, the Supreme Court of New York has held that the dispute with which this suit is concerned is *not* covered by the arbitration provision of the agreement. The plaintiffs have not, therefore, entrusted to their union representative the rights which they now seek to enforce.

As to the merits of the plaintiff's claims, the defendant takes the bold position that the collective bargaining contract conferred upon the employees no rights which survived the contract. It says, at page 27 of its memorandum:

> Even if the Elmhurst operations had continued but the collective bargaining agreement had expired, the seniority status of plaintiffs would not have survived the termination of that agreement. For it is only by reason of existing provisions in the agreement that provisions relating to the seniority have any application. When such provisions no longer exist, seniority no longer exists.

*   *   *   *   *

We think the defendant's language, quoted above, is not supportable. Suppose an employee had completed five years of service in October, 1957. Under the seniority provision of the collective bargaining agreement, he thinks that he has earned, and acquired, by continuous service, valuable insurance against unemployment; that by reason of having worked continuously for this company longer than many of his fellow workmen, he could not be laid off unless the lay-off cut deep into the working force; that even if he should be reached in a lay-off, he would be sure to be re-employed if at any time within three years after the lay-off his name should be reached on the seniority list, for re-employment. As we have seen, the defendant's position is that the employee had not acquired any such rights.

Rights embodied in a collective bargaining contract negotiated by a union "inure to the direct benefit of employees and may be the subject of a cause of action." . . . If one has in October a right to demand performance of the corresponding obligation at any relevant time within a period of three years, it would be strange if the other contracting party could unilaterally terminate the right at the end of three weeks. Of course the employee owning the right, or his authorized union agent, could bargain away the employee's right. Nothing of that kind occurred in the instant case.

*   *   *   *   *

. . . Those who had 15 years of service and had reached the age of 45 at the time of their discharge were advised by the defendant that they had vested rights

Exhibit 2—Continued

to retirement benefits and would begin to receive payments when they reached the age of 65.

These rights to retired pay, though their realization will extend far into the future, and though they arise solely and only out of the terms of the union agreement with the defendant, have been treated as "vested" rights and are being voluntarily honored by the defendant. This was, we suppose, because the employees had earned these rights by compliance with the terms of the contract, and the fact that the contract was not renewed, and that other workmen in the future might not have the opportunity to earn similar rights, was irrelevant. We think the plaintiff employees had, by the same token, "earned" their valuable unemployment insurance, and that their rights in it were "vested" and could not be unilaterally annulled.

. . . [Judge Palmieri] held that the rights were not enforceable except in the Elmhurst plant, and therefore denied recovery. With deference, we disagree with this conclusion.

The union contract, in its preamble, recited that it was made by the defendant company

    for and on behalf of its plant facilities located at Corona Avenue and 94th

    Street, Elmhurst, Long Island, New York.

If this narrow geographical description is treated as setting fixed boundaries upon the scope of the contract, difficulties immediately arise. If the plant moved from 94th Street to 93d Street in Elmhurst, an entire structure of valuable legal rights would tumble down. *A fortiori* if the plant moved to a site a few miles or a good many miles away, the consequence would be the same. But one would be obliged to wonder why so catastrophic a consequence should follow a mere change in physical location. And it would be hard to conjure up a reason why it should. . . .

*   *   *   *   *

We can see no expense or embarrassment to the defendant which would have resulted from its adopting the more rational, not to say humane, construction of its contract. The plaintiffs were, so far as appears, competent and satisfactory employees. They had long since completed the period of probation prescribed in the union contract. It would seem that they would have been at least as useful employees as newly hired applicants. The defendant's Bethelehem plant was a new plant. There could not have been an existing union representative or a collective bargaining agreement there, at the time the plant was opened.

In the circumstances, no detriment to the defendant would have resulted from a recognition by the defendant of rights in its employees corresponding with their reasonable expectations. In that situation, a construction of the contract which would disappoint those expectations would be irrational and destructive.

It follows from what we have said that the plaintiffs were entitled to be employed at the defendant's Bethlehem plant, with the seniority and reemployment rights which they had acquired at the Elmhurst plant. . . .

*   *   *   *   *

LUMBARD, Chief Judge (Dissenting):

*   *   *   *   *

It is immaterial to the resolution of the question before us that the employment of competent and satisfactory employees is suddenly terminated, or even that the employer has acted ungenerously, as indeed it has. We are called upon

Exhibit 2—Continued

to construe the contract upon which the parties agreed and not to substitute for it one with more humane or less destructive terms.

*   *   *   *   *

The federal cases hold that seniority is not inherent in the employment relationship but arises out of the contract. . . . If rights are to persist beyond the terms of the collective-bargaining agreement, the agreement must so provide or be susceptible of such construction. . . .

The agreement we are here called upon to interpret did not expressly provide for any retention of seniority rights beyond the termination of the collective-bargaining agreement. The employees claim, however, that by agreeing to rehire on the basis of seniority for two or three years after layoff, the employer undertook not only to retain seniority rights after the expiration of the agreement but to extend existing seniority privileges to any other location to which the work then done at Elmhurst would be assigned. Relocation of an employer's plant does not, of course, automatically terminate all rights under a collective-bargaining agreement; whether such rights continue depends on the terms of the contract. . . . The issue here is whether this collective-bargaining agreement gave the employees the right to "follow the work" to the new site. I would hold that it did not.

The closing of the Elmhurst plant and the removal of the defendant's operations to a new location were concededly done in good faith and were not wholly unforeseeable. As Judge Palmieri points out, it is not uncommon for the parties to extend beyond a single plant the area in which seniority rights are to apply. Surely unions are now fully of age and are able to protect themselves and their members at the bargaining table. The consequences of dismissing the plaintiffs' case might indeed be unfortunate and even "catastrophic" from their point of view, but it is hardly "irrational and destructive" for a court to leave the parties as they are if they have never seen fit to provide otherwise.

MORRIS AIRWAYS COMPANY*

Company Background

Having acquired nearly eight years of valuable military and civilian flight experience in both fixed-wing and helicopter aircraft, Glynn Morris of Albuquerque, New Mexico, began making plans toward the achievement of his boyhood dream—the ownership and management of a commercial airline to service the Southwest.

Consultation with prominent businessmen revealed to Morris that the entire area might be in the initial stages of an economic boom. Perhaps most noticeable was the marked development and expansion of New Mexico's nuclear and atomic energy industry. The four main locations of this activity were:

1. Albuquerque, with almost 200,000 residents, lay at the hub of the state's "nuclear industrialization." The adjacent establishment of the Sandia (N.M.) Field Command for the Defense Atomic Support Agency and the Air Force's Special Weapons Development Laboratory at nearby Kirtland Air Force Base attracted a number of technically oriented civilian contractors.

2. Los Alamos, some 60 miles to the north of Albuquerque, was the site of the Atomic Energy Commission's Weapons Development Laboratory. Located close to the capital city of Santa Fe, Los Alamos has grown in population to almost 20,000 because of increased public and private spending.

3. Clovis is the site of the Air Force's Special Weapons Logistical Center. Although 200 miles east of Albuquerque, Clovis' contribution as a major source of special support materiel made its day-to-day communications with the large nuclear centers imperative.

4. Alamagordo, situated 155 miles directly south of Albuquerque, was the home of White Sands Proving Ground and its auxiliary Holloman Air Force Base.

Having decided that these four centers were his best market areas, Morris began discussions with aircraft suppliers to find the necessary helicopters and fixed-wing aircraft to best meet his needs. Low cost and flexibility of function were the main requirements. In a matter of a short time, Morris located three serviceable aircraft, specifically:

1. One Beach H18 twin-engine, fixed-wing aircraft:
   a) Speed: 210 miles per hour;
   b) Maximum payload: 2,000 lbs. (or passenger equivalence);

---

    c) Power source: 350 hp. engines;
    d) General condition: Used, but operable after minor repairs; only 220 hours since its last major overhaul;
    e) Selling price: $35,000.

2. One Hewes model 5000 helicopter:
    a) Speed: 125 miles per hour;
    b) Maximum payload: 1,600 lbs. (or passenger equivalence);
    c) Power source: Allyson 250–C18 turbine engines powering a single four-bladed rotor motor;
    d) General condition: Used, but immediately operable with no requirement for minor repairs; zero time on engines;
    e) Selling price: $32,000.

3. One Kamon UH–2A helicopter:
    a) Speed: 135 miles per hour;
    b) Maximum payload: 2,800 lbs. (or passenger equivalence);
    c) Power source: GE T58–8 turbine engines powering twin, intermeshing, contrarotating four-bladed rotors;
    d) General condition: Used, in need of minor repairs; 350 hours on installed engine since last major overhaul;
    e) Selling price: $93,000.

The two helicopters were intended to be the backbone of Morris' taxi service, with the smaller Hewes directed toward the shortest operations.

The next step for Morris was to find two other full-time pilots and the necessary complement of ground employees. The two pilots acquired were former acquaintances, Harry Foiles (recently retired from the Air Force), and Buzz Collins, who had flown Search and Rescue helicopter missions in Korea with Morris. Only Collins and Morris were qualified in both helicopter and fixed-wing aircraft. Foiles was qualified to fly only helicopters.

While it was Morris' eventual intention to organize his own ground maintenance and handling crew, he contracted-out all repair requirements to the Albuquerque Municipal Airport's aircraft maintenance pool until such time as he felt it necessary to engage MAC in these activities. In addition, Morris avoided hiring an administrative staff in the early stages of operations by accepting the burden of these duties himself. Nevertheless, Morris did take on Dick Ziegler, a certified public accountant, on a part-time basis to assist him in capital expansion, cost control, tax submission, and the like.

Initial Operations

Morris Airways began operations 20 months ago with the acquisition of several short-term commercial contracts. Profit margins were low, but valuable experience was obtained in the scheduling and operating of a short-haul airline.

Shortly after the company was founded, Morris placed a bid on, and was awarded, a five-year government contract to provide air service to the New Mexico area. Revenues to MAC were fixed and guaranteed at $60,000 yearly, in return for which the company was to provide passenger service from Kirtland Air Base, 7 miles outside Albuquerque, to three primary destinations in New Mexico:

1. The Los Alamos Sunport;
2. The Alamagordo Air Terminal; and
3. The Clovis Air Force Base.

There was to be no cross-routing between the three destinations. Scheduling was to be strictly between Kirtland and each separate airfield. Annual average passenger quotas were established as follows:

	Los Alamos	Alamagordo	Clovis
From Kirtland Air Force Base	1,800	2,600	2,000

Based on five-year projected revenues, Morris made an initial estimate of his gross profit margin, which proved to be quite encouraging.[1]

Annual Cash Receipts		Annual Cash Disbursements	
Contracted revenue	$60,000	Operating costs	$25,000
	......	Bank notes due	17,500
Total receipts	$60,000	Total disbursements ...	$42,500
		Gross profit margin (receipts less disbursements)	$17,500

Operations under the Government Contract

During the first few months of operations, Morris experienced the normal, day-to-day difficulties characteristic of a new business enterprise. However, after a few months, he felt that he had achieved an efficient scheduling of pilots and aircraft.

Morris personally flew the twin-engine Beach on the more proximate Los Alamos and Alamagordo runs—carrying equal customer proportions to each location. Although intuitively Morris felt that the Beach would be better suited for the longer hauls (especially to Clovis), the aircraft's higher speed enabled him to return to the central facility at Kirtland Air Force Base more quickly. In short, he believed that this decreased return time put him in a better position to oversee the company's entire operations.

While Morris flew the Beach, Harry Foiles operated the Hewes helicopter for total servicing of the Alamagordo area, and Collins was assigned the heavy-duty Kamon helicopter. Morris preferred to have Collins concentrate primarily on servicing the distant Clovis Air Force

---

[1] *Note:* Total contracted passenger sales (6,400) coincided with the total annual seating capacity of Morris Airways:

Aircraft	Annual Seating Capacity
Beach	2,000 passengers
Hewes	1,600 "
Kamon	2,800 "
Total	6,400 passengers

Base because the Kamon's workhorse capability was better suited for longer hauls than the Hewes, and the distant runs had a less strenuous effect on Collins than would be the case with Foiles, who is 56 years old. Overflow traffic to Los Alamos—averaging about 800 passengers annually—was allocated to Collins.

In summary, Morris Airways' scheduling within the "nuclear net" was:

Pilot	Aircraft	Destination	Distance	Annual Passengers
Morris	Beach	Los Alamos	62 miles	1,000
		Alamagordo	155 miles	1,000
Foiles	Hewes	Alamagordo	155 miles	1,600
Collins	Kamon	Los Alamos	62 miles	800
		Clovis	200 miles	2,000

Reassessment of Operating Conditions

Upon completion of the first year of operations, Morris was pleased to find that the company was acquiring a favorable reputation for its record in federal service. Several letters of recommendation had been received from prestigious public officials regarding the line's efficiency and reliability.

However, while these conditions justified Morris' optimistic outlook, he also states that "there were definite indications that the line's continued growth was in peril. In particular, MAC was experiencing considerable difficulty in generating a sufficient profit margin with which to finance its capital expansion."

The first year's operations had generated the following:

Operating revenues			$60,000
Less: Operating expenses	$39,000		
Bank notes due	17,500	56,500	
Cash generated		$ 3,500	

Morris realized that with the increasing shortage of domestic airline pilots, wages for both Foiles and Collins would have to be raised in the near future. In addition, major engine and turbine change were to be provisioned for both the Beach and Kamon during the coming year.

In an effort to pinpoint which specific areas of MAC operations were most costly, Morris instructed Dick Ziegler, his administrative assistant, to devote his entire attention to the matter.

After an intensive 10-day study, Ziegler submitted a unitized cost breakdown to Morris. He found transportation costs per unit (defined as a "seat-mile" in this instance) from the central point of departure,

Kirtland Air Force Base, to each terminal area by specifically designated aircraft to be as shown:

Aircraft	Los Alamos	Alamagordo	Clovis
Beach	$0.07/unit	$0.05/unit	$0.02/unit
Hewes	$ .01/unit	$ .02/unit	$ .03/unit
Kamon	$ .02/unit	$ .04/unit	$ .05/unit

Ziegler next proceeded to calculate the number of seat-miles made by each aircraft to each destination over the first year of operations. He then was able to determine total costs incurred by Morris Airways for the year.

Aircraft	Seat-Miles per Year to:		
	Los Alamos	Alamagordo	Clovis
Beach	62,000	155,000	0
Hewes	0	248,000	0
Kamon	49,600	0	400,000

COST OF EQUIPMENT

Aircraft	Los Alamos		Alamagordo		Clovis		Total
Beach	62,000 (.07)	+	155,000 (.05)	+	0	=	$12,090
Hewes	0	+	248,000 (.02)	+	0	=	4,960
Kamon	49,600 (.02)	+	0	+	400,000	=	20,992
Grand Total						=	$38,042

It was readily apparent to Ziegler that the main cause of the high costs incurred by Morris Airways was a misallocation of aircraft resources. As an example, he noted that there were costly engine and turbine maintenance expenses sustained by the twin-engine Beach. He felt that these expenses were attributable to the plane's frequent takeoffs and landings at the shorter Los Alamos and Alamagordo airstrips.

Ziegler presented his findings to Morris along with the recommendation that Morris hire a recognized operations researcher to assist in finding a solution to the high-cost situation facing Morris Airways. He further suggested that Dr. K. F. Heinrich, who is on the staff of a leading eastern university, would be a good choice. Dr. Heinrich, who was vacationing in the area, is the author of "Decision Paradigms and Their Application to Transportation Problems."

Consulting by Dr. Heinrich

The following week, Morris contacted Heinrich by telephone and the latter came to his office. The two men spent approximately three hours together, during which time, according to Morris,

I described the background of my company, and the tight financial position I face. I covered the cost figures that Ziegler worked up, something of the qualifications and personal characteristics of my pilots, the industrial and growth characteristics of this area, and so on. I also tried to familiarize him with the really tough job I have in managing the airline—the fact that I must fly in an employee category, but that thinking about a million other things and supervision of current operations both require much time. I told him that it meant a great deal to me to arrange my own flying trips so that I could be at home base for my work as president. In that conversation, Heinrich seemed pleasant. He seemed to want to spend most time finding out how Ziegler arrived at his cost figures, and we called Dick in for about half our conversation. At the end of the conversation, we arrived at a fee of $350 a day for his services, and it really floored me to find that is what these kinds of experts are getting. Also, I made the very strong point that I wanted him to lead me through all of his thinking when he makes the recommendation. After all, I didn't think I could afford to make a major change in how we are operating based simply on the short study of some college professor using formulas. I must say that, at the end of that conversation, I didn't know much about what he was going to do.

Morris also explained to the case writer that, in addition to his wanting to fly shorter routes to be at the headquarters for managerial duties, there was another reason. He felt that with all of the pressure of finance, public relations, and government contracts, his flying ability was not as "alert and precise as it might be. I simply feel more relaxed on the two shorter routes, and Clovis seems more pressure. Also, I do not want to change back and forth from the Beach to the helicopters. It is true I have a license for both, but changing to such different aircraft is simply an added burden to upset the week's work and my peace of mind."

Dr. Heinrich subsequently worked in Morris' office for five days. His initial step was to audit all of the cost and capacity characteristics of the various aircraft that had been prepared by Ziegler. In agreement with Ziegler's calculations, Heinrich proceeded to construct his transportation model.

During the week at Morris Airways, I recognized immediately what I originally concluded in the first conversation with Glynn Morris. The problem is a well-known one in operations research—quite simple, in fact. We have had a great amount of experience in allocation of resources by what we call the transportation problem method. Of course, it has the problem of assumptions I mentioned in my report to Morris, but as long as these are recognized as such, the optimization process is quite simple. And it yields a final strategy that is much more logical than seat-of-the-pants judgment. Morris came in frequently while I was working, and I explained essentially the same things that appear in the technical appendix to my report.

Incidentally, that technical appendix has a history. I wrote a report which appears as the covering letter to the final report. [EDITOR'S NOTE: This is the memorandum in Exhibit 1.] Morris had asked me not to spend too much time writing a long and detailed report, because he did not feel like paying me the additional time. However, after I was back at the ranch, he called and said that he simply could not buy the recommendations without understanding more about how I arrived at the strategy. He said that if I would undertake to explain clearly and simply the decision method, he would gladly pay for whatever time it took to write an explanation. The technical appendix which appears in the present report is that explanation. Believe it or not, it is difficult to write that appendix—it took me three drafts and two days' work to try to put into terms easily understandable by a man like Morris the more technical aspects of the decision method.

My problem was simply to select a strategy of transporting MAC passengers from home base to each terminal area in a manner which would meet the constraints and remain within the capacities of aircraft. In short, I sought the optimum allocation of his resources.

After Morris received the new report with the technical appendix, together with Dr. Heinrich's bill for $2,500, he

. . . felt as annoyed as I ever get. The more I thought about it, the madder I got. Look at one of these sentences in his clear and simple explanation: "This step applies the iterative routine of matrix algebra to obtain the optimum cost solution to the problem as given." And look at this: ". . . what is done is to take the information supplied in Matrix A and rearrange the values to that of the cells." On the one hand, I think the guy knows what he is doing, but on the other hand, I just know that he doesn't know enough about my operation for me to upset the whole company on the sheer basis of having read explanations like this. Everything from weather, mechanical troubles, sudden expenses on a given trip, and morale of the pilots has to be considered. Also, if I make any changes in equipment such as modification in seating or updating of the aircraft, I'm right back in the same boat—I have to hire a total stranger, who is not even a businessman, to tell me to do something that may or may not be good business practice, even if it is good math.

It is really a frustrating feeling. Heinrich was a nice guy, civil, and no doubt an expert. I just know he must have something here, and I want to run an up-to-date company with all of the most modern methods. The only thing that I have against him is that in all of our conversations he had two faults. His attention seemed to wander when I was telling him about the broad variety of facts across the business, and he seemed interested when we were talking about Ziegler's cost figures or his own formulas. That's the first fault—when I was talking to him. The second one was when he was talking to me. He absolutely could not keep from using language like those quotes I just read, and when I asked him to say it in another way, he generally ended up by using still other similar words. Don Fowler, the local banker, has a son at home for the holidays from Princeton. When I told him about my difficulties, he said that Dr. Heinrich has a disease that is called "quantiphobia" at Princeton!

I just don't know whether to put this thing into effect or to forget the whole episode. And I certainly don't feel like hiring a permanent consultant to take over my business.

Exhibit 1

To: Mr. Glynn Morris, President
         Morris Airways Company
FROM: K. F. Heinrich
RE: Minimizing Operating Expense

After a careful first-hand examination of the Morris Airways Company, I have found your aircraft utilization, with particular regard to routing, to be substantially less than optimal. I have arrived at an optimal, least-cost solution, enunciated in the quantitative appendix to this letter, which will effectively

Exhibit 1—Continued

reduce your present operating costs by some $16,650. To accrue these benefits, however, you must reschedule your aircraft in the following manner:

Aircraft	Present Routes		Recommended Routes	
Beach	Los Alamos	(1,000 passengers)	Clovis	(2,000 passengers)
	Alamagordo	(1,000 passengers)		
Kamon	Los Alamos	(800 passengers)	Los Alamos	(1,000 passengers)
	Clovis	(2,000 passengers)	Alamagordo	(1,000 passengers)
Hewes	Alamagordo	(1,600 passengers)	Remains the same	

It is intended that these changes be effected as soon as possible.

Now, a few words about the methodology used to support my findings. You may recall from our conversations that the "transportation method" as an allocational tool exemplifies decision making under certainty. Or stated otherwise, for a "feasible solution" to be derived, I have assumed to possess complete knowledge of the below-listed interacting variables:

1. The annual capacities of each aircraft.
2. The contractual passenger requirements of each terminal area.
3. The distances between these terminals.
4. The cost of traveling a single "seat-mile" to each individual air terminal by each type of MAC aircraft.

Although I went to great pains to verify all pertinent information while in Albuquerque this week, it must be pointed out that the above variables may in fact be quite temporary in nature. For instance, factors (1) and (2) above would be altered substantially in the event of such occurrences as an accident causing major repairs, the loss of a pilot, of the modification of certain contractual provisions. Also, unit costs, as represented by number (4) above, are probably in a constant state of change. Because of these inherent limitations of the model, I must define my feasible solution to be a set of individual allocations which, simultaneously, at a given point of time, removes all existing surpluses and satisfies all existing deficiencies. Therefore, as a result of the potential changes of interacting key factors (especially unit costs), it is imperative that the model's supporting variables be continually updated.

In view of this requirement for continuous revision, I recommend that you consider the possibility of hiring an operations researcher on a part-time basis. The State University's industrial engineering department would provide an interesting starting point for a talent search; you might expect to pay between $4,000 and $6,000 annually for the appropriate individual's services. Eventually, with the growth of Morris Airways, computerization might have to be considered.

In conclusion, if these measures and those found in detail in the appendix are followed, the success of Morris Airways in the future can be safely predicted.

KLAUS HEINRICH, PH.D.

TECHNICAL APPENDIX

Step I: After a careful analysis of the essential interactive variables, shipping units (*a* or aircraft), receiving units (*n* or destinations), and unit trip costs (*sm* or seat miles; s = number of seats in any given a; m = number of miles to any given n), Matrix A was constructed and total costs for MAC were computed as of October of last year.

MATRIX A

Aircraft	Los Alamos62	Alamagordo155	Clovis200	Capacity
Beach	62,000 (0.07)	155,000 (0.05)	(0.02)	2,000
Hewes	(0.01)	248,000 (0.02)	(0.03)	1,600
Kamon	49,600 (0.02)	(0.04)	400,000 (0.05)	2,800
Contracted traffic:	1,800	2,600	2,000	= 6,400

Total Cost: 62,000 ($0.07) + 155,000 ($0.05) + 248,000 ($0.02)
+ 49,600 ($0.02) + 400,000 ($0.05) = $38,042

Step II: This step applies the iterative routine of matrix algebra to obtain the optimum minimal cost solution to the problem as given. Essentially, what is done is to take the information supplied in Matrix A and rearrange the "seat-mile" values so that the cells in the new matrix with the smallest cost values are fully utilized, and that the cells containing the highest costs are avoided. Matrix A is obviously not the best solution, since two of the highest cost cells in that matrix (Beach–Los Alamos) and (Kamon–Clovis) are being used quite extensively, and the low cost cells (Beach–Clovis) and (Hewes and Kamon–Los Alamos) are not being used at all. The method to be used below takes on the task of rearranging the given variables in such a fashion as to minimize the sum of cell products (total costs), while at the same time holding to the constraints of plane capacities and contracted traffic.

Moving from Matrix A, circle the costs in those cells in which we distributed seat-miles. Then evaluate all noncircled cells as possible lower-cost alternatives by using the following movement system: Starting in any one of the cells not containing a circled cost figure, move horizontally to a circled cell. Then alternate vertical and horizontal moves, moving to circled cells only, until a closed loop with the cell started from can be completed. The fewest possible movements should be used in returning to the cell to be evaluated; circled cells in the path of completing the closed loop can be bypassed. Once the closed loop is detected, the specific noncircled cell under consideration can be evaluated by summing the values of the cells forming the loop in the following manner: Change the signs of all costs in the circled cells forming the loop; add those cells arrived at horizontally; and subtract all those cells arrived from a vertical direction. Matrix B and the accompanying evaluation demonstrates this procedure.

MATRIX B

Aircraft	Los Alamos62	Alamagordo155	Clovis200	Capacity
Beach	⑦ (0.07)	⑤ (0.05)	−8 (0.02)	2,000
Hewes	−3 (0.01)	② (0.02)	−6 (0.03)	1,600
Kamon	② (0.02)	+4 (0.04)	⑤ (0.05)	2,800
Traffic:	1,800	2,600	2,000	= 6,400

EVALUATION OF MATRIX B

Cell 13* $= +(-7) - (-2) + (-5) - (-2) = -8$
Cell 23 $= +(-2) - (-5) + (-7) - (-2) + (-5) - (-3) = -6$
Cell 32 $= +(-2) - (-7) + (-5) - (-4) = +4$
Cell 21 $= +(-2) - (-5) + (-7) - (-1) = -3$

* Cell code: first digit represents row; second digit represents column.

The optimal solution has been achieved if the noncircled numbers evaluated in Matrix B are all equal to or greater than zero. If one or more of the noncircled numbers is negative, we must find another feasible solution in the following way:

   a) Select the cell containing the largest negative number (cell 13).
   b) Shift seat-miles from cell 11 to cell 13.
   c) So that traffic requirements will still be met, shift an equal number of seat-miles from cell 33 to cell 31. We thus arrive at Matrix C.

MATRIX C

Aircraft	Los Alamos[62]	Alamagordo[155]	Clovis[200]	*Capacity*
Beach	(0.07)	155,000 (0.05)	200,000 (0.02)	2,000
Hewes	(0.01)	248,000 (0.02)	(0.03)	1,600
Kamon	111,600 (0.02)	(0.04)	200,000 (0.05)	2,800
Traffic:	1,800	2,600	2,000	= 6,400

Total Cost = 155,000 ($0.05) + 200,000 ($0.02) + 248,000 ($0.02)
                      + 111,600 ($0.02) + 200,000 ($0.05) = $28,942

Step III: Repeat the above procedure until a matrix which contains no negative numbers is constructed. Such a matrix is found below in Matrix D; the optimal total cost is also calculated.

MATRIX D

Aircraft	Los Alamos[62]	Alamagordo[155]	Clovis[200]	*Capacity*
Beach	(0.07)	(0.05)	400,000 (0.02)	2,000
Hewes	(0.01)	248,000 (0.02)	(0.03)	1,600
Kamon	111,600 (0.02)	155,000 (0.04)	(0.05)	2,800
Traffic:	1,800	2,600	2,000	= 6,400

Total Cost = 400,000 ($0.02) + 248,000 ($0.02) + 111,600 ($0.02)
                      + 155,000 ($0.04) = $21,392

NORTH EUROPEAN REGION OCEAN TRANSPORTATION DIVISION

After World War II, a special division was established for the purpose of centralizing and controlling all ocean cargo movements for all branches of the Armed Forces, called the Ocean Transportation Division (OTD). The new division was designed to reduce the costs of ocean transportation by coordinating cargo shipments by the various services to ports around the world. Because of the worldwide military commitments, cargo shippers are located all over the world and vary in size from the large service-operated ports stateside to the small operations of the military advisory groups located in small emerging nations.

The organization structure of OTD consists of a central headquarters in Washington, D.C., and five regional headquarters located around the world. Each regional headquarters serves several countries for military cargo movement. There are from 5 to 60 military cargo shippers (one for each major port used within a region). These cargo shippers (or shipper services as they are properly called) can be Army, Air Force or Navy (including Marine Corps) representatives.

Each of the five regional offices is staffed primarily with U.S. government civil service personnel, a few military (usually Navy) personnel who hold the top positions, and several local national personnel who serve as clerks, translators, and in other nontechnical positions. Each office has basically the same organizational structure which corresponds to the central headquarters staff in Washington, D.C. The North European Region, referred to as NOREUR OTD, with headquarters in Rotterdam, had a standard structure as shown in Exhibit 1, which was recommended for all regional offices by the OTD headquarters in Washington, D.C. The positions of Commanding Officer and Executive Officer are held by a Navy captain and a Navy lieutenant commander respectively. The Administration/Personnel section and the Comptroller/Supply section were each headed by Navy lieutenants; the offices of each were staffed by a total of 15 Navy enlisted personnel. The top position in the Operations section, the primary section in NOREUR OTD, had been unstaffed since it was vacated during the Korean War to provide more personnel for the Far Eastern regional headquarters. The Executive Officer doubled as Operations Officer. No change in this arrangement was anticipated. The Ship Scheduling Officer was a U.S. Navy lieutenant who had three en-

Exhibit 1

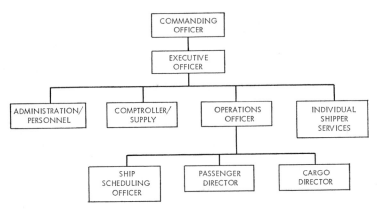

listed under him, and the Passenger Director was a civil servant who had one enlisted and two local Dutch nationals under him. The Cargo Director was a civil servant who was assisted by eight Navy enlisted men and six local Dutch civilians.

The individual shipper service units in 26 countries offered cargo by type, amount, destination, and required delivery date to the NOREUR OTD headquarters. The Cargo Director at NOREUR OTD could combine cargo lifts from various shipper services and schedule government-owned shipping for the large-quantity, high-priority, moving cargo or arrange for U.S. flag commercial shipping for the small lots. Where U.S. flag shipping was not available, appropriate foreign flag service would be negotiated by NOREUR.

Cargo is allowed to accumulate at a port until a large enough lot is available to justify use of government-owned shipping. The local shipper services cannot load or arrange shipment of any cargo without clearance from the NOREUR OTD headquarters, i.e., from the Cargo Director in that headquarters. Occasionally, some friction between the demands of the shipper services and the planning and clearance of cargo by the regional headquarters arises, but NOREUR OTD has the final word. NOREUR OTD had developed a procedure for handling all incoming requests for cargo clearance so that there was a minimum of confusion.

Though no two shipments were identical in all respects, there was a certain amount of standardization in handling cargo clearances that lent some predictability to the operation both for the shipper services and for the NOREUR Cargo Director. The shipper services knew that the Cargo Director was governed by requirements and regulations of the Washington headquarters, as well as by specific contracts negotiated between the various shipping companies and OTD. They also knew that the Cargo Director was restricted in his operations by the availability of government-owned and/or commercial shipping for every cargo lift.

From its inception, the organizational structure of NOREUR OTD had not changed. Mr. Newtall, the Cargo Director, had been with this regional office since it was created in 1949. He had an English wife and did not desire to leave northern Europe even though he had been offered better jobs in the United States. Mr. Newtall, because of his extensive experience in this job, was considered an expert in military ocean transportation. Due to the complexity of knowledge required to fill his position, he limited his vacation time to 10 days at a time. When he took home leave to the United States every two years, another cargo specialist from New York or Washington would take his place. No one in NOREUR OTD except Mr. Newtall was qualified to clear and arrange shipments of cargo.

In March of 1965, Lieutenant Commander (LCDR) Hawthorne arrived at this office for duty as Executive Officer. When he arrived at the office, he met Captain Williams, who had commanded this office for over a year. He welcomed LCDR Hawthorne to Holland and to the Rotterdam office, telling him that he was lucky to have this assignment away from the pressures of duty in Washington or at sea. He said:

> This place is nicknamed "Sleepy Hollow" and from my year's experience here that's a fair evaluation. George [Newtall] over there in cargo, is king around here. He's been here for years and knows more about military cargo shipping than anyone in Washington. You don't need to touch that operation in there, it's smooth and George never lets us get into trouble. I don't know much about his job, but it doesn't matter because if anything comes up that you need to know about, George will brief you. You might keep a close watch on the Admin. and Comptroller officers, since you should be able as a naval officer to control their type of work.

Captain Williams introduced LCDR Hawthorne to the staff and then excused himself "to run some errands" in town. Since afternoons were fairly quiet except for the normal working routine, Captain Williams usually took in what he called a little field work (golf).

Captain Williams did not schedule many inspections, and he was very liberal with his liberty and leave policy. Captain Williams felt that everyone should enjoy his tour of duty in Europe, seeing as much as possible as long as required work was completed in the office. The enlisted men shared the work load whenever any of them went on leave. Captain Williams was pleased with the flexibility and capability of his enlisted men in being able to do each other's job.

In the following six months, LCDR Hawthorne tried to learn about cargo operations and ship scheduling, but both Mr. Newtall and Lt. Barrett (who was Ship Scheduling Officer) were usually too occupied to explain all the workings of their jobs. As Mr. Newtall put it:

> Don't worry about cargo; it's too complex for you to learn in your two-year tour anyway, and it won't do you any good after you leave here. If anything happens to me, Lt. Barrett can take over until they get a replacement for me. He's a sharp boy and has learned a lot about cargo operations in the last two years.

Lt. Richfield in Comptroller/Supply and Lt. Ellis in Administration/ Personnel had about a year each to complete their tours at NOREUR OTD. Lt. Richfield felt that he was fully occupied with his duties as Comptroller/Supply officer, and Lt. Ellis felt the same about his duties as Administration/Personnel officer. Both recognized that their functions were required to support Mr. Newtall's work, which was the essence of NOREUR, and both of them ensured that Mr. Newtall's work received priority in their sections.

Mr. Newtall's operations frequently depended on assistance from Administration in preparing replies to letters and issuing instructions to the shipper service units. Occasionally, when the work load was heavy in cargo, Lt. Ellis would temporarily loan one or two of his men to Mr. Newtall. One of the enlisted men in Administration once remarked that he was not always sure whether he was working for Lt. Ellis or Mr. Newtall, since he was assigned to cargo so often.

Mr. Newtall's primary association with Comptroller/Supply was in the preparation of payments to the commercial shipping companies. Lt. Richfield was responsible for all disbursing functions out of the Rotterdam office. When invoices from shipping companies arrived, they were given to Mr. Newtall for certification. When certified, they were delivered to the Comptroller's office where a clerk would check the computations on an adding machine. Disbursing vouchers were prepared for Lt. Richfield's signature, and after he signed them, they were forwarded to a central disbursing office in Heidelburg, Germany, where checks were prepared and mailed to the various shipping companies.

Lt. Richfield rarely questioned the billings once Mr. Newtall had certified them. However, Lt. Richfield once asked Mr. Newtall how much checking he did on the invoices, since he was interested in taking one of his men off the adding machines to do other work and could not see the point of the invoices being checked for computational errors in cargo and again in supply. Mr. Newtall replied that he didn't have the time or the personnel to check all of these figures. He noted that the shipping companies were meticulous about preparing invoices, and he said that occasionally they bill a little too high, sometimes a little too low, but that it all comes out in the long run. He said that he just certified them whenever they were placed on his desk without wasting time to read them.

In October 1965, Captain Williams was relieved by Captain Reese. Captain Reese, after observing operations, felt that Mr. Newtall was the key to the operations and in January 1966, in anticipation of an inspection from the Washington staff in February, he appointed Mr. Newtall as Operations Officer to oversee not only cargo but also Ship Scheduling and Passenger operations. Captain Reese told LCDR Hawthorne that his job was to ensure that the other two sections were ready for this inspection. LCDR Hawthorne felt that he should have been responsible for preparing the whole staff for the inspection, but Captain Reese assured him that this new arrangement was only for the next month and would optimize the use of personnel in making preparations.

The inspection team included the Washington counterparts to each of the NOREUR OTD staff members. The inspection, as always, included a considerable amount of informal exchange at each level. Each officer, and especially Mr. Newtall, obtained valuable information from his counterpart on how Washington wanted things done.

After the inspection, Captain Reese noted how pleased he was with the results and said that he planned to make some changes in the organizational structure of the staff to accommodate the personnel presently serving on the staff. However, as a result of the Washington inspection team's visit to all European and Mediterranean offices, a large reorganization of OTD was planned. Several major planning meetings were held in Washington, London, and Heidelburg, and Captain Reese attended all of them accompanied by Mr. Newtall. The reorganization took place in May 1966 and included the transfer of Captain Reese to London. One of his old friends, Captain Downey, arrived in Rotterdam to replace him. Captain Reese did not have the opportunity to complete his planned reorganization within the NOREUR OTD staff but had let it continue essentially as it was at the time of the February inspection.

Captain Downey was proceeded by his reputation as being a tough, stringent, but fair man. He reported from the Washington headquarters of OTD and knew most of the operations at NOREUR. After two days in his new position, Captain Downey called LCDR Hawthorne, Mr. Newtall, Lt. Barrett, Lt. Richfield, Lt. Ellis, and Mr. Odette (the Passenger Director) together and made the following remarks.

From a cursory inspection of this office in the past two days, I'm somewhat disturbed with the disorganized appearance. The work flow seems to be chaotic, in speaking to the exec, he doesn't know what's going on in cargo, and no one has briefed me on anything since I arrived. Maybe you don't have any problems; however, I saw two messages yesterday afternoon: one on some cargo in Hamburg that has been held there for over four months awaiting shipping instructions from us; a second message indicating that the government refueling contract in St. Nazaire has expired. I consider these as two problems that our office is directly responsible for, and yet no one has even mentioned them to me. I want to know what is being done about these problems. If you have other problems hidden in desk drawers, I want to know about them before they can damage our operations. Whenever possible, use completed staff work; I consider that the most efficient way of handling this operation. Yesterday afternoon, there were nine enlisted men with the afternoon off for running errands—can we afford to have that many away every afternoon? If we can, we have too many men. There's a war in Vietnam, and believe me, they could use another nine men in OTD Saigon. What I'm trying to get at, gentlemen, is that this organization needs some tightening. It seems to be dependent on one man in cargo who is doubling as Operations Officer, and I'm not convinced that one man should. . . .

"I'm on top of everything in operations," Mr. Newtall interrupted. "Cargo operations are closely tied to ship scheduling; it should all be placed under my cognizance for maximum coordination. In order to make any changes after two days, you should at least. . . ."

"Mr. Newtall, before you interrupted me, I had intended to note that I desired to observe this operation for one month before making any organizational changes. Everyone except LCDR Hawthorne and Mr. Newtall is excused."

Captain Downey continued, "LCDR Hawthorne, I want you as Operations Officer starting right now. I want a daily briefing on all extraordinary problems with your recommended solutions; you may bring the cognizant person in charge of a section to assist you if necessary. Mr. Newtall, I expect you to be on top of cargo operations at all times, and I expect you to live up to your fine reputation as a cargo specialist."

Mr. Newtall returned to his desk and muttered that he might as well retire now rather than wait until 1971, since he had been stripped of his responsibility. "It doesn't appear that Captain Downey will appreciate anyone's efforts. Pretty soon, he'll be in here trying to run cargo operations. I certainly don't intend to cut him in on all the operations over here; he'll only slow down the whole procedure."

At the end of the first week, Lt. Ellis remarked to Lt. Barrett that he was glad to see a commanding officer that took an interest in the office. "Just this morning, I had to see him about revising our staff organization manual, and he understood the problems of issuing a new one. He gave me some guidelines and offered some good suggestions. Don't worry about going in to see him. It's easy to talk to him."

After three weeks, Captain Downey wrote to Captain Reese and included these comments in his letter:

I'm surprised at how long operations ran so smoothly here over the past three or four years. It looks good on the surface, but I feel like I'm sitting on a keg of TNT that could explode at any minute. I don't sense that I have control over the operations of this staff, but I believe things are changing. Hawthorne will never make a decent exec or Operations Officer. I'm afraid I don't trust Newtall as much as you did either.

Two weeks later, Lt. Richfield came into Mr. Newtall's office with an invoice from the Eastern Atlantic Shipping Company which Mr. Newtall had certified that morning.

"Mr. Newtall, did you mean to certify this invoice for $20,000 on a 26-pound box of hand grenades?"

"What do you mean? Let's see that. There must be some mistake." Mr. Newtall read over the invoice and then went to the effective shipping contract between OTD and the Eastern Atlantic Shipping Company, where he read the following from the ammunition rates section:

Effective 1 January 1959, the above ammunition rates are subject to the application of a $20,000 minimum to cover the costs of additional insurance required and of more expensive handling charges inherent in ammunition loading and discharging.

Mr. Newtall flushed, "They have never done this to us before. How are we going to tell Downey about this?"

APPENDIX

Appendix

THE MANAGERIAL MIND *

⁋ Is the thinking of business executives characterized by certain well-defined qualities and attitudes, as is the thinking of scientists, lawyers, and other professional men?

⁋ How does the "managerial mind" resemble the "scientific" or "professional" mind with respect to attitudes about facts, numbers, theory, consistency, change, risk, and other questions?

⁋ In what ways does the "managerial mind" differ from or fall short of the intellectual qualities that we usually associate with doctors, lawyers, and scientists?

⁋ What is the significance of these similarities and differences for businessmen and for business educators?

In the philosophy of science, art, and the professions we find fairly clear statements about the qualities of the "scientific mind," the "creative mind," the "engineering mind," or the "legal mind." But we do not find such statements about the "managerial mind." To be sure, the men who manage the affairs of the world in industry, government, and the armed services are not scientists or artists or doctors. But in failing to state with some clarity the qualities of the managerial mind, we have denied both individual executives and society some very practical advantages.

The professional manager sits by while others enunciate the noble qualities of the scientific or artistic mind, as if there were no realization that management decision making also can be complicated and intellectually difficult. And there is little recognition of standards which promote competence in management, as there is in the established professions, so that efforts to motivate and train men for administration are handicapped. Moreover, business schools lack the kind of clear, balanced concept of goals that has proved such an asset to professional schools.

Note that I am not writing about ability. Nor am I writing about decision-making skills. Almost everyone—even a novelist here and there—recognizes that a good manager has these. My concern here is with common qualities of thinking, with attitudes, biases, predispositions—in short, with those patterns of thought that enable us to characterize the executive and to predict how he will go about handling a problem, if not how he will decide it.

For my purpose here, it is unnecessary to define all facets of the professional mind. We need only agree that a professional is a man who uses his mind and the knowledge of other people's minds to accomplish results in the real world of action. He is concerned with understanding the environment or natural order, predicting what will happen in it as it operates, and in most cases con-

* By Charles E. Summer, Jr. Reprinted from *The Harvard Business Review*, January–February, 1959, by permission of the publisher.

trolling it. It is this orientation toward *action* and *results* and *solving action problems* that identifies the intellectual qualities of a professional.

The question of whether or not management is becoming a profession is also beside the point here. It stands to reason, however, that if mental qualities similar to those presented in this article are developed and accepted as standards, management will come much *nearer* to the status of a profession. Yet it will never be quite like any profession that we know today. The managerial mind is developing many similarities to scientific, engineering, medical, and legal minds, but also some differences. It is going its own way, working in an independent direction. Of course, this is as it should be, but the fact that the pattern is a strange one may explain why so many people have been so slow in recognizing the new intellectual stature of management.

One more thing: in this discussion we shall be concerned only with the intellectual qualities of the manager. While these are vitally important, it should be remembered that other attributes are also important—moral, aesthetic, and creative qualities, for example, or knowledge and wisdom gained from experience. Indeed, from time to time the nonintellectual qualities may be a good deal more important than the intellectual ones, both from the point of view of the company and of society at large.

EMPIRICAL QUALITIES

The empirical qualities of the managerial mind are not new, in and of themselves. But they are combined in a different way, and they are given different emphasis, than in the case of the medical mind, say, or the engineering mind. What is especially noticeable is that the executive typically does not pursue any one kind of empirical reasoning to an extreme. Here, as elsewhere in this discussion, we shall find that no single attitude or predisposition dominates. Each seems to be followed in moderation, with the emphasis on the blend—on a way of thinking in its entirety, rather than on the individual ingredients.

THE FACTUAL ATTITUDE

Alfred North Whitehead, the great philosopher and mathematician, tells us that scientists have always had a bias for observational and experimental investigation.[1] Galileo's insistence on "irreducible and stubborn facts" led to a distrust of reasoning to the point where even today there is among some scientists the feeling that those whose methods involve patient observation of facts through experiments or analysis of past experience are "greater" than those whose methods rely primarily on reason and logic.

This first empirical quality, which might be called the factual attitude, is particularly valuable in the world of managerial action, where the manager has to cause or control specific events in his problem situation. It is too bad if either quick conclusions or imaginative speculations yield decisions that are not in accordance with the real world of problems and facts.

The factual attitude is very much in evidence in the annals of management. For example, when General Motors first decided to go into the diesel engine business, management got extensive facts on what kind of small locomotive was required and what it would take to design, produce, and sell such a product; then it methodically proceeded to base its actions on this evidence. Again, the

---

[1] *Science and the Modern World* (New York, New American Library Edition, 1948), pp. 9, 17.

careful long-range planning of many companies today attests to the importance of the factual attitude.[2]

Conversely, there are many examples of unsatisfactory results when facts are *not* gathered carefully before making decisions. For example, a number of studies show that the primary reason for failure of new businesses is optimistic speculation of owners who fail to be as factual as possible about projected sales, operating problems, capital requirements, and so on.

However, the factual attitude can be overdone. If the administrator is too possessed with the necessity of patience in getting *all* of the facts, he may fail on two counts: (1) In many decisions the facts bearing on a problem cannot be known. (2) Even if the various kinds of needed facts could be known, there may not be enough time to dig all of them out patiently.

What is needed, therefore, is a modified form of the factual attitude, one that says, in effect, *"Have patience and a desire to get the facts, be reluctant to jump to conclusions, but do not hesitate to use such reasoning and judgment as you must if lack of facts or lack of time prevents thorough research of a problem."*

In this respect the managerial mind is not unlike the medical or legal mind; the doctor must make decisions at times on the spur of the moment, and the lawyer may have to advise a client before a question of law can be settled by the courts or the legislature. But a modified factual attitude would do little credit to an aeronautical engineer or a research chemist. Here, in other words, we have the first in a series of likenesses and contrasts between management and the established professions.

THE QUANTITATIVE ATTITUDE

A second empirical quality might be called the quantitative attitude. Philosophers of science tell us that scientists have a distinct "innate prejudice" for selecting only those facts in the environment which can be *measured*. One writer has noted: "Kepler's deepest conviction was that nature is essentially mathematical, and all his scientific life was an endeavor to discover nature's mathematical harmonies. Galileo, also, had no doubt that mathematics is the one true key to natural phenomena."[3] That this preference exists strongly even today is attested to by biologists, physicists, anthropologists, and others.

The quantitative attitude satisfies two important needs of the scientist. It helps him to be objective, and it enables him to "prove" his relationships or laws —for instance, what will happen to x units of y variable if b variable changes by z units.

This mathematical predisposition can also be of value to the executive. It can result in improved ways of doing things. The budget is an example, as are standard costs and financial ratios. Operations research, digital computers, probability and game theory, systems theory, automation, and such social sciences as applied anthropology are all adding to the possibilities for being "scientific" in the sense of measuring the consequences of managerial decisions.

Efforts to quantify complex business problems have so often been successful that almost every businessman is familiar with at least a few of them—as for example:

---

[2] For a documentation of many companies' experience, see *Long-Range Planning for Management*, edited by David W. Ewing (New York, Harper & Brothers, 1958).

[3] J. W. N. Sullivan, *The Limitations of Science* (New York, New American Library Edition, 1949), p. 128.

- The work done in chemical process plants in scheduling complicated flows of by-products through linear equations.
- The efforts of Thomas Malone, a weather expert for The Travelers Insurance Companies, and oil industry people to show what quantification can do to help control inventories of heating fuel, schedule refinery runs, schedule tanker shipments, and even plan capital investment.

Most businessmen have also had numerous opportunities to learn what may happen if management does *not* have a quantitative predisposition—cases like that of the new owner of a large newspaper in the Midwest who discovered that the previous publisher had been losing money every year for 15 years on a job-order printing business, simply because he "hated figures" and failed to separate job printing from the newspaper in a quantitative fashion; or instances of companies continuing unprofitable lines, or continuing to serve territories and customers which cost more than their profit contribution, simply because nobody had time to worry with figures when there were more glamorous things to do.

Interestingly enough, the quantitative attitude can be of great assistance in the executive's human relations. The objectivity of numbers, rather than subjective emotion, is one road by which the individual can be understood by, and influenced by, others. This has been pointed out by social scientists, and it seems to fit the facts in the world of business, as evidenced, for instance, by General Electric's stress on the "authority of facts" as contrasted with the "authority of command."

Unlike the scientific mind, however, the managerial mind can give only qualified emphasis to the use of numbers; the beauty and preciseness of measurement can be admired only up to a point. Otherwise the decision maker may delay things while the patient dies, the war is lost, or the firm misses its opportunity. Business organizations may need certain people who are deeply, zealously interested in quantification, but the one who receives quantitative facts and has to incorporate them into judgmental actions in a limited time should not possess this temperament in excessive degree.

Perhaps the modified predisposition for the manager would be something like: *"Strive patiently and creatively to prove the results of your decision by searching for variables that can be measured, but do not let yourself be enchanted by mathematical systems to the point where you postpone or shun judgment when action is necessary."*

Here, by the way, we see an interesting difference in the managerial mind from the mind of most professional groups. *Parts* of the company organization can be as deeply committed to quantitative techniques as any scientists are, and the policy-making executive himself may *once* have been closely associated with such projects; but when he is making decisions as a member of top management, he must vigorously resist the temptation to become beholden to any one point of view. This is a problem which is generally insignificant for scientists, lawyers, doctors, and so on. They work in homogeneous groups. By contrast, the heterogeneity of a business organization requires a very high order of judgment and mental discipline on the part of the manager. Indeed, far from making him unprofessional, this may really do a great deal to *justify* professional status for the manager.

LOGICAL QUALITIES

In spite of what appears to be a bias among some men of science for the factual, most scientists recognize the necessity for a delicate interaction and balance between experiment and observation, on the one hand, and speculation and reasoning, on the other. The scientist will, of course, speculate and theorize in the same mathematical and physical terms as he observes and proves, but a difference in approach is involved.

THE THEORETICAL ATTITUDE

The first quality of the deductive mind seems to be a faith and belief in the similarity and harmony of events over time. With this goes an interest in searching out *concepts* that catalogue these events into the same meaning, and an interest in reasoning out laws that govern what happens to one concept when another changes. This is the theoretical attitude; and while it is most often associated in the popular mind with science, it has many uses in business. Thus:

We have a concept called "inventory" and other concepts called "current assets," "current liabilities," "current ratio," and "bank loans." The financial executive may know that when the inventory goes up and is paid for with bank loans, the current ratio decreases as current assets and current liabilities are increased by the same amount. He can deduce other future events from these relationships: when the inventory is sold and the cash used to build a building, this converts current assets to fixed assets, and the current ratio decreases. He then deduces what will happen to other parts of the business when the current ratio declines; there is a whole chain of effects.

There are hundreds of these concepts and relationships in the functions of finance, sales, personnel, manufacturing, and the rest.

Now the really great minds in mathematics and deductive physics are minds which have peculiarly strong predispositions of this nature. Albert Einstein made this clear when he said:

"I believe with Schopenhauer that one of the strongest motives that lead men to art and science is escape from everyday life with its painful crudity and hopeless dreariness, from the fetters on one's own ever shifting desires."[4]

In other words, by inventing new concepts abstracted from the problems, events, and situations in the real world around us, the scientist escapes to what is, for him, a more pleasant world of theory and reason.

This kind of attitude can be most valuable to the professional "on the firing line." In cutting through the complex difficulty of running a business or an army, one is completely lost if he cannot catalogue the confusion of facts and problems into a more simplified meaning so that his mind can handle them. Instead of reacting to someone else's theory as "egghead," or quickly saying, "Give me facts not theory," many a businessman has found it helpful to ponder the operations researcher's "model" of the firm, the economist's "laws" for the economy, and the social scientist's hypothesis about the relation between morale, participation, and decentralization. Indeed, I wonder if business leaders and business schools might not do well to support more of the kind of training (both in logic and semantics) that encourages interest in "theory spinning" and the use of theory in practice.

Of course, in order to prevent the professional manager from resting too long on "Cloud 9" rather than in the real world, the theoretical attitude, too, needs modifying. Perhaps it could be stated thus: *"Reasoning and quiet thought, and use of theory from others, can be valuable in professional practice, provided I maintain a healthy distrust and a willingness to abandon theoretical concepts if they do not fit my specific problem."*

---

4 Albert Einstein, *Essays in Science* (New York, Philosophical Library, 1934), p. 2.

Predisposition for Truth

A second logical quality that is useful to the professional executive might be termed the predisposition for truth.

The attitude of Aristotelian logic is one that says, "I must define my terms precisely, and test each statement, before using them as premises in arguments and drawing any conclusions." The modern semanticists, who have developed a supplementary method, would declare, "Every word must be tested and traced to the abstract characteristics that connect the word to the object it represents in the real world; only then do we know what is truth."

The quality of an executive's thinking and the workability of his ideas are dependent upon the truth and preciseness of statements with which he reasons. Thus, the concept of truth is not as "long hair" as it sounds; on it rests the possibilities of executive decisions working or not working.

Like the other qualities of mind taken from science and logic, this attitude must be modified for the professional manager. Oftentimes, he must deal with fuzzy concepts, and he cannot take the time to retire to a cloister and reduce his problem to fundamental truth. The logician, seeing an ambiguous object and unable to identify it, may refuse to deal with it—"morale," for instance—unless its identity can be thoroughly investigated. The executive, on the other hand, must sometimes grab whatever concepts he can use as factors in his problem.

The modified attitude toward truth might sound something like this: *"I must be as precise in reasoning from facts and premises as time will allow, and I must search out premises and conclusions that are true, but I must not shrink from the problem because some statements are impossible to define precisely."* To illustrate:

Suppose that the president of a small but growing company is faced with hiring more and more people and assigning them work, all of which must be coordinated to achieve the goals of this growing business. In assigning a pattern of work and decision making, he reasons that he should create departments for the operating work (planning and deciding the details of jobs, explaining and clarifying work, appraising results, receiving information from the workers themselves in order to appraise, and so on), and either hire staff assistants or decentralize the managing to the departments themselves. He may further reason that the choice between these alternatives is best determined by certain factors: human needs, the speed necessary for decision, the coordination required between parts of the work flow, and other matters.

A few writers have given *some* precision to the meaning of the terms just used—"department," "planning," "staff," and so on. But semanticists and others urge the executive to seek out and use more precise and fundamental terms, such as would give a concrete, clearly defined reality to the kind of decentralization, to the authority of staff men, to the role of the department in the revised organization picture, and so forth. Obviously this would be a major and impractical undertaking, especially at this stage of the development of management.

Accordingly, the modified attitude toward truth would lead the executive to do only the best he can in the time he has available, and to go ahead and use the terms that have proved to be the *most useful* tools in his thinking. He could not take a leave of absence and retire to build deductive models, or search out more fundamental premises.

The fuzziness of so many management terms and concepts points up a shortcoming of the executive mind that has no parallel in the sciences and professions (with the possible exception of a few areas of the law). The situation suggests that one of the main goals of business scholarship should be to increase both our experimental and deductive knowledge of business practices and policies to the end that the words we use symbolize reality more accurately than they now do. I wonder, for example, if members of faculties of business schools should not have some time (or more time) for model building, just as they should have time for gathering "practical" facts from the business world. As both types of knowledge become available to future executives over the years, the compromise with the scientist's predisposition for truth will become less pronounced.

CONSISTENCY

A third logical quality of the professional executive is a modified version of the "validity" attitude in formal logic. So far we have been talking about whether *statements* of fact are "true" or "false" in the executive's reasoning. Now, we turn to whether or not the *arguments* in his reasoning are valid—that is, whether the premises as stated are consistent among themselves rather than contradictory, and whether the statement of conclusions and decisions is consistent with the statements of premises.

An excellent example of logical form in industry is the way decisions are prepared by management for action by the board of directors of Standard Oil Company of New Jersey: projects are usually prepared in the form of proposals (conclusions) with supporting statements as to the positive and negative results of the action. This is a deductive form and is the reverse of another sequence that is often used elsewhere—the classical form of inductive argument, where a series of statements is built up from lower-order statements based on facts and then is followed by a conclusion.

The reasons why the manager must emphasize consistency *within limits* are similar to those mentioned in connection with the attitude about truth. Both logic and semantics, as disciplines of the mind, may take long, patient reflection, away from the day-to-day pressures of operating decisions. And too often that amount of time simply does not exist.

The discipline of mind which the manager needs should be something like this: *"Clear, precise reasoning from premises to conclusions is necessary if my professional decisions and proposed actions are to be workable. However, I cannot expect to discover scientific laws in every decision through strictly valid arguments, and sometimes it will be necessary to substitute 'reasonableness' in a broad sense for syllogistic precision in thinking."*

IN DEFENSE OF MODIFICATION

It is not always clear to observers why businessmen must modify the traditional logical attitudes as much as they do. For instance, if the manager were to take time and insist on more truth and consistency, might he not save time for everybody in the end? Personally, I doubt it. Let me illustrate:

> Last year I attended an executive program designed for top managers from a cross section of companies and from the government. A nationally known writer on logic and clear thinking was discussing the pitfalls and fallacies that are common if one does not make use of precise syllogistic logic. His thesis seemed to be an exhortation for executives to use such reasoning.
>
> In the question period which followed, the speaker was caught by the audience in two rather definite errors in his own thinking—errors of "overgeneralization"—and he seemed quite unprepared to handle his predicament.

The reason was: he did not see that by standing in front of a group and answering questions he was transformed from a logician and a thinker to a man of action. He saw the necessity for acting by answering as helpfully as possible, and he acted.

Now this man, had he been a precise logician first and foremost, instead of a logician equally interested in helping this group of executives, would have declined to answer questions until he had time to state them clearly, retire from the platform for as long a period as needed, and think through an answer. In the case in point, he tried to be both a scholar and a man of action at the same time; hence his trouble.

The lesson to be learned from this episode is clear. If decisions are reasoned sloppily with low degrees of validity and truth, the executive can make them in the time period required but they may be unworkable. On the other hand, if he insists on such high degrees of validity and truth that he is removed from his job into long periods of abstract thought, he may have to stay on the platform and say "I don't know" to every question, and never get going with actions at all. Somewhere in between is the only practical course—but this requires another set of quite different qualities.

QUALITIES OF ACTION

We turn now to a group of action-centered qualities which discipline the managerial mind. Those accustomed to thinking in a scientific way may immediately challenge these qualities and say, "They are not intellectual." Since this misconception is one which prevents both professionals and university teachers who teach professionals from seeing the importance of action-centered qualities and consciously trying to develop them, a word is needed to say why they *are* intellectual in nature.

Any belief or predisposition which influences the way a person thinks, the sequences involved in mental thought, or the way he attacks a problem can be thought of as an intellectual attitude. This is one of the meanings of the phrase "disciplined way of thinking." A scientist has one set of predispositions or beliefs, an artist another set, professionals another set, and so on.

In the discussion that follows, we shall look at a set of attitudes that influence the way the action-centered mind works as it tries to be factual and rational. We shall see great variances between the managerial mind and the scientific mind, but important similarities in the intellectual biases of executives, lawyers, and doctors.

Desire to Change Things

Remembering Einstein's statement, quoted earlier, about how the scientist and artist try to escape from the world of current action, we might say that the professional has a somewhat opposite desire to *take actions* that have results. The lawyer wants to win cases as well as to present a brilliant argument. The surgeon wants to cure people as well as to know anatomy. The architect wants to build buildings, the engineer to build bridges, the army general to win campaigns. And the executive wants to get output.

There are a number of ways in which executives have been observed to demonstrate this quality. Some have moved from a comfortable, safe, high-status position in a well-run company to accept a position with a company that is in trouble, is lagging behind its competitors, or is "worn-out." Such tough problem situations may be viewed as a challenge. In the same way, the executive who takes pleasure in turning his attention to the "messy" departments in his division may be exhibiting this quality. It also shows up, on a more modest plane, in the desire to make improvements in an otherwise good situation, or in an "itch to do something new." Frequently this leads to innovations which show immediate results—witness, for example, the record of the Prudential Insurance Company in the last few years.

To be sure, the desire to change things may be more characteristic of "chiefs" than of "braves." For example, William H. Whyte, Jr. would say that the "organization man"[5] does not feel much like departing from tested experience, and Chris Argyris would say that people who start out "healthy," with a desire to grow and to produce innovations, instead tend to adapt to the organizaion and become apathetic and disinterested in the company and its goals.[6] Both of these are probably overstatements, but the warning is a legitimate one. Certainly it is management at *all levels* that needs a disposition toward action, since small improvements in processes and techniques can add up to the equivalent of "big" innovations.

This desire to change things in the real world is perhaps quite different from that of the pure scientist who wants to be basic, factual, logical, and to contribute to the truth and validity of knowledge. The scientist may in fact want to change things—but, if so, he is not overly concerned about just when. It may be in the very distant future. For example, Arthur Burns, former adviser to the President of the United States, has stated his preference for *long-run* results accomplished through scholarly ideas, rather than *current* results obtained through operating as a professional economist in government.[7]

TIMELY ACTION

Top executives, in addition to desiring to change things in the real world, should have a predisposition for timely action. John L. Burns, president of Radio Corporation of America, a man with a doctorate in physical science, has put the attitude this way: "I'd rather be president than be right"—by which he means simply that when timeliness and speed of decision are necessary, truth and validity must sometimes rank secondary.

There seem to be at least two ways in which an executive can fail to demonstrate this vital quality of timeliness:

(1) He can insist on a deluge of facts without any forthright conclusion. Examples of this are familiar to most businessmen (although seldom recorded). It is also interesting to note that military history is full of cases where commanders refused to act because they demanded more facts. General McClellan, for instance, made this mistake when he followed Lee into Virginia.

(2) The executive can postpone action for a long time on the grounds that "we have to wait and see." What he may really mean is that he is afraid to make a move until all the facts are in. By the time they are in, of course, it will probably be too late to accomplish much.

---

[5] *The Organization Man* (New York, Simon and Schuster, Inc., 1956).
[6] *Personality and Organization: The Conflict Between the System and the Individual* (New York, Harper & Brothers, 1957); and "The Organization: What Makes It Healthy?" HBR November–December 1958, p. 107.
[7] "An Economist in Government," Columbia University Forum, Winter 1957, p. 4.

Judgmental Qualities

The term "judgment" is one that has caused much confusion. It is usually described only in the most general terms. F. R. Collbohm, president of the Rand Corporation, for instance, recently said: "What is Judgment? Judgment is just experience."[8] Certainly judgment is based to a great extent on experience, but describing it so simply does not, in my opinion, do the term justice. The role of judgment can be made more meaningful if the word is broken down and analyzed.

Executives and all men of action must many times try to make meaning out of their problems and solve them without doing certain things that the scientist or logician does in his patient search for truth and validity. For each of the scientific devices by which scholars eliminate risk from their thinking, there is a corresponding judgment or risk that the man of action often must take if he is to accomplish results in the real world. These various kinds of judgment can be looked at as conceptual judgment, quantity judgment, weight judgment, and whole problem judgment:

❡ *Conceptual judgment* results from the fact that the executive cannot reduce the ideas he works with to fundamental concepts, either by science (experimentation and generalization) or by logic (reasoning backward to fundamental premises). The physicist deals with forces and mass, atoms and electrons; the chemist deals with atoms and molecules; and the anatomist deals with corpuscles and cells. On the other hand, the management of a company like General Foods must deal with such big, multifaceted symbols as "customer service," "product line," "duplication of effort," "jobbers," and others in order to reason out its policy of a single sales force selling a product line to customers.

Use of such imprecise or "sloppy" variables in a problem is an attempt by the managerial mind to create "big" thinking tools to include a host of other minor variables. If the problem *could* be broken down to fundamental variables (which it cannot), it would be so complex it could not be solved.

❡ The nature of *quantity judgment* and *weight judgment* have been mentioned already. The managements of Du Pont and General Motors cannot say, "If we decentralize 68,000 decisions to the divisions, morale will go up 5 degrees, speed of decision will increase 35 miles per hour, or development of lower executives will accelerate at a rate of 16 foot-pounds per minute." Rather, the managerial mind makes an estimate of such factors as the cost of employing general executives to head independent divisions, a second estimate of the effect of the proposal on decision speed, increased motivation, and so on, and then reaches a decision.

❡ *Whole problem judgment* results from the fact that the executive cannot eliminate all of the thousands of factors in a problem, narrow it down to two or three factors, and then triumphantly say that the value of such-and-such a policy or course of action can be *proved*.

Shortly after the Korean War, the International Business Machines Corporation was confronted with a problem of whether initially to produce a small or large number of Model 650 computers. Now, if the company's president, Thomas Watson, had been a scientist instead of an executive, then he might have proved that "if manufacturing costs are held constant, capital investment expenditure is held constant, sales and advertising methods are held constant, number of plant

---

[8] "Scientific Aids to Decision-Making: A Perspective," American Management Association, General Management Series, No. 187 (1957), p. 43.

personnel is held constant, and materials costs are held constant, a change of 180 in computer output will yield $5 million in sales." Even if this were a triumphant truth, and 180 computers did sell for $5 million, the discovery would be almost useless, for manufacturing-unit cost *would* go down, the number of plant personnel *would* vary, and so forth.

Accordingly, the executive must try to grapple with thousands of chain effects, both inside and outside the company, when he makes a major decision. In doing so, he takes a judgmental risk of being wrong in his evaluation of the relationships.

SUSPICION OF SCIENCE

One of the most difficult balances to maintain in the managerial mind is that between respect for scientific theory and a healthy suspicion of it. In business there is a long history of fads which have come and gone. They stand as evidence that both "good" and "bad" science are offered to the businessman, and that the former can be used both effectively and ineffectively. To indicate the range of possibilities:

❡ As far back as 1850, Jeremy Bentham tried to help the English government make policies for running the country by his "felicific" calculus. His purpose was to enable the Parliament to choose between alternative laws by measuring the pleasures and pains each inflicted on the population.

❡ Frederick Taylor's scientific management has been pursued vigorously by many companies. At times past, a large number of companies applied it as a formula.

❡ Just before World War II, a consultant named Charles E. Bedeaux convinced the managements of a large number of corporations that his Bedeaux System of wage payments could equate human effort and "rest" with technology and output. Among the companies using his theory were American Rolling Mills, Campbell Soup, Diamond Match, General Electric, Du Pont, Eastman Kodak, Swift, Postum, and Goodrich.[9]

Today, many competent social scientists and mathematicians are trying to help management solve problems. We read of studies which indicate that productivity can be increased if employees "participate," or that morale can be increased by less authority and pressure from supervisors. Yet I know of one company where a study of this kind was performed (and published), which today believes there "is something wrong" with such formulas.

Perhaps the key to such misunderstandings between scientists and professionals lies in the "closed system" idea versus the "whole problem" concept. Social scientists frequently stress that their mission is to help the executive *understand* his problem, and not to tell him what to do.[10] They are no more physically or mentally able to tell the executive what to do than the executive is himself. But behavioral scientists can help to illuminate the human variables just as the engineer, accountant, marketing-research man, and others isolate the variables associated with technology, costs, consumer preferences, and the numerous other factors that get mixed into the decision-making picture.

What I am saying is that both scientists and managers should have a reluctance to think that scientific formulations can solve action problems in all of their complexity. A manager errs if he grabs onto "participation" or "scientific

---

9 *The New Yorker,* September 22, 1945, p. 30.

10 See Edward C. Bursk, "Opportunities for Persuasion," HBR September–October 1958, p. 111.

management" or the "Bedeaux System" and employs it as a formula for an action problem. Scientists also err if they write their publications so as to *imply* that their understandings will work on a broad and general basis, without adjustment or change, in the world of action.

One reason for a healthy suspicion of theory is that usually it is impossible, or impractical, to quantify the variables in a decision. Certainly "morale" and, as many executives know, even "profit" cannot be *precisely* measured.

In advanced research with computers, in the more sophisticated econometric formulas, and in operations research models, the mathematician usually either (1) selects only a few variables that can be measured and leaves the other variables to the executive for judgment; (2) includes more variables but weights them arbitrarily, as is done in some of the business games now popular; or (3) looks for and attacks only those problems which lend themselves to a high degree of quantification. In any of these three cases, both the scientist and the manager can understand each other better if they appreciate the proper use and limitation of quantitative science.

I do not mean that the executive should take a pessimistic view of the progress in social science and in operations research. The long, patient identification of fundamental variables, their quantification, and the fitting together of theory will yield better solution of problems over the years. But we must be patient and realize that, while we are moving, there is still a long way to go.

OBJECTIVITY AND VALUES

The scientist strives above all for something called "objectivity." This is the belief that his mission is the patient and dispassionate study of the environment—of the basic facts in nature and of the way different factors influence one another. The professional manager seeks objectivity, too, but under different conditions. For example, the search for factual and logical truth is not his highest governing objective when timing of actions and results are also important. Again, unlike most scientists, he is willing boldly to enter debates on moral and ethical questions, and to have research influenced, stopped, or changed by subjective factors.

Why does the manager or the lawyer allow himself to be influenced more by moral and ethical considerations than the scientist? The answer, it seems to me, does not have so much to do with personalities and tradition as with the time dimension in which these men work. In most professions the practitioners are faced immediately with the results of their decisions; hence they are naturally impelled to take moral and ethical values into consideration along with objective "facts." To illustrate:

- The doctor, believing in value of human life, keeps a patient alive in the midst of suffering.
- The lawyer, believing in the right of every person to have his case presented and understood, defends the criminal.
- The business executive, believing in the dignity of individuals, may refrain from firing an aged employee.

By contrast, scientists often do not have to face immediate results. Whether or not results are "good" or "bad" to their way of thinking may not be known for years, if ever. Those who worked with quantum and relativity theories did not know whether the atomic bomb would be used on Hiroshima or whether atomic power plants would be constructed to heat and light the homes of mankind.

If progress in science operated so that one day a scientist worked in his laboratory and the results of his work were available to use in the everyday world the next day, perhaps he too would incorporate nonrational values into his research.

CONCLUSION

A better understanding of the qualities of the managerial mind ought to stimulate business education and management training. For the executive on the job it would add meaning and nobility of purpose to the tasks of getting things done through people. And it would help in the crystallization of standards for the businessman to measure up to.

How does a person develop the qualities earlier described in this article? Generally speaking, it seems to me that he makes the greatest progress when he can:

1. Become acquainted with the substantive knowledge available and with the particular attitudes and predispositions that disinguish the successful manager.

2. Observe the mistakes executives make when they do not apply these qualities.

3. Experience successes and failures of this kind himself in the presence of his colleagues or superiors.

As for formal training methods, management might take a cue from law. In developing qualities of the legal mind, law school moot courts and the study of precedent have been most helpful. Similarly, in training the managerial mind, Socratic questioning, along with skillful teaching of theory, should be helpful. The study of cases is excellent, provided it exposes the executive or student in all three of the ways just mentioned. The type of oral examination currently used for scholarly degrees suggests a kind of discussion that can effectively force thinking through *action* issues and create an awareness of mistakes in fact and logic. Finally, business games ought to be useful in developing the logical and empirical as well as action qualities earlier discussed.[11]

Of course, there is nothing quite as compelling as the example of business leaders in the field. The more they can personally demonstrate the qualities of the managerial mind, and the more they can make it a living reality, the more meaningful will be the efforts of everyone in adding to the stature of management.

---

11 See G. R. Andlinger, "Business Games—Play One!" HBR March–April 1958, p. 115; and "Looking Around: What Can Business Games Do?" HBR July–August 1958, p. 147.

INDEXES

INDEX OF CASES

INDEX OF AUTHORS

This book has been set in 10 point Baskerville, leaded 2 points, and 9 point Baskerville, leaded 1 point. Part and chapter numbers and titles are in 18 point Deepdene italic. The size of the type page is 27 by 47 picas.